ASPEN PUBLISHERS

D1323452

# CONSTITUTIONAL LAW

**TWENTY-SIXTH EDITION**

## STEVEN L. EMANUEL

Harvard Law School, J.D. 1976
Member, NY, CT and MD bars

# The *Emanuel Law Outlines* Series

Wolters Kluwer

Law & Business

AUSTIN   BOSTON   CHICAGO   NEW YORK   THE NETHERLANDS

Printed in the United States of America.

1 2 3 4 5 6 7 8 9 0

ISBN 978-0-7355-7049-8

This book is intended as a general review of a legal subject. It is not intended as a source for advice
for the solution of legal matters or problems. For advice on legal matters, the reader should consult
an attorney.

## About Wolters Kluwer Law & Business

Wolters Kluwer Law & Business is a leading provider of research information and workflow solutions in key specialty areas. The strengths of the individual brands of Aspen Publishers, CCH, Kluwer Law International and Loislaw are aligned within Wolters Kluwer Law & Business to provide comprehensive, in-depth solutions and expert-authored content for the legal, professional and education markets.

**CCH** was founded in 1913 and has served more than four generations of business professionals and their clients. The CCH products in the Wolters Kluwer Law & Business group are highly regarded electronic and print resources for legal, securities, antitrust and trade regulation, government contracting, banking, pension, payroll, employment and labor, and healthcare reimbursement and compliance professionals.

**Aspen Publishers** is a leading information provider for attorneys, business professionals and law students. Written by preeminent authorities, Aspen products offer analytical and practical information in a range of specialty practice areas from securities law and intellectual property to mergers and acquisitions and pension/benefits. Aspen's trusted legal education resources provide professors and students with high-quality, up-to-date and effective resources for successful instruction and study in all areas of the law.

**Kluwer Law International** supplies the global business community with comprehensive English-language international legal information. Legal practitioners, corporate counsel and business executives around the world rely on the Kluwer Law International journals, loose-leafs, books and electronic products for authoritative information in many areas of international legal practice.

**Loislaw** is a premier provider of digitized legal content to small law firm practitioners of various specializations. Loislaw provides attorneys with the ability to quickly and efficiently find the necessary legal information they need, when and where they need it, by facilitating access to primary law as well as state-specific law, records, forms and treatises.

Wolters Kluwer Law & Business, a unit of Wolters Kluwer, is headquartered in New York and Riverwoods, Illinois. Wolters Kluwer is a leading multinational publisher and information services company.

# Dedication

To Jeffrey Howard Emanuel,

No longer even close to being
the littlest Emanuel

# Abbreviations Used in Text

**CASEBOOKS**

Sullivan & Gunther — Kathleen Sullivan & Gerald Gunther, *Constitutional Law* (Foundation Press, 16th Ed. 2007)

L,K,&C — Lockhart, Kamisar, Choper, Shiffrin & Fallon, *Constitutional Law — Cases, Comments, Questions* (West Publ., 8th Ed. 1996)

S,S,S,T&K — Stone, Seidman, Sunstein, Tushnet & Karlan, *Constitutional Law* (Aspen, 5th Ed. 2005)

**HORNBOOKS AND OTHER AUTHORITIES**

Chemerinsky — Erwin Chemerinsky, *Federal Jurisdiction* (Little, Brown & Co., 2d Ed. 1994)

Ely — John Ely, *Democracy and Distrust* (Harvard Univ. Press, 1980)

Engdahl — David Engdahl, *Constitutional Power: Federal and State* (West Publ., Nutshell Series, 1974)

N&R — Nowak & Rotunda, *Constitutional Law* (West Publ., 5th Ed. 1995)

Schwartz — Bernard Schwartz, *Constitutional Law: A Textbook* (MacMillan Publ., 2nd Ed. 1979)

Tribe — Lawrence Tribe, *American Constitutional Law* (Foundation Press, 2nd Ed. 1988)

U.S.L.W. — *U.S. Law Week*, Supreme Court sections (BNA)

# SUMMARY OF CONTENTS

# TABLE OF CONTENTS

Chapter 1

# INTRODUCTION

Chapter 2

# THE SUPREME COURT'S AUTHORITY

Chapter 3

# FEDERALISM AND FEDERAL POWER GENERALLY

Chapter 4

# THE FEDERAL COMMERCE POWER

Chapter 5

# OTHER NATIONAL POWERS

Chapter 6

# TWO LIMITS ON STATE POWER:
# THE COMMERCE CLAUSE AND CONGRESSIONAL ACTION

Chapter 7

# INTERGOVERNMENTAL IMMUNITIES & INTERSTATE RELATIONS

Chapter 8

# SEPARATION OF POWERS

Chapter 9

# DUE PROCESS OF LAW

Chapter 10

# EQUAL PROTECTION

Chapter 11

# MISCELLANEOUS CLAUSES:
# 14TH AM. PRIVILEGES & IMMUNITIES; TAKING;
# CONTRACTS; RIGHT TO BEAR ARMS;
# EX POST FACTO; BILL OF ATTAINDER

Chapter 12

# STATE ACTION

Chapter 13

# CONGRESSIONAL ENFORCEMENT
# OF CIVIL RIGHTS

Chapter 14

# FREEDOM OF EXPRESSION

Chapter 15

# FREEDOM OF RELIGION

Chapter 16

# JUSTICIABILITY

# Preface

Thanks for buying this book.

This new edition includes coverage of the Supreme Court's term that ended in June 2008. That term included the landmark case on the Second Amendment (*D.C. v. Heller*), a major case on separation-of-powers and habeas corpus (*Boumediene*) and an important case on the free-speech aspects of campaign finance (*Davis v. F.E.C.*), all of which are extensively covered here.

Here are some of this book's special features:

- **"Casebook Correlation Chart"** — This chart, located just after this Preface, correlates each section of our Outline with the pages covering the same topic in the four leading Con Law casebooks.

- **"Capsule Summary"** — This is a 92-page summary of the key concepts of Constitutional Law, specially designed for use in the last week or so before your final exam.

- **"QuizYourself"** — Either at the end of the chapter, or after major sections of a chapter, we give you short-answer questions so that you can exercise your analytical muscles. There are over 100 of these questions, each written by me.

- **"Exam Tips"** — These alert you to what issues repeatedly pop up on real-life Con Law exams, and what factual patterns are commonly used to test those issues. We created these Tips by looking at literally hundreds of multiple-choice and essay questions asked by law professors and bar examiners. You'd be surprised at how predictable the issues and fact-patterns chosen by profs really are!

I intend for you to use this book both throughout the semester and for exam preparation. Here are some suggestions about how to use it:[1]

1. The book seems (and is) *big*. But don't panic. The actual text includes over 60 pages of *Quiz Yourself* short-answer questions, plus lots of *Exam Tips*. Anyway, you don't have to read everything in the book — there are lots of special features that you may or may not decide to take advantage of.

2. During the semester, use the book in preparing each night for the next day's class. To do this, first read your casebook. Then, use the *Casebook Correlation Chart* to get an idea of what part of the outline to read. Reading the outline will give you a sense of how the particular cases you've just read in your casebook fit into the overall structure of the subject. You may want to use a yellow highlighter to mark key portions of the *Emanuel*.

3. If you make your own outline for the course, use the *Emanuel* to give you a structure, and to supply black letter principles. You may want to rely especially on the *Capsule Summary* for this purpose. You are hereby authorized to copy small portions of the *Emanuel* into your own outline, provided that your outline will be used only by you or your study group, and provided that you are

---

1. The suggestions below relate only to this book. I don't talk about taking or reviewing class notes, using hornbooks or other study aids, joining a study group, or anything else. This doesn't mean I don't think these other steps are important — it's just that in this Preface I've chosen to focus on how I think you can use this outline.

the owner of the *Emanuel*.

4. When you first start studying for exams, read the *Capsule Summary* to get an overview. This will probably take you about one day.

5. Either during exam study or earlier in the semester, do some or all of the *Quiz Yourself* short-answer questions. You can find these quickly by looking for *Quiz Yourself* entries in the Table of Contents. When you do these questions: (1) record your short "answer" on the small blank line provided after the question, but also: (2) try to write out a "mini essay" on a separate piece of paper. Remember that the only way to get good at writing essays is to write essays.

6. Three or four days before the exam, review the *Exam Tips* that appear at the end of each chapter. You may want to combine this step with step **5**, so that you use the Tips to help you spot the issues in the short-answer questions. You'll also probably want to follow up from many of the Tips to the main outline's discussion of the topic.

7. The night before the exam: (1) do some *Quiz Yourself* questions, just to get your thinking and writing juices flowing; and (2) re-scan the *Exam Tips* (spending about 2-3 hours).

Good luck in your Con Law course. If you'd like any other publication of Aspen Publishers, you can find it at your bookstore or at **http://lawschool.aspenpublishers.com**.

Steve Emanuel
Larchmont NY
August 2008

# CASEBOOK CORRELATION CHART

(**Note:** general sections of the outline are omitted from this chart. **NC** = not directly covered by this casebook.)

| Emanuel's Constitutional Law Outline (*by chapter and section heading*) | Sullivan & Gunther **Constitutional Law** (16th ed. 2007) | Stone, Seidman, Sunstein, Tushnet & Karlan **Constitutional Law** (5th ed. 2005) | Rotunda, **Modern Constitutional Law** (8th ed. 2007) | Cohen, Varat & Amar **Constitutional Law** (12th ed. 2005) | Chemerinsky, **Constitutional Law** (2d ed. 2005) |
|---|---|---|---|---|---|
| CHAPTER 2 **THE SUPREME COURT'S AUTHORITY** | | | | | |
| I. Review of Acts of Congress (*Marbury v. Madison*) | 1-15 | 29-51 | 1-9 | 25-37 | 1-9 |
| II. Review of State Court Decisions | 15-21 | 51-60 | 9-28 | 44-56 | 9-10 |
| III. Congress' Control of Federal Court Jurisdiction | 28-29 | 77-89 | 28-38 | 37-43 | 24-30 |
| IV. The Supreme Court's Jurisdiction Today | NC | 159-162 | 28-29 | 48-49, 56-59 | NC |
| CHAPTER 3 **FEDERALISM AND FEDERAL POWER GENERALLY** | | | | | |
| I. The Concept of Federalism | 60-62 | 70-74, 165-169 1584-1588 | NC | 127-134 | 109-112 |
| II. *McCulloch v. Maryland* | 62-76 | 61-77 | 71-82 | 134-143 | 99-109 |
| III. State Oversight of the Federal Government — the Term Limits Problem | 77-81 | 163-165, 354-355 | 453-476 | 143-148 | 90-91 |
| CHAPTER 4 **THE FEDERAL COMMERCE POWER** | | | | | |
| I. The Commerce Clause Generally | 82-83 | 177-185 | NC | 162-163 | 112-113 |
| II. Cases Prior to 1933 | 83-91 | 170-175, 185-192 | 168-186 | 162-166 | 113-118, 125-129 |
| III. Court Barriers to the New Deal | 91-96 141-178 | 192-200 | 186-192 | 166-169 | 118-124 |
| IV. The Modern Trend | 96-126 | 175-177, 200-229 | 192-203, 220-249 | 169-193 | 129-144, 153-176 |
| V. The Tenth Amendment as a Limit on Congress' Power | 126-143 | 330-356 | 250-283 | 221-256 | 144-152, 176-197 |
| CHAPTER 5 **OTHER NATIONAL POWERS** | | | | | |
| I. The Taxing Power | 150-155 | 280-283 | 203-207 | 193-196 | 198 |
| II. The Spending Power | 155-166 | 283-296 | 208-220 | 196-203 | 198-207 |
| III. The War, Treaty, and Foreign Affairs Powers | 167-173 | 296-299, 330-333 | 324-350 | 203-213 | 327-331 |
| CHAPTER 6 **TWO LIMITS ON STATE POWER: THE COMMERCE CLAUSE AND CONGRESSIONAL ACTION** | | | | | |
| I. The Dormant Commerce Clause —Regulation | 174-222 | 229-273 | 83-139 | 148-162, 275-354 | 381-431 |
| II. State Taxation of Interstate Commerce | 240 | 273-275 | 157-167 | 271-275 | NC |
| III. Congressional Action - Preemption and Consent | 229-240 | 275-278 | 149-157 | 377-392 | 366-381 |

# CASEBOOK CORRELATION CHART (continued)

| Emanuel's Constitutional Law Outline *(by chapter and section heading)* | Sullivan & Gunther **Constitutional Law** (16th ed. 2007) | Stone, Seidman, Sunstein, Tushnet & Karlan **Constitutional Law** (5th ed. 2005) | Rotunda, **Modern Constitutional Law** (8th ed. 2007) | Cohen, Varat & Amar **Constitutional Law** (12th ed. 2005) | Chemerinsky, **Constitutional Law** (2d ed. 2005) |
|---|---|---|---|---|---|
| **CHAPTER 7** **INTERGOVERNMENTAL IMMUNITIES AND INTERSTATE RELATIONS** | | | | | |
| I. Tax Immunities | 240-241 | NC | 80-82 | NC | NC |
| II. Federal Immunity from State Regulation | 241-242 | NC | NC | NC | NC |
| III. State Immunity from Federal Regulation | 241-242 | 330-356 | NC | 221-256 | NC |
| IV. Interstate Relationships | 22-229, 242-243 | 252-253, 825-826 | 139-148 | 354-368, 469-471 | 432-443 |
| **CHAPTER 8** **SEPARATION OF POWERS** | | | | | |
| I. Domestic Policy and the Separation of Powers | 245-260, 291-306 | 357-375, 417-429 | 290-297, 341-349, 408-423 | 393-400, 423-442 | 271-280, 287-292, 299-307 |
| II. Foreign Affairs and the War Powers | 260-291 | 375-405 | 284-324 | 400-404 | 320-327 |
| III. Appointment and Removal of Executive Personnel (Including Impeachment) | 306-320 | 429-445 | 424-452 | 442-453 | 307-320 |
| IV. Legislative and Executive Immunity | 320-338 | 405-417 | 365-407 | 453-464 | 280-287, 354-364 |
| **CHAPTER 9** **DUE PROCESS OF LAW** | | | | | |
| I. The Bill of Rights and the States | 354-361 | 717-724, 734-741 | 496-501 | 467-468, 471-474, 489-512 | 446-448, 458-468 |
| II. Substantive Due Process — Before 1934 | 362-375 | 741-757 | 477-492 | 513-523 | 521-539 |
| III. Substantive Due Process — The Modern Approach to Economic and Social-Welfare Regulation | 375-384 | 757-768 | 492-496 | 523-533 | 539-558 |
| IV. Substantive Due Process — Protection of Non-Economic Rights | | | | | |
| Early non-economic cases | 413-414 | 845 | 851-853 | 582-584 | 839-842, 847-850 |
| *Griswold v. Connecticut* | 415-423 | 845-857 | 854-862 | 584-590 | 850-858 |
| *Roe v. Wade* | 424-429 | 857-869 | 864-872 | 621-633 | 858-866 |
| Modification of *Roe* by *Casey* | 434-443 | 884-904 | 876-895 | 633-659 | 867-878, 897-901 |
| Post-*Roe* developments | 429-434, 443-450 | 869-884, 904-916 | 862, 872-876, 896-899 | 659-663 | 901-905, 878-896 |
| Family Relations | 450-456 | 916-929 | 863-864 | 590-621 | 821-839, 842-847 |
| Sexuality, Incl. Homosexuality | 456-469 | 929-949 | 899-922 | 664-676 | 920-932 |
| The Right to Die | 469-480 | 950-965 | 922-943 | 676-689 | 905-920 |
| Rights of the Mentally Retarded | 469 | NC | NC | NC | NC |
| V. Procedural Due Process | 273-282, 480-485 | 967-988 | 307-324, 501-537 | 404-422, 534-536, 1098-1130 | 332-342, 1006-1043 |

# CASEBOOK CORRELATION CHART (continued)

| Emanuel's Constitutional Law Outline *(by chapter and section heading)* | Sullivan & Gunther **Constitutional Law** (16th ed. 2007) | Stone, Seidman, Sunstein, Tushnet & Karlan **Constitutional Law** (5th ed. 2005) | Rotunda, **Modern Constitutional Law** (8th ed. 2007) | Cohen, Varat & Amar **Constitutional Law** (12th ed. 2005) | Chemerinsky, **Constitutional Law** (2d ed. 2005) |
|---|---|---|---|---|---|
| **CHAPTER 10** **EQUAL PROTECTION** | | | | | |
| I. Introduction | 486-487 | 504-506, 516-519 | NC | 690-697 | 617-623 |
| II. Economic and Social Laws — The "Mere Rationality" Test | 613-638 | 501-523, 666-689 | 642-649 | 697-712, 918-935 | 623-646, 807-813 |
| III. Suspect Classifications, Especially Race | 487-517 | 447-500, 523-576 | 649-686 | 712-754, 800-824 | 646-706 |
| IV. Affirmative Action and "Benign" Discrimination | 517-571 | 576-622 | 686-734, 979-993 | 825-901, 960-997 | 706-751 |
| V. Classifications Based on Sex | 572-604 | 622-666 | 755-778 | 754-800 | 752-789 |
| VI. Classifications Based on Alienage | 604-608 | 689-700 | 734-748 | 901-911 | 789-804 |
| VII. Illegitimacy | NC | 713-714 | 749-755 | 911-918 | 804-807 |
| VIII. Mental Retardation and Mental Illness | 608-613 | 710-713 | 788-789 | 918-926 | 810-811 |
| IX. General Principles of Middle-Level Scrutiny | NC | NC | NC | NC | NC |
| X. Fundamental Rights | 614, 638-643, 651-673, 1162-1167 | 700-710, 768-844 | 778-850 | 935-936, 998-1096 | 811-821, 935-1006 |
| **CHAPTER 11** **MISCELLANEOUS CLAUSES: 14TH AM. PRIVILEGES & IMMUNITIES; TAKING; CONTRACTS; EX POST FACTO; BILLS OF ATTAINDER** | | | | | |
| I. The 14th Amendment's Privileges and Immunities Clause | 340-354 | 724-733 | 477-483, 843 | 474-486 | 448-458 |
| II. The "Taking Clause" | 384-408 | 989, 1004-1047 | 555-575 | 551-582 | 574-616 |
| III. The "Contract Clause" | 408-413 | 989-1004 | 544-555 | 469, 536-551 | 558-574 |
| IV. *Ex Post Facto* Laws | NC | NC | NC | NC | NC |
| V. Bills of Attainder | NC | NC | 537-544 | NC | NC |
| **CHAPTER 12** **STATE ACTION** | | | | | |
| I. Introduction | 675-680 | 1584-1589 | 576-583 | 1131-1137 | 469-474 |
| II. The "Public Function" Approach | 680-683 | 1626-1648 | 583-595 | 1137-1146 | 474-487 |
| III. "Nexus" — The Significance of State Involvement | 683-697 | 1589-1626 | 595-641 | 1146-1180 | 487-518 |
| **CHAPTER 13** **CONGRESSIONAL ENFORCEMENT OF CIVIL RIGHTS** | | | | | |
| II. Congress' Power to Reach Private Conduct | 697-707 | 327-330 | 962-974 | 1184-1197 | 207-211 |
| III. Congress' Power to Remedy Constitutional Violations, or to Modify Constitutional Rights | 707-740 | 299-327 | 944-962, 974-979 | 1197-1247 | 211-222, 235-258 |

# CASEBOOK CORRELATION CHART (continued)

| Emanuel's Constitutional Law Outline (by chapter and section heading) | Sullivan & Gunther **Constitutional Law** (16th ed. 2007) | Stone, Seidman, Sunstein, Tushnet & Karlan **Constitutional Law** (5th ed. 2005) | Rotunda, **Modern Constitutional Law** (8th ed. 2007) | Cohen, Varat & Amar **Constitutional Law** (12th ed. 2005) | Chemerinsky, **Constitutional Law** (2d ed. 2005) |
|---|---|---|---|---|---|
| **CHAPTER 14** **FREEDOM OF EXPRESSION** | | | | | |
| I. General Themes | 741-753, 936-941, 943-946 | 1049-1061 | NC | NC | 1045-1084, 1126-1127 |
| II. Advocacy of Illegal Conduct | 753-790 | 1061-1108 | 994-1007 | 1257-1291 | 1151-1173 |
| III. Overbreadth and Vagueness | 1080-1096 | 1142-1151, 1421 | 1556-1557 | 1291-1308 | 1084-1092 |
| IV. Regulation of Context — "Time, Place and Manner" | 791-805, 824-842,- 965-1036, 1121-1123 | 1108-1124, 1234-1343, 1442-1483, 1577-1579 | 1025-1066, 1095-1123 | 1308-1319, 1398-1416, 1463-1519, 1573-1578, 1600-1606, 1684-1688 | 1111-1125, 1132-1136, 1173-1189, 1193-1202, 1222-1252, 1342-1384, 1436-1438 |
| V. Symbolic Expression | 947-965, 992-996 | 1367-1387 | 1123-1128, 1284-1303 | 1566-1578 | 1314-1325, 1384-1388 |
| VI. Defamation and Invasion of Privacy | 805-824 | 1163-1185 | 1199-1233 | 1319-1335 | 1189-1193, 1283-1314 |
| VII. Obscenity | 842-903 | 1208-1234 | 1338-1390 | 1351-1398 | 1109-1111, 1202-1222, 1231-1233 |
| VIII. Commercial Speech | 903-935 | 1185-1208 | 1168-1199 | 1416-1462 | 1252-1283 |
| IX. Regulation in the Context of Political Campaigns | 1137-1140, 1167-1205 | 1387-1420 | 1303-1338 | 1616-1654 | 1325-1342 |
| X. Some Special Contexts | 941-943, 1036-1047, 1066-1080, 1140-1146 | 1343-1367, 1421-1437 | 1066-1095 | 1519-1565, 1679-1684 | 1129-1132, 1136-1137, 1384-1395 |
| XI. Freedom of Association, Denial of Public Jobs or Benefits, and Unconstitutional Conditions | 1047-1065, 1118-1120, 1128-1137, 1146-1162 | 1099-1103, 1420-1442 | 1234-1284 | 1580-1600, 1654-1677 | 1127-1129, 1137-1150, 1395-1416 |
| XII. Special Problems Concerning the Media | 1096-1117, 1126-1128, 1205-1245 | 1125-1162 | 1007-1025, 1128-1168 | 1308-1319, 1335-1351, 1688-1724 | 1092-1109, 1301-1314, 1416-1452 |
| **CHAPTER 15** **FREEDOM OF RELIGION** | | | | | |
| II. The Establishment Clause | 1289-1370 | 1485-1549, 1566-1581 | 1391-1486, 1496-1498 | 1725-1822 | 1456-1486 |
| III. The Free Exercise Clause | 1256-1289 | 1549-1566 | 1486-1514 | 1578-1580, 1822-1845 | 1486-1560 |
| **CHAPTER 16** **JUSTICIABILITY** | | | | | |
| II. Advisory Opinions | 30-32 | 91-92 | 38-44 | 59-62 | 31-34 |
| III. Standing | 32-47 | 92-119 | 1526-1576 | 62-89 | 34-66 |
| IV. Mootness | 47-48 | 158-159 | 1519-1526 | 89-92 | 72-77 |
| V. Ripeness | 47-48 | 158-159 | 1515-1519 | 92-102 | 67-72 |
| VI. The 11th Amendment, and Suits Against States | 143-159 | 310-327 | 44-46 | 256-269 | 222-235, 258-269 |
| VII. Political Questions | 49-59, 643-651 | 119-158 | 46-70, 332-336, 795-807 | 102-123, 936-960 | 77-98 |

# CAPSULE SUMMARY

This Capsule Summary is intended for review at the end of the semester. Reading it is not a substitute for mastering the material in the main outline. Numbers in brackets refer to the pages in the main outline where the topic is discussed. The order of topics is occasionally somewhat different from that in the main outline.

CHAPTER 1

# INTRODUCTION

## I. THREE STANDARDS OF REVIEW

**A. Three standards:** There are three key *standards of review* which reappear constantly throughout Constitutional Law. When a court reviews the constitutionality of government action, it is likely to be choosing from among one of these three standards of review: (1) the *mere rationality* standard; (2) the *strict scrutiny* standard; and (3) the *middle-level review* standard. [2]

**1. Mere rationality:** Of the three standards, the easiest one to satisfy is the *"mere rationality"* standard. When the court applies this "mere rationality" standard, the court will *uphold* the governmental action so long as two requirements are met:

**a. Legitimate state objective:** First, the government must be pursuing a *legitimate governmental objective*. This is a very broad concept — practically any type of health, safety or "general welfare" goal will be found to be "legitimate."

**b. Rational relation:** Second, there has to be a *"minimally rational relation"* between the means chosen by the government and the state objective. This requirement, too, is extremely easy to satisfy: only if the government has acted in a completely *"arbitrary and irrational"* way will this rational link between means and end not be found.

**2. Strict scrutiny:** At the other end of the spectrum, the standard that is hardest to satisfy is the *"strict scrutiny"* standard of review. This standard will only be satisfied if the governmental act satisfies two very tough requirements:

**a. Compelling objective:** First, the *objective* being pursued by the government must be *"compelling"* (not just "legitimate," as for the "mere rationality" standard); and

**b. Necessary means:** Second, the *means* chosen by the government must be *"necessary"* to achieve that compelling end. In other words, the "fit" between the means and the end must be extremely tight. (It's not enough that there's a "rational relation" between the means and the end, which is enough under the "mere rationality" standard.)

**i. No less restrictive alternatives:** In practice, this requirement that the means be "necessary" means that there must not be any *less restrictive* means that would accomplish the government's objective just as well.

**3. Middle-level review:** In between these two review standards is so-called *"middle-level"* review.

**a. "Important" objective:** Here, the governmental objective has to be *"important"* (half way between "legitimate" and "compelling").

      **b.** **"Substantially related" means:**   And, the means chosen by the government must be ***"sub-stantially related"*** to the important government objective. (This "substantially related" standard is half way between "rationally related" and "necessary").

**B.** **Consequences of choice:**   The court's choice of one of these standards of review has two important consequences: [3]

    **1.** **Burden of persuasion:**   First, the choice will make a big difference as to who has the ***burden of persuasion***.

      **a.** **Mere rationality:**   Where the governmental action is subject to the "mere rationality" standard, the ***individual*** who is attacking the government action will generally bear the burden of persuading the court that the action is unconstitutional.

      **b.** **Strict scrutiny:**   By contrast, if the court applies "strict scrutiny," then the ***governmental body*** whose act is being attacked has the burden of persuading the court that its action is constitutional.

      **c.** **Middle-level review:**   Where "middle level" scrutiny is used, it's not certain how the court will assign the burden of persuasion, but the burden will usually be placed on the government.

    **2.** **Effect on outcome:**   Second, the choice of review standard has a very powerful effect on the ***actual outcome***. Where the "mere rationality" standard is applied, the governmental action will ***almost always be upheld***. Where "strict scrutiny" is used, the governmental action will ***almost always be struck down***. (For instance, the Supreme Court applies strict scrutiny to any classification based on race, and has upheld only one such strictly scrutinized racial classification in the last 50 years.) Where middle-level scrutiny is used, there's roughly a 50-50 chance that the governmental action will be struck down.

      **a.** **Exam Tip:**   So when you're writing an exam answer, you've got to concentrate exceptionally hard on choosing the correct standard of review. Once you've determined that a particular standard would be applied, then you might as well go further and make a prediction about the outcome: if you've decided that "mere rationality" applies, you might write something like, "Therefore, the court will almost certainly uphold the governmental action." If you've chosen strict scrutiny, you should write something like, "Therefore, the governmental action is very likely to be struck down."

**C.** **When used:**   Here is a quick overview of the entire body of Constitutional Law, to see where each of these review standards gets used: [3]

    **1.** **Mere rationality:**   Here are the main places where the "mere rationality" standard gets applied (and therefore, the places where it's very hard for the person attacking the governmental action to get it struck down on constitutional grounds):

      **a.** **Dormant Commerce Clause:**   First, the "mere rationality" test is the main test to determine whether a state regulation that affects interstate commerce violates the ***"Dormant Commerce Clause."*** The state regulation has to pursue a legitimate state end, and be rationally related to that end. (But there's a second test which we'll review in greater detail later: the state's interest in enforcing its regulation must also outweigh any ***burden*** imposed on interstate commerce, and any discrimination against interstate commerce.)

      **b.** **Substantive due process:**   Next comes ***substantive due process***. So long as no "fundamental right" is affected, the test for determining whether a governmental act violates substantive due process is, again, "mere rationality." In other words, if the state is pursuing a legitimate objective, and using means that are rationally related to that objective, the state will not be found to have violated the substantive Due Process Clause. So the vast bulk of ***economic regulations***

(since these don't affect fundamental rights) will be tested by the mere rationality standard and almost certainly upheld.

    **c. Equal protection:** Then, we move on to the *equal protection* area. Here, "mere rationality" review is used so long as: (1) *no suspect* or *quasi-suspect classification* is being used; and (2) *no fundamental right* is being impaired. This still leaves us with a large number of classifications which will be judged based on the mere rationality standard, including: (1) almost all economic regulations; (2) some classifications based on alienage; and (3) rights that are not "fundamental" even though they are very important, such as food, housing, and free public education. In all of these areas, the classification will be reviewed under the "mere rationality" standard, and will therefore almost certainly be upheld.

    **d. Contracts Clause:** Lastly, we find "mere rationality" review in some aspects of the *"Obligation of Contracts"* Clause.

**2. Strict scrutiny:** Here are the various contexts in which the court applies *strict scrutiny*: [4]

    **a. Substantive due process/fundamental rights:** First, where a governmental action affects *fundamental rights*, and the plaintiff claims that his *substantive due process* rights are being violated, the court will use strict scrutiny. So when the state impairs rights falling in the *"privacy"* cluster of marriage, child-bearing, and child-rearing, the court will use strict scrutiny (and will therefore probably invalidate the governmental restriction). For instance, government restrictions that impair the right to use contraceptives receive this kind of strict scrutiny.

    **b. Equal protection review:** Next, the court uses strict scrutiny to review a claim that a classification violates the plaintiff's *equal protection* rights, if the classification relates either to a *suspect classification* or a *fundamental right*. "Suspect classifications" include *race*, *national origin*, and (sometimes) *alienage*. "Fundamental rights" for this purpose include the right to *vote*, to be a *candidate*, to have access to the *courts*, and to *travel interstate*. So classifications that either involve any of these suspect classifications or impair any of these fundamental rights will be strictly scrutinized and will probably be struck down.

    **c. Freedom of expression:** Next, we move to the area of *freedom of expression*. If the government is impairing free expression in a *content-based way*, then the court will use strict scrutiny and will almost certainly strike down the regulation. In other words, if the government is restricting some speech but not others, based on the *content of the messages*, then this suppression of expression will only be allowed if necessary to achieve a compelling purpose (a standard which is rarely found to be satisfied in the First Amendment area). Similarly, any interference with the right of *free association* will be strictly scrutinized.

    **d. Freedom of religion/Free Exercise Clause:** Lastly, the court will use strict scrutiny to evaluate any impairment with a person's *free exercise* of religion. Even if the government does *not intend* to impair a person's free exercise of his religion, if it substantially burdens his exercise of religion the government will have to give him an *exemption* from the otherwise-applicable regulation unless denial of an exemption is necessary to achieve a compelling governmental interest.

**3. Middle-level review:** Finally, here are the relatively small number of contexts in which the court uses middle-level review: [5]

    **a. Equal protection/semi-suspect:** First, middle-level review will be used to judge an *equal protection* claim, where the classification being challenged involves a *semi-suspect* trait. The two traits which are considered semi-suspect for this purpose are: (1) *gender*; and (2) *illegitimacy*. So any government classification based on gender or illegitimacy will have to be "substantially related" to the achievement of some "important" governmental interest.

> b.  **Contracts Clause:**   Second, certain conduct attacked under the Obligation of Contracts Clause will be judged by the middle-level standard of review.
>
> c.  **Free expression/non-content-based:**   Finally, in the First Amendment area we use a standard similar (though not identical) to the middle-level review standard to judge government action that impairs expression, but does so in a ***non-content-based*** manner. This is true, for instance, of any content-neutral ***"time, place and manner"*** regulation.

# THE SUPREME COURT'S AUTHORITY AND THE FEDERAL JUDICIAL POWER

## I.  THE SUPREME COURT'S AUTHORITY AND THE FEDERAL JUDICIAL POWER

**A.** *Marbury* **principle:**   Under *Marbury v. Madison*, it is the Supreme Court, not Congress, which has the authority and duty to declare a congressional statute unconstitutional if the Court thinks it violates the Constitution. [8-9]

**B.  Supreme Court review of state court decision:**   The Supreme Court may review state court opinions, but only to the extent that the decision was decided ***based on federal law.*** [10-11]

> **1.  "Independent and adequate state grounds":**   Even if there is a federal question in the state court case, the Supreme Court may not review the case if there is an "***independent and adequate***" state ground for the state court's decision. That is, if the same result would be reached even had the state court made a different decision on the federal question, the Supreme Court may not decide the case. This is because its opinion would in effect be an "advisory" one. [11]
>
> > a.  **Violations of state and federal constitutions:**   If a state action violates the ***same clause*** of both state and federal constitutions (e.g., the Equal Protection Clause of each), the state court decision may or may not be based on an "independent" state ground. If the state court is saying, "This state action would violate our state constitution whether or not it violated the federal constitution," that's "independent." But if the state court is saying, "Based on our reading of the constitutional provision (which we think has the same meaning under both the state and federal constitutions), this state action violates both constitutions," this is ***not*** "independent," so the Supreme Court may review the state court decision. [12]
>
> **2.  Review limited to decisions of highest state court:**   Federal statutes limit Supreme Court review to decisions of the ***highest state court available***. But this does not mean that the top-ranking state court must have ruled on the ***merits*** of the case in order for the Supreme Court to review it. All that is required is that the case be heard by the highest state court ***available*** to the petitioner. (*Example:* A state trial court finds a particular state statute to be valid under the federal Equal Protection Clause. An intermediate appellate court in the state affirms; the highest state court refuses to hear an appeal from the affirmance. As a matter of both the federal judicial power and federal statutes, the Supreme Court may hear this case, because the intermediate appellate court was the highest court "available" to the petitioner.)

**C.  Federal judicial power:**   Article III, Section 2 sets out the federal judicial power. This includes, among other things: (a) cases arising under the ***Constitution*** or the ***"laws of the U.S.*** *"* (i.e., cases posing a "federal question"); (b) cases of ***admiralty***; (c) cases between ***two or more states***; (d) cases between ***citizens of different states***; and (e) cases between a state or its citizens and a ***foreign country or foreign citizen***. Note that this does ***not*** include cases where both parties are citizens (i.e., residents) of the same state, and no federal question is raised. [12]

## II. CONGRESS' CONTROL OF FEDERAL JUDICIAL POWER

A. **Congress' power to decide:** *Congress* has the general power to **decide what types of cases the Supreme Court may hear**, so long as it doesn't expand the Supreme Court's jurisdiction beyond the federal judicial power (as listed in the prior paragraph.) [*Ex parte McCardle*] [13-14]

B. **Lower courts:** Congress also may decide what **lower federal courts** there should be, and what cases they may hear. Again, the outer bound of this power is that Congress can't allow the federal courts to hear a case that is not within the federal judicial power. [14]

> **Example 1:** Congress may cut back the jurisdiction of the lower federal courts pretty much whenever and however it wishes. Thus Congress could constitutionally eliminate diversity jurisdiction (i.e., suits between citizens of different states), even though such suits are clearly listed in the Constitution as being within the federal judicial power.

> **Example 2:** But Congress could not give the lower federal courts jurisdiction over cases between two citizens of the same state, where no federal issue is posed. The handling of such a case by the federal courts would simply go beyond the federal judicial power as recited in the Constitution.

CHAPTER 3

# FEDERALISM AND FEDERAL POWER GENERALLY

## I. THE CONCEPT OF FEDERALISM

A. **The federalist system:** We have a *"federalist"* system. In other words, the national government and the state governments co-exist. Therefore, you always have to watch whether some power being asserted by the federal government is in fact allowed under the Constitution, and you must also watch whether some power asserted by the states is limited in favor of federal power. [19]

B. **Federal government has limited powers:** The most important principle in this whole area is that the federal government is one of **limited, enumerated powers**. In other words, the three federal branches (Congress, the executive branch, and the federal courts) can only assert powers **specifically granted** to them by the United States Constitution. So any time Congress passes a statute, or the President issues, say, an Executive Order, or the federal courts decide a case, you've got to ask: What is the enumerated, specified power in the U.S. Constitution that gives the federal branch the right to do what it has just done? (This is very different from what our Constitution says about the powers of *state* governments: state governments can do whatever they want as far as the U.S. Constitution is concerned, unless what they are doing is **expressly forbidden** by the Constitution.) [19]

1. **No general police power:** The most dramatic illustration of this state/federal difference is the general *"police power."* Each state has a general police power, i.e., the ability to regulate solely on the basis that the regulation would enhance the welfare of the citizenry. But there is **no general federal police power**, i.e., no right of the federal government to regulate for the health, safety or general welfare of the citizenry. Instead, each act of federal legislation or regulation must come within one of the very specific, enumerated powers (e.g., the Commerce Clause, the power to tax and spend, etc.).

a. **Tax and spend for general welfare:** Congress *does* have the right to "lay and collect taxes … to pay the debts and provide for the … general welfare of the United States. … " (Article I, Section 8.) But the phrase "provide for the … general welfare" in this sentence modifies "lay and collect taxes … to pay the debts. … " In other words, the power to tax and spend is subject to the requirement that the general welfare be served; there is no ***independent*** federal power to provide for the general welfare.

C.  **"Necessary and Proper" Clause:**  In addition to the very specific powers given to Congress by the Constitution, Congress is given the power to "make all laws which shall be ***necessary and proper*** for carrying into execution" the specific powers. The "Necessary and Proper" Clause means that if Congress is seeking an ***objective*** that is within the specifically enumerated powers, then Congress can use ***any means*** that is: (1) ***rationally related*** to the objective Congress is trying to achieve; and (2) is not specifically forbidden by the Constitution. [21-23]

D.  **Can't violate specific constitutional provision:**  Even where congressional action appears to fall within a specific grant of power, the federal action may not, of course, violate some ***other*** specific constitutional guarantee. In other words, congressional (or other federal) action must satisfy ***two*** tests to be constitutional: (1) it must fall within some specific grant of power under the Constitution; and (2) it must not violate any specific constitutional provision. [20]

CHAPTERS 4, 5 AND 8
# POWERS OF THE FEDERAL GOVERNMENT; THE SEPARATION OF POWERS

## I.  POWERS OF THE THREE FEDERAL BRANCHES

A.  **Powers of the three branches:**  Here is a summary of the powers of the ***three branches*** of the federal government:

  1.  **Congress:**  Here are the main powers given to Congress [20]:

    a.  **Interstate commerce:**  Congress has the power to ***regulate interstate commerce***, as well as foreign commerce.

    b.  **Taxing and spending:**  Congress has the power to ***tax*** and the power to ***spend***.

    c.  **DC:**  Congress can regulate the ***District of Columbia***.

    d.  **Federal property:**  Congress has power to regulate and dispose of ***federal property***.

    e.  **War and defense:**  Congress can ***declare war***, and can establish and fund the armed forces.

    f.  **Enforcement of Civil War amendments:**  Congress can ***enforce*** the ***post-Civil War amendments***. (For instance, under its power to enforce the Thirteenth Amendment's abolition of slavery, Congress can ban even private intrastate non-commercial conduct.)

  2.  **President:**  Here are the main powers of the President:

    a.  **Execution of laws:**  The President holds the ***"executive power."*** That is, he ***carries out*** the laws made by Congress. It is his obligation to make sure the laws are "faithfully executed."

    b.  **Commander in Chief:**  He is ***Commander in Chief*** of the armed forces. So he directs and leads our armed forces (but he cannot declare war — only Congress can do this.)

    c.  **Treaty and foreign affairs:**  The President can make ***treaties*** with foreign nations (but only if two-thirds of the Senate approves). He appoints ***ambassadors.*** Also, he effectively controls our ***foreign policy*** — some of this power over foreign policy stems from his right to appoint ambassadors, but much is simply ***implied*** from the nation's need to speak with a single voice in foreign affairs (so that congressional involvement in the details of foreign affairs will generally not be appropriate).

d. **Appointment of federal officers:** The President appoints all *federal officers*. These include *cabinet members*, *federal judges* and *ambassadors*. (But the Senate must approve all such federal officers by majority vote.) As to "*inferior* [federal] officers," it's up to Congress to decide whether these should be appointed by the President, by the judicial branch, or by the "heads of departments" (i.e., cabinet members). (But Congress can't make these lower-level appointments itself; it may merely decide who *can* make these appointments.)

e. **Pardons:** The President can issue *pardons*, but only for federal offenses. (Also, he can't pardon anyone who has been impeached and convicted.)

f. **Veto:** The President may *veto* any law passed by both houses (though this veto may be *overridden* by a 2-3's majority of each house.) If the President doesn't veto the bill within 10 days after receiving it, it becomes law (unless Congress has adjourned by the 10th day after it sent him the bill — this is the so-called "pocket veto").

3. **Judiciary:** The federal *judiciary* may decide "cases" or "controversies" that fall within the federal judicial power. See the section on "Federal Judicial Power" in the chapter called "The Supreme Court's Authority and the Federal Judicial Power," above.

## II. THE FEDERAL COMMERCE POWER

A. **Summary:** Probably Congress' most important power is the power to "*regulate Commerce* … among the several states." (Art. I, §8.) This is the "Commerce power." [27]

> **Exam Tip:** Any time you have a test question in which Congress is doing something, first ask yourself, "Can what Congress is doing be justified as an exercise of the commerce power?" Most of the time the answer will be "yes."

B. **Summary of modern view:** There seem to be *four broad categories* of activities which Congress can constitutionally regulate under the Commerce power:

1. **Channels:** First, Congress can regulate the use of the *"channels"* of interstate commerce. Thus Congress can regulate in a way that is reasonably related to highways, waterways, and air traffic. Presumably Congress can do so even though the activity in question in the particular case is completely intrastate. [44]

2. **Instrumentalities:** Second, Congress can regulate the *"instrumentalities"* of interstate commerce, even though the particular activities being regulated are completely intrastate. This category refers to people, machines, and other "things" used in carrying out commerce. [44]

> **Example:** Probably Congress could say that every truck must have a specific safety device, even if the particular truck in question was made and used exclusively within a single state.

3. **Articles moving in interstate commerce:** Third, Congress can regulate *articles moving* in interstate commerce. [44]

> **Example:** The states and private parties keep information about the identities of drivers. Since this information gets exchanged across state lines (e.g., from states to companies that want to sell cars), the information is an article in interstate commerce and Congress may regulate how it's used. [*Reno v. Condon*]

4. **"Substantially affecting" commerce:** Finally, the biggest (and most interesting) category is that Congress may regulate those activities having a *"substantial effect"* on interstate commerce. [*U.S. v. Lopez.*] As to this category, the following rules now seem to apply: [44]

a. **Activity is commercial:** If the activity itself is arguably *"commercial,"* then it doesn't seem to matter whether the *particular instance* of the activity directly affects interstate commerce, as long as the instance is part of a general class of activities that, ***collectively***, substantially affect interstate commerce. So even purely intrastate activities can be regulated if they're directly "commercial." This is especially true where Congress regulates the intrastate commercial activities as part of a ***broad scheme*** to regulate interstate commerce in the same activity. [44]

**Example:** In the federal Controlled Substances Act (CSA), Congress outlaws all distribution and possession of marijuana. California then makes it legal under state law for a Californian to cultivate marijuana for her own personal medicinal use. The U.S. seeks to prevent P, a Californian, from taking advantage of this state-law loophole. P asserts that the application of the CSA to bar P from personally cultivating marijuana for her own personal medical use is beyond Congress' Commerce powers.

*Held*, Congress' Commerce powers extended to this regulation of P's own cultivation and use. Marijuana is a commercial commodity, and the CSA was regulating interstate commerce in that commodity. Congress reasonably feared that if it exempted personal — and thus "intrastate" — cultivation and use of marijuana for medical purposes, some of the marijuana so cultivated would be illegally drawn into the interstate market, jeopardizing Congress' overall scheme of banning the drug. So the private cultivation of marijuana by people like P, even though purely an intrastate activity, fell within Congress' Commerce power. [*Gonzales v. Raich*] [40]

b.  **Activity is not commercial:** But if the activity itself is ***not "commercial,"*** then there will apparently have to be a ***pretty obvious connection*** between the activity and interstate commerce. [45]

**Example 1:** Congress makes it a federal crime to possess a firearm in or near a school. The act applies even if the particular gun never moved in (or affected) interstate commerce. *Held*, in enacting this statute Congress went beyond its Commerce power. To fall within the Commerce power, the activity being regulated must have a "substantial effect" on interstate commerce. The link between gun-possession in a school and interstate commerce is too tenuous to qualify as a "substantial effect," because if it did, there would be essentially no limit to Congress' Commerce power. [*U.S. v. Lopez*]

**Example 2:** Congress says that any woman who is the victim of a violent gender-based crime may bring a civil suit against the perpetrator in federal court. *Held*, Congress went beyond its Commerce power. Although it may be true that some women's fear of gender-based violence dissuades them from working or traveling interstate, gender-based violence is not itself a commercial activity, and the connection between gender-based violence and interstate commerce is too attenuated for the violence to have a "substantial effect" on commerce. [*U.S. v. Morrison*]

i.  **Jurisdictional hook:** But where the congressional act applies only to particular activities each of which has a direct link to interstate commerce, then the act will probably be within the Commerce power. Thus the use of a ***"jurisdictional hook"*** will probably suffice. (*Example*: Suppose the statute in *Lopez* by its terms applied only to in-school gun possession if the particular gun had previously moved in interstate commerce. This would probably be enough of a connection to interstate commerce to qualify.) [43]

c.  **Little deference to Congress:** The Court ***won't*** give much ***deference*** (as it used to) to the fact that Congress ***believed*** that the activity has the requisite "substantial effect" on interstate commerce. The Court will basically decide this issue for itself, from scratch. It certainly will no longer be enough that Congress had a ***"rational basis"*** for believing that the requisite effect existed — the effect must *in fact* exist to the Court's own independent satisfaction. [*Lopez.*] [45]

    **d. Traditional domain of states:** If what's being regulated is an activity the regulation of which has *traditionally* been the *domain of the states*, and as to which the states have expertise, the Court is less likely to find that Congress is acting within its Commerce power. Thus *education*, *family law* and *general criminal law* are areas where the court is likely to be especially suspicious of congressional "interference." [45]

        **i. National solution:** However, the fact that the activity has traditionally fallen within the states' domain can be *outweighed* by a showing that a *national solution* is needed. This would be so, for instance, where one state's choice heavily affects other states. Regulation of the *environment* is an example, since air and water pollution migrate across state boundaries. The same would be true of regulation of *drug trafficking* (e.g., Congress can regulate forbid cultivation of marijuana, because otherwise, Congress' national ban on the drug might be undermined; see *Gonzales v. Raich*). [40]

**C. The Tenth Amendment as a limit on Congress' power:** The *Tenth Amendment* provides that "the powers not delegated to the United States by the Constitution, nor prohibited by it to the States, are reserved to the States respectively, or to the People." This Amendment today seems to place a small but possibly significant limit on Congress' ability to use its commerce power to *regulate the states*. [47-53]

    **1. Generally-applicable law:** If Congress passes a *generally applicable law*, the fact that the regulation *affects the states* has virtually no practical significance, and the Tenth Amendment never comes into play. If the regulation would be valid if applied to a private party, it is also valid as to the state. [49]

        **Example:** Congress passes minimum-wage and overtime provisions, which are made applicable to all businesses of a certain size. The statute contains no exemption for employees of state-owned mass transit systems. *Held*, the regulation even of state employees here is a constitutional exercise of the commerce power, and is not forbidden by the Tenth Amendment. [*Garcia v. San Antonio Metropolitan Transit Authority*]

    **2. Use of state's law-making mechanisms:** But the Tenth Amendment *does* prevent Congress from interfering in certain ways with a state's *law-making processes*. Congress may not simply "commandeer the legislative processes of the states by directly *compelling them to enact and enforce a federal regulatory program.*" [*New York v. United States*] [50-53]

        **Example:** Congress provides that each state must arrange for the disposal of toxic waste generated within its borders, or else be deemed to "take title" to the waste and thereby become liable for tort damages stemming from it. *Held*, the congressional scheme violates the Tenth Amendment. Congress may not force a state to enact and enforce a federal regulatory program, and this is in effect what Congress has tried to do here. *New York v. United States*, *supra*.

    **a. Administrative actions:** Similarly, Congress may not compel a state or local government's *executive branch* to perform functions, even ones that are easy-to-do and involve no discretion.

        **Example:** Congress can't order local sheriffs to perform background checks on applicants for handgun permits. [*Printz v. U.S.*] [51]

## III.  THE TAXING AND SPENDING POWERS

**A.  Taxing power:**  Congress has the power to "***lay and collect taxes***." (Art. I, §8.) This is an independent source of congressional power, so it can be used to reach conduct that might be beyond the other sources of congressional power, like the Commerce Clause. [57]

　　**1.  Regulation:**  Congress can probably ***regulate*** under the guise of taxing, so long as there's some real revenue produced. [58-59]

　　**2.  Limits on taxing power:**  There are a few ***limits*** which the Constitution places upon the taxing power:

　　　　**a.  Direct taxes:**  "Direct taxes" must be allocated among the states in proportion to population. This provision is of little practical importance today.

　　　　**b.  Customs duties and excise taxes must be uniform:**  All ***customs duties*** and ***excise taxes*** must be ***uniform*** throughout the United States. (*Example:* Congress may not place a $.10 per-gallon federal excise tax on gasoline sales that take place in New Jersey, and a $.15 per-gallon tax on those that take place in Oklahoma.) [58]

　　　　**c.  No export taxes:**  Congress may not tax any ***exports*** from any state. (*Example:* Congress may not place a tax on all computers which are exported from any state to foreign countries.) [58]

**B.  Spending power:**  Congress also has the power to "pay the debts and provide for the common defense and general welfare of the United States." (Art. I, §8.) This is the "***spending***" power. [59]

　　**1.  Independent power:**  This is an independent power, just like the Commerce power. So Congress could spend to achieve a purely local benefit, even one that it couldn't achieve by regulating under the Commerce power.

　　**2.  Use of conditions:**  Congress may place ***conditions*** upon use of its spending power, even if the congressional purpose is in effect to regulate. Conditions placed upon the doling out of federal funds are usually justified under the "Necessary and Proper" Clause (which lets Congress use any means to seek an objective falling within the specifically-enumerated powers, as long as the means is rationally related to the objective, and is not specifically forbidden by the Constitution). [59]

　　　　**Example:** Suppose Congress makes available to the states certain funds that are to be used for improving the states' highway systems. Congress provides, however, that no state may receive any of these funds unless the state has by statute imposed a speed limit of no higher than 55 mph on all state roads. Even without reference to the Commerce Clause, this is a valid use of congressional power. That's because by the combination of the spending power and the "Necessary and Proper" Clause, Congress is permitted to impose conditions (even ones motivated solely by regulatory objectives) on the use of federal funds.

**C.  "General Welfare" Clause:**  Although, as noted above, Congress can "provide for the common defense and general welfare of the United States," the reference to "general welfare" does ***not*** confer any independent source of congressional power. In other words, no statute is valid solely because Congress is trying to bring about the "general welfare." Instead, the phrase "for the general welfare" describes the circumstances under which Congress may use its "taxing and spending" power. So if Congress is ***regulating*** (rather than taxing and spending), it must find a specific grant of power (like the Commerce Clause), and it's not enough that the regulation will promote the general welfare. [60]

## IV.  THE SEPARATION OF POWERS

**A.  Separation of powers generally:**  Let's now review some of the major practical consequences that come from the fact that each federal branch gets its own set of powers. These practical consequences are collectively referred to as *"separation of powers"* problems. [110-117]

1.  **President can't make the laws:** The most important single separation of powers principle to remember is that the *President cannot make the laws*. All he can do is to *carry out the laws* made by Congress. [110]

    **Example:** During the Korean War, Pres. Truman wants to avert a strike in the nation's steel mills. He therefore issues an "executive order" directing the Secretary of Commerce to seize the mills and operate them under federal direction. The President does not ask Congress to approve the seizure. *Held*, the seizure order is an unconstitutional exercise of the lawmaking authority reserved to Congress. [*Youngstown Sheet & Tube v. Sawyer*]

    a.  **Line Item Veto:** The principle that the President can't make the laws means that the President can't be given a *"line item veto."* That is, if Congress tries to give the President the right to veto individual portions of a statute (e.g., particular expenditures), this will violate the Present-ment Clause. (The Presentment Clause says that bills are enacted into law by being passed by both Houses, then being presented to the President and signed by him.) [*Clinton v. City of New York*] [113]

    b.  **Congress' acquiescence:** But the scope of the President's powers may be at least somewhat expanded by *Congress' acquiescence* to his exercise of the power. This congressional acqui-escence will never be *dispositive*, but in a close case, the fact that Congress acquiesced in the President's conduct may be enough to tip the balance, and to convince the Court that the Pres-ident is merely carrying out the laws rather than making them. [111]

    c.  **Implied powers:** Recall that Congress' powers are somewhat expanded by the "Necessary & Proper" clause — Congress can pass any laws reasonably related to the exercise of any enu-merated power. There's no comparable "Necessary & Proper" clause for the President. But the effect is the same, because of the inherent vagueness of the phrase "shall take care that the laws be faithfully executed..." The Constitution does specifically enumerate some of the Pres-ident's powers (e.g., the pardon power, the commander-in-chief power, etc.) But this specific list is not supposed to be exclusive. Instead of giving a complete list of the President's powers (as is done for Congress), the Constitution gives the President this general "executive" or "law carrying out" power.

        i.  **Consequence:** Consequently, so long as the President's act seems reasonably related to carrying out the laws made by Congress, the Court won't strike that act merely because it doesn't fall within any narrow, enumerated Presidential power. (*Example:* Nothing in the Constitution expressly gives the President prosecutorial discretion (the power to decide whom to prosecute), yet he clearly has this power, because it's part of the broader job of "carrying out the law".)

    d.  **Delegation:** Congress may *delegate* some of its power to the President or the executive branch. This is how federal agencies (which are usually part of the executive branch) get the right to formulate *regulations* for interpreting and enforcing congressional statutes. If Con-gress delegates *excessively* to federal agencies (by not giving appropriate standards), the dele-gation can be struck down — but this is very rare.

2.  **War powers:** Be alert for separation-of-powers issues when the President's *war-related powers* are at stake.

    a.  **Can't declare war:** The President is the Commander-in-Chief of the armed forces. But *only Congress, not the President, can declare war.* The President can commit our armed forces to repel a sudden attack, but he cannot fight a long-term engagement without a congressional declaration of war. [119]

b.  **Congress' ambiguous grant of power to President:**    Presidents sometimes assert that Congress has *intended to delegate* to the President a certain wartime power (e.g., power to commit our armed forces to a particular foreign conflict). The Court now requires relatively *explicit proof* that Congress has intended to give the President a certain war-related power; if it does not find such proof, the Court is likely to hold that the President has exceeded his Commander-in-Chief, executive, or other enumerated powers.

   **Example:** After the 9/11 attacks, Congress passes a Resolution saying that the President may "use all necessary and appropriate force against those ... [who] planned ... or committed ... the attacks." The President argues that by this Resolution, Congress intended to give him the power to set up "military commissions" to try enemy combatants, including D, without the usual pro-defendant procedures found in courts martial. *Held*, Congress did not intend to give the President this power, so he doesn't have it, and his proposed commission to try D is therefore unconstitutional. [*Hamdan v. Rumsfeld*] [112, 120]

c.  **Habeas corpus:** The constitutional right of prisoners — including foreign prisoners of war — to make a *habeas corpus petition* reflects separation-of-powers principles. Under the *"Suspension Clause"* of Art. I, § 9, cl. 2, the government (i.e., the executive branch) may not suspend habeas corpus — the right of a state or federal prisoner to prove to a federal judge that the prisoner is being held in violation of the constitution or federal law — except "when in Cases of Rebellion or Invasion the public Safety may require it." [124]

   **Example:** At the President's urging after 9/11, Congress passes a law that foreigners held by the military as enemy combatants at the U.S. base in Guantanamo Bay, Cuba may not use a habeas corpus petition to a federal district judge to contest the legality of their imprisonment. (Instead, such prisoners are required to appeal to the federal Court of Appeals for the D.C. Circuit, but that court is limited to reviewing the record of the military tribunal that made the enemy-combatant classification, and can't examine newly-discovered evidence.) The Ps, foreigners captured abroad, held at Guantanamo and classified as enemy combatants, seek a ruling that the law unconstitutionally takes away their right to show by habeas petition that they were misclassified as an enemy combatant.

   *Held*, for the Ps. The law violates the Suspension Clause, because the appeal procedure in the law is not an adequate substitute for habeas corpus, and even foreigners imprisoned by the U.S. have habeas rights. Separation-of-powers principles make it vital that the judicial branch keep the power to hear habeas challenges to the executive branch's authority to imprison a person. [*Boumediene v. Bush*]. [125]

3.  **Treaties and executive agreements:**    As noted, the President has the power to enter into a *treaty* with foreign nations, but only if two-thirds of the Senate approves. Additionally, the Court has held that the Constitution implicitly gives the President, as an adjunct of his foreign affairs power, the right to enter into an *"executive agreement"* with a foreign nation, without first getting express congressional consent. [61-62]

4.  **Appointment and removal of executive personnel:**    The President, not Congress, is given the power to *appoint federal executive officers*. This is the "Appointments" Clause. [127-133]

a.  **General scheme:**    More specifically, the scheme is that only the President, not Congress, may appoint "principal," i.e., *high-level* federal officers. Congress cannot appoint "inferior," i.e., *lower-level* federal officials either, but it may say which of three other entities — the President, the Courts, or the Cabinet — may appoint these lower officials. [127-128]

b.  **Congress can't appoint federal executives:**    The most important thing for you to remember about the appointment of federal officers is that *Congress has no power to directly appoint federal executive officers*. [128]

**Example:** Congress establishes the federal Election Commission, which enforces federal campaign laws. The Commission has power to bring civil actions against violators. The statute establishing the Commission allows Congress to appoint a majority of the Commission's members. *Held*, the tasks performed by the Commission are primarily executive, and its members are "officers of the United States." Therefore, the members must be appointed by the President, not Congress. [*Buckley v. Valeo*]

c. **Removal of federal executives:** The power to **remove** federal executive officers basically rests with the President. The President may remove any executive appointee **without cause**. The only exceptions are that the President must **have cause** in order to remove: (1) an officer who is appointed pursuant to a statute specifying the length of the term of office; or (2) an officer who performs a **judicial** or **quasi-judicial** function. [129-130]

**Example:** The President may remove an ambassador at any time, without cause.

i. **Removal by Congress:** Conversely, **Congress** may **not** remove an executive officer. This is true whether the officer is a "principal" or "inferior" one. [*Bowsher v. Synar*] However, Congress can to some extent **limit** the **power of the President** to remove an officer, if Congress specifies a term of office and then provides that removal is allowable only for cause. (*Example:* Congress may say that the Special Prosecutor — an executive officer — may only be removed by the Executive Branch for "good cause" or other inability to perform his duties. [*Morrison v. Olson*]) [130-132]

ii. **Impeachment:** Separately, Congress may remove any executive officer by *impeachment*, discussed below.

d. **Impeachment:** Congress can remove any "officer" of the U.S. (President, Vice President, Cabinet members, federal judges, etc.) by **impeachment**. The House must vote by a **majority** to impeach (which is like an indictment). Then, the Senate conducts the trial; a two-thirds vote of the Senators present is required to convict. Conviction can be for treason, bribery, and other "high crimes and misdemeanors." Probably only serious crimes, and serious non-criminal abuses of power, fall within the phrase "high crimes and misdemeanors." [132-133]

5. **Removal of federal judges:** Federal *judges* cannot be removed by *either* Congress or the President. Article III provides that federal judges shall hold their office during "good behavior." This has been held to mean that so long as a judge does not act improperly, she may not be removed from office. The only way to remove a sitting federal judge is by formal *impeachment* proceedings, as noted above.

a. **Non-Article III judges:** However, the above "life tenure" rule applies only to garden-variety federal judges who hold their positions directly under Article III. Congress is always free to establish what are essentially **administrative** judgeships, and as to these, lifetime tenure is not constitutionally required.

B. **Legislative and executive immunity:**

1. **Speech and Debate Clause:** Members of Congress are given a quite broad immunity by the "Speech and Debate" Clause: "For any speech or debate in either house, [members of Congress] shall not be questioned in any other place." This clause shields members of Congress from: (1) civil or criminal suits relating to their legislative actions; and (2) grand jury investigations relating to those actions. [134]

2. **Executive immunity:** There's no executive branch immunity expressly written into the Constitution. But courts have recognized an implied executive immunity based on separation of powers concepts. [134-136]

   **a. Absolute for President:** The President has *absolute* immunity from civil liability for his *official* acts. [*Nixon v. Fitzgerald*] [134] (There's *no* immunity for the President's *unofficial* acts, including those he committed before taking office. [*Clinton v. Jones*])

   **b. Qualified for others:** But all other federal officials, including presidential aides, receive only *qualified* immunity for their official acts. (They lose this immunity if they violate a "clearly established" right, whether intentionally or negligently.) [*Harlow v. Fitzgerald*] [135]

**3. Executive privilege:** Presidents have a qualified right to refuse to disclose confidential information relating to their performance of their duties. This is called "*executive privilege*." [136-138]

   **a. Outweighed:** Since the privilege is qualified, it may be outweighed by other compelling governmental interests. For instance, the need for the President's evidence in a *criminal trial* will generally outweigh the President's vague need to keep information confidential. [*U.S. v. Nixon*] [136-138]

CHAPTER 6

# TWO LIMITS ON STATE POWER: THE DORMANT COMMERCE CLAUSE AND CONGRESSIONAL ACTION

## I. THE DORMANT COMMERCE CLAUSE

**A. Dormant Commerce Clause generally:** The *mere existence* of the federal commerce power *restricts the states* from *discriminating against*, or *unduly burdening*, interstate commerce. This restriction is called the "*Dormant Commerce Clause*." [68]

**1. Three part test:** A state regulation which affects interstate commerce must satisfy *each* of the following three requirements in order to avoid violating the Dormant Commerce Clause:

   **a.** The regulation must pursue a *legitimate state end*;

   **b.** The regulation must be *rationally related* to that legitimate state end; and

   **c.** The regulatory *burden* imposed by the state on interstate commerce must be *outweighed* by the state's interest in enforcing its regulation.

   **d. Summary:** So to summarize this test, it's both a "*mere rationality*" test (in that the regulation must be rationally related to fulfilling a legitimate state end) plus a separate *balancing test* (in that the benefits to the state from the regulation must outweigh the burdens on interstate commerce). [72]

**2. Discrimination against out-of-staters:** Above all else, be on the lookout for *intentional discrimination against out-of-staters*. If the state is promoting its residents' *own economic interests*, this will not be a legitimate state objective, so the regulation will virtually automatically violate the Commerce Clause.

   **Example:** New York refuses to let a Massachusetts wholesaler set up a receiving station in New York, from which he can buy New York milk to sell it to Massachusetts residents. New York is worried that this will deprive New Yorkers of enough milk. *Held*, this restriction violates the Dormant Commerce Clause — New York is protecting its own citizens' economic interests at the expense of out-of-staters, and this is an illegitimate objective. [*H.P. Hood & Sons v. DuMond*]

3. **Health/safety/welfare regulations:** Regulations that are truly addressed to the state's ***health, safety and welfare*** objectives are usually "legitimate." (But again, this cannot be used as a smoke-screen for protecting residents' own economic interests at the expense of out-of-staters.)

4. **Balancing test:** When you perform the balancing part of the test (to see whether the benefits to the state from its regulation outweigh the unintentional burdens to commerce), pay special attention to whether there are ***less restrictive means*** available to the state: if the state could accomplish its objective as well (or even almost as well) while burdening commerce less, then it probably has to do so. [73-73]

   > **Example**: Wisconsin can't ban all out of state milk, even to promote the legitimate objective of avoiding adulterated milk — this is because the less restrictive means of conducting regular health inspections would accomplish the state's safety goal just as well. [*Dean Milk Co. v. Madison*]

   a. **Lack of uniformity:** A measure that leads to a ***lack of uniformity*** is likely to constitute a big burden on interstate commerce. For instance, if various states' regulations are ***in conflict***, the Court will probably strike the minority regulation, on the grounds that it creates a lack of uniformity that substantially burdens commerce without a sufficiently great corresponding benefit to the state.

5. **Some contexts:** The most standard illustrations of forbidden protectionism are where the state says, *"You can't bring your goods into our state,"* or *"You can't take goods out of our state into your state."* Here are some other contexts where Dormant Commerce Clause analysis may be important:

   a. **Embargo of natural resources:** Laws that prevent ***scarce natural resources*** from moving out of the state where they are found are closely scrutinized. Often, this is just protectionism (e.g., a state charges higher taxes on oil destined for out-of-state than for in-state use.) But even if the state's interest is ***conservation*** or ***ecology***, the measure will probably be struck down if ***less-discriminatory alternatives*** are available. [80]

   b. **Environmental regulations:** Similarly, the states may not ***protect their environment*** at the expense of their neighbors, unless there is no less-discriminatory way to achieve the same result. (*Example:* New Jersey prohibits the importing of most solid or liquid waste into the state. *Held*, this violates the Commerce Clause. Even if the state's purpose was to protect the state's environment or its inhabitants' health and safety, the state may not accomplish these objectives by discriminating against out-of-staters. [*Philadelphia v. New Jersey*]) [82-84]

   c. **"Do the work in our state":** Statutes that pressure out-of-state businesses to ***perform certain operations*** within the state are likely to be found violative of the Dormant Commerce Clause. Such statutes will probably be found to unduly burden interstate commerce. [80-81]

6. **Discrimination by city against out-of-towners:** The dormant Commerce Clause also prevents a ***city or county*** from protecting its own local economic interests by discriminating against both out-of-state and out-of-town (but in-state) producers. (*Example:* Michigan allows each county to decide that it will not allow solid wastes generated outside the county to be disposed of in the county. County X responds by barring both non-Michigan waste and waste generated in Michigan by counties other than X. *Held*, this scheme violates the Dormant Commerce Clause because it is an attempt to protect local interests against non-local interests. The regulation is not saved merely because it discriminates against in-state but out-of-county waste producers as well as out-of-state producers. [*Fort Gratiot Sanitary Landfill v. Mich. Dept. of Nat. Res.*] [78]

7. **Market participant exception:** But there is one key ***exception*** to the Dormant Commerce Clause rules: if the state acts as a ***market participant***, it ***may*** favor local over out-of-state interests. (*Example:* South Dakota owns a cement plant. It favors in-state customers during shortages. *Held*,

this does not violate the Commerce Clause, because the state is acting as a market participant. [*Reeves v. Stake*]) [84-86]

**B. State taxation of interstate commerce:**   Just as state regulation may be found to unduly burden (or discriminate against) interstate commerce, so state ***taxation*** may be found to unduly burden or discriminate against interstate commerce, and thus violate the Commerce Clause. To strike a state tax as violative of the Commerce Clause, the challenger must generally show either: [86-88]

  **1. Discrimination:**   That the state is ***discriminating*** against interstate commerce, by taxing in a way that unjustifiably benefits local commerce at the expense of out-of-state commerce. [87]

  **2. Burdensome:**   Or, that the state's taxing scheme (perhaps taken in conjunction with other states' taxing schemes) unfairly ***burdens*** interstate commerce even though it doesn't discriminate on its face. One way this can happen is if the tax leads to ***unfair cumulative taxation***. The test is whether, if every state applied the same tax, commerce would be unduly burdened.

> **Example:** North Dakota requires every out-of-state mail order vendor who sends mail into the state to collect N.D. use tax on any sales made to N.D. buyers, even if the vendor has no in-state employees. *Held*, this taxing scheme violates the Commerce Clause, because it unduly burdens interstate commerce. If this scheme were allowable, all 6,000 taxing jurisdictions in the U.S. could impose local-tax-collection requirements on all out-of-state vendors, making compliance virtually impossible. [*Quill Corp. v. North Dakota*] [87]

## II. CONGRESSIONAL PRE-EMPTION AND CONSENT; THE SUPREMACY CLAUSE

**A. Congressional pre-emption and consent:**   The discussion above relates only to the "Dormant" Commerce Clause, i.e., the situation in which Congress has not attempted to ***exercise*** its commerce power in a particular area. Now, we consider what happens when Congress does take action in a particular area of commerce. [88]

**B. Pre-emption:**   Congress can ***preempt*** the states from affecting commerce. There are two ways it can do this:

  **1. Conflict:**   First, the congressional statute and the state action may be in ***actual conflict***. If so, the state regulation is automatically invalid. [88] There are two types of direct conflicts:

   **a. Joint compliance impossible:**   First, it may be ***impossible to obey both the state and federal regulations simultaneously.*** (*Example:* Suppose the state requires a certain type of labelling on cereal boxes, and the FDA regulations (done pursuant to Congress' authorization) require a different type of labelling. Since the box can't practically contain both types of labelling, the state's labelling requirement is invalid under the Supremacy Clause.) [88]

   **b. Conflicting objectives:**   Second, the ***objectives*** behind the two sets of regulations may be inconsistent. Here, too, the state regulation must fall even though the regulated party could theoretically comply with both sets simultaneously. [88]

  **2. Federal occupation of field:**   Congress may also pre-empt state regulation not because there is an actual conflict between what Congress does and what the states do, but because Congress is found to have made the decision to ***occupy the entire field***. This is always a question of congressional intent. [89-90]

**C. Consent by Congress:**   Conversely, Congress may ***consent*** to state action that would otherwise violate the Commerce Clause. Congress may even allow a state to discriminate against out-of-staters. [90-91]

**D. The Supremacy Clause:** Article VI, Clause 2, states that "This Constitution, and the Laws of the United States which shall be made in Pursuance thereof … shall be the supreme Law of the Land. … " This is the *"Supremacy Clause."* The rules governing preemption in Commerce-Clause cases (discussed above) derive from the Supremacy Clause. [88]

    **1. Direct conflict:** The most natural application of the Supremacy Clause is that if a state law is *inconsistent with* a valid federal law covering the same subject matter, the state law is invalid.

        **Example:** Congress passes a statute stating that no person shall be required to retire earlier than the age of 65. State X passes a law stating that any university located in State X may require its tenured professors to retire at the age of 60. Assuming that the federal law is a constitutionally-valid exercise of congressional powers (which certainly seems to be the case), the law of State X is invalid under the Supremacy Clause — in the case of a conflict between a federal statute and a state law, the state law must give way.

    **2. Federal silence:** Cases in which there is a direct conflict between a federal law and a state law (as in the above example) are fairly easy to spot as violations of the Supremacy Clause. But the Supremacy Clause may also be violated if the state legislates or regulates in an area that has been *"preempted"* by federal regulation. In other words, if Congress has manifested an intent to *occupy an entire field*, then any state regulation in that field — even if it does not directly conflict with federal regulation — will be found to be invalid because of the Supremacy Clause. Our discussion just above of pre-emption in commerce cases is one illustration of this general congressional power to pre-empt state regulation by occupying a whole field.

CHAPTER 7
# INTERGOVERNMENTAL IMMUNITIES; INTERSTATE RELATIONS

## I. TAX AND REGULATORY IMMUNITIES

**A. Several types of immunities:** There are several kinds of *immunities* produced by our federalist system: [97]

    **1. Federal immunity from state taxation:** The federal government is immune from being *taxed by the states*. [98-98]

        **a. "Legal incidence" standard:** This immunity applies only if the *"legal incidence"* of the tax — not just the practical burden — falls on the federal government. [98]

        **Example:** Suppose a private contractor doing work for the federal government under a cost-plus contract is required to pay a state tax. The fact that the burden of this tax will be passed on to the federal goverment under the contract won't be enough to trigger the immunity. This is so because on these facts, the "legal incidence" of the tax is not on the U.S.

    **2. State immunity from federal taxation:** The *states* have *partial immunity* from federal taxation. What this means is that the federal government can't tax property used in or income from a state's performance of its *basic governmental functions* (*Example:* The federal government probably can't put a property tax on a state's public parks). [98]

    **3. Federal immunity from state regulation:** The federal government is essentially free from *state regulatory interference*. (*Example:* A state cannot set the laws for conduct on a military post located within the state, unless Congress consents.) [99]

    **a. Federal contractors:** State regulation of a federal *contractor* (one performing a contract on behalf of the federal government) may also violate the federal immunity from state regulation. However, as in the state taxation context, the states have greater leeway to regulate federal contractors than to regulate the federal government directly. In general, a state may regulate federal contractors as long as the regulation does not interfere with *federal purposes* or *policies*. For instance, a state regulation that has the effect of *increasing the cost* borne by the federal government under the contract might be invalid as a violation of this immunity.

  **4. State immunity from federal regulation:** The converse immunity, immunity of the *states* from *federal* regulation, exists only in a very theoretical way. In general, federal regulation of the states is valid. However, if a federal regulatory scheme had the effect of preventing the states from exercising their *core functions*, this might be found to be a violation of the Tenth Amendment. [99]

## II. THE INTERSTATE PRIVILEGES AND IMMUNITIES CLAUSE

**A. Interstate Privileges and Immunities:** Article IV of the Constitution says that "the Citizens of each State shall be entitled to all Privileges and Immunities of Citizens in the several States." This is the *"interstate" Privileges and Immunities Clause.* (Be sure you distinguish this from the Privileges and Immunities Clause of the Fourteenth Amendment, which prevents a state from denying certain rights of "national citizenship" (like the right to travel).) [100]

  **1. Standard:** The interstate Privileges and Immunities Clause prevents a state from *discriminating against non-residents*. But it only operates with respect to rights that are *fundamental* to *national unity*. [100]

    **a. What rights are fundamental:** The rights that are "fundamental in the national unity" are all related to *commerce*. Thus the right to *be employed*, the right to *practice one's profession*, and the right to *engage in business* are all fundamental, and are therefore protected by the interstate Privileges and Immunities Clause.

    **Example:** Alaska requires that Alaskan residents be given an absolute preference over non-residents for all jobs on the Alaska oil pipeline. *Held*, since access to employment is a right fundamental to national unity, Alaska's decision to prefer its own citizens over out-of-staters impairs the out-of-staters' rights under the interstate Privileges and Immunities Clause, and is invalid. [*Hicklin v. Orbeck*, the "Alaska Hire" case] [100]

  **2. Two-prong test:** Even if a state does impair an out-of-stater's exercise of a right fundamental to national unity, the state impairment is not necessarily invalid. But the state will lose unless it satisfies a two-pronged test:

    **a. "Peculiar source of evil":** First, the state must show that out-of-staters are a *"peculiar source of the evil"* the statute was enacted to rectify. [101]

    **b. Substantial relation to state objective:** Second, the state must show that its solution (the discriminatory statute) is *"substantially related"* to this "peculiar evil" the out-of-staters represent. Generally, to meet this prong the state must show that there are no *less discriminatory alternatives* that would adequately address the problem. (For instance, in *Alaska Hire*, had Alaska been able to show that there was no other way to combat unemployment than to absolutely prefer in-staters, it would have met this prong.) [101]

  **3. No "market participant" exception:** Recall that a state is immune from Commerce Clause violations if it's acting as a *market participant*. But there's *no* such market participant exception for the Privileges & Immunities Clause. (Thus even if, in the *Alaska Hire* case, Alaska had been hiring the workers itself, its absolute preference for residents would have violated the clause.) [101-103]

4. **Distinguished from Equal Protection:** When a non-resident is discriminated against, he may also have an Equal Protection claim. But there are two key differences:

    a. **Aliens and corporations:** The Equal Protection Clause can apply to *corporations* and to *aliens*; the Privileges & Immunities Clause can't. [103]

    b. **Strict scrutiny:** Conversely, the level of scrutiny given to the state's action is much tougher under Privileges & Immunities Clause than under Equal Protection Clause. Under Equal Protection, non-residency isn't a suspect classification, and therefore the discrimination must just meet a standard of "mere rationality." Under the Privileges & Immunities Clause, by contrast, the statute must survive what amounts to *strict scrutiny* — the non-residents must be a "peculiar source of the evil," and there must not be less-discriminatory alternatives available. [103]

    c. **Tactical tip:** Wherever possible, couch the attack as Privileges & Immunities, rather than Equal Protection, since the level of scrutiny usually makes a dispositive difference.

CHAPTER 9
# THE DUE PROCESS CLAUSE

## I. INTRODUCTION

A. **Two major principles:** For the rest of this outline, we'll be talking about rights guaranteed to individuals by the Constitution. Before we get into the individual rights, there are two general principles that are crucial to remember: [145-146]

1. **Protected against the government:** First, practically all of the individual rights conferred by the Constitution upon individuals *protect only against government action*. They do *not* protect a person against acts by other private individuals. (*Example:* Suppose P is a woman who's two months pregnant, and none of the private hospitals in her state will perform an abortion. P's substantive due process right to an abortion has not been violated, because the government has not interfered with that right.)

    **Note:** The only exception to the "government action only" rule is the Thirteenth Amendment's ban on slavery, which *does* apply to private conduct.

2. **Not directly applicable to states:** The other general principle to remember is the central role of the Fourteenth Amendment's *Due Process* Clause. Many of the important individual guarantees are given by the Bill of Rights (the first ten amendments). For instance, the First Amendment rights of free expression and freedom of religion fall into this category. But the Bill of Rights does *not directly* apply to the states. However, the Fourteenth Amendment's Due Process Clause (which does apply to the states) has been interpreted to make nearly all of the Bill of Rights guarantees applicable to the states — these individual guarantees are "incorporated" into the Bill of Rights. "Incorporation" is discussed further below.

## II. THE 14TH AMENDMENT GENERALLY

A. **Text of 14th Amendment:** Section 1 of the 14th Amendment provides, in full, that: "All persons born or naturalized in the United States, and subject to the jurisdiction hereof, are citizens of the United States and of the State wherein they reside. No State shall make or enforce any law which shall abridge the privileges and immunities of citizens of the United States; nor shall any State deprive any person of life, liberty, or property, without due process of law; nor deny to any person within its jurisdiction the equal protection of the laws." [146]

1.  **Three rights:**   So in one sentence we have three major rights: (1) the right to due process; (2) the right to equal protection; and (3) the right to the privileges and immunities of national citizenship.

B.  **The Bill of Rights and the states:**   One of the major functions of the 14th Amendment's Due Process Clause is to make the ***Bill of Rights*** — that is, the first 10 amendments — applicable to the states. [145]

  1.  **Not directly applicable to states:**   The Bill of Rights is not ***directly*** applicable to the States. The Supreme Court held early on (in 1833) that the Bill of Rights limited only the federal government, not state or municipal governments. [146]

  2.  **Effect of due process clause:**   But enactment of the 14th Amendment in 1868 effectively changed this. The 14th Amendment directly imposes on the states (and local governments as well) the requirement that they not deprive anyone of "life, liberty or property" without due process. Nearly all the guarantees of the Bill of Rights have been interpreted by the Supreme Court as being so important that if a state denies these rights, it has in effect taken away an aspect of "liberty."

  3.  **Application of Bill of Rights to states:**   The Supreme Court has never said that due process requires the states to honor the Bill of Rights as a whole. Instead, the Court uses an approach called ***"selective incorporation"***. Under this approach, each right in the Bill of Rights is examined to see whether it is of ***"fundamental"*** importance. If so, that right is "selectively incorporated" into the meaning of "due process" under the 14th Amendment, and is thus made binding on the states. [146-148]

  4.  **Nearly all rights incorporated:**   By now, nearly ***all rights contained in the Bill of Rights*** have been incorporated, one by one, into the meaning of "due process" (and thus made applicable to the states). [147] The only major Bill of Rights guarantees ***not*** incorporated are:

      a.  **Grand jury:**   The 5th Amendment's right not to be subject to a criminal trial without a ***grand jury indictment*** (so that a state may begin proceedings by an "information," as some states do); and

      b.  **Right to jury in civil cases:**   The 7th Amendment's right to a ***jury trial*** in ***civil*** cases.

  5.  **"Jot-for-jot" incorporation:**   Once a given Bill of Rights guarantee is made applicable to the states, the ***scope*** of that guarantee is interpreted the ***same way*** for the states as for the federal government. The Court has rejected "the notion that the 14th Amendment applies to the states only a 'watered-down' ... version of the individual guarantees of the Bill of Rights." [*Malloy v. Hogan*] [147-148]

      **Example:** The 4th Amendment right not to be subject to an unreasonable search or seizure is interpreted the same way whether the case involves federal or state police — thus if on a given set of facts the FBI would be found to have violated the 4th Amendment, so would local police.

C.  **The federal Due Process Clause:**   We'll generally be discussing the *14th* Amendment's due process clause, which binds the states. But keep in mind that there is also a due process clause in the *5th* Amendment, that is binding on the *federal* government. Both clauses have been interpreted the same way, so that any state action that would be forbidden by the 14th Amendment Due Process Clause is also forbidden to the federal government via the 5th Amendment Due Process Clause. (For instance, exactly the same limits apply to federal and state regulations that impair the right to have an abortion.)[148]

## III.  SUBSTANTIVE DUE PROCESS — ECONOMIC AND SOCIAL WELFARE REGULATION

A. **Substantive due process generally:**  There are two quite different functions that the Due Process Clause serves. Most obviously, it imposes certain *procedural* requirements on governments when they impair life, liberty, or property. (We'll be talking about this "procedural due process" area below.) But the Due Process Clause also limits the *substantive power* of the states to regulate certain areas of human life. This "substantive" component of the Due Process Clause derives mainly from the interpretation of the term *"liberty"* — certain types of state limits on human conduct have been held to so unreasonably interfere with important human rights that they amount to an unreasonable (and unconstitutional) denial of "liberty." [148]

> **Exam Tip:** Any time your fact pattern suggests that a state or federal government is *taking away* some thing or value that could be considered "life," "liberty," or "property," then entirely apart from the issue of whether the government has used proper procedures, you must ask the question: Has the government by carrying out this taking violated the individual's *substantive* interest in life, liberty, or property?

1. **Non-fundamental rights:**  There's an absolutely critical distinction that you must make right at the outset, when you're analyzing a substantive due process problem. That's the distinction between *fundamental* and *non-fundamental* rights. If a right or value is found to be "non-fundamental," then the state action that impairs that right only has to meet the easy *"mere rationality"* test. In other words, it just has to be the case that the state is pursuing a *legitimate governmental objective*, and is doing so with a means that is *rationally related* to that objective.

   a. **Economic regulation:**  Nearly all *economic* regulation (and most *"social welfare"* regulation) will turn out to implicate only non-fundamental rights, and will almost certainly be upheld under this easy-to-satisfy mere rationality standard. So anytime you can't find a fundamental right being impaired, you should presume that the measure does not violate substantive due process.

2. **Fundamental rights:**  But if a state or federal government is impairing a *"fundamental"* right, then it's a different ball game entirely: here, the court uses *strict scrutiny*. Only if the governmental action is *"necessary"* to achieve a *"compelling"* governmental objective, will the government avoid violating substantive due process.

3. **Significance of distinction:**  So 95% of the battle in analyzing a substantive due process problem is deciding whether the right in question is "fundamental" or not. Once you know that, you pretty much know how the case will come out — if the right is not "fundamental," there's almost certainly no substantive due process problem; if the right *is* fundamental, then strict scrutiny will almost certainly result in the measure being invalidated. So as you prepare for your exam, it's worth devoting some significant mental effort to remembering which rights are fundamental.

B. **Economic and social-welfare regulation:**  It is very easy for state *economic regulation* to survive substantive due process attacks. *Since 1937, the Court has not struck down an economic regulation for violating substantive due process.* [154]

1. **Two requirements:**  Today, an economic statute has to meet only two easily-satisfied requirements to be in conformity with substantive due process [154]:

   a. **Legitimate state objective:**  The state must be pursuing a *legitimate state objective*. But virtually any health, safety or "general welfare" goal comes within the state's *"police power"* and is thus "legitimate."

    **b.** **Minimally rationally related:** Second, there must be a *"minimally rational relation"* between the means chosen by the legislature and the state objective. To put it another way, the Court will presume that the statute is constitutional unless the legislature has acted in a completely *"arbitrary and irrational"* way.

  **2.** **Other (non-economic) non-fundamental rights:** Outside the economic area, the same rule applies as long as no *fundamental right* is being affected: the state must merely be pursuing a legitimate state objective by rational means. So most *"social welfare"* legislation merely has to meet this very easy standard. We discuss below what rights are "fundamental" — in summary, these rights relate to sex, marriage, child-bearing and child-rearing, all components of the general "right to privacy." (By contrast, practically no economic rights are "fundamental" — the sole exception may be the right to practice a profession or calling, and even this is not certain.)

    **a.** **General rule:** For now, the important thing to remember is that if the right does *not* fall within this grouping of "fundamental" rights, the state must merely act rationally in pursuit of some health, safety or other "general welfare" goal. [155]

    **Example:** New York sets up a prescription drug reporting scheme, whereby the names and addresses of all patients who receive prescriptions for certain drugs must be reported by doctors, and are placed on a central computer. Some individuals claim that this regulation infringes on their right to avoid government collection of private matters. *Held,* the statute does infringe on a patient's right to keep prescription information secret. But this right is not "fundamental." Therefore, the statute will be sustained as long as the state is acting in pursuit of a legitimate state objective, and has chosen a rational means. Here, these requirements are satisfied. [*Whalen v. Roe*].

    **b.** **Regulation struck down even though right is non-fundamental:** Where the right being regulated is non-fundamental, and the review is therefore mere-rationality, the regulation will usually, *but not always*, be sustained. Most dramatically, regulations that *interfere with sexual expression*, though given mere-rationality review, may be *struck down* as totally irrational.

    **Example:** Laws criminalizing sodomy, enforced principally against gays, have been struck down as failing the rational-relation test, on the theory that they demean homosexuals and interfere with their autonomy, in a way that the Court has deemed "illegitimate." [*Lawrence v. Texas*] [185]

## IV.  SUBSTANTIVE DUE PROCESS — REGULATIONS AFFECTING FUNDAMENTAL RIGHTS

**A.** **Fundamental rights generally:** The rest of our discussion of substantive due process will be solely about fundamental rights. [156]

  **1.** **Strict scrutiny:** If a state or federal regulation is impairing a fundamental right, the court *strictly scrutinizes* the regulation. Here is what it means in practical terms for the Court to apply strict scrutiny to a state or federal regulation that impairs a fundamental right: (1) the objective being pursued by the state must be *"compelling"* (not just "legitimate" as for a non-fundamental right); and (2) the means chosen by the state must be *"necessary"* to achieve that compelling end. In other words, there must not be any *less restrictive means* that would do the job just as well (if there were, then the means actually chosen wouldn't be "necessary"). [156]

    **a.** **Burden of proof:** When strict scrutiny is used, there is an important impact on *who bears the burden of persuasion*. In the usual case in which strict scrutiny is not being used, the person attacking the statute has the burden of showing that the state is pursuing an illegitimate objective, or that the state has chosen a means that is not rationally related to its objective. But if strict scrutiny is used because a "fundamental" right is involved, the burden of proof shifts: now, it's up to the state to show that it's pursuing a compelling objective, and that the means it chose are "necessary" to achieve that objective.

2.  **Rights governed:**   The only rights that have been recognized as "fundamental" for substantive due process purposes are ones related to the loose category ***"right to privacy."*** Sometimes this area is said to involve the "right to ***autonomy***" — what we're really talking about is usually a person's right to ***make his own decisions*** about ***highly personal matters***. This right of privacy or autonomy derives indirectly from several Bill of Rights guarantees, which collectively create a ***"penumbra"*** or ***"zone"*** of privacy. [156]

    a.  **List:**   The list of rights or interests falling within this "right to privacy" or "right to autonomy" include actually just a few related areas: ***marriage***, ***child-bearing***, and ***child-rearing***. So anytime you're looking at a particularly narrow interest and you have to decide whether it's "fundamental," first ask yourself, "Does it fall within the areas of marriage, child-bearing, or child-rearing?" If not, it's probably not "fundamental."

        i.  **Illustrations:**   So the right to ***use birth control***, to ***live together with your family***, to ***direct the upbringing*** and ***education*** of your children, to ***marry*** — these are some (probably most) of the specific interests that are "fundamental."

        ii.  **Non-illustrations:**   By contrast, an interest that does not fall within one of these areas probably is not fundamental — for instance, an adult's interest in having consensual sex outside of marriage seems not to be "fundamental." (The right to ***abortion*** used to be "fundamental," but now seems to be only "quasi-fundamental" after *Planned Parenthood v. Casey*.)

B.  **Birth control:**   Individuals' interest in ***using birth control*** is "fundamental." So whether a person is married or single, he or she has a fundamental interest in contraception, and the state cannot impair that interest without satisfying strict scrutiny. (*Example:* Planned Parenthood cannot be prohibited from supplying condoms or diaphragms to single or married adults who want them. [*Griswold v. Connecticut*]) [158-161]

    1.  **Minors:**   We still don't know whether ***minors*** have a fundamental right to contraception. If this comes up on your exam, just say that there is plausible logic behind viewing a minor's interest in contraception as being either "fundamental" or "non-fundamental." [182]

C.  **Abortion:**   The right of ***abortion*** is the primary example of a right protected by substantive due process. But the right of abortion as it stood under *Roe v. Wade* has been largely overhauled — and ***cut back*** — by ***Planned Parenthood of Southeastern Pennsylvania v. Casey*** (1992). [163-169]

    1.  **The right today:**   In this post-*Casey* world, here is what seems to be the status of abortion: A woman has a constitutionally-protected privacy interest in choosing to have an abortion ***before viability***. However, the state has a somewhat countervailing interest in ***protecting "potential life,"*** even before viability. This conflict seems to yield the following results:

        a.  **No right to ban:**   The state does not have the right to ***ban*** all pre-viability abortions. Also, the state may not even forbid all pre-viability abortions except those necessary to save the life or health of the mother. [169]

        b.  **Regulation:**   However, the state has a far greater ability to ***regulate*** the abortion process than it did before *Casey*. The state may regulate only if it does not place an ***"undue burden"*** on the woman's right to choose a pre-viability abortion. A regulation will constitute an "undue burden" if the regulation "has the purpose or effect of placing a ***substantial obstacle*** in the path of a woman" seeking a pre-viability abortion. [169]

c. **Not a fundamental right that will be strictly scrutinized:** Apparently, abortion is *no longer a fundamental right*, and restrictions on it are *no longer to be strictly scrutinized*. This represents a huge departure from the law as it stood under *Roe v. Wade*.

2. **What constitutes "undue burden":** Most state regulation will apparently *not* constitute an "undue burden," and will thus be sustained.

> **Example 1 (informed consent):** The state may impose an elaborate "informed consent" provision, whereby at least 24 hours before performing an abortion, the physician must inform the woman of the nature of the procedure, the health risks of both abortion and childbirth, the probable gestational age of the fetus, the availability of state-printed materials, etc. *Casey*. [166]

> **Example 2 (partial-birth procedure):** The federal government may outlaw the "partial birth" abortion method, without giving an exception for cases in which the physician believes that the procedure may be needed to safeguard the woman's health. The ban on this procedure is not an undue burden, because Congress has made a credible finding of fact that the partial-birth method is never necessary for the woman's health. *Gonzales v. Carhart* (2007). [175]

3. **Consent:** Even after *Casey*, the state is limited in the extent to which it can require the *consent* of third parties before an abortion is performed.

   a. **Spousal consent:** The state may *not* give a pregnant woman's *spouse* a *veto right* over the woman's abortion decision. [*Planned Parenthood v. Danforth*] In fact, the state may not even require that the woman *notify* her spouse of her intent to get an abortion, even if the state exempts cases of spousal sexual assault or threatened bodily injury. [*Casey*] [166]

   b. **Parental consent:** The state *may* require that an *unemancipated* woman under the age of 18 obtain *parental* consent. The state may also require that this parental consent be "informed," even if this requires an in-person visit by the parent to the facility, and even if it involves a 24-hour waiting period. [167]

      i. **Court hearing:** But if the state does require parental consent, it must give the girl an opportunity to persuade a judge that an abortion is in her best interests. This is a *"judicial bypass."*

      ii. **Emancipation or maturity:** The state must also allow an individualized judicial hearing at which the girl may persuade the court that she is in fact sufficiently *mature* or *emancipated* that she is able to make this decision for herself. If the girl proves this, the abortion must be allowed even if the judge believes that the abortion is not in the girl's best interest.

4. **Public funding:** States may refuse to give *public funding* (e.g., Medicaid) for abortions even though they give such funding for other types of operations. Also, states may prohibit public hospitals from performing abortions. [171-173]

5. **Abortion counseling:** The government may, as a *condition of funding* family-planning clinics, insist that the doctor or other professional *not recommend abortion*, and not refer clinic patients to an abortion provider. [*Rust v. Sullivan*] [172]

6. **Types of abortion:** The state has substantial freedom to place regulations on the *types* of abortions that may be performed.

> **Example:** The federal government may completely outlaw the "partial birth" abortion method, without giving an exception for cases in which the physician believes that the procedure may be needed to safeguard the woman's health. The ban on this procedure is rationally related to the achievement of several state goals, including safeguarding unborn life and making it less likely that a woman will later have profound regret over the particular abortion

method she selected. Also, the ban does not constitute an undue burden on the woman's right to abort, because Congress has made a credible finding of fact that the partial-birth method is never necessary for the woman's health. *Gonzales v. Carhart* (2007). [175]

**D. Family relations:** Whenever the state interferes with a person's decision about how to live his *family life* and *raise his children*, you should be on the lookout to see whether a fundamental right is being interfered with. [182-185]

1. **Right to live together:** For instance, *relatives* have a fundamental right to *live together*. [182-183]

    **Example:** A city may not enact a zoning ordinance that prevents first cousins from living together, because the right of members of a family — even a non-nuclear family — to live together is "fundamental," and any state interference with that right will be strictly scrutinized. [*Moore v. East Cleveland*]

    **Note:** What the Court was protecting in *Moore* was clearly the right of *families* to live together, not the more general right to live with whomever one wants outside of ties of blood and marriage. Thus the Court had previously held [*Belle Terre v. Borass*] that unrelated people had no "fundamental right" to live together, and in *Moore* the Court pointed out that families' rights to live together were different, and much stronger.

2. **Upbringing and education:** Similarly, a parent's right to direct the *upbringing* and *education* of his children is "fundamental."

    **Example 1:** The state may not require parents to send their children to public schools. Parents have a fundamental right to determine how their children will be educated. [*Pierce v. Soc. of Sisters*] [157]

    **Example 2:** A parent has a fundamental interest in deciding who will spend time with the child. Therefore, the state may not award visitation rights to a child's grandparents over the objection of the child's fit custodial parent, unless the state first gives "special weight" to the parent's wishes. [*Troxel v. Granville*]

    a. **Right to continue parenting:** There's also probably a fundamental right to *continue parenting* — so the state can't take away your child just because it thinks a foster home would be "better" for the child. (Even if there's child abuse, the parent still has a fundamental right to parent, but here the state's interest in protecting the child would be "compelling," so putting the child in foster care would probably satisfy strict scrutiny.)

    b. **No relationship:** If a parent has *never married* the other parent, and has never *developed a relationship* with the child (e.g., they have never lived together), then there is probably *not* a fundamental right to continue to be a parent. (So the state may, for instance, deny the non-custodial unwed parent who has never participated in the child's upbringing the right to block an adoption of the child. [*Quilloin v. Walcott*] [185]

3. **Right to marry:** The *right to marry* is also fundamental, so again the state can only interfere with this right by passing strict scrutiny. (*Example:* A state may not forbid anyone from remarrying unless he is not current on all support payments from his prior marriage. [*Zablocki v. Redhail*]) [184]

**E. Adult sex:** There is no general fundamental right to engage in *adult consensual sexual activity*. Therefore, the Court will generally review restrictions on adult consensual sexual activity under the *mere-rationality* test.

1.  **Rational-relation review "with bite":** However, although the Court will generally review restrictions on adult sexual activity under the mere-rationality test, the Court will sometimes ***strike down*** the regulation on the grounds that it interferes with people's sexual autonomy. [185]

    a.  **Homosexual sodomy:** Most dramatically, the Court has ***struck down*** all state laws that ***criminalize homosexual sodomy***, on the grounds that such laws "***demean the lives of homosexual persons***," and thus violate their substantive due process rights. Gays now have "the full right to engage in their [homosexual] conduct without intervention of the government." [*Lawrence v. Texas*] [185]

2.  **Other sexual conduct:** Notwithstanding *Lawrence v. Texas*, the state can almost certainly prohibit, and punish, such adult consensual sexual activities as ***adultery, incest, bestiality and bigamy***, on the grounds that these activities are provably ***harmful***, and their prohibition is therefore not merely an irrational expression of the majority's "moral disapproval." (On the other hand, it's not so clear that states may criminalize ***fornication*** — the Court might hold that this activity is so widespread and unharmful that attempts to ban it should be treated as being as irrational as bans on gay sex.) [193]

3.  **Married people's conduct:** But where the parties are ***married*** (to each other), there probably *is* a fundamental right to have even "deviant" sex, as long as it's not physically dangerous and is consensual. For instance, the state probably may not prohibit oral sex in marriage, since that would fall within the marriage area of the fundamental right to privacy.

F.  **The "right to die," and the right to decline unwanted medical procedures:** The law of "right to die" and "right to pull the plug" is developing. Here's what we know already:

1.  **Can't be forced to undergo unwanted procedures:** A competent adult has a 14th Amendment liberty interest in ***not being forced to undergo unwanted medical procedures***, including artificial life-sustaining measures. It's not clear whether this is a "fundamental" interest. (*Example:* P, dying of stomach cancer, has a liberty interest in refusing to let the hospital feed him through a feeding tube.) [194]

2.  **State's interest in preserving life:** The state has an important ***countervailing interest in preserving life.***

3.  **"Clear and convincing evidence" standard:** In the case of a now-incompetent patient, the state's interest in preserving life entitles it to say that it won't allow the "plug" to be "pulled" unless there is ***"clear and convincing evidence"*** that the patient would have voluntarily declined the life-sustaining measures. [*Cruzan v. Missouri*] [194]

    **Example:** P is comatose, hospitalized, being fed through a tube, and kept breathing through a respirator. P's parents want the hospital to discontinue the tube-feeding and respirator. *Held,* the state may insist that if the parents can't show "clear and convincing evidence" that during her conscious life P showed a desire not to be kept alive by such artificial measures, the measures must be continued. [*Cruzan, supra*]

    a.  **Living wills and health-care proxies:** But probably the states must honor a ***"living will"*** and a ***"health-care proxy."*** In a living will, the signer gives direct instructions. In a health-care proxy, the signer appoints someone else to make health care decisions. [196]

4.  **No "right to commit suicide":** Terminally-ill patients do ***not*** have a general liberty interest in ***"committing suicide."*** Nor do they have the constitutional right to ***recruit a third person*** to help them commit suicide. [*Washington v. Glucksberg*] [198-201]

    **Example:** A state may make it a felony for a physician to knowingly prescribe a fatal dose of drugs for the purpose of helping the patient commit suicide.

G. **Other possible places:** Here are a couple of other areas where there might be a fundamental right.

   1. **Reading:** You probably have a fundamental right to ***read what you want***. (*Example*: A state cannot forbid you from reading pornography in the privacy of your own home, even though it can make it criminal for someone to sell you that pornography.) [*Stanley v. Georgia*] [202]

   2. **Physical appearance:** You may have a fundamental right to control your ***personal appearance***. (*Example:* If the public school which you are required to attend forces you to cut your hair to a length of no more two inches for boys and four inches for girls, this might violate a "fundamental right." But this is not clear.) [194]

H. **Final word:** Deciding whether the right in question is "fundamental" is, as noted, the key to substantive due process analysis. But it's not the end of the story. Even if you decide that the right is "fundamental" you've still got to carry out the strict scrutiny analysis: it might turn out that the state's countervailing interest is indeed "compelling" and the means chosen is "necessary" to achieve that interest. (*Example:* A state has a compelling interest in taking a child away from an abusive parent and putting him into foster care.)

   1. **Non-fundamental:** Conversely, even if the right is not "fundamental," you've still got to apply the "mere rationality" standard, and you might decide that the state is being so completely irrational that the state action is a violation of substantive due process anyway.

# V. PROCEDURAL DUE PROCESS

A. **Introduction:** We turn now to the other main aspect of the 14th Amendment's Due Process Clause: this is the requirement that the state act with adequate or fair ***procedures*** when it deprives a person of life, liberty or property. Here, the emphasis is on the particular case presented by the particular person — has the government handled his particular situation fairly? Our discussion is divided into two main questions: (1) has the individual's life, liberty or property been "taken"?; and, if so, (2) what process was "due" him prior to this taking?

   1. **Life, liberty or property:** The most important single thing to remember about procedural due process is that there cannot be a procedural due process problem unless government is taking a person's ***life***, ***liberty*** or ***property***. In other words, there is ***no general interest in having the government behave with fair procedures***. (*Example:* A city hires for an opening on its police force. The city can be as arbitrary and random as it wants, because as we'll see, an applicant for a job has no liberty or property interest in obtaining the job. Therefore, the city doesn't have to give the applicant a hearing, a statement of reasons why she didn't get the job, a systematic test of her credentials, or any other aspect of procedural fairness.) [211]

   2. **Distinction between substance and procedure:** Always distinguish between "substantive" due process and "procedural" due process. Procedural due process applies only where ***individual determinations*** are being made.

      **Example:** Suppose a state passes a law that says that no person with child support may marry. This statute raises an issue of substantive due process — unless this means of enforcing child support payments is necessary to achieve a compelling state interest, the state may not use that method at all, against anyone. Separately, even if this "ban on marriage" could pass this substantive due process hurdle (which it apparently can't, based on past Supreme Court cases like *Zablocki v. Redhail*) the state still must use *adequate procedures* before enforcing the ban *against a particular person*. For instance, the state must probably provide a person with ***notice*** that the ban will be applied, and a ***hearing*** at which he can show that the ban shouldn't apply to him because (for instance) he's fully paid up. The obligation to use fair procedures always applies *"one case at a time,"* and governs the application of government action to a particular person in a particular situation.

**B. Liberty:**   Remember that *"liberty"* is one of the things the government cannot take without procedural due process. What *is* "liberty" for due process purposes? [212]

    **1. Physical liberty:**   First, we have the interest in *"physical"* liberty. This liberty interest is violated if you are *imprisoned*, or even if you are placed in some other situation where you do not have physical freedom of movement (e.g., juvenile and/or civil commitment).

    **2. Intangible rights:**   Also, a person has a liberty interest in being able to do certain intangible things not related to physical freedom of movement. There's no complete catalog of what interests fall within this "intangible" aspect of liberty. Here are some examples, however: (1) the right to drive; (2) the right to practice one's profession; (3) the right to raise one's family. But one's interest in having a *good reputation* is not "liberty" (so the state can call you a crook without giving you due process — see *Paul v. Davis.*) [215]

**C. Property:**   The government also can't take *"property"* without procedural due process. Here are the things that may be "property" for procedural due process purposes: [212]

    **1. Conventional property:**   First, of course, we have "conventional" property (i.e., personal and real property). Thus the government cannot impose a monetary fine against a person, or declare a person's car forfeited, without complying with procedural due process.

        **a. Debt collection:**   Certain kinds of *debt collection* devices involve "property." For instance, if the state lets private creditors *attach* a person's bank account prior to trial (which means that the owner can't get at the funds), even that temporary blockage is a "taking" of property. Similarly, if the state lets a private creditor *garnish* a person's wages, that's a taking of property. On the other hand, if the state simply passes a law that lets creditors use *self-help* to repossess goods, there's no governmental taking of property when the creditor repossesses. (The due process requirement applies only where it is *government* that does, or at least is involved in, the taking of liberty or property).

    **2. Government benefits:**   *Government benefits* may or may not constitute "property" rights. Generally, if one is just *applying* for benefits and hasn't yet been receiving them, one does *not* have a property interest in those benefits. (*Example:* If P applies for welfare, and has never gotten it before, the government does not have to comply with procedural due process when it turns P down. Therefore, the government doesn't have to give P a statement of reasons, a hearing, etc.)

        **a. Already getting benefits:**   But if a person has *already been getting the benefits*, it's probably the case that he's got a property interest in *continuing* to get them, so that the government cannot *terminate* those benefits without giving him procedural due process. [*Goldberg v. Kelly*] [213] (But state law can change even this — for instance, if the state statute governing welfare benefits says that "benefits may be cut off at any time," you probably don't have a property interest in continuing to get those benefits, so you have no claim to due process.)

    **3. Government employment:**   A government *job* is similar to government benefits.

        **a. Applicant:**   If you're just *applying* for the job, you clearly do *not* have a property interest in it.

        **b. Already have job:**   If you already have the job, then the court looks to *state law* to determine whether you had a property interest in the job.

            **i. Ordinarily at-will:**   Ordinarily, under state law a job is *terminable at will*; if so, the jobholder has no property right to it, so he may be fired without due process. [214]

      ii.  **Legitimate claim of entitlement:**  If either a statute or the public employer's ***practices*** give a person a ***"legitimate claim of entitlement"*** to keep the job, then she's got a property interest. (*Example*: If a public university follows the publicized custom of never firing anybody from a non-tenured position without cause except on one year's notice, then a non-tenured teacher has a property right to hold his non-tenured job for a year following notice. [*Perry v. Sindermann*]) [214]

**D.**  **Process required:**  If a person's interest in property or liberty is being impaired, then she is entitled to due process. But ***what procedures*** does the person get? There is no simple answer. [215]

    **1.**  **Court proceedings:**  Where a person is a litigant in a formal ***judicial proceeding***, a quite full panoply of procedural safeguards is constitutionally required for "due process." The state is required to give the litigant the right to a ***hearing***, the right to ***call witnesses***, the right to ***counsel***, the right to a ***fair and objective trial***, and the right to an ***appeal***. (Other constitutional provisions aside from the Due Process Clause give additional procedural safeguards. For example, the Sixth Amendment confers a right to jury trial in criminal cases, the right to appointed counsel if one is indigent, and a right to confront witnesses against oneself.) [216]

        **a.**  **Punitive damages:**  In some circumstances the award of ***punitive damages*** may violate the defendant's due process rights. [217-218]

            **i.**  **Ratio of actual to punitive:**  A punitive damages award will violate due process if it is ***"grossly excessive."*** [*BMW of North America v. Gore*]

                **(1)**  **Ratio of punitive to compensatory:**  One of the most important factors in whether an award of punitive damages is grossly excessive is the ***ratio*** of the ***punitive damages*** to the ***actual damages.*** A punitive award that is ***more than nine times*** the compensatory award probably won't satisfy due process. [State *Farm Mut. Automobile Insur. Co. v. Campbell*].

            **ii.**  **Reprehensibility:**  Another of the key factors in the due process analysis is the ***reprehensibility*** of the defendant's conduct — the more reprehensible the conduct, the higher the amount of punitive damages that may be awarded without violating due process.

            **iii.**  **Conduct vis a vis strangers to the litigation:**  Only the defendant's conduct ***towards the plaintiff***, not its conduct towards ***strangers to the litigation,*** may be taken into account by the jury in setting the amount of punitive damages. [*Philip Morris USA v. Williams*].

    **2.**  **Non-judicial proceeding:**  Where the property or liberty interest is being impaired in something ***other*** than a judicial proceeding, the state does ***not*** have to give the individual the full range of procedural safeguards that would be needed for a court proceeding. Instead, for any particular procedural safeguard that the plaintiff says she should get (e.g., the right to a hearing), the court conducts a ***balancing*** test: the strength of the plaintiff's interest in receiving the procedural safeguard is weighed against the government's interest in avoiding extra burdens. [*Mathews v. Eldridge*] [216-217]

        **Examples:** If *A* has been receiving welfare benefits, these benefits may not be terminated without giving *A* an evidentiary hearing, because a wrongful termination of welfare benefits, even temporarily, is likely to lead to extreme hardship, without a large countervailing benefit to the government. [*Goldberg v. Kelly*] By contrast, a tenured employee who is being fired from a government job gets fewer procedural safeguards — he gets notice of the charges and an opportunity to present some evidence, but not a full adversarial evidentiary hearing with right to counsel; this is because the government's interest in being able to fire unsatisfactory employees quickly is factored into the balance. [*Cleveland Board of Ed. v. Loudermill*]

CHAPTER 10
# EQUAL PROTECTION

## I.  EQUAL PROTECTION GENERALLY

**A.  Text of clause:**  The Equal Protection Clause is part of the 14th Amendment. It provides that "[n]o state shall make or enforce any law which shall ... deny to any person within its jurisdiction the equal protection of the laws." [233]

   **1.  General usage:**  The Clause, like all parts of the 13th, 14th and 15th Amendments, was enacted shortly after the Civil War, and its primary goal was to attain free and equal treatment for ex-slaves. But it has always been interpreted as imposing a ***general*** restraint on the governmental use of classifications, not just classifications based on race but also those based on sex, alienage, illegitimacy, wealth, or any other characteristic.

   **2.  State and federal:**  The direct text of the Clause, of course, applies only to state governments. But the federal government is also bound by the same rules of equal protection — this happens by the indirect means of the Fifth Amendment's Due Process Clause. So if a given action would be a violation of Equal Protection for a state, that same action would be unconstitutional if done by the federal government (though in this situation, if you wanted to be scrupulously correct, you would call it a violation of the Fifth Amendment's Due Process Clause). [235]

      **a.  Government action only:**  The Equal Protection Clause, and the Fifth Amendment's Due Process Clause, apply ***only to government action***, not to action by private citizens. This is commonly referred to as the requirement of ***"state action,"*** and is discussed further below.

         **Example:**  D, a large private university, refuses to admit African American students. No government participates in this decision. The university's conduct cannot be a violation of the Equal Protection Clause, because there is no "state action."

   **3.  Making of classes:**  The Equal Protection Clause is only implicated where the government ***makes a classification***. It's not implicated where the government merely decides which of two classes a particular person falls into. (For instance, if Congress says that you don't receive Social Security if you work more than 1,000 hours per year, then it's made a classification that distinguishes between those who work more than 1,000 hours and those who work less — this classification can be attacked under the Equal Protection Clause. But an administrative determination that a particular person did or did not work 1,000 hours is not a classification, and cannot be attacked under the Equal Protection Clause, only the Due Process Clause.) [235]

   **4.  "As applied" vs. "facial":**  Here is some nomenclature: If P attacks a classification that is clearly written into the statute or regulation, he is claiming that Equal Protection is violated by the statute or regulation ***"on its face."*** If P's claim is that the statute does not make a classification on its face, but is being ***administered*** in a purposefully discriminatory way, then he is claiming that the statute or regulation is a violation of equal protection ***"as applied."*** (*Example:* A statute that says "you must be a citizen to vote" creates a classification scheme "on its face" — citizens vs. non-citizens. But if P claims that in actual administration, blacks are required to prove citizenship but whites are not, then his equal protection claim would be on the statute "as applied.")

      **a.  Same standards for both:**  Either kind of attack — facial or "as applied," — may be made. Both follow essentially the same principles. For instance, if no suspect classification or fundamental right is involved, the classification scheme will violate the Equal Protection Clause if it's not rationally related to a legitimate state objective, whether the scheme is on the face of the statute or merely in the way the statute is applied.

5. **What the Clause guarantees:** The Clause in essence guarantees that *people who are similarly situated will be treated similarly.* [237]

> **Example:** Consider racial segregation in the public schools. Such segregation gives a different treatment to two groups that are similarly situated, African Americans and whites. Therefore, it violates the Equal Protection rights of African Americans. (Of course, this reflects a judgment that there are no meaningful differences between blacks and whites that relate to public education. If the issue were, say, compulsory medical screening for sickle cell anemia, blacks and whites might not be similarly situated).

    a. **Dissimilar:** The Equal Protection Clause also guarantees that people who are *not* similarly situated will not be treated similarly. But this aspect is rarely of practical importance, because courts are rarely convinced that differences in situation require differences in treatment by the government.

6. **Three levels of review:** Recall that in our discussion of substantive due process, we saw that depending on the circumstances, one of two sharply different standards of review of governmental action was used, the easy "rational relation" test or the very demanding "strict scrutiny" standard. In the Equal Protection context, we have two tests that are virtually the same as these two, plus a third "middle level" of scrutiny. Let's consider each of the three types of review: [240]

    a. **Ordinary "mere rationality" review:** The easiest-to-satisfy standard of review applies to statutes that: (1) are *not based on a "suspect classification"*; (2) do not involve a *"quasi-suspect"* category that the Court has implicitly recognized (principally gender and illegitimacy); and (3) don't impair a *"fundamental right."* This is the so-called *"mere rationality"* standard. Almost every *economic regulation* will be reviewed under this easy-to-satisfy standard. (This is similar to the ease with which economic regulation passes muster under the substantive due process clause). Under this easiest "mere rationality" standard, the Court asks only "whether it is conceivable that the classification bears a rational relationship to an end of government which is not prohibited by the Constitution." [240]

        i. **Standard summarized:** So where "mere rationality" review is applied, the classification must satisfy two easy tests: (1) government must be pursuing a *legitimate governmental objective*; and (2) there must be a *rational relation* between the classification and that objective. Furthermore, it's not necessary that the court believe that these two requirements are satisfied; it's enough that the court concludes that it's *"conceivable"* that they're satisfied.

    b. **Strict scrutiny:** At the other end of the spectrum, the Court will give *"strict scrutiny"* to any statute which is based on a *"suspect classification"* or which impairs a *"fundamental right."* (We'll be discussing below the meaning of these two terms, "suspect classification" and "fundamental right"). A classification based on *race* is a classic example of a "suspect class"; the right to *vote* is an example of a fundamental right. [241]

        i. **Standard:** Where strict scrutiny is invoked, the classification will be upheld only if it is *necessary* to promote a *compelling* governmental interest. Thus not only must the objective be an extremely important one, but the "fit" between the means and the end must be extremely tight. This strict scrutiny test is the same as for substantive due process when a "fundamental right" (e.g., the right to privacy) is involved.

    c. **Middle-level review:** In a few contexts, the Court uses a *middle level* of scrutiny, more probing than "mere rationality" but less demanding than "strict scrutiny". This middle level is mainly used for cases involving classifications based on *gender* and *illegitimacy*. [241]

    **i.**   **Standard:**   This middle-level test is usually stated as follows: the means chosen by the legislature (i.e., the classification) must be *substantially related* to an *important governmental objective*. So the legislative objective must be *"important"* (but not necessarily "compelling," as for strict scrutiny), and means and end must be *"substantially related"* (easier to satisfy than the almost perfect "necessary" fit between means and end in strict scrutiny situations).

**7.**   **Importance:**   Con Law essay exams very frequently test the Equal Protection Clause because: (1) it's open-ended, so it applies to a lot of different situations; (2) there are often no clear right or wrong answers under it, so it gives the student a good chance to show how well she can articulate arguments on either side; and (3) it's one of the two or three most important single limitations on what government can do to individuals.

    **a.**   **Test tip:**   Therefore, any time you're asked to give an opinion about whether a particular governmental action is constitutional, make sure to check for an equal protection violation.

# II. ECONOMIC AND SOCIAL LAWS — THE "MERE RATIONALITY" TEST

**A.**   **Non-suspect, non-fundamental rights (economic and social legislation):**   First, let's examine the treatment of classifications that do *not* involve either a *suspect class* or a *fundamental right*. Most *economic* and *social-welfare* legislation falls into this category. [241]

**1.**   **Mere rationality:**   Here, as noted, courts use the "mere rationality" standard. In other words, as long as there is some *rational relation* between the classification drawn by the legislature and some *legitimate legislative objective*, the classification scheme will not violate the Equal Protection Clause. [241]

> **Example:** Suppose the Muni City Council, in order to cope with a budget deficit, increases the fares on all city-operated buses from $1 to $2. Statistical evidence shows that 80% of people who ride the Muni bus system on a typical day have incomes below the city-wide median. At the same time the City Council increases the bus fares, it refuses to raise the annual automobile inspection fee; car owners on average have higher-than-median incomes. P, a bus passenger, sues Muni, arguing that it is a violation of his equal protection rights for the city to increase bus fares for the poor while not increasing inspection fees for the affluent.
>
> A court would apply the "mere rationality" standard to this regulation, because poverty is not a suspect class, and no fundamental right is at issue here. Since the City Council could rationally have believed that Muni's deficit would be better handled by raising bus fares, and because the Council could rationally have decided to tackle its deficit problem one phase at a time, the constitutional challenge will almost certainly lose.

    **a.**   **Need not be actual objective:**   One thing this "mere rationality" standard means is that the "legitimate government objective" part of the test is satisfied even if the statute's defenders come up with merely a *"hypothetical"* objective that the legislature "might have" been pursuing. The government does not have to show that the objective it's pointing to was the one that *actually motivated* the legislature. [243-244]

    **b.**   **No empirical link:**   Also, there does not have to in fact be even a "rational relation" between the means chosen and the end — all that's required is that the legislature *"could have rationally believed"* that there was a link between the means and the end.

    **c.**   **Loose fit:**   Finally, a very *loose fit* between means and end will still be O.K.

2. **Conclusion:** Therefore, if you decide that a particular government classification does not involve a suspect category or a fundamental right, and should thus be subjected to "mere rationality" review, you should almost always conclude that the classification survives equal protection attack.

3. **Non-suspect classes:** Here is a partial list of classifications that have been held *not* to involve a suspect or quasi-suspect class:

   a. **Age:** Classifications based on *age*.

   **Example:** Suppose that a state requires all state troopers over 50 to retire, in order preserve a physically fit police force. Because age is not a suspect or quasi-suspect classification, the "mere rationality" test will be used. Because there is some slight overall relation between age and fitness, this requirement is satisfied, so the retirement rule does not violate equal protection. [*Mass. Board of Retirement v. Murgia*]

   b. **Wealth:** Classifications based upon *wealth*.

   **Example:** Suppose that a state provides that no low-income housing project may be built in any community unless a majority of the voters approve it in a popular referendum. A resident who would like to live in the low-income housing that would be built if allowed challenges the statute on equal protection grounds. Even if P shows that the statute was motivated by a desire to discriminate against the poor, P's constitutional challenge will probably fail. Because wealth is not a suspect or quasi-suspect class, the court will use "mere rationality" review, and will uphold the statute if it finds that the legislature could reasonably have believed that its statute might help achieve some legitimate state objective, perhaps letting communities avoid the greater governmental cost that arguably accompanies concentrations of low-income residents.

   c. **Mental condition:** Classifications based upon *mental illness* or *mental retardation*.

   **Example:** A city makes it harder for group homes for the mentally retarded to achieve zoning permission than for other group living arrangements to do so. This classification, based upon mental status, will not be treated as suspect or quasi-suspect, and will thus be subject only to "mere rationality" review. (However, such a zoning procedure was found to violate even "mere rationality," in [*City of Cleburne v. Cleburne Living Center*].)

   d. **Sexual orientation:** Classifications based on *sexual orientation.* Thus states face only mere-rationality review if they treat *homosexuals* differently from heterosexuals.

      i. **Mere rationality "with bite":** But the Court now seems to review anti-gay legislation a bit more skeptically than most legislation not involving a semi-suspect or suspect class, even though gays still don't have suspect or semi-suspect status. [250]

      **Example:** Colorado amends its constitution to prohibit any state or local law that protects homosexuals against discrimination on the basis of their sexual orientation or conduct. *Held*, this amendment violates gays' equal protection rights — it's not even minimally rational, and is motivated solely by animus towards gays. [*Romer v. Evans*]

## III. SUSPECT CLASSIFICATIONS, ESPECIALLY RACE

A. **Suspect classifications:** At the other end of the spectrum, we apply *strict scrutiny* for any classification that involves a *"suspect class."* [252]

   1. **Race and national origin:** There are only three suspect classes generally recognized by the Supreme Court: (1) *race*; (2) *national origin*; and (3) for some purposes, *alienage*. So be on the

C
A
P
S
U
L
E

S
U
M
M
A
R
Y

lookout for a classification based on race, national origin, or alienage. For other classifications, you can safely assume that these are not suspect. [252]

2.  **Purposeful:** One of the most important things to remember about strict scrutiny of suspect classifications is that this strict scrutiny will only be applied where the differential treatment of the class is *intentional* on the part of the government. If the government enacts a statute or regulation that merely has the unintended incidental *effect* of burdening, say, African Americans worse than whites, the court will *not* use strict scrutiny. [*Washington v. Davis*] *This is probably the most frequently-tested aspect of suspect classifications.* [253-258]

    **Example:** Suppose a city gives a standardized test to all applicants for the local police force. The city and the test designers do not intend to make it harder for African Americans than for whites to pass the test. But it turns out that a lot fewer African Americans pass than whites, even though the applicant pools otherwise seem identical. This differential will not trigger strict scrutiny, because the government did not intend to treat African Americans differently from whites.

    a.  **Circumstantial evidence:** However, remember that an intent to classify based on a suspect class can be proven by *circumstantial*, not just direct, evidence. For instance, if a particular police force picks new officers based on a personal interview conducted by the police chief, and over five years it turns out that only 1% of African American applicants receive jobs but 25% of whites do (and there is no apparent objective difference in the black versus white applicant pools), this statistical disparity could furnish circumstantial evidence of purposeful discrimination, which would then allow a court to apply strict scrutiny to the selection procedures.

3.  **Invidious:** In addition to the requirement that the discrimination be "purposeful," it must also be *"invidious,"* i.e., based on prejudice or tending to denigrate the disfavored class. This requirement is what has caused race, national origin, and (for some purposes) alienage to be the only suspect classes — these involve the only minorities against whom *popular prejudice is sufficiently deep.* [258]

    a.  **Rationale:** Why do we give especially close scrutiny to governmental action that disadvantages very unpopular minorities? Because ordinarily, groups will protect themselves through use of the *political process*, but: (1) these particular groups don't usually have very much political power, because the past discrimination against them has included keeping them out of the voting system; and (2) even if the minority votes in proportion to its numbers, the majority is very likely to vote as a block against it, because of the minority's extreme unpopularity.

    b.  **"Discrete and insular" minority:** A famous phrase to express this concept, from a footnote in a Supreme Court opinion, is *"discrete and insular minorities"* — discrete and insular minorities are ones that are so disfavored and out of the political mainstream that the courts must make extra efforts to protect them, because the political system won't. [259]

    c.  **Traits showing suspectness:** Here are some traits which probably make it more likely that a court will find that a particular class is suspect:

        i.  **Immutability:** If the class is based on an *immutable* or unchangeable trait, this makes a finding of suspectness more likely. Race and national origin qualify; wealth does not. The idea seems to be that if you can't change the trait, it's especially unfair to have it be the basis of discrimination. [259]

        ii. **Stereotypes:** If the class or trait is one as to which there's a prevalence of false and disparaging *stereotypes*, this makes a finding of suspectness more likely. Again, race, national origin and alienage seem to qualify, at least somewhat better than, say, wealth. [259]

    **iii. Political powerlessness:** If the class is ***politically powerless***, or has been subjected to ***widespread discrimination*** (especially official discrimination) historically, this makes it more likely to be suspect.

   **d. "Separate but equal" as invidious:** Even if a classification involves a group that has frequently been discriminated against, the classification's defenders may argue that their particular use of the classification is not "invidious" because it's not intended to disadvantage the class. ***Affirmative action*** is one example where this argument might be raised. Another context in which the requirement that the discrimination be "invidious" arises is the ***"separate but equal"*** situation; in this context, the defenders of the classification claim that although both classes are treated differently, the unpopular class is being treated no "worse." In general, the Court now seems to hold that discrimination based on race or national origin is ***"per se" invidious***; for instance, the argument that the races are being treated "separately but equally" will almost never serve as a successful defense to an Equal Protection problem. [262]

    **Example:** Virginia forbids interracial marriage. It claims that blacks aren't disfavored, because whites are blocked from marrying blacks just as much as blacks are blocked from marrying whites. *Held*, the statute's legislative history shows that it was enacted to protect the "racial purity" of whites, so the classification is invidious and violates Equal Protection. [*Loving v. Virginia*]

**4. Strict equals fatal:** Once the court does decide that a suspect classification is involved, and that strict scrutiny must be used, that scrutiny is almost always ***fatal*** to the classification scheme. For instance, no purposeful racial or ethnic classification has survived strict scrutiny since 1944. [260]

   **a. "Necessary" prong:** Sometimes, this is because the state cannot show that it is pursuing a "compelling" objective. But more often, it's because the means chosen is not shown to be ***"necessary"*** to achieve that compelling objective. A means is only "necessary" for achieving the particular objective if there are ***no less discriminatory alternatives*** that will accomplish the goal as well, or almost as well.

    **Example:** Suppose Pearl Harbor occurred today, and the U.S. government once again put any citizen of Japanese ancestry into an internment camp. Presumably this would not be a "necessary" means of dealing with the danger of treason and sabotage, because less discriminatory alternatives like frequent document inspections and/or loyalty oaths would be almost as effective as virtual imprisonment.

**5. Some examples:** Here are two contexts in which claims have been made (and in most instances accepted) that a suspect class has been intentionally discriminated against in violation of Equal Protection:

   **a. Child custody and adoption:** Some notion of "racial compatibility" or "racial purity" may motivate state officials to differentiate based on race in ***child custody*** and ***adoption*** proceedings. In general, the practical rule is that the state may not impose flat rules that handle child custody and adoption differently based solely on the race of the child and parents. [264]

    **Example:** Mother and Father are divorced, and Mother is given custody of Child. All are white. Mother then marries Husband, who is African American. The family court transfers custody to Father, on the grounds that Child will be socially stigmatized if she grows up in an interracial family. *Held*, this custody decision can't survive strict scrutiny — government may not bow to private racial prejudices. [*Palmore v. Sidoti*]

   **b. Political process:** Actions taken by government that relate to the ***political process***, and that are intended to disadvantage racial or ethnic minorities, often run afoul of Equal Protection. [263]

C
A
P
S
U
L
E

S
U
M
M
A
R
Y

**Example:** A state requires that in every election, each candidate's race must appear on the ballot. *Held*, this violates Equal Protection because it was motivated by a desire to keep African Americans out of office. [*Anderson v. Martin*]

6. **Segregation:** The clearest example of a classification involving a suspect class and thus requiring strict scrutiny is *segregation*, the maintenance of physical separation between the races.

   a. **General rule:** Official, intentional segregation based on race or national origin is a violation of the Equal Protection Clause. As the result of *Brown v. Board of Education*, even if the government were to maintain truly "separate but equal" facilities (in the sense that, say, a school for blacks had as nice a building, as qualified teachers, etc., as a school for whites), the intentional maintenance of separate facilities *per se* violates the Equal Protection Clause. [264-268]

   b. **Education and housing:** The two areas where official segregation is most often found are *education* and *housing.*

      i. **Education:** Thus if a school board establishes attendance zones for the purpose of making one school heavily African American and/or Hispanic, and another school heavily white, this would violate Equal Protection.

      ii. **Housing:** Similarly, government may not intentionally segregate in housing. For example, it's a violation of Equal Protection for a city to do its *zoning* in such a way that all *government-subsidized housing* is built in the heavily black part of town, if the intent of this zoning practice is to maintain racial segregation.

   c. **Must be *de jure*:** But it's critical to remember that there is a violation of equal protection only where the segregation is the result of *intentional government action*. In other words, the segregation must be *"de jure,"* not merely *"de facto."* [268]

   **Example:** School district lines are drawn by officials who have no desire to separate students based on race. Over time, due to housing choices made by private individuals, one district becomes fully African American, and the other all-white. Even though the schools are no longer racially balanced, there has been no equal protection violation, because there was no act of intentional separation on the part of the government. *Cf. Bd. of Ed. v. Dowell.* [269]

   d. **Wide remedies:** If a court finds that there has been intentional segregation, it has a wide range of *remedies* to choose from. For instance, it can bus students to a non-neighborhood school, or order the redrawing of district boundaries. But whatever remedy the court chooses, the remedy must *stop* once the effects of the original intentional discrimination have been eradicated. (Then, if because of housing patterns or other non-government action, the schools become resegregated, the court may *not* reinstitute its remedies.)

## IV. RACE-CONSCIOUS AFFIRMATIVE ACTION

A. **Race-conscious affirmative action:** You're more likely to get an exam question about race-conscious *affirmative action* than about official discrimination against racial minorities. If you see a question in which government is trying to help racial or ethnic minorities by giving them some sort of preference, you should immediately think "equal protection" and you should think "strict scrutiny." [273]

   1. **Public entity:** Be sure to remember that there can only be a violation of equal protection if there's *state action*, that is, action by the federal government or by a state or municipality. In general, the use of affirmative action by private entities does *not* raise any constitutional issue (except perhaps where a judge orders a private employer to implement a race-conscious plan). But any time you have a fact pattern in which a police department, school district, public university, or

other governmental entity seems to be intentionally preferring one racial group over another, that's when you know you have a potential equal protection problem.

2. **Strict scrutiny:** It is now the case that ***any affirmative action program that classifies on the basis of race will be strictly scrutinized***. [*Richmond v. Croson*] So a race-conscious affirmative action plan, whether it's in the area of employment, college admissions, voting rights or anywhere else, must be adopted for the purpose of furthering some "compelling" governmental interest, and the racial classification must be "necessary" to achieve that compelling governmental interest. [277]

   a. **Past discrimination:** Since a race-conscious affirmative action plan will have to be in pursuit of a "compelling" governmental interest, probably the only interests that are likely to qualify are: (1) the government's interest in ***redressing past discrimination***; and (2) a ***university's*** interest in ***student-body diversity***. So if the government is merely trying to get a ***racially-balanced work force***, to make African Americans ***more economically successful***, or any other objective that is not closely tied to one of these two objectives, you should immediately be able to say, "The government interest is not compelling, and the measure flunks the strict scrutiny test." [278-279]

   b. **Clear evidence:** Even if the government's trying to redress past discrimination, there's got to be ***clear evidence*** that this discrimination in fact occurred.

      i. **Societal discrimination:** Redressing past discrimination "***by society*** as a whole" will ***not*** suffice. There must be past discrimination closely related to the problem, typically discrimination ***by government***. [279]

   c. **Quotas:** One device that is especially vulnerable to Equal Protection attack is the racially-based ***quota***. A racially-based quota is an inflexible number of admissions slots, dollar amounts, or other "goodies" set aside for minorities. For instance, it's a quota if the state says that 1/2 of all new hires in the police department must be African American, or if it says that 20% of all seats in the public university's law school class will be set aside for African Americans and Hispanics. Probably ***virtually all racially-based quotas will be struck down even where the government is trying to eradicate the effects of past discrimination*** — the Court will probably say that a quota is not "necessary" to remedy discrimination, because more flexible "goals" can do the job. [279]

   d. **Congress:** It doesn't make any (or at least much) difference that the affirmation action program was enacted by ***Congress*** rather than by a state or local government. Here, too, the Court will apply strict scrutiny if the program is race-conscious. [*Adarand Constructors, Inc. v. Pena*].

      i. **Possibly greater deference:** However, the Court might give slightly greater ***deference*** to a congressional finding that official discrimination had existed in a particular domain, or that a particular race-conscious remedy was required, than it would to a comparable finding by a state or local government. (We don't know yet whether this greater deference would occur.)

B. **Some contexts:**

1. **Preferential admissions in higher education:** Any scheme which gives a preference to one racial group for ***admission*** to a public university has to be strictly scrutinized. However, such preferences will not necessarily be invalidated as the result of this strict scrutiny. Here are what seem to be the main rules governing affirmative action in public-university admissions, as the result of the twin landmark 2003 cases of *Grutter v. Bollinger* [282] and *Gratz v. Bollinger* [286]:

   [a] Race-conscious admissions measures will ***receive strict scrutiny***, and thus must be narrowly-

tailored to achieve a compelling objective;

**[b]** The pursuit of *diversity in the student body* can be a *compelling objective*;

**[c]** A *one-student-at-a-time evaluation* in which the student's race is merely one factor among various ones considered is *sufficiently narrowly-tailored*; but

**[d]** Mechanical approaches resembling *quotas*, such as automatically awarding an applicant a fixed number of *points* towards admission based on his race, are *not narrowly-tailored* and therefore violate equal protection.

**Example 1 (valid):** The Univ. of Mich. Law School evaluates each applicant's entire file, weighing such variables as undergraduate GPA, LSAT scores, and the contribution the applicant will make to diversity in the student body. The school treats as a major "plus" factor an applicant's membership in one of three historically-discriminated-against groups, blacks, Hispanics and Native Americans. The school does so to create a "critical mass" of these minority students, so that they will participate without feeling isolated.

*Held* (by a 5-4 vote), this form of affirmative-action is constitutional. The interest in a diverse student body is a compelling one, and the approach here — in that it relies on an individualized, non-mechanical evaluation of each applicant — is narrowly tailored to achieve that interest. [*Grutter v. Bollinger*] [282]

**Example 2 (invalid):** The Univ. of Michigan undergraduate college awards pre-measured "points" to applicants for various attributes (e.g., up to 5 points for being an outstanding artist or student leader). Every black or Hispanic applicant automatically gets 20 points for diversity. 100 points are needed for admission. The extra 20 points for minority-group status has the effect that virtually every minimally-qualified black or Hispanic applicant is admitted, whereas many well-qualified non-minority applicants are rejected.

*Held* (by 6-3), this form of affirmative action is unconstitutional, because it is not narrowly-tailored to the achievement of the compelling interest in student-body diversity. The scheme here is a mechanical one that is equivalent to a quota, not an individualized-evaluation scheme like the one approved in *Grutter*. And the fact that "near-misses" can be flagged for individualized review does not save the scheme. [*Gratz v. Bollinger*] [286]

**Note:** *Grutter* and *Gratz* were decided by a Court in which Justice O'Connor voted with the majority in each decision. Now that O'Connor has been replaced by Alito (who is far more hostile to race-conscious government action in the name of affirmative action), it's not at all clear that the Law School's individualized "racial-diversity-as-a-plus" plan approved in *Grutter* would be approved today, in light of the 2007 *Parents Involved* decision, discussed immediately *infra*.

**2.** **Admissions to public schools by race-conscious means:** *No individual student's race may be considered in making that student's public high-school or elementary school assignment,* if the district is not combatting prior official segregation. *Parents Involved in Community Schools v. Seattle School District No. 1* (2007).

**Example:** The Seattle school system adopts a "tiebreaker" plan for allocating spaces to incoming ninth graders who want to attend certain racially-imbalanced oversubscribed high schools. One of the tiebreakers is that as between a white and nonwhite student seeking admission to the same oversubscribed high school, the one who will lessen the target school's degree of racial imbalance (compared with district-wide percentages) will get the slot. Thus a black student will be selected over a white student if the target school already has a materially higher percentage of white students in it than the overall district white percentage. Seattle has never been found to have officially practiced school segregation; racial imbalance in the target schools schools is due to racially-imbalanced residential housing patterns.

*Held*, the race-conscious plan here must be strictly scrutinized, and will be struck down. Five members of the Court believe that it is not narrowly-tailored to meet any governmental objective. The decisive fifth member of the Court (Kennedy) believes that reducing school-by-school racial imbalance and increasing diversity in the student population are compelling governmental interests, but that the plan here — based on labelling each student as "white" or "non-white" — is not necessary to achieve those interests, because the district has not shown that methods not involving the "crude" binary racial classification of each students (e.g., race-conscious drawing of school-attendance zones) cannot adequately achieve these same objectives. *Parents Involved in Community Schools v. Seattle School District No. 1, supra.*

3. **Minority set-asides:** *Minority set-asides*, by which some percentage of publicly-funded contracts are reserved for minority-owned businesses, will be subjected to scrutiny and generally struck down. That's true whether the set-aside is enacted by Congress or by a state/local government. [299-308]

4. **Employment:** Anytime a public *employer* gives an intentional preference to one racial group, strict scrutiny will probably be called for. [308]

   a. **Layoffs:** If the employer intentionally prefers blacks over whites when it administers *layoffs*, that preference will almost certainly be unconstitutional. [*Wygant v. Jackson Bd. of Ed.*] [311]

   b. **Hiring:** A racial preference in *hiring* is almost as hard to justify (though it might pass muster if that particular public employer had clearly discriminated against African Americans in the past, and there seemed to be no way short of a racial preference in hiring to redress that past discrimination).

   c. **Promotions:** A race-based scheme of awarding *promotions* to cure past discrimination (so that African Americans eventually get promoted to the levels that they would have been at had there not been any discrimination in the first place) is the easiest to justify, since it damages the expectations of whites the least. But even this will have to satisfy strict scrutiny. [311]

5. **Drawing of election districts:** A *voter* who thinks she has been disadvantaged by the drawing of *electoral districts* in a race-conscious (or other "group-conscious") way may bring an equal protection suit against the government body that drew the district lines. But the plaintiff must show either: (1) that the lines were drawn with the *purpose* and *effect* of *disadvantaging the group* of which P is a part; or (2) that *race* was the *"predominant factor"* in how the district lines were drawn. [312-318]

   a. **"Partisan gerrymander" claims almost impossible to win:** The first of these types of claims — "my group has been systematically disadvantaged" — is used to attack *"partisan gerrymanders,"* gerrymanders based on political factors rather than racial factors. These claims are *almost impossible to win.* [*Vieth v. Jubelirer; League of United Latin Amer. Citizens v. Perry*] [313-315]

      i. **Lack of political power over many elections:** For one thing, the mere fact that in one or two election cycles the plaintiff group does not get nearly the same percentage of seats as it has of the total electorate can never by itself suffice to win an Equal Protection challenge to a partisan gerrymander. At the very least, the Ps must show that they lack political power, and have been *fenced out of the political process*, over *many elections.*

      ii. **Never successful:** *No partisan-gerrymander claim has ever succeeded.* See, e.g., *League of United Latin Amer. Citizens v. Perry*, where a congressional-district gerrymander was upheld even though the lower court found (and the Supreme Court agreed) that "the single-minded purpose of the [party ruling the state legislature] in enacting the [gerry-mander] was to **gain partisan advantage.**" [314-315]

    **b. Race as predominant factor:** But the second type of attack — "race was the predominant factor in drawing district lines" — has a **much better chance of success.** If the court concludes that **race** was indeed the **predominate factor** in how the electoral district lines were drawn, the court will **strictly scrutinize** the lines, and probably strike them down. Legislatures may "take account" of race in drawing district lines (just as they take account of ethnic groups, precinct lines, and many other factors), but they may not make race the predominant factor, unless they can show that using race in this way is necessary to achieve a compelling governmental interest (e.g., eradication of prior official voting-rights discrimination). The desire to create the maximum number of "majority black" districts will not by itself be a "compelling" interest. [*Miller v. Johnson*] [317]

    **6. Law enforcement and other operational areas:** Even where government's own **operational needs** are arguably aided by a race-conscious policy, the Court will strictly scrutinize this use of race. Thus race-conscious government decisions in such operational areas as **law enforcement, prison administration** and the **military** will be strictly scrutinized.

        **Example:** A state prison system racially segregates new prisoners in cell assignments, believing that this cuts down on gang-related violence. *Held*, the race-conscious policy must be strictly scrutinized, even though the state believes that its policy does not prefer one race over another. [*Johnson v. California*] [320]

# V. MIDDLE-LEVEL REVIEW (GENDER, ILLEGITIMACY AND ALIENAGE)

**A. Middle-level review generally:** A few types of classifications are subjected to "middle-level" review, easier to satisfy than strict scrutiny but tougher than "mere rationality." [322]

    **1. Standard:** Where we apply the middle-level standard, the government objective must be **"important,"** and the means must be **"substantially related"** to that objective.

        **a. No hypothetical objective:** One important respect in which mid-level review differs from "mere rationality" review concerns the state **objectives** that the Court will consider. Recall that in the case of the easy "mere rationality" review, the Court will consider virtually **any objective that might have conceivably motivated** the legislature, regardless of whether there's any evidence that that objective was in fact in the legislature's mind. But with "intermediate-level" review, the Court will **not** hypothesize objectives; it will consider only those objectives that are shown to have **actually motivated the legislature.**

    **2. What classes:** There are two main types of classifications that get middle-level review: (1) **gender**; and (2) **illegitimacy**. We also consider **alienage** here, because it has aspects of both strict scrutiny and mere rationality, so it's kind of a hybrid.

**B. Gender:** The most important single rule to remember in the entire area of middle-level scrutiny is that **sex-based classifications get middle-level review.** [*Craig v. Boren*] So if government intentionally classifies on the basis of sex, it's got to show that it's pursuing an important objective, and that the sex-based classification scheme is substantially related to that objective. [323-324]

        **Example:** City sets the mandatory retirement age for male public school teachers at 65, and for female teachers at 62. Because this classification is based upon gender, it must satisfy middle-level review: City must show that its sex-based classification is substantially related to the achievement of an important governmental objective. In this case, it is unlikely that City can make this showing.

1. **Benign as well as invidious:** The same standard of review is used whether the sex-based classification is *"invidious"* (intended to harm women) or *"benign"* (intended to help women, or even intended to redress past discrimination against them). [258]

2. **Male or female plaintiff:** This means that where government classifies based on sex, the scheme can be attacked either by a *male* or by a *female*, and either gender will get the benefit of mid-level review.

   > **Example:** Oklahoma forbids the sale of low-alcohol beer to males under the age of 21, and to females under the age of 18. *Held*, this statute violates the equal protection rights of males aged 18 to 20, because it is not substantially related to the achievement of important governmental objectives. [*Craig v. Boren*] [323-324]

3. **Purpose:** Sex-based classifications will only be subjected to middle-level review if the legislature has *intentionally* discriminated against one sex in favor of the other. (This is similar to the requirement for strict scrutiny in race-based cases.) If, as the result of some governmental act, one sex happens to suffer an *unintended burden* greater than the other sex suffers, that's not enough for mid-level review.

   > **Example:** Massachusetts gives an absolute preference to veterans for civil service jobs. It happens that 98% of veterans are male. *Held*, this preference does not have to satisfy mid-level review because the unfavorable impact on women was not intended by the legislature. Therefore, the preference does not violate equal protection, since it satisfies the easier "mere rationality" standard. [*Personnel Admin. of Mass. v. Feeney*]

4. **Stereotypes:** Be on the lookout for *stereotypes*: if the legislature has made a sex-based classification that seems to reinforce stereotypes about the "proper place" of women, it probably cannot survive middle-level review. (*Example:* Virginia maintains Virginia Military Institute as an all-male college, because of the state's view that only men can handle the school's harsh, militaristic method of producing "citizen soldiers." *Held*, this sex-based scheme does not satisfy mid-level review, because it stems from traditional ways of thinking about gender roles; there are clearly *some* women who are qualified for and would benefit from the VMI approach, and these women may not be deprived of the opportunity to attend VMI. [*U.S. v. Virginia*]) [326-329]

5. **"Exceedingly persuasive justification":** Although the Supreme Court still gives gender-based classifications only mid-level, not strict, scrutiny, the Court now applies that scrutiny in a very tough way. The Court now says that it will require an *"exceedingly persuasive justification"* for any gender-based classification, and will review it with *"skeptical scrutiny."* [*U.S. v. Virginia, supra.*] [322]

C. **Illegitimacy:** Classifications disadvantaging *illegitimate children* are "semi-suspect" and therefore get middle-level review. [344]

1. **Claims can't be flatly barred:** Therefore, the state can't simply bar unacknowledged illegitimate children from bringing wrongful death actions, from having any chance to inherit, etc. Such children must be given at least *some reasonable opportunity* to obtain a *judicial declaration of paternity* (e.g., in a suit brought by their mother). Once they obtain such a declaration, they must be *treated equivalently to children born legitimate.*

   > **Example:** Pennsylvania passes a statute of limitations saying that no action for child support may be brought on behalf of an out-of-wedlock child unless the action is brought before the child turns 6. *Held*, the statute violates the child's equal protection

rights. Since the classification is based on out-of-wedlock status, it will be upheld only if it is substantially related to an important governmental objective. Concededly, Pennsylvania has an interest in avoiding the litigation of stale or fraudulent claims. But the 6-year statute of limitations is not "substantially related" to the achievement of that interest. [*Clark v. Jeter*]

**D. Alienage:** Alienage might be thought of as a "semi-suspect" category. In fact, though, alienage classifications, depending on the circumstances, will be subjected either to ***strict scrutiny*** or to ***mere rationality*** review (so there's only middle-level review as a kind of "average").

1. **Distinguished from national origin:** Be careful to distinguish "alienage" from "national origin": if a person is discriminated against because he is ***not yet a United States citizen,*** that's "alienage" discrimination. If, on the other hand, he's discriminated against because he is a naturalized citizen who originally came from Mexico (or whose ancestors came from Mexico), that's discrimination based on "national origin." Remember that national origin always triggers strict scrutiny, whereas alienage does not necessarily do so.

2. **General rule:** Subject to one large exception covered below, discrimination against aliens is subject to ***strict scrutiny***. [338]

   **Example 1:** A state cannot deny welfare benefits to aliens, because such a classification based on alienage cannot be shown to be necessary to the achievement of a compelling state interest. [*Graham v. Richardson*]

   **Example 2:** A state cannot prevent resident aliens from practicing law, because such a classification cannot survive strict scrutiny. [*In re Griffiths*]

3. **"Representative government" exception:** But the major exception is that strict scrutiny does not apply where the discrimination against aliens relates to a ***"function at the heart of representative government."*** Basically, this means that if the alien is applying for a ***government job***, and the performance of this job is ***closely tied in with politics, justice or public policy***, we use only ***"mere rationality"*** review. So government may discriminate against aliens with respect to posts like ***state trooper***, ***public school teacher***, or ***probation officer***. See, e.g., [*Ambach v. Norwick*]. [339]

   a. **Low-level government jobs:** But don't make the mistake of thinking that because what's involved is a government job, strict scrutiny automatically fails to apply. If the job is ***not*** closely tied in with politics, justice or public policy — something that is true of most ***low-level jobs*** — then strict scrutiny applies.

      **Example:** Strict scrutiny would almost certainly be applied to a city ordinance that said that no resident alien may work for the city government as a sanitation worker.

4. **Education of illegal aliens:** A last quirky rule in the area of alienage is that if a state denies ***free public education*** to ***illegal aliens***, this will be subjected to intermediate-level review, and probably struck down. [*Plyler v. Doe*] (But this comes from a combination of the fact that the plaintiffs were aliens and also that they were children. If a state discriminates against ***adult*** illegal aliens, we don't know whether something higher than middle-level review will be applied.) [340-343]

**E. Other unpopular groups:** Discrimination against ***other unpopular groups*** might conceivably be subjected to middle-level review. For instance, discrimination against the ***elderly*** or the ***disabled*** might possibly trigger mid-level review, but the Court has not addressed this question. (This would be a good gray area for an exam question — you could argue both the pros and the cons of applying mid-level review to these unpopular, frequently-discriminated-against groups.)

1. **Homosexuals:** Similarly, *gays* may eventually get the benefit of what is effectively mid-level review. In fact, *Romer v. Evans*, which struck down an anti-gay Colorado enactment, purports to apply mere-rationality review but seems more like mid-level review. [248]

F. **Congressional affirmative action plans:** Finally, remember that there's one other area where the Court uses mid-level review: affirmative action programs established by *Congress*.

# VI.  FUNDAMENTAL RIGHTS

A. **Fundamental rights generally:** Now, let's look at the second way strict scrutiny can be triggered in equal protection cases: there will be strict scrutiny not only when a "suspect classification" is used, but also when a *"fundamental right"* is burdened by the classification the government has selected. Whenever a classification burdens a "fundamental right" or "fundamental interest," the classification will be subjected to strict scrutiny *even though the people who are burdened are not members of a suspect class*. [350]

1. **"Fundamental" defined:** "Fundamental" means something absolutely different in this Equal Protection context than it means in the Substantive Due Process context. Remember that in due process, the fundamental rights are ones related to privacy. Here, the fundamental rights are related to a variety of other interests protected by the Constitution, but generally having nothing to do with privacy. [350]

2. **List:** The short list of rights that are "fundamental" for equal protection strict scrutiny purposes is as follows: (1) the right to *vote*; (2) maybe the right to be a *political candidate*; (3) the right to have access to the *courts* for certain kinds of proceedings; and (4) the right to *migrate interstate.* [343]

B. **Voting rights:** The right to *vote* in state and local elections is "fundamental," so any classification that burdens that substantially burdens right to vote is often strictly scrutinized. [354- 361]

1. **The "related to voter qualifications" issue:** In deciding whether to use strict scrutiny, the Court seems to place great weight on whether the voting regulation is *reasonably related to determining voter qualifications.*

   a. **If not reasonably related to voter qualifications:** If the Court decides that the regulation is *not* reasonably related to determining voter qualifications, then the Court *uses strict scrutiny*, and will probably strike down the regulation.

   b. **If reasonably related to voter qualifications:** If, on the other hand, the Court decides that the regulation *is* reasonably related to determining voter qualifications, then the Court generally does *not* use strict scrutiny. Instead, it uses some less stringent review method (typically, an intermediate-level *balancing test*), and is likely to *uphold* the measure.

2. **Not reasonably related to voter qualifications:** Here are various types of regulations that the Court has found to be *not reasonably related to determining voter qualifications*, and as to which it has therefore *applied strict scrutiny.* [355-357]

   a. **Poll tax:** *Poll taxes* are not reasonably related to determining voter qualifications. Therefore, a poll tax, no matter how minor, creates an inequality in the right to vote that must be strictly scrutinized, and struck down as an Equal Protection violation. [*Harper v. Virginia Bd. of Elections*]

   b. **Ballot restricted to "interested voters":** The requirement that voters *own property* or otherwise have some *"special interest"* is ordinarily not related to voter qualifications, and is thus usually given strict scrutiny.

      **Example:** A New York statute limits school district elections to persons who either: (1) own or lease property within the district; or (2) are parents of children in the district's public schools. *Held*, the statute must be strictly scrutinized, and will be struck down because it is not necessary to promote a compelling state interest. [*Kramer v. Union Free School District No. 15*]

   **i. Exception for "special purpose" body:**   However, if the Court finds that the governmental unit for which elections are being held has a *limited purpose* which *disproportionately affects* only one group, the franchise may be limited to that group. Thus *"special purpose bodies"* may restrict the vote to persons who are directly affected by the body's activities.

   **Example:** Votes for a special-purpose *"water storage district"* can be limited to landowners, and can be on a "one acre, one vote" basis. [*Ball v. James*]

   **c. Duration-of-residence requirements:**   A requirement that voters have *resided within the state* for *more than a certain time* prior to Election Day are strictly scrutinized, if the requirement goes beyond what's reasonably required to ensure that the voter really is a local resident.

   **Example:** A state limits the right to vote to people who have resided in the state for at least one year before the election. *Held*, the requirement will be strictly scrutinized and struck down. Such a duration-of-residence requirement violates both the voter's fundamental right to vote and his right to travel. [*Dunn v. Blumstein*]

   **i. Fifty-day statutes:**   But *shorter* residency requirements (e.g., 50 days) have been *upheld*, on the theory that these are merely methods of ensuring that the person *really is a resident.*

**3. Reasonably related to voter qualifications:**   If the Court finds that the regulation *is reasonably related to voter qualifications*, the Court reviews it by a *less-than-strict-scrutiny* standard (some form of *intermediate-level* review). [357-359]

   **a. Voter identification requirements:**   For example, a state requirement that every voter *present a photo ID* has been *upheld* under this non-strict-scrutiny standard, as a means of protecting the "integrity and reliability of the electoral process." [*Crawford v. Marion County Election Board* (2008)]

   **b. Denial of vote to felons:**   Many states deny the vote to *felons*, even ones who have served their sentence and finished any parole. Such disenfranchisement has been *upheld.* [*Richardson v. Ramirez*].

   **c. Burden on right to vote by limiting voter's choices:**   Where state regulation of voting merely has the effect of *"burdening"* the right to vote, by *limiting the voter's choices*, the Court does *not* use strict scrutiny, and merely balances the degree of burden against the magnitude of the state's interest.

   **Example:** A state may completely ban all *write-in votes*. So long as the state gives candidates reasonable access to the ballot (thus preserving each voter's interest in having a reasonable choice of candidates), the state is not required to protect each voter's interest in being able to vote for any candidate of his choosing. [*Burdick v. Takushi*]

**C. Ballot access:**   The right to be a *political candidate*, and to have your name on the ballot, seems to be "quasi-fundamental." [361]

**1. Two invalid restrictions:**   The two kinds of ballot restrictions that the Supreme Court does seem to give strict or almost strict scrutiny to are:

   **a. Unfair to new parties:**   Restrictions that are unfair to *new, not-yet-established political parties*. (*Example:* A rule saying that a minor party can get its candidate on the ballot only if it presents signatures from 15% of the voters, holds a formal primary, and has an elaborate party structure, violates Equal Protection. [*Williams v. Rhodes*]) [362]

b. **Based on wealth:** Ballot access limits that are based on **wealth**. (*Example:* A $700 candidate filing fee, which the state refuses to waive for an indigent candidate, violates Equal Protection. [*Lubin v. Panish*])

2. **Candidate eligibility rules:** But reasonable rules concerning the eligibility of the individual candidate, that don't fall into either of these two categories — unfair to new parties, or based on wealth — seem to be generally **upheld** by the Court. Thus a state may set a **minimum age**, or may require that the candidate have **resided for a certain period of time** in the state or district where he is seeking office.

D. **Court access:** Access to the **courts** is sometimes a "fundamental right," so that if the right is burdened by a state-imposed classification, that classification will sometimes be closely scrutinized. Basically, what it comes down to is that if the state imposes a **fee** that the rich can pay but the poor cannot, and the access relates to a **criminal** case, strict scrutiny will be used. (*Example:* The state cannot charge an indigent for his trial transcript in a criminal case. [*Griffin v. Illinois*] Similarly, the state must provide him with free counsel on appeal.) [364-366]

1. **Civil litigation:** When **civil** litigation is involved, access to the courts is usually **not** fundamental. Only for various family-law proceedings (e.g., **divorce, paternity suits, termination of parental rights)** is the state barred from charging fees. [*Boddie v. Connecticut*] [366-367]

E. **Right to travel:** The so-called **"right to travel"** is generally a "fundamental" right. This term "right to travel" is misleading — it's really the right to **change one's state of residence or employment.** So any time the state imposes a classification that burdens one's right to change her state of residence or employment, that classification will be strictly scrutinized. [367-369]

1. **Duration of residence:** This mainly means that if the state imposes a substantial **waiting period** on newly-arrived residents, before they can receive some **vital governmental benefit**, this will be strictly scrutinized.

   **Example:** Pennsylvania denies welfare benefits to any resident who has not resided in the state for at least a year. *Held*, this one-year waiting period impairs the "fundamental right of interstate movement" so it must be strictly scrutinized, and in fact invalidated. [*Shapiro v. Thompson*]. [367-368]

2. **Vital government benefit:** But the key phrase here is **"vital government benefit"** — if the benefit is **not** vital, then the state may impose a substantial waiting period. (*Example:* A one-year waiting period before a student can qualify for low in-state tuition at the public university probably does not burden a fundamental right, and thus does not need to be strictly scrutinized.)

F. **Necessities:** The right to **"necessities"** is **not** fundamental. So if the state distributes necessities in a way that treats different people differently (or if it distributes the money to be used to buy these things differentially), there will be no strict scrutiny because there is no fundamental right. [370]

1. **Education:** For instance, one does not have a fundamental right to a **public school education**. Therefore, the state may allow or even foster inequalities in the distribution of that public school education, without violating any fundamental right, and thus without having to pass strict scrutiny. [*San Antonio School Dist. v. Rodriguez*] [351-354]

   **Example:** The Ps claim that Texas' system of financing public education violates equal protection, because districts with a high property tax base per pupil consistently spend more on education than those with a low base are able to do.

   *Held*, education is not a fundamental right. Therefore, Texas' scheme merely has to undergo "rational relation" review. Because the use of property taxes to finance education is a rational way of achieving the legitimate state goal of giving each local school district a large measure of control over the education its residents get, this "mere rationality" standard is satisfied. *San Antonio School Dist. v. Rodriguez, supra.*

    **a.**  **Complete deprivation:**  Actually, it's still possible that a ***complete deprivation*** of public education might be held to be a violation of a "fundamental" right. If a state simply refused to give any public education *at all* to some groups of residents, this might be such a large deprivation that it would amount to a violation of a fundamental right, and thus be subject to strict scrutiny. [352]

  **2.**  **Food, shelter:**  There is no fundamental right to the material ***"necessities of life."*** Thus ***food***, ***shelter***, and ***medical care*** are not "fundamental" for equal protection purposes. Therefore, the state may distribute these things unevenly. Similarly, the state may give some people but not others money for these things without having to survive strict scrutiny. (*Example:* The state can give a smaller per capita welfare payment to big families than small families, without having the scheme subjected to strict scrutiny. This is because the food and shelter for which the payments are used are not "fundamental rights." [*Dandridge v. Williams*]) [370]

CHAPTER 11
# MISCELLANEOUS CLAUSES

## I.  FOURTEENTH AMENDMENT PRIVILEGES AND IMMUNITIES

**A.**  **Privileges and Immunities Clause Generally:**  The Fourteenth Amendment has its own "Privileges and Immunities" Clause: "No state shall make or enforce any law which shall abridge the privileges or immunities of citizens of the United States." [382]

  **1.**  **National rights only:**  But this clause is very narrowly interpreted: it only protects the individual from state interference with his rights of ***"national"*** citizenship. The most important of these rights of "national" citizenship are: (1) the right to ***travel from state to state*** (which as we saw is also protected by the Equal Protection Clause); and (2) the right to ***vote in national elections***.

  **2.**  **Right to change state of residence:** The clause is most relevant where a state treats ***newly-arrived residents less favorably*** than those who have resided in-state for a longer time: this violates the "right to travel," protected by the clause. (*Example:* If a state gives newly-arrived residents lower welfare payments than ones who have been residents longer, this is a violation of the "right to travel" protected by the 14th Amendment P&I clause. [*Saenz v. Roe*]) [383]

  **3.**  **Strict scrutiny:** The Court gives ***strict scrutiny*** to state laws that interfere with the rights of national citizenship. [*Saenz v. Roe*]

## II.  THE "TAKING" CLAUSE

**A.**  **The "Taking" Clause Generally:**  The Fifth Amendment contains the "Taking" Clause: "*[N]or shall private property be taken for public use, without just compensation*."

  **1.**  **General meaning:**  The gist of the Taking Clause is that the government may take private property under its "power of eminent domain," but if it does take private property, it must ***pay a fair price***. This is true even if the property is taken to serve a compelling governmental interest. [384]

  **2.**  **Taking vs. regulation:**  The government (whether it's federal or state) must pay for any property that it "takes." On the other hand, if it merely ***"regulates"*** property under its police power, then it does not need to pay (even if the owner's use of his property, or its value, is substantially diminished). [385-393]

**a. Land use regulations:** Usually the problem of distinguishing between a compensable "taking" and a non-compensable "regulation" occurs in the context of *land-use regulation*.

**b. Guidelines:** Here are some guidelines about when a land-use regulation will avoid being a taking:

**i. No denial of economically viable use:** A land-use regulation must not "deny an owner *economically viable use* of his land," or it will be considered a taking. However, few land use regulations are likely to be found to deny the owner all economically viable use of his land. For instance, if a particular 3-story building is made a landmark, the fact that the owner can't tear down the building to build a skyscraper doesn't deprive him of "all economically viable use". But if the state were to *permanently* deny the owner the right to *build any dwelling* on the land, this *would* probably constitute a denial of all economically viable use. [386]

**Example:** The state of South Carolina, in order to protect against coastal erosion, prohibits landowners from building any permanent habitable structure at all on certain parcels. P owns 2 vacant parcels (for which he paid $1 million), on which the building ban applies. *Held*, by the Supreme Court, if this regulation indeed prevents P from making any "economically viable use" of the parcels (something for the state court to decide on remand), there has been a "taking" for which the state must pay compensation, even if the state was just trying to protect the health and safety of its citizens. [*Lucas v. South Carolina Coastal Council*] [387]

**Note 1:** Most zoning, environmental laws and landmark-preservation laws will satisfy this don't-deny-all-economically-viable-uses rule, and will thus *not* be takings, merely non-compensable regulations.

**Note 2:** If a land-use law merely *temporarily* prevents all economically viable use of a parcel, this will not necessarily constitute a taking — *all surrounding circumstances* must be considered to determine whether the interference with use is significant enough to constitute a taking. For instance, a 2- or 3-year *moratorium on development* of a particular parcel, until a permanent land-use scheme can be enacted by government, might not constitute a taking even though for that period an affected owner can't make any economically viable use of her parcel. [*Tahoe-Sierra Preservation Council v. Tahoe Regional Planning Agency*] [387-388]

**ii. Permanent physical occupation:** If the government makes or authorizes a *permanent physical occupation* of the property, this will *automatically* be found to constitute a taking, no matter how minor the interference with the owner's use and no matter how important the countervailing governmental interests. (*Example:* The state requires landlords to permit cable TV companies to install their cable facilities in the landlord's buildings. *Held*, this compulsory cabling was a taking because it was a permanent physical occupation, even though it didn't really restrict the owner's use of his property or reduce its value. [*Loretto v. Teleprompter*]) [385]

**iii. Diminution in value:** The more drastic the *reduction in value* of the owner's property, the more likely a taking is to be found. But a very drastic diminution in value (almost certainly much more than 50%) is required. [386]

**iv. Landmark:** *Landmark preservation schemes*, just like zoning and environmental regulations, will rarely be found to constitute a taking. This is especially true where the designation of a particular building to landmark status occurs as part of a *comprehensive* city-wide preservation scheme. (*Example:* New York City didn't carry out a taking when it designated Grand Central Station as a landmark; this was true even though this designation prevented the owner from constructing a 55-story office building above the Terminal. [*Penn Central v. New York City*]) [390]

3. **Requirement of "public" use:** The Taking Clause says that private property shall not be taken *"for public use"* unless just compensation is paid. This language has been interpreted by the Supreme Court as prohibiting the taking of private property for *private use, even if just compensation is made*. Thus the government cannot simply take private property from one person, and give it to another, without any public purpose.

   a. **"Public use" construed broadly:** However, the Supreme Court has construed the requirement of a "public use" quite *broadly*. Here are two principles illustrating just how broadly the Court stretches the phrase:

   ❑ So long as the state's use of its eminent domain power is "*rationally related* to a *conceivable public purpose*," the public use requirement is satisfied. *Hawaii Housing Authority v. Midkiff*. [393]

   ❑ The property *need not be open to the general public after the taking.* Therefore, the fact that the property is *turned over to some private user* does not prevent the use from being a public one as long as the public can be expected to derive some benefit (e.g., economic development) from the use. [394]

   **Example:** The City of New London, as part of an economic-development plan for the City's waterfront area, condemns 15 houses owned by the Ps. The properties are not blighted. The plan contemplates turning the properties over to private developers. The Ps claim that this is not a "public use," and thus violates their rights under the Fifth Amendment even if "just compensation" is paid.

   *Held*, for the City. Even though the properties are being turned over to private developers (not made available to the public), and even though the properties were not blighted, this is still a "public use" as the term is used in the Fifth Amendment. [*Kelo v. New London*] [394]

## III. THE "CONTRACT" CLAUSE

A. **The "Contract" Clause:** The so-called "Contract" Clause (Art. I, §10) provides that "no state shall ... pass any ... law impairing the obligation of contracts." The clause effectively applies to both federal and state governments. The Clause has a different meaning depending on whether the government is impairing its own contracts or contracts between private parties. [395]

   1. **Public contracts:** If the state is trying to escape from its *own financial obligations*, then the Court will *closely scrutinize* this attempt. Here, the state attempt to "weasel" will be struck down unless the modification is "*reasonable* and *necessary* to support an *important* public purpose" (basically *middle-level review*). [396]

   2. **Private contracts:** But when the state is re-writing contracts made by *private parties*, the judicial review is not so stringent. Here, even a *substantial* modification to contracts between private parties will be allowed so long as the state is acting "*reasonably*" in pursuit of a "legitimate public purpose." So we apply what is basically "mere rationality" review in this situation. (*Example:* If a state's economy is in shambles with widespread home mortgage foreclosures, the state probably may temporarily order a lower interest rate on home mortgages, or impose a moratorium on mortgage repayments, without violating the Contract Clause.) [397-399]

   a. **Incidental effect on contracts:** Even this "mere rationality" standard applies only where the state takes an action that is *specifically directed* at contractual obligations. If the state applies a *"generally applicable rule of conduct"* that has the *incidental by-product* of impairing contractual obligations, the Contract Clause *does not apply at all*. [400]

**Example:** Suppose Manco, a manufacturing company located outside the state of Texahoma, contracts with Disposal Corp., which operates a toxic waste disposal facility within Texahoma. The contract runs through the year 2000, and allows Manco to deliver up to 1,000 tons of toxic waste per year to the dump. The Texahoma legislature then enacts a statute that, effective immediately, prohibits anyone from disposing of any additional toxic wastes within the state. Even though this enactment has an effect on the Manco-Disposal contract, it does not trigger Contract Clause review at all, because the statute affects contracts as an incidental by-product, rather than being specifically directed at contractual obligations.

# IV. THE SECOND AMENDMENT "RIGHT TO BEAR ARMS"

A. **Text of the Amendment:** The Second Amendment provides: "A well regulated Militia, being necessary to the security of a free State, the right of the people to *keep and bear Arms*, shall *not be infringed*." [400]

B. **Applicable to private individuals:** The *Amendment* confers on *private individuals* a right to keep basic firearms, including handguns, *at home for self-defense*. [*District of Columbia v. Heller* (2008)] [400-401]

> **Example:** Washington D.C. makes it a crime to keep any type of handgun at home. It also makes it a crime to keep a non-gun (e.g., a rifle) at home unless the weapon is kept unloaded and inoperable (e.g., by a trigger lock). *Held*, both provisions violate the Second Amendment right of private individuals to keep at home operable firearms of the type that were kept by private citizens for self-defense in 1791. [*Heller, supra.*] [401-405]

1. **State and local governments:** The Second Amendment clearly applies to the *federal* government (since Washington D.C., the jurisdiction at issue in *Heller*, is an arm of the federal government). It's not yet clear whether whether the Amendment is applicable to states and cities. But the Court will likely ultimately conclude that the Amendment is *incorporated* into the meaning of due process for purposes of the 14th Amendment, and is thus *applicable to the states and their sub-divisions (i.e., counties and cities)*. [405]

2. **Review standard to be used:** It's unclear what *standard* the court will use for reviewing governmental restrictions that impair Second Amendment rights (*Heller* didn't decide this). The most likely outcome is that *mid-level review*, under which the question is whether the means chosen by government is *"substantially related"* to the achievement of an *"important"* governmental interest, will ultimately be used. [406]

3. **Some regulation allowed:** It seems likely that despite *Heller*'s broad reading of the Second Amendment, all governments will be allowed to exercise *substantial regulation of gun possession.* So, for example:

   a. **Licensing requirements:** *Licensing requirements* will probably *not* be found to violate the Second Amendment as long as the procedures for obtaining a license are not unreasonably burdensome, and are directed towards keeping guns out of the hands of people who do not have a Second Amendment right to possess them. [407]

   > **Example:** Licensing requirements that deny gun permits to felons and the mentally ill — and that give government a reasonable amount of time to check whether the applicant falls into these categories — are probably valid even after *Heller*.

     **b.**  **Concealed-carry permits:**  Similarly, the Amendment will probably be found not to prohibit governments from banning the ***carrying of concealed weapons in public places.*** [407]

     **c.**  **Modern weapons:** Probably the Amendment won't be found to block governments from banning the possession of ***modern weapons*** that are much more ***advanced and dangerous*** than those existing in 1791. So ***machine guns, assault rifles*** and ***sawed-off shotguns*** probably may still be banned. [407]

## V.   *EX POST FACTO* LAWS

**A. Constitutional prohibition:**  Article I prohibits both state and federal governments from passing any "ex post facto" law. An *ex post facto* law is a law which has a ***retroactive punitive effect****.* So government may not ***impose a punishment*** for conduct which, at the time it occurred, was ***not punishable****.* Also, government may not ***increase*** the punishment for an offense over what was on the books at the time of the act. [408]

> **Example:** On June 1, Joe smokes a cigarette in a public building. On June 10, the state legislature makes it a crime, for the first time, to smoke in a public building. Because of the ban on *ex post facto* laws, Joe cannot be convicted of the June 1 smoking, since it was not a crime at the time he did it. The same would be true if the legislature on June 15 increased the penalty for such smoking over what it was on June 1.

    **1.**  **Criminal only:**  The ban on *ex post facto* laws applies only to measures that are ***"criminal"*** or ***"penal,"*** not to those that are civil. Basically, this means that only measures calling for ***imprisonment*** will come within the *ex post facto* ban (so a measure that imposes, say, ***disbarment***, or one that imposes ***deportation***, can be made retroactive, since these sanctions are civil). See, e.g., *Galvan v. Press*.

## VI. BILLS OF ATTAINDER

**A. Generally:**  Art. I prohibits both the federal government and the states from passing any ***"bill of attainder."*** A bill of attainder is a legislative act which "applies either to named individuals or to easily ascertainable members of a group in such a way as to ***punish*** them without a ***judicial trial***." (*Example:* Congress prohibits the payment of salaries to three named federal agency employees, on the grounds that they are engaged in subversive activities. This is an invalid bill of attainder, since it applies to named or easily-identified individuals, and punishes them without a judicial trial. [*U.S. v. Lovett*]) [409]

CHAPTERS 12 AND 13

# THE "STATE ACTION" REQUIREMENT; CONGRESS' ENFORCEMENT OF THE CIVIL WAR AMENDMENTS

## I.   STATE ACTION

**A. State action generally:**  Virtually all of the rights and liberties guaranteed by the Constitution to individuals are protected only against interference by the government. We summarize this rule by referring to the requirement of ***"state action."*** But sometimes, even a ***private individual's act*** will be found to be "state action" that must comply with the Constitution. There are two main doctrines that may lead a private act to be classified as state action; if ***either*** of these doctrines applies, then the private action is "state action" even if the other doctrine would not apply. The two doctrines are the ***"public function"***

doctrine and the *"state involvement"* doctrine. [417-420]

**B. "Public function" doctrine:** Under the *"public function"* approach to state action, if a private individual (or group) is entrusted by the state to perform functions that are *governmental in nature*, the private individual becomes an *agent of the state*, and his acts constitute state action. [421-425]

   **1. Political system:** The *electoral process* is a "public function," and is thus state action. Therefore, the carrying out of *primary elections* is state action, even if the acts are directly carried out by "private" political parties. (*Example:* A state convention of Democrats (in essence, a "private" political party) rules that only whites may vote in the Texas Democratic Primary. *Held*, this racial restriction is "state action", and therefore violates the 15th Amendment. The primary is an integral part of the election scheme, and the running of elections is traditionally a "public function", so the running of the primary is state action even though it is directly carried out by private groups. [*Smith v. Allwright*]) [421]

      **a. Company town:** Similarly, operation of a *"company town"* is a "public function," and thus is state action, because towns are usually operated by the government. [421-423]

         **i. Shopping centers not a public function:** But operation of a *shopping center* is *not* the equivalent of operating a company town, so a person does not have any First Amendment rights in the shopping center. [*Hudgens v. NLRB*] [422]

      **b. Parks:** Operation of a *park* is usually deemed a governmental function, so generally the operation of a park will constitute "state action" under the "public function" doctrine. Therefore, even if the park is being operated by private persons, it must still obey constitutional constraints (e.g., it can't be operated for whites only). [*Evans v. Newton*]. [423]

   **2. The "exclusively public" requirement:** Apparently, the function must be one that traditionally has been *"exclusively"* a public function, in order for the "public function" doctrine to apply. [423-425]

      **Example:** A warehouseman has a warehouseman's lien on goods stored with him, to cover unpaid storage charges. He sells the goods pursuant to the warehouseman's lien, and the owner claims that due process was required because the resolution of disputes is a "public function". *Held*, the warehouseman's lien and sale was not a "public function" because the resolution of disputes between private individuals is not traditionally an "exclusively" governmental activity — for instance, the parties might have agreed to private arbitration. [*Flagg Bros. v. Brooks*]. [424]

**C. "State involvement" doctrine:** Even if the private individual is not doing something that's traditionally a "public function," his conduct may constitute state action if the state is *heavily involved* in his activities. This is the *"state involvement"* branch of state-action doctrine. Here are some of the ways in which the state and private actor can be so closely involved that the private person's acts become state action: [425]

   **1. Commandment:** The state may become responsible for the private party's actions because it *commanded*, i.e., required, the private party to act in that way. (*Example:* The state enforces a private agreement among neighbors that none will sell his house to a black. Because the state has lent its state judicial enforcement mechanism to this otherwise private contract, the combination of enforcement and private discrimination violates equal protection. [*Shelley v. Kraemer*] [425-428]

   **2. Encouragement:** If the state *"encourages"* the private party's actions, then the private action will be converted into state action. (*Example:* The voters of California amend their constitution to prohibit the state government from interfering with any private individual's right to discriminate when he sells or leases residential real estate. This amendment immediately results in the repeal of two state Fair Housing statutes. *Held*, this state-constitutional amendment amounts to governmental "encouragement" of private discrimination. Therefore, the resulting private discrimination will be imputed to the state, and the state constitutional provision violates the 14th Amendment. [*Reitman v. Mulkey*]) [428]

3. **Symbiosis:**   There is state action if there exists between the state and private actor a **"symbiotic"** relationship, i.e., a relation between the two that is **mutually beneficial**. (*Example:* A Wilmington, Delaware city agency owns and runs a parking garage complex. The agency gives a 20 year lease to a privately-operated restaurant located in the complex. The restaurant refuses to serve African Americans. *Held*, African Americans who are refused service have had their equal protection rights violated. The relation between the restaurant and the publicly-run garage was so close and symbiotic — the garage wouldn't have been able to operate viably without rents from the restaurant — that the restaurant's actions must be imputed to the state, and therefore constitute state action. [*Burton v. Wilmington Parking Authority*]) [428-429]

4. **Entanglement or entwinement:**   State action may arise from the fact that the state is so **"entangled"** or **"entwined"** with a private actor that even though the state might not directly benefit from the private actor's conduct, the conduct will still be treated as state action. This is true where the state and the private party **act together** to carry out the action being challenged. [429-432]

> **Example 1:** A state allows a private litigant — either a civil litigant or a defendant in a criminal case — to use peremptory challenges to exclude jurors on racial grounds. This conduct constitutes state action, and therefore violates the Equal Protection Clause. [*Edmondson v. Leesville Concrete Co.*; *Georgia v. McCollum*] [431]

> **Example 2:** A state recognizes a private association of high schools as being the regulator of high school interscholastic sports. Most members of the association are public high schools within the state, and these schools are active in the association affairs as part of the schools' official business of running athletic programs. Because the association's activities are deeply entwined with state affairs, the association's conduct is state action. [*Brentwood Academy v. Tenn. Secondary School Athl. Assoc.*] [432]

   a. **Mere acquiescence not enough:**   But if the state merely **acquiesces** in the private party's discrimination, this won't be enough of a state involvement to convert the private actor's conduct into state action. [432]

   > **Example:** The state regulates all utilities. A private utility cuts off plaintiff's service without notice or a hearing, and this fact is known to the state, which does not object. *Held*, the utility's conduct was not state action, because the state merely acquiesced in that conduct, rather than actively participating in it. [*Jackson v. Metropolitan Edison Co.*]

   b. **Licensing:**   Similarly, the fact that the state has **licensed** a private person is generally not enough to convert the private person's conduct into state action. [429-430]

   > **Example:** A private club refuses to serve African Americans. Even though the state has given the club one of a limited number of liquor licenses, this act of licensing is not enough to turn the club's action into state action. [*Moose Lodge v. Irvis*]

## II. CONGRESSIONAL ENFORCEMENT OF CIVIL RIGHTS

A. **Congressional enforcement of civil rights:**   Congress has special powers to enforce the post-Civil War amendments, i.e., the Thirteenth, Fourteenth, and Fifteenth Amendments. [439-441]

   1. **13th Amendment:**   The Thirteenth Amendment **abolishes "slavery"** and **"involuntary servitude."**

2.  **14th Amendment:** The Fourteenth Amendment requires the states to give *"due process," "equal protection,"* and *"privileges and immunities."*

3.  **15th Amendment:** The Fifteenth Amendment bars the states from denying *voting rights* on the basis of race, color or previous condition of servitude.

B.  **Congress' power to reach private conduct:** The special enforcement powers let Congress reach a lot of *private conduct* that it could not reach by means of any other congressional power. [441-446]

1.  **14th and 15th Amendments:** When Congress enforces the Fourteenth and Fifteenth Amendments, it has some, but not unlimited, power to reach private conduct. So Congress could, for instance, make it a crime for somebody to *interfere with a state official* who is trying to guarantee another person's equal protection rights or voting rights. (*Example:* Congress can make it a crime for D to prevent a school principal from allowing African Americans to enroll in an all white school.) [441-444]

    a.  **Can't reach purely private discrimination:** But Congress under the Fourteenth Amendment *cannot* simply make it a crime for one private person to practice ordinary racial discrimination against another. [441] (Congress would instead have to use its power to regulate interstate commerce; this is the basis on which the 1964 Civil Rights Act, forbidding racial discrimination in places of public accommodation, was upheld. [*Katzenbach v. McClung*])

2.  **13th Amendment:** But the *13th* Amendment is different. §1 of the 13th Amendment provides that "neither slavery nor involuntary servitude, except as a punishment for crime … shall exist within the United States." §2 gives Congress the power to "enforce this [amendment] by appropriate legislation." The 13th Amendment, unlike the 14th and 15th, is *not explicitly limited to governmental action.* Indeed, that's the most important thing to remember about the 13th Amendment, and its principal use today — it's practically the only clause in the entire Constitution that prevents one private citizen from doing something to another. So the 13th Amendment gives Congress important authority to reach certain private conduct that it couldn't reach through the 14th and 15th Amendments. [444-446]

    a.  **"Badges of slavery":** If the 13th Amendment only meant that Congress could take special action to ensure that slavery itself, in its most literal sense, shall be wiped out, the Amendment wouldn't be of much practical use today. But instead, the Supreme Court has held that the Amendment allows Congress also to stamp out the *"badges and incidents"* of slavery. In fact, Congress has the power to determine what the "badges and incidents of slavery" are, so long as it acts rationally — once Congress defines these "badges and incidents", it can then forbid them. [444-446]

        **Example:** In 1866, Congress passes a statute, 42 U.S.C. §1982, which provides that "all citizens of the United States shall have the same right, in every state and Territory, as is enjoyed by white citizens thereof to inherit, purchase, lease, sell, hold and convey real and personal property." In a modern case, the Ps argue that the statute prevents D (a private developer) from refusing to sell them a house solely because they are African American.

        *Held*, this statute applies to block discrimination by D, a private citizen. Furthermore, the statute is constitutional under the 13th Amendment. §2 of the 13th Amendment, which gives Congress enforcement powers under that amendment, gives Congress the power to make a rational determination of *what the badges and incidents of slavery are.* Here, Congress could have rationally concluded that barriers to enjoyment of real estate, and discrimination in housing, are relics of slavery. [*Jones v. Alfred H. Mayer Co.*] [444-446]

    b.  **Ancestry, ethnic discrimination:** As we've just seen, the 13th Amendment clearly lets Congress prevent private discrimination against African Americans, on the grounds that it's a "badge or incident" of slavery. *All other racial minorities are also protected* — Congress could probably even bar private racial discrimination against *whites* based on the 13th Amendment (though the Court has never explicitly decided this). But it's not clear whether private discrimination based on **non-racial grounds** (e.g., **ancestry**, **ethnic background**, religion, sex, etc.) can be barred by Congress acting pursuant to the 13th Amendment. [445]

    **c.** **Must have statute:** The application of the 13th Amendment to a broad range of "badges and incidents of slavery" applies only where Congress has used its **enforcement** powers by passing a **statute** that relies on the Amendment. If private citizen A discriminates against B on the basis of race, but the type of discrimination is not one that Congress has outlawed, then the 13th Amendment's "naked" or "self-executing" scope **won't** be enough to reach that discrimination. Probably actual **peonage** — the keeping of a person as a slave — is the only type of private racial discrimination that is directly barred by the 13th Amendment in the absence of a congressional statute. [445]

**C.** **Congressional power to modify constitutional rights:** Congress does **not** have the power to **redefine the scope** of the rights protected by the Civil War amendments in a way that is different from the way the Supreme Court would define their scope. [449]

    **1.** **No power to redefine scope:** This is true whether Congress is trying to **expand** or **contract** the right. [449-451]

        **Example:** The Supreme Court issues a decision defining the First Amendment Establishment Clause more narrowly than the Court had previously defined that clause. Congress doesn't like this decision. It therefore passes the "Religious Freedom Restoration Act," which in effect says that all state and local governments must refrain from any action that would have violated the Establishment Clause under the earlier, now-overruled, cases. *Held*, Congress has no power to either expand or contract the scope of constitutional rights, so the Act is an unconstitutional exercise of congressional power. [*Boerne v. Flores*]

**D.** **Congress' remedial powers:** The Thirteenth, Fourteenth and Fifteenth Amendments each has a specific provision giving Congress the power to **"enforce"** that amendment. See, e.g., § 5 of the Fourteenth Amendment, giving Congress the power to enforce the amendment **"by appropriate legislation."**

    **1.** **Remedial powers:** Under this enforcement power, Congress may **prohibit** certain actions that **don't directly violate** these amendments, if it reasonably believes that these actions would or might **lead** to violations of the amendments. That is, Congress has **broad "remedial" or "prophylactic" powers.** [448]

        **Example:** Congress may use its 15th Amendment remedial powers to ban voter literacy tests in states with a history of voting rights violations, even though such tests aren't themselves necessarily unconstitutional. This is so because Congress reasonably fears that such tests **may lead** to violations of the 15th Amendment. [*South Carolina v. Katzenbach*]

# III. FEDERAL ATTEMPTS TO STOP STATES FROM DISCRIMINATING

**A.** **"Congruent and proportional":** When Congress purports to use its enforcement powers to prohibit acts that it fears might lead to constitutional violations, Congress' action must be **"congruent and proportional"** to the threatened violation. If not, the congressional action is **invalid** under the enforcement powers. [*Boerne v. Flores*] [451]

    **1.** **Significance:** The most important consequence of this principle is that if Congress wants to let private individuals **sue the states** in federal district court for money **damages** for state violations of a federal anti-discrimination statute, two conditions must be satisfied:

[1] Congress must ordinarily have before it evidence of ***widespread past constitutional violations by the states*** of the sort that Congress is trying to prevent; and

[2] the remedy picked by Congress must be ***"congruent and proportional"*** to the state violations that Congress is trying to prevent.

Otherwise, Congress' action cannot be justified by its Civil-War-Amendments enforcement powers. And only those powers (not, say, the Commerce power) are sufficient to let Congress overcome states' ***Eleventh Amendment immunity from private federal-court damage suits.*** [451-452]

> **Example:** In the Age Discrimination in Employment Act (ADEA) Congress makes the states, when they act as employers, obey the same age-discrimination rules as private employers. And Congress authorizes state employees to sue the states in federal court for money damages for ADEA violations committed by the state. Congress says it has acted under authority of its 14th Amendment §5 remedial powers, to prevent violations by the states of older state employees' equal protection rights.
>
> *Held*, Congress went beyond the scope of its §5 remedial powers, because there was no evidence that the states routinely violated older workers' equal protection rights. Therefore, Congress' regulation was not a "congruent and proportional" response to any threatened constitutional violations, making the regulation not authorized under Congress' § 5 remedial powers. Consequently, the states are free to assert their Eleventh Amendment immunity from private damage suits (which immunity can properly be overcome only by Congress' use of its § 5 remedial powers, not by its use of other powers like the Commerce power). [*Kimel v. Fla. Bd. of Regents*] [452-453]

a.  **Area receiving heightened scrutiny:** But if the federal statute that creates the right of the plaintiff to sue a state for damages deals with an area that involves ***either a suspect or semi-suspect class or a fundamental right, Congress has more freedom.*** *S*ince the Court applies some form of ***heightened scrutiny*** to these areas, the Court will be much more likely to find that Congress' decision to allow a damages suit ***meets the "congruent and proportional" requirement*** and is thus constitutional. [454-455]

> **Example:** Congress lets state employees sue in federal court for damages for violations of the federal Family and Medical Leave Act (FMLA), which allows employees to take unpaid leave to care for a sick family member. A state that is sued for FMLA damages by its employee argues that the state has Eleventh Amendment immunity from such suits.
>
> *Held*, for the employee. Congress acted properly here. FMLA was enacted to deal, in part, with widespread state and private *gender* discrimination with regard to leave policies. Since gender discrimination receives heightened (mid-level) equal protection review, Congress can use its 14th Amendment § 5 enforcement powers against the states on less of a showing of state discrimination than where the type of discrimination being addressed gets only mere-rationality review (e.g., the *age* discrimination at issue in *Kimel, supra.*) Therefore, Congress had before it enough evidence of state gender-oriented leave discrimination to make Congress' response in enacting FMLA a "congruent and proportional" response to the discrimination it found. This made Congress' use of its 14th Amendment § 5 enforcement power proper. And by the use of that power Congress was able to overcome the otherwise-applicable Eleventh Amendment immunity of the states from private federal-court damage suits. [*Nevada Dept. of Human Res. v. Hibbs*] [454-455]

b.  **Right to prohibit direct constitutional violations:** Also, if the state conduct that the plaintiff is complaining of was an ***actual violation*** by the state of the plaintiff's ***constitutional rights,*** Congress can grant the plaintiff the right to recover damages against the state in federal court without worrying about whether the federal statute is congruent-and-proportional to the overall pattern of constitutional violations that Congress was trying to prevent. [*U.S. v. Georgia*]

**Example:** P is a disabled prisoner in a state-run prison, who seeks damages from the state for violating his rights under a federal disability-discrimination statute by not accommodating his disability (e.g., by putting him in a cell too small to turn his wheelchair around).

*Held*, if the state conduct P is alleging was a direct violation of P's equal protection rights, then Congress has the power to give P a damages remedy even if the federal statute in question does not meet the congruent-and-proportional requirement. That's because Congress clearly has the power, under its Fourteenth Amendment § 5 enforcement powers, to overcome a state's Eleventh Amendment immunity from private damage suits for state conduct that directly violates the plaintiff's constitutional rights. [*U.S. v. Georgia*]

CHAPTER 14
# FREEDOM OF EXPRESSION

## I. GENERAL THEMES

**A. Text of First Amendment:** The First Amendment provides, in part, that "Congress shall make no law ... abridging the ***freedom of speech***, or of the press; or the right of the people peaceably to assemble, and to petition the Government for a redress of grievances." [464]

    **1. Related rights:** There are thus several distinct rights which may be grouped under the category "freedom of expression": freedom of ***speech***, of the ***press***, of ***assembly***, and of ***petition***. Additionally, there is a well-recognized "freedom of ***association***" which, although it is not specifically mentioned in the First Amendment, is derived from individuals' rights of speech and assembly.

**B. Two broad classes:** Whenever you consider governmental action that seems to infringe upon the freedom of expression, there's one key question that you must always ask before you ask anything else. That question is, "Is this governmental action '***content-based***' or '***content-neutral***'?" If the action is "content-based," the government's action will generally be subjected to strict scrutiny, and the action will rarely be sustained. On the other hand, if the action is "content-neutral", the government's action is subjected to a much less demanding standard, and is thus much more likely to be upheld. [464-466]

    **1. Classifying:** A governmental action that burdens a person's expression is "content-based" if the government is aiming at the ***"communicative impact"*** of the expression. By contrast, if the government is aiming at something other than the communicative impact of the expression, the government action is "content-neutral", even though it may have the *effect* of burdening the expression.

        **Example 1 (content-based):** Virginia forbids pharmacists to advertise the prices of prescription drugs, because it's afraid that the public will buy drugs at the lowest available price and will therefore receive low-quality goods and services. This government ban is "content-based", since the speech is being regulated because of the government's fears about how consumers will respond to its *communicative impact.* Therefore, the government's ban will be strictly scrutinized, and is in fact violative of the First Amendment. [*Virginia Pharmacy Bd. v. Virginia Consumer Council*] [466]

        **Example 2 (content-neutral):** A city forbids the distribution of all leaflets, because it wishes to prevent littering. This ban is "content neutral" — the government is banning all leaflets, regardless of their content, and the harm sought to be avoided (littering) would exist to the same extent regardless of the message in the leaflets. Therefore, the government action is subject to less rigid review — more or less "intermediate level review" (though it was still struck down on these facts.) [*Schneider v. State*] [466]

    **a. Tip:** Here's a tip to help you decide whether a given governmental action is content-based or not: would the harm the government is trying to prevent exist to the same degree if the listeners/readers ***didn't understand English***? If the answer is "no," the action is probably content-based.

    **Example:** Suppose a consumer in the prescription-drug case above didn't speak English. He wouldn't suffer the harm the state was trying to prevent — being induced to buy bad drugs or bad service for a cheap price — even if he saw or read the advertising, so it's clearly the content of the communication that the state is objecting to. But in the case of the ban on littering, even a whole city of non-English-speakers would suffer the same harm — littered streets — so the ban is content-neutral.

    **b. Motive counts:** When a court decides whether a regulation is content-based or content-neutral, ***motives*** count for everything — the question is what the state really ***intends*** to do. If the court believes that the state intends to inhibit certain speech because of its message, the court will treat the statute as content-based (and strictly scrutinize it) even though it is neutral on its face.

**C. Analysis of content-based government action:** Once we've determined that a particular government action impairing expression is "content-based", we then have to determine whether the expression falls within a category that is ***protected*** by the First Amendment.

    **1. Unprotected category:** If the speech falls into certain pre-defined ***unprotected*** categories, then the government can basically ban that expression completely based on its content, without any interference at all from the First Amendment. [469]

        **a. Listing:** The main "unprotected" categories are: (1) ***obscenity***; (2) ***fraudulent misrepresentation***; (3) ***defamation***; (4) ***advocacy of imminent lawless behavior***; and (5) ***"fighting words"***.

        **b. Not totally unprotected:** But even speech falling within an "unprotected category" receives one small First Amendment protection: government must regulate in a basically ***content-neutral*** way. (*Example:* The state may ban all "fighting words." But it may not choose to ban just those fighting words directed at the listener's race, religion, or other enumerated traits. [*R.A.V. v. City of St. Paul*])

    **2. Protected category:** All expression not falling into one of these five pre-defined categories is "protected". If expression is protected, then any government ban or restriction on it based on its content will be ***presumed to be unconstitutional***. The Court will subject any content-based regulation of protected speech to ***strict scrutiny*** — the regulation will be sustained only if it (1) serves a ***compelling governmental objective***; and (2) is ***"necessary,"*** i.e., drawn as ***narrowly as possible*** to achieve that objective (since a broader-than-needed restriction wouldn't be a "necessary" means.) [467-469]

    **Example:** A District of Columbia statute bans the display of any sign within 500 feet of a foreign embassy, if the sign would bring the foreign government into "public disrepute". *Held*, this regulation is content-based, since a sign is prohibited or not prohibited based on what the sign says. Therefore, the regulation must be strictly scrutinized, and cannot be upheld. Even if the government's interest in protecting the dignity of foreign diplomats is compelling — which it may or may not be — the statute is not "necessary" to achieve that interest, since a narrower statute that only banned the intimidation, coercion or threatening of diplomats would do the trick. [*Boos v. Barry*]. [469]

        **a. Religious speech gets equal protection:** The requirement of content-neutrality is now so strong that it seems to take precedence over the ***Establishment Clause*** (which protects separation of church and state). Thus if the government allows private speech in a particular forum, it may not treat *religiously-oriented* speech *less favorably* than non-religiously-oriented speech.

**Example:** If a public university gives funding for student publications on various topics, the requirement of content-neutrality means that the university must give the same funding to a student publication whose mission is to proselytize for Christianity. [*Rosenberger v. Univ. of Virginia*.]

**D. Analyzing content-neutral regulations:** Now, let's go back to the beginning, and assume that the government restriction is *content-neutral*.

1. **Three-part test:** Here, we have a *three-part test* that the government must satisfy before its regulation will be sustained if that regulation substantially impairs expression [472-473]:

    a. **Significant governmental interest:** First, the regulation must serve a *significant governmental interest.*

    b. **Narrowly tailored:** Second, the regulation must be *narrowly tailored* to serve that governmental interest. So if there's a somewhat *less restrictive* way to accomplish the same result, the government must use that less-intrusive way. (*Example:* Preventing littering is a significant governmental interest. But the government can't completely ban the distribution of handbills to avoid littering, because the littering problem could be solved by the less restrictive method of simply punishing those who drop a handbill on the street. [*Schneider v. State*])

    c. **Alternative channels:** Finally, the state must *"leave open alternative channels"* for communicating the information. (*Example:* Suppose a city wants to ban all billboards. If a political advertiser can show that there's no other low-cost way to get his message across to local motorists, this billboard ban might run afoul of the "alternative channels" requirement.)

2. **Mid-level review:** This three-part test basically boils down to *mid-level* review for content-neutral restrictions that significantly impair expression (as opposed to strict scrutiny for content-based restrictions).

**E. Overbreadth:** The doctrine of *overbreadth* is very important in determining whether a governmental regulation of speech violates the First Amendment. A statute is "overbroad" if it bans speech which could constitutionally be forbidden but *also* bans speech which is protected by the First Amendment. [483-486]

1. **Standing:** To see why the overbreadth doctrine is important, let's first consider how a litigant attacks the constitutionality of a statute *outside* the First Amendment area. Here, the litigant can only get a statute declared unconstitutional if he can show that it's unconstitutional in its *application to him*. But the overbreadth doctrine lets a litigant prevail if he can show that the statute, applied according to its terms, would violate the First Amendment rights of *persons not now before the court*. So overbreadth is really an exception to the usual rule of "standing" — under the usual standing rules, a person is not normally allowed to assert the constitutional rights of others, only his own.

2. **"Substantial" overbreadth:** In cases where the statute is aimed at *conduct* that has expressive content (rather than aimed against pure speech), the overbreadth doctrine will only be applied if the overbreadth would be *"substantial"*. In other words, the potential unconstitutional applications of the statute must be reasonably numerous compared with the constitutional applications. [485-486]

**F. Vagueness:** There is a second important First Amendment doctrine: *vagueness*. A statute is unconstitutionally vague if the conduct forbidden by it is so *unclearly defined* that a reasonable person would have to *guess at its meaning*. [486]

1. **Distinguish from overbreadth:** Be careful to *distinguish vagueness from overbreadth:* they both leave the citizen uncertain about which applications of a statute may constitutionally be imposed. But in overbreadth, the uncertainty is hidden or "latent," and in vagueness the uncertainty is easily apparent. [486]

   **Example:** Statute I prohibits anyone from "burning a U.S. flag as a symbol of opposition to organized government." Statute II prohibits anyone from "burning a U.S. flag for any purpose whatsoever." Statute I is probably unconstitutionally vague, because there's no way to tell what the statute means by "symbols of opposition to organized government." Statutue II is unconstitutionally overbroad — it's obviously not vague, since it's perfectly clear that it bans *all* flag burning. But since by its terms it appears to apply to constitutionally-protected conduct (e.g., burning that's intended as a political expression), and since there's no easy way to separate out the constitutional from unconstitutional applications, it's overbroad.

## II. ADVOCACY OF ILLEGAL CONDUCT

A. **Advocacy of illegal conduct:** Remember that one of our "unprotected categories" is the *advocacy of imminent illegal conduct*. The government can ban speech that advocates crime or the use of force if (but only if) it shows that two requirements are met [474-483]:

   1. **Intent:** The advocacy must be *intended* to incite or produce "imminent lawless action"; and

   2. **Likelihood:** The advocacy must in fact be *likely* to incite or produce that imminent lawless action.

## III. TIME, PLACE AND MANNER REGULATIONS

A. **Time, place and manner generally:** Let's now focus on regulations covering the *"time, place and manner"* of expression. This is probably the area of Freedom of Expression on which you are most likely to be tested, since these kinds of regulations are quite often found in real life. When we give you the rules for analyzing "time, place and manner" restrictions below, assume that the speech that is being restricted is taking place in a *public forum*. (If it's not, then the government has a somewhat easier time of getting its regulation sustained; we'll be talking about these non-public forum situations later.) [490]

   1. **Three-part test:** A "time, place and manner" regulation of public-forum speech has to pass a *three-part test* to avoid being a violation of the First Amendment [492]:

      a. **Content-neutral:** First, it has to be *content-neutral*. In other words, the government can't really be trying to regulate content under the guise of regulating "time, place and manner".

         **Example:** City enacts an ordinance allowing parades or demonstrations "to protest governmental policies" to be conducted only between 10 a.m. and 4 p.m. No such restrictions are placed on other kinds of parades or demonstrations. Even though this restriction is ostensibly merely a "time, place and manner" restriction, it violates the requirement of content-neutrality, because the restriction applies to some expressive conduct but not others, based on the content of the speech.

      b. **Narrowly tailored for significant governmental interest:** Second, it's got to be *narrowly tailored* to serve a *significant governmental interest*. (We saw this above when we were talking more generally about the analysis of all content-neutral restrictions on speech.) This basically means that not only must the government be pursuing an important interest, but there must not be some significantly *less intrusive* way that government could achieve its objective.

**Example**: Suppose the government wants to prevent littering on the streets. Even though prevention of littering is an important governmental objective, the government may not simply ban all distribution of handbills, because there is a significantly less restrictive means of achieving this objective — a direct ban on littering — so the ban on handbills is not "narrowly tailored" to achieving the anti-littering objective.)

c. **Alternative channels:** Finally, the state must "leave open *alternative channels*" for communicating the information.

**Example:** City is a medium-sized city, with six public parks and many streets. City enacts an ordinance stating that any parade or demonstration, no matter what the content of the message, shall take place only in Central Park or on Main Street. City argues that its limited budget for police security, and the greater ease of handling crowds in these two places than in other places, justify the ordinance. Even though this time, place and manner restriction is apparently content-neutral and is arguably narrowly tailored for a significant governmental interest, it probably violates the "leave open alternative channels" requirement because it puts off limits for parades and demonstrations the vast majority of locations within City.

2. **Application to conduct:** These rules on when the state may regulate the "time, place and manner" of expression apply where what is being regulated is pure speech. But much more importantly, these rules apply where the state is regulating *"conduct"* that has an expressive component. *So the state can never defend on the grounds that "We're not regulating speech, we're just regulating conduct."* [492-493]

**Example**: It's "conduct" to hand out handbills, or to form a crowd that marches down the street as part of a political demonstration. But since both of these activities have a major expressive component, the state cannot restrict the conduct unless its satisfies the three-part test described above, i.e., the restriction is content neutral, it's narrowly tailored to achieve a significant governmental interest, and it leaves open alternative channels.

3. **"Facial" vs. "as applied":** A "time, place and manner" regulation, like any other regulation impinging upon First Amendment rights, may be attacked as being either "facially" invalid or invalid "as applied." Thus even a time, place and manner restriction that has been very carefully worded to as to satisfy all three requirements listed above may become unconstitutional *as applied to a particular plaintiff*. [497]

**Example:** A City ordinance provides that any parade or demonstration participated in by more than five people shall be held only after the purchase of a permit, which shall be issued by the City Manager for free to any applicant upon two days notice. The City Manager normally issues such permits without inquiring into the nature of the demonstration planned by the applicant. P, who is known locally as an agitator who opposes the current city government, applies for a permit. The City Manager denies the permit, saying, "I don't like the rabble rousing you've been doing." Even though the ordinance on its face is probably a valid time, place and manner restriction, the application of the ordinance to P's own permit request violates P's First Amendment rights, because that application is not being carried out in a content-neutral manner.

B. **Licensing:** Be especially skeptical of governmental attempts to require a *license* or *permit* before expressive conduct takes place. [494-498]

1. **Content-neutral:** Obviously, any permit requirement must be applied in a *content-neutral* way. (*Example:* Local officials give permits for speeches made for purposes of raising money for non-controversial charities, but decline to give permits for demonstrations to protest the racism of local officials. The requirement of content neutrality in the licensing scheme is not being satisfied, and the scheme will be automatically struck down.) [494]

2. **No excess discretion:** Also, the licensing scheme must set forth the grounds for denying a permit *narrowly* and *specifically*, so that the discretion of local officials will be curtailed. (*Example*: A municipal ordinance cannot require a permit for every newspaper vending machine where the permit is to be granted on "terms and conditions deemed necessary by the mayor" — the grounds for denying a permit must be set forth much more specifically, to curb the official's discretion. [*Lakewood v. Plain Dealer Publ. Co.*]) [495]

3. **Narrow means-end tailoring:** Finally, the permit *mechanism* must be *closely tailored* to the *objective* that the government is trying to achieve.

> **Example:** A village bans any "canvasser" from going onto residential property for the purpose of promoting any "cause" without first getting a Solicitation Permit from the mayor. The village defends the ordinance on the grounds that it helps prevent fraud, and protects residents' privacy. *Held*, this ordinance is invalid on its face, because it's not tailored to the village's stated interests. For instance, the ordinance applies even to religious and political proselytizing unaccompanied by fund-raising, which poses little risk of fraud. Conversely, the interest in protecting residents' privacy could be just as well achieved by letting residents post No Solicitation signs that it would be an offense to ignore. [*Watchtower Bible and Tract Soc. v. Stratton*] [496]

4. **Reasonable means of maintaining order:** But if these three requirements — content-neutral application, limited administrative discretion and close means-end fit — are satisfied, the permit requirement will be *upheld* if it is a *reasonable means of ensuring that public order is maintained.* [497]

> **Example:** A requirement that a permit be obtained before a large group of people may march would probably be upheld as a reasonable way of maintaining order, if the requirement is applied in a content-neutral way and is drafted so as to apply without exception to *all* large marches.

5. **Right to ignore requirement:** Assuming that a permit requirement is unconstitutional, must the speaker apply, be rejected, and then sue? Or may he simply speak without the permit, and then raise the unconstitutionality as a defense to a criminal charge for violating the permit requirement? The answer depends on whether the permit is unconstitutional on its face or merely as applied. [497-498]

  a. **Facially invalid:** If the permit requirement is unconstitutional *on its face*, the speaker is *not* required to apply for a permit. He may decline to apply, speak, and then defend (and avoid conviction) on the grounds of the permit requirement's unconstitutionality.

  b. **As applied:** But where the permit requirement is not facially invalid, but only unconstitutional *as applied to the speaker*, the speaker generally does *not* have the right to ignore the requirement — he must apply for the permit and then seek prompt judicial review, rather than speaking and raising the unconstitutionality-as-applied as a defense. (However, an exception to this rule exists where the applicant shows that *sufficiently prompt judicial review* of the denial was *not available.* )

C. **Right to be left alone:** People have no strong *right to be left alone*, and the government therefore can't regulate broadly to protect that right. As a general rule, it's *up to the unwilling listener* (or viewer) *to avoid the undesired expression.* [498]

**Example:** A city can't make it a misdemeanor to walk up and down the street handing advertising brochures to people without the recipient's express consent. (It's up to the recipient to decline the handbill.)

1.  **Captive audience:** But if the audience is *"captive"* (unable to avert their eyes and ears), this makes it *more likely* that a fair degree of content-neutral regulation *will be allowed*. (However, the fact that the audience is captive is just one factor in measuring the strength of the state interest in regulating.) [499]

    > **Example:** A state may make it a crime to approach close to a woman who is entering an abortion clinic, if the approacher's purpose is to orally "counsel or educate" the woman and the woman does not consent to the approach. [*Hill v. Colorado*].

D.  **Canvassing:** A speaker's right to *canvass*, that is, to go around ringing doorbells or giving out handbills, receives substantial protection. [500-503]

    1.  **Homeowner can say "no":** The individual listener (e.g., the homeowner), is always free to say, "No, I don't want to speak to you about becoming (say), a Jehovah's Witness." The city can then make it a crime for the speaker to persist.

    2.  **City can't give blanket prohibition:** But the *government* cannot say "No" *in advance* on behalf of its homeowners or other listeners. [501]

        > **Example:** A city passes an ordinance providing that "All doorbell ringing for the purpose of handing out handbills is hereby forbidden." *Held*, such an ordinance violates the First Amendment, even if (as the city claims) it is a content-neutral ordinance designed to protect unwilling listeners, such as those who work nights and sleep days. The most the city can do is to provide that once the individual homeowner makes it clear he doesn't want to be spoken to, the speaker must honor that request. [*Martin v. Struthers*]

    3.  **Time, place & manner:** But the authorities may impose "time, place & manner" limits on canvassing, if these limits: (1) are content-neutral; (2) serve a significant governmental interest; and (3) leave open adequate other channels for communication. (*Example:* A town might prohibit canvassing after 6:00 PM, if its policy is truly content-neutral (e.g., it wasn't enacted for the purpose of silencing Jehovah's Witnesses), is enacted to protect homeowners' night-time tranquility, and allows solicitation to take place at other times.)

E.  **Fighting words:** One of our other "unprotected categories" consists of *"fighting words."* "Fighting words" are words which are likely to make the person to whom they are addressed commit an *act of violence*, probably against the speaker. Expression that falls within the "fighting words" category can be flatly banned or punished by the state. [*Chaplinsky v. New Hampshire*] [503-504]

    > **Example**: D picks out one member of his audience and calls him a liar, racist and crook. D can be arrested for this speech, because these are words which might well provoke a reasonable person to whom they are addressed into physically attacking D.)

    1.  **Limits:** But the "fighting words" doctrine is tightly limited:

        a.  **Anger not enough:** It's not enough that the speaker has made the crowd angry; they must be so angry that they are *likely to fight*. [503]

        b.  **Crowd control:** The police must *control* the angry crowd instead of arresting the speaker if they've got the physical ability to do so. (In other words, the police can't grant the hostile crowd a "heckler's veto.") [504]

        c.  **Dislike of speaker's identity:** The doctrine doesn't apply where it's the mere *identity* or *lawful acts* of the speaker, rather than his threatening words, that moves the crowd to anger. (*Example*: If D is a black civil rights worker speaking in a small southern town with a history of racial violence, the fact that members of the audience are ready to attack D because they hate all black civil rights activists will not suffice to make D's speech "fighting words" — here the anger is not really coming from the speaker's particular threatening words, but from his identity and his lawful advocacy of change.) [504]

**F. Offensive language:** Language that is ***"offensive"*** is nonetheless protected by the First Amendment. [506-508]

    **1. Profanity:** This means that even language that is ***profane*** may not be banned from public places. (*Example*: D wears a jacket saying "Fuck the Draft" in the L.A. County Courthouse. D cannot be convicted for breaching the peace. The state may not ban language merely because it is "offensive," even if profane. [*Cohen v. Calif.*]) [506-507]

        **a. Sexually-oriented non-obscene language:** This protection of "offensive" material also means that messages or images that are ***sexually-oriented*** but not obscene are, similarly, protected.

        **Example:** Congress bans the use of the Internet to display any "indecent" language or images which may be accessed by minors. *Held*, this statute is unconstitutional, because it restricts the First Amendment rights of adults to receive indecent-but-not-obscene material. [*Reno v. ACLU*] [523]

    **2. Racial or religious hatred:** Similarly, this means that messages preaching ***racial or religious hatred*** are protected (at least if they don't incite imminent violence or come within the "fighting words" doctrine). (*Example*: A member of the American Nazi Party tells a predominantly-Jewish audience, "Jews are the scum of the earth and should be eliminated." D cannot be punished for, or even restricted from, saying these words.) [508-508]

    **3. Limits:** But offensive language *can* be prohibited or punished if: (1) the audience is a ***"captive"*** one (e.g., the speech occurs on a city bus or subway); or (2) the language is ***"obscene,"*** under the formal legal definition of this term (lewd and without socially redeeming value).

**G. Regulation of "hate speech":** Government efforts to regulate ***"hate speech"*** — for instance, speech attacking racial minorities, women, homosexuals, or other traditionally disfavored groups — may run afoul of the First Amendment for being content-based. [509-516]

    **1. Three rules:** Here are the general rules about how a state may go about banning hate speech:

        ❑ **General ban:** A ban on speech or conduct intended or likely to incite anger or violence based solely on ***particular listed topics or motives*** — such as race, color, religion or gender hatred — is ***impermissibly content-based.*** That's true even if all the speech/conduct banned falls within an ***"unprotected"*** category such as, here, ***"fighting words."*** [*R.A.V. v. St. Paul*] [510]

        **Example:** City bans only those "fighting words" that evoke hatred or conflict based on race, ethnicity or gender (not fighting words based on, say, the listeners' political affiliation). This enactment is content-based, in that it selects speech for proscription based on its content. Therefore, the statute will be strictly scrutinized, and struck down for not being sufficiently narrowly-tailored to achieve the compelling state interest in avoiding dangerous physical conflict. (However, a state could ban *all* fighting words — it just can't select fighting words based only on certain types of hatred.) [*R.A.V.*] [510]

        ❑ **Worst examples:** However, a state ***may*** impose a content-based ban on ***particular instances*** of unprotected speech if the ban forbids ***only the very worst examples*** illustrating ***the very reason the particular class of speech is unprotected.***

        **Example:** The state may choose to criminalize just the very most dangerous "fighting words," just the very most obscene obscene images, etc. [*R.A.V.*]

        ❑ **Penalty-enhancement statutes:** Also, a state may identify particular generally-applicable criminal proscriptions, and may then choose to punish ***more severely*** those criminal acts that happen to be motivated by hate than those not motivated by hate. This is called the *"penalty enhancement"* approach. [*Wisconsin v. Mitchell*] [513]

**Example:** For instance, from within the overall class of acts that constitute arson (all of which are defined as crimes), the state may punish arson more seriously if it's motivated by bias against particular groups.

❏ **All intimidating acts:** Finally, a state may select a particular type of expressive act (e.g., cross-burning), and punish *all instances* where that act is done with a purpose of *intimidating or threatening* someone, even though the state doesn't punish other types of intimidating or threatening acts. [*Virginia v. Black*] [513]

**Example:** A state may choose to ban all cross-burnings that are done with intent to intimidate another. That's true even if the state chooses not to criminalize other types of expressive activity that are done with intent to intimidate another (e.g., burning that other in effigy).

**H. Injunctions against expressive conduct:** Where the restriction on expression is in the form of an *injunction* issued by a judge, there is a special standard of review. When a court issues an injunction that serves as a kind of "time, place and manner" restriction, the injunction will be subjected to slightly *more stringent* review than would a generally-applicable statute or regulation with the same substance: the injunction must "*burden no more speech than necessary* to serve a significant governmental interest." [*Madsen v. Women's Health Center, Inc.*] [516]

**I. The public forum:** Let's turn now to the concept of the *"public forum."* [526-537]

  **1. Rules:** Here are the rules concerning when the fact that speech occurs in a public forum makes a difference, and how: [526]

    **a. Content-based:** If a regulation is *content-based*, it makes no difference whether the expression is or is not in a public forum: strict scrutiny will be given to the regulation, and it will almost never be upheld.

    **b. Neutral "time, place & manner":** It's where a regulation is *content-neutral* that the existence of a public forum makes a difference; especially regulations on "time, place & manner" are less likely to be upheld where the expression takes place in a public forum. [526]

      **i. Non-public forum:** When expression takes place in a *non-public forum*, the regulation merely has to be *rationally related* to some *legitimate governmental objective*, as long as equally effective alternative channels for the expression are available.

      **ii. Public forum:** When the expression takes place in a *public forum*, by contrast, the regulation has to be *narrowly drawn* to achieve a *significant governmental interest* (roughly *intermediate-level* review). It is necessary, but not sufficient, that the government also leaves alternative channels available. [526]

**Example 1 (public forum speech):** A city says, "No political campaign messages may be presented in handbills distributed on city streets." Since this rule impairs communications in a public forum (city streets), the city will have to show that its ordinance is necessary to achieve a significant governmental interest, which it probably can't do (anti-littering won't be enough, for instance). The city can't say, "Well, TV or radio ads will let the same message be given" — the existence of alternative channels for the communication is necessary, but is not enough, when the expression takes place in a public forum.

**Example 2 (non-public forum speech):** A city says, "No political campaign messages may be displayed on privately-owned billboards, even with the consent of the owner." Here, no public forum is involved. Therefore, as long as adequate alternative channels are available (which they probably are, e.g., radio & TV ads), the city only has to show that its regulation is rationally related to some legitimate governmental objective. The city can probably meet this burden (e.g., by pointing to the objective of beautifying the city).

2. **What are public forums:** What places, then, are public forums?

   a. **"True" or "traditional" public forums:** First, there are *"true"* or *"traditional"* public forums. These are areas that are public forums by custom and tradition, not by virtue of any particular government policy. The classic examples are: (1) *streets;* (2) *sidewalks;* and (3) *parks*. [529]

   b. **"Designated" public forums:** There's a second type of public forum: places that the government has *decided to open up* to a broad range of expressive conduct.

   Some possible Examples:

   ❏ places where *government meetings* take place that the government has decided to open to the public at large (e.g., a school board meeting held in a school auditorium);

   ❏ places that government has decided may be used by a broad range of people or groups (e.g., school classrooms after hours, under a policy that lets pretty much any group use them, or a municipal theater that any group may rent).

   These are called *"designated"* public forums. [529]

   i. **Same rules:** The *same rules* apply to designated public forums as apply to true public forums, except that government can *change its mind* and remove the designation (in which case the place becomes a non-public forum that can be subjected to much broader viewpoint-neutral regulation, as described below).

   c. **Non-public-forums:** Still other public places are not at all associated with expression traditionally, so they can be treated as *non-public forums. Here, the government regulation just has to be rationally related* to some *legitimate governmental objective*, as long as the interference with speech is not "substantial." And if alternative channels are available, then this fact alone usually *makes* the interference "insubstantial." So we basically use "mere rationality" review for content-neutral "time, place & manner" regulations of non-public-forum expression that leave open alternative channels of communication. [530-537]

   i. **All expression banned:** Often, even a regulation that completely *bans* expression in a particular non-public forum will be found to satisfy this "mere rationality" test. Or, the government can choose to forbid discussion of certain subjects (but *not certain viewpoints*).

   **Example:** A publicly-owned airport terminal is not a public forum. Therefore, the government may ban face-to-face solicitation of funds in the terminal, because such a ban is rationally related to the legitimate governmental objectives of reducing congestion and combatting fraud. (However, a total ban even on literature distribution will not be upheld, because this ban does not even satisfy the "mere rationality" standard.) [*Int'l Soc. for Krishna Consciousness v. Lee*]

   ii. **Illustrations of non-public-forums:** Here are some illustrations of facilities that, even though they are owned by the government, are not public forums: *airport terminals*, *jails*, *military bases*, the insides of *courthouses*, and *governmental office buildings*. [534-537]

   iii. **Limited public forums:** Some places are referred to by the Court as *"limited public forums."* These are government property that the government has decided to *open only to a particular set of topics or purposes*. A limited public forum is treated *just like a non-public forum*: the government merely has to be rational, and viewpoint-neutral, in its regulation. (But the requirement of viewpoint-neutrality has real impact, especially in cases where government tries to keep out religious material.) [529]

**Example:** A school district allows an elementary school to be used after hours by any community group that wishes to put on a program about current affairs. However, the district says that "programs of primarily religious content" are excluded. The Good Christians Club wants to hold a discussion of how practicing Christians should view recent events in the Middle East, to be followed by a prayer for peace in that region. The district's program is a "limited public forum," and is to be treated like a non-public forum. Since the proposed program concerns the appropriate topic (current affairs), the school district cannot exclude it on the grounds of its religious orientation, because that would be illegal viewpoint-discrimination. [Cf. *Good News Club*] [531]

**J. Access to private property:** In general, a speaker does not have any First Amendment right of *access* to another person's *private property* to deliver his message. Most significantly, a person does not have a First Amendment right to speak in *shopping centers*. [*Hudgens v. NLRB*] (*Example:* State trespass laws may be used to prevent a person from conducting an anti-war demonstration or a religious proselytizing campaign at her local privately-owned shopping center.) [537-540]

## IV.  REGULATION OF SYMBOLIC EXPRESSION

**A. Symbolic expression:**  Let's consider *"symbolic expression,"* i.e., expression that consists solely of *non-verbal* actions. [540-546]

   **1. Standard:**  We use essentially the same rules to analyze restrictions on symbolic expression as we do for restrictions that apply to verbal speech, or to verbal speech coupled with conduct. Thus: (1) any attempt by government to restrict symbolic expression because of the *content* of the message will be strictly scrutinized and almost certainly struck down; (2) any restriction on the *time, place or manner* of symbolic expression will have to be *narrowly tailored* to a *significant governmental objective* and will have to *leave open alternative channels*. [540]

     **Example:** The Ds (high school students) wear armbands to school, in the face of a school policy forbidding students from wearing such armbands. Because school officials were motivated by a desire to suppress particular messages — anti-war messages — the ban must be strictly scrutinized, and is struck down. [*Tinker v. Des Moines Schl. Dist.*] [543]

   **2. Flag desecration:**  The most interesting example of government regulation of symbolic expression is *flag desecration* statutes. The main thing to remember is that if a statute bans flag desecration or mutilation, and either on the statute's face or as it is applied, the statute is directed only at particular *messages*, it will be invalid. (*Examples:* Both the Texas and federal flag burning statutes have been struck down by the Supreme Court. In the case of the federal statute, the Court concluded that Congress was trying to preserve the flag as a "symbol of national unity." The statute was therefore content-based, so the Court struck it down. [*U.S. v. Eichman*]) [546]

## V.  DEFAMATION AND INVASION OF PRIVACY

**A. Defamation:**  The First Amendment places limits on the extent to which a plaintiff may recover tort damages for *defamation.* [553]

   **1. *New York Times v. Sullivan* test:**  Most importantly, under the rule of *New York Times v. Sullivan*, 376 U.S. 254 (1964), where P is a *public official*, he may only win a defamation suit against D for a statement relating to P's official conduct if P can prove that D's statement was made either "with *knowledge* that it was false" or with *"reckless disregard"* of whether it was true or false.

These two mental states are usually collectively referred to as the ***"actual malice"*** requirement. [554-556]

> **Example**: The *New York Times* runs an ad saying that P — the Montgomery, Alabama police commissioner — has terrorized Dr. Martin Luther King by repeatedly arresting him. Even if these statements are false, P cannot recover for libel unless he can show that the *Times* knew its statements were false or acted with reckless disregard of whether the statements were true or false. [*N.Y. Times v. Sullivan, supra*].

2. **Public figures:** This rule of *Times v. Sullivan* — that P can only recover for defamation if he shows intentional falsity or recklessness about truth — applies not only to public "officials" but also to public ***"figures"***. Thus a well known college football coach, and a prominent retired Army general, were public figures who had to show that the defendant acted with actual malice. [*Assoc. Press v. Walker*] [555]

   a. **Partial public figure:** Someone who voluntarily ***injects himself*** into a public controversy will be a public figure for ***just that controversy*** — thus an anti-abortion activist might be a public figure for any news story concerning abortion, but not for stories about, say, his private life unrelated to abortion.

   b. **Involuntary public figure:** Also, some people may be ***"involuntary"*** public figures. (*Example:* A ***criminal defendant*** is an involuntary public figure, so he cannot sue or recover for a news report about his crime or trial unless he shows actual malice).

3. **Private figure:** If the plaintiff is a ***"private"*** (rather than "public") figure, he does ***not*** have to meet the *New York Times v. Sullivan* "actual malice" rule. [*Gertz v. Robert Welch, Inc.*]. On the other hand, the First Amendment requires that he show at least ***negligence*** by the defendant — the states may not impose strict liability for defamation, even for a private-figure plaintiff. *Id.* [556-556]

   a. **No punitive damages:** Also, a private-figure plaintiff who shows only negligence cannot recover ***punitive*** damages — he must show actual malice to get punitive damages. *Id.*

B. **Intentional infliction of emotional distress:** The *Times v. Sullivan* rule applies to actions for intentional infliction of ***emotional distress*** as well as ones for defamation. Thus a public-figure plaintiff cannot recover for any intentional infliction of emotional distress unless he shows that the defendant acted with actual malice. (*Example*: *Hustler* Magazine satirizes religious leader Jerry Falwell as a drunken hypocrite who has sex with his mother. *Held*, Falwell cannot recover for intentional infliction of emotional distress unless he shows that *Hustler* made a false statement with knowledge of falsity or with reckless disregard of falsity. [*Hustler Magazine v. Falwell*]) [558]

C. **Falsity:** The First Amendment also probably requires that the plaintiff (whether or not she is a public figure) must show that the statement was ***false***. [559]

# VI. OBSCENITY

A. **Obscenity:** Another of our "unprotected categories" is ***obscenity***. Expression that is obscene is simply ***unprotected*** by the First Amendment, so the states can ban it, punish it, or do whatever else they want without worrying about the First Amendment. [560-566]

B. **Three-part test:** For a work to be "obscene," all three parts of the following test must be met [561]:

1. **Prurient interest:** First, the average person, applying today's community standards, must find that the work as a whole appeals to the ***"prurient"*** interest;

2. **Sexual conduct:** Second, the work must depict or describe in a "patently offensive way" particular types of *sexual conduct* defined by state law; and

3. **Lacks value:** Finally, the work taken as a whole, must lack "serious literary, artistic, political or scientific value."

[*Miller v. Calif.*]

C. **Significance:** So something will not be "obscene" unless it depicts or describes *"hard core sex"*. (For instance, mere *nudity*, by itself, is not obscene.) [562]

D. **Materials addressed to minors:** It will be much easier for the state to keep erotic materials out of the hands of *minors*. Probably even minors have some First Amendment interest in receiving sexually explicit materials, but this is typically *outweighed* by the state's compelling interest in protecting minors against such material. So the distribution of non-obscene but sexually explicit materials may basically be forbidden to minors (provided that the regulations do not substantially impair the access of adults to these materials). [563]

1. **Adult's rights impaired:** But if a measure aimed at minors *does* substantially impair the access of adults to material that's "indecent" but not obscene, the measure will be struck down. (*Example:* If Congress outright bans all "indecent" material on the Internet (as it has done), out of a fear that the material will be seen by minors, the measure will be found to violate the First Amendment rights of adults. [*Reno v. ACLU*]) [523]

E. **"Pandering":** The issue of whether the material appeals primarily to prurient interests may be influenced by the manner in which the material is *advertised* — if the publisher or distributor plays up the prurient nature of the materials in the advertising, this will make it more likely that the materials will be found to appeal mostly to prurient interests and thus to be obscene. The advertisement itself, and expert testimony about the likely effect of the advertising, may be admitted into evidence to aid the determination on obscenity. (The marketing of materials by emphasizing their sexually provocative nature is often called *"pandering."*) [566]

F. **Private possession by adults:** The mere *private possession* of obscene material by an adult may *not* be made criminal. [*Stanley v. Georgia*]. [562]

**Example:** While police are lawfully arresting D at his house on a robbery charge, they spot obscene magazines on his shelf. D may not be criminally charged with possession of pornography, because one has both a First Amendment right and a privacy right to see or read what one wants in the privacy of one's own home.

1. **Child pornography:** However, the states *may* criminalize even private possession of *child pornography*. [*Osborne v. Ohio*] [564]

2. **No right to supply to consenting adults:** Also, the state may punish a person who *supplies* pornography even to consenting adults. In other words, there is a right to *have* pornography for one's own home use, but not a right to supply it to others for their home use. [563]

# VII. COMMERCIAL SPEECH

A. **Commercial speech generally:** Speech that is *"commercial"* — that is, speech advertising a product or proposing some commercial transaction — gets First Amendment protection. But this protection is in some ways *more limited* than the protection given to non-commercial (e.g., political) speech.[567]

1. **Truthful speech:** *Truthful* commercial speech gets a pretty fair degree of First Amendment protection. The government may restrict truthful commercial speech only if the regulation (1) *directly advances* (2) a *substantial governmental interest* (3) in a way that is *"no more extensive than*

*necessary"* to achieve the government's objective. So basically, we apply *mid-level review* to government restrictions based on the content of commercial speech (whereas we apply strict scrutiny to content-based restrictions on non-commercial speech). [573]

> **Example:** Virginia forbids a pharmacist from advertising his prices for prescription drugs. Virginia must show that it is pursuing a "substantial" governmental interest, and that materially-less-restrictive alternatives are not available. Here, the state's desire to prevent price-cutting that will lead to shoddy service is not strong enough to qualify as "substantial," so the measure must be struck down on First Amendment grounds. [*Virginia Pharmacy Board v. Virginia Consumer Council*] [567-569]

2. **False, deceptive or illegal:** On the other hand, *false or deceptive* commercial speech may be *forbidden* by the government. Similarly, speech which proposes an *illegal transaction* may be forbidden (e.g., advertisements for cocaine). [573]

   a. **Harmful:** But if the product or service is *harmful* but *lawful*, the state *may not limit* advertising about it any more than the state may limit advertising about a non-harmful product — the right to ban product X does not necessarily include the "lesser" right to regulate speech about product X. (*Example:* Congress is free to ban casino gambling entirely. But if Congress allows such gambling, it may not limit advertising of casino gambling unless the limitation passes the mid-level review standard, summarized above, that applies to regulation of truthful commercial speech. [*Greater New Orleans Broadcasting v. U.S.*]) [578]

3. **No overbreadth:** The *overbreadth* doctrine does *not apply* in commercial speech cases, because advertisers are thought not likely to be "chilled" by overly broad governmental regulation of speech. Therefore, a commercial enterprise that is protesting a regulation of speech must show that the regulation infringes the enterprise's own speech, not merely that the regulation would curtail speech not now before the court. [581]

B. **Advertising of lawful but harmful products:** Sellers of products that are *lawful* but *harmful* receive the *same protection as any other commercial speaker*. That is, the fact that government could completely *ban* the product does *not* mean that government can automatically curtail truthful advertising about the product. Therefore, regulation of advertising about the product must be substantially related to an important govermental objective, and the court will require a fairly tight fit between means and end.

   **Example:** A state bans all outdoor tobacco advertising, on the theory that this will help minors be less attracted to tobacco products. (Tobacco cannot legally be sold to minors in the state). *Held*, the regulation is invalid — it unduly interferes with the rights of tobacco vendors, and their adult customers, to exchange truth information about tobacco. [*Lorillard Tobacco v. Reilly*] [579]

C. **Lawyers:** The qualified First Amendment protection given to commercial speech means that *lawyers* have a limited right to advertise. Thus a state may not ban all advertising by lawyers or even ban advertising directed to a particular problem. See, e.g., *Bates v. State Bar of Ariz.* (Thus a lawyer can advertise, "If you've been injured by a Dalkon shield, I may be able to help you.") [569-570]

1. **In-person solicitation:** On the other hand, the states may ban certain types of *in-person solicitation* by lawyers seeking clients (e.g., solicitation of accident victims in person by tort lawyers who want to obtain a contingent-fee agreement. [*Ohralik v. Ohio St. Bar Ass'n.*]) [569]

2. **Direct mail:** Similarly, the states may ban lawyers from *direct-mail* solicitation of accident victims, at least for a 30-day period following the accident. [*Florida Bar v. Went For It*]

## VIII.  REGULATION IN THE CONTEXT OF POLITICAL CAMPAIGNS

**A.  Campaign spending, generally:**  The state or federal governments can regulate *campaign spending* to some extent, but other campaign regulations would violate the First Amendment. [583-597]

**B.  Contributions:**  *Contributions* made by individuals or groups to candidates, political parties, or Political Action Committees may be limited.

> **Example 1:** Congress may constitutionally prevent anyone from contributing more than $1,000 to a candidate for federal office, in order to curb actual or apparent corruption. [*Buckley v. Valeo*] [584-590]

> **Example 2:** Congress may prevent national political parties from receiving more than $2,000 from any donor, thus outlawing unregulated "soft money" donations. That's because such donations give the appearance that large donors get special access to office-holders, a type of corruption that Congress may constitutionally combat. [*McConnell v. F.E.C.*] [592]

> **1.  Lower limit:**  But contribution limits may not be made *so low* that they substantially interfere with candidates' and parties' ability to *run a competitive election campaign.*

> > **Example:** Vermont prevents any individual or political party from contributing more than $400 to the campaign of any candidate for governor during any two-year period. *Held*, this limit is so low that it violates the free speech and free association rights of individuals and parties (though no majority of the Court can agree on the precise test for "how low is too low"). *Randall v. Sorrell.* [586-590]

**C.  Expenditures:**  But an individual's *independent* campaign-related *expenditures* (whether he's a candidate or not) may *not* be limited at all.

> **Example 1:** A candidate may not be prevented from spending as much of his own money on getting elected as he wishes. [*Buckley v. Valeo; Randall v. Sorrell*]

> **Example 2:** Similarly, private citizen X may spend as much money to try to get Y elected as he wishes, as long as X spends the money in a truly independent manner rather than contributing it to Y or coordinating with Y on how it should be spent. [*Buckley v. Valeo*] [585]

**D.  Corporate issue ads:** Government may *not* prevent corporations (including non-profits) from running *genuine "issue ads,"* even if those ads specifically mention candidates and are run near election time.

> **Example:** Congress prohibits making an "electioneering communication" (an "EC") within 30 days prior to a federal primary election. An ad is deemed an EC if it mentions a particular candidate, even if the ad doesn't expressly urge the listener to vote for or against that candidate. A non-profit corporation, Wisconsin Right to Life, wants to run an ad saying, "Call Senator Feingold and tell him to oppose the filibustering of President Bush's judicial nominees." The ad is a prohibited EC, and WRTL contends that the ban violates WRTL's free-speech rights.

> *Held*, for WRTL: the ban here was unconstitutionally applied to WRTL's ad. Regulation of the contents of an ad that is a genuine issue ad — as opposed to a disguised campaign ad — will be strictly scrutinized. The ad here was a genuine issue ad, so the regulation will be strictly scrutinized. Since it is not necessary to achieve the admittedly compelling interest in reducing corruption, it must be struck down. *FEC v. Wisconsin Right to Life* (2007) [593-595].

## IX.  SOME SPECIAL CONTEXTS

**A.  Public school students:**  Students in *public schools* have a limited right of free speech. The student's right to speak freely has to be *balanced* against the administration's right to carry out its educational mission and to maintain discipline. [597]

1.  **Allowable regulation:**   Thus a school may ban profanity. It may also ban the school newspaper from running stories that would disturb the school's *educational mission* (e.g., stories about sex and birth control that the principal reasonably believes are inappropriate for younger students at the school). [*Hazelwood Sch. Dist. v. Kuhlmeier*]

    a.  **Advocacy of illegal drug use:**  Also, schools may ban the *advocacy of illegal drug use,* even where the advocacy does not pose an immediate threat to discipline or the school's educational mission. [*Morse v. Frederick*]

2.  **Non-allowable regulation:**   But school officials may *not* suppress students' speech merely because they disagree with that speech on ideological or political grounds. (*Example:* School officials may not ban the wearing of anti-war armbands [*Tinker v. Des Miones Schl Dist.*).

B.  **Group activity:**  The rights of a *group* to engage in *joint expressive activity* get special First Amendment protection, generally called the *"freedom of association"*. (*Example*: Groups have the right to get together to bring law suits, or to conduct non-violent economic boycotts. Therefore, they cannot be prevented from doing these things by state rules against fomenting litigation or conducting boycotts. [*NAACP v. Button*]) [603]

C.  **Government as speaker or as funder of speech:** So far, we've looked only at the role of government as the regulator of speech by non-government actors. But sometimes, *government itself wishes to speak*.  And sometimes, government wishes to give *financial support* to certain speech by others.  In these two contexts — government as speaker, and government as funder of speech — government seems to have at least *somewhat greater ability to prefer one viewpoint over another* than it does when it merely regulates. [604]

1.  **Government as speaker:** When government wishes to *be a speaker itself*, it is pretty clear that government may *say essentially what it wants*, and is not subject to any real rule of viewpoint neutrality. [604]

    **Example:** Government can pay for ads attacking smoking as a health hazard, without having to pay for opponents' ads saying that the dangers of smoking are overrated.

2.  **Government as funder of third-party speech:** It's not clear how viewpoint-neutral government has to be when it acts as *funder of speech by third parties.*

    a.  **Broad-based programs:** Where government operates a program that by its terms seems to be *broad-based* (open to all comers or to a large number of speakers), government probably has to be viewpoint-neutral.

        **Example:** Where government offers a cheaper mailing rate to publications, it can't give the rate to publications whose message it approves of and deny it to those it disapproves of.

    b.  **Competitive awards:** But suppose that government gives *awards* to a *few speakers* on account of their special artistic or technical merit, and does this as part of a competitive process. Here, probably government *can* take into account the speaker's message in deciding who should get the award, at least where the award process doesn't seem designed to punish unpopular views. (However, the rules in this area are very unclear.) [605]

## X.  FREEDOM OF ASSOCIATION, AND DENIAL OF PUBLIC BENEFITS OR JOBS

A.  **Freedom of association generally:**   First Amendment case law recognizes the concept of *"freedom of association"*. In general, the idea is that if an individual has a First Amendment right to engage in a particular expressive activity, then a ***group*** has a "freedom of association" right to engage in that same activity as a group. [608]

1.  **Right not to associate:** Individuals and groups also have a well-protected ***"right not to associate."*** Thus any government attempt to make an individual give ***financial support*** to a cause she dislikes, or to make a group ***take members*** whose presence would interfere with the group's expressive activities, will be ***strictly scrutinized***. [609-613]

    **Example 1:** Where public school teachers are required to pay union dues, a teacher has a freedom-of-association right not to have the dues used to support ideological causes the teacher dislikes. [*Abood v. Detroit Bd. of Ed.*]

    **Example 2:** The Boy Scouts can't be forced (by a state anti-discrimination law) to accept an openly-gay male as a scoutmaster, because this would significantly interfere with the Scouts' First Amendment-protected message that homosexuality is immoral. [*Boy Scouts of America v. Dale*]

B.  **Illegal membership:** The freedom of association means that ***mere membership in a group or association may not be made illegal***. Membership in a group may only be made part of an offense if: (1) the group is ***actively engaged in unlawful activity***, or ***incites others*** to ***imminent lawless action***; and (2) the individual ***knows*** of the group's illegal activity, and specifically intends to further the group's illegal goals. (*Example*: Congress cannot make it a crime simply to be a member of the American Communist Party. On the other hand, Congress can make it a crime to be a member of a party that advocates imminent overthrow of the government, if the member knows that the party so advocates and the member intends to help bring about that overthrow.) [613]

C.  **Denial of public benefit or job:** Freedom of expression also prevents the government from ***denying a public benefit or job*** based on a person's association. [613-620]

    1.  **Non-illegal activities:** If a person's activities with a group could not be made ***illegal***, then those activities may generally not be made the basis for denying the person the government job or benefit.

        **Example 1**: A state may not refuse to hire a person as a teacher merely because he is a member of the American Communist Party, since the state could not make it illegal to be a member of the ACP.

        **Example 2:** At a time when Republicans are in power, a state may not refuse to hire Democrats for non-policy-making jobs like police officer or clerk. [*Rutan v. Republican Party of Illinois*].

    2.  **No right/privilege distinction:** There is no constitutional distinction between a ***"right"*** and a ***"privilege."*** Even if, say, a particular public benefit or job is defined by the state to be a "privilege," the state may not deny that job or benefit on the basis of the applicant's constitutionally-protected membership in a group or organization. [613]

    3.  **Loyalty oath:** Government may generally not require an applicant to sign a ***loyalty oath***, unless the things that the applicant is promising in the loyalty oath not to do are things which, if he did them, would be grounds for punishing him or denying him the job. (*Example*: You cannot be required to sign a loyalty oath that you are not a member of the Communist Party in order to get a teaching job. But you can be required to sign an oath that you will not advocate the forcible overthrow of our government.) [615]

    4.  **Compulsory disclosure:** Similarly, the government may not force you to ***disclose*** your membership activities (or require a group to disclose who its members are), unless it could make that mem-

bership illegal. (*Example*: The state cannot require the Communist Party to furnish a list of its members.) [620-622]

5.  **Some exceptions:** There are some *exceptions* to the general rule that associational activities that couldn't be outlawed directly also can't be made the basis for public hiring or benefits decisions. In general, these exceptions are for conduct which, although it includes protected expression, directly (and negatively) relates to *performance of the job*.

    a.  **Partisan political activities:** For instance, civil servants can constitutionally be forced to choose between their jobs and engaging in *partisan political activities*, since there's a very strong government interest in making sure that civil servants can do their jobs without being coerced into campaigning for or contributing to their elected bosses. [*CSC v. Letter Carriers*].

    b.  **Patronage hirings:** Similarly, some public jobs may be awarded as *patronage appointments*, ones the performance of which is *reasonably related to a person's politics*. [614]

        **Example:** Even though I have a First Amendment right to be a Democrat, the Republican Congressman representing my district doesn't violate my rights when, on the basis of my political beliefs, he declines to hire me as, say, a speech writer, a high advisor, or some other post with a *heavy political content*.

        On the other hand, if I'm a Democrat, and there's a Republican governor in power, he can't block me from getting a government job as a clerk or secretary or police officer — the old fashioned "patronage" system whereby all public jobs could be restricted to supporters of the party in power has been outlawed as a violation of freedom of association, and only jobs with a heavy political content, like speech writer, say, or Chief of Staff, can be based on party membership.

        i.  **Independent contractors:** The same rule — that party affiliation may be used if and only if the performance is reasonably related to one's politics — applies to people and companies doing work for government on an *independent-contractor* basis. [615] (*Example:* P has a contract to haul trash for City. Even if the contract is at-will, City can't decline to renew it on the grounds that P belongs to the wrong political party or has supported the Mayor's opponent. )

    c.  **Speech critical of superiors or otherwise inappropriate:** An employee gets limited protection for speech or associational activities that are *critical of superiors*, or that the employer believes are *inappropriate for the workplace*. Where such speech involves a matter of *"public concern,"* the court will *balance* the speech rights of the employee and the government's interest as employer in promoting efficiency on the job. [*Connick v. Myers*] [615-617]

        **Example:** P, a government clerical worker, hears that John Hinckley has tried to shoot Pres. Reagan, and says, "If they go for him again, I hope they get him." P is fired for the remark. *Held*, for P. This remark was intended as political commentary and was thus on a matter of "public concern," so P could not be fired unless the remark heavily affected P's job performance, which it did not. [*Rankin v. McPherson*]

        i.  **Not a matter of public concern:** But where the speech does *not* involve a matter of public concern, *Connick* and *Rankin, supra*, do *not* apply, and the court gives great *deference* to the employer's judgment.

        ii.  **Must not be part of employee's job function:** Also, even the limited protection given to employee speech on matters of public concern doesn't apply where the speech occurs as *part of the employee's job functions* — here, the employee gets no First Amendment protection at all, no matter how important the issue on which the employee is speaking.

**Example:** P, a supervising lawyer in a District Attorney's Office (D), is called on to investigate whether an affidavit prepared by a deputy sheriff to obtain a search warrant was properly done. P writes a memo to his supervisor concluding that the affidavit was improperly done. The supervisor retaliates against him for what he says in the memo.

*Held*, for D. "[W]hen public employees make statements **pursuant to their official duties**, the employees are **not speaking as citizens** for First Amendment purposes, and **the Constitution does not insulate their communications from employer discipline.**" Here, because P's investigation and the ensuing memorandum were part of his job responsibilities, D had the right to regulate the content and manner of P's speech. *Garcetti v. Ceballos* [618]

# XI. SPECIAL PROBLEMS OF THE MEDIA

**A.** **The media (and its special problems):**   Here is a brief review of some special problems related to the *media*: [625-642]

   1. **Prior restraint:**   In general, the government will not be able to obtain a **prior restraint** against broadcasters or publishers. In other words, only in exceptionally rare circumstances may the government obtain an **injunction** against the printing or airing of a story, and the government will almost never be allowed to require that a publisher or broadcaster obtain a **permit** before it runs a story. [627-631]

      **Example**: The *New York Times* may not constitutionally be enjoined from publishing part of the Pentagon Papers, even though these government-prepared materials might contain information that is useful to our enemies or that would embarrass the U.S. [*N.Y. Times v. U.S.*]

      a. **Gag order:**   This means that a judge may generally not impose a **gag order** on the media ordering it not to disclose a certain fact about a pending trial. [631-633]

         i. **Participants:**   But the judge may usually order the **participants** not to speak to the press. For instance, a state may prevent a lawyer from making any statement which would have a "substantial likelihood of materially prejudicing" a trial or other court proceeding. [*Gentile v. State Bar of Nevada*] [633]

   2. **Subpoenas by government:**   The press does not get any special protection from government demands that the press **furnish information** which other citizens would have to furnish. In particular, if a reporter has information that is of interest to a **grand jury**, the reporter may be required by subpoena to disclose that information to the grand jury even though this would cause him to violate a promise of confidentiality to a source. [*Branzburg v. Hayes*] (But the state is always free to enact a "shield law" making such subpoenas illegal under some or all circumstances.) [633-635]

   3. **Right of access:**   The press does not get any general **right of access** to information held by the government. [638-640]

      a. **Right to attend trials:**   However, the media does have a constitutionally protected right to **attend criminal trials**. This right is not absolute — the government can close the media (and the public) out of a trial if it shows that there is an "overriding" government interest being served by a closed trial, and that that interest cannot be served by less restrictive means. [*Richmond Newspapers v. Virginia*] [639]

         i. **Showing rarely made:** But this showing will rarely be made, so that as a practical matter the press is usually entitled to attend a criminal trial. (*Example:* A state statute automatically bars the press from hearing any trial testimony by a minor who was allegedly the victim of a sex crime. *Held*, the statute unduly interferes with the public's right of access to criminal trials. [*Globe Newspapers v. Sup. Ct.*])

ii. **Other proceedings:** Probably the media also has a qualified constitutional right to attend other proceedings, like *civil trials* and *pre-trial proceedings*. [*Gannett Co. v. DePasquale*]. [639]

4. **Disclosure of confidential or illegally-obtained information:** Government may generally *not* prohibit the media from disclosing information that goverment believes ought to be *secret*. If a media member *lawfully* obtains information about a matter of public significance, government may punish disclosure of the information only if government has "a *need* of the *highest order,*" which it will rarely be found to have. [*Smith v. Daily Mail*] [636-637]

**Example:** A broadcaster may not be held civilly liable for *publishing the name of a rape victim*, if the broadcaster learns the name from reading a publicly-filed indictment. [*Cox Broadcasting v. Cohn*]

a. **Where publisher has acted illegally:** If the *publisher itself* has *acted illegally* in obtaining the information, then government *may make it a crime* to punish the information, no matter how newsworthy it is. (*Example:* A newspaper reporter breaks into a private home to steal an audiotape, then publishes a transcript of the tape. The newspaper may constitutionally be punished for the publication.)

b. **Where private party has acted illegally but publisher has not:** On the other hand, the fact that the secret information was originally *obtained illegally* by a person *acting independently* of the eventual publisher is *not* enough to allow publication to be made criminal, at least where the material has significant newsworthiness.

**Example:** X, a private individual acting alone, intercepts and tapes a cellphone conversation between the Ps (two teachers' union officials) who are discussing their upcoming negotiation with a school board. The interception violates federal wiretapping laws. X anonymously mails the tape to a radio station, which broadcasts it. The Ps sue the station. *Held*, the station may not constitutionally be held liable for damages to the officials, because the station did not participate in the illegality, and the strong First Amendment interest in disseminating this newsworthy material outweighs the admittedly strong interest in safeguarding cellphone conversations. [*Bartnicki v. Vopper*] [636]

CHAPTER 15
# FREEDOM OF RELIGION

## I. INTRODUCTION

A. **Two clauses:** There are two quite distinct clauses in the First Amendment pertaining to religion.[656]

1. **Establishment Clause:** First, we have the *Establishment* Clause. That clause prohibits any law "respecting an establishment of religion." The main purpose of the Establishment Clause is to prevent government from *endorsing* or *supporting* religion.

2. **Free Exercise:** The second clause is the *Free Exercise* Clause. That clause bars any law "prohibiting the free exercise of religion." The main purpose of the Free Exercise Clause is to prevent the government from *outlawing* or seriously *burdening* a person's pursuit of whatever religion (and whatever religious practices) he chooses.

B. **Applicable to states:** Both the Establishment and the Free Exercise Clauses by their terms only restrict legislative action by *Congress*. However, both clauses have been interpreted to apply also to the *states*, by means of the Fourteenth Amendment's due process clause. Therefore, you don't have to worry whether the government action in question is federal or state — the same standards apply to each. [657]

C.  **Conflict:**   Occasionally, the Establishment and Free Exercises Clauses seem to *conflict* on particular facts. That is, a religious group may be asking for some government benefit; if the benefit is given, there may be an Establishment Clause problem. Yet if the benefit is not given, this may be a burdening of religion. When the two clauses seem to conflict, the *Free Exercise* Clause dominates. In other words, if a particular benefit or accommodation to religion is arguably required by the Free Exercise Clause, then when government grants that accommodation or benefit it is not violating the Establishment Clause.

> **Example:** A public university makes meeting rooms available to all sorts of student groups. If the university allows religious groups to use the room, there might be an Establishment Clause problem. But if it doesn't allow religious groups to use the rooms, while allowing non-religious groups to do so, there might be a Free Exercise Clause problem. Consequently, it will not be an Establishment Clause violation for the university to allow the religious groups to use the rooms. [656]

## II.  THE ESTABLISHMENT CLAUSE

A.  **General rule:**   The overall purpose of the Establishment Clause is to put a *wall between church and state*. In other words, the government must stay out of the business of religion, and religious groups must to some extent stay out of the business of government. [657-658]

1.  **Some examples:**   Here are some things that would clearly be forbidden by the Establishment clause:

a.  **Official church:**   Congress cannot establish an "official religion of the United States". In fact, Congress probably couldn't even declare that "the American people believe in God," because the Establishment Clause means that government may not prefer or endorse religion over non-religion.

b.  **Go to church:**   The government cannot force people to worship. In fact, the state can't even intentionally *encourage* people to worship — for example, it cannot decide that it wants to promote church attendance, and then give people a special tax deduction that applies to church donations but not to other charitable donations. (But it could, as Congress does, give a *general* tax deduction for charitable contributions, and let contributions to churches be eligible. This would be allowable because the government is treating religion the same as non-religion, not preferring religion over non-religion.)

c.  **Preference of one religion over another:**   The government cannot intentionally *prefer one religion over another religion.* For instance, a state may not decide that since Christians are in the majority, it will allow tax deductions for contribution to Christian churches but not for contributions made, say, to synagogues.

d.  **Participate:**   Government may not actively *participate* in religious affairs, or allow religious organizations to have a special participation in government affairs. For instance, Congress probably could not constitutionally use public officials and public polling places to run an election to determine the next head of the American Presbyterian Church — this would be an undue governmental entanglement in religious affairs.

B.  **Three-part test:**   Government action that has some relationship to religion will violate the Establishment Clause unless it satisfies *all three parts* of the following test (known as the "*Lemon*" test, from *Lemon v. Kurtzman*) [658]:

1. **Purpose:** First, the government action must have a *secular legislative purpose*. In other words, there must be some governmental purpose that has nothing to do with religion. (If there is both a religious and a non-religious purpose, then this prong is probably satisfied.)

   **Example:** Alabama passes a statute saying, "Every public school student shall have the opportunity to engage in silent prayer or meditation for at least two minutes at the start of every school day." If there is evidence that the legislature was *motivated* solely by a desire to help students pray, then the statute will be struck down (and in fact such an Alabama statute was struck down. [*Wallace v. Jaffree*]) This is true even if many of the students who take advantage of the statute engage in non-religious meditation — if the sole purpose was to aid religion, that's enough to make the government action void.

2. **Effect:** Second, the governmental action's principal or *primary effect* must *not be to advance* religion. (But *incidental effects* that help religion do not violate this prong.)

3. **Entanglement:** Finally, the governmental action must not foster an *excessive governmental entanglement* with religion. (*Example:* Massachusetts lets a church veto the issuance of a liquor license to any premises located within 500 feet of the church. *Held*, this statute violates the Establishment Clause, because it entangles churches in the exercise of governmental powers. [*Larkin v. Grendel's Den*])

C. **Religion and the public schools:** If the government tries to introduce religion into the *public schools*, it is probably violating the Establishment Clause. [658-666]

1. **Instruction:** Thus the government may, of course, not conduct religious instruction in the public schools. In fact, it can't even allow privately-employed religious teachers to conduct classes on the public schools' premises during school hours. [658-661]

   a. **Accommodation:** However, it's probably allowable for the government to allow students to *leave school early* to attend religious instruction somewhere else. It's also probably acceptable for government to let religious groups have access to school facilities, as long as non-religious groups are given equal access. Remember our example of the university that lets all kinds of student groups, including religious groups, use meeting rooms — that's permissible.

2. **Prayer reading:** The official *reading of prayers* in the public schools will virtually always be unconstitutional. See, e.g., *Engel v. Vitale*. That is, it will almost always turn out to be the case that either the sole purpose, or the primary effect, of the prayer reading is to advance religion. [661-663]

   a. **Moment of silence:** Even the setting aside of a *"moment of silence"* at the beginning of the school day will generally violate the Establishment Clause, since a moment-of-silence statute will usually turn out to have been solely motivated by the legislators' intent to advance religion, or will at least have the primary effect of advancing religion. (But this will always turn on the actual purpose and effect of the particular statute — there's no absolute *per se* rule against moments of silence. [*Wallace v. Jaffree*] [661]

   b. **Prayer reading at graduation:** Similarly, the school may not conduct a prayer as part of a *graduation ceremony*, at least where school officials can fairly be said to be sponsoring the religious message. [*Lee v. Weisman*] [662-663]

   c. **Student-selected speakers don't solve problem:** The school can't easily get around prayer-reading problems by having the student body *elect a student speaker,* and then having that speaker decide whether to give a prayer. As long as the school's process can be reasonably viewed as supporting school prayer, the fact that a student-body election intervenes is irrelevant. [*Santa Fe Indep. Sch. Dist. v. Doe*] [663]

3. **Curriculum:** The state may not design or modify the ***curriculum*** of its schools in order to further religion at the expense of non-religion, or to further one set of religious beliefs over others. (*Example*: A state may not forbid the teaching of evolution. [*Epperson v. Ark.*] Similarly, it probably may not demand that "creationism" be taught in addition to evolution, since "creationism" is mainly a religious doctrine the teaching of which would have the primary effect of advancing religion. [*Edwards v. Aguillard*]) [664-666]

4. **Equal treatment of religion and non-religion:** But it's not a violation of the Establishment Clause for government to treat religion and non-religion ***equally*** in the schools (and government may in fact be *required* to do this because of free-speech principles.) (*Example*: If a public university funds non-religiously-oriented student publications, it must fund an evangelical Christian publication on the same terms. [*Rosenberger v. Univ. of Virginia.*] )

D. **Sunday closing laws:** Laws requiring ***merchants*** to be ***closed on Sundays*** generally do ***not*** violate the Establishment Clause. The reason is that these "blue laws" have a primarily secular effect and purpose — they permit everyone (Christian, non-Christian and atheist alike) to have a uniform day of rest. [*McGowan v. Md.*]. [666-667]

E. **Ceremonies and displays:** Any time your exam question involves a governmentally-sponsored ***ceremony*** or ***display***, beware of Establishment Clause problems. [669-678]

1. **Ceremonies:** Thus a ***ceremony*** put on by the government may not have the sole purpose or primary effect of advancing religion. (For instance, as noted above, the government may not normally conduct a prayer as part of a high school graduation ceremony.) [669-670]

    a. **Long-standing tradition:** However, if a particular ceremony has a ***long historical tradition*** going back to the time when the Constitution was enacted, then it will probably be allowable, especially outside of the public-school context. (*Example*: The practice of opening a session of the legislature with a prayer by the legislative chaplain dates back to colonial days, so presumably the authors of the Bill of Rights thought that it did not violate the Establishment Clause. Therefore, the practice will be upheld. [*Marsh v. Chambers*])

    b. **Incidental references:** Similarly, the Establishment Clause probably is not violated when the ceremony has an ***incidental reference*** to God or to a religious theme. (*Example*: The Pledge of Allegiance, with the phrase "One nation, under God," is probably allowable.)

2. **Religious displays:** Where a ***display*** with religious themes is either put on by the government, or put on by private groups using government property, there is a potential Establishment Clause problem. The problem usually arises where there is a "Christmas" display, "Easter" display, etc. Ask yourself this question: Would a reasonable observer seeing the display conclude that the government was ***endorsing*** religion? If so, there is a violation of the Establishment Clause. [670-678]

    a. **Context:** *Context* is very important. If there is one religious symbol, but it is surrounded by primarily-secular symbols, then the display would be taken as a whole and probably does not violate the Establishment Clause.

    **Example:** For instance, if a nativity scene is surrounded by reindeer, Santa Claus, "Season's Greetings" banners, etc., then as a whole the display would seem to be primarily secular, and the nativity scene won't be a violation of the Establishment Clause. [*Lynch v. Donnelly*]. But if the nativity scene or other primarily-religious symbol stands by itself, then that display probably will have a primarily religious effect, and thus violate the Establishment Clause.

    b. **History:** The ***history*** behind the display is also very important. The longer the display has been around without objection or controversy, the less likely it is to be an Establishment Clause violation.

**Example:** In Case 1, a display of text of the Ten Commandments has existed for 40 years without objection, before the present suit, and was originally donated as part of an anti-juvenile-delinquency campaign. *Held*, no Establishment Clause violation. [*Van Orden v. Perry*] In Case 2, a display of the text of the Ten Commandments is recent, and replaced two other recent displays that were from the beginning criticized on Establishment Clause grounds. *Held*, an Establishment Clause violation. [*McCreary County v. ACLU of Kentucky*]. [671-675]

F. **Intentional preferences between denominations:** The government may not intentionally *prefer one religion over another*, or one sect over another. [678-680] That's true even if government thinks that it's merely trying to "accommodate" a particular religion.

> **Example:** The New York legislature creates a special school district whose residents consist solely of members of a particular orthodox Jewish sect, the Satmar Hassidim. The purpose and effect of the special district is to let the Satmars get public funding for a public school in their village to educate their handicapped children. *Held*, the district violates the Establishment Clause, because it was created in a way that singled out the Satmars for a special preference not made available to other groups (and also because it amounted to a delegation of state authority to a group chosen according to a religious criterion.) [*Bd. of Educ. of Kiryas Joel Village v. Grumet*] [678-679]

1. **Unintended effect:** But a regulation that has the incidental unintended *effect* of helping one religion or sect more than another, or hurting one more than another, does not generally violate the Establishment Clause.

2. **Preference of religion over non-religion:** In theory, government can't even "accommodate" *religion generally*, by giving religion in general a preference over non-religion. But in practice, the Court is *less likely to object* to a special accommodation of religion generally than to an accommodation of a particular sect.

> **Example:** In a federal statute, the Religious Land Use and Institutionalized Persons Act (RLUIPA), the federal government orders prison officials to go out of their way to accommodate the religious needs of all prisoners (e.g., by giving them opportunities for group worship and the right to adhere to the dress mandates of their religion). *Held*, even though comparable accommodations are not given to similar needs/desires that are not mandated by religious belief, RLUIPA (at least on its face) does not violate the Establishment Clause. [*Cutter v. Wilkinson*] [680]

G. **Aid to religious schools:** Whenever your fact patterns shows that the government is giving some sort of *financial aid* to religious schools, you must immediately think "Establishment Clause". And, of course, you must apply the three-part test. [680-688]

1. **General principles:** In general, here are some things to look for when you analyze aid to religious schools:

   a. **Benefit to all students:** A government program that benefits *all students*, at public, private non-parochial and parochial schools alike, is much more likely to pass muster than aid which goes overwhelmingly to parochial-school students;

   b. **Colleges:** Aid to religious *colleges* is easier to justify than aid to high schools or, especially, elementary schools; and

   c. **Aid to parents:** Aid given to *parents* in a way that permits them to choose what school to use the aid at is more likely to be sustained than aid given directly to the *school.*

2. **Transportation:** Programs by which parents may have their children *transported* free to religious schools are probably constitutional, as long as the transport program also covers public and private non-parochial students. [*Everson v. Bd. of Ed.*] [682]

3. **Textbooks and equipment:**  Similarly, ***textbooks*** and ***equipment*** (e.g., computers) may be loaned to parochial school students as long as loans on the same basis are made to public school and private non-parochial students. But only books and materials that are ***strictly secular*** may be used (e.g., Bibles can't be lent out). [*Bd. of Ed. v. Allen; Mitchell v. Helms*] [682]

4. **Teachers:**  The state ***may*** send ***public school teachers*** into parochial schools, even to teach basic academic subjects, as long as what's taught is free of: (1) religious content and (2) influence from the parochial school's administration. [*Agostini v. Felton*] [683-683]

5. **Tuition vouchers:**  The state may give ***tuition vouchers*** to parents to enable them to pay religious-school tuition, if the vouchers may also be used in non-religious private schools. That's true even if the tuition is used to cover the costs of educating the children in core religious doctrine, and even if the benefits overwhelmingly go to the parents of religious school students. [*Zelman v. Simmons-Harris*] [684-687]

## III.  THE FREE EXERCISE CLAUSE

**A. Free Exercise generally:**  Let's now turn to the second clause relating to religion, the Free Exercise Clause. Under this clause, the government is barred from making any law "prohibiting the free exercise" of religion. The Free Exercise Clause prevents the government from getting in the way of people's ability to practice their religions. [688-689]

1. **Conduct vs. belief:**  The Free Exercise Clause of course prevents the government from unduly burdening a person's abstract "beliefs". (*Example:* Congress cannot ban the religion of voodooism merely because it disapproves of voodooism or thinks that voodooism is irrational.) But the Clause also relates to ***conduct***.

   a. **Non-religious objectives:**  Free Exercise problems most typically arise when government, acting in pursuit of ***non-religious objectives***, either: (1) forbids or burdens conduct which happens to be ***required*** by someone's religious belief; or conversely, (2) compels or encourages conduct which happens to be ***forbidden*** by someone's religious beliefs.

   **Example (government forbids conduct dictated by belief):** The military prohibits any soldier from wearing a hat (other than a regular military cap) while on duty. This order prevents orthodox Jewish soldiers from wearing yarmulkes, which their religion requires them to wear at all times. (On these facts, the Supreme Court held that the Jewish officer-plaintiffs had a free exercise right that was being burdened, but that this right was outweighed by the need to defer to the military's judgment that discipline and uniformity require the ban on all non-standard headgear. [*Goldman v. Weinberger*])

   **Example (government compels or encourages conduct forbidden by the belief):** The state awards unemployment compensation only to jobless workers who make themselves available for work Monday through Saturday. This rule has a non-religious purpose (making sure that only those whose employment is truly involuntary collect). But the statute strongly encourages conduct that violates the religious beliefs of some persons (e.g., Seventh Day Adventists, for whom Saturday is the Sabbath). Therefore, the rule raises significant free exercise problems. (In fact, the statute was held to violate the Free Exercise Clause as applied to Seventh Day Adventists. [*Sherbert v. Verner*]. The case is discussed below.)

**B. Intentional vs. unintentional burdens:**  The Free Exercise Clause prevents the government from unduly interfering with religion whether the government does so ***intentionally*** or ***unintentionally***.

1. **Intent:**  If the interference with religion is ***intentional*** on government's part, then the interference is subjected to the ***most strict scrutiny***, and will virtually never survive. [689-690]

**Example:** The Ps practice Santeria, a religion involving animal sacrifice. D (the local city council), motivated by the citizenry's dislike of this religion and of the sacrifices, outlaws all animal sacrifice (but exempts Kosher slaughter). *Held*, the Ps' Free Exercise rights have been violated. D has acted with the purpose of outlawing a practice precisely because the practice is motivated by religion, so D's act must be most strictly scrutinized. Because there is no compelling state objective here, and because any state objective that the state is pursuing (e.g., maintenance of public health) could be achieved by less discriminatory means, the law fails this strictest scrutiny. [*Church of the Lukumi Babalu Aye v. Hialeah*]

   a.  **Perhaps limited to "punishments":** However, this rule of strict scrutiny probably applies only to criminal or civil *"sanctions"* — in essence *punishments* — that are imposed for the purpose of disfavoring religious practices, not to government conduct that merely *withholds some generally-applicable benefit* so the benefit cannot be used in connection with a religiously-motivated activity.

   **Example:** A state gives merit scholarships to college-bound student with a certain G.P.A., but excludes anyone who wants to use the scholarship to study for the ministry. *Held*, this exclusion doesn't violate the Free Exercise clause, because it doesn't involve a criminal or civil sanction, merely a refusal by government to grant an affirmative benefit to subsidize an "essentially religious endeavor." [*Locke v. Davey*] [691]

2. **Unintentional burden:** If government *unintentionally burdens* religion, the Free Exercise Clause is still applied. Here, however, the government action is not per se illegal. Instead, the Court traditionally uses a somewhat less stringent form of strict scrutiny. (But there are signs that the Court is cutting back on this strict scrutiny for unintentional burdens on religion. For instance, if the government makes certain conduct a *crime*, and this unintentionally burdens the exercise of religion, the Court does not use strict scrutiny, and instead uses "mere rationality" review.) [691-697]

C. **Coercion required:** The Free Exercise Clause only gets triggered where government in some sense *"coerces"* an individual to do something (or not to do something) against the dictates of his religion. If the government takes an action that *unintentionally happens to make it harder for you to practice your religion* — but without coercing you into taking or not taking some action as an individual — the Free Exercise Clause *does not apply.* [698]

   **Example:** The federal government, without intending to affect any religious practice, wants to build a road. The effect will be to destroy Native American ritual grounds.

   *Held*, there is no impairment of free exercise rights, because the Native American plaintiffs are not being coerced into doing or not doing anything — external reality is simply being changed in a way that makes it harder for them to practice their religion. (But if government *forbade* the Native Americans from using existing grounds to pray on, this *would* be a violation, because the Native Americans would be coerced into not taking some action of their own.) [*Lyng v. Northwest Indian Cemetery Ass'n*]

D. **Denial of benefits:** One way the government may be found to have interfered with a person's free exercise of religion is if the government *denies the person a benefit* solely because of that person's religious beliefs or practices. (*Example:* A state may not forbid practicing members of the clergy from holding elective state office, because this imposes a burden on the exercise of a religious belief. [*McDaniel v. Paty*])

E. **Exemptions required:** Because strict scrutiny is traditionally given even to unintentional impairments of religion, government *must give an exemption* to avoid such an unintentional interference with religion, if this could be done *without seriously impairing some compelling governmental interest.* (*Example:* P is denied unemployment benefits because he refuses to work on Saturday, his religion's holy day. *Held*, the state must exempt P from the requirement of Saturday work as a condition to unemployment benefits, since an exemption will not seriously undermine any compelling governmental interest. [*Sherbert v. Verner*]) [692-694]

1. **Criminal prohibition:** But there's a special, recent, rule in the area of ***criminal prohibitions***: A ***generally applicable criminal law*** is ***automatically enforceable***, regardless of how much burden it causes to an individual's religious beliefs (assuming that the government did not *intend* to disadvantage a particular religion when it enacted its law). [696-697]

    **Example:** A state may make it a crime to possess the drug peyote, and may enforce this rule against Native Americans who use peyote as a central part of their religious rituals. [*Employment Div. v. Smith*]

2. **No serious impairment required:** Also, even where no criminal prohibition is involved, government does ***not*** have to tolerate a ***serious impairment*** of some ***compelling*** governmental goal — here, no exemption needs to be given, because strict scrutiny is satisfied. (*Example:* Even if a religiously-affiliated university honestly believes that its religion bars African Americans and whites from studying together, government need not tolerate interference with its compelling goal of eliminating racial discrimination, so government does not need to exempt the university from anti-discrimination laws.)

3. **Cutting back:** In any event, all of free exercise law seems to be in the process of being scaled back, so the general rule that government must give an exemption where this can be done without seriously impairing a compelling governmental interest, may be on its way out.

F. **Conscientious objection:** Probably Congress ***must*** (as it does) give an exemption for military service for ***conscientious objectors*** (i.e., those who believe that all war is evil). [698]

1. **Selective c.o.'s:** But Congress need not give an exemption to "selective" c.o.'s (i.e., those who do not believe that all war is evil, but who believe that the particular war in which they are being asked to fight is evil). [*Gillette v. U.S.*]

G. **Public health:** Government may have to sacrifice its interest in the ***health*** of its citizenry, if individuals' religious dictates so require. [699]

1. **Competent adult:** Where the case involves a ***competent adult***, and only that adult's own health is at stake, government may probably not force treatment on the individual over his religious objection. (*Example:* A state probably can't force a Jehovah's Witness to accept a blood transfusion or other life-saving medical care over that person's religious objections.)

2. **Child:** However, where the patient is a ***child*** whose parents object on religious grounds, the state may probably compel the treatment.

3. **Danger to others:** Also, if the case involves not only a health danger to the person asserting a religious belief, but also a health danger to ***others***, then government probably does not have to give an exemption. (*Example:* P may be forced to undergo a vaccination over his religious objections. [*Jacobsen v. Mass.*])

H. **What constitutes a religious belief:** Only *bona fide* "religious beliefs" are protected by the Free Exercise Clause. But "religious beliefs" are defined very ***broadly***. [699]

1. **Non-theistic:** For instance, ***non-theistic*** beliefs are protected. That is, the belief need not recognize the existence of a supreme being. (*Example:* Public officials cannot be forced to take an oath in which they say that they believe that God exists. [*Torcaso v. Watkins*])

2. **Unorganized religions:** Similarly, ***unorganized*** or obscure religions get the same protection as the major religions. In fact, even if a person's religious beliefs are followed ***only by him***, he's still entitled to free exercise protection.

3. **Sincerity:** A court will not sustain a free exercise claim unless it is convinced that the religious belief is *"genuine"* or *"sincere."* (The fact that the belief or practice has been observed by a religious group for a long period of time may be considered in measuring sincerity. But the converse — absence of a long-standing practice — does not mean that the belief is insincere.)

   a. **Unreasonableness:** The court will *not* consider whether the belief is "true" or *"reasonable"*. Even a very "unreasonable" belief (that is, a belief that most people might consider unreasonable) is not deprived of protection, so long as it is *genuine*. [*U.S. v. Ballard*] (*Example:* The practice of voodoo, including sticking pins into dolls representing one's enemies, might be considered by most of us to be "unreasonable." But as long as such a practice is part of a person's genuine set of beliefs and religious practices, it will not be deprived of protection merely because most find it unreasonable.)

# CHAPTER 16

# JUSTICIABILITY

## I. JUSTICIABILITY GENERALLY

A. **List:** In order for a case to be heard by the federal courts, the plaintiff must get past a series of procedural obstacles which we collectively call requirements for *"justiciability"*: (1) the case must not require the giving of an *advisory opinion*; (2) the plaintiff must have *standing*; (3) the case must not be *moot*; (4) the case must be *ripe* for decision; and (5) the case must not involve a non-justiciable *political question*. [710]

## II. ADVISORY OPINIONS

A. **Constitutional "case or controversy" requirement:** Article III, Section 2 of the Constitution gives the federal courts jurisdiction only over "cases" and "controversies." The federal courts are therefore prevented from issuing opinions on *abstract* or *hypothetical* questions. This means that the federal courts may not give *"advisory opinions"*. In other words, the federal courts may not render opinions which answer a legal question when no party is before the court who has suffered or faces specific injury. [710]

> **Example:** Suppose that both houses of Congress approve a bill, but the President has doubts about the bill's constitutionality. The President may *not* go to a federal court and ask the federal court whether the bill is constitutional, so that he may decide whether to veto it. If the federal court were to give its opinion about whether the bill was constitutional, at a time when no party who had been or might soon be injured by the unconstitutionality was before the court, this would be an "advisory opinion" that would violate the constitutional "case or controversy" requirement.

1. **Declaratory judgments sometimes allowed:** But *declaratory judgments* are sometimes allowed, and are not forbidden by the rule against advisory opinions. A declaratory judgment is a judicial decision in which the court is not requested to award damages or an injunction, but is instead requested to state what the legal effect would be of proposed conduct by one or both of the parties. [711]

   a. **Requirements:** But the plaintiff is not entitled to get a declaratory judgment on just any question about what the legal consequence of the particular conduct would be. If the declaratory judgment action raises only questions that are very *hypothetical* or *abstract*, the federal court is likely to conclude that what's sought here is an illegal advisory opinion, because no specific, concrete controversy exists.

# III.  STANDING

**A.  Function of a standing requirement:**   Probably the most important rule about when the federal courts may hear a case is that they may do so only when the plaintiff has *"standing"* to assert his claim. By this, we mean that the plaintiff must have a significant *stake* in the controversy. [711-713]

> **Example:** Suppose that during the Vietnam War, P, a federal taxpayer, becomes convinced that, since Congress has never formally declared war, P's tax dollars are being used to support an unconstitutional war. If P were to sue the federal government in federal court to have the war effort enjoined on this ground, the court would not hear his claim — he would be found to lack "standing," since (as we'll see in detail later) a person whose only connection with the controversy is that he is a taxpayer will almost never be deemed to have standing to claim that tax dollars are being used illegally.

**B.  Requirement of "injury in fact":**   The key concept behind the law of standing is simple: the litigant must show that he has suffered an *"injury in fact."* At its broadest level, the standing requirement means that the plaintiff must show that *he has himself been injured* in some way by the conduct that he complains of. [712]

**C.  Who is kept out:**   The standing rules tend to keep two main types of cases *out* of the federal courts: [713]

  **1.  Non-individuated harm:**   First, we have cases in which the harm suffered by the plaintiff is *no different* from that suffered by very large numbers of people not before the court. (*Example:* Suppose P's only connection with the suit is that he is a federal "citizen" or a "taxpayer" who is injured the same as any other citizen or taxpayer by the fact that the government is spending tax dollars illegally or otherwise violating some law. P does not have standing.)

  **2.  Third parties' rights:**   Second, we have cases where the rights claimed to be violated are not the rights of the plaintiff, but instead the rights of *third parties* who are not before the court. (But there are some important exceptions to the general rule that the plaintiff can't complain of government actions that violate someone else's rights.)

**D.  Taxpayer and citizen suits:**   Here is the single most important context in which standing problems arise: suits that are brought by federal *"citizens"* or *"taxpayers"* arguing that their general rights as citizens or taxpayers are violated by governmental action. [713-715]

  **1.  Taxpayer suits:**   Suppose that the plaintiff contends that: (1) he is a federal *taxpayer*; and (2) his tax dollars are being spent by the government in some illegal way. May the plaintiff pursue this suit in federal court? In general, the answer will be, *"no."* The fact that a person's federal taxes are used to fund an unconstitutional or illegal government program is simply not a sufficient connection with the governmental action to confer standing on the plaintiff. [*Frothingham v. Mellon*]. [713]

    **a.  One exception:**  There is one very narrow exception: a federal taxpayer has standing to sue to overturn a *congressional tax or spending program* that violates the *Establishment Clause*. [*Flast v. Cohen*] [713]

      **i.  Tightly limited:**  But this "*Flast* exception" is extremely *tightly limited:* it applies only to *congressional* spending that violates the Establishment Clause, not even to *Executive-Branch* spending that might violate the Clause. [*Hein v. Freedom from Religion Foundation*] [714]

    **b.  State taxpayers:**   A *state* taxpayer, like a federal taxpayer, does *not* have federal-court standing to litigate the legality of the state's expenditures. [*DaimlerChrysler Corp. v. Cuno.*] [714]

c. **Municipal taxpayer:** But a *municipal* taxpayer definitely *does* have standing to litigate the legality of his city's expenditures. [714]

2. **Citizen suits:** Suppose now that plaintiff argues that he is a federal *"citizen"*, and that as such he has the right to have his government act in accordance with the Constitution. Assume that P has no direct connection with the governmental act he's complaining about (he's merely claiming that, like every other citizen, he has the right to have the federal government obey the Constitution). In this "citizen suit" situation, P will *not have standing*. The Court has always held that one federal citizen's interest in lawful government is no different from the interest of any other citizen, and that an individual litigant relying on citizenship has not shown the *"individualized"* injury-in-fact that is required for standing. [715]

E. **Cases not based on taxpayer or citizen status:** Now suppose that the plaintiff is not arguing that his standing derives from his status as citizen or taxpayer. In other words, we're now talking about the vast bulk of ordinary law suits. [715-718]

1. **Three requirements:** Here, there are three standing requirements that the plaintiff must meet: (1) he must show that he has suffered (or is likely to suffer) an *"injury in fact"*; (2) the injury he is suffering must be *concrete* and *"individuated"*; and (3) the action being challenged must be the *"cause in fact"* of the injury. [715]

2. **"Injury in fact":** The plaintiff must show that he either *has suffered*, or *will probably suffer*, some concrete *"injury in fact."* [715]

a. **Non-economic harm:** This "injury in fact" requirement is pretty loosely applied. For instance, the harm does not have to be *economic* in nature. (*Example:* A group of people who use a national forest claim that the construction of a recreation area in the forest will violate federal laws. To get standing, the plaintiffs point to the injury to their "esthetic and environmental well-being" which would result from the construction. *Held*, this esthetic and environmental injury satisfies the "injury in fact" requirement, even though the harm is non-economic and in fact very intangible. [*Sierra Club v. Morton*]) [715]

b. **Imminent harm:** If P has not *already* suffered the injury in fact, he must show that the future injury is not only probable but *"concrete"* and *"imminent."* In other words, a vague sort of harm that may come about in the indefinite future will not suffice. (*Example:* The Ps challenge a federal regulatory action that they say will endanger certain species abroad. The Ps say that they have in the past, and will in the future, travel abroad to visit the habitats of these species. *Held*, the Ps lack standing, because the lack of specific information about their future plans means the harm to them is not sufficiently concrete or imminent. [*Lujan v. Defenders of Wildlife*]) [715]

c. **Remedy:** In addition to showing an "injury in fact," P must show that the injury would be *remedied* by a favorable court decision. [715]

3. **Individuated harm:** The harm that has been or will be suffered by the plaintiff has to be *"individuated."* That is, it can't be the same harm as suffered by every citizen, or every taxpayer.

a. **Large number:** But the harm may still be found to be "individuated" even though there are a *large number* of people suffering the harm. [716]

i. **Same harm:** But remember that if the harm complained of by the plaintiff is truly the same harm as suffered by every citizen or every taxpayer in the country, the harm will not be sufficiently "individuated," and the plaintiffs won't have standing.

b. **Organizations and associations:** What about organizations and associations — does the organization itself have to suffer the harm, or can it merely assert that its *members* will suffer or have suffered the required harm? In general, the answer is that organizations and associations will be able to sue on behalf of their members. However: (1) the members have to be people who would have **standing in their own right** (so that an organization of citizens or tax-payers could not complain of harm that is suffered by all citizens or taxpayers); (2) the inter-ests being asserted by the organization in the lawsuit must be **related to the organization's purpose** (so that an environmental group could probably not try to pursue its members' inter-ests in, say, an effective criminal justice system); and (3) the case cannot be one which requires the **participation of individual members.** [*Hunt v. Wash. Apple Advt'g. Comm.*]. These three requirements are pretty liberally applied. [716]

4. **Causation:** Finally, the action that the plaintiff is complaining about must be the *"cause in fact"* of his injury. Actually, this causation requirement breaks down into two sub-requirements:

(1) P has to show that the challenged action was a *"but for"* cause of his injury, that is, that the injury would not have occurred unless the challenged action had taken place; and

(2) P must show that a favorable decision in the suit will probably *redress* the injury to him. [717-718]

5. **Perhaps easier test for states:** When the suit is brought by a *state*, the injury-in-fact and causa-tion requirements are probably interpreted a bit *less stringently.*

**Example:** Massachusetts sues to force the EPA to regulate auto emissions. The state's reason-ing is that (1) such regulation will or may slow the speed of global warming "over the next century" (even though non-U.S. sources will concededly grow their own emissions dramati-cally during this period); and (2) without the slowing, the state's coastal lands will or may be eroded by rising sea levels. *Held*, Mass. has met the injury-in-fact and causation requirements, in part because Mass. is acting as a sovereign state protecting the interests of its citizens. [*Mass. v. EPA*, 2007] [719]

F. **Third-party standing:** One of the key functions of the standing doctrine is that this is how courts apply the general rule that a litigant normally may **not assert the constitutional rights of persons not before the court**. (This principle is sometimes called the rule against use of "constitutional *jus tertii*," — *jus tertii* means "rights of third persons" in Latin.) [720]

**Example:** Zoning laws enacted by the city of Penfield, N.Y., intentionally exclude the build-ing of low-income housing. The Ps are residents of nearby Rochester, who claim that because Penfield has refused to allow low- and middle-income housing, the taxes of these Rochester residents have risen, since Rochester has to subsidize or build more low-income housing than it would have to build than had Penfield not practiced exclusionary zoning.

*Held*, these Rochester residents lack standing. It is true that their higher taxes are an "injury in fact" to them. But Penfield's zoning laws do not apply to these Rochester residents, and therefore do not violate *their* rights. And the Rochester residents may not claim that the rights of **other people not before the court** have been violated (e.g., people who would have moved to Penfield had exclusionary zoning not been practiced). [*Warth v. Seldin*]) [717-718]

1. **Not constitutionally required:** This rule against the assertion of third-party rights is **not** man-dated by the Article III "case or controversy" requirement. In other words, it is not a rule imposed by the Constitution on the federal courts; instead, it is a rule of *"prudence,"* a policy decision adopted by the Supreme Court. [721]

2. **Exceptions:** Since the rule against asserting third-party rights is not required by the Constitution, the Supreme Court is free to make whatever *exceptions* it wishes to the doctrine.

   a. **Associations:** One exception is that an *association* will normally be allowed to raise the rights of its *members*. For instance, if a group of people would be injured by damage to the air they breathe and the water they drink, an organization of which they are members (e.g., the Sierra Club) would typically be allowed to sue on their behalf. [716]

    **b. Overbreadth:** Another sort of exception to the rule against third-party standing is the First Amendment *overbreadth* doctrine, which we covered earlier in our discussion of freedom of expression. Remember that the basic idea behind overbreadth is that even where a statute could constitutionally be applied to the plaintiff's conduct, if he can show that the statute would unconstitutionally restrict the expression of *some other person not before the court,* the court may hear the lawsuit and strike down the statute. We allow overbreadth in the *First Amendment area* but not elsewhere because statutes that purport to restrict expression in an overbroad manner will have a *"chilling effect"* on citizens' general willingness to exercise their freedom of speech. [721]

**G. "Prudential" standing:** We just saw that the rule against third-party standing is not dictated by the Article III "case or controversy" requirement, and is instead the result of *"prudential"* considerations. More generally, the federal courts retain the right to refuse to hear *any* case on such prudential-standing grounds, even cases falling outside the pure third-party-standing area.

    **Example:** P is the father of a daughter, X, who attends public-school. P claims that the school's policy of reciting the Pledge of Allegiance violates his First Amendment right to have his daughter be instructed in P's atheistic beliefs without government interference. (X's mother, who is divorced from P, opposes the suit.) *Held*, because the suit involves domestic relations questions -- typically avoided by the federal courts -- and also involves X's rights in a highly controversial matter, the Court's prudential-standing policies dictate that the federal courts not hear the case. [*Elk Grove v. Newdow*] [721]

# IV. MOOTNESS

**A. General rule:** A case may not be heard by the federal courts if it is *"moot."* A case is moot if it raised a live controversy at the time the complaint was filed, but *events occurring after the filing* have deprived the litigant of an ongoing stake in the controversy. [722]

    **Example:** P sues D, a state university, claiming that the university's law school admissions program is racially discriminatory. P is permitted to attend the law school while the case is being litigated. By the time the case arrives at the Supreme Court for review, P is in his final year of law school, and the university says that he will be allowed to graduate regardless of how the case is decided. *Held*, the case is moot. Therefore, the appeal will not be decided. [*DeFunis v. Odegaard*]

    **1. Constitutional basis for:** Apparently the rule that the federal courts may not decide "moot" cases is *required* by the Constitution. That is, deciding a case when the parties no longer have a live controversy would amount to issuing an advisory opinion, in violation of Article III's "case or controversy" requirement.

**B. Exceptions:** Nonetheless, the courts recognize a few situations where a case that would appear to be "moot" will nonetheless be heard. [722]

    **1. "Capable of repetition, yet evading review":** For instance, a case will not be treated as moot if the issue it raises is *"capable of repetition, yet evading review."* This "capable of repetition, yet evading review" doctrine takes care of situations in which, if the case were to be declared moot, a *different person* might be injured in the *same way* by the same defendant, and his claim, too, would be mooted before review could be had. [723]

        **Example:** P, a pregnant woman, attacks the constitutionality of Texas' anti-abortion law. She brings the suit as a class action, in which she is the named plaintiff and other pregnant women who want abortions are unnamed members. By the time the case reaches the Supreme Court, P is no longer pregnant.

*Held*, the case should not be dismissed as moot. A pregnancy will almost always be over before the usual appellate process is complete. Therefore, if the Court insisted that the named plaintiff who starts the suit must still be pregnant by the time the suit gets to the Supreme Court, no plaintiff could ever get to that Court. So the constitutionality of the Texas anti-abortion law is "capable of repetition, yet evading review." [*Roe v. Wade*]

2. **Voluntary cessation by defendant:**  The case will generally not be treated as moot if the defendant *voluntarily ceases* the conduct that the plaintiff is complaining about. So if the plaintiff is seeking an injunction, the defendant can't usually get the case dismissed on mootness grounds merely by saying that he has voluntarily stopped the conduct that the plaintiff is trying to get an injunction against — unless the defendant shows that there is no reasonable likelihood that he will return to his old ways, the court will let the action go forward. [723]

3. **Collateral consequences:**  Finally, a case will not be moot even if it is mostly decided, if there are still *collateral consequences* that might be adverse to the defendant. For instance, suppose that a criminal defendant has already served his sentence by the time his attack on the constitutionality of his conviction comes before the federal court. The case will not be moot, because there will probably be future collateral consequences to the defendant from his conviction (e.g., he will lose the right to vote, his reputation or employability will be damaged, etc.) [723]

# V. RIPENESS

A. **Ripeness problem generally:**  You can think of the problem of ripeness as being the opposite of mootness. A case is moot, as we've just seen, because it *no longer* involves an actual controversy. By contrast, a case is not yet ripe (and therefore not yet decidable by a federal court) if it has *not yet become sufficiently concrete* to be easily adjudicated. [723]

**Example:** The Hatch Act prohibits federal executive-branch employees from getting involved in "political management or … political campaigns." The plaintiffs are federal civil servants who want to attack the constitutionality of the Hatch Act. The plaintiffs claim that they want to engage in prohibited political activities. But they concede that they have not yet engaged in such activities.

*Held*, the plaintiffs' claims are not yet ripe. The problem is not that the Ps have not yet violated the statute. Rather, the problem is that the plaintiffs have not been adequately specific about the *precise acts* that they wish to carry out. (If the Ps would specify in detail what they want to do, their suit might not be unripe even though they haven't yet violated the act.) [*United Public Workers v. Mitchell*]. [723]

B. **Uncertain enforcement of criminal statute:**  One common ripeness problem arises where the plaintiff attacks the constitutionality of a statute and says that he has violated the statute, but it is clear that the statute is *rarely enforced* and probably will not be enforced in this particular situation. Here, the rules are pretty blurry — suffice it to say that if the court believes that it is *very unlikely* that the statute will be enforced against the plaintiff either for the activity he has already done or similar activity he is likely to do in the future, the court will probably treat the case as being not ripe.

**Example:** Connecticut forbids the distribution of contraceptives. Two married couples and a physician challenge the law's constitutionality, and allege that they have violated the law. *Held*, the case is not ripe, because the statute has been on the books for 80 years with only one reported prosecution, so there does not exist the required "clear" threat that the plaintiffs will be prosecuted. [*Poe v. Ullman*] [724]

1. **Specific threatened harm required:** But for a case to be ripe, it is not necessary that the litigant have *already suffered* harm. It will be enough that there is a *reasonable probability* of harm. However, the anticipated harm has to be fairly *specific*. [724]

# VI. THE ELEVENTH AMENDMENT AND SUITS AGAINST THE STATES

A. **The Eleventh Amendment generally:** The *Eleventh Amendment* specifically bars any federal suit "against any one of the *states* by citizens of another state, or by citizens or subjects of any foreign state." [725]

   1. **Damage suits against states:** The Eleventh Amendment has been held to bar most types of *damage suits* against a state.

      a. **Plaintiff not a citizen of defendant state:** By its own terms, the Amendment clearly applies to suits against a state brought by citizens of a *different state* or by foreigners. (*Examples:* A citizen of Missouri may not bring a damage suit against the state of Illinois. Nor may a British subject bring a damage suit against the state of Illinois.)

      b. **Suit by citizen of defendant state:** The Eleventh Amendment has been *interpreted* to apply also to bar a damage suit where the plaintiff is a *citizen of the defendant state*. [*Hans v. Louisiana*] (*Example:* Suppose P is an employee of the Delmarva state legislature. He is then fired, in apparent violation of his employment contract. P brings a suit for contract damages against Delmarva, in federal court. This suit would be a violation of the Eleventh Amendment, as broadly interpreted by the Supreme Court.)

   2. **Suits by states or federal government:** The Eleventh Amendment does *not* bar federal suits brought by *one state* against another state, or by the *federal government* against a state.

   3. **No counties or cities protected:** Only the *state itself*, not its *subdivisions*, such as *counties* or *cities*, is protected by the Eleventh Amendment. (*Example:* P, a county worker, is fired. He brings a federal suit for contract damages against the county. Since the suit is not against the state *per se*, the Eleventh Amendment does not apply, even though the county is in essence a subdivision of the state.)

   4. **No bar against injunctions:** The Eleventh Amendment essentially bars only suits for *damages*. That is, it does not bar most suits for *injunctions*. For instance, if a private litigant sues a state official to enjoin him from taking acts which would violate the plaintiff's *constitutional* or *federal-law* rights, the Eleventh Amendment does not apply and the suit may proceed. [*Ex parte Young*]

   5. **Congress can't override:** *Congress* generally *can't change* the "no federal-court suits against the states" principle behind the 11th Amendment, even if it wants to and expressly says it's doing so. [*Seminole Tribe v. Florida*] [726-728]

      **Example:** Congress passes a statute saying any state *can* be sued in federal court by private citizens for violating, say, federal patent or environmental laws. This statute won't have any effect — a federal court still can't hear a private suit against a state for damages for violating the federal law. [*Florida Prepaid v. Coll. Sav. Bank*] [728]

      a. **Exception for remedial powers:** But there's an *exception* — if Congress is acting properly pursuant to its *remedial powers* under the 13th, 14th or 15th Amendment, it may *abrogate* the states' 11th Amendment immunity.

B. **States' sovereign immunity:** The states have a constitutionally-guaranteed *sovereign immunity* from certain proceedings brought by private parties.

1. **Suit in states' own courts:** Thus the states have constitutional sovereign immunity from private damage suits brought against the state in the ***state's own courts.*** This is true even if the suit is based on a ***congressionally-granted federal right.*** [728-728]

   **Example:** Congress passes a valid statute saying that state employees must receive premium pay for overtime just as private-sector employees do. Employees of Maine sue the state in Maine courts on this right. *Held,* the Constitution's structure incorporates the doctrine of sovereign immunity, and that doctrine allows Maine to avoid hearing the employees' suit, even if Congress has expressly said that the states must hear such suits. [*Alden v. Maine*] [728]

2. **Proceeding before federal administrative agency:** Similarly, the states have sovereign immunity from being required to respond to a private complaint before a ***federal administrative agency.*** [*Federal Maritime Comm. v. So. Car. St. Ports Auth.*] [729]

# VII. POLITICAL QUESTIONS

A. **The doctrine generally:** The final aspect of justiciability is the requirement is that the case not involve the decision of a **"political question."** This rule is even more vague than the other justiciability rules we've talked about already. The doctrine does ***not*** mean that federal courts will not decide a case that involves politics. It doesn't even mean that courts will refuse to decide cases where political issues are right at the heart of the controversy. Instead, the court will decline to hear a case on political question grounds only if it thinks that the doctrine of ***separation of powers*** requires this, or if it thinks that deciding the case would be unwise as a policy matter. [729]

1. **Two of the factors used:** Two of the factors that seem to be very important in whether a case will be found to involve a non-justiciable political question are:

   a. **Commitment to another branch:** First, the fact that the case presents an issue which has been committed by the Constitution to ***another branch of the federal government***, i.e., to Congress or to the President instead of the courts.

   b. **Lack of standards:** Second, the fact that there are no manageable ***standards*** by which a court could resolve the issue.

B. **"Commitment to other branches" strand:** The courts will refuse to decide a case on political-question grounds if the case raises an issue the determination of which is clearly committed by the Constitution to ***another branch of the federal government.*** [730-732]

   **Example:** D, a federal judge, claims that the Senate has used improper procedures in convicting him following his impeachment, because the case was heard before a committee of Senators rather than the full Senate (though the full Senate voted, after receiving a transcript of the committee proceedings). D claims that this violates the Impeachment Clause, which says that "the Senate shall have sole Power to try all Impeachments." *Held,* the case presents a nonjusticiable political question, because the Constitution has given the Senate, not the courts, the power to decide what constitutes a "trial." [*Nixon v. U.S.*]

1. **Other impeachment issues:** The same principle probably applies to ***all*** aspects of the impeachment process. Thus if the House voted to impeach the President and the Senate voted to convict, the Supreme Court would probably refuse to review either of these decisions on "commitment to other branches" political-question grounds (so that if the President tried to get the Supreme Court to hear his argument that the crime for which he was impeached and convicted was not within the constitutionally-defined category of "high crimes and misdemeanors," the Court would probably refuse to consider the merits of this argument).

**2. Rare:** It is quite rare for a case to be declined on the grounds that it involves a question committed to some other branch of government.

**C. "Lack of judicially manageable standards":** The second major factor that may lead the court to decide that there is a non-justiciable political question, is that there are no *manageable standards* by which the courts can resolve the issue. [732]

> **Example:** Article IV, Section 4 provides that "the United States shall guarantee to every state in this union a republican form of government." Some unhappy Rhode Island citizens stage a rebellion. Ultimately, various Rhode Islanders ask the federal courts to decide which of two competing factions is the lawful government of the state.
>
> *Held*, the Court cannot decide this question, because it presents a political question. There are no criteria by which a court could determine whether a particular "government" was "Republican." [*Luther v. Borden*]

**D. Reapportionment:** Let's now look in some detail at the federal cases on *legislative reapportionment*. [733-736]

**1. One person, one vote rule:** The landmark case of *Baker v. Carr,* and cases following it, establish the so-called *"one person, one vote"* principle: any governmental body, whether it's a federal one (like congressional districts) or a state one (like a state legislature) must be apportioned on a *population* basis, so that *all voters have essentially the same voting power.* If a governmental electoral scheme does not comply with this "one person, one vote" principle, it violates the *equal protection* rights of the under-represented voters. [*Reynolds v. Sims*]. [733-734]

    **a. Justiciable:** Such cases raising the "one person, one vote" argument are *justiciable*. The Court has rejected the argument that these cases raise non-justiciable political questions. [*Baker v. Carr*] [733]

    **b. Both houses of state legislature:** One of the consequences of the "one person, one vote" principle is that if a state has a bicameral (two-house) legislature, *both* houses must be elected based on population. Thus, paradoxically, the U.S. Constitution prohibits a state from having one body that awards seats without reference to population (e.g., a house that gives the same number of votes to each county), even though the U.S. Senate is built upon exactly this kind of non-population-based scheme!

**2. How much equality is required:** The rules for *how much equality is required* vary depending on whether we're talking about a congressional districting scheme or, instead, a state or local districting scheme. [735]

    **a. Congressional:** For *congressional districts*, the districts have to be *almost precisely equal.* Even a scheme where one congressional district within a state was only 1% more populous than another has been struck down. States must make a "good-faith effort to achieve *precise mathematical equality*" in the drawing of congressional districts. [*Kirkpatrick v. Preisler*]

    **b. State and local:** *Much greater deviation* from mathematical equality is allowed where what is being apportioned is *state legislatures* or *local governmental bodies*. So for example, a *10%* or smaller deviation between the voting power of a voter in one district versus a voter in another will generally be *upheld*. [*White v. Regester*] Even greater disparities will be allowed if there are good reasons for them. (For instance, suppose a state wants not to have to redraw its county boundaries, and wants to have each county elect its own representative to the state Assembly. This desire to "respect pre-existing political boundaries" will probably justify, say, a 15% or even 20% disparity in per-person voting power.)

**3.   Gerrymandering:**   Consider *gerrymandering*, that is, the process by which the strength of a particular voting bloc is curtailed by restricting its members to carefully and artificially-constructed districts.

   **a.   "Partisan gerrymandering" cases hard to win:**   First, consider *"partisan gerrymandering"* cases, i.e., cases arguing that a group is being disadvantaged based on its *political* rather than racial status. These cases are almost impossible for the plaintiffs to win. See C-39 *supra*. (In fact, a near-majority of the Court believes that such cases aren't even *justiciable*. [*Vieth v. Jubelirer*] [736].)

   **b.   Racial minority:**   But if a *racial or ethnic minority* can show that the gerrymandering scheme was intentionally designed to hurt, and did hurt, that minority, the plaintiffs' case *will* be justiciable, and probably winnable. For instance, if the state legislature draws districts for the state senate in a way that intentionally gives African Americans control of 5% of the districts when African Americans constitute 10% of the state population, African American voters have a good chance of winning an equal protection suit. [315]

C
A
P
S
U
L
E

S
U
M
M
A
R
Y

<small>CHAPTER 1</small>

# INTRODUCTION

## I. ROADMAP OF CONSTITUTIONAL LAW

**A. Roadmap:** Here is a very brief "roadmap" of Constitutional Law, giving you the names of the major doctrines/clauses, and the flavor of how each operates:

1. **Federalism:** First, we'll be covering various aspects of *"federalism."* Federalism means that the federal and state governments co-exist. Some of the main principles stemming from federalism are:

   a. **Limited, enumerated powers:** The powers of the federal government are *limited* to those that are *enumerated* in the Constitution. [Chap. 3]

   b. **Separation of powers:** Each of the three branches of the federal government (Congress, the President and the Judiciary) has its own enumerated powers, and one branch may not take actions reserved by the Constitution to one of the other branches. This is the doctrine of *"separation of powers."* [Chap. 8]

   c. **Congress' Commerce power:** The most important power given to Congress is the power to regulate *"commerce."* [Chap. 4]

2. **Dormant Commerce Clause:** Under the *"Dormant* Commerce Clause," the mere existence of the federal commerce power *restricts the states* from *discriminating against,* or unduly *burdening, interstate commerce.* [Chap. 6]

3. **Due Process Clause:** The *"Due Process Clause"* of the 14th Amendment has two different types of effects: [Chap. 9]

   a. **Substantive due process:** It limits the *"substantive"* power of the government to regulate certain areas of human life (e.g., child-bearing);

   b. **Procedural due process:** It imposes certain *"procedural"* requirements on government when it takes an individual's *"life, liberty or property."* (*Example:* Before government can take away food stamps you've been receiving, it must give you a hearing.)

4. **Equal Protection Clause:** The *"Equal Protection Clause"* of the 14th Amendment prevents government from making certain types of *"classifications,"* mainly ones that unfairly treat similarly-situated people differently. (*Example:* The Equal Protection Clause is what prohibits governments from running racially segregated schools.) [Chap. 10]

5. **Freedom of Expression:** The First Amendment protects *"speech"* against government interference. This includes the freedom of individuals to engage in *political protest,* the freedom of the *press* to publish, the freedom of individuals to *"associate"* with whomever they wish, and more. As you might expect, this "freedom" is far from absolute — often, government will be able to restrict free expression in some way or another (e.g., by requiring a permit before a large political demonstration takes place, or by prohibiting someone from advocating that a crime be committed). [Chap. 14]

6. **Freedom of Religion:** The First Amendment also protects *"freedom of religion."* There are two distinct clauses in the First Amendment dealing with religion: [Chap. 15]

    **a.** **Establishment Clause:** The *"Establishment"* Clause prevents government from "establishing" an official religion. That is, government may not **endorse** or **support** religion generally, or a particular religion.

    **b.** **Free Exercise Clause:** The *"Free Exercise"* Clause prevents government from **outlawing** or seriously **burdening** a person's pursuit of whatever religion (and whatever religious practices) he chooses.

## II.   THREE STANDARDS OF REVIEW

    **A.** **Three standards:** There are three key **standards of review** which reappear constantly throughout Constitutional Law. When a court reviews the constitutionality of government action, it is likely to be choosing from among one of these three standards of review: (1) the **mere rationality** standard; (2) the **strict scrutiny** standard; and (3) the **middle-level review** standard.

        **1.** **Mere rationality:** Of the three standards, the easiest one to satisfy is the *"mere rationality"* standard. When the court applies this "mere rationality" standard, the court will **uphold** the governmental action so long as two requirements are met:

            **a.** **Legitimate state objective:** First, the government must be pursuing a **legitimate governmental objective**. This is a very broad concept — practically any type of health, safety or "general welfare" goal will be found to be "legitimate."

            **b.** **Rational relation:** Second, there has to be a *"minimally rational relation"* between the means chosen by the government and the state objective. This requirement, too, is extremely easy to satisfy: only if the government has acted in a completely *"arbitrary and irrational"* way will this rational link between means and end not be found.

        **2.** **Strict scrutiny:** At the other end of the spectrum, the standard that is hardest to satisfy is the *"strict scrutiny"* standard of review. This standard will only be satisfied if the governmental act satisfies two very tough requirements:

            **a.** **Compelling objective:** First, the *objective* being pursued by the government must be *"compelling"* (not just "legitimate," as for the "mere rationality" standard); and

            **b.** **Necessary means:** Second, the *means* chosen by the government must be *"necessary"* to achieve that compelling end. In other words, the "fit" between the means and the end must be extremely tight. (It's not enough that there's a "rational relation" between the means and the end, which is enough under the "mere rationality" standard.)

                **i.** **No less restrictive alternatives:** In practice, this requirement that the means be "necessary" means that there must not be any **less restrictive** means that would accomplish the government's objective just as well.

        **3.** **Middle-level review:** In between these two review standards is so-called *"middle-level"* review.

            **a.** **"Important" objective:** Here, the governmental objective has to be *"important"* (half way between "legitimate" and "compelling").

b. **"Substantially related" means:** And, the means chosen by the government must be *"substantially related"* to the important government objective. (This "substantially related" standard is half way between "rationally related" and "necessary").

B. **Consequences of choice:** The court's choice of one of these standards of review has two important consequences:

1. **Burden of persuasion:** First, the choice will make a big difference as to who has the *burden of persuasion*.

   a. **Mere rationality:** Where the governmental action is subject to the *"mere rationality"* standard, the *individual* who is attacking the government action will generally bear the burden of persuading the court that the action is unconstitutional.

   b. **Strict scrutiny:** By contrast, if the court applies *"strict scrutiny,"* then the *governmental body* whose act is being attacked has the burden of persuading the court that its action is constitutional.

   c. **Middle-level review:** Where *"middle level"* scrutiny is used, it's not certain how the court will assign the burden of persuasion, but the burden will usually be placed on the government.

2. **Effect on outcome:** Second, the choice of review standard has a very powerful effect on the *actual outcome*. Where the "mere rationality" standard is applied, the governmental action will *almost always be upheld*. Where "strict scrutiny" is used, the governmental action will *almost always be struck down*. (For instance, the Supreme Court applies strict scrutiny to any classification based on race, and has upheld only one such strictly scrutinized racial classification in the last 50 years.) Where middle-level scrutiny is used, there's roughly a 50-50 chance that the governmental action will be struck down.

C. **When used:** Here is a quick overview of the entire body of Constitutional Law, to see where each of these review standards gets used:

1. **Mere rationality:** Here are the main places where the "mere rationality" standard gets applied (and therefore, the places where it's very hard for the person attacking the governmental action to get it struck down on constitutional grounds):

   a. **Dormant Commerce Clause:** First, the "mere rationality" test is the main test to determine whether a state regulation that affects interstate commerce violates the *"Dormant Commerce Clause."* The state regulation has to pursue a legitimate state end, and be rationally related to that end. (But there's a second test which we'll review in greater detail later: the state's interest in enforcing its regulation must also outweigh any *burden* imposed on interstate commerce, and any discrimination against interstate commerce.)

   b. **Substantive due process:** Next comes *substantive due process*. So long as no "fundamental right" is affected, the test for determining whether a governmental act violates substantive due process is, again, "mere rationality." In other words, if the state is pursuing a legitimate objective, and using means that are rationally related to that objective, the state will not be found to have violated the substantive Due Process Clause. So the vast bulk of *economic regulations* (since these don't affect fundamental rights) will be tested by the mere rationality standard and almost certainly upheld.

    **c. Equal protection:** Then, we move on to the ***equal protection*** area. Here, "mere rationality" review is used so long as: (1) ***no suspect*** or ***quasi-suspect classification*** is being used; and (2) ***no fundamental right*** is being impaired. This still leaves us with a large number of classifications which will be judged based on the mere rationality standard, including: (1) almost all economic regulations; (2) some classifications based on alienage; and (3) rights that are not "fundamental" even though they are very important, such as food, housing, and free public education. In all of these areas, the classification will be reviewed under the "mere rationality" standard, and will therefore almost certainly be upheld.

    **d. Contracts Clause:** Lastly, we find "mere rationality" review in some aspects of the ***"Obligation of Contracts"*** Clause.

**2. Strict scrutiny:** Here are the various contexts in which the Court applies ***strict scrutiny***:

    **a. Substantive due process/fundamental rights:** First, where a governmental action affects ***fundamental rights***, and the plaintiff claims that his ***substantive due process*** rights are being violated, the Court will use strict scrutiny. So when the state impairs rights falling in the ***"privacy"*** cluster of marriage, child-bearing, and child-rearing, the Court will use strict scrutiny (and will therefore probably invalidate the governmental restriction). For instance, government restrictions that impair the right to use contraceptives receive this kind of strict scrutiny.

    **b. Equal protection review:** Next, the Court uses strict scrutiny to review a claim that a classification violates the plaintiff's ***equal protection*** rights, if the classification relates either to a ***suspect classification*** or a ***fundamental right***. "Suspect classifications" include ***race***, ***national origin***, and (sometimes) ***alienage***. "Fundamental rights" for this purpose include the right to ***vote***, to have access to the ***courts***, and to ***travel interstate***. So classifications that either involve any of these suspect classifications or impair any of these fundamental rights will be strictly scrutinized and will probably be struck down.

    **c. Freedom of expression:** Next, we move to the area of ***freedom of expression***. If the government is impairing free expression in a ***content-based way***, then the court will use strict scrutiny and will almost certainly strike down the regulation. In other words, if the government is restricting some speech but not others, based on the ***content of the messages***, then this suppression of expression will only be allowed if necessary to achieve a compelling purpose (a standard which is rarely found to be satisfied in the First Amendment area). Similarly, any interference with the right of ***free association*** will be strictly scrutinized.

    **d. Freedom of religion/Free Exercise Clause:** Lastly, the court will use strict scrutiny to evaluate any impairment with a person's ***free exercise*** of religion. Even if the government does ***not intend*** to impair a person's free exercise of his religion, if it substantially burdens his exercise of religion, the government will have to give him an ***exemption*** from the otherwise-applicable regulation unless denial of an exemption is necessary to achieve a compelling governmental interest.

3. **Middle-level review:** Finally, here are the relatively small number of contexts in which the court uses middle-level review:

   a. **Equal protection/semi-suspect:** First, middle-level review will be used to judge an *equal protection* claim, where the classification being challenged involves a *semi-suspect* trait. The two traits which are considered semi-suspect for this purpose are: (1) *gender*; and (2) *illegitimacy*. So any government classification based on gender or illegitimacy will have to be "substantially related" to the achievement of some "important" governmental interest.

   b. **Contracts Clause:** Second, certain conduct attacked under the Obligation of Contracts Clause will be judged by the middle-level standard of review.

   c. **Free expression/non-content-based:** Finally, in the First Amendment area we use a standard similar (though not identical) to the middle-level review standard to judge government action that impairs expression, but does so in a *non-content-based* manner. This is true, for instance, of any content-neutral *"time, place and manner"* regulation.

# THE SUPREME COURT'S AUTHORITY

## *ChapterScope*

This Chapter examines several aspects of the Supreme Court's authority. The most important concepts in this Chapter are:

- **Supreme Court review:** It is the ***Supreme Court, not Congress,*** which has the authority and duty to review the ***constitutionality*** of statutes passed by Congress, and to invalidate the statute if it violates the Constitution.

- **Review of state court decisions:** The Supreme Court may review state court decisions, but only to the extent that the decision was based on ***federal law.***

  - ❏ **"Independent and adequate state grounds":** Even if there *is* a federal question in a state court case, the Supreme Court may not review the case if there was an ***"independent and adequate" state ground*** for the state court's decision. (That is, if the same result would be reached even if the state court had made a different decision on the federal question, the Supreme Court may not decide the case.)

- **Federal judicial power:** The federal judicial power is set forth in Art. III, Section 2 of the U.S. Constitution. The federal judicial power includes (a partial listing):

  - ❏ cases arising under the ***Constitution*** or under ***federal statutes***;

  - ❏ cases of ***admiralty***;

  - ❏ cases between ***two or more states***;

  - ❏ cases between citizens of ***different states***; and

  - ❏ cases between a state or its citizens and a ***foreign country*** or ***foreign citizens.***

  The federal judicial power does ***not*** include cases where both parties are citizens (i.e., residents) of the same state, and no federal question is raised.

- **Congress' control of federal judicial power:** Congress has some meaningful control over the federal judicial power:

  - ❏ **Control of Supreme Court docket:** Congress has the general power to decide ***what types*** of cases the ***Supreme Court*** may hear, so long as it doesn't expand the Court's jurisdiction beyond the federal judicial power summarized above.

  - ❏ **Lower courts:** Congress may also decide what lower ***federal courts*** there should be, and what cases they may hear.

# I.　REVIEW OF ACTS OF CONGRESS (*MARBURY V. MADISON*)

**A.　The *Marbury* case itself:**　Which branch of the federal government shall have the *final say in interpreting the Constitution*? That is the principal question resolved by Chief Justice John Marshall's opinion in *Marbury v. Madison*, 1 Cranch 137 (1803), perhaps the cornerstone of American constitutional law.

1.　**Historical background:**　The background of the case was a political struggle between John Adams and the Federalists, and his successor Thomas Jefferson and the Republicans. Just before leaving office, Adams appointed a number of new judges, including several justices of the peace for the District of Columbia. Commissions for these justices of the peace had been signed by Adams, but not yet delivered by the time he left office. The Jefferson Administration then refused to honor the appointments for which commissions had not actually been delivered prior to the end of Adams' term.

2.　**Subject of suit:**　Several of the would-be justices of the peace, including William Marbury, brought suit directly in the Supreme Court. They sought a writ of mandamus compelling Jefferson's Secretary of State (James Madison) to deliver their commissions.

3.　**Marshall's decision:**　Justice Marshall's opinion dealt with a number of issues, of which only the last gives the case its present significance.

　　a.　**Right to commission:**　First, Marshall decided that Marbury and the other justices did indeed become entitled to their commissions once these had been signed by the President (and sealed by the Secretary of State, who was none other than Marshall himself!) Marshall could have short-circuited the whole problem by ruling that delivery was required for validity, but he did not take this route.

　　b.　**Remedy:**　Secondly, Marshall had to decide whether Madison's failure to deliver the commissions entitled the plaintiffs to some sort of remedy. Marshall distinguished between political acts, which are not reviewable by the courts, and acts specifically required by law, which are reviewable. The refusal to deliver the commissions, Marshall ruled, fell into this latter category.

　　c.　**Mandamus not allowed:**　Lastly, Marshall had to decide whether the particular remedy sought by the plaintiffs, an application for a writ of mandamus directly to the Supreme Court, could be granted.

　　　　i.　**Judiciary Act allows:**　The then-effective Judiciary Act provided that the Supreme Court would have jurisdiction "to issue ... writs of mandamus ... [to] persons holding office under the authority of the United States." Thus the Act itself explicitly authorized the relief being sought by the plaintiffs.

　　　　ii.　**At odds with Constitution:**　However, Marshall concluded, this grant of jurisdiction was in conflict with Article III, §2, of the Constitution, which grants the Supreme Court original jurisdiction only "[i]n all Cases affecting Ambassadors, other public Ministers and Consuls, and those in which a State shall be Party." Since issuance of mandamus is not among the types of cases as to which original jurisdiction is conferred on the Supreme Court, Marshall held, the congressional statute was at odds with the Constitution.

　　d.　**Supremacy of Constitution:**　This brought Marshall to the holding for which *Marbury v. Madison* is principally known today. If the Supreme Court identifies a ***conflict*** between a constitutional provision and a congressional statute, ***the Court has the authority (and the duty) to declare the statute unconstitutional and to refuse to enforce it***. Therefore, Marshall concluded, the requested writ of mandamus could not be issued. In reaching this conclusion, Marshall made two interlocking arguments:

i. **Constitution is paramount:** The very purpose of a written constitution is to establish a fundamental and paramount law. It follows from this that any act of the legislature repugnant to the Constitution must be void.

ii. **Who interprets:** "It is emphatically the ***province and duty of the judicial department to say what the law is***." That is, it is the ***court, not the legislature***, which must make the determination whether, in a particular case, an act of Congress is in conflict with the Constitution. To deny the permissibility of judicial review of the constitutionality of a congressional statute would be to say that the courts "must close their eyes on the constitution, and see only the law. This doctrine would subvert the very foundation of all written constitutions."

4. **Criticism of *Marbury*:** Because of its key importance, *Marbury v. Madison* has been subject to a huge amount of analysis and criticism. Only one of these lines of criticism is of interest to us here.

a. **Who determines constitutionality:** Most critics are willing to concede Step One of the two arguments above, i.e., that the Constitution is superior to statutes and that where there is a conflict, the Constitution must be respected. But Step Two is what all the shouting is about: ***the critics argue that nowhere in the Constitution is it stated that the courts, not Congress, ought to decide whether a given statute does in fact conflict with the Constitution.***

i. **Congress could decide:** Thus it is possible to imagine a system in which we would still have our written Constitution, acknowledged to be the supreme law of the land, but in which *Congress* (not the courts) would have the final say in interpreting that Constitution. Congress would be seen as having the duty to make sure that no act promulgated by it exceeded the Constitution; but Congress' interpretation of the presence or absence of a conflict, not the courts', would be the method of enforcing constitutional limits. See Tribe, p. 25.

ii. **Assumption, not conclusion:** Many, perhaps most, commentators believe that this criticism is well-taken, at least in the sense that the Constitution nowhere states that courts are to have the last say on whether a conflict between statute and Constitution exists. However, one answer to the critics is to say that Marshall was making an ***assumption***, rather than a deduction, when he stated that courts have the ultimate right to interpret constitutionality. That is, the Constitution can be classified as being "indeterminate" as to who has the final say. When viewed in this way (which is Tribe's approach; *id.*), Marshall's assumption is at least as reasonable as the contrary one (that Congress, not the courts, should decide constitutionality) — this contrary assumption is also nowhere to be found in the Constitution.

iii. **Judicial independence:** Furthermore, if one is merely trying to decide which assumption to make, there are some practical reasons why judicial interpretation, rather than legislative interpretation, might be a better means of construing the Constitution. Federal judges are appointed for life, and are thus free of day-to-day political pressures. Since Congress generally responds to the ***majority's*** will, and since one of the key functions of the Constitution is to protect the rights of ***minorities***, the relatively apolitical judiciary will interpret the Constitution in a way more sensitive to this minority-protection goal.

## II.  REVIEW OF STATE COURT DECISIONS

**A.  General principles of review:**   When the Supreme Court reviews the judgment of a state court, it is of course exercising its appellate, rather than its original, jurisdiction. Article III, §2, provides that the Supreme Court's appellate jurisdiction may be regulated and limited as Congress shall provide. (See *infra*, p. 12). Since the original Judiciary Act was enacted in 1789, the Supreme Court's appellate review of state court judgments has always been limited to the ***federal questions*** decided by the state courts. Tribe, p. 162.

  **1.  No review of state law issues:**   Thus the Supreme Court may determine whether a state court has reached a decision that is not in conformity with the Constitution; but it may ***not review state court decisions that merely adjudicate questions of state law***. How the Court determines whether a state court decision is limited to state law questions is a problem discussed more extensively below; the main point is that the Supreme Court's review of state court judgments is limited to ***questions of federal law***.

**B.  *Martin v. Hunter's Lessee:***   Recall that in *Marbury v. Madison*, the Court held that it had the power to review acts of Congress for constitutionality. In the later case of ***Martin v. Hunter's Lessee***, 1 Wheat. 304 (1816), the Court confronted the similar, and perhaps even more important question, of whether the Supreme Court is constitutionally authorized to review the constitutionality of ***state court decisions.***

  **1.  Virginia's argument:**   *Martin* involved the issue of whether a particular Virginia statute conflicted with a federal treaty. The Virginia courts took the position that if litigation commenced in state courts, then it was up to the state court to say whether the state action violated the federal constitution, and the U.S. Supreme Court had no right to review whatever conclusion the state court reached.

  **2.  Supreme Court's holding:**   The Supreme Court flatly rejected the Virginia courts' view, and held that the Court could ***review the constitutionality of a decision by a state's highest court***. There were two principal strands to the Court's opinion, which was written by Justice Story:

   **a.  Sovereignty argument rejected:**   First, the Virginia court's assertion that it was "sovereign" was rejected, on the grounds that the federal Constitution cut back upon state sovereignty in numerous respects. There was no reason to presume that state judiciaries were immune from this set of limitations.

   **b.  Uniformity:**   Secondly, Story wrote, there is a need for ***uniformity*** in decisions throughout the nation interpreting the Constitution. "[I]f there were no revising authority to control these jarring and discordant judgments, and harmonize them into uniformity, the laws, the treaties and the constitution of the United States would be different in different states. ... "

3. ***Cohens v. Virginia:*** *Martin v. Hunter's Lessee* dealt with Supreme Court review of state civil cases. The Supreme Court's right to review state ***criminal cases*** for constitutionality was similarly upheld, in ***Cohens v. Virginia***, 6 Wheat. 264 (1821).

C. **Recent state challenges to Supreme Court authority:**   Even though the Supreme Court's right to review the constitutionality of state supreme court decisions has been firmly established since *Martin* and *Cohens*, numerous state challenges to that right have arisen since then.

1. **Desegregation:**   The most recent serious such challenge came in response to the Supreme Court's school desegregation decisions, beginning with *Brown v. Board of Education, infra,* p. 265. For instance, in *Cooper v. Aaron,* 358 U.S. 1 (1958), Arkansas state officials claimed that they were not bound by a lower federal court desegregation order. The Supreme Court went out of its way to state that "the federal judiciary is supreme in the exposition of the law of the Constitution," and that the Supreme Court's interpretation of the Constitution is binding on state legislatures and executive and judicial officers. State challenges such as the one in *Cooper v. Aaron* are generally viewed as not involving any serious issue of constitutional law. See N&R, p. 19.

D. **Independent and adequate state grounds:**   The federal judicial power extends, by Article III, §2, to "all Cases, in Law and Equity, arising under this Constitution, the Laws of the United States, and Treaties. ... " On its face, this language seems to allow for Supreme Court review of state court decisions in any case where a federal question was involved, regardless of how the state court disposed of that federal question. Also, nothing in this clause seems to prevent the Supreme Court from reviewing all of the issues raised in any case, so long as a federal question is present.

1. **Statutory basis:**   However, as noted, the Supreme Court's appellate jurisdiction exists only as provided by Congress. The limitations presently in force are discussed *infra,* p. 15. For the moment, it is sufficient to note that the mere fact that a federal question is involved in a case is ***not sufficient*** to entitle the Supreme Court to review it. Furthermore, even if the Supreme Court is entitled to review a case, it will generally adjudicate ***only the federal issues***. (Tribe, at p. 163, suggests that if Congress attempted to give the Supreme Court the right to issue on matters of state law decisions which would be binding under the Supremacy Clause, this would be an interference with state sovereignty violative of the Tenth Amendment.)

2. **Independent and adequate state ground:**   Suppose that a state supreme court upholds a state statute against a federal constitutional attack. This would seem to be by itself enough to bring the case within the Supreme Court's congressionally-granted appellate jurisdiction (see *infra,* p. 12). But another doctrine, that of the "***independent and adequate state ground***," may nonetheless prevent the Supreme Court from reviewing the constitutionality of the state statute.

   a. **How doctrine works:**   The federal judiciary may decide only those cases presenting a "justiciable" controversy; one consequence is that the Supreme Court ***may not render an advisory opinion***. (See *infra,* p. 710). Suppose now that the state supreme court decision rested upon two grounds, each of which would have been sufficient to produce the same result: (1) a determination that the state statute does not violate the federal Constitution; and (2) a determination that, even if the state statute being attacked were invalid, the party attacking it would lose the case anyway. In this situation, a Supreme Court determination that the state statute violated the U.S. Constitution would have ***no effect*** upon the ultimate outcome of the case (since the party attacking the statute would lose anyway); therefore the Court's opinion would, in effect, be advisory. For this reason, the Supreme Court has repeatedly held that it will not review a state court decision otherwise falling within its appellate jurisdiction if that state decision rests upon an "independent and adequate state ground."

3. **State substantive law:**   Sometimes, the state ground may be ***substantive***. For instance, the state court may hold that a state statute ***violates both the state and federal constitutions***. However, the holding that the state constitution is violated may be achieved in one of two ways: (1) the state court may have independently interpreted the state constitutional provision, without relying directly on federal cases construing the federal constitutional provision; or (2) the state court may have interpreted the state constitutional provision as being ***co-extensive*** with the comparable federal constitutional provision, and then attempted to follow the relevant federal case law. In the latter situation, the Supreme Court may find that an independent and adequate state ground really ***did not exist***.

4. **State rules of procedure:**   In the "substantive state law" situation discussed immediately above, it is generally clear that the state ground is "adequate," and the real issue is whether it is "independent" of the federal ground. But the state ground may, by contrast, be ***"procedural."*** That is, because of some state procedural rule, the state court may simply fail to reach a federal issue. In this situation, the state procedural rule is clearly independent of the federal question, but it is not necessarily ***"adequate."***

   a. **Meaning of "adequacy":**   The mere fact that the state court itself recites that state procedural grounds bar consideration of the federal claim does not automatically render those grounds "adequate." Instead, the Supreme Court will review the procedural grounds. In several different types of situations, the Supreme Court is likely to hold that the state procedural grounds are ***not "adequate,"*** and therefore do not foreclose Supreme Court review of the federal issues:

      i. **"Fundamental fairness":**   Most importantly, a state procedural rule must at least meet the requirement of ***"fundamental fairness*.*"* This is a requirement imposed on the states by the Fourteenth Amendment Due Process Clause (see *infra*, p. 143).

   b. **Narrow review:**   But modern cases indicate that the present Supreme Court will seek to ***respect***, rather than disregard, state procedural rules wherever possible. For instance, the Court has held that in a federal *habeas corpus* proceeding (a collateral attack, brought in federal district court, upon a prior state criminal conviction), state procedural rules will be given serious respect.

# III.   CONGRESS' CONTROL OF FEDERAL COURT JURISDICTION

A. **The problem generally:**   To what extent may Congress ***curtail the jurisdiction*** of the Supreme Court, or of the lower federal courts? If one looks solely at Article III, the only direct grant of jurisdiction to any particular court is that the Supreme Court shall have original jurisdiction in cases involving ambassadors, ministers and consuls, and cases in which a state is a party.

1. **Limits indicated by Article III:**   Article III itself suggests that Congress may place certain limits both on the Supreme Court's appellate jurisdiction and on the jurisdiction of the

lower federal courts. First, Article III, §2 states that in all cases not falling within the Supreme Court's original jurisdiction (but falling within the federal judicial power), the Supreme Court shall have "appellate Jurisdiction both as to Law and Fact, ***with such Exceptions, and under such Regulations as the Congress shall make.***" Similarly, the lower federal courts do not even exist until Congress creates them; Article III, §1, provides that federal judicial power shall vest in the Supreme Court and "in such inferior Courts as the Congress may from time to time ordain and establish."

**B.** ***McCardle* case:**    The Supreme Court has confirmed that Congress does indeed have at least some power to control the boundaries of the Supreme Court's appellate jurisdiction. The principal case so holding is ***Ex parte McCardle***, 74 U.S. 506 (1869).

1. **Facts of *McCardle*:**    McCardle was imprisoned by a military government imposed by Congress as part of post-Civil War Reconstruction. He brought a *habeas corpus* action in federal circuit court, charging that the Reconstruction Acts under which he was imprisoned were unconstitutional. The circuit court rejected his claim, and he then appealed under an 1867 congressional statute, authorizing the grant of *habeas corpus* by federal circuit courts and also authorizing appeal to the Supreme Court in such cases.

2. **Congress restricts appeal:**    After the Supreme Court heard arguments in the *McCardle* case, but before it handed down its decision, Congress passed a law repealing the portion of the 1867 Act which allowed appeals to the Supreme Court. (Congress did this out of fear that the Court would hold in *McCardle* that the Reconstruction Acts were unconstitutional.) Thus Congress purported to deprive the Supreme Court of its right to decide the *McCardle* case and any other *habeas corpus* case coming to it by appeal from the circuit courts.

3. **Holding:**    The Supreme Court ***upheld*** Congress' restriction of the Court's jurisdiction. The opinion noted that the appellate jurisdiction of the Supreme Court is conferred "with such exceptions and under such regulations as Congress shall make." The limitation enacted by Congress here was such an exception. Therefore, the Court concluded, it had no jurisdiction to decide the case.

4. **Limited withdrawal:**    Observe that in the statute involved in *McCardle*, Congress was not completely withdrawing the Supreme Court's right to hear *habeas corpus* cases. Rather, it was withdrawing that right only where the Supreme Court got the case by appeal from the lower courts; under the jurisdictional statutes of the time, an ***original petition*** for *habeas corpus* could be commenced in the Supreme Court itself. See Schwartz, p. 21. Furthermore, even if only the lower courts had jurisdiction, this would still not be leaving the litigant without the possibility of federal *habeas corpus* relief; the lower court decision would simply be final.

   a. **Limited significance:**    Thus *McCardle* does not by any means stand for the proposition that Congress may strip the federal courts in their entirety of the right to issue *habeas corpus* relief; such congressional action would probably be a violation of prisoners' Fourteenth Amendment right to due process.

5. **Neutral:**    Also, note that the congressional statute in *McCardle* operated in a ***neutral manner***. That is, appeal to the Supreme Court was not allowed either to the government or to a private party; thus in a future case, it might be the government which suffered because of the statute. The fact that the congressional restriction of jurisdiction would not always

favor the same side makes that curtailment less objectionable constitutionally. See N&R, p. 34.

**C. Limits on congressional power:** But Congress ***does not have unlimited power*** to tamper with the Supreme Court's appellate jurisdiction.

1. ***Klein case:*** An important Supreme Court case from the same era as *McCardle* shows that there are some limitations to Congress' power to modify the Supreme Court's appellate jurisdiction. ***U.S. v. Klein***, 80 U.S. 128 (1872).

   a. **Facts of *Klein*:** Klein sued in the Court of Claims under a federal statute allowing citizens who had abandoned property to federal troops during the Civil War to recover compensation for it, if they could satisfy a loyalty requirement. Klein won in the Court of Claims, on the strength of earlier cases holding that a general presidential pardon satisfied the statutory requirement that the claimant not have been a supporter of the Confederacy. Before the government's appeal was heard in the Supreme Court, Congress passed a new statute providing that a presidential pardon would show the opposite (that the claimant *had* supported the Confederacy); the statute also provided that the Court of Claims and the Supreme Court were both without jurisdiction to decide cases where a pardon had been granted.

   b. **Statute struck down:** The Supreme Court in *Klein* struck down the statute as ***unconstitutional***, on the grounds that it violated the separation of powers and invaded the judicial function. The Court argued that this was not a valid and *bona fide* denial of appellate jurisdiction in a ***whole class*** of cases; instead, it was merely a "means to an end," i.e., a way "to deny to pardons granted by the President the effect which this Court had adjudged them to have."

   c. **Standard set by *Klein*:** Thus *Klein* seems to stand for the proposition that "[A]ny jurisdictional limitation must be ***neutral***; that is, Congress may not decide the merits of a case under the guise of limiting jurisdiction." N&R, p. 36.

2. **Practical limitation:** Observe that there is also a ***practical*** limitation upon Congress' ability to cut back on the appellate jurisdiction of the Supreme Court. If Congress is motivated by hostility to a particular Court decision, then it might be defeating its own purpose by restricting the Court's subsequent ability to hear similar cases — the adverse precedent will be ***left on the books***. Furthermore, without Supreme Court jurisdiction in an area, the individual courts of appeals will be left to go their own ways, destroying national uniformity of the law in that area. See Sullivan & Gunther, p. 83.

**D. Modern congressional controls on federal jurisdiction:** In the twentieth century, Congress has acted to cut back on lower federal court and Supreme Court jurisdiction in a number of special situations. None of these curtailments has been found to be unconstitutional.

1. **Forum left open:** When Congress has acted to restrict the jurisdiction of either the Supreme Court or the lower federal courts, it has generally ***not entirely deprived litigants*** of a judicial remedy. For instance, often the ***state courts*** are left with jurisdiction. But if Congress curtailed federal jurisdiction in such a way that a litigant was completely deprived of the right to have his case heard in ***any court***, the congressional scheme would probably be unconstitutional; thus Congress could probably not deprive the federal courts of the right to hear a certain type of case falling within the federal courts' exclusive jurisdiction (e.g., bankruptcy cases).

## IV. THE SUPREME COURT'S JURISDICTION TODAY

**A. Limited scope of discussion:** A full discussion of the jurisdiction of the Supreme Court is beyond the scope of this outline. We will discuss mainly how the Court selects its docket.

**B. *Certiorari:*** Until recently, there were two ways a case could get to the Supreme Court: "appeal" and "*certiorari*". If a case fell within the Court's appeals jurisdiction, in theory the Court had to hear the case and decide it (though it often did so by means of a "summary disposition," which had almost no precedential value because it did not involve an opinion.) But in 1988, Congress virtually eliminated the Court's appeals jurisdiction. Therefore, nearly all cases now come to the Court by ***"writ of certiorari"***.

  **1. Grounds for grant of *certiorari:*** The Court's decision on whether to grant *certiorari* is ***completely discretionary***. Since *certiorari* is now the sole means by which cases get to the Court, this means that the Court has ***full control*** over what cases it will hear and decide.

   **a. Rules:** However, the Court's decision whether to grant *certiorari* is not completely unguided. The Court has adopted formal Court Rules, which list several types of reasons which may lead the Court to grant *certiorari*. These include: (1) a ***conflict*** between ***different federal courts of appeal*** (e.g., the Second Circuit disagrees with the Ninth Circuit); (2) a conflict between the ***highest courts of two states***, or between a state's highest court and a federal court of appeals; (3) a state court or federal court of appeals decision on an ***important question*** which has not yet been settled by the Supreme Court. See Supreme Court Rule 17(1). In all of these situations, the issue triggering the decision to grant *certiorari* will of course be one of ***federal*** law.

  **2. Four votes needed:** The votes of ***four*** of the nine Justices are needed to grant *certiorari*.

   **a. Denial not precedent:** A ***denial*** of *certiorari* is ***not a decision on the merits***, and is therefore ***not a precedent*** which may be cited in other cases.

---

*Quiz Yourself on*
### *THE SUPREME COURT'S AUTHORITY (ENTIRE CHAPTER)*

1. The Constitution of the state of Ames contains a due process clause whose language is identical to the Due Process Clause of the U.S. Constitution's Fourteenth Amendment. Tom was a teacher in the Town of Aaron, in Ames. Because Tom's status was that of "probationary teacher," the custom in Aaron was that Tom could be fired at the end of any school year without cause. Tom was fired without cause. He sued Aaron in Ames state court. His suit was premised on the argument that his firing violated the Ames due process clause, in that he was not given a hearing before being fired. The Ames state court agreed, and the highest appeals court in Ames affirmed. Now, the Town of Aaron has appealed the case to the U.S. Supreme Court. May the U.S. Supreme Court hear the case? Give your reasons. _____

2. Same basic fact pattern as prior question. Now, however, assume that Tom in his Ames state court litigation asserted that his firing violated both the Ames constitution's due process clause and the federal Due Process Clause. The state trial court agreed with Tom that both constitutional provisions were violated, and the Ames Supreme Court affirmed the trial court decision in all respects. The trial court's decision on the state-constitution issue was based solely upon the court's reading of prior Ames state court decisions that in turn relied upon the intent of Ames voters in adopting the Ames due process clause. The portion of the decision relating to the federal constitution relied on U.S. Supreme Court cases construing the federal Due Process Clause. May the U.S. Supreme Court review the decision of the Ames Supreme Court?

3.  Congress, in an effort to streamline the federal judiciary, passes a statute eliminating diversity jurisdiction (i.e., jurisdiction over cases brought by a citizen of one state against a citizen of another state). The legislation would prevent diversity suits from being brought in federal district court, so that they would have to be brought in state court. (The legislation does not directly change the Supreme Court's appellate jurisdiction, so that the Supreme Court can continue to review the judgments of state courts, including state court suits that turn on a federal question.) Is the congressional legislation constitutional? _____

*Answers*

1.  **No, because the case does not involve a federal question.** The federal judicial power extends, by Article III, Section 2, to cases arising under the U.S. Constitution and federal laws. That power does not extend to cases decided solely on state-law grounds. Here, although the Ames due process clause may have mirrored the language of the U.S. Constitution's Due Process Clause, the state decision was solely based on the Ames courts' interpretation of the Ames constitution. Since no federal issue was involved, the Supreme Court has no jurisdiction (whether by appeal or by certiorari).

2.  **No.** In contrast to the prior question, here at least a decision on an issue of federal law (the meaning of the U.S. Constitution) was part of the state court decision. However, the federal judicial power does not extend to Supreme Court review of any state court case for which there is an *"independent and adequate state ground."* Because Tom's firing would be unlawful even without any finding that the federal Constitution had been violated (since the state constitution was found to have been violated as well), an independent and adequate state ground exists here. (If the Ames state court decision on the meaning of the Ames constitution's due process provision had derived in part from the court's belief that the clause should mean the same thing as it means in the federal Constitution, the state ground would not be truly "independent." But the facts make it clear that the finding on the meaning of the state constitution here derived solely from Ames state-law sources.)

3.  **Yes.** The Constitution gives Congress full control over the jurisdiction of the lower federal courts. In fact, these lower federal courts do not even exist until Congress creates them; Article III, Section 1 grants the federal judicial power to the Supreme Court and to "such inferior courts as Congress may from time to time ordain and establish." This language has been interpreted to mean that Congress may also define the cases that may be heard by the lower federal courts, and that Congress may do this by refusing to let the lower federal courts hear cases that fall within the general federal judicial power (e.g., cases between citizens of different states).

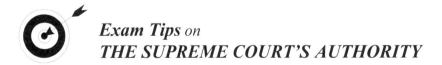

*Exam Tips on*
## THE SUPREME COURT'S AUTHORITY

If the facts describe a lawsuit that takes place in federal court (or a state-court lawsuit that is eventually heard by the U.S. Supreme Court) be alert to *limits* on the *federal judicial power:*

☞ If the facts involve a state-court suit that is heard by the *Supreme Court* on *certiorari*, be sure that the state-court decision was *based on federal law*.

☞ Be alert to the possible existence of an ***independent and adequate state ground***. That is, if the state court decided some issue of state law in a way that would have been enough to dispose of the case, there is no federal issue that is vital to the case, and the Supreme Court may not decide the federal issue. In particular, be alert for fact patterns where a ***state*** and ***federal constitutional provision*** cover the ***same territory*** — the state court might have decided the state issue as solely a matter of state law, in which case there would be no federal issue necessary to the case.

☛ If a fact pattern involves an attempt by ***Congress*** to ***limit the power*** of either the Supreme Court or the lower federal courts, the main things to remember are:

☞ Congress can within limits ***cut back*** on the kinds of cases the Supreme Court may hear, but cannot ***expand*** the case load beyond the categories set forth as the federal judicial power in the Constitution; and

☞ Congress may cut back, perhaps even completely eliminate, the ***lower federal courts***; as with the Supreme Court, Congress may not ***expand*** the lower courts' dockets beyond the bounds of the constitutional federal judicial power.

# CHAPTER 3

# FEDERALISM AND FEDERAL POWER GENERALLY

## *ChapterScope*

In this brief chapter, we examine the following concepts:

- **Federal system:** The U.S. has a *federal* system. The national government, and the government of each of the states, coexist.

- **Federal government has limited powers:** The federal government is one of *limited, enumerated,* powers. That is, the three branches of the federal government may only assert those powers *specifically granted* by the U.S. Constitution.

  ❏ **"Necessary and Proper" Clause:** However, Congress does have the power to make all laws that are *"necessary and proper"* for carrying out its enumerated powers. So if Congress is seeking an *objective* that falls within the specifically enumerated powers, Congress may use *any means* that is *rationally related* to the objective being sought, and that is not specifically forbidden by the Constitution.

## I. THE CONCEPT OF FEDERALISM

**A. Nature of federalism:** The United States has a *federalist* system. That is, the national government, and the government of each of the states, coexist. This chapter, and the several that follow, are devoted to the implications of this fact. Thus we will be examining the limits on federal power imposed in favor of state power, and conversely the limits on state power in favor of federal power.

**B. Federal government has limited powers:** The fundamental attribute of federal power under the U.S. Constitution is that the federal government is one of *limited, enumerated, powers.* That is, the three branches of the federal government can only assert those powers *specifically granted by the U.S. Constitution.*

    **1. Comparison with state power:** This limited-power concept should be contrasted with the nature of state power. The power of state governments might be called "inherent" — a state government, at least as far as the federal Constitution is concerned, holds a general "police power", i.e., the power to protect the health, safety or general welfare of state residents. An action by a state government is *valid* under federal law unless it violates some *specific limitation* imposed by the U.S. Constitution. A federal action, by contrast, *must fall within one of the enumerated powers* listed in the Constitution.

        **a. No general police power:** In other words, there is *no general federal police power*, i.e., no right of the federal government to regulate for the health, safety or general welfare of the citizenry. Instead, each act of federal legislation or regulation must come within one of the very specific, enumerated powers (e.g., the Commerce Clause, the power to tax and spend, etc.).

    **i.** **Tax and spend for general welfare:** Congress *does* have the right to "lay and collect taxes … to pay the debts and provide for the … general welfare of the United States. … " (Article I, Section 8.) But the phrase "provide for the … general welfare" in this sentence modifies "lay and collect taxes … to pay the debts. … " Thus the power to tax and spend is subject to the requirement that the general welfare be served; there is no *independent* federal power to provide for the general welfare.

  **2.** **Review of government action:** Thus for an action by the federal government to be valid, it must meet *two* distinct requirements: (1) it must fall within one of the powers *specifically enumerated* within the Constitution as being given to the federal government; and (2) it must *not violate any particular limitation* on federal power given in the Constitution (e.g., the limitations contained in the Bill of Rights.)

    **Example:** Congress, stating that it is acting on behalf of the general welfare of U.S. citizens, passes a law making it a federal crime for any person to read any type of pornographic material in his house. Unless the measure can be shown to fall within the commerce power (*infra*, p. 27), the measure will almost certainly be found by the courts to be invalid, since it is not within any power specifically given to the federal government by the Constitution (and since the power to legislate "on behalf of the general welfare" is not one of the enumerated powers.) (Also, the measure will probably be found to violate one or more specific limitations in the Bill of Rights, including the "right of privacy" inferred by modern Supreme Court decisions. See *Stanley v. Georgia*, *infra*, p. 562.)

**C.** **Specific powers:** The principal grant of specific federal powers is in Article I, §8. That section contains 18 clauses which grant power to *Congress*. (Grants of power to the judicial and executive branches are contained in other parts of the Constitution.)

  **1.** **Congressional powers:** Among the more important powers given to the Congress by Article I, §8, are the power to:

    a.  lay and collect *taxes*;

    b.  provide for the *defense* of the country;

    c.  *borrow money* on the credit of the U.S.;

    d.  *regulate commerce* with foreign nations, and *among the* several states;

    e.  regulate *immigration* and *bankruptcy*;

    f.  establish *post offices*;

    g.  control the issuance of *patents* and *copyrights*;

    h.  *declare war*;

    i.  pass all laws needed to govern the *District of Columbia* and federal *military enclaves* (e.g., military bases); and

    j.  "make all Laws which shall be *necessary and proper* for *carrying into Execution* the foregoing Powers, and all other Powers vested by this Constitution in the Government of the United States. … " This is the so-called "*necessary and proper*" clause.

  **2.** **Other sources:** Other parts of the Constitution provide additional grants of power to the various branches of the federal government. Article II defines the powers and duties of the

President. Article III confers the federal judicial power (and also gives Congress power to control Supreme Court jurisdiction). Other grants of power are scattered throughout the document (e.g., Article IV, §3 gives Congress power over U.S. territories and federal property.) Finally, many of the ***amendments*** specifically give Congress the power to enact supporting legislation (e.g., §5 of the Fourteenth Amendment.) See N&R, p. 128.

3. **Foreign affairs power:** One exception has been recognized to the general rule that only enumerated powers may be exercised by the federal government. Nothing in the Constitution explicitly gives the federal government the power to regulate ***foreign affairs*** (though Article I, §8, gives Congress the right to "regulate Commerce with foreign Nations"). The federal government's right to conduct foreign affairs is generally considered to be implied by the nature of the federal union, and by the impracticability of having each of the several states conduct its own foreign policy. N&R, pp. 133-34.

## II. *McCULLOCH v. MARYLAND*

A. **Doctrine of implied powers:** Although the federal government may act only where it is affirmatively authorized to do so by the Constitution, the authorization does not have to be ***explicit***. That is, by the doctrine of "***implied powers***," the federal government (especially Congress) may validly exercise power that is ***ancillary*** to one of the powers explicitly listed in the Constitution, so long as this ancillary power does not conflict with specific Constitutional prohibitions (e.g., those of the Bill of Rights). See Tribe, p. 301.

B. ***McCulloch* and "necessary and proper" clause:** This notion of implied powers is itself explicitly stated in the ***"necessary and proper"*** clause of Art. I, §8: Congress may "make all Laws which shall be necessary and proper for carrying into Execution" the specific legislative powers granted by Art. I, §8, or by other parts of the Constitution. The first case to make an important interpretation of "necessary and proper" was the landmark case of ***McCulloch v. Maryland***, 17 U.S. 316 (1819).

1. **Setting of *McCulloch*:** Congress chartered the second Bank of the United States in 1816. The Bank was designed to regulate the currency and help solve national economic problems. However, it soon encountered substantial political opposition, mostly as the result of the Panic of 1818 and corruption within the various branches of the Bank. As a result, a number of states enacted anti-Bank measures.

   a. **The Maryland Act:** One of these anti-Bank statutes, enacted by Maryland, was at the center of the *McCulloch* dispute. Maryland imposed a tax upon all banks operating in the state that were not chartered by the state. The measure was intended to discriminate against the national Bank, and its Maryland branch. The state then brought suit against the Bank and its cashier (McCulloch) to collect the tax. The Supreme Court held the tax constitutionally invalid in *McCulloch*.

2. **Structure of opinion:** The opinion, one of the most significant ever written by Marshall, had two main portions: (1) a determination that the chartering of the Bank was within the constitutionally-vested power of the federal government; and (2) a finding that since the Bank was constitutionally chartered, Maryland's tax upon it was unconstitutional. At this juncture, we examine only the first of these two parts; the second is discussed *infra*, p. 98.

3. **Constitutionality of the Bank:** In concluding that the Bank was constitutionally chartered, Marshall first disposed of Maryland's argument that the powers of the national gov-

ernment were delegated to it by the states, and that these powers must be exercised in subordination to the states. Marshall concluded that the powers come ***directly from the people***, not from the states *qua* states.

4.  **Grant need not be explicit:**   Marshall then turned to the issue of whether the constitutional grant of the particular power (here, the power to charter a bank or a corporation) was required to be made ***explicitly*** in the Constitution. Marshall concluded that particular powers could be ***implied*** from the explicit grant of other powers: "A constitution, to contain an accurate detail of all the subdivisions of which its great powers will admit, and of all the means by which they may be carried into execution, would partake of the prolixity of a legal code, and could scarcely be embraced by the human mind. … ***[W]e must never forget that it is a constitution we are expounding*.**"

    a.  **Corporation allowed:**   More specifically, Marshall found that Congress had the power to create a corporation (in this case, the Bank), if this was incidental to the carrying out of one of the constitutionally-enumerated powers, such as the power to ***raise revenue***.

    b.  **"Necessary and proper" clause:**   Marshall relied upon the "necessary and proper" clause as a justification for Congress' right to create a bank or corporation even though such a power was not specifically granted in the Constitution. In perhaps the most significant part of the opinion, he ***rejected*** the contention that "necessary" meant "absolutely necessary" or "indispensable." Instead, he stated that: "let the end be legitimate, let it be within the scope of the constitution, and all means which are ***appropriate***, which are ***plainly adapted*** to that end, which are not prohibited, [and which are consistent] with the letter and spirit of the constitution, are constitutional."

        i.   **Summary:**   Thus so long as the means is ***rationally related*** to a constitutionally-specified object, the means is also constitutional (assuming that it does not violate any specific prohibition, such as those from the Bill of Rights.)

    c.  **Support for conclusion:**   To support his liberal interpretation of "necessary and proper," Marshall pointed to a number of situations where Congress' power to carry out constitutionally-specified objectives had been liberally interpreted. For instance, the Constitution does not contain any specific grant of the power to ***punish*** the violation of federal laws, yet this power had always been inferred. Similarly, the power "to establish post offices and post roads" had been substantially expanded, to include the federal prohibition on mail theft. Yet these exercises of power could not be termed "indispensable" to a carrying out of the constitutionally-specified ends.

    d.  **Separation of powers rationale:**   Marshall also based his opinion upon ***separation-of-powers*** principles: An examination by the judicial branch into the "degree of necessity" justifying a statute would be an invasion of Congress' domain. Thus Marshall felt that the Supreme Court should strike down a law as being beyond the powers of Congress only where it was ***quite clear*** that no constitutionally-specified object was being pursued; in any closer case, the final decision should be left to Congress, not the courts.

5.  **Conclusion:**   Marshall thus concluded that the act chartering the national bank was valid, because it bore a reasonable relationship to various constitutionally-enumerated powers of the government (e.g., the power to collect taxes, to borrow money, to regulate commerce, etc.).

    **a. Maryland tax invalid:**   Marshall then went on to find the Maryland tax invalid, because it interfered with the exercise of a valid federal activity. See *infra*, p. 98, for a discussion of this part of the opinion.

6. **The modern import of *McCulloch:***   The standard set forth in *McCulloch* is still in force today. The courts will not strike down a congressional action so long as Congress has employed a means which is not prohibited by the Constitution and which is ***rationally related*** to objectives that are themselves within constitutionally-enumerated powers. Tribe, p. 303.

    **a. Motive irrelevant:**   As a corollary, the Court will show great deference to Congress, and will generally ***not*** inquire into the legislators' ***motives***. Thus as long as the legislation is rationally related to ***one*** constitutionally-enumerated motive which Congress was or might have been pursuing, the fact that other ends not within the enumerated powers of Congress might also be achieved does not invalidate the power. Tribe, *id.* at 302-03. (But legislative motive may be relevant in determining whether certain constitutional prohibitions, such as the equal protection clause's ban on racially-discriminatory laws, have been violated. See, e.g., *Arlington Heights v. Metropolitan Housing Corp.*, *infra*, p. 256.)

    **b. Early twentieth century deviation:**   This principle of deference to Congress was not followed during the late nineteenth and early twentieth centuries. Instead, until about 1937, the Supreme Court adhered to the view that certain areas were, as a constitutional matter, to be left to state regulation, and that congressional legislation purporting to affect these matters should be stricken. These decisions relied principally on the Tenth Amendment, and generally involved the scope of the Interstate Commerce Clause. This aberrant phase is detailed more fully in the chapter on interstate commerce, particularly pp. 28-33.

# III. STATE OVERSIGHT OF THE FEDERAL GOVERNMENT — THE "TERM LIMITS" PROBLEM

A. **Issue generally:**   What power do the individual states, as states, have to restrict the federal government? The answer has always been thought to be "essentially none." For instance, if Congress passes an unpopular statute, a vote by all 50 state legislatures purporting to repeal the statute would be irrelevant.

B. **The term-limits problem generally:** In fact, the kind of question posed in the prior paragraph had long been thought to be of only theoretical interest. But the problem became very practical in 1995, when the Court had to decide the "term limits" problem. In a nutshell, the problem was, may the states ***limit the terms of members of Congress***? The Court answered ***"no,"*** but only after exposing a deep split among the Court's members as to the proper division of authority between the states and the federal government.

C. **The term-limits case:**   The term-limits case was ***U.S. Term Limits, Inc. v. Thornton***, 514 U.S. 779 (1995), which was decided by a 5-4 vote.

    1. **Facts:**   The voters of Arkansas modified the Arkansas State Constitution to prohibit any person from appearing on the ballot for Congress from that state if he or she had previously served three terms in the House or two in the Senate. This provision was similar to

term limit provisions that had been adopted — either by statute or state constitutional amendment — in 22 other states.

2. **Federal constitutional provisions:** The case had to be decided against the backdrop of several federal constitutional provisions dealing directly with federal elections.

   a. **Qualifications Clauses:** Most importantly, the *"Qualifications Clauses"* set specific requirements for membership in Congress: Art. I, §2, cl. 2 requires each member of the House to be at least 25 years old, to have been a citizen of the U.S. for at least 7 years, and to be a resident of the state from which she is elected. Similarly, Art. I, §3, cl. 3, governing Senate membership, requires 30 years of age, 9 years of national citizenship, and residence in the state. The key question in *Thornton* became, do these clauses state the *exclusive* requirements for membership in Congress, or are they merely "minimum requirements" that the states may supplement?

3. **Majority strikes down:** A 5-member majority of the Court, in an opinion by Justice Stevens, ***struck down*** the Arkansas provision as being beyond the states' constitutional authority. A contrary ruling would undermine the whole framework of federalism, Stevens wrote: "Permitting individual States to formulate diverse qualifications for their congressional representatives would result in a patchwork of state qualifications, ***undermining the uniformity and the national character*** that the Framers envisioned and sought to ensure."

   a. **Congress can't add additional qualifications:** The majority began by reaffirming the holding of *Powell v. McCormack* (see *infra*, p. 731), a 1969 case which established that *Congress* couldn't add qualifications for membership in the House or Senate to those contained in the Qualifications Clauses.

   b. **States can't add qualifications either:** Stevens then went on to say that the states may not add qualifications for membership in Congress any more than Congress may. Here, Stevens rejected Arkansas' two-part argument: (1) the Constitution nowhere explicitly denies the states this power; and (2) therefore, under the Tenth Amendment, the states have this power. (The Tenth Amendment provides: "The powers not delegated to the United States by the Constitution, nor prohibited by it to the States, are reserved to the States respectively, or to the people." See *infra*, p. 47.)

      i. **Not an "original power":** There were two problems with this syllogism, according to Stevens. First, the Tenth Amendment only lets the states *retain* powers they already had before enactment of the Constitution, and the power to add qualifications for federal elections was not an "original power" that the states had before enactment, because there was no federal government or electoral system at all.

      ii. **Intended as exclusive source of qualifications:** Second, even if there had been such an original power, Stevens wrote, the Framers intended the Constitution to be the ***sole source of qualifications*** for membership in Congress. Enactment of the Constitution therefore ***divested*** the states of whatever power to add qualifications they might have had.

      iii. **Democratic principles:** Finally, Stevens argued that ***"democratic principles"*** dictated that the states not be permitted to add qualifications for membership in the national legislature. The right to choose representatives "belongs not to the States, but to the people. … The Framers … conceived of a Federal Government directly responsible to the people, possessed of direct power over the people, and ***chosen directly, not by States, but by the people.*** ... The Congress ... is ***not a confederation of nations*** in which separate sovereigns are represented by appointed delegates, but is instead a body composed of representatives of the people."

4. **Concurrence by Kennedy:** The swing vote was by Justice Kennedy, who wrote a concurrence agreeing with the majority's core reasoning.

5. **Dissent by Thomas:** Justice Thomas (joined by Rehnquist, O'Connor and Scalia) dissented. His view of the matter stemmed from a view of federal power that was diametrically opposed to the majority's. For Thomas, "the ultimate source of the Constitution's authority is the ***consent of the people of each individual State***, not the consent of the undifferentiated people of the nation as a whole."

---

*Quiz Yourself on*
## FEDERALISM AND FEDERAL POWER (ENTIRE CHAPTER)

4. Congress, pursuant to its power to establish and regulate copyrights, has decided that there is far too much counterfeiting of copyrighted musical recordings. Therefore, Congress has passed a statute making it a felony, punishable by up to five years in prison, to give a "bootlegged" (i.e., not authorized by the copyright owner) CD or MP3 recording to any other person, even if it is the donor's neighbor or relative, and even though no compensation is charged. Dennis, charged with a violation of this statute, asserts that it is unconstitutional because it is beyond the scope of Congress' authority. Should the Court agree with Dennis' assertion, and why? _____

---

*Answer*

4. **No, because the statute is valid under the "Necessary and Proper" Clause.** *McCulloch v. Maryland*, 17 U.S. 316 (1819), establishes that when Congress is acting in pursuit of a constitutionally-specified objective, the means chosen merely has to be ***rationally related*** to the objective, not "necessary" to the objective's attainment. Here, Congress is exercising its enumerated power to regulate copyrights. Congress could rationally have believed that even non-profit-motivated transfers of copyright-violating recordings contribute to the general decline of copyright protection, and that felony punishment for such transfers is a reasonable way of combatting the problem. The Court will show great deference to Congress' choice of the means to attain constitutionally-enumerated objectives, so the statute here will certainly be sustained.

---

 *Exam Tips on*
## FEDERALISM AND FEDERAL POWER GENERALLY

Issues covered by this Chapter are often hidden in a fact pattern. Here are some things to watch out for:

☛ Most importantly, any time your fact pattern tells you that Congress (or, for that matter, the Executive or Judicial Branch) is doing something, be sure that the action taken falls within one of the ***enumerated*** powers.

☛ Remember that there is ***no general federal police power***.

   ☞    It's true that Congress has the power to ***tax*** and ***spend*** for the "general welfare." But Congress ***doesn't*** have a general power to ***legislate*** for the "general welfare."

   ☞    Therefore, if your fact pattern indicates that Congress is ***regulating*** rather than taxing or spending, it is not enough that Congress is acting for the "general welfare"; it must be regulating pursuant to some other enumerated power, typically the commerce power or the post-Civil War amendments.

☛ Once you identify an enumerated power that might be relied upon by Congress, invoke the "Necessary and Proper" Clause. Under this clause, Congress may use ***any means*** that is: (1) ***rationally related*** to the exercise of the enumerated power; and (2) not specifically ***forbidden*** by the Constitution.

CHAPTER 4

# THE FEDERAL COMMERCE POWER

*ChapterScope*

This Chapter examines Congress' power to "regulate commerce … among the several states." This is the "commerce power." The most important concepts in this Chapter are:

- **Test for commerce power:** A particular congressional act comes within Congress' commerce power if both of the following are true:

  ❑ **Substantially affects commerce:** The activity being regulated *substantially affects commerce*; and

  ❑ **Reasonable means:** The *means* chosen by Congress is *"reasonably related"* to Congress' objective in regulating.

- **Conclusion:** Where Congress thinks that what it is doing falls within its commerce power, the Court rarely disagrees, especially where the activity being regulated is itself "commercial."

- **The Tenth Amendment as a limit on Congress' power:** The *Tenth Amendment* ("the powers not delegated to the United States by the Constitution, nor prohibited by it to the States, are reserved to the States respectively, or to the People") occasionally limits Congress' ability to use its commerce power to *regulate the states*.

## I.  THE COMMERCE CLAUSE GENERALLY

- **A. Introduction:**  Article I, §8 of the Constitution gives Congress the power "to regulate Commerce with foreign Nations, and among the several States, and with the Indian Tribes."

  1. **Foreign and Indian regulation:**  Congress' power to regulate foreign trade and trade with Indian tribes is not of great interest to us here. It is sufficient to note that since the adoption of the Constitution, the Supreme Court has always recognized full power on Congress' part to regulate these matters, since there is no countervailing interest in them on the part of the states. See N&R, pp. 133-134.

  2. **Commerce among the states:**  Congress' power to regulate commerce *among the states*, by contrast, is of paramount importance — it is upon the commerce power that many, perhaps most, congressional activities are based.

- **B. Limitation on states vs. limitation on Congress:**  The Commerce Clause serves two distinct functions: (1) it acts as a *source of congressional authority*; and (2) it acts, implicitly, as a *limitation* on *state legislative power*. In this chapter, we examine the commerce power solely as a source of congressional authority; its function as a limitation on state power is treated in a separate chapter beginning *infra*, p. 67.

- **C. Chronological approach:**  Our approach to the federal commerce power will be a chronological one, so that development of the power may be clearly seen. Our discussion begins with the landmark commerce-power case of *Gibbons v. Ogden*, proceeds through the late nineteenth and early twentieth century cases, and then details the ever-broadening scope of the commerce power since 1937. Finally, the modern treatment of some particular subject-matter areas (civil rights, criminal law and regulation of state government activities) is detailed.

## II.  CASES PRIOR TO 1933

A.  **The groundwork — *Gibbons v. Ogden:*** The first major case construing the Commerce Clause was a Marshall opinion, ***Gibbons v. Ogden***, 9 Wheat. 1 (1824). Although the *Gibbons* opinion contained some discussion of the Commerce Clause as a limitation upon state powers, its principal interest is for its broad-sweeping view of ***congressional power*** under that clause.

1.  **Facts of *Gibbons:*** Ogden acquired, by grant from the New York legislature, monopoly rights to operate steamboats between New York and New Jersey. Gibbons began operating steamboats between New York and New Jersey, in violation of Ogden's monopoly; Gibbons' boats were licensed, however, under a federal statute. Ogden obtained an injunction in a New York court ordering Gibbons to stop operating his boats in New York waters.

2.  **Holding:** When the case came to the Supreme Court, Justice Marshall found the injunction against Gibbons invalid, on the ground that it was based upon a monopoly that conflicted with a valid federal statute, and thus violated the Supremacy Clause.

3.  **Broad view of commerce power:** In reaching this conclusion, Marshall took a broad view of Congress' powers under the Commerce Clause. Under that clause, he said, Congress could legislate with respect to ***all*** "commerce which concerns more States than one." "Commerce," he concluded, included not only buying and selling, but ***all "commercial intercourse."***

    a.  **May affect intrastate matters:** Ogden apparently argued that insofar as his New York-granted monopoly affected his rights in New York waters, this monopoly was superior to any federal rights regarding those New York waters. But Marshall answered that the congressional power to regulate interstate commerce included the ability to ***affect matters occurring within a state***, so long as the activity had some commercial connection with another state. Thus federal law could affect New York waters, if voyages beginning in New York ended in New Jersey. (But Marshall conceded that "[t]he completely internal commerce of a State … may be considered as reserved for the State itself.")

    b.  **May be used to "utmost extent":** In the most important portion of his opinion, Marshall stated that ***no area of interstate commerce is reserved for state control***. That is, the mere existence of the states does not by itself act as a limit upon Congress' power to govern commercial matters that affect more than one state: "This power, like all others vested in Congress, is complete in itself, may be exercised to its utmost extent, and acknowledges no limitations, other than are prescribed in the constitution."

        i.  **Tenth Amendment no bar:** Thus Marshall implicitly rejected the argument that the Tenth Amendment (which provides that "[t]he powers not delegated to the United States by the Constitution, nor prohibited by it to the States, are reserved to the States respectively … ") acts as an independent limit on Congress' power to regulate interstate commerce.

4.  **Limits on state power:** The other portion of Marshall's opinion in *Gibbons* dealt with New York's right to grant a monopoly, and with whether this monopoly was invalid under

the Supremacy Clause. This aspect of the opinion is discussed in the treatment of limitations on state power, *infra*, p. 69.

**B. Inactive:** From *Gibbons* until the late nineteenth century, the Supreme Court had practically no occasion to consider Congress' powers under the Commerce Clause. It was not until enactment of the Interstate Commerce Act (in 1887) and the Sherman Antitrust Act (in 1890) that Congress' powers under the Commerce Clause were again seriously scrutinized by the Court. When this scrutiny did occur, the result was much more hostile to congressional power than it was in the Marshall *Gibbons* approach.

    **1. Economic regulation vs. police power:** Between about 1880 and 1937, the Supreme Court reviewed (and frequently struck down) two different types of congressional legislation premised upon the commerce power: (1) economic regulatory laws; and (2) "police power" regulations, i.e., those directed at moral or general welfare issues. We consider each of these areas in turn.

**C. Economic regulation:** The Supreme Court's review of ***economic regulatory laws*** from about 1880 to 1937 was characterized by what has been called a ***"dual federalism"*** approach. That is, the Court felt that there were areas of economic life which, under the Tenth Amendment, were to be ***left to state regulation***, and other areas of activity which were properly the preserve of the federal government. These two areas were viewed as being essentially ***non-overlapping*** — either an area was proper for state regulation, or for congressional regulation, but not for both.

    **1. "Substantial economic effects":** During this period from 1880 to 1937, congressional regulation was found to fall within the Commerce power so long as the activities being regulated had a ***"substantial economic effect"*** upon interstate commerce.

        **a. The Shreveport Rate Case:** The best-known example of this "substantial economic effect" approach was the so-called Shreveport Rate Case, *Houston E. & W. Texas Railway Co. v. U.S.*, 234 U.S. 342 (1914). In that case, the Interstate Commerce Commission, after setting rates for transport of goods between Shreveport, Louisiana and various points in Texas, sought to prevent railroads from setting rates for hauls ***totally within*** Texas which were less per mile than the Texas-to-Shreveport rates. The Commission's theory was that Shreveport competed with certain Texas cities for shipments from other parts of Texas, and that the lower Texas intrastate rates were unfairly discriminating against the Texas-to-Shreveport interstate traffic. The railroads countered that it was beyond Congress' power to control intrastate rates of an interstate carrier.

            **i. Commission upheld:** The Court rejected the railroads' challenge, and upheld the ICC's right to regulate intrastate charges, at least of interstate carriers. The opinion held that the commerce power necessarily included the right to regulate "all matters having such a ***close and substantial relation*** to interstate traffic that control is essential or appropriate to the security of that traffic. ... ." The fact that the activity being regulated was intrastate did not place it beyond congressional control, since the ***ultimate object*** was protection of interstate commerce.

    **2. "Current of commerce" theory:** Apart from the "substantial economic effects" rationale for sustaining congressional action, Justice Holmes developed the ***"current of commerce"*** rationale. Under this theory, an activity could be regulated under the commerce power not because it had an ***effect*** on commerce, but rather, because the activity itself could be viewed as being "in" commerce or as being part of the "current" of commerce. *Swift & Co. v. U.S.*, 196 U.S. 375 (1905).

D. **"Police power" regulations and the commerce-prohibiting technique:**     In  cases  like *Shreveport Rate, supra*, Congress attempted to regulate local activities directly. But Congress also developed a separate technique; instead of regulating intrastate activities directly, Congress used the technique of ***prohibiting interstate transport*** of certain items or persons. This "commerce-prohibiting" technique was used not only for pure economic regulatory matters, but also for "***police power***" or "***moral***" regulation. During the first two decades of the twentieth century, the Court was substantially more sympathetic to this "commerce-prohibiting/ police power" technique than to direct regulation of intrastate affairs.

1. **The Lottery Case:**   For instance, when Congress passed the Federal Lottery Act, which prohibited the interstate shipment of ***lottery tickets***, the Court upheld the statute in *Champion v. Ames* ("*The Lottery Case*"), 188 U.S. 321 (1903). The majority opinion began with the assumption that lotteries were clearly an "evil" which it was desirable for Congress to regulate; since Congress regulated only the interstate shipment of these evil articles, it could not be said to be interfering with intrastate matters reserved for state control. (But a four-Justice dissent contended that only commerce itself could be regulated, and that lottery tickets were not "articles of commerce.")

2. **Regulation of intrastate affairs:**   Once it became apparent that the Court looked favorably upon the commerce-prohibiting technique as a means of asserting national police power, Congress took a significant additional step: it began to regulate ***intrastate*** activities as a ***means of enforcing*** bans on interstate transport. Even this extension was generally favorably viewed by the Supreme Court.

   **Example:** Congress passed the Pure Food and Drug Act of 1906. Acting under the Act, federal officials seized a shipment of adulterated eggs after they had arrived in the state of their destination. The right to seize adulterated eggs once they had arrived at their destination was "certainly appropriate to the right to bar them from interstate commerce, and completes its purpose, which is not to merely prevent the physical movement of adulterated articles, but the use of them. ... " *Hipolite Egg Co. v. U.S.*, 220 U.S. 45 (1911).

3. **The Child Labor Case:**   But the Supreme Court was more hostile to congressional interference with the ***employer-employee relationship***. The Justices were particularly unwilling to allow congressional legislation which was pro-labor, and which the Justices saw as being an unwarranted interference with the free-market system. This was most dramatically illustrated in ***The Child Labor Case, Hammer v. Dagenhart***, 247 U.S. 251 (1918).

   a. **Holding in case:**   In that case, the Court voted, 5-to-4, to strike down a federal statute which prohibited the interstate transport of articles produced by companies which employed children younger than certain ages or under certain conditions.

   b. **Rationale:**   The majority distinguished this statute from other police power/commerce-prohibiting statutes which the Court had upheld; in those cases, the Court argued, the interstate transportation being prohibited was ***part of the very evil*** sought to be prohibited (e.g., the prohibition on the interstate shipment of lottery tickets, where the tickets themselves were viewed as evil.) Here, by contrast, the goods shipped in interstate commerce were themselves harmless; it was only the employment of child labor which was an evil, and this employment was not directly related to interstate commerce.

    **i.  Powers reserved to states:**  The majority reasoned further that if a prohibition on interstate commerce were permitted in this situation, all manufacturing intended for interstate shipment would be brought under federal control, encroaching unconstitutionally on the authority of the states.

  **c.  Holmes' dissent:**  But it was the classic dissent by Justice Holmes that in the long run became the more significant opinion in *Hammer*. Holmes argued that so long as the congressional regulation falls within power specifically given to the Congress (here, the power to regulate interstate commerce), the fact that it has a collateral effect upon local activities otherwise left to state control does not render the statute unconstitutional.

    **i.  Tenth Amendment of no force:**  Thus Holmes' dissent implicitly rejected the Tenth Amendment as a source of limitations on federal authority — so long as congressional action technically comes within a constitutionally-enumerated power, it is valid *no matter how substantially* it impairs the states' ability to regulate what would otherwise be local affairs. This highly restrictive view of the Tenth Amendment became the *majority view* beginning in 1937, and has endured to the present. See *infra*, pp. 47-53.

## III.  COURT BARRIERS TO THE NEW DEAL

**A.  The New Deal threatened:**  When Congress and President Roosevelt began implementing the New Deal in 1933, the Supreme Court's view of congressional power under the Commerce Clause stood in an ambiguous state. The "commerce-prohibiting" technique was of doubtful validity, in view of *Hammer v. Dagenhart*. The validity of the "effect upon commerce" rationale was unclear: The *Shreveport Rate Case* (*supra*, p. 29) indicated that intrastate activity having a substantial practical effect on interstate commerce could be regulated; but other cases suggested that there must be a "direct" and "logical" relationship between the intrastate activity being regulated and interstate commerce. Within a few years, it became apparent that the direct-and-logical requirement would carry the Court, and that a majority of the Court would strike down congressional regulation of any area which the majority felt was reserved by the Tenth Amendment to state control.

**B.  The *Schechter Poultry* ("Sick Chicken") case:**  The decision which caused the greatest public uproar during the New Deal was *Schechter Poultry Corp. v. U.S.*, 295 U.S. 495 (1935), the "Sick Chicken" case. At issue in the case was the validity of the National Industrial Recovery Act (NIRA). The NIRA authorized the President to adopt "codes of fair competition" for various trades or industries; the codes regulated such items as minimum wages and prices, maximum hours, collective bargaining, etc. See Sullivan & Gunther, p. 135.

  **1.  Facts of *Schechter*:**  The *Schechter* case involved the conviction of Schechter Poultry Corp. on charges of violating the wage and hour provisions of the New York Metropolitan Area Live Poultry Industry Fair Competition Code. Although the vast majority of poultry sold in New York came from other states, Schechter itself bought within New York City, and resold its stock *exclusively to local dealers*.

  **2.  Act held unconstitutional:**  The Supreme Court held the NIRA *unconstitutional* as applied to *Schechter*.

a.  **Not in "current of commerce":**   Schechter's activities were not within the "current" or "stream" of commerce, because the interstate transactions ended when the shipments reached Schechter's New York City slaughter-houses (unlike the cattle in the *Swift* case, which were ultimately reshipped out of state after being slaughtered).

b.  **Not "affecting commerce":**   Nor was the "affecting commerce" rationale applicable; what was required was a ***direct***, not indirect, effect on commerce. Although Schechter's wage and price policies might have forced interstate competitors to lower their own prices, this impact was much too indirect to allow for congressional control.

C.  **The *Carter Coal* case:**   The facts of *Schechter* made it a particularly weak case for the government, so the decision was not as damaging as was popularly perceived. A much more significant blow to the New Deal was delivered in ***Carter v. Carter Coal Co.***, 298 U.S. 238 (1936). That case was a challenge to the Bituminous Coal Conservation Act of 1935, which set maximum hours and minimum wages for workers in coal mines.

1.  **Held unconstitutional:**   The Act was found not to be a valid use of the commerce power. The Court returned to the distinction (espoused in *Knight*) between "production" and "commerce." Production, which was what was being regulated here, was a "purely local activity," even though the materials produced would nearly all ultimately be sold in interstate commerce. Nor did the production "directly affect" interstate commerce; the issue was not the ***extent*** of the effect produced on interstate commerce, but the existence or non-existence of a ***direct logical relation*** between the production and the interstate commerce.

    a.  **Local evil:**   Furthermore, the Court held, the issue was the link between the employer-employee relationship (the precise matter being regulated) and interstate commerce; it could not be said that this relationship had a sufficiently direct effect upon interstate commerce. Also, the employer-employee relationship was a "local relation," and whatever evils currently characterized that relationship in the coal industries were all "***local evils*** over which the federal government has no legislative control."

2.  **Cardozo dissent:**   The majority opinion did not give separate consideration to the validity of other aspects of the Act, such as the setting of minimum and maximum prices on coal sales. The majority viewed these price rules and the wage-hour rules as being inescapably intertwined, so that the invalidity of the latter made the entire Act invalid. But a dissent by Justice Cardozo contended that at least the price rules were valid, even as applied to intrastate sales. He argued that the prices for intrastate coal sales had such a direct impact on those for interstate sales that regulation of the latter could not be successfully carried out without regulation of the former. Justices Brandeis and Stone joined this dissent, and Chief Justice Hughes agreed in a separate opinion that the price regulations were valid. Thus on the price issue, the decision was a narrow 5-4 one.

D.  **The Court-packing plan:**   The *Carter* decision was a body-blow to the New Deal, since it implied that all attempts to deal with what the Court perceived as "local problems," including probably all employer-employee problems, would be struck down. President Roosevelt waited until after the 1937 election to launch a counterattack. When he did so, it was principally in the form of the infamous ***Court-packing plan.***

1.  **How the plan was to work:**   Roosevelt's proposal sought congressional authority for him to appoint an additional federal judge for each judge who was 70 years old and had served on a court for at least 10 years. The plan was to apply to all levels of the federal

judiciary, and provided for a maximum of 15 members on the Supreme Court, i.e., an additional six Justices. (Not by coincidence, there were six Supreme Court Justices over the age of 70 in 1937. See Sullivan & Gunther, p. 140.)

2. **Plan defeated:** The plan stirred enormous political controversy. Those opposed to it contended that "its practical operation would be to make the Constitution what the executive or legislative branches of the Government choose to say it is — an interpretation to be changed with each change of administration." (Senate Judiciary Committee Report, June 14, 1937, in Sullivan & Gunther, p. 141.) The plan was ultimately defeated, in mid-1937.

   a. **Practical effect:** However, by that time the Supreme Court had materially "reformed" itself. The retirement of Justice Van Devanter was enough to form a new majority, and the Court decided the important *NLRB v. Jones & Laughlin* case (*infra*, p. 33) in favor of the validity of the NLRA; all this occurred while the debate on the Court-packing plan was still in progress. Thus President Roosevelt made a plausible claim to have lost the battle but won the war.

# IV.  THE MODERN TREND

A. **The modern trend generally:** The modern trend in Supreme Court Commerce-Clause analysis began in the Court's 1937 decision, *NLRB v. Jones & Laughlin Steel Corp.* (*infra*.) Beginning with that case, the Court showed a vastly greater willingness to defer to legislative decisions. Under present doctrines, the Court will uphold commerce-based laws if the Court is convinced that the activity being regulated *"substantially affects"* interstate commerce. In fact, in only one case since 1937 has the Court found that Congress went beyond its Commerce Clause powers (the *Lopez* case, *infra*, p. 36).

   1. **Three theories:** The Court expanded the reach of the Commerce power by recognizing three theories upon which a commerce-based regulation may be premised: (1) an expanded *"substantial economic effect"* theory; (2) a *"cumulative effect"* theory; and (3) an expanded *"commerce-prohibiting" protective* technique. Each of these is considered in turn.

B. **Expanded "substantial economic effect":** Recall that in pre-1937 cases, the Court had insisted upon a "direct" and "logical" relationship between the intrastate activity being regulated and interstate commerce. But beginning in ***NLRB v. Jones & Laughlin Steel Corp.***, 301 U.S. 1 (1937), the Court substantially loosened the nexus required between the intrastate activity being regulated and interstate commerce.

   1. **Facts of *Jones & Laughlin:*** The *Jones & Laughlin* case tested the constitutionality of the National Labor Relations Act of 1935 (NLRA). The case involved the NLRB's attempt to prevent Jones & Laughlin (a large integrated steel producer) from engaging in "unfair labor practices" by the discriminatory firing of employees for union activity.

   2. **NLRA upheld:** In *Jones & Laughlin*, a majority of the Court held that the NLRA, as applied to Jones & Laughlin, lay within the commerce power. The Court noted that while Jones & Laughlin manufactured iron and steel only in Pennsylvania, it owned mines in two other states, operated steamships on the Great Lakes, held warehouses in four states, and sent 75% of its product out of Pennsylvania.

      a. **Conclusion:** Because of this multi-state network of operations, the Court concluded, a labor stoppage of the Pennsylvania intrastate manufacturing operations would have a *substantial effect on interstate commerce*. Therefore, labor relations at the Pennsylvania plants could constitutionally be regulated by Congress.

   b. **"Current of commerce" rationale not needed:**   The Court expressly declined to rely on the "current of commerce" theory. The Court indicated that "current of commerce" cases (such as *Swift, supra,* p. 29) were merely particular, not exclusive, illustrations of the commerce power.

   c. **Tenth Amendment rejected as limitation:**   The Court implied, though it did not expressly state, that the Tenth Amendment would no longer act as an independent limitation on federal commerce-clause powers.

3. **Practical consequence:**   The abandonment of the "current of commerce" rationale, begun in *Jones & Laughlin,* now makes it irrelevant whether the activity being regulated occurs before, during or after the interstate movement. So long as the regulated activity has a *"substantial economic effect"* upon interstate commerce, that activity may occur substantially before the interstate movement (e.g., steel production in the *Jones & Laughlin* case, where the steel might not have been shipped out of state for months after its production) or even long *after* the interstate commerce. See Tribe, p. 309.

   a. **Effect must be "substantial:**  In fact, for many years after *Jones & Laughlin,* observers wondered whether the regulated activity's effect on interstate commerce even had to be "substantial"; the Court's pronouncements on this issue were ambiguous. But in the landmark 1995 case of *U.S. v. Lopez, infra,* p. 36, a majority of the Court decided that a "substantial" effect on interstate commerce *is* indeed required.

C. **The "cumulative effect" theory:**   The second major expansion of Commerce Clause power might be termed the "*cumulative effect*" theory. That theory provides that Congress may regulate not only acts which *taken alone* would have a substantial economic effect on interstate commerce, but also an entire *class* of acts, if the class has a substantial economic effect (even though one act within it might have virtually no interstate impact at all.) As a result of this "cumulative effect" principle, it is not only the type of regulation sustained in *Jones & Laughlin* (regulation of a large steel producer, where that producer's labor problems would *by themselves* have a substantial effect on interstate commerce) which may be regulated. See Tribe, pp. 310-11.

1. *Wickard v. Filburn:*   The case which established this "cumulative effect" principle was *Wickard v. Filburn,* 317 U.S. 111 (1942). This case (the facts of which are almost like a law school examination question in their far-fetchedness), is probably the *furthest* the Court has ever gone in sustaining Commerce-Clause powers, at least in the economic, as opposed to "police power," area.

   a. **Facts of *Wickard:***   *Wickard* involved the Agricultural Adjustment Act of 1938, which permitted the Secretary of Agriculture to set quotas for the raising of wheat on every farm in the country. The Act allowed not only the setting of quotas on wheat that would be sold interstate and intrastate, but also quotas on wheat which would be *consumed on the very farm where it was raised*. Wheat raised in excess of the quota was subject to a per-bushel penalty.

      i. **Home consumption:**  Filburn, the plaintiff in *Wickard,* owned a small farm in Ohio. He challenged the government's right to set a quota on the wheat which he raised and consumed on his own farm, on the grounds that this was a purely local activity beyond the scope of federal control.

**b. Statute upheld:**   But a unanimous Court (whose composition had changed radically from the days of the *Carter Coal* case just six years before) *upheld* the Act, even as it applied to home-consumed wheat. The Court reasoned as follows:

    **i. Consumption has market effect:**   First, the consumption of home-grown wheat is a large and variable factor in the economics of the wheat market. The more wheat that is consumed on the farm where it is grown, the less wheat that is bought in commerce (i.e., from other farmers), whether interstate or not.

    **ii. Cumulative effect:**   Plaintiff's own effect on the market, by his decision to consume wheat grown himself, might be trivial. But this decision, "taken together with that of *many others similarly situated*, is far from trivial. ... " That is, home-grown wheat "supplies a need of the man who grew it which would otherwise be reflected by purchases in the open market," and the home-grown wheat thus "competes with wheat in commerce." Protection of the interstate commercial trade in wheat clearly falls within the commerce power, and the regulation of home-grown wheat is *reasonably related to protecting that commerce.*

**c. Still good law:** *Wickard* is *still good law.* In a 2005 case, the Court relied extensively on *Wickard* to hold that Congress had the power to forbid cultivation and consumption of home-grown marijuana for medical purposes. In that case, *Gonzales v. Raich*, 545 U.S. 1 (2005), the Court said that "*Wickard* ... establishes that Congress can regulate purely intrastate activity that is not itself 'commercial,' in that it is not produced for sale, if it concludes that failure to regulate that class of activity would undercut the regulation of the interstate market in that commodity." The case is discussed further *infra*, p. 40.

**D. The commerce-prohibiting technique (police power regulations):**   Recall that apart from the "affecting commerce" line of cases, another pre-1933 line of cases dealt (ambiguously) with Congress' right to use *prohibitions* on the *interstate transportation* of items or people in furtherance of "*police power*" or "*general welfare*" regulations. This commerce-prohibiting technique, like the "affecting commerce" principle, was substantially broadened shortly after 1937.

  **1. *Darby* reverses *Hammer*:**   Recall that in the *Child Labor Case*, *Hammer v. Dagenhart* (*supra*, p. 30), the Court held that Congress could not prohibit the interstate sale of the products of child labor. *Hammer* was flatly overruled in *U.S. v. Darby*, 312 U.S. 100 (1941).

    **a. Minimum wage regulations upheld:**   In *Darby*, the Court unanimously upheld the Fair Labor Standards Act of 1938, which set minimum wages and maximum hours for employees engaged in the production of goods for interstate commerce. The Act not only prohibited the shipment in interstate commerce of goods made by employees employed for more than the maximum hours or not paid the prevailing rates, but it also made it a federal crime to employ workmen in the production of goods "for interstate commerce" at other than the prescribed rates and hours.

    **b. Direct ban upheld:**   The Court first upheld the direct ban on interstate shipments; it disposed of the argument that manufacturing conditions are left for exclusive state control, by stating that "[t]he power of Congress over interstate commerce [can] neither be enlarged nor diminished by the exercise or non-exercise of state power. ... The [Tenth Amendment] states but a truism that all is retained which has not been surrendered."

    **i.** **Tenth Amendment irrelevant:** Thus the Tenth Amendment will *no longer act as an independent limitation on congressional authority over interstate commerce.* (See *infra*, pp. 47-53 for a summary of the present status of the Tenth Amendment.) As the result of *Darby*, Congress is completely free to impose whatever conditions it wishes upon the privilege of engaging in an activity that substantially affects interstate commerce, so long as the conditions themselves violate no independent constitutional prohibition (e.g., the Equal Protection Clause of the Fourteenth Amendment.) See Tribe, pp. 311-312.

    **c.** **Motive irrelevant:** The Court also disavowed any interest in Congress' *motive*: "The motive and purpose of a regulation of interstate commerce are matters for the legislative judgment upon the exercise of which the Constitution places no restriction and over which the courts are given no control."

        **i.** **Present rule:** The irrelevance of motive remains a feature of Commerce Clause, and most other sorts, of constitutional analysis. (But motive may be relevant where a preferred right, such as the right of free expression or freedom from racial discrimination, is concerned. See, e.g., pp. 253 and 464 *infra*.)

    **d.** **Reasonable means to achieve end:** Finally, the Court in *Darby* upheld the portion of the Act making it a crime to employ workers engaged in interstate commerce in violation of the wage/hour provisions.

        **i.** **Rationale:** Given Congress' right to impose direct prohibitions or conditions on interstate commerce, Congress "may choose the *means reasonably adapted to the attainment of the permitted end*, even though they involve control of intrastate activities." Thus the outright criminalization of employer conduct was a reasonable means of *implementing* the prohibition on interstate shipments.

        **ii.** **Bootstrap:** This portion of the *Darby* opinion has been referred to as a "super-bootstrap suggestion"; see Gunther & Sullivan (13th Ed.), pp. 195-96. If it is taken seriously, it means that Congress may attack any problem (even one of overwhelmingly local concern) by prohibiting all interstate activity associated in any way with it; then, the local activity itself could be prohibited as a means of implementing the ban on interstate transactions.

**E.** **Some limits still exist (*U.S. v. Lopez*):** But some limits *still exist* on Congress' Commerce Clause powers, as the result of a landmark 1995 decision. In *U.S. v. Lopez*, 514 U.S. 549 (1995), the Court for the first time in 60 years *invalidated a federal statute on the grounds that it was beyond Congress' Commerce power*.

    **1.** **Gun-Free Schools:** The statute was the Gun-Free School Zones Act of 1990, in which Congress made it a federal crime "for any individual knowingly to possess a firearm at a place that the individual knows, or has reasonable cause to believe, is a school zone."

        **a.** **Little connection to commerce:** The statute clearly had less explicit connection to interstate commerce than most federal statutes premised on the Commerce power. For instance:

**i.** **No findings:** The statute did not include explicit findings by Congress that the activity being regulated (possession of guns in schools) affected commerce.

**ii.** **No jurisdictional nexus:** Perhaps more important, the statute did not include a "jurisdictional nexus." For instance, Congress could have made it a crime only to possess a gun that had moved in (or otherwise affected) interstate commerce. (Congress often uses this "jurisdictional" approach to carry out the "commerce-prohibiting" technique; see, for instance, the 1964 Civil Rights Act, discussed *infra*, p. 46, regulating restaurants that buy food a substantial part of which has moved in interstate commerce.) But this isn't what Congress did here — instead it banned even possession of a gun that had never traveled in, or even affected, interstate commerce.

**2.** **Statute struck down:** By a 5-4 vote, the Court struck down the statute. The majority opinion was by Chief Justice Rehnquist, joined by Justices O'Connor, Scalia, Kennedy and Thomas.

**a.** **"Substantial" effect required on Commerce:** The majority opinion first resolved a prior uncertainty, by holding that it is not enough that the activity being regulated merely "affects" interstate commerce. Instead, the activity must "***substantially*** affect" interstate commerce.

**b.** **Requisite effect not present:** Then, the majority concluded that the possession of guns in schools had not been demonstrated to "substantially affect" commerce.

**i.** **Not commercial:** The majority seemed to think that it was important that the particular activity being regulated — possession of guns in schools — ***was not itself a "commercial" activity***. The majority distinguished *Wickard v. Filburn, supra*, p. 34 (which it called "perhaps the most far reaching example of Commerce Clause authority over intrastate activity. ... ") from the activity at issue here, saying that *Wickard* "involved economic activity in a way that the possession of a gun in a school zone does not." Also, unlike the wheat-growing regulation in *Wickard*, the regulation here was not part of a "larger regulation of economic activity, in which the regulatory scheme could be undercut unless the intrastate activity were regulated."

**ii.** **Government's argument:** The federal government, in defending the statute, had argued that gun possession in schools *does* have a "substantial effect" on commerce. The government asserted the following syllogism: (1) possession of a firearm in a school may result in violent crime; and (2) violent crime affects the functioning of the national economy in several ways (e.g., (a) the costs of crime are insured against, and thus spread across state lines because of the interstate nature of the insurance market; (b) violent crime reduces individuals' willingness to travel to areas of the country they believe are unsafe; and (c) violent crime in the schools reduces the schools' ability to educate their students, who thus become less economically-productive.)

**iii.** **Argument rejected:** But the majority rejected this argument, essentially because it ***proved too much***. For instance, under the "economic productivity" argument, "Congress could regulate any activity that it found was related to the economic productivity of individual citizens: family law (including marriage, divorce, and child custody), for example." In general, under the government's approach, "[I]t is difficult to perceive ***any limitation on federal power***, even in areas such as criminal law enforcement or education where States historically have been sovereign. Thus, if we were to accept the Government's arguments, we are hard-pressed to posit any activity that Congress is without power to regulate."

    **iv. Parade of horribles:** The majority went on to describe some of the types of federal regulation that would fall within the Commerce power, if the government's approach were accepted: "Congress could mandate a ***federal curriculum*** for local elementary and secondary schools because what is taught in local schools has a significant 'effect on classroom learning,' and that, in turn, has a substantial effect on interstate commerce." Similarly, "Congress could … look at ***child rearing*** as 'fall[ing] on the commercial side of the line', because it provides a 'valuable service — namely, to equip [children] with the skills they need to survive in … the workplace.' " Such results would make the Commerce power limitless.

    **v. Summary:** In summary, the majority said, "To uphold the Government's contentions here, we would have to pile inference upon inference in a manner that would bid fair to convert congressional authority under the Commerce Clause to a ***general police power*** of the sort retained by the States." Prior cases may have extended the Commerce power to great lengths, "but we decline here to proceed any further." To uphold the act here "would require us to conclude … that there never will be a distinction between what is truly national and what is truly local.…"

**3. Concurrences:** There were two concurrences, one by Justice Kennedy (joined by Justice O'Connor) and the other by Justice Thomas. Kennedy's concurrence suggested that he and O'Connor are less eager than Rehnquist (or, probably, Scalia and Thomas) to cut back the Court's prior Commerce Clause interpretations. He said that he had "some pause" about joining the majority's opinion, and that this was a "necessary though limited holding."

    **a. Commercial transactions untouched:** More than Rehnquist, Kennedy seemed eager to leave untouched prior cases holding that Congress has full power to regulate what are truly commercial transactions, even if the transaction being regulated is a very local one: *stare decisis* "mandates against returning to the time when congressional authority to regulate undoubted commercial activities was limited by a judicial determination that those matters had an insufficient connection to an interstate system. Congress can regulate in the commercial sphere on the assumption that we have a single market and a unified purpose to build a stable national economy."

        **i. Not commercial:** But the activity being regulated here, Kennedy said, was not essentially commercial.

        **ii. Traditionally left to states:** Furthermore, Kennedy suggested, activities that had ***traditionally*** been ***left to the states*** to regulate should be further off-limits to the federal commerce power than activities that had not been so limited. Education was one of those traditional concerns of the States. To allow the federal government to interfere would "foreclose the States from experimenting and exercising their own judgment … " in this area traditionally left to them.

**4. Dissent:** There were four dissenters (Stevens, Souter, Breyer and Ginsburg), who wrote three separate opinions. The principal one was by Justice Breyer, in which all three of the other dissenters joined.

a. **"Rational basis" test:** For Breyer, the test was "whether Congress could have had a *rational basis* for finding a significant (or substantial) connection between gun-related school violence and interstate commerce." (The majority had not mentioned "rational basis" — to the majority, the question was whether there actually *was* a substantial connection, not merely whether Congress could rationally have believed that there was.) With the issue formulated this way, Breyer had no trouble concluding that the answer was yes.

   i. **Government's arguments accepted:** Breyer accepted the Government's arguments on this point. There was ample evidence available to Congress that gun-related violence in the schools interfered with the quality of education. And there was also extensive evidence that education was intimately tied to the economic viability of not only individuals but whole areas (since "many firms base their location decisions upon the presence, or absence, of a work force with a basic education.")

b. **Majority's view rejected:** Breyer vehemently objected to the majority's approach.

   i. **Contrary to case law:** First, Breyer found that approach contrary to modern cases upholding congressional action regulating activities that (in his opinion) had less connection with interstate commerce than the guns-in-schools at issue here. For instance, he thought that a single instance of racial discrimination at a local restaurant, found regulable in *Katzenbach v. McClung, infra*, p. 46, had no greater connection with interstate commerce than the instance of gun possession being regulated here.

   ii. **Commercial/non-commercial distinction rejected:** Second, Breyer rejected the majority's distinction between "commercial" and "non-commercial" transactions, believing that the line would prove hard to draw. He also thought that the majority drew the line in the wrong place here — if the majority was holding that education as a whole was a non-commercial activity, the majority was mistaken because "Congress … could rationally conclude that schools fall on the commercial side of the line."

   iii. ***Stare decisis*:** Finally, Breyer believed that the majority was unwise to "threaten … legal uncertainty in an area of law that, until this case, seemed reasonably *well settled*."

5. **Violence against women (*Morrison*):** An important 2000 case suggests that *Lopez* will be a major obstacle whenever Congress relies on its Commerce power to regulate conduct that is essentially non-commercial. Just as *Lopez* held that Congress can't ban gun possession in schools, this next case says that Congress *can't broadly regulate violence against women. U.S. v. Morrison,* 529 U.S. 598 (2000).

a. **Facts:** In *Morrison*, Congress was concerned that the states' judicial systems were not taking gender-motivated violence against women sufficiently seriously. Congress therefore passed the Violence Against Women Act of 1994, 42 U.S.C. s. 13981. The Act announced that all persons within the U.S. "shall have the right to be free from crimes of violence motivated by gender." To enforce that right, the Act then said that a woman who was a victim of such a gender-motivated violent crime could bring a civil suit against the perpetrator in federal court. A female student at Virginia Tech who said she had been raped by two members of the school's football team sued them under the Act. They defended by arguing that the act was beyond Congress' powers, including its Commerce power.

b. **Holding:** By the same 5-4 split as in *Lopez*, the Court agreed with the defendants that the Act was beyond Congress' Commerce power. The majority opinion by Chief Justice Rehnquist relied principally on the fact that the activity being regulated was essentially ***non-economic***: "Gender-motivated crimes of violence are not, in any sense of the phrase, economic activity. While we need not adopt a categorical rule against aggregating the effects of any noneconomic activity … Thus far in our Nation's history our cases have upheld Commerce Clause regulation of intrastate activity only where that activity is economic in nature."

   i. **Congressional findings not enough:** Rehnquist conceded that here, unlike in Lopez, there were ***detailed findings*** by Congress detailing the effect of the conduct being regulated on interstate commerce; for instance, Congress had found that gender-motivated violence deterred potential victims from traveling interstate or from being employed in interstate businesses. However, Rehnquist seemed to give virtually no deference to these findings, because they made for too attenuated a causal chain: "If accepted [this] reasoning would ***allow Congress to regulate any crime*** as long as the nationwide, aggregated impact of that crime has substantial effects on employment, production, transit, or consumption. Indeed, if Congress may regulate gender-motivated violence, it would be able to ***regulate murder or any other type of violence*. …**"

   ii. **Local vs. national distinction:** Rehnquist concluded by relying on the ***distinction between local and national activities:*** "The Constitution requires a distinction between what is truly national and what is truly local … The regulation and punishment of intrastate violence that is not directed at the instrumentalities, channels, or goods involved in interstate commerce has always been the province of the States."

c. **Dissent:** There were two dissents, one by Justice Souter and the other by Justice Breyer. The dissenters were especially critical of the majority's rejection of Congress' factual findings. They also criticized the majority's view that where an activity is basically non-commercial its aggregate affects on commerce cannot suffice. Justice Breyer pointed out that the economic/noneconomic distinction would be a hard one to implement reliably. (E.g., "Would evidence that desire for economic domination underlies many brutal crimes against women save the present statute?"). He also argued that there was no reason for attaching such importance to that distinction in situations where non-commercial local activities have a large *effect* on interstate commerce. (E.g., "If chemical emanations through indirect environmental change cause identical, severe commercial harm outside a State, why should it matter whether local factories or home fireplaces release them?")

6. **Regulation of non-commercial activity as part of broad regulation of commercial activity:** Conversely, when Congress is engaged in a ***broad regulation of a commercial activity***, even after *Lopez* and *Morrison* it may regulate ***purely non-commercial and intrastate instances of that activity,*** if it ***reasonably believes that failure to regulate these instances would jeopardize the success of the overall regulatory scheme.*** Thus in ***Gonzales v. Raich***, 545 U.S. 1 (2005), Court concluded by 6-3 that Congress, as part of its over-

all ban on the cultivation and sale of marijuana, could forbid even the purely ***intrastate and noncommercial cultivation*** of ***marijuana*** for ***medical purposes.***

a. **Facts:** Congress had since the 1970s classified marijuana as a Schedule 1 drug (drugs with high potential for abuse and lack of any accepted medical use), and had made it a crime to manufacture distribute or possess any Schedule I drug. Congress did so in the Controlled Substances Act (CSA). California then, in 1996, by means of a voter-approved Proposition, established an exemption from criminal prosecution for physicians who recommended marijuana to a patient for medical purposes, as well as for patients and primary caregivers who possessed or cultivated marijuana for medicinal purposes with the recommendation or approval of a physician. (Eight other states also authorized use of marijuana for medicinal purposes.)

   i. **How suit arose:** The two plaintiffs in *Gonzales* were California residents who suffered from very serious medical ailments that they sought to treat with marijuana. (One of them, Monson, grew her own marijuana, which was confiscated by federal Drug Enforcement Administration agents.) The plaintiffs then sued for an injunction barring the enforcement of the CSA against them, on the theory that Congress did not have the power, under the Commerce Clause or any other grant of authority, to regulate the interstate, noncommercial cultivation and possession of marijuana for personal medical purposes. The Ninth Circuit agreed with the plaintiffs, on the basis of *Lopez* and *Morrison*.

b. **Plaintiffs lose by 6-3:** By a 6-3 vote, the Court held against the Ps, concluding that Congress' Commerce clause powers gave it the right to regulate ***even the purely intrastate and noncommercial cultivation of marijuana.*** The majority opinion was by Justice Stevens.

   i. **Reliance on *Wickard*:** Stevens relied heavily on *Wickard v. Filburn* (*supra*, p. 34). There, the Court had concluded that when Congress was attempting to regulate the production (and thus pricing) of wheat that moved in interstate commerce, Congress could also regulate farmer Filburn's cultivation of 12 acres of wheat for consumption on his own farm. Stevens asserted that *Wickard* "thus establishes that Congress ***can regulate purely intrastate activity that is not itself 'commercial,'*** in that it is not produced for sale, if it concludes that ***failure to regulate that class of activity would undercut the regulation of the interstate market in that commodity.***"

   ii. **Application to facts:** Stevens believed that this *Wickard* principle easily fit the facts of the marijuana cultivation here. "Like the farmer in *Wickard*, [plaintiffs] are cultivating, for home consumption, a fungible commodity for which there is an established, albeit illegal, interstate market." And, just as Congress in *Wickard* rationally feared that "when viewed in the aggregate, leaving home-consumed wheat outside the regulatory scheme would have a substantial influence on price and market conditions," so, here, Congress had "a rational basis for concluding that leaving home-consumed marijuana outside federal control would similarly affect price and market conditions." That is, Congress, in passing the CSA, rationally believed that if cultivation of home-grown marijuana were permitted for medicinal consumption, the high demand in the interstate market would ***draw that*** *home-grown marijuana into the interstate market*, frustrating Congress' purpose of banning interstate commerce in marijuana.

iii. ***Lopez* and *Morrison* distinguished:**   Stevens distinguished *Lopez* and *Morrison*. In those two cases, the parties making the "no congressional authority" argument asserted that a particular statute or provision fell outside Congress' commerce power *in its entirety*. For instance, in *Lopez*, the Gun-Free School Zones Act *did not regulate any economic activity at all,* and did not contain any requirement that possession of a gun have any connection to past or future commercial activity. Here, by contrast, Congress' regulation of marijuana grown for home consumption was merely one of many *"essential part[s] of a larger regulation of economic activity*, in which the regulatory scheme could be undercut unless the interstate activity were regulated' " (quoting language from *Lopez*).

iv. **"Economic activity":**   Indeed, for Stevens, the activities regulated by the CSA, unlike those regulated in *Lopez* (gun possession near schools) and *Morrison* (violence against women), were *"quintessentially economic."* "Economics," he noted, refers to the "production, distribution and consumption of commodities." Since the CSA regulated the "production, distribution, and consumption of commodities for which there was an established, and lucrative, interstate market[,]" and since the Court had long recognized that prohibiting the *intrastate* manufacture or possession of an article of commerce was a rational means of regulating interstate commerce in that product, the intrastate regulation here easily fell within Congress' commerce powers.

v. **Scalia's concurrence:** Justice Scalia concurred. Unlike the majority, he relied on the *necessary and proper clause* (*supra*, p. 21): he believed that Congress could regulate even noneconomic local activity that did not "substantially affect" interstate commerce, if "that regulation is a *necessary part of a more general regulation of interstate commerce."* Since Congress could reasonably conclude that its objective of barring marijuana from the interstate market might be undercut if local growing for medical purposes was allowed, a ban on that local activity was necessary to the success of the overall regulatory scheme.

vi. **Dissent:** Justice O'Connor, joined by Chief Justice Rehnquist and (for the most part) by Justice Thomas, *dissented*. She objected that the majority's approach "allows Congress to regulate intrastate activity without check, so long as there is some implication by legislative design that regulating intrastate activity is essential ... to the interstate regulatory scheme." She believed that the majority's method reduced *Lopez* to "nothing more than a *drafting guide:* Congress should have described the relevant crime [in *Lopez*] as 'transfer or possession of a firearm anywhere in the nation' — thus including commercial and noncommercial activity ... Had it done so ... we would have sustained its authority to regulate possession of firearms in school zones."

Instead, O'Connor would have treated the possession and use of homegrown marijuana for medical purposes as being a *separate class of activity* that had not been shown to have even "a discernible, let alone substantial, impact on the national illicit drug market." Consequently, she would have distinguished that marijuana use from the wheat being consumed in *Wickard*, and would have found it to be beyond Congress' commerce powers.

7. **Significance:** So what is the significance of *Lopez* and the cases decided under it?

    a. **Effect must be "significant":** The activity being regulated must be one that *"significantly"* affects commerce — an *incidental effect* on commerce is *not* enough.

    b. **Commercial transactions:** Where the transaction being regulated is itself a clearly *commercial or economic one*, the Court will probably continue to allow Congress to regulate that transaction, even if it's a completely *intrastate* one, as long as it's part of a *class* that, in the aggregate, substantially affects interstate commerce. Thus in *Gonzales v. Raich*, the growing of medicinal marijuana for the grower's own use, even though purely local, was commercial in nature, and was reasonably believed by Congress to be an activity that might in the aggregate substantially affect interstate commerce (by leading to diversions of the drug into the interstate market); therefore, it could be regulated.

        i. **Non-commercial:** But where the activity in being regulated is essentially a *non-commercial* one, the Court apparently will *not* regard the aggregate impact of that activity on interstate commerce as being sufficient, unless either: (1) the causal link is extremely short and direct; or (2) the item being regulated, although non-commercial, crosses state lines or enters the stream of interstate commerce. (Thus in *Morrison*, the fact that some women failed to travel interstate or work for interstate businesses because they feared violence was too indirect an impact on interstate commerce to count.)

    c. **Findings:** The fact that Congress has made particular *findings* that an activity substantially affects interstate commerce may make some difference, but is unlikely to be dispositive very often. For instance, Congress actually made the express finding that guns adversely affected interstate commerce (it did this after the 1990 Act in question in *Lopez*, in connection with a different statute), and the *Lopez* majority was unswayed. Similarly, in the statute struck down in *Morrison*, Congress had made quite detailed findings that gender-based violence adversely affects interstate commerce, but again the majority essentially disregarded these findings. So legislative findings will at most tip a *close case* over the line into the "regulable" category.

    d. **Jurisdictional hooks:** Where Congress drafts the statute in a way that requires a *"jurisdictional hook"* between the particular activity and commerce, the act is still quite likely to be found within the Commerce power.

    **Example:** Suppose Congress makes it a crime to possess near a school a gun that moved in interstate commerce at some point in its career (and Congress doesn't purport to criminalize possession of a gun made and used within a single state up to the point of the arrest). There's a very good chance the statute would be upheld.

    e. **Examples of questionable provisions:** Here are various statutory provisions (some hypothetical, others real-life) that would be open to *serious question* under *Lopez*, especially if not accompanied by congressional findings of fact showing a clear link between the activity being regulated and interstate commerce:

        ❑ Congress makes it a crime for a *felon to possess a firearm*, without reference to whether the firearm ever travelled in interstate commerce. After *Morrison*, this one could go either way — firearms are certainly items of commerce (even if the particular one in question didn't travel interstate), but possession of firearms by felons isn't a commercially-related activity.

❑ Congress makes it a crime to *interfere with a person's efforts to obtain "reproductive health services,"* including abortions, in the Freedom of Access to Clinic Entrances ("FACE") Act. FACE is probably not supported by the Commerce power, because an interference with a person's attempt to get, say, an abortion does not "substantially affect" commerce.

❑ Congress prohibits states from *awarding marriage licenses* to anyone under the age of 18. This is a hypothetical statute, so of course it hasn't been tested. But it's hard to believe that the statute could be valid.

❑ Congress makes it a federal crime for a person to *physically injure his or her spouse*. *Morrison* makes it virtually impossible for this statute to be valid.

**Note:** Observe that all of these examples involve congressional attempts to *regulate activities* that are *not clearly commercial*.

**F.  Summary of modern view:**  Let us summarize the modern Court's view of Congress' Commerce power, in light of *Lopez*. There seem to be *four broad categories* of activities which Congress can constitutionally regulate:

1.  **Channels:** First, Congress can regulate the use of the *"channels"* of interstate commerce. Thus Congress can regulate in a way that is reasonably related to highways, waterways, and air traffic. Presumably Congress can do so even though the activity in question in the particular case is quite intrastate.

2.  **Instrumentalities:** Second, Congress can regulate the *"instrumentalities"* of interstate commerce, "even though the threat may come only from intrastate activities." *Lopez*. This category refers to people, machines, and other "things" used in carrying out commerce. So, for instance, presumably Congress could say that every truck must have a specific safety device, even if the particular truck in question was made and used exclusively within a single state.

3.  **Articles moving in interstate commerce:** Third, Congress can regulate *articles moving* in interstate commerce. For instance, in *Reno v. Condon*, 528 U.S. 141 (2000), the Court said that computerized information about motorists was an "article of commerce" whose release into the "interstate stream of business" made the information an appropriate subject for congressional regulation. (Apparently this would have been so even if the information did not "substantially affect" commerce, as described in the next paragraph.)

4.  **"Substantially affecting" commerce:** Finally, the biggest (and most interesting) category is that Congress may regulate those activities having a *"substantial effect"* on interstate commerce. *Lopez*. As to this category, the following rules now seem to apply:

    a.  **Real bite:** The requirement of a "substantial" effect has *real bite*.

        i.  **Activity is commercial:** If the activity itself is arguably *"commercial,"* then it doesn't seem to matter whether the *particular instance* of the activity directly affects interstate commerce, as long as the instance is part of a general class of activities that, collectively, substantially affect interstate commerce. Thus in the *Gonzales v. Raich* type of situation — P's own marijuana-growing activities are in a sense "commercial," but are entirely intrastate; however, when aggregated with all other local medicinal-marijuana-growing activities P's activities might undermine Congress' interstate-regulatory scheme — Congress can regulate even the solely-intrastate events.

    **ii. Activity is not commercial:** But if the activity itself is *not "commercial,"* then there will apparently have to be a *pretty obvious connection* between the activity and interstate commerce. (We know from *Lopez* that the link must be more obvious than the link between guns-in-schools and commerce; and we know from *Morrison* that the link must be more obvious than the one between gender-based violence and commerce). This is probably the main legacy of *Lopez* and *Morrison*.

  **b. Little deference to Congress:** The Court *won't* give much *deference* (as it used to) to the fact that Congress *believed* that the activity has the requisite "substantial effect" on interstate commerce. The Court will basically decide this issue for itself, from scratch. It certainly will no longer be enough that Congress had a *"rational basis"* for believing that the requisite effect existed — the effect must *in fact* exist to the Court's own independent satisfaction.

  **c. Traditional domain of states:** If what's being regulated is an activity the regulation of which has *traditionally* been the *domain of the states*, and as to which the states have expertise, the Court is less likely to find that Congress is acting within its Commerce power. Thus *education*, *family law* and *general criminal law* are areas where the Court is likely to be especially suspicious of congressional "interference."

    **i. National solution:** However, the fact that the activity has traditionally fallen within the states' domain can be *outweighed* by a showing that a *national solution* is needed. This would be so, for instance, where one state's choice heavily affects other states. Regulation of the *environment* is an example, since air and water pollution migrate across state boundaries.

**G. Federal criminal laws:** A broad reading of Congress' Commerce Clause powers has been applied in a number of decisions involving federal *criminal* statutes.

  **1. Ban on marijuana cultivation:** Thus the Court upheld the Congress' power to criminalize even the purely local, non-profit-oriented growing of medicinal marijuana in *Gonzales v. Raich*, *supra*, p. 40. As we saw, the Court used the "cumulative effect" rationale: (1) the sale of marijuana as a whole had an effect on interstate commerce, and (2) Congress reasonably feared that its entire regulatory scheme would be undermined if Congress were required to exempt purely local non-profit medicinal cultivation, since some of this supposedly-local supposedly-nonprofit marijuana might leak into the interstate market and substantially affect it.

  **2. Commerce-prohibiting technique:** Federal criminal statutes have also frequently made use of the *"commerce-prohibiting technique"* (see *supra*, p. 35), by banning the *interstate transportation* of persons or items in a matter incident to some criminal activity. See, e.g., the Mann Act, which prohibits the interstate transportation of women for immoral purposes, and the Dyer Act, which makes it a federal crime to transport a stolen vehicle across state lines.

  **3. Statutory interpretation:** As *Perez*, *supra*, illustrates, the Supreme Court will uphold the constitutionality of criminal statutes affecting even seemingly local activities, if Congress has shown a clear intent to encompass such activities. But as a matter of *statutory* *interpretation*, the more local the activities of the defendant, the more likely the Court is to conclude that Congress *did not intend* to reach those activities.

**H. Civil rights legislation:**  A key use of the federal commerce power has been in *civil rights* legislation. Thus Title II of the 1964 Civil Rights Act bans discrimination in places of public accommodation. This ban applies against all but the very most localized, small hotels or restaurants. It does this by covering any establishment which *serves interstate travelers,* or (in the case of a restaurant) which buys *food,* a substantial portion of which "has *moved in commerce.*"

    **1. The Court decisions:**  Any doubts about the constitutionality of the 1964 Act were put to rest by two 1964 Supreme Court decisions upholding it. Both, but especially the second discussed below, involved what might be termed "local" enterprises.

        **a. *Heart of Atlanta* case:**  In *Heart of Atlanta Motel v. U.S.*, 379 U.S. 241 (1964), the plaintiff was a motel located in downtown Atlanta, which refused to rent rooms to blacks.

            **i. Contacts with interstate travel:**  The motel was near two interstate highways, derived 75% of its occupancy from out-of-state guests, and solicited business in national media.

            **ii. Holding:**  The Supreme Court held that the motel could constitutionally be reached by the Civil Rights Act, under the Commerce Clause. The Court took note of Congress' findings that racial discrimination discouraged travel on the part of a substantial portion of the black community, and that such discrimination could therefore be regulated by Congress in the aggregate. Furthermore, the Court held, "[t]he power of Congress to promote interstate commerce also includes the power to regulate the local incidents thereof, including local activities in both the States of origin and destination, which might have a substantial and harmful effect upon that commerce." The Court quoted a prior decision, to the effect that "if it is interstate commerce that feels the pinch, it does not matter how local the operation that applies the squeeze."

            **iii. Police-powers motive acceptable:**  Nor was the Court troubled by the fact that Congress' *motive* for this legislation was not purely economic, but rather, principally moral and social.

        **b. *Katzenbach v. McClung:***  The other early Civil Rights Act case, *Katzenbach v. McClung*, 379 U.S. 294 (1964), demonstrates even more clearly the Court's approval of the use of the Commerce Clause to reach what seemed to be overwhelmingly local activities.

            **i. Facts:**  *Katzenbach* involved a Birmingham, Alabama restaurant called Ollie's Barbecue. The restaurant was relatively far from any interstate highway or train or bus station, and there was no evidence that an appreciable part of its business was in serving out of state travellers. However, 46% of the food purchased by the restaurant during the previous year had been bought from a supplier who had bought it from out of state. (Recall that the Civil Rights Act applies to any restaurant a substantial portion of whose food has moved in commerce.)

            **ii. Application of Act upheld:**  The Court *upheld* the Act as applied to the restaurant. As in the *Heart of Atlanta* case, the Court observed that unavailability of accommodations dissuaded blacks from travelling in interstate commerce. The Court returned to the *Wickard v. Filburn* rationale: even though Ollie's itself was small, and the value of food it purchased from out of state had only an insignificant effect on commerce, the restaurant's discriminatory conduct was representative of a great deal of similar conduct throughout the country, and this conduct in the aggregate clearly had an effect on interstate commerce. Therefore, Congress was entitled to regulate the individual case.

    **iii. Deference to Congress' findings:** Nor did the fact that the bill contained ***no congressional findings*** about the impact of restaurant discrimination on commerce render the Act unconstitutional. The Court would not scrutinize the facts to make a *de novo* determination of whether restaurant discrimination affected commerce. Rather, "where we find that the legislators, in light of the facts and testimony before them, have a ***rational basis*** for finding a chosen regulatory scheme necessary to the protection of commerce, our investigation is at an end." Such a rational basis was present here.

  **2. Effect of *Lopez* and *Morrison*:** It's not clear whether *U.S. v. Lopez, supra,* p. 36, and *U.S. v. Morrison, supra,* p. 39, would change the result in either *Heart of Atlanta* or *Katzenbach v. McClung. Katzenbach* seems to be the more constitutionally suspect of the two. We know from *Lopez* that the disinclination of businesses to locate in districts containing gunfire-ridden schools is not a sufficient connection with interstate commerce. And we know from *Morrison* that the reluctance of women who fear gender-based violence to travel or work interstate is not a sufficient connection. So racial discrimination in accommodations, and its chilling effect on blacks' willingness to travel interstate, might also not be sufficient, if today's Court were revisiting *Katzenbach.* However, the core activity being regulated in *Katzenbach* — the furnishing of restaurant meals — is clearly "commercial" in a way that possessing a gun in a school is not. On balance, *Katzenbach* would probably be decided the same way today, because of the more obviously commercial nature of the activity being regulated.

# V. THE TENTH AMENDMENT AS A LIMIT ON CONGRESS' POWER

  **A. Apparent irrelevance of Tenth Amendment:** For nearly 40 years following the *Carter Coal* decision (*supra,* p. 32), the Supreme Court did not invalidate a single federal statute on the grounds that it violated state or local government sovereignty. This sustained stretch led most observers to conclude that the Tenth Amendment was completely dead as an independent check upon federal power under the Commerce Clause.

  **B. Once again irrelevant:** As of this writing, it does indeed seem to be the case that the Tenth Amendment places relatively few practical limitations upon the exercise of federal power under the Commerce Clause. However, for the period 1976-85, the Supreme Court treated the Tenth Amendment as imposing an important limit on federal power — this Amendment was held to bar the federal government from doing anything that would impair the states' ability to perform their "traditional functions." Then, in 1985, the line of cases establishing this limit was ***flatly overruled*** by the Supreme Court, in one of the most amazing reversals of doctrine in modern Supreme Court history.[1] Before the 1985 reversal can be understood, some understanding of the prior line of cases is needed.

1. *National League of Cities:* Like a bolt out of the blue, the Supreme Court in 1976 gave the Tenth Amendment practical significance in *National League of Cities v. Usery*, 426 U.S. 833 (1976). In that case, the Court held that the Tenth Amendment barred Congress from making federal minimum-wage and overtime rules applicable to state and municipal employees. The vote was 5-4.

   a. **Rationale:** The five-justice majority conceded that the minimum-wage/overtime rules, as applied to state employees, clearly affected commerce. Thus these wage/hour regulations could unquestionably be constitutionally applied to private employers, under the commerce power. But when these wage/hour rules were applied to state employees, they violated the independent requirement, imposed by the Tenth Amendment, that "Congress may not exercise power in a fashion that *impairs the States' integrity* or their *ability to function effectively in the federal system*." The wage/hour rules violated this requirement in two ways.

      i. **Cost:** First, the wage/hour provisions impaired the states' ability to function effectively purely as a matter of *cost*: compliance would have cost the states and their municipal subdivisions substantial sums.

      ii. **Removal of discretion:** Secondly, the new rules stripped the states of their discretion to decide how they wished to allocate a fixed pool of funds available for salaries.

   b. **Summary:** Thus if the wage/hour rules were allowed to stand, the majority reasoned, Congress would have the right to make "fundamental employment decisions" regarding state employees, and "there would be little left of the States' 'separate and independent existence.' "

C. **Overruling of *National League of Cities*:** *National League of Cities* was on tenuous ground from the day it was decided. The fifth vote came from Justice Blackmun, who stated in his concurrence that he was "not untroubled by certain possible implications of the Court's opinion." All it took to overturn the decision in *National League of Cities* was for Justice Blackmun to abandon his never-passionate attachment to the principle of that case. In *Garcia v. San Antonio Metropolitan Transit Authority*, 469 U.S. 528 (1985), he joined with the four Justices who had dissented in *National League of Cities* (Brennan, White, Marshall and Stevens) to repudiate that case. By a 5-4 majority, the Court stated that *National League of Cities* "is *overruled*."

1. **Facts:** In view of the sweeping nature of the holding in *Garcia*, the facts would ordinarily seem to be of little significance. However, they apparently seemed to Justice Blackmun to make the failings of the *National League of Cities* approach especially clear. The issue in *Garcia* was whether the minimum-wage and overtime provisions of the federal Fair Labor Standards Act (the same statute at issue in *National League of Cities*) should apply to employees of a municipally-owned and-operated *mass-transit system*. Under *National League of Cities* and cases later decided under it, this issue translated into the issue: Is municipal ownership and operation of such a transit system a "traditional governmental function?"

---

1. Then, this reversal was partially "re-reversed," in several cases from the 1990s that established that Congress cannot directly command the states to enact or enforce federal policies; see *New York v. U.S.* (p. 50) and *Printz* v. U.S. (p. 51).

2. **Difficulty of line-drawing:** The majority opinion, by Justice Blackmun, contended that the 8-year period following *National League of Cities* had shown that it was "difficult, if not impossible, to identify an organizing principle" that would distinguish between those functions that are "traditional governmental functions" and those that are not. For instance, federal courts of appeal had held that the licensing of automobile drivers was a "traditional governmental function" (as to which the Tenth Amendment therefore protected state sovereignty from federal control), but that the regulation of traffic on public roads was not.

3. **The problem of subjectivity:** An additional, but related, problem was that the *National League of Cities* approach inevitably led to judicial subjectivity. "Any rule of state immunity that looks to the 'traditional,' 'integral,' or 'necessary' nature of governmental functions inevitably ***invites an unelected federal judiciary to make decisions about which state policies it favors and which ones it dislikes.***"

4. **Procedural safeguards:** Yet, the *Garcia* majority insisted, its rejection of *National League of Cities* did *not* mean that there are no limitations upon the federal government's right to use its delegated powers to impair state sovereignty. However, state sovereign interests are protected by ***"procedural safeguards inherent in the structure of the federal system,"*** not by "judicially created limitations on federal power."

    a. **Examples of structural protection:** For instance, the requirement that each state have two Senators, the fact that the states are given general control over electoral qualifications for federal elections, and the fact that the states have a special role in presidential elections by means of the electoral college, are all indications that the ***structure of the federal government*** has been constitutionally arranged so as to protect state sovereignty.

5. **Dissent:** The four dissenters in *Garcia* asserted that the majority approach "effectively reduces the Tenth Amendment to meaningless rhetoric when Congress acts pursuant to the Commerce Clause."

    a. **Powell's dissent:** Justice Powell, writing the principal dissent, contended that *National League of Cities* was correctly decided and that it articulated a workable standard. The *Garcia* majority's approach, by contrast, established no effective standard at all, in his opinion. Powell was especially troubled by the fact that under the majority approach, "federal political officials, invoking the Commerce Clause, are the ***sole judges of the limits of their own power.*** … " He contended that the majority position was inconsistent with the rule, in force since *Marbury v. Madison* (*supra*, p. 8), that it is up to the federal judiciary to "say what the law is" with respect to the constitutionality of congressional actions.

D. **Significance of case:** *Garcia* appears to mean that once Congress, acting pursuant to its Commerce power, regulates the states, the fact that it is a state being regulated ***has virtually no practical significance — if the regulation would be valid if applied to a private party, it is also valid as to the state.***

1. **Political process:** This is not quite the same as saying that there are no constitutional protections against congressional interference with state sovereignty. Rather, the majority is saying that whatever limits exist inhere in the structure or process of congressional lawmaking.

**2. Later cases cut back:** Several post-*Garcia* cases seem to be ***cutting back*** the apparently-broad scope of *Garcia*. *New York v. United States* (discussed immediately *infra*) and *Printz v. U.S.* (*infra*, p. 51) both place limits on the extent to which Congress can force state or local governments to ***make or enforce laws***. And *Alden v. Maine* (*infra*, p. 728) blocks Congress from forcing the states to ***hear damage suits*** against themselves in ***state courts***, even on federally-created claims. So the principle that there are some limits on the way Congress can regulate a state remains very much alive after *Garcia*.[2]

**E. Use of state's lawmaking mechanisms:** One aspect of state sovereignty is a state's ability to ***make and apply law***, through legislative, judicial, and administrative functions. Even after *Garcia*, there are limits to Congress' right to interfere with these state legislative or executive processes, and Congress will violate the Tenth Amendment if it exceeds those limits. In a pair of cases, the Court has held that the federal government may not: (1) compel a state to ***enact*** or enforce a particular ***law*** or type of law; or (2) compel state/local officials to perform federally-specified ***administrative*** tasks. Holding (1) occurred in *New York v. United States*, 505 U.S. 144 (1992). Holding (2) occurred in *Printz v. U.S.*, 117 S. Ct. 2365 (1997).

**1. Waste disposal case:** *New York v. United States, supra*, dramatically illustrates the principle that Congress may not simply force a state to ***enact a certain statute*** or to ***regulate*** in a certain manner.

   **a. Regulatory scheme:** Congress enacted the Low-Level Radioactive Waste Policy Amendments Act of 1985. The Act attempted to force each state to make its own arrangements for disposing (either in-state or out-of-state) of the low-level radioactive waste generated in that state. The Act tried to do this with several types of incentives. Most significant was the ***"take title"*** incentive, whereby any state which did not arrange for disposal of its waste would be required to "take title" to the waste (upon request by the waste generator), and would be liable for damages in connection with disposal of this waste.

   **b. New York attacks statute:** New York, unlike most states, made little progress in solving its waste disposal problems, because local residents of each community where the state proposed to put disposal sites fiercely objected. New York then sued the federal government, arguing that the "take title" provision violated the Tenth Amendment, by effectively forcing the state to regulate in a particular area.

   **c. Tenth Amendment found violated:** A majority of the Court agreed that the "take title" provision violated the Tenth Amendment: Congress may not simply ***"commandee[r] the legislative processes of the States*** by directly ***compelling them to enact and enforce*** a federal regulatory program."

      **i. Explanation:** New York was being put to the choice of two "unconstitutionally coercive regulatory techniques": it could either choose to regulate on its own by

---

2. In fact, two cases from the late 1990s together strip *Garcia* of most of its practical significance. Under *Seminole Tribe of Florida v. Florida* (*infra*, p. 727), Congress does not have authority to abrogate the 11th Amendment and thus to allow state employees to sue the state in federal court for violating the federal wage-and-hour laws that *Garcia* said apply to the states. And under the just-mentioned *Alden v. Maine* (*infra*, p. 728), Congress can't force the states to waive their sovereign immunity and therefore to hear such employee suits in the state's own courts. So *Garcia* gives state employees a federal right, but the two later cases block individual employees from any state-court or federal-court *remedy* for violation of that right (though the federal government could still be the plaintiff in a federal-court suit to redress a violation).

making arrangements for disposal of waste generated inside the state, or be forced to indemnify waste-generators against tort damages. Because Congress could not employ either of these methods alone, it could not escape the problem by giving the state a choice between the two.

**d. Dissent:** Three members of the Court (White, joined by Blackmun and Stevens) dissented. White argued that this was not an instance where Congress was forcing its will upon the states. Rather, he said, Congress had responded to a request by many of the states to ratify a compromise worked out among themselves, so that the waste-disposal problem could be solved. "The Court's refusal to force New York to accept responsibility for its own problem inevitably means that some other State's sovereignty will be impinged by it being forced, for public health reasons, to accept New York's low-level radioactive waste. I do not understand the principle of federalism to impede the National Government from acting as referee among the States to prohibit one from bullying another."

**e. Alternative methods:** Is Congress powerless to make each state deal with its radioactive waste (or any other specific problem)? Probably not. Justice White's dissent suggests several methods that are apparently still open to Congress, notwithstanding *N.Y. v. U.S.*

   **i. Spending power:** First, Congress clearly may condition the ***receipt of federal funds*** on a state's solving the problem (provided that the funds in question have something to do with the problem; for instance, Congress probably cannot hold back federal Medicare funds until the state complies, because spending for medical expenses has little if anything to do with solving the radioactive waste problem.)

   **ii. Threat of regulation:** Second, Congress could ***directly regulate*** the conduct in question, and could therefore take the less drastic step of telling the states that this direct regulation will follow if the states do not take care of the problems themselves. (For instance, Congress' commerce power would entitle it to say, "No state may ship radioactive waste outside of its own border." Congress could therefore say, as a lesser exercise of this power, "Any state which does not make its own arrangements for disposing of waste, whether in-state or out-of-state, shall be required to keep its waste within its own borders.")

   **iii. Summary:** In summary, Congress may have to be a little more clever about how it accomplishes its regulatory purposes — and it will not be able to escape the ***"political heat"*** for unpopular decisions by forcing state officials to make those decisions. But Congress, by careful use of its enumerated powers (including the spending and commerce powers) can achieve practically any regulatory end it wants without running afoul of the Tenth Amendment.

**2. No commandeering of executive branch:** *N.Y. v. U.S.* limits Congress' power to "commandeer the *legislative* processes of the States. . . ." In a post-*N.Y.* case, the Court has held that Congress may, similarly, not compel a state or local government's ***executive*** branch to perform functions. And that's true even if the functions are fairly ministerial and easy-to-perform, and even if the compulsion is only temporary. ***Printz v. U.S.***, 117 S. Ct. 2365 (1997).

a. **Brady bill's provision:** In 1993, Congress enacted the "Brady Bill," aimed at controlling the flow of guns. As a temporary 5-year measure, the law ***ordered local law enforcement officials*** to ***conduct background checks*** on prospective purchasers, until a national computerized system for doing these checks could be phased in. Printz, a county sheriff in Montana, objected to the background-check requirement and sued. He argued that under *New York v. U.S.*, Congress could not force him to conduct background checks on the federal government's behalf.

b. **Decision:** By a 5-4 margin, the Court agreed with the plaintiff. Justice Scalia's majority opinion noted that in *N.Y. v. U.S.*, the Court had said that the federal government "may not compel the States to enact or administer a federal regulatory program." Scalia then concluded that the background-check portion of the Brady bill violated this prohibition.

   i. **Rationale:** Scalia ***rejected*** the dissent's distinction between compelling a state to ***make policy*** (such as the compelled enactment of a regulatory scheme, like the "take title" scheme at issue in *N.Y. v. U.S.*) and compelling state executive-branch officers to perform ***ministerial tasks*** (such as the background checks at issue here). Even if no policy-making was involved here, this did not prevent Congress' action from being an intolerable incursion into state sovereignty: "It is an essential attribute of the States' retained sovereignty that they remain ***independent and autonomous within their proper sphere of authority*** . . . . It is no more compatible with this independence and autonomy that their officers be 'dragooned' . . . into administering federal law, than it would be compatible with the independence and autonomy of the United States that its officers be impressed into service for the execution of state laws."

   ii. **Basis unclear:** It's not clear whether Scalia believed that any *particular* constitutional provision had been violated. He seemed to be relying on a general, non-textual, principle of state sovereignty, rather than on any specific clause (e.g., the Tenth Amendment, which he referred to only occasionally and in passing). But two concurring opinions specifically said that the background-check requirement violated the ***Tenth Amendment.***

c. **Dissents:** Four Justices dissented in *Printz*.

   i. **Justice Stevens' dissent:** The main dissent was by Justice Stevens. He first pointed out that the federal commerce power gave Congress the authority to regulate handguns. He then concluded that this being so, the ***"necessary and proper" clause*** gave Congress the right to implement its regulation by temporarily requiring local police officers to perform the ministerial step of identifying persons who should not be entrusted with handguns. This was especially true, he said, since Congress could have required *private citizens* to help with such identification: "The [Tenth] Amendment provides no support for a rule that immunizes local officials from obligations that might be imposed on ordinary citizens."

d. **Control over purse strings:** Again (as in *N.Y. v. U.S.*) presumably Congress could get around the problem by conditioning the state's or local government's ***receipt of federal funds*** on its officials' willingness to do the federal bidding. Only compulsion, not a voluntary *quid pro quo*, seems foreclosed by the majority's analysis.

3. **Significance:** So *New York v. U.S.* and *Printz* seem to stand for the propositions that Congress may ***not*** (1) ***force a state to legislate or regulate in a certain way;*** or (2) require state ***executive-branch*** personnel to perform even ***ministerial functions***.

   a. **Distinguished from *Garcia* situation:** How does the rationale of these cases fit in with the rationale of *Garcia*? *Garcia* seems to apply mainly to ***generally applicable*** federal lawmaking; that case holds that where Congress passes a generally applicable law (e.g., a minimum wage law that applies to ***all*** or nearly all businesses), the Tenth Amendment does not entitle a state's own operations to an exemption, merely because it is a state that is being regulated along with all the other private entities. But where the federal government tries to force a state or local government to ***enact legislation*** or ***regulation***, or tries to force state or local ***officials*** to perform particular governmental functions, this is not part of a generally-applicable federal scheme, and is instead directed specifically at the state's basic exercise of sovereignty: the state's right to carry out the business of government. The federal government may not use such coercion, *N.Y. v. U.S.* and *Printz* say.

---

*Quiz Yourself on*
## THE FEDERAL COMMERCE POWER *(ENTIRE CHAPTER)*

5. Congress makes it a federal felony for any individual to place a bet with another individual on a sporting event, or to propose such a bet. The statute is written broadly, so as to cover two friends who bet with each other primarily for purposes of friendship rather than profit. The House and Senate Committee Reports on the bill show that Congress believed that ostensibly "friendly" betting creates a climate that is tolerant of gambling, which in turn increases the interstate gambling profits of organized crime, a multi-million dollar nationwide problem. Devon is charged with violating the statute by placing a bet on the Super Bowl with her best friend, Elaine. They made the bet face to face within a single state.

   **(a)** If Devon challenges the constitutionality of the statute on the grounds that it goes beyond Congress' enumerated powers, what enumerated power should the prosecutors point to in defending the statute's constitutionality? _____

   **(b)** Is the statute in fact constitutional? State your reasons. _____

6. After several years of rising unemployment nationally, and falling wage levels, Congress passes a statute prohibiting the employment of any person under the age of 19. Congress' intent is to keep teenagers in high school or college, where they may or may not learn something but will at least not be competing with adults for jobs, thus allowing wage rates to rise. The state of Alahoma employs many 17- and 18-year-olds, for such posts as cleaners in state parks and apprentice state troopers. Alahoma estimates that its total payroll costs will rise by 8% if it is required to obey the new federal statute (which by its terms applies to government as well as private-sector employees).

   **(a)** Assuming that the federal statute falls within Congress' power to regulate commerce, what is the strongest argument that Alahoma can make as to why the Constitution requires that the state's own hiring be exempted from the statute? _____

   **(b)** Will this argument succeed? _____

7. Congress has concluded that cigarette smoking raises the nation's annual health care budget 15% above what it would otherwise be. Congress has therefore enacted a statute that requires each state to: (1) place a

tax of at least 10% on the sale of cigarettes (in addition to existing federal cigarette taxes); (2) compile a registry of every premises in the state where cigarettes are sold, and audit those premises quarterly to make sure they're collecting the tax; (3) modify its health-care-financing scheme so that the state does not pay any hospital or doctor for the costs of treating any condition found to be caused by cigarette smoking; and (4) modify its tort law so as to treat cigarettes as a "defective product" for which strict liability is allowed under state tort law. Congress does not allocate any funds for the carrying out of these objectives. It provides that if a state is found not to be in compliance one year after enactment of the act, the federal district courts for that state shall have authority to direct the legislature and agencies of the state to comply, and to hold state officials in contempt if they do not comply.

**(a)** If you are given the job of arguing on behalf of a state that this provision is an unconstitutional infringement of your state's sovereignty, what constitutional provision should you point to? _____

**(b)** Will your argument succeed? _____

**(c)** If you are charged with improving the likelihood that the federal scheme will pass muster, what fundamental change will you urge to be made in that scheme? _____

———————————————

*Answers*

5. **(a) Congress' power to regulate commerce.**

   **(b) Probably, but this is no longer as certain as it once was.** Before the 1995 decision in *U.S. v. Lopez*, it was enough that there was a "rational basis" for Congress' belief that a regulated activity "affects" interstate commerce. But *Lopez* establishes that the activity which Congress is regulating must *in fact* have a ***"substantial effect"*** on interstate commerce.

   Where an activity is "commercial," the Court still seems willing to find regulation of it to be within Congress' commerce power even if the particular act is wholly intrastate, as long as the act is part of a ***class*** of activities which, collectively, substantially affect interstate commerce. The bet here seems to qualify — the bet is probably itself a "commercial" transaction (i.e., one primarily motivated by the desire to make a profit), and private bets taken as a group probably have a substantial effect on interstate commerce (e.g., they are often made over interstate phone lines, they contribute to the use of interstate "handicapping" services and interstate money transfers, etc.) Once the Court finds that the activity substantially affects commerce, the Court requires only that the means selected by Congress be "rationally related" to the objective being sought. Here, prohibition of the damaging activity — friendly sports betting — would certainly seem to be a reasonable means of combatting that activity. The scenario seems a lot like that in *Gonzales v. Raich*, where the Court held that Congress could regulate a purely intrastate but commercially-oriented activity regarding a commodity (personal cultivation of marijuana for one's own medicinal uses) because such regulation was reasonably tied in to Congress' regulation of the interstate commercial aspects of that same commodity.

6. **(a) The Tenth Amendment.** That Amendment provides that "the powers not delegated to the United States by the Constitution, nor prohibited by it to the States, are reserved to the States respectively, or to the People." Alahoma could make a plausible argument that Congress, by precisely detailing whom the state may hire, has interfered with the sovereignty reserved to the state by the Tenth Amendment.

   **(b) No, probably.** At one time, Alahoma would probably have succeeded with this argument, because of *National League of Cities v. Usery*, which held that the Tenth Amendment prevented Congress from regulating the states in a way that might impair their "ability to function effectively in the federal system"; state employees were exempted from federal wage/hour regulations on this theory. But *National League of Cities* was overruled in *Garcia v. San Antonio Metropolitan Transit Authority. Garcia* seems to mean that when Congress, acting pursuant to its commerce power, regulates the states as part of a generally applicable regulatory scheme, the fact that it is a state being regulated has no practical significance — if the regulation would be valid where applied to a private party, it is also valid as to the state. Consequently, since Congress would almost certainly have the power to set a minimum age for employment in the private sector (on the theory that this directly affects commerce, because of its effect on unemployment and wage limits), the state is not entitled to an exemption.

**7. (a) The Tenth Amendment.**

**(b) Yes.** The Tenth Amendment does not have very huge scope in light of *Garcia* (see previous question), but it has some. In particular, Congress may not simply "commandee[r] the legislative processes of the States by directly compelling them to enact and enforce a regulatory program." *New York v. U.S.* Thus in *New York v. U.S.*, *supra*, the Court held that Congress could not force states to regulate nuclear waste. So, here, the Court would almost certainly conclude that Congress may not force a state to enact a specific regulatory framework for dealing with the cigarette/health care problem. Nor may Congress force state official to carry out administrative tasks (such as the audits of cigarette vendors here); see *Printz* and *Mack*. Congress is always free to regulate health care directly, but it may not thrust onto the states the job of doing this.

**(c) Supply federal funds, and make the loss of those funds the only penalty for failure to comply.** Congress is always free to use its power to tax and spend for the general welfare in order to carry out a regulatory scheme. Furthermore, it may do this by giving an incentive to the states to get them to do the regulating. See, e.g., *South Dakota v. Dole* (Congress may induce states to prevent underage drinking by withholding federal highway funds from states that don't prohibit drivers under age 21 from drinking). So long as the only penalty is loss of funds that are related to the congressional program, there should not be a constitutional problem. Probably Congress cannot cut off funds that have no relation to the regulatory scheme desired by Congress; thus Congress probably couldn't cut off all educational funding to states that refuse to enact the cigarette/health care scheme.

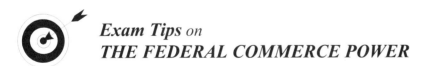

# *Exam Tips on*
# *THE FEDERAL COMMERCE POWER*

Any time your fact pattern involves an action by Congress, you've got to keep the Commerce Clause in mind. In particular:

☛ Whenever you've got to decide whether a congressional statute falls within an enumerated power, ***check the Commerce Clause first***. It encompasses a broader variety of congressional action than any other congressional power.

☛ Remember that the Court takes a fairly ***deferential*** view on the issue of whether a particular action falls within the commerce power. So long as a regulated activity ***"substantially affects"*** interstate commerce, the regulation will be found to fall within the commerce power.

☞ For instance, even if a particular commercial activity being regulated seems to take place solely *intrastate*, the Court will usually find that when all similar activities are considered as a *class*, they have a cumulative effect on interstate commerce. (*Example:* Remember *Gonzales v. Raich*, where the Court upheld Congress' right to ban intrastate cultivation of marijuana for one's own medicinal use because exemption of such cultivation might damage Congress' scheme banning interstate marijuana distribution.)

☞ Also, remember that Congress may ban or regulate interstate transport as a way of dealing with local problems.

☞ However, look out for congressional regulation of activities that are ***not really commercial***. Here, there's a much better chance that the Court will find that the activity does ***not*** substantially affect interstate commerce. Cite to *U.S. v. Lopez* in this situation.

*Examples* of attempts to regulate activities that probably ***don't substantially affect interstate commerce***, so that the regulation is probably *invalid*:

❑ Congress prescribes the curriculum public schools must use.

❑ Congress makes it a federal crime to commit a gender-based violent crime against a woman (see *U.S. v. Morrison*).

❑ Congress bans marriage under the age of 18.

☞ But if there's a "jurisdictional hook" — like a ban only on those machine guns that passed in interstate commerce — the regulation is probably O.K.

☛ Be alert for fact patterns where Congress is regulating ***the states***. Such regulation raises a ***Tenth Amendment*** issue:

☞ So long as Congress has merely passed a ***generally applicable*** law, this law can apply to the states just as it does to private individuals, and there is no Tenth Amendment violation. (*Example:* Minimum wage laws may be applied to state workers just as to private workers.)

☞ But Congress may not directly compel the states to enact or enforce a federal regulatory program. [*New York v. United States; Printz*] When Congress does this, it violates the Tenth Amendment. (But Congress may single out the states for regulation when the states are acting as market participants. [*Reno v. Condon*]

# Chapter 5

# OTHER NATIONAL POWERS

## *ChapterScope*

The previous chapter covered the Commerce Clause, clearly the most important source of federal power. This chapter considers other sources of federal authority:

- **Taxing power:** Under the "*taxing* power," Congress is given a far-reaching ability to tax in order to raise revenue.

  - **Taxation as regulation:** Congress may also *regulate* via taxation.

- **Spending power:** Under the "*spending* power," Congress may "provide for the common Defense and general Welfare of the United States. ... "

  - **Conditional spending:** Congress may place *conditions* on its spending power as a kind of regulation. This is true even if Congress could not regulate in an area directly (because the area regulated would be of such completely local concern that the commerce power would not be triggered). Conditions placed upon the doling out of federal funds are usually justified under the "Necessary and Proper" Clause.

    - **"General Welfare" Clause:** There is *no* independent congressional power to pursue the *"general welfare."* The only relevance of general welfare is that Congress when it taxes and spends must be pursuing the general welfare (a requirement that has very little independent significance today).

- **War power:** Congress is given the power to *declare war*, and to tax and spend for national defense.

- **DC:** Congress can regulate the *District of Columbia*.

- **Federal property:** Congress can regulate and dispose of *federal property* (e.g., federal parks).

- **Enforcement of Civil War amendments:** Congress can *enforce* the *post-Civil War amendments* (13th, 14th and 15th).

## I. THE TAXING POWER

A. **Several provisions on tax:** Several constitutional clauses relate to the power of the federal government to tax. The basic power is given in Article I, §8: "The Congress shall have Power To lay and collect Taxes, Duties, Imposts and Excises. ... "

   1. **Independent federal power:** This power to tax is an independent source of federal authority. That is, Congress may tax activities or property that it might not be authorized to regulate directly under any of the enumerated regulatory powers (e.g., the Commerce Clause.) Tribe, p. 318.

      **Example:** Congress could enact a national marriage tax, which would be payable by any couple getting married. Marriage is an area which may be beyond direct federal legislative regulation (unless some tie-in to interstate commerce were devised), but the power to tax stands on its own and does not derive from the commerce power or any other power. (However, if it were absolutely clear that Congress was not trying to raise revenues, but was instead trying to dissuade marriage, by putting, say, a $10,000 tax on it, the Supreme Court might conceivably hold that the tax was a disguised regulation that failed to fall within any of the other enumerated powers. The tax-as-disguised-regulation problem is discussed *infra*, pp. 58-59).

B. **Special rules on taxes:**  In addition to the general enabling provision just discussed, the Constitution imposes several specific limits and rules on the taxing power. These are as follows:

   1. **Uniform indirect taxes:**  Article I, §8 requires that "all Duties, Imposts and Excises shall be uniform throughout the United States. ... " This requirement merely means that the tax structure may not discriminate among the states; it does not matter that specific individuals are not taxed uniformly. Tribe, p. 318. The requirement applies to "indirect" taxes, that is, ones which tax an activity (e.g., the carrying on of a business) rather than taxing property.

   2. **Apportionment of direct taxes:**  A more specific, and burdensome, requirement is imposed with respect to so-called "direct" taxes. Article I, §2 provides that "direct Taxes shall be apportioned among the several States which may be included within this Union, according to their respective Numbers. ... " Thus direct taxes must be arranged in such a way that the revenue produced by them comes from each state in proportion to its share of the nation's overall population.

      a. **"Direct" defined:**  There has been substantial dispute over the years about what exactly is a "direct" tax. In general, taxes on ***real property*** are virtually the only kind of tax likely to be imposed today that would be considered "direct." Provisions of the 1894 Income Tax Act were held to be direct (and therefore invalid because not apportioned by population) since they taxed income from real estate and personal property. However, the Sixteenth Amendment, passed in 1913, provides that "Congress shall have power to lay and collect taxes on incomes, from whatever source derived, without apportionment among the several States. ... " This Amendment has essentially put to rest the need to distinguish between "direct" and "indirect" taxes.

   3. **No duty on exports:**  The final tax-related rule imposed by the Constitution is that no ***duty*** may be imposed on ***exports***. Article I, §9.

C. **Regulatory effect:**  Nearly any measure enacted in the form of a tax will have at least an incidental ***regulatory effect***. For instance, if an excise tax on cigarettes is enacted, people may smoke, on average, fewer cigarettes. If the regulatory impact of the tax is one which could be ***achieved directly***, by use of one of the other enumerated powers (e.g., the Commerce Clause), the fact that the tax has this regulatory effect is not of constitutional significance.

   1. **Disguised regulation:**  If, however, the regulatory effect is one which could ***not*** have been achieved directly (e.g., the subject matter is so purely local that it could not be reached under the Commerce Clause, and there is no other enumerated power which applies), then it is possible that the tax may be stricken as an ***invalid disguised regulation.***

   2. **Modern rules:**  The "tax vs. regulation" issue has become somewhat less important in recent years, since almost all regulation could be sustained under the Commerce power anyway (and thus a tax statute could be sustained as a "necessary and proper" means of implementing the Commerce power, even if invalid under the enumerated taxation

power). However, the following rules are probably applicable: (1) a tax that produces substantial revenue will almost certainly be sustained, and the Court will not inquire into Congress' motive in enacting it; (2) *regulatory provisions* that accompany the tax are valid if they bear a reasonable relation to the tax's enforcement; (3) a tax which regulates directly through its rate structure is valid (e.g., tax of 1/4 cent per pound on white oleomargarine versus 10 cents per pound on yellow oleomargarine). See Tribe, p. 320.

    a. **Possibly invalid tax:** The one type of tax which might be held to be a regulatory tax (invalid if not authorized under some other power) is a tax enacted together with specified conditions, and written in such a way that the tax does not apply at all unless the taxpayer has violated the conditions. *Id.* at 222.

        **Example:** Suppose Congress passes the Marriage Tax Act of 2000. One portion of the Act contains detailed definitions of a "taxable marriage," defined to include any marriage in which either party is under the age of sixteen, or both parties are under the age of eighteen. Another portion of the Act provides for a tax of $2,000 on any "taxable marriage."

        The Supreme Court might find this measure to be a regulatory tax (and hence invalid if not authorized under another power, probably the Commerce power.) This is because the detailed conditions (the portions defining "taxable marriage") cannot really be said to be an aid to enforcement of the tax, but are rather the conditions which trigger the very application of the Act. However, if the Act produced more than trivial revenue, the Court might sustain it anyway; the Court is probably unlikely to review the legislative history of the Act to determine its "true" purpose.

# II. THE SPENDING POWER

    A. **The spending power generally:** Article I, §8, gives Congress the power "[t]o lay and collect Taxes ... to pay the Debts and provide for the common Defence and general Welfare of the United States. ... " The power to spend is thus linked to the power to tax — money may be raised by taxation, and then spent "for the common Defence and general Welfare of the United States."

    B. **Not limited to enumerated powers:** Prior to 1937, it was not clear whether Congress could spend for whatever purpose it wished (so long as the "general welfare" was being served), or whether Congress could only spend in order to carry out one of the other enumerated powers listed in Article I, §8. Then, in *U.S. v. Butler*, 297 U.S. 1 (1936), the Court held that *no such limitation exists* — the spending (and taxing) powers are themselves enumerated powers, so Congress may spend (or tax) to achieve the general welfare, even though no other enumerated power is being furthered.

        1. **Facts of *Butler*:** *Butler* involved the validity of the Agricultural Adjustment Act of 1933, a New Deal measure which sought to raise farm prices by cutting back agricultural production. The scheme was to be carried out by authorizing the Secretary of Agriculture to contract with farmers to reduce their acreage under cultivation in return for benefit payments; the payments were in turn to be made from a fund generated by the imposition of a "processing tax" on the processing of the commodity.

        2. **Separate spending power:** The Court first concluded that the power to "tax and spend for the general welfare" existed as a power *separate and distinct* from the other powers

enumerated in Article I, §8. Thus the taxing-and-spending power stood on equal footing with, say, the power to regulate interstate commerce. By this standard, there was no difficulty with the Agricultural Adjustment Act.

3. **Not usable for regulation:** But the Court rejected the contention that Congress had an independent power to "provide for the general welfare" apart from the power to tax and spend. Thus Congress *may not regulate in a particular area merely on the ground that it is thereby providing for the general welfare*; it is only *taxing and spending* which may be done "for the general welfare." Otherwise, the Court noted, the federal government would be one of "general and unlimited powers," rather than enumerated and limited ones.

4. **Can't regulate for general welfare:** The most important principle for which *U.S. v. Butler* stands today is that Congress has *no power* to *regulate* for the purpose of providing for the *"general welfare."* Congress may *spend* for the general welfare, it may *tax* for the general welfare, but it may not regulate for the general welfare. (For this reason, a congressional regulatory scheme has to be justified as a reasonable means of carrying out *some other enumerated power*, typically the commerce power. See *supra*, p. 27.)

5. **Other constitutional provisions as limits:** A federal spending program may still be found invalid because it runs afoul of other, specific, federal constitutional provisions protecting individuals. For instance, Congress could not violate the Due Process Clause of the Fifth Amendment, even as part of an otherwise-valid spending program in furtherance of the "general welfare."

   a. **Achievement of otherwise disallowed objectives:** Suppose that Congress could not achieve objective X by direct regulation, since that would lie beyond its enumerated powers. May Congress use its *conditional* spending power to achieve that result *indirectly*, say by depriving the states of money if *they* do not achieve the regulatory result? The answer is, *"yes,"* so long as the action by the state does not violate the constitutional rights of any individual.

   **Example:** Congress, in order to prevent drivers under the age of 21 from drinking, withholds federal highway funds from states that permit individuals younger than 21 to purchase or possess in public any alcoholic beverage. South Dakota attacks the statute on the grounds that this condition interferes with its own exclusive powers under both the Tenth and Twenty-First Amendments.

   *Held*, the statute is valid. Even if, *arguendo*, direct congressional setting of the drinking age for the entire country would be unconstitutional, Congress' indirect use of its conditional spending power to achieve the same results is permissible. Only if, by the use of that conditional spending power, Congress induced the states to pass laws that would *themselves* violate the constitutional rights of individuals would that congressional action be unconstitutional. *South Dakota v. Dole*, 483 U.S. 203 (1987).

6. **"General welfare" still required:** A federal spending program must still be for the "general welfare." However, this requirement seems to have almost *no bite* at present.

## III.  THE WAR, TREATY AND FOREIGN AFFAIRS POWERS

A. **War power:** Congress is given the power to *declare war*, and to *tax and spend for national defense*. Also, it is explicitly given the right to "raise and support Armies" and to provide and maintain a navy. All of these powers are given by Article I, §8. The President, by contrast, is made the Commander in Chief of the Armed Forces. (Article II, §2.) Thus Congress and the President in effect split the war powers.

1.  **Separation of powers:** This division raises important questions of the separation of powers. (E.g., may the President commit armed forces to battle without express congressional authorization?) However, these questions are deferred until a separate chapter on separation of powers, *infra*, p. 109.

2.  **Federalism:** The war powers raise important issues regarding *federalism*.

    a.  **Economic regulation:** These issues of federalism have principally arisen in a context of *economic regulations* promulgated during wartime. The right to promulgate such regulations as an adjunct to the war powers was broadly construed by the Supreme Court in *Woods v. Miller Co.*, 333 U.S. 138 (1948).

        i.  *Woods* **case:** *Woods* involved the constitutionality of the Housing and Rent Act of 1947, by which Congress sought to impose rent controls because of the post-war housing shortage. The Court held that even though actual combat had terminated, a state of war still technically existed. Furthermore, the shortage directly resulted from the war; therefore, Congress could act to combat the shortage, under its power to take all "necessary and proper" steps to enforce an enumerated power (the power to declare war).

3.  **Impact on private citizens:** The war powers sometimes permit Congress to *regulate private behavior* without the need to rely on broad powers like the commerce or the taxing-and-spending powers. Indeed, when Congress does purport to act under its war powers, the Supreme Court will give the resulting action maximum judicial *deference*, and will be extremely reluctant to hold that the congressional action is unconstitutional.

    > **Example:** In a recent case, *Rumsfeld v. FAIR*, 547 U.S. 47 (2006), the Court upheld the constitutionality of the "Solomon Amendment," under which Congress said that any university could receive certain federal funding only if all parts of the university, including its law school, gave the same on-campus access to military recruiters as to other recruiters. A group of law schools argued that the Solomon Amendment infringed their First Amendment rights by forcing the schools to accommodate the anti-gay message of military recruiters. At the outset of its opinion, a unanimous court noted that Congress' war powers "include[] the authority to *require campus access for military recruiters.*" That is, as an adjunct to its war powers Congress could simply have required every law school and university to host military recruiters, without giving the schools the choice between giving access or foregoing the funding. In the course of finding that the Solomon Amendment was constitutional, the Court noted that *"judicial deference [to Congress] is at its apogee when Congress legislates under its authority to raise and support armies."*

B.  **The treaty power:** Like the war powers, the *treaty power* is divided between two branches of the federal government. The President may make a treaty, but it must be ratified by two-thirds of the Senate. Article II, §2.

    1.  **Equivalent of federal statute:** A validly-ratified treaty is the rough equivalent of a *federal statute*. Thus when a conflict arises between a valid treaty and a valid congressional

statute, ***whichever was enacted later*** controls, under the rule that "the last expression of the sovereign will must control." See Tribe, p. 226.

2.  **Independent source of authority:**   The power to ratify treaties is in effect an enumerated legislative power, just like the specific powers listed in Article I, §8. Thus even though a subject area might not otherwise be within congressional control, if it falls within the scope of an otherwise valid treaty, it will be valid as a "necessary and proper means" of exercising the treaty power. It will also be binding on the states, under the Supremacy Clause.

> **Example:** Congress attempts to regulate the killing of migratory birds within the United States. This statute is struck down as not being within any enumerated congressional authority. A treaty is then enacted between the U.S. and Great Britain, governing migration of birds between the U.S. and Canada; the act prohibits the killing or capture of certain birds within the United States. The state of Missouri claims that the treaty invades rights guaranteed to it under the Tenth Amendment.
>
> *Held*, the treaty and its regulations are valid, and do not violate any state's Tenth Amendment rights. The treaty power is explicitly given to Congress, and thus furnished authority for this particular treaty. Furthermore, migration of wild birds is a national problem, best dealt with by a national solution; therefore, no Tenth Amendment rights of individual states will be allowed to stand in the way of such a solution. *Missouri v. Holland*, 252 U.S. 416 (1920).

3.  **May not violate constitutional guarantees:**   A treaty may not violate any distinct constitutional prohibitions or guarantees (e.g., the Bill of Rights). See, e.g., *Reid v. Covert*, 354 U.S. 1 (1957), holding that "no agreement with a foreign nation can confer power on the Congress, or on any other branch of Government, which is free from the restraints of the Constitution."

4.  **Executive agreements:**   The Constitution's only reference to international agreements is to the treaty power, the exercise of which, as noted, requires ratification by the Senate. However, the Constitution does not explicitly prohibit the President from entering into international agreements without Senate consent, and presidents have traditionally frequently done so. These unratified agreements are usually called ***"executive agreements."***

   a.  **Status of executive agreements:**   The precise status of such agreements is unclear. It seems settled that they are not *per se* unconstitutional; for instance, if such an agreement is enacted within the scope of an enumerated presidential power, it will surely be upheld. Thus Tribe (pp. 170-71) cites the example of an armistice agreement justified by use of the President's commander-in-chief power.

   b.  **Cannot override congressional act:**   An executive agreement, unlike a treaty, ***cannot override*** a prior act of Congress. Tribe, p. 171.

   c.  **Superior to state law:**   But such an agreement, like a treaty, will have ***priority over conflicting state laws***, because the Constitution as a general principle vests all control over international affairs in the federal government. *Id.*

C.  **Power over foreign affairs:**   Neither Congress nor any other branch of the federal government is explicitly given power over "***foreign affairs***" as such. However, the Supreme Court has always recognized that Congress and the executive branch have power over foreign affairs, even where no enumerated power is applicable. That is, the Court has recognized a "general constitutional principle" that foreign affairs are the proper province of the federal government. Support for this proposition comes from several constitutionally-imposed limitations on state interference with foreign affairs (e.g., the bans on states' making of treaties, and on their laying of import or export duties, both imposed by Article I, §10).

    **1. State action improper:** Thus "all state action, whether or not consistent with current federal foreign policy, that has significant impact on the conduct of American diplomacy is *void* as an unconstitutional infringement upon an exclusively federal sphere of responsibility." Tribe, p. 230.

# IV. OTHER POWERS

    **A. Other federal powers:** It is not profitable to examine in detail all of the constitutionally-enumerated sources of federal authority. However, a brief listing of some of the other sources of federal authority is as follows:

    **B. Congressional powers:** Some of the powers given to *Congress* are:

        **1. Money:** To *coin money*, and to regulate its value (Art. I, §8);

        **2. Bankruptcy:** To establish laws governing *bankruptcy (id.)*;

        **3. Post offices:** To establish *post offices (id.)*;

        **4. Copyrights and patents:** To control the issuance of *copyrights* and *patents (id.)*;

        **5. Federal property:** To govern the District of Columbia, and all other *federal properties (id.)*;

        **6. Immigration and naturalization:** To control *naturalization* (and implicitly, *immigration*) of aliens *(id.)*;

        **7. Civil War Amendments:** To enforce, "by appropriate legislation," the Thirteenth, Fourteenth and Fifteenth Amendments (all arising out of the Civil War). See *infra*, p. 439.

        **8. Constitutional amendments:** To *propose*, by a two-thirds vote, a *constitutional amendment* for ratification by three-fourths of the states (Art. V). (The holding of a constitutional convention is an alternative, but one which has never been used since the Constitution's original ratification.)

    **C. Powers of the executive:** The powers of the *executive branch* will not be reviewed here. However, some of these powers are discussed in the treatment of separation of powers, beginning *infra*, p. 110. See also the discussion of the President's role in the treaty-making process, *supra*, p. 61.

    **D. Judicial powers:** The powers of the federal *judiciary* are spelled out in Article III, §2. These powers, discussion of which is generally reserved for the course in federal courts, include the power to decide:

        1. cases *arising under the Constitution or under federal* laws;

        2. cases involving *ambassadors* and other diplomats;

        3. cases involving *admiralty* and *maritime* issues;

        4. cases in which the *U.S. is a party*;

5.  cases *between two or more states*, between *a state and* citizens of another state, or between *citizens of different states*; and

6.  cases between *a state or its citizens and foreign states* or citizens.

> **Note:** Observe that although all of these types of cases fall within the federal courts' constitutionally-vested power, Congress has the right to "regulate" the jurisdiction of the lower federal courts, and to make "exceptions" to that jurisdiction. This has resulted in a substantial curtailment of the theoretically-available powers of the federal judiciary, as a practical matter. This area is more extensively discussed *supra*, pp. 12-14.

*Quiz Yourself on*

## OTHER NATIONAL POWERS *(ENTIRE CHAPTER)*

8.  Congress has decided that breast implants, even of the less-dangerous saline variety, are undesirable. Congress has therefore placed a tax of $2,000 on any breast implant, to be paid by the surgeon at the time of implantation. The legislative history of the statute shows that Congress' principal purpose was to discourage the use of such implants, and that Congress did not believe the measure would produce very much revenue. In its first year, the Act produced collections of about $1 million. Doc, a surgeon specializing in implants, sues to have the statute declared unconstitutional on the grounds that it is beyond the powers of Congress. Is Doc's suit likely to succeed? If so, state why. _____

9.  Congress, after concluding that the states have lagged behind in educating school children to be tolerant towards homosexuals, enacts a program providing a small subsidy to any public elementary school that conducts a program teaching a better understanding of, and tolerance of, gay people.

    **(a)** Putting aside the commerce power, what constitutional provision best supplies constitutional authority for this statute? _____

    **(b)** A parent whose child is about to receive such instruction sues to have the provision found unconstitutional, on the grounds that it encourages homosexuality and thus detracts from the general welfare of the nation. Assuming that the federal court hearing the case concludes that the measure will probably make the nation worse off than it was before, will this constitutional attack on the statute succeed? _____

10. Congress, alarmed about the dramatic rise in teenage pregnancies, passes the Underage Procreation Act of 1994. That Act requires any person under the age of 17 to obtain a federal permit before becoming pregnant. The permit is granted to any woman who shows that she has received one hour of counselling about the dangers of teen pregnancy from a state-licensed social worker. Violators are to be fined. A 16-year-old woman who wishes to become pregnant files suit to attack the statute's constitutionality on the grounds that it is beyond Congress' enumerated powers. The federal government defends the statute on the grounds that it is a proper exercise of Congress' power to regulate for the "general welfare." Will the plaintiff's attack on the statute succeed? (Ignore any issues relating to a woman's constitutional right to privacy or right to become pregnant. Assume that the Court decides that nothing in the activity being regulated affects interstate commerce.) _____

*Answers*

8.  **No.** The fact that the principal purpose of a tax is regulatory rather than revenue-raising does not pose a

constitutional problem today. So long as the tax produces at least non-trivial revenue, and does not run afoul of any explicit constitutional limitation on the taxing power (e.g., the prohibition on export duties in Art. I, Section 9), the tax will be found to be within Congress' general power to "lay and collect taxes. ... " Art. I, Section 8.

9. **(a) The spending power.** Art. I, Section 8 gives Congress power to "lay and collect Taxes ... to pay the Debts and provide for the ... general Welfare of the United States. ... " This language includes the "spending" power, although the word "spend" is not used.

**(b) No.** It is true that the spending power of Art. 1, Section 8 is phrased specifically in terms of providing for the "general welfare" of the nation. However, the requirement that a federal spending program be for the "general welfare" has almost no bite at present — certainly, the Court is not entitled to substitute its own judgment of what would be "best" in lieu of Congress'.

10. **Yes.** There is *no federal "police power."* That is, Congress does not have the right to *regulate "for the general welfare."* Congress' only powers regarding the general welfare are the right to tax and to spend to achieve that welfare. Since nothing in the statute provides for either a tax or an expenditure, the statute is not supported by the taxing and spending power or any other enumerated power. Normally, a federal regulatory scheme could be supported by the commerce power (since the Court takes an extremely expansive view of what activity can be found to "affect commerce"), but the facts tell us to ignore the commerce power here.

---

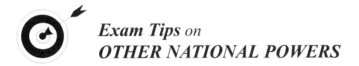

*Exam Tips on*
**OTHER NATIONAL POWERS**

Here are some of the ways issues discussed in this chapter can appear on exams:

☞ Professors sometimes test on the blurry line between taxing and regulation. Your fact pattern might give you a *tax* that is principally for *regulatory purposes*. If so, you can rely on the taxation power as an independent source of congressional power (distinct from the Commerce Clause, for instance) — so long as the tax produces at least a non-trivial amount of revenue, and its regulatory scheme seems *rationally related* to the collection of the tax itself, it's a valid exercise of the tax power.

☞ Occasionally, you will be tested on the procedural requirements for a *treaty*. Remember that the President may propose a treaty, but it does not become effective until *ratified* by two-thirds of the Senate.

&#9759; Also, keep in mind that even where the President cannot get a treaty ratified, the President may create an international agreement as an *"Executive Agreement."* (An Executive Agreement is essentially an agreement entered into between the President and some other country but not ratified by the Senate.) An Executive Agreement can't override a prior act of Congress, but is superior to state law.

&#9759; Your fact pattern may involve *foreign affairs* without any war and without any treaty. In this situation, you should pose the question whether the action falls within the enumerated powers. The answer, typically, is that there is no power over foreign affairs expressly given to either the President or the Congress, but the Court has recognized an implicit power of both branches over this domain. For instance, your fact pattern might involve an attempt by Congress to prevent Americans from travelling abroad, to prevent aliens from visiting this country, or some other aspect of foreign affairs not falling within a specifically-enumerated power.

☛ Be on the lookout for questions involving congressional regulation of the ***District of Columbia***. Congress has a special enumerated power to govern the District of Columbia, so it may regulate there in purely local matters (which would not fall, say, within the commerce power).

☛ Similarly, remember that Congress can govern all ***federal property***. Fact patterns frequently involve national parks, national monuments, military bases, and other types of federal property. In all of these areas, Congress has complete regulatory power, so you do not need to worry about whether the activity being regulated falls within the commerce power or any other general congressional power.

CHAPTER 6

# TWO LIMITS ON STATE POWER: THE COMMERCE CLAUSE AND CONGRESSIONAL ACTION

*ChapterScope*

This Chapter examines two federalism-based limits on state and local power: (1) the so-called "dormant" Commerce Clause; and (2) ways in which Congress may block the states from legislating in particular areas. The most important concepts in this Chapter are:

- **Dormant Commerce Clause:** The *mere existence* of the federal commerce power *restricts the states* from *discriminating against*, or *unduly burdening*, interstate commerce. This restriction is called the "dormant Commerce Clause."

  - **Three part test:** A state regulation which affects interstate commerce must satisfy *each* of the following three requirements in order to avoid violating the dormant Commerce Clause:

    - The regulation must pursue a *legitimate state end;*

    - The regulation must be *rationally related* to that legitimate state end; and

    - The regulatory *burden* imposed by the state on interstate commerce must be *outweighed* by the state's interest in enforcing its regulation.

  - **Intentional discrimination:** Courts especially frown on *intentional discrimination* against out-of-staters. If the state is promoting its residents' own economic interests, this will not be a legitimate state objective, so the regulation will almost always be found to violate the Commerce Clause.

  - **Market participant exception:** There is one key *exception* to the dormant Commerce Clause rules: if the state acts as a *market participant*, it *may* favor local over out-of-state interests.

- **Preemption:** Congress can *preempt* the states from affecting commerce. There are two ways it can do this:

  - **Conflict:** First, the congressional statute and the state action may be in *actual conflict*. If so, the state regulation is automatically invalid.

  - **Federal occupation of field:** Congress may also pre-empt state regulation not because there is an actual conflict between what Congress does and what the states do, but because Congress is found to have made the decision to *occupy the entire field*.

  - **Consent by Congress:** Conversely, Congress may *consent* to state action that would otherwise violate the Commerce Clause. Congress may even allow a state to discriminate against out-of-staters.

- **The Supremacy Clause:** Under the *"Supremacy Clause"* of the Constitution, the Constitution and federal laws *take priority* over any conflicting state law.

## I.   THE DORMANT COMMERCE CLAUSE — REGULATION

**A. Negative implications of federal power:**   Prior chapters of this book have been devoted to limitations on the federal powers. We turn now to limitations on *state power* embodied in the Constitution.

   **1. Express limits:**   Some limitations on state action are explicitly set forth in the Constitution; for instance, Article I, §9 flatly prohibits any state from imposing an export duty.

   **2. Implied limits:**   With respect to most areas in which the Constitution gives the federal government authority, however, that document does not say anything about whether the states may exercise similar power in the area. For instance, does the Constitution's grant to Congress of the power to issue patents mean that a state cannot give a different kind of protection to inventors?

   **a. No general rule:**   The "negative implications" to be drawn from a constitutional grant of power to Congress have generally been resolved by the Supreme Court on an *area-by-area basis*. Thus a finding of no preemption in the patent context would not necessarily mean the same finding in, say, the bankruptcy area.

**B. Negative implications of the Commerce Clause:**   There is only one power whose grant in the Constitution has given rise to substantial litigation concerning states' powers: this is the Commerce Clause. The issue which has been posed over and over again in the so-called *"dormant* Commerce Clause" cases is: Does the mere fact that the Constitution gives Congress the power to regulate interstate commerce *prevent a state* from taking a particular action which affects interstate commerce, assuming that Congress has not actually exercised its power in the subject area in question (so that no Supremacy-Clause questions are involved)? In other words, the controversy in the dormant Commerce Clause cases focuses not on what Congress *has* done, but on what it *might* have done.

   **1. No simple test:**   As we shall see, no easy answer or test for solving this question has been devised.

**C. Traditional approach:**   The early Supreme Court could have adopted either of two extreme views on the significance of the dormant Commerce Clause for state regulation.

   **1. Great freedom to states:**   It could have held that where Congress has remained silent as to a particular subject matter, the states are completely free to regulate, no matter what the burden on or discrimination against interstate commerce.

   **2. Exclusive federal terrain:**   Alternatively, the Court could have held that Congress' power to regulate interstate commerce is *exclusive*, so that even if Congress has chosen not to act in a certain area affecting interstate commerce, the states are not entitled to act.

   **3. Middle ground:**   But rather than adopting either of these two extreme positions, the Court has always chosen something of a *middle ground*, though the precise nature of that middle position has varied through the years. Essentially, the Court's approach has always been to *weigh* the *state interest in regulating its local affairs* against the *national interest* in *uniformity* and in an *integrated national economy.*

   **4. Congress has ultimate say:**   Because the limitations on state authority imposed by the dormant Commerce Clause are not explicitly stated in the Constitution, but are rather derived by negative implication, limitations on state commerce-related conduct imposed by the Court *may always be reversed by Congress.*

    **a. States given greater freedom:** Thus if the Court holds that a particular type of state action unduly burdens interstate commerce, Congress may pass a law explicitly allowing the state to interfere with commerce in this manner.

    **b. Stricter standard:** Conversely, if the Court holds that a particular type of state action, although it affects interstate commerce, does not burden it unduly, Congress may reverse this ruling either by stating that it intends to *preempt the entire field* to which the state regulation relates, or by passing a statute which *explicitly conflicts* with the state rule.

    **c. Summary of Court's role:** To put it another way, the Supreme Court's role in this area is limited to *interpreting congressional silence*. See Tribe, p. 404.

**D. Early interpretations:** From its earliest days, the Supreme Court has given great weight to the purposes behind the Commerce Clause: the creation and nurturing of a *common market* among the states, and the *abolition of trade barriers.*

    **1. Failure of Articles of Confederation:** The pre-Constitution *Articles of Confederation* had failed largely because the states fought destructive *trade wars* against each other. Tribe, p. 404. These trade wars arose principally from the fact that state governments were too responsive to local economic interests — each state government tended to pursue the interests of its own constituents, at the expense of citizens of other states. *Id.*

    **2. Prevention of economic balkanization:** Therefore, under the Constitution, the power of the federal judiciary, interpreting the Commerce Clause, had to be used to prevent this *"economic balkanization."*

    **3. Congress' silence:** Also, the Supreme Court has always well recognized that the fact that Congress has not chosen to speak out in a particular area does not mean that it tacitly approves of state regulation of that area. Congress is simply too busy, with too many pressing matters on its legislative docket, for there to be any assurance that state regulations which burden or discriminate against interstate commerce will be overturned by congressional action. Tribe, p. 402. Therefore, the Supreme Court has always been intensely conscious of its own obligation to *keep the channels of interstate commerce free of state-originated impediments.*

    **4. *Gibbons v. Ogden:*** The first Supreme Court case interpreting the meaning of congressional silence in a commerce context was *Gibbons v. Ogden*, 22 U.S. (9 Wheat.) 1 (1824). Other aspects of this case, the opinion in which was written by Chief Justice Marshall, are discussed *supra*, p. 28.

        **a. Factual summary:** To summarize briefly the facts, New York had granted an exclusive steamboat operating license which was ultimately owned by Ogden. Gibbons obtained a federal license to operate his vessel between New York and New Jersey, but was enjoined by the New York courts from sailing it in New York waters because of Ogden's monopoly. Gibbons argued that the New York monopoly violated the federal commerce power.

        **b. Holding:** After giving a broad definition of "commerce" (see *supra*, p. 28), Marshall went on to hold that the New York monopoly was invalid because it *conflicted with the federal commerce power.* He took two steps to reach this conclusion:

i. **Meaning of congressional silence:** Gibbons' counsel had argued that the federal commerce power was *exclusive*; that is, that the states had no right to take any action which affected interstate commerce. Marshall conceded that there was "great force" in this argument, and that he was "not satisfied that it has been refuted." However, he avoided an explicit ruling on the argument, and assumed, without deciding, that the states could regulate commerce in a particular way if there was no actual conflict between the state regulation and an act of Congress.

ii. **Actual conflict:** But then, Marshall found that there was indeed an *actual conflict* between New York's action and a law of Congress: the federal licensing law, in Marshall's view, conflicted with the New York monopoly, and the New York monopoly had to fall under the *Supremacy Clause.*

iii. **Effect of silence not adjudicated:** Thus Marshall never made any dispositive holding in *Gibbons* about the effect of congressional silence on the States' regulatory powers.

5. **State "police power" allowed:** But a few years after *Gibbons*, Marshall appeared to concede that a state could sometimes affect interstate commerce as an incidental consequence of its exercise of its "police powers." In *Willson v. The Black Bird Creek Marsh Co.*, 27 U.S. (2 Pet.) 244 (1829), Delaware authorized the construction of a dam on a creek which flowed into the Delaware River. Because the dam blocked navigation of the creek, the owners of a federally-licensed ship broke the dam in order to pass through the creek, and were sued by the dam's owners.

a. **Holding:** Marshall held in favor of the dam company. First, he found that there was no actual conflict between Delaware's permitting the dam and any act of Congress. (Observe that Marshall seemed to retreat from the view he expressed in *Gibbons*, that congressional licensing of a vessel constituted congressional action which was specifically in conflict with a state's attempt to regulate the use of its waterways.) Then, he found that Delaware's action was not "repugnant to the power to regulate commerce in its dormant state."

i. **Rationale:** In so concluding, Marshall apparently reasoned that Delaware was not acting for the *purpose* of regulating interstate commerce, but rather, was attempting to protect the *health* of nearby inhabitants, and to increase the value of property adjoining the creek. Marshall implied, though he did not explicitly state, that a state's attempt to regulate matters of health or local property concerns would normally not be construed as interfering with the dormant federal commerce power.

ii. **Non-discriminatory:** Notice that Delaware's action in allowing the dam to be built was *not discriminatory* against interstate commerce; that is, both vessels travelling solely in intrastate traffic, as well as those engaged in interstate voyages, were equally barred from navigating the dammed-up creek. Absence of discrimination against interstate commerce has continued to be an important factor in those cases in which the Court has held that state regulation is permissible even though it affects interstate commerce.

E. **Rise of the "local" vs. "national" distinction:** The *Black Bird Creek* case, and other cases which followed it, turned mainly on the distinction between state regulation which principally governed interstate commerce (which was not allowed, even where Congress was silent) and state regulations which were construed to be "police power" regulations and therefore upheld (e.g., health and safety measures). However, the "regulation of commerce" and "police power" labels were more conclusory than analytical; if the Court wished to uphold the regulation, it termed it a "police power" one. See Tribe, p. 406.

1. **The *Cooley* case:** But in 1851, the Court embarked on a new way of looking at the dormant Commerce Clause problem, a view which continues to have great significance at present. Instead of focusing on whether the state was regulating commerce or using its "police powers," the Court focused on ***whether the subject matter being regulated was "local" or "national."*** In *Cooley v. Board of Wardens of the Port of Philadelphia*, 53 U.S. (12 How.) 299 (1851), the Court affirmed a Pennsylvania law which required ships entering or leaving the port of Philadelphia to hire a local pilot.

   a. **"Local" vs. "national" problem:** The Court refused to hold either that Congress had an exclusive right to make regulations affecting interstate commerce, or that the states had a complete right to regulate interstate commerce in areas where Congress had remained silent. Instead, ***some but not all*** state regulation affecting interstate commerce was permissible. The states were free, the *Cooley* Court held, to regulate those aspects of interstate commerce that were of ***such a local nature as to require different treatment from state to state***. But the states could not regulate aspects of interstate commerce which, because of their nature, required a ***uniform national treatment*** (which only Congress could provide).

   b. **Application to facts of *Cooley*:** On the facts of *Cooley* itself, the Court found Pennsylvania's regulation was permissible, because pilotage in local harbors was a subject appropriate for local control (at least if that local control did not conflict with an explicit congressional action). In reaching this conclusion, the Court relied on a congressional statute adopted many years previously allowing pilotage to be regulated by the states.

2. **Aftermath of *Cooley*:** There were at least two major shortcomings to the *Cooley* doctrine. First, it was not at all easy to distinguish between those "subjects" that required uniform national regulation, and those that needed diverse local regulation. Secondly, and probably more importantly, the *Cooley* test, since it looked solely to the "subject" being regulated, did not consider how extensively the states' regulation ***impacted*** interstate commerce.

   a. **Significance of impact:** To remedy this second shortcoming, in post-*Cooley* years, the Court looked closely at the actual impact the state regulation had on interstate commerce. "***What the states did***, and ***not what subject they did it to***, came to be seen as the crucial question in deciding whether state action was compatible with the [C]ommerce [C]lause." Tribe, p. 408.

      i. **"Direct" vs. "indirect" impact:** In taking impact into account, the Court distinguished between "***direct***" and "***indirect***" impact on interstate commerce; a state regulation having direct impact on interstate commerce was not acceptable (even though Congress remained silent), but one having only an indirect impact was permissible.

   b. **Legacy of *Cooley*:** But during the time of this "direct" vs. "indirect" test, and up through to the present, the basic policy behind *Cooley* has remained in effect; the dormant Commerce Clause blocks ***some but not all*** state regulations which affect interstate commerce, and the resolution of particular cases turns on, roughly speaking, a balancing between the state interest in regulating local affairs and the national interest in uniformity. Tribe, p. 407.

**F. Modern approach:** The distinction between "direct" and "indirect" effects upon interstate commerce has proven to be no more satisfactory than the "effect on commerce" vs. "police power" distinction. In recent years, the Supreme Court has shifted to a more complex series of tests. A state regulation which affects interstate commerce must meet *each* of the following requirements in order to be upheld:

1.   the regulation must pursue a *legitimate state end;*

2.   the regulation must be *rationally related* to that legitimate end; and

3.   the regulatory *burden* imposed by the state on interstate commerce, and any *discrimination* against interstate commerce, must be *outweighed* by the state's interest in enforcing its regulation. See Tribe, p. 408.

**G. Application of the test:** While these three requirements are somewhat vague, and the Court has tended to decide dormant Commerce Clause cases on very much of a case-by-case basis, there are at least some general observations that can be made about how the Court will apply each of the three tests:

1.   **Meaning of "legitimate state end":** The Court has sharply distinguished between measures that are designed for promotion of health, safety and welfare objectives, on the one hand, and those that are designed for furtherance of *economic benefits*, on the other.

     a.   **Health, safety and welfare:** If the state is acting to further health, safety or "general welfare" objectives, the Court is quite likely to hold that these objectives constitute "legitimate state ends." This is really the "police power" rationale which has been used by the Court ever since the *Black Bird Creek* case (*supra*, p. 70). (However, the Court will not accept at face value a state's contention that it is acting for these purposes, if there is substantial evidence that the state's real purpose is for economic advantage.)

     b.   **Economic advantage:** The Court is *much more skeptical* of a state regulatory scheme where the state's objective is to promote the *economic interests* of its *own residents*. Protection of a state's economic interests is generally *not considered to be a legitimate state objective*, where pursuit of that objective materially affects interstate commerce.

2.   **Rational means to end:** The second requirement, that the means used have a *rational relation* to the (legitimate) end, usually has *less "bite"* than the first requirement. The Court has been fairly careful not to substitute its judgment for that of the legislature in determining whether the regulation is a good way of attaining the end. A mere "rational relation" between means and end is *all* that is required; it is *not* required that the means used be the *best* way of achieving that end, or the way which least affects interstate commerce.

     a.   **Deference to legislative fact finding:** In judging whether there is a requisite "rational relation," the Court will also give *due deference to any "facts" found by the state legislature*; that is, the Court will not conduct its own *de novo* inquiry into the facts.

**b. Similarity to review of Congress' actions:** In general, the Court's role is similar to the one it follows when evaluating whether an act of Congress falls within the commerce power (*supra*, p. 33).

3. **Balancing test:** Once the first two tests (legitimate end, and rationally-related means) have been met, the Court generally performs a rough *"balancing" test*, but one skewed towards a finding of constitutionality. "Where the statute regulates even-handedly to effectuate a legitimate local public interest, and its effects on interstate commerce are only incidental, it will be upheld unless the burden imposed on such commerce is *clearly excessive* in relation to the putative local benefits." *Pike v. Bruce Church, Inc.*, 397 U.S. 137 (1970). Thus in the case of legislation that is non-discriminatory (even if somewhat burdensome to interstate commerce), the state regulation achieves a *presumption of constitutionality*. But this presumption can be overcome by a *clear showing* that the national interest in uniformity or in free commerce outweighs the state benefit.

   a. **Less-restrictive alternatives:** In performing this balancing test, the Court has sometimes considered not only the objectives which the state is pursuing, but also the *necessity of the means* which the state has used to achieve this objective: if the objective could have been achieved by means *less burdensome* (or less discriminatory) to interstate commerce, the Court is more likely to find that the national interest in free commerce outweighs the state's interest. See Tribe, pp. 426-27.

      i. ***Dean Milk* case:** For instance, in *Dean Milk Co. v. City of Madison*, 340 U.S. 349 (1951) (discussed *infra*, p. 77), local regulations preventing importation of milk were struck down. Even though the state's objective (protection of residents against adulterated milk) was permissible, and the regulatory scheme (prohibiting importation so that only regularly-inspected local plants could sell milk) was rationally related to that objective, the safety objective could have been achieved by less burdensome means (e.g., sending of inspectors to out-of-state pasteurization plants to make quality checks, at the out-of-state producers' expense).

   b. **"Local" vs. "national" subject matter:** Recall the "local" vs. "national" distinction made by the *Cooley* case (*supra*, pp. 71-71). Although this distinction is no longer explicitly made in Supreme Court cases, it is implicit in the balancing process: if the matter being regulated is overwhelmingly of local concern, it is much more likely that the state interest in controlling its own affairs will be found to outweigh the national interest in uniformity and free commerce. Tribe. p. 437.

4. **Scope of following discussion:** The remainder of our treatment of state regulation and the dormant Commerce Clause is organized according to the type of regulation being pursued by the state. Five major subject areas are considered: (1) regulation of transportation; (2) regulation of incoming trade; (3) regulation of outgoing trade (including exportation of scarce resources); (4) attempts to compel out-of-staters to perform business activities within the state; and (5) regulation of the environment.

H. **Regulation of transportation:** When states have regulated the *instrumentalities* of interstate commerce (generally, *railroads* and *highways*), they have usually done so in the name of public safety objectives, rather than to benefit local economic interests. Therefore, the existence of a legitimate state objective is generally not in doubt, and the Supreme Court's scrutiny of such measures has usually focused on the second and third of the tests listed above (i.e., rational relation between the means and the safety objective, and balancing benefit to the state against burden on commerce).

1.  **Absence of discrimination as factor:**  The Court has been much more likely to find that a transportation regulation does not violate the dormant Commerce Clause where the evidence is that it is *not discriminatory* against interstate commerce, either in *intent* or in *effect*. That is, even though the measure may create burdens on interstate commerce, if *similar burdens are created on intrastate activities*, the Court is likely to take the position that in-state political processes supply a sufficient check against abuse.

    a.  *Barnwell* **case:**  For instance, in *South Carolina State Highway Dept. v. Barnwell Bros., Inc.*, 303 U.S. 177 (1938), South Carolina prohibited the use on state highways of trucks wider than 90 inches or weighing more than 20,000 pounds. There was clear evidence that the vast majority of trucks used in interstate commerce exceeded one or both of these limitations, so the regulation clearly burdened interstate commerce.

        i.  **Measure upheld in** *Barnwell*:  Yet the Supreme Court, in an opinion by Justice (later Chief Justice) Stone, *upheld the regulation* against Commerce Clause attack. The Court stressed that the regulations were *applicable to interstate and intrastate traffic alike*, and "[t]he fact that they affect alike shippers in interstate and intrastate commerce in large number within as well as without the state is a *safeguard against their abuse*. ... "

2.  **Balancing test:**  Even where a transportation regulation pursues a legitimate state objective (e.g., public safety) in a rational manner, the Court will usually apply a *balancing test*, weighing the benefit to the state from the regulation against the burdens it places on interstate commerce. However, the Court has been reluctant to substitute its judgment for that of state legislatures; therefore, it has usually tried to perform this "balancing" in a way that is fairly deferential to state policies.

    a.  **Slight safety improvement:**  Thus the balance has generally been struck in favor of interstate commerce interests and against state safety interests only where the regulation's contribution to safety is *so marginal* or *so speculative* that there is little doubt in the Court's mind that the safety interest is outweighed by the burdens on commerce.

3.  **Look for discrimination before doing balancing test:**  A plaintiff attacking a transportation regulation on Commerce Clause grounds has a far greater chance of prevailing by showing *discrimination* against out-of-staters than by showing merely that the scheme's burdens outweigh its benefits. It seems probable that a majority of the present Supreme Court is now *unwilling* to use balancing, and will automatically *uphold* a transportation regulation, if the safety interests asserted by the state are more than "slight" or "problematic." Conversely, the Supreme Court remains very quick to strike down any transportation regulation that seems to the Court to be motivated by *discriminatory* or protectionist impulses. See, e.g., *Kassel v. Consolidated Freightways Corp.*, 450 U.S. 662 (1981) (Iowa statute prohibiting 65-foot-long trucks is struck down, but at most four members of the Court seem to use a balancing test, and the remainder decide the case based on whether there is a clear discriminatory purpose).

4.  **Cumulative and contradictory burdens:**  A particular regulation, even though it may seem to be non-discriminatory and non-burdensome when viewed in isolation, may be part of a discriminatory or burdensome *mass* of regulations imposed by *many states*. This may occur either because many states impose regulations that *contradict* each other, or

even because many states impose regulations that are not contradictory, but that become burdensome if compliance with all is required. Such a set of multiple regulations is by nature discriminatory in effect against interstate commerce, since only those enterprises that do business in many states will suffer from this problem. The problem is especially likely to occur in the case of regulation of interstate transport.

a. **Actual conflict:** When an actual *conflict* between the regulations of two or more states is shown, the Court is likely to strike down at least one of the conflicting rules, on the grounds that the need for *national uniformity* outweighs the individual state's interest in regulating its own highways, railroads, etc.

**Example:** An Illinois statute requires trucks operating in that state to be equipped with contoured rear-fender mudguards. At least 45 other states which have mudguard requirements permit a straight, rather than contoured, mudguard, and one state (Arkansas) explicitly requires a straight mudguard. Thus a particular truck could not be operated in both Arkansas and Illinois (at least without re-welding a new mudguard onto it each time).

*Held*, the Illinois statute violates the dormant Commerce Clause. "This is one of those cases — few in number — where local safety measures that are nondiscriminatory place an unconstitutional burden on interstate commerce." If the Illinois mudguard were so clearly superior in safety to the straight mudguard, it might be the straight-mudguard regulations which would have to give way; but the safety advantage of the Illinois curved mudguard is far from clear. Therefore, it is Illinois which must conform. *Bibb v. Navajo Freight Lines, Inc.*, 359 U.S. 520 (1959).

b. **Cumulative burden:** *Bibb* involved, at least in part, an actual conflict between the regulations of two states. But even where no actual conflict exists, it may be the case that the differing regulations of two or more states may place a large *cumulative burden* on interstate commerce. In this situation, the Court is likely to strike down one or more of the measures.

**Example:** Suppose that many states each impose different limits on the length of trains. The train-length limits are not contradictory; a railroad can simply follow the shortest limit, and thus operate in all states with the same length trains. However, such national compliance with the rule of the most restrictive state would probably be held to be a violation of the Commerce Clause, because it gives the most restrictive state authority beyond its own borders. See *Southern Pacific Co. v. Arizona*, 325 U.S. 761 (1945), so holding.

5. **Discriminatory intent or effect:** It is vital to remember that, in any regulation of transportation (or other aspect of commerce), the existence of an *intent to discriminate* against interstate commerce, or even an unintended discriminatory effect, will make it dramatically more likely that the Court will strike the measure as violating the dormant Commerce Clause. See, e.g., *Kassel v. Consolidated Freightways Corp.*, *supra* p. 74.

I. **State barriers to incoming trade:** Many cases have involved state regulations which, either intentionally or otherwise, place *barriers upon the importing of goods into the state*. As a general rule, the test to which these regulations will be subjected depends on the nature of the state interest being served:

1. **Protection of economy:**   If the purpose of the regulation is to ***protect in-state producers*** from competing out-of-state commodities, or otherwise to ***strengthen the local economy***, the Court will generally ***strike the measure***, without even inquiring whether the benefit to the state outweighs the national interest in free commerce. N&R, pp. 295-296. Protection of local economic interest is thus viewed as an "illegitimate" aim, so that Test One of the three tests described *supra*, p. 72, is failed, and the inquiry goes no further.

   a. **Small size of discrimination irrelevant:**   Even if the discrimination against out-of-state commodities is ***small***, the Court will strike it down if it is motivated by a desire to protect in-state interests — the ***mere fact*** of discrimination, not the ***magnitude*** of it, is what counts.

2. **Health and safety regulations:**   If, however, the state is in good faith pursuing ***health*** or ***safety*** objectives, then the Court will generally balance the benefit to the state against the burdens to interstate commerce. In conducting this balancing test, the degree to which the regulation has a discriminatory effect (even though an unintended one), and the extent to which less burdensome or less discriminatory alternatives are available, will be considered. *Id.* at 231.

3. ***Baldwin* case:**   The classic illustration of an impermissible protection of local economic interests at the expense of interstate commerce is ***Baldwin v. G.A.F. Seelig, Inc.***, 294 U.S. 511 (1935).

   a. **Facts of *Baldwin:***   *Baldwin* involved a New York attempt to set minimum prices to be paid by New York milk dealers to New York milk producers. The statute also prohibited retail sales in New York of out-of-state milk, if the milk had been purchased at a lower price than the one set for purchases within New York. The avowed purpose of the statute was to make sure that New York's farmers could earn an adequate income.

   b. **Act stricken:**   The act was held unconstitutional by the Supreme Court, in an opinion by Justice Cardozo. The statute "set a barrier to traffic between one state and another as effective as if custom duties, equal to the price differential, had been laid upon the [goods]."

      i. **Danger of interstate rivalries:**   Cardozo's opinion observed that "[i]f New York, in order to promote the economic welfare of her farmers, may guard them against competition with the cheaper prices of Vermont, the door has been opened to rivalries and reprisals that were meant to be averted by subjecting commerce between the states to the power of the nation. … [The Constitution] was framed upon the theory that ***the peoples of the several states must sink or swim together. … ***"

   c. **No political check:**   Observe that the situation in *Baldwin* was one of those where ***only*** out-of-staters were burdened (at least directly). Thus the possibility of abuse was heightened by the fact that no strong constituency within New York was likely to fight against the regulation. (It is true that consumers might ultimately have ended up being burdened, by having to pay higher prices, but this was probably an indirect, camouflaged, effect. See N&R, p. 295-296.)

4. **Valid health objective not sufficient:**   The New York regulation in *Baldwin, supra,* was clearly designed to foster the purely economic interests of New York residents. The Court is at least somewhat more sympathetic where the state regulation of incoming goods, while it burdens interstate commerce, is in good faith designed to protect the ***safety or***

*health* of residents. But even in the case of such safety or health regulations, the Court will either implicitly or explicitly perform a "***balancing test,***" weighing the state's interest in its regulatory scheme against the national interest in unburdened, free-flowing interstate commerce. A crucial part of this balancing is often whether there are ***less burdensome alternatives*** which the state might have adopted.

a. **The *Dean Milk* case:** Thus in ***Dean Milk Co. v. Madison***, 340 U.S. 349 (1951), the city of Madison, Wisconsin made it unlawful to sell any milk that had not been processed and bottled within five miles of the city. The city claimed (perhaps correctly) that the measure was not intended to discriminate against out-of-state milk producers, but was rather designed to permit inspection of pasteurization quality control so as to guard against adulterated milk. The regulation was attacked by an Illinois corporation which distributed milk in both Illinois and Wisconsin.

b. **Statute stricken:** The Supreme Court agreed that the Madison regulation unduly burdened interstate commerce. The Court conceded that the regulation might have been motivated by *bona fide* safety and health concerns. But the regulation nonetheless discriminated against interstate commerce (in the sense of a discriminatory ***effect***). Nor did the fact that companies within Wisconsin, but more than five miles from Madison, were also discriminated against save the regulation from unduly burdening commerce, in the Court's view.

c. **Reasonable non-discriminatory alternatives:** The real crux of the Court's holding in *Dean Milk* was that ***reasonable non-discriminatory alternatives***, which would have protected the local interest in unadulterated milk, ***could have been implemented***. For instance, Madison could have sent its inspectors to out-of-state plants, and could have passed the cost onto the producers. Alternatively, Madison could have agreed to be bound by the standards of neighboring areas, provided that those standards were at least as high as Madison's own.

d. **Dissent:** Three Justices dissented, principally on the grounds that a good faith effort to promote local safety and health objectives should not be stricken merely because the Court believes that some less-burdensome alternative could produce as good a result.

5. **Intentional discrimination (the *Washington Apple* case):** Although the Court has occasionally stricken barriers to incoming trade that are not enacted for discriminatory purposes (e.g., the *Dean Milk* case), the Court is, as noted, much more likely to strike down a statute whose clear purpose is to ***favor local economic interests*** by discriminating against out-of-state interests. This is what really happened, for instance, in *Hunt v. Washington Apple Advertising Commission*, 432 U.S. 333 (1977).

a. **Facts of *Hunt*:** North Carolina required that all closed containers of apples shipped into or sold within the state bear the applicable U.S. grade or no grade at all. A group of Washington state apple growers attacked the North Carolina statute, since it prohibited the display in North Carolina of Washington's stringently-policed apple grades. The Washington manufacturers had to either obliterate the printed labels on containers shipped to North Carolina, or repack apples bound for North Carolina in special containers.

b. **Holding:** The Court found that the North Carolina statute unconstitutionally burdened interstate commerce. More significantly, it also ***discriminated*** against Washington growers, since it raised the costs of doing business for Washington producers but not North Carolina ones; Washington growers had to repack their apples or obliterate their labels, whereas North Carolina growers were unaffected. Furthermore, whereas North Carolina had no grading requirements at all, Washington state had very strict ones; the North Carolina statute hurt Washington by stripping from it the competitive advantages it had earned through its rigorous and well-known inspection and grading system.

    **i.  Intentional:** The Court attached substantial weight to the fact that the North Carolina scheme was apparently ***intentionally*** discriminatory. There was evidence that it was the North Carolina apple growers who were responsible for the passage of the statute. Also, the state's declared purpose for the statute (to safeguard consumers against fraud) was suspect, since: (1) the statute applied only to the labels of closed shipping containers, and retail sales are generally not made while the apples are still in their shipping containers; and (2) the state permitted the sale of apples with no grading at all.

**6.  Discrimination by city against out-of-towners:** Suppose a ***city*** or ***county*** tries to protect its own local economic interests by discriminating not only against out-of-***state*** producers, but also out-of-town producers in the ***same state***. Is it open to the city/county to argue, "The fact that we discriminate against other in-state but non-local producers shows we're not discriminating against interstate commerce"? The short answer is ***"no"***: if the locality is protecting its own local interests at the expense of out-of-staters, the protectionism is not saved by the fact that it also comes at the expense of in-staters who are not local.

**7.  Facially neutral statutes and the meaning of "discrimination" (*Exxon v. Maryland*):** A statute which is evenhanded on its face may nonetheless turn out to be ***disproportionately burdensome*** to some or all out-of-state businesses. Where this disproportionate impact is truly ***accidental***, and does not directly derive from the fact that the burdened firms are out-of-staters, the Court will normally ***uphold*** the statute. This is what happened in ***Exxon Corp. v. Governor of Maryland***, 437 U.S. 117 (1978).

    **a.  Facts of *Exxon* case:** Maryland passed a law prohibiting oil producers or refiners from operating retail gas stations in Maryland. The law was enacted because of evidence that gas stations operated by producers and refiners had received preferential treatment during the 1973 oil shortage. Since no gas is produced or refined in Maryland, the rule against vertically-integrated operations ***affected out-of-state companies exclusively.*** Conversely, the vast majority (but not all) of the non-integrated retailers, who were not harmed and were probably helped by the statute, were in-state business people.

        **i.  Statute attacked:** Exxon and several other out-of-state integrated oil companies sued. They made a three-pronged Commerce Clause argument: (1) that the measure impermissibly discriminated against interstate commerce; (2) that the measure unduly burdened such commerce; and (3) that because of the nationwide nature of oil marketing, only the federal government may regulate retail gas sales.

    **b.  Statute upheld:** The Court upheld the statute against each of these attacks.

        **i.  No discrimination:** First, the opinion (by Justice Stevens) held that the statute did not discriminate against interstate commerce. Most significantly, not all out-of-state companies were affected by the statute; Sears Roebuck, for instance, was an out-of-state company which was selling gas at retail within Maryland, yet was not involved in refining it and was therefore not affected by the statute. The mere fact that the entire burden of the statute fell on *some* out-of-state companies was insufficient to establish that "interstate commerce" was discriminated against.

    ii. **Not burdened:** Similarly, the Court found that interstate commerce was not impermissibly burdened by the statute. The opinion conceded that the statute might cause sales volume to shift from refiner-operated stations to independent dealers. But, the Court held, the Commerce Clause "protects the interstate market, not particular interstate firms, from prohibitive or burdensome regulation." Furthermore, the Court noted, in all probability the same percentage of gasoline would come from out-of-state suppliers after the statute as before it (i.e., 100%), so that the flow of goods in the interstate market would not be decreased.

    iii. **Not preempted:** Finally, the Court quickly dismissed the contention that because the market for gasoline is nationwide, no state may regulate its retail marketing. The dormant Commerce Clause may preempt an entire field from state regulation only when *lack of national uniformity* would impede the flow of interstate goods. What the plaintiffs were complaining of here was not a lack of uniformity, but rather that many or all of the states would pass exactly the sort of divestiture law that Maryland did. Thus the problem was not one of national uniformity.

  **8.** **Personal mobility:** Commerce Clause analysis has also been used to strike down state limits on *individuals'* ability to *migrate* from state to state. Thus in *Edwards v. California*, 314 U.S. 160 (1941), the Court invalidated a law making it a misdemeanor to bring into California an indigent non-resident. (The law was aimed at stemming the flow of "Okies" during the Dust Bowl years.) A majority found that the law was an unconstitutional burden on commerce. (Four Justices concurred, but on the basis of the Privileges and Immunities Clause of the Fourteenth Amendment, discussed *infra*, p. 382).

**J.** **State barriers to outgoing trade:** Another important group of Commerce Clause cases involves attempts by a state to regulate or restrict the *export* to other states of agricultural products, scarce natural resources, or other commodities. The cases in this area are hard to reconcile. However, the following general observations may be made:

  **1.** **"Local" vs. "national" subject:** The *Cooley* distinction (*supra*, pp. 71-71) between subject areas of primarily *"local"* concern and "national" concern continues to be of importance in the export area. If the subject matter being regulated is of *primarily local concern*, and the effect on interstate commerce is *incidental*, the regulation is fairly likely to be sustained, even if it is motivated by local economic concerns rather than public safety and health purposes. However, all of this assumes that the regulation does *not discriminate*, in either purpose or effect, against interstate commerce (although it may burden that commerce).

  **2.** **Discrimination important:** The presence or absence of *discrimination* continues to be an important factor in the outgoing trade cases, as in the other areas we have already examined. If the burden of a particular regulation falls on in-state and out-of-state persons alike, the Court is much more likely to sustain it than if the burden falls more heavily on out-of-staters (whether by design or by accident). This is especially true where the state interest being pursued is an *economic,* rather than public health or safety, one.

**Example:** New York refuses to give a Massachusetts milk distributor a license to operate an additional milk receiving station in New York (he already has three). The state reasons that such a new receiving station will divert additional New York milk to Massachusetts consumers. The state argues that such a diversion will: (1) dangerously increase the costs, and decrease the volume, of other distributors (who will lose their suppliers to the new plant); and (2) thereby make it likely that there will be a shortage of milk for the local New York market during peak seasons.

*Held*, the license refusal violates the Commerce Clause. What New York is seeking here is economic advantage, not really the health or safety of the consuming public. This goal of economic security may not be pursued by discriminating against other states. If New York is allowed to withhold its milk from the interstate markets, fatal interstate rivalries will develop. (E.g., Michigan might provide that automobiles cannot be taken out of that state until local dealers' demands are fully met; Ohio might then refuse to export tires to retaliate for Michigan's auto monopoly.) *H.P. Hood & Sons v. DuMond*, 336 U.S. 525 (1949).

3. **Embargo of natural resources:** The most significant, and troublesome, of the barrier-to-outgoing-trade cases are those in which a state attempts to ***prevent exportation of scarce natural resources***, either to keep them from being used at all right now, or to restrict their use to in-state residents.

   a. **Strict scrutiny approach:** Courts give relatively ***strict scrutiny*** to measures which, whether by design or by accident, keep such scarce resources from moving interstate. This strict review is often imposed even where the state's interest is a valid conservation or ecological one, rather than a crude desire to keep economic benefits in-state.

   b. **Less discriminatory alternatives:** A key feature of this stricter scrutiny is that the regulation will generally be upheld only if ***less-discriminatory alternatives*** for achieving the state's interest are unavailable.

      **Example:** Oklahoma bars the export for sale of any minnows which are procured from the natural waters of the state. (The statute does not apply to hatchery-bred minnows.)

      *Held*, the statute violates the Commerce Clause. The statute discriminates on its face against out-of-state commerce. Therefore, the burden falls on Oklahoma to justify it under a balancing test, and the state must show that non-discriminatory alternatives are not adequate to preserve the state interest. Here, regardless of the unquestioned validity of the state's interest in conservation and protection of wild animals, no attempt to use non-discriminatory measures was made. (For instance, the state could have set limits on the number of minnows which could be taken by any dealer, rather than completely prohibiting export of minnows, and placing no restrictions at all on capture of minnows for in-state sale.) *Hughes v. Oklahoma*, 441 U.S. 322 (1979).

K. **Local-processing requirements:** The Supreme Court has been especially suspicious of state regulations which pressure out-of-state businesses to ***perform certain operations*** within the state. Most often, these regulations require that agricultural products or natural resources produced in the state also be ***processed*** in the state.

   **Example:** Arizona requires that all Arizona cantaloupes be packed in Arizona. The regulation is applied to prevent a California company from shipping uncrated cantaloupes from its Arizona ranch to its California packing plant. The purpose of the requirement is to enhance the reputation of (and demand for) Arizona's cantaloupes, which are of high quality.

*Held*, statute invalid. The state's interest in enhancing the reputation of Arizona cantaloupes is legitimate (though tenuous). However, this interest is clearly outweighed by the national interest in unencumbered commerce. "[T]he Court has viewed with particular suspicion state statutes requiring business operations to be performed in the home State that could more efficiently be performed elsewhere. Even where the State is pursuing a clearly legitimate local interest, this particular burden on commerce has been declared to be virtually *per se* illegal." *Pike v. Bruce Church, Inc.*, 397 U.S. 137 (1970).

1. **Local processing of garbage:** A state or local government may not even require that its own ***garbage*** be ***locally processed***, as a result of *C & A Carbone, Inc. v. Clarkstown*, 511 U.S. 383 (1994). Such a local-processing requirement discriminates against firms that could have done the processing out-of-state.

   a. **Facts:** In *Carbone*, the town of Clarkstown enacted a "flow control" ordinance. The practical effect of the ordinance was to require that any trash generated in the town be taken to a particular "waste transfer station," which charged a tonnage fee for all trash it processed.

      i. **How it came about:** The town had been required by the state to set up the waste transfer station. Instead of building the station itself, the town induced a local entrepreneur to build it, and promised the entrepreneur a certain volume of trash to process. The town then required residents to take their trash there, as a means of delivering the guaranteed volume.

   b. **Holding:** The Court held that the flow control ordinance violated the Commerce Clause. The majority described the ordinance as a "local processing ordinance," whose purpose and effect was to hoard trash processing jobs (and the income from those jobs) within the town. The ordinance thus discriminated against interstate commerce — it deprived out-of-state firms of the opportunity to do the processing. As a discriminatory "protectionist" statute, the ordinance was virtually *per se* invalid.

      i. **Consequence to in-staters irrelevant:** To the majority, it did not matter that lots of *in-state* trash processors were also deprived of the ability to process Clarkstown's trash. A government-authorized monopoly was no less discriminatory against out-of-state commerce than would be a more typical ordinance protecting all local producers against all out-of-state producers, such as the ordinance struck down in *Pike, supra*.

   c. ***Carbone* not applicable where government owns the facility:** But *Carbone* does ***not*** apply where government awards a monopoly to a ***government-owned facility*** rather than the type of privately-owned facility at issue in *Carbone*. See *United Haulers Ass'n v. Oneida-Herkimer Solid Waste Management Auth.*, 550 U.S. ___ (2007).

      i. **Facts of *United Haulers*:** *United Haulers* involved a flow-control ordinance virtually indistinguishable from the one in *Carbone*, except that the garbage-transfer station that all residents were required to use was owned by a ***public agency*** rather than a private company as in *Carbone*. The government monopoly resulted in residents' being required to pay higher fees for trash removal.

ii. **Preference upheld:** A majority of the court believed that this distinction between private and public ownership of the transfer station made a critical difference – unlike in *Carbone*, the majority in *United Haulers* concluded that the counties' "all trash must be brought to our facility" ordinance did not discriminate against interstate commerce, and did not violate the dormant commerce clause. The majority thought that the public/private distinction was constitutionally significant for two reasons:

❏ First, regulations by which government takes a monopoly on the performance of an activity — especially in an area where the function has been a "traditionally government activity" — raise ***fewer fears of protectionism*** than where government favors a local privately-owned business. For one thing, any higher costs from the government-owned monopoly are "likely to fall upon the very people who voted for the [monopoly-causing] laws," whereas in the usual discrimination-in-favor-of-local-businesses scenario much of the burden of the regulation falls on out-of-staters who cannot vote.

❏ Second, if the traditional strict scrutiny were applied to government regulations that conferred a monopoly on government, the result would be an "unprecedented and unbounded ***interference by the courts*** with state and local government." Local voters here chose the government to be the exclusive provider of waste management services, and the dormant commerce clause should not be used as a "roving license for federal courts to decide what activities are appropriate for state and local government to undertake, and what activities must be the province of private market competition."

iii. **Significance:** So *Carbone* remains in force — and bars government from preferring a local privately-owned business over out-of-staters, at least with respect to trash processing – but under *United Haulers* government is permitted to go into the waste management business itself and then to require that all citizens use the government-owned facility.

L. **Environmental regulation:**   States' attempts to ***control their environment*** have sometimes been attacked as violative of the Commerce Clause. As the result of a case on garbage disposal, it appears that the Court will now strictly scrutinize any discriminatory or protectionist state action, even if it was enacted in furtherance of environmental or other ***non-economic*** motives. Only if ***no less-discriminatory alternatives*** are available will the Court uphold such a statute.

1. **Summary:**   To put it another way, a state may no longer maintain or improve its environment at the expense of its neighbors' environmental or economic interests, unless no reasonable alternative is available.

2. **The *New Jersey Garbage* Case:**   The garbage disposal case was *City of Philadelphia v. New Jersey*, 437 U.S. 617 (1978). The case involved a New Jersey statute prohibiting the importing of most solid or liquid waste into the state. The law was enacted in response to the use of New Jersey landfills for disposal of waste from cities in Pennsylvania and New York. Several New Jersey operators and out-of-state users of the landfill sites (including

Philadelphia) sued to have the statute invalidated on the ground that it discriminated against interstate commerce.

a. **Statute stricken:** The Supreme Court (by a 7-2 vote) struck the statute as violative of the Commerce Clause. The majority opinion, by Justice Stewart, concluded that the law was "basically a protectionist measure," rather than a way of resolving legitimate local concerns.

    i. **Purpose unclear:** The opinion declined to decide whether the main purpose of the statute was to protect the state's environment and its inhabitants' health and safety (as New Jersey claimed) or to stabilize the costs of waste disposal for New Jersey residents at the expense of out-of-state interests (as the plaintiffs claimed).

    ii. **Discriminatory means:** It was unnecessary to decide this issue because "the evil of protectionism can reside in *legislative means* as well as legislative ends." Since New Jersey had chosen a discriminatory means of furthering its objectives (whatever those objectives were), it was a protectionist measure. That is, "it imposes on out-of-state commercial interests the full burden of conserving the State's remaining landfill space. … [It is an] attempt by one State to isolate itself from a problem common to many by erecting a barrier against the movement of interstate trade."

b. **Per se rule of invalidity:** In striking the statute, the Court suggested, though it did not explicitly state, that the same "virtually *per se* rule of invalidity" which had previously been applied in cases of protectionism should be extended to non-economic regulations such as the one at hand. See 92 HARV. L. REV. 57.

c. **Quarantine laws distinguished:** The Court's opinion attempted to distinguish *quarantine* laws (i.e., laws preventing the importation of diseased or otherwise dangerous livestock or goods into a state), which had often been upheld by the Court. Such quarantine laws banned the importation of materials which, *at the moment of importation*, were hazardous. Here, by contrast, the solid waste whose importation was prohibited by New Jersey endangered health (if at all) only when buried in landfill sites, by which time there was no valid reason to differentiate between out-of-state and domestic garbage. *Id.* at 54.

d. **Dissent:** A two-Justice dissent, authored by Justice Rehnquist, contended that the quarantine law cases supported the New Jersey law. He saw no reason why New Jersey "may ban the importation of items whose movement risks contagion, but cannot ban the importation of items which, although they may be transported into the State without undue hazard, will then simply pile up in an ever increasing danger to the public's health and safety." The dissent found it reasonable for New Jersey to guard against a worsening of its own waste disposal problem by banning the addition of out-of-state waste.

e. **Criticism of quarantine distinction:** The majority's distinguishing of the quarantine cases does not seem convincing. One commentator has suggested what he contends to be a better way of distinguishing between the quarantine and waste-disposal situations: whereas the typical quarantine case had a limited economic impact (e.g., a few out-of-state cattlemen were prevented from transporting their cattle), waste disposal is "an integral part of modern industrial processes," and raises much more serious problems, so that " '[T]he peoples of the several states must sink or swim together … ' even in their collective garbage." Tribe, pp. 425-26.

3. **Taxation of out-of-state waste:** Some states have responded to the *Philadelphia* case by trying to ***tax*** out-of-state waste rather than forbidding it. If the state really taxes out-of-state and in-state waste ***equally***, then there is probably no violation of the Commerce Clause. But the Court is extremely vigilant to ensure that any such taxing scheme is ***not discriminatory***. For instance, a state may not impose a flat ***per-ton*** tax on out-of-state waste, and then claim that this tax "compensates" for general income-tax revenues that are collected from in-staters and used to defray the cost of in-state waste. See *Oregon Waste Systems, Inc. v. Dep't of Environmental Quality*, 511 U.S. 93 (1994).

4. **Non-protectionist legislation:** Although ecological legislation which is purposefully discriminatory appears to be virtually "*per se* invalid" under the *Philadelphia* case, this is not true for environmental acts which merely ***burden*** (without discriminating against) interstate commerce. For instance, the Supreme Court sustained a state law which banned non-returnable milk containers made of plastic (but permitted non-returnable milk containers made of other substances, principally cardboard cartons), in ***Minnesota v. Clover Leaf Creamery Co.***, 449 U.S. 456 (1981).

   a. **Burden on out-of-state firms:** The Court sustained the statute even though the plastic used for milk cartons was made solely by non-Minnesota firms, whereas pulpwood, used for making the cardboard containers, was a major Minnesota product. The Court concluded that the statute was not simple "protectionist" legislation camouflaged in a recitation of environmental purposes.

M. **State as purchaser or subsidizer:** All of the cases considered so far involved state action that was purely regulatory. But suppose the state acts as a ***market participant***, spending money to run a proprietary enterprise, or to subsidize private businesses. Is the state barred from discriminating against interstate commerce, or unduly burdening it, as it would be if its actions were solely regulatory? Where the state acts as a market participant, dormant Commerce Clause analysis will ***not*** be applied, and the state may favor local citizens over out-of-state economic interests.

   **Example 1:** Maryland, in an effort to rid the state of abandoned cars, purchases crushed auto hulks at an above-market price. The state refuses to buy hulks from out-of-state sellers. *Held,* Maryland did not violate the Commerce Clause. The Commerce Clause simply does not apply when a state, in its role as participant in a market, favors its own citizens. *Hughes v. Alexandria Scrap Corp.*, 426 U.S. 794 (1976).

   **Example 2:** A state-owned cement plant favors in-state customers in times of shortage. *Held,* this preference does not violate the Commerce Clause. When states act as proprietors, they are free of dormant Commerce Clause limitations. *Reeves v. Stake*, 447 U.S. 429 (1980).

1. **Summary of market-participant exception:** So the *"market participant"* exception to the dormant Commerce Clause is pretty ***narrow***: it applies only where state or local government, acting as a market participant, ***chooses to deal with in-staters rather than out-of-staters in direct transactions.*** So a government-owned entity may ***prefer in-state buyers*** when government sells, ***may prefer in-state sellers*** when government buys, and the like.

a. **Does not affect state's acts as regulator:** Importantly, the market-participant exception does ***not*** permit the state to ***regulate*** in a way that discriminates against out-of-staters, even if the state is *also* acting as market participant.

   i. **Effect on "downstream" participants:** For example, the market-participant exception does not apply where the state tries to use its market clout to regulate transactions ***involving parties that are not dealing directly*** with the state-owned market-participant entity. Thus a state market-participant cannot, for instance, try to regulate ***"downstream"*** from its own transactions, by saying to its customers, "We'll sell to you [or buy from you] only if you, in turn, discriminate against out-of-staters."

      **Example:** Alaska sells timber from state-owned lands at below-market prices. The state requires each buyer to promise that it will process the timber inside Alaska before the timber is exported. A non-Alaska firm with no Alaska processing facilities attacks the local-processing rule as violative of the dormant Commerce Clause. The state defends on the grounds that it is a "market participant" that is merely selling a commodity it owns.

      *Held*, for the plaintiff. The market-participant exception does not apply here, for several reasons. One reason is that the exception will apply only where the effects of the state's terms are *limited to the particular market in which the state is participating*, not to a broader one. Here, the state is trying to engage in "downstream regulation" of the timber-processing market (i.e., trying to affect the conduct of parties with whom the state is not dealing directly), and the market-participant exception does not apply to immunize that downstream regulation from dormant Commerce Clause attack. ***South-Central Timber Development, Inc. v. Wunnicke***, 467 U.S. 82 (1984).

b. **Lesser scrutiny where state has own market-participating entity:** However, even where the market-participant exception does not directly apply, the fact that the state's regulation takes the form of a decision to ***conduct the entire activity via its own government-owned entity*** seems to make it more likely that the regulation will ***pass*** commerce clause scrutiny, as the result of a 2007 decision. In *United Haulers Ass'n v. Oneida-Herkimer Solid Waste Management Auth.* (discussed more fully *supra*, p. 81), the Court found no dormant commerce clause violation where a county required that all residents have their trash processed at a county-owned transfer station. The majority did not rely on the market-participation exception. But the fact that the government was electing to perform the entire activity at its own facility rather than preferring a privately-owned one made the critical difference for the majority, mainly because the majority believed that cases in which government takes over a function entirely are less likely to be motivated by protectionism than where government prefers local businesses over out of staters.

   i. **Consequence:** So even though the market-participant exception does not expressly apply where the government is wearing a "regulator" hat rather than making business-owner-type decisions about with whom it will deal, *United Haulers* suggests that the government's regulations will get gentler review when those regulation are in a domain in which the state has chosen to act as a market participant. That's especially true if the area is one – like waste management -- that is a domain in which governments have ***traditionally*** performed the market activity in question.

2. **Privileges and Immunities attack:**   In any case in which out-of-staters are discriminated against by the state acting as a "market participant," the state's actions may be vulnerable to an attack based on the ***Privileges and Immunities Clause*** of Article IV ("The Citizens of each State shall be entitled to all the Privileges and Immunities of Citizens in the several States.") The Supreme Court has held that there is no "market participant" exception to the Privileges and Immunities Clause. See *United Building and Construction Trades Council v. Camden*, *infra*, p. 102, holding that this Clause might be violated by an ordinance providing that at least 40% of any work force on a city-funded construction project must consist of city residents.

# II.  STATE TAXATION OF INTERSTATE COMMERCE

A. **Compared with regulation:**   Just as state regulation may violate the dormant Commerce Clause, so may certain types of state ***taxation***. This is most likely to happen where a state tries to tax operations of a business that operates in more than one state. Many of the same issues are involved in the two situations; for instance, a tax may be stricken on the grounds that it discriminates against interstate commerce, or on the grounds that an interstate business is being subjected to unfair cumulative taxation.

B. **Limited scope:**   The Supreme Court has decided literally hundreds of state taxation cases involving the Commerce Clause, and most of the decisions are confusing and hard to reconcile. No attempt will be made here to give full treatment to this subject area. Instead, a few of the general principles which the Court has applied will be discussed.

C. **General principles:**   For a multi-state company to succeed in a challenge to a particular state tax, it will generally have to make one of the three following showings: (1) that the company's business activity does not have a ***sufficient connection*** with the taxing state; (2) that the tax ***discriminates against interstate commerce***; or (3) that the tax has led to an unfair ***cumulative burden*** (e.g., it is not fairly apportioned as between the company's in-state and out-of-state activities, or it is unrelated to services rendered by the taxing state).

D. **Minimum contacts:**   Not only because of the Commerce Clause, but also because of the ***Due Process Clause*** of the Fourteenth Amendment, a non-domiciliary company may not be taxed ***at all*** unless there are "***minimum contacts***" between the company and the taxing state. This is a threshold matter, which must be resolved even before examining whether the particular tax involved is equitable.

> **Example:** Iowa has a net income tax, which it applies to corporations. In the case of a corporation doing business in more than one state, the percentage of corporate net income attributable to Iowa (and thus taxed by Iowa) is determined by taking the ratio of Iowa sales to total gross national sales. ABC Corp., a New Jersey corporation, sends one salesman into Iowa for one week during the year; the salesman makes sales in Iowa equal to one-half of one percent of the company's total national gross sales for that year. The Supreme Court would probably hold that ABC's contacts with Iowa are so minimal that Iowa may not tax the company's net income ***at all***. Thus even though the apportion formula (Iowa sales as a percentage of total national sales) may be a fair

way of apportioning net income, no tax could be levied against ABC. This would be true as a matter of both the Commerce and Due Process Clauses.

1. **Not too much bite:** The requirement of "minimum contacts" does not have too much practical "bite" in the context of state taxation of interstate commerce — the dormant Commerce Clause (insofar as it bans both discrimination and undue burdening of commerce) usually is much more likely to lead to invalidation of a tax scheme than is the lack of minimum contacts. Also, any tax that fell on an out-of-stater who did not have minimum contacts would probably also represent a discrimination against or unfair burden on interstate commerce.

E. **No discrimination:** The state may not tax in a way which *discriminates* against interstate commerce, i.e., in a way which unjustifiably benefits local commerce at the expense of out-of-state commerce. Tribe, pp. 453-54.

1. **Facially discriminatory statutes:** Sometimes, the taxing statute can be seen *on its face* to be discriminatory. For instance, if the taxing scheme explicitly charges a *higher tax rate* (regardless of the type of tax) with respect to goods manufactured outside the state than for those manufactured within it, this will probably be found to be discriminatory against interstate commerce, and therefore *per se* violative of the Commerce Clause.

2. **Burdensome but facially neutral statutes:** Even a *facially neutral* statute, however, may nonetheless place a *greater burden* on interstate businesses than on intrastate ones; in such a situation, the tax will be *stricken* as discriminatory.

   a. **"Drumming" license fees:** For instance, many states and towns at one time or another have exacted license fees for so-called "drumming," i.e., the *door-to-door selling* of items which are to be delivered at some future time (e.g., magazine subscriptions). While such licensing schemes theoretically apply to interstate and intrastate businesses alike, an interstate business is much more likely to make its sales through door-to-door solicitation than is a local business (which can sell out of a store or office). Thus such drummer licensing schemes have generally been stricken.

F. **Cumulative burdens:** Even a non-discriminatory tax may nonetheless violate the Commerce Clause if the taxpaying company can show that the taxing scheme would expose it to *unfair cumulative taxation*, and thus unduly *burden* interstate commerce.

1. **Administrative complexity:** The main way in which taxation may unduly burden interstate commerce is if it would create undue *administrative complexity* for the taxpayer conducting interstate operations. The Supreme Court begins to look at a tax provision by saying to the taxing jurisdiction, in effect, "If we let you do it, we'll have to let every jurisdiction do it." If having all jurisdictions enact the same tax scheme would be administratively unworkable, the tax will be struck down even though the burden imposed by the particular jurisdiction whose tax is being considered at the moment would not be unworkable.

   **Example:** North Dakota attempts to require all mail order merchants who send mail into North Dakota to collect a North Dakota use tax on sales made to North Dakota buyers, even if the merchant has no employees in the state and conducts no direct business operations there.

   *Held*, this taxing scheme violates the Commerce Clause, because it unduly burdens interstate commerce. If the scheme here were upheld, "similar obligations might be imposed by the Nation's 6,000-plus taxing jurisdictions … 'Many variations in rates of tax, in allowable exemptions, and in administrative and record-keeping requirements could entangle [a mail-order house] in a virtual welter of complicated obligations.' " *Quill Corp. v. North Dakota*, 504 U.S. 298 (1992).

    **a.** **"Substantial nexus" requirement:** To prevent the problem of thousands of jurisdictions all taxing the same interstate business, the Court has required that there be a ***"substantial nexus"*** between the taxpayer and the jurisdiction that is imposing the tax. *Quill Corp. v. North Dakota*, *supra*. (The mere sending of advertising mail into the jurisdiction does not constitute the required "substantial nexus," *Quill* holds.)

## III.  CONGRESSIONAL ACTION — PREEMPTION AND CONSENT

  **A.** **Federal preemption generally:** The aspect of the Commerce Clause which we have been examining thus far in this chapter is its "dormant" aspect, i.e., its force as a negative implication where Congress has not acted. A different, but surprisingly similar, set of problems is presented when Congress ***does exercise its power***: To what extent does this exercise of valid congressional power restrict what the states may do?

    **1.** **Supremacy Clause:** In the case of a direct, obvious, conflict between a federal and state statute, the resolution is clear: the state statute is simply invalid. The ***Supremacy Clause*** of Article VI provides that in case of a conflict, state law must yield to federal law. Federal law is said to have "***preempted***" state law.

    **2.** **Unclear cases:** But much more likely to arise is the situation where the federal and state actions involve similar or identical subject matter, but there is no clear-cut conflict. In this situation, no single rule gives a way of deciding whether the state rule must fall. Rather, the Supreme Court has applied a number of general principles to determine whether the Supremacy Clause is relevant. Some of these principles are quite similar to rules applied in dormant Commerce Clause cases.

    **3.** **Not limited to Commerce Clause:** The problems of conflict between federal and state regulations often arise in Commerce Clause contexts. But these problems may also arise in other contexts (e.g., where Congress acts under its power to control immigration and naturalization, as in *Hines v. Davidowitz*, discussed *infra*, p. 90). These problems of preemption have been treated in this chapter on the Commerce Clause because they involve a similar need to balance national and local concerns.

  **B.** **Actual conflict:** As noted, in cases of an actual clear-cut conflict between congressional and state regulation, the state statute is invalid.

    **1.** **Joint compliance impossible:** For instance, it may be impossible to obey the state and federal regulations simultaneously. Thus in *McDermott v. Wisconsin*, 228 U.S. 115 (1913), Wisconsin's syrup-labeling rules were such that if out-of-state syrup was labeled so as to comply with the federal Food and Drugs Act, the syrup would be mislabeled under Wisconsin law. The Court barred enforcement of the Wisconsin regulations.

    **2.** **Conflicting objectives:** Even if the federal and state regulations do not conflict upon their face (and thus compliance with both is not impossible), it may be that the ***objectives*** behind the two regulations are inconsistent. In this case, too, the state regulation must fall.

3. **Conflicting tactics:** Finally, even if the federal and state regulations are pursuing a common objective, the *tactics* employed by the two may be sufficiently conflicting that the court will conclude that the state regulation must give way. For instance, if Congress and a state are trying to eliminate the same evil, but the state uses *blunter, less-calibrated,* methods, the court may find a conflict.

   a. **Foreign relations:** The Court is especially likely to find a conflict when a state takes an action that affects *foreign policy.* There is a presumption that the federal government (and in particular the President) needs to "speak with one voice" in matters of foreign policy, so the Court will be quick to conclude that a state regulation that seems intended to influence other nations conflicts with federal foreign policy, even if the state is pursuing the same ultimate objective as the federal government. Two cases from the early 21st century illustrate this tendency.

      **Example:** Congress passes a statute imposing limited sanctions on Burma (Myanmar), in an attempt to induce Burmese authorities to allow democracy and to end human-rights abuses. The federal statute calls on the President to engage in dialogue with Burma, and to coordinate with other nations in trying to bring about change in Burma. Massachusetts then enacts a law barring state entities from buying goods or services from any company that does business with Burma. The Mass. statute is attacked on the grounds that it conflicts with, and is therefore preempted by, the federal statute.

      *Held,* the Mass. statute is pre-empted. "The fact of a common end hardly neutralizes conflicting means[.]" Sanctions "are drawn not only to bar what they prohibit but to allow what they permit, and the inconsistency of sanctions here undermines the congressional calibration of force." Furthermore, the state sanctions here "compromise the very capacity of the President to speak for the Nation with one voice in dealing with other governments." *Crosby v. National Foreign Trade Council,* 530 U.S. 363 (2000).

C. **Federal occupation of the field:** A federal-state conflict (whether in statutory provisions, or in purposes) is only one of two ways in which congressional action may render state action invalid. The other way is for Congress to "*occupy the field*" for the federal government. If Congress has made such a decision to occupy the field (i.e., if it has *"preempted" the entire subject area*), state action in that area must fail no matter how well it agrees with the federal action and policies. Tribe, p. 497.

   1. **Tests for preemption:** The preemption issue is one of congressional intent; Congress could, if it wished, enact one narrow regulation in a broad subject area, yet evince a clear intent to preempt the entire subject area against state regulation. But Congress rarely makes its intent so clear, and the Court must work by inference. Recent Supreme Court decisions indicate that Congress will be deemed to have preempted an area only where either its *intent* is *unmistakable*, or where "the *nature* of the regulated subject matter permits no other conclusion. ... " *Florida Lime & Avocado Growers v. Paul,* 373 U.S. 132 (1963).

   2. **Broad federal coverage of area:** Where the existing federal regulatory scheme is *broad,* and *covers most of the subject area*, the Court is much more likely to find federal preemption than where the federal scheme is less comprehensive. Tribe, p. 497.

3. **Field traditionally left to states:** Subject matter areas ***traditionally left to the states*** are less likely to be found to be the subject of federal preemption. This means that if the subject area is usually viewed as "local" rather than "national," preemption is unlikely to be found. This is especially true in cases involving ***health*** and ***safety*** regulations.

4. **National matters:** Conversely, areas ***traditionally left to federal control***, such as foreign relations, bankruptcy, patent and trademark, admiralty, immigration, etc., will normally be found to be federally preempted.

5. **Effect of federal agency:** Where Congress has set up a ***federal agency*** and given it broad regulatory powers in a particular subject area, this may indicate a congressional intent to preempt the field. For instance, the broad authority given to the National Labor Relations Board and the Federal Communications Commission have led to findings that particular aspects of labor law and communications law have been federally preempted. See Tribe, p. 502. But even where a federal regulatory agency has broad regulatory powers, a particular state regulation in that area may be found to be so "local" that it is not preempted. See Tribe, p. 504.

   a. **Federal licensing scheme:** The fact that the federal government has ***licensed*** a particular aspect of interstate commerce usually does ***not*** automatically mean that state regulation of that aspect of commerce is preempted. The Court will look to the goals of the federal and state policies to see if there is a true conflict. Tribe, p. 506.

      **Example:** Congress extensively regulates the nuclear power industry, through power delegated to the Nuclear Regulatory Commission (NRC), which licenses and inspects all nuclear power plants. California passes a law conditioning the construction of any new nuclear plant in the state upon a finding by a state agency that when the plant produces nuclear waste, there will be "adequate storage facilities and means of disposal" for that waste. A utility claims that Congress has preempted the entire field of nuclear regulation.

      *Held*, California's regulation is valid. The federal system of licensing and inspecting nuclear plants was set up solely to deal with ***safety*** issues, and with the construction and operation of nuclear plants. Since California asserts (and the Court accepts) that its statute was aimed at the ***economic*** problems of storing and disposing of waste, not safety problems, the California statute does not come within the area preempted by Congress. (But if California placed a moratorium on nuclear construction because of safety concerns, or sought to regulate the way in which nuclear plants are constructed and operated, these actions *would* fall within the area preempted by Congress.)

      Nor was there an actual conflict between California's refusal to allow plants to be built until the nuclear-waste issue was resolved and the NRC's decision to grant licenses while uncertainty remained; here, too, NRC action merely indicates that construction is safe, not that it is economically sound. Since the NRC could not ***force*** a utility to build a power plant, simultaneous compliance with both the NRC's rules and California's is possible. *Pacific Gas & Electric Co. v. State Energy Comm'n*, 461 U.S. 190 (1983).

D. **Federal consent to state laws:** We turn now to an obverse problem: To what extent may Congress affirmatively ***consent*** to state action which would otherwise be an unconstitutional violation of the Commerce Clause?

1. **Generally allowable:** Early decisions, including *Cooley v. Board of Wardens, supra,* p. 50, suggested that Congress did *not* have the power to consent to what would otherwise be state encroachments on the congressional commerce power. But the more modern view has been that Congress *may affirmatively consent to state interference with interstate commerce.* See Tribe, pp. 524-25; N&R, pp. 286-287.

    a. **Rationale:** One rationale for giving Congress the right to give such consent is that the ban on state interference with interstate commerce stems from the danger that each local part of the national economy will protect its own interests at the expense of the other parts; when Congress acts, by contrast, it is the "whole" rather than any individual part which is consenting to the interference with commerce, so that all affected parties are presumably represented in the political process. See N&R, pp. 281-282.

2. **Discrimination:** Thus the Court has allowed Congress to authorize a state to discriminate overtly against out-of-state corporations.

    **Example:** Congress passes the McCarran-Ferguson Act, which reserves to the states the power to regulate insurance, and which provides that no federal statute shall be construed to invalidate any state insurance law or tax, unless the federal statute specifically relates to insurance. A New Jersey insurance company sues to overturn a South Carolina tax of 3% on premiums received from all South Carolina insurance underwriting; the tax does not apply to South Carolina insurance firms.

    *Held,* even though the tax is "discriminatory" and would thus be invalid under ordinary Commerce Clause analysis, the tax is valid under the McCarran Act. Congress itself would have the power to discriminate against interstate commerce and in favor of local trade; there is no reason why such discrimination cannot be conducted by Congress in conjunction with the states. *Prudential Insurance Co. v. Benjamin,* 328 U.S. 408 (1946).

---

*Quiz Yourself on*
## TWO LIMITS ON STATE POWER *(ENTIRE CHAPTER)*

11. The City of Fairhaven is located in the state of North Texarkansas. The border with the neighboring state of South Texarkansas is three miles south of the Fairhaven city limits. After a serious outbreak of food poisoning, traced to improperly butchered meat, the Fairhaven City Council passed an ordinance forbidding the sale within Fairhaven of any meat not killed at a slaughterhouse inspected by the Fairhaven Department of Sanitation. All evidence suggests that the Fairhaven ordinance was in fact motivated solely by health and safety objectives, not by any desire to favor local producers. Fairhaven Sanitation inspectors survey all slaughterhouses within a 70-mile radius of the city, but do not attempt to cross the boundary to inspect South Texarkansas slaughterhouses. South Texarkansas, at the state level, conducts its own inspections of slaughterhouses for sanitation, using standards that are closely similar to those used by the Fairhaven inspectors.

    Chopem, the owner of a butcher shop in Fairhaven, sells meat purchased from a slaughterhouse in South Texarkansas. Chopem was charged with selling meat that had not been slaughtered in a Fairhaven-inspected slaughterhouse. Chopem would like to get the charges dismissed on the grounds that the statute, as applied here, violates the U.S. Constitution.

**(a)** What is the strongest argument that Chopem can make for the unconstitutionality of the Fairhaven ordinance? _____

**(b)** Will this constitutional attack succeed? State your reasons. _____

12. The state of New Wales has a single nuclear power plant. Because the power plant has been in operation for over 20 years, it is now time for the plutonium used in the plant to be disposed of. The safest and cheapest way to do this is to bury it in a lead-enclosed structure 200 feet below the surface. Because residents of the state are worried that their state will become a "toxic dumping ground" if strict measures are not taken, the New Wales state legislature has enacted the following statute: "No plutonium imported into this state after 1994 may be buried anywhere within the confines of this state." The effect of this statute is to permit the state's existing utility to make a one-time disposal of its pre-1994 plutonium by the burial method described above. The owners of a nuclear reactor located in South Brunswick, the state directly east of New Wales, have attacked the new statute on the grounds that it violates the Commerce Clause because it prevents them from shipping their spent plutonium into New Wales and burying it there. Assume that Congress has not spoken on the issue of nuclear-waste disposal at all. Should the court hearing this action agree with the plaintiff? _____

13. The state of Rouge decided to build a new and large state office building. Quarries in Rouge had for years produced fine granite. However, in recent years, the in-state granite industry had begun to suffer because of high costs. In an effort to give a shot in the arm to the local industry, the Rouge legislature provided that all granite used in the new building should be purchased from in-state granite producers, even though the price would inevitably be higher than if the materials were bought from out-of-staters. A granite producer in a neighboring state has sued Rouge in federal District Court, asserting that Rouge's preference for in-staters violates the Commerce Clause. Should the court agree with the plaintiff's argument? _____

14. The state of Sylvan, in order to raise money to repair its existing highways and build new ones, has imposed a flat "axle tax" on any truck travelling more than 100 miles on Sylvan highways during any calendar year. The tax is $200 per axle. (The typical truck has two axles.) If all trucks were required to pay their fair share of maintaining the state's highways, the fairly-allocated cost for a truck driven full time (at least 20,000 miles per year) within the state would be approximately $500 per year. Trucker is a trucking company located in a state adjacent to Sylvan. Trucker's one truck drives about 200 miles a year in Sylvan, carrying goods into and out of the state.

**(a)** What is Trucker's best argument for attacking the constitutionality of the taxing scheme as applied to it? _____

**(b)** Will this attack succeed? _____

15. Same facts as Question 12 (on plutonium disposal). Now, assume that Congress has passed the following statute: "Any state may define the circumstances, if any, under which nuclear waste products [defined to include plutonium] may be buried or otherwise disposed of within the confines of that state." If the New Wales statute is attacked on the grounds that it violates the dormant Commerce Clause, should the Court find the statute invalid? _____

*Answers*

**11. (a) That the ordinance unreasonably burdens interstate commerce.**

**(b) Yes.** The dormant Commerce Clause prevents a state or local government from placing ***undue burdens*** on interstate commerce. Most violations of the dormant Commerce Clause occur when government acts in a "protectionist" manner, i.e., with an intent to favor the economic interests of local residents over out-of-staters. But even a non-protectionist "neutral" regulation will be found to violate the dormant Commerce Clause if it amounts to an ***unreasonable burden*** on commerce. This can be true, for instance, of regulations that are enacted for the good-faith purpose of protecting the safety or health of local residents. The Court performs a "balancing test," weighing the state or local government's interest in its regulatory scheme against the national interest in unburdened free-flowing interstate commerce. A major part of this balancing is whether there were ***less burdensome alternatives*** which the government might have adopted.

Here, since South Texarkansas conducts a similar inspection, Fairhaven could simply have accepted the results of South Texarkansas's inspection without materially compromising its own health standards. Therefore, the Fairhaven ordinance will probably be found to have been an "unreasonable" burden on commerce. See *Dean Milk Co. v. Madison.* (The fact that Fairhaven is a municipality rather than a state, and its ordinance might have discriminated against out-of-town but in-state slaughterhouses, i.e., those beyond the 70-mile inspection radius, does not save the ordinance from a dormant Commerce Clause attack.)

**12. Yes.** Any state or local action that is taken for a ***protectionist purpose*** — that is, for the purpose of preferring in-state economic interests over out-of-state interests — will be ***strictly scrutinized***. This is true even where the measure is taken for what are basically environmental or other non-economic motives. Thus in *City of Philadelphia v. New Jersey* (a garbage disposal case), the Court held that one state could not ban the importation of another's garbage, unless there were no less-discriminatory alternatives. Here, New Wales is clearly preferring local nuclear plant operators to out-of-state operators. New Wales clearly has a less-discriminatory alternative (allow importation, and simply limit the total amount of plutonium that may be buried in the state), so the measure would almost certainly be struck down.

**13. No.** Ordinarily, if a state prefers the economic interests of in-staters over out-of-staters, we have a classic violation of the Commerce Clause. But there is an important exception: where the state acts as a ***market participant***, spending its money to acquire goods or services, dormant Commerce Clause analysis is not applied, and the state may favor local interests over out-of-staters. Here, Rouge is clearly spending its own money, so it is free to limit that money to acquisitions from in-state producers. See, e.g., *Hughes v. Alexandria Scrap Corp.*; *Reeves v. Stake.*

**14. (a) That the tax operates as an undue burden on interstate commerce.**

**(b) Yes, probably.** A state may impose a tax that operates "on" interstate commerce. That is, an interstate business may be required to pay to a state the business' fair share of services supplied by that state to the business' operations in the state. So Trucker can be required to pay its fair share of the construction costs of highways it uses. But in determining whether the tax is fair, the Court requires "internal consistency." That is, the Court determines what would happen if all states taxed interstate operators the same way the state in question is doing; if this "all states" approach would produce a tax that is out of all proportion to the fair value of state services supplied to the payor, the tax is likely to be struck down as unreasonable. Here, each trucker who comes into the state for more than a trivial distance is required to pay the same amount as a truck that drives full time on Sylvan's roads, an approach that would make interstate trucking impossibly expensive if applied by all other states. See *American Trucking Assoc. v. Scheiner*, 483 U.S. 260 (1987), striking down such a flat "axle tax."

**15. No.** Dormant Commerce Clause analysis is only to be performed when Congress has not expressly allowed the type of discrimination against out-of-staters in question. Here, by the federal statute, Congress has in effect allowed a state to prefer its own citizens over out-of-staters.

## Exam Tips on
## TWO LIMITS ON STATE POWER

Issues involving the dormant Commerce Clause and congressional pre-emption can often be well-hidden in a fact pattern; you must be especially vigilant to spot these issues. Here are some particular things to look for:

☛ Remember that one main branch of dormant Commerce Clause analysis is the **"burden"** branch: if a state's regulations would burden interstate commerce, the regulation will be struck down unless the burdens are **outweighed** by the state's interest in enforcing its regulation. Thus you must use a **balancing test** to evaluate "burden" problems. Also:

   ☞ Look for **conflicts** between the laws of two or more states. The existence of conflicting regulations is likely to be an undue burden on commerce, since a business operating in multiple states would find it difficult or impossible to comply with all of the conflicting regulations.

   ☞ Be on the lookout for regulations affecting **transportation**, especially **trucking**. These are classic scenarios where the states have differing regulations and commerce is directly affected because goods have to pass from state to state.

   ☞ Remember that you must do a "burden" analysis even where the state seems totally **even-handed**, and is not showing any protectionism.

      ☞ A common instance of state regulations that are even-handed but nonetheless unduly burdensome are **health** and **safety** regulations. If the state (or local government) insists on performing its own inspection of goods that are imported from elsewhere, this is likely to be an undue burden on commerce even if the state is truly pursuing health and safety rather than protectionism.

☛ Remember that the other main branch of dormant Commerce Clause analysis is the **"protectionist"** branch — if the state is intentionally **discriminating** against out-of-staters, in order to promote its residents' **own economic interests**, this is not a legitimate state objective, so the regulation will almost **automatically** violate the Commerce Clause.

Here are some ways to spot protectionism:

   ☞ Look for rules **restricting** the **export** of **"good stuff"** produced inside the state. This is especially likely where **natural resources** are the "good stuff" (e.g., a rule saying, "No more than x% of coal mined from the state may be exported").

☞ Look for rules barring the *import* of *"bad stuff"* (e.g., "No out-of-state garbage or toxic waste may be buried in our state").

☞ Look for rules whose effect is to *limit imports* of *"good stuff"* because the state is trying to *boost demand* for *in-state-produced* good stuff (e.g., "Coal-fired utilities located in this state must buy at least 10% of their coal from in-state mines").

☛ Remember that the dormant Commerce Clause does not apply at all where the state is a *market participant*. Therefore, be on the lookout for instances where the state is *operating a factory*, *purchasing goods*, or otherwise *directly engaging in commercial transactions* for its own account (as opposed to regulating the commercial transactions done by private parties).

☛ Don't forget that *local ordinances*, not just state rules, can violate the dormant Commerce Clause. This is true even where the ordinance discriminates against out-of-town in-staters as well as out-of-staters.

☛ Remember that *taxes* can be a violation of the dormant Commerce Clause (DCC) just as readily as regulations can be. We have the same two branches of analysis for taxes:

☞ Thus if the state is *discriminating* against interstate commerce by taxing it less favorably than in-staters, this will be a DCC violation.

☞ Alternatively, a tax scheme will violate the DCC if the scheme unfairly *burdens* commerce even though it doesn't discriminate against out-of-staters on its face. One common type of illustration: the state puts a *flat tax* on some activity, regardless of its degree of connection with the state. (*Example:* The state puts a flat annual tax on all trucks entering the state even occasionally, which has the effect of taxing out-of-state trucks much more heavily per mile than in-state trucks.) In considering the burden, consider whatever the fact pattern tells you about the tax policies of *other states* — inconsistencies can make the whole scheme burdensome even though each state's scheme is not burdensome when viewed in isolation.

☛ Separately, be on the lookout for *congressional pre-emption* problems. Remember that this is an aspect of the Supremacy Clause; if Congress has acted in a particular respect or occupied a particular domain, the states are often precluded from regulating.

☞ Be on the lookout for a fact pattern telling you that there are federal and state statutes dealing with the *same subject area*. This is a clue to pre-emption problems.

☞ Where the fact pattern gives you federal and state laws that are in the same subject area, check first for a *direct conflict*. If a person or business could not simultaneously obey both the state and federal regulation, then obviously the state regulation must fall. Most fact patterns are *not* of this "direct conflict" type, however.

☞ More commonly, you'll see a fact pattern where there are federal and state statutes dealing with the same activity, and the state statute is *more stringent* than the federal statute. Obviously, a person can obey both (simply by obeying the more stringent state statute). Here, ask yourself whether Congress meant to say, "We're setting a minimum standard, and we'll let the states be more stringent," or meant to say instead, "We're regulating this way, and we don't want states interfering with our scheme by being more stringent." Remember that it is always a question of *what Congress intended*.

☞    Finally, be on the lookout for a federal statutory scheme that seems to deal with an ***entire broad area***. Where Congress has acted in this way, this may represent Congress' intent to ***"occupy the whole field,"*** in which case even a state regulation dealing with an aspect of the problem that is not addressed in the federal regulatory scheme may be pre-empted. Commonly, this happens in fact patterns involving ***nuclear power*** and ***immigration*** — the existence of a broad federal regulatory scheme in these areas may well prevent the states from enacting even non-conflicting regulations dealing with these subjects.

CHAPTER 7

# INTERGOVERNMENTAL IMMUNITIES AND INTERSTATE RELATIONS

## *ChapterScope*

This Chapter, like the ones before it, examines several aspects of federal-state relationships and inter-state relationships. As before, the emphasis is on federalism, and the limits it places both on state and federal power. The most important concepts in this Chapter are:

- **Several types of immunities:** There are several types of *immunities* produced by our federal-ist system. The most important are:

  - **Federal immunity from state taxation:** The *federal* government is immune from being *taxed by the states*.

  - **State immunity from federal taxation:** The *states* have *partial immunity* from *federal* taxation.

  - **Federal immunity from state regulation:** The federal government is essentially free from *state regulatory interference.*

  - **State immunity from federal regulation:** The states generally are *not* immune from fed-eral regulation. However, if a federal regulatory scheme had the effect of preventing the states from exercising their *core functions*, this might be found to be a violation of the Tenth Amendment.

- **Interstate privileges and immunities:** The *"Privileges and Immunities"* Clause of Article IV says that "the Citizens of each State shall be entitled to all Privileges and Immunities of Citizens in the several States." This clause means that a state may not *discriminate against non-residents*.

  - **Rights fundamental to national unity:** But this clause only operates with respect to rights that are *fundamental* to *national unity*. Thus only rights related to *commerce* are covered: the right to *be employed*, the right to *practice one's profession*, and the right to *engage in business* are the prime examples.

## I. TAX IMMUNITIES

A. **Federal and state immunity:** It has long been established that the federal government is *immune* from taxation by any state, unless Congress has consented to such taxation. Likewise, it has always been accepted that a *state*, at least in the performance of its *essential government functions*, is *immune from federal taxation*. However, the scope of this state immunity has been significantly narrowed in recent years. Although the rules in the federal immunity and state immunity situations are similar, there are enough differences to warrant separate treat-ment of the two.

**B. Federal immunity from state taxation:**    The principle that the federal government is *immune from taxation by any state* derives from *McCulloch v. Maryland*, 4 Wheat. 316 (1819) (discussed *supra*, pp. 21-23).

    **1. Holding of *McCulloch*:**    Recall that *McCulloch* held that the Bank of the United States was immune from a Maryland tax against it. This conclusion was essentially the result of the following syllogism: (1) the power to tax is the power to destroy; (2) if state taxation were permitted to destroy or harm the Bank, the federal government's exercise of its powers under the Constitution (especially the "Necessary and Proper" and Spending Clauses) would be thwarted; and (3) the federal Constitution must be preserved against such state interference.

    **2. Broad rationale:**    More generally, the theory behind federal immunity from state taxation is that a government may not tax those it does not represent, so that a state may not tax the entire nation. See Tribe, p. 512.

    **3. Modern "legal incidence" test:**    Federal immunity from state taxation exists only in those situations where the "*legal incidence*" of the tax is on the United States (or upon one of its instrumentalities, such as a federally-sponsored entity like a VA hospital).

        **a. Meaning of "legal incidence":**    "Legal incidence" means "*obligation to pay*," not "economic burden." Thus if a private contractor or other non-government entity is required to pay the state tax, the fact that the burden of this tax might be *passed on* to the government is *not enough* to confer tax immunity. Only where the government entity is *directly required to make the payment* will there be federal immunity from state taxation.

        **b. Employees not immune:**    *Employees* of the federal government are *not* immune from state taxation. See *Graves v. New York ex rel. O'Keefe*, 306 U.S. 466 (1939).

    **4. Congressional control:**    Congress may, whenever it wishes, explicitly *confer additional immunity* from state taxation upon other persons or entities.

    **5. Congressional waiver:**    Conversely, Congress may *waive* its constitutionally-derived immunity whenever it sees fit.

**C. State immunity from federal taxation:**    Similar, though not identical, principles control the *immunity of states* from *federal* taxation. The federal government may not tax in a way which would "interfere unduly with the State's performance of its sovereign functions of government." *New York v. United States*, 326 U.S. 572 (1946) (Stone, C.J., concurring).

    **1. Source of limitation:**    The Constitution nowhere explicitly provides that the states shall be immune from federal taxation of essential government functions. Rather, the state immunity is implied from the *Tenth Amendment's* preservation of state autonomy.

    **2. Essential functions:**    Thus the federal government may generally not impose a significant tax on property used in or income received from a state's performance of its *basic governmental functions*. For instance, it is doubtful that the federal government may include a state's *public schools* or *public parks* within a general property tax, or its revenues from state taxes within a general federal income tax. See *New York v. United States*, *supra* (Stone, C.J., concurring).

3. **Non-essential function:** But where a state government engages in a function that is not at the core of traditional governmental functions, the federal government may tax that function as part of a non-discriminatory, generally-applicable tax.

4. **Employees not covered:** As in the case of state taxation of the federal government, state *employees*, and other persons doing business with the state, will generally *not be immune* from federal taxation.

## II.  FEDERAL IMMUNITY FROM STATE REGULATION

A. **Federal immunity from regulation:** The freedom of the federal government from state regulation is governed by principles similar to those in the taxation context. That is, the federal government is essentially *immune from state regulatory interference*.

> **Example:** Suppose a state attempts to apply its criminal code to actions that take place on a U.S. military base located within the state. Such a state regulation of the federal government would be found unconstitutional, assuming that Congress did not consent to it.

B. **Sources of immunity:** This federal immunity from state regulation, like federal immunity from state taxation, derives from *McCulloch v. Maryland* (*supra*, p. 21). The theory is that a government may not control those whom it does not represent; thus a state may not control the entire nation. See Tribe, p. 512.

1. **Who is covered:** Generally, only the United States and its instrumentalities will be free of state regulation. However, sometimes a federal employee will be free of state regulation while acting in the course of his federal duties. See, e.g., *Johnson v. Maryland*, 254 U.S. 51 (1920), reversing the conviction of a post office employee for driving a truck without a state license.

2. **Congress' consent:** Again, keep in mind that Congress is always free to *consent* to state regulation of federal instrumentalities. This is frequently done, for instance, with respect to the law governing *military posts* and other federal enclaves. Thus Congress has made the changing body of state criminal law applicable to federal enclaves; the Court found this to be constitutional in *U.S. v. Sharpnack*, 355 U.S. 286 (1958).

## III.  STATE IMMUNITY FROM FEDERAL REGULATION

A. **Exits only theoretically:** The immunity of the *states* from *federal* regulation exists only in a very theoretical way. In general, federal regulation of the states is *valid*.

1. **Interference with core functions:** However, if a federal regulatory scheme had the effect of preventing the states from exercising their *core functions*, this might be found to be a violation of the *Tenth Amendment*.

> **Example:** Suppose Congress enacted a statute that said, "No state may have its own criminal code, and the only crimes that may be defined in the United States are those defined in the federal criminal code." The Supreme Court might well hold that this federal regulation so interfered with a traditional state core function — enactment and enforcement of a criminal code — that the Tenth Amendment was violated.

**Note:** The Tenth Amendment, and the limited extent to which it may prevent the federal government from regulating the states, is discussed *supra*, pp. 47-53. See especially *Garcia v. San Antonio Metropolitan Transit Authority*, *supra*, p. 48.

## IV.  INTERSTATE RELATIONSHIPS

A.  **Interstate relationships generally:**   We now examine two aspects of *interstate* relationships: (1) the Privileges and Immunities Clause; and (2) interstate collaboration, including compacts.

B.  **The Privileges and Immunities Clause:**   Article IV, §2, cl. 1 of the Constitution provides: "The Citizens of each State shall be entitled to all Privileges and Immunities of Citizens in the several States."

1.  **Function:**   This *interstate* Privileges and Immunities Clause (to be distinguished from the Privileges and Immunities Clause of §1 of the Fourteenth Amendment) *prevents states from discriminating against out-of-state individuals*. As the Supreme Court has put it, the clause "was designed to insure to a citizen of State A who ventures into State B the same privileges which the citizens of State B enjoy." *Toomer v. Witsell*, 334 U.S. 385 (1948). Like the Commerce Clause, the interstate Privileges and Immunities Clause is an attempt to "help fuse into one Nation a collection of independent, sovereign States." *Id.*

2.  **"Citizenship" vs. "residence":**   The Privileges and Immunities Clause speaks of "citizens" of other states. But as a practical matter, discrimination against non-*residents* is what is barred.

    a.  **Corporations and aliens not protected:**   The one practical effect of the use of the word "citizens" within the Clause is that *corporations* and *aliens* are not protected by the Clause. (In contrast, observe that both corporations and aliens are protected by the Equal Protection and Due Process Clauses of the Fourteenth Amendment.)

3.  **Test for P&I violation:**   Even where a state does discriminate against out-of-staters, it is relatively hard for the out-of-staters to establish a violation of the Privileges and Immunities Clause.

    a.  **Only "fundamental rights" covered:** First, only rights that are *"fundamental to national unity"* are covered. The rights that meet this "fundamental to national unity" standard are all related to *commerce*.

        i.  **Examples:** The right to be *employed*, the right to *practice one's profession*, and the right to *engage in business* are all fundamental, and are therefore protected.

            **Example:** Alaska requires that Alaskan residents be given an absolute preference over non-residents for all jobs on the Alaska oil pipeline. *Held*, the preference violates the Privileges and Immunities Clause. Access to employment is a right fundamental to national unity. Since the statute cannot survive the two-part standard applicable to discrimination against out-of-staters (described below), the preference is invalid. *Hicklin v. Orbeck* (the "Alaska Hire" case), 437 U.S. 518 (1978).

        ii.  **Recreational use:**   Conversely, *non-economic* rights are generally *not* "fundamental to national unity," and thus not protected by the Privileges and Immunities Clause. For example, the right to engage in *recreational* activities is not protected by the clause.

> **Example:** Montana allows Montana residents to purchase a license for hunting elk and other animals for $30, while non-residents are charged $225. *Held*, this scheme does not violate the Privileges and Immunities Clause, because the right to recreation is not a right that is fundamental to national unity. *Baldwin v. Montana Fish and Game Comm'n,* 436 U.S. 371 (1978).

b. **Two-part test:** Once the Court concludes that a "fundamental right" *is* at stake, then the Court applies a *two-part test* to determine whether the discrimination against non-residents is acceptable. The plaintiff (who is attacking the discrimination against out-of-staters) will win if *either* of the following is shown:

   i. **"Peculiar source of evil":** First, the discrimination will violate the Privileges and Immunities Clause unless non-residents are a *"peculiar source of the evil"* which the law was enacted to remedy.

   > **Example:** In the "Alaska Hire" case, *supra*, Alaska argued that its employment preference for residents was a reasonable response to high unemployment rates. But the Court held that the state did not show that the non-residents were a "peculiar source of the evil" (unemployment), because much of the unemployment came from the fact that too many residents were untrained or lived too far from job opportunities, and the influx of out-of-staters seeking jobs was just a small part of the problem.

   ii. **"Substantial relationship" test:** Second, the plaintiff will win if the discrimination against non-residents *does not bear a "substantial relationship" to the problem* the statute is attempting to solve.

   > **Example:** In "Alaska Hire" this prong was not satisfied, either — a blanket and absolute preference for all qualified residents over all non-residents was not *sufficiently "closely tailored"* to the unemployment problem. (In other words, if there is a *less discriminatory alternative* that would solve the problem, the requisite "substantial relationship" between the discrimination against out-of-staters and the problem will not be found to exist.)

   > **Note:** Once a "right fundamental to national unity" is shown to be at stake, the Supreme Court uses something close to *strict scrutiny*: the burden is on the state to show both that non-residents are a peculiar source of the evil, and that the discrimination bears a substantial relationship to the problem being solved.

4. **Practice of law:** The right to *practice law* is a sufficiently important and "fundamental" right that this privilege may not be limited to state residents. Thus in *Supreme Court of New Hampshire v. Piper*, 470 U.S. 274 (1985), the Supreme Court held that New Hampshire could not restrict the right to practice to those who resided within the state.

5. **No "market participant" exception for state:** Recall that where a state is acting as a *"market participant,"* it is not subject to the Commerce Clause's prohibition on discrimination against interstate commerce. (See *supra*, p. 84.) It can plausibly be argued that a similar "market participant" exception should exist to render the Privileges and Immunities Clause inapplicable where the state discriminates against out-of-state residents for *government jobs*. However, the Court has held that there is *no "market participant" exception to the Privileges and Immunities Clause*. The Court reached this conclusion in ruling that the clause applied to a Camden, New Jersey ordinance which required that at

least 40% of the work force on any construction project funded by the city must reside in the city. (The Court did not hold that the ordinance violated the clause; it remanded for a determination on this issue.) **United Building and Construction Trades Council v. Camden**, 465 U.S. 208 (1984).

    **a.  Grounds for distinction:**  The majority reasoned that the rationale for a "market participant" exemption in the privileges and immunities context was not nearly as strong as in the Commerce Clause context. The Commerce Clause deals only with regulation, and a state acting as "market participant" is simply not regulating. But the Privileges and Immunities Clause bars *any* type of state conduct, regulatory or otherwise, which discriminates against out-of-staters on matters of fundamental concern.

    **b.  Factor to be considered:**  Nonetheless, the Court indicated, the fact that the discriminatory conduct consists of the state's expenditure of its own funds is *a non-dispositive factor* which militates in favor of upholding the action against a privileges and immunities attack.

    **c.  Discrimination against municipal residence barred:**  The Supreme Court broke other major new ground in the *Camden* case: it held that the Privileges and Immunities Clause bars discrimination based on *municipal residence*, just as it bars such discrimination based on state residence. The Court conceded that a regulation that discriminates against out-of-towners burdens some in-staters as well as out-of-staters. But it reasoned that in-staters "at least have a chance to remedy at the polls any discrimination against them. Out-of-state citizens have no similar opportunity," so that there is a violation of the Privileges and Immunities Clause as to them.

    **d.  "Substantial reason" may justify:**  The Court emphasized in *Camden* that the ban on discrimination against out-of-staters is *not absolute*; all that is required is that there be a *tight fit* between the particular discrimination used and a significant evil that the state is combatting. Here, Camden claimed that it was attempting to reverse widespread local unemployment and "middle-class flight." The Court remanded to the trial Court for a consideration of whether this was an appropriate purpose, and whether the particular discriminatory measure chosen was sufficiently closely linked to attainment of that objective. But the Court implied that, especially since the City was spending its own funds, the City would prevail if it could show that emigration was indeed a "peculiar source" of the City's economic decline.

    **e.  Local residence requirements generally:**  Thus after *Camden*, municipalities may still be able to require that all or a specified portion of their employees live within the city limits. Such provisions will be subjected to privileges and immunities scrutiny, but if the city can show that out-of-towners are a peculiar source of the significant evil at which the discriminatory measure is aimed, the measure will still be upheld. For instance, if a city can show that a particular spending program was created *for the purpose* of reducing local unemployment (e.g., a program giving summer jobs to inner-city youths) a ban on those not living within the city limits, including those living out-of-state, would probably survive privileges and immunities attack.

**6.  Distinguished from equal protection:**  Where a nonresident is discriminated against, the case may be actionable under the *Equal Protection Clause* as well as under the Privileges and Immunities Clause. There are two principal differences between these two types of claims:

a. **Aliens and corporations:** First, as noted, an ***alien*** or ***corporation*** may not take advantage of the Privileges and Immunities Clause, but may take advantage of the Equal Protection Clause.

b. **Not suspect classification:** Secondly, nonresidency (unlike alienage) has thus far not been held by the Court to be a "suspect classification" for equal protection purposes. Therefore, a state scheme which discriminates against nonresidents is not subject to *strict* equal protection scrutiny, and must just meet a standard of "mere rationality." (See *infra*, p. 240.)

    i. **Strict scrutiny:** Where a privileges and immunities attack is lodged, by contrast (assuming that a right fundamental to national unity is involved), the functional equivalent of ***strict scrutiny*** is given, since nonresidents must be shown to be a "peculiar source" of the evil, and there must be a relatively close fit between the evil and the state's solution to it.

C. **Interstate compacts:** No state may enter into any "treaty, alliance, or confederation. ... " Article I, §10, cl. 1. However, by negative implication, Clause 3 of that same section allows certain interstate agreements: "No state shall, ***without the consent of Congress*** ... enter into any agreement or compact with another state or with a foreign power. ... " Such *"interstate compacts"* are a frequently-used device for insuring cooperation among two or more states.

1. **When congressional consent necessary:** Despite the literal wording of Clause 3 (quoted above), ***not every agreement between states requires congressional consent***. Rather, congressional consent is required only where the interstate combination "tend[s] to the increase of political power in the States, which may encroach upon the just supremacy of the United States. ... " *Virginia v. Tennessee*, 148 U.S. 503 (1893).

a. **Illustrations:** Thus if two states were to agree that one would cede part of its territory to the other, this agreement would probably require congressional consent, since it would increase the power of the latter in the House. But a reciprocal tax agreement (whereby each consenting state would agree not to tax residents of other states) would not affect the national government, and would not require congressional consent.

---

*Quiz Yourself on*

## INTERGOVERNMENTAL IMMUNITIES & INTERSTATE RELATIONS
*(ENTIRE CHAPTER)*

16. Arms Co. is a government military contractor. Its sole business is to manufacture M-16 rifles, all of which are then sold by it to the U.S. government. Arms Co.'s contract with the U.S. government is of a "cost plus fixed fee" variety. Okra, the state in which Arms Co. is located, has enacted a generally-applicable sales tax on all wholesale sales of tangible property made within the state. Okra applies this tax to Arms Co., with the result that Arms Co. must pay a tax of 8% on all goods bought by it for use in the manufacture of the M-16 rifle. The net effect of this tax is to increase by 4% the price paid by the U.S. government to Arms Co. for each M-16 rifle.

    **(a)** If Arms Co. wishes to attack the constitutionality of the Okra sales tax as applied to its purchase of materials for use in the M-16, what is its best argument? _____

    **(b)** Will this argument succeed? _____

17. The state of River provides that no physician may practice within the state unless that physician resides in

the state. The state has enacted this rule because its legislators believed (with at least some rationality) that doctors are frequently called upon to give emergency service after hours, and doctors who live out-of-state will be, on the whole, less able to do this than those who live in-state. Doc, a person who has satisfied all other requirements for a license to practice in River (e.g., passage of the national medical boards), lives in the neighboring state of Lake.

**(a)** If Doc wishes to challenge River's residency requirement on constitutional grounds, what is his best argument? _____

**(b)** Will this argument probably succeed? _____

*Answers*

**16. (a) That the tax violates the federal immunity from state taxation.**

**(b) No.** It is true that the federal government is itself immune from taxation by any state. See *McCulloch v. Maryland*. But this immunity generally does not extend to federal government employees or to contractors who work for the federal government. It does not matter that the "economic incidence" of the tax falls on the federal government — as long as it is not the federal government itself that is being ***directly obliged*** to pay the tax, the fact that the economic burden of the tax may fall on the federal government is irrelevant.

**17. (a) That the requirement violates the Privileges and Immunities Clause of Article IV.**

**(b) Yes.** Art. IV, Section 2, provides that "the Citizens of each State shall be entitled to all Privileges and Immunities of Citizens in the several States." This Clause prevents states from discriminating against out-of-state individuals. It applies only to rights that are "fundamental to national unity." The right to practice one's profession has been found to be such a right. Once such a "fundamental right" is shown to be at stake, then the defenders of the statute will lose unless they show that non-residents are a "peculiar source of the evil" which the law was enacted to remedy, and that there are no less discriminatory alternatives that would satisfactorily solve the problem.

Here, the unavailability of physicians after-hours may be an important problem, but it is unlikely the state can show that non-residents are a "peculiar source of the evil" (since resident physicians will also frequently be unavailable after hours). Furthermore, it is highly unlikely that there are no less discriminatory alternatives; for instance, the state could simply require that each physician be reachable after hours and have a method of furnishing service within a certain period of time. Therefore, the statute will almost certainly be found to violate at least one of the two required tests, and will thus be struck down. See *Supreme Court of New Hampshire v. Piper*, holding that a state requirement that lawyers practicing within the state reside within it violated the P&I Clause.

*Exam Tips* on
## *INTERGOVERNMENTAL IMMUNITIES AND INTERSTATE RELATIONS*

Here are things to watch for in connection with the two main topics from this Chapter, intergovernmental immunities and Art. IV's Privileges and Immunities Clause:

☛ If your fact pattern shows that a ***federal tax*** is being applied directly to an activity conducted by a ***state government***, consider whether the limited state immunity from federal taxation is being violated.

   ☞ Typical fact patterns raising this issue are: the federal government requires every user, including states, to pay a fee for ***federally-sponsored services*** (e.g., a tax on airplanes to support the air traffic controller system), or the federal government applies a ***general tax*** on certain ***wages*** (e.g., a payroll tax applicable to state as well as private-sector employees).

   ☞ Remember the general rule: the only real state immunity from federal taxation is that the federal government may not tax in a way which ***substantially interferes*** with a state's performance of its ***basic governmental functions***.

      ☞ Thus if the federal government is taxing a state's public parks or schools, you might have a violation of the state immunity.

      ☞ But in the vast majority of situations, including virtually all situations where the federal tax is a ***generally applicable*** tax, there will be ***no*** interference with basic governmental functions and thus no violation of state immunity. (*Example*: The federal government can tax all airplanes, including state-operated ones.)

☛ Conversely, any time you spot a ***state tax*** that is applied to an activity somehow connected with the ***federal government***, consider whether this violates the ***federal immunity from state taxation:***

   ☞ The federal government is certainly immune from ***direct*** taxation by any state. For instance, if your fact pattern involves a state or local property tax on, say, a post office, that's a clear violation.

   ☞ But most exam fact patterns do *not* involve a "direct" tax on a federal instrumentality. Instead, the state taxes a ***private party***, in a way that (arguably) increases the federal government's costs. The classic illustration is a tax on the operations of a ***contractor*** who is performing tasks for the federal government on a cost-plus basis. Here, the rule is that it doesn't matter whether the economic burden is passed onto the federal government; as long as the ***"legal incidence"*** of the tax is ***not*** on the federal government, there is ***no violation*** of the federal immunity. (*Example:* A state may impose a sales tax on materials used by a real estate contractor who is building a post office for the U.S. on a cost-plus basis, since the legal incidence of the tax is not on the federal government.)

☛ Similarly, be on the lookout for state *regulations* that affect the federal government. Such a fact pattern raises the issue of whether the federal immunity from state regulation is being violated.

☞ Typically, federal immunity from state regulation arises where the states are attempting to regulate a *federal enclave*, such as a post office or military post. Even if the state is regulating in a generally-applicable way, federal enclaves are *immune* from this regulation unless Congress has expressly consented to it. (*Example:* A state may not impose its criminal code on a military base, unless Congress consents.)

☛ If your facts show that the *federal government* is *regulating a state*, consider whether the state immunity from federal regulation is being violated.

☞ Here, you should almost always conclude that the state immunity is *not* being violated. State immunity from federal regulation is exceptionally narrow. Only if a federal regulation prevents a state from exercising its *core functions* will there be a violation. (If you do find a violation, it is essentially a violation of the Tenth Amendment.) It is unlikely you will see a fact pattern where the federal regulatory interference with state functioning is so great that this test is satisfied.

☛ Issues involving Article IV's *Privileges and Immunities Clause* are easily hidden.

☞ You should be looking for fact patterns where there is *discrimination* against *out-of-staters*. When you see such discrimination, your first instinct will be to see if there is a violation of the dormant Commerce Clause, and you will also want to examine the possibility of an equal protection violation. But don't forget to check for an Article IV P&I violation, since where that clause applies, the standard of review is very tough.

☞ When you do see a state discriminating against out-of-staters, the most important thing to remember about Article IV P&I is that it applies only to rights that are *"fundamental to national unity."* Essentially, the only rights covered are rights related to *commerce*.

☞ In general, for the "fundamental to national unity" standard to be satisfied, your fact pattern will usually involve an individual who is a *U.S. citizen*, *resides out of state*, and is either *totally blocked* from following his *chosen profession or job* in the state, or is subjected to a *higher license fee* than is charged to in-staters. (*Example:* A state law preventing citizens of other states from practicing law or medicine in the state would involve a right "fundamental to national unity," and would in fact violate the Article IV P&I Clause.)

☞ If you conclude that the right in question *is* fundamental to national unity, then be sure to articulate the correct standard for review. Something akin to strict scrutiny is used: the state *loses* unless it can prove *both* that: (1) non-residents are a *"peculiar source of the evil"* which the discrimination against out-of-staters is attempting to remedy; and (2) the discrimination bears a *"substantial relationship"* to the problem the discriminatory statute is attempting to solve. Usually, you should conclude that the state has *failed* to satisfy one or both of these tests (the "peculiar source of evil" test is especially hard for the state to satisfy).

☞ There is one context in which you should always conclude that a right "fundamental to national unity" is *not* involved: where what is involved is the pursuit of *recreation*. Thus your fact pattern will frequently involve an out-of-stater's right to *hunt*, *fish*, use tennis courts, etc.; typically the out-of-stater will either be entirely blocked from doing these things, or charged a much higher fee than in-staters. Even if the ban on out-of-staters is total, you should still conclude that Article IV's P&I is *not* violated, because commerce is not involved and thus there is no right fundamental to national unity. (But if the out-of-stater wants to hunt, fish, etc. as a *professional* who will earn most of his living that way, then this analysis probably will not apply, and the P&I Clause will apply.)

☞ When you spot discrimination against out-of-staters that seems to trigger the Article IV P&I Clause, you typically will want to compare the application of the P&I Clause with the Equal Protection Clause. Keep in mind the important differences between how these two clauses apply to discrimination against out-of-staters:

   ☞ *Aliens* and *corporations* do *not* get to use the Article IV P&I Clause (since it applies only to "national citizenship," and neither aliens nor corporations are "United States citizens.")

   ☞ On the other hand, once the P&I Clause does apply, something like *strict scrutiny* is applied, and the out-of-stater will almost always win. By contrast, under Equal Protection Clause analysis, non-residency is *not* a suspect classification, so a state can usually discriminate against out-of-staters without violating the Equal Protection Clause as long as the state regulation is rationally related to a legitimate state objective. Often, the state will be able to satisfy this easy standard.

☞ Be sure to specify that it is the *Article IV* P&I Clause, *not* the Fourteenth Amendment P&I Clause that you're talking about. The Fourteenth Amendment P&I Clause is extremely limited, and is virtually never used. Especially on multiple choice questions, be careful not to pick a response stating that the challenged action is a violation of "the Fourteenth Amendment's Privileges and Immunities Clause" — professors love to slip this in as a trick answer.

CHAPTER 8

# SEPARATION OF POWERS

## *ChapterScope*

A prior Chapter (*supra*, p. 57) summarized the general boundaries of the powers of the three federal branches. Here, we examine closely certain *conflicts* between branches, especially between the Executive and Legislative Branches. Here are the most important concepts in this Chapter:

- **President/Congress boundary line:** Many separation-of-powers conflicts involve the boundary line between the President (Executive Branch) and Congress (Legislative Branch). Here are some of the more important principles concerning this boundary line:

  - ❑ **President can't make the laws:** The President cannot make the laws. All he can do is to *carry out the laws* made by Congress.

  - ❑ **Declaration of War:** Only *Congress*, not the President, can *declare war*.

  - ❑ **Appointments:** The President, not Congress, has the power to *appoint* federal executive officers.

    - ❑ **Removal by Congress:** Just as Congress may not directly appoint federal executive officers, it may not *remove* an executive officer, except by the special process of *impeachment*.

  - ❑ **Removal of federal judges:** Federal *judges* cannot be removed by *either* Congress or the President.

- **Other issues:** The other main separation-of-powers area involves issues of *immunity* and *executive privilege*:

  - ❑ **"Speech and Debate" Clause:** Members of Congress are given a quite broad immunity by the *"Speech and Debate"* Clause. This clause shields members of Congress from: (1) civil or criminal suits relating to their legislative actions; and (2) grand jury investigations relating to those actions.

  - ❑ **Executive immunity:** Courts recognize an implied *executive* immunity from civil actions.

    - ❑ **Absolute for President:** The President has *absolute* immunity from civil liability for his official acts.

    - ❑ **Qualified for others:** All other federal officials, including presidential assistants, receive only *qualified* civil immunity.

  - ❑ **Executive privilege:** Presidents have a qualified right to refuse to disclose *confidential information* relating to the performance of their duties. This is called *"executive privilege."*

    - ❑ **Outweighed:** Since the privilege is qualified, it may be outweighed by other compelling governmental interests (e.g., the need for the President's evidence in a criminal trial).

# I.   DOMESTIC POLICY AND THE SEPARATION OF POWERS

**A.  General problem:**   There are a few powers which are explicitly granted by the Constitution to the President. These are enumerated in Article II, §2, and will not be listed here. They include, for instance, the President's status as Commander-in-Chief of the armed forces and his treaty-making power.

  **1.  Implied powers:**   But unlike the Congress, whose powers are much more closely delineated (by Article I, §8), much of the President's power, in both the domestic and foreign spheres, is *implied*. This process of implication has been derived mostly from Article II, §1, which provides, in relevant part, "The executive Power shall be vested in a President. … " If the Supreme Court concludes that a presidential action is properly regarded as being part of the "executive" (rather than judicial or legislative) sphere, that action will not be rendered unconstitutional merely by the fact that it does not fall within any specific constitutionally-enumerated power. See Tribe, pp. 210-211.

**B.  No right to "make laws":**   Despite its willingness to infer the existence of broad presidential authority, the Supreme Court has adhered to one over-arching limitation on presidential power: *The President may not make laws*; he may only *carry them out*. The best-known case evidencing this limitation is *Youngstown Sheet & Tube Co. v. Sawyer*, 343 U.S. 579 (1952) (the *Steel Seizure Case*).

  **1.  Facts of *Youngstown Sheet*:**   During the Korean War, President Truman sought to avert a strike in the nation's steel mills. He therefore issued an executive order directing his Secretary of Commerce to seize the mills and operate them under federal direction. Congressional approval of the seizure order was not requested. The steel companies sought an injunction to prevent the seizure.

  **2.  Supreme Court strikes down seizure:**   The Court *struck down the seizure order*, concluding that it was an unconstitutional exercise of the lawmaking authority reserved to Congress. Although the decision was 6-3, four of the six Justices on the majority side wrote separate concurring opinions, making it difficult to summarize the "doctrine" of the case.

   **a.  Black's opinion:**   Justice Black's opinion for the Court flatly stated that the President's seizure order, coming as it did without the consent of Congress, was a clear usurpation of congressional lawmaking power. The order could not be justified under the "Commander-in-Chief" power; the taking of private property in order to keep labor disputes from stopping production of war materiel was too far removed from the actual "theater of war" in which the President had the right to set policy. Nor could the seizure be justified under the President's power to see that the laws are faithfully executed — the very language of the clause shows that the President must merely carry out the laws, not make them.

   **b.  Concurring opinions:**   But the four concurring opinions, unlike Justice Black's opinion for the Court, attached principal importance to the fact that Congress had previously, and repeatedly, *explicitly rejected* plant seizure as a means of handling labor disputes. Justice Jackson's concurrence, probably the best known of the four, contended that the President's powers "are not fixed but *fluctuate*, depending on their disjunction or conjunction with those of Congress." He conceived of three categories:

    **i.** where the President acts pursuant to express or implied ***authorization*** of Congress, in which case his authority is at its maximum;

    **ii.** where the President acts in the ***absence*** of either a congressional ***grant or denial*** of authority, in which case "there is a zone of twilight in which he and Congress may have ***concurrent*** authority, or in which its distribution is uncertain"; and

    **iii.** where the President acts in ***contradiction*** to the express or implied will of Congress; in this case, his power is ***"at its lowest ebb."*** Jackson felt that the steel seizure fell into this third category, and that it could therefore not be constitutionally justified.

  **c.** **Dissent:** Three Justices dissented in *Youngstown Sheet & Tube*. They contended that temporary seizure was justified because of the emergency nature of the situation, and in order to preserve temporarily the *status quo* until Congress could act.

**3.** **Implied acquiescence by Congress:** Congress may sometimes be found to have ***impliedly acquiesced*** in the President's exercise of power in a certain area. Where such acquiescence exists, this fact may be enough to tip the balance in favor of a finding that the President acted within the scope of his constitutional authority.

  **a.** ***Dames & Moore* case:** The Court relied on such a theory of implied congressional acquiescence when it upheld President Carter's power to take certain actions for the purpose of obtaining the release of American hostages from Iran, in ***Dames & Moore v. Regan***, 453 U.S. 654 (1981).

    **i.** **Facts:** As part of the settlement of the hostage situation, President Carter took a number of actions affecting the claims of American creditors against Iran. The action which posed the most difficult constitutional issue was his ***suspension*** of all contractual claims against Iran then pending in American courts; such claims were to be later arbitrated by an international tribunal.

    **ii.** **Suspension upheld:** The Court found that the claims suspension was ***within*** the President's constitutional authority. While Congress had never explicitly delegated to the President the power to suspend such claims, it had ***implicitly authorized*** that practice by a long history of ***acquiescing*** in similar presidential conduct. (For instance, Congress had implicitly approved the use of executive agreements between the President and foreign powers to ***settle*** claims.)

    **iii.** **Limited scope:** The Court carefully stressed the limited scope of its holding. It was not holding that the President has constitutional authority to settle or suspend *all* claims; the Court was simply deciding that where such settlement or suspension is a "necessary incident to the resolution of a major foreign policy dispute," *and* Congress has acquiesced in that type of presidential action, the action will be deemed within the President's constitutional authority.

    **iv.** **Not dispositive:** In any event, the fact that Congress has impliedly consented to Presidential action will almost certainly not ***by itself*** bring the action within the scope of his constitutional authority; it will merely be a ***factor*** in the analysis of close cases. In *Dames & Moore*, the President's general executive authority in foreign policy matters (and perhaps his Commander-in-Chief powers) were probably also part of the equation.

**b. Implied acquiescence not found (*Hamdan v. Rumsfeld*):** But the Court will not always be quick to find that Congress has implicitly acquiesced in the President's exercise of power. For instance, in a 2006 decision involving the President's wartime powers, the Court *rejected* President George W. Bush's claim that, in the aftermath of the 9/11 terror attacks, Congress had implicitly granted him power to set up *"military commissions"* to try Al Qaeda members for war crimes. See *Hamdan v. Rumsfeld*, 126 S.Ct. 2749 (2006), which is also discussed *infra*, p. 120.

   **i. Facts in brief:** Shortly after the 9/11 attacks, Congress passed a Joint Resolution called the Authorization for Use of Military Force ("AUMF"). The AUMF authorized the President to "use *all necessary and appropriate force* against those nations, organizations, or persons he determines planned, authorize, committed or aided the terrorist attacks ... in order to prevent any future acts of international terrorism[.]" President Bush then issued an executive order (the "November 13 Order") providing that with respect to any non-citizen who the President determines is or was a member of Al Qaeda, that person should be tried by a "military commission." The November 13 Order also provided that the procedures to be followed by these military commissions would give substantially less protection to defendants than they would get if they were tried by a court martial conducted under the rules set out in a federal statute called the Uniform Code of Military Justice (UCMJ). (For details about these differences, see *infra*, p. 120.)

   **ii. Issue:** The issue in *Hamdan* was whether the accused, Hamdan — who the administration alleged had been Osama bin Laden's driver and bodyguard — could properly tried by military commission under these less-protective procedures. The administration argued that Congress, by passing the AUMF, had implicitly granted the President power to conduct such trials by commission. Hamdan argued that (1) Congress had not meant the AUMF to authorize military commissions and therefore (2) the use of such commissions was to be governed by the UCMF, a pre-AUMF statute, which barred the use of commissions unless they followed the procedures for courts martial "insofar as practicable."

   **iii. Hamdan wins:** By a 5-3 vote, the Court *sided with Hamdan.* The majority believed that Congress had not intended, in passing the AUMF, to repeal the UCMJ's rule barring military commissions that did not use the UCMJ's courts martial procedures where these were "practicable." The majority cited an earlier case saying that "repeals by implication are not favored."

   **(1) Reference to *Youngstown*:** *Hamdan* shows that Justice Jackson's three-part analysis in *Youngstown Sheet & Tube* remains important. Justice Kennedy, who in a concurrence supplied the key fifth vote for the plaintiff, quoted extensively from Jackson's analysis. Kennedy believed that what the administration was trying to do here with military commissions was incompatible with Congress' intent in the UCMJ. Consequently, he believed that the case fell within Jackson's *third category*: cases in which "the President takes measures *incompatible with the expressed or implied will of Congress,"* and in which the President's power is therefore *"at its lowest ebb."*

   **iv. Significance:** So *Hamdan* suggests that, especially in the controversial area of the President's wartime powers, the Court will be reluctant to conclude that a vague or ambiguous congressional statute constitutes implicit acquiescence in the President's exercise of the authority in question — if Congress wants to authorize the President to exercise a particular wartime power, it will have to confer that authority relatively ***explicitly***.

**C. President's veto power:** Article I, §7, gives the President the power to ***veto*** any bill passed by Congress. If the measure is vetoed, the veto can be overridden (and the measure enacted into law) only by a ***two-thirds vote*** in each house. There are several major separation-of-powers issues concerning the presidential veto power: (1) To what extent does the President have the ability to make a "pocket veto"? (2) Can the President constitutionally be given a "line-item veto"? and (3) To what extent does the so-called "legislative veto" violate the President's veto power?

1. **The "pocket veto":** Article I, §7 provides that ordinarily, if the President fails within ten days either to sign a bill or to veto it and return it to the house in which it originated (so that a possible override attempt can be made), the bill becomes law. However, that section also provides that if Congress by its ***adjournment*** has ***prevented*** return of the vetoed legislation, the statute cannot go into effect unless the President signs it. In this situation, the President is given an ***absolute*** veto power (i.e., one which cannot be overridden); this is known as a ***"pocket veto."***

2. **The "line item" veto:** Nearly every president since Grant has coveted the ***"line item veto."*** This is the ability to veto a particular part of a bill — typically, a single item of spending — rather than the entire bill. In 1997, President Clinton became the first U.S. President to receive essentially this power from Congress. However, the Supreme Court quickly ruled that the line item veto as implemented by Congress violated the Presentment clause of the Constitution, in ***Clinton v. City of New York***, 524 U.S. 417 (1998).

   a. **How the line-item veto worked:** The Line Item Veto Act gave the President the power to ***"cancel"*** any of several types of provisions contained in new statutes enacted by Congress, including any "item of new direct spending" and any "limited tax benefit." The Act allowed the President to sign an entire bill (containing multiple provisions) into law, and then to "cancel" any individual spending or limited-tax-benefit item he wished, provided that he did so within five days after enactment. At that point, the only way Congress could restore the vetoed item was re-enact it as a separate "disapproval bill," which the President could again veto. The net effect of the Act was to let the President plus one-third of Congress (the percentage necessary to uphold the president's veto of the disapproval bill) veto any individual item of spending or limited tax benefit.

   b. **Majority strikes down:** By a 6-3 vote, the court found that the Line Item Veto Act ***violated the Presentment clause,*** Art. I, §7, cl. 2. The majority opinion was by Justice Stevens.

      i. **The Presentment clause:** The Presentment clause provides that after a bill has passed both houses of Congress, but before it has become a law, it must be presented to the president; if he approves it, "he shall sign it, but if not he shall return it, with his objections to that house in which it shall have originated, who shall . . . proceed to reconsider it." (The President's "return" of the bill is what is commonly known as a presidential "veto.")

    **ii. Violates Presentment clause:** The majority concluded that the Line Item Veto Act failed to follow the Presentment clause's method of enacting or repealing statutes. The process laid down in that clause was, the majority concluded, the *only* way authorized in the Constitution to enact or repeal a bill. The Act failed to follow this procedure in at least two ways: (1) the President's "return" of the bill (his veto of it) occurred *after* the bill had been signed into law, rather than before, as the Presentment clause requires; and (2) the cancellation could apply to only *part* of the bill, whereas the Presentment clause requires veto of the *entire* bill.

    **iii. Net effect is to let President write new bill:** The net effect of the act was to produce "truncated versions of . . . bills that passed both Houses of Congress," Stevens said. The resulting bills were not the product of the " *'finely wrought' procedure* that the Framers designed." If the act were valid, "it would authorize the President to *create a different law* — one whose text was not voted on by either House of Congress or presented to the president for signature." Stevens noted that he was not expressing any opinion about the wisdom of the procedures reflected in the act; however, if the President was to play a different role in the process of enacting legislation, that change would have to come about through a constitutional amendment.

  **c. Kennedy concurrence:** The majority opinion by Justice Stevens concentrated on the narrowly-technical requirements of the Presentment clause, and did not explore the *separation-of-powers* problems that the Line Item Veto Act might pose. But a concurrence by Justice Kennedy did discuss those separation-of-powers problems. Kennedy acknowledged that the act was intended to help restrain congressional spending, something that Congress seemed to have trouble doing on its own. However, he said, "failure of political will does not justify unconstitutional remedies." The act "establishes a new mechanism which gives the President the sole ability to hurt a group that is a visible target, in order to disfavor the group or to extract further concessions from Congress." This "enhances the President's powers beyond what the Framers would have endorsed."

  **d. Dissent:** Three Justices — Breyer, O'Connor and Scalia — dissented in *Clinton v. New York*. The dissenters rejected the majority's core assertion that the Line Item Veto Act enabled the President to repeal or amend statutes. The President's use of his power to cancel a spending item was *not a repeal or amendment of a statute*, they said — the statute itself remains fully in force following the President's "cancellation" action. Instead, Congress had merely given the President the *discretion to spend or not spend an appropriated item*, something it had done many times in the past without problems. As Scalia put it, "[T]here is not a dime's worth of difference between Congress' authorizing the President to cancel a spending item, and Congress' authorizing money to be spent on a particular item at the President's discretion. And the latter has been done since the Founding of the Nation." Scalia concluded that the Act did not truly give the President a line item veto; the title of the act ("Line Item Veto Act") "has succeeded in *faking out the Supreme Court*."

  **e. Multiple bills as solution:** One way in which Congress might achieve essentially the result it was trying for in the Line Item Veto Act would be to make sure that each item of federal spending is embodied in a *separate bill* — that way, the President could simply veto any item he wished by vetoing the bill that contained that item and only that item. However, this approach would require literally thousands of spending bills per session, each of which would have to be separately produced, and separately voted on by Congress. Nonetheless, some members of Congress have asserted, following the *Clinton* decision, that advances in computer technology make this approach a viable option.

3. **The legislative veto:**   The so-called "*legislative veto*" is a device which enables Congress to monitor actions by the executive branch, including federal administrative agencies. Typically, such a legislative veto provision is included as part of a congressional statute delegating certain powers to federal agencies. If, after an agency takes a certain action (usually, issuance of a regulation), Congress disagrees, the veto provision in the original bill allows one or both houses to cancel that administrative action by means of a *resolution*. The resolution is not presented to the President (as a statute must be), and he does not receive the opportunity to veto it.

   a. **Veto ruled unconstitutional:**   In one of the most important constitutional law decisions of the 1980's, the Supreme Court held that a typical one-house legislative veto was *unconstitutional*, because it violated both the President's veto power and the bicameral structure of Congress. *Immigration and Naturalization Service (INS) v. Chadha*, 462 U.S. 919 (1983).

      i. **Facts:**   Article I, §8 of the Constitution gives Congress the right to establish rules of naturalization and, by implication, immigration. Congress has always possessed, and has frequently exercised, the power to allow an alien who would otherwise be deportable under existing immigration rules to remain in the country; typically, this has been done by means of a "private bill" applicable to one or a few particular aliens. In an effort to relieve itself of the burdens of considering numerous private bills, Congress delegated to the Attorney General, in the Immigration and Nationality Act, the authority to suspend deportation of aliens in certain situations. However, in order to retain some control over this delegated power, Congress reserved to itself a legislative veto over each decision by the Attorney General suspending deportation. The veto could be exercised by a resolution passed by *either* house within a certain time after the Attorney General's decision to suspend deportation. Chadha, the plaintiff, was one of several aliens as to whom the House of Representatives used its veto power to reverse the Attorney General's suspension of deportation.

      ii. **Veto provision stricken:**   The Supreme Court *struck down* this legislative veto as a violation of two distinct constitutional requirements. First, the veto violated the Presentment Clause (Art. I, §7, cl. 2), which requires that every bill be presented to the President for his signature, so that he may have the opportunity to veto it. Secondly, this particular veto provision, since it could be exercised by a *single house*, violated the *bicameral* requirement of Article I, §§1 and 7, by which both houses must pass a bill before it can become law.

      iii. **Essentially legislative act:**   The real issue in the case was whether the House's issuance of the legislative veto here itself constituted the exercise of *legislative power*. Not all acts by a house fall into this category, and only the ones that do require presentment and bicameral approval. However, in the Court's view the overruling of the Attorney General's decision on a deportation matter did constitute the exercise of legislative power, since it had the "purpose and effect of altering the legal rights, duties and relations of persons … outside the legislative branch."

    **iv. Consequence:** Consequently, Congress could reverse the Attorney General's decision on a deportation matter only by ***passing a law***, in the constitutionally-prescribed manner (passage by both houses, presentment to the President and either signature by him or the overriding of his veto). The fact that the legislative veto mechanism may be a more "efficient" means of controlling administrative action was irrelevant.

**b. Dissent:** Two Justices, White and Rehnquist, dissented in *Chadha*. The main dissent was by Justice White, who argued that a house's use of the legislative veto was simply not the functional equivalent of passing a law. The legislative veto "no more allows one House of Congress to make law than does the presidential veto confer such power upon the President."

    **i. Administrative agencies' lawmaking function:** In White's view, executive agencies engage in a sort of "lawmaking" function, and no one contends that every agency decision of a lawmaking nature need be confirmed by subsequent vote of both houses of Congress and by presidential signature. "If Congress may delegate lawmaking powers to independent executive agencies, it is most difficult to understand Article I as forbidding Congress from also reserving a check on legislative power for itself." In White's view, it was "enough that the ***initial*** statutory authorizations comply with the Article I requirements."

    **ii. Change in status quo:** Finally, White argued that the legislative veto provision in this case did not violate the separation-of-powers principles behind the bicameral and presidential-veto requirements. White contended that the net result of Congress' delegation of authority to the Attorney General plus its reservation of veto power was that "[a] departure from the status quo occurs only upon the ***concurrence of opinion*** among the House, Senate, and President." That is, if the determination that an alien is deportable is viewed as a change in the legal status quo, this change can be consummated only with the approval of ***each*** of the three actors (assuming that the Attorney General is treated as embodying the President's authority). This result preserved the required separation of powers, in White's opinion.

**c. Significance:** *Chadha* thus makes the one-house legislative veto completely unusable. If the House or Senate wants to reserve power to undo the action of an administrative agency, both houses will have to pass the same bill and present it to the President for a possible veto.

**d. Two-house veto provisions:** In the vast majority of instances, legislative veto clauses allowing a veto only where ***both houses*** act concurrently are ***just as unconstitutional*** as a single-house veto provision, since both types of clauses ***deprive the President of his veto power.***

    **i. Single-house actions approved by Constitution:** There are four actions which the Constitution permits a ***single house*** to take, without possibility of presidential veto. In these four situations, a single-house legislative veto would presumably be ***constitutional***. For instance, since the Senate alone is given the power to approve or disapprove presidential appointments (Art. II, §2, Cl. 2), the Senate could presumably pass a resolution that all presidential appointments shall be deemed approved by the Senate if that body does not vote to reject them within a certain period of time. (However, such a provision might be attacked on the theory that it delegates to the Executive Branch powers which must be affirmatively exercised by the Senate itself.)

**D. Special prosecutor:** Obviously a key element of the President's constitutional power is the power to *enforce the law*, including the power to investigate and prosecute violations of the law. Consequently, it might be thought that any congressional interference with the President's untrammeled right to enforce the laws would be vulnerable to a separation-of-powers argument. But the Supreme Court has recently upheld the Ethics in Government Act, which lets the Judicial rather than Executive Branch appoint a *special prosecutor* to investigate and prosecute crimes by high executive officials, and which restricts the Executive Branch's right to fire such a prosecutor. See *Morrison v. Olson*, discussed further *infra*, pp. 129-130. The *Morrison* case seems to mean that the present Court will allow a fairly significant limitation to be placed by Congress upon the President's previously-untrammeled power to enforce the law.

**E. Interference with, or undue delegation to, the Judicial Branch:** So far in this section, we have focused mainly on the boundary line between Congress and the Executive Branch, and have looked at how separation-of-powers principles prevent Congress from delegating law-making power to the President (see *Youngstown Sheet*, *supra*, p. 110) or interfering with the President's powers (e.g., his veto power; see *INS v. Chadha*, *supra*, p. 115). Similar separation-of-powers issues can be presented by action that takes place at the boundary line between Congress and the *Judicial Branch*, or the boundary between the Executive and Judicial Branches.

Basically, the same very general rule applies: the *Judicial Branch's role cannot be abridged by action of one of the other branches*, and conversely, functions that are the *appropriate job of the other two branches cannot be given instead to the Judicial Branch*. (Separation issues relating to the Judicial Branch actually don't arise very often.)

1. **Delegation of legislative powers:** However, Congress *does* have considerable flexibility in *assigning* to the Judicial Branch tasks that might be considered law-making ones, at least where the subject matter relates to the *role of the courts*. This principle is illustrated by *Mistretta v. U.S.*, 488 U.S. 361 (1989).

   a. **Sentencing commission:** *Mistretta* involved the U.S. Sentencing Commission, set up by Congress to develop mandatory guidelines that federal judges would have to apply in setting sentences for federal crimes. Congress provided that of the seven voting members (all to be appointed by the President with the advice and consent of the Senate), at least three must be *federal judges*. The plaintiffs claimed that this was an unconstitutional delegation of law-making power to the Judicial Branch. That is, the plaintiffs argued, Congress was assigning to the judges on the Commission not the job of interpreting the law (the proper judicial role), but the job of making *sentencing policy*, a classic legislative function.

   b. **Delegation attack rejected:** The Court *rejected* this claim of unconstitutional delegation of law-making authority to the Judicial Branch. It is true, the Court said, that non-judicial duties may generally not be given to the Judicial Branch. But there are some exceptions, and this was one. Because the judiciary plays the major role in sentencing, allowing some judges to participate in the making of guidelines for sentences does not threaten the "fundamental structural protections of the Constitution."

## II.  FOREIGN AFFAIRS AND THE WAR POWERS

A.  **Special presidential role in foreign affairs:**  The Constitution gives the President substantially greater authority with respect to *foreign affairs* than with respect to domestic ones. Article II, §2, explicitly enumerates a number of powers given to him in this area (e.g., the Commander-in-Chief power, the treaty-making power and the right to appoint ambassadors). But even more generally, the need to present a clear and unified face to the world dictates that the President bear a special role in implementing the nation's foreign policy.

1.  *Curtiss-Wright* **case:**  This special role was emphasized in *U.S. v. Curtiss-Wright Export Corp.*, 299 U.S. 304 (1936). In *Curtiss-Wright*, a joint resolution of Congress authorized the President to ban the sale of arms to countries engaged in a particular conflict. President Roosevelt proclaimed such an embargo, and Curtiss-Wright was charged with conspiring to sell arms to Bolivia, one of the countries to which the embargo extended. Curtiss-Wright challenged the joint resolution as being an unconstitutionally broad *delegation* of legislative power to the President.

   a.  **Upheld by Supreme Court:**  The Supreme Court *upheld* the resolution, and the resulting presidential embargo. The Court stressed the "very delicate, plenary and exclusive power of the President as the sole organ of the federal government in the field of international relations. ... " The need for negotiation, plus the President's special access to sources of information, required "a degree of discretion and freedom from statutory restriction which would not be admissible were domestic affairs alone involved." Here, for instance, the President would be better able than Congress to determine whether Bolivia was in fact engaged in the conflict. Thus the delegation to the President was not unconstitutionally broad, regardless of whether such delegation would be permissible with respect to a domestic issue (a question which the Court did not decide).

   b.  **In accord with Congress' intent:**  Observe that the presidential embargo in *Curtiss-Wright* was in accord with congressional intent; in fact, the very point of the defendant's argument was that there was excessive *harmony* between Congress and the President (i.e., excessive delegation). If, however, the President acted in an area where Congress had been *silent*, or where Congress had manifested a *contrary intent*, the President's power to make international policy would presumably be less broad. This is certainly the theory behind Justice Jackson's concurrence in the *Youngstown Sheet & Tube* case (*supra*, pp. 110-111).

   c.  **Delegation problems generally:**  The *Curtiss-Wright* case was really about the proper limits of delegation of power by Congress to the President. A full discussion of delegation doctrine is more properly made in the course on Administrative Law. However, the following general propositions can be stated:

      i.  **International vs. domestic:**  Broader delegation of lawmaking power by Congress to the President will be tolerated in the area of international affairs than in the domestic area; this is the explicit holding of *Curtiss-Wright*; and

ii. **Delegation rules relaxed:** Even in the domestic area, the limits on delegation by Congress to the President or to administrative agencies have been substantially relaxed since the late 1930's. In general, the more precise the *standards* laid down by Congress to guide the executive branch or administrative agencies, the less likely it is that excessive delegation will be found.

2. **Executive agreements:** Recall that by Article II, §2, the President may enter into treaties only upon a two-thirds vote of the Senate. Presidents have often used the device of the *"executive agreement"* to avoid the need for Senate ratification. This device presents some separation-of-powers difficulties, which are discussed briefly *supra*, p. 62.

B. **The war powers:** The Constitution gives both Congress and the President special powers with respect to *war*:

❏ *Congress* is given the power to "*declare War* ... and make Rules concerning *Captures on Land and Water.*" Art. I, § 8, cl. 11. Congress is also given the power to *"raise and support Armies"* (*id.*, cl. 12); to "define and punish ... Offences against the Law of Nations," (*id.*, cl. 10), and to "make Rules for the Government and Regulation of the *land and naval Forces*" (*id.*, cl. 14).

❏ On the other hand, the *President* is made the *"Commander in Chief"* of the *armed forces.* Art. II, § 2, cl. 1. (Also, more generally, "the *executive Power*" is "vested" in the President. Id., § 1.)

So the basic idea is that Congress declares war and maintains the armed forces, but the President, by use of his Commander-in-Chief power executive powers, carries out any war that is so declared.

We consider here two areas in which the division of war powers between Congress and the President has raised important separation-of-powers questions: (1) the President's right to *commit our armed forces abroad* without congressional approval; and (2) the President's right to *detain and try enemy combatants* who have been captured.

1. **Commitment of the armed forces abroad:** The extent to which the President may use his Commander-in-Chief powers to *commit the use of American armed forces abroad*, without a congressional declaration of war, has sparked great controversy during the last two decades.

    a. **Courts silent:** Although the President has committed American armed forces to military action without a declaration of war at numerous times during our history, the courts have rarely passed on the constitutionality of such action. Generally, Congress has tacitly acquiesced in such action, so that no litigation has arisen.

    b. **Sudden attack:** It is settled that the President may commit our armed forces to *repel a sudden attack* upon the United States itself.

    c. **Attack on allies:** It is not clear whether the President may commit forces, without congressional approval, where it is an *ally* of the U.S., rather than the U.S. itself, that is attacked.

    d. **Preemptive strike:** Similarly, the President's right to order a *preemptive strike* in anticipation of an enemy attack is unclear. Since in this situation there would probably not be time for Congress to consider the wisdom of military action, a presidentially-ordered preemptive strike would be likely to be found constitutional.

**e. Defense treaties:** In many instances, the United States is one of several signatories to a collective ***defense treaty***, pledging us to come to the aid of any treaty member who is attacked. Since the treaty has itself been ratified by the Senate, it can be argued that this constitutes sufficient authorization for the President to commit troops when another treaty signatory is in fact attacked.

     **i. Criticism:** But Tribe (p. 233 and n. 14) points out that treaty approval by the ***Senate*** is not the same thing as a declaration of war by ***Congress*** (i.e., both houses). He therefore concludes that the treaty may not be relied upon for a prolonged troop commitment, but could be used "in support of a harried ally until Congress has had ample time" to review the matter. *Id.*

**f. Delegation by Congress:** Congress sometimes ***delegates*** to the President in advance the discretion to commit the armed forces. The best known example of this is the Gulf of Tonkin Resolution, enacted by Congress in 1964 during the early stages of the Vietnam War. The Resolution stated that "[t]he United States is ... prepared, ***as the President determines***, to take all necessary steps, including the use of armed force, to assist any member or protocol state" of SEATO.

     **i. Possibly overbroad delegation:** It may be argued that such a ***broad delegation*** of Congress' war-making powers is unconstitutional. Tribe (p. 234) suggests that the test for the constitutionality of such a delegation should be the same as in other delegation contexts, i.e., whether there are "***articulated standards***" to guide the President. The Gulf of Tonkin Resolution seemed nearly empty of guidelines.

**2. Power to establish military commissions:** Probably the most important separation-of-powers case concerning the war powers in recent decades was a 2006 case involving the President's power to set up ***"military commissions"*** for trying captured alleged terrorists. The case was ***Hamdan v. Rumsfeld***, 126 S.Ct. 2749 (2006). The case yielded a major defeat for President George W. Bush's expansive view of the President's war powers.

**a. Facts:** The accused in *Hamdan*, Salim Hamdan, was a citizen of Yemen who was captured in Afghanistan shortly after 9/11 by U.S. military forces who were fighting with the Taliban. The government asserted that Hamdan had served as Osama bin Laden's "bodyguard and personal driver," and that through this and other means Hamdan had assisted Al Qaeda in planning terrorist attacks including the 9/11 attacks. The core issue in the case was whether Hamdan could be tried by the use of very pro-government procedures before a "military commission" for the war crime of conspiracy to commit terrorist acts.

     **i. Military commissions:** Shortly after 9/11, President Bush issued an executive order (the "November 13 Order") saying that if any non-citizen who the President determined is or was a member of Al Qaeda or a terrorist was to be tried for war crimes, that person should be tried by a "military commission." The November 13 Order provided that the procedures to be followed by such military commissions would give much less protection to defendants than they would get if they were tried by a court martial conducted under the rules set out in a federal statute called the Uniform Code of Military Justice (UCMJ). For instance, the accused and his counsel could in certain circumstances be ***excluded from the proceeding*** or even barred from ***learning what evidence was presented***. Also, any evidence having "probative value to a reasonable person" could be admitted even if it was ***hearsay***

or was *obtained through coercion*. Neither live testimony nor witnesses' written out-of-court statements needed to be sworn. All of these provisions were in sharp contrast to the more pro-defendant provisions that apply to courts martial under the UCMJ.

**(1) "Uniform procedures" rule in UCMJ:** The UCMJ appeared to bar the use of military commissions unless they followed the same procedures used in courts martial "insofar as practicable." This was known as the *"uniformity principle."*

b. **Dispute:** The main issue in *Hamdan* was whether Hamdan could be tried before a military commission operating under the pro-government rules mandated by the President's November 13 Order. Hamdan argued that the uniformity principle prevented this result. The President's legal team countered by arguing that

[1] Congress had *overruled the uniformity principle* by adopting, after 9/11, the Authorization for Use of Military Force ("AUMF"), which authorized the President to "use all necessary and appropriate force against those nations, organizations, or persons he determines planned, authorized, committed or aided the terrorist attacks[.]"

[2] In the absence of the uniformity principle, the President's general Commander-in-Chief powers gave him the right to use military commissions that followed different procedures than used in courts martial; and

[3] In any event, even if the uniformity principle applied, the President had adequately demonstrated that it was not "practicable" to use court-martial procedures against accused terrorists like Hamdan, because it would be too hard to get convictions if these stringent procedures were insisted upon.

c. **President loses:** By a 5-3 vote,[1] the Court *found against the President*: Hamdan could not be tried by a military commission operating under the pro-government procedures announced in the President's November 13 Order. The decision turned mainly on matters of statutory and treaty interpretation, but the case showed that a majority of the Court had a much *narrower view of the President's wartime powers* in ambiguous circumstances than did President Bush.

i. **Majority finds uniformity principle still applies:** Five justices believed that the UCMJ imposed the uniformity principle, that the AUMF was not intended by Congress to overrule the uniformity principle, and that the president had not shown that it was "impracticable" to use uniform rules — i.e., the relatively pro-defendant courts-martial procedures — in the military commission trying Hamdan.[2] Justice Stevens wrote a lengthy opinion so concluding, in which he was

---

1. Newly-appointed Chief Justice Roberts did not participate, because, prior to his appointment, he had written the Court of Appeals decision being appealed. Since that lower-court decision found for the President, it is nearly certain that with Roberts' participation, the vote would have been 5-4 against the President rather than 5-3.

2. For more about this issue, see *supra*, p. 112.

joined on all points by Justices Souter, Ginsburg and Breyer, and on key points by Justice Kennedy.

    **(1) Broad language:**  Stevens wrote in broad terms, making it clear that he believed the case involved important constitutional principles. For instance, Stevens' final sentence said that "the Executive is bound to ***comply with the Rule of Law*** that prevails in this jurisdiction."

    **(2) Rationale:**  Stevens did not believe that the President had shown that it was ***"impracticable"*** to apply the standard court martial rules to Hamdan's trial. The President had never actually made any "official determination" that it was impracticable to apply the rules for courts martial. And Stevens could see no reason for a finding of impracticability. Stevens was most disturbed by the absence of what he called "one of the most fundamental protections" afforded to the accused in courts martial: the ***right to be present.***

  **ii.  Kennedy concurrence:**  On this main argument about whether the uniformity principle still applied, Stevens got the needed fifth vote in the form of a concurrence by Justice Kennedy. Kennedy believed that trials by military commission raise ***"separation-of-powers concerns of the highest order,"*** because these courts "carry the risk that offenses will be ***defined, prosecuted, and adjudicated by executive officials without independent review."*** Such "concentration of power" ***"puts personal liberty in peril of arbitrary action by officials***, an incursion the ***Constitution's three-part system is designed to avoid."***

As discussed previously (see supra, p. 112), Kennedy believed that the three-part scheme of Justice Jackson in *Youngstown Sheet & Tube* should be used to analyze the case, and that here, the President had taken "measures incompatible with the express or implied will of Congress" (quoting Jackson). Therefore, under the Jackson approach the President's power was "at its lowest ebb," and must yield to Congress' intent that military commissions obey the uniformity principle. The uniformity principle, in turn, required that the commissions' procedures deviate from those used in courts martial only if the use of the courts-martial procedures was "impracticable," and Kennedy, like Stevens, could not see any impracticability in using those procedures.

    **(1) Get consent of Congress:**  But Kennedy emphasized that his conclusion was based on interpretation of congressional statutes. Therefore, he invited the administration to ***go back to Congress*** and ***request a change in those statutes*** (e.g., the provision in the UCMJ imposing the uniformity principle).

  **iii. Dissents:**  Justices Thomas, Scalia and Alito ***dissented***. The main dissent was by Justice Thomas, who said that the court's opinion "openly flouts our well-established duty to ***respect the Executive's judgment in matters of military operations and foreign affairs."*** Unlike the majority, he believed that the President here was using his Commander-in-Chief authority "with the complete support of Congress." Thomas therefore believed that this case fell within the first category of Justice Jackson's concurrence in *Youngstown Sheet and Tube*: situations where the President acts "pursuant to an express or implied authorization from Congress," in which case his actions are, according to Jackson, "supported by the strongest of presumptions and the widest latitude of judicial interpretation, [so that] the burden of persuasion ... rest[s] heavily upon any who might attack it."

**(1) Rationale:** Thomas thought that the AUMF passed by Congress after 911 constituted an authorization to use military commissions like the one here. He also believed that even if the AUMF had not been passed, the UCMJ's uniformity principle did not mean that procedures used in military commissions must be the same as those used in courts martial.

d. **Significance:** *Hamdan* does not seem to set forth any new principles of constitutional law. However, it does seem to say a couple of significant things about the scope of the President's wartime powers in the eyes of the present Court:

❏ If it is unclear whether Congress has **acquiesced** to the President's proposed course of conduct, the Court will **not be quick to conclude that acquiescence has occurred.** A majority, albeit a bare one, of the Roberts Court seems to be saying that vague or broad congressional authorizations (e.g., the AUMF's grant of power to the President to use "all necessary and appropriate force" to combat those who instituted the 9/11 attacks) will not be found to displace prior, more specific, limits on the President's wartime authority.

❏ The Court seems quite concerned to make sure that the **joint roles of Congress and the President** are scrupulously **respected** in this wartime-powers area.

e. **Congress' response:** Congress responded to the *Hamdan* decision by passing the **Military Commissions Act of 2006.** The MCA explicitly gave the President much of the authority that President Bush unsuccessfully claimed in *Hamdan* that he already had. The Act allowed the President to set up a new form of military commissions that do not have to obey many of the rules that the *Hamdan* Court found to be required in the commissions at issue there. For example, the MCA made many of the pro-defendant provisions of the UCMJ, which are applicable to courts martial, specifically inapplicable to the new military commissions. The inapplicable UCMJ rights included various aspects of the right against self-incrimination, the right not to have secret and hearsay evidence admitted against one, and the right to cite any part of the Geneva Conventions in one's defense.[3]

i. **Limited judicial review:** The MCA also limited the judicial review to which defendants convicted in a military commission are entitled. This aspect of the MCA was later found by the Supreme Court to be an unconstitutional suspension of the writ of *habeas corpus*, in *Boumediene v. Bush*, discussed *infra*, p. 125.

---

3. Four members of the *Hamdan* court thought that the military commissions at issue there would violate Common Article 3 of the **Geneva Conventions**. That Article requires that prisoners be sentenced by a "regularly constituted court according all the judicial guarantees which are recognized as indispensable by civilized people." (The four Justices thought that the military commissions didn't meet this regularly-constituted-court standard, in part because the defendants did not have the right to be present at the trial or be privy to all evidence against them.) In enacting the MCA, Congress apparently recognized that it could not unilaterally reinterpret the Geneva Conventions to allow conduct that a plurality of the Court thought would be Convention violations (the Conventions are a treaty to which the U.S. is a party, so Congress can't unilaterally change the document's meaning). Congress therefore seems to have tried do the next-best thing, which was to deprive defendants in new-style military commissions of the right to *assert* violations of the Convention in their defense case.

3. **Habeas corpus, and the rights of enemy combatants to it (*Boumediene*):** The post-9/11 war on terror has also caused the Supreme Court to focus on the separation-of-powers implications of the *"writ of habeas corpus."* As we'll see below (p. 125), in a 2008 case, *Boumediene v. Bush*, the Court, relying on separation-of-powers principles, has concluded that non-citizens detained as enemy combatants at Guantanamo Bay, Cuba, have the constitutional right to use the habeas process to challenge in federal district court the lawfulness of their imprisonment.

   a. **Nature of the habeas writ:** For centuries, Anglo-American law has generally entitled prisoners to use the "writ of habeas corpus." In American law, the right of habeas corpus is basically the right of a state or federal prisoner to go to a federal district court and argue that the prisoner is being held in violation of the federal Constitution or federal law. "Habeas corpus" is Latin for "You have the body," and the idea is that the prisoner can force the "jailer" (i.e., the governmental body that is imprisoning the prisoner) to *justify* to the federal judge hearing the habeas petition *why the imprisonment is proper.*

      i. **Suspension Clause:** The right to bring a habeas corpus petition is granted by the Constitution. This occurs by means of Art. I, s. 9, cl. 2 (the *"Suspension Clause"*), which says that "The privilege of the Writ of Habeas Corpus shall not be suspended, unless when in Cases of Rebellion or Invasion the public Safety may require it." Under post-Civil War Supreme Court cases, the right applies to *both state and federal prisoners.*

      ii. **Federal judge can order release:** If a prisoner properly brings a habeas proceeding,[4] the federal judge is authorized to conduct her own factual inquiry into the case. Then, if the judge concludes that the prisoner is indeed being held in violation of the Federal Constitution or federal law, the judge has the power to order the prisoner released.

   b. **Applicability to enemy combatants:** Prior to 9/11, it had never been clear whether a *non-U.S. citizen* held by U.S. military authorities as an enemy combatant was entitled to bring a federal habeas corpus proceeding, in which the prisoner could have a federal district judge review the legality of his detention.

      i. **Combatant Status Review Tribunals:** Beginning soon after 9/11, the U.S. military detained hundreds of non-U.S. citizens (aliens) in combat areas like Afghanistan and Bosnia. U.S. forces designated many of these as *"enemy combatants,"* and brought them to the U.S. base at Guantanamo Bay, Cuba, where they were held, sometimes for years. At Guantanamo, the Defense Department conducts *Combatant Status Review Tribunals (CSRTs)* to determine whether each detainee was properly classified as an enemy combatant. In the CSRTs, detainees have limited rights compared with the rights they would have if subjected to a traditional U.S. criminal trial — for instance, they do not have the right to counsel, they do not have the right to full knowledge of the charges against them, and hearsay evidence is fully admissible against them.

---

4. Congress has imposed many restrictions on habeas proceedings, especially in connection with state-court convictions. For instance, there is a one-year statute of limitations on such proceedings, and the state-court decision is entitled to a large degree of deference.

ii. **No habeas, according to administration:** The Bush administration took the position that once a prisoner at Guantanamo was declared an enemy combatant and the decision was upheld in the CSRT proceeding, the prisoner could be detained indefinitely (for at least so long as the war on terror continued). The administration also contended that such an enemy combatant was not entitled to bring a habeas corpus challenge to his imprisonment.

iii. **Congress agrees:** In two statutes, Congress agreed with the administration's view that enemy combatants should not have habeas rights. First, in the Detainee Treatment Act of 2005 (DTA), Congress said that no court would have jurisdiction to hear an application for habeas corpus brought by any alien detained by the military at Guantanamo. Instead, the sole jurisdiction to review any decision by a CSRT that a prisoner was indeed an enemy combatant was given to the federal Court of Appeals for the District of Columbia. And the D.C. Court of Appeals was *limited in the facts that it could consider* on the appeal — for instance, it *could not consider newly-discovered evidence* that the prisoner was not in fact an enemy combatant, as the court could presumably have done in a true habeas proceeding.

(1) **MCA:** Then, in the Military Commissions Act of 2006 (MCA), Congress said that these jurisdiction-stripping provisions of the DTA were to be applied not just prospectively, but also to cases that were already "in the pipeline" when the DTA was enacted.[5]

c. **The *Boumediene* case:** Several Guantanamo prisoners were able to get to the Supreme Court on two issues regarding the DTA's and MCA's jurisdiction-stripping rules: (1) Did a foreign national held at Guantanamo — which is not officially U.S. territory — have the constitutional right to bring a habeas petition? and (2) if so, did the procedures specified by Congress in the DTA and the MCA violate the prisoners' habeas rights? In ***Boumediene v. Bush***, 128 S.Ct. 2229 (2008), by a 5-4 vote, the Court answered *"yes"* to both of these questions. Consequently, all prisoners held as enemy combatants at Guantanamo — and probably held at other foreign military bases that are under the full control of U.S. authorities — *have the right to challenge the legality of their detention in federal district court.*

i. **Facts:** The petitioners in *Boumediene* were foreigners taken prisoner by the U.S. in foreign countries such as Bosnia and Afghanistan, as part of the U.S.'s post-9/11 anti-terrorist activities. The petitioners were then brought to Guantanamo and classified as enemy combatants by military CSRT tribunals. They argued that when Congress took away their habeas rights and said they could appeal only by using the special D.C. Court of Appeal process set forth in the DTA, Congress violated their Suspension Clause rights.

ii. **Majority opinion:** Justice Kennedy allied with the four liberal members of the court (Stevens, Souter, Breyer and Ginsburg) to form a majority that found for the petitioners. Kennedy's majority opinion concluded that the MCA's stripping of federal-court jurisdiction over cases brought by foreign nationals detained at

---

5. This provision of the MCA was enacted to reverse the Court's holding in *Hamdan v. Rumsfeld, supra,* p. 120, that the no-habeas provision of the DTA was not intended to be retroactive to cases already pending when the DTA was enacted.

Guantánamo *violated the Suspension Clause.* To reach that conclusion, he took several steps:

(1) **"No sovereignty over the territory" argument:** The Bush administration argued that because Guantanamo is not officially U.S. territory (it's leased from Cuba), the constitutional right of habeas does not extend to detentions there. But Kennedy concluded that, since the U.S. has "complete jurisdiction and control over the base," the country *"maintains de facto sovereignty* over this territory." If the detentions occurred at a temporary military base in, say, an occupied foreign country (as happened in a Supreme Court case involving a U.S.-administered prison in allied-occupied Germany in 1950), Kennedy said, the fact that the detention was in foreign territory might prevent habeas rights from attaching. But here, "in every practical sense Guantanamo is *not abroad*; it is within the *constant jurisdiction* of the United States"; therefore, *habeas rights apply as if the prison were on U.S. soil.*

(2) **Not a substitute:** Kennedy then addressed the issue of whether the procedures here violated the Suspension Clause. For there not to be a violation, the federal court review of the results of the CSRT proceeding would have to represent an adequate substitute for habeas corpus. And that, in turn, would mean, Kennedy said, that the federal court must have "the means to correct errors that occur during [the CSRT] proceeding." But under the DTA, the reviewing court (the D.C. Court of Appeals) was *not permitted to consider any evidence outside the CSRT record* — the court's role was limited to determining whether the CSRT had followed appropriate standards and procedures. So the reviewing court could not, for instance, *consider exculpatory evidence that wasn't presented in the CSRT* (e.g., *newly-discovered* evidence). This lack of authority to consider anything beyond the CSRT record meant that the D.C. Circuit review was *not an "adequate substitute"* for habeas corpus, making the review procedures a violation of the Suspension Clause.

(3) **Separation of powers:** Kennedy emphasized *separation-of-powers principles* in rebutting the dissents' suggestion that his opinion unwisely curtailed the president's Commander-in-Chief powers. The exercise of those powers is, he said, "vindicated, not eroded, when confirmed by the Judicial Branch. Within the constitution's separation-of-power structure, few exercises of judicial power are as legitimate or as necessary as the *responsibility to hear challenges to the authority of the executive to imprison a person."*

iii. **Dissents:** Four justices dissented, in two opinions, one by Chief Justice Roberts and the other by Justice Scalia.

(1) **Roberts:** Roberts' dissent argued that the system devised by Congress here — review by the D.C. Court of Appeals of the CSRT tribunals' conclusions — was an *adequate substitute* for habeas corpus, and therefore did not violate the Suspension Clause. Roberts believed that the CSRT proceedings should themselves be viewed as *part* of the habeas-like review process. Since exculpatory evidence could be admitted in front of the CSRT, the combination of the CSRT process and the D.C. Court of Appeals' review was more than adequate to

replace habeas. The majority was striking down "greater procedural protections than have ever been afforded alleged enemy detainees — whether citizens or aliens — in our national history." And, Roberts concluded, the majority's decision, while giving detainees few if any significant extra rights, would cause the American people to "lose a bit more control over the conduct of this nation's foreign policy to *unelected, politically unaccountable judges.*"

**(2) Scalia:** Scalia's dissent predicted more dire consequences than Roberts' did. For Scalia, the majority opinion "will make the war [on terror] harder on us. It will almost certainly *cause more Americans to be killed.*" Scalia feared that whatever new rules were implemented to give habeas rights to alien enemy combatants, those new rules would impose a higher standard of proof. And that higher standard would be applied in connection with events that occurred on foreign battlefields, as to which proof would be difficult under the best of circumstances. This higher standard would likely lead to an increase in the number of enemy fighters returned to combat against Americans.

For Scalia, the majority's holding meant that the Supreme Court was *improperly second-guessing Congress and the President on military matters.* As a consequence, "[H]ow to handle enemy prisoners in this war will ultimately lie with the branch that *knows least* about the national security concerns that the subject entails." The majority opinion "most tragically ... sets our military commanders the impossible task of proving to a civilian court, under whatever standards this Court devises in the future, that evidence supports the confinement of each and every enemy prisoner."

# III. APPOINTMENT AND REMOVAL OF EXECUTIVE PERSONNEL (INCLUDING IMPEACHMENT)

**A. The President's power of appointment:** The President, not Congress, is given the power to *appoint federal officers*. Article II, §2 (the "Appointments" Clause) provides that the President shall "nominate, and by and with the Advice and Consent of the Senate, shall appoint Ambassadors ... Judges of the Supreme Court, and all other Officers of the United States. ... " That section goes on to provide that "the Congress may by Law vest the Appointment of such inferior Officers, as they think proper, in the President alone, in the Courts of Law, or in the Heads of Departments."

**1. Interpretation:** This means that *Congress may not appoint federal officials*.

    **a. "Principal" officers:** In the case of *"principal"* officers of the United States (i.e., top-level officers), the President nominates a candidate, and the Senate must, as a constitutional matter, decide whether to approve the nomination. As to such officers, Congress may not take away the President's right of appointment.

        **i. Cabinet members:** *Members of the Cabinet* and *ambassadors* are examples of top-level federal officers. Therefore, Congress cannot take away or even limit the President's right to make such appointments (though the Senate has the right and duty to approve or disapprove such appointments).

**b. Lower-level officials:**   In the case of ***lower-level*** federal officials (the ones that Article II, Section 2 refers to as "inferior officers"), Congress does have the right to limit the President's right of appointment. Congress cannot make such appointments itself. But it may give the power of appointment to: (1) the President; (2) the judiciary; or (3) the heads of departments (i.e., Cabinet officials), bringing appointments in class (3) indirectly within the President's power.

**c. Dividing line:**   The Supreme Court has established the dividing line between "principal" and "inferior" officials in a way that leaves few if any employees other than Cabinet officials, ambassadors, and federal judges as "principal" officers. In *Morrison v. Olson*, 487 U.S. 654 (1988), the Court held that ***Special Prosecutors*** are "inferior" officers, as to whom the President need not be given appointment power. Therefore, Congress may constitutionally delegate to the ***judiciary*** the job of appointing such prosecutors, who are named to investigate allegations of wrongdoing against members of the executive branch.

   **i. Consequence:**   Since such special prosecutors have fairly broad investigatory and litigation powers, and may be removed only for cause, the Court's judgment that they are nonetheless "inferior" probably means that almost every federal official below Cabinet level will similarly be held to be an "inferior" one whom Congress may require to be appointed by one other than the President. (The *Morrison* case is discussed further *infra*, pp. 129-130).

**2. No appointments by Congress:**   A key aspect of the Appointments Clause is that Congress itself ***may not make any appointments*** of federal officials, whether "principal" or "inferior." The most it may do is, in the case of lower-level officials, to prescribe the ***procedures*** by which the executive or judicial branch shall make appointments. These "procedures" may, however, include fairly detailed qualifications regarding age, experience, etc. N&R, p. 272.

   **a. Supporting employees appointable by Congress:**   Congress may, however, make its own appointments of persons to exercise "powers … essentially of an investigative and informative nature." See *Buckley v. Valeo*, discussed *infra*. Thus Congress or one of its committees might appoint a staff to make an investigation into a particular matter, e.g., the investigative staff of the Senate Watergate Committee.

**B. *Buckley v. Valeo* (the *Election Law* Case):**   The principal modern case on the Appointments Clause is ***Buckley v. Valeo***, 424 U.S. 1 (1976), where the Court invalidated the composition of the Federal Election Commission, established by the Federal Election Campaign Act. The Act provided that a majority of the FEC's members were to be appointed by the President Pro Tem of the Senate and the Speaker of the House.

**1. Wide powers:**   The FEC was given broad powers to enforce the Act, including the right to bring civil actions against violators. The Commission was also given extensive rule-making authority.

**2. Holding:**   The Court held that the tasks performed by the FEC were executive in nature, and could only be exercised by "Officers of the United States." Since Congress had no constitutional right to appoint such federal officers, the Commission as presently constituted was invalid, and could not exercise most of its statutorily-granted powers.

a. **Definition of "Officer of U.S.":** The Court defined "Officer of the United States" to include "any appointee exercising ***significant authority*** pursuant to the laws of the United States. ... "

C. **The President's right to remove appointees:** Apart from setting out the process for impeachment, *infra*, pp. 132-134, the Constitution does not state whether and when the President, Congress, or both, may ***remove*** federal appointees and employees. (Article III, §1, does provide that federal judges may not be removed except for misconduct.) Accordingly, it has been left to the Supreme Court to determine the extent of the President's right to make such removals.

1. **Quasi-legislative and quasi-judicial officers:** Where a federal appointee holds a ***quasi-judicial*** or ***quasi-legislative*** role, Congress may ***limit*** or completely ***block*** the President's right of removal. Thus in *Humphrey's Executor v. U.S.*, 295 U.S. 602 (1935), the Court found that congressional control over the removal of quasi-legislative and quasi-judicial officials was necessary in order to preserve their independence from the executive branch. Therefore, the Court upheld the Federal Trade Commission Act, which limited the President's right to remove federal trade commissioners.

   a. **Congress silent:** In the quasi-legislative or quasi-judicial situation dealt with by *Humphrey's Executor*, the President may remove ***only if Congress has explicitly conferred the right of removal***. See *Wiener v. U.S.*, 357 U.S. 349 (1958), holding that congressional silence as to whether the President could remove a member of the War Claims Commission (a quasi-judicial entity) meant that the President could ***not*** do so. The tasks of the Commissioners were such that they required "absolute freedom from Executive interference."

2. **Purely executive officers:** Until 1988, the rule seemed to be that if a ***purely executive officer*** had been appointed by the President, Congress may not limit the President's right to remove that officer. But in a case upholding a statute setting up a system of special prosecutors to investigate alleged wrongdoing by executive officials, the Court seems to have changed this rule. The rule now seems to be that Congress *may* limit the President's right to remove even a purely executive officer, so long as the removal restrictions are not "of ***such a nature that they impede the President's ability to perform his constitutional duty***. ... " *Morrison v. Olson*, 487 U.S. 654 (1988).

   a. **Facts:** The statute in *Morrison* required the Attorney General to investigate any allegations of wrongdoing against certain high level members of the Executive Branch (including members of the Cabinet), and to apply to a special federal court (the "Special Division") for the appointment of a ***special prosecutor*** if he found "reasonable grounds to believe that further investigation or prosecution is warranted." Once the special prosecutor was appointed, she could only be removed by the Attorney General, and only "for good cause, physical disability, mental incapacity, or any other condition that substantially impairs the performance of [her] duties."

   b. **Holding:** By a 7-1 vote, the Court held that neither the removal provisions nor the act taken as a whole so restricted the President's powers as to violate the separation-of-powers principle. Because the Attorney General could terminate the special prosecutor for "good cause," the Executive Branch "retains ample authority to assure that the counsel is competently performing her statutory responsibilities. ... "

   i.   **Law taken as whole:**   Similarly, the Act taken as a whole did not unconstitution-
        ally take away the President's executive powers, even though his freedom to con-
        trol the special prosecutor was somewhat limited. True, the President could not
        select the prosecutor, determine her jurisdiction or remove her except for cause.
        But the Act reserved to the President the right to decide whether to apply for
        appointment of a prosecutor, imposed on the prosecutor the obligation to abide by
        Justice Department policy "except where not possible," and as noted, allowed the
        Attorney General to remove her for cause. These powers gave the Executive
        Branch "sufficient control over the [special prosecutor] to ensure that the President
        is able to perform his constitutionally assigned duties."

   ii.  **Dissent:**   The sole dissenter, Justice Scalia, contended that the separation-of-pow-
        ers principle required that the President maintain ***complete*** control over the inves-
        tigation and prosecution of violations of law. Since even by the majority's
        reasoning the President's control over the special prosecutor was curtailed, in Sca-
        lia's view the Act was clearly a violation of the constitutionally-required separa-
        tion of powers.

c.   **Significance:**   *Morrison* seems to have major significance for the separation-of-pow-
     ers doctrine. It is hard to imagine a more purely executive function than the right to
     investigate and prosecute violations of law. The case thus seems to stand for the prop-
     osition that the Executive Branch may be deprived of the power to appoint, and the
     untrammeled power to remove, an "inferior officer," even where the appointment
     relates to purely executive powers. Apart from the issue of restricting the President's
     right of removal, the case seems to herald a Court that will view even fairly substantial
     interference with the President's ability to exercise unfettered control over executive
     functions as not being violative of the separation of powers.

d.   **Top-level officers:**   It is not clear whether the rationale of *Morrison* would even
     allow Congress to limit the President's right to appoint or remove ***"principal officers"***
     of the United States, such as Cabinet officers. Recall that the *Morrison* Court deter-
     mined that the special prosecutor was an "inferior" officer rather than a "principal"
     officer. It probably continues to be the case after *Morrison* that Congress may not take
     away the President's right to appoint such principal officers — the President's right to
     make such appointments seems directly and unequivocally guaranteed by the
     Appointments Clause of Article II. Also, even post-*Morrison,* the Court would proba-
     bly be much less willing to allow Congress to limit the President's right to define the
     duties of such principal officers, or to allow Congress to limit the President's right to
     discharge such an officer.

     **Example:** For instance, a statute purporting to require that the Secretary of State be
     named by a special court, or a statute requiring the President to seek congressional
     approval before dismissing his Secretary of Defense, would still almost certainly be
     struck down on Appointments Clause and separation-of-power principles, respectively
     — the difference is that these Cabinet officials are "principal" officers, whereas the
     special prosecutor in *Morrison* was an "inferior" officer.

D.   **Removal by Congress:**   Let us turn now to the converse problem: May Congress ***reserve to
     itself*** the power to remove an ***executive*** officer? The brief answer to this question is "***no***." The

practical impact of this rule was demonstrated in a very significant constitutional ruling striking down the Gramm-Rudman deficit control statute. ***Bowsher v. Synar***, 478 U.S. 714 (1986).

1. **Facts:** The Gramm-Rudman Act, Congress' attempt to reduce federal budget deficits, set a "maximum deficit amount" for each of the fiscal years 1986-91. The size of the maximum allowable deficit was reduced each year, until it was to become zero in 1991. In any year in which the deficit exceeded the maximum deficit amount, the Act required across-the-board cuts in federal spending to meet the targeted amount. These cuts were "automatic" in the sense that they were essentially pro-rata (half to defense programs and the other half to non-defense programs).

   a. **Role of Comptroller General:** Most relevant to our discussion here, the Act gave a key role to the Comptroller General of the U.S. in carrying out the automatic cut provisions. The Comptroller was to review budget estimates given to him by two federal agencies, and then submit to the President a report stating on a program-by-program basis how much needed to be cut. The President was then required to issue an order mandating the reductions specified by the Comptroller. Congress could then, by special legislation, reduce spending to eliminate the need for some or all of the cuts; if it did not do so, the cuts called for in the presidential order were to be automatically carried out.

   b. **Right to remove Comptroller:** By separate, much older, legislation, Congress reserved to itself the right to remove the Comptroller General from office for five specified reasons ("permanent disability," "inefficiency," "neglect of duty," "malfeasance," or "a felony or conduct involving moral turpitude"). In the 80-odd years since the post of Comptroller General was established, Congress had never exercised, or even made a serious move to exercise, this removal power.

2. **Statute struck down:** By a 7-2 vote, the Court struck down the automatic-reduction provisions of the Act. In doing so, the Court applied the following reasoning: (1) the Act uses the Comptroller's "executive powers"; (2) executive powers may not be vested by Congress in itself or its agents, because Congress is limited to legislative rather than executive functions; (3) because Congress can remove the Comptroller, he is an agent of Congress; therefore (4) the Comptroller may not constitutionally exercise the executive powers given to him in the Act; and (5) the Act's automatic budget reduction mechanism, which is based on the Comptroller's exercise of his executive powers, must be invalidated. (See the accurate summary of the majority's reasoning given by Justice White in his dissent in *Bowsher*.)

3. **Nature of removal power:** The most novel aspect of the majority's reasoning is its assertion that the ***retention by Congress of the right to remove an executive officer*** for certain specified types of cause ***converts that officer into an agent of Congress***. The majority stressed that several of the types of cause ("inefficiency," "neglect of duty," and "malfeasance") are "very broad and, as interpreted by Congress, could sustain removal of a Comptroller General for any number of actual or perceived transgressions of the legislative will." Also, it was not clear to the majority that there could be judicial review of any removal. Furthermore, there was evidence that both Congress and the Comptroller General himself view him as being "an office of the Legislative Branch."

4. **Concurrence:** Justices Stevens and Marshall, who concurred, agreed with the majority that the Comptroller was an agent of Congress. But they disagreed that it was Congress'

right to remove him that made him such — rather, it was the fact that the bulk of his duties are directed at, and for the benefit of, Congress instead of the executive branch.

5. **Dissents:** Justices White and Blackmun dissented.

     a. **White's dissent:** White contended that Congress' retention of the right to remove the Comptroller for specified causes did not convert him into an agent of Congress. To him, "the question is whether there is a genuine threat of 'encroachment or aggrandizement of one branch at the expense of the other'. ... Common sense indicates that the existence of the removal provision poses no such threat to the principle of separation of powers."

6. **Constitutional significance:** What is the constitutional significance of *Bowsher*? It establishes that ***Congress may not reserve the right to remove an executive officer for cause***, at least where the definition of "cause" is fairly ***broad*** (e.g., "inefficiency," "neglect of duty," or "malfeasance," three of the causes listed in the Act).

     a. **Narrower grounds:** Presumably the retention of ***narrower grounds*** for removal of an executive officer (e.g., "permanent disability" or "commission of a felony or conduct involving moral turpitude," the two other grounds for removal of a Comptroller, to which the Court seemed not to object) would be ***allowed***. Furthermore, nothing in the decision seems to have any impact on Congress' right to remove an executive officer by ***impeachment*** (see *infra*, below).

7. **Relation to Election Law case:** When viewed together with *Buckley v. Valeo* (the *Election Law Case* discussed *supra*, p. 128), *Bowsher* represents a sharpening of the limits on Congress' control over executive appointments — just as *Buckley* prevents Congress from ***appointing*** executive officers, so *Bowsher* prevents it from removing them. (But *Morrison v. Olson, supra*, pp. 129-130, demonstrates that Congress *may* entrust to the judiciary the right to appoint all but top-level executive officers, and may limit the President's right to remove such officers.)

E. **Impeachment:** The standards for ***impeachment*** are set forth in Article II, §4 of the Constitution: "[t]he President, Vice President and all civil Officers of the United States, shall be removed from Office on Impeachment for, and Conviction of, Treason, Bribery, or other ***high Crimes and Misdemeanors***."

1. **Procedure for impeachment:** The term "impeachment" itself refers to the decision by the ***House of Representatives*** to subject the President, or other federal official, to a trial in the Senate. See Art. I, §2, Cl. 5. A House vote to impeach is thus similar to a grand jury indictment; it is not a conviction, but merely the necessary pre-condition to a trial.

     a. **Trial in Senate:** If the House votes (by a ***majority*** vote) to impeach, the trial itself occurs in the Senate, and a ***two-thirds vote*** of those Senators present is required to convict. Art. I, §3, Cl. 6. In the case of impeachment of a President, the Chief Justice presides over the trial.

2. **Sparingly used:** The impeachment power has been sparingly used throughout our nation's history. Only three Presidents, Andrew Johnson, Richard Nixon and Bill Clinton, have been the subject of serious impeachment efforts. Presidents Johnson and Clinton were impeached by the House, and escaped conviction in the Senate. President Nixon resigned after three articles of impeachment had been voted against him by the House Judiciary Committee, but before the full House could vote on the impeachment issue.

3. **Meaning of "high crimes and misdemeanors":** Because the constitutional phrase "high Crimes and Misdemeanors" is inevitably somewhat vague, its meaning has been subject to great dispute.

   a. **Serious crimes:** Some have argued that only "serious indictable crimes" may serve as the basis for impeachment. See Gunther & Sullivan (13th Ed.), p. 411-12.

   b. **Abuse of power:** Others have contended that any serious *abuse of the powers* of the presidency may serve as the basis for a President's impeachment, even if the offense would not be a crime.

   c. **Majority view:** Many commentators reject the Nixon view that only crimes may be impeachable. However, they also reject the view that *any* crime is necessarily an impeachable offense.

      **Example:** Suppose the President deliberately and maliciously decided to weaken our national defenses. This would probably not violate any criminal statute, but it should be considered grounds for impeachment. Tribe, p. 294.

      **Example:** During President Clinton's impeachment, his defenders made a plausible argument that the minor crime of perjury in a civil deposition, at least where it concerned a peripheral matter (whether Pres. Clinton had had sex with someone not a party to the litigation, Monica Lewinsky) should not be treated as an impeachable offense. The Senate, by voting to acquit him despite relatively clear evidence that perjury occurred, seems to have accepted this argument.

4. **Effect of resignation:** The fact that a federal officer has *resigned* does not bar the use of subsequent impeachment proceedings against him. The same is true of a *pardon*: thus the pardon of President Nixon by his successor, Gerald Ford, would not have prevented the use of impeachment proceedings against Nixon.

5. **Criminal liability:** The Constitution explicitly provides that an impeachment conviction has no immediate effect other than to remove the officer from office (and to disqualify him from holding any other federal office). Art. I, §3, Cl. 7. But that same Clause provides that "the Party convicted shall nevertheless be liable and subject to Indictment, Trial, Judgment, and Punishment, according to Law." Consequently, following the impeachment conviction a *criminal prosecution* may be brought against the impeached officer, based on the same set of facts as the impeachment. A criminal conviction in this situation does not constitute double jeopardy. Tribe, p. 296.

   a. **No pardon power:** Furthermore, a criminal conviction following an impeachment cannot be avoided by use of the pardon power. Art. II, §2, Cl. 1 gives the President the power to grant pardons "except in Cases of Impeachment." Thus had President Nixon been convicted by the Senate, Gerald Ford would not have been able to pardon him from criminal liability (at least with respect to offenses of which he was convicted in the Senate).

6. **Reviewability by Court:** Once the Senate has convicted in an impeachment trial, it is not clear whether the *Supreme Court* may review the conviction. There are no Supreme Court precedents on point.

   a. **Pros and cons:** The traditional view is that an impeachment conviction presents a *non-justiciable political question*. The contrary view is that the Supreme Court may review an impeachment conviction to determine at least some issues, for instance, whether an adequate definition of "high Crimes and Misdemeanors" was applied. The traditional view is probably the correct one, in light of a recent case, *Nixon v. U.S.*, 506 U.S. 224 (1993) (involving a different Nixon, Walter Nixon, a federal judge) — the Court held there that the question of what procedures validly constitute a "trial" of an impeachment case by the Senate was a non-justiciable political question. See *infra* p. 731.

## IV.  LEGISLATIVE AND EXECUTIVE IMMUNITY

**A. Scope of discussion:**   We examine now several facets of ***immunity*** held by the various branches of the federal government. In particular, we examine: (1) Congress' immunity from civil and criminal suits and from grand jury investigations; (2) the civil and criminal immunity of the executive branch; and (3) the doctrine of "executive privilege," and the related issue of protection of state secrets.

**B. Congress and the Speech and Debate Clause:**   Article I, §6, provides that "for any Speech or Debate in either House, [members of Congress] shall not be questioned in any other Place." In general terms, this so-called Speech and Debate Clause shields members of Congress from: (1) ***civil or criminal suits*** relating to their ***legislative actions***; and (2) ***grand jury investigations*** relating to those actions.

   **1. Rationale:**   The Speech and Debate Clause serves important separation-of-powers functions: for instance, it protects members of Congress against executive officials (e.g., Justice Department officials) who might seek unduly to influence congressional conduct by conducting criminal prosecutions or grand jury investigations. More generally, it serves the related function of assuring that members of Congress are not distracted from their duties by being called into court to defend their actions. See Tribe, p. 370.

**C. Executive immunity:**   The Speech and Debate Clause has no counterpart in the Constitution giving any sort of immunity to members of the ***Executive*** Branch. However, as a common-law matter, the courts have recognized certain types of executive immunity.

   **1. Judicial process:**   As the result of *U.S. v. Nixon* (discussed more extensively *infra*, p. 136), there does not seem to be any general doctrine making the President or other members of the Executive Branch immune from ***judicial process*** (e.g., subpoenas). In the *Nixon* case, the Supreme Court affirmed a federal district court order that the President turn over the Watergate tapes. Although the Supreme Court did not explicitly discuss the issue of presidential (or other executive official) amenability to judicial process, *Nixon* seems to stand for the proposition that there is no general immunity from such process.

   **2. Civil liability of President for official acts:**   The President has ***absolute immunity*** from ***civil liability*** for his ***official acts***, as the result of ***Nixon v. Fitzgerald***, 457 U.S. 731 (1982), a 5-4 decision.

      **a. Facts:**   Fitzgerald, the plaintiff, contended that he had been fired from his Defense Department job in retaliation for testimony in which he had criticized military cost overruns. His suit charged Nixon and several Nixon Administration officials with violating his First Amendment and statutory rights.

b. **Holding:** In an opinion by Justice Powell, the Court held that the President is entitled to **absolute immunity** from civil damage actions for all acts within the *"outer perimeter"* of his authority. Since the President has authority to prescribe the manner in which the business of the armed forces will be conducted, including the authority to dismiss personnel, Nixon was immune from liability for the firing of Fitzgerald *even if he caused it maliciously or in an illegal manner.*

c. **Dissent:** Four members of the Court dissented vigorously. The principal dissent, by Justice White, contended that there was no reason to depart from the usual rule that absolute immunity "attaches to particular functions — not to particular offices." The majority's approach, White argued, *"places the President above the law* [and] is a reversion to the old notion that the King can do no wrong."

3. **Civil immunity of presidential assistants:** Do presidential **assistants** get a similar absolute immunity from civil suits for their official acts? The brief answer is *"no." Harlow v. Fitzgerald*, 457 U.S. 731 (1982), a companion case to *Nixon v. Fitzgerald.*

   a. **Qualified immunity granted:** But presidential assistants do get fairly broad *"qualified* immunity." Essentially, a presidential assistant has immunity from civil suit for conduct arising out of her performance of her office, except where the official has violated a *"clearly established"* right.

      **Example:** Suppose a cabinet official fires a subordinate, on the grounds that the subordinate is openly gay. Suppose further that at the time of the firing, there is no clearly established law about whether the federal government may fire a person for being gay. Even if, immediately after the firing, the Supreme Court decides that such firings are illegal, the cabinet official will benefit from his qualified immunity. This is because, at the moment of the firing, he was not violating a "clearly established" right.

4. **No presidential immunity for non-official acts:** *Fitzgerald* only established immunity for *official* presidential acts, i.e., those that are within the "outer perimeter" of the President's job. There is *no immunity* — not even qualified immunity — for acts that the President takes that are completely *unrelated to the carrying out of his job.* This was the holding of *Clinton v. Jones*, 117 S. Ct. 1636 (1997).

   a. **Paula Jones case:** *Clinton v. Jones* involved a private damages suit by Paula Jones against President Clinton, filed while Clinton was in office. Jones claimed that while she was employed by the state of Arkansas and Clinton was Governor of Arkansas, Clinton made illegal sexual advances to her. Clinton argued that a President should have "temporary immunity" — to last while he is in office — against virtually all civil litigation arising out of events that occurred before he took office.

   b. **Claim rejected:** But the Court unanimously *rejected* this claim. The Court noted that the rationale for immunity for *official* acts of the President and other officials was that such immunity "serves the public interest in enabling such officials to perform their designated functions effectively *without fear* that a particular decision may give rise to personal liability." This rationale did not apply to the President's unofficial acts, including any acts he took before he became President. Therefore, there was no policy reason for allowing even temporary immunity for unofficial acts.

5. **Criminal prosecution:** There is *no* executive immunity, either of a common-law or constitutional nature, from *criminal* prosecution. Tribe, p. 268.

    **a. Delay:** However, a strong argument may be made that, at least in the case of the President, the Constitution's provision of impeachment as the means of removing federal officers bars any criminal prosecution of such officials until ***after they have been removed from office.*** In the case of the President, Tribe states that "[t]he question must be regarded as an open one. ... " Tribe, p. 269.

        **i. People other than the President:** In the case of the Vice-President and other federal officers, criminal prosecution prior to impeachment seems to be permissible. For instance, Vice-President Agnew was indicted by a federal grand jury on bribery and tax evasion charges prior to his resignation, although the Supreme Court did not pass on the "no prosecution prior to impeachment" argument. *Id.* at 268-69.

**D. "Executive privilege":** Several Presidents have invoked what they described as the doctrine of "***executive privilege***" to justify their refusal to ***disclose information*** which they claimed to be confidential. The only Supreme Court case to give any definitive scope to the doctrine was ***U.S. v. Nixon***, 418 U.S. 683 (1974), the famous "Watergate Tapes" case. In *Nixon*, the Court recognized in general terms a constitutionally-based doctrine of executive privilege, but held that the privilege was only a ***qualified*** one, which was overcome on the facts of *Nixon* by the needs of a pending criminal investigation.

    **1. Facts:** In March of 1974, a federal grand jury indicted seven Nixon aides on charges of conspiracy to obstruct justice and other Watergate-related offenses. The President was named as an unindicted co-conspirator. The Watergate Special Prosecutor then persuaded the federal trial court to issue a subpoena *duces tecum* to the President requiring him to produce various tapes and documents relating to certain meetings involving the President; these documents and tapes were to be used during the trial of the indictments. The President released transcripts of some of the tapes, but refused to produce the tapes themselves, and moved to quash the subpoena. The trial court rejected the President's claim of privilege, and the matter was heard by the Supreme Court on an expedited basis.

    **2. Holding:** Although the Supreme Court upheld the general doctrine of executive privilege, the Court held that in this case, ***the privilege did not apply,*** and ordered the President to comply with the subpoena.

        **a. Court, not President, decides:** First, the Court rejected the President's claim that "the separation of powers doctrine precludes judicial review of a President's claim of privilege." The Court quoted Justice Marshall's statement, in *Marbury v. Madison* (*supra*, p. 9) that it is the duty of the judicial branch to "say what the law is." Thus the **Court**, not the President, must evaluate claims of presidential privilege.

        **b. Privilege exists:** The Court then held that there was indeed a privilege for ***"confidentiality of Presidential communications in the exercise of Article II powers*. ... "** The Court noted that confidentiality was required by the fact that "those who expect public dissemination of their remarks may well temper candor with a concern for appearances and for their own interests to the detriment of the decision-making process." Therefore, the Court concluded, the privilege of confidentiality "can be said to derive from the supremacy of each branch within its own assigned area of constitutional duties."

        **c. Privilege only qualified:** However, the Court rejected the President's claim that the executive privilege was an absolute one. At least where the claim of privilege was (as in the present case) a **general** one, and not related to a particular need to protect "military, diplomatic, or sensitive national security secrets," the Court held that the privilege was merely a **qualified** one. As such, it was **outweighed** by the need to **develop all relevant facts in a criminal trial.**

    **i.** **Rationale:** The Court observed that both the President's claim of privilege, and the criminal justice system's need for access to all relevant evidence, were of constitutional dimension. However, the latter outweighed the former, in part because the Court did not believe that the possibility of infrequent subpoenas like the one here would often have an adverse impact on the candor of discussions to which Presidents are parties.

    **d.** **Duty of trial court:** The President was therefore ordered to deliver the subpoenaed tapes and documents to the federal district court. However, the district court was ordered to perform a close *in camera* (i.e., non-public) examination of all of the materials. Statements that were both admissible and relevant to the criminal prosecution were to be isolated, and all other statements were to be disregarded and kept secret.

**3.** **Scope of *Nixon* holding:** The precise scope of the *Nixon* Court's holding is unclear.

    **a.** **Status in criminal proceedings:** Where, as in the *Nixon* case itself, the presumptively privileged material is sought by the **prosecution** for use in a criminal case, the Court's opinion seems to mean that the qualified privilege will always be outweighed by the needs of the criminal justice system (at least if military, diplomatic or national security secrets are not involved).

        **i.** **Possibly more limited scope of holding:** But the Court may not have meant for the privilege to carry so little weight. Tribe suggests that the Court may have meant that only materials which were "**essential**" to the trial (rather than merely relevant and admissible) will be deemed non-privileged. Tribe, p. 281.

    **b.** **Criminal defendant:** Where privileged information is sought by a **defendant** in a criminal proceeding (rather than by the prosecution, as in *Nixon*), the reasons for overriding the claim of privilege seem to be even more compelling. Due process demands that a defendant have access to all information relevant to his defense. Also (at least in a federal prosecution) the executive branch, which controls the prosecution, always has the option of dropping the case rather than releasing the privileged information. See Tribe, p. 282.

    **c.** **Civil suits:** The *Nixon* case did not touch at all on the fate of presidential privilege in **civil** proceedings. Tribe suggests that civil proceedings should be placed on the **same footing** as criminal ones, and therefore that "[a] showing that presumptively privileged information is needed in a civil trial should be sufficient to overcome the presumption." Tribe, p. 283.

    **d.** **State secrets:** The *Nixon* Court made it clear that "military, diplomatic, or sensitive national security secrets" would be placed upon a different footing from a mere "general" claim of confidentiality (as in *Nixon* itself). It remains to be seen how such "**state secret**" matters will be handled. In cases where external evidence demonstrates to the court's satisfaction that a state secret **is** indeed involved, the Court may well decide, even without an *in camera* inspection, that the presidential privilege outweighs the needs of the judicial system. Where a court is not satisfied, from external evidence, that a state secret is really involved, an *in camera* inspection may be necessary; however, once the Court decides that sensitive matters of state are at issue, it will probably give substantially greater weight to the privilege than in the "general" confidentiality situation. See generally Tribe, pp. 284-85.

e. **Congressional inquiries:**  Another area carefully left untouched by the *Nixon* Court is the conflict between a presidential claim of privilege and the needs of a ***congressional inquiry***. For instance, had the *Nixon* case involved the Senate Watergate Committee's subpoena for tapes, rather than a subpoena stemming from a grand jury investigation, it is not at all clear whether the result would have been the same. The need to prevent Congress from usurping the President's functions certainly presents an additional separation-of-powers concern not present in the judicial-proceedings situation. The precise weighing of a claim of privilege against congressional needs must be regarded as an open question.

f. **Assertion by non-incumbents:**  *U.S. v. Nixon*, of course, involved an assertion of executive privilege by the ***incumbent*** President. In a subsequent case, also related to Richard Nixon, the Court held that the qualified privilege could also be asserted by a ***non-incumbent***. In *Nixon v. Administrator of General Services*, 433 U.S. 425 (1977), the Court held that Nixon could assert executive privilege with respect to his presidential papers, which were to be entrusted to succeeding administrations for archiving under congressionally-prescribed guidelines.

   i. **Privilege not violated:**  However, the Court held that the guidelines, at least insofar as they permitted an Executive Branch employee to screen the materials and return items of a personal nature to the ex-President, did not violate his executive privilege. The Court's decision was influenced in part by the fact that neither of the two succeeding administrations supported Nixon's claim of privilege, thus suggesting that the functioning of the Executive Branch was not threatened by the archiving and screening process.

---

*Quiz Yourself on*
**SEPARATION OF POWERS** *(ENTIRE CHAPTER)*

**18.** Congress passes the Personal Communications Services Act of 1999. The PCSA authorizes the FCC to award to private applicants, based on competitive bid, various pieces of radio spectrum for use in a new method of providing cellular phone service. The PCSA provides that any spectrum award by the FCC shall become permanently effective 90 days after it is first made, unless Congress has within the 90-day period enacted a Joint Resolution cancelling the particular award. According to the statute, such a Joint Resolution is to take effect immediately, without further action by any government official. The FCC then awards a particular spectrum license to Comm Co. Sixty days after this award, Congress passes a Joint Resolution purporting to cancel the award to Comm Co.

   **(a)** If Comm Co. wishes to attack the constitutionality of the Joint Resolution stripping it of its license, what is the best argument it can make?  _____

   **(b)** Will this constitutional attack succeed?  _____

**19.** The Caribbean island of Grenoble is a small but strategically important ally of the United States. Grenoble holds a popular election, but the military refuses to allow the democratically elected president to take office. The military then begins to seize the property of American businesses located in Grenoble. The President of the the U.S., concerned that U.S. strategic interests are endangered, and invoking his powers as Commander in Chief, sends 20,000 U.S. troops onto the island. This action is taken after the President confers with congressional leaders, but with no other congressional action. With Congress still inactive, fighting continues for six months, due to the Grenoble military's well-entrenched status. A member of Congress, Senator Piper, then brings suit for a declaratory judgment that the President has acted unlawfully in using U.S. forces in this manner.

**(a)** What is the best argument that Senator Piper can make against the constitutionality of the President's actions? _____

**(b)** Will Piper's attack succeed? Assume there's no existing relevant federal legislation. _____

20. Congress has established the Federal Truck Safety Board (FTSB). In the statute setting up the FTSB, Congress has provided that the Director of the FTSB shall be appointed by the President, without the need for House or Senate confirmation. The enabling legislation also provides that at any time, without cause, the House and Senate, acting together in the form of a Joint Resolution, may remove the Director. The Director is given certain powers, including the ability to issue an order suspending certain types of truck traffic if the Director concludes that the suspension is needed to protect the safety of interstate commerce.

In the 30 years since the FTSB was set up, Congress has played no role in the appointment or removal of the FTSB's Director. The incumbent, Derrick, was appointed 10 years ago. Recently, there have been a rash of accidents on the highway involving trucks of more than six feet in width. Derrick has decided that such wide trucks are dangerous, and has, therefore, issued an order suspending any truck of that width or greater from moving on the federal highways across a state border. Truck Co., owner of many extra-wide trucks, wishes to challenge the constitutionality of Derrick's action.

**(a)** What is the best grounds on which Truck Co. can challenge the constitutionality of Derrick's order?

_____

**(b)** Will this attack succeed? _____

21. Jessica was the White House Press Secretary. After she had served for one year, the President summarily fired her, without giving any reasons. Jessica sued the President for damages in federal court, alleging that he fired her in violation of a federal statute, Title VII. Jessica's claim is that the President made sexual advances to her, and fired her in retaliation for her refusal to entertain those advances. (Title VII does indeed prohibit sexual harassment of the sort charged here.) The President has moved to dismiss the suit on the broad grounds that he has absolute immunity from civil liability for any official act done by him during his term of office, and that the court must dismiss the case without considering whether the allegations are true or false. Should the President's motion be granted? _____

---

*Answers*

**18. (a) That the Resolution violates the Presentment Clause, by which the President is given the opportunity to veto any bill.**

**(b) Yes.** The scheme described here is a classic two-house *"legislative veto,"* under which Congress attempts to keep oversight over administrative action by reserving the power to cancel that administrative action by means of a Resolution. The scheme here, insofar as it calls for the Joint Resolution to take effect immediately, deprives the President of his opportunity to veto any bill. Therefore, the scheme is invalid. See *INS v. Chadha* (The theory behind the invalidity of the legislative veto is that the Resolution is itself the exercise of legislative power, so it must be carried out by the same procedures as for any other legislative act, i.e., passage by a majority of each house and presentment to the President for his signature).

**19. (a) That it violates Congress' sole power to declare war.**

**(b) Yes, probably.** It is true that Article II, Section 2, explicitly grants the President the power of Commander in Chief of the U.S. Armed Forces. However, the President must use this power subject to oversight by Congress. In particular, the power to "declare war" is given solely to Congress, in Art. I, Section 8. While the President may, without a declaration of war, probably commit our troops to repel an immediate emergency, it is very unlikely that the President may wage a prolonged ground war, without a declaration of war, especially where the United States has not been directly attacked.

Also, the 2006 decision in *Hamdan v. Rumsfeld* indicates that in cases where the President asserts broad power to act in wartime, and it is not clear that Congress has acquiesced to what the President is doing, the Court will favor Congress over the President. So here, probably the Court will say that the President's action violates Congress' sole power to declare war.

**20. (a) That by retaining the right to remove Derrick, Congress has improperly vested executive functions in its own agent.**

**(b) Yes, probably.** Congress and its agents can only exercise "legislative power," not "executive power." The FTSB Director's powers are clearly executive — the Director is carrying out the laws (by determining what is required for safety) rather than "formulating" the laws. Congress, by retaining the right to remove the Director without cause, converted the post of Director into an agent of Congress, thus in effect taking executive powers onto itself. Therefore, Derrick is not permitted to exercise his statutory powers, including issuance of the order. See *Bowsher v. Synar*, striking down certain powers of the Comptroller General on the similar analysis that Congress improperly converted him into an agent of Congress by retaining the power to remove him.

**21. Yes.** The President does indeed have absolute immunity from civil liability for his official acts. See *Nixon v. Fitzgerald*. This immunity applies even if the official act was done illegally or maliciously. If the President did in fact fire Jessica for the reasons she states, the President has clearly violated Title VII, which bans various forms of sexual discrimination, including sexual harassment. However, since the President was clearly acting within the "outer perimeter" of his duties as President (that is, when he fired his Press Secretary he was clearly acting within the bounds of his Presidential authority), the illegality of his actions is irrelevant for civil damage purposes. (Observe that if the conduct charged here had been carried out by any other federal government official, the immunity would have merely been a "qualified" one, since the conduct charged here violated a "clearly established" right. See *Harlow v. Fitzgerald*.)

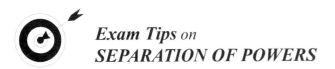

*Exam Tips on*
*SEPARATION OF POWERS*

Separation-of-powers problems are usually pretty easy to spot. The harder part, usually, is to say something intelligent about how the issue should be resolved, since the law in this area is very hazy. Here are some particular things to watch for:

☛ Whenever your fact pattern indicates that the President is issuing an *"executive order,"* consider whether this may amount to the ***making of law*** rather than the mere carrying out of law. If so, the President is probably treading on Congress' domain. (But remember that if Congress acquiesces, even implicitly, to the President's exercise of power, then the problem disappears. See, e.g., *Dames & Moore v. Regan.*)

☞ Always remember that "legislation" cannot go into effect unless the President has been given the opportunity to ***veto*** the bill. Therefore, if your fact pattern has Congress do something by a one-house or concurrent ***resolution***, determine whether what Congress is doing amounts to lawmaking; if so, the action is unlawful. (See, e.g., *INS v. Chadha*, the "legislative veto" case.)

☞ One of the most common separation-of-powers issues involves the President's power as Commander in Chief to ***commit the use of American armed forces abroad***. The general rule, of course, is that only Congress, not the President, may declare war.

    ☞ However, the President may commit our armed forces even without a declaration of war in order to ***repel a sudden attack***, and probably to defend an ally with whom we have a treaty. But if you conclude that one of these exceptions applies, note in your answer that the President probably has the obligation to consult with Congress after the fact, and to bring our troops back if Congress has not passed a declaration of war within, say, a couple of months.

☞ Any time your fact pattern involves the ***appointment*** or the ***firing*** of a ***federal official***, be alert to possible separation-of-powers problems.

    ☞ The President, not Congress, has the power to appoint federal officers. Federal officers include ambassadors, federal judges, Cabinet members, agency heads, etc.

    When the President appoints a ***"principal"*** officer of the United States (i.e., a top-level officer), the appointment does not take effect until the Senate "advises and consents," i.e., approves. This applies to members of the Cabinet, ambassadors and federal judges.

    ☞ The most frequently-tested area involving appointment of federal officers involves ***removal*** of officers once they have been appointed.

        ☞ Congress may ***not*** itself ever remove a federal officer, ***except by impeachment***. (*Example:* If Congress decided that it did not like the Secretary of State, it could not pass a law stripping him of his office, even if Congress were able to override the President's veto. Impeachment is the only method by which Congress could remove this officer.) Congress ***may limit the President's right to remove*** a federal official, at least a lower-ranking official. Probably Congress may ***not*** severely limit the President's right to fire high-level officers. (*Example:* Congress probably may not pass a law stating, "The Secretary of State shall serve for at least four years, and may not be removed by the President before expiration of this term.")

☞ ***Impeachment*** is occasionally tested.

    ☞ Keep in mind the procedural rules: by majority vote, the House decides whether to "impeach" (which is like an indictment). Then, the Senate conducts a trial, at which a two-thirds vote is necessary for conviction.

☞ Your fact pattern may involve the issue of whether the President or another federal official may only be removed for crimes, or may also be removed for non-criminal "abuses of power." The constitutional phrase is "high crimes and misdemeanors," but it is not clear what this means.

☛ Issues relating to *immunity* of the various branches are sometimes tested:

☞ If a *member of Congress* is sued (either civilly or criminally), or called before a grand jury, be alert to the possibility that the member may be protected by the *"Speech or Debate"* Clause, which is basically a form of immunity.

☞ There is a common-law immunity for the *President* and other members of the *Executive Branch*.

☞ Members of the Executive Branch other than the President get only *qualified* immunity from civil suits. (Focus on whether the right violated by the official was "clearly established" at the time he acted; if it was, he can be liable, if not, he'll be immune.)

☞ Remember that there is *no* Executive-Branch immunity from *criminal* prosecutions.

☛ If your fact pattern involves a President or other Executive-Branch member who wants to *decline to disclose* material, consider the possibility that the doctrine of *"executive privilege"* may apply. If you discuss the doctrine, remember that the privilege is merely a *qualified* one, which can be outweighed by other interests (e.g., the need to develop all facts at a criminal trial). Also, mention that claims of executive privilege are justiciable — that is, the Court will typically decide these claims, rather than avoiding them as non-justiciable political questions.

CHAPTER 9

# DUE PROCESS OF LAW

## *ChapterScope*

This Chapter examines principally the Due Process Clause of the *Fourteenth* Amendment, which imposes the obligation of due process on the states. As you read, keep in mind that there is also a *Fifth* Amendment Due Process Clause, which applies only to the federal government; in general, anything that the Fourteenth Amendment Due Process Clause would require the states to do, the Fifth Amendment Due Process Clause requires the federal government to do. Here are the key concepts in this Chapter:

- **Due Process Clause generally:** The Fourteenth Amendment provides (in part) that "no state shall make or enforce any law which shall … deprive any person of *life*, *liberty*, or *property*, without due process of law. … " This is the Fourteenth Amendment's Due Process Clause.

- **The Bill of Rights and the states:** One of the major functions of the Fourteenth Amendment's Due Process Clause is to make the ***Bill of Rights*** — that is, the first ten amendments — applicable to the states.

  - ❏ **Not directly applicable to states:** The Bill of Rights is not *directly* applicable to the states — the Bill of Rights as originally drafted limited only the *federal* government, not state or municipal governments.

  - ❏ **Application of Bill of Rights to states:** But the Fourteenth Amendment, enacted in 1868, essentially changed this rule. That amendment requires that the states not deprive anyone of "life, liberty or property" without due process. Nearly all the guarantees of the Bill of Rights have been interpreted by the Supreme Court as being so important that if a state denies these rights, it has in effect taken away an aspect of "liberty."

  - ❏ **Selective incorporation:** The Supreme Court has never said that due process requires the states to honor the Bill of Rights as a whole. Instead, the Court uses an approach called ***"selective incorporation."*** Under this approach, each right in the Bill of Rights is examined to see whether it is of "fundamental" importance. If so, that right is "selectively incorporated" into the meaning of "due process" under the Fourteenth Amendment, and is thus made binding on the states.

    - ❏ **Nearly all rights incorporated:** By now, nearly *all rights* contained in the Bill of Rights have been incorporated, one by one, into the meaning of "due process." The only major Bill of Rights guarantees *not* incorporated: (1) the Fifth Amendment's right not to be subject to a criminal trial without a ***grand jury indictment*** (so a state may begin proceedings by an "information" rather than indictment); and (2) the Seventh Amendment's right to a ***jury trial*** in ***civil cases***.

    - ❏ **"Jot-for-jot" incorporation:** Once a given Bill of Rights guarantee is made applicable to the states, the *scope* of that guarantee is interpreted the *same way* for the states as for the federal government.

- **Substantive due process generally:** One function of the Due Process Clause is to limit the *substantive power* of the states to regulate certain areas of human life. That is, certain types of state limits on human conduct are held to so unreasonably interfere with important human rights that they amount to an unconstitutional denial of "liberty." This use of due process analysis is called "substantive due process" analysis.

❏ **Non-fundamental rights:** In doing substantive due process analysis, courts distinguish between *fundamental* and *non-fundamental* rights. If a right or value is found to be "non-fundamental," then the state action that impairs that right only has to meet the easy "mere rationality" test. That is, the state must merely be pursuing a *legitimate governmental objective*, and be doing so with a means that is *rationally related* to that objective.

  ❏ **Economic regulation:** Nearly all *economic* regulation (and most *"social welfare"* regulations) implicates only non-fundamental rights, and is thus usually upheld under this easy "mere rationality" standard.

❏ **Fundamental rights:** But if a state or federal government is impairing a *"fundamental"* right, then the Court uses *strict scrutiny*: only if the governmental action is *"necessary"* to achieve a *"compelling"* governmental objective, will the government avoid violating substantive due process.

❏ **Significance of distinction:** The single most important thing to do when analyzing a substantive due process problem is thus to determine whether the right in question is "fundamental." If the right is not fundamental, there's almost certainly no substantive due process problem. If the right *is* fundamental, then strict scrutiny will almost certainly result in the measure's being invalidated.

■ **Economic and social-welfare regulation:** It is very easy for state *economic* and *social-welfare* regulation to survive substantive due process attack. The state must merely be pursuing a legitimate state objective by rational means. Virtually every state enactment that does not implicate a fundamental right will be upheld under this standard.

■ **Fundamental rights generally:** If a state or federal regulation *does* impair a fundamental right, then the Court *strictly scrutinizes* the regulation.

❏ **Test used:** Here is the test used by courts applying strict scrutiny where a state or federal regulation impairs a fundamental right: (1) the objective being pursued by the state must be *"compelling"*; and (2) the means chosen must be *"necessary"* to achieve that compelling end. In other words, there must not be any *less restrictive means* that would do the job just as well.

  ❏ **Burden of proof:** Strict scrutiny also shifts the *burden of persuasion*. That is, when a fundamental right is involved, it's up to the state to show that it's pursuing a compelling objective and that the means chosen are "necessary" to achieve that objective — it's not up to the plaintiff to show that the state fails to meet these tests.

❏ **Rights governed:** The only rights that are "fundamental" for substantive due process purposes are ones related to the *"right of privacy"* or *"right of autonomy"*:

  ❏ **Birth control:** Individuals' interest in *using birth control* is "fundamental." So the state can't impair that interest without satisfying strict scrutiny.

  ❏ **Abortion:** Similarly, *abortion* is a right protected by substantive due process. (However, the state has a somewhat countervailing interest in protecting "potential life," so that not all restrictions on the right of abortion will be subjected to strict scrutiny.)

❏ **Family relations:** A person's decisions about how to live her *family life* and *raise her children* are also usually "fundamental." Thus the right of relatives to *live together*, a parent's right to direct the *upbringing* and *education* of his children, and the right to *marry* are all fundamental. Therefore, these rights can be impaired only if the state can pass strict scrutiny.

■ **Procedural due process:** The Due Process Clause protects not only "substantive" rights as discussed above, it also requires that the state act with adequate or fair *procedures* when it deprives a person of life, liberty or property.

❏ **Life, liberty or property:** There cannot be a procedural due process problem unless the government is taking a person's *life, liberty or property*. There is *no general interest* in having the government behave with fair procedures.

❏ **Property:** Most procedural due process problems involve the issue of whether the thing being taken constitutes "property."

❏ **Government benefits:** *Government benefits* may or may not constitute "property" rights. Generally, if one is just *applying* for benefits, one does *not* have a property interest in those benefits. But if a person has *already been getting* the benefits, usually he's got a property interest in *continuing* to get them, so the government cannot *terminate* those benefits without giving him procedural due process. The same analysis generally applies to government *jobs*: if you're just applying for the job, you don't have a property interest in it, but if you already have the job, then you may have a property interest, which entitles you to fair procedures before the job can be taken away.

❏ **Process required:** Once you determine that a person's interest in property or liberty is being impaired, you have to determine exactly *what procedures* the person is entitled to get.

❏ **Non-judicial proceedings:** Usually, the issue arises in a non-judicial proceeding (e.g., taking away someone's government job or government benefits). In general, in a non-judicial proceeding, the state does *not* have to give the individual the full range of procedural safeguards needed for a court proceeding. Instead, the court conducts a *balancing* test to determine the required procedures — the strength of the plaintiff's interest in receiving a particular procedural safeguard is weighed against the government's interest in avoiding extra burdens from having to give that safeguard. Thus in a particular situation the government may or may not have to give, say, a hearing, depending on the strength of the plaintiff's interests and the burden to the state in giving the hearing.

# I.   THE BILL OF RIGHTS AND THE STATES

**A. The Bill of Rights generally:**   The first ten amendments to the Constitution, all adopted in 1791, are commonly called the *Bill of Rights*. Their principal purpose is to protect the individual against various sorts of interference by the federal government.

1. **Not applicable to the states:** The Supreme Court decided fairly early that the guarantees of the Bill of Rights *were not directly binding upon state governments*. In *Barron v. The Mayor and City Council of Baltimore*, 32 U.S. (7 Pet.) 243 (1833), an opinion by John Marshall, the Court reasoned that "[h]ad the framers of [the Bill of Rights] Amendments intended them to be limitations on the powers of the state governments, they would have … expressed that intention … in plain and intelligible language." This conclusion has generally been accepted as being historically justified. See, e.g., N&R, p. 339-340.

   a. **Consequence:** As a consequence of the *Barron* holding, however, neither the Supreme Court nor the lower federal courts was able to exercise significant control over the substance of state legislation, or the procedures by which a state law was administered. For instance, in *Barron* itself, the City of Baltimore (a subdivision of the State of Maryland) ended up being able to divert a stream in a way that ruined plaintiff's wharf; the "Taking" Clause of the Fifth Amendment was not applicable to a state government. What little control over state government existed was exercised mainly through the Contract Clause of Article I, §10 (discussed *infra*, p. 395).

B. **Enactment of the Civil War Amendments:** The relative lack of constitutional restrictions on relations between state governments and individuals was drastically changed by the enactment of the three Civil War Amendments, the Thirteenth, Fourteenth and Fifteenth. Each of these three was enacted for the purpose of barring discrimination by states against individuals, especially blacks.

   1. **Fourteenth Amendment:** Of greatest interest to us here is the Fourteenth Amendment, especially §1. §1 provides, in full, as follows:

      "All persons born or naturalized in the United States, and subject to the jurisdiction thereof, are citizens of the United States and of the State wherein they reside. No State shall make or enforce any law which shall abridge the privileges or immunities of citizens of the United States; nor shall any State deprive any person of life, liberty, or property, without due process of law; nor deny to any person within its jurisdiction the equal protection of the laws."

C. **Due process of law and "incorporation":** Shortly after the Fourteenth Amendment was enacted, the Supreme Court seems to have implicitly rejected the notion that that Amendment automatically made applicable to the states all of the Bill of Rights guarantees (which had previously been binding solely on the federal government). See Gunther & Sullivan (13th Ed.), p. 431. But exactly what effect the Fourteenth Amendment had on the states' obligation to honor the Bill of Rights remained quite unsettled until well into this century. Most of the litigation on this issue has involved the *criminal procedure* aspects of the Bill of Rights.

   1. **Two contrasting views:** There have been two main contrasting views espoused by members of the Court on this issue: the "*selective incorporation*" or "fundamental rights" approach, and the "*total incorporation*" approach. The former has always held a majority on the Court, but proponents of the latter view have triumphed in practice, although not in doctrine.

   2. **"Selective incorporation" or "fundamental rights" view:** The "*selective incorporation*" approach denies that the entire Bill of Rights is made applicable to the states via the Fourteenth Amendment. Instead, the term "liberty" as used in that Amendment is to be interpreted by judges without regard to the Bill of Rights. Only those aspects of liberty that are in some sense "*fundamental*" are protected by the Fourteenth Amendment against

state interference. (That is, those parts of the Bill of Rights which are of fundamental importance are "selectively incorporated" into the Fourteenth Amendment.) For this reason, the selective incorporation approach is sometimes called the "*fundamental rights*" approach.

3. **"Total incorporation" view:** The contrary view, that *all* of the guarantees specified in the Bill of Rights are made applicable to the states by the Fourteenth Amendment's Due Process Clause, is usually referred to as the "*total incorporation*" view.

4. **Modern approach:** As noted, the selective incorporation/fundamental rights approach has always held a majority on the Court. The Court today incorporates into the Fourteenth Amendment any guarantee which is "fundamental in the context of the [judicial] processes *maintained by the American states*." *Duncan v. Louisiana*, 391 U.S. 145 (1968).

   a. **Right to jury trial:** Thus in *Duncan*, the Court held that the Fourteenth Amendment guaranteed the right to a jury trial in state criminal prosecutions for which the potential sentence was two years in jail. A criminal process which was fair and equitable but used no juries was easy to imagine, the Court noted, but in the American scheme, where the jury is extensively used, and very serious punishments are generally imposed only after a right to a jury trial, the jury plays a fundamental role which the Fourteenth Amendment must safeguard.

   b. **Nearly all guarantees incorporated:** Although the Court has continued to adhere, in theory at least, to the selective incorporation/fundamental rights approach, the Warren Court speeded up the process by which individual Bill of Rights guarantees were incorporated into the Fourteenth Amendment. Today, *virtually the entire Bill of Rights* has been incorporated into the Fourteenth Amendment (and thereby made applicable to the states), one guarantee at a time.

      i. **Exceptions:** The only important Bill of Rights guarantees not incorporated into the Fourteenth Amendment are the Fifth Amendment's prohibition of criminal trials without a grand jury indictment, and the Seventh Amendment's right to jury trial in civil cases. (Application to the states of the Eighth Amendment's prohibition on excessive bail and on excessive fines has only been implicit. See N&R, pp. 340-341).

         (1) **Second Amendment:** We don't yet know whether the newly-recognized *Second Amendment* right of private individuals to keep firearms at home for self-defense (see *infra*, p. 401) will be incorporated and thus made applicable to the states. It seems likely, however, that the right will be incorporated.

   c. **"Jot-for-jot" or "bag and baggage" incorporation:** Once the Court determines that a particular Bill of Rights guarantee is incorporated into the Fourteenth Amendment, is the *scope* of that guarantee the same when applied to the states as when applied to the federal government? Some members of the Court, at various times, have argued that the answer should be "no." But a majority of the Court has always believed that once a particular guarantee is applied to the states, its *contours should be the same* as in its federal application. This majority view has sometimes been characterized (by those not holding it) as the "*jot-for-jot*" or "*bag and baggage*" approach to incorporation. See the dissent in *Crist v. Bretz*, 437 U.S. 28 (1978).

    **i.  Illustration:** An example of the prevailing "jot-for-jot" approach is *Malloy v. Hogan*, 378 U.S. 1 (1964): "[T]he prohibition of unreasonable searches and seizures of the Fourth Amendment ... and the right to counsel guaranteed by the Sixth Amendment are ... to be enforced against the states under the Fourteenth Amendment according to the ***same standards*** that protect those personal rights against federal encroachment. ... The Court has rejected the notion that the Fourteenth Amendment applies to the states only a ***'watered-down' subjective version*** of the individual guarantees of the Bill of Rights."

    **d.  Anomaly on jury trial right:** There is one anomalous situation in which a Bill of Rights guarantee is presently interpreted to have a different scope in state proceedings than in federal ones. In *Apodaca v. Oregon*, 406 U.S. 404 (1972), the Court upheld the constitutionality of ***non-unanimous jury verdicts*** in state criminal cases, even though jury verdicts in federal criminal cases must be unanimous.

**D.  The Fifth Amendment's Due Process Clause:** Throughout this chapter, we'll be referring almost exclusively to the Due Process Clause of the *Fourteenth* Amendment. But there is another Due Process Clause: the ***Fifth*** Amendment states that "No person shall be ... deprived of life, liberty, or property, without due process of law..."

    **1.  Binding on federal government:** The Fifth Amendment, since it is part of the Bill of Rights, binds the federal government. Observe that the language of the Fifth Amendment's Due Process Clause is virtually identical to that of the Fourteenth Amendment's Due Process Clause, except as to which government is bound.

    **2.  Same interpretation:** Court decisions have interpreted the two clauses ***identically***. That is, if a given type of conduct would be a due process violation when carried out by a state, it's equally forbidden to the federal government. It's important, however, to state which Amendment is triggered: the Fourteenth Amendment governs state action and the Fifth Amendment governs federal action.

# II.  SUBSTANTIVE DUE PROCESS — BEFORE 1934

**A.  Introduction:** The Due Process Clause of the Fourteenth Amendment reads as follows: "Nor shall any State deprive any person of life, liberty, or property, without due process of law[.]"

If this language is analyzed literally, it sounds like a limitation that relates solely to ***procedures***. However, the clause came to be interpreted as a limitation upon the ***substantive power*** of state legislatures to regulate various areas of economic and non-economic life.

    **1.  Meaning of "liberty":** Courts' willingness to review (and often invalidate) the substance of state legislation has taken place principally through interpretation of the term ***"liberty,"*** as used in the Due Process Clause. For instance, if a given state regulation is found to be an undue interference with a private person's "freedom of contract," or with his "right to privacy," the regulation is stricken as a taking of "liberty" without due process of law.

    **2.  Substantive due process:** The doctrine relying on the Fourteenth Amendment to invalidate a substantive state regulation is commonly called the ***"substantive due process"*** doctrine.

3. **Growth, abandonment and rebirth:** The present section of this outline, and the two which follow it, trace: (1) the rise of substantive due process from the late nineteenth century until the 1930s; (2) the doctrine's abandonment (at least with respect to economic regulation) in the late 1930s; and (3) its fairly dramatic rebirth as a means for vindicating a broad range of ***non-economic*** interests (especially the so-called ***"right to privacy"***).

B. **Early history of substantive due process:** When the Fourteenth Amendment was first enacted, it was not clear whether it would be found to limit states' substantive, as opposed to procedural, powers.

   1. ***Slaughterhouse Cases:*** In fact, in a case decided shortly after the Fourteenth Amendment was enacted, the Court seemed reluctant to conclude that that Amendment might limit states' powers. In the ***Slaughterhouse Cases***, 83 U.S. (16 Wall.) 36 (1873), the Court had to decide whether Louisiana could give a monopoly on New Orleans-area slaughterhouses to a particular company. The Court held that this monopoly did ***not*** violate the Due Process Clause. Although one of the dissenters argued that a statute prohibiting a large group of citizens from pursuing a lawful employment deprived them of both liberty and property without due process of law, the majority curtly rejected this contention, apparently on the theory that the Due Process Clause protects only against procedural unfairness.

   2. **Rise of substantive due process:** But within just a few years after the 1873 *Slaughterhouse* decision, pressures on the Court to review the ***substance*** of state economic regulation proved compelling. There were several reasons why this occurred:

      a. **"Natural rights" theory:** First, even before the Civil War, many English and American philosophers espoused the ***"natural law"*** doctrine. This doctrine held that certain rights (especially the right to own property and the right to contract freely) were "fundamental" or "natural" rights, i.e., rights which derived not from any constitution or legal system but simply from the nature of things. It was only a short step to the view that if a legislature enacted a law which restricted these "natural rights," the statute was a deprivation of "liberty" and/or "property" without due process of law.

      b. **Laissez-faire economic theory:** The nation's rapid post-Civil War economic development coincided with the rise in ***"laissez faire"*** economic theory, according to which industrial growth and national well-being would be maximized by ***minimizing government interference with business.*** This "laissez faire" theory was related to so-called ***"social Darwinism,"*** a doctrine which asserted that, in socio-economic life, as in evolution of species, only the fittest would and should survive.

      c. **Enactment of Fourteenth Amendment:** Finally, enactment of the Fourteenth Amendment, with its explicit guarantee of due process protection of liberty and property against state action, came to be viewed by the Court as a "peg" on which substantive review of state law could be hung. This occurred despite the initial rejection of this view by the majority in the *Slaughterhouse Cases.*

   3. **Increasing scrutiny:** In two important post-*Slaughterhouse Cases* decisions, the Supreme Court sustained state regulations, but indicated its willingness to engage in substantive review in some circumstances.

      a. **Regulation of "private" contracts:** In *Munn v. Illinois*, 94 U.S. 113 (1877), the Court deferred to the legislature's judgment as to an issue which the Court found to be "public" rather than "private" (the rates charged by grain elevators); but the Court indicated that in "mere private contracts," the judiciary would determine what regulations were "reasonable."

    **b. Violations of "fundamental law":** And in *Mugler v. Kansas*, 123 U.S. 623 (1887), even though the Court sustained a state ban on alcoholic beverages, the opinion indicated that legislation would be valid under the states' "police powers" only if it truly related to protection of the public health, safety or morals, and only if it did not violate "rights secured by the *fundamental law.*"

**4. Liberty of contract:** Then, in 1897, the Court finally used substantive due process review to invalidate a state statute. In *Allgeyer v. Louisiana*, 165 U.S. 578 (1897), the Court struck down a Louisiana statute which prohibited anyone from obtaining insurance on Louisiana property from any company not licensed in Louisiana.

    **a. Rationale:** The Court held that the statute violated the Fourteenth Amendment's Due Process Clause because it prevented the defendant (who had bought insurance from an out-of-state firm) from exercising his *freedom of contract*. The guarantee of "liberty" in the Fourteenth Amendment, the Court stated, protected not only physical liberty, but also such intangibles as the right to live and work where one wishes, to earn one's livelihood "by any lawful calling," and to enter any contracts necessary to accomplish any of these goals. While the state's police power might allow it to prohibit certain activities or contracts, that power did not extend to barring contracts, like this one, which were both made and to be performed outside of the state.

**C. *Lochner* and its aftermath:** The 40 years after *Allgeyer* saw an enormous Supreme Court trend towards striking down state legislation on due process and similar constitutional grounds. Between 1899 and 1937, 159 Supreme Court decisions (not counting civil rights cases) held state statutes unconstitutional under the Due Process and Equal Protection Clauses; another 25 were struck down under the Due Process Clause coupled with some other constitutional provision. L,K&C, p. 439.

**1. The *Lochner* case itself:** The best known, and from today's perspective most infamous, of these cases was *Lochner v. New York,* 198 U.S. 45 (1905). In *Lochner*, the Court struck down as an abridgement of *"liberty of contract,"* and therefore a violation of due process, a New York law which limited the hours which a bakery employee could work to 10 per day and 60 per week.

    **a. Two defenses of statute:** The statute was defended on two grounds: (1) that it was a valid labor law; and (2) that it protected the health and safety of the workers.

    **b. Not valid labor law:** The Court quickly rejected the labor law justification for the statute. The police power extended only to protection of the "public welfare." The readjustment of bargaining power between bakery employees and their employers, the Court implied, was not of sufficiently public (as opposed to private) concern, especially in view of the law's infringement of the "liberty of contract." (The Court suggested that if bakers were not as intelligent as other workers, or for some reason needed unusual protection, the statute might be valid as a labor law; but the Court found no reason to believe that bakers as a class needed such special protection.)

    **c. Not safety or health measure:** Nor did the Court accept the "health and safety" rationale advanced for the statute. The Court did not find bakers to be an especially endangered group (as it had found miners to be in a case a few years previously). And long working hours did not affect the *public* health and safety by making the baked goods less fit to eat. In any event, the Court indicated, any interest the state had in guarding the wholesomeness of the baked goods could be satisfied by measures which interfered less with freedom of contract, e.g., inspecting premises, requiring that washrooms be furnished, etc.

**d. Legislature's motives suspected:** The *Lochner* majority clearly disbelieved that the legislature had in fact acted in part for safety and health reasons. The law's natural effect was to regulate labor conditions, not to protect anyone's health and safety. The Court thus implied that only the legislature's *actual motive*, not a hypothetical motive, would be looked to in evaluating a statute subjected to substantive due process attack.

**e. No deference to legislative fact finding:** Another key element of the *Lochner* Court's holding was its *refusal to defer to legislative findings of fact*. The Court insisted on reaching its own conclusions on the factual issue of whether the health and safety of bakers, or of the bread-eating public, needed special protection. For instance, the Court stated that "[i]n our judgment it is not possible in fact to discover the connection between the number of hours a baker may work in the bakery and the healthful quality of the bread made by the workman."

**f. Dissent:** Four Justices dissented in *Lochner.*

   **i. Harlan's dissent:** One dissent, authored by Justice Harlan, argued that there was enough evidence that the statute would promote the health and safety of bakers that the legislature's judgment on this issue should have been accepted.

   **ii. Holmes' dissent:** The other dissent, a very famous one by Justice Holmes, contended that the Court had no right to impose its own views about correct economic theory on legislatures. He made one of the most famous remarks in constitutional law: "The Fourteenth Amendment does not enact Mr. Herbert Spencer's social statics," a reference to a then popular "social Darwinism"/"laissez faire" theory. Holmes went on to say that "[a] constitution is not intended to embody a particular economic theory, whether of paternalism and the organic relation of the citizens of the state or of laissez faire." "Liberty," as the term is used in the Fourteenth Amendment, should be found to be violated only when "a rational and fair man necessarily would admit that the statute … would infringe fundamental principles as they had been understood by the traditions of our people and our law." By that test, Holmes contended, the statute was valid.

**g. Analysis of *Lochner* test:** Observe that the *Lochner* majority's test was an extremely stringent one in at least two respects:

   **i. Close fit:** First, it required a *very close "fit"* between the statute and its objectives. In the majority's words, there had to be a "real and substantial" relationship between the statute and the goals which it was to serve. This tight fit was absent in *Lochner* because bakers could have been protected by less restrictive measures, e.g., more frequent inspections, required bathrooms, etc.

   **ii. Limited objectives:** Second, only certain legislative *objectives* were acceptable. Regulation of health and safety was permissible, but *readjustment of economic power* or economic resources was *not.* Thus to the extent that the New York law in *Lochner* was merely a "labor law" which readjusted bargaining power, rather than a true health regulation, it served an impermissible objective. See Tribe, pp. 570-74.

2. **Relation to fundamental interests:**   Even today, strict due process scrutiny is used by the Court where a "fundamental interest" is at stake. Perhaps the *Lochner* Court's mistake was in treating "freedom of contract" as a "fundamental interest," so that the counterbalancing state interest had to be subjected to strict-scrutiny rather than minimal-rationality review. Gunther & Sullivan (13th Ed.), pp. 466-67.

3. **Other decisions of the *Lochner* era:**   The period from about 1900 to 1937 was characterized, as noted, by widespread invalidation of economic legislation on substantive due process grounds. But not every statute directly affecting economic rights was overturned.

   a. **Maximum hours:**   Consider laws setting maximum work hours, for instance. The *Lochner* case, of course, invalidated maximum-hour statutes as they pertained to bakers. But the Court was willing to allow such laws where it found that the benefited class for some reason ***needed special protection***, beyond that given to workers in general.

      i. **Women:**   Thus in *Muller v. Oregon*, 208 U.S. 412 (1908), the Court sustained a law barring the employment of ***women*** in a factory or laundry for more than ten hours in a day; the decision viewed women as members of a weaker class "disadvantage[d] in the struggle for subsistence," and therefore needing special protection.

         (1) **"Brandeis brief" technique:**   By the way, *Muller* saw the first use of the "Brandeis brief" technique. This type of brief (named after then-lawyer Louis Brandeis, who used it in *Muller*) contained extensive documentation to demonstrate the requisite link between the legislative end and the means used to achieve it (e.g., in *Muller*, the special weaknesses and needs of women, and the extra protection which a ten-hour maximum work day would give them).

   b. **Minimum wages:**   On the other hand, the Supreme Court in the *Lochner* era struck down a ***minimum wage*** law for women. *Adkins v. Children's Hospital*, 261 U.S. 525 (1923). The Court did this even though it had previously accepted maximum-hour laws for women (in *Muller, supra*). Again, the rationale was "freedom of contract," and again, Justice Holmes dissented.

      i. **Reconciliation:**   One explanation of the apparent inconsistency between *Muller* and *Adkins* is that maximum hour rules could be seen as promoting a legitimate health objective, whereas it was hard to see minimum wage rules as promoting anything other than a lessening of economic inequality. See Gunther & Sullivan (13th Ed.), pp. 472-73, n. 3; Tribe, p. 573, n. 22.

## III.   SUBSTANTIVE DUE PROCESS — THE MODERN APPROACH TO ECONOMIC AND SOCIAL-WELFARE REGULATION

A. **Initial decline of Lochnerism:**   *Lochner*, and the judicial philosophy behind it, were subjected to intense criticism in the three decades which followed that case. In addition to this criticism, the election of Franklin Roosevelt, and his New Deal programs, convinced many people of the need for aggressive legislative programs to ensure the nation's economic survival. Such large-scale government intervention in economic affairs was clearly at odds with the *Lochner* "freedom of contract" philosophy.

1.  **Shift in Court personnel:**  Turnover in the Court's personnel, together with Roosevelt's threat of Court-packing, contributed to a philosophical shift towards greater deference to legislative intervention in economic affairs. See Tribe, p. 449.

2.  ***Nebbia* case:**  The decline of Lochnerism was presaged by *Nebbia v. New York*, 291 U.S. 502 (1934), where the Court sustained a New York regulatory scheme for fixing milk prices. The Court did not explicitly reject the *Lochner* philosophy. However, the majority noted that due process required only that "[t]he law shall not be unreasonable, arbitrary or capricious, and that the means selected shall have a real and substantial relation to the object sought to be attained … " A state was free "to adopt whatever economic policy may reasonably be deemed to promote public welfare, and to enforce that policy by legislation adapted to its purpose." (The *Nebbia* majority also explicitly rejected the contention that only businesses involving a special "public interest," such as utilities or monopolies, could be subjected to governmental price regulation.)

    a.  **Significance:**  *Nebbia's* requirement of a substantial means-end relationship was essentially the test of *Lochner*. But the *Nebbia* Court was clearly determined not to impose upon legislatures its own views about correct economic policy, as the *Lochner* Court had done.

3.  ***West Coast Hotel Co. v. Parrish:***  But it was not until several years after *Nebbia* that the Supreme Court explicitly overruled one of the major *Lochner*-era precedents. This occurred in **West Coast Hotel v. Parrish**, 300 U.S. 379 (1937), where the Court upheld a state minimum wage law for women, and thereby explicitly overruled the *Adkins* case (*supra*, 152).

    a.  **Rationale:**  The Court mentioned the state's interest in protecting the health of women. But it gave substantial weight to the state's interest in redressing women's ***inferior bargaining power*** as well. The Court conceded that the minimum wage law interfered with "freedom of contract," but unlike *Adkins* (or *Lochner*), the decision concluded that a readjustment of economic bargaining power in order to enable workers to obtain a living wage was a legitimate limitation on that freedom of contract.

B.  **Judicial abdication in economic cases:**  *Nebbia* explicitly (and *West Coast Hotel* implicitly) preserved the requirement of a "real and substantial relation" between an economic regulation and a legitimate state objective. But cases following *West Coast Hotel* virtually abandoned even this degree of scrutiny between means and ends in economic cases.

1.  ***Carolene Products:***  The year after *West Coast Hotel*, the Court made it clear that a ***presumption of constitutionality*** would be applied in the case of an economic regulation subjected to due process attack. In *U.S. v. Carolene Products Co.*, 304 U.S. 144 (1938), the Court sustained against a due process attack a federal prohibition on the interstate shipment of "filled" milk, i.e., skimmed milk mixed with non-milk fats.

    a.  **Rationale:**  The Court noted that Congress had acted upon findings of fact (e.g., committee reports) showing a public health danger from the filled milk. But even in the absence of explicit legislative findings, the Court held, "[t]he existence of facts supporting the legislative judgment is to be ***presumed***, for regulatory legislation affecting ordinary commercial transactions is not to be pronounced unconstitutional unless … it is of such a character as to preclude the assumption that it rests upon some rational basis within the knowledge and experience of the legislators." This test might be characterized as a "*minimum rationality*" standard, coupled with a *presumption of constitutionality.*

2. **Lessening of scrutiny:**  But even the relatively mild scrutiny of *Carolene Products* was abandoned by the Supreme Court in subsequent economic regulation cases.

   a. **Hypothetical reasons to support act:**  For instance, the court has frequently been willing to *hypothesize* reasons which would support the legislature's action, even though there is *no evidence* whatsoever that these reasons *in fact motivated* the lawmakers.

      i. **Illustration:**  Thus in **Williamson v. Lee Optical Co.**, 348 U.S. 483 (1955), the Court upheld an Oklahoma statute which, *inter alia*, prevented opticians from fitting eyeglass lenses into frames (even old lenses into new frames) without a prescription from an ophthalmologist or optometrist. The statute was a rational health measure, the Court found, because the legislature "*might have concluded*" that in some instances prescriptions were necessary to permit accurate fitting, or that "eye examinations were so critical, not only for correction of vision, but also for detection of latent ailments or diseases, that every change in frames and every duplication of a lens should be accompanied by a prescription from a medical expert." Similar hypothetical justifications were given for restrictions on advertising by opticians.

      ii. **Consequence:**  A consequence of the Court's tendency to hypothesize reasons in support of economic legislation is that one who attacks such legislation has the burden of rebutting not only reasons given by the legislature, but also all reasons which the legislature "might have" considered. Some of these hypothetical reasons may not even surface until the Court writes its opinion, making the job of attacking such legislation difficult indeed. See N&R, p. 388.

   b. **Complete abandonment of scrutiny:**  Even less scrutiny was given by the Court in *Ferguson v. Skrupa*, 372 U.S. 726 (1963), where a Kansas law prohibiting non-lawyers from engaging "in the business of debt adjusting" was sustained. Justice Black stated that the Court had "abandoned the use of the 'vague contours' of the Due Process Clause to nullify laws which a majority of the Court believed to be economically unwise." The Court would now "refuse to sit as a '*superlegislature*' to weigh the wisdom of legislation.' "

      i. **Criticism:**  Tribe (p. 582) refers to *Ferguson* as a case where a state law was upheld against due process attack "for virtually no substantive reason at all."

C. **Summary of modern approach:**  In summary, the modern Court has *withdrawn almost completely from the business of reviewing state legislative economic regulation for substantive due process violations.* Not since 1937 has the Court struck down an economic regulation for violating substantive due process, and the present members of the Court all seem in agreement with this withdrawal. See L,K&C, p. 449.

   1. **"Minimum rationality" standard:**  Assuming that the objective being pursued by the legislature in an economic regulation falls within the state's "police power" (now extremely broadly defined to include virtually any health, safety or "general welfare"

goal), all that is required is that there be a ***minimally rational relation*** between the means chosen and the end being pursued. Or, as the Supreme Court put it in *Duke Power v. Carolina Environmental Study Group, Inc.*, 438 U.S. 59 (1978), there will be a presumption of constitutionality unless the legislature has acted in an "***arbitrary and irrational***" way.

2. **"Social welfare" legislation:** The highly deferential "mere rationality" standard of review applies not only in the case of economic regulation, but also in the case of "***social welfare***" legislation, so long as "fundamental" constitutional rights are not impinged. See, e.g., *Whalen v. Roe*, 429 U.S. 589 (1977), where the Court sustained New York's maintenance of a computerized data base of users of certain prescription drugs; the scheme was held to be an "orderly and rational legislative decision," and therefore not violative of substantive due process.

   a. **Distinguished from "fundamental" rights:** But where a law in the economic or "social welfare" area impinges on something the Court has found to be a "***fundamental right***," a substantially higher level of scrutiny is applied. The most important fundamental right, at least in substantive due process cases, has turned out to be the broadly-defined "***right of privacy***." Privacy cases are discussed extensively beginning at p. 156, *infra*.

---

*Quiz Yourself on*

## SUBSTANTIVE DUE PROCESS — ECONOMIC AND SOCIAL-WELFARE REGULATION

22. The legislature of the state of Utopia was worried about the large number of consumers being abused by the harassing tactics of debt collectors. A committee of the legislature investigated, and discovered that the vast majority of complaints involved debt collection techniques used by non-lawyers. Therefore (and at the urging of the state Bar Association), the Utopia legislature passed a statute providing that no person not admitted to the Bar of the State of Utopia may engage in the business of collecting debts owed by consumers. Kneecap, a non-lawyer debt collector, wishes to challenge the statute's constitutionality.

    **(a)** Putting aside any possible First Amendment issues, what right held by Kneecap is most likely to have been violated by the Utopia statute? _____

    **(b)** With respect to the right you listed in your response to (a), what is the standard for determining whether the right has been violated? _____

    **(c)** Will Kneecap's attack on the statute succeed? _____

---

*Answer*

22. **(a) Kneecap's substantive due process rights have been violated.**

    **(b) Whether the statute bore a rational relation to a legitimate state objective.**

    **(c) No.** Where a state statute regulates a purely economic matter, and does not involve any fundamental right, all that is required is that the means chosen be rationally related to a legitimate governmental objective. Here, the objective of reducing the harassment of consumer debtors falls within the state's police power, and is clearly "legitimate." The relation between the means chosen (ban on all non-lawyer collections) and achievement of the objective of reducing harassment is tenuous. But so long as the legislature could rationally have **believed** that non-lawyers were worse offenders on average than lawyers, the requisite "rational relation" between means and end is satisfied. In fact, for over 50 years, no state economic regulation has been overturned for substantive due process purposes, assuming an absence of a fundamental right. (The right to engage in the business of debt collection will almost certainly be held not to be "fundamental," a status limited in substantive due process cases to the "right to privacy," i.e., the areas of sex, marriage, child-bearing and child-rearing.)

# IV.  SUBSTANTIVE DUE PROCESS — PROTECTION OF NON-ECONOMIC RIGHTS, INCLUDING "FUNDAMENTAL" RIGHTS

A.  **Overview:**  We turn now to those cases, mostly modern, in which the Supreme Court has in effect given substantive due process protection for certain **non-economic** rights. In contrast with the economic rights area, where the Supreme Court has virtually abstained from meaningful due process review since the late 1930s (see *supra*, p. 154), the Court has been surprisingly willing, during the last fifteen or so years, to strike down legislation which it finds to violate important non-economic interests.

1.  **"Two-tier" scrutiny:**  This dichotomy stems from the fact that the Court has applied *two* (or more) different *standards of review* in substantive due process cases. In the case of economic rights, the Court has required merely that there be a *rational relation* between the statute and a legitimate state objective. But where the Court finds that a *"fundamental right"* is impaired by a statute, it has applied a scrutiny that is stricter in two respects:

    a.  the state's *objective* must be *"compelling,"* not merely "legitimate"; and

    b.  the *relation* between that objective and the means (i.e., the means-end "fit") must be very close, so that the means can be said to be *"necessary"* to achieve the end.

2.  **Comparison with equal protection:**  This two-tier scrutiny is used in very much the same way in *equal protection* cases; differential treatment of groups will be sustained if it is rationally related to a legitimate state goal, unless either the classification impairs a "fundamental right," or the classification itself is found to be "suspect." See *infra*, p. 234.

3.  **Which rights are "fundamental":**  In the substantive due process area, the rights which the Supreme Court has found to be *"fundamental"* have tended to be in the related areas of *sex, marriage, child-bearing* and *child-rearing*.

    a.  **Right to "privacy":**  Generally, the Court has treated most of the interests it has found to be fundamental as falling within the broad category of the *"right to privacy."* However, as will be seen below, the Court's use of the term "privacy" often differs substantially from what we normally consider this term to mean. In many instances (e.g., the child-bearing situation), a more descriptive term might be the right to *"personal autonomy."*

4.  **Significance of two tiers:**  The significance of the Court's decision to place a particular "right" into the "fundamental" or "non-fundamental" side of the line is even greater than might at first be supposed.

    a.  **Non-fundamental right:**  Where the right is found not to be fundamental, so that a "legitimate" state objective, and a rational relation between the means chosen and that objective, are all that is required, the Court's deference to the legislative judgment is so extreme that there is ***virtually no scrutiny at all***. As noted, for instance, in the economic area no statute has been invalidated on substantive due process grounds in over 50 years.

b. **Fundamental right:**   By contrast, if the right is found to be fundamental, the scrutiny is so strict that few statutes impairing it can meet the double test of showing that the state's objective is "compelling," and that it cannot be achieved in a less burdensome way.

c. **Significance:**   Thus the Court's decision on "fundamentalness" tends to be ***virtually dispositive*** of whether the statute is sustained or invalidated.

5. **Relevance of "liberty":**   In some of the cases discussed below, the Supreme Court does not expressly state that it is using the doctrine of substantive due process. Nonetheless, these cases are usually treated as being, at bottom, substantive due process holdings. This is so because these decisions are properly viewed as holding that the right in question (whatever it is) is part of the ***"liberty"*** guaranteed against state action by the Fourteenth Amendment. For instance, Justice Stewart's concurrence in *Roe v. Wade*, *infra*, p. 161, stated that the prior *Griswold* decision (striking down state barriers to birth control by married couples) "can be rationally understood only as a holding that the Connecticut statute substantively invaded the 'liberty' that is protected by the Due Process Clause of the Fourteenth Amendment."

6. **Scope of following discussion:**   Most of the discussion which follows is concerned with two principal areas: ***birth control*** and ***abortion*** (*infra*, pp. 158 and 161, respectively). Then, aspects of family relations (*infra*, p. 182) and other privacy/autonomy-related issues (including sexuality, *infra*, p. 185) are treated. We then conclude with a more complete discussion of the process by which the Court deems a particular right to be fundamental or non-fundamental (*infra*, p. 205).

B. **The early non-economic cases:**   Although vindication of non-economic rights by use of the substantive due process doctrine has become of great practical importance only in recent years, several much older cases make similar use of the doctrine. The best known are *Meyer v. Nebraska*, 262 U.S. 390 (1923) and *Pierce v. Society of Sisters*, 268 U.S. 510 (1925).

1. *Meyer:*   In *Meyer*, the Supreme Court struck down a state law which prohibited the ***teaching of foreign languages*** to young children. The Court held that the term "liberty," as used in the Fourteenth Amendment, included many non-economic, but nonetheless important, rights; the right of teachers to teach, and that of students to ***acquire knowledge***, were among these. The Court applied what appears to have been a "mere rationality" test (rather than any kind of strict scrutiny), but nonetheless concluded that the statute was "without reasonable relation to any end within the competency of the State."

2. *Pierce:*   In *Pierce*, the Court struck down a state statute requiring children to attend public schools, and thus preventing them from attending private and parochial ones. This decision rested on the "liberty of parents and guardians to direct the upbringing and education of children under their control." The Court denied the power of the state to "standardize its children" by forcing them to accept only public instruction.

3. *Skinner:*   A third case was decided on equal protection grounds, but was motivated by substantive-due-process-like concerns. In *Skinner v. Oklahoma*, 316 U.S. 535 (1942), the

Court invalidated an Oklahoma statute which provided for compulsory sterilization of persons convicted three times of felonies showing "moral turpitude," but which did not apply to such "white-collar" crimes as embezzlement. The Court objected to the discrimination between, say, grand larceny and embezzlement, but it emphasized that its reason for strictly scrutinizing the discrimination was that "marriage and procreation are fundamental to the very existence and survival of the race."

    **a.**   **Probable modern view:**  If a statute like the one in *Skinner* arose today, it would almost certainly be struck down on substantive due process/"right of privacy" grounds, even without regard to equal protection. Given the Supreme Court's acceptance of the fundamental importance of procreation in *Griswold* (birth control) and *Roe v. Wade* (abortion), it is almost inconceivable that the state would be permitted to sterilize any group (with the possible exception of convicted rapists).

        **i.**   **Sterilization of mental defectives:**  A law allowing involuntary sterilization of institutionalized ***mental defectives*** would also almost surely be struck down today. Yet such a statute was upheld, in one of the less glorious moments of the Supreme Court, in *Buck v. Bell*, 274 U.S. 200 (1927); Justice Holmes justified the statute with the remark that "three generations of imbeciles are enough."

**C. Birth control (the *Griswold* case):**  The first major modern-era case which used a substantive-due-process-like approach to protect a fundamental right was ***Griswold v. Connecticut***, 381 U.S. 479 (1965), the famous ***contraceptives*** case.

    **1.**   **Facts of *Griswold*:**  The statute at issue in *Griswold* was a Connecticut law which forbade the use of contraceptives (and made this use a criminal offense); the statute also forbade the aiding or counseling of others in their use. The defendants were the director of the local Planned Parenthood Association and its medical director. They were convicted of counseling ***married persons*** in the use of contraceptives. No users, married or single, were charged in the case.

    **2.**   **Majority strikes statute:**  The Court, by a 7-2 vote, ***struck down*** the statute. The majority opinion, authored by Justice Douglas, declined to make explicit use of the substantive due process doctrine. Instead, the opinion found that several of the Bill of Rights guarantees protect the privacy interest and create a "***penumbra***" or "zone" of privacy. The Court then concluded that the right of married persons to use contraceptives fell within this penumbra.

        **a.**   **Examples:**  Thus the Court claimed that the First Amendment, by its explicit protection of the freedoms of speech and of the press, has "emanations" which create a "penumbra"; it is this penumbra which protects, for instance, the freedom of association, a freedom not explicitly mentioned in the Constitution. Similarly, the Court found, the Fourth Amendment's ban on unreasonable searches has a penumbra which protects privacy interests, as do the Third, Fifth and Ninth Amendments. Collectively, these Amendments establish a zone in which "privacy is protected from governmental intrusion."

        **b.**   **Why statute was invalid:**  Douglas' majority opinion did not specify exactly how the Connecticut ban on contraceptives violated this penumbra of privacy. But a good part of the rationale seemed to have to do with the privacy implications of ***proof*** in prosecutions. Thus the Court asked: "Would we allow the police to search the sacred precincts of marital bedrooms for telltale signs of the use of contraceptives?" Douglas concluded that "[t]he very idea is repulsive to the notions of privacy surrounding the marriage relationship."

3. **Concurrences:**   There were three separate concurring opinions in *Griswold*. All agreed with the Douglas opinion's basic conclusion that the Connecticut statute violated the Fourteenth Amendment interest in liberty, but each reached this conclusion by different means.

a. **Goldberg's Ninth Amendment view:**   Justice Goldberg believed that the Fourteenth Amendment Due Process Clause protected all "fundamental" rights, whether or not these were explicitly listed in the Bill of Rights. He contended that the ***Ninth Amendment*** (which provides that "[t]he enumeration in the Constitution, of certain rights, shall not be construed to deny or disparage others retained by the people") supported this view, because it "shows a belief of the Constitution's authors that fundamental rights exist that are not expressly enumerated in the first eight Amendments. ... " Just as the Ninth Amendment showed that certain rights not enumerated in the Bill of Rights were protected as against the ***federal*** government, so (he argued) the Fourteenth Amendment should be found to protect against state action fundamental rights, including some not enumerated in the Bill of Rights. Goldberg found the right of "marital privacy" to be among such fundamental rights, and argued that the statute unconstitutionally violated that right, because it was not necessary for the fulfilling of a "compelling" state objective.

b. **Harlan "ordered liberty" approach:**   Justice Harlan's concurrence was essentially in accord with Justice Goldberg's. As he had done several times before, he argued that the Fourteenth Amendment Due Process Clause does not merely incorporate the specific Bill of Rights guarantees, but instead "stands ... on its own bottom," to protect those basic values "implicit in the concept of ordered liberty." He then relied on his prior dissent in *Poe v. Ullman*, 367 U.S. 497 (1961), which had contended that the same Connecticut statute violated the due process interest in marital privacy.

i. **No protection outside of marriage:**   Harlan's *Griswold/Poe* opinions stopped carefully short of finding a general right to privacy for sexual relations. He explicitly rejected the idea that adultery, homosexuality, fornication and incest were protected by the same right to privacy. He distinguished these from the marital relations situation by noting that the state allows (even encourages) the marital relation, and should therefore not be permitted to use the criminal law to regulate the intimate details of that relation. By contrast, the state completely forbids the other types of sexual relations, so that it may permissibly regulate the details of those forbidden relations as well.

c. **White's means-end test:**   Justice White's concurrence focused on the means-end relationship. He would apparently have upheld the statute had it been "reasonably necessary for the effectuation of a legitimate and substantial state interest." But the Connecticut statute, which supposedly served the state's policy against promiscuity and illicit sex, was drawn too broadly: there was no need to ban the use of birth control by married couples in order to achieve this objective. Thus White would presumably have upheld the ban as applied to the use of birth control by unmarried couples.

4. **Dissent:**   Justices Black and Stewart each wrote a separate dissent. Black reiterated his familiar argument that only those rights explicitly protected by a specific Bill of Rights (or other constitutional) provision were protected by the Fourteenth Amendment; he felt that

no "right of privacy," in the broad and general way the majority used that term, was protected by any specific provision. Justice Stewart similarly failed to find a right of privacy in any specific guarantee, and also rejected the Goldberg Ninth Amendment rationale (claiming that it limited only the powers of the federal government).

    **a. Stewart reverses view:** But Justice Stewart, as noted *infra*, p. 163, ultimately changed his view of *Griswold*, and concluded that the statute was properly invalidated as a substantive invasion of the Fourteenth Amendment Due Process Clause's "liberty" interest.

**5. Criticism of majority:** The majority opinion in *Griswold* has been criticized on a number of counts. Three of these are as follows:

    **a. "Penumbra" theory illogical:** Justice Douglas, in articulating his "penumbra" theory, points to particular aspects of the right of privacy in the First, Third, Fourth and Fifth Amendments. He then appears to conclude that under the collective penumbra of these Amendments, a ***general***, complete, right of privacy must also dwell. (And it is this general right of privacy which was necessary to decide *Griswold* as the Court decided it; the privacy aspects explicitly addressed by those Amendments don't deal with the *Griswold* type of problem.) Yet the logic of Douglas' jump from the specific privacy aspects to the general right of privacy is suspect: it could be argued that "[w]hen the Constitution sought to protect private rights it specified them; [the fact] that it explicitly protects some elements of privacy, but not others, suggests that it did not mean to protect those not mentioned." 74 COLUM. L. REV. 1410 (quoted in L,K&C, p. 522.)

    **b. No search at issue:** Douglas' main privacy rationale in *Griswold* was that enforcement of the statute would require possible searches of the marital bedroom, and other public inquisition into intimate details. But the heart of the case was the ***giving of counseling*** about birth control use, not the search of the marital bedroom or other inquisition. Thus the Court's search rationale seems disingenuous, and seems to be a way of forcing the facts to fit within the more traditional Fourth Amendment-like meaning of "privacy." The true meaning of *Griswold*, in fact, becomes clear in light of the later decision in *Eisentadt v. Baird*, discussed below.

    **c. The property/personal rights distinction:** The Douglas opinion declined to use substantive due process analysis, and explicitly rejected the choice of using a *Lochner*-type approach. Instead, Douglas used the "penumbra" theory as a way of protecting "personal" rights (like the right of privacy), while not having to give equally strict scrutiny to "economic" or "property" rights. Yet the penumbra theory ***seems to be equally applicable to many property rights.***

        **i. Contract rights:** For instance, since the Constitution explicitly provides against the impairment of the obligation of contracts, it seems fair to say that the Contract Clause has a "penumbra" which includes a constitutional right to enter into contracts (the dreaded "liberty of contract" that was at the basis of *Lochner*). Similarly, the Fifth Amendment's right not to have one's property taken without due process would seem to include more broadly-defined property rights within its penumbra. See 64 MICH. L. REV. 235 (quoted in L,K&C, p. 522).

    **ii. No reason for not covering property rights:** Yet neither *Griswold* nor any Court decision since then offers a principled rationale for applying the penumbra theory to personal rights but not to "property" or "economic" ones.

**D. Post-*Griswold* contraceptive law:** Developments since *Griswold* make it clear that that case ultimately means much more than that married persons may not be prevented from using birth control — it means that ***no person***, single or married, may be prohibited from using contraception, or otherwise be subjected to undue interference with ***decisions on procreation***. As the Court said in a post-*Griswold* case, "[r]ead in light of its progeny, the teaching of *Griswold* is that the Constitution protects individual decisions in matters of child-bearing from unjustified intrusion by the state." *Carey v. Population Services Int'l*, discussed *infra*, p. 181.

    **1. *Eisenstadt v. Baird*:** Much of the expansion of the meaning of *Griswold* came in **Eisenstadt v. Baird**, 405 U.S. 438 (1972), where the Court invalidated a statute which, by permitting contraceptives to be distributed only by registered physicians and pharmacists, and only to married persons, ***discriminated against the unmarried.***

        **a. Rationale:** In striking down the statute, the majority invoked equal protection as well as substantive due process grounds. The Court observed that "[w]hatever the rights of the individual to access to contraceptives may be, the rights must be the same for the unmarried and the married alike. … If the right of privacy means anything, it is the right of the ***individual***, married or single, to be free from unwarranted government intrusion into matters so fundamentally affecting a person as the decision whether to bear or beget a child." (Emphasis in original.)

    **2. Private place no longer required:** What might be called the right of "***reproductive autonomy***" (see Tribe, p. 1339), protected by both *Griswold* and *Eisenstadt*, now exists ***even in non-private situations***. In the post-*Eisenstadt* case of *Carey v. Population Services Int'l* (discussed further *infra*, p. 181), the Court noted that the constitutionally-protected privacy interest in, *inter alia*, procreation and child-rearing "is not just concerned with a particular place, but with a protected intimate relationship. Such protected privacy extends to the doctor's office, the hospital, the hotel room or as otherwise required to safeguard the right to intimacy involved."

    **3. Non-marital relationships:** Just as *Eisenstadt* broadened at least the contraceptive aspect of privacy to non-married couples, the Supreme Court has begun to recognize ***a general right of privacy in sexual or procreational matters*** outside the bounds of marriage. This happened in *Lawrence v. Texas*, *infra*, p. 185, in which the Court held that state bans on sodomy violate the substantive due process rights of homosexuals, becauset there is "an autonomy of self that includes ... certain intimate conduct."

**E. Abortion generally:** The right of privacy which the Court found to exist in *Griswold* has been extended to the ***abortion*** context. The case recognizing that the right of privacy limits a legislature's freedom to proscribe or regulate abortion was the landmark case of *Roe v. Wade*, 410 U.S. 113 (1973). That case has since been interpreted in a long line of decisions and, most recently, cut back in important ways in *Planned Parenthood v. Casey* and *Gonzales v. Carhart*, cases decided in 1992 and 2007 respectively. We will first review *Roe v. Wade*, then *Casey*, then various sub-topics relating to abortion including *Gonzales*.

**F. *Roe v. Wade*:** In **Roe v. Wade**, 410 U.S. 113 (1973), the Court held that a woman's right to privacy is a "***fundamental***" ***right*** under the Fourteenth Amendment. Therefore, the legislature has only a limited right to regulate — and may not completely proscribe — abortions. The actual result of the case was to invalidate, on privacy grounds, Texas' nearly-complete ban on abortions.

1.  **Precise holding in *Roe*:**  The actual holding of *Roe* was remarkably specific, almost legislative. In an opinion by Justice Blackmun, the Court divided pregnancy into three *trimesters*, and prescribed a different rule for each:

    a.  **First trimester:**  During the first trimester, a state ***may not ban, or even closely regulate, abortions***. The decision to have an abortion, and the manner in which it is to be carried out, are to be left to the pregnant woman and her physician.

        i.  **Rationale:**  The Court's rationale for this approach was that at present, the mortality rate for mothers having abortions during the first trimester is lower than the rate for full-term pregnancies. Therefore, the state has no valid (or at least no compelling) interest in protecting the mother's health by banning or closely regulating abortions during this period. (But the state may require that abortions be performed only by licensed physicians.)

    b.  **Second trimester:**  During the second trimester, the state may protect its interest in the ***mother's health***, by regulating the abortion procedure in ways that are "reasonably related" to her health. Such regulation might include, for instance, a requirement that the operation take place in a hospital rather than a clinic. (The Court implied that during this second trimester, the risk of maternal death through abortion was higher than that in full-term pregnancies.)

        i.  **No protection of fetus:**  But the state may protect only the mother's health, ***not the fetus' life***, during this period. Therefore, a flat ban on second trimester abortions is not permitted. Nor may the state regulate in ways that protect the fetus rather than the mother's health.

    c.  **Third trimester:**  At the beginning of the third trimester, the Court stated, the fetus typically becomes "***viable***." That is, it has a "capability of meaningful life outside the mother's womb." Therefore, after viability the state has a "***compelling***" interest in protecting the fetus. It may therefore regulate, or ***even proscribe***, abortion. However, abortion ***must be permitted*** where it is necessary to preserve the ***life or the health*** of the mother.

2.  **Rationale of *Roe*:**  The *Roe* decision was premised upon the ***right of privacy***. The Court pointed to *Griswold*, as well as to other privacy-derived holdings (e.g., *Pierce v. Society of Sisters* and *Meyer v. Nebraska*, both *supra*, p. 157, recognizing freedom in child-rearing and education). This right of privacy, which the Court found to be part of the "liberty" guaranteed by the Fourteenth Amendment, was "broad enough to encompass a woman's decision whether or not to terminate her pregnancy."

    a.  **Standard of review:**  In fact, the Court held, a woman's interest in deciding this issue herself was a "***fundamental***" one, which could only be outweighed if: (1) there was a "***compelling state interest***" in barring or restricting abortion; and (2) the state statute was "***narrowly drawn***" so that it fulfilled only that legitimate state interest.

    b.  **Countervailing state interest:**  The Court found that the state had two interests which, in particular circumstances, might be compelling: protecting the health of the mother, and protecting the viability of the fetus. The former would only be compelling after the first trimester (when the abortion-related dangers outweigh the live-birth-related ones); the latter only applied during the last trimester, when the fetus was viable. From these two postulates the Court drew its three-part rule, summarized above.

    **i. Fetus not person:** The Court explicitly rejected the argument that the state had a compelling interest, even before viability, in ***protecting the fetus as a "person"*** as that term is used in the Fourteenth Amendment. The Court reached this conclusion largely on historical grounds.

**3. Concurrences:** There were two concurrences in *Roe*, by Justices Stewart and Douglas.

    **a. Stewart's concurrence:** The Stewart concurrence reversed that Justice's dissenting position in *Griswold*, and accepted both *Griswold* and *Roe* as substantive due process cases; these and other decisions "make clear that freedom of personal choice in matters of marriage and family life is one of the liberties protected by the Due Process Clause of the Fourteenth Amendment."

    **b. Douglas' concurrence:** Justice Douglas wrote that the Fourteenth Amendment protected "freedom of choice in the basic decisions of one's life respecting marriage, divorce, procreation, contraception, and the education and upbringing of children." Douglas conceded that this freedom of choice was subject to regulation where there was a compelling state interest, but found that Texas' nearly-complete proscription of abortion in *Roe* went beyond such state interest.

**4. Dissent:** Justices White and Rehnquist wrote separate dissents.

    **a. White's dissent:** Justice White objected to what he called the Court's imposition of its own value scheme, preferring the "convenience, whim or caprice of the putative mother [over] the life or potential life of the fetus" prior to viability. He thought that the relative weights which should be assigned to these two interests should be left to "the people and to the political processes."

    **b. Rehnquist's dissent:** Justice Rehnquist argued that only a ***"mere rationality"*** test, not a strict scrutiny one, should be applied; in his view, at least some of the abortion prohibitions and regulations forbidden by the majority could meet this minimum rationality standard. Also, he criticized the majority's three-part result as being "judicial legislation."

**G. The modification of *Roe* by *Casey*:** *Roe* has been ***partially overruled***. This occurred in probably the Court's most important[1] post-*Roe* abortion decision, ***Planned Parenthood of Southeastern Pennsylvania v. Casey***, 505 U.S. 833 (1992). In *Casey*, a majority of the Court declined to overrule *Roe v. Wade* explicitly. However, important aspects of *Roe* — including abortion's status as a ***"fundamental right,"*** the state's almost complete inability to ***regulate first-trimester abortions***, and in fact the whole ***trimester framework*** of *Roe* — were all ***overturned***. As a result of *Casey*, the states ***may restrict abortion*** so long as they do not place ***"undue burdens"*** on the woman's right to choose.

**1. Pennsylvania statute:** At issue in *Casey* was a Pennsylvania statute which placed a number of significant restrictions on abortion, such as a requirement that the woman ***wait for 24 hours*** after receiving from a doctor certain information about abortion, and a requirement that a married woman ***notify her husband*** of her intent to abort. Several of

---

1. Another contender for "most important post-*Roe* abortion decision" is *Gonzales v. Carhart*, the partial-birth abortion decision discussed *infra*, p. 175.

these restrictions were clearly unconstitutional judged by the standards of the Court's post-*Roe* decisions.

2. **Three blocs:** There were three distinct voting blocs in *Casey*. First, two traditionally "liberal" Justices — Stevens and Blackmun (the author of *Roe*) — voted to reaffirm *Roe* completely. Second, a four-Justice "conservative" bloc — Chief Justice Rehnquist, and Justices White, Scalia and Thomas — voted to overturn *Roe* completely. The "swing" votes were supplied by a middle-of-the-road bloc consisting of Justices O'Connor, Souter and Kennedy, who voted to reaffirm the "central principle" of *Roe v. Wade*, but to allow state regulation that did not "unduly burden" the woman's freedom to choose. Thus the Court decided by 5-4 to maintain *Roe v. Wade* as precedent, but by 7-2 to allow states to regulate more strictly than *Roe* and its progeny had allowed.

3. **The joint opinion:** The three "centrist" Justices — O'Connor, Souter and Kennedy — formed a *plurality* opinion, which spoke for the Court on all points. This opinion must be closely read, since it is now effectively the law of the land. Interestingly, the plurality opinion was written by all three Justices *jointly*, rather than by a single Justice with others joining in the opinion. We will refer to this plurality opinion as the "joint opinion."

   a. *Roe* **reaffirmed:** The joint opinion began by stating broadly that it was *reaffirming* the *"essential holding* of *Roe v. Wade*." The opinion saw this "essential holding" as having three parts: (1) a recognition of "the right of the woman to choose to have an abortion before viability and to obtain it without undue interference from the state"; (2) a confirmation of the State's power to restrict abortions after fetal viability, if the law contains exceptions for pregnancies endangering the woman's life or health; and (3) a recognition of the state's "legitimate interests from the outset of the pregnancy in protecting the health of the woman and the life of the fetus. ... "

      i. **Rationale:** The joint opinion appeared to agree not only with the "essential holding" of *Roe*, but with the constitutional analysis that gave rise to that decision. It remains settled, the three Justices wrote, "that the Constitution places limits on a State's right to interfere with a person's most basic decisions about family and parenthood[.]" Cases upholding the right to use contraception (such as *Griswold*, *supra*, p. 158) continue to be relevant to the abortion situation as well: both the contraception and the abortion contexts "involve personal decisions concerning not only the meaning of procreation but also human responsibility and respect for it."

      ii. **Decision personal to the woman:** The joint opinion emphasized that the special nature of the abortion decision required that it be left to the woman alone, for it impacts upon her in a *uniquely personal way*. "The liberty of the woman is at stake in a sense unique to the human condition and so unique to the law. The mother who carries a child to full term is subject to anxieties, to physical constraints, to pain that only she must bear. ... Her suffering is too intimate and personal for the State to insist, without more, upon its own vision of the woman's role, however dominant that vision has been in the course of our history and our culture. The destiny of the woman must be shaped to a large extent on her own conception of her spiritual imperatives and her place in society."

   b. *Stare decisis*: However, the joint opinion also suggested that its authors might *not* have endorsed the principles of *Roe v. Wade* if the issue were appearing before the

Court for the first time. The opinion referred to "the reservations any of us may have in reaffirming the central holding of *Roe.*" But, the joint opinion held, what tipped the scales in favor of reaffirming *Roe* was the force of **stare decisis**, the doctrine that says that courts should not lightly overturn precedent. Where a constitutional decision has not proven "unworkable," and where overturning it would damage reliance interests, *stare decisis* dictated that the decision not be overturned.

    **i.  Shouldn't overrule under fire:** The *legitimacy* of the Court would be undermined if it were to overrule *Roe,* the joint opinion suggested. "Where, in the performance of its judicial duties, the Court decides a case in such a way as to resolve the sort of **intensely divisive** controversy reflected in *Roe* … its decision has a dimension that the resolution of the normal case does not carry. It is the dimension present whenever the Court's interpretation of the Constitution calls the contending sides of a national controversy to end their national division by accepting a common mandate rooted in the Constitution." In this respect, the only other comparable case from "our lifetime" was *Brown v. Board of Education.* If the Court overruled *Roe* without a compelling reason to do so, it would be seen as **surrendering to political pressure**, a result that would "subvert the Court's legitimacy beyond any serious question."

**c.  The "undue burden" standard:** But what the joint opinion gave, it partly took away. Two aspects of *Roe* and the cases interpreting it should be **abandoned**, the three Justices held: the *"trimester framework"* of *Roe*, and (at least implicitly) the principle that any pre-viability abortion regulation must survive **strict scrutiny**.

    **i.  Trimester approach rejected:** The joint opinion noted that *Roe* used a trimester approach to govern abortion regulations: almost no regulation at all was permitted during the first trimester of pregnancy; regulations designed to protect the woman's health (but not to further the state's interest in potential life) were permitted during the second trimester; during the third trimester, because the fetus was now viable, the state could prohibit abortion as long as the life or health of the mother was not at stake. But the joint opinion did not agree that the trimester approach was a necessary method of safeguarding a woman's right to choose. The biggest vice of the trimester approach was that it "undervalues the State's interest in potential life," because it completely ignores that interest during the first two trimesters.

    **ii.  The "undue burden" standard:** In place of the trimester approach, the joint opinion articulated a new *"undue burden"* standard: "Only where state regulation imposes an undue burden on a woman's ability to make [the decision whether to abort] does the power of the State reach into the heart of liberty protected by the Due Process Clause." A state regulation will constitute an "undue burden" if the regulation "has the purpose or effect of placing a **substantial obstacle** in the path of a woman seeking an abortion of a nonviable fetus." Under this standard, if state regulations merely "create a **structural mechanism**" by which the state may "express profound respect for the life of the unborn," and do not place a substantial obstacle in the woman's path, the regulations will be upheld. Similarly, the state may regulate to further the **health or safety of the woman**, as long as the regulation does not unduly burden the right to abortion. After viability, the state may proscribe all abortions not needed to protect the health or life of the mother (a holding that does not represent any change from *Roe* or later cases).

**iii. Fundamental rights and strict scrutiny:**   The joint opinion implicitly rejected *Roe*'s view that the right to abortion is a "fundamental" right, and *Roe*'s concomitant rule that every pre-viability restriction on this fundamental right must survive ***strict scrutiny***. The opinion did not discuss either the "fundamental rights" or "strict scrutiny" issue, but it is clear that the opinion did not in fact apply strict scrutiny to the Pennsylvania statute (and applied the "undue burden" test instead). So we must assume that ***abortion is no longer a fundamental right***, and restrictions on it are ***no longer to be strictly scrutinized***.

**d. Application to Pennsylvania statute:**   The plurality then applied its new "undue burden" analysis to the Pennsylvania statute. All but one of the Pennsylvania restrictions were ***upheld*** as not being unduly burdensome:

**i. Informed consent:**   The Pennsylvania statute contained an elaborate ***"informed consent"*** requirement, which the joint opinion ***upheld***. First, at least ***24 hours*** before performing an abortion, a physician must inform the woman of the nature of the procedure, the health risks of both abortion and childbirth, and the "probable gestational age of the unborn child." (The waiting period was subject to an exception for "medical emergencies," defined as situations where an immediate abortion is required to avert serious risk of death or major bodily impairment to the woman.) Second, either a physician or a qualified non-physician must inform the woman of the availability of state-printed materials describing the fetus and providing information about non-abortion alternatives (e.g., adoption, child support, etc.)

**(1) No undue burden found:** The joint opinion found that these informed consent requirements ***did not "unduly burden"*** the woman's right to choose to abort. The closest question came as to the 24-hour waiting period; here, the joint opinion relied mainly on the absence of any strong findings by the district court that the increased costs and potential delays which might stem from this waiting period were truly "substantial" obstacles.

**ii. Spousal notification:**   But the joint opinion ***struck down*** the Pennsylvania statute's ***"spousal notification"*** provision. Under that provision, a married woman could not receive an abortion without signing a statement that she had notified her spouse that she was about to undergo the procedure. The provision contained several exceptions, including one for the situation where the pregnancy was the result of spousal ***sexual assault*** (provided that the assault was reported to the police within 90 days), and one applicable if the woman believed that notifying her husband would cause him or someone else to inflict ***bodily injury*** upon her.

**(1) Struck down as undue burden:** The joint opinion found that this spousal notification requirement was a ***substantial obstacle*** to abortion for some women: many fear that they will be ***psychologically abused*** by the husband, or that he will abuse their ***children*** (neither situation was covered by an exception in the notification requirement); others may fail to be able to use the exception for sexual assaults because they will be terrified to report the episode to the police, as was required for the use of that exception. The fact that the overwhelming majority of married women *do* notify their husbands was irrelevant; what counted was that as to that small percentage who do not voluntarily notify the spouse, the requirement that they do so was a substantial impediment.

**(2) Outmoded view of role of women:** The three Justices concluded their ruling on the spousal-notification requirement by asserting that the requirement reflected an outmoded view of the position of women in society: the requirement "embodies a view of marriage consonant with the common-law status of married women but repugnant to our present understanding of marriage and of the nature of the rights secured by the Constitution. Women do not lose their constitutionally protected liberty when they marry."

iii. **Parental consent:** The joint opinion ***upheld*** the statute's ***parental consent*** provision, by which except in medical emergencies, an unemancipated young woman under 18 may not obtain an abortion unless she and one of her parents provides informed consent. The statute allowed for a "judicial bypass," by which a court could authorize performance of the abortion without parental consent, if the judge determined that the young woman had given informed consent and that an abortion would be in her best interest.

**(1) Rationale for upholding:** The three Justices had little trouble upholding this provision, because it matched other "parental consent with possibility of judicial bypass" provisions that the Court had previously upheld (see the cases summarized *infra*, pp. 169-171). One difference was that here, the parent's consent must be shown to have been ***informed*** (which under the statute required the parent to listen to the alternatives to abortion and to hear about available state literature, 24 hours before the procedure). But the three Justices believed that the parental informed consent requirement was constitutional just as the requirement that an adult woman give her own informed consent was now constitutional; neither represented an "undue burden" on the right of abortion.

4. **The Stevens and Blackmun opinions:** Justices Stevens and Blackmun each wrote a separate opinion, concurring in part and dissenting in part. Each agreed that *Roe v. Wade* should be maintained as precedent, but each disagreed with the plurality as to how tightly the states may regulate abortion, and each believed that some of the Pennsylvania regulations upheld by the plurality were unconstitutional.

a. **Stevens:** Justice Stevens agreed with the joint opinion that the state has a legitimate interest in protecting potential life. But he did not believe that this interest was directly protected by the Constitution, and believed it was therefore a less weighty interest than the woman's constitutional liberty interest in deciding whether to bear a child. Stevens believed that the state could "express a preference for normal childbirth," but that the state could not force the woman to receive the state's obviously pro-life materials just at the moment she was considering her decision.

b. **Blackmun:** The separate opinion by Justice Blackmun, the author of *Roe*, was notably personal. Blackmun wrote in deeply emotional and metaphorical language not usually seen in Supreme Court decisions: as the result of recent prior court decisions, he said, "All that remained between the promise of *Roe* and … darkness … was a single, flickering flame. … But now, just when so many expected the darkness to fall, the flame has grown bright." Blackmun argued that the standard imposed by *Roe v. Wade* — that any regulation of abortion be subject to **strict scrutiny** — should be maintained, which he believed the "undue burden" standard did not do. Similarly, he believed that *Roe*'s trimester framework should be maintained. For Blackmun, *all* of the challenged regulations were infirm: the pre-abortion counseling requirement, the 24-hour waiting period, the requirement that consent by a minor's parent be "informed" (which the trial court found would require an in-person visit by the parent to the facility), the detailed record-keeping and disclosure provisions — none of these, in Blackmun's view, could survive strict scrutiny.

5.   **Dissents:**   There were four **dissenters** in *Casey*. Chief Justice Rehnquist wrote one dissent, in which Justices White, Scalia and Thomas joined. Justice Scalia wrote another dissent, in which Rehnquist, White and Thomas joined.

   a.   **Rehnquist dissent:**   Paradoxically, Rehnquist's dissent read in some ways more like a declaration of victory than a protest against defeat. He argued that the joint opinion "retains the outer shell of *Roe v. Wade* … but beats a wholesale retreat from the substance of that case." By contrast, he said, he and the other dissenters "believe that *Roe* was wrongly decided, and that it can and should be overruled. … " The dissenters would have upheld *all* the challenged provisions of the Pennsylvania statute.

      i.   **Not a fundamental right:**   To Rehnquist, the right to terminate a pregnancy was not, and should not have ever been declared to be, **"fundamental."** Abortion was quite different from marriage, procreation and contraception (other rights found to be "fundamental"), because it involved the termination of life and was thus a unique situation. Nor was the right to abort rooted in the historical traditions of the American people, which Rehnquist believed was the only way in which a right could become fundamental. Rehnquist believed that a woman's interest in having an abortion is a form of liberty protected by the Due Process Clause, but that since that interest was not a fundamental right, the states could regulate it "in *ways rationally related to a legitimate state interest*."

      ii.   **Application to statute:**   Given Rehnquist's belief that the regulations merely needed to be "rationally related to a legitimate state interest," it was not surprising that he found them all to be valid. For instance, the spousal notice requirement was a "rational attempt by the State to improve truthful communication between spouses and encourage collaborative decision making, and thereby fosters marital integrity."

   b.   **Scalia's dissent:**   Justice Scalia's dissent was a scornful, almost personal, attack on the joint opinion. To Scalia, the right to terminate an unwanted pregnancy was simply not a liberty interest protected in any way by the U.S. Constitution. "I reach [this conclusion] for the same reason I reach the conclusion that **bigamy** is not constitutionally protected — because of two simple facts: (1) the constitution says absolutely nothing about it, and (2) the long standing traditions of American society have permitted it to be legally proscribed." The non-historically-oriented factors relied on by the majority to support abortion's special protected status — for instance, the fact that it is among "a person's most basic decisions" and involves "a most intimate and personal choice"

— could be applied equally to homosexual sodomy, polygamy, adult incest and suicide, "all of which can constitutionally be proscribed because it is our own unquestionable constitutional tradition that they are proscribable."

    **6. Significance of case:** So what is the significance of *Casey*?

        **a. Abortion as protected interest:** Post-*Casey*, a woman's right to decide whether to terminate her pregnancy remains an interest that receives *special constitutional protection*. For example, it seems completely clear that a state may not simply *forbid* all abortions, or even all abortions occurring in, say, the second trimester. Similarly, it seems clear that a state may not forbid all pre-viability abortions except those necessary to save the life or health of the mother. Any such regulation seems to be an "undue burden" on abortion.

        **b. Regulations easier to sustain:** On the other hand, state provisions that in some way *regulate* the abortion process are much more likely to be sustained than they were prior to *Casey*. The Court's 2007 decision upholding a federal ban on so-called "partial birth abortions" in *Gonzales v. Carhart* (*infra*, p. 175) confirms that both the state and federal governments have far greater scope to regulate the abortion process than they did before *Casey*.

        **c. Future of *Roe*:** Even the preservation of the "central holding" of *Roe v. Wade* seems to hang by a single vote, which as of 2007 belongs to Justice Kennedy.

        **d. Additional discussion:** We discuss the Court's likely future path on abortion in more detail *infra*, p.175.

**H. Post-*Roe* developments, generally:** Post-*Roe* abortion cases have centered around several areas, the most important of which are: (1) requirements that persons other than the pregnant woman *consent* to the operation before it may be performed; (2) limits on *public funding* of abortions; and (3) bans on particular types of *procedures*. In reading the following discussion of these issues, consider that most of these cases were decided before *Planned Parenthood v. Casey* and *Gonzales v. Carhart* (*infra*, p. 175*)*, and might be decided differently today in view of the present Court's "undue burden" approach, which makes state regulations on abortion much more likely to be upheld.

**I. Consent:** A number of states have enacted statutes, usually after the *Roe v. Wade* decision, which impose requirements that third persons *consent* to a woman's decision to get an abortion, or which require *notice* to such third persons. The Supreme Court has decided a number of major cases in this area.

    **1. No absolute veto allowed (*Danforth*):** The first, and most important, of these cases was *Planned Parenthood of Missouri v. Danforth*, 428 U.S. 52 (1976), where the Supreme Court barred the states from giving a pregnant woman's *spouse* or parents, in most instances, an *absolute right to veto* the woman's decision to obtain an abortion.

        **a. Statute invalidated:** The statute struck down in *Danforth* barred abortions unless the operation was consented to by the woman's spouse or (if she was unmarried and under 18) by her parents.

        **b. Husband's consent:** The Court flatly *rejected* the requirement of consent by the husband. Both parents have rights at stake, but since the woman is more directly affected by the pregnancy, the Court concluded, she should have the deciding vote. Also, since the state itself cannot proscribe abortions during the early stages of pregnancy, it cannot delegate this power to the husband by allowing him to veto the procedure.

    **c.**  **Effect of *Casey*:**  The principal holding in *Danforth* — that the states may not give a pregnant woman's spouse an absolute veto right over the woman's abortion decision — seems still to be good law. In *Planned Parenthood v. Casey, supra,* p. 163, the Court struck down a requirement that the woman's spouse be ***notified*** of the woman's intent to get an abortion. Even this lesser requirement of notice (as distinguished from consent, at issue in *Danforth*) was found to be an "undue burden" upon abortion, and this restriction was, indeed, the only restriction that the Court struck down in *Casey.* So the state may not require spousal consent.

        **i.**  **Effect of *Gonzales*:** Even the 2007 decision in *Gonzales v. Carhart,* p. 175, upholding the federal ban on "partial birth" abortions, doesn't seem to change this result. A majority of the Court that decided *Gonzales* seems likely to uphold procedural limits on the abortion process, but nothing in the *Gonzales* opinion indicates that five Justices are ready to say that a pregnant woman's spouse gets a veto over her right to abort.

  **2.**  **Parental consent reexamined:**  In numerous cases decided in the last 30 or so years, the Court has reexamined the circumstances under which the state may require ***parental consent*** before allowing a ***minor*** to procure an abortion. See *Bellotti v. Baird,* 443 U.S. 622 (1979); *Akron v. Akron Center For Reproductive Health* (other aspects of which are discussed *infra,* p.174); *Planned Parenthood v. Casey* (*supra,* p. 163). As the result of these cases, the following rules seem to govern consent for minors' abortions:

    **a.**  **No automatic right to abortion:**  Where a minor is found to be ***insufficiently mature or emancipated*** to make the abortion decision for herself, the state ***may require parental consent.***

        **i.**  **Informed consent by parents:**  When the state requires parental consent, it may insist that that consent be ***"informed."*** More precisely, the state may insist that the parent listen to a presentation by the doctor about the alternatives to abortion, about the probable gestational age of the daughter's fetus, about the availability of state-printed literature, etc. Also, the state may apparently insist that this parental informed consent take place as part of an ***in-person*** visit by the parent to the facility where the abortion will be performed, and may insist that at least 24 hours elapse between the visit and the procedure. See *Planned Parenthood v. Casey, supra,* p. 163.

    **b.**  **Court hearing:**  If the state does require parental consent, it must also give the girl an opportunity to ***persuade a court*** that, although she is not sufficiently mature or emancipated to make the decision for herself, an abortion is nonetheless ***in her best interests.*** If she does make such a showing, the court must override the parental veto. This procedure is sometimes called a ***"judicial bypass".***

        **i.**  **Consent of both parents:**  If the state supplies the "judicial bypass," it may require the consent of ***both*** parents where the girl does not use the bypass. This is true even if one parent does not live with the girl.

    **c.**  **Emancipation or maturity:**  The state must provide for an ***individualized judicial hearing*** in which the girl may persuade the court that she is in fact sufficiently ***mature***

or *emancipated* that she is able to make this decision for herself. If the court concludes that she is mature or emancipated, it must allow the operation whether or not the court feels it is in the girl's best interest.

     **d. Effect of *Gonzales*:** But *Gonzales v. Carhart* (*infra*, p. 175) indicates that states can probably go further in requiring parental approval than the above earlier cases suggest. In *Gonzales*, the Court emphasized that government has an interest in protecting women by helping them anticipate that if they have an abortion, they may *later regret* having done so. This rationale seems especially applicable to the area of abortion by minors, and suggests that a majority of the present Roberts Court may well hold that the states may weaken some of the pre-*Gonzales* limits on the parental veto rights over a minor's abortion, such as the requirement that a judicial bypass be available.

   **3. Notice and consultation (*H.L. v. Matheson*):** Some states, seeing their ability to require parental consent in minor-abortion cases curtailed by *Danforth* and *Bellotti*, have taken a different route: they require that *notice* be given to the parents before an operation is performed on a minor. Most of these statutes have the express purpose of promoting "consultation" between the minor and her parents (even if the statute does not purport to give the parents veto power over the minor's decision to obtain the abortion). In *H.L. v. Matheson*, 450 U.S. 398 (1981), the Court **upheld** such a notice requirement, when applied to a young woman who is ***neither emancipated*** (i.e., living on her own) ***nor mature enough*** to make the abortion decision herself.

     **a. Equivalent to consent:** Post-*Matheson* cases suggest, though they do not explicitly hold, that requiring *notice* to parents is constitutionally the equivalent of requiring *consent* by the parents. For instance, the Court has held that a state may not require that notice be given to both parents unless the state supplies a "judicial bypass" as an alternative; this holding (in *Hodgson v. Minnesota*, 497 U.S. 417 (1990)) parallels the Court's holdings in the consent area. Nothing in *Planned Parenthood v. Casey* suggests that the Court there saw the matter any differently — so probably under *Casey* the states may only require parental notice and consultation if they supply a judicial bypass, and if they exempt from the requirement any mature or emancipated woman.

       **i. Weakened by *Gonzales*:** But again, *Gonzales v. Carhart* (*infra*, p. 175) seems likely to weaken this principle that the states may only require parental notice and consultation if a judicial bypass is supplied.

**J. Public funding of abortions:** While *Roe v. Wade* held that the decision on whether or not to procure an abortion (at least before viability) belongs solely to the woman, not to the legislature, this line of reasoning was not followed by the Court in its decisions on whether ***public funding*** of abortions is required. In two post-*Roe* decisions, the Court held that the government may pay for the expenses of childbirth, yet refuse to pay the expenses of abortion: (1) where the abortion is non-therapeutic (i.e., not necessary for the health of the mother); and (2) even where the abortion *is* necessary for the health, or even the life, of the mother. In a third post-*Roe* case, the Court held that the state may prohibit the use of any ***public facility*** or public staff to perform abortions.

   **1. Non-therapeutic abortions (the *Maher* case):** In 1977, the Court held that the states may refuse to provide Medicaid funding for ***non-therapeutic*** abortions, i.e., those where the operation is not necessary to protect the mother's life or health. Although the Court simultaneously decided three cases relating to this issue, the most important is *Maher v.*

*Roe*, 432 U.S. 464 (1977). In *Maher*, the Court held that Connecticut could constitutionally refuse to give Medicaid financing for non-therapeutic abortions, ***even though it gave Medicaid financing for the expenses of ordinary childbirth***. The decision was 6-3.

    **a. Interpretation of *Roe*:** In reaching this conclusion, the majority interpreted *Roe* to mean ***not*** that a woman had a fundamental right to an abortion, but merely that she had a fundamental right to be free of "unduly burdensome interference with her ***freedom to decide*** whether to terminate her pregnancy." The Connecticut statute here placed no obstacles in the pregnant woman's path, but merely failed to alleviate a pre-existing obstacle (her poverty). The fact that Connecticut may have made the alternative to abortion more attractive by subsidizing it was not at all the same thing as placing a direct obstacle in the path to abortion.

**2. Funding of medically-necessary abortions (*Harris v. McRae*):** An even more troubling abortion-funding question was posed to the Court in 1980: may the states or federal government refuse to fund ***medically-necessary*** abortions? Here, too, the Court answered "yes," in *Harris v. McRae*, 448 U.S. 297 (1980).

    **a. Statute sustained:** A bitterly divided Court, by a 5-4 vote, sustained various federal funding limitations, including one that refused to allow Medicaid funding where the mother's health (but not life) was in jeopardy without an abortion, and another that refused to grant an exception even for cases of rape and incest.

        **i. Rationale:** The majority relied heavily on the *Maher* analysis: funding of other medically-necessary expenses but not ones relating to abortion left an indigent pregnant woman ***no worse off*** than she would have been had there been no funding of any medical expenses. The existence of a constitutionally-protected right did not obligate the government to grant the funds needed to exercise that right.

**3. Use of public facilities and staff (*Webster*):** *Maher* and *Harris* both stand for the proposition that the government need not give assistance to women desiring to exercise their constitutional right to an abortion. A more recent case carries this principle even further: in ***Webster v. Reproductive Health Services***, 492 U.S. 490 (1989), the Court held that a state may prohibit all use of ***public facilities*** and ***publicly-employed staff*** in abortions.

    **a. Holding:** A five-justice majority (Rehnquist, White, O'Connor, Scalia, and Kennedy) believed that this no-public-facilities-or-staff rule was ***constitutional***. To them, the principle was the same as in *Maher* and *Harris*: the state's refusal to allow public employees or public hospitals to participate in abortions "leaves a pregnant woman with the same choices as if the State had chosen not to operate any public hospitals at all."

**4. Abortion counseling:** *Maher*, *Harris* and *Webster* were all cases holding that the government need not give assistance to women who want to exercise their constitutional right to an abortion. The most recent case in this sequence goes even further: it holds that the government may, as a condition of funding family-planning clinics, insist that the doctor or other professional ***not recommend abortion***, and ***not refer clinic patients to an abortion provider. Rust v. Sullivan***, 500 U.S. 173 (1991).

    **a. Facts:** Title X of the Public Health Service Act provides federal funding for family-planning clinics. The Act provides that none of the funds appropriated under it "shall be used in programs where abortion is a method of family planning." The Secretary of

Health and Human Services enacted regulations enforcing this prohibition with a vengeance. According to the regulations, a Title X project "may not provide counselling concerning the use of abortion as a method of family planning or provide referral for abortion as a method of family planning." Thus if a woman comes to a Title X clinic looking for birth control information, and tests performed at the clinic disclose that she is pregnant, the clinic doctor may not recommend an abortion, may not list abortion as a possible method of dealing with the woman's situation, and may not refer the woman to an abortion provider.

b. **Holding:**   A five-justice majority in *Rust* believed that these tight limits ***did not violate*** a pregnant woman's right to an abortion. The majority believed that the right-to-abortion argument was completely disposed of by *Maher*, *Harris* and *Webster*. Congress' refusal to "fund abortion counselling and advocacy" merely left a pregnant woman with the same choices as if the government had chosen not to fund family-planning services at all.

c. **Dissent:**   On the right-to-abortion claim in *Rust*, there were three dissenters (Blackmun, joined by Marshall and Stevens). The dissenters of course disagreed with the correctness of *Maher*, *Harris* and *Webster* in the first place. But beyond this, they believed that what was being asserted here in *Rust* was "the right of a pregnant woman to be free from affirmative governmental ***interference*** in her decision," an even more uncontrovertible right than the basic right to abortion. A Title X client would now be receiving physician's advice that was strictly controlled by the government; the client "will reasonably construe [her physician's words] as professional advice to forego her right to obtain an abortion." A woman who listens to this government-controlled advice would thus *not* be left in the same position as she would have been in if there had been no government funding, and thus no clinic and no professional advice, in the first place.

d. **Free expression issue:**   The plaintiffs in *Rust* also made a First Amendment claim — Title X doctors argued that the regulations interfered with their own freedom of expression. The majority rejected this claim as well. This aspect of the case is discussed *infra*, p. 613.

K. **Types of abortion allowable:**   A state's restrictions on the ***types*** of abortions which may be used, or the procedures surrounding the performance of abortions, may run afoul of *Roe v. Wade*. However, these restrictions are exactly the sort that are more likely to be upheld today, after *Planned Parenthood v. Casey* (*supra*, p. 163) made it much easier than it had been under *Roe* for a state to regulate abortion. Indeed, in 2007, in *Gonzales v. Carhart*, the Court for the first time ***upheld a complete ban on a particular method*** of abortion – the so-called "partial birth" method – as we'll see shortly below.

1. ***Danforth:***   In ***Planned Parenthood of Missouri v. Danforth***, 428 U.S. 52 (1976) (other aspects of which are discussed *supra*, p. 169), the Supreme Court struck down a Missouri requirement that the little-utilized prostaglandin method be used rather than the much more common saline amniocentesis method.

   a. **Rationale:**   The Court reasoned that the prostaglandin method was so largely unavailable in Missouri that the regulation had the effect of blocking most abortions after the first trimester.

     **b.** **Effect of *Casey* and *Gonzales*:** Under *Planned Parenthood v. Casey*, a state may not regulate pre-viability abortions in a way that would impose an "undue burden" on such abortions. If a state forbade a heavily-used method (e.g., D&C or saline), even the post-*Casey* Court might well hold that this constituted an "undue burden" on abortion, and was thus a violation of the constitutionally-protected interest in deciding whether to terminate her pregnancy. On the other hand, the proscription of a little-used method might not be an "undue burden"; *Gonzales v. Carhart,* the 2007 case approving a federal ban on the lightly-used "partial birth" method, suggests that the Missouri ban on the seldom-used prostaglandin method, struck down in *Danforth*, would probably be upheld today.

**2.** **Hospitalization for second-trimester abortions:** The Court has held that the state *may not impose a blanket rule that all abortions after the first trimester be performed in a hospital*. In *Akron v. Akron Center For Reproductive Health, Inc.*, 462 U.S. 416 (1983), the Court concluded that such a requirement, which had the effect of barring abortions in "outpatients facilities that are not part of an acute-care, full-service hospital" (i.e., licensed clinics) unconstitutionally infringed on the abortion right recognized in *Roe*.

     **a.** **Effect of *Casey* and *Gonzales*:** But the later cases of *Planned Parenthood v. Casey* (*supra*, p. 163) and *Gonzales v. Carhart* (*infra*, p. 175) suggest that this holding — that the states may not require all abortions after the first trimester to be performed in a hospital — is likely to be overturned eventually.

**3.** **The health of the mother, and the "partial birth" abortion method:** The most significant holdings about the regulation of particular abortion methods are a pair of rulings on legislative attempts to ban the *"partial birth"* abortion method. In the first of these, *Stenberg v. Carhart*, the Court struck down by 5-4 a Nebraska statute; then, seven years later and after a change in Court personnel, the Court *upheld* a very similar federal statute by 5-4, in *Gonzales v. Carhart*.

     **a.** ***Stenberg* (the 2000 case):** In the first case of the partial-birth-abortion pair, ***Stenberg v. Carhart***, 530 U.S. 914 (2000), the Court held that if a particular abortion method may be *safer for the mother* in some circumstances, the state may not flatly ban the method, and must instead *allow a maternal-health exception* to the ban.

         **i.** **Facts of *Stenberg*:** In *Stenberg*, the Nebraska legislature made it a felony to perform a "partial birth abortion" unless the procedure was necessary to save the life of the mother. A "partial birth abortion" was defined as "an abortion procedure in which the person performing the abortion partially delivers vaginally a living unborn child before killing the unborn child and completing the delivery." The principal procedure against which the statute was designed was the so-called "D&X" procedure. In a D&X abortion, the fetus is drawn partly out of the uterus so that the physician can reach the skull, puncture it, vacuum its contents, and thereby bring the now-smaller skull through the birth canal. The D&X procedure is rarely used except after the 16th week.

         **ii.** **Holding:** By a 5-4 vote, the court *struck down* the Nebraska statute. The majority opinion, by Justice Breyer, found two distinct faults with the statute:

             **(1)** **Lack of health exception:** First, the statute did not contain an exception allowing the procedure where it was *necessary to protect the health* (as opposed to the life) of the mother.

**(2) Might cover D&E method:** Second, the majority concluded, the language of the statute was ambiguous, and might be construed by Nebraska courts and prosecutors to also cover the more-common D&E method. The mere *possibility* that the statute might be so construed was enough to constitute an ***"undue burden"*** on women's abortion rights, because practitioners might be reluctant to use the clearly-constitutionally-protected D&E method for fear that they would be prosecuted for a felony.

iii. **Dissent:** Significantly, the four dissenters included Justice Kennedy, even though he had been part of the joint opinion in *Casey* that more or less reaffirmed the right to abortion.

**(1) Physicians as healers:** Kennedy believed that the state had a significant interest in ensuring that its physicians were ***viewed by society as healers***, and that that interest was well served by forbidding a procedure that bore a strong "resemblance to ***infanticide***."

**(2) No real safety issue:** He also believed that the plaintiffs had not demonstrated that lack of the D&X method would ever deprive a woman of a safe abortion, so forbidding the procedure did not place an undue burden in a woman's path.

**(3) No overbreadth:** Finally, Kennedy believed that the majority was twisting the statutory words to reach its conclusion that the ban might also reach the more common and clearly constitutionally-protected D&E procedure (which would make the statute unconstitutionally "overbroad"). In his view standard rules on statutory construction made it clear that the statute did not reach that procedure.

b. ***Gonzales v. Carhart* (the 2007 case):** By 2007, Justice O'Connor, who had been part of the majority in *Stenberg*, had retired, and had been replaced by Justice Alito. That turned out to make a critical difference, because the Court by a 5-4 vote ***upheld,*** in ***Gonzales v. Carhart***, 550 U.S. __ (2007), a federal ban on partial-birth abortions that was very similar to the Nebraska ban struck down in *Stenberg*.

i. **Facts:** Congress made it a crime to carry out an abortion by a procedure that the *Gonzales* Court referred to as an "intact D&E."[2] Congress defined the crime of performing a "partial-birth abortion" (the term used in the statute itself) as requiring two intentional steps by the physician:

❑ First, the physician causes a still-living fetus to begin to be ***delivered*** until either (a) in a head-first delivery, the ***entire head*** of the fetus is outside the mother's body; or (b) in the case of a breech delivery, any part of the fetus' ***body past its naval*** is outside the mother's body; and

❑ Second, the physician performs an ***"overt act"*** on the partially-delivered fetus for the purpose of killing it. (The overt act must be something other than the mere completion of the delivery — typically, the overt act consists of the phy-

---

2. "Intact D&E" seems to be essentially the same procedure as the one at issue in *Stenberg*, which the Court there called the "D&X" procedure. However, as we'll see Congress defined the prohibited procedures somewhat more tightly than Nebraska had in *Stenberg*.

sician's use of scissors to make an opening at the base of the fetus's skull, through which a surgical catheter evacuates the skull contents.)

**(1) Distinction from Nebraska statute:** Congress enacted the federal ban in response to the *Stenberg* decision, in a clear attempt to overcome some of the *Stenberg* majority's objections to the Nebraska statute. Consequently the federal statute differed from the Nebraska statute in several ways (though the majority and dissent in *Gonzales* sharply disagreed about how significant these differences were):

❏ Unlike the Nebraska Legislature, Congress made various *factual findings* about the procedure it was banning, including that there was a "moral, medical, and ethical consensus" that the partial-birth procedure "is a gruesome and inhumane procedure that is *never medically necessary.*"

❏ Whereas the Nebraska statute seemed to cover any procedure that involved "delivering a living unborn child, or *a substantial portion thereof,*" the federal statute could be triggered only if what was delivered was either the entire head or the lower body from the feet past the navel. This was an arguably important distinction, because the Nebraska statute was relatively vague, and could plausibly have been interpreted to cover (on account of the "substantial portion" clause) a procedure in which only one arm or one leg had been delivered, whereas the federal statute was not susceptible to that interpretation.

❏ Also, the federal statute, by requiring *two steps* before a prohibited abortion would be deemed to have occurred — a partial live birth followed by a *later overt act* of killing — made it pretty clear that the standard *constitutionally-protected* late-term D&E procedure (in which the fetus is killed inside the uterus, and then individual parts are separated and removed one at a time) is *not covered by the statute.* The *Stenberg* majority had concluded that the Nebraska statute was drafted broadly enough to cover the standard D&E procedure, and that even the mere possibility of this interpretation was enough to constitute an undue burden; so Congress, by introducing the two-step / overt-act definition, had pretty clearly overcome this problem.

One respect in which the federal statute did *not* differ from the Nebraska statute, however, was that like the Nebraska act, the federal act *did not contain an exception* allowing the partial-birth procedure where it was necessary to *protection the mother's health* (though there *was* an exception to protect the mother's life).

**ii. Attack on statute:** The suits in *Gonzales*[3] were *"facial attacks"* rather than "as applied" ones — that is, the plaintiffs were claiming that *all* applications of the statute should be ruled unconstitutional, whether or not application of the statute to

---

3. The case consisted of two separate suits that were consolidated before the Supreme Court.

the plaintiff's own behavior or proposed behavior would be unconstitutional. (See p. 484 for a discussion of the facial / as-applied distinction.)[4]

- **iii. Supreme Court upholds the statute:** The Supreme Court concluded by a 5-4 vote that the federal statute was ***not invalid on its face.*** The majority opinion was by Justice Kennedy, who served as the swing vote as he has so often done in recent years, and who as a dissenter in *Stenberg* would have found the Nebraska statute constitutional too. Kennedy's opinion (which was joined by Roberts, Scalia, Thomas and Alito), ***did not overrule Stenberg***, and instead ***distinguished*** it.

  - **(1) Not vague:** Kennedy first concluded that the federal act was not void for vagueness. Unlike the Nebraska statute struck down in *Stenberg* — which ambiguously prohibited delivery of a "substantial portion" of the fetus — the federal statute here gave precise "anatomical landmarks" (head and navel, respectively) to establish a clear dividing line between forbidden abortion methods and permitted ones.

  - **(2) Does not bar standard D&E's:** Next, Kennedy concluded that the statute did not ban standard late-term D&E abortions (i.e., ones in which the fetus was dead and dismembered before being removed from the uterus). So any over-breadth problem was eliminated.

  - **(3) Not an undue burden:** Finally, Kennedy concluded that the statute ***did not impose an undue burden*** on a woman's right to control her reproductive destiny. In reaching this conclusion, he seemed to endorse legislative goals and methods that no prior post-*Roe* decision had approved:

    - ❏ Citing *Casey*, Kennedy said that Congress was free to legislate to "show its ***profound respect for the life within the woman,"*** and to further government's "legitimate interest in ***regulating the medical profession*** in order to ***promote respect for life***, including ***life of the unborn***."

    - ❏ He then laid out a chain of reasoning by which, he said, the ban here would ***fulfill this legitimate interest*** without constituting an ***undue burden*** on the right of abortion:

      - **(a)** "Some women ***come to regret their choice*** to abort the infant life they once created and sustained ... Severe depression and loss of esteem can follow";

      - **(b)** The abortion doctor might not ***disclose*** to the woman the "precise details" of the means by which an intact D&E might be performed;

      - **(c)** A woman who learns ***post-operatively*** the precise details of the procedure "must ***struggle with grief*** more anguished and sorrow more profound when she learns, only after the event, what she once did not know: that she allowed a doctor to pierce the skull and vacuum the fast-developing brain of her unborn child, a child assuming the human

---

4. The suit in *Stenberg*, too, had been a facial attack, and had led to a ruling by the Supreme Court that the Nebraska statute could not be enforced against *anyone*.

form";

(d) A "necessary effect" of Congress' ban on the partial-birth procedure "will be to encourage some women to **carry the infant to full term**, thus **reducing the absolute number of late-term abortions**";

(e) "The medical profession ... may **find different and less shocking methods** to abort the fetus in the second trimester," thus avoiding the tendency of the partial-birth method to (in Congress' words) "undermine[] the public's perception of the appropriate role of a physician during the delivery process, and pervert[] a process during which life is brought into the world";

(f) Finally, the federal statute's failure to supply a **mother's-health exception** did **not create an undue burden.** There was "documented medical disagreement whether the act's prohibition would ever impose significant health risks on women." Prior non-abortion decisions by the Court had given state and federal legislatures "wide discretion to pass legislation in areas where there is medical and scientific **uncertainty**." The standard urged by those attacking the statute — that a mother's-health exception was constitutionally required "if substantial medical authority" supported the proposition that the ban might endanger some women's health – was "too exacting a standard to impose on the legislative power ... to regulate the medical profession."

(4) **As-applied challenge still available:** But Kennedy emphasized that the Court was deciding only this broad *facial* challenge — which he said could succeed only if the plaintiff showed that the act would be unconstitutional in a "large fraction of relevant cases." If in any case involving a particular plaintiff, the lack of a mother's-health exception meant that the mother's health would be placed in jeopardy, an *"as-applied"* challenge could still be brought.

iv. **Concurrence:** In a brief concurrence, Justice Thomas (joined by Scalia), repeated his view that "the Court's abortion jurisprudence, including *Casey* and *Roe v. Wade*, ... has **no basis** in the Constitution."

v. **Dissent:** Justice Ginsburg wrote a long and passionate dissent, in which she was joined by Stevens, Souter and Breyer.

(1) **Lack of mother's-health exception:** Ginsburg objected especially to the statute's lack of an exception where the **mother's health** was at stake. She noted that this was the first time since *Roe* that the Court had "blessed a prohibition with no exceptions safeguarding a woman's health." She pointed to evidence produced at trial that the banned partial-birth method was **safer** for many women, including those with "uterine scarring, bleeding disorders, heart disease, ... compromised immune systems [or] certain pregnancy-related conditions[.]" Therefore, she thought, the Supreme Court should not blithely defer to Congress' findings that there was a medical consensus that the banned procedure is never necessary to protect a woman's health, a finding that the lower

courts had found to be (in her words) "unreasonable and not supported by the evidence."

**(2) No fetus saved:** Ginsburg noted that the Court was upholding a law that ***"saves not a single fetus*** from destruction," since another abortion method could always be used. Therefore, the law did not in fact further one of the goals that the Court claimed it furthered, the goal of "preserving and promoting fetal life."

**(3) "Regret" rationale criticized:** Ginsburg also criticized the Court's ***"emotional distress"*** rationale, that is, the theory that government was properly acting to spare women the emotional pain of learning the details of the procedure only after it had been carried out. She pointed out that the Court was not permitting government to require that women be ***accurately informed*** of the risks of the procedure (something that *Casey* had already allowed); instead, the Court was "depriv[ing] women of the ***right to make an autonomous choice***, even at the expense of their safety." She concluded that "this way of thinking ***reflects ancient notions about women's place*** in the family and under the Constitution — ideas that have long since been discredited."

**(4) As-applied:** Finally, Ginsburg was deeply troubled by the majority's insistence that ***as-applied challenges***, rather than the present facial attack, were the proper means to handle those cases where women's health was in fact at stake. Virtually all of the Supreme Court's post-*Roe* abortion cases had been facial attacks. She argued that forcing women to wait for as-applied challenges "jeopardizes women's health and places doctors in an untenable position." For instance, if a woman had a particular medical condition that had not been the subject of a prior as-applied challenge, the treating physician would not have any clarity about whether the woman would have a constitutional right to have the partial-birth procedure, and therefore the physician would ***risk prosecution*** and imprisonment if she performed the procedure.

**(5) "Chip away" at right:** Ginsburg closed by saying that the statute, and the Court's defense of it, "cannot be understood as anything other than an effort to ***chip away at a right*** declared again and again by this Court[.]"

vi. **Significance:** Here are some broad guidelines, in light of *Gonzales*, about whether and how government can regulate particular abortion methods:

❏ Government may sometimes ***completely ban*** a particular method (e.g., the partial-birth method); all that seems to be required is that the ban not constitute an "undue burden" on women, which it will not apparently constitute if ***another reasonably-safe method*** is available;

❏ When government decides whether to ban a particular method, it may take into account what it perceives as ***risks to the mental health of women*** who might elect that method and then ***come to regret it;*** therefore, government may apparently ban "more regrettable" procedures in favor of "less regrettable" ones;

❏ As long as the legislature has made credible findings that there is medical uncertainty about whether the prohibited procedure is ever necessary to safeguard a woman's health, government need not draft the statute so as to give an *exemption* from its ban for cases where in the physician's opinion the *mother's health would be better served* by allowing use of the method.

**L. Future of abortion regulation:** The *Gonzales* decision suggests that the Roberts Court will make it *significantly easier* than it has ever been since the decision in *Roe* for governments to *restrict abortion.*

1. **Changes:** Here are some of the respects in which *Gonzales* seems to make it easier for legislatures to regulate abortion:

   ❏ Government's concern for a pregnant woman's *emotional health* is now recognized as an important interest, justifying the state's attempt to prevent types of procedures that the woman is likely later to regret;

   ❏ Government's desire to *reduce the number of abortions* is itself recognized as a *legitimate goal*, justifying measures whose effect will be to reduce the number of abortions;

   ❏ Government's desire to *regulate the medical profession* so as to uphold "the public's perception of the appropriate role of a physician during the delivery process" is a legitimate goal, again justifying restrictions on abortion practices;

   ❏ A statute that forbids certain types of abortions apparently *need not preserve an exception for cases in which the physician believes that the mother's health is at risk*, at least where the legislature makes credible findings of fact that alternative equally-safe methods are available;

   ❏ *Facial attacks* will be *harder to win* than before — after a new regulation is enacted, the Court's preference will apparently be to let the statute go into force, and to wait for an "as applied" attack in which a particular pregnant woman or doctor claims that the plaintiff's own rights have been infringed. This means that newly-enacted restrictive statutes are more likely to "remain on the books" not only before but even after a successful as-applied attack than would have been true before *Gonzales.*

2. **Future of the "undue burden" standard:** It's not clear whether a majority of the present court is still in favor of the *Casey "undue burden"* standard, by which any regulation found to be a substantial burden on abortion will be struck down. Kennedy's opinion in *Gonzales* did not say whether he favored maintaining the undue-burden standard; the opinion merely said that the opinion would "assume" *Casey's* validity.[5] Kennedy was part of the 3-justice plurality in *Casey,* which advocated the undue-burden test. It seems likely that he, as the swing vote on this issue, will continue to pay at least lip service to the prohibition on undue burdens, but will be slow to find that any particular restriction constitutes an undue burden.

---

5. As Kennedy's majority opinion in *Gonzales* noted, two members of the Court, Thomas and Scalia, had previously stated their disagreement with *Casey.* It seems likely that the two newest members of the Court, Roberts and Alito, have no love for *Casey* and the undue-burden standard either. Therefore, the survival of the undue-burden test pretty clearly depends on Kennedy's vote.

**3. Possible legislative responses:** Here are some of the types of statutes that, if enacted by Congress or a state legislature, would likely be **upheld** by the Roberts court in light of *Gonzales*:

❑ Provisions requiring that the woman be given **extensive warnings**, including detailed descriptions of how the procedure will be performed or what its consequences will be. (*Example:* South Dakota has passed a statute requiring that pregnant women be told that they will be aborting "a whole, separate, unique living human being," and that they be warned in writing of the increased risk of "depression and related psychological distress" and of "suicide ideation and suicide." S.D. Codified Laws § 34-23A-10.1.) Such "informed consent" provisions would presumably be justified by the state's interest, recognized in *Gonzales*, in protecting women's later emotional health and in reducing the number of abortions.

❑ Mandatory **ultrasound examinations** for women who are proposing to have an abortion, with the woman required to look at the fetus in the film. Again, this could be justified on the theory that the state is entitled to guard against the woman's later change of heart and consequent emotional distress.

❑ **Waiting periods** before an abortion can be performed, again on the "prevent later emotional distress" theory.

❑ More-stringent **parental consent** provisions for minor women. For instance, probably the consent of **both** parents may be required. It may also be the case that the state may dispense with the need to furnish an exception for a "mature and emancipated" woman under the age of 18. And states may well be entitled to make the procedure for a "judicial bypass" more burdensome (e.g., by limiting the factors that the court may consider in deciding whether an abortion would be in the young woman's best interests.).

❑ Stricter **licensing requirements** for doctors and clinics. For instance, a state might require that all abortions be performed in a hospital, and with the patient staying overnight. So *Akron v. Akron Center, supra,* p. 174, would likely be decided differently post-*Gonzales.*

❑ Bans on particular abortion methods, including **abortion-causing drugs.** For instance, there is nothing in *Gonzales* that suggests that Congress could not ban, say, any physician from prescribing use of a drug whose intended effect would be to kill a fetus that was more than two days old. As long as Congress made findings that there were alternative equally-safe methods of abortion available, and as long as Congress concluded that the ban would help reduce the total number of abortions and thus the incidence of post-abortion maternal regret, this kind of ban would seem to pass the two main requirements under *Casey* and *Gonzales*: (1) be rationally related to the achievement of a legitimate governmental interest, and (2) not cause an undue burden on the right to abortion.

All in all, there seem to be ample opportunities for legislatures to "chip away at [the] right" to abortion, as Ginsburg feared in her *Gonzales* dissent.

**M. Post-*Roe* regulation of contraception (*Carey* case):** Only one Supreme Court case after *Roe v. Wade* has dealt with the regulation of **contraception**. In that case, **Carey v. Population Services Int'l**, 431 U.S. 678 (1977), the Court struck down a New York statute which: (1) prohibited anyone but a licensed pharmacist from distributing contraceptives to persons over 16; and (2) entirely prohibited the sale or distribution of contraceptives to minors under the age of 16, except by prescription.

1. **Pharmacists-only rule:**    The rule allowing only pharmacists to distribute contraceptives to adults was subjected to *strict scrutiny* (because it bore on the "fundamental" right to decide whether or not to procreate). Since the limitation reduced access to contraceptives, and lessened price competition, that restriction had to be justified by some "compelling" state interest. The interests advanced by the state (e.g., protecting health) were not compelling, so the provision was struck down. Six Justices agreed on this point.

2. **Ban on sale to minors:**    As to the complete ban on non-prescription sales of contraceptives to minors, seven Justices agreed that the ban violated the right of privacy, but they were split 4-3 as to the appropriate rationale.

N. **Family relations:**    One of the most striking expansions of substantive due process doctrine in recent years has been in the area of *family relations*. In a number of cases, individuals' desires to live together, to marry, or to raise their children in a certain way have come face to face with the state's desire to regulate zoning, marriage, child-rearing or other areas of public concern.

   1. **"Fundamental rights" frequently found:**    In general, the Supreme Court has in recent years found that a person's decision about how to conduct his family life often rises to the level of a "fundamental right." Consequently, the state may interfere with such a decision only when it shows that the interference is necessary for the fulfillment of a compelling public interest.

   2. **Zoning and the "non-nuclear family":**    Thus the government may not pass *zoning regulations* which impair the ability of family members to reside together, even if the family is an "extended" rather than "nuclear" one. In *Moore v. East Cleveland*, 431 U.S. 494 (1977), the Court struck down a zoning ordinance which allowed only members of a single "family" to live together.

      a. **"Family" defined:**    The ordinance's definition of "family" was a restrictive one, which prevented the plaintiff from living with her two grandsons, who were first cousins. (She would have been permitted to live with two grandsons had they been brothers rather than cousins.)

      b. **Extended family protected:**    A four-Justice plurality opinion (authored by Justice Powell) concluded that the right of members of a family, even a non-nuclear one, to live together was a liberty interest, and that state impairment of that interest must be "examine[d] carefully." Although the state interests advanced in support of the ordinance were legitimate ones (e.g., preventing overcrowding, traffic congestion and burdens on the local school system), these interests were only marginally advanced by the ordinance.

      c. **Dissents:**    Four Justices dissented in *Moore*. Several of the dissenters contended that the right of members of an extended family to live together was not "fundamental," and that therefore a "mere rationality" test, rather than heightened scrutiny, should be applied. The dissenters also warned that reference to "traditional values" would lead to widespread and standardless judicial invalidation of state legislative action.

      d. **Stevens' deciding vote:**    Only four Justices followed the Powell analysis. The plaintiff won because Justice Stevens concurred on the grounds that the ordinance had no substantial relation to any state interest, and violated the plaintiff's *property* rights. Thus it is unclear whether a case involving the rights of extended family members to reside together as lessees rather than landowners would yield the same result.

   **e.** ***Moore* distinguished from *Belle Terre*:**  The *Moore* plurality took pains to distinguish that case from *Belle Terre v. Borass*, 416 U.S. 1 (1974), where a majority of the Court upheld a zoning restriction which excluded most groups of **unrelated** people from living together. The *Belle Terre* majority found that unrelated persons had no "fundamental" right to live together. (In particular, no fundamental right of association or privacy was found to be involved.)

   **i.** **Reconciliation:**  Comparing *Moore* and *Belle Terre* illustrates that it is *family relations, not the right of individuals to choose with whom they live*, that the Court has honored with "fundamental rights" status.

**3.** **Child-rearing:**  Parents clearly have a substantive due process right to direct the *upbringing and education of their children.*

   **a.** **Older holdings:** The Court has long recognized this right. See, e.g., *Pierce v. Society of Sisters (supra*, p. 157), holding that parents' substantive due process right to direct their children's education was violated by a rule requiring all children to **attend public schools** rather than private schools.

   **b.** **Right to decide who visits the child:** A recent example of a parent's right to direct the upbringing her child came in ***Troxel v. Granville***, 530 U.S. 57 (2000), where most members of the Court seemed to agree that a parent has a fundamental due process interest in *determining which people outside the nuclear family will have access to the children.*

   **i.** **Facts:** In *Troxel*, a state-court judge ordered the mother of two minor girls to give monthly *visitation privileges* to the girls' paternal **grandparents**. The judge did so under a state statute that allowed a court to "order visitation rights for any person when visitation may serve the best interest of the child."

   **ii.** **Plurality:** There was no majority opinion in *Troxel*. But at least six members of the Court appeared to believe that the compulsory visitation here violated the mother's due process rights. A four-Justice plurality said that "the liberty interest at issue in this case — the interest of parents in the care, custody, and control of their children — is perhaps the *oldest of the fundamental liberty interests recognized by this Court*" (citing *Meyer v. Nebraska* and *Pierce*). The plurality went on to say that the visitation statute as applied in this case "unconstitutionally infringes on that fundamental parental right." The plurality did not suggest that the custodial parent's decision on visitation issues must always be respected by the state. But the opinion did say that where a parent is fit, a court deciding whether to grant visitation rights "must accord at least *some special weight* to the parent's own determination" about whether the proposed visitation would be in the child's best interests.

   **iii.** **Concurrences:** Two other justices who concurred, Souter and Thomas, agreed with this analysis. In fact, Justice Thomas said that to the extent the Court's precedents recognized a parent's fundamental interest in determining the details of child-rearing, he would apply ***strict scrutiny*** to infringements of that interest. (The plurality did not say what standard of review it was using.)

    **iv. Significance:** So at least six present members of the Court seem to be on record as saying that a parent (at least a fit custodial parent) has a ***fundamental liberty interest*** in controlling the ***care and custody of her child***, and that the state's machinery for ordering visitation rights must attach ***significant weight*** to the ***custodial parent's judgment*** on visitation matters.

**4. Right to marry (*Zablocki v. Redhail*):** The ***right to marry*** is viewed by the Supreme Court as being "fundamental"; substantial interferences with that right will therefore not be sustained merely because they are "rational." ***Zablocki v. Redhail***, 434 U.S. 374 (1978).

    **a. Facts of *Zablocki*:** In *Zablocki*, the plaintiff attacked a Wisconsin law which required that any parent who was under court order to support a minor child not in his custody meet two requirements before being permitted to remarry: (1) payment of all court-ordered support; and (2) a demonstration that the child was not currently, and was not likely to become, a public charge (i.e., supported by welfare). Plaintiff attacked the statute on both equal protection and substantive due process grounds.

    **b. Statute stricken:** The Court voted 8-1 to strike the statute. Five Justices, in an opinion by Marshall, felt that the right to marry was a sufficiently fundamental one that a "direct and substantial" interference with it should be subjected to strict scrutiny. (The Marshall opinion was, ultimately, an equal protection opinion, but its discussion of "fundamental rights" and strict scrutiny is highly relevant to substantive due process law.)

    **c. State interest here not compelling:** Applying strict scrutiny to the statute at issue, Justice Marshall concluded that the state's interests were "legitimate and substantial," but that the state's method of furthering these interests ***unnecessarily interfered*** with the fundamental right to marry.

        **i. Less restrictive collection devices:** For instance, rather than using the denial of a marriage license as a kind of "collection device" to assure that support payments were made, the state could have used less drastic compliance methods (e.g., wage assignments, civil contempt proceedings, etc.)

    **d. Indirect interference is not subject to test:** The Marshall opinion was careful to note that where a regulation had some incidental effect upon the ability to marry, but did ***not "significantly"*** interfere with that ability, only a ***"mere rationality"*** test would be used. For instance, the opinion distinguished *Califano v. Jobst*, 434 U.S. 47 (1977), where the Court had applied a mere rationality test to a Social Security Act provision which cut off benefits to a dependent child upon the parent's marriage to someone not covered by the Act. In the *Jobst* situation, the social security provision did not place a "direct legal obstacle in the path of persons desiring to get married," and did not "significantly discourage" marriage, according to Marshall.

    **e. Gay marriage:** Although conventional marriage is "fundamental," as *Zablocki* shows, the right of persons of the ***same sex*** to marry, or to enter some other socially-recognized ceremony of commitment, has so far ***not*** been viewed by the Court as fundamental. However, the Court's decision in *Lawrence v. Texas*, *infra*, p. 185, striking down anti-sodomy laws, makes it more likely than previously that the Court will some day recognize some sort of a right by gay people to enter into a marriage or a marital-like status. See *infra*, p. 191.

5. **Right of natural father:**   Under the family law of most states, the father of a legitimate child may block that child's adoption. But most states do not give a similar veto right to the natural father of a child born ***out of wedlock***, unless the father has "legitimated" his child (by obtaining a court order). In *Quilloin v. Walcott*, 434 U.S. 246 (1978), a Georgia law following this pattern was challenged by an unwed father who had attempted to block the adoption of his eleven-year-old son (whom he had never legitimated or had custody of) by the child's stepfather. The Supreme Court unanimously ***rejected*** the challenge.

    a. **Due process conclusion:**   The Court held that the statute did not violate the Due Process Clause. The Court reasoned that the state had a legitimate interest in preserving existing family units; since the plaintiff had never lived with the child, or sought custody of him, the statute as applied here preserved existing families and was therefore arguably in the best interests of the child.

    b. **Father lives with child:**   The father in *Quilloin* had never ***lived with*** his child. Where a man has fathered a child out of wedlock but has lived with the child for some substantial period, or has formed a ***significant relationship*** with the child, it is not so clear that a state can deprive the father of a veto power over the child's adoption. In fact, a majority of the present Court seems to believe that an unwed father who has lived with or has developed a substantial relationship with the child has a substantive due process right to maintain that relationship.

        i. ***Michael H* case:** Thus in *Michael H. v. Gerald D.*, 491 U.S. 110 (1989), five justices seemed to agree with the proposition that "Although an unwed father's biological link to his child does not, in and of itself, guarantee him a constitutional stake in his relationship with that child, such a link combined with a substantial parent-child relationship will do so." (The quoted remark was by a four-Justice plurality; a fifth Justice, Stevens, seemed to agree with this statement, though he believed, unlike the plurality, that the state here had done what was required to protect that interest.)

O. **Sexuality, including homosexuality:**   A person's ***sexual conduct*** — apart from any issues of procreation or family life — will now receive substantive due process protection, as the result of a strikingly important 2003 decision ***invalidating*** a Texas law ***criminalizing homosexual sodomy***. In that case, ***Lawrence v. Texas***, 539 U.S. 558 (2003), the majority opened by saying that "liberty presumes an ***autonomy of self*** that includes freedom of thought, belief, expression, and ***certain intimate conduct***. The instant case involves ***liberty of the person*** both in its spatial and ***more transcendent dimensions***."   While the case directly holds only that states may not criminalize private homosexual conduct between consulting adults, the expansive language used by the majority suggests that the present Court is willing to recognize a fairly broad autonomy/liberty interest in ***private consensual adult sexual conduct*** generally. The case is especially significant because it squarely overruled a fairly fresh precedent, the Court's 1986 decision in ***Bowers v. Hardwick***, 478 U.S. 186 (1986).

1. ***Bowers v. Hardwick*:** Before we can understand the significance of *Lawrence*, we must understand what the Court did in *Bowers*, the decision that *Lawrence* overruled. In *Bowers,* the plaintiff, who was openly gay, challenged a Georgia statute making it a crime to

perform or submit to "any sexual act involving the sex organs of one person and the mouth or anus of another[.]" The statute did not on its face distinguish between heterosexual and homosexual behavior. Violations were punishable by a prison sentence of up to 20 years!

**a.  Statute upheld:**  By a 5-4 vote the Court in *Bowers* **upheld** the statute against the plaintiff's substantive due process attack. The majority, in an opinion by Justice White, phrased the issue as being "whether the Federal Constitution ***confers a fundamental right upon homosexuals to engage in sodomy[.]* "

   **i.  Not a fundamental right:**  The majority asserted that the Court had regarded and should regard as "fundamental" only those liberties that are either "implicit in the concept of ordered liberty" or "deeply rooted in this Nation's history and tradition." Homosexual sodomy was not such a liberty under either of these formulations, the majority found. In view of the fact that, until 1961, all 50 states outlawed sodomy, and 24 still did, any claim that the right to practice sodomy was "implicit in the concept of ordered liberty" or "deeply rooted in this Nation's history and tradition" was "at best, ***facetious.*"

   **ii.  Privacy of home irrelevant:**  The plaintiff in *Bowers* asserted that whatever right the state might have to police public sexual practices, conduct occurring in the ***privacy of the home*** should be protected; he relied on *Stanley v. Georgia (infra,* p. 562), in which the Court had held that a person could not be convicted of possessing and reading obscene material in the privacy of his own home. The majority ***rejected*** this argument on the grounds that *Stanley* was based on the First Amendment, not the Fourteenth.

      **(1)  "Parade of horribles":**  The majority believed that plaintiff's *Stanley*-based argument, insofar as it claimed a constitutional protection for all voluntary sexual conduct between consenting adults in the home, would make it logically impossible to protect the claimed right to homosexual conduct "while leaving exposed to prosecution ***adultery, incest,*** and other sexual crimes even though they are committed in the home." The majority was "unwilling to start down that road."

**b.  Blackmun's dissent:**  A dissent by Justice Blackmun (in which Brennan, Marshall, and Stevens joined) disagreed not only with the result reached by the majority but with the proper framework for analyzing the Georgia statute.

   **i.  What case is about:**  The case was not about "a fundamental right to engage in homosexual sodomy" as the majority argued, said the dissenters. Rather, it was about the much broader ***"right to be let alone."*** The statute was not limited to homosexual sodomy; by its terms, heterosexual conduct was equally covered.

   **ii.  Two strands to privacy right:**  The dissenters then noted that this "right to be let alone" had two different strands recognized in prior Court decisions: (1) a right to be free of governmental interference in making certain private ***decisions*** (the "decisional" aspect of the privacy right); and (2) the right to privacy of certain ***places*** without regard to the activities that go on there (the "spatial" aspect). The dissenters believed that the Georgia statute violated each of these aspects.

      **(1)  Decisional aspects:**  As to the "decisional" aspect, the dissenters contended that "sexual intimacy is 'a sensitive, key relationship of human existence, central to family life, community welfare, and the development of the human personality' " and that "much of the richness of a relationship will come from the freedom an individual has to choose the form and nature of these intensely personal bonds." The majority decision did not merely refuse to recognize a fundamental right to engage in homosexual sodomy — "what the Court has really refused to recognize is the ***fundamental interest all individuals have in controlling the nature of their intimate associations with others***."

    **(2) Protection for the home:**  Furthermore, activities that take place in one's ***own home*** deserve special protection, the dissenters argued. "The right of an individual to conduct intimate relationships in the intimacy of his or her own home [is] the heart of the Constitution's protection of privacy."

2. ***Lawrence* overrules *Bowers*:** That's where constitutional law on homosexual conduct stood for 17 years until 2003, when *Lawrence* came along to overturn *Bowers*.

3. **Facts of *Lawrence*:** *Lawrence* came about when the Houston Police entered the apartment of one of the two Ds through an unlocked door. (The police were responding to a reported disturbance involving a weapon. Although the Supreme Court's opinion doesn't say so, the neighbor who made the report was later convicted of filing a false report.) The police discovered the two Ds, both men, having sex.

    a. **Texas anti-sodomy statute:** The Ds were charged with violating a Texas statute that made it a crime to "engage[] in deviant sexual intercourse with another individual of the same sex." "Deviate sexual intercourse" was defined to include (i) any contact between the genitals of one person and the mouth or anus of another, or (ii) the penetration of the genitals or anus of another by an object. The Ds were not only arrested but held in custody overnight, then tried, convicted, and fined.

4. **Majority opinion:** Justice Kennedy, joined by four other justices (Stevens, Souter, Ginsburg and Breyer), delivered the opinion for the Court in *Lawrence*. That opinion found that the Texas statute violated the Ds' substantive due process rights, and concluded that *Bowers* had been wrongly decided. (Justice O'Connor supply a sixth vote for striking down the statute, but on equal protection grounds, as described below.)

    a. **Review of older cases:** Kennedy's opinion began by reviewing a number of the Court's older substantive-due-process cases that touched on sexual conduct, and that emphasized some form or another of a right to privacy. Kennedy noted that *Griswold* (*supra*, p. 158), in the course of striking down state restrictions on contraception, had described the protected interest as a right to privacy, and had emphasized the "protected space of the marital bedroom." Similarly, he noted that when *Eisenstadt v. Baird* (*supra*, p. 161) had struck down prohibitions on the distribution of contraceptives to unmarried persons, the Court had said that the right of privacy included "the right of the *individual*, married or single, to be free from unwarranted governmental intrusion into matters so fundamentally affecting a person as the decision whether to bear or beget a child." And, Kennedy observed, *Roe v. Wade* had recognized that "the protection of liberty under the Due Process Clause has a substantive dimension of fundamental significance in defining the rights of the person."

    b. **Review of *Bowers*:**  Against this backdrop, Kennedy reviewed the *Bowers* decision. He noted that the majority's decision in *Bowers* phrased the issue as "whether the Federal Constitution confers a fundamental right upon homosexuals to engage in sodomy[.]" But, Kennedy now concluded, that very phrasing of the issue "discloses the Court's own failure to appreciate the extent of liberty at stake. To say that the issue in *Bowers* was simply the right to engage in certain sexual conduct ***demeans the claim*** the individual put forward, just as it would demean a married couple were it to be said marriage is simply about the right to have sexual intercourse." Laws like the one in *Bowers* and the one here "have more far-reaching consequences, touching upon the ***most private human conduct, sexual behavior***, and in the ***most private of places, the home***."

i.   ***Bowers' historical analysis wrong:***  Kennedy then concluded that *Bowers* was wrong when it concluded that American laws banning homosexual conduct "have ***ancient roots***." Kennedy's own historical analysis was that "American laws targeting same-sex couples did not develop until the last third of the 20th-century." At the very least, the historical conclusions in *Bowers* were "overstated."

ii.  **Emerging recognition of liberty interest in sex:**  Kennedy believed that American "laws and traditions in the ***past half century***" were the ones that were of "most relevance here." And that recent body of law showed "an ***emerging awareness*** that liberty gives ***substantial protection*** to adult persons in ***deciding how to conduct their private lives in matters pertaining to sex***." Kennedy asserted that this "emerging recognition" "should have been apparent when *Bowers* was decided."

iii. **Europe:**  Perhaps most startlingly, Kennedy attached great weight to the fact that ***other countries*** had, even before *Bowers*, reached the conclusion that government ought not to bar private homosexual conduct. For instance, he pointed out, the ***European Court of Human Rights*** had, almost five years before *Bowers*, held that a Northern Ireland law forbidding consensual homosexual conduct violated the European Convention on Human Rights.

iv.  **Post-*Bowers* developments:**  Post-*Bowers* developments, too, had cast doubt on *Bowers'* validity, Kennedy said. For instance, whereas 25 states had laws prohibiting homosexual sodomy at the time of *Bowers*, that number had now been reduced to 13. And even in those states, there was now a "pattern of non enforcement" as to consulting adults acting in private. Furthermore, post-*Bowers* decisions by the Court, in *Planned Parenthood v. Casey* (*supra*, p. 163) and *Romer v. Evans* (*infra*, p. 245) had caused ***"serious erosion"*** of *Bowers*. For instance, *Romer* had concluded that the anti-gay legislation there was "born of animosity towards the class of persons affected" and had no rational relation to any governmental purpose. *Romer* was obviously relevant here, he said, because "when homosexual conduct is made criminal by the laws of the State, that declaration in and of itself is an invitation to ***subject homosexual persons to discrimination both in the public and in the private spheres***." Continuing *Bowers* as precedent ***"demeans the lives of homosexual persons."***

c.   **Conclusion:**  Kennedy concluded that ***"Bowers was not correct when it was decided, and it is not correct today.*** It ought not to remain binding precedent." Therefore, it was now overruled. The Ds "are ***entitled to respect for their private lives.*** The state ***cannot demean their existence or control their destiny*** by ***making their private sexual conduct a crime.*** The right to liberty under the Due Process Clause gives them ***the*** *full right to engage in their conduct without intervention of the government.* ... The Texas statute *furthers no legitimate state interest* which can justify its intrusion into the *personal and private life of the individual*."

> **i. What isn't covered:** Kennedy also stressed that there were various types of statutes that were *not covered* by the *Lawrence* decision: "The present case does not involve *minors*. It does not involve *persons who might be injured or coerced* or who are situated in relationship where *consent might not be easily refused.* It does not involve *public conduct* or *prostitution*." And, he said, it "does not involve whether the government must give formal recognition to any relationship that homosexual persons seek to enter," an obvious reference to the issue of *gay marriage*.

> **d. Rational basis review:** Notice that while Kennedy's opinion is filled with broad-reaching language about the importance of the interest being served (e.g., that the right to liberty under the due process clause protects the "full right to engage in [sexual] conduct without intervention of the government"), the opinion does *not* classify the interest in pursuing homosexual conduct as being a *fundamental* interest. Instead, the opinion applies *rational-basis review*, and strikes down the statute on the grounds that it *"furthers no legitimate state interest."*

**5. O'Connor's concurrence:** Justice O'Connor concurred that the Texas statute was invalid. However, she reached this conclusion on *equal protection* rather than due process grounds. The Texas statute here applied only to sodomy between same-sex partners, not to sodomy between opposite-sex partners. Thus Texas was treating the same conduct differently "based solely on the participants." Texas justified its statute as furthering the "promotion of morality." But, O'Connor concluded, *"moral disapproval"* of a group like homosexuals, like a "bare desire to harm" a group, is "an interest that is *insufficient to satisfy rational basis review* under the Equal Protection Clause."

> **a. Conduct versus status:** Texas defended its statute on the grounds that it did not discriminate against homosexual persons, but only against "homosexual conduct." But O'Connor rejected this distinction: "The conduct targeted by this law is conduct that is closely correlated with being homosexual ... '[T]here can hardly be more palpable discrimination against a class than making the conduct that defines the class criminal.' " (O'Connor declined to opine about whether a statute that criminalized *both* homosexual and heterosexual sodomy would violate substantive due process — it was enough for her that the present statute violated equal protection by treating the two classes differently.)

**6. Scalia's dissent:** Justice Scalia, joined by Chief Justice Rehnquist and Justice Thomas, dissented. He criticized the majority for applying "an *unheard-of form of rational-basis review* that will have far-reaching implications beyond this case."

> **a. *Stare decisis*:** Scalia began by arguing that the majority was wrong to find that *stare decisis* (respect for precedent) did not control here — Scalia believed that the factors relied on by the majority to justify departing from *stare decisis* (e.g., that the earlier decision had been subject to "substantial and continuing" criticism) applied just as well to *Roe v. Wade,* in which the majority had relied on *stare decisis* in refusing to overrule.

b.  **History of anti-sodomy laws:**   Next, Scalia took issue with the majority's conclusion that laws like the one upheld in *Bowers* and the one struck down here were not deeply rooted in history. To Scalia, the relevant fact was that our nation "has a longstanding history of laws *prohibiting sodomy in general* — regardless of whether it was performed by same-sex or opposite-sex couples." Therefore, he said, *Bowers*' conclusion that homosexual sodomy was not a deeply-rooted fundamental right was "utterly unassailable."

c.  **Foreign nations' approach irrelevant:**   Scalia was especially critical of the majority's reliance on the fact that *foreign nations* had decriminalized homosexual sodomy. In evaluating a constitutional entitlement, what counts is solely the values and history of *this country,* he said; he quoted approvingly a remark from Justice Thomas in another case that "this Court ... *should not impose foreign moods, fads, or fashions on Americans.*"

d.  **Rational relation:**   Scalia then turned to the core of the majority's position, that the law here was not rationally related to the promotion of a legitimate state interest. The Texas statute here "seeks to further the belief of its citizens that certain forms of sexual behavior are '*immoral and unacceptable*'." But this was the same interest, he said, that was furthered by "criminal laws against *fornication, bigamy, adultery, adult incest, bestiality,* and *obscenity.*" Therefore, "if, as the Court asserts, the promotion of majoritarian sexual morality is not even a *legitimate* state interest, *none of the above-mentioned laws can survive rational-basis review.*"

e.  **"Homosexual agenda":**   Scalia closed with an angry invective-filled passage of the sort that has increasingly characterized his dissents in recent years. The majority's opinion was "the product of a law-profession culture, that has largely signed on to the so-called *homosexual agenda*[.]" The Court had, he said, "taken sides in the *culture war*, departing from its role of assuring, as *neutral observer*, that the democratic rules of engagement are observed." He said that he had "nothing against homosexuals, or any other group, promoting their agenda through normal democratic means." But here, the Court was inappropriately allowing gays to *achieve judicially* what they had been *unable to achieve politically* in Texas.

   i.  **Gay marriage:**   Scalia was especially fearful that the majority's logic would lead inexorably to a constitutionally-recognized right to *homosexual marriage*. "If moral disapprobation of homosexual conduct is 'no legitimate state interest' [as the majority said] ... what justification could there possibly be for denying the benefits of marriage to homosexual couples exercising [quoting the majority] '[t]he liberty protected by the Constitution'?" A distinction between heterosexual and homosexual marriage certainly could not be justified as an encouragement of *procreation*, since the sterile and the elderly are allowed to marry. *Lawrence* did not involve the issue of homosexual marriage (as the majority insisted it didn't) "only if one entertains the belief that *principle and logic have nothing to do with the decisions of this Court.*"

7.  **Significance:**   *Lawrence* obviously represents a significant change in the majority's view of how the due process clause applies to government attempts to regulate human sexuality. Although restrictions on adult sexual conduct occurring in private will ostensibly continue to be judged by the rational-relation standard, it seems undeniable that that standard will

be applied with *more "bite"* when the state's justification is a general sense of sexual morality rather than some specific objective harm from the forbidden conduct.

Here's a brief look at some particular issues on which *Lawrence* is likely to have an impact:

a.  **Anti-sodomy laws that apply to heterosexuals as well as gays:**  The Texas statute struck down in *Lawrence* applied only to *same-sex* sodomy. What is the opinion's effect on statutes that prohibit sodomy whether by same-sex or *different-sex* couples?[6] It seems nearly certain that Justice Kennedy's opinion meant to hold *these statutes, too, invalid* as violative of substantive due process. In explaining why he was not deciding *Lawrence* on equal protection grounds, he stated, "Were we to hold the [Texas] statute invalid under the Equal Protection Clause some might question whether a prohibition would be valid if drawn differently, say, to prohibit the conduct both between same-sex and different-sex participants." It's hard to see what this remark could mean except that the majority's due process holding applies *even where the statute bars different-sex sodomy as well.* Certainly the central logic of the Kennedy opinion — that making private consensual adult sex between persons of the same sex unconstitutionally interferes with their private life — applies even where the statute theoretically applies to different-sex sodomy as well.

b.  **Gay marriage:**  As Justice Scalia's dissent indicates, a big question is whether the logic of *Lawrence* dictates that a state's refusal to recognize *gay marriage* constitutes a substantive due process violation. Kennedy's opinion takes pains to reserve this question for another day, saying that the opinion "does not involve whether the government must give formal recognition to any relationship that homosexual persons seek to enter." When this question is eventually posed to the Court — as seems almost inevitable — the answer could go either way:

   i.  **In favor of right to gay marriage:**  There are certainly statements in Kennedy's opinion that seem to apply almost as well to gay marriage as they do to gay sexuality. Consider, for instance this passage: "When sexuality finds overt expression in intimate contact with another person, the conduct can be but one element in a personal bond that is more enduring. The liberty protected by the Constitution allows homosexual persons the right to make this choice." Would it not be the case that, like " intimate contact," another "element" of the "personal bond that is more enduring" between two gay people is the ability to have *society recognize* that the two have indeed created that bond? If "marriage" (or at least some sort of social recognition of the fact that two people are a couple) is another key "element" of this "enduring personal bond," wouldn't the "liberty protected by the Constitution" allow gays "the right to make this choice," too?

   ii. **Against right to gay marriage:**  But there are other elements of Kennedy's *Lawrence* opinion that suggest grounds for the Court to draw a line short of requiring states to recognize gay marriage.

      (1) **Ban on gay marriage doesn't criminalize anything:**  For instance, the thrust of the opinion is that criminalizing sodomy makes the basic form of gay

---

6. At the time *Lawrence* was decided, nine states had such statutes, in addition to four that barred only same-sex sodomy.

sexuality *criminal*, and "*demeans the lives* of homosexual persons." A state's refusal to recognize gay marriage does not directly criminalize any conduct, and it is at least questionable whether the unavailability of gay marriage "demeans the lives" of gay people who would wish to marry.

(2) **Rational-relation analysis:** Furthermore, let's remember that *Lawrence* still purports to be applying *rational relation analysis,* not some form of mid-level or strict scrutiny. In other words, so long as a refusal to recognize gay marriage is a rational means of achieving some legitimate state objective, the refusal ought to be upheld against substantive due process attack. Notwithstanding Justice Scalia's assertion to the contrary in his dissent, it's hard to see why a state couldn't plausibly defend its refusal to recognize gay marriage with the following syllogism: (1) society's special recognition of marriage is in part an attempt to further the goal of *encouraging men who father children to take a long-term interest in the welfare of those children*; (2) straight men are far more likely to father children (and thus more likely to be encouraged by the availability of marriage to take a long-term interest in the child) than are gay men, even though some of the latter do indeed father children; and (3) when a social policy is evaluated by the rational-relation test, the fit between the end (encouraging fathers to take care of their children for the long term) and the means (giving special social status to marriage) need not be very tight — it's enough that the legislature *could plausibly have thought that there was some connection* between means and end, and certainly the fit between the availability of marriage and the strengthening of paternal bonds satisfies this undemanding standard. Keep in mind also that if the state's legitimate objective is to combat an "evil," the rational-relation test permits the state to tackle that evil *"one step at a time"* (see *infra*, p. 242) — so here, if the state is tackling the evil of fathers' abandonment of their children, the fact that the state has chosen to tackle that evil solely by offering different-sex marriage and not by the additional step of offering same-sex marriage ought not to be fatal.

(3) **"Deeply rooted":** Yet another possible ground for distinguishing the gay-marriage issue from bans on sodomy arises out of the different treatment of these two issues *historically*. In *Lawrence*, Kennedy concluded that *Bowers* was at least "overstating" the matter when it said that proscriptions against sodomy have "ancient roots." On the other hand, it certainly seems accurate to say that since ancient times, and throughout American history, societies have defined "marriage" as a status that can *only exist between a man and a woman.* The present five-justice majority that decided *Lawrence* is not likely to view the historically-narrow definition of marriage as being conclusive, but this factor certainly seems to cut against a finding that a state's refusal to recognize gay marriage violates substantive liberty.

iii. **Refusal to recognize gay marriage that occurred in another state:**   The initial battleground concerning gay marriage probably will *not* take the form of an assertion by gay plaintiffs that they have an affirmative right to compel their own state to perform a marriage ceremony. Instead, what's most likely to happen is that a gay couple will get married in jurisdiction *A*, then claim that jurisdiction *B* is required to treat that marriage as valid. Since mid-2003, same-sex marriages have apparently been legal in Canada; a gay couple could get married in Canada, then move to, say, Texas and demand that the marriage be considered valid there. If some American state eventually allows same-sex marriages (Vermont already allows same-sex "civil unions" that confer many of the same benefits), then the constitutional requirement of ***"full faith and credit"*** will put additional weight behind the argument that State *B* cannot refuse to recognize a same-sex marriage that was validly contracted in State *A*.[7]

c.   **Other restrictions on gays:** There are other restrictions that some states place upon gays that may also violate substantive due process rights.

   i.   **Family-law rules:** This seems especially true of ***family-law*** rules that discriminate against gays.

      (1)   **Adoption:**   For example, Florida ***prohibits adoption*** by gays, even where the child is a relative of the gay person who is seeking to adopt. Opponents of this ban would seem to have a powerful argument that the ban was enacted out of animosity towards or moral disapproval of gays, exactly the sort of motive that *Lawrence* says is illegitimate. On the other hand, defenders of the ban could argue that children are better off being raised by a married couple, and that the ban on gay adoption is a rational — even though not perfectly fitting (since single people can adopt in Florida) — method of advancing that objective.

      (2)   **Custody decisions:**   Similarly, some states give a large preference in ***custody disputes*** to a non-gay parent over a gay one. Again, such a preference seems vulnerable to the *Lawrence*-type objection that it is motivated by a baseless animosity towards gays rather than by any legitimate social objective.

   ii.   **Employment, including gays in the military:**   Another area of discrimination that is cast in doubt by *Lawrence* is ***public employment***. The most dramatic example is our nation's present ban on gays in the ***military***. The Pentagon justifies its ban (the "don't ask, don't tell" policy) on the grounds that "unit cohesion" will be weakened if openly gay soldiers are officially tolerated. But there is a powerful argument that the Pentagon's policy is the product of the very sort of majoritarian moral disapproval of homosexuality that *Lawrence* found to be irrational. On the other hand, the Supreme Court has a long tradition of giving ***great deference to the military*** in matters involving military life, and that deference may be just enough to induce the *Lawrence* majority to conclude that the military is not irrational in its fears about cohesion.

d.   **Prohibitions on adultery, fornication, etc.:**   Justice Scalia warned in *Lawrence* that if a society's "moral disapproval" of particular conduct was no longer a valid reason for criminalizing that conduct, laws against ***fornication, bigamy, adultery, adult incest, bestiality,*** and ***obscenity*** would all be invalid. However, this is probably one

---

7. In 1996, Congress passed the federal Defense of Marriage Act, which authorizes a state to ignore any same-sex marriage granted by another state. However, if the Court decided that there was a substantive due process right to same-sex marriage, the federal act would be almost certainly held unconstitutional. Consequently, in the immediate aftermath of *Lawrence* some conservatives began calling for a constitutional amendment banning gay marriage.

instance in which Scalia is *crying wolf.* With the possible exception of fornication, every type of conduct in that list involves *provable harm* that often results from the conduct. Under a rational-relation analysis, the mere fact that the state can even articulate some plausible danger posed by the conduct (beyond the mere conclusory assertion that the conduct is morally repugnant) ought to be enough to *satisfy* the rational-relation standard.

**P.   The "right to die":**   Should a *terminally ill* or *comatose* patient have the right to choose to *"die with dignity"?* The so-called *"right to die"* is really a series of sub-issues, on which the law is just starting to develop. The Supreme Court has issued two major decisions, one on the "right to *decline unwanted medical procedures*" (*Cruzan v. Missouri Dept. of Health, infra,* p. 194) and the other on the "right to *commit suicide*" (*Washington v. Glucksberg, infra,* p. 198).

As the result of these two decisions, there are several major propositions that we can recite at this point:

❏   A competent adult has a Fourteenth Amendment "liberty" interest in *not being forced to undergo unwanted medical procedures*, including artificial life-sustaining measures.

❏   The state has an important countervailing interest in *preserving life.* At the very least, this interest entitles the state to require, before it allows "pulling the plug," *"clear and convincing evidence"* that a now-incompetent patient would have voluntarily declined the life-sustaining measures.

❏   Terminally-ill patients do *not* have a general liberty interest in *"committing suicide."* Nor do they have the right to *recruit a third person* to help them commit suicide (e.g., a physician who would prescribe a fatal does of drugs).

Virtually everything else in this "right to die" area remains unsettled.

**1.   The *Cruzan* case:**   The Supreme Court's sole "right to decline artificial life-sustaining measures" case so far was the important 1990 case of *Cruzan v. Missouri Department of Health*, 497 U.S. 261 (1990).

    **a.   Facts:**   Nancy Cruzan suffered severe brain damage in an automobile accident. Since 1983, she had lain in a "persistent vegetative state," i.e., a coma in which she had no awareness or cognition but continued to breathe without a respirator. All medical authorities agreed that there was virtually no chance that she would ever become conscious again or be aware of her surroundings. She was kept alive by means of a *feeding and hydration tube* implanted in her stomach. She was cared for in a Missouri state hospital, and the state was paying for her care.

    **b.   The claim:**   Nancy's parents asked the hospital to end the artificial nutrition and hydration procedures. Everyone agreed that she would die if these procedures were terminated. But the hospital refused to do this without a court order. Nancy's parents claimed in court that Nancy had a Fourteenth Amendment due process right not to be kept alive by unwanted medical procedures, and that before her accident she had told friends that she would not want to be kept alive in such a comatose condition. But the Missouri Supreme Court, interpreting the state's "living will" statute, concluded that even if Nancy had such a Fourteenth Amendment right, the right could be exercised under state law only by "clear and convincing" evidence that Nancy would not have wanted the life-sustaining procedures used here. The court concluded that such clear and convincing evidence was not present, and it thus denied Nancy's parents' claim.

c. **Supreme Court affirms:** The U.S. Supreme Court, by a 5-4 vote, agreed that Missouri's continuation of the life-sustaining procedures here did ***not violate*** Nancy's Fourteenth Amendment rights. The majority opinion, by Chief Justice Rehnquist, turned largely on procedural issues:

  i. **Right exists:** The majority opinion began by holding that "a competent person has a constitutionally protected ***liberty interest*** in ***refusing unwanted medical treatment*** . ... " The majority thought that this interest might be outweighed by the state's interest in preserving life in at least some instances, but was willing to assume (without deciding) that a competent person would have a right to refuse lifesaving hydration and nutrition, and that this right would outweigh any countervailing state interest.

  ii. **"Clear and convincing" standard:** But the problem, the majority wrote, was that Nancy was obviously not a competent person who could make a present informed and voluntary choice to discontinue the lifesaving procedures. So the question became, may Missouri require that such procedures be discontinued only when there is ***"clear and convincing"*** evidence that this is what Nancy would have wanted? The court answered ***"yes"*** to this question — Missouri's interest in safeguarding human life was strong enough that the state was entitled to "guard against potential abuses" by imposing the "clear and convincing" standard.

  iii. **Standard not satisfied:** The majority then concluded that the Missouri Supreme Court had not committed "constitutional error" when it decided that here there was no clear and convincing evidence that Nancy would have wanted the hydration and the nutritive procedures stopped. The evidence consisted mainly of Nancy's statements to a housemate, about a year before the accident, that she would not want to live as a "vegetable."

  iv. **No "substituted judgment" required:** Finally, the majority held that no constitutional doctrine required Missouri to accept the "substituted judgment" of Nancy's close family members, if there was no proof that the views of these members reflected what Nancy's own views were or would have been.

d. **Dissent:** Four members of the Court dissented in *Cruzan*. The principal dissent was by Justice Brennan (joined by Marshall and Blackmun). Brennan contended that Nancy not only had a constitutionally-protected liberty interest in declining unwanted medical procedures, but that this interest far outweighed any general countervailing state interest in preserving life.

  i. **Stevens' dissent:** Justice Stevens, in a separate dissent, argued that where the patient had made no prior expression of intent, the patient's "best interests," not the state's general policy in favor of preserving life in all instances, must control.

e. **Scalia's concurrence:** Justice Scalia was the only member of the Court who did not believe that there was a constitutionally-protected interest in refusing unwanted medical treatment. In a concurrence, Scalia argued that the right to refuse unwanted medical procedures, asserted on behalf of Nancy, was equivalent to a ***"right to commit*** *suicide*," and that our nation's law and constitutional tradition gave the states unquestioned power to prohibit suicide.

    **f.**  **Family wins on remand:** By the way, on remand a Missouri judge heard new evidence presented by Nancy's family, which he decided was "clear and convincing evidence" that Nancy would not have wanted to be kept alive under these circumstances. The judge therefore permitted disconnection of the feeding tube, and Nancy died soon thereafter.

    **g.**  **Significance:** So *Cruzan* establishes two major propositions: (1) a competent adult has a constitutionally-protected Fourteenth Amendment liberty interest in declining unwanted medical procedures (though we don't know whether this interest may sometimes be outweighed by the countervailing general state interest in preserving life); and (2) where the patient is incompetent, the state may constitutionally refuse to allow these medical procedures to be terminated except where there is "clear and convincing evidence" that this is what the patient would have wanted. Many other issues remain unsettled, some of which are briefly touched upon below.

  **2.**  **Incompetent patient, no expression of wishes:** Where the patient is *incompetent* to express present wishes (e.g., the patient is in a coma as Nancy Cruzan was), the first question to ask is: has the patient previously expressed *clear wishes* either: (a) that she does not want medical treatment under circumstances like those now existing; or (b) that she wishes some designated other person (e.g., a family member) to make such decisions for her in the event of incapacity? If the answer to this question is "no" (as it was in *Cruzan*), then we know from *Cruzan* that the state may refuse to discontinue the procedures even though all concerned agree that the best interest of the patient would be to discontinue the treatment.

  **3.**  **Living wills and other clear expressions of intent:** Suppose the patient has, prior to becoming incompetent, signed a *"living will,"* or given some other extremely clear expression of desire not to undergo specified medical procedures. (A "living will" is a document in which the signer specifies what treatments are or are not desired in the event of certain medical conditions. Such documents typically state that the signer does not want to be kept alive by artificial feeding or respiration techniques in the event that he is in an irreversible coma.) *Cruzan* suggests, even if it does not expressly hold, that the state is constitutionally *required to honor the patient's wishes* in this situation. Eight members of the Court (all but Justice Scalia) agreed in *Cruzan* that a competent adult has a constitutionally-protected liberty interest in declining unwanted medical procedures. While there is some chance that a majority of the court might conclude that this liberty interest is outweighed by the state's general interest in preserving life, this seems unlikely judging from the tone of the opinions in *Cruzan*. So probably the state is constitutionally required to respect a living will or other *clear expression of intent*.

  **4.**  **Document delegating decision-making:** Another kind of document is likely to become increasingly relevant: the *"health-care proxy."* Whereas in a living will the signer typically attempts to state his own wishes for future situations (e.g., "I don't want artificial feeding if I'm in an irreversible coma"), the health-care proxy attempts to *appoint another person* to make these decisions. Thus a proxy might simply state, "In the event that I should become comatose, I entrust to my spouse Herbert all decisions about what lifesaving or other medical treatments shall be given to me."

a. **Not answered in *Cruzan*:** We don't know from *Cruzan* whether the Constitution requires that such a proxy be honored. The majority in *Cruzan* expressly stated that "we are not faced in this case with the question of whether a State might be required to defer to the decision of a surrogate if competent and probative evidence establishes that the patient herself had expressed a desire that the decision to terminate life-sustaining treatment be made for her by that individual."

b. **Legislative response:** Many states have responded to *Cruzan* by expressly recognizing such health-care proxies. See, for instance, New York's statute, summarized in *The New York Times*, July 2, 1990, A1.

c. **Prediction:** It seems probable that if a competent adult has the constitutional right to decline unwanted medical assistance, that competent adult also has the right to delegate to another the job of exercising this right in the event of incompetence. But even if this is true, the states probably have a great deal of scope in deciding what ***evidentiary standards*** such a proxy must satisfy. For instance, a state can probably require (as New York does) that any such proxy be signed in the presence of two witnesses, and that the surrogate be allowed to withdraw nutrition and hydration (as opposed to more extraordinary treatments) only if the patient has specifically so requested.

5. **Child:** Where the patient is a ***child***, the issues are even murkier. Since a child can hardly be expected to have left "clear and convincing" evidence of whether she wanted lifesaving medical treatment, *Cruzan* is not directly relevant. It is unclear whether the state may, over the objection of parents, continue to hydrate and feed a child who is in an irreversible coma. The court may conclude, notwithstanding *Cruzan*, that the state must give the parents or a court-appointed guardian the right to make such decisions, so that the child's constitutional rights are not nullified.

6. **Right to commit suicide:** Suppose that the patient is a competent adult who desires to die. If the adult wishes simply to "pull the plug," i.e., terminate life-preserving medical treatment, *Cruzan* seems to hold or at least strongly suggest that the state may not deny that privilege. A distinct, and tougher, issue is whether the state may forbid a competent adult from taking ***active steps*** to ***commit suicide***.

Thus suppose a patient suffering from terminal cancer desires to commit suicide by taking, say, an overdose of barbiturates. May the state forbid this conduct? And, more interestingly, may the state ***forbid others***, including ***doctors***, from ***assisting*** in this conduct? The answer to both questions is now generally ***"yes,"*** as the result of a landmark 1997 pair of Supreme Court decisions.

a. **Background:** In 1996, two federal Courts of Appeal held that there *was* a constitutional right for a terminally ill patient to receive the assistance of a physician in committing suicide. The two courts split on the rationale.

i. **Due process:** The Ninth Circuit held that Washington's ban on physician-assisted suicide violated the ***Due Process Clause***. The court opined that the ban violated the patient's substantive due process "liberty interest in controlling the time and manner of one's death."

ii. **Equal protection:** The Second Circuit struck down New York's assisted-suicide ban on ***equal protection*** grounds. The court noted that New York allowed patients to order their doctor to end artificial life-sustaining measures (i.e., to "pull the plug"), but forbade the doctors to prescribe life-ending medication. According to the court, there was not even a rational basis for making that distinction.

**b.   Supreme Court reverses:** But the Supreme Court disagreed, unanimously reversing each of these decisions. We'll focus here on the Court's decision reversing the Ninth Circuit's due process ruling. That decision came in ***Washington v. Glucksberg***, 117 S. Ct. 2258 (1997).[8]

**c.   Statutory ban:** *Glucksberg* involved Washington's ban on "promoting a suicide attempt." The state defined this crime as "knowingly caus[ing] or aid[ing] another person to attempt suicide," and made it a felony.

**d.   Rehnquist's majority opinion:** Justice Rehnquist wrote the Court's opinion in *Glucksberg*. Four other Justices (O'Connor, Scalia, Kennedy and Thomas) joined his opinion. The remaining four Justices agreed with the result (that the Washington statute was not unconstitutional) but not necessarily with Rehnquist's reasoning.

    **i.   Broad level of generality:** Rehnquist phrased the issue at a very high level of generality: "whether the 'liberty' specially protected by the Due Process Clause includes a ***right to commit suicide*** which itself includes a right to ***assistance*** in doing so." (Thus Rehnquist rejected the Ninth Circuit's narrower phrasing of the issue: "whether there is a liberty interest in determining the time and manner of one's death.")

    **ii.   No historical right:** To answer this question, Rehnquist began by canvassing past and present laws on the subject. He noted that "for over 700 years, the Anglo-American common-law tradition has punished or otherwise disapproved of both suicide and assisting suicide." And, today, he noted, in virtually every state — and in almost every western democracy — it was a crime to *assist* in suicide. Although the states had begun to re-examine this prohibition in light of modern medical technology, the prohibition remained on the books practically everywhere, he pointed out.[9]

    **iii.   Not a fundamental right:** Rehnquist then concluded that any due process liberty interest in ***committing suicide*** was certainly ***not a "fundamental"*** interest.

        **(1)   Rationale:** He noted that the Court had always been reluctant to expand the list of fundamental due process interests "because guideposts for responsible decisionmaking in this uncharted area are scarce and open-ended." Only rights or interests that were ***"deeply rooted in this Nation's history and tradition"*** could be fundamental. And, in view of the nearly universal past and present prohibition of suicide or assisting suicide, the asserted interest in committing suicide did not come close to meeting this "deeply rooted" test.

        **(2)   *Cruzan* distinguished:** Rehnquist then distinguished the interest recognized in *Cruzan, supra*, from the one asserted here. *Cruzan* may have recognized a lib-

---

8. For our brief discussion of the Court's other decision (*Vacco v. Quill*), reversing the Second Circuit's equal protection ruling, see p. 238 *infra*.

9. As of this writing (July, 2007), Oregon is the only state to expressly provide a right to physician-assisted suicide: in 1994 Oregon voters approved a ballot initiative that legalized physician-assisted suicide for competent, terminally-ill adults.

erty interest in declining unwanted life-sustaining treatment, but that interest "was not simply deduced from abstract concepts of personal autonomy." Rather, the interest recognized in *Cruzan* derived from "the common-law rule that forced medication was a battery, and the long legal tradition protecting the decision to refuse unwanted medical treatment." So the right recognized in *Cruzan* was "entirely consistent with this Nation's history and constitutional traditions." The interest in committing suicide with another's assistance "may be just as personal and profound as the decision to refuse unwanted medical treatment, but it has never enjoyed similar legal protection."

iv. **State's interest in regulation was "rational":** Having decided that the liberty interest in assisted suicide was not "fundamental," Rehnquist then turned to the issue of whether there were any limitations at all on the state's right to ban such suicides. Rehnquist actually ducked the issue of whether there was a *non-fundamental* liberty interest in assisted suicide. Instead, he seemed to say that even if such a non-fundamental interest existed, the state merely had to show that its ban was "rationally related to legitimate government interests." Rehnquist quickly concluded that the state easily satisfied this test.

(1) **Interest in preserving human life:** First, Rehnquist said that the state had an ***"unqualified interest in the preservation of human life."*** He noted that many people who desire to commit suicide are clinically depressed (often because of untreated pain), and that of this group many who receive proper treatment withdraw their suicide request. "Thus, legal physician-suicide could make it more difficult for the State to protect depressed or mentally ill persons, or those who are suffering from untreated pain, from suicidal impulses."

(2) **Protecting integrity of medical profession:** Also, the state had an interest in protecting the ***integrity of the medical profession:*** physician-assisted suicide could "undermine the trust that is essential to the doctor-patient relationship by blurring the time-honored line between healing and harming."

(3) **Protecting the vulnerable:** Next, Rehnquist wrote, the state had an interest in ***"protecting vulnerable groups*** — including the poor, the elderly, and disabled persons — from abuse, neglect and mistakes." There was a "real risk of ***subtle coercion*** and ***undue influence*** in end-of-life situations." Apart from the state interest in combatting coercion, the state had an interest in protecting these vulnerable groups from societal prejudice: the state's suicide ban "reinforces its policy that the lives of terminally ill, disabled and elderly people must be no less valued than the lives of the young and healthy. . . ."

(4) **Slippery slope:** Finally, the state could rationally fear that legalizing physician-assisted suicide would set it down a ***slippery slope*** towards "voluntary and perhaps even involuntary ***euthanasia.***" For instance, family members would inevitably begin to participate in the suicide, if the patient was unable to self-administer the drugs. And the experience of the Netherlands — the only western nation to allow even voluntary euthanasia — suggested that voluntary euthanasia had led to the *in*voluntary variety for such groups as severely disabled newborns and elderly persons with dementia. Thus recognizing a right to

physician-assisted suicide for the competent, terminally-ill patient "is likely, in effect, a much broader license, which could prove extremely difficult to police and maintain."

**(5) State interests were rational:** These various interests were, Rehnquist wrote, "unquestionably important and legitimate." And Washington's outright ban on assisted suicide was "at least reasonably related" to the promotion of these interests.

**v.   The concurrences:** There were several concurrences. Several Justices agreed only with the result reached by Rehnquist, and believed that the issue had been incorrectly phrased by him.

**vi.  O'Connor's concurrence:** Justice O'Connor, concurring, supplied the critical fifth vote in support of Rehnquist's opinion. She agreed that there was "no generalized right to 'commit suicide.'" But she seemed to leave open the possibility that a terminally-ill patient suffering great pain might have a ***limited right*** to have a physician prescribe medication to ***alleviate that suffering***, even where this would hasten death. O'Connor thought that there was no need to address that question here, since Washington (and New York, the state whose statute was at issue in the companion case) did not forbid such prescriptions.

**vii. Stevens' concurrence in the result:** Justice Stevens, although he concurred in the result, disagreed with the majority's reasoning. Stevens agreed that statutes like those of Washington and New York were not *always* unconstitutional, so that the plaintiffs' facial attack on the statutes had to fail. However, Stevens believed that "there are situations in which an interest in hastening death is legitimate . . . ***I am also convinced that there are times when it is entitled to constitutional protection***."

**viii. Souter's concurrence in the result:** Justice Souter, concurring in the result only, would have applied a somewhat different test for determining whether the statute violated plaintiffs' substantive due process rights. He saw the issue as whether the statute sets up "one of those ***'arbitrary impositions'*** or ***'purposeless restraints'*** at odds with the Due Process Clause." In Souter's view, if a statute did this, it would violate due process even if it didn't burden a fundamental interest, and even if it wasn't wholly irrational. In other words, Souter seemed to be advocating a ***"sliding scale"*** approach to due process (though he didn't use that phrase), by which the stronger the individual's interest, the stronger the state's countervailing interest had to be.

**(1) Legislature has greater competence:** In any event, Souter agreed that for the present, the legislature's judgment recognizing that a right to assisted suicide posed major dangers, should not be disturbed. But he left open the door for some future claim, when the factual realities were better understood.

**ix.  Breyer's concurrence in result:** Justice Breyer, like Stevens and Souter, agreed only with the Court's result, not its analysis. Breyer disagreed with Rehnquist's description of the plaintiffs' claimed liberty interest as a "right to commit suicide with another's assistance." Breyer said that he couldn't be precise about what the plaintiffs' interest truly consisted of, but that his formulation "would use words roughly like a *'right to die with dignity,'*" and that "at its core would lie *personal control over the manner of death*, professional medical assistance, and the *avoidance of unnecessary and severe physical suffering — combined*."

**(1) More direct challenge:** So Breyer, like several of the concurring Justices, thought that in a different case, the Court might some day have occasion to find that a state's ban on assisted suicide infringed a constitutional right. He suggested, for instance, that this might be the case if a state prohibited physicians from dispensing drugs needed to avoid pain at the end of life.

**e. Significance:** So where does *Glucksberg* leave us?

**i. No generalized "right to commit suicide":** Clearly, the case establishes that there is no *generalized* right to commit suicide, let alone a right to enlist the assistance of others in doing so. And, in fact, it's pretty clear that even the class of "terminally ill patients in severe pain" do not have such a generalized right.

**ii. Right to be free of pain:** But *Glucksberg* (and *Quill*, the New York case decided at the same time) were *facial* challenges, essentially claims that the statute couldn't constitutionally be applied to *any* terminally-ill competent patient. The Court has carefully left the door open to *"as applied"* claims. Thus a future plaintiff might well succeed with a claim that a particular state ban on suicide or suicide-assistance has infringed *that particular patient's* autonomy-based due process interest. For instance a terminally-ill, competent patient, whose pain can't be reduced by any method that wouldn't bring about death, might well succeed with a constitutional claim if the state prevented him from getting any relief.

**(1) Five Justices leave open possibility:** Five members of the Court (O'Connor, Stevens, Souter, Ginsburg and Breyer) seemed to explicitly leave open the possibility that such an "as applied" claim might succeed.

**Example:** Suppose that a state passed the following statute: "It shall be a felony for a physician to prescribe a substance for the purpose of alleviating a patient's pain, if the physician knows or should reasonably know that the ingestion of the substance is likely to cause the patient's life to end sooner than it would end without such ingestion." (The Washington statute in *Glucksberg*, and the New York statute in *Quill*, did *not* contain this sort of prohibition.)

Suppose further that P is a terminally-ill patient whose severe pain cannot not be dealt with in any way other than by giving him a large dose of painkiller that will hasten his death. It seems probable that a majority of the Court would conclude that the statute, as applied to P, violates his substantive due process rights. This statute would probably, in the words of Justice Breyer, infringe P's liberty interest in *"personal control over the manner of death*, professional medical assistance, and the *avoidance of unnecessary and severe physical suffering — combined*."

**iii. States free to permit:** Lastly, it is of course the case that the states are *free to permit assisted suicide*, if they want to. See, e.g., the Oregon voter initiative, *supra*, p. 198, permitting assisted suicide in some circumstances.

**Q. Other assorted autonomy issues:**   The "autonomy" branch of right-to-privacy law has raised a number of other interesting issues, on most of which the Supreme Court has not yet spoken. Some of these are as follows:

1. **Autonomy of mental processes:**   The autonomy branch of the right to privacy probably encompasses an individual's right to what might be called ***"freedom of thought processes."*** That is, the courts have recognized certain limits on what the government may do to ***shape the minds*** of individuals.

   a. **"Mandatory incantation":**   Thus the government does not generally have the right to condition receipt of benefits upon what Tribe (pp. 1315-16) calls "mandatory incantation." For instance, a state may not require a flag salute and recitation of the Pledge of Allegiance as a condition of receiving public education. *West Virginia State Bd. of Educ. v. Barnette*, 319 U.S. 624 (1943) (discussed further *infra*, p. 598).

   b. **Freedom of inquiry:**   Similarly, the government may not generally restrict students' ***freedom of inquiry***. See, e.g., *Meyer v. Nebraska (supra*, p. 157) (state may not ban teaching of foreign languages, at least in private schools); see also *Board of Education v. Pico, (infra*, p. 598) (First Amendment bars school board from removing books from school library for "narrow[ly] partisan or political [reasons].") However, a state is probably substantially free to limit the subject matter that is studied as part of the ***required curriculum*** in the public schools, so long as no other constitutional provision is violated (e.g., the separation of church and state, as violated by public-school prayer sessions, discussed *infra*, p. 658).

   c. **Private use of pornography:**   Similarly, a person has the constitutional right to possess and use ***pornographic*** or other objectionable materials in private. See *Stanley v. Georgia*, 394 U.S. 557 (1964) (discussed more fully *infra*, p. 562). This is true even where the material could be completely banned from ***sale.***

   d. **Drug statutes distinguished:**   But the government does have the right to make possession of specified ***drugs*** illegal, even though what makes the drug objectionable is its effect upon mental processes (e.g., LSD or marijuana).

2. **Rights of committed mentally retarded:**   ***Mentally retarded persons*** who have been ***involuntarily committed*** have been recognized by the Court to have the substantive due process right to be kept in a ***safe environment***, and not subjected to ***undue bodily restraint***. In addition, such persons may have a limited right to ***training***. *Youngberg v. Romeo*, 457 U.S. 307 (1982).

3. **Prohibition of risk-taking:**   Attempts by the state to control the ***amount of risk*** to which an individual may expose himself, may be questioned on autonomy/privacy grounds.

   a. **Motorcycle helmet rules:**   The best-known, and most criticized, example of a government attempt to limit risk-taking is the requirement that ***motorcyclists wear helmets***, a requirement imposed by statute in many states. Helmet requirements have generally been upheld.

   b. **Seat belts:**   Similarly, laws requiring that motorists wear ***seat belts*** have been challenged on autonomy/privacy grounds. These attacks, too, have generally failed.

4. **The right to travel:**   The ***"right to travel"*** from state to state is sometimes viewed as being part of the constitutionally-protected "right to privacy." For instance, Tribe (pp. 1378-80) includes this right within his chapter called "rights of privacy and personhood."

However, because the right-to-travel cases (especially *Shapiro v. Thompson*) have often involved equal protection considerations, our discussion of the right is postponed until the chapter on equal protection. See *infra*, p. 367.

5. **Right to occupation:** The right to *engage in one's chosen occupation* could be viewed as one of the elements of privacy/autonomy. Recall that since the demise of *Lochner*, the courts have been reluctant to give more than minimal substantive-due-process weight to "economic" rights. Nonetheless, in at least some kinds of situations, state interference with the right to practice one's chosen occupation is being subjected to more than minimal scrutiny.

   a. **Arbitrary deprivation:** The state may not prevent someone from practicing his chosen occupation for *completely arbitrary reasons*. Thus in *Schware v. Board of Bar Examiners of New Mexico*, 353 U.S. 232 (1957), the Court held that state qualifications to practice law "must have a rational connection with the applicant's fitness or capacity," and that plaintiff's prior membership in the Communist Party did not have such a rational connection with his fitness to practice law.

   b. **Equal protection:** Similarly, rules which deprive members of a *narrow* (and perhaps generally disadvantaged) *group* from practicing a profession are subject to attack, on both substantive due process and equal protection grounds. Thus in *Hampton v. Mow Sun Wong*, 426 U.S. 88 (1976), the Court held that the right to work in the federal Civil Service was important enough to be classed as an "interest in liberty." Consequently, Civil Service Commission rules barring aliens from the civil service could be upheld only if they were "justified by reasons which are properly the concern of [the Civil Service Commission]." Under this test, which appeared to be more than a "mere rationality" one, the rules could not be sufficiently justified, and were therefore violative of Fifth Amendment due process.

R. **No right to be protected from privately-imposed harm:** Virtually all of the substantive due process claims we have examined so far are ones in which the plaintiff was asserting the right to be free of *governmentally-imposed restrictions* that impair his life, liberty, or property. Suppose, however, that a person's life, liberty, or property are threatened not by the government itself, but by a *private person*; can one have a substantive due process right to be *protected by the government* from this third-party interference?

In a pair of cases, the Supreme Court has essentially answered *"no"* to this question. As the Court said in the first of those cases, *DeShaney v. Winnebago County Department of Social Services*, 489 U.S. 189 (1989), "[T]he Due Process Clauses generally confer *no affirmative right to governmental aid*, even where such aid may be necessary to secure life, liberty, or property interests of which the government itself may not deprive the individual."

1. *DeShaney***:** The tragic facts of *DeShaney, supra,* pose the problem with utmost clarity. P was a boy who was repeatedly beaten by his father, to the point of permanent, severe retardation. The Ds were county social-welfare officials who received repeated complaints that P was being beaten, had reason to believe that this was the case, but did nothing to help P. (In fact, at one point the state took custody of P temporarily, then returned him to his father.) P's lawsuit argued that the Ds had deprived P of his liberty without due process of law, by failing to intervene to protect him from his father.

   a. **Claim rejected:** By a 6-3 vote, the Court *rejected* P's claim. The purpose of the Due Process Clause, the majority said, is "to protect the people from the State, not to ensure that the State protect[s] them from each other." Thus the Due Process Clause does not impose any duty upon the state to provide substantive services within its borders, whether these services are safety-protection, medical services, adequate housing, or anything else. The state's obligation under the Due Process Clause is simply to avoid affirmatively injuring a citizen's life, liberty or property without due process.

2. ***Castle Rock***: The later case of *Castle Rock v. Gonzales*, 545 U.S. 748 (2005) posed a related question: may government by its ***express pronouncements*** in a statute ***give a citizen an affirmative right of protection*** against third-party harm, such that that right *will* constitute a substantive due process property interest? The Court's answer was that such a result is theoretically possible, but that it will ***rarely occur***, and in any event did not occur in the case at hand.

   a. **Facts:** *Castle Rock*, like *DeShaney*, involved tragic facts. P (Mrs. Gonzales) obtained from a Colorado court a ***restraining order*** compelling her estranged husband to stay away from P and her three daughters. Several weeks after being served with the order, the husband kidnapped the three daughters in violation of the order. Over the next five hours, P repeatedly asked the Town of Castle Rock police to arrest the husband, but the police refused to do so, apparently due to a policy of not normally making arrests for violation of restraining orders. Later that night, the husband came to the police station and was killed in a gunbattle with police; inside his truck, the murdered bodies of his three daughters were found.

   b. **P's claim:** P sued the town on the theory that she had had a due process property interest in having the police enforce the restraining order, and that the police, by their policy of not enforcing restraining orders, had deprived her of this property interest without due process.

      i. **Colorado statute:** In making this claim, P was not relying on the broad assertion (as had been made in *DeShaney*, *supra*) that government has a generalized duty to protect its citizens by making an arrest where there is probable cause to do so. Instead, P relied on a very specific and recently-passed Colorado statute designed to reduce domestic abuse; the statute provided that a peace officer "shall use every reasonable means to enforce a restraining order," and "shall arrest ... a restrained person when the peace officer has information amounting to probable cause that ... the restrained person has violated or attempted to violate any provision of a restraining order[.]" P asserted that this very specific statutory language demonstrated that Colorado intended to give her a due-process-protected property right.

   c. **Claim rejected:** By a vote of 7-2, the Court concluded that Colorado ***had not in fact conferred upon P a due-process-protected property interest*** in having the police enforce the restraining order. In an opinion by Justice Scalia, the Court reasoned that P's claim of a property interest failed in three distinct respects:

      i. **Not mandatory:** First, the Colorado statute did not truly make enforcement of restraining orders ***mandatory***. "A well established tradition of police ***discretion*** has long coexisted with apparently mandatory arrest statutes ... [A] true mandate of police action would require some stronger indication [of mandatoryness] from the Colorado Legislature" than was present here.

ii. **No entitlement to enforcement:** Second, even if the statute should be interpreted to make enforcement of restraining orders "mandatory," this would not necessarily mean that Colorado had intended to give a private person in P's position "an entitlement to enforcement of the mandate." Scalia reasoned that "Making the actions of government employees obligatory can serve various legitimate ends other than the conferral of a benefit on a specific class of people."

iii. **Not a property interest:** Finally, even if Colorado had meant to confer a true entitlement on P, it was not necessarily the case that this entitlement would amount to a "property" interest for due-process purposes. Nearly all the cases in which the Court had recognized a government entitlement as constituting "property" (cases like *Roth, supra*) had involved entitlements that constituted *direct* substantive benefits to the plaintiff (e.g., welfare payments, or a job). Here, the benefit sought by P was an *indirect* one — the right to have government take some action (an arrest) vis a vis a third person, not vis a vis the right-holder. Scalia suggested that any entitlement to an indirect benefit from government's taking an action against a third person was not properly viewed as a due-process "property" interest.

iv. **Conclusion:** In summary, Scalia said, *Castle Rock* and *DeShaney* taken together mean that "the benefit that a third party may receive from *having someone else arrested* for a crime generally *does not trigger protections under the Due Process Clause*, neither in its procedural nor in its 'substantive' manifestations." He added that this result "reflects our continuing reluctance to treat the 14th Amendment as a '*font of tort law.*'"

**S. Looking back on the "fundamental value" approach:** Let us now briefly recapitulate the Court's current approach to substantive due process. The Court is willing to subject to more than minimal "mere rationality" review only those legislative acts which materially impair a *"fundamental right."*

1. **Economic rights:** "Economic" rights are rarely found to be "fundamental" (though there are some hints that the right to practice one's chosen vocation may sometimes be viewed as fundamental).

2. **Non-economic rights:** Within the *non-economic* sphere, the Burger and Rehnquist Courts have been most likely to label a right as fundamental if it falls within what Prof. Ely refers to as "the 'area' (at least the Court sees it as an area) of *sex-marriage-child-bearing-childrearing*. ... " 92 HARV. L. REV. 11.

   a. **Middle-class values:** Within this "area," the Court has been much more likely to protect what might be seen as *traditional, middle-class* values, than it has the values of more isolated segments.

      i. **Illustrations:** For instance, the Court has given fundamental status to a number of rights exercised within the context of a *traditional marriage* (e.g., the right to use contraceptives — *Griswold v. Connecticut, supra*, pp. 158-161). By contrast, the Court has refused to grant fundamental status to the right of consenting adults to engage in homosexual activity (*Bowers v. Hardwick, supra*, p. 185).[10]

      ii. **Zoning:** Even the Court's substantive due process decisions in the area of *zoning* show a willingness to protect the family (e.g., *Moore v. City of East Cleveland supra*, pp. 182-183, protecting the extended family) but not a willingness to protect the right of unrelated individuals to live together (*Village of Belle Terre v. Borass, supra*, p. 183).

---

*Quiz Yourself on*

## SUBSTANTIVE DUE PROCESS — PROTECTION OF NON-ECONOMIC RIGHTS

**23.** The state of Aha has enacted a statute that proscribes what the statute refers to as "unnatural sexual acts." The acts described include oral sex. The statute applies to conduct between married persons as well as to conduct between unmarried persons, but contains an exemption for conduct that takes place in a dwelling that is the residence of one or both parties. Joe and Martha Danzig, a married couple, were vacationing at the Happy Times Motel, when a state police officer burst into the room acting on a tip (reasonable-seeming but erroneous) that the couple was using drugs. The officer happened to see Joe and Martha engaging in oral sex at that moment, and arrested them.

**(a)** If Joe and Martha want to challenge the charges on constitutional grounds, what is their best argument? _____

**(b)** Will this argument succeed? _____

**24.** A number of states have enacted regulations bearing on specific aspects of abortion. Consider the following:

**(a)** The state of Aloha provides that no abortion may be performed within the state if at the moment of the procedure the fetus is more than three months old.

**(b)** The state of Brie provides that no abortion may be performed on a married woman unless she signs an affidavit that she has notified her spouse. However, the prohibition does not apply if the married woman instead signs an affidavit that she and her husband are not living together, or that her husband is not the father of the child, or that she has not given notice because she fears that he will abuse her if he finds out that she is planning an abortion. The statute is challenged by P, a woman who is two months pregnant, wants an abortion, and does not want to notify her spouse (with whom P lives, whom she believes to be the father of the child, and who is not likely to abuse her if she tells him she wants an abortion).

**(c)** The state of Caledonia provides that no abortion may be performed on a woman under the age of 18, unless one parent of the woman has received one hour of counselling about alternatives to abortion, and this mandatory counselling has been followed by a 24-hour waiting period. The young woman may avoid the need for parental consent by taking advantage of a procedure under which she is entitled to try to persuade a judge that either: (i) an abortion is in her best interests; (ii) she is living apart from her parents and is effectively emancipated; or (iii) abortion is made necessary by a medical emergency.

State whether each of these provisions is constitutional. (Assume that the suits in (a) and (c) are attacks on the face of the statute, and that the attack in (b) is "as applied"). _____

**25.** In recent years, in the state of North Rockland, there has been an increase in the number of marginally-

---

10. However, the 2003 decision in *Lawrence v. Texas* (*supra*, p. 185), overruling the result in *Bowers*, at least gives a more stringent form of rational-relation review to restrictions on homosexual sex, though *Lawrence* did not change *Bowers'* classification of the interest in having same-gender sex as non-fundamental. Perhaps *Lawrence* will prove to be the start of a willingness by the Court to give somewhat increased protections to sexual/intimacy/procreative interests falling outside the traditional marriage context.

funded, educationally-inadequate private schools, as well as a rise in the number of parents who have been teaching their children at home rather than sending them to the public schools. The North Rockland legislature has, therefore, just passed a statute providing that every child between the age of 6 and 16 must be educated in the state's public schools. Parents who do not comply face criminal punishment. The statute does not allow any exceptions for even educationally-sound private schools or educationally-sound home instruction. Paula, the parent of a seven-year-old son, wishes to educate him at home. Paula was until last year a first-grade teacher in a state public school, and all concerned agree that she is well qualified to teach her child at home provided that she does so full time, which she expects to do. Paula has sued to overturn the statute, as applied to her and her son, on substantive due process grounds.

    **(a)** What standard of review should the court use in deciding Paula's suit? _____

    **(b)** Will the statute be found constitutional as applied to Paula and her son? _____

26. The state of Centuria has a criminal statute prohibiting "sodomy," defined to include any instance in which one person's mouth or anus touches another person's genitals. Century Village, a town in Centuria, has a school-board regulation providing that any person who the school board finds to have violated any state statute involving moral turpitude shall be dismissed, and further providing that a violation of the sodomy ban shall be deemed to constitute moral turpitude. Darwin, a non-tenured teacher at Century Village High School, was involved in a sexual relationship with Fred. After Darwin broke up the relationship, Fred sent a video to the Century Village school board, showing Darwin and Fred involved in conduct of the sort proscribed by the Centuria criminal statute. The school board viewed the video, concluded that Darwin had violated the statute, and dismissed Darwin. In recent years, the statute has rarely been enforced, and on those rare occasions has been enforced principally against same-sex sodomy. Darwin has now attacked his firing on the grounds that it violates his substantive due process rights. Assume that issues of procedural due process are ignored.

    **(a)** What standard should the court use for deciding Darwin's challenge? _____

    **(b)** Was Darwin's firing constitutional? _____

27. The town of Tinsel originally did not have any written regulation concerning the beard or hair styles of fire fighters. At the time Jordan was hired onto the fire fighting force, he had a beard and hair that was neatly combed but of shoulder length. After Jordan had been on the force two years, Tinsel enacted a regulation providing that no male firefighter could wear a beard or hair extending below his neck. Jordan has challenged this regulation as violating his substantive due process rights. Tinsel has defended the regulation on the grounds that: (i) uniformity of hairstyle is necessary to generate a feeling of esprit de corps among firefighters; and (ii) facial hair and long hair are more likely to catch fire even if the person dons the usual safety equipment.

    **(a)** What standard should the court use in deciding whether Jordan's substantive due process rights have been violated? _____

    **(b)** Is the regulation constitutional? _____

28. Two years ago, Pedro signed a "living will," in which he directed that in the event he should ever be in a persistent vegetative state, with no real likelihood of improvement, he should not be artificially respirated or hydrated. Pedro was then in a car accident, and lapsed into a deep coma (a persistent vegetative state) from which, all the doctors who have seen him agree, he is very unlikely to emerge. The hospital where he is being kept is willing to disconnect the respirator and hydration unit, but only if Wanda, Pedro's wife, signs a form agreeing with this step and waiving her right to sue. Wanda refuses to sign this document,

arguing that although pulling the plug may well be what Pedro wanted (she does not dispute that he signed the living will while competent) she herself is opposed on moral and religious grounds to pulling the plug. Pedro's brother has been appointed Pedro's guardian *ad litem*, and has brought suit for a court order directing the hospital to discontinue life support even without Wanda's consent.

**(a)** What is the strongest constitutional argument that Pedro's brother can make as to why the plug should be pulled? _____

**(b)** Should the court order that the plug be pulled? _____

**(c)** Now, suppose that Pedro, instead of having had a car accident, is in the last stages of terminal cancer, and is in extreme pain. He is competent, and wishes to have his physician, Doctor, prescribe a fatal dose of morphine so that Pedro can commit suicide. The state makes it a crime to help anyone commit suicide, no matter what the circumstances. Doctor goes to court to seek a declaratory judgment that the ban on assisting suicide is unconstitutional as applied to these facts. Should the court grant Doctor's request? _____

---

*Answers*

**23. (a) That the charges violate the defendants' substantive due process right to "privacy."**

**(b) Yes, probably.** The Supreme Court has held that every individual has a "zone of privacy," and that government action which invades that zone will be found to violate the individual's substantive due process rights unless the government action is necessary to achieve a compelling governmental objective (strict scrutiny). The Supreme Court has never explicitly held that the sexual acts of a married couple, taken in private, fall within the zone of privacy for all purposes. However, the Court has held (in *Griswold v. Connecticut*) that the right to privacy is violated when the state interferes with a couple's attempts to use birth control. Later cases suggest that state interferences with a married couple's sexual intimacy would similarly violate the right to privacy, assuming that the conduct took place in private (even if it took place in a hotel room or other non-residential but non-public setting). See, e.g., *Lawrence v. Texas*, the homosexual-sodomy case, where the majority opinion refers to "an emerging awareness that liberty gives substantial protection to adult persons in deciding how to conduct their private lives in matters pertaining to sex." In summary, since Joe and Martha are married and were performing the activity in private, their conduct probably fell within the protected zone of privacy. (It is a bit less clear that their "right of privacy" argument would prevail if they had been unmarried, or engaged in an adulterous relationship.)

**24. (a) Unconstitutional.** *Planned Parenthood v. Casey* and *Gonzales v. Carhart* make it substantially easier than it was formerly for the states to regulate abortion. Nonetheless, even under these cases, the states may not place **"undue burdens"** on the right of abortion. A state regulation will constitute an undue burden if the regulation has the purpose or effect of placing a "substantial obstacle" in the path of a woman seeking an abortion of a ***non-viable fetus***. *Casey*. Since a four- or five-month-old fetus is certainly not viable even under present medical advances, the blanket prohibition on abortions during this time frame would likely be found to be a "substantial obstacle" and thus an "undue burden," even given the Roberts Court's more-circumscribed view of abortion rights. (But a state probably could bar all abortions past the moment of viability.)

**(b) Unconstitutional, probably.** *Casey* struck down a spousal notification provision. The provision here, while it may contain slightly more escape hatches, would likely be found to be a substantial obstacle to the plaintiff (who is not covered by any of the escape hatches). Notice that the attack here is "as applied" rather than "on the face" of the statute. That is, the suit argues that the statute directly violates the rights of the plaintiff, rather than asking the Court to prevent the statute from being enforced against anyone because it violates the rights of persons not before the Court. Even the Roberts Court that decided the *Gonzales* partial-birth-abortion case would likely find that the statute acts as an undue burden *upon P*, even if that Court wouldn't allow a facial attack on the spousal notification provision. (*Gonzales* indicates that the Court will allow facial attacks only if the plaintiffs prove that the statute would be unconstitutional "in a large fraction of relevant cases"; the plaintiffs in a facial attack might not be able to make this "large fraction" showing, given the various escape hatches.)

**(c) Constitutional.** A provision much like the one here was upheld in *Casey*. In particular, the Court held in *Casey* that states may require the parent to listen to alternatives to abortion, and may establish a 24-hour waiting period following this mandatory counselling. The Court in the post-*Casey* case of *Gonzales v. Carhart* — upholding a federal ban on partial-birth abortions — emphasized the state's strong interest in warning women of the likely emotional regret that they may come to feel after an abortion, so *Gonzales* makes it even more likely that the Court would uphold the provision here than would have been the case before *Gonzales*.

25. **(a) Strict scrutiny, probably.** That is, the statute will probably be struck down unless shown to be ***necessary*** to achieve a ***compelling*** state interest. The question is really whether the right to make core decisions about how one's children shall be educated is a ***"fundamental"*** right. The Supreme Court has not addressed this issue directly in recent years. However, several cases (discussed further in part (b) below) suggest that the Court would hold that the right to direct the education of one's children is indeed "fundamental," in which case strict scrutiny must be applied to any governmental regulation that substantially impairs that right.

**(b) No, probably.** In *Pierce v. Society of Sisters* (a 1925 case), the Court struck down a state statute requiring children to attend public schools. The decision seems to have been on substantive-due-process-like grounds, and seems to have applied essentially strict scrutiny. Similarly, in more recent years, the Court has held that parents have a fundamental right to decide who may visit the child; *Troxel v. Granville*.

Assuming that the right to choose how one's children are to be educated is in some sense fundamental, it is very unlikely that the statute here could survive strict scrutiny. Ensuring a good education for children is certainly an important state objective, and probably a "compelling" one. However, it is highly unlikely that foreclosing all options other than public schools is a "necessary" means of attaining that objective. For instance, allowing a program of home instruction by one who is clearly a qualified elementary school teacher certainly seems to be an adequate way to assure a good education. And the state could adopt a monitoring program to make sure that home study programs satisfy a minimum quality standard. So the statute will probably flunk strict scrutiny, if strict scrutiny is applied.

26. **(a) The "rational relation," not "strict scrutiny," standard.** The Supreme Court has held that a state may not criminalize sodomy defined in this way. *Lawrence v. Texas* (2003) (p. 185). But in reaching this conclusion, the Court applied the easier-to-satisfy rational-relation standard. However, the Court found that such a ban on sodomy — generally enforced only against homosexual sodomy — could not satisfy even the rational-relation test, because it pursued only the illegitimate aim of expressing moral disapproval of homosexuality. The Court would presumably use the same rational-relation standard in evaluating whether a public body may fire a person for engaging in such sodomy.

**(b) No, probably.** Although the Court would (as noted in part (a) above) probably apply the rational-relation standard to the school-board regulation here, it is likely that the regulation would be found invalid even under that relatively easy-to-satisfy standard. The essence of the regulation is that one who violates a state statute forbidding a particular act of turpitude may be fired. Since the underlying state statute is no longer valid in light of *Lawrence*, it is hard to believe that the Court would find that it was rational for the school board to fire someone for violating this no-longer-valid statute. This is especially likely given that the governmental objective that the school district seems to be pursuing here — punishing gay people for "moral turpitude" — is the very one that *Lawrence* found to be illegitimate.

**27. (a) The "rational relation" standard, not strict scrutiny.** The choice of standard depends on whether the right of a firefighter to wear a beard, etc., is found to be "fundamental." In a case almost completely on point, *Kelley v. Johnson*, the Supreme Court held that a policeman's right to wear his hair as he wished was not "fundamental," and that the hair-length regulation there should be judged on a rational relation standard.

**(b) Yes, probably.** Assuming that the rational relation standard is used, the regulation here almost certainly passes muster. The town certainly has a legitimate interest in preserving *esprit de corps* and promoting safety. The contribution of short hair to fulfillment of these objectives may be questionable, but it is certainly "rational." (For instance, the town could reasonably have believed that long-haired male firefighters would not fit in as well.) Certainly the comparable hair-length regulation in *Kelley* was found to be rationally related to a legitimate governmental objective, and was thus upheld, so the same result is likely here.

**28. (a) That Pedro's substantive due process rights would be violated by forcing him to be kept on artificial life support.**

**(b) Yes, probably.** The Supreme Court has never explicitly faced the issue of whether a person who signs a living will has a substantive due process (or other constitutional) right to have that directive obeyed. But in *Cruzan v. Missouri Dept. of Health*, the Court suggested that a competent adult has a constitutionally-protected liberty interest in declining unwanted medical procedures. The Court might well hold that this interest is a "fundamental" one. If so, the state would have the right to decline to obey the directive only if the refusal was necessary to achieve some compelling governmental interest.

It is highly unlikely that there is any compelling governmental interest here that could only be achieved by keeping Pedro on life support. Certainly Wanda's interest in preserving her own religious or moral objectives would be unlikely to outweigh Pedro's right to control his own destiny. Therefore, the Court will probably order that the plug be pulled even without Wanda's consent (and the Court will probably immunize Hospital from suit by Wanda). (But *Cruzan* does recognize that the states have a significant governmental interest in requiring *clear evidentiary proof* about what the patient's wishes really are, so that if Pedro had not signed the living will, the state could probably refuse to accept, say, weak oral testimony from relatives about what Pedro "would have wanted.")

**(c) No, probably.** The Supreme Court decided in *Washington v. Glucksberg* that state prohibitions on assisted-suicide are not facially invalid, because there is no general right to commit suicide or to enlist another's assistance in doing so. *Glucksberg* seems to apply even where the plaintiff is a competent, terminally-ill person who desires escape from pain. However, it's possible that Pedro or his doctor could convince the Court that his "as applied" challenge (as opposed to the broad "facial" challenge that lost in Glucksberg) is narrow enough that he should win: he could argue that where a fatal dose of medication is the *only way* he can escape unbearable pain, it's a violation of his personal autonomy to be denied that relief. (See Justice Breyer's concurrence in *Glucksberg*, recognizing a "right to die with dignity," which he said would encompass "personal control over the manner of death, professional medical assistance, and the avoidance of unnecessary and severe physical suffering — combined." It seems pretty clear that Breyer would give Pedro the relief he seeks on these facts.)

# V. PROCEDURAL DUE PROCESS

A. **Introduction:** We turn now to an element of due process that is quite distinct from that with which the previous part of this chapter was concerned. The requirement that the government act with "*procedural* due process" derives, like the requirement of substantive due process, from the Due Process Clauses of the Fifth Amendment (in the case of the federal government) and the Fourteenth Amendment (in the case of the states). Recall that both clauses prevent the government from depriving any person of "*life, liberty*, or *property*, without due process of law."

1. **State rules:** In the following discussion, unless otherwise noted, we are talking about the Fourteenth Amendment Due Process Clause, and limits on *state* action. However, the same rules generally apply to the federal government via the Fifth Amendment.

2. **No interest in governmental regularity** *per se:* It is crucial to understand that the Due Process Clause *does not bar the government from procedural irregularities per se. Only when "life," "liberty" or "property" are being taken* is the government required to act with procedural correctness. If none of these interests is implicated by a particular government act, the government may act *as arbitrarily or unfairly as it wishes* (at least insofar as the Due Process Clause is concerned). As one commentator has put it, "Procedural due process … is evidently not a free standing human interest." 62 CORNELL L. REV. 452 (quoted in L,K&C, p. 626.)

   **Example:** Suppose a state government announces that it will hire a new secretary for the head of a state agency. P is superbly qualified. The state interviews P, but awards the job to X, who can't type, but who is the daughter of a prominent local politician. Even if P can prove that the state's action was utterly arbitrary or unfair, P has not established any violation of her procedural due process rights. The reason is that P did not have any "property" or "liberty" interest in the job opening (see *infra*, p. 212), so there was simply no protected interest on which any procedural due process rights could hang.

   a. **Significance:** Thus most of our discussion of procedural due process will focus on the issue of just what types of interests are deemed to be ones in "liberty" or "property," such that they may not be impaired without procedural due process? (Interests in "life" are imperiled by government action only in relatively rare circumstances, principally capital punishment; there, the interest in "life" is so clearly at stake that it is obvious that the government must act with procedural correctness.)

      i. **Distinguished from substantive due process:** The need to focus carefully upon exactly what constitutes "liberty" and "property" in the procedural due process area contrasts sharply with the practice in the substantive due process area. In the latter context, it has rarely been an issue in the Supreme Court's decisions whether "liberty" or "property" was implicated; "liberty" has been assumed to include "just about every interest of significance to an individual." Gunther (12th Ed.), p.

583. (Of course, if the interest involved is not deemed "fundamental," only a very small state justification is necessary to support its impairment; but the interest in "liberty" or "property" is nonetheless assumed to exist in virtually every substantive due process situation.)

b. **Three-part historical analysis:** The Supreme Court's definition of "liberty" and "property" has undergone marked variation over the years. Our treatment divides the Court's approach to defining these terms into three major stages: pre-1970, early 1970s and post-1972.

c. **What process is due:** After a comprehensive discussion of the meaning of "liberty" and "property," we turn to a much shorter analysis of a second issue: Once it is determined that a particular government action implicates an interest in "liberty" or "property," *what "process" is due*? That is, must a hearing be given? Must counsel be permitted?, etc.

3. **Individual adjudications:** One important difference between procedural due process and substantive due process is that a right to the former will only exist where the government action at issue involves an ***individualized determination.***

a. **Illustration of substantive question:** Thus suppose a state establishes broad, mechanical, requirements (e.g., age, education, residence) which must be met before one may be licensed to practice a certain profession. These requirements will be tested solely by use of a substantive due process analysis (i.e., is a fundamental interest at stake; if not, does the rule have some rational relation to a legitimate state objective?)

b. **Illustration of procedural question:** On the other hand, if a state imposes requirements against which each individual must be carefully, and subjectively, evaluated, the need for procedural due process may also be triggered. Thus if the professional licensing procedure requires an evaluation of "good moral character," the elements of procedural due process (e.g., the right to be heard, the right to an explanation, etc.) must be given. See Tribe, p. 682-83.

c. **Simultaneously valid and invalid:** Thus a regulation may simultaneously be valid from the viewpoint of substantive due process and invalid from the perspective of procedural due process.

B. **"Liberty" and "property" before 1970:** The Supreme Court has, historically, taken a broad view of what constitutes "liberty" and "property." As the Court said in *Meyer v. Nebraska (supra*, p. 157), the interest in "liberty" includes "not merely freedom from bodily restraint but also the right of the individual to **contract**, to engage in any of the common **occupations** of life, to acquire useful knowledge, to marry, establish a home and bring up children [and] to worship God according to the dictates of … conscience." Although the Court has never defined "property" explicitly, this term, too, has always been interpreted liberally.

1. **Public benefits:** But before 1970, there was one notable area in which the Court was reluctant to find that a "liberty" or "property" interest existed. This was the area of ***benefits flowing from the public sector***, including ***government employment*** and monetary benefits (e.g., ***welfare***). The Court traditionally took the view that such items were a ***"privilege"*** not a "right," and that they could therefore be withdrawn without procedural regularity. This view is sometimes referred to as the "right/privilege dichotomy." See Tribe, pp. 680-81.

a. **Constitutionally impermissible reasons:** However, even under this traditional view that public-sector benefits were privileges, not rights, it was apparently the case that these privileges could not be withdrawn for *reasons violative of other constitutional protections*. For instance, it was clear prior to 1970 that the government could not fire a worker for exercising his right to free speech off the job.

   i. **Right to hearing:** A separate issue is whether a worker's mere *claim* that he has been fired or denied government benefits for such unconstitutional reasons entitles him to a due process hearing. The Supreme Court has still not explicitly decided whether such a mere claim of unconstitutional action, without additional evidence, suffices to trigger the need for procedural due process. Tribe, p. 682 and n. 34.

C. **Growth in the '70s of "entitlements":** During the early 1970s the Supreme Court held that many types of government benefits previously thought to be mere "privileges" rather than "rights" were *in fact interests in liberty or property*, which could therefore not be taken without procedural due process.

   1. **Welfare benefits (*Goldberg v. Kelly*):** The first, and perhaps most important, of these decisions was *Goldberg v. Kelly*, 397 U.S. 254 (1970), in which the Court held that a *welfare recipient* must be given an "evidentiary hearing" before his benefits may be terminated. Welfare payments, for a person statutorily entitled to receive them, were not "mere charity," but were a *right* protected by the Constitution against arbitrary withdrawal.

D. **Narrowing of "entitlements" theory:** But the expansionary process described above posed a real risk: more and more transactions by state and federal governments might be deemed to impair liberty or property interests, until the entire day-to-day activities of those governments were rendered completely subject to constitutional review (and until the judicial system was drowned by due process claims). Consequently, after the early 1970s the Burger Court began to curtail the types of public benefits which would be deemed to create an interest in liberty or property. This scaled-back view of what constitutes liberty or property remains basically in effect today.

E. **The tenure cases (*Roth* and *Perry*):** The best-known example of the Court's cutting back is *Board of Regents v. Roth*, 408 U.S. 564 (1972), a *university tenure* case. But a companion case, *Perry v. Sindermann*, 408 U.S. 593 (1972), seemed to put an important brake on the retreat in *Roth*.

   1. *Roth:* In *Roth*, plaintiff was given a non-tenured one-year contract to teach at Wisconsin State University. The University declined, without giving reasons, to hire him after the one-year period. Under Wisconsin law, decisions on hiring for non-tenured positions were left totally to the discretion of University officials. The Supreme Court held that plaintiff's interest in being rehired was not an interest in "liberty" or "property," and that he therefore had no right to procedural due process.

      a. **Rationale:** The Court's opinion emphasized that the "weight" (i.e., the importance) of the plaintiff's interest was irrelevant; it was the "nature" of that interest that counted.

      b. **Not a "liberty" interest:** Plaintiff's interest was not one in "liberty," the Court said, because the state's decision not to rehire plaintiff did not include charges which might damage his reputation (e.g., a charge of dishonesty or immorality), nor was he barred from a broader class of employment (e.g., all other jobs in state universities.) Had either of these things occurred, the Court indicated, plaintiff's "liberty" would have been affected, and he would have had the right to procedural due process.

    **i.   Change in law:**   However, the Court's suggestion that damage to plaintiff's reputation would have been sufficient to invoke a "liberty" interest is probably no longer good law. In the later case of *Paul v. Davis,* (discussed *infra*, p. 215), the Court held that a person's interest in reputation alone is not a constitutionally-protected liberty interest.

   **c.   Not "property" interest:**   Nor was plaintiff's interest in being rehired a "property" interest. Such an interest did not exist merely because the individual had a "need" for a benefit, or even a "unilateral expectation" of it; rather, he must have had a *"legitimate claim of entitlement"* to it.

    **i.   Scope defined by state law:**   Whether or not such a "legitimate claim of entitlement" to the benefit existed was, the Court held, to be determined *by reference to state law*. Since Wisconsin law made it clear that rehiring decisions in non-tenured cases were to be completely discretionary, plaintiff had no such entitlement.

   **d.   Present enjoyment required:**   The *Roth* Court observed that the Fourteenth Amendment due process protection of property applied to interests "that a person has *already acquired* in specific benefits." This remark seems to mean that *unless a person is already enjoying a benefit, he has no procedural due process rights* (at least arising from the "property" as opposed to "liberty" branch) if the benefit is denied to him.

    **i.   Initial application:**   Thus where the state turns down an *initial application* for such benefits as welfare, government employment or parole, it may be the case that no procedural due process rights attach, even though the applicable statute or precedents make the applicant eligible for the benefit. But the Supreme Court has never squarely focused on this issue.

   **e.   Marshall's dissent:**   Justice Marshall, one of three dissenters in *Roth*, advocated the extraordinary view that "every citizen who applies for a government job is entitled to it unless the government can establish some reason for denying the employment," and that this entitlement constituted a Fourteenth Amendment "property" right.

**2.   *Perry v. Sindermann*'s contrasting view:**   Despite *Roth*'s severe approach, the companion case, *Perry v. Sindermann*, indicates that *informal practices or customs* may be sufficient to create a *legitimate claim of entitlement* to a benefit.

   **a.   Facts:**   The plaintiff in *Perry*, like the one in *Roth*, was untenured. However, he had taught for ten years, and alleged that the college where he worked had a "*de facto*" tenure program, and that the college administration had created an "understanding" that he had tenure under that program.

   **b.   Holding:**   The Court held that plaintiff was entitled to a hearing on his *de facto* tenure claim, and that such a claim, if proven, gave plaintiff a property interest. Such an interest will be found to exist if there are "mutually explicit understandings" supporting a claim of entitlement.

**F.   Breadth of injury is weighed:**   The *breadth* of the public benefit denied is likely to be considered by the Court, especially in public employment cases. For instance, a governmental decision not to hire or rehire a person for one particular government job is much less likely to be held to be violative of a "liberty" or "property" interest than is a decision that the individual may not hold *any* government job. See *Board of Regents v. Roth, supra*, p. 213.

**G. Freedom from arbitrary procedures:** Some commentators have suggested that the courts should recognize, as a *substantive aspect of liberty*, certain elements of procedural fairness. Professor Van Alstyne, for instance, advocates recognizing *"freedom from arbitrary adjudicative procedures"* as an element of "liberty." 62 CORNELL L. REV. 487 (quoted in L,K&C, p. 635). Similarly, Rabin, 44 U. CHI. L. REV. 60 advocates a "right to a *reasoned explanation* of government conduct that is contrary to the expectations the government has created by conferring a special status upon an individual." (Quoted in L,K&C, p. 646.)

  **1. Significance:** These proposals would effectively amount to making procedural due process a "free standing" right which can exist without the presence of any unrelated liberty or property interest. The Supreme Court has never indicated any willingness to do this. See *supra*, p. 211.

**H. Narrowing of protected "liberty" interests:** In *Bishop*, as noted, the Court appeared to limit constitutionally-protected "property" interests to those which exist under an explicit provision of state law or contract; other sources of substantive property rights (e.g., justifiable expectations, a common-law tradition, etc.) seemed to have been excluded. Very much the same kind of cutting back has also taken place in the definition of *"liberty,"* principally as the result of *Paul v. Davis*, 424 U.S. 693 (1976).

  **1. Facts of *Paul*:** Plaintiff, after being arrested for shoplifting, was listed as an "active shoplifter" in a flyer which the police circulated to hundreds of local merchants. After the shoplifting charges were dismissed, plaintiff sued the police under 42 U.S.C. §1983 (*infra*, p. 440), which allows recovery from public officials for violation of constitutional rights.

  **2. Holding:** By a 5-3 vote, the Supreme Court held that plaintiff's *interest in his reputation,* by itself, was *not a constitutionally-protected "liberty" or "property" interest.*

  **3. Federalism considerations:** The majority view in *Paul* seems to have been motivated largely by a desire to *avoid the federalization of tort law*, and to keep suits alleging wrongdoing by state government officials from deluging the federal court system.

**I. Rights of students:** The Court has not cut back on the definition of "liberty" and "property" in all contexts. For instance, it has given an expansive reading to these terms in the *school* environment. Thus in *Goss v. Lopez*, 419 U.S. 565 (1975), the Court held that a suspension from public school constituted deprivation of a constitutionally-protected property interest. (*Goss'* holding as to the type of procedure required in the suspension situation is discussed *infra*, p. 222.)

**J. What process is due:** Once a court concludes that a constitutionally-protected "liberty" or "property" interest has been impaired, the issue becomes: *What process is due?* While full consideration of this question is generally covered in other courses (particularly *Administrative Law*), a brief outline of the Courts' treatment of the issue is given here.

  **1. Traditional adversary model:** The early 1970s saw the Supreme Court require an extremely broad set of procedural protections before the government could take away what the Court found to be a "property" interest. For instance, in *Goldberg v. Kelly*, 397 U.S. 254 (1970) (also discussed *supra*, p. 213), the Court held that an *evidentiary hearing* was required before welfare benefits could be terminated. In *Goldberg* and cases following it, the Court seemed to be moving towards a view that in order for the government to take administrative action which might affect a person's "property" or "liberty" interest, the full panoply of procedural safeguards typically imposed in court proceedings was required.

   a. **Wide range of procedures:**   This approach, if followed to its logical conclusion, would have guaranteed not only the right to a hearing, but such protections as the right to *call witnesses*, the right to *counsel*, the right of *cross-examination*, the right of *judicial review*, etc.

2. **Withdrawal towards a "balancing" test:**   Provision of such a full set of guarantees any time a "property" or "liberty" interest was at issue would obviously have been extremely expensive, time-consuming, and perhaps administratively impossible. Therefore, in the late 1970s, just as the Court cut back on its notion of what constitutes a "property" or "liberty" interest (see *supra*, p. 213), so it cut back on its interpretation of exactly what procedures are required where a liberty or property interest is at issue.

   a. **Balancing test:**   The Court's present view may be summarized as calling for use of a *"balancing test,"* in which the costs of requiring a particular set of procedures will be weighed against the benefits from the use of those procedures.

   b. **Illustrated in *Mathews*:**   This balancing test was first formulated in *Mathews v. Eldridge*, 425 U.S. 319 (1976). In holding that disability benefits could be terminated without a prior evidentiary hearing (a sharp contrast with the holding in *Goldberg v. Kelly*, the welfare benefits case), the Court listed the factors to be balanced.

      i. **One side of equation:**   On one side of the equation are: (1) the strength of the private interest that would be affected by the official action (so that the bigger the individual's stake in the outcome, the more safeguards would be required), and (2) the "risk of an erroneous deprivation of such interest through the procedures used, and the probable value, if any, of additional or substitute procedural safeguards." These two factors are presumably to be multiplied together in some way.

      ii. **Other side of equation:**   On the other side of the equation is "the government's interest, including the function involved and the fiscal and administrative burdens that the additional or substitute procedural requirement would entail."

      iii. **Mathematical form:**   Thus the *Mathews* balancing test might be expressed in the following mathematical terms, where "A" is the additional procedural safeguard to which the individual asserts that he is entitled: procedural safeguard, *A*, will be required if and only if

      (amount at stake for individual) *x* (likelihood that administrative error will be reduced by using *A*)  <  cost to the government of granting A

   c. **Application in *Mathews*:**   The Court applied this equation in *Mathews* as follows:

      i. **Lower stake:**   First, unlike the welfare payments at issue in *Goldberg*, the disability payments were less likely to be the individual's sole source of income, so his stake was lower than in *Goldberg*.

      ii. **Value of safeguard:**   Second, the value of an evidentiary hearing was less than in *Goldberg*, because the disability issue turned upon a medical assessment of the worker's physical or mental condition, which assessment could probably be evaluated through written documents rather than oral testimony.

**iii. Burden on government:** Thirdly, the burden of supplying a full administrative hearing was likely to be substantial, and the cost of it "may in the end come out of the pockets of the deserving since resources available for any particular program of social welfare are not unlimited."

**iv. Conclusion:** Therefore, the Court concluded, no evidentiary hearing was required before termination of disability benefits.

**d. Firing of tenured employee:** Where the protected interest being terminated is a ***public-sector job***, the required procedural safeguards are similarly determined by a balancing test. Thus in *Cleveland Bd. of Ed. v. Loudermill*, 470 U.S. 532 (1985) (discussed more extensively *infra*, p. 221), the Court weighed a tenured employee's interest in retaining his employment against the government's interest in having a quick way to fire unsatisfactory employees; the Court also factored in "the risk of an erroneous termination."

    **i. Conclusion:** The *Loudermill* Court then concluded that although "some kind of a hearing" was required prior to the discharge of the plaintiff, that hearing was required to include only "oral or written notice of the charges against him, an explanation of the employer's evidence, and an opportunity to present his side of the story." It did ***not*** include the right to a ***full evidentiary hearing*** of the sort imposed in the welfare-benefits context in *Goldberg v. Kelly, see supra*, p. 213. Requiring a full adversarial evidentiary hearing would "intrude to an unwarranted extent on the government's interest in quickly removing an unsatisfactory employee."

**3. Traditional court proceedings:** When a person's life, liberty or property is at stake in a traditional civil or criminal ***lawsuit***, the range of procedural protections required by the Constitution is at its broadest. Certainly as a matter of practice, and probably as a matter of constitutional due process, the state may not take life, liberty or property as the result of a lawsuit — even if the suit is brought by a private party against another private party — without granting such protections as the right to call witnesses, the right to counsel, the right of cross-examination, and the right of judicial review. A meaningful treatment of what constitutes due process in the litigation context is beyond the scope of this outline.

**a. Unlimited discretion:** One aspect of the right to due process in the litigation context is that a litigant has the right to be free of excessive ***discretion*** on the part of ***juries***. For instance, when a state allows juries to award tort damages against a defendant, the state must give at least some guidance to the jury on when it may allow an award, and in what amount.

**b. Punitive damages:** In some circumstances the award of ***punitive damages*** may violate the defendant's due process rights.

    **i. Ratio of actual to punitive:** A punitive damages award will violate due process if it is ***"grossly excessive."*** *BMW of North America v. Gore*, 517 U.S. 559 (1996).

        **(1) Ratio of punitive to compensatory:** One of the most important factors in whether an award of punitive damages is grossly excessive is the ***ratio*** of the ***punitive damages*** to the ***actual damages***. The Court has said that "*few awards* [significantly] exceeding a ***single-digit ratio*** between punitive and compensatory damages ... will satisfy due process." *State Farm Mut. Automobile Insur. Co. v. Campbell*, 123 S.Ct. 1513 (2003).

**Example:** In one of the few cases in which the Supreme Court has found that a punitive damages award was so excessive that it violated the defendant's due process right, the court attached a lot of weight to the fact that the punitive award to P was *500 times* the amount of his actual harm as determined by the jury. *BMW of North America, supra.*

   **ii. Reprehensibility:** Another of the key factors in the due process analysis is the *reprehensibility* of the defendant's conduct — the more reprehensible the conduct, the higher the amount of punitive damages that may be awarded without violating due process. *State Farm Mut. Automobile Insur. Co. v. Campbell, supra.*

   **iii. Conduct vis a vis strangers to the litigation:** Only the defendant's conduct *towards the plaintiff*, not its conduct towards *strangers to the litigation,* may be taken into account by the jury in setting the amount of punitive damages. *Philip Morris USA v. Williams*, 127 S.Ct. 1057 (2007).

**Example:** P (Jesse Williams), a smoker, sues D (a large tobacco manufacturer) for fraud in having knowingly and falsely led P to believe that smoking was safe. P's attorney tells the jury to "think of how many other Jesse Williams in the last 40 years in the state of Oregon there have been. [Cigarettes] are going to kill ten [of every hundred]." The judge refuses D's request that the jury be instructed that in assessing punitive damages, the jury should not punish D for the impact of its alleged misconduct on other persons, who may bring lawsuits of their own. The jury awards P $821,000 in compensatory damages and $79.5 million in punitive ones.

*Held*, for D, which is entitled to a new trial. "[T]he Constitution's Due Process Clause forbids a State to use a punitive damages award to punish a defendant for injury that it conflicts upon nonparties [who are] strangers to the litigation." That's so because a defendant threatened with punishment for injury to a non-party has no opportunity to respond (e.g., by showing that the other victim is not entitled to damages because she did not rely on the defendant's statements.) Furthermore, permitting punishment for injuring a nonparty victim "would add a near standard-less dimension to the punitive damages equation." *Philip Morris USA, supra.*

**4. Detention of "enemy combatants" who are citizens:** One context in which the Court has made use of the *Mathews* balancing test for determining what process is due is the *detention of "enemy combatants" during war.* In one of the first cases exploring the President's powers in the post-9/11 war on terrorism, the Court held that if a U.S. citizen is to be held as an enemy combatant, he is entitled to due process, including at a minimum the *right to counsel*, and the right to *go before a neutral decisionmaker* to challenge his designation as enemy combatant. *Hamdi v. Rumsfeld*, 542 US. 507 (2004).

   **a. Facts:** The prisoner in *Hamdi* was Yaser Hamdi, an American citizen who was captured in Afghanistan in 2001 by the Northern Alliance, a coalition fighting alongside U.S. troops to oust the Taliban. The Alliance turned Hamdi over to the U.S. military, which labeled him an "enemy combatant" based mostly on the fact that he had been associated with the Taliban and had surrendered his rifle to the Alliance. The military transferred him to a naval brig in South Carolina. The Bush administration asserted that by designating Hamdi as an enemy combatant, the executive branch obtained the power to hold him in confinement indefinitely, without formal charges or proceedings, so long as the war in which he had been seized continued.

**b. Ruling against government:** Although the Court's rationale was badly splintered, eight members of the Court concluded that the U.S. did not in fact have the power that the government contended it had, i.e., the power to hold Hamdi without counsel, without charges and without opportunity for some sort of trial.

    **i. O'Connor's plurality opinion:** Justice O'Connor, writing for herself and three other justices (Rehnquist, Kennedy and Breyer) wrote a plurality opinion concluding that Hamdi had the right to due process, at least with respect to pursuing his claim that he was not in fact an "enemy combatant."[11] In determining to what procedural protections Hamdi was entitled, O'Connor said, the ***balancing test of Mathews v. Eldridge applied.*** That is, the government's interest in the nation's security needed to be balanced against Hamdi's interest in not being deprived of liberty without due process.

        **(1) Government's interest:** O'Connor conceded that the government had a strong interest in "ensuring that those who have in fact fought with the enemy during a war do not return to battle against the United States." She also agreed with the Bush administration that the government's interest in being free to wage a war without the distraction of litigation would be impeded by having to follow a system of trial-like procedures — including discovery into the details of military operations and national defense — before someone captured on the battlefield could be declared an enemy combatant.

        **(2) Citizen's interest:** But Hamdi had strong countervailing interests: the "fundamental nature of a citizen's right to be free from involuntary confinement by his own government without due process of law."

        **(3) Minimum procedures:** O'Connor then spelled out some of the procedural protections to which she believed Hamdi was entitled under the *Mathews* balancing test, if he wished to challenge the correctness of his classification as an enemy combatant:

           ❑ He was entitled to ***"notice of the factual basis* for his classification"** (as an enemy combatant);

           ❑ He was entitled to "a ***fair opportunity*** to ***rebut the government's factual assertions*** before a ***neutral decisionmaker***";

           ❑ He had the right of ***access to counsel*** in connection with the proceedings.

        **(4) Open questions:** But O'Connor also tried not to tie the government's hands unduly. The Court was not being confronted with any particular set of procedures that the government was proposing to use — indeed, the government

---

11. Hamdi claimed that he never bore arms against the United States, that he arrived in Afghanistan to do relief work less than two months before 9/11, and that he was trapped there when the U.S. military campaign began.

was contending that it did not have to use *any* procedures at all, and could simply detain Hamdi indefinitely on its own say so. However, O'Connor speculated about certain respects in which procedures *less protective* than the ones guaranteed for a standard criminal trial might nonetheless *suffice* in Hamdi's upcoming challenge to his status as enemy combatant, due to the need to "alleviate [the proceedings'] uncommon potential to burden the Executive at a time of ongoing military conflict." Here are some of O'Connor's speculations:

❏   *Hearsay* "may need to be *accepted* as the most reliable available evidence from the Government";

❏   The Constitution "would not be offended by a *presumption in favor of the government's evidence,*" as long as that presumption "remained a *rebuttable* one" and as long as "fair opportunity for rebuttal were provided." Thus once the government put forth "credible evidence" that Hamdi was indeed an enemy combatant, the burden could shift to Hamdi to prove the contrary. (In a criminal case, by contrast, the government would have to prove each element of the crime not just by "credible evidence" but by proof beyond a reasonable doubt.)

❏   Whatever procedures are due, they would *not* be due at the moment a citizen was initially captured on the battlefield; instead, the procedures would be due only when the government decided to *continue to hold* those it had captured. (By the time of the Court's decision in *Hamdi*, for instance, Hamdi had already been held for over two years without any kind of hearing.)

❏   Finally, O'Connor said, it was *not* necessarily the case that a *federal district court* would have to be the one to hear Hamdi's challenge to his confinement. Instead, she said, "there remains the *possibility* that the standards we have articulated could be met by an appropriately authorized and properly constituted *military tribunal.*"

ii.   **Souter and Ginsburg concur in judgment:**   Justices Souter and Ginsburg, concurring only in part, disagreed with the plurality's conclusion that Hamdi's detention was authorized at all. But they agreed that if he *was* to be detained, he would certainly have *at least those procedural due process rights that the plurality was willing to give him*. In fact, these two justices indicated that they would give Hamdi even *more* procedural protections than the plurality — for instance, they *disagreed* that the government could be given the benefit of a *presumption* that Hamdi was an enemy combatant, or that litigating the issue before a *military tribunal* might constitutionally substitute for Hamdi's right to bring a habeas corpus petition in federal court.

iii.   **Scalia and Stevens dissent:**   Two additional Justices, Scalia and Stevens, dissented from the Court's basic holding that a citizen could be held in wartime by the executive branch without full recourse to the traditional right to challenge his imprisonment by means of a habeas corpus petition. Therefore, they strongly disagreed with the plurality's suggestion that Hamdi was due something less than the full-dress procedural due process protections given to any other imprisoned citizen. They criticized the plurality's "unheard-of system in which the citizen rather than the Government bears the burden of proof, testimony is by hearsay rather than live witnesses, and the presiding officer may well be a 'neutral' military officer rather than judge and jury."

    **iv. Summary:** So eight members of the Court (all but Thomas) believed that the executive branch could not detain a citizen accused of being an enemy combatant unless the citizen was given *substantial due process protections* to allow him to challenge the enemy-combatant designation — at a minimum, protections like *notice of the details* of the charge, a right to rebut the charge before a n*eutral decisionmaker*, and the *right to counsel*. Indeed, four members of the court (Souter, Ginsburg, Scalia and Stevens) seemed to believe that the *full or nearly-full range of protections* that would be given to any citizen imprisoned while accused of a crime were due to a citizen held on such enemy-combatant charges.

        **(1) Wartime not that different:** *Hamdi* also illustrates that, for the present Court, even the fact that the nation is effectively *at war* will not allow the executive branch to dispense with basic due process requirements when it imprisons one of its own citizens. This marks a quite dramatic turnaround from the view of the World War II court in the 1944 Japanese exclusion case (*Korematsu v. U.S.*, discussed *infra*, p. 261), where the Court held that all citizens of Japanese ancestry on the West Coast could effectively be imprisoned to prevent them from committing espionage and sabotage. As Justice O'Connor put it in her plurality opinion in *Hamdi*, "[A] state of war is *not a blank check for the President* when it comes to the rights of the Nation's citizens."

**5. Legislature's right to limit procedures:** The Court in *Mathews v. Eldridge* (*supra*, p. 216), although it took a limited view of procedural protections, did seem to be applying constitutional criteria in making its decision. But suppose that the *legislature itself*, in creating a statutory entitlement, *attempts to define the procedures* under which the right may be denied or cut off. Do these legislative principles control?

    **a. No right to limit procedures:** The answer is *"no."* Even where the legislature creates the property or liberty interest in question, *it is not free to establish procedures for terminating that right* — " 'Property' cannot be defined by the procedures provided for its deprivation any more than can life or liberty. The right to due process 'is conferred, not by legislative grace, but by constitutional guarantee.' ... [O]nce it is determined that the Due Process Clause applies, 'the question remains what process is due.' ... The answer to that question is not to be found in the ... statute [creating the property right.]" *Cleveland Bd. of Ed. v. Loudermill*, 470 U.S. 532 (1985).

        **i. Application to facts in *Loudermill*:** The plaintiff in *Loudermill* was, under state law, a "classified civil servant," who could only be terminated for cause. The statute setting out this tenure provided for administrative review following discharge, but did not allow for any kind of hearing before termination. As the *Loudermill* Court made clear, the procedures to which the *Loudermill* plaintiff was entitled were to be judged by independent constitutional standards, not merely by whether they complied with the state statutory scheme. Since the constitution requires at least *"some kind of a hearing"* prior to the deprivation of any significant property interest, plaintiff here was denied due process. (But only notice of the charges and some kind of opportunity to respond before termination, not a full evidentiary hearing of the sort found necessary in *Goldberg v. Kelly, supra*, p. 213, before welfare payments may be cut off, were required. This aspect of *Loudermill* is discussed *supra*, p. 217.)

6.  **Educational cases:** Issues about what process is due have surfaced repeatedly in cases involving public ***education***. A brief summary of the Court's major holdings is as follows:

    a.  **Disciplinary suspension:** Where a student is ***suspended*** for disciplinary reasons for more than a trivial period, due process requires that he be given "oral or written notice of the charges against him and, if he denies them, an explanation of the evidence the authorities have and an opportunity to present his side of the story." *Goss v. Lopez*, 419 U.S. 565 (1975). (In *Goss*, a ten-day suspension was held to be clearly more than trivial.)

    b.  **Academic dismissal:** By contrast, where a student is dismissed for ***academic*** (as distinguished from disciplinary) reasons, no hearing is necessary, since this type of decision is more subjective, and less suited to formal judicial or administrative decision making. *Board of Curators v. Horowitz*, 435 U.S. 78 (1978) (involving dismissal of a medical student because of poor clinical performance and personal hygiene).

7.  **Rationales for due process:** The Supreme Court's cases on what process is due reflect strongly the notion that the principal reason for procedural safeguards is to ***prevent inaccurate decisions***. This notion implies that if the means by which a decision is made does not introduce an unacceptably high risk of error, the procedure is valid, no matter how little chance to participate is given the adversely-affected individual.

    a.  **Participation and explanation:** But a number of commentators have argued that a separate, quite distinct, value should be furthered by procedural safeguards: the right of the individual to have his ***autonomy respected***, by being permitted to ***participate in the decision***, and by receiving a ***reasoned explanation*** of adverse conduct. See Tribe, p. 713, and Rabin, 44 U. CHI. L. REV. 74-79 (quoted in L,K&C, p. 646-47). See also Van Alstyne, 62 CORNELL L. REV. 483 (quoted in Tribe, *loc. cit.*), urging the recognition of "***freedom from arbitrary adjudicative procedures***" as a substantive element of one's liberty."

        i.  **Significance:** These three commentators all share the view that procedures in which the individual participates are an ***end in themselves***, not merely a means to assure correct decisions.

        ii. **Not likely to be accepted:** However, nothing in the Supreme Court's decisions suggest any likelihood that this "procedure as an end in itself" approach is likely to prevail in the near future.

---

*Quiz Yourself on*
## *PROCEDURAL DUE PROCESS*

29. The town of Corinth advertised an opening for a position as secretary to the City Clerk. The ad described the job briefly, and said nothing about the criteria that would be used to fill it. Jane Brown applied for the job. She was given a typing test, and then an interview with George Crako, the City Clerk. Crako chose

somebody else for the job. Brown asked for a statement of why she didn't get the job, but the Clerk's office refused to respond.

Brown later heard from the grapevine that Crako had told someone else in the department that he thought Brown was probably the best at performing the technical tasks, but that he had declined to hire her because he had heard she was gay. Brown, who was not gay, realized that Crako was probably thinking of another member of the community, Jane Browne, who was widely known to be gay. Brown asked for a hearing at which she could present what she called "information which would cause the Clerk to reverse his decision," but town officials again refused. Brown has now sued, arguing that the procedures used to fill the opening deprived her of her Fourteenth Amendment due process rights. Should the court find in Brown's favor? _____

30. Tenant, a single mother who was receiving Welfare, resided in a public housing project owned by the city of Pretoria. She had lived in the building for over 10 years, pursuant to a series of two-year leases. The rules of the housing project, posted on a bulletin board in the complex, stated that "customarily, residents who are well behaved and current on all of their obligations will be offered the opportunity to renew their leases upon their expiration." There is no statute or other body of state or local law bearing on whether one in Tenant's position is entitled, as a contractual matter, to a renewal. At the end of Tenant's current two-year term, she was not offered the opportunity to renew her lease. Instead, the apartment was given to a woman who turned out to be the niece of Pretoria's Buildings Commissioner, who would not have been given an apartment had the ordinary informal allocation procedures that had previously been followed in the housing project been followed here. Tenant was at no time given an explanation for why she wasn't permitted to renew, or a hearing regarding the decision.

**(a)** If Tenant wishes to challenge the city's handling of her tenancy on constitutional grounds, what is the strongest argument she can make? _____

**(b)** Will this argument succeed? _____

31. Netsville High School, a public high school, was known for its strong boys' and girls' tennis teams. The administration caused to be published in the school newspaper an invitation for tryouts. This invitation included the following sentence: "All students in good academic standing have the right to compete for the 7 spots on each team. These spots will be awarded to the best players." Priscilla, a high school freshman, had not been on the team previously. However, she had had some strong results in non-school tournaments the summer before her freshman year. During tryouts, the head coach watched Priscilla play only briefly. He very quickly reached the conclusion that her game was not mature enough to make her a varsity player. After one day of practice, he cut her from the team. He did not give her any statement of reasons, or opportunity to present her view of why she should make the team; he merely stated that she was "not good enough." The coach awarded team spots exclusively to those who had been on the team in prior years, including at least one girl whom Priscilla had soundly beaten in a non-school tournament the summer before. Priscilla has sued the school board, arguing that the procedures by which she was dropped from the team violated her due process rights to be awarded a post if she was one of the "best players."

Assuming that Priscilla can demonstrate that most tennis coaches would have found her to be one of the seven strongest players trying out for the team, should the judge order the coach to reconsider her status? _____

---

*Answers*

**29. No.** The Fourteenth Amendment's Due Process Clause only prevents the government from depriving a person of "***life***, ***liberty***, or ***property*** without due process of law." Unless Brown can show that she had a "liberty" or "property" interest that was impaired, she will not even get to the point of being allowed to show that fair procedures were not followed. In other words, the Due Process Clause does not bar the government from procedural irregularities per se, only procedural irregularities in connection with the taking of life, liberty or property. It is very clear that a person applying for an initial government position has no liberty or property interest in the position, so the government may turn the applicant down for totally arbitrary or irrational reasons (so long as the reasons are not themselves violations of independently-guaranteed constitutional rights, such as refusing to hire a person because she is, say, black). So the fact that the Clerk's decision was completely "wrong," in the sense that he had the wrong person in mind, is completely irrelevant. We never get to the question of what type of process (e.g., right to a statement of reasons, or right to a hearing) would have been due.

30. **(a) That it violated her right not to have her "property" taken without due process, and that this right included the right to a hearing.**

    **(b) Yes, probably.** The core issue is whether Tenant had a ***"property" interest*** in her apartment. The Court has held that even ***informal practices or customs*** may be sufficient to create a ***legitimate claim of entitlement*** to a benefit. See, e.g., *Perry v. Sindermann* (in which a college was found to have created a de facto tenure program that created in P, a college professor, the "understanding" that he would be entitled to tenure). Here, the statement regarding the customary right of renewal was probably enough to create in Tenant such a legitimate claim of entitlement to renew, in view of the lack of any other law bearing on whether Tenant did indeed have such a right. (If there were a statute or body of case law holding that as a matter of state law there is no right to renew despite a seeming indication to the contrary in a housing project's rules and regulations, then this body of state law would be dispositive, and Tenant would not have any "property" interest.)

    If Tenant indeed had a legitimate entitlement to being allowed to renew provided that she was in good standing, then she was presumably entitled to at least a hearing before this property interest could be taken away. (The precise procedures that would have to followed are not clear, but for a right as important as the right to continue to live in subsidized housing, it is likely that some sort of hearing and statement of reasons, however informal, would be required.)

31. **No, probably.** The facts are enough to establish that Priscilla indeed probably had a "property" interest (albeit a weak one) in being awarded a spot if she was in fact one of the best seven players. That is, the notice in the newspaper probably was sufficient to constitute a binding offer on the part of the school to award a place to anyone who tried out and proved that she was indeed among the seven best players, and this contract was enough to give rise to a "property" interest. However, the case really turns on exactly what procedures were "due" to Priscilla when it came time to determine whether she was in fact one of the seven best players. The Supreme Court uses a ***balancing test*** for deciding whether a particular set of procedures should be required once a property interest (or liberty interest) is at stake. On one side is placed the amount at stake for the individual, multiplied by the likelihood that administrative error will be reduced by using the procedure in question; on the other side is the cost to the government of granting that procedure.

    Here, the amount at stake for Priscilla is relatively weak, compared with, say, the right to continue receiving welfare benefits or the right to keep one's job. The likelihood that "administrative errors" would be reduced by requiring, say, a statement of reasons before anyone is cut, or a right to present one's case, is relatively small — a coach would still have to be the decision-maker, and that decision would still be based principally on what the coach saw, so that a hearing and statement of reasons are unlikely to reduce error by much. Conversely, there is a substantial cost to the government (here, the school board) in having to set up detailed, judicially-challengeable procedures for awarding every spot on an athletic team. Consequently, the court is very likely to decide that such litigation-like procedures as a statement of reasons and an opportunity to present one's case are not worth their cost.

(On the other hand, probably an applicant who has a property interest in being allowed to compete for a spot on the team at least has the right to marginally "fair" procedures, so that, for instance, an applicant who could show that the coach favored the coach's own child or own private-coaching pupils might be able to show that her procedural rights had been violated.)

## Exam Tips *on* DUE PROCESS OF LAW

In virtually any fact pattern where an individual or company is not permitted to do something, you must be alert to the possibility that there is a ***due process*** violation. A large portion of all complex-fact-pattern essay questions will raise at least one due process issue. Here are the most important things to keep in mind:

☛ Determine whether it is an issue of ***substantive*** DP or ***procedural*** DP that you're faced with.

   ☞ In a ***substantive*** DP problem, the government is completely taking away a whole group's ability to do something, and there is no issue of whether the particular plaintiff falls into the governmentally-defined group or not. (*Example:* The state says, "No woman may have an abortion after the third month of pregnancy." If the facts make it clear that P is a woman who is four months pregnant, we have a substantive DP problem, not a procedural DP problem.)

   ☞ In a ***procedural*** DP problem, the overall issue is whether P as an individual does or does not fit into the legislatively-defined group, and the sub-issue is what if any individualized, case-specific, procedures must be followed before the government can determine which group P falls into. (*Example:* A city says, "Public school teachers may only be fired for acts of moral turpitude." If there is an issue about whether P did or did not commit such an act, then we're dealing with procedural due process, i.e., the procedures used to determine whether P did or did not commit such an act.)

☛ If you're dealing with a ***substantive*** DP problem, decide immediately whether the right at issue is ***fundamental*** or non-fundamental.

   ☞ Remember that the only rights that are fundamental for substantive DP purposes are those that involve the ***"right of privacy"*** or ***"right of autonomy."*** The key examples are:

      ☞ The right to ***marry***.

      ☞ The right to ***bear*** (or decide ***not*** to bear) ***children***.

      ☞ The right to decide how to ***rear*** one's children.

☞ Perhaps the right to decline **unwanted medical treatment** (and possibly the right to **commit suicide** if competent and terminally ill).

☞ Possibly, the right to control one's **dress** and **personal appearance**.

☞ If you conclude that the right is "fundamental," state that the court must **strictly scrutinize** the regulation. The state **bears the burden** of defending its regulation. The state loses unless **both** the following are true:

☞ The state is pursing a **"compelling"** (not just "legitimate") objective; and

☞ The means chosen by the state are **"necessary"** to achieve that compelling end. (If there are **less restrictive means** that would do the job just as well, or almost as well, then the means chosen aren't "necessary.")

☞ By contrast, if you conclude that the right involved is **non-fundamental**, then state that **"mere rationality"** review is used. That is, it just has to be the case that the state is:

☞ Pursuing a **legitimate governmental objective**; and

☞ Doing so with a means that is **rationally related** to that objective.

☞ If the government regulation is essentially **economic**, you should almost certainly conclude that the rights involved are non-fundamental, and apply mere rationality. The same is true of most health, safety or other "social welfare" legislation — unless it treads on one of those narrow areas (marriage, child-bearing, child-rearing, "right-to-die"), it's non-fundamental, and you should be using "mere rationality" review.

☞ Be sure to distinguish between the **Fifth** Amendment's DP Clause and the **Fourteenth** Amendment's DP Clause. If the regulation is imposed by the **federal** government, the relevant clause is the Fifth Amendment. If the regulating is being done by a state or local government, the Fourteenth Amendment is the relevant one.

☞ Here's an overview of some of the most testable issues relating to the substantive due process protection given to **fundamental** rights:

☞ Most regulations restricting access to **contraception** will be strictly scrutinized and will fail. However, it is not clear that **minors** have a substantive DP right to birth control without parental consent — this makes a good testable issue.

☞ A pregnant woman's interest in **abortion**, of course, gets some substantive DP protection. Your professor will expect you to know that this is so, as a general proposition. The particular sub-issues she is likely to test you on are:

☞ Whether the state may require that the woman's **spouse** be given notice prior to the abortion (the answer is *"no"*);

☞ Whether a **minor** may be required to have **parental consent** (the answer is generally *"yes,"* but there must be a "judicial bypass" offered as an alternative); and

☞ Whether **late-term** abortions may be tightly regulated (the answer generally seems to be *"yes"*).

*Note*: In general, when you're analyzing an abortion problem, remember to say that as a result of *Planned Parenthood v. Casey*, the standard is whether the regulation ***"unduly burdens"*** the woman's interest in deciding whether to have the baby or not. Also, in any case involving regulations on the abortion process (rather than outright bans), mention that under the recent *Gonzales v. Carhart* partial-birth-method decision, the Court has grown more likely to uphold regulations that are justifiable by a desire to spare the woman from later regret about her decision to use a particular method.

☞ If the regulation interferes with ***sexual*** activities, distinguish between interferences with the rights of ***married*** couples, and virtually all other types of sex.

    ☞ Thus if your facts involve a government attempt to make certain practices unlawful when practiced between members of a ***married*** couple in ***private***, you should usually be applying strict scrutiny, and you should conclude that the interference violates substantive DP.

    ☞ Where the activity consists of ***homosexual sex***, you should conclude that (1) the activity is ***not*** "fundamental," and the regulation is therefore not to be strictly scrutinized; but that (2) the ***"mere rationality"*** review that's used should have real ***"bite,"*** and should be used to ***strike down*** as "irrational" any regulation that seems motivated solely by the majority's ***"moral disapproval."***

    **Example:** If government bans "sodomy" in a way that restricts gay sexual activity, say that even under mere-rationality review the measure must be struck down as an irrational substantive due process violation of the right to sexual expression. Cite to *Lawrence v. Texas*.

    ☞ If the activity consists of sex between ***unmarried heterosexual*** adults (or adults who are married but not to each other), again conclude that the activity is not fundamental, and the regulation is therefore not to be strictly scrutinized (and is to be given "mere rationality" review). But allude to the possibility that it may be struck down anyway under this mere-rationality review, as reflecting just the majority's irrational "moral disapproval." Cite to *Lawrence v. Texas* for this point.

    ☞ If the activity is by unmarried ***minors***, it is especially clear that it is not "fundamental," and may be extensively regulated (or probably even forbidden) by the state.

☞ If the state has placed restrictions on a person's right to decline ***unwanted medical attention***, say that a fundamental interest is probably at stake.

    ☞ If the state is declining to honor a properly-prepared ***living will*** or ***health care proxy*** (delegating the health care decision to another person if the patient is incompetent), conclude that the state is violating substantive DP.

    ☞ But where there is no living will or health care proxy, and the patient is incompetent, the state does ***not*** violate substantive DP by setting very high ***evidentiary standards*** before concluding that the medical care is really unwanted. Cite to the *Cruzan* case in this kind of situation (where the Court held that the state may require "clear and convincing evidence" that the incompetent really would not have wanted the medical attention).

☞ If the patient is terminally ill (and competent) and the issue is whether a relative or doctor may ***assist in the patient's suicide***, indicate that whatever due process interest the patient may have in committing suicide is certainly ***not fundamental***, and that the state's countervailing interest in preventing the suicide is stronger. Therefore, the state ***may make it a crime*** to attempt suicide, or to assist another in committing suicide.

☞ Here are some other contexts where you might find that fundamental interests are being impaired in violation of substantive DP:

☞ The state has impaired parties' right to ***get married*** to each other (e.g., by disallowing marriage until one party pays some fine or satisfies a back obligation like child support — see *Zablocki v. Redhail*).

☞ Relatives are being prevented from ***living together*** (e.g., by restrictive ***zoning*** rules such as the no-cousins rule in *Moore v. East Cleveland*).

☞ Parents are being deprived of freedom to choose how their child is to be ***educated*** (e.g., a state statute banning home-study or private-school education, or unduly restricting these alternatives) or how the child is to be ***raised at home*** (e.g., a state court order compelling a mother to give lengthy visitation rights to the child's paternal grandparents).

☞ Adults are unfairly restricted in their attempts to ***adopt*** a child (e.g., by a requirement that the ***race*** of the parent and child, or the ***religion*** of the parent and child, ***match***).

☞ Whenever you have government denying a person a job, license, benefit, etc., consider whether the individual was entitled to ***procedural due process***, and if so, whether the requirements of procedural DP were complied with.

☞ First, make sure that there is ***government action*** in the denial. (*Example:* If the facts tell you that a private employer is firing someone, you never get to the issue of procedural due process because there is no state action.)

☞ Next, check to make sure that what is being denied is ***"life," "liberty"*** or ***"property."***

☞ You'll never have to worry about "life" being taken unless your fact pattern deals with the death penalty in criminal cases.

☞ Here are some typical situations where "liberty" is at stake:

☞ P is deprived of the right to ***drive***;

☞ P is denied a ***license*** that she needs in order to practice her profession (e.g., law, medicine, accounting, teaching, or even truck-driving or tour-guiding);

☞ P is deprived of the right to ***raise his family***, because of charges of child abuse or neglect.

☞ Most commonly, though, you'll see fact patterns suggesting that *"property"* may have been taken.

   ☞ Many situations involve government *benefits*. If you are *already* getting the benefit, the government is probably depriving you of a "property" interest if it tries to *terminate* the benefit. On the other hand, if you are first *applying* for the benefit, then you probably do not yet have a property interest, so the government probably does not have to use procedural DP — it can arbitrarily or irrationally reject your application.

   ☞ Here are some typical kinds of government benefits that pop up on exam questions:

      ❑ receipt of *welfare* payments;

      ❑ right to occupy *public housing*;

      ❑ right to take certain *courses* in public school, or to participate in *extracurricular activities* sponsored by the public school.

   ☞ Remember that a key part of the analysis is whether state law, or perhaps even government custom, gives P a *"legitimate claim of entitlement"* to have the benefit continue. (*Example:* If a statute, regulation or even an informal document like a benefit handbook indicates the circumstances under which a particular benefit will be granted or continued, then a person is likely to have a "property" interest in the benefit on the terms provided in the statute, regulation, etc.)

   ☞ When you're dealing with a state or local government *job*, the same analysis applies: if you've already got the job, you may or may not have a "legitimate claim of entitlement" to it (depending on what state law says about how and when you can be fired). If you do have a legitimate claim of entitlement, then you have a "property" interest that can only be taken away by complying with procedural DP. If you don't have a legitimate claim, then you have no procedural DP rights either.

   ☞ If P's claim is that government owed P a duty to *protect P from some private third-party's bad deeds*, probably P did *not* have a property or liberty interest in receiving that help from government, even if some statute required government to give that help. (*Example*: A statute says that police "shall arrest" anyone who violates a protective order. P asks the police to protect her by arresting her husband, H, who has just violated such an order. The police refuse, giving H the chance to murder P's children. P has not been deprived of a property or liberty interest. *Castle Rock v. Gonzales.*)

☞ If you've decided that P has a "property" or "liberty" interest that is being taken away, you know that P is entitled to some sort of procedural DP. Now, you must decide exactly *what procedures* are due to P.

   ☞ Here, remember to do a *balancing* test: for each procedural safeguard that may or may not be due, weigh the state's interest in making a prompt disposition against the damage to P in being denied the safeguard. (*Example:* If P is a school teacher who is suspended based on suspicions that he has sexually abused a student, P's interest in being given a formal hearing with counsel *before* the suspension is clearly outweighed by the system's need to get him out of the classroom quickly. By contrast, where the state wants to cut off P's welfare benefits, he's probably entitled to a hearing before any suspension, because the cost to the state of a delay is not very great, and the damage to P from an erroneous determination would be great.)

☞ If P has been awarded *punitive damages* against D, consider the possibility that the award is so excessive (or so inappropriately takes account of harm done by D to persons not present in the litigation) that the award violates D's due process rights.

☞ Some of the procedural safeguards that you should consider are (in ascending order of the burden that they typically put on the state):

❑ the right to receive a *statement of reasons* why the benefit is being cut off;

❑ the right to a *hearing* at which P can plead her case;

❑ the right to have *counsel present* at the hearing;

❑ the right to *appeal* the adverse decision to a higher body.

In general, you should conclude that P has the right to counsel and appeal only where the proceedings are criminal or quasi-criminal, but you should be relatively quick to conclude that P has a right to a statement of reasons or a hearing, even in a non-criminal situation such as loss of a job or loss of a financial benefit.

CHAPTER 10

# EQUAL PROTECTION

*ChapterScope*

The Equal Protection Clause is part of the Fourteenth Amendment. It provides that "no state shall make or enforce any law which shall … deny to any person within its jurisdiction equal protection of the laws." Here are the key concepts concerning equal protection:

■ **Classifications:** The Clause imposes a *general* restraint on the governmental use of *classifications*, not just classifications based on race but also those based on sex, alienage, illegitimacy, wealth, or any other characteristic.

■ **Federal government:** The direct text of the Clause applies only to state governments. But the *federal* government is also bound by the same rules of equal protection — the Fifth Amendment's Due Process Clause is interpreted to bar the federal government from making any classification that would be a violation of the Equal Protection Clause if done by a state.

■ **Government action only:** The Equal Protection Clause (and the Fifth Amendment's Due Process Clause) apply *only to government action*, not to action by private citizens. This is the requirement of *"state action."*

■ **"As applied" vs. "facial":** There are two different types of attacks a plaintiff may make on a classification:

❏ **Facial:** If P attacks a classification that is clearly written into the statute or regulation, he is saying that the statute or regulation violates equal protection *"on its face."*

❏ **"As applied":** If P's claim is that the statute/regulation does not make a classification on its face, but is being *administered* in a purposefully discriminatory way, then he is claiming that the statute/regulation is a violation of equal protection *"as applied."*

■ **What the Clause guarantees:** The Clause in essence guarantees that *people who are similarly situated will be treated similarly*.

■ **Three levels of review:** There are three levels of review that are used in judging whether governmental classifications violate the Equal Protection Clause:

❏ **Strict scrutiny:** At one end of the spectrum, the Court gives *"strict scrutiny"* to any statute that is based on a "suspect classification" or that impairs a "fundamental right." Where strict scrutiny is invoked, the classification will be upheld only if it is *necessary* to promote a *compelling* governmental interest. The three suspect classes are *race*, *national origin* and (for some purposes) *alienage*. The rights that are "fundamental" are principally the right to *vote*, the right to have access to the *courts*, and the right to *migrate interstate*.

❏ **Middle-level review:** In a few situations, the Court uses a *middle level* of review, less demanding than "strict scrutiny." This level is used for *"semi-suspect"* classifications, i.e., those based on *gender* and *illegitimacy*. Under mid-level review, the means chosen by the legislature (i.e., the classification) must be *substantially related* to an *important* governmental objective.

❏ **Ordinary "mere rationality" review:** At the easiest-to-satisfy end of the spectrum, we have the "mere rationality" standard. This standard applies to all classifications that are not based on a "suspect" or "semi-suspect" classification (i.e., that do not involve race, national origin, alienage, gender or legitimacy) and do not impair a "fundamental right" (i.e., do not impair the right to vote, access the courts or migrate interstate). Under this standard, the classification will be upheld so long as it is conceivable that the classification bears a ***rational relationship*** to a ***legitimate*** governmental objective. Almost every classification survives this easy review.

  ❏ **Economic regulation:** Almost every ***economic*** and ***tax*** classification is reviewed under this easy standard.

■ **Suspect classifications:** When a classification involves a ***suspect class*** (race, national origin and, for some purposes, alienage), here are the key features of how courts do their review:

❏ **Purposeful:** Strict scrutiny will only be applied where the differential treatment of the class is ***intentional*** on the part of the government. If the government enacts a statute or regulation that merely has the unintended incidental ***effect*** of burdening, say, blacks worse than whites, the Court will ***not*** use strict scrutiny.

❏ **Strict equals fatal:** Once the Court decides that a suspect classification is involved and that strict scrutiny must be used, the scrutiny is almost always ***fatal*** to the classification scheme. For instance, only one purposeful racial or ethnic classification has survived strict scrutiny by the Supreme Court since 1944.

❏ **Segregation:** The clearest example of a classification involving a suspect class and thus requiring strict scrutiny is ***segregation***, the maintenance of physical separation between the races. Official, intentional segregation based on race or national origin is a violation of the Equal Protection Clause.

■ **Race-conscious affirmative action:** Government programs that attempt to ***assist*** racial or ethnic ***minorities*** (i.e., ***affirmative action*** programs), and that do so in an explicitly race- or ethnically-conscious way, are strictly scrutinized just the same as those that purposefully ***disadvantage*** minorities.

■ **Gender:** ***Sex-based*** classifications get ***middle-level review***. If government intentionally classifies on the basis of sex, government must show that it is pursuing an ***important*** objective, and that the sex-based classification scheme is ***substantially related*** to that objective.

❏ **Benign as well as invidious:** The same standard of review is used whether the sex-based classification is "invidious" (intended to harm women) or ***"benign"*** (intended to help women, or even intended to redress past discrimination against them).

■ **Illegitimacy:** Classifications disadvantaging ***illegitimate*** children are "semi-suspect" and therefore get middle-level review.

■ **Alienage:** Alienage classifications are subjected either to ***strict scrutiny*** or to ***mere rationality*** review, depending on the circumstances.

❏ **General rule:** Usually, discrimination against aliens is subject to ***strict scrutiny.***

❏ **"Representative government" exception:** But strict scrutiny does not apply where the discrimination against aliens relates to a ***"function at the heart of representative govern-***

*ment."* This means that government may discriminate against aliens with respect to *jobs* that are closely tied in with politics, justice or public policy, including posts like state trooper, public school teacher or probation officer.

■ **Fundamental rights:** There will be strict scrutiny not only when a "suspect classification" is used, but also when a *"fundamental right"* is burdened by the classification selected by the government. Whenever a classification burdens a "fundamental right," the classification will be subjected to strict scrutiny *even though the people who are burdened are not members of a suspect class*.

&#10063; **Voting:** The right to *vote* in state and local elections is "fundamental," so any classification burdening that right will be strictly scrutinized (e.g., a poll tax, or an unduly long residency requirement before voting is allowed).

&#10063; **Court access:** Access to the *courts* is sometimes a "fundamental right." For instance, if the state imposes a *fee* that the rich can pay but the poor cannot, and the access relates to a *criminal case*, strict scrutiny is used. (*Example:* The state must give an indigent in a criminal case a free trial transcript, and free counsel on appeal.)

&#10063; **Right to travel:** The *"right to travel"* — which is really the right to *change one's state of residence or employment* — is "fundamental."

    &#10063; **Duration of residence:** Thus if the state imposes a substantial *waiting period* on newly-arrived residents, before they can receive some *vital governmental benefit* (e.g., *welfare* payments), the scheme will be strictly scrutinized.

&#10063; **Necessities:** There is no fundamental right to material *"necessities of life."* Thus *food, shelter and medical care* are not "fundamental," and the state may distribute these things unevenly. Similarly, one does not have a fundamental right to a *public school education*; therefore, the state may impose inequalities in the distribution of that education, without having to pass strict scrutiny.

# I. INTRODUCTION

A. **Historical overview:** The Fourteenth Amendment provides that "[n]o State shall make or enforce any law which shall … deny to any person within its jurisdiction the equal protection of the laws."

1. **Historical purpose:** This Clause, like all parts of the Thirteenth, Fourteenth and Fifteenth Amendments, was enacted shortly after the Civil War, and its primary goal was to secure free and equal treatment for ex-slaves. But from the beginning, the courts interpreted the Clause to "impose a *general* restraint on the use of classifications, whatever the area regulated, whatever the classification criterion used." Gunther (10th Ed.), p. 676.

2. **Clause before Warren Court:** Prior to the Warren Court, the Equal Protection Clause played only a very minor role with respect to classifications based on grounds other than race and national origin. So long as the *means* used by the legislature (i.e., the classification) *reasonably related* to the legislature's purpose, the statute was upheld. Very little attention was paid to whether the legislature's purpose was itself valid. Gunther & Sullivan (13th Ed.), p. 629.

a. **Contrast with due process:** Contrast this limited view of the Equal Protection Clause with the broad reading given to the Due Process Clause during the early part of this century (see *supra*, p. 148). The Court was much more likely to strike an economic or social-welfare statute on substantive due process grounds than on the grounds that the classifications made in the statute denied equal protection.

3. **Key clause in Warren Court:** But under the *Warren Court*, the Equal Protection Clause gained new "bite," and became the most important clause for ensuring a broad range of individual rights against legislative encroachment.

    a. **Strict scrutiny:** The principal way in which the Clause gained new vitality in the Warren years was by means of a broadened view of when a statutory classification should be subjected to "*strict scrutiny*," i.e., a scrutiny more demanding than the "mere rationality" test generally applied in earlier years. Whereas pre-Warren Courts applied strict scrutiny only to statutes classifying on the grounds of race or national origin, the Warren Court was willing to impose strict scrutiny wherever either the classification was a "*suspect*" one (because it discriminated against a politically powerless or unpopular minority) or that classification had an impact on a "*fundamental right*" or interest. Once strict scrutiny was applied to a particular law, the law would be upheld only if it was *necessary to achieve a compelling* governmental interest.

    b. **Suspect classification:** In actual fact, the Warren Court found only race and national origin to be suspect classifications. But there were hints that other classifications might also be subjected to some sort of heightened review (e.g., illegitimacy). Sullivan & Gunther, p. 642.

    c. **"Fundamental rights":** The real change made by the Warren Court was in the development of the "*fundamental rights*" branch of strict scrutiny. If the Court concluded that a statute had a material impact on a fundamental right or interest, it subjected the statute to strict scrutiny, even though the classification itself was not "suspect." The grounds by which the Warren Court determined that an interest was "fundamental" were never quite clear; the actual list of such fundamental rights seemed to be restricted principally to the areas of *voting, criminal appeals* and *interstate travel*. Sullivan & Gunther, p. 642.

4. **Burger/Rehnquist Court:** The *Burger/Rehnquist Court* has *not* made wholesale cutbacks in the Warren equal protection approach. But the present Court has *declined to expand* the Warren doctrine in the ways that Warren-era opinions suggested might ultimately evolve. For instance, neither the list of classifications deemed "suspect" nor the list of fundamental rights has been materially broadened. (But where a classification is deemed by the Warren Court to be "suspect" or to involve a fundamental right, the Burger/Rehnquist Court's scrutiny does seem to be quite strict.[1])

    a. **Middle-level scrutiny:** The most interesting development during the Burger/Rehnquist years has been the emergence of what is sometimes called "*middle-level*" or

---

1. Race-conscious affirmative action in *university admissions* seems to be the one exception to this general rule that Burger/Rehnquist strict scrutiny is quite strict. Although the Rehnquist court says that it is applying standard strict scrutiny to such race-conscious schemes, most observers believe that the scrutiny used in *Grutter v. Bollinger, infra*, p. 282, was significantly less stringent in fact than the Court has applied in other cases where the strict-scrutiny label was used.

"*intermediate-level*" scrutiny. Most clearly in the area of gender-based classifications, but also probably in the areas of *illegitimacy* and *alienage* classifications, statutes are not subjected to strict scrutiny, but are given a scrutiny more rigorous than the extreme deference with which general economic and social-welfare classifications are treated.

    **i.   Not formally labeled:** No majority of the Burger/Rehnquist Court has ever formally admitted that it is following a middle level of scrutiny in these situations. But a number of times the Court has stated its standard of review in terms that clearly suggest such an intermediate level of review. See, e.g., *Craig v. Boren,* discussed *infra,* p. 323.

  **b.   Lowest level has some "bite":** Also, *occasionally*, even the so-called "mere rationality" or lowest-level of review has *some bite* under the Burger/Rehnquist Court, as it almost never did in previous Courts. Thus a statute will occasionally be found to be so completely lacking in rationality that, even when viewed under a mere rationality standard, it violates equal protection. See, e.g., *Lawrence v. Texas* (striking down anti-sodomy laws as irrational, under the due process clause), *supra,* p. 185.

**B.  Operation of the Clause:** The following is a broad summary of the present operation of the Equal Protection Clause:

  **1.  State and federal actions:** The guarantee of equal protection applies to actions by *both* the *state* and *federal* governments. However, the federal guarantee comes from a distinct source.

    **a.  State and local governments:** The Equal Protection Clause of the Fourteenth Amendment itself applies only to *state and local governments* ("[n]o state shall deny … "). Local governments are deemed to be subdivisions of the state, and therefore fall within the ban.

    **b.  Federal government:** Nothing in the Constitution explicitly requires that the federal government provide equal protection of the laws. But where the federal government makes a classification which, if it were by a state, would violate the Fourteenth Amendment's Equal Protection Clause, the Court has treated this as a violation of the Fifth Amendment's Due Process Clause (a clause which is, of course, directly applicable to the federal government.) See, e.g., *Bolling v. Sharpe,* 347 U.S. 497 (1954). See also N&R, pp. 595-597.

      **i.   Special rule for Congress:** The normal rule is that equal protection standards are *identical* for the federal and state governments, so that a federal action which would constitute a violation of equal protection if done by the state will also be a Fifth Amendment Due Process violation. However, the present Court seems willing to grant *acts of Congress* slightly greater deference than acts of state legislatures, in two areas: classifications burdening *aliens* (because of Congress' authority to determine the conditions of immigration) and classifications relating to the *military* (because of the federal government's war power.)

  **2.  Applies only to making of classes:** The Equal Protection Clause prevents governments from making improper classifications. What makes a classification "proper" is, of course, the subject of this Chapter. But it should be noted that if a classification scheme is proper, the issue of *which class a particular individual belongs in* is *not* an equal protection matter. Instead, this will be a matter of statutory interpretation and, possibly, the Due Process

Clause. The Equal Protection Clause itself applies only to the **making** of the classifications, not to the adjudication of individual situations. N&R, p. 597.

   a.  **Caveat:**  But a statute which, on its face, does not draw any classifications may nonetheless be **applied** in a way that indicates that classes **are in fact being drawn** in the **administrative process**. In such a situation, the courts will examine the administratively-derived classifications just as they would review ones which were apparent on the face of the statute.

   **Example:** Suppose that a state passes a statute instituting a literacy test for voters in statewide elections. Even though the statute does not draw any impermissible classifications on its face, if it is applied by local officials in a way that purposefully discriminates against blacks (i.e., treats blacks as one class and whites as another, and penalizes the former), the Equal Protection Clause is violated. But a court review of the determination that a **particular voter** is in fact illiterate would be carried out pursuant to the Due Process Clause, not the Equal Protection Clause.

3.  **"As applied" vs. "facial" attacks:**  Notice that in the above "Caveat," we referred to how a statute is "applied." This points up the need to make an important distinction between **"as applied"** attacks on statutes and **"facial"** attacks. (The distinction exists for all sorts of attacks on statutes, but here, we're concentrating on the Equal Protection Clause, so we'll use illustrations involving that Clause.)

If P attacks a classification that is clearly written into the statute or regulation, he is claiming that Equal Protection is violated by the statute or regulation **"on its face,"** without the need to examine how it is applied to P. If P's claim is that the statute does not make a classification on its face, but is being **administered** in a purposefully discriminatory way, then he is claiming that the statute or regulation is a violation of equal protection **"as applied."**

   **Example:** A statute that says "you must be a citizen to vote" creates a classification scheme "on its face" — citizens vs. non-citizens. P might therefore attack this statute on its face, arguing that the classification written into the language of the statute is always invalid, i.e., invalid without reference to how it is applied in any particular concrete situation, such as P's own situation.

   By contrast, if P claims that in actual administration, blacks are required to prove citizenship but whites are not, then his equal protection claim would be on the statute "as applied."

   a.  **Same standards for both:**  Either kind of attack — facial or "as applied" — may be made. Both follow essentially the same principles. For instance, if no suspect classification or fundamental right is involved, the classification scheme will violate the Equal Protection Clause if it's not rationally related to a legitimate state objective, whether the scheme is on the face of the statute or merely in the way the statute is applied.

   b.  **Why distinction matters:**  However, it is considerably **harder for P to prevail with a facial attack.** When P makes an "as applied" attack, P can win if P can show that the statute cannot constitutionally be applied *against P* — the fact that the statute could be constitutionally applied to some other hypothetical person or situation won't save it from being found invalid in P's suit. By contrast, at least in theory, if P makes a facial attack, P can generally win only if P shows that there are **no circumstances in which the statute is valid.** See *U.S. v. Salerno*, 481 U.S. 739 (1987) ("A facial challenge to a legislative Act is, of course, the most difficult challenge to mount successfully, since the challenger must establish that no set of circumstances exists under which the Act would be valid.") [2]

4. **What the Clause guarantees:** The Equal Protection Clause, at bottom, guarantees two things: (1) that people who are similarly situated will be treated similarly; and (2) that people who are *not* similarly situated will not be treated similarly. Tribe, p. 1438.

> **Examples:** As an example of a violation of (1), consider intentional racial segregation in the public schools — this is a failure to treat people who are similarly situated (blacks and whites, at least with respect to public education, though perhaps not with respect to, say, sickle-cell anemia) similarly to each other. As an example of a violation of (2), consider Tribe's (p. 1438) hypothetical statute requiring voters to come to the polls personally regardless of their physical capacity to do so — Tribe suggests that this would be a denial of the equal protection right of the handicapped to be treated differently with respect to voting.

    a. **Difficulty of establishing (2):** Most successful equal protection challenges involve a violation of (1), that is, a refusal to treat similarly-situated persons similarly. In any given situation, there may be, but there is not necessarily, a requirement of (2), that is, that the government treat *differently*-situated persons differently. Most claims that wealth/poverty classifications (*infra*, p. 370) violate equal protection are claims of this variety, i.e., claims that the government's demand for payment for goods or services (e.g., poll taxes) or its refusal to pay for benefits (e.g., appellate transcripts for indigent defendants) fail to treat rich and poor differently. However, claims of this (2) type have been hard to raise successfully; in the wealth/poverty area, for instance, such claims have been sustained only where certain narrowly-defined "fundamental rights" are impaired. See Tribe, p. 1439, n. 19.

5. **Must look at statute's objectives:** What does it mean to say that two persons are "similarly situated" or "differently situated"? Obviously, two persons may be similarly situated in some respects and differently in others. For instance, a randomly-selected black person and white person might be similarly situated in many respects (e.g., their right to vote or obtain a job) but differently situated in others (e.g., their statistical susceptibility to sickle-cell anemia). In nearly all instances, the "differentness" or "sameness" of people in the context of equal protection analysis is determined by reference to the *objectives of the statute* being analyzed.

> **Example:** The California "statutory rape" law makes men criminally liable for intercourse with a woman under eighteen but does not make women liable for intercourse under any circumstances. Whether this statute violates equal protection (by treating men and women differently for criminal liability purposes) must be determined by looking at the legislature's *objective* in enacting, or maintaining, the statute.
>
> Here, the principal purpose was to discourage illegitimate teenage pregnancies. The legislature could reasonably have concluded that men are differently situated from

---

2. In reality, the Supreme Court doesn't seem to treat facial challenges quite as strictly as this formulation would suggest — often the Court seems to uphold a facial challenge even though there are at least some applications of the statute that would be constitutional. See 46 Stan. L. Rev. 235, 236 (1994). But there's no doubt that facial challenges are harder to win than as-applied challenges.

women, because the woman already has the deterrent of an unwanted pregnancy. The statute therefore roughly "equalizes" the deterrence on the sexes. Thus it is only by looking at the goal of preventing teenage pregnancy that the "sameness" or "differentness" of men and women who engage in the forbidden intercourse may be evaluated. See *Michael M. v. Superior Court*, 450 U.S. 464 (1981) (discussed in more detail *infra*, p. 275).

   a.   **Intent and causation:** Common-sense concepts like ***"intent"*** and ***"causation"*** may furnish the legislature with a valid basis for treating groups differently. For instance, where two actions produce the same result, the legislature does not violate equal protection where it criminalizes one action and not the other, if one action was taken with intent to produce the result, and the other action was not.

   **Example:** New York state makes it a felony for a doctor (or anyone else) to help even a terminally-ill patient commit suicide, such as by knowingly prescribing a fatal dose of drugs. But New York does not make it a crime at all for a doctor to "pull the plug," i.e., to withdraw artificial life-sustaining medical treatment at the patient's request. A group of doctors claims that since both assisted-suicide and plug-pulling "hasten death," it violates the equal protection rights of patients not on life-support to forbid the former but not the latter. The Second Circuit Court of Appeals agrees.

   *Held* (by the Supreme Court), there is no equal protection violation. The distinction between assisting suicide and withdrawing life-sustaining treatment "comports with fundamental legal principles of causation and intent." A doctor who at the patient's request withdraws life-sustaining treatment does not necessarily intend (in the sense of desire) that the patient die; the doctor may be doing this only for the purpose of respecting the patient's dignity in not having useless medical procedures performed upon him. But one who knowingly helps a patient to commit suicide by prescribing fatal quantities of drugs *does* intend primarily to cause the death. This distinction is certainly a rational one, so making it does not violate equal protection. *Vacco v. Quill*, 117 S. Ct. 2293 (1997).

6.   **Over- and under-inclusive classifications:**   Consider now the usual equal protection claim that persons who are similarly situated have been treated differently (i.e., a type (1) claim, as organized *supra*, p. 237). The way most classifications work is that they ***identify a trait*** present in some people, and presume a certain connection between that trait and the legislative goal. This goal may be either the prevention of a harm or the furthering of a good; for our discussion here, we will presume that it is a prevention of a harm. (The analysis would be the same for furthering of a good.)

   a.   **Classic analysis:**   Tussman and tenBroek, in a famous article in 37 CALIF. L. REV. 341 (1949) (partially reprinted in Sullivan & Gunther, pp. 645-46), described the five ways in which the Trait upon which the legislature has based its classification might relate to the Harm (which they called the "Mischief"). Of these, nos. (3), (4) and (5) are the most important, since they are the most likely to occur in real situations.

   b.   **Sample fact situation:**   To illustrate each of the five possible relations between Trait and Harm, we will consider the statute construed in *Massachusetts Board of Retirement v. Murgia*, discussed *infra*, p. 249. That statute required all uniformed state police to retire at the age of 50. The purpose of the statute was to help keep the police force free of officers whose physical health would not be sound enough for them to perform their duties.

    **i.**   **Perfect fit:**   There might be a ***"perfect fit"*** between the Trait and the Harm. This would be the case if all officers under 50 are in good health, and all older than 50 are in poor health.

    **ii.**  **Perfect lack of correlation:**   Conversely, there might be a perfect *lack* of correlation between Trait and Harm. This would be the case if all officers under 50 are in poor health and all over 50 are in good health.

    **iii.**  **"Under-inclusive:"**   It might be the case that all persons who have the Trait contribute to the Harm, but that persons without the Trait *also* contribute to the Harm. Such a classification scheme is called ***"under-inclusive."*** For instance, if all officers over 50 are in poor health, but some officers under 50 are also in poor health, the scheme is under-inclusive.

    **iv.**  **"Over-inclusive":**   Conversely, all persons who contribute to the Harm might have the Trait, but some people who have the Trait might not contribute to the Harm. In this situation, the classification is said to be ***"over-inclusive."*** In the retirement example, the classification is over-inclusive if all officers in poor health are over 50, but some officers over 50 are in good health. Another example of an over-inclusive classification is the ***quarantine***, in which all persons who could have been exposed to a disease are kept confined; the quarantine will normally encompass all persons who might contribute to the Harm (i.e., actual carriers of the disease), but will inevitably also burden persons without the Harm (i.e., the uninfected).

    **v.**   **Over- and under-inclusive:** The final type of classification is one which has attributes of both (iii) and (iv), i.e., one which is *both over- and under-inclusive*. Although this sounds impossible, it is in fact probably the most common type of classification. The way this occurs is that the classification is over-inclusive as to some groups of people but under-inclusive as to others. In the retirement example, for instance, it is almost certainly the case that some officers over 50 are healthy (so that the statute is over-inclusive as to these healthy older-than-50 people), and at the same time that some officers who are under 50 are unhealthy (so that the statute is under-inclusive as to these sick younger-than-50 officers).

**7.**  **Significance:**  Although these categories are useful ways of labeling what a given classification is doing, attaching the correct label says very little about whether the Court will find the classification to be violative of equal protection or not.

    **a.**  **Pros and cons of under-inclusiveness:**  The Court rarely, in practice, invalidates an ***under-inclusive*** law. See Tribe, p. 1440, n. 4.

        **i.**  **Rationale:**  The Court has often justified this reticence by asserting that legislatures are permitted to solve problems ***"one step at a time,"*** i.e., to regulate certain aspects of a harm without regulating all. Or, as the idea was expressed in *Railway Express Agency v. New York*, 336 U.S. 106 (1949) (discussed *infra*, p. 242), "[i]t is no requirement of equal protection that all evils of the same genus be eradicated or none at all. ... "

**ii. Political accountability:** However, a plausible argument can be made that under-inclusive laws should be subjected to some real judicial review, because of the way such laws fit into the process of political decisionmaking. A famous footnote by Justice Stone in *U.S. v. Carolene Products Co.* (discussed *infra*, p. 259) suggested a stricter standard of review for laws which manifest prejudice against "discrete and insular minorities." A failure to grant some realistic review of under-inclusive legislation may give legislatures an incentive to burden only such powerless minorities, rather than taking full political accountability for a measure which burdens all similarly-situated people equally. See Tribe, p. 998. As Justice Jackson put it in *Railway Express*, "Nothing opens the door to arbitrary action so effectively as to allow … officials to pick and choose only a few to whom they will apply legislation and thus to escape the political retribution that might be visited upon them if larger numbers were affected."

**b. Pros and cons of over-inclusiveness:** There are equally conflicting rationales concerning the scrutiny which should be given to ***over-inclusive*** laws:

**i. Political accountability:** The "political accountability" rationale, which suggests careful scrutiny of under-inclusive laws, clearly does not apply to over-inclusive ones — since more people than necessary are being burdened by the classification, there seems little danger that discrete and insular minorities are being singled out to enable the legislature to escape accountability for its actions.

**ii. Unfair burdens:** But on the other hand, while the worst that can be said for under-inclusive laws is that they fail to burden some who ought logically to be burdened, an over-inclusive law actually ***places a burden on one on whom it should not fall***. See 82 HARV. L. REV. 1086 (quoted at L,K&C, pp. 1253-54.) The notion that unfair burdens are worse than unfairly-escaped ones makes strong intuitive sense, and suggests that over-inclusive laws should be given at least moderately strict review.

**8. Summary of present standards of review:** Traditionally, there has been a "two-tiered" model of equal protection review. Either a statute was subjected to the lower tier (in which case the scrutiny was minimal and the statute almost always upheld) or it was subjected to "strict" scrutiny (and generally invalidated). Since 1970, there have been strong hints of a middle standard, as noted above. A rough summary of the present Court's standards for reviewing statutes under equal protection challenges is as follows:

**a. Ordinary "mere rationality" review:** The least probing standard of review applies to statutes which are not based upon a "suspect classification," and do not involve the "quasi-suspect" categories implicitly recognized by the Court (principally gender and illegitimacy). The statutes reviewed under this lowest-level scrutiny are generally ones which involve mainly ***economic issues***. Just as the Court has, ever since the decline of the *Lochner* philosophy, declined to give more than minimal substantive due process review to economic legislation, so it has declined to impose very searching review of such legislation under the Equal Protection Clause.

**i. The test:** Therefore, in this least-scrutiny area, the Court "will ask only whether it is ***conceivable*** that the classification bears a ***rational relationship*** to an end of government which is ***not prohibited*** by the Constitution." N&R, p. 601. This test is sometimes called (and will be called here) the ***"mere rationality"*** standard.

b. **Strict scrutiny:** At the other end of the spectrum, the Court will give *"strict scrutiny"* to any statute which is based upon a *"suspect classification"* or which impairs a *"fundamental right."* (The meaning of these two terms is discussed extensively beginning *infra,* p. 252.) Classifications based on *race* are a classic example of a "suspect" class; the right to *vote* is an important example of a fundamental right.

  i. **The test:** Where strict scrutiny is invoked, the classification will be upheld only if it is *necessary* to promote a *compelling* governmental interest. Thus not only must the objective be an extremely important one, but the "fit" between the means and the end must be extremely tight.

c. **Middle-level review:** In a few situations, the Court has engaged in scrutiny that is more probing than the "mere rationality" test, but less rigid than classical "strict scrutiny." This has happened principally in cases involving classifications based on *gender* and *illegitimacy*, and in some cases involving access to the judicial process. N&R, p. 602-603. Classifications based on *alienage* are also sometimes viewed as being based on this middle-level review.

  i. **Test:** Where the middle level of review is applied, the test is usually stated as follows: the means chosen by the legislature (i.e., the classification) must serve *important governmental objectives* and must be *substantially related* to achievement of those objectives. See, e.g., *Craig v. Boren,* 429 U.S. 190 (1976), a sex-discrimination case discussed *infra,* p. 323. In this middle-level situation, therefore, the legislative objective must be an important one (but not necessarily "compelling") and the fit between means and end must be reasonably tight (not almost perfect, as in a strict scrutiny situation).

# II. ECONOMIC AND SOCIAL LAWS — THE "MERE RATIONALITY" TEST

A. **Deferential review:** As noted, where neither a suspect class nor a fundamental right is implicated, the Court will review a classification with extreme deference, and with a heavy presumption of constitutionality. Most general "economic" and "social welfare" legislation falls within this limited review category.

  1. **Mere rationality:** The standard for lowest-level review is generally phrased in terms of *"mere rationality."* That is, the statute will not be stricken if it's conceivable that there is some *rational relation* between the means selected by the legislature and a *legitimate* legislative objective.

B. **Broad reading of "legitimate public objective":** Although the legislature's "purpose" or *"objective"* in enacting a statute must be "legitimate," the courts give *extreme deference* to the legislature's right to define its objectives. Thus of the relatively few cases in which general economic and social policy has been struck down on equal protection grounds in the last fifty years, even fewer have been based upon a finding that the legislature's "objective" was not "legitimate."

  1. **Search for objectives:** The Court often reviews various "conceivable" objectives which *might have* motivated the legislature, if it is not clear from the legislative history what the precise objectives were. (See *infra,* p. 243.) So long as there is at least one conceivable

objective which is legitimate and which is rationally related to the means selected, the possibility that another, illegitimate, objective might have motivated the legislature will be ignored by the Court.

2.  **Great deference:**   Furthermore, any objective that does not strike the Court as being grossly unfair or totally irrational will be upheld. The fact that the Court thinks that the objective behind the legislation is *unwise* will not be sufficient to make it "illegitimate."

3.  **Not all objectives legitimate:**   Yet not every objective that motivates a legislature will be found by the Supreme Court to be "legitimate." In *Metropolitan Life Ins. Co. v. Ward*, 470 U.S. 869 (1985), the Court invalidated, on equal protection grounds, an Alabama statute that taxed out-of-state insurance companies at a higher rate than in-state ones. Alabama argued that the statute was a reasonable means of achieving its objective of promoting its domestic insurance industry. But the Court (by a 5-4 vote) concluded that "promotion of domestic business by *discriminating against nonresident competitors* is not a legitimate state purpose."

C.  **"One step at a time" approach:**   A key feature of "mere rationality" review is that legislation will not be invalidated merely because the legislature dealt with only one part of a problem. That is, the legislature may deal with a problem *"one step at a time."* This is really another way of saying that a statute which is "under-inclusive" is not necessarily invalid.

> **Example:** A New York City traffic regulation bans the placing of advertising on vehicles, except that the owner of a vehicle is permitted to advertise his own products. The purpose of the regulation is to reduce traffic hazards. The act is challenged on the theory that a vehicle carrying advertising for the vehicle's owner is no less distracting than a vehicle carrying advertising for others. Also, the challengers point out that other traffic hazards (e.g., "vivid displays on Times Square") have not been banned.
>
> *Held*, the regulation is not a violation of equal protection. "It is no requirement of equal protection that all evils of the same genus be eradicated or none at all … " *Railway Express Agency v. New York*, 336 U.S. 106 (1949).
>
> But a concurrence contended that the majority's rationale was an invitation to arbitrary action, since this kind of under-inclusive act (which the concurrence described as "regulation of the few") would allow legislators to "choose only a few to whom they will apply legislation and thus to escape the political retribution that might be visited upon them if larger numbers were affected." Instead, the concurrence contended, the statute should be upheld because "[t]here is a real difference between doing in self-interest and doing for hire, so that it is one thing to tolerate action from those who act on their own and it is another thing to permit the same action to be promoted for a price."

1.  **Support for a "step-by-step" view:**   In support of the view that a problem may be attacked "one step at a time," the following arguments have been made: (1) a contrary rule might "preclude a state from undertaking any program of correction until its resources were adequate to deal with the entire problem"; and (2) there might be a legislative majority in favor of attacking one aspect of the problem, but not other aspects, so that an "all or nothing" rule might "restrict the state's opportunities to experiment." 82 HARV. L. REV. 1085 (quoted in L,K&C, p. 1252).

**D. Determining a statute's "purpose":** Before a court can determine whether the purpose of a statute is "legitimate," and that there is a sufficiently close link between means and end, it must somehow determine what the "purpose" is. The Supreme Court seems always to have agreed that so long as *one* of the purposes of the statute is legitimate, and sufficiently closely linked to the means, the statute will be valid under lowest-level review. But the Court has vacillated over the years about where to look to find the possible purposes.

1. **"Actual" legislative purpose:** Obviously, if the statute itself, either within its text, or in its preamble, contains a statement of purpose, that statement will control. Similarly, if the legislative history of the bill discloses a purpose, that will control. In these two situations, the Court is relying on the legislature's *"actual"* purpose.

   a. **Combination of goals:** The legislature will often have *more than one* objective in mind when it passes a statute. It seems clear that so long as the challenged classification is rationally related to *any one* of these actual objectives, the statute will be sustained, even if it is not rationally related to the others (or the others are not "legitimate" objectives).

2. **"Conceivable basis" standard:** The quest for the legislature's "actual" purpose may be complicated by either of two possibilities: (1) that neither the statute nor its legislative history discloses *any* clear purpose; or (2) that apart from the stated purpose(s) there may have been other objectives which, either solely or in combination with the stated purpose(s), in fact induced the legislature to pass the bill. One way in which the Court has dealt with these possibilities is by being willing to consider *any purpose which the statute's defenders* (i.e., the litigant seeking to have the statute upheld) can assert as having been *the* or even *a*, consideration which *"may"* have motivated the legislature. If the Court agrees that this purpose "may" have motivated the legislature, and that purpose is "legitimate" and rationally related to the means used by the legislature, the statute will be upheld *even if there is no "hard" evidence that that purpose was in fact a motivation* to the legislature.

   a. **Illustration from Burger Court:** For instance, in *U.S. Railroad Retirement Bd. v. Fritz*, 449 U.S. 166 (1980), six members of the Court held that so long as there was a "plausible" reason for Congress to have made the classification scheme it did, lowest-level equal protection review was satisfied; it was *"constitutionally irrelevant whether this reasoning in fact underlay the legislative decision,"* since the Court had "never insisted that a legislative body articulate its reasons for enacting a statute."

      i. **Dissenter's view in *Fritz*:** But two dissenters in *Fritz*, Brennan and Marshall, took a sharply different view on this issue. They believed that "a challenged classification may be sustained only if it is rationally related to the achievement of an *actual* legitimate governmental purpose," and that "any *post hoc* justifications preferred by Government attorneys" should be viewed skeptically. (Justice Stevens concurred with the majority, but believed that a purpose should be considered only if it was either an "actual" one or else a "legitimate purpose that we may reasonably presume to have motivated an impartial legislature.")

   b. **Facts of *Fritz*:** The facts of *Fritz* show that whether or not one insists on an "actual" legislative purpose may sometimes make a difference in the outcome. In *Fritz*, Congress modified a prior scheme, by which persons who worked long enough for both railroad and non-railroad employers could obtain retirement benefits under both the railroad and social security systems. In order to preserve the solvency of the railroad retirement system, Congress eliminated this double-benefit "windfall."

i. **Order of employment significant:** To accomplish this, Congress set up four classes; depending on the class into which he fell, a person got either full windfall, reduced windfall, or no windfall benefits at all. At issue in *Fritz* was that portion of the scheme which, within the class of persons who had worked for railroads more than ten years but less than twenty-five, and who had not yet retired when the act took effect, gave different treatment to those who had worked first for a non-railroad employer than to those who had worked first for a railroad. A person in the former situation received at least a reduced windfall; one in the latter received none. Thus the order of jobs was the sole basis for the statutory distinction.

ii. **Majority view:** The majority, as noted, was willing to accept any proffered statutory "purpose," whether actually relied upon by the legislature or not. They reasoned that Congress "may" have been attempting to preserve limited windfall benefits only for "career" railroad employees, and that persons still working in railroading (as a second career) when the act went into force were more likely to be "career" railroad workers than those who had left railroading before the act came into force. Since this was a "plausible reason" for Congress' action, it was sufficient to save the statute.

iii. **Dissent:** But the dissent, since it required an "actual" legislative purpose, reached an opposite result. By looking to the legislative history, the dissent concluded that Congress' actual intent was *not* to eliminate any "vested" benefit, and that Congress did not intend to deprive members of plaintiff's class of their windfall (which the dissent called an "earned benefit"). Thus, in the dissent's opinion, the classification was not rationally related to any actual government purpose.

c. **Inconsistent purpose:** Since, under the *Fritz* majority's view, any "conceivable" purpose advanced by a statute's defender will, if it rationally relates to the classification, be sufficient to validate the statute, a side effect is probably that the Court may consider even those "conceivable" purposes which, the statute's text and history show, *could not have been* the *"actual"* purpose of the statute.

3. **Court's own imagination:** On occasion, the Court has gone even further than in *Fritz*, and has simply used *its own imagination* to derive theoretical objectives which the legislature "might have" been pursuing when it enacted the statute. Here, too, if this hypothetical purpose is adequate, the statute has been upheld. When the Court has been inclined to proceed in this manner, it has stated that it will overturn statutory classifications "only if no grounds can be *conceived* to justify them." *McDonald v. Board of Election*, 394 U.S. 802 (1969).

4. **Pros and cons of "actual" purpose requirement:** The commentators have disagreed about the wisdom of requiring an "actual" legislative objective, rather than one hypothesized *post hoc* by a defender of the statute or by the Court itself.

a. **Pros:** Professor Gunther has argued that no objective should be considered unless it has been articulated by a representative of the state (either by the legislature itself, or at least, say, the attorney general's office). Such a rule would, Gunther contends, "be indirect pressure on the legislature to state its own reasons for selecting the particular means and classifications [and would thus] improve the quality of the political process [by] encouraging a fuller airing in the political arena of the grounds for legislative action." 86 HARV. L. REV. 46 (quoted in L,K&C, p. 1251).

    **b.  Cons:**  But several difficulties with this view have been articulated.

        **i.  Anti-democratic:**  The strongest of these is that an "actual purpose" requirement, since it sends the judiciary on a vague quest for the motivations of multiple politicians pursuing differing objectives, "leaves the judiciary free to strike legislation it finds politically objectionable by attributing to the legislature either an illegitimate purpose or a purpose that, though legitimate, is too far removed from the means selected to withstand even minimum scrutiny." 95 HARV. L. REV. 160. The result may well be "anti-democratic," in a manner similar to the striking of economic and social welfare legislation on substantive due process grounds during the *Lochner* era.

        **ii.  Different results for same statute.**  A second difficulty is that, if the "actual purpose" standard is applied, when two states adopt identically-worded statutes for differing "purposes," *one state's statute might be valid and the other invalid*. Such a result certainly seems anomalous and confusing. Also, if a statute is struck down because it has an inadequate "actual purpose," what happens if the legislature reenacts it accompanied by recitations of an adequate actual purpose? It seems hypocritical of the courts to require legislatures to go through such a charade.

**E.  Legal disabilities motivated by "animus" towards unpopular groups:**  Occasionally, the Court has examined legislation that it finds to have been motivated by *"animus"* or *"hostility"* towards a *politically-unpopular group*. The Court has been willing to *strike down* such legislation even though only "mere rationality" review is used. In so doing, the Court has used one or both of the following rationales: (1) that the desire to harm an unpopular group cannot be a "legitimate governmental objective"; or (2) that to the extent some apparently legitimate state objective is cited by the statute's defenders, the means drawn are so poorly linked to achievement of that objective that not even a "rational relation" between means and end is present.

    **1.  Ban on protection of gays:**  By far the most important case in which the Court has used this "intent to harm the unpopular" analysis is ***Romer v. Evans***, 517 U.S. 620 (1996), a case in which the Court *struck down* a Colorado constitutional amendment that would have *prevented the state or any of its cities from giving certain protections to gays or lesbians*. The Court found that the measure flunked "mere rationality" review on two separate grounds: there was no legitimate state interest in fact being served, and the means chosen by the state were not rationally related to the (possibly legitimate) interest that the state asserted.

        **a.  Facts:** The Colorado provision, known as "Amendment 2," modified the Colorado constitution to provide that neither the state nor any subdivision (including state agency, city or school district) shall "enact, adopt or enforce any statute, regulation, ordinance or policy whereby *homosexual, lesbian or bisexual orientation*, *conduct*, practices or relationships shall constitute or otherwise be the basis of or entitle any person or class of persons to have or claim any *minority status*, quota preferences, *protected status* or *claim of discrimination*."

i. **Bans anti-discrimination laws:** The main practical impact of Amendment 2 was that it prevented both the state legislature and any city from passing statutes or ordinances that would *protect gays and lesbians from discrimination*. For instance, the cities of Aspen, Boulder and Denver had all passed (prior to the enactment of Amendment 2) ordinances barring discrimination against gays in housing, employment, education, public accommodations, and the like; each of these ordinances would apparently have been wiped out by Amendment 2. Only by re-amending the state constitution — something requiring a state-wide referendum — could gays obtain any protection against discrimination on the basis of sexual orientation.

b. **Holding:** By a 6-3 vote, the Court struck down Amendment 2, even though the majority used only "mere rationality" review. The opinion by Justice Kennedy relied on several grounds:

   i. **Gays not put in "same position" as others:** Colorado defended the amendment on the grounds that it merely (in Kennedy's words) "puts gays and lesbians in the *same position* as all other persons" and "does no more than deny homosexuals *special rights*." But Kennedy found this interpretation "implausible." The amendment in fact singled gays out for *worse* treatment than other groups: "Homosexuals, by state decree, are put in a solitary class with respect to transactions and relations in both the private and governmental spheres. The amendment withdraws from homosexuals, but no others, specific legal protection from the injuries caused by discrimination . . . ."

      (1) **Wide protection of other groups:** Kennedy noted that existing state and municipal laws in Colorado protected many groups, not just the racial, ethnic or gender groups to which the U.S. Supreme Court has given heightened Equal Protection review. For instance, various ordinances protected persons from discrimination based on "age, military status, marital status, pregnancy, parenthood, custody of a minor child, political affiliation, [or] physical or mental disability of an individual or of his or her associates. . . ." So Amendment 2 was not simply withdrawing special rights from gays, it was "*forbidd[ing] them] the safeguards that others enjoy or may seek without constraint. . . .* These are protections taken for granted by most people either because they already have them or do not need them. . . ."

   ii. **Desire to harm is not a legitimate interest:** Kennedy then asserted that Amendment 2 "seems inexplicable by anything but *animus toward the class that it affects*. . . ." He quoted approvingly a prior case: "If the constitutional conception of 'equal protection of the laws' means anything, it must at the very least mean that a *bare . . . desire to harm a politically unpopular group cannot constitute a legitimate governmental interest.*" Amendment 2, by identifying persons by a single trait and then denying them equal protection across the board, was "unprecedented in our jurisprudence" and "not within our constitutional tradition." Central to the guarantee of equal protection is "the principle that government and each of its parts remain *open on impartial terms to all who seek its assistance.*"

   iii. **"Protection of liberties of landlords or employers" rationale is rejected:** Colorado argued that Amendment 2 was rationally related to the protection of *other* *citizens' freedom of association*, in particular the freedom of landlords or employers who have personal or religious objections to homosexuality. Kennedy did not reject this as a legitimate state interest. But he found the *means-end fit* to be fatally loose: "The breadth of the Amendment is so far removed from these particular justifications that we find it impossible to credit them."

    **iv. Conclusion:** Kennedy concluded by saying that "Amendment 2 classifies homosexuals not to further a proper legislative end but to make them *unequal to everyone else*. This Colorado cannot do. A State *cannot so deem a class of persons a stranger to its laws*."

**c. Dissent:** The dissent, by Justice Scalia (joined by Rehnquist and Thomas) was unusually vitriolic. Scalia accused the majority of *"tak[ing] sides in the culture wars,"* and said that its striking down of the Amendment was "an act, not of judicial judgment, but of political will."

    **i. No singling out:** Scalia rejected the majority's view that Amendment 2 singled out homosexuals for unfavorable treatment. All the Amendment did was to say to gays that "they may not obtain preferential treatment without amending the state constitution." If it was a violation of equal protection to force gays to resort to the state-constitutional-amendment level when others don't have to, then it would also violate equal protection, Scalia wrote, to force any group to "have recourse to a more general and hence more difficult level of political decisionmaking than others." He posed the example of a state law prohibiting the award of municipal contracts to relatives of mayors or city councilmen: "Once such a law is passed, the group composed of such relatives must, in order to get the benefit of city contracts, persuade the state legislature — unlike all other citizens, who need only persuade the municipality. It is ridiculous to consider this a denial of equal protection. . . ."

    **ii. Inconsistent with *Bowers*:** Scalia also believed that the majority's reasoning was inconsistent with *Bowers v. Hardwick* (see *supra*, p. 185), in which the Court had held that states may make homosexual conduct a crime. "If it is constitutionally permissible for a State to make homosexual conduct criminal, surely it is constitutionally permissible for a State to enact other laws merely disfavoring homosexual conduct," and Amendment 2 was at most a very slight disfavoring of that conduct, in his view.[3]

    **iii. Not politically unpopular:** Scalia noted in passing that it was "nothing short of preposterous to call 'politically unpopular' a group which *enjoys enormous influence in American media and politics*." And he accused the majority of siding with the "views and values of the lawyer class," whose tolerant views of homosexuality are reflected by the fact that law schools require interviewers to pledge their willingness to hire homosexuals.

    **iv. Rationally related:** Lastly, Scalia believed that the Amendment was in fact reasonably related to a legitimate governmental interest. That interest was the prevention of "*piecemeal deterioration of the sexual morality* favored by a majority of Coloradans." And a measure that merely denied homosexuals "preferential treatment" was surely an appropriate means of achieving that end.

---

3. Of course, the post-*Romer* case of *Lawrence v. Texas*, *supra*, p. 185, has overruled *Bowers*.

**d. Significance:** *Romer* has already proven to be just the first step in applying some kind of ***heightened review*** to government action that disfavors homosexuals. In the later case of *Lawrence v. Texas*, the Court applied a similar type of "rational relation review with bite" to strike down on substantive due process grounds all laws that criminalize homosexual sodomy in private between consenting adults. Taken together, *Romer* and *Lawrence* suggest that a majority of the present Court will take a jaundiced view of any regulations that seem to be motivated principally by hostility towards or disapproval of gays. (See the extended discussion of other gay-rights issues that may soon be litigated, *supra*, pp. 190-193)

   **i. Other contexts:** Beyond the gay-rights area, *Romer* may have an impact on any other provision which the Court finds to be motivated by ***hostility towards a politically unpopular group***. For instance, if a state or city were to specifically deny emergency health care or other government benefits to ***illegal aliens*** (not a suspect or semi-suspect class), such a denial might fall within the rationale of *Romer*. See *NY Times*, May 21, 1996, A1.

**2. Discrimination against out-of-staters:** *Romer* is not the first case in which the Court has held that the objective being pursued by the government was not "legitimate." Another cluster of "illegitimate objective" cases has involved measures that discriminate against ***out-of-staters***. Here, too, the Court has purported to use "mere rationality" review, but its refusal to find the asserted state interest to be legitimate has led to a striking down of the provision.

   **a. *Metropolitan Life:*** Thus in *Metropolitan Life Insurance Co. v. Ward*, 470 U.S. 869 (1985), the Court held that a desire to promote in-state insurance companies at the expense of insurers based out-of-state was not legitimate. So the Court struck down Alabama's higher tax on out-of-state insurers.

   **b. Benefits based on length of residence struck down:** Similarly, the award of money or other benefits based on ***length of residence*** within the state has been struck down several times by the Court, even though only "mere rationality" analysis was used. See, e.g., *Zobel v. Williams*, 457 U.S. 55 (1982) (Alaskan scheme, by which residents were paid $50 for each year they had resided in the state, invalidated).

**F. Highly deferential standard:** But cases like *Romer v. Evans, Metropolitan Life*, etc. in which "mere rationality" review nonetheless leads to invalidation under the Equal Protection Clause, have been the exception rather than the rule in the Burger/Rehnquist Court. Not only *U.S. Railroad Retirement Bd. v. Fritz, supra*, p. 243, but several other recent cases, show that the Court will give ***great deference*** to the legislature in cases involving mere economic and social legislation.

**1. Means-end link need not be empirical:** One aspect of this deference is in the doctrine that there need not be ***in fact*** a link between the means selected by the legislature and a legitimate objective. All that is required is that the legislature ***"could rationally have believed"*** that there was such a link.

   **Example:** A state statute bans the sale of milk in plastic non-returnable containers, but allows such sale in other types of non-returnable containers, including paperboard cartons. Several justifications are proffered in support of the bill, including: (1) that the elimination of plastic cartons will encourage use of environmentally-superior containers; (2) that banning just plastic containers will cause less economic dislocation within the milk industry than banning both plastic and paperboard simultaneously; and (3) that the law will help to conserve energy. The statute's challengers attempt to show that the statute will not in fact achieve any of these three objectives.

*Held*, the statute is not a violation of the Equal Protection Clause. Whether or not the statute will *in fact* achieve any of its objectives is **irrelevant**. The only question is whether the legislature "could rationally have decided" that it would meet these objectives. The burden is on the statute's challengers to show that "the legislative facts on which [a] classification is apparently based could not reasonably be conceived to be true by the governmental decision-maker." Here, whether the classification scheme would meet one or more of these objectives was **at least debatable**. By that fact alone, it cannot be said that the legislature acted irrationally, and the statute must be upheld. *Minnesota v. Clover Leaf Creamery Co.*, 449 U.S. 456 (1981).

2. **Mathematical exactitude not required:**  Since all that is required is that the means-end relationship be close enough that its rationality is **"debatable,"** a **very loose fit between means and ends will be acceptable**. For instance, in **Massachusetts Bd. of Retirement v. Murgia**, 427 U.S. 307 (1976), a Massachusetts statute required state police officers to retire at age 50. All parties conceded that the objective of the statute was to maintain a physically-fit police force. The statute was upheld, even though some (perhaps many) officers over 50 were not in poor physical health, making the statute over-inclusive. The link between being over 50 and being physically unfit was **not so attenuated as to be irrational**. And the fact that better means of measuring physical health were available and were in fact being used (e.g., annual physical examinations) did not mean that the less-than-best means selected by the statute was impermissible.

    a. **Not suspect class:**  The decision in *Murgia* turned largely on the fact that the Court **declined** to treat the classification based on **age** as a **"suspect"** class, on the theory that old age "marks a stage that each of us will reach if we live out our normal span ... " (Justice Marshall, in dissent, argued that the age classification should be subjected to **middle-level** scrutiny, because older workers "constitute a class subject to repeated and arbitrary discrimination in employment." In Marshall's view, the statute certainly could not survive such middle-level scrutiny, because of its over-inclusiveness.)

        i. **Still not suspect:**  A post-*Murgia* case shows that the Supreme Court still views age as not being a "suspect" class. See *Gregory v. Ashcroft*, 501 U.S. 452 (1991), upholding a scheme by which state judges are required to retire at age 70. The Court held that it was not irrational for the state to distinguish between judges older and younger than 70, nor was it irrational for the state to distinguish between judges and other state employees of the same age, who were not subject to mandatory retirement.

3. **Likelihood of bias:**  There are some traits which the Court has recognized as being so unpopular that classifications based upon them should be subject to "strict" scrutiny (as in the case of "suspect" classifications like race and national origin) or subject to "middle-level" scrutiny (including classifications based on illegitimacy and, for slightly different reasons, gender). (These higher levels of scrutiny are discussed extensively beginning at p. 252, *supra*.) But what about traits that are unpopular, **but not extremely so?** While the Court has never explicitly adjusted its "mere rationality" standard to reflect the presence of such a "moderately suspect" class, there are some indications that the Court is now tak-

ing into account the *likelihood of bias* against a moderately-unpopular class, such as the *mentally retarded* or *gays and lesbians*.

   a.  **Mentally retarded:**  For instance, in *City of Cleburne v. Cleburne Living Center*, 473 U.S. 432 (1985), the Court struck down a Texas city's denial of a special use permit for the operation of a group home for the *mentally retarded*. The Court refused to treat mental retardation as an explicitly "quasi-suspect" classification like gender or illegitimacy (see *infra*, p. 344). Yet while purporting to apply a "mere rationality" standard, the Court quite clearly gave the challenged classification a more rigorous review than it has given to purely economic regulations (see, e.g., *Fritz, supra*, p. 243). Since the Court conceded that "there have been and there will continue to be instances of discrimination against the retarded that are in fact invidious ... ," it seems apparent that the Court's more-rigorous-than-usual application of the "mere rationality" standard was motivated by historical and current prejudice against the retarded.

      i.  **"One step at a time" approach declined:**  One clue to the fact that more than the ordinary highly-deferential standard of review was being applied in *Cleburne* came from the fact that the Court rejected the defendant city's argument that the proposed home would be unsafe because it was on a "five hundred year flood plain" and because it would have too many people living in it for its size — the Court saw no reason why these arguments justified discriminating between the home for the retarded and, say, a nursing home or a home for convalescents, which could be located in exactly the same place without a special use permit. Yet the Court has historically allowed reform to take place *"one step at a time"* (see *supra*, p. 242), so it is hard to see why the city should have been required to protect, say, nursing home patients in order to protect the retarded. (Justice Marshall, dissenting from the majority's refusal to apply intermediate-level scrutiny, made this argument to show that the majority was really applying heightened scrutiny without admitting it.)

   b.  **Illegitimate purpose:**  Slightly higher-level scrutiny of classifications involving unpopular groups may also be accomplished by the Court's refusal to treat a proffered legislative *purpose* as being *"legitimate."*

      i.  **Anti-gay laws:** For instance, it now appears that *disapproval of gay lifestyles* will be found to be an "illegitimate" objective. Recall that in *Romer v. Evans*, *supra*, p. 245, the Court found that Colorado's constitutional amendment forbidding laws that protect gays against discrimination did not pursue any legitimate justification. Similarly, in the substantive due process case of *Lawrence v. Texas*, *supra*, p. 185, the Court found that a ban on sodomy, enforced principally against gays, pursued only the <u>il</u>legitimate objective of expressing majoritarian disapproval of homosexuality.

G.  **Summary of present Court's position:**  In summary, the Supreme Court now seems to be taking a generally deferential equal protection approach to economic and social legislation. However, this deference is not complete. The principal features of the present Court's review in these areas may be summarized as follows:

1.  **Purpose need not be actual:**  The law will be upheld if the means chosen by the legislature bear a *rational relation* to *any conceivable* legitimate legislative purpose (at least if proffered by any representative of the state, and perhaps even if thought of only by mem-

bers of the Court); this will be so even though there is no evidence that this was the *actual* purpose motivating the legislature.

2. **Means-end link:** It is not necessary that there be an *actual*, empirical, link between the means selected by the legislature and the (actual or theoretical) legislative objective. All that is necessary is that the legislature could *"rationally have believed"* that there was a link between the means and the end. And the legislature will be deemed to have been capable of such a belief so long as it is "debatable" whether such a means-end link exists (even though the Court suspects that it probably does not.)

3. **Unpopular trait:** Finally, if the classification involves an unpopular trait or affiliation, thereby suggesting bias on the part of the majority, the Court may subject the statute to a slightly more probing review, even where neither "strict" nor "middle level" scrutiny is appropriate. Examples are statutes that single out the *mentally retarded* (*City of Cleburne*), and those directed at *gays and lesbians* (*Romer v. Evans*).

---

*Quiz Yourself on*

## EQUAL PROTECTION — ECONOMIC & SOCIAL-WELFARE LAWS

32. The state of Chartreuse has delegated to the state bar association the job of determining requirements for the practice of law. Until recently, the bar association imposed no continuing legal education requirements. However, there has been a large rise in the number of malpractice actions against lawyers in the state, some of which appear to derive from the fact that lawyers have not kept pace with changing legal principles. Also, there has been a rise in the disdain with which the public in Chartreuse holds lawyers. The bar association, therefore, imposed a mandatory continuing legal education requirement of 12 course-hours per year. The state imposes on doctors a continuing education requirement of only 4 hours per year. There is strong evidence that, in general, changes in medicine happen faster than changes in law. Amos, a lawyer in Chartreuse, has challenged the continuing legal education requirement on the grounds that by imposing a much higher requirement on lawyers than on doctors, the state has violated his equal protection rights. Assume that the state bar association's conduct constitutes state action.

    **(a)** What standard should the court use to test whether the legal education requirement satisfies the demands of equal protection? _____

    **(b)** Will Amos' attack succeed? _____

33. The town of Solon established a regulation that all members of the fire department must retire at the age of 50. The Town Council enacted the regulation after reading a news report that in a neighboring town, a 53 year-old firefighter with a bad back was unable to carry a child out of the fourth floor of a burning building, leading to the child's death. The Town Council members reasoned that on average, those over 50 are less able to perform the highly demanding physical functions of firefighting than those under 50. Prentice is the Chief of the Solon Fire Department. His duties are exclusively desk-bound. He has just turned 50, and has challenged the retirement regulation, as applied to him, on the grounds that it violates his right to equal protection. Will Prentice's attack on the regulation succeed? _____

---

*Answers*

32. **(a) The court should ask whether the classification is rationally related to a legitimate state objective.**

**(b) No.** Unless there is a suspect or semi-suspect class involved, or a fundamental right, the Supreme Court will uphold a state legislative classification against equal protection attack so long as the classification scheme bears a ***rational relation*** to some ***legitimate legislative objective***. The desire to have lawyers be better trained, and to increase public confidence and reduce suits, certainly seem to constitute legitimate governmental objectives. The link between the classification system chosen and the objective being pursued does not have to be a close one. In fact, there does not need to be an actual empirical link between means and end, merely a ***rational belief*** on the part of the legislature that there is a link between means and end. Here, a bar association (acting as a government body) certainly could rationally have believed that lawyers who take mandatory legal education will be more up to date, and thus less likely to make mistakes through outmoded training. The fact that doctors might need refresher courses even more than lawyers will be ignored by the court, because reform may take place ***"one step at a time"*** (i.e., the government does not commit an equal protection violation every time it addresses one aspect of a problem without solving all related aspects).

33. **No.** As in the prior question, the threshold issue is what standard of review the court will give to the challenged classification. Unless a suspect or quasi-suspect class, or a fundament right, is at issue, the court will use the "mere rationality" standard. The Supreme Court has held repeatedly that age is not a suspect or semi-suspect class. See, e.g., *Mass. Bd. of Retirement v. Murgia* (police officers may be required to retire at age 50). Therefore, the Court applies mere rationality review to age-based classifications such as the one here. The goal of assuring that each firefighter is fit for the particular duties of the profession is clearly a legitimate one. There is some question about whether the means chosen (outright ban on all over-50 firefighters) is a good way to accomplish that objective, since there are less drastic alternatives (e.g., testing of each applicant, or an exemption for those who perform only desk duties). But all that is required between means and end is a ***rational relation***. Here, the blanket-ban approach was certainly a rational way of assuring physical fitness, even though it was not the best possible approach or even a very well-tailored one. The classification will be upheld unless it is completely irrational, which this one is certainly not.

# III.  SUSPECT CLASSIFICATIONS, ESPECIALLY RACE

A. **Suspect classes generally:**  We turn now to "suspect" classifications, i.e., statutory classifications which, because they give distinct treatment to a group that has historically been the victim of discrimination, are subjected to "strict scrutiny."

   1. **Race and national origin:**  The paradigmatic example of a suspect classification is, of course, ***race***. The other principal example is ***national origin***.

   2. **Alienage:**  Some Court cases appear to make ***alienage*** a suspect classification as well, but more recent cases make such large exceptions to the strict scrutiny of alienage classifications that alienage is probably more properly viewed as involving "middle-level" scrutiny; the subject is therefore discussed along with other middle-level scrutiny classes *infra*, p. 337.

   3. **Five subject areas:**  In our treatment of suspect classes, five principal subject areas are addressed: (1) What groups have been so frequently the object of discrimination and prejudice that classifications disfavoring them should be labelled as "suspect"? (2) To what extent must discrimination be shown to be "purposeful" before it is outlawed by the Equal

Protection Clause? (3) How rigorous must "strict" scrutiny be? (4) How does one demonstrate that public facilities (especially schools) have been *racially segregated*, and what are the remedies for such segregation? and (5) To what extent may the government make *"benign"* use of suspect classifications (i.e., the problem of "affirmative action")?

**B. Groups covered:** Classification based on *race* is, of course, the classic example of a "suspect" classification, because of our nation's long history of both public and private racial discrimination. In addition to blacks (the group Congress of course intended most explicitly to assist by means of the Equal Protection Clause), *any other racial group* may, if made the object of a classification intended to disfavor that group, invoke strict scrutiny. See, e.g., *Yick Wo v. Hopkins, infra*, p. 254, treating as suspect administrative discrimination against Asians.

   **1. National origin:** Apart from blacks, Asians, and other minorities that are clearly racially distinct, a classification based on *national origin* is also suspect. Thus in *Hernandez v. Texas*, 347 U.S. 475 (1954), discrimination against *Mexican-Americans* with regard to jury service was treated in the same way that discrimination against blacks would have been.

   **2. Extension in *Croson*:** Discrimination against *any* racial group will merit strict scrutiny, even if that group has never been the subject of widespread discrimination. A majority of the Supreme Court so concluded in *City of Richmond v. J.A. Croson Co.*, discussed extensively *infra*, p. 299. So if a city discriminates in favor of, say, black contractors at the expense of white contractors, this discrimination must be subjected to strict scrutiny (and probably struck down), as happened in *Croson*.

      **a. Ethnic groups:** Probably the rationale of *Croson* means that any intentional discrimination against a particular *ethnic* group also must be strictly scrutinized, even if the group has not been the victim of widespread prejudice or discrimination. Thus if Whites of Anglo-Saxon Protestant descent were discriminated against in favor of other groups (e.g., Whites of Italian or Mediterranean descent), strict scrutiny would presumably be required even though White Anglo-Saxon Protestants have historically rarely been discriminated against.

   **3. Other classes:** Thus far, the Court has not treated as fully "suspect" classifications based on any grounds other than race and national origin. (But see the discussion of classes treated as "semi-suspect," e.g., sex and illegitimacy, pp. 321 and 344.)

      **a. Wealth:** Of special significance has been the Court's refusal to treat classifications based on *wealth* as "suspect." This refusal is discussed *infra*, p. 370.

**C. "Purposeful" discrimination:** A classification will not be deemed to be "suspect," and therefore subject to strict scrutiny, unless the Court finds that there was a legislative *intent* to discriminate against the disfavored group. That is, the mere fact that a law has a less favorable impact on a minority group than it has on the majority is not sufficient to constitute a violation of equal protection. As is discussed in more detail below, a demonstration of disproportionate *impact* is *a factor* in the equal protection analysis, but it can never by itself suffice; proof of *intentional* discrimination is required.

   **1. Three ways to show purpose:** Purposeful discrimination may appear in any of three ways: (1) the law discriminates *on its face*, i.e., by its explicit terms; (2) the law, although neutral on its face, is *administered* in a discriminatory way; and (3) the law, although it is neutral on its face and is applied in accordance with its terms, was enacted with a purpose of discriminating, as shown by the law's legislative history, statements made by legislators, the law's disparate impact, or other circumstantial evidence of intent.

2. **Some examples:** Following are some examples of statutes found to have been "purposefully discriminatory," and therefore violative of the Equal Protection Clause:

> **Example — facially discriminatory:** A state statute provides that "all white male persons who are twenty-one years of age who are citizens of this State shall be eligible to serve as jurors." P, a black, is convicted of murder by a jury from which all blacks have been removed pursuant to the statute.
>
> *Held*, the act on its face discriminates against blacks, and therefore violates the Equal Protection Clause. *Strauder v. West Virginia*, 100 U.S. 303 (1880).

> **Note:** Where a law is found to discriminate "on its face," the Court will ***not*** require that it be shown to have had an actual discriminatory ***impact*** in the case at hand. Thus in *Strauder*, P was not required to show that he would not have been convicted by a jury containing blacks, or even to show that some blacks would have been seated on the jury had the statute not been in force. The mere ***risk*** of discriminatory impact was sufficient, given the facial discrimination.

> **Example — discrimination in administration:** A San Francisco ordinance bars the operation of hand laundries in wooden buildings, except with the consent of the Board of Supervisors. The Board gives permits to all but one of the non-Chinese applicants, but to none of nearly 200 Chinese applicants.
>
> *Held*, although the ordinance is neutral on its face, there was discrimination in its administration, and this discrimination violates the Equal Protection Clause. *Yick Wo v. Hopkins*, 118 U.S. 356 (1886).

> **Example — discriminatory purpose shown by circumstantial evidence:** Burke County, Georgia elects its five-member Board of Commissioners via an at-large system. Whites are only in a slight majority in the voting-age population, but no black has ever been elected to the Board.
>
> *Held*, although the at-large system was facially neutral (and although it was not originally adopted, in 1911, for discriminatory purposes), it has been maintained by the state legislature for discriminatory purposes, and has a discriminatory impact on the county's black citizens. In addition to the fact that no black has ever been elected to the Board (which would not by itself be sufficient to show discriminatory purposes), (1) the history of discrimination against blacks with respect to party affairs, primary and general elections; (2) the unresponsiveness of the county's elected officials to the needs of the black community; and (3) the fact that the state legislature's maintenance of the at-large system was basically due to the county's own state representatives (who desired to maintain a system that excluded black participation), all support an ***inference*** of intentional discrimination. *Rogers v. Lodge*, 458 U.S. 613 (1982).

3. **Proving discriminatory purpose:** If a statute is shown to discriminate on its face, no showing of discriminatory purpose will be necessary. And if those making a discriminatory-administration claim can show that administrators to whom discretion is entrusted have applied the law in a way that is disadvantageous to the suspect class, no additional showing of legislative or administrative motive will be necessary (though the defenders of

the law can attempt to rebut the case with an innocent explanation of the disparate administration). In the third situation, however, that of the law which is facially neutral and is applied according to its terms, the difficulties of proving "discriminatory purpose" are much greater.

a. **No general rule:** There is no general rule that describes exactly how one demonstrates an intent to discriminate on the part of the legislature. Like proof of any other sort of intent, the use of *circumstantial evidence* is required.

b. ***"De jure" vs. "de facto" discrimination:*** In any situation where a discriminatory purpose is found to exist, the discrimination is termed ***"de jure"*** (roughly "by law"). If, on the other hand, a law is found not to result from a discriminatory purpose, then the discrimination will be termed ***"de facto"*** (even if a discriminatory *effect* has resulted). The most common use of the terms, of course, is to describe the two types of ***public school segregation*** (with *de jure* segregation being the only judicially redressable one; *infra*, p. 268).

4. **General requirement of purpose (*Washington v. Davis*):** Prior to 1976, it was not completely clear that an intent to discriminate *was* in fact required, if there was a discriminatory *impact* upon a suspect class. But in that year, ***Washington v. Davis***, 426 U.S. 229, set forth an explicit requirement that an intent to discriminate be found before an equal protection racial discrimination claim would be upheld.

a. **Facts of *Washington v. Davis*:** *Washington v. Davis* involved a suit brought by unsuccessful black applicants for positions as Washington, D.C. policemen. They had failed a written test of verbal ability and reading comprehension, which blacks failed *four times as frequently* as whites. The plaintiffs claimed that this differential impact made the hiring process violative of equal protection even though those who composed or selected the test had no intent to discriminate against blacks. (The plaintiffs also produced evidence suggesting that performance on the test did not necessarily correlate with job performance.)

b. **Holding:** The Supreme Court held that racial discrimination violative of the Equal Protection Clause exists only where it is a product of a *discriminatory purpose*. While a showing of disproportionate racial impact is *a* factor in ascertaining intent, *it can never by itself be sufficient to prove discriminatory intent*. Here, other facts, including the D.C. Police Department's affirmative efforts to recruit more black policemen, negated any finding of a discriminatory purpose in the use of the test (which was used throughout the federal Civil Service).

i. **Comparison to Title VII:** The *Washington* Court conceded that under Title VII of the 1964 Civil Rights Act, a hiring practice which disqualifies a substantially disproportionate number of blacks will be stricken, even without a showing of discriminatory intent. But the Court declined to establish a "no-intent" standard where the source of the discrimination claim was simply the Equal Protection Clause, as distinguished from a specifically-worded congressional statute.

ii. **Rationale:** The Court was especially concerned that absence of an intent requirement might invalidate "a whole range of tax, welfare, public service, regulatory, and licensing statutes that may be more burdensome to the poor and to the average black than to the more affluent white." In a footnote, the Court listed numerous statutory schemes that might be open to attack under such a standard, including such items as sales taxes, bridge tolls, minimum wage laws and professional licensing requirements.

5. **Other areas of application:**   The principle of *Washington v. Davis* has been extended beyond the public employment context, to include such areas as ***jury selection, zoning*** and ***public housing***, and ***voting rights***. It seems apparent that no matter what the subject area, a statute will not be held to establish an impermissible suspect classification merely because of a disproportionately harsh impact on blacks or other minorities.

6. **Need not be sole motive:**   Although a discriminatory purpose is required for invocation of strict scrutiny, such a purpose need not be the ***sole*** purpose of the statute. It is enough that that purpose was a ***"motivating factor"*** in the legislature's decision to enact the statute. *Arlington Heights v. Metropolitan Housing Corp.*, 429 U.S. 252 (1977).

   a. **Two motivations:**   Thus if there were two purposes that motivated the legislature to enact a statute, and only one of these was discriminatory against the suspect class, the presence of the second, non-discriminatory motive, will not immunize the statute from strict scrutiny. So long as the legislature would not have passed the statute had the discriminatory motive not been present, the existence of the other motive makes no difference. Cf. *Hunter v. Underwood*, 471 U.S. 222 (1985) (where voting law was enacted to disenfranchise both blacks and poor whites, the fact that disenfranchisement of blacks was a "but-for" motivation for the law was enough to make it a violation of the Fourteenth Amendment).

   b. **Shifting burden of proof:**   In fact, the plaintiff only needs to show that an intent to discriminate was a "motivating" or "substantial" factor in the legislature's enactment decision. Once he does this, the burden then shifts to the defendant to show that the statute ***would have been passed anyway***, even without that intent. If the defendant succeeds in showing this, the requirement of proof of discriminatory purpose will be deemed not satisfied.

      i. **Restatement:**   To put it another way, the issue is whether a discriminatory motive was a ***"but for"*** cause of the enactment, but the burden of proof is on the defendant once a *prima facie* showing of "motivating factor" has been made by a plaintiff. Thus in *Hunter v. Underwood, supra*, the requisite discriminatory purpose was shown by the fact that a desire to disenfranchise whites would not have been sufficient to lead to the enactment — the attempt to disenfranchise blacks was the "but for" cause of the enactment.

   c. **Must be "because of" not "in spite of":**   It follows from this requirement of "but for" causation that the statute must have been enacted ***"because of"*** a desire to bring about a discriminatory impact, ***not merely "in spite of"*** the probability of such an impact. This principle was established in a sex-discrimination case, ***Personnel Administrator of Mass. v. Feeney***, 422 U.S. 256 (1979), but it seems clear that this rule will be applied in racial discrimination cases as well.

      i. **Facts of *Feeney*:**   In *Feeney*, P, a woman, challenged a Massachusetts civil service statute which gave an ***absolute hiring preference*** to any veteran who obtained a passing score on a competitive exam. Since, at the time the suit was brought, over 98% of the veterans in Massachusetts were men, the preference operated overwhelmingly to the benefit of males and to the detriment of females.

    **ii. Holding:** The Supreme Court held that the statute was not intentionally gender-based, either overtly or covertly. A significant number of *men* were also non-veterans. Therefore, "[t]oo many men are affected by [the law] to permit the inference that the statute is but a pretext for preferring men over women."

    **iii. "In spite of" not enough:** The Court was willing to accept the plaintiff's contention that the legislature in fact knew that the law would be heavily unfavorable to women. But it rejected her further syllogism that, because a person "intends the natural and foreseeable consequences of his voluntary actions," the inevitable disproportionate impact proved an intent to discriminate. "Awareness of consequences" was *not* sufficient to prove "discriminatory purpose"; only if the legislature chose its course *"because of,"* and *not* merely *"in spite of,"* its adverse effects upon women, could there be said to have been intentional discrimination. And the Court found no evidence that the disparate effect upon women was, in the legislature's mind, anything more than a foreseeable but undesired inevitable by-product of the basic decision to favor veterans. Therefore, the preference did not violate the Equal Protection Clause.

**7. Passage of time:** Suppose that a legislature enacts, for discriminatory motives, a provision that disadvantages a suspect class. It is apparently the case that *no matter how long a time elapses*, that provision continues to be a violation of equal protection so long as it has a discriminatory impact.

    **a. Extension of principle:** Thus in theory even a pre-Civil War statute shown to have been enacted for the purpose of disadvantaging blacks could be struck down today if the law were shown to currently disfavor blacks.

**8. Use of statistics:** Since disproportionate impact will be considered as *a* factor in measuring discriminatory intent (though it can never be the sole factor), the equal protection claimant will often attempt to use *statistical analysis* to show the degree of disproportionate impact. In general, the Court has *allowed* such statistical proof.

    **a. Heavy weight in subjective discretion cases:** Statistical evidence will be especially persuasive where the claim is that an *individual selection process* is being discriminatorily performed by administrative officials. See N&R, pp. 622-624. In this situation, it is difficult to gauge the subjective intent of the administrators in any other manner; also, there is less reason for the courts to defer to these officials' subjective decisions than there is to defer to the legislature's own acts.

    **Example:** When court officials have selected panels of *prospective jurors* by using questionnaires, in-person screening or other factors by which the officials become aware of each prospective juror's race, proof of major statistical deviation from the voting population's racial makeup has generally been enough to establish a *prima facie* case of discrimination. But where the selection process does not involve any discretion by the officials (e.g., random selection from tax lists) the occurrence of statistical underrepresentation of minorities has not been enough to make even a *prima facie* case of discrimination. N&R, p. 623.

    **b. Prosecutors' peremptory challenges:** Statistics are similarly one of the ways to prove discrimination by *prosecutors* in their use of *peremptory challenges*.

    **i.  Race-based challenges not allowed:** Peremptory challenges enable either side to excuse a certain number of potential jurors "without cause." Prosecutors may not use such challenges based solely on the race of the juror. For instance, a prosecutor may not, in the trial of a black defendant, exclude all black jurors on the theory that such jurors are more likely to side with a black defendant than a white juror would be. *Batson v. Kentucky*, 476 U.S. 79 (1986).

        **(1)  Statistical proof:** Statistical proof — i.e., proof that the prosecution has consistently declined to seat black jurors in trials of black defendants — is one way to show that the prosecution has violated this general principle.

        **(2)  Other methods:** But other ways of showing impermissible racial bias, not involving statistics, also exist. For instance, ***within the defendant's own case***, the prosecutor's questions during voir dire, or even the pattern of his use of challenges, may support an inference of discrimination. Once the inference of discrimination arises, the burden shifts to the prosecution to explain away the racial exclusion. *Batson, supra.*

        **(3)  Gender-based challenges:** By the way, a state may no longer allow litigants to make ***gender-based*** peremptory challenges, either. See *J.E.B. v. Alabama*, discussed further *infra*, p. 332.

   **c.  Voting rights:** Statistical evidence can also be important in establishing a discriminatory purpose in ***voting rights*** cases. For instance, in *Rogers v. Lodge*, 458 U.S. 613 (1982), black voters attacked an at-large voting scheme; they argued that use of this arrangement (rather than a series of electoral districts) was intended to dilute the black vote. The Court held that proof of discriminatory purpose, not just effect, was needed. But the Court noted that although blacks composed nearly 54% of the population and 38% of the registered voters in the county, no black had ever been elected to the county Board of Commissioners. The Court affirmed the trial court's finding that the requisite proof of discriminatory purpose had been made — the fact that no black had ever been elected was "important evidence of purposeful exclusion" (though there was other evidence of purposeful discrimination as well).

**9.  Consequence of finding of "discrimination":** Suppose that the Court does conclude that the legislature or administration acted in an intentionally discriminatory way in enacting or applying a statute. The state might try to show, in rebuttal, that the same statute ***could*** have been enacted for perfectly legitimate reasons.

   **a.  Probably unsuccessful:** The present Court will not regard this rebuttal as relevant; if a discriminatory purpose was a substantial factor in the enactment, the statute will be ***stricken*** even though a properly-motivated legislature might also have enacted it.

   **b.  Distinction:** This is one of the differences between a statute subjected to strict scrutiny and one which, because it involves only general economic or social welfare considerations, is subjected to a "mere rationality" analysis — in the latter case, any legitimate objective, whether in fact relied upon by the legislature or not, will probably suffice. (See *supra*, p. 244.)

**D.  Other requirements for strict scrutiny:** For discrimination to be subject to strict scrutiny, it is not sufficient that it be "purposeful." It must also be of an especially ***"invidious,"*** or ***preju-***

*dicial*, sort. In practice, this has meant that the discrimination must be on the grounds of either *race* or *national origin*.

1. ***Carolene Products* footnote:** The basic theory behind strict scrutiny for these types of discrimination remains that expressed by Justice Stone in his *Carolene Products* footnote: "Prejudice against **discrete and insular minorities** may be a special condition, which tends seriously to curtail the operation of those political processes ordinarily to be relied upon to protect minorities, and which may call for a correspondingly more searching judicial inquiry." *U.S. v. Carolene Products Co.*, 304 U.S. 144 (1938).

   a. **Tribe's formulation:** Or, as Tribe has put the idea, special judicial protection is given to those groups which, because of "widespread, insistent prejudice against them," occupy the position of *"perennial losers in the political struggle."* Tribe, p. 1454.

2. **Immutability:** It is sometimes suggested that a classification is more likely to be treated as suspect if it is based upon an *immutable* trait, which race and natural origin certainly are. (Immutability also goes some of the way towards explaining the middle-level scrutiny given to classifications based on alienage, illegitimacy and gender, all discussed beginning *infra*, p. 321.)

   a. **Criticism:** However, it is not obvious why the fact of immutability should make a difference. As Professor Ely has pointed out, "[c]lassifications based on physical disability and intelligence are typically accepted as legitimate, even by judges and commentators who assert that immutability is relevant." Ely, p. 150.

3. **Stereotypes:** It is also often suggested that the prevalence of *stereotypes* concerning a group makes it more likely that classifications disadvantaging that group will be found to be "suspect." See, e.g., Justice Blackmun's statement in *Bakke* (*infra*, p. 281) that "[r]acial and ethnic distinctions where they are stereotypes are inherently suspect and call for exacting judicial scrutiny."

   a. **Criticism:** However, the term "stereotype" really means little more than an imperfect generalization. Since almost all legislation involves an imperfect generalization (in the sense that nearly all statutes are under- or over-inclusive or both), it would never do to impose strict scrutiny on any legislation based on a stereotype.

   b. **Incidence of falseness:** Perhaps generalizations whose *incidence of falseness is unduly high* are what should be strictly scrutinized. However, determining what is "too high" is difficult. For instance, as Ely suggests, if a generalization were used to determine who should be subject to capital punishment, virtually *any* occurrence of falsity would be intolerably high; by contrast, if the legislature is trying to identify persons susceptible to heart attacks in order to keep them from piloting commercial aircraft, a high rate of false generalization, perhaps well over 50%, would be appropriate. Ely, p. 156.

   c. **Ely's solution:** Ely suggests that "[t]he cases where we ought to be suspicious are not those involving a generalization whose incidence of counterexample is 'too high,' but rather those involving a generalization whose incidence of counterexample is *significantly higher than the legislative authority appears to have thought it was*." *Id.* at 157.

4. **Modern Court's view:** One Supreme Court case, in discussing why the class of "close relatives" should not be treated as suspect, gave a catalogue of factors the modern Court will view as leading towards strict scrutiny: "As a historical matter, [close relatives] have not been **subjected to discrimination**; they do not exhibit **obvious, immutable,** or **distinguishing characteristics** that define them as a **discrete group**; and they are not a **minority** or **politically powerless**." *Lyng v. Castillo*, 477 U.S. 635 (1986).

E. **How strict is "strict scrutiny":** Once the decision to apply strict scrutiny has been made, the statute will be upheld only if it is found to be **necessary** (not merely appropriate) to the attainment of some **compelling** (not merely desirable) governmental objective. As Professor Gunther has put it, this scrutiny has generally been "'strict' in theory and 'fatal' in fact." 86 HARV. L. REV. 8.

1. **Rationale for strict scrutiny:** Both the requirement of a "compelling" objective and that of "necessary" means to that objective can be seen as aspects of the same judicial goal: to assure that suspect classifications are used only in those very rare situations where the high cost of sanctioning official invidious discrimination is outweighed by the even higher cost of not doing so.

    a. **Weightiness of objective:** An additional reason for requiring, in strict scrutiny cases, that the state objective be "compelling" is that such a requirement represents **a way of ferreting out discriminatory purposes**. Even if the means-end fit is perfect (i.e., the means is the only way of establishing that particular end), if the end that is advanced as a justification is insubstantial, one can legitimately suspect that this end is merely a **pretext**, and that what really motivated the decision was, say, racial prejudice. See Ely, p. 148.

        i. **Illustration:** For instance, suppose a school principal seats African Americans on one side of the stage at a graduation ceremony, and whites on the other, and justifies the choice by claiming that this arrangement is more esthetically appealing. The objective here is so trivial that one could fairly suspect that it was a pretext to cover racial discrimination. See Brest, *Processes of Constitutional Decision-Making*, p. 489 (1975) (quoted in Ely, p. 148).

    b. **"Necessary" means:** The requirement that the means selected (the suspect classification) be "necessary" to attainment of the goal expresses the view that **less discriminatory alternatives** must **always** be used if they are available to attain the goal. In fact, less discriminatory alternatives may sometimes be required to be used even if they will **not** achieve the compelling goal **quite as well** as the discriminatory means. That is, some degree of sacrifice of the legislative objective may be required in the name of equality of treatment.

2. **Strict scrutiny nearly always fatal:** As an illustration of the strictness with which "strict scrutiny" is applied, consider that only once since 1944 has the Supreme Court upheld a governmental classification based on a racial or national-origin classification to which strict scrutiny was applied.

    a. **May be changing:** However, as the present Supreme Court has expanded the use of strict scrutiny, it may, paradoxically, have become **easier** for a measure to survive that scrutiny. Thus in *Adarand Constructors* (*infra*, p. 305), a case applying strict scrutiny to race-based federal affirmative action programs, the Court went out of its way to "dispel the notion that strict scrutiny is 'strict in theory, but fatal in fact.'"

i. **Affirmative action in admissions:** The one post-1944 instance in which a race-based governmental classification has actually survived strict scrutiny by the Court illustrates that strict scrutiny may now be less likely to be fatal. That instance involved the use of affirmative action in ***university admissions.*** See *Grutter v. Bollinger* (*infra*, p. 282), a 2003 case in which the Court upheld the University of Michigan Law School's right to give an admissions preference to black and Hispanic applicants in order to obtain a "diverse" entering class, as long as this preference was granted as part of an individualized evaluation process that treated race as merely one "plus factor" among others.[4]

ii. **Voting Rights Act:** Another context in which race-conscious governmental action might survive strict scrutiny is the ***drawing of race-conscious electoral districts*** where the use of race is required by a federal statute called the ***Voting Rights Act*** (VRA), which strives to prevent the dilution of the racial strength of minority groups in jurisdictions that have previously discriminated against minorities' voting rights. The Court has never actually upheld race-conscious district lines after strict scrutiny in a VRA case, but six members of the *Roberts* court indicated that the government would have a compelling interest in drawing race-conscious lines where the VRA so required; see *League of United Latin American Citizens v. Perry*, 126 S.Ct. 2594 (2006), other aspects of which are discussed further *infra*, p. 314.

3. ***Korematsu:*** Before 2003's *Grutter* decision, the last case in which a racial or ethnic classification ***survived*** strict scrutiny was ***Korematsu v. U.S.***, 323 U.S. 214 (1944), the infamous ***Japanese Exclusion Case.*** (Ironically, *Korematsu* was the first case in which race was explicitly referred to as a "suspect" criterion.)

a. **Facts:** *Korematsu* involved a post-Pearl Harbor military order excluding all persons of Japanese ancestry from certain areas of the West Coast, and resulting in their effective imprisonment. The order was applied against citizens as well as non-citizens.

b. **Holding:** The Court upheld the order, despite its suspectness. It did so on the theory that there was a ***compelling need*** to prevent espionage and sabotage, and that there was no practical and sufficiently rapid way for the military to distinguish the loyal from the disloyal.

c. **Dissent:** Three Justices dissented in *Korematsu*. The strongest dissent was that of Justice Murphy, who argued that the majority's view relied on the "assumption that all persons of Japanese ancestry may have a dangerous tendency to commit sabotage and espionage. ... " He contended that individualized loyalty hearings, at least for those persons who were American citizens, could have been held. Another dissenter, Justice Jackson, pointed out that no attempt was made anywhere in the United States to exclude German or Italian aliens (thus suggesting that the order was based at least in part on racial prejudice, though Justice Jackson did not explicitly so charge).

---

4. But the post-*Grutter* case of *Parents Involved in Community Schools v. Seattle School District No. 1* (*infra*, p. 291), in which the Court struck down the use of race in public-school pupil assignments, suggests that strict scrutiny in the Roberts Court will generally still be very strict indeed.

**d. Criticism:** Commentators have almost universally scorned *Korematsu* as one of the worst betrayals of Americans' constitutional rights in the Supreme Court's history. See sources cited in L,K&C, p. 1263, n. c.

   **i. Military necessity:** Obviously, even the *Korematsu* Court would not have upheld a racial distinction like the one at issue there, if it were not for (what the Court perceived as) extreme emergency. What is most troubling about the decision is not the Court's conclusion that the governmental objective was compelling (since prevention of espionage and sabotage clearly was), but rather, the Court's loose definition of means "necessary" to achieve that objective.

**4. "Separate but equal" treatment:** Strict scrutiny has traditionally been reserved for those classifications which operate to the ***disadvantage*** of a racial or ethnic minority. But suppose that a classification ***utilizes*** race, but does not explicitly disadvantage either blacks or whites. In this situation, claims that there has been "equal application of the law" have usually failed; the school desegregation cases (including the rejection of the "separate but equal" theory, *infra*, p. 264) are the most notable example.

   **Example 1:** A Virginia statute prohibits marriage between a white and a non-white. The state rebuts an equal protection attack by contending that the statute applies "equally" to whites and blacks, since members of each race are punished to the same degree.

   *Held*, the statute violates equal protection. The statute contains a racial classification, and the fact that it has "equal application" does not immunize it from strict scrutiny. Since the legislative history shows that the statute was enacted to "preserve the racial integrity" of citizens (i.e., whites), the statute has only an invidious, discriminatory, purpose, and has no "legitimate overriding" one. ***Loving v. Virginia***, 388 U.S. 1 (1967).

   **Example 2:** Seattle's public-school system, in order to reduce school-by-school racial imbalance, sometimes makes the decision whether to allow a student to transfer into a particular school based solely on whether that student would improve the racial balance in the school.

   *Held*, this race-based scheme, even though it is not intended to systematically disadvantage any race, must be strictly scrutinized (and will be struck down). *Parents Involved in Community Schools v. Seattle School District No. 1*, infra, p. 291.

   **a. Special traits:** There may, however, be ***special traits*** applicable to one race or ethnic group which, if they serve as the basis for a classification, do not necessarily lead to invidious discrimination.

      **i. Alcohol susceptibility:** For instance, there is respectable evidence that American Indians and Eskimos are abnormally susceptible to ***alcohol***; a number of states therefore bar the sale of alcohol to these races. While the Supreme Court has never decided the issue, the Court might well hold that such a classification is not invidious, and does not disadvantage the races at which it is directed. If so, such a statute would probably be upheld.

      **ii. Sickle-cell test:** Similarly, a state might require that all African Americans undergo testing for ***sickle-cell anemia***. Again, such a statute would probably be upheld on the theory that it is benign rather than invidious. See L,K&C, p. 1264, n.

2. The same would presumably be true of a requirement that persons of Jewish ancestry undergo testing for Tay Sachs disease.

   iii. **Overbreadth:** However, these statutes could be subject to attack on an *overbreadth* theory, i.e., a theory that the government may not use racial groups as a substitute for an individualized determination. Such an argument seems unlikely to succeed where individualized treatment would be impractical (e.g., testing all racial groups for all genetic defects, even though a particular defect could almost never occur in most of the races). But where individualized judgments *are* feasible, the Court may well insist upon them even though the use of race as an initial screening device makes matters simpler.

   iv. **Relation to affirmative action:** This issue of "special traits" is related to the much broader issue of "affirmative action," i.e., the extent to which racial classifications may be used to advantage, rather than disadvantage, the minority race. The affirmative action area is discussed more fully *infra*, p. 273.

5. **Racial classes and the political process:** The Court has not hesitated to strictly scrutinize, and strike down, uses of racial classes as part of the *political process.*

   a. **Identification of candidates:** For instance, the Court struck down a law requiring each *candidate's race* to appear on the ballot, in *Anderson v. Martin*, 375 U.S. 399 (1964). The *Anderson* Court apparently believed that, in light of private attitudes towards African Americans at that time and place, the statute was designed to help white candidates.

   b. **More difficult procedures:** Similarly, legislation which, for a racially discriminatory purpose, *modifies the political process* to make certain types of political action more difficult, will be subject to strict scrutiny. Thus in **Hunter v. Erickson**, 393 U.S. 385 (1969), after the Akron City Council adopted a fair housing ordinance, the voters amended the city charter to prohibit any ordinance dealing with racial discrimination in housing, unless it had first been approved by a majority of the voters.

      i. **Holding:** The Supreme Court held that this charter amendment was violative of equal protection, on the theory that it: (1) was an "explicitly racial classification," and (2) clearly made it more difficult to enact antidiscrimination ordinances than other types of ordinances (which automatically passed into law following enactment by the Council).

6. **Other areas:** Some other areas in which the state has used racial classifications are as follows:

   a. **Security:** Prison officials sometimes *separate prisoners by race* in order to quell racial tensions or riots. However, *Johnson v. California*, discussed *infra*, p. 320, holds that a prison system's decision to routinely segregate newly-arrived prisoners by race must be *strictly scrutinized*.

   b. **Official records:** The state may keep official statistics by race, if, but only if, the statistics serve some useful purpose (e.g., a sociological one). Thus the recording of the race of a husband and wife in every divorce has been upheld (*Tancil v. Woolls*, 379 U.S. 19 (1964)), but the keeping of separate lists of blacks and whites in voting and tax records was held to be without useful purpose, and therefore violative of equal protection, in a companion case (*Virginia Board of Elections v. Hamm*, 379 U.S. 19 (1964)).

c. **Child custody and adoption:**   Some states take race into account in decisions on *adoption* and *child custody*. The use of racial considerations for these purposes will certainly be subject to strict scrutiny, and few if any such uses will survive that review.

    i. **Child custody:**   The one case decided by the Supreme Court in this area concerned child custody. In *Palmore v. Sidoti*, 466 U.S. 429 (1984), two white parents were divorced, and custody of the child was given to the mother. The mother then married an African American, and the Florida courts transferred custody to the father on the grounds that if the daughter remained with her mother and stepfather, she would become "vulnerable to peer pressures [and] suffer from the social stigmatization that is sure to come." The Supreme Court unanimously reversed, finding that the Florida court's order could not survive strict scrutiny. The Court conceded that the private biases on which the Florida court relied were probably real ones, but held that the law *may not, directly or indirectly, give effect to such private prejudices*. (In strict scrutiny terms, the Court apparently held that the state's goal of awarding custody based on the "best interests of the child" was a sufficiently compelling one, but that bowing to private prejudices was not a necessary means of accomplishing that goal.)

    ii. **Adoption:**   If a state were to impose a rule that in *adoption* situations, the adoptive parent and the child must be of the same race, there is little doubt that the rationale of *Palmore* would dictate that the state rule be struck down. It is less clear whether race may be considered as *one factor among many*. The rationale of *Palmore* would appear to mean that the possibility of prejudice and social rejection may not be considered by adoption authorities even as one factor among many. However, the broader interest in ensuring that the adoptive parents and child are culturally compatible, and that the child will feel a sense of unity with the adoptive parents, might well be recognized as a compelling one.

F. **Segregation and its remedies:**   Most of the racial classifications discussed above imposed fairly direct, visible, burdens on racial or ethnic minorities. But some, like the miscegenation statute in *Loving v. Virginia*, purported to treat all races "identically," even though they used a racial classification. The most important example of government action which classifies by race, but which, superficially at least, does not explicitly disadvantage minorities, is *segregation*, i.e., the maintenance of physical separateness between the races.

1. **Summary of issues:**   Since 1954, officially-sanctioned segregation not only in the public schools but in other areas has been treated as a *clear violation of equal protection*. Therefore, the principal issues related to segregation have been not whether intentional segregation violates the Constitution, but rather: (a) How does one distinguish between "intentional," or *de jure*, segregation (which is unconstitutional) and unintentional, or *de facto*, segregation (which is not)? and (b) What are the *remedies* for official segregation? Prior to a discussion of these issues, however, some history is in order.

2. **The "separate but equal" doctrine (*Plessy v. Ferguson*):**   Initially, the Supreme Court's view was that *"separate but equal" treatment did not violate equal protection*. This doctrine was formulated in *Plessy v. Ferguson*, 163 U.S. 537 (1896), where the Court upheld a Louisiana law calling for separate-but-equal accommodations for white and black railroad passengers.

**a. Rationale:** The majority reasoned that laws such as this one related only to "social" equality, not to political or civil equality. Social equality was not, the Court held, a goal of the Equal Protection Clause, and could be attained only through ***voluntary action*** by individuals, not by statutes.

    **i. Not badge of inferiority:** Also, the Court reasoned, the law itself did not "stamp ... the colored race with a badge of inferiority." If African Americans felt inferior under the law, "it is not by reason of anything found in the act, but solely because the colored race chooses to put that construction upon it."

**b. Dissent:** The first Justice Harlan, in a classic dissent, argued that the law did indeed violate equal protection. Although it appeared facially neutral, "[e]very one knows that [it] had its origin in the purpose, not so much to exclude white persons from railroad cars occupied by blacks, as to exclude colored people from coaches occupied by or assigned to white persons." The statute therefore interfered with the personal freedom of African Americans.

    **i. "Color blindness":** Harlan then added, in an oft-cited remark, that "***our Constitution is color-blind***." Some have argued that Harlan meant this remark to include "benign" or "reverse" discrimination based on race.

**3. *Brown v. Bd. of Ed.:*** *Plessy v. Ferguson's* validation of "separate but equal" segregation remained the law until 1954. (However, in a series of pre-1954 cases involving graduate school education, the Court found that facilities available to African Americans were not in fact "equal" to those given to whites.) Then, in ***Brown v. Board of Education***, 347 U.S. 483 (1954), the Court explicitly ***rejected the "separate but equal" doctrine***, at least insofar as public education was concerned.

**a. Rationale:** The Court reasoned that even where all-black and all-white schools were equal in terms of "tangible" factors, intangible factors necessarily prevented children who were restricted to all-black schools from receiving equal educational opportunities. In particular, racial segregation "generates [in African American students] a feeling of inferiority as to their status in the community that may affect their hearts and minds in a way unlikely ever to be undone. ... Separate educational facilities are ***inherently unequal.***"

    **i. Expert opinion:** In reaching this conclusion, the Court also relied on the findings of psychologists and educators who had concluded from their research that segregation gave African American pupils a sense of inferiority, which in turn impaired their motivation to learn and their success at learning.

    **ii. Fourteenth Amendment's history irrelevant:** One factor upon which the *Brown* Court did ***not*** particularly rely was the ***legislative history*** of the Fourteenth Amendment itself. The Court noted that, at the time that Amendment was adopted, blacks in the South were not educated at all, and even in the North there was no compulsory public education system for whites, let alone blacks. Therefore, nothing in the legislative history of the Amendment gave the Court any real clue about what Congress intended with respect to school segregation. Instead, the Court decided to focus on public education as it stood in 1954, not as it stood when the Amendment was adopted in 1868.

**b. Also applicable to federal government:** On the same day as *Brown* was decided, the Court held that the ***federal government*** could not be permitted to operate racially-segregated schools any more than could the states. In *Bolling v. Sharpe*, 347 U.S. 497 (1954), the Court held the racial segregation of the District of Columbia public schools to be in violation of the Fifth Amendment's Due Process Clause. The Court concluded that such segregation was not reasonably related to any proper governmental objective, and thus was an arbitrary deprivation of African American students' liberty. Given that such conduct by the ***states*** was not constitutionally permissible, "[i]t would be unthinkable that the same Constitution would impose a lesser duty on the Federal Government."

4. **Criticism of empirical basis:** A casual reading of *Brown v. Bd. of Ed.* gives the impression that the Court was relying principally upon ***social science*** and ***empirical evidence***, i.e., factual evidence that segregation indeed harms African American students. But if that is the basis for the Court's decision, it may be criticized. As one commentator has said, "I would not have the constitutional rights of Negroes — or of other Americans — rest on any such flimsy foundation as some of the scientific demonstrations in these records. [Behavioral science findings] have an uncertain expectancy of life." 30 N.Y.U. L. REV. 157-58.

   **a. Possibility of new evidence:** For instance, one could imagine new findings suggesting that, where there are truly equal tangible facilities, African American students do ***better*** in segregated schools than as a minority in a school where they are subject to hostility, and possibly violence, from the white majority. See Wechsler, *Toward Neutral Principles of Constitutional Law*, 73 HARV. L. REV. 33.

   **b. Change in African Americans' views:** Furthermore, since such a psychologically-focused theory turns on African Americans' own feelings about segregation, such a theory would presumably no longer be valid if a majority of black students or parents in a given community preferred separation. Constitutional requirements could then theoretically vary from town to town, depending on the views of local African Americans; such a result would not foster the uniformity and predictability usually considered desirable in constitutional (or other) law.

5. **Other public facilities:** Although *Brown* by its terms applied only to schools, the Court extended its rejection of the "separate but equal" doctrine to many ***other public facilities*** during the following ten years.

6. **Implementation of *Brown (Brown II)*:** The Court in *Brown*, by pronouncing official segregation to be a violation of equal protection, did not by that pronouncement alone do much to modify the actual educational patterns of Kansas or any other state. It was only by a long series of "implementation" decisions that a significant reduction in school segregation came about. The first of these implementation decisions was a continuation of *Brown* itself; in *Brown v. Board of Education*, 349 U.S. 294 (1955), the so-called ***Brown II*** decision, the Court did several significant things:

   **a. Lower federal courts:** It gave the ***federal district courts*** primary responsibility for supervising desegregation because of their "proximity to local conditions" and the "possible need for further hearings."

   **b. Equitable principles:** The Court gave no precise guidelines for carrying out desegregation. Instead, it directed the district courts to use *"**general equitable principles.**"*

c. **"All deliberate speed":** A plaintiff whose constitutional rights have been violated by state action would normally be entitled to **immediate** relief. But, apparently because it feared the chaos and violence that might develop if attempts were made to carry out desegregation instantly, the Court authorized the district courts to take into account the public interest in eliminating desegregation "in a systematic and effective manner." However, the burden of proving any need for delay was placed upon the school boards, and the lower courts were ordered to implement desegregation "with *all deliberate speed.*"

7. **Aftermath of *Brown*:** For almost a decade after *Brown*, the Supreme Court rarely intervened in the desegregation process, leaving this to the federal district courts and to local politics. However, in *Cooper v. Aaron*, 358 U.S. 1 (1958) (discussed *supra*, p. 11), where the governor of Arkansas had used the National Guard to block desegregation of a Little Rock high school, all nine Justices refused to grant to the Little Rock Board of Education a 2 1/2 year delay in desegregation. The Court refused to allow the constitutional rights of African American children to be compromised by actions of the governor and the legislature, even though the school board itself had made good-faith efforts to desegregate.

8. **Specific rules for desegregating:** Then, beginning in a 1963 case, the Court began to lay down much more specific guidelines concerning what means were acceptable for implementing desegregation. Some of the important principles which emerged from this line of cases are as follows.

   a. **Minority-to-majority transfer invalid:** Some school districts rezoned to create schools that would be initially desegregated, but then permitted any student whose race was in a minority in a particular school to transfer to a school where he would be in the majority. These *"minority-to-majority" transfer plans* were invalidated in *Goss v. Board of Education*, 373 U.S. 683 (1963), on the grounds that such schemes "inevitably lead toward segregation of the students by race."

   b. **Closing of public schools:** A county's scheme to *close its public schools* rather than comply with a desegregation order, and then to fund white-only private schools through state and local tax credits and grants, was rejected in *Griffin v. County School Board*, 377 U.S. 218 (1964). The Court indicated that a county could under some circumstances close its public schools, but that it could not do so for an *unconstitutional purpose*, which avoiding desegregation obviously was.

   c. **"Freedom of choice" plans rejected:** Many districts adopted *"freedom of choice"* plans, under which any student could attend the school of his choice. In *Green v. County School Board*, 391 U.S. 430 (1968), a small school district had about a 50% African American population, two schools, and little residential segregation. After the "freedom of choice" plan had been in operation for three years, no white child had chosen to go to the formerly black school, and 85% of the black students remained in that school.

      i. **Holding:** In these circumstances, the Court held, the plan did not adequately desegregate the schools. Once a school system had been officially segregated, the Constitution required that it be converted to a "unitary, non-racial system of public education."

      ii. ***Green's* focus on effect, not cost:** *Green* is probably most significant not for the fact that it rejected "freedom of choice" plans, but for the fact that it was the first case in which the Supreme Court attached explicit importance to the *effect* of desegregation measures, and not merely to the *intent* with which those measures were enacted. Once official segregation existed, *good intentions* on the part of the school board *were not sufficient*; whatever affirmative measures were needed to bring about a unitary, non-racial system must be implemented. This doctrine has essentially continued in force to date.

9. *Swann v. Charlotte-Mecklenburg:* Perhaps the most important case giving guidance to the district courts and school boards concerning the techniques of desegregation came in *Swann v. Charlotte-Mecklenburg Board of Education*, 402 U.S. 1 (1971). In *Swann*, the Court made the following rulings:

   a. **Must have *de jure* segregation:** The federal courts may not order a school board to adjust the racial composition of any of its schools (*no matter how great the racial imbalance as between schools*) unless there has been a finding that there was *officially-maintained* (i.e., intentional or *de jure*) segregation. Thus a federal court may not order *de facto* segregation, no matter how severe, to be cured by adjustment of racial balance. (However, the Court noted, the school board itself could constitutionally exercise *discretion* to adjust racial balances, "in order to prepare students to live in a pluralistic society. ... ")

   b. **Racial quotas:** Once official segregation is found, the court may, in determining the appropriate remedy, consider what the *ratio* is of black students to white students for the district as a whole. While the court may *not* require that every school in the district have *precisely that ratio*, the district-wide ratio may be considered as a "useful starting point in shaping a remedy."

   c. **Single-race schools:** The fact that one or more schools that are completely or almost completely *single-race remain* in a district does *not* necessarily mean that desegregation has not yet been accomplished. But such schools must be carefully scrutinized by the court, and it is up to the school board to show that the racial concentration in these schools is not due to official segregation but to other causes (e.g., residential patterns).

   d. **Rezoning:** *Rezoning*, i.e., the redrawing of attendance zones, is a *permissible* technique for remedying segregation. Furthermore, the new zones do *not* necessarily have to be either "compact" or *contiguous*. Thus the Court approved, in *Swann* itself, a system of *"pairing"* and *"clustering"* schools from non-contiguous parts of the city. The effect of this scheme was to combine predominantly African American schools with predominantly white schools, so as to bring racial balance to each school in the pair or cluster.

      i. **Not usable for *de facto* cases:** Again, the Court emphasized that such an order could never be given to remedy *de facto* segregation; it was only because the school authorities presented the lower court with a "loaded gameboard" that this kind of alteration of attendance zones was permissible.

   e. **Busing:** The Court also *approved busing* as a means of bringing about desegregation. "Desegregation plans cannot be limited to the walk-in school." The scheme ordered in *Swann* was valid, because it did not result in excessive amounts of busing, compared with the amount being done voluntarily by the district prior to the desegregation order.

i. **Danger to health or education:** However, the Court indicated that a busing scheme would not be upheld if "the time or distance of travel is so great as to risk either the health of the children or significantly impinge on the educational process."

f. **Later unintentional imbalances allowed:** *Swann* and later cases establish that once the effects of official segregation have been even ***temporarily remedied***, later imbalances caused by ***changing residential patterns*** or other non-official conduct may not be cured by federal court order. (The school board itself, of course, always remains free to cure such imbalances as a matter of discretion; the board simply cannot be forced by a federal court to do so.)

i. **Illustration:** A post-*Swann* case illustrates this principle, and demonstrates that court-supervised desegregation will not necessarily ever lead to a desegregated school system. In *Board of Education v. Dowell*, 498 U.S. 237 (1991), the Court held that as long as the school board had complied in good faith with the desegregation decree (which it had apparently done for the six prior years), and as long as the vestiges of past *de jure* discrimination had been eliminated ***"to the extent practicable,"*** the desegregation decree should be lifted and the school district allowed to revert to a system of neighborhood schools. This was true even though, evidence showed, 33 of the 64 elementary schools would then be either more-than-90% black or more-than-90% white. (If the present residential segregation was due to the prior official school segregation, then obviously the Supreme Court's "vestiges of past discrimination removed" standard would not be satisfied. But if the residential segregation was due primarily to ***people's personal choices about where to live***, then, the Supreme Court indicated, the court desegregation order would have to be lifted and the district could revert to neighborhood — and thus *de facto* segregated — schools.) See more about ending federal-court supervision of desegregation, *infra*, p. 272.

10. **Desegregation in the North:** For the first twenty years following *Brown*, virtually all of the Supreme Court's school desegregation cases involved the South, where segregation was generally ***required by law*** at the time *Brown* was decided. These cases thus presented the Court with little need to distinguish between *de jure* and *de facto* segregation, or to prescribe methods for determining whether a school board had intended to segregate — all racial imbalance which the Court evaluated could be linked quite directly to statutorily-required segregation. But then, starting in 1974, the Court began to hear cases involving claimed segregation in the ***North***, where there was virtually no statutorily-authorized segregation at the time of *Brown v. Bd. of Ed.* In a series of Northern cases, the Court attempted to lay down some rules for dealing with a number of new issues, most of them relating to the *de facto/de jure* distinction.

11. ***Keyes* (the Denver case):** The first Northern case was ***Keyes v. School District #1***, 413 U.S. 189 (1973), involving the Denver system. Segregation in Colorado had never been statutorily required. But the district court found that Denver school authorities had used gerrymandered attendance zones, school construction policies, and other devices to purposely keep one part of the city's school system, the Park Hill area, racially segregated. The Supreme Court then made the following rulings for dealing with this and other cases where there was no statutorily-mandated segregation:

a. ***De jure* requirement maintained:** The Court repeated that only *de jure* segregation, not *de facto* segregation, could be redressed by court action, and emphasized that *de jure* segregation would be found to exist only where there was a ***purpose or intent*** to segregate.

b. **Segregation of one part of district:** The most important aspect of *Keyes* is in the Court's treatment of the ***effects*** of a finding that there was intentional segregation as to ***one substantial part*** of a ***larger*** metropolitan district. Such a finding could, the Court held, have one or both of the following effects:

i. **Dual system:** The finding of intentional segregation of a substantial portion of the district would create a ***prima facie case*** that there was a "dual" school system, i.e., that the ***entire district*** was segregated. This *prima facie* demonstration of a dual system could be rebutted only if the school board showed that the segregated part should be viewed as a ***separate, unrelated*** area, and that segregation in that one part had no effect on the others.

ii. **Probative of segregative intent:** Even if the school board succeeded in showing that the district was divided into unrelated areas, the finding of segregative intent as to one area (the Park Hill area) would create a ***presumption*** that segregated patterns in the other areas were intentional, not coincidental. This presumption, in turn, could only be rebutted if the school board showed either that: (1) segregative intent was not in fact one of the motivating factors in the board's actions as to these other areas (it would not be enough to show that some hypothetical "innocent" motivation "could" have produced those actions by the board); or (2) past segregative acts by the school board did not "create or contribute to the current segregated condition" of the schools. Thus the board would have to prove ***either lack of intent***, or ***lack of a causal connection*** between intent and segregation.

c. **Summary:** Thus, as a practical matter, a plaintiff who is able to show segregative intent as to one portion of a large school district enjoys an enormous tactical advantage over his adversary: the burden of proof is shifted entirely to the school board to explain away segregated conditions in other portions of the district.

d. **African Americans and Hispanics aggregated:** The *Keyes* Court defined as segregated any school having a ***combined*** predominance of African Americans ***and Hispanics***. It did so on the theory that these groups had suffered "identical discrimination in treatment," at least in the Southwest. This conclusion had the effect of identifying more segregated schools than if African American enrollment alone were considered.

12. **Interdistrict remedies:** Many of the country's big-city school districts are now predominantly African American. If a city's school system is shown to be *de jure* segregated, may a federal judge order a remedy which ***includes suburban school districts***? In ***Milliken v. Bradley***, 418 U.S. 717 (1974), the Court answered this question, for most purposes, in the ***negative***. The case was decided by a 5-4 split.

a. **Facts:** The school district for the city of Detroit is predominantly African American. The Detroit suburbs, consisting of numerous towns each having its own school district, are predominantly white. A federal trial judge, after concluding that the city had practiced *de jure* segregation, concluded that a Detroit-only desegregation plan would not be effective, since many schools would remain more than 75% African American.

He therefore ordered that 53 surrounding suburban communities participate in the desegregation plan.

**b.** **Majority holding:** Justice Burger, writing for a majority of the Court, reversed. He cited the general principle of equity that "[t]he scope of the remedy is determined by the nature and extent of the constitutional violation." Thus there could be a cross-district remedy *only if there had been a cross-district wrong*, i.e., segregation in Detroit that *caused an effect in the suburbs*, or vice versa.

   **i.** **Practical problems:** Burger also pointed to the practical problems that would result from a cross-district desegregation order. Difficult jurisdictional issues would arise regarding the right to levy taxes, the right to establish attendance zones, the authority to locate and construct new schools, etc. And such consolidation would weaken the strong tradition of local control over public education.

   **ii.** **State's role irrelevant:** The majority also rejected the dissent's argument (an argument also advanced by the district court), that there had been significant participation by the *state of Michigan* in the Detroit segregation. Even assuming that this was so (which the majority denied), the constitutional right of black students in Detroit was merely "to attend a unitary school system *in that district*."

**c.** **Dissent:** The four dissenters in *Milliken* produced two opinions, the main one by Justice White.

   **i.** **White's dissent:** White's dissent stressed that the city of Detroit was a *subdivision of the state*, and that it was the state, not the locality, that must "respond to the command of the Fourteenth Amendment." Justice White simply saw no historical support for a rule that desegregation remedies must stop at the district line.

**13. Segregated colleges and universities:** So far, we've spoken only about segregation in the context of elementary schools up through high schools. Where government has intentionally segregated in a *college or university*, the same basic rule applies: this *de jure* segregation violates the Equal Protection Clause and must be dismantled. See *U.S. v. Fordice*, 505 U.S. 717 (1992).

**14. State and congressional efforts to curb busing:** Several states have attempted to *limit* the use of *busing* as a judicially-ordered desegregation tool. The Supreme Court has issued two opinions concerning the states' right to do this.

**a.** **Law stricken in Seattle case:** In a case involving a Seattle busing plan, *Washington v. Seattle School Dist. No. 1*, 458 U.S. 457 (1982), the state's effort to nullify the busing plan was ruled *unconstitutional.*

   **i.** **Facts:** Seattle enacted a plan to undo *de facto* segregation in its schools by, *inter alia*, use of mandatory busing. The State of Washington then enacted, by initiative, a law *preventing local school districts* from enacting busing plans (but not purporting to limit a court's right to order busing as a remedy for *de jure* segregation).

   **ii.** **Law held violative of equal protection:** By a 5-4 vote, the Court held the state initiative violative of equal protection. The majority opinion, written by Justice Blackmun, relied on *Hunter v. Erickson* (*supra*, p. 263), and held that the *reallocation of governmental decision-making power must be done in a racially-neutral manner*. Since the issue of mandatory busing had strong racial overtones, the state could not strip local school boards of the right to decide busing matters, yet leave these boards with control over other local school matters. The state law was unconstitutional because it made it "more difficult for certain racial and religious minorities … to achieve legislation that is in their interest."

b. **California case allows limits on remedies:**   But in a companion case from California, the Court *upheld* an *amendment to the state constitution* which had the effect of preventing judicially-ordered busing in cases of *de facto* segregation. *Crawford v. Los Angeles Board of Education*, 458 U.S. 527 (1982).

   i. **Facts:**  *Crawford* arose from an earlier California Supreme Court opinion which had interpreted the equal protection clause of the *state* constitution to bar *de facto*, not just *de jure*, school segregation. The California Constitution was then amended to prevent state courts from ordering mandatory busing unless a federal court would order such busing to redress a violation of the federal Equal Protection Clause (i.e., unless the segregation were found to be *de jure*.)

   ii. **Amendment upheld:**  Eight members of the Court found this amendment to be constitutional. The majority's basic rationale was that California, having gone further in enforcing the right to racially-balanced schools than the federal Constitution required, should be *free to return* in part to the federal standard. The majority did not see this as a case in which the *Hunter v. Erickson* principle was applicable, since the political decision-making process with respect to busing had not been modified; this was simply a case in which an anti-discrimination or desegregation law had been modified, *something which a state has always been permitted to do.*

   iii. **Absence of discriminatory intent:**  Had the amendment clearly been enacted by voters for discriminatory *purposes*, the Court suggested, that fact might have made the amendment unconstitutional. But there was no evidence that such a purpose, rather than, say, a desire to have the benefits of neighborhood schooling, motivated most voters.

c. **Distinction between two cases:**  One central theme that emerges from a comparison of the *Washington* and *Crawford* cases is that only the *reallocation of decision-making power*, not the mere elimination of a desegregation or anti-discrimination policy, will be found unconstitutional. Desegregation laws and remedies, like, say, fair housing ordinances, may be repealed at any time. But the power to make decisions about racially-linked issues may not be reallocated in a way that makes it harder for minorities to obtain favorable disposition of such issues (as, for instance, by depriving them of the ability to win at the local level, something they had accomplished in Seattle).

15. **Ending District-Court supervision:**  More than 50 years have now passed since *Brown v. Board of Ed.* Some school districts have been under federal-court supervision for desegregation for nearly that entire time. When does that supervision end? It ends when the school district has been "*restored to unitary status.*" That is, supervision (and constitutionally-mandated desegregation efforts) must end as soon as the *effects* of the *official* segregation have been eliminated. Supervision will *not* necessarily last until the system is truly integrated.

a. **Neighborhood re-segregation:**  So the fact that *neighborhoods* have become *re-segregated* (after school desegregation began) based *on private housing decisions*, and that this has led to re-segregated local schools, can't be used to justify extending federal-court supervision.

    **b. White flight:** Similarly, the fact that busing or other desegregation methods have caused ***whites*** to ***flee*** the school district entirely for the surrounding suburbs, leaving the former *de jure* segregated city system heavily minority, can't be used to delay the end of judicial supervision. See *Missouri v. Jenkins*, 515 U.S. 70 (1995).

    **c. Use of race for pupil assignments:** Once unitary status has been restored, any use of race in making pupil assignments will be strictly scrutinized, as if the official segregation had never occurred. That's what happened in the Louisville portion of *Parents Involved in Community Schools v. Seattle School District No. 1*, *infra*, p. 291 — the fact that de facto segregated housing patterns had caused individual schools to become racially isolated once again was not a reason to allow race-conscious pupil assignments to occur, a majority of the Court believed.

# IV. AFFIRMATIVE ACTION AND "BENIGN" DISCRIMINATION

  **A. "Benign" discrimination generally:** We live in a world in which governments, universities, major corporations, etc., are all trying (or at least claim to be trying) to reverse the effects of past discrimination. Yet, past discrimination often cannot be reversed without treating people differently, based upon explicit consideration of the very criterion on which the past discrimination was based (e.g., race or sex).

    **1. Problem:** Not surprisingly, such attempts to remedy past discrimination (sometimes called ***"benign"*** or ***"reverse"*** discrimination, and more frequently, ***"affirmative action"***) present major constitutional questions in their own right. Probably the most important is: What standard should be used to review the "benign" use of a "suspect" classification, such as race? Since classifications which disadvantage a racial minority will be strictly scrutinized, and may be justified only where they are "necessary" to fulfill a "compelling" governmental objective (see *supra*, p. 260), is the same strict scrutiny required of "affirmative action" attempts based on race?

       **a. Strict scrutiny:** The answer is ***"yes"***, the same strict scrutiny is required of "affirmative action" attempts based on race as is required of race-based classifications that disadvantage a minority. This is the result of the landmark decision in *City of Richmond v. J.A. Croson Co.*, discussed *infra*, p. 299.

    **2. Sex considered before race:** Before we begin our discussion of the benign use of racial classifications, however, we will discuss the benign use of ***sexual*** classes. Although discrimination against women is not viewed with the same extremely high level of suspicion as is discrimination against African Americans (compare *supra*, p. 252 with *infra*, p. 321), the reverse discrimination precedents in the sexual area laid important groundwork for *Croson* and other racial affirmative action cases.

  **B. Benign use of sex classes:** Where a sexual classification ***disadvantages*** women, it is subjected to "middle-level" scrutiny. That is, the gender-based classification must be "substantially" related to the achievement of "important" governmental objectives. (See *Craig v. Boren, infra*, p. 323.) Perhaps surprisingly, statutes which make sexual classifications which ***favor*** women, even if enacted solely to remedy past anti-female discrimination, are judged by exactly the same formal standard: the statute will be stricken if the sex-based criterion is not substantially related to an important governmental objective. Thus to put it colloquially, the legislature gets no explicit "brownie points" for attempting to remedy past sexual discrimination.

1. **"Means" aspect most important:**   However, there is a sense in which a statute that favors women in an attempt to remedy past discrimination may implicitly be subject to gentler review. The Supreme Court has generally acknowledged that the aim of remedying a particular type of past sexual discrimination is itself a worthy and "important" governmental objective. Thus most of the pro-women statutes have passed or failed the Court's middle-level scrutiny principally on whether the *means* part of the test was satisfied, i.e., whether there was a "substantial relationship" between the statute and the discrimination which was to be remedied.

   a. **Alimony:**   Thus an Alabama statute which allowed *alimony* to be awarded only against men was stricken by the Court because of its weakness in the "means," rather than the "end," part of the test. In *Orr v. Orr*, 440 U.S. 268 (1979), the Court recognized that the statute helped serve an important governmental objective, namely, compensating women for discrimination during marriage. But an outright ban on alimony awards against women was *not substantially related* to the worthy objective.

      i. **Rationale:**   The Court observed that the relative financial need of the parties was already required to be considered as part of the divorce process, so that there was no need to use sex as an automatic "proxy for financial dependence." Furthermore, the only women who would be given extra protection by the statute were those who were *not* financially needy; thus the statute's main effect was at odds with its stated purpose.

2. **Difficulty of verifying "benignness":**   Observe that it is not always so easy to verify whether discrimination that is claimed to be "benign" really *is*. For instance, a legislature which takes the general view (as Alabama's apparently did, in *Orr, supra*) that women invariably need to be protected may, although claiming that it is helping them by special legislation, in actuality be *reinforcing a negative and untrue stereotype of them.*

3. **Attempt to remedy past discrimination:**   Where a gender classification is used in an attempt to remedy *specific, objectively-verifiable* past discrimination against women (rather than to perpetuate stereotypes of women's dependency), the statute is much more likely to be upheld.

   a. **Remedy for job discrimination:**   Thus in *Califano v. Webster*, 430 U.S. 313 (1977), the Court unanimously upheld a Social Security Act provision which in computing a wage earner's "average monthly wage" (upon which benefits are based) allowed women to exclude three more lower-earning years than a man could.

      i. **Rationale:**   The Court found that this provision was not the result of "archaic and overbroad generalizations" about women, but was rather the result of prior objectively-verifiable discrimination which had barred most women from all but the lowest-paying jobs. Thus the measure directly, even though only partially, remedied past discrimination.

   b. **Blurry line:**   But the line between remedying past discrimination, and merely viewing women stereotypically as incapable of earning a living, may sometimes be quite blurry. For instance, the same year as *Califano v. Webster*, the Court struck down a provision of the Social Security Act which paid benefits to a widow of a covered worker, but paid them to a widower only if he proved dependency on his deceased wife. ***Califano v. Goldfarb***, 430 U.S. 199 (1977). The plurality opinion felt that the provision was not a defensible attempt to help women because they were needier; it was simply an attempt to aid "dependent spouses of deceased wage earners, coupled with a presumption that wives are usually dependent." The plurality found this presumption of dependency impermissible.

   i.  **Criticism:**  It is hard to see why the presumption in *Webster* (that women have usually received lower wages) is any less objectionable than the presumption in *Goldfarb* that most women are dependents. Each presumption is probably true in most cases though not in all. Perhaps the different result really stems from the fact that one presumption is ***harder to prove or disprove*** in a ***particular case*** than the other. A widow (or a widower) could relatively easily prove dependence on the deceased spouse; therefore, the *Goldfarb* presumption was unnecessary. A woman would find it much more difficult to prove that she had been the victim of lower wages due to employment discrimination, by contrast; therefore, the presumption in *Webster* could not easily have been replaced by a case-by-case determination.

   ii.  **Not necessarily benign:**  Notice that the discrimination in *Goldfarb* was ***not necessarily "benign,"*** i.e., not necessarily favorable to women. It favored widows over widowers, but a working wife was actually disfavored over a working husband, in that the working wife received for her social security taxes less protection for her spouse than did the working husband. Thus there was not an especially strong reason for the Court to treat this as a statute which favored women and which therefore might be entitled to somewhat less rigorous scrutiny. (However, as stated above, even in true "benign" sex discrimination cases, the formal standard of review seems to be the same as in cases involving anti-women statutes.)

4. **Statutory interpretation or remand:**  The equal protection problem in *Goldfarb* could have been solved ***either*** by requiring case-by-case determination of dependency for survivors of ***both*** sexes, or by ***not*** requiring it for survivors of ***either*** sex.

   a.  **Remove classification:**  Sometimes the Court itself, as a matter of statutory interpretation, may completely remove the sex-based classification (e.g., by completely eliminating the need for case-by-case determination of dependency or, conversely, by making that dependency determination mandatory for both sexes.) This will generally happen only where federal legislation is involved.

   b.  **Remand:**  Where a state statute is at issue, the Court will typically ***remand to the legislature*** for the latter to make the decision about which way to modify the statute; this is what happened in *Wengler v. Druggist's Mutual Ins. Co.*, 446 U.S. 142 (1980).

5. **Statutory rape:**  A necessary (though not sufficient) condition for "benign" sex discrimination to be legal is that men and women be ***differently situated***, in a way relevant to the statute's purpose. Of all the possible differences between the sexes, the clearest ones are of course ***biological***. For instance, the fact that only women may become pregnant led a majority (albeit a bare one) of the Court to declare California's ***statutory rape law valid***, even though it applied only to male defendants, in ***Michael M. v. Superior Court***, 450 U.S. 464 (1981).

a. **Nature of statute:**   The statute involved in *Michael M.* made it a crime to have sexual intercourse with a female under the age of eighteen. Thus only men could be liable for "statutory rape" (more precisely, "unlawful sexual intercourse").

b. **Plurality upholds statute:**   A four-Justice plurality upheld the statute (with Justice Blackmun, concurring in the judgment, supplying the fifth vote.) The plurality acknowledged that, since the statute discriminated based on sex, it could be upheld only if the classification bore a "substantial relationship" to "important governmental objectives" (the "middle-level scrutiny" standard of *Craig v. Boren, infra*, p. 323). This test could only be met if men and women were situated differently, in a way that was relevant to the statutory purpose.

   i. **Statutory purpose:**   The plurality found it obvious that the purpose of the statute was to ***prevent illegitimate teenage pregnancies***. This purpose was also, the plurality held, an "important governmental objective."

   ii. **Substantial relation:**   The fighting issue in the case, however, was whether there was a ***substantial relation*** between this important objective and the classification chosen. The plurality felt that there was, for two reasons: (1) Since only women can become pregnant, the male had no direct disincentive from having sex with an unmarried minor. The statute therefore served to "roughly 'equalize' the deterrence on the sexes." (2) Enforcement of the statute was more feasible if the girl was exempted from prosecution, since a successful prosecution would normally require her testimony, which she would generally not give if she might be subjected to prosecution.

c. **Dissent:**   Four Justices dissented, in opinions written by Justices Brennan and Stevens. The dissenters believed that, even if prevention of illegitimate pregnancy was the statute's goal (something they were not convinced of), the male-only prosecution scheme ***did not substantially advance*** that objective. They felt that a statute which applied equally to the woman would be a still stronger deterrent (even assuming that ***enforcement*** might be more difficult.) As Justice Stevens put it, "the fact that a class of persons is especially vulnerable to a risk that a statute is designed to avoid is a reason for making the statute applicable to that class."

6. **Draft registration of women:**   The federal government's historical refusal to require the ***draft registration*** or ***conscription*** of women might be viewed as "benign" sex discrimination. In ***Rostker v. Goldberg***, 453 U.S. 57 (1981), the Court ***upheld male-only draft registration***. However, the Court did not view the case as involving affirmative action but rather, military necessity.

   a. **Facts:**   The draft registration process is simply a way of maintaining an inventory of available personnel who may be drafted in the event of a military emergency. An actual draft, in turn, would almost certainly be principally for the purpose of drafting ***combat*** troops. At least until the Persian Gulf War, the policy of both Congress and the armed services had been that women should not serve in combat. The issue in *Rostker* (at least for the majority) was whether the policy against use of women in combat was sufficient to allow Congress to decline to require registration of women.

   b. **Majority upholds exclusion:**   Six Justices held that the exclusion of women from registration was ***not*** a violation of equal protection. The majority did not clearly articulate the test to which it was subjecting the regulation. However, it rejected the government's request that a "mere rationality" standard be used, and implied that it was applying the "heightened scrutiny" (i.e., middle-level scrutiny) standard of *Craig v. Boren*.

  c. **Factors:** In upholding the exclusion of women despite this middle-level scrutiny, the majority relied upon the following factors:

   i. **Deference to Congress in military affairs:** In the area of ***military affairs***, Congress' authority is extremely broad, and the courts should show even greater-than-usual deference to congressional decisionmaking.

   ii. **Not unthinking stereotype:** Congress gave careful, and reasoned, consideration whether to register women. In contrast to several other legislative schemes previously reviewed by the Court, the decision not to register women was not the "accidental by-product of a traditional way of thinking about women."

   iii. **Not eligible for combat:** As noted, women were currently not eligible for combat. (The constitutionality of this restriction was not before the Court.) According to the majority, the purpose of registration is to prepare for the possible drafting of combat troops. Since women would not be drafted for combat posts under the present scheme, the government was justified in not registering them. Because of the combat restrictions, this was a case in which men and women "are ***simply not similarly situated*** for purposes of a draft or registration for a draft."

 7. **New "exceedingly persuasive justification" standard:** It's not clear whether gender-based schemes that the Court finds to be truly "benign" or compensatory will have to meet the same tough standard that non-benign gender-based enactments now have to meet. In *U.S. v. Virginia, infra*, p. 326, the Court held that gender-based schemes like the one there (maintenance of all-male status for the Virginia Military Institute) could be sustained only if the state showed an ***"exceedingly persuasive justification"*** that the Court would look at with "skeptical scrutiny." But the scheme in that case was clearly not a "benign" one, or one that was motivated by a desire to redress past discrimination; it was instead an old scheme that (the Court found) derived from stereotypes about gender roles. It's too soon to tell whether this new, tougher version of mid-level review will be applied to schemes that attempt to reverse prior discrimination against one sex or the other.

C. **Race:** We turn now to the "benign" use of ***racial*** classifications. Just as in the sex-based area, the scrutiny is the same "middle level" one for both "benign" and non-benign discrimination, so race-based classification will receive the same ***strict*** scrutiny whether the classification is supposedly "benign" (i.e., an attempt to help previously disadvantaged racial minorities) or invidious (an attempt by the white majority to hurt African American or other racial minorities). This is the result of *City of Richmond v. J.A. Croson Co.*, discussed *infra*, p. 299.

*Croson* does not mean that a race-based classification will always be struck down. For instance, a governmental body that had previously discriminated against African-Americans in a very clear way might be able to institute a race-based scheme to eradicate the effects of that discrimination. Similarly, a university that wants to obtain a "diverse" class may give a preference to applicants from underrepresented minorities, as long as this is done as part of an individualized process; see *Grutter v. Bollinger, infra*, p. 282. However, any race-based classification will clearly face a ***presumption of unconstitutionality***, even if it is motivated by affirmative action concerns.

1. **Significance:** Therefore, a race-conscious affirmative action plan, whether it is in the area of employment, college admissions, voting rights or anywhere else, must be adopted for the purpose of furthering some *"compelling"* governmental interest, and the racial classification must be *necessary* to achieve that compelling governmental interest. The only governmental objectives that have so far been endorsed by the Court as possibly supporting race-conscious affirmative action are (1) the *redressing of clear past discrimination* and (2) the pursuit of *diversity* in a *student body.* The former is the kind of affirmative action on which we will be focusing here.

2. **Past discrimination:** When government institutes an affirmative action plan to accomplish the objective of redressing past racial discrimination, two key questions arise: (1) what kind of *proof* must there be that there's really been past discrimination? and (2) *who is it* who must have discriminated? So far, the Supreme Court hasn't given much guidance on these issues. A reasonable guess would go like this:

    a. **No findings needed:** As to question 1 — what kind of proof of discrimination is needed — there must be *quite strong and specific evidence of past discrimination* against African Americans or other racial minorities whom the plan is helping. It's not enough that the government has a general belief that there's been discrimination. Nor is it enough that African Americans are in some sense *"under-represented"* among the job-holders, students, contractors, or whatever "goody" is in issue.

        **Example:** The Richmond, Virginia City Council notices that less than 1% of the city's construction contracts have been awarded to minority-owned businesses in the past five years. It therefore infers that general contractors have discriminated against minority-owned firms, and requires that henceforth, 30% of the dollar amount of all City-funded construction projects must go to minority-owned firms.

        *Held*, this racially-based classification must be subjected to strict scrutiny, and will only be upheld if necessary to achieve a compelling governmental purpose. If there were clear evidence of past racial discrimination by general contractors, the City would have a compelling interest in having its tax dollars not used to support such discrimination by private firms. But here, the city did not have "hard" evidence of such past discrimination. The fact that black-owned firms got only a tiny share of contracts, and made up only a tiny portion of the local contractors' association, was not enough to prove such past discrimination — there was no evidence that there really were more black-owned firms than this, and "the relevant statistical pool for purposes of demonstrating discriminatory exclusion must be the number of minorities qualified to undertake the particular task." *City of Richmond v. J.A. Croson Co.*, 488 U.S. 469 (1989), discussed extensively *infra*, p. 299.

        i. **Formal findings probably not necessary:** On the other hand, it's probably not necessary that there be a formal *"finding"* by a court that this discrimination took place. So for instance, if a particular police force had statistically far fewer African Americans than would be expected based on the number of qualified African Americans in the local labor force, this might be enough to demonstrate that there was discrimination; in that case, the police department might be able to voluntarily put in a plan that gave African Americans some preference in the hiring process. Similarly, the department might be able to settle a discrimination suit by agreeing to put in such a plan. But there does have to be quite clear evidence of past discrimination, not mere supposition.

b. **Discrimination by whom:** Now for Question 2 — *who* must have discriminated? Obviously, a race-conscious affirmative action plan is most likely to be upheld if the past discrimination was by the ***particular government entity in question.*** If the past discrimination was not by the particular governmental entity involved in the present case (e.g., the particular governmental employer), but was in the same ***general domain*** (e.g., the ***same industry***), this probably also justifies a race-conscious remedy. For instance, in *Croson, supra,* the required "compelling" government objective would have been shown by hard evidence that general contractors had discriminated against black-owned contracting firms, even had the City itself not discriminated. On the other hand, ***the mere fact that there has been general "societal" discrimination is not enough to justify race-conscious measures.***

3. **Quotas:** One device that is especially vulnerable to Equal Protection attack is the racially-based ***quota***. A racially-based quota is an inflexible number of admissions slots, dollar amounts, or other "goodies" set aside for minorities. (For more about the definition of "quota," see sub-paragraph (a) below.) In the aftermath of the decision in *Richmond v. Croson*, it seems probable that ***virtually all racially-based quotas will be struck down even where the government is trying to eradicate the effects of past discrimination*** — the Court will probably say that a quota is not "necessary" to remedy discrimination, that more flexible "goals" can do the job.

> **Example:** Recall the facts of *Croson* — Richmond tried to remedy what it saw as past discrimination against black-owned contracting firms by giving them 30% of future city contracts. Even if there had been hard evidence that there really was discrimination in the past (evidence that Richmond didn't have), and thus even had Richmond been acting in pursuit of a compelling objective (getting rid of past discrimination), Richmond would probably still have lost, because the 30% requirement was a hard-and-fast one, i.e., a quota. A majority of the Court would probably have said that a flexible goal would have done the job just as well — the City could have required general contractors to show that they "tried" to assign 30% of the contracts to black-owned firms, without automatically penalizing them if they failed. Since a flexible goal would have done as well, the quota wasn't "necessary", and Richmond would (probably) have lost.

a. **What is a "quota":** What, then, will be considered to be a ***"quota"***? Apparently the term will now be quite ***narrowly-construed*** following the affirmative-action-in-admissions decision in *Grutter v. Bollinger, infra*, p. 282. The majority opinion there says that "properly understood, a 'quota' is a program in which a certain ***fixed number or proportion of opportunities*** are '*reserved exclusively* for certain minority groups.' ... Quotas 'impose a fixed number or percentage which ***must be attained***, or which ***cannot be exceeded***'." A program that merely contains aspirational ***"goals"*** does ***not*** thereby become a quota. Nor does a program become a quota merely because membership in a certain group is made a ***"plus factor"*** — even a very strong plus factor — as long as the plus factor is administered as part of ***individualized evaluations***.

   i. **Point system:** On the other hand, a system that automatically assigns a certain fixed number of ***"points"*** for a certain race or ethnicity ***will*** be treated by the present court as being the equivalent of a quota, even though no particular slots are reserved exclusively for members of the minority group. That's the lesson of the Court's other recent affirmative-action-in-admissions case, *Gratz v. Bollinger, infra*, p. 286.

4. **Court-ordered vs. voluntary:** Some affirmative action plans are ***ordered by a court*** to remedy past discrimination; other plans are ***voluntarily adopted*** by a public entity to remedy past discrimination. Does it make any difference to the constitutionality of the plan whether it's court-ordered or voluntary? The answer is not yet clear — court-ordered race-conscious remedies may be spared the strict scrutiny given to voluntary plans put in place by legislatures or executive officials, perhaps on the theory that a court-ordered remedy is less likely to constitute disguised political patronage than, say, a legislature's plan.

5. **Some contexts:** Let us now turn to some special contexts in which affirmative action has been challenged as being itself a violation of the equal protection rights of the white majority. The contexts which we will examine include: (1) school desegregation; (2) voting rights; (3) preferential admissions; (4) minority set-asides; and (5) employment.

D. **Desegregation:** The theory that the Constitution requires that all government action be "color-blind" was rejected quite early in one area, that of **school desegregation**. In *Swann v. Charlotte-Mecklenburg Board of Education*, 402 U.S. 1 (1971) (discussed extensively *supra*, p. 268), the Court explicitly upheld the use of race-conscious pupil assignments in order to remedy past intentional segregation.

1. **Effect of *Croson*:** But even in the school desegregation area, *Richmond v. Croson*, (*infra*, p. 299) will probably make race-conscious remedies much harder to justify. The Court will presumably apply strict scrutiny to any race-conscious remedy for discrimination, such as pupil assignments or teacher assignments that explicitly take account of race. The Court will have to be satisfied that the race-conscious measure is "necessary" to eradicate the prior segregation, and this may be a hard burden to satisfy.

   a. ***De facto* segregation:** Now suppose that a school district is trying to remedy ***de facto*** segregation. Here, it is even more clear that any race-conscious remedy will be strictly scrutinized, and probably invalidated, in light of *Croson*. First, the Supreme Court might not even agree that maintaining racially-balanced schools (where the racial imbalance is *de facto* rather than *de jure*) is a "compelling" objective. Even if this objective were found to be compelling, the court would be likely to hold that there are race-neutral alternatives that would cure the problem with acceptable speed, so that race-conscious methods (such as a race-based pupil assignment scheme like the one described in the above example) are not "necessary" to fulfill that objective.

E. **Preferential admissions:** Next, let's turn to ***admissions*** to colleges and universities. As the result of a pair of very major 2003 decisions involving the University of Michigan, we now know that: (1) public universities and colleges ***may explicitly consider minority racial status*** as a factor that increases the odds of admission; but that (2) these institutions ***may not award "points" for minority status***, or otherwise pursue ***mechanical quota-like schemes,*** and must instead evaluate each candidate as part of a ***"holistic" review*** that treats race as ***merely one factor among others***. The two cases are ***Grutter v. Bollinger***, 539 U.S. 306 (2003) (upholding by 5-4 the University of Michigan Law School's "race as one factor among many" approach) and ***Gratz v. Bollinger***, 539 U.S. 244 (2003) (striking down as a violation of equal protection, by a 6-3 vote, Michigan's undergraduate scheme, by which members of favored racial and ethnic groups got an automatic 20 points of the 100 points needed for admission).

1. ***Bakke* decision:** Before we analyze the two Michigan decisions, we need to review the court's only prior decision on affirmative action in the University context, ***Regents of Univ. of California v. Bakke***, 438 U.S. 265 (1978). The case is now significant principally for Justice Powell's opinion, which provided the swing vote even though no other justice joined its reasoning fully, but which was adopted 25 years later by the pro-affirmative-action majority in *Grutter*.

   a. **Facts:** The admissions procedure at the University of California-Davis Medical School reserved 16 seats in each entering class of 100 for disadvantaged minority students. Only African Americans, Hispanics, and Asian-Americans could compete for these places.

      i. **Suit against plan:** Allan Bakke, a white, sued the University, claiming that the admissions scheme violated the Equal Protection Clause, as well as Title VI of the 1964 Civil Rights Act. Bakke contended that his grade point average and MCAT scores were higher than those of some persons accepted for the minority slots.

   b. **Supreme Court's holding:** No majority opinion emerged from the Supreme Court's consideration of the case. The nine Justices wrote six separate opinions, and no more than four Justices agreed in their reasoning.

      i. **Justice Powell:** It fell to Justice Powell to form a majority. He agreed with four other Justices (Brennan, White, Marshall and Blackmun) that a university should be permitted to ***take into account*** an applicant's membership in a racial minority as part of the admissions process. But he believed that a racial ***"quota"*** system, i.e., the explicit reservation of places which could only be filled by minorities, was ***unconstitutional***. His holding on this issue, coupled with the belief of the remaining four Justices that the Davis program was invalid for statutory rather than constitutional reasons, led to the striking down of the mechanical Davis approach.

         (1) **Powell rationale:** Justice Powell believed that ***any racial or ethnic classification***, regardless of the class against which it is directed or the reason for it, must be subjected to ***strict scrutiny***. Powell concluded that (1) the need to obtain "the ***educational benefits*** that flow from an ***ethnically-diverse*** student body" was a compelling state interest; but (2) it was ***not necessary*** (and therefore not permissible) to use a ***quota*** scheme like Davis', where certain seats were reserved ***exclusively*** for members of particular races; instead, this goal could be pursued by considering an applicant's minority status as merely ***one factor*** in the admissions process (the so-called "Harvard plan").

         (2) **Individual treatment:** Powell stressed that a Harvard-type "weigh all factors" scheme, unlike the Davis quota scheme, "treats each applicant ***as an individual*** in the admissions process." This key distinction by Powell — contrasting individualized asssessment of each applicant (constitutionally acceptable) with the reservation of particular "slots" for minorities (unacceptable) — was later adopted by a ***majority*** of the Court, in *Grutter v. Bollinger, infra*.

2. **Aftermath of *Bakke*:** *Bakke* remained the Court's only pronouncement on race-conscious affirmative action in university admissions until 2003. During the quarter-century

following *Bakke*, lower courts were deeply confused and split about whether Powell's opinion represented the law of the land in light of *Croson*'s later adoption of strict scrutiny for race-conscious affirmative action plans.

3. ***Grutter* and *Gratz* together:** *Grutter* and *Gratz* answered this question by effectively ***adopting Powell's approach in Bakke,*** and by holding that:

[a] Race-conscious admissions measures will ***receive strict scrutiny***, and thus must be narrowly-tailored to achieve a compelling objective;

[b] The pursuit of ***diversity in the student body*** can be a ***compelling objective***;

[c] A ***one-student-at-a-time evaluation*** in which the student's race is merely one factor among various ones considered is ***sufficiently narrowly-tailored***; but

[d] Mechanical approaches resembling ***quotas***, such as automatically awarding an applicant a fixed number of ***points*** towards admission based on his race, are ***not narrowly-tailored*** and therefore violate equal protection.

We consider each of the two cases in turn.

4. ***Grutter*:** In *Grutter*, the Court ***upheld*** by a 5-4 vote the University of Michigan Law School's admission process, in which the school pursued the objective of diversity by subjectively adding race into the mix when a student's entire application was considered. Justice O'Connor wrote the Court's opinion, in which she was joined by Justices Stevens, Souter, Ginsburg and Breyer.

a. **Facts:** The Law School was (and is) an elite, highly-selective one, which at the time in question received more than 3500 applications each year for a class of around 350 students. The Law School's admissions policy required admissions officials to ***read each applicant's entire file.*** Admission was based upon undergraduate grades, LSAT scores, and a number of "soft" variables (e.g., enthusiasm of recommenders, quality of the undergraduate institution, difficulty of undergraduate courses taken, etc.) One of the soft variables was the extent to which the applicant's presence would ***contribute to "diversity"*** at the school. There were (according to the official admissions policy cited by O'Connor) "many possible bases" for an applicant's contribution to student-body diversity. But one type of diversity was singled out in the official policy: "***racial*** and ***ethnic*** diversity with special reference to the inclusion of students from groups which have been ***historically discriminated against***, like ***African-Americans***, ***Hispanics*** and ***Native Americans***, who without this commitment ***might not be represented in our student body in meaningful numbers.***"

i. **"Critical mass":** The Law School defended its race-conscious admissions policy principally on the grounds that the school was seeking to enroll a " **'*critical mass'*** of [underrepresented] minority students." The school's officials testified that "critical mass" meant ***"meaningful representation,"*** which in turn meant "a number that encourages underrepresented minority students to ***participate*** in the classroom and ***not feel isolated.***"

ii. **Numbers:** The school ***denied*** that there was ***any particular number***, percentage or range of numbers or percentages that constituted critical mass. During the years in question, the percentage of students in each class that were members of the three favored groups (black, Hispanic and Native American) varied from 13.5% to

20.1%. The Law School denied that this was a quota, but did acknowledge that consideration of race significantly increased the numbers of minorities who attended. For instance, the Law School put on testimony (apparently unrebutted by P) indicating that had race not been considered, underrepresented minority students would have comprised 4% of the class that entered in 2000 rather than the actual figure of 14.5%. The school acknowledged that at the height of the admissions season, the admissions staff frequently consulted *"daily reports"* that kept track of the racial and ethnic composition of the class to date.

**b. Plaintiff's argument:** P was a white Michigan resident who unsuccessfully applied to the Law School. Her undergraduate GPA and her LSAT scores were, she claimed, higher than those of many minority applicants who were accepted. Consequently, she alleged, the Law School's use of race as what P termed a "predominant" factor constituted a denial of equal protection to her.

**c. O'Connor's majority opinion:** Justice O'Connor's opinion *applied strict scrutiny* to the Law School's consideration of race as an admissions factor, but concluded that the school's method was *sufficiently narrowly tailored* to achieve the compelling interest in maintaining diversity.

    **i. Adoption of Powell *Bakke* opinion:** O'Connor began by summarizing Justice Powell's opinion in *Bakke*, which she said "approved the university's use of race to further only one interest: 'the attainment of a diverse student body'." She declined to decide whether Powell's opinion was binding on the Court as precedent; instead, she said, her opinion for the Court *"endorse[s]* Justice Powell's view that *student body diversity is a compelling state interest* that can *justify the use of race* in university admissions."

    **ii. Strict scrutiny required:** Next, O'Connor recited the Court's prior holdings that all racial classifications imposed by government must undergo strict scrutiny, and are constitutional "only if they are narrowly tailored to further compelling governmental interests."

    **iii. Diversity as a compelling interest:** O'Connor then concluded that the Law School had "a *compelling interest* in obtaining a *diverse student body*." She noted that the Law School itself had concluded that such diversity was essential to the school's educational mission. And, she said, the Court had a "tradition of giving a degree of *deference* to a university's academic decisions."

        **(1) "Critical mass" of minority students:** An aspect of the Law School's push for a diverse class was its attempt to "enroll a *'critical mass'* of minority students." Having such a critical mass would have a number of benefits, according to the Law School (to whose conclusions the Court was paying deference): the promotion of *"cross racial understanding"*; the breaking down of *racial stereotypes*; and the promotion of *livelier and more-enlightening classroom discussion* because students have "the greatest possible *variety of backgrounds*."

        **(2) Societal benefits:** Furthermore, O'Connor said, the *benefits* from a broadly diverse class, including one with a critical mass of underrepresented minorities, *extended to society as a whole*. For instance, she noted, many large

American ***businesses*** had told the Court in *amicus curia* briefs that "the skills needed in today's increasingly global marketplace can only be developed through exposure to widely diverse people, cultures, ideas, and viewpoints."

**iv. Narrowly-tailored:** O'Connor next turned to the even-more-contentious issue of whether the particular race-conscious methods adopted by the Law School were ***sufficiently narrowly-tailored*** to the achievement of the compellingly-important objective of obtaining diversity in the student body.

**(1) No quotas:** O'Connor began by adopting Powell's position in *Bakke* that a race-conscious program ***cannot use a quota system.*** O'Connor defined "quota" somewhat narrowly: a quota was "a program in which a certain ***fixed number or proportion of opportunities*** are '***reserved exclusively*** for certain minority groups' "; quotas "impose a fixed number or percentage which must be attained, which cannot be exceeded," and "insulate the individual from comparison with all other candidates for the available seats."

**(2) Michigan's plan not a quota:** By this test, the Law School's approach was ***not*** a forbidden quota, O'Connor said. The Law School's plan was much more like the "Harvard plan" that Powell had approved of in *Bakke* than it was like the plan struck down in *Bakke*. Harvard made, in O'Connor's words, "flexible use of race as a 'plus' factor," as did Michigan Law School.

**(3) "Holistic" review:** Also, the actual ***process*** by which the Law School ***evaluated*** each application was inconsistent with a quota. The Law School, O'Connor said, "engages in a ***highly individualized, holistic review*** of each applicant's file, giving serious consideration to ***all the ways*** an applicant might contribute to a diverse educational environment." The school did ***not*** give any ***"mechanical, predetermined diversity 'bonuses'*** based on race or ethnicity" (as the Court found that the undergraduate admissions scheme at Michigan did, in the companion case of *Gratz*, *infra*.)

**(4) Race-neutral alternatives:** Finally, O'Connor considered whether the Law School's approach failed to be narrowly tailored because of the availability of ***race-neutral alternatives*** for achieving the desired diversity. O'Connor agreed that narrow tailoring "require[s] serious, good faith ***consideration*** of ***workable*** race-neutral alternatives that will achieve the diversity the university seeks." But she asserted that that "narrow tailoring ***does not require exhaustion of every conceivable race-neutral alternative,"*** only those alternatives that would ***serve the governmental interest "about as well."*** She agreed with the Law School that the various race-neutral alternatives that had been proposed were ***not workable ones***. For instance, the type of ***"percentage plan"*** advocated by the Bush administration — under which all students above a certain class-rank threshold in every school in the state would be guaranteed admission — would not work for graduate and professional schools, and would probably preclude individualized assessments of each student's contribution to other, non-racial, types of diversity.

> **v. "Sunset" after 25 years:** But O'Connor cautioned that race-conscious admissions policies "must be *limited in time*." She noted that it had been 25 years since Justice Powell's opinion in *Bakke*, and she wrote that "We expect that *25 years from now*, the use of racial preferences will *no longer be necessary*[.]"

**d. Dissents:** The four dissenters — Chief Justice Rehnquist and Justices Kennedy, Scalia and Thomas — each produced a separate dissent.

**e. Rehnquist's dissent:** The principal dissent was by Chief Justice Rehnquist, in which the other three dissenters also joined. Rehnquist seemed not to object to the majority's belief that a diverse student body could be a compelling governmental objective. But he very much disputed the majority's conclusion that the Law School's approach was a narrowly-tailored method of achieving that objective. Instead, he believed, the Law School's pursuit of "critical mass" was a *"veil,"* which when stripped revealed "a *naked effort to achieve racial balancing.*"

> **i. Pursuit of racial balance:** In support of his assertion that the Law School was really pursuing racial balancing, Rehnquist reproduced statistics that he said showed that "the percentage of the admitted applicants who were members of [the three favored] minority groups *closely tracked* the percentage of individuals in the school's *applicant pool* who were from the same groups." Thus in 1995, when 9.7% of the applicant pool was African-American, 9.4% of the admitted class was African American; in 2000, by contrast, when 7.5% of the applicant pool was African-American, 7.3% of the class was African-American. He concluded that "the Law School has managed its admissions program, not to achieve a 'critical mass,' but to *extend offers* of admission to members of selected minority groups *in proportion to their statistical representation in the applicant pool.*" This, he said, was "precisely the type of *racial balancing* that the Court itself [in the majority opinion] calls 'patently unconstitutional'."

**f. Kennedy's dissent:** Like Chief Justice Rehnquist, Justice Kennedy believed that the majority was not in fact applying strict scrutiny. He accused the majority of giving only a "perfunctory" review of the Law School's policy, which he characterized as using critical mass as a "delusion ... to mask its attempt to *make race an automatic factor* in most instances and to achieve *numerical goals indistinguishable from quotas.*"

> **i. Small fluctuations:** Kennedy's belief that the school was engaged in "racial balancing" was supported by what he said was the *small year-to-year variation* in minority enrollment. For instance, during a four-year period (1995 to 1998), the percentage of enrolled minorities "fluctuated only by .03%, from 13.5% to 13.8%." He was especially disturbed by fact that admissions officers "consulted ... *daily reports* which indicated the composition of the incoming class along racial lines." He unfavorably compared the Law School's approach to that of a group of amicus highly-selective colleges (the "Little Ivy League colleges"), which did not "keep ongoing tallies of racial or ethnic composition of their entering students," and at which there was consequently a quite large year-to-year fluctuation in the number of matriculating minority students.

g. **Thomas' dissent:**  Justice Thomas (joined by Justice Scalia) wrote a long, highly personal, dissent that seemed to stem partly from his own negative personal experience with affirmative action.

    i. **Not a compelling interest:**  Unlike Rehnquist and Kennedy, Thomas did ***not*** even accept the position that the Law School had a ***compelling interest*** in pursuing diversity in its student body.

    ii. **Affirmative action bad for its beneficiaries:**  Thomas then attacked affirmative action, of the sort practiced by the Law School, as being ***bad for its beneficiaries.*** "The Law School *tantalizes* unprepared [minority] students with the promise of a University of Michigan degree and all of the opportunities that it offers. These ***overmatched students take the bait,*** only to find that they ***cannot succeed*** in the cauldron of competition." Furthermore, he wrote, even the "handful" of black students each year who would have been admitted in the absence of racial discrimination are damaged by the policy: "Who can differentiate between those who belong and those who do not? The majority of blacks are admitted to the law school because of discrimination, and because of this policy ***all are tarred as undeserving.***"

h. **Scalia's dissent:**  Justice Scalia, in a brief dissent (in which Justice Thomas joined) made it clear that he, like Thomas, rejected even the proposition that the Law School's pursuit of a diverse student body was a compelling state interest. He saw Michigan's interest as merely being an "interest in maintaining a 'prestige' law school whose normal admissions standards disproportionately exclude blacks and other minorities." He argued that "if that is a compelling state interest, everything is."

5. ***Gratz:***  The same day as the Court decided *Grutter*, it decided ***Gratz***, which involved affirmative-action admissions policies at the University of Michigan's main ***undergraduate*** College in Ann Arbor.

a. **Facts:**  There were several different affirmative-action schemes, used by the College in different years, at issue in *Gratz*. For procedural reasons, most of the Supreme Court's eventual analysis concerned the school's policy after 1998. Under that policy, the school used a "selection index," in which ***points were awarded*** for various characteristics, up to a maximum of 150 points. A minimum of 100 points was needed for admission. An applicant was entitled to an ***automatic 20 points*** for membership in an ***underrepresented racial or ethnic minority group*** (the same three groups — blacks, Hispanics and Native Americans — as in the Law School plan at issue in *Grutter*). The significance of these extra 20 points was great: the University conceded that "the effect of automatically awarding 20 points is that ***virtually every qualified underrepresented minority applicant is admitted.***" By contrast, the award given for most other types of non-academic traits was much smaller: a student with "extraordinary *artistic* talent" rivaling that of Monet or Picasso, for instance, or the most outstanding national high school ***student leader***, could receive ***at most five points.*** Students who didn't get enough points but came close could be ***manually flagged*** for ***in-person review*** of the file, which might lead to admission.

b. **Rehnquist's majority opinion:**  Chief Justice Rehnquist's majority opinion (joined by O'Connor, Scalia, Kennedy and Thomas) concluded that this ***point system*** was ***unconstitutional***, in that it was ***not narrowly tailored*** to achieve the school's interest in educational diversity.[5] Because Justice Breyer concurred in the result, the vote was 6-3 to strike the point system.

i.  **Does not conform to Powell's opinion:** Rehnquist believed that the College's point system did ***not*** meet the requirements of Justice Powell's *Bakke* opinion. The essence of Powell's approach was that race could be deemed a "plus," but was not to be "decisive"; each applicant was to be evaluated as an ***individual***, and each characteristic of that applicant was to be considered. The College's point system was not at all the kind of system that Powell had in mind, Rehnquist said. For instance, the automatic award of 20 points had the effect of making race decisive "for virtually every minimally qualified underrepresented minority applicant."

ii.  **Flagging not a solution:** The fact that an applicant who failed to get the requisite points but came close could have her application ***flagged*** for special individualized review ***did not remedy*** these flaws. Flagging would only come into play if the student failed to get enough points to be automatic admitted. Because the 20 points for minority racial status virtually guaranteed admission to minimally-qualified minorities, such minorities would never be near-misses, would therefore never be flagged, and thus never subjected to individualized review.

iii.  **Large numbers not a defense:** Finally, Rehnquist rejected the College's argument that the ***large volume of applications*** received by the school made a Powell-style individualized review of each file impractical: "[T]he fact that the implementation of a program capable of providing individualized consideration might present ***administrative challenges*** does ***not*** render constitutional an otherwise problematic system."

c.  **O'Connor's concurrence:** Justice O'Connor wrote a concurrence, in which Justices Thomas and Breyer joined. Since O'Connor wrote the majority opinion in *Grutter* upholding the Law School's affirmative action plan, her *Gratz* concurrence is important in that it spells out how and why she thought the College's unacceptable plan differed from the Law School's acceptable one.

i.  **Predetermined points:** O'Connor principally objected to the fact that ***far fewer points*** were available for diversity characteristics other than the race-oriented ones, and to the fact that the point values were completely ***hard-wired*** at the outset. Thus she pointed out that diversity contributions like "leadership," "personal achievement" and geographic diversity were capped at much lower levels than membership in an underrepresented race (e.g., 5 points maximum for leadership, compared with the 20 automatic points for being black or Hispanic.) Furthermore, "by setting up ***automatic, predetermined point allocations***" for all of the diversity characteristics, the system "ensures that the diversity contributions of applicants ***cannot be individually assessed***." This was in "sharp contrast" to the Law School's plan, under which admissions officers were able to "make ***nuanced judgments*** with respect to the contributions each applicant is likely to make to diversity of the incoming class."

d.  **Breyer's concurrence in result:** Justice Breyer concurred briefly in the result, giving a sixth vote to strike down the point-based system. However, Breyer did not join

---

5. The majority also rejected a "standing" argument advanced by the dissenters.

the majority's opinion (though he did agree with the reasoning in O'Connor's concurrence).

e. **Dissent:**  Three justices — Stevens, Souter and Ginsburg — dissented in *Gratz*. Justice Stevens dissented only on procedural grounds — he believed that the plaintiffs lacked standing, and that the Court should therefore not have heard the case at all. Therefore, only two Justices, Souter and Ginsburg, went on record as believing that the college's point system was constitutional.

f. **Souter's dissent:**  Justice Souter (whose dissent was joined by Justice Ginsburg) seemed to be say that only true quotas of the sort condemned by Powell's *Bakke* opinion should be struck down, and that the point-based scheme here was not such a quota.

    i. **Narrow view of "quota":**  Souter took a far narrower view of what constituted a forbidden quota than did the majority: the sort of quota condemned by Powell, he said, was one "which 'insulated' all non minority candidates from the competition for certain seats" and "effectively told nonminority applicants that [quoting *Bakke*] 'no matter how strong their qualifications ... they are never afforded the chance to compete with applicants from the preferred groups for the [set-aside] special admission seats.' " The College's plan here, by contrast, "lets all applicants compete for all places," and "values an applicant's offering for any place not only on grounds of race, but on grades, test scores, strength of high-school," etc. Therefore, a nonminority applicant who scored high in several of these other categories could "readily garner a selection index exceeding that of a minority applicant who gets the 20-point bonus." Furthermore, there were a few non-race-oriented characteristics (e.g., athletic ability, or socio-economic disadvantage) that could yield the same 20 points as membership in an underrepresented minority group.

g. **Ginsburg:**  Justice Ginsburg wrote a separate dissent (joined by Souter and in part by Breyer).

    i. **Legacy of discrimination:**  Ginsburg emphasized that "the effects of centuries-old law-sanctioned inequality remain painfully evident in our communities and schools." Consequently, she thought, "government decision makers may properly distinguish between policies of *exclusion* and *inclusion.* ... Actions designed to burden groups long denied full citizenship stature are not sensibly ranked with measures taken to hasten the day when entrenched discrimination and its after effects have been extirpated."

6. **Significance of the two cases:**  So what, then, have we learned from what Justice Scalia correctly referred to as the "split double  header" of *Grutter* and *Gratz*?

a. **Core principle of affirmative action preserved:**  Most importantly, the core principle of *affirmative action* in higher education to ensure a *racially-diverse class* is *preserved*. As long as admissions officers *individually evaluate* the contribution that each applicant will make towards a diverse class — not just racially diverse, but diverse in other aspects such as life experiences, special talents, etc. — the fact that membership in an underrepresented racial or ethnic minority is given great weight will not constitute a violation of equal protection rights of applicants who are not members of those underrepresented minority groups. This is the core result of *Grutter*.

**i. Effect of Seattle case:** However, the post-*Grutter* case of *Parents Involved in Community Schools v. Seattle School District No. 1*, *infra*, p. 291, striking down the use of race in making public-secondary-school pupil assignments, suggests that at least four members of the Roberts Court, and maybe a fifth (Kennedy) would not allow public higher-education institutions to consider each individual student's race as part of the admissions decision. Since Kennedy would not have upheld the Law School's plan in *Grutter*, and since O'Connor's pro-affirmative-action vote in *Grutter* has since been replaced by the more conservative Alito's vote, it seems likely that *Grutter* would ***not be decided the same way*** by the present Roberts Court.

**b. Can't use points:** In contrast to the "individualized consideration of race among various factors" system that the Court approved in *Grutter*, a system that the Court perceives as being ***"mechanical"*** rather than ***"holistic"*** is ***vulnerable***. Most obviously, any system in which a certain pre-defined number of ***"points"*** is automatically given for membership in a particular minority group will pretty clearly be unconstitutional under *Gratz*. The result in *Parents Involved in Community Schools v. Seattle School District No. 1*, *infra*, p. 291 — striking down the mechanical use of race in public-secondary-school pupil assignments — makes this even clearer.

**7. Open questions:** Here are some questions which the *Grutter* and *Gratz* opinions raise:

**a. Expansion to other contexts:** Will the core principle of *Grutter* — that pursuit of diversity is a compelling objective, which may be achieved by race-conscious means — be extended to ***other contexts*** beyond university admissions?

**i. Faculty:** For instance, within the educational context, may public higher-education institutions treat underrepresented-minority status as a plus factor when they assemble their ***faculty***? The need for "educational diversity" in the sense of presenting varying viewpoints would seem just as applicable to university faculty selection as to student-body selection. And the deference that the *Grutter* majority gave to the presumed greater expertise of educators would seem to be just as applicable to faculty selection. So perhaps *Grutter* will be expanded to allow public universities to consider the race of prospective faculty members as one factor in the hiring or tenure decision.

**(1) Public secondary schools:** On the other hand, it seems ***less likely*** that the Court will accept race-conscious faculty selection's being extended to, say, the public ***secondary-school*** context. The post-*Grutter/Gratz* case of *Parents Involved in Community Schools v. Seattle School District No. 1*, *infra*, p. 291 — which was decided after Justice O'Connor was replaced by Justice Alito — suggests that a majority of the present Roberts Court is uncomfortable with the use of racial preferences in the public secondary-school area. Four members of the present Court (Roberts, Thomas, Scalia and Alito) would almost certainly strictly scrutinize, and strike down, the use of race in selecting public school faculty. Therefore, the outcome would likely turn on Justice Kennedy's views, and his vote in *Parents Involved* to strike down the use of race in *pupil* assignments probably means that he would look unfavorably on any consideration by a public school district of an individual *faculty* applicant's race.

ii. **Non-educational employment:** Outside of the educational context, a similar question arises: where a particular workforce — or the population being served by a workforce — is heavily integrated, to what extent may public employers treat race as a plus factor when choosing bosses? The issue is presented by such work forces as the ***armed services***, the ***police departments*** of highly-integrated cities, and the ***correction-officer corps*** in heavily-minority ***prisons***.

> **Example:** According to an amicus brief filed in *Grutter* by a large group of retired high-ranking military officers, as of 2002 22% of enlisted persons in the armed services were black and 10% were Hispanic. The presence of these two groups in the officer corps, by contrast, was significantly smaller (e.g., 9% of officers were black in 2002). Suppose the Army, in making officer-promotion decisions, promotes blacks and Hispanics materially more rapidly in order to achieve this goal of a more diverse officer corps. What result?
>
> Again, the post-*Grutter/Gratz* case of *Parents Involved, infra*, p. 291, suggests that a majority of the Roberts Court today would strictly scrutinize, and likely invalidate, any scheme in which a public employer like, say, the Army, considered an individual applicant's race as a meaningful factor in the employment decision. However, it is possible that Justice Kennedy, as the present holder of the likely swing vote, would vote to allow the applicant's race to be treated as "one factor among many."

b. **"Gentler" strict scrutiny?** Does *Grutter* indicate that in some instances the Court will now use a ***"gentler"*** form of strict scrutiny? The *Grutter* majority claimed to be applying ordinary strict scrutiny. But the majority certainly did not seem to be insisting on the kind of very tight means-end fit that the Court usually demands in strict-scrutiny cases. The extreme deference given to university officials' conclusion that there were no race-neutral means that could do the job almost as well was a particularly dramatic illustration that this was not the usual strict review.

    i. **Change to Roberts Court:** But whatever "gentleness" was present in the version of strict scrutiny applied in *Grutter* seems to have ***vanished*** with Justice O'Connor's replacement by Justice Alito in 2006. The post-*Grutter* case of *Parents Involved* (*infra*, p. 291) suggests that in the Roberts Court, strict scrutiny will not be very gentle, and little deference will be given to government officials' views about whether there are race-neutral means that can do the job. (In *Seattle*, five justices gave very little deference to the judgment by school board members that only race-conscious means would suffice to prevent racial isolation in public schools.)

c. **Centrality of O'Connor, and her replacement by Alito:** Notice just how central to the whole affirmative-action debate ***Justice O'Connor*** was. Had she voted the other way in *Grutter*, we would presumably have had a 5-4 majority for at least the proposition that the heavy weight given by the Law School to underrepresented minority status was effectively a quota rather than a narrowly-tailored means of achieving diversity. Now that Justice O'Connor has been replaced by Justice Alito, the Court's tolerance for race-conscious university admissions may well turn out to have been short-lived. Such a shift is suggested by the 2007 decision in *Parents Involved, infra*, p. 291, in which as we'll see the Court refused to allow race-conscious pupil-assignment policies in public elementary and secondary schools. The swing vote on such affirmative action questions has passed from Justice O'Connor to Justice Kennedy.

    **d.  Impact on private universities:**  What impact, if any, will *Grutter* and *Gratz* have on the admissions practices of **private universities**? You might think that the answer would be "none," since in the absence of state action (see *infra*, p. 417), there can be no equal protection violation. However, various federal **statutes** prohibit racial discrimination in various contexts. Therefore, if a particular practice would constitute an equal protection violation under *Gratz*, that same practice would, or at least might, violate a federal statute barring "racial discrimination." For instance, in the education context a federal statute known as "Title VI" bars any educational institution receiving federal funds (as virtually all universities do) from discriminating based on race or ethnicity. Therefore, if the admissions office of a private college were to pursue an affirmative action plan based on a point system comparable to the one struck down in *Gratz*, it is likely that the system would be found to be a violation of Title VI. Conversely, a "holistic" system like the one upheld in *Grutter* is presumably now immunized against Title VI attack if used by a private school receiving federal funds.

**F.  Admissions to public secondary schools by race-conscious pupil-assignments (the *Parents Involved* case):**  To what extent may a **public school system** make **race-conscious pupil-assignment decisions** in order to combat racial imbalances in the district's schools? As a result of a 2007 decision that was the Roberts Court's first consideration of affirmative action, **no individual student's race may be considered in making that student's school assignment.** The case, **Parents Involved in Community Schools v. Seattle School District No. 1**, 552 U.S. __ (2007), was a bitter 5-4 split, with Justice Kennedy siding with the four conservative members of the Court in striking down the race-conscious school-assignment plans from Seattle and Louisville, Kentucky at issue there. The case marks an important extension of the Court's recent tendency to strictly scrutinize, and usually invalidate, race-conscious affirmative action decisions by governments.

    **1.  The assignment plans:**  Both Seattle's and Louisville's race-conscious pupil-assignment plans were essentially **voluntary** as opposed to court-ordered. Seattle had never been under court order to desegregate its schools. Louisville had once been under such a court order, but prior to the use of the plan at issue court supervision had ceased because the district had been found to have eradicated the vestiges of official segregation. Both districts enacted plans that **occasionally took account of race,** in an effort to prevent individual schools from becoming **racially isolated**.

        **a.  Seattle plan:**  Under the Seattle plan, **race served as a "tiebreaker"** for the assignment of incoming ninth graders to certain of the city's high schools. Ninth graders were asked to state their preferences; if a school was "oversubscribed" (more students listed it as their first choice than there were slots), a series of tiebreakers was used. The first tiebreaker gave a preference to students with a sibling already enrolled at the school.

        The next tiebreaker was what the litigation was about. In the district as a whole, 41% of students were white, and 59% "nonwhite" (a designation that apparently included Asian Americans, African Americans and Latinos). But due to housing patterns, the north end of the city was predominantly white and the south end predominantly nonwhite. If the school in question was not within 10 points of the district-wide white/

nonwhite ratio, the tiebreaker went in favor of *an applicant whose race would bring the school into better balance.* So, for instance, if a school was more than 51% white (i.e., more than 10 percentage points above the 41% district-wide percentage of whites), the tiebreaker would go in favor of a black applicant over a white applicant. Out of a total of about 20,000 high school students in a typical year, about 300 were affected by the race-based tiebreaker (see the dissent of Justice Breyer). The plaintiff was a nonprofit corporation consisting of parents of students who had been or might be denied admission to their first-choice high school on account of the student's race.

b.  **The Louisville plan:**  In Louisville, a federal court dissolved a prior desegregation order in 2000, finding that the system had been desegregated to the extent feasible. The following year, the school district continued to use the pupil-assignment rules at issue (which had been put into effect during the desegregation-order years), in an attempt to prevent individual schools from becoming racially isolated due to housing patterns. About 34% of the district students were black; most of the remaining 66% were white. The plan allowed students to transfer from their initially-assigned school to another, but a transfer was not allowed if the transferee school had a black enrollment of less than 15% or more than 50% and the *transfer would worsen the imbalance.* The plaintiff was an individual, Crystal Meredith, who sought to transfer her kindergartener son Joshua from an assigned school 10 miles from his house to a school that was only 1 mile from his house; he was denied the transfer on the grounds that the transferee school he selected was outside the 15-50% racial guidelines, and his presence would worsen the imbalance.

2.  **Both plans ruled invalid:**  The court ruled that both the Seattle plan and the Louisville plan *violated the equal protection clause by considering race.* Four members of the Court, led by Chief Justice Roberts, concluded that *any* use of race in the context of school assignments would be unconstitutional. (I refer to this bloc as the *"plurality."*) Another four-member bloc, led by Justice Breyer's dissent, asserted that both plans were constitutional. The case therefore turned on *Justice Kennedy's concurrence*; he concluded that the taking into account of racial considerations would *not always* be unconstitutional in the school-assignment context, but that the particular plans here — which involved *categorizing each student by race* and then making some students' assignments depend on that race — was an unconstitutional use of race.

3.  **The Roberts plurality opinion:**  Chief Justice Roberts' plurality opinion was joined in full by Justices Scalia, Thomas and Alito. He concluded that both the Seattle and Louisville plans failed the requisite strict scrutiny on two grounds: first, the districts were *not pursuing a compelling governmental interest*, and second, the race-conscious *means* chosen by the districts were *not narrowly tailored to meet* whatever governmental interests they were designed to pursue.

a.  **Strict scrutiny required:**  Roberts began by summarizing the standard that the Court's emerging conservative majority had  imposed for race-conscious affirmative action plans in cases like *Gratz* (*supra*, p. 286) and *Adarand* (p. 305): "When the government distributes burdens or benefits on the basis of individual racial classifications, that action is reviewed under strict scrutiny. ... In order to satisfy this searching standard of review, the school districts must demonstrate that the use of individual racial classifications in the assignment plans here under review is 'narrowly tailored' to achieve a 'compelling' government interest."

**b.** **No compelling interest being pursued:** Roberts began by examining the issue of what governmental interests being pursued by the two cities could be considered "compelling." There were only two governmental interests, Roberts said, that the Court had recognized in prior school cases as being "compelling": *"remedying the effects of past intentional discrimination"* and "the interest in *diversity in higher education"* recognized in *Grutter* (*supra.* p. 282).

**i.** **Past intentional discrimination:** Roberts rapidly dismissed the first of these objectives from the present cases: the Seattle school system had never been shown to be segregated by law and had never been under a court-ordered desegregation decree; and the Louisville system had been found to have eradicated all vestiges of official segregation prior to the use of the race conscious plan under analysis here. So neither city could justify its plan based on combating the effects of past intentional discrimination.

**ii.** **Educational diversity:** Roberts spent far more time explaining why he believed that neither plan could be found to have been enacted in support of the second objective, the interest in *diversity*. The objective upheld in *Grutter* was *not "focused on race alone,"* he said, but was rather the interest in "*all factors* that may contribute to student body diversity," including such factors as a student's having lived or traveled abroad, fluency in several languages, overcoming of personal adversity, community service, and the like. Here, by contrast, "When race comes into play, it is decisive by itself. It is *not simply one factor* weighed with others in reaching a decision, as in *Grutter*; it is <u>the</u> factor."

**(1)** **(White / nonwhite distinction:** Even worse, Roberts said, both plans manifested only a *"limited notion of diversity,"* viewing race exclusively in white/nonwhite terms (Seattle) or black/other terms (Louisville). For instance, under the Seattle plan, a school with 50% Asian-American students and 50% white would be considered "balanced" but one that was 30% Asian-American, 25% African-American, 25% Latino and 20% white would not. Roberts could not see how this classification scheme could be said to be in pursuit of an enrollment that was "broadly diverse," the objective upheld in *Grutter*.

**iii.** **Directed to "racial balance":** Roberts also rejected the school districts' argument that the race conscious plans here pursued a compelling interest in a *racially integrated learning environment*, in which students would learn more and become better socialized. Roberts declined to decide whether pursuit of educational benefits flowing from racial diversity might ever be a compelling interest because, he said, the plans here pursued *"only ... racial balance, pure and simple,* an objective this Court has repeatedly condemned as *illegitimate."* Accepting racial balancing as a compelling state interest, he said, "would justify the *imposition of racial proportionality throughout American society,"* a tactic that would have *"no logical stopping point."*

**c.** **Lack of tight means-end fit:** Even if the interests being pursued by the school districts were compelling, Roberts went on to say, the particular race-conscious *means* selected by the districts were not *necessary for achieving those interests.* In both cities, the use of the racial guidelines resulted in the *shifting of only a few students*, suggesting to Roberts that "other means would be effective." Furthermore, he said, cases like *Grutter* had interpreted the requirement of narrow tailoring to require "serious, good faith consideration of workable and race-neutral *alternatives*"; the districts here had flunked that requirement, by failing to show that they had even considered race-neutral methods.

d. **Mantle of *Brown*:**   Roberts then argued that the plurality's position, not the dissent's, was true to the legacy of *Brown v. Board of Education*. "It was not the inequality of the facilities but the fact of *legally separating children on the basis of race* on which the Court relied to find a constitutional violation" in *Brown*. Even the plaintiffs in *Brown*, he said, had argued (and he quoted from their 1953 brief) that "the Fourteenth Amendment prevents states from according differential treatment to American children on the basis of their color or race." In sum, he wrote, *"The way to stop discrimination on the basis of race is to stop discriminating on the basis of race."*

4. **The Kennedy concurrence:**   Justice Kennedy, in a concurring opinion, supplied the key fifth vote to strike down the Seattle and Louisville plans. But he *disagreed* sharply with the plurality's view that a school system may *never take race into account* as part of a voluntary system of pupil assignments.

a. **Diversity as a compelling educational goal:**   Kennedy agreed with the plurality that since both plans "classify individuals by race and allocate benefits and burdens on that basis," the plans were to be subjected to strict scrutiny. But Kennedy rejected the plurality's conclusion that the districts had not identified any compelling interest that they were pursuing. For Kennedy, "*diversity*, depending on its meaning and definition, *is a compelling educational goal* a school district may pursue." (At the end of his opinion, Kennedy was even more specific about what interests should be deemed compelling: a school district had a compelling interest in both "*avoiding racial isolation*" and in "achiev[ing] a *diverse student population.*" As to the latter, "race may be one component of that diversity, but other *demographic* factors, plus *special talents and needs*, should also be considered.")

b. **Not narrowly tailored:**   But Kennedy voted to strike the plans because, even if they were enacted in pursuit of a compelling objective, they did not manifest the *tightness of means-end fit* required under strict scrutiny. In the case of Seattle, for instance, even accepting as appropriate goals Seattle's desire to reduce racial isolation and promote the educational benefits of diversity, Kennedy could not see how Seattle's use of the *white / non-white distinction as the sole racial classification* furthered those goals. Less than half of Seattle's student body was white, yet the district had used "the *crude racial categories of 'white' and non-white' "* as the basis for its assignment decisions.

Kennedy cited with approval the plurality's criticism that under the Seattle plan, a school with 50% Asian-American students and 50% white students, and with no black, Native-American or Latino students, would qualify as balanced, whereas a school with 30% Asian-American, 25% African-American, 25% Latino and 20% white students would not. "Far from being narrowly tailored to its purposes, this system threatens to defeat its own ends[.]" "Individual racial classifications" like the ones used here, he said later in his opinion, were permissible "only if they are a *last resort* to achieve a compelling interest," and neither district had satisfied this last-resort standard.

c.  **Plurality criticized:**  But Kennedy also believed that the *plurality* had *gone much too far in its insistence on complete color-blindness.* He criticized Roberts' *"all-too-unyielding insistence that race cannot be a factor* in instances when, in my view, it *may be taken into account."* The plurality opinion, he said, was "too dismissive of the *legitimate interest* government has in ensuring all people have *equal opportunity* regardless of their race."

Kennedy was especially unwilling to accept the plurality's apparent belief that "the Constitution requires school districts to *ignore the problem of de facto resegregation* in schooling." If the plurality was suggesting that the Constitution required that state and local authorities "must *accept the status quo of racial isolation* in the schools," the plurality was *"profoundly mistaken."*

  i.  **Right to consider race:**  Kennedy believed that school authorities were entitled to use "race-conscious measures" to address the goal of offering "an *equal educational opportunity* to all of their students." But authorities had to *"address the problem in a general way* and *without treating each student in different fashion solely on the basis of a systematic, individual typing by race."*

   (1)  **Allowable methods:**  Kennedy pointed to several *race-conscious methods* that a school district *might use* without running afoul of his "no individual typing by race" rule:

   ❏  "strategic *site selection* of new schools" based on consciousness of neigborhood demographics;

   ❏  "drawing *attendance zones* with a general recognition of the demographics of neighborhoods";

   ❏  "allocating *resources for special programs*";

   ❏  *"recruiting students and faculty* in a targeted fashion" and

   ❏  "tracking enrollments, performance, and other statistics by race."

   (2)  **Rationale:**  Kennedy believed that these methods, although they were race conscious, did not need to be strictly scrutinized because they "do not lead to different treatment based on a *classification that tells each student he or she is to be defined by race*[.]"

d.  **Summary:**  In sum, Kennedy was willing to allow some use of race in the student assignment process, but not the broad use of race, including *student-by-student classification*, that the dissent would allow. The dissent's approach, he said, had "no principled limit and would result in the *broad acceptance of governmental racial classifications in areas far afield from schooling*." Kennedy stressed "the dangers presented by individual [racial] classifications," dangers that he said "are not as pressing when the same ends are achieved by *more indirect means*." He was especially worried about the *mechanics* by which any direct-classification process would have to work: "When the government classifies an individual by race, it must first *define what it means to be of a race*.  Who exactly is white and who is nonwhite? To be forced to live under a *state-mandated racial label* is inconsistent with the *dignity of individuals* in our society." By contrast, the race-conscious methods he was willing to allow — drawing attendance zones in a race-conscious manner, race-conscious site selection, etc. — did not pose these problems to the same degree because they did not "rely on differential treatment based on ***individual classifications***."

5. **The dissent:** The principal dissent was by Justice ***Breyer***, who was joined by Stevens, Souter and Ginsburg.[6] Breyer disagreed with virtually every step of the plurality's analysis, saying that the plurality's views "threaten a ***surge of race-based litigation***," violated long-established precedent, and were likely to jeopardize *Brown*'s promise of progress towards racial equality.

   a. **De jure / de facto distinction rejected:** At the outset, Breyer rejected the importance the plurality gave to the distinction between de jure and de facto segregation. Both Seattle and Louisville had had racially segregated schools, and had long struggled to reduce that racial isolation. For Breyer, the fact that Seattle had never been under a formal court finding of official segregation, and that Louisville's official segregation had been declared eradicated, should not have deprived either district of the power to make voluntary use of race-conscious factors in pupil assignments. Instead, Breyer believed, under a "long-standing and unbroken line of authority," the Court had interpreted the Equal Protection clause to *permit* local school boards to use race-conscious criteria to promote racial integration, even if the clause did not *require* them to use such methods. For Breyer, the plurality's insistence on color-blindness was at odds with the equal protection clause's purpose; the purpose of the clause was to ***bring the races together***, and it was nonsensical to treat race-conscious government action taken in furtherance of that purpose with the ***same intense scrutiny as action taken to keep the races apart***.

   b. **Gentler form of strict scrutiny:** Breyer also believed that the plurality was misinterpreting the legal standard set by recent cases on raced-based affirmative action, like *Adarand* and *Grutter*. He conceded that those cases seemed to require that strict scrutiny be applied to all race-based classifications. But he thought that in practice, these cases applied a far more forgiving form of strict scrutiny to "racial classifications that seek to ***include***" than to "racial classifications that harmfully ***exclude***." And he believed that the plans here were entitled to the more forgiving version of scrutiny, because what was at issue here was "not a context that involves the use of race to decide ***who will receive goods or services*** that are normally distributed on the basis of merit and which are in short supply" but instead, a context of "racial limits that seek, not to keep the races apart, but to ***bring them together***." Therefore, Breyer said, he thought that the plan should be given merely a ***"careful review,"*** not a review that was " 'strict' in the traditional sense of that word[.]"

   c. **Meets even true strict review:** But even if full-fledged strict scrutiny were applied, Breyer said, the plans here passed muster: they were ***narrowly tailored*** to the achievement of a ***compelling objective***.

---

6. Justice Stevens wrote his own, briefer, dissent. He found Roberts' reliance on *Brown* to be a "cruel irony," and noted that "history books do not tell stories of white children struggling to attend black schools." For Stevens, the racial classifications here should be viewed differently than the ones struck down in *Brown*, because the ones here "do not impose burdens on one race alone and do not stigmatize or exclude." Stevens closed by lamenting that "It is my firm conviction that no Member of the Court that I joined in 1975 would have agreed with today's decision."

i. **Compelling objective:** Breyer characterized the interest being pursued by the school boards as the interest in ***"promoting or preserving greater racial 'integration' of public schools."*** He thought that this interest was in turn motivated by several sub-interests: (1) a ***historical*** interest in "setting right the consequences of prior conditions of segregation"; (2) an ***educational*** interest in "overcoming the adverse educational effects produced by and associated with ***highly segregated schools***" and (3) a ***democratic*** interest in "helping our children learn to ***work and play together*** with children of different racial backgrounds." He then asked rhetorically, "If an educational interest that combines these three elements is not 'compelling', what is?"

ii. **Narrow tailoring:** Kennedy next turned to whether the race conscious means chosen by the school boards here were ***"narrowly tailored"*** towards achievement of this compelling objective in preserving integration. He thought that the answer was yes, even under "the strictest 'tailoring' test." He listed several factors in support of this conclusion:

(1) First, the use of race-conscious criteria here was only a small part of the decision-making process in school assignments, a process that depended mainly on other, non-racial, elements. The plans depended mainly on the non-racial factor of ***student choice***, and race was used only to set "the ***outer bounds*** of ***broad ranges.***" This made the plans less like a quota and more like the kinds of "useful starting points" that the Court had previously approved.

(2) Second, he thought that the use of race here was more narrowly tailored than the use of race approved in *Grutter*: here, "race becomes a factor only in a ***fraction*** of students' ***non-merit-based*** assignments," whereas in *Grutter*, race affected "***large numbers*** of students' ***merit-based*** applications."

(3) Finally, the history behind each plan showed that it was the product of the district's long efforts to "enhance student choice, while diminishing the need for mandatory busing"; each plan thus made ***less use of race*** than the plans it replaced, demonstrating how hard the districts had tried to use race in the most narrowly-tailored way that would still accomplish the objective of integration.

iii. **Criticism of Kennedy's methods:** Breyer rejected Kennedy's assertion that other race-conscious means would have sufficed. The history of integration efforts in these two cities as well as in the rest of the country demonstrated, he said, that the types of measures cited by Kennedy — "strategic site selection," "drawing neighborhood attendance zones on a racial basis", and the like — ***did not get the job done***, at least not without being accompanied by very burdensome race-based measures like forced busing.

iv. **Warning of "race-based litigation":** Breyer warned that the plurality's approach "threaten[s] a ***surge of race-based litigation.***" He asserted that "hundreds of state and federal statutes and regulations use racial classifications for educational or other purposes," and that all of these uses would now be subject to attack in litigation. Furthermore, the plurality's approach was taking away a vital weapon in local school boards' efforts to resist racial isolation: "Yesterday, school boards had available to them a full range of means to combat segregated schools. Today, they do not."

   **v.   Legacy of *Brown*:**   Finally, Breyer asserted that his side, not the plurality, was being faithful to the real meaning of *Brown v. Board of Education*.  It was, Breyer said, a "cruel distortion of history to compare Topeka, Kansas, in the 1950s to Louisville and Seattle in the modern day[.]"  *Brown* had made a promise of racial equality, a promise which American society had not yet achieved; the plurality's position, he feared, "would break that promise."  And, he predicted, "This is a decision that the Court and the Nation will come to regret."

6. **Significance:**   So what is the significance of the *Parents Involved v. Seattle* case?

   a.   **Direct impact:** The direct impact on the operation of the nation' public schools will probably ***not be great***, for a couple of reasons:

   ❏   There remain five votes (Kennedy plus the four dissenters) for allowing school boards to ***take account of race***, and to ***pursue racial integration***, as long as ***individual students are not assigned on the basis of the student's own race***.  So, for instance, school districts remain free take account of race while using tools like school-siting decisions and the drawing of attendance zones to promote racial integration. Most school districts had, even before the *Parents Involved* decision, declined to use tools that required a racial classification of each student, so the case changes nothing for these districts.

   ❏   Perhaps more importantly, nothing in the *Parents Involved* decision seems to prevent school districts from promoting school-by-school diversity so long as only ***non-racial grounds*** are used for measuring diversity.  Most promising is the use of ***socioeconomic status*** ("SES"), a factor already used by many districts.  For instance, the fact that a student qualifies for the free or reduced-cost federally-financed ***school lunch program*** gives districts a way to promote socio-economic integration: assignment and transfer policies can be implemented so as to place the same ratio of school-lunch and non-school-lunch (i.e., poor and non-poor) students in each of a district's schools. Because minority students tend to be on average from poorer families, such an SES-based program will also tend to reduce school-by-school racial isolation while being beyond reproach from an equal protection standpoint. See, e.g., *N.Y. Times*, June 29, 2007, p. A25 (quoting a commentator's statement that SES-based plans produce "a fair amount of racial integration that's legally bullet-proof").

   b.   **Indirect impact:**  But the case is more significant for what it shows about the rightward drift of the Court from the Rehnquist era to the Roberts era. *Parents Involved* is the Court's first affirmative action decision since Justice O'Connor was replaced by Alito, and that seems to have made a key difference — Justice O'Connor voted with the majority to allow consideration of race in law school admissions in *Grutter*, whereas Justice Alito voted with the plurality in *Parents Involved* (and would almost certainly have voted with the dissent in *Grutter*). *Parents Involved* seems to establish the proposition that for a majority of the present Court, any use of racial classifications, no matter how indirect, will be subjected to the traditional, deeply-biting, variety of strict scrutiny, and likely invalidated.

**G. Minority set-asides by states and cities:**   Congress and many states and cities have enacted so-called minority *"set-aside"* programs, by which some fixed percentage of publicly-funded *construction projects* must be set aside for minority-owned businesses. Where such a program is enacted by a city or state (as opposed to the federal government), such set-aside programs will be subjected to **strict scrutiny**, and will often be found unconstitutional. This is exactly what happened in the landmark case of ***Richmond v. J.A. Croson Co.***, 488 U.S. 469 (1989), the first case in which a majority of the Court finally agreed on what level of review should be applied to race-conscious affirmative action programs. Because of the significance of *Croson*, it is worth going into the facts and holding in some detail.

1.  **Facts:**   The city of Richmond, Virginia, enacted a Minority Business Utilization Plan. The plan required prime contractors on construction contracts funded by the city to sub-contract at least 30% of the dollar amount of the contract to one or more Minority Business Enterprises, or MBEs. To be an MBE, a business had to be at least 51% owned by minority group members. "Minority group members" were defined to include African Americans, Hispanics, Asians, Indians, Eskimos and Aleuts. An MBE need not be based in the Richmond area: it could be anywhere in America, and still qualify under the set-aside program.

    a.  **Rationale:**   The City Council declared that its plan was designed to overcome the effects of past discrimination against African Americans in the Richmond-area construction industry, and was thus "remedial" in nature. The Council said it wanted to "promot[e] wider participation by minority business enterprises in the construction of public projects."

    b.  **Waiver:**   A prime contractor could obtain a waiver from the MBE requirement, but only if he showed that there were no qualified MBEs available and willing to participate in the contract.

2.  **Evidence before the Council:**   The Council had before it some evidence that there had been extensive racial discrimination in the construction industry:

    a.  **None by city:**   There was no evidence that the *city itself* had ever discriminated with respect to construction.

    b.  **No contracts:**   However, there was evidence before the Council that even though Richmond was 50% black, only .67% of the city's prime construction contracts had been awarded to minority businesses in the prior five years.

    c.  **Associations:**   Also, most of the contractors' associations active in the area had virtually no minority businesses within their membership.

    d.  **Congressional plan:**   Lastly, the Council had before it reports issued by Congress, at the time Congress enacted a similar minority set-aside program for federal public works projects. Those congressional findings contained strong evidence that there had been extensive discrimination against African American construction concerns nation-wide.

3.  **Nature of the claim:**   The plaintiff in *Croson* was a white-owned prime contractor seeking a contract to install toilets in the city jail. P claimed that he was unable to find an MBE who could supply 30% of the work at acceptable cost. P sued the city, claiming that the set-aside violated its right to equal protection of the law.

4. **Holding:**   The opinion for the Court was written by Justice O'Connor. On some points, she spoke for only a plurality. But on the key point, she spoke for a majority: ***any governmental action that is explicitly race-based must be "necessary" to achieve a "compelling" governmental interest.*** In other words, the majority held, race-based affirmative action plans must be subjected to the same ***strict scrutiny*** as are governmental actions that intentionally discriminate ***against*** racial minorities.

   a. **Rationale:**   Justice O'Connor seemed to assert three distinct reasons why race-conscious affirmative action plans must be subjected to strict scrutiny:

      i. **No way to tell:**   First of all, there is no easy way to tell which racial classifications are truly "benign" or "remedial" and which ones are ostensibly benign, but in reality motivated by "illegitimate notions of racial inferiority or simple racial politics." (For instance, since the measure here was enacted by a City Council that had a black majority, it might well have been merely a successful political attempt to get more of the economic pie.) Use of strict scrutiny, Justice O'Connor said, would help "smoke out" the illegitimate use of race by insisting on a compelling governmental objective and a very tight fit between the means chosen and that objective. (See *supra*, p. 260, for a discussion of how strict scrutiny helps to "smoke out" illegitimate objectives.)

      ii. **Stigmatic harm:**   Second, O'Connor asserted, classifications based on race "carry a danger of ***stigmatic harm***." That is, the group "benefitted" by an affirmative action program (e.g., African American contractors in Richmond) might in the long run be harmed, because society will believe that the favored group is less competent and cannot succeed without special protection.

      iii. **Can't get beyond race:**   Finally, she argued, unless race-conscious affirmative action plans are strictly scrutinized, as a society we will never achieve our goal of becoming truly ***race-neutral***. Justice O'Connor accused Justice Marshall's dissent (discussed below) of advocating a "watered-down version of equal protection review [that] effectively assures that race will always be relevant in American life. … "

   b. **As applied to Richmond plan:**   Strict scrutiny clearly required that the Richmond plan be struck down, Justice O'Connor thought.

      i. **Objective:**   Although Richmond claimed to be pursuing the objective of overcoming past racial discrimination in construction, there was not nearly adequate proof that this discrimination had in fact occurred. For instance: (1) there was no direct evidence of discrimination by ***anyone*** in the Richmond construction industry (merely "an amorphous claim that there has been past discrimination"); (2) there was no evidence that there would be more minority contracting firms had there not been past societal discrimination; and (3) there was no showing of how many MBEs in the local labor market could have done the work (a relevant factor, since "where special qualifications are necessary, the relevant statistical pool for purposes of demonstrating discriminatory exclusion must be the number of minorities ***qualified to undertake the particular task***").

      ii. **Inadequacy of evidence:**   The evidence pointed to by the city and by the dissenters was inadequate to make the requisite showing of clear past discrimination, O'Connor thought. For instance: (1) the fact that only .67% of publicly-funded prime construction contracts in prior years had been given to African American contractors was irrelevant, because there was no showing that **qualified MBEs** represented more than this tiny fraction of overall qualified construction firms in the Richmond area; (2) the fact that MBE membership in local contractors' associations was extremely low did not prove discrimination, because "[B]lacks may be disproportionately attracted to industries other than construction"; and (3) the fact that Congress had previously (in adopting a federal minority set-aside program upheld in a prior Court decision) made legislative findings that there was a lot of discrimination against African Americans in the construction industry **nationwide**, was almost irrelevant, since the degree of discrimination would vary from market to market, and what was relevant was how much discrimination there was in the **Richmond market**.

    **iii. Conclusion:** In conclusion, Richmond, like any other public entity that wants to use race-conscious affirmative action measures, "must identify [the] discrimination, public or private, with some specificity before [it] may use race-conscious relief."

  **c. Tailoring:** Not only did Richmond not show that it had a compelling need to redress past discrimination, it also was unable to show that its plan was **narrowly tailored** to this remedial objective. For instance, there was no showing that **race-neutral** means (e.g., city financing for small firms without regard to the race of their owners) would not increase minority participation adequately. Similarly, the 30% quota was not narrowly tailored to any goal. (True, Richmond was 50% black; but there was no showing that qualified African American firms could or would get 30% of the work in the absence of discrimination, so the 30% quota was not a narrowly tailored way of redressing past discrimination even if that discrimination had been adequately shown.)

  **d. Sometimes might survive:** Justice O'Connor did not believe that **all** race-conscious remedial plans would necessarily fail this strict scrutiny test. If there was clear evidence of discrimination either by the government or perhaps even by private parties, eradication of this discrimination might be a sufficiently compelling objective. For instance, had there been clear evidence of discrimination by specific general contractors in the Richmond area, eliminating the effects of this discrimination might have been a "compelling" objective, and some sort of race-conscious plan might have been a sufficiently-narrowly-tailored means of correcting that discrimination.

    **i. Statistical inference:** Furthermore, Justice O'Connor noted, if there was a "significant **statistical disparity** between the number of qualified minority contractors willing and able to perform a particular service and the number of such contractors actually engaged by the locality or the locality's prime contractors," then an **inference** of discrimination might arise, even in the absence of direct proof of discrimination by a particular contractor against a particular sub-contractor on a particular project.

**5. Array of judges:** Five members of the Court in *Croson* agreed with the key proposition that all race-conscious measures, even supposedly "remedial" ones, must be subjected to strict scrutiny. Three justices (Rehnquist, White, and Kennedy) joined O'Connor's opinion on this point; a fifth, Scalia, said in a concurrence that he agreed with this proposition (though he would go even further than O'Connor, and would not allow race-conscious measures *ever* as a means of remedying past discrimination committed by anyone other than the government itself).

6. **Stevens' concurrence:** Justice Stevens, in a concurrence, seemed to agree with the basic holding that where the government institutes a race-conscious measure for remedial purposes, that measure must be subjected to strict scrutiny. But he saw the majority opinion as having an underlying premise that "a governmental decision that rests on a racial classification is never permissible except as a remedy for a past wrong," and he disagreed with that premise. That is, he thought that there might be some legitimate public purposes, other than relief of past discrimination, that might be served by race-conscious measures (e.g., "In a city with a recent history of racial unrest, the superintendent of police might reasonably conclude that an integrated police force could develop a better relationship with the community and thereby do a more effective job of maintaining law and order than a force composed only of white officers"). He agreed with the majority that Richmond's plan should be held invalid in part because the class of persons benefitted by the ordinance was not limited to victims of discrimination — for instance, it included persons who had never been in business in Richmond.

7. **Dissent:** Three justices bitterly dissented. The principal dissent was by Justice Marshall, joined by Justices Brennan and Blackmun.

   a. **Standard:** The dissenters sharply disagreed with the majority's assertion that strict scrutiny was the appropriate standard for measuring race-conscious remedial plans. They believed that ***intermediate level*** scrutiny was the appropriate one: "[R]ace-conscious classifications designed to further remedial goals 'must serve important governmental objectives and must be substantially related to achievement of those objectives. ... ' "

   b. **Rationale:** Marshall asserted that "[a] profound difference separates governmental actions that themselves are racist, and governmental actions that seek to remedy the effects of prior racism or to prevent neutral governmental activity from perpetuating the effects of such racism." By adopting the strict scrutiny standard, the majority "signals that it regards racial discrimination as largely a phenomenon of the past." Marshall, by contrast, did not believe that the country was "anywhere close to eradicating racial discrimination or its vestiges."

   c. **Minority control of Richmond:** Marshall conceded that the fact that Richmond now had a population and a City Council that were both mostly African American was a factor to be considered in determining the appropriate level of scrutiny. But he disagreed that this should be dispositive. A city that had recently come under minority control was likely to be the very kind of city that would have the most prior discrimination to rectify; certainly that was true of Richmond. Furthermore, the affirmative action plan here was voted for not only by the black city council majority, but also by one of the four white council members, with a second one abstaining.

   d. **Important objective:** Under Marshall's intermediate-level standard of review, the Richmond plan was clearly constitutional. Unlike the majority, he thought that the fact that less than 1% of public construction contracts had gone to minority-owned prime contractors strongly suggested (though it didn't directly prove) discrimination. Also, Marshall would have given substantial weight to the descriptive testimony of Richmond's leaders that the small presence of minorities in construction stemmed from past exclusionary practices. He would have given substantial weight to the fact that there were practically no minority members of area trade associations. And perhaps most importantly, he would have given great weight to the congressional findings of past nationwide discrimination in the construction industry. All of this evidence taken together made a strong showing that past discrimination had caused the present lack of minority participation in the Richmond construction industry, and therefore made the goal of promoting minority participation in that industry an "important" one.

   e.  **"Substantially related":**  Also, Marshall thought, the particular 30% set-aside was "substantially related" to achieving this objective. The set-aside applied only to public contracting dollars, and amounted to merely 3% of overall Richmond-area contracting. Also, the Richmond plan did not interfere with any vested right of a contractor to a particular contract; instead, it operated almost entirely prospectively, and was therefore less damaging than a plan which took away a contract already awarded to a white contractor. Finally, while the 30% set-aside was in a sense a quota, it was merely a "half-way" measure — it set a percentage about half-way between the present percentage of Richmond-based minority contractors (nearly zero) and the percentage of minorities in Richmond (50%).

**8.**  **Significance:**  What does *Croson* signify about the constitutionality of the many hundreds of minority set-aside programs enacted by states and cities across the country? The Richmond plan was probably unusually vulnerable, because of the relative weakness of the findings of past discrimination, the relatively high (30%) set-aside, and the relatively narrow procedures for obtaining a waiver. But the case will undoubtedly make it dramatically harder for other set-aside programs to pass constitutional muster as well.

   a.  **Findings:**  Governmental bodies that want to pursue set-asides (or other race-conscious remedial plans) will have to make ***very precise*** legislative findings that there has been past discrimination.

      i.  **Discrimination by governmental body:**  If there are specific findings that the ***governmental body itself*** has practiced intentional racial discrimination, eradication of the effects of this discrimination will presumably constitute a "compelling" governmental objective. However, governmental bodies will rarely voluntarily make such findings about their own conduct, because of the public relations and legal liability problems this would entail.

      ii.  **Discrimination by others:**  If the government entity comes up with clear evidence that ***others*** (even private parties) have practiced discrimination in the past, and shows a danger that non-remedial government activity would compound the effects of that discrimination, apparently avoiding this will also suffice as a "compelling" governmental objective. For instance, if Richmond had had clear evidence of past discrimination by prime contractors, Richmond would apparently have been entitled to reason, "If we award city construction funds without making an affirmative attempt to eradicate the effects of this prior private discrimination, we will be ourselves compounding the effects of this past discrimination, and we have a compelling interest in not doing so."

      iii.  **Societal discrimination:**  Clearly, it is not enough for the governmental body to come up with findings of past ***societal discrimination***. For instance, no matter how clear the evidence was that there had been widespread racial discrimination by society as a whole in the Richmond area, this would have been irrelevant — what counted was discrimination *in the construction industry*.

    **iv. Inference:** It will also be possible to prove past discrimination by *inference*. Generally, this can be done by statistics. But the statistics will have to be much more carefully worked out than they were in the Richmond case. For instance, it will not be enough to show that only a tiny percentage of, say, construction contracts go to African American firms. Instead, the government will apparently have to show fairly precisely how many *qualified* minority firms there are, and will have to demonstrate that these firms are getting a much smaller percentage of the work than their numbers would indicate — only then can a statistical inference of discrimination be made. Of course, since widespread discrimination will tend to prevent minority firms from existing in the first place, it will be a rare instance where there will be qualified minority firms in existence, who are nonetheless receiving very disproportionately little work.

  **b. Other objectives:** The curing of past intentional discrimination is almost the *only* objective that will be found "compelling" and thus justify a race-conscious set-aside plan. For instance, a governmental body's desire to improve the general economic status of its poorer citizens will virtually never justify a race-conscious plan.

    **i. Pursuit of educational diversity:** The only other objective that the Court has ever found to be a "compelling" one that may justify race-conscious measures is the pursuit of *diversity* in an *educational setting*. Recall that in *Grutter v. Bollinger, supra*, p. 282, a bare five-justice majority found that a public law school had a compelling interest in seeking broad diversity — including but not limited to racial and ethnic diversity — in its entering class. (We will have to wait and see whether the pursuit of racial/ethnic diversity can be compelling in other contexts, such as in university faculty hirings, or non-education-related hirings by such organizations as the armed forces and police departments. See *supra*, p. 289.)

  **c. Narrowly tailored:** The requirement that the means chosen be very *"narrowly tailored"* to meet the compelling governmental objective will also make it very hard for minority set-asides to pass muster.

    **i. Quota:** Probably a rigid *quota* will almost always be invalid. Thus even had Richmond set aside only 10% of its contracts for minorities (the figure used by Congress, as opposed to the 30% figure actually used by Richmond), it is hard to imagine that the case would have turned out differently. The Court would almost always conclude that a less rigid plan would have been adequate.

    **ii. Race-neutral plans:** Probably the requirement of narrow tailoring means that the government must first either try out, or at least consciously eliminate, *race-neutral* means before using race-conscious means. Thus the Richmond City Council would presumably have to have either tried race-neutral methods (like giving a preference for small or new construction firms, regardless of the race of their owners), or at least come up with specific findings as to why such race-neutral means would not succeed, before it could be allowed to use race-conscious methods.

      **(1) Race-neutral means of achieving educational diversity:** On the other hand, the requirement of narrow tailoring seems to have been somewhat *weakened* in the main affirmative-actions-in-admissions case, *Grutter v. Bollinger,* *supra*, p. 282. There, the majority certainly examined whether workable race-neutral means of attaining diversity were available, such as a race-blind lottery system open to all minimally-qualified candidates. But the Court did not insist that the University ***try out*** these race-neutral methods first, or even that the university conduct some sort of formal ***fact-finding*** to determine whether these alternative methods might be workable. Instead, the Court seemed to give broad ***deference*** to the university's assertion in the litigation itself that these methods would prove unworkable. However, there is not yet any indication that outside of the diversity-in-admissions context, there will be any weakening of the requirement that race-neutral methods be carefully evaluated by the defendant before race-conscious means are used.

    **iii. Goals:** Probably set-asides will at least have to be replaced by less rigid, *"soft"* racial preferences, if racial preferences are to be allowed at all. For instance, Richmond would have had a better chance if it had expressed a *"goal"* or *"preference"* for minorities that would remain in force until 30% of contracts were awarded to minority-owned firms, instead of the hard and fast "quota" which it used. Similarly, a city might fare better if it allowed consideration of race as *one factor* among many to be considered when the city decides who should get a contract. But even a "goal" or "one factor among many" plan will probably be struck down if there is no clear evidence of past discrimination, and no showing that race-neutral means would be inadequate. [7]

**H. Set-asides by Congress:** The rules are the same for minority set-asides imposed by ***Congress***, though this has been true only since mid-1995. In ***Adarand Constructors, Inc. v. Pena***, 515 U.S. 200 (1995), the Court overturned prior law and announced that ***strict scrutiny must be applied to race-based affirmative action schemes imposed by Congress***, just as it is applied to those imposed by state and local governments.

    **1. Pre-*Adarand* law (*Metro Broadcasting*):** *Adarand* overruled a prior case, *Metro Broadcasting, Inc. v. FCC,* 497 U.S. 547 (1990), which had applied intermediate level review, not strict scrutiny, in judging whether "benign" race-conscious action by Congress violated the equal protection rights of non-minorities.

    **2. Facts of *Adarand*:** The minority preference at issue in *Adarand* was subtle but nonetheless real. Plaintiff (Adarand) was a white-owned construction firm that had bid for a subcontract to supply guardrails to a federal highway project in Colorado. P's bid was the lowest. But the general contractor took a bid from a minority-owned firm that qualified under federal regulations as a Disadvantaged Business Enterprise (DBE). The prime contractor was not *required* to award the sub-contract to a minority-owned DBE, but it received a financial incentive (10% of the amount of the sub-contract, or 1.5% of the amount of the prime contract, whichever was less) for doing so.

---

7. Again, ***university admissions*** present a slight exception. The use of goals for minority enrollment to achieve diversity in the student body (rather than to remedy past discrimination) was officially endorsed by the court in *Grutter, supra,* p. 282. But *Grutter* also demonstrates that, as the main text suggests, soft "goals," as opposed to rigid quotas, are far more likely to be found to be an acceptably narrowly-tailored means of achieving whatever compelling interest justifies the use of race-conscious decision making.

a. **Whites can be DBE's:** Small white-owned firms could also be DBE's. But a firm owned by an African American, Hispanic or certain other ethnic minority (as well as a firm owned by a woman) was automatically, though rebuttably, ***"presumed"*** to be disadvantaged. A firm owned by a white male, by contrast, had to prove disadvantage by "clear and convincing evidence." In any event, P in *Adarand* could not or did not gain DBE status, and the winning bidder for the sub-contract did.

3. **Strict scrutiny applied:** The Court in *Adarand* overruled *Metro Broadcasting*, and held that ***congressionally-authorized race-conscious affirmative action programs must be subject to strict scrutiny.*** In other words, the rule of *Richmond v. Croson, supra* — that race-conscious "reverse discrimination" may be upheld only if "necessary" to achieve a "compelling" governmental interest — applies to congressional statutes the same as it applies to the actions of state and local governments. On this issue, the vote was 5-4; the Court's opinion was by Justice O'Connor (joined by Rehnquist, Kennedy, Thomas and Scalia).

   a. **Rationale:** O'Connor believed that *Metro Broadcasting* should be overruled because it departed from what she said was one of the core principles of the Court's pre-*Metro* cases on affirmative action: the principle of ***"congruence,"*** that "equal protection analysis in the Fifth Amendment area [applicable to the federal government] is the same as that under the Fourteenth Amendment [applicable to state and local government]." No matter what level of government is involved, "[W]henever the government treats any person unequally because of his or her race, that person has suffered an injury that falls squarely within the language and spirit of the Constitution's guarantee of equal protection."

      i. **Other principles undermined:** O'Connor also believed that *Metro*'s application of the more lenient "mid-level review" to congressional actions undermined two other core principles: ***skepticism*** of all racial classifications, and ***consistency*** of treatment irrespective of the race of the burdened or benefited group. The three core principles of congruence, skepticism and consistency "derive from the basic principle that ***the Fifth and Fourteenth Amendments ... protect persons, not groups.***"

   b. **Strict scrutiny not necessarily fatal:** But O'Connor went out of her way to assure that the use of strict scrutiny did ***not*** necessary mean that the governmental action being reviewed would be struck down: "we wish to ***dispel*** the notion that strict scrutiny is '***strict in theory, but fatal in fact***.'" She suggested that if government is responding to "the ***lingering effects of racial discrimination*** against minority groups," and does so in a ***"narrowly tailored way,"*** even race-conscious methods may survive.

   c. **Particular regulation not addressed:** The Court's opinion did not decide whether the particular set-aside regulations at issue could survive strict scrutiny. Instead, the Court remanded the issue to the lower courts. O'Connor suggested that on remand, the lower courts should consider whether the governmental interest being served was ***"compelling,"*** whether ***race-neutral*** means might have been effective to achieve that interest, and whether the remedy was appropriately ***short-lived*** so as not to "last longer than the discriminatory effects it is designed to eliminate."

4. **Concurrences:** Two members of the majority would have gone even further than O'Connor. Both Scalia and Thomas indicated in concurrences that they would have ruled that race-conscious affirmative action can ***never*** be justified. As Thomas put it, "government-sponsored racial discrimination based on benign prejudice is just as noxious as discrimination inspired by malicious prejudice. In each instance, it is racial discrimination, plain and simple."

5. **Dissents:** The four Justices in the minority wrote three dissents. Perhaps the most interesting dissent was the one by Justice Stevens, since he had voted with the majority in *Croson* to apply strict scrutiny to state and local affirmative action programs.

   a. **Good motives less suspect:** Stevens rejected the majority's "consistency" principle: "There is no moral or constitutional equivalence between a policy that is designed to perpetuate a caste system and one that seeks to eradicate racial subordination. … The consistency that the Court espouses would ***disregard the difference between a 'No Trespassing' sign and a welcome mat.*** It would treat a Dixiecrat Senator's decision to vote against Thurgood Marshall's confirmation in order to keep African Americans off the Supreme Court as on a par with President Johnson's evaluation of his nominee's race as a positive factor."

   b. **"Congruence" derided:** Stevens also believed that there were at least two strong reasons for rejecting the majority's "congruence" principle, and for giving ***more deference*** to race-based affirmative action efforts by Congress than to state and local programs.

      i. **Special enforcement powers:** First, Congress' powers concerning matters of race were "***explicitly enhanced***" by §5 of the 14th Amendment (which gives Congress the power to "enforce, by appropriate legislation, the provisions of the 14th Amendment"). By contrast, the states' use of race-conscious measures was what the Amendment was specifically directed *against*.

      ii. **Entire nation's representatives:** Second, "federal affirmative-action programs represent the will of our ***entire Nation's elected representatives***, whereas a state or local program may have an impact on ***nonresident entities*** who played no part in the decision to enact it." Just as Congress may burden interstate commerce even though the individual states may not (see *supra*, p. 68), so Congress should have greater leeway to use race to combat the effects of past discrimination, Stevens argued.

6. **Significance of *Adarand*:** Here is a summary of what *Adarand* seems to establish, and what it leaves unresolved:

   a. **Federalizes *Croson*:** Most importantly, *Adarand* ***"federalizes"*** *Croson*: the federal government must satisfy the same "strict scrutiny" standard for race-based affirmative actions as must state and local governments. That is, government may use race only in a way that is "narrowly tailored" to achieve some "compelling" governmental objective.

   b. **"Compelling" interest and "narrowly-tailored means":** *Adarand* doesn't tell us much new about what governmental objectives are "compelling," or about how to tell whether the means chosen are sufficiently "narrowly tailored." Clearly the prevention of ***ongoing discrimination*** in the particular area being regulated (e.g., the awarding of highway construction sub-contracts in a particular city) will qualify, but it's not clear what other objectives would suffice.

c. **Applies to non-set-aside contexts:** *Adarand* does not just apply to minority set-asides or to contracting. It applies equally to *educational admissions*, *employment*, and any other domain. For instance, a congressionally-funded scholarship fund that gave a preference to African American and Hispanic students would presumably be subjected to strict scrutiny.

d. **Possible greater deference to Congress:** Even though *Adarand* makes the "same" test (strict scrutiny) applicable across all levels of government, the Court may be willing to grant Congress *greater deference* than it would to a state or local government body. For instance, the Court might be quicker to accept a congressional finding that there had been discrimination in a particular domain — or a finding that the discrimination could only be redressed through race-conscious means — than it would be to accept such a finding from a state or local legislature.

   i. **Nationwide findings:** Similarly, Congress may be entitled to make findings on a *national* rather than local basis. If so, it could be relatively easy for Congress to protect some widesweeping programs.

   ii. **Degree of congressional involvement needed:** If Congress does get greater deference compared with state and local governments, the action probably has to be one taken fairly directly by *Congress itself*, not one taken by a federal *administrative agency* acting under broad congressional guidelines.

e. **Degree of outcome-determinativeness:** The degree to which the minority preference *determines the outcome* will presumably be part of the equation when the Court decides whether the program is sufficiently narrowly-tailored. A modest preference like that in *Adarand* (in essence, an at-most-10% advantage given to minority subcontractors, with the final decision left to the prime contractor) is likely to be easier to justify than a flat quota or set-aside (e.g., a commandment to prime contractors, "You may not receive this contract unless x% of the sub-contracts go to minority firms.").

   i. **Presumptions:** Similarly, *rebuttable* presumptions are more likely to pass muster than *irrebuttable* rules. Thus the scheme in *Adarand* (where a minority-owned firm is presumed to be economically and socially disadvantaged, and a firm owned by a white male is presumed not, but either presumption can be overturned by particularized evidence) is more likely to survive than a flat rule stating "All black-owned firms shall be conclusively deemed to be disadvantaged, and no white-male-owned firm shall be deemed disadvantaged."

f. **"Diversity" as an objective:** It remains unclear whether the pursuit of racial *diversity* can ever by itself be a "compelling objective." The best guess is that a majority of the present Court will ultimately conclude that pursuit of racial diversity, without more, is *not* a compelling objective. (However, where diversity is tied to a more specific objective — like assuring that a police force has some common bonds with, and understanding of, the minority neighborhoods it polices — a compelling interest might be found.)

I. **Hiring, lay-offs, and promotions:** Are race-conscious affirmative action programs constitutional when they relate to *hiring*, *lay-offs*, *promotions*, and other *job-related* decisions? Voluntary arrangements by a private company do not raise any constitutional issue, since no state action is present. Constitutional issues do, however, arise when a race-conscious employment policy is either:

❏ voluntarily entered into by a ***public employer***; or

❏ ***imposed*** upon either a public or private employer ***by a court*** as a remedy for a judicial finding of prior discrimination.

No case raising these issues has been decided by the Supreme Court since the decision in *Croson*, requiring strict scrutiny for all race-conscious affirmative action measures. Here is what can be said at present about affirmative action plans in the employment area:

1. **Standard:** A race-conscious plan in the employment area, like a race-conscious plan adopted by government in any context, must be ***strictly scrutinized,*** as the result of *Croson*. That is, the government objective must be a "compelling" one, and the means chosen must be very "narrowly tailored" to that objective — "narrowly tailored" seems to mean that there must be no feasible less-restrictive alternative. Thus the employer must either have tried race-neutral methods, or at least come up with a convincing argument as to why such race-neutral methods would not suffice.

2. **Governmental objective:** The Court has now either adjudicated or alluded in dictum to five possible governmental objectives in the employment area, only some of which are sufficiently important to survive scrutiny:

   a. **Redress of past discrimination:** The redress of ***past discrimination*** by the ***particular employer*** enacting the affirmative action program is sufficiently compelling to pass muster with all or nearly all members of the Court.

      i. **Broader discrimination:** Furthermore, it will sometimes suffice that there is evidence of past discrimination in a particular ***industry***, rather than on the part of a particular employer.

   b. **"Societal" discrimination:** On the other hand, the remedying of "***societal***" discrimination, i.e., discrimination by society as a whole, does ***not*** constitute an objective that is important enough to justify use of race-conscious measures.

   c. **Encouragement of "diversity":** It is possible that the goal of promoting "***racial diversity***" in a workforce may sometimes be a sufficiently weighty goal.

      i. **Admissions context as precedent:** We now know, of course, of that the goal of promoting racial diversity in a ***university student body*** can be a compelling governmental interest; that's the core holding of *Grutter v. Bollinger, supra*, p. 282. We will have to see whether promoting racial diversity in a ***workforce*** as opposed to student body can sometimes similarly be compelling. Perhaps where the ***constituency served*** by a workforce is highly ***integrated***, attaining racial diversity among the work force itself will be deemed especially weighty, as in the case of an inner-city police force or a corrections staff serving a highly integrated prison population. Similarly, where a public workforce itself is highly integrated, having an integrated ***leadership*** at the top of that workforce may be deemed to be compelling, as in the case of the officer corps of our nation's very-integrated armed forces; see Justice O'Connor's opinion for the court in *Grutter*, relying heavily on an amicus brief by various retired military leaders that argued for the need to use affirmative action to ensure an integrated officer corps.

d.  **Balanced workforce:**   The goal of assuring a "*balanced workforce*," by itself, clearly will *not* justify use of race-conscious employment policies. Thus even where, say, a public employer has a smaller percentage of minorities in its workforce than are present in the relevant local labor force, the goal of bringing minority participation up to the labor-pool average will not suffice, in the absence of evidence of discrimination by that particular employer, or at least discrimination by the industry or union covering the labor market in question.

e.  **Furnishing of "role models":**   The goal of supplying "role models" to minority students is probably *not* a goal adequate to support race-conscious measures. That is, although it may be appropriate to seek some degree of diversity on a high school faculty, it is almost certainly not permissible to give preferences to minorities for the purpose of increasing minority representation on the faculty to match the percentage of minority students.

3.  **Narrowly tailored means:**   On the "means" side of the equation, employment cases have focused on three broad classes of methods for achieving the various objectives discussed above: (1) goals and "quotas" in hiring; (2) protections against lay-offs; and (3) preferences in promotions.

a.  **Hiring goals:**   Explicitly race-conscious "*hiring goals*" are generally permissible when they are an attempt to redress *clear past discrimination* by the employer who is using them.

**Example:** Employer, who has been found by a court to have discriminated against African Americans in the past, is ordered by the court to make best efforts to ensure that 18% of all new employees it hires are African American. African Americans make up 18% of the local labor force for the type of worker commonly employed by Employer. This type of "hiring goal" will probably be found to be constitutional.

i.  **Non-victims as beneficiaries:**   It does not matter that *non-victims* benefit from the hiring goals. Thus on the facts of the above example, even if it were shown that few or none of the African Americans who obtained jobs from Employer had ever been discriminated against on racial grounds (either by Employer or by other companies), the scheme would remain valid.

ii.  **Quotas:**   However, "hiring goals" are not the same thing as "*quotas*." Quotas are probably *not constitutional* even where used by an employer who has discriminated in the past. While the difference between a "hiring goal" and a "quota" is fuzzy, the difference mainly relates to *flexibility*. A hiring goal is flexible in the sense that the employer does not adopt a hard-and-fast rule that a particular percentage of new hires *must* belong to the minority, no matter what their relative qualifications. Similarly, if the program is under the supervision of a court, in order to avoid a presumptively unconstitutional quota the court must grant a temporary waiver to the employer if there is a plausible reason why the employer was not able to meet the goals.

iii.  **Absolute bar to majority advancement:**   The goals cannot act as an *absolute bar to majority advancement*. Thus a goal calling, even briefly, for 100% of new hires to belong to the minority would presumably be unconstitutional, no matter how egregiously the employer had discriminated in the past, and no matter how far the percentage of minorities in the employer's workforce fell below the percentage in the overall local workforce.

iv.  **Temporary:**   The goals must be ***temporary.*** That is, they must expire as soon as the percentage of minorities in the employer's workforce equals the percentage in the relevant labor force, since at that point the result of past discrimination has presumably been eliminated. Thereafter, it does not matter if the minority participation in the employer's workforce drops ***below*** the percentage in the local labor pool, so long as there is no evidence of actual discrimination. (Remember that race-conscious affirmative action programs cannot be used to achieve the objective of a racially balanced workforce; see *supra*, p. 310.)

v.  **Percentage of places reserved:**   It may be unconstitutional for the goals to call for reservation, even temporarily, of a ***higher*** percentage of places in the employer's workforce than minorities occupy in the local labor force. This is an issue on which the Court has not yet taken an explicit position.

vi.  **Tested against race-neutral means:**   Race-conscious hiring goals will probably always be tested against possible ***race-neutral*** methods. Thus if the employer cannot show that it has considered and rejected for good reason race-neutral means, the race-conscious hiring goal will probably be struck down. For instance, the employer will normally have to show that it has considered ***more aggressive recruiting*** of minority workers, special training programs for new workers regardless of race, or other methods apart from race-based selection procedures, before the employer may use race-conscious hiring goals.

b.  **Lay-offs:**   Preferential protections against ***lay-offs*** are far harder to justify, as a constitutional matter, than are hiring preferences. Since lay-offs affect a worker's present job, rather than merely one of several possibilities for future employment, the harm suffered by "innocent" members of the majority is far greater than in the hiring-preference case. See, e.g., *Wygant v. Jackson Bd. of Educ.*, 476 U.S. 267 (1986) (plurality opinion). Therefore, it seems unlikely that there is any scheme for giving minorities preferential protection against lay-offs that would be supported by a majority of the Court.

c.  **Promotion preferences:**   Preferences in ***promotions*** of existing employees fall somewhere between hiring preferences and lay-off preferences in terms of the disruption to the lives of existing employees. Therefore, they are somewhat harder to justify than hiring goals but easier than lay-off preferences. A preferential promotions plan is most likely to survive constitutional scrutiny where it is a closely calibrated attempt to ***restore*** minority workers to the senior positions they ***would have had*** in the employer's workforce had the past discrimination never occurred.

4.  **Significance of context:**   The ***context*** in which the employment preference occurs is also significant:

a.  **Judicial finding:**   Where the employer, whether public or private, is found by a court to have discriminated in the past, and the preference scheme is one ordered by the court, the above analysis controls. That analysis would probably also control if the employer settled a serious discrimination suit by agreeing to the preference scheme, but this has not been definitively established.

b. **Voluntary arrangement by private party:** Where the preference scheme is a *voluntary* one enacted by a *private* employer which has *discriminated* in the past, there is no constitutional problem at all because there is no state action.

c. **No past discrimination:** Where the scheme is enacted by a private employer for some purpose other than the remedying of past discrimination by that employer (e.g., to maintain a balanced workforce, or to remedy "societal" discrimination), there is similarly no constitutional problem. (However, there may be problems with Title VII, the main federal anti-discrimination *statute*.)

d. **Voluntary arrangement by public employer:** Where a *public* employer *voluntarily* enacts preferences without evidence that it has discriminated in the past, the Court will presumably *strictly scrutinize* the preference. While this strict scrutiny will make it hard for the voluntary plan to survive, it has a respectable chance of surviving if: (1) there is strong statistical evidence of an imbalance that could not have happened by chance; (2) there is some evidence of discrimination by the industry or unions in the relevant market (even if not evidence of discrimination by the particular employer); and (3) race or sex is merely made "one factor" in the hiring or promotion decision.

J. **Drawing of election districts:** The process by which the boundaries of *election districts* are drawn has often led *groups of voters* to claim unconstitutional reverse racial discrimination. When election districts are drawn by state legislatures or other government bodies, those drawing the lines almost always take race into account, just as they take account of party affiliation, ethnic breakdown, and other demographics. In light of *Richmond v. Croson, supra,* p. 299, at first glance it would seem that once the plaintiff could show that she had been disfavored by the racially-conscious drawing of election district boundaries, the Court would strictly scrutinize the boundaries. But this is generally not in fact the case. A plaintiff will succeed with a reverse discrimination claim regarding electoral districting only by showing either: (1) that the lines were drawn with the *purpose* and *effect* of *disadvantaging the group* of which the plaintiff is a part; or (2) that *race* was the *"predominant factor"* in how the district lines were drawn. We consider each of these types of attacks in turn.

1. **"Partisan gerrymander" claims:** Traditionally, the type of claim most frequently brought by groups believing themselves to have been disadvantaged by the district-drawing process has been an equal protection claim based upon *"dilution of voting strength."* In this type of claim, the plaintiffs argue that their group's ability to elect representatives of their choice has been weakened by the drawing of boundary lines that advantage some other group.

These claims are typically directed at *"partisan gerrymanders,"* i.e. the drawing of districts in a highly artificial way for the principal purpose of disadvantaging a particular political group.[8]

---

8. Here, we're assuming that the claim is that the gerrymander was principally based on some factor *other than race,* such as *membership in a particular political party.* As to racially-motivated gerrymanders, which are easier to attack, see *infra,* p. 315. In our present discussion, we are talking about garden-variety political-party-based gerrymanders in which, say, Republicans try to disadvantage Democrats, or vice versa.

**Example:** In most states, the boundary lines for congressional districts are drawn by the state legislature. Let's assume that the legislature in State X is controlled by Democrats, and that the state has 14 congressional districts. Let's further assume that 51% of the state's registered voters are Democrats and 49% are Republicans ( and let's pretend that there are no independents.) If the congressional districts were drawn in a non-partisan and essentially random way, most of the time the state would elect seven Democrats to Congress and seven Republicans. Now, however, let's assume that through some quirk of local politics the State X legislature is so completely controlled by Democratic legislators that the Democrats have the ability to enact any districting plan they want, so long as it meets the requirement of mathematical equality (i.e., that each district have the same population, in accordance with the Supreme Court's "one-person, one-vote" rule, described *infra*, p. 733).

When it next comes time to redraw congressional district boundaries,[9] the Democrats spring into action. They propose a redistricting plan that packs most Republican voters into four districts in each of which at least 75% of the voters are Republican. Conversely, Democratic voters are spread out so that they have a narrow but clear majority in the other 10 districts. Let's also assume that this map drawing is done in such a way as to create very oddly shaped districts, to disrespect political subdivisions (e.g., by splitting cities), and to ignore natural geographical features (e.g., by putting both sides of a river in the same district while splitting a neighborhood). Then, the Democrats use their control of the state legislature to enact the redistricting plan, over the fierce objection of the Republicans. If the Democrats have drawn their lines well, and if voters vote on party lines, the Democrats will have 10 of the 14 members of the state's congressional delegation, verses the seven seats that would be produced by a neutral plan. This is a classic "partisan gerrymander."

a. **Nearly impossible to win:** Claims attacking such partisan-gerrymandered districts are ***virtually impossible to win.*** In the final years of the Rehnquist Court, four Justices believed that such claims were ***non-justiciable***, and should thus not be heard at all. Of the five members of that Court who were theoretically willing to hear such claims, all agreed that the standards for winning such a claim should be very demanding, but the five could not even agree among themselves on just what the standards should be. See *Vieth v. Jubelirer*, immediately *infra* and p. 736. In any event, no plaintiff in recent generations has succeeded in winning a partisan-gerrymandering Equal Protection claim at the Supreme Court level.[10]

b. **No agreement on standards (*Vieth v. Jubelirer*):** In ***Vieth v. Jubelirer***, 541 U.S. 267 (2004), apart from the four members of the Rehnquist Court who said that partisan-gerrymandering claims were not even justiciable all, the remaining five members could not agree among themselves on what the standards for a gerrymandering claim should be. Here is a very brief summary of the views of several of those five Justices on what the plaintiff in a partisan gerrymandering case should have to show:

---

9. This normally happens every 10 years, shortly after the 1990, 2000, etc. Census.

10. Nothing in the Roberts Court's early going has changed the difficulty of winning a partisan gerrymander claim. See, e.g., *League of United Latin Amer. Citizens v. Perry*, 126 S.Ct. 2594 (2006), discussed further *infra*, p. 314, where the plaintiffs failed with a partisan-gerrymander claim.

    **i.**  **Stevens:**  Justice Stevens would let the plaintiff win if she could show that "the legislature *allowed partisan considerations* to *dominate and control* the lines drawn, *forsaking all neutral principles."* So if "the only possible explanation for a district's bizarre shape is a naked desire to increase partisan strength," Stevens would find the district a violation of Equal Protection. (Stevens thought that under this test, there would be "only a few meritorious claims," but that "extreme abuses" would be prevented.)

    **ii.**  **Souter:**  Justice Souter proposed a complex five-element standard for a prime facie case. Space prevents us from summarizing all the elements. But, for instance, Souter would require the plaintiff to show that the district in which she resided "paid little or no heed to those *traditional districting principles [like] contiguity, compactness, respect for political subdivisions,* and *conformity with geographic features like rivers and mountains."* The plaintiff would also have to "establish *specific correlations* between the district's deviations from traditional districting principles and the distribution of the population of his group." For instance, if P was complaining that the lines were drawn in a way that split particular towns and communities, P would have to show that "Democrats tended to fall on one side and Republicans on the other."

    **iii.**  **Kennedy:**  Justice Kennedy couldn't say what the precise standard ought to be, but thought that a standard based on the *First Amendment* might work better than one based on the Equal Protection clause. That is, Kennedy thought that the Court should try to use First Amendment *free-association* principles to protect the disfavored voters' right not to be discriminated against on account of their association with the disfavored political party.

  **c.**  **Mid-decennial redistricting:**  Plaintiffs' difficulties in winning partisan-gerrymander claims are further illustrated by a 2006 case involving *"mid-decennial redistricting."* In *League of United Latin American Citizens v. Perry*, 126 S.Ct. 2594 (2006), the Court declined to overturn what was perhaps the most nakedly partisan redistricting plan to come before the Court in many years.

    **i.**  **Facts:**  *Perry* involved Texas' congressional redistricting in the aftermath of the 2000 Census. During the 1990s, the Republican Party had large growth in Texas. Nonetheless, in the 2000 election (conducted with district lines based on the 1990 Census), Republicans captured only 13 congressional seats (versus 17 for the Democrats), even though Republicans carried 59% of the votes in statewide elections that year.

      **(1)**  **Deadlock after 2000 census:**  By the time the 2000 Census results came in, Republicans controlled the governorship and the state Senate, but Democrats still had the state House of Representatives. Because of this deadlock, the Legislature could not agree on the required redistricting plan. Instead, a court-ordered redistricting plan (called Plan 1151C) was put into place. Plan 1151C did very little to redraw the pro-Democrat 1990s districting lines, and in the 2002 congressional elections based on that plan, the Democrats kept a 17-15 Democratic majority in the Texas delegation, even though the state had turned sharply Republican.

(2) **Republicans get control of the House:** But in 2003, the Republicans finally got control of the state House of Representatives and thus ***control of both houses.*** The now-Republican-controlled legislature immediately enacted a redistricting plan for congressional districts ("Plan 1374C") about which the federal trial court later said, "the ***single-minded purpose*** of the Texas Legislature in enacting [the new plan] was to ***gain partisan advantage."*** Plan 1374C was spectacularly successful for the Republicans: in the next congressional election they went from 15 seats in the state delegation to 21, while the Democrats went from 17 down to 11.

ii. **Plan upheld:** The Supreme Court handily ***upheld*** the Republicans' Plan 1374C against the claim that it was an unconstitutional partisan gerrymander.[11] The Court was badly split on the rationale, with no more than two justices agreeing on any particular rationale. But most importantly, only two members of the Court believed that the Texas plan here was unconstitutional.

   (1) **Kennedy's opinion:** Justice Kennedy, who wrote the main opinion in *Perry*, thought that the plan here was constitutional for a variety of reasons, including the fact that "there is nothing inherently suspect about a legislature's decision to replace mid-decade a court-ordered plan with one of its own." He also noted that the Republicans' plan made the party balance in the congressional delegation "more congruent to statewide party power" than the prior court-ordered plan had done, thus making the Republican plan arguably "fairer" than the court-ordered one.

   (2) **Four more votes:** No other Justice joined Justice Kennedy's rationale. But four members agreed with his conclusion that the plan was constitutional, and two additional members declined to say whether they thought it was constitutional or not. Only two members — Stevens and Breyer — voted to strike the plan as an unconstitutional gerrymander.

iii. **Conclusion:** So following *Vieth* and *Perry*, it's hard to see how plaintiffs in a partisan-gerrymandering case can ever convince a majority of the Court that a particular partisan gerrymander would violate the plaintiffs' Equal Protection rights.

2. **"Racial gerrymanders" violate Equal Protection:** Until the mid-1990s, "partisan gerrymandering" claims (described above) seemed to be the only way in which voters could bring an equal protection attack against the race-conscious drawing of election districts. But the Supreme Court has since held that there is a second type of equal protection claim under which voters may attack the drawing of electoral districts: if the plaintiffs can show that the use of ***race*** was the ***"predominant factor"*** in drawing the district lines, the districting scheme will be subjected to ***strict scrutiny.*** The Court has referred to such schemes as ***"racial gerrymanders."*** This second type of equal protection claim was recognized in a pair of cases, one in 1993 and the other in 1995. And, in contrast to partisan-gerrymander cases, racial-gerrymander cases have often proved to be winnable by the plaintiffs.

---

11. The Court did strike down one aspect of the plan, the redrawing of a West Texas district, on the grounds that the redrawing had weakened the voting power of a minority group there (Latinos) in violation of the Voting Rights Act (see *infra*, p. 318).

a. **The "facially irrational" theory (*Shaw v. Reno*):** The first racial-gerrymandering decision by the Court was ***Shaw v. Reno***, 509 U.S. 630 (1993). By a 5-4 vote, the Court held that if the plaintiffs could show that the districting scheme was "so ***irrational*** on its face that it can only be understood as an effort to segregate voters into separate voting districts because of their race," strict scrutiny would be triggered, and the districting struck down unless it was shown to be "narrowly tailored to further a compelling governmental interest."

   i. **Bizarre shape:** The majority in *Shaw* seemed to concentrate on the ***shape*** of the district. The district at issue in *Shaw* was in fact strangely-shaped and non-compact. Because North Carolina's African American population is relatively dispersed, a long, narrow, irregularly-shaped district was the only way to create two districts that would be majority-black in the state, a goal the state legislature was willing to achieve and the Voting Rights Act may have required. The district as drawn was 160 miles long, and in some places was only as wide as the interstate highway.

      (1) **Remanded:** The Court remanded for a determination of whether this district was so bizarre as to violate the Court's new standard. Later, in *Shaw v. Hunt*, 517 U.S. 899 (1996) (also discussed *infra*, p. 317), the Court held that the district *did* violate the standard.

   ii. **Significance of shape unclear:** The *Shaw* decision left it unclear whether a bizarre shape was a requirement for showing an illegal "racial gerrymander," or whether instead *any* racially-motivated districting scheme would be strictly scrutinized, with bizarre shape merely being one possible indicator of racial motive.

   iii. **Rationale:** In any event, the majority in *Shaw* made it clear that 5 members of the Court thought that "racial gerrymanders" were bad, and constitutionally suspect, policy. There were two reasons. First, the drawing of district lines based mainly on race would have a ***socially-divisive impact*** on ***voters***, resembling "***political apartheid***" and "***balkaniz[ing]***" us into competing racial factions." Second, racially-motivated districting sends a bad message to the ***officials*** elected from the gerrymandered districts, that their primary obligation is to ***represent only the members of the racially-dominant group*** rather than the whole constituency.

b. **"Predominant factor" test (*Miller v. Johnson*):** The next racial-gerrymandering case, ***Miller v. Johnson***, 515 U.S. 900 (1995), then made it clear that a bizarre shape is ***not*** a requirement for such a claim, and that all the plaintiffs must prove is that race was a "***predominant factor***" in the drawing of the district lines. Once the plaintiffs make this showing, the Court will use strict scrutiny. *Miller*, like *Shaw*, was a 5-4 vote.

   i. **Kennedy's opinion:** The majority opinion in *Miller*, by Justice Kennedy, spoke in broad terms: "Just as the state may not, absent extraordinary justification, segregate citizens on the basis of race in its public parks, buses, golf courses, beaches, and schools," so it may not "separate its citizens into different voting districts on the basis of race."

   ii. **Facts:** The facts in *Miller* illustrate at least one scenario in which an illegal racial gerrymander will be found. Because Georgia had previously been found to have discriminated against African Americans in voting, it was subject to the "pre-clearance" provisions of the federal Voting Rights Act. Under these provisions, any redistricting plan had to be pre-approved by the Justice Department. The Justice Department (the majority found) took the position that any redistricting plan must create at least three majority-black districts. After initially resisting, the Georgia legislature eventually came up with a plan that included three such districts, including the district at issue here (the 11th). In the litigation, the state essentially conceded that the drawing of the lines for the 11th was done mostly for racial reasons, because of the need to produce three majority-black districts to satisfy the Justice Department. The fact that the district was relatively **compact**, and no more "irregular" or "bizarre" in its shape than many districts, was not enough to save it, given the race-conscious motives with which it was drawn.

iii. **Flunks strict scrutiny:** Because the districting had been done primarily for racial reasons, the Court applied strict scrutiny. The majority found that the lines for the 11th district flunked because the state was not pursuing any "compelling" interest. If the drawing of three majority-black districts had really been necessary to redress past discrimination, the Court suggested, the requisite compelling interest might have been found. But here, the only interest the majority found was the interest in satisfying the Justice Department's rules. And these rules, the majority concluded, were not necessary for eliminating past anti-black discrimination in the state.

iv. **O'Connor's concurrence:** Justice O'Connor, who in a concurrence supplied the vital fifth vote to strike the districting plan, suggested that she might make it harder than the other four members of the majority would for plaintiffs to win such challenges. She characterized the standard for those challenging race-conscious districts as being a "demanding one" — plaintiffs must show that the State has "relied on race in **substantial disregard of customary and traditional districting practices**." Only "**extreme instances** of gerrymandering" would be subjected to strict scrutiny, she said.

v. **Dissent:** As in *Shaw*, four Justices dissented. The principal dissent, by Justice Ginsburg, argued that the majority was unduly expanding *Shaw*. Ginsburg objected to the use of strict scrutiny whenever race was a "predominant factor" — she believed that this would open the door to federal litigation over the legitimacy of any districting plan that even took account of race.

c. **Additional districts struck down:** A pair of 1996 cases shows that majority-minority districts will in fact frequently be struck down under *Shaw* and *Miller*. See *Bush v. Vera*, 517 U.S. 952 (1996) and *Shaw v. Hunt*, 517 U.S. 899 (1996). In this pair of cases, the Court struck down **all four** of the districts whose constitutionality it considered, on the grounds that in each, race was the predominant factor.

d. **Significance:** So what do *Shaw* and *Miller*, taken together, mean for the future of voting rights? Here are some thoughts:

i. **Race-consciousness still allowed:** States are not prevented from being "race conscious" when they draw lines, as long as race does not become the ***"predominant factor."*** If, as seems likely, the Court goes only as far as Justice O'Connor is willing to go, plaintiffs will have to show that the state "relied on race in substantial disregard of customary and traditional districting practices." So if race is heavily considered, but so are such (traditional) objectives as protecting incumbents, keeping "communities of interest" (e.g., large urban neighborhoods) together, using county and precinct lines, and not diluting the voting strength of other ethnic groups (e.g., Irish Americans), the plan may survive.

**(1) Race as predominant factor:** But the fact that the people drawing the district lines consider other factors in addition to race certainly ***won't immunize*** the districting scheme from being invalidated for making race the "predominant factor." The Supreme Court will take a very detailed look at exactly *how* the line-drawers went about their business, and won't hesitate to find that race was the most important factor. For instance, in *Bush v. Vera, supra,* p. 317, a plurality of the Court attached great weight to the fact that the legislature used maps and computer programs that ***provided racial data at the block-by-block level***, but other data (e.g., incumbency and political affiliation) only on a broader basis; this fact helped convince these Justices that race was more important to the line-drawers than all other factors taken together, including incumbency.

ii. **Minority districts vulnerable:** "Majority-minority" districts are clearly more vulnerable than they were before *Shaw* and *Miller*. Any plan that seems to have been motivated principally by a desire to create the maximum possible number of such districts will be open to attack.

**(1) Compliance with Voting Rights Act:** But a majority of the Court now believes that ***compliance with the Voting Rights Act can*** supply the requisite "compelling" state objective to support intentional creation of majority-minority districts. This is demonstrated by a post-*Shaw/Miller* 2006 case, *League of United Latin American Citizens v. Perry,* 126 S.Ct. __ (2006), in which six members of the Court agreed that compliance with the VRA can be a compelling state objective that justifies drawing race-conscious district lines. So if the creation of one or more majority-minority districts were in fact necessary to comply with the VRA's requirement that the political processes be ***"equally open to minorities,"*** a solid six-justice majority of the Roberts Court would apparently uphold the districts even though race was in some sense the predominant factor.

iii. **Dispersed racial majority:** Districting authorities will find it toughest to avoid a violation where African Americans or other racial minorities are ***widely dispersed***. For instance, the plan struck down in *Miller* was weakened by the fact that it reached from the outskirts of Atlanta in the middle of the state to Savannah, on the coast 260 miles away. By contrast, districts that are relatively ***compact***, and that consist completely of neighborhoods within a single large city, are more likely to survive.

K. **Harm to members of minority:** Thus far, we have implicitly assumed that race-conscious affirmative action programs disadvantage only the majority, if they disadvantage anyone. But suppose that such a program, while it perhaps benefits ***most*** members of the previously-disadvantaged minority, ***harms certain members of the minority class***. Does the existence of this harm render the plan a violation of equal protection? So far, the Supreme Court has not had to face this issue.

1. **Housing:** One area in which the question may arise involves attempts to prevent *"tipping"* in residential areas. Such attempts have generally taken one of two forms: (1) the expenditure of public funds to create a program of *"benign steering"* in which prospective purchasers are shown homes solely in areas where they will contribute to integration rather than segregation (e.g., African Americans would not be shown homes in areas already containing more than, say, 40% blacks); (2) actual racial *quotas* in *public housing projects.*

   a. **No clear rule for "benign steering":** With respect to the *"benign steering"* programs, there have been very few decisions. But it seems probable that such plans would be *upheld*, since the plans do not prevent members of the minority from living wherever they wish — the plans simply use public funds in a way that encourages integration.

   b. **Absolute quotas:** Absolute racial quotas for public housing projects, on the other hand, seem more difficult to justify, since such quotas will lead to a person's being absolutely deprived of a particular good (an apartment in a particular project) solely on the ground of his race. Probably the majority's opinion in *Richmond v. Croson* (see *supra*, p. 299), casting doubt on whether a racial preference is ever truly "benign", means that an absolute racial quota for public housing projects will be strictly scrutinized and in fact struck down.

2. **Racial balance in schools:** Similarly, suppose that a school board, in an attempt to maintain integration in an area that seems to be suffering from "white flight," decrees that only a limited percentage of African Americans living in a particular school district may attend the neighborhood school, but that all whites may.

   a. **Effect of *Croson*:** Recall that *Richmond v. Croson* (*supra*, p. 299) apparently requires strict scrutiny of *any* race-conscious government decision. Although preventing "white flight" might be found to be a compelling governmental objective, it is doubtful that a majority of the Court would conclude that an explicitly race-conscious plan that permits all white students in a neighborhood to attend their local school, but deprives African Americans of this right, is a "necessary" means of solving the white flight problem. (Instead, a majority of the Court would probably conclude that magnet schools, anti-racist public relations programs, and other race-neutral means could and must be used to deal with the problem.)

   b. **Voluntary one-race schools:** As a twist on the usual integration problems, suppose that African American (or Hispanic or other minority) students decide that *they* wish to have a segregated school, dormitory or facility limited to their own race. May the majority accede?

      i. **Possible justification:** Such voluntary segregation could be justified on the grounds that it promotes racial pride and cohesiveness on the part of groups which have been the victims of long discrimination and consequent poor self-image.

      ii. **Criticism:** Yet making a school or dormitory off-limits to whites certainly deprives them of a good solely on the grounds of race. *Richmond v. Croson* (*supra*, p. 299) certainly seems to require that such single-race facilities must be subjected to *strict scrutiny*. If strict scrutiny were applied, it seems unlikely that the Court would find that one-race facilities were a *necessary* means of promoting racial pride or cohesiveness among minorities. Special courses in black culture, a representative proportion of minority instructors, etc., certainly seem like adequate and less-intrusive ways of achieving the same result.

**L. Law enforcement, prison administration and military operations:**   Governments sometimes make race-conscious decisions not in order to redress past discrimination, but in order to further *operational* needs, especially in the *law-enforcement, prison administration* and *military* contexts. The Supreme Court's only modern-era decision in these areas — which applied strict scrutiny to a state's policy of racial segregation in the *cell assignments of recently-arrived prisoners* — suggests that race-conscious policies will be *strictly scrutinized* despite governments' operational needs in these contexts. That ruling came in *Johnson v. California*, 543 U.S. 499 (2005).

1. **Facts of *Johnson*:** *Johnson* involved California's unwritten policy under which, when prisoners entered a new correctional facility, they were racially segregated in double cells for up to 60 days. (After the initial up-to-60-day period, prisoners were allowed to choose their own cellmates.) The state defended this segregative practice as being "necessary to prevent violence caused by racial gangs."

2. **Subjected to strict scrutiny:** Of the eight members of the Court who expressed an opinion (Chief Justice Rehnquist did not participate), six agreed that the state's policy *must be strictly scrutinized.* In an opinion by Justice O'Connor, the Court remanded the case to the lower courts for a determination whether the segregative policy could survive the strict scrutiny standard.

   a. **Applies to all classifications:** O'Connor noted that the Court had held that " '*all* racial classifications [imposed by government] ... must be analyzed by a reviewing court under strict scrutiny' " (quoting *Adarand*, supra).

   b. **"Benign" use irrelevant:** California defended its segregation policy on the grounds that it was a "neutral" one that "neither benefits nor burdens one group or individual more than any other group or individual." But O'Connor quickly dismissed this rationale: the Court had "rejected the notion that separate can ever be equal – or 'neutral' – 50 years ago in *Brown v. Board of Education*," and there was no reason to resurrect that notion now.

   c. **Might increase racial hostility:** Indeed, O'Connor said, the use of racial classifications in prison housing assignments might well *"breed further hostility* among prisoners and reinforce racial and ethnic divisions. By perpetuating the notion that race matters most, racial segregation of inmates 'may exacerbate the very patterns of [violence that it is] said to counteract.' " She noted that virtually all other states and the federal government "manage their prison systems without reliance on racial segregation." And she rejected the argument that the operational needs of prison administration dictated a different result: "[C]ompliance with the 14th Amendment's ban on racial discrimination is not only consistent with proper prison administration, but also bolsters the legitimacy of the entire criminal justice system."

      i. **Might still survive:** O'Connor emphasized that the Court was not deciding whether California's policy here could *survive* the required strict scrutiny — that would be left to the courts below. But she noted that "prisons are dangerous places, and the special circumstances they present may justify racial classifications in some contexts."

3. **Dissent:** Justice Thomas, joined by Justice Scalia, dissented in *Johnson*. Thomas thought that "The Constitution has always demanded less within the prison walls," and believed that the Court should adopt a ***"deferential standard*** for reviewing prisoners' constitutional claims."

4. **Other contexts:** *Johnson* suggests that the present Court will ***apply strict scrutiny*** to any race-conscious government policy, even in the demanding operational areas of law enforcement, prison administration and the military. However, it is probably the case that in these areas, race-conscious schemes have a better chance of surviving the requisite strict scrutiny than in many other areas. Here are some domains in which the issue might arise:

    a. **Police:** ***Police departments*** have sometimes preferred black applicants to white ones not in order to remedy past discrimination, but in order to have more African American policemen available for duty in predominantly-black neighborhoods, where it is felt that African American officers will have better rapport. Such a plan might even survive the strict scrutiny presumably required by *Croson* and *Johnson*.

    b. **Prison guards:** Similarly, there have been attempts to hire more minorities as ***prison guards***, in order to match more closely the racial composition of the prison population. Such a plan might well be sustained, on the grounds that the state's interest in reducing racial strife in the prison system is a compelling state interest.

    c. **Officer corps in military:** The U.S. armed forces, too, have adopted explicitly-race-conscious means to develop more minority officers (e.g., by relaxing admissions criteria for the military academies). Given the heavily integrated rank-and-file in the military (e.g., 32% of rank-and-file were black or hispanic in 2002), and the much lower percentage of minority officers, it seems likely that the present Court would approve limited race-conscious methods. See Justice O'Connor's opinion for the court in *Grutter*, *supra*, p. 282, commenting favorably (albeit in dictum) on the armed services' use of affirmative action to ensure an integrated officer corps.

# V. CLASSIFICATIONS BASED ON SEX

A. **Introduction:** When examining a racially-conscious statute, it is generally not too difficult to ascertain whether the statute was intended as "benign" affirmative-action legislation designed to benefit a disadvantaged minority, or was, rather, garden-variety discrimination *against* a racial minority. But when one examines a statute which classifies by ***gender***, it will usually be much more difficult to decide whether the statute is "benign" (i.e., beneficial to women) or not.

1. **Prior cases:** Many of the cases arguably involving benign sex-based classifications were discussed *supra*, p. 273, in conjunction with the general discussion of affirmative action. We turn now to the remainder of the sex-classification cases. The statutes in many of these cases may seem neither more nor less "benign" than those considered previously, so that the prior materials should be reviewed together with the ones which follow.

2. **Rarely outright hostility:** The reason for the difficulty of determining "benignness" is that legislatures have almost never acted out of ***hostility*** or ***ill-will*** towards women. Nearly all gender-based legislative classifications have evolved out of some kind of desire to ***"protect"*** women.

a. **Early laws:** Early statutes typically did so on the theory that a woman's place was *at home raising children*, and that women therefore needed to be protected from a whole list of dangers lurking in the male-dominated world outside the home: alcohol, physical labor, jury duty, etc.

b. **Later laws:** A second group of laws, generally enacted after 1960, were protective in another way: they attempted to *undo the effects* of past paternalistic attitudes which had curtailed opportunities for women.

c. **Intermediate standard throughout:** Perhaps surprisingly, the Court today ostensibly applies a *single* standard to all gender-based classifications, whether these are found to be truly compensatory or merely paternalistic and stereotypical: *any gender-based classification must be "substantially related" to "important" governmental objectives.* This is, of course, the *intermediate level* of scrutiny, also applicable to illegitimacy and, perhaps, alienage. (See *supra*, p. 241.)

   i. **"Exceedingly persuasive justification":** But the Court will now, as the result of a 1996 case, apparently apply intermediate scrutiny in a quite *rigorous* way, which makes it *closer to strict scrutiny* than to "mere rationality" review. As the result of *U.S. v. Virginia, infra*, p. 326, the defenders of a gender-based scheme must show an *"exceedingly persuasive justification"* for the scheme, and the Court will apply *"skeptical scrutiny."* The Court still officially applies the intermediate-level test ("substantially related to an important governmental objective"), but apparently the government won't often pass this test.

   ii. **Stereotypical thinking vs. attempt to reverse discrimination:** A gender-based scheme is especially likely to be invalidated where it is an older one that arguably stems from a *traditional, stereotypical* way of thinking about gender roles, rather than a newer one that is intended to *combat past discrimination* against women. See *U.S. v. Virginia, infra*, p. 326 (all-male status of Virginia Military Institute struck down, based in part on the state's stereotypical views of the skills and interests of men vs. women).

B. **Traditional deference by Court:** Until 1971, the Supreme Court treated classifications based on gender as not meriting any special scrutiny, so that the highly deferential "mere rationality" test was applicable. Thus a statute was upheld if the Court could find it to be *rationally related* to some *legitimate state objective*, usually the preservation of women's "proper role."

> **Example:** A Michigan law provides that no woman may obtain a license to tend bar unless she is the wife or daughter of the male owner of a licensed tavern. The state argues that bartending by women may cause "moral and social problems" but that oversight of the barmaid by her husband or father will minimize these problems.
>
> *Held*, statute upheld. The state could forbid *all* women from working in bars. This is so despite the possibility that public attitudes have changed, since "[the] Constitution does not require legislatures to reflect sociological insight, or shifting social standards. … " Furthermore, it was not irrational for the legislature to conclude that the social and moral problems posed by having women tend bar would be less grave where the barmaid's husband or father was available to supervise. Therefore, the statute is not invalid. *Goesaert v. Cleary*, 335 U.S. 464 (1948). (*Goesaert* was later explicitly disapproved by the Supreme Court, in *Craig v. Boren, infra*, p. 323.)

**C. Stricter review:** But in the early 1970's, the Court began to give more than trivial review to gender-based classifications.

1. ***Reed:*** This occurred first in *Reed v. Reed*, 404 U.S. 71 (1971), where a statute preferring men over women as administrators of estates was struck down. The Court purported to apply the traditional "mere rationality" standard. But in rejecting the state's contention that the preference reduced the workload of probate courts by eliminating hearings on the merits, the Court was clearly putting more bite into the traditional standard than it had done previously.

2. **Explicit strict scrutiny:** The "mere rationality" standard for gender-based classifications was then explicitly ***rejected*** by the Court in *Frontiero v. Richardson*, 411 U.S. 677 (1973). In fact, that case went virtually to the other extreme, with a plurality holding that classifications based on sex, "like classifications based upon race, alienage, or national origin," are "inherently suspect and must therefore be subjected to strict judicial scrutiny."

3. **Retreat to "intermediate scrutiny":** The Court then settled (permanently, it now appears) on an *"intermediate"* level of scrutiny for gender-based classifications, whether "benign" or not. This standard was formulated in ***Craig v. Boren***, 429 U.S. 190 (1976).

   a. **Facts of *Craig:*** *Craig v. Boren* was a successful challenge to an Oklahoma statute which forbade the sale of "3.2% beer" (supposedly non-intoxicating) to males under the age of 21, and to females under the age of 18. The constitutional claim was that the statute denied equal protection to males aged 18 to 20.

   b. **Standard articulated:** The Court articulated the applicable standard as being that "classifications by gender must serve ***important*** governmental objectives and must be ***substantially*** related to achievement of those objectives."

      i. **New standard not explicit:** The majority did not explicitly announce that it was applying a new standard different from either the traditional "mere rationality" test or the "strict scrutiny" reserved for suspect classifications and fundamental rights. In fact, the Court purported merely to be applying standards established in previous cases, including *Reed* and *Frontiero*. But the concurring and dissenting opinions clearly viewed the majority as having formulated a third, ***middle***, level of scrutiny.

   c. **Defense of statute:** Oklahoma defended the statute on the grounds that it promoted traffic safety, since, statistically, 18- to 20-year-old males were arrested for drunken driving much more frequently than females in the same age group. (2% of males and .18% of females in that age group were arrested for drunk driving.)

   d. **Insufficient correlation:** The majority found this statistically-based defense ***insufficient***.

      i. **Maleness not "proxy":** First, since such a small portion even of *males* in the relevant age group were convicted of drunken driving, maleness could not serve as a "proxy" for drinking and driving.

      ii. **Non-intoxicating beverage:** Secondly, even if 18- to 20-year-old males did drive while drunk with a sufficiently greater frequency than similarly-aged females, this did not establish that the state's regulation of *3.2%* beer was reasonable, since that beverage was supposedly non-intoxicating.

      **iii. Only sale prohibited:**  Lastly, the statute only prohibited the ***selling*** of the beer to males, not their ***drinking*** it once they acquired it (perhaps via a purchase by an 18- to 20-year-old female companion).

      **iv. Poor overall fit:**  Thus, overall, the *"fit"* between the ***means*** of regulation selected (ban on sale of 3.2% beer to 18- to 20-year-olds) and the ***end*** sought to be achieved (promotion of traffic safety) was simply ***too tenuous*** to constitute the required *"substantial relation"* between means and end.

  **e. Dissent:**  Justice Rehnquist, dissenting, argued that the case should be judged according to a "mere rationality" standard. He apparently would not have objected to intermediate-level scrutiny for discrimination ***against women***, but saw no reason why discrimination against ***males*** should be given any greater scrutiny than that given to the great majority of other statutes attacked on equal protection grounds.

      **i. Means-end "fit":**  Rehnquist also objected to the majority's conclusion that the statute was invalid because the ***fit*** between being an 18- to 20-year-old male and driving while drunk was unduly tenuous. In his opinion, what counted was not the relative size of the percentage of young males who drank, but ***whether this percentage was higher than for females***. Since there was evidence that, however few young males were arrested for drunken driving, it was far more proportionately than the number of females, he found the connection between regulation of 3.2% beer and promotion of traffic safety "rational," meriting upholding of the statute.

  **f. "Exceedingly persuasive justification":** But the "intermediate" level of review is today ***quite difficult to meet***. A 1996 case holds that the state must show an *"exceedingly persuasive justification"* for a gender-based scheme, and that the courts must give "skeptical scrutiny" to such a scheme. See *U.S. v. Virginia*, *infra*, p. 326. So even though intermediate-review remains the official standard, it's a standard that's closer to strict scrutiny than to mere-rationality.

**D. Middle-level review not always fatal:**  However, the intermediate-level scrutiny now given to gender-based classifications, although substantially more probing that the traditional "mere rationality" standard, has by no means proven to be universally fatal to the statutes examined.

  **1. Most interests "important":**  Almost every governmental interest urged in support of a gender-based statute has been found *"important"* and therefore sufficient to meet the first prong of the test. The sole exceptions have been: (1) *"administrative convenience"* (see, e.g., *Frontiero*, *supra*, p. 323; *Wengler v. Druggists' Mutual Ins. Co.*, *supra*, p. 275); and (2) providing women, but not men, with "a choice of educational environments" (rejected as a rationale for a single-sex admissions policy in *Mississippi University for Women v. Hogan, infra*, p. 329).

    **a. Must be "actual" objective:** But to qualify as an important governmental objective, the objective must be one that *"actually"* motivated the legislature, as opposed to one that is articulated after the gender-based scheme was adopted. See *U.S. v. Virginia* (the VMI case), *infra*, p. 326 ("a tenable justification must describe actual state purposes, not rationalizations for actions in fact differently grounded").

  **2. "Substantially related":**  The requirement that the means chosen be *"substantially related"* to the end has had considerably more bite. But it, too, has frequently been satisfied.

**Example 1:** In *Michael M. v. Superior Court*, 450 U.S. 464 (1981) (discussed more fully *supra*, p. 275), the Court held that California could constitutionally make men but not women liable for sexual intercourse with a partner under the age of 18. The state's asserted purpose of protecting against teenage pregnancy was deemed important, and punishing the man but not the woman was held to be "substantially" related to achievement of that end — only women could become pregnant, so that a criminal sanction against men "equalized" the deterrence on the sexes. Also, women would be less likely to report statutory violations if they themselves could be punished, so that a gender-neutral statute might be unenforceable.

**Example 2:** Congress was permitted to require that only men register for the draft, in *Rostker v. Goldberg*, 453 U.S. 57 (1981) (discussed more extensively *supra*, p. 276). Since the purpose of draft registration was to facilitate eventual drafting of combat troops, and since only men were eligible for combat, the male-only registration scheme was "closely related" to the purpose of the statute.

**Note:** One can disagree about whether the means chosen in *Michael M.* and *Rostker* are indeed substantially related to the ends sought to be achieved by those two statutes. But if one accepts the majority's characterization of the aims of those two statutes, it does seem that ***neither*** was enacted as "the accidental by-product of a ***traditional way of thinking about females***" (*Califano v. Webster, supra*, p. 274.) It is the latter sort of statute, typically enacted more than 60 years ago, that is the sort most likely to fail to withstand intermediate-level scrutiny. See, e.g., *U.S. v. Virginia*, discussed immediately below.

a.  **Some imprecision allowed:** Even if the fit between the means chosen by the legislature and the governmental objective is ***far from perfect***, the Court may nonetheless conclude that there *is* the required "substantial relation" between means and end. A good illustration of the imprecision that the Court will tolerate came in ***Nguyen v. INS***, 533 U.S. 53 (2001), where the Court held that Congress could make it easier for the out-of-wedlock child of an American mother to achieve citizenship than for such a child of an American father.

    i.  **The statutory scheme:** Congress has set up some detailed rules for determining the citizenship of a child who is born abroad, and out of wedlock, to parents one of whom is an American citizen and the other of whom is not. These rules make it easier for the child to become an American citizen if the American parent is the mother. When the American parent is the mother, the child is ***automatically*** deemed an American citizen at birth. But when the American parent is the father, the child will become a citizen only if, before the child turns 18, the father's paternity is legally established by one of several specified means (e.g., the father acknowledges paternity in writing under oath, or a court finds paternity).

    ii. **Holding:** By a 5-4 vote, the Court ***upheld*** this scheme against an equal protection claim by the son of an American father who never took any of the legitimating steps before the son turned 18. The majority reasoned that by imposing the requirement of one of three legitimating steps before the child was 18, Congress was promoting parent-child bonding by requiring "that an ***opportunity for a parent-child relationship occur*** during the ***formative years*** of the child's minority." And the fact that none of the legitimating steps would *necessarily* indicate that a parent-child bond had developed did not mean that the requisite substantial relation between means and end was absent, for "***none*** of our gender-based classification equal protection cases have required that the statute under consideration must be ***capable of achieving its ultimate objective in every instance.***"

    **iii. Dissent:** Justice O'Connor, dissenting in *Nguyen*, argued that there was not even close to a substantial relation between the means chosen by Congress and Congress' supposed objectives. For instance, with respect to the supposed congressional interest in making sure that there was an "opportunity" for father-child bonds, she contended that the way to promote that objective would have been to require that there actually *be* a real father-child relationship, not to require that *proof* of that relationship be obtained by the time the child was 18. Instead, O'Connor believed, Congress' scheme was based on an "overbroad sex-based generalization," and reflected "a ***stereotype*** ... 'that mothers are significantly more likely than fathers ... to develop caring relationships with their children.' "

**E. Stereotypical thinking rejected:** The Court is especially likely to strike down a gender-based classification system that seems to be based on ***faulty generalizations*** or ***stereotypes*** about the ***differing abilities and interests of the two sexes***. Such generalizations were at the heart of the Court's conclusion in ***U.S. v. Virginia***, 518 U.S. 515 (1996), that Virginia's publicly-operated men-only military academy, Virginia Military Institute, violated equal protection.

    **1. Facts:** Virginia had operated VMI as a men-only institution since its founding in 1839; the school's purpose was and is to develop "citizen-soldiers." VMI was the only single-sex school among Virginia's 15 public universities. Virginia's principal defense of its single-sex policy was that three aspects of VMI's approach — its extremely rigorous physical training, its technique of depriving students of privacy, and its "adversative" approach (under which entering students are extensively hazed, in a manner comparable to Marine Corps boot camp) — would have to be materially changed if the school were made co-ed. Instead, the state sought to create a less rigorous program for women — but still one in theory devoted to developing citizen-soldiers — at a pre-existing all-women private liberal arts college, Mary Baldwin College.

    **2. Holding:** By a surprisingly broad 7-1 majority, the Court held that: (1) Virginia's policy of excluding women from VMI was a violation of women's equal protection rights; and (2) the program at Mary Baldwin College was not sufficiently comparable to the VMI program to redress the injury. The majority opinion by Justice Ginsburg was a sweeping one:

        **a. No "overbroad generalizations":** Ginsburg began by noting that gender-based classifications "must not rely on ***overbroad generalizations*** about the different talents, capacities or preferences of males and females. . . . [Gender-based] classifications may not be used, as they once were . . . to create or perpetuate the legal, social, and economic inferiority of women."

        **i. Suitable for some women:** Ginsburg rejected Virginia's claim that the VMI program would have to be materially changed if women were admitted. It may be true that, as Virginia asserted, *most* women wouldn't like the rigorous, adversative martial VMI program, and would prefer a more cooperative program. But the experience of women in the U.S. military academies, and in the U.S. military, suggested that these fears were overblown. In any event, there were clearly *some* women for whom the existing VMI program was an attractive and suitable program, and Virginia could not deprive these unusual women of the opportunity to attend VMI. "*[G]eneralizations about 'the way women are,'* estimates of what is appropriate for *most women*, no longer justify denying opportunity to women whose talent and capacity place them *outside the average description*."

ii. **Diversity policy:** Virginia had also defended its men-only rule as being in further-ance of a state policy of "diversity in educational approaches." But the majority rejected this objective as well, concluding that this was not an "*actual* state pur-pose," given that Virginia had no women-only public universities, and that the no-women policy at VMI dated from a time when Virginia did not offer any sort of public higher education for women.

b. **Mary Baldwin program insufficient:** The majority then concluded that the proposed women-only program at Mary Baldwin would *not constitute an adequate remedy* for the equal protection violation caused by VMI's men-only status. To remedy an equal protection violation, the solution would have to "place [victims] in the *position they would have occupied in the absence of discrimination*," and "to eliminate [so far as possible] the discriminatory effects of the past." The Mary Baldwin program would not be in any way the equivalent of VMI: it would not give its students the same intense military and leadership training (for instance, it would not use the adversative method); it would not have a student body or faculty of the same quality; it would not benefit from the same strong alumni ties, etc. It would, in sum, be a *"pale shadow"* of VMI.

c. **"Exceedingly persuasive justification" needed:** The majority opinion was also nota-ble for the *stricter tone* with which it applied mid-level scrutiny. The Clinton Admin-istration had asked the Court to change course, and apply strict scrutiny, instead of traditional mid-level review, in gender cases. The majority did not do this. But it said that sex-based classifications would have to undergo *"skeptical scrutiny,"* and would be upheld only if the state demonstrated an *"exceedingly persuasive justification"* for any gender-based governmental action.

   i. **Objective must be one that really motivated state:** Perhaps the most important aspect of the new "skeptical scrutiny" is that when the government articulates a justification for the gender-based classification, this justification "must describe *actual state purposes*, not rationalizations for actions in fact differently grounded." Thus when Virginia asserted that its policy fulfilled the objective of diversity-in-education, the Court's response was not that this wasn't an important objective (or that the men-only program wasn't closely related to achieving that objective), but that this wasn't the state's *real* objective, merely a pretext.

3. **Dissent:** The lone dissenter was Justice Scalia. (Even Chief Justice Rehnquist concurred in the result, though not in the majority's full reasoning; Justice Thomas recused himself because his son was attending VMI.)

   a. **Objection to majority's standard:** Scalia objected first to the majority's choice of standard. He claimed that while the majority admitted to having changed the tradi-tional intermediate level of review, it was in fact substituting a new and improper "exceedingly persuasive justification" standard that contradicted the reasoning of the Court's prior gender cases. In Scalia's view, this standard was an *"unacknowledged adoption* of what amounts to (at least) *strict scrutiny*."

b. **Satisfies mid-level review:** Scalia believed that operation of VMI as an all-male school *satisfied mid-level review* when that standard was properly applied. The state had an important interest in achieving the educational diversity provided by single-sex colleges. And when Virginia elected to have an all-male school that used the adversative model (VMI) and an all-female school that used the cooperative model (the new Mary Baldwin program), it had selected a strategy that was "substantially related" to the achievement of that interest in diversity.

c. **End of single-sex public education:** Scalia said that the majority's approach "ensures that *single-sex public education is functionally dead*." In fact, he said, this approach even endangered *private* single-sex colleges, since the government's furnishing of all-important financial assistance (e.g., tax deductions for private donations) might be held to be state action in support of discrimination, as it had been in cases involving private racially-discriminatory colleges.

4. **Significance:** The VMI decision looks as though it will prove highly significant:

a. **New standard:** Justice Scalia seems to be correct in observing that the "exceedingly persuasive justification" standard is tougher than the traditional mid-level review. However, it does not seem as though the Court will apply full-bore strict scrutiny to gender-based classifications. Instead, the Court will apparently still require only that the means chosen be substantially related to achievement of an important governmental objective (the traditional mid-level test), but will apply that test in a way that is at least marginally more demanding than before.

   i. **Real objective:** For instance, the Court will apparently now insist that the objective being advanced be one that *actually motivated the government* when it devised the system, a requirement that the Court has traditionally applied in strict scrutiny cases but not necessarily in mid-level cases.

   ii. **Suspicion of stereotypes:** Furthermore, the Court seems to be exceptionally intolerant of anything that strikes it as being *stereotypical thinking* about the differences between the sexes. Even if there is respectable scientific evidence that *most* women *are* different from most men in a particular way, this will apparently not support a gender-based classification. Thus the majority did not really dispute evidence advanced by Virginia that far fewer women than men would like the adversative method — but this didn't matter: as long as there were *some* women who didn't fall within that (arguably correct) generalization, it was a violation of these women's equal protection rights to not have the same opportunity as was given to men.

b. **Single-sex public education:** It's too soon to tell whether the VMI case means that practically all single-sex public education is dead. It may well be that if a single-sex program is designed for the purpose of *remedying past discrimination* against women (or curing the particular problems faced by women), it will be easier to sustain, even though the Court has not expressly said that it will treat remedial classifications less stringently.

c. **Tax and loan breaks for private schools:** It's also too soon to tell whether even *private* same-sex schools are doomed if they *get substantial government support*. The Court's prior race-discrimination cases suggest that the furnishing of indirect government assistance to private schools that racially discriminate amounts to government support of racial discrimination in violation of the 14th Amendment. But the majority may well decline to apply the same standard to sex discrimination, perhaps somehow relying on the theory that mid-level review means that greater ties between government action and private discrimination must be shown before the government action is treated as itself discriminatory.

   **d.   "Separate but equal":** It also remains to be seen whether a state can maintain a pair of single-sex schools, one for men and one for women, on the theory that the two are ***"separate but equal."*** The Court in the VMI case held that an all-women's military training course that Virginia proposed to set up at Mary Baldwin College was not sufficiently comparable to the all-male Virginia Military Institute to satisfy the requirements of equal protection. The VMI case seems to mean that: (1) a pair of single-sex schools (one for each sex) can *theoretically* pass equal protection scrutiny, if the two schools are truly equal; but that (2) it will be very hard, as a *practical* matter, for the state to show that the two are so substantially equal that the new "exceedingly persuasive justification" standard will be satisfied.

**F.   Remedial statutes:** If the Court finds that a gender-conscious statute represents an attempt to ***remedy past discrimination*** against women, both prongs of the intermediate-level test will almost certainly be found to be satisfied.

   **1.   Redress for lower earnings:** For instance, in *Califano v. Webster*, 430 U.S. 313 (1977) (*supra*, p. 274), the Court upheld a Social Security provision by which a female worker's "average monthly wage" (against which social security benefits are calculated) could exclude three more lower-earning years than a male worker's. The Court found this provision to be a strictly remedial one, whose purpose was one of "redressing our society's long standing disparate treatment of women," not one of "role-typing" women by casually assuming that they are "the weaker sex" or are "more likely to be child-rearers or dependents."

   **2.   Remedy must be specific:** But it is not enough that the statute is intended to improve the position of women. It must also be the case that this improvement comes ***in a particular narrowly-defined sphere***, in which women have ***previously been disadvantaged***. An especially vivid illustration of this rule came in ***Mississippi University for Women v. Hogan***, 458 U.S. 718 (1982), in which the Court struck down Mississippi's policy of barring men from the University's School of Nursing.

      **a.   Facts of *MUW v. Hogan*:** The Mississippi University for Women (MUW) is a state university that has enrolled only women since its establishment in 1884. The School of Nursing was not established until 1971. The nursing school, like the other university departments, allowed men to audit courses but not to take them for credit. The plaintiff, Hogan, was denied admission to the degree program at the nursing school, which was located in the town where he lived and worked. There were co-ed degree programs at other Mississippi-supported nursing schools, but he would have had to commute a substantial distance to attend any of them.

      **b.   Holding:** A five-Justice majority (in one of the first opinions authored by Justice O'Connor) ***struck down*** the women-only policy of the nursing school. The majority opinion applied the intermediate level of scrutiny prescribed by *Craig v. Boren*; Justice O'Connor then added her own gloss on that standard, arguing that an "exceedingly persuasive justification" must be shown for any sex-based classification. The statute was unable to survive this scrutiny.

    **c.** **Not affirmative action:** Most significantly, Justice O'Connor rejected the state's assertion that the single-sex admissions policy ***compensated for discrimination*** against women and was therefore "educational affirmative action." Such a "compensatory purpose" justification would be valid, the Justice stated, only if members of the sex benefitted by the classification "actually suffer a ***disadvantage related to the classification.***" In the present case, this would have required a showing that women were disadvantaged ***in the field of nursing***, not merely in the general sphere of education or employment.

        **i.** **Nursing as woman's field:** The state made no such showing regarding nursing. In fact, Justice O'Connor noted, the evidence was just the contrary: nursing in Mississippi (as well as in the rest of the country) was widely viewed as exclusively a woman's job. Thus the single-sex policy of the nursing school in fact merely ***perpetuated a stereotype about proper roles for women***, and had nothing to do with compensation for past discrimination.

**G. Discriminatory purpose required:** In the sex-discrimination cases which we have examined so far, there was usually little dispute about whether the statute was intended to classify on the basis of sex. Most of the statutes explicitly mentioned sex, and the main issue was whether the classification was justifiable. But it is important to remember that, in sex-discrimination cases as in race-discrimination ones, the plaintiff is nonetheless required to show a ***discriminatory purpose***, not merely a discriminatory ***effect.***

    **1.** *Feeney:* One illustration of this requirement is *Personnel Administrator of Massachusetts v. Feeney*, 442 U.S. 256 (1979) (discussed more fully *supra*, p. 256). In *Feeney*, the Court held that Massachusetts' absolute veterans' preference for civil service jobs did not violate equal protection, even though over 98% of the veterans in Massachusetts were men. Only "purposeful discrimination" against women could give rise to an equal protection violation — "[T]he Fourteenth Amendment guarantees equal laws, not equal results." (The fact that Massachusetts legislators may have ***foreseen*** that the statute would operate to women's extreme detriment was not enough; an equal protection claim could be valid only upon proof that the legislature acted in part "because of," not merely "in spite of" adverse effects on women.)

    **2.** **Use of biological factors:** A legislature's use of ***biological factors*** may similarly cause a disparate effect upon the two sexes. Again, only if there is proof that the disparate effect was ***intended*** by the lawmakers will the statute be struck down on equal protection grounds. ***Geduldig v. Aiello***, 417 U.S. 484 (1974), purports to be an illustration of this principle.

        **a.** **Facts:** *Geduldig* involved a provision of California's disability insurance system which excluded coverage for "disability that accompanies normal pregnancy and childbirth."

        **b.** **Holding:** The Court held that the statute did not violate the Equal Protection Clause. There was no evidence that the distinction based on pregnancy was a pretext designed to effect invidious discrimination against women. Therefore, the legislature's choice of conditions to be covered or not covered needed simply to satisfy the "mere rationality" test. The state's legitimate interests in keeping the insurance system solvent and in making benefits adequate for those conditions covered, were rationally related to the means chosen (exclusion of pregnancy-related conditions).

3. **Explicit differentiation by sex:** But where the statute itself *explicitly differentiates* based on sex, the Court will give heightened scrutiny to a justification based on biological considerations.

    a. **Parents of illegitimate children:** For instance, a New York statute giving the mother of an illegitimate child, but not the father, the right to *veto the child's adoption*, was invalidated by the Court (5-4) in *Caban v. Mohammed*, 441 U.S. 380 (1979). The father, mother and child in *Caban* had lived together for several years as a family. The majority concluded that New York could not deny the father the right to block an adoption by withholding consent, if it gave this right automatically to the mother; there was no "universal difference," at every stage of a child's development, between the closeness of the father-child relationship and that of the mother- child one.

        i. **Other adoptions:** But the majority emphasized that the state was free to differentiate between mothers and fathers as to adoptions taking place while the child was *still an infant*, or where the child was past infancy but the father had *not participated* in its rearing.

    b. **Wrongful death action:** But not all schemes which treat the father of an illegitimate child less favorably than the mother will be struck down. For instance, in *Nguyen v. INS* (*supra*, p. 325), a 2001 case, the Court upheld a federal statute that allowed a mother who is a U.S. citizen to automatically confer U.S. citizenship on her illegitimate child, while a father who is a citizen must take one of several affirmative steps before the child turns 18 in order to confer citizenship. The majority relied heavily on the theory that the mother automatically establishes ties to the child merely by giving birth and being present at the birth, whereas the father does not have such automatic ties.

4. **Co-ed bathrooms and lockerrooms:** Public bathrooms, lockerrooms, sleeping quarters and other facilities related to *intimate bodily functions* of course generally remain sex-segregated. The Court has not explicitly dealt with this sort of segregation, but there is little reason to believe that such facilities-separation would be struck down as violative of equal protection.

    a. **Privacy argument:** Perhaps the best argument against a finding of an equal protection violation in this context is that sex-segregated facilities such as these are not expressions of invidious discrimination, but rather, expressions of the recognized desire for *sexual privacy*. Recall that the Court has recognized a substantive, constitutionally-protected, "right of privacy" (*supra*, p. 156), which seems to be applicable in this situation.

H. **"As applied" challenges:** So far, nearly all of the challenges to gender-based classifications we have considered have been "facial" ones, i.e., ones directed to gender-based classifications that are present in the text of the statute or regulation itself. But remember that the Equal Protection Clause also allows for *"as applied"* challenges — if the plaintiff can show that government has *enforced* a neutral-sounding provision in a way that discriminates against one or the other gender, this discrimination, too, will have to satisfy mid-level review.

1. **Peremptory challenges:**   Consider, for instance, statutes that allow for civil or criminal litigants to use *peremptory challenges*, by which potential jurors may be dismissed without any showing of cause. The Court has held that the use of peremptory challenges to *exclude all women* from a jury cannot survive mid-level review, and thus violates equal protection. *J.E.B. v. Alabama*, 511 U.S. 127 (1994).

    a. **Rationale:** The Court phrased the issue as being "whether discrimination on the basis of gender in jury selection substantially furthers the State's legitimate interest in achieving a fair and impartial trial." It then answered "no," concluding that the assumption that women jurors will have certain types of attitudes in certain cases (such as the paternity case that was at issue in *J.E.B.*) reinforced stereotypical assumptions about women. So, just as a state may not permit litigants to strike jurors peremptorily on the grounds of race (see *Batson v. Kentucky*, discussed *supra*, p. 258), so the state may not allow gender-based strikes.

*Quiz Yourself on*

## EQUAL PROTECTION — SUSPECT CLASSES, AFFIRMATIVE ACTION AND CLASSIFICATIONS BASED ON SEX

34. The state of Minnetonka has enacted an adoption statute that specifies the criteria to be used when public agencies make adoption placements. (No private adoptions are permitted in the state.) According to the statute, the "racial compatibility" between the child and the adoptive parents is the most important factor to be considered, though many other factors are also to be considered. Peter and Jill, a white couple in their 40's, wished to adopt a child. They learned that a large number of African American children were being raised in state-sponsored orphanages, because no homes could be found for them. The couple applied to a state adoption agency, requesting to adopt any African American child under the age of four, who was currently living in an orphanage. The adoption agency replied, "Because applicable statutes require us to give racial matching heaviest weight in making adoption placements, and because you are seeking a relatively young child who may well be placeable with a racially-compatible, i.e., African American family in the future, we cannot grant your request." Peter and Jill have sued in federal court for a ruling that the statute providing for race-matching violates their equal protection rights. They have presented evidence that African American children are staying longer in orphanages than white children who are otherwise similar, and that this lengthier stay is due in part to the heavy statutory weight placed on race-matching.

    **(a)** By what standard should the court test the constitutionality of the race-matching statute as it applies to Peter and Jill? _____

    **(b)** Should the court agree with Peter and Jill's contention that their equal protection rights have been violated? _____

35. Carolene High School, a public high school, has for years maintained special remedial reading classes. Students can take these classes in lieu of the regular English class, if they are shown to have learning disabilities or otherwise shown to be behind on their reading skills. Students of African American ancestry make up 12% of the student body of the high school. Forty-five percent of the students in the remedial reading program are African American. Because of reduced federal aid to education and a local recession, the school board has reluctantly concluded that it must reduce expenditures. Therefore, it has cancelled

the remedial reading program, which is about 15% more expensive per student than the regular English program. The school board has not cut funding for the honors English program, which similarly costs about 15% more per student than regular English. About 9% of the students in the honors English program are African American. All of the evidence is that the school board made the decision it did on the honest belief that the honors program accomplishes more per dollar and strengthens the school system more, than does the remedial reading program. Carl, an African American student enrolled in the remedial reading program, has now challenged the termination on the grounds that it violates his right to equal protection.

   **(a)** What standard should the court use in deciding Carl's challenge? _____

   **(b)** Will Carl's challenge succeed? _____

36. Smithville is a small town located near the Canadian border. A significant minority of the children attending Smithville High School are American citizens of French-Canadian descent. The school board has just canceled the honors French program. The decision was made by the school principal, an American of Anglo-Saxon descent, who told school board members, "If we keep running an extensive French program, we'll just attract more Americans of French-Canadian ancestry to the town, and soon they'll be a majority." Since the school board was completely dominated by Anglo-Saxon Americans, they concurred with the decision. Jacques, an American student at the school of French-Canadian descent, has sued the school district, arguing that the cancellation has violated his constitutional rights.

   **(a)** What standard of review should the court use to judge the school district's cancellation decision?
_____

   **(b)** Will Jacques' challenge succeed? _____

37. Same facts as prior question. Now, however, assume that the town of Smithville, and its school board, both contain a majority of Americans of French-Canadian descent. The board has now voted to dramatically expand the French program, and to cancel the honors English program. Strong evidence suggests that the board was motivated by a desire to attract more French-Canadian Americans into town, and to solidify this group's majority over Anglo-Americans. Does either of your answers to question 41 change here, and if so, how? _____

38. The city of Monroe enacted an ordinance providing that 10% of all procurements of office supplies in the city for the coming year must be purchased from office supply companies majority-owned by either African Americans or Hispanics, the two largest ethnic groups in the city. African Americans and Hispanics together make up a substantial minority (approximately 40%) of the city's population. The City Council did not conduct legislative hearings or investigations prior to enacting the bill. However, minutes of the Council's deliberations show that Council members enacted the bill primarily because they felt that minority business people, especially in the office supply industry, had had less general economic opportunity than white-owned firms, and that the 10% set-aside was the best way to increase the opportunities for minority owned companies. At the moment the bill was enacted, firms owned by African Americans or Hispanics amounted to approximately 10% of the total office supply companies in the city, but these companies did only about 4% of the total office supply business in the city, since the average minority-owned firm was much smaller than the average white-owned firm.

   Anglo Office Supply, a white-owned office supply firm, has challenged the Monroe set-aside on equal protection grounds.

   **(a)** What standard should the court use in evaluating the constitutional sufficiency of the set-aside?

**(b)** Will Anglo's attack succeed? _____

39. The Oneanta state legislature mandated that any employer with five or more employees grant a paid six-month maternity leave to any woman who gave birth while on the company's payroll. The legislature imposed no requirements regarding paid or unpaid family leave for men who had just had a child. In deciding to enact the measure, the legislators relied principally on evidence that various rising social problems, such as drugs and crime, were caused in part by the rise in working women and a consequent failure of mothers to bond with their infants. Frank, the father of a newborn infant who wished to have a paid paternity leave, has challenged the statute on the grounds that it violates his equal protection rights.

   **(a)** What standard should the court apply in evaluating Frank's challenge to the maternity-leave statute?

_____

   **(b)** Will Frank's attack succeed? _____

40. Congress was dismayed by statistics indicating that although African Americans and Hispanics now compose approximately 15% of America's university-age population, these two groups comprise only 7% of enrollees at colleges and universities nationally. Most members of Congress believed that the shortfall was due to the residual effects of past official discrimination by state and local governments, including public university systems. Therefore, Congress enacted a statute providing that any college or university receiving federal funds was required to treat an applicant's African American or Hispanic status into account as a "positive factor," and to "make best efforts" to enroll as high a percentage of African American and Hispanic students as are present in the school-age population for the geographical area being served by that college or university. The statute further provided that statistics regarding actual enrollments would be treated as follows: a university would be rebuttably presumed to have failed to comply with the statute if the number of African American and Hispanic students actually enrolled was less than 80% of what would be predicted from the pool of recent high school graduates in the region from which the university draws the bulk of its enrollees. The statute's preamble recited Congress' belief that enrollment disparities stemmed in major part from past governmental discrimination, but neither the statute nor the statute's legislative history described the particulars of this discrimination (e.g., whether it was national, whether it was by universities or other governmental actors, etc.) Penny, a white female with good grades and test scores, was denied admission to Statesville University, a large and prestigious public university. She sued the University, pointing out that her grades and test scores were above the average for those accepted at the University, and arguing (correctly, as a factual matter) that but for the federally-required racial preference, she would probably have been admitted. She therefore contends that the federal statute violates her equal protection rights.

   **(a)** What standard should the court use in deciding whether the federal statute violates Penny's equal protection rights? _____

   **(b)** Will Penny's attack succeed? _____

———————

*Answers*

34. **(a) The court should apply strict scrutiny, and ask whether the statute is necessary to achieve a compelling governmental objective.**

   **(b) Yes, probably.** The Supreme Court has generally given strict scrutiny to any race-based classification scheme, even if it does not appear to be enacted for the purpose of disadvantaging African Americans. In a somewhat analogous situation involving child custody, the Court held that child custody decisions could not be made by taking into account race-matching or social prejudices; see *Palmore v. Sidoti*. So unless the mandatory consideration of race here is shown to be a necessary method of achieving a compelling state objective, it will be struck down. The state undoubtedly has a compelling interest in guaranteeing that a child be raised by a family that will be compatible. All other factors being equal, a racial match probably will make it easier for the child to develop a strong sense of identity. However, it is hard to see where the mandatory first-preference for a racial match is a "necessary" means of achieving state objectives, especially in light of evidence that it may keep children in institutional care longer. Therefore, the odds are that the court will find that the "necessary means" part of the equation has not been satisfied, and will strike down the mandatory first preference. (But a scheme merely requiring that race be considered as one factor among many, without making it the most important factor, probably would survive even strict scrutiny.)

35. **(a) The court should use the mere rationality standard, not the strict scrutiny standard.**

**(b) No, probably.** Race is a "suspect category," and classifications based on race are therefore ordinarily subject to strict scrutiny. However, strict scrutiny will only be applied where the court finds that there was a governmental ***intent*** to discriminate against the disfavored group. The mere fact that a law has a less favorable ***effect*** on a racial minority than it has on the majority is ***not*** sufficient to trigger strict scrutiny. Disparate effect can be used as circumstantial evidence of an intent to discriminate, but such evidence is not dispositive. Here, the facts tell us that an intent to disfavor African American students was not present on the part of the school board. Therefore, strict scrutiny will not be applied, and instead the "rational relation" standard will be used. Under this standard, the classification will be upheld so long as it is rationally related to the achievement of a legitimate state objective. Here, cutting an expensive program is certainly rationally related to saving money for the school system, and saving money is certainly a legitimate state of objective in a time of economic hardship.

36. **(a) Strict scrutiny.** Classifications based on ***national origin*** are suspect. Similarly, classifications based on ethnic ancestry are suspect. So whether the French-Canadians are being discriminated against because they or their ancestors came from another country, or because they are part of a different ethnic group that speaks a different language, they are clearly a suspect class. Since all the evidence indicates that the decision was made for the purpose of disadvantaging members of this group (i.e., the disadvantage was not merely an inadvertent effect of action taken for some other reason), the requisites for strict scrutiny have been satisfied.

**(b) Yes.** Once strict scrutiny is applied, the challenged classification will only be upheld if it is necessary to achieve a compelling governmental objective. Preventing a particular group of citizens from becoming a majority in a town or school system is certainly not a compelling state objective (and probably not even a "legitimate" objective). Therefore, even if the challenged classification is a "necessary" means of achieving that objective, the classification must fall.

37. **No.** Discrimination against ***any*** racial, ethnic or national-origin group will be strictly scrutinized, even if that group has traditionally not been the victim of widespread prejudice or discrimination. Thus even discrimination against whites of Anglo-Saxon Protestant descent will be strictly scrutinized. This is the result of *City of Richmond v. J.A. Croson Co.*, striking down a minority set-aside program that disadvantaged whites. So the analysis, and outcome, should be exactly the same as in the prior question.

38. **(a) Strict scrutiny.**

**(b) Yes.** The facts here are fairly similar to those of *Richmond v. Croson*. That case makes it clear that any race-based affirmative action scheme will be strictly scrutinized, and will thus be struck down unless it is necessary to achieve a compelling governmental objective. Here, the scheme has at least two shortcomings, each of which is probably separately fatal. First, the city is not trying to remedy past official discrimination, or even explicitly trying to remedy past unofficial discrimination — the facts tell us merely that there has been an inequality of "economic opportunity," which is not the same as racial discrimination. In the absence of a legislative finding of discrimination in the office supply industry in the city of Monroe itself, any attempt to give a racial preference would probably be struck down regardless of how that preference was carried out. Secondly, the plan here is essentially a *quota* — it allocates a particular fixed percentage of city contracts for minority-owned firms. Rarely if ever will quotas be found to be a "necessary" means of redressing even clear past discrimination — certainly a city needs to consider, and probably try, less restrictive measures first, such as voluntary goals, an outreach program to solicit more bids from minority-owned firms, or some other means that is less hard-and-fast than an absolute set-aside.

39. **(a) Mid-level scrutiny, i.e., whether the statute is "substantially related" to the achievement of an "important" governmental objective.** (*U.S. v. Virginia* says that gender-based classifications will now need an "exceedingly persuasive justification," and will be "skeptically scrutinized," but the case seems not to officially reject mid-level scrutiny, merely to indicate that mid-level scrutiny will now be applied in a rigorous way.)

**(b) Yes, probably.** Government classifications involving suspect or semi-suspect claims are evaluated by the same standard regardless of whether the purpose is to discriminate against the traditionally disfavored class or to redress past discrimination. In other words, there is no easier standard for "affirmative action." Thus the Supreme Court applies the same mid-level review to all gender-based classes, whether the classification is old-fashioned discrimination against women or affirmative action designed to improve the lot of women. In both cases, the gender-based classification will be upheld only if it is substantially related to the achievement of important governmental objectives.

Here, encouragement of bonding between parent and newborn child is probably an "important" governmental objective. However, a court would probably conclude that there is no "substantial relation" between a mother-only parental-leave program and achievement of this objective. It is highly likely that whatever social problems are caused by not having either parent at home during a child's infancy, those problems can be redressed as well or almost as well by having the father be at home. Therefore, a scheme that entitled either parent, but not both parents, to take a paid maternity leave would accomplish the legislative purposes as well or almost as well as the mother-only scheme. Consequently, the court will probably, thought not certainly, strike down the statute.

In general, courts are likely to strike down any statute that reflects *stereotypes* about the "proper place of women." See, e.g., *U.S. v. Virginia*, finding Virginia's belief that VMI's intense military training program is unsuitable for women to be an unconstitutional generalization about "the way women are." The scheme here — which implies that a mother's place, but not a father's place, is to be home with the newborn infant — reflects similar stereotypical thinking.

40. **(a) Strict scrutiny — the statute must be necessary to achieve a compelling governmental objective.**

**(b) Yes, probably.** There are three key issues here: (1) whether the fact that the preference was enacted by *Congress* rather than by a state or local government should change the standard for judicial review; (2) whether Congress' attempt to *wipe out past discrimination* renders the measure constitutionally acceptable; and (3) whether the Court's decision in *Grutter v. Bollinger*, allowing race-conscious university admissions, affects the answer.

As to the first issue — whether the fact that the preference was enacted by **Congress** rather than by a state or local government should change the standard for judicial review — the answer is *"no."* Because of the decision in *Adarand Constructors v. Pena*, strict scrutiny will be given to race-conscious congressionally-enacted affirmative action plans. Since the statute clearly classifies on the basis of race, it falls within this rule.

As to the second issue -- whether Congress' desire to wipe out past governmental discrimination renders the measure acceptable -- the answer is again *"no."* The eradication of past governmental discrimination is indeed probably a "compelling" goal. However, the preference probably would *not* be found to be *"necessary"* for the rooting out of the effects of past governmental discrimination. Congress did not make detailed *findings* about which geographical regions this discrimination exists in, or about which governmental units (e.g., universities versus other governmental actors) caused it. Also, there is no indication that Congress considered *race-neutral means* (e.g., use of "socio-economic" criteria rather than racial ones) as a possible way to solve the problem. The "rebuttable presumption" used here is better than an outright quota, but *Adarand*, which involved a similar presumption-based scheme, suggests that racially-based presumptions will nonetheless be hard to justify (though the *Adarand* Court didn't actually decide whether the preference there survived strict scrutiny.) Also, the Court might give slightly greater deference to Congress than it would to a state or local body. Nonetheless, the best guess is that the statute here would be struck down.

As to the final issue — whether the Court's decision in *Grutter v. Bollinger*, allowing race-conscious university admissions, changes the outcome — the answer once again is *"no."* Race-conscious affirmative action was allowed in *Grutter* because the majority was satisfied that the University there was pursuing the compelling goal of achieving diversity in the student body, and doing so in a narrowly-tailored way by use of individualized evaluations of each applicant. Here, there is no indication that Congress was seeking true diversity in each student body — Congress seems to have been nakedly pursuing *"racial balancing"* (i.e., making the portion of minority students at each university mirror the local student-age population), and the *Grutter* majority opinion makes it clear that this is not a legitimate objective. The numerically-based presumption of illegality just makes things worse, since such a presumption is more like the point system struck down by the Court in *Gratz v. Bollinger* than it is like the individualized evaluations upheld by the Court in *Grutter*. The Court's post-*Gratz* decision in *Parents Involved in Community Schools v. Seattle School District*, where a majority struck down pupil-assignment plans that gave a preference to students whose presence would lessen the racial imbalance in the target public school, further buttresses the conclusion that the racial preference here would be found to be in essence an illegitimate quota or "racial balancing" plan.

# VI. CLASSIFICATIONS BASED ON ALIENAGE

A. **Alienage generally:**  Recall that in deciding whether or not to treat a particular type of classification as "suspect," the Court has given substantial weight to whether the class which is disadvantaged is a "discrete and insular minority," i.e., a minority which is politically powerless and which has historically been discriminated against. (See *supra*, p. 259.) We have already seen that race, and its close relative national origin, have been treated by the Court as suspect classifications (*supra*, p. 252). In general, the Court has also purported to apply strict scrutiny to classifications disadvantaging *aliens*. However, the status of alienage classifications is much less clear than those of race and national origin.

1. **Definition:** "Alienage," as the term is used by the Court, means "***not having U.S. citizenship***." Thus the term is not co-extensive with "national origin," since (1) discrimination against a person because he is of a particular national origin might occur even if he is a citizen (e.g., discrimination against a Mexican-American); and (2) discrimination against aliens often takes the form of discrimination against *all* aliens, without regard to their country of origin.

2. **Powerless and discriminated against:** Aliens as a class do seem to bear the two principal traits which make a minority "discrete and insular." It seems clear that aliens as a class are "***politically powerless***," since they are not permitted to vote. And it is at least arguable that there has been traditional discrimination against aliens (though much of this is probably more easily explained as either discrimination against persons of particular national origins, or discrimination against undocumented, i.e., "illegal," aliens).

   a. **Not "immutable":** But one factor often relied upon by the Court in establishing that a given classification is "suspect" is lacking in the case of aliens: "***immutability.***" Thus in the case of race and national origin (and also in the cases of sex and illegitimacy, both subject to intermediate-level scrutiny), the trait is ***beyond the power of the individual to change it.*** But in the case of an alien, at least one who is legally in this country, there will normally come a time when he becomes ***eligible for citizenship***; at that moment, of course, his alienage is no longer immutable.

      i. **Significance:** The "mutability" of the alienage trait may explain, at least in part, the wavering quality of the Court's commitment to strict-scrutiny treatment for the trait. This seems, for instance, to have been a sub-theme in the majority's handling of *Ambach v. Norwick, infra*, p. 339, involving two aliens who were already entitled to citizenship but who declined to claim it.

3. **Federal preemption:** Unlike nearly all the other classifications typically reviewed under equal protection analysis, those based on alienage raise significant questions of ***federal supremacy*** and ***preemption***. This is because the Constitution vests in the federal government full authority to deal with issues of immigration.

   a. **Consequence:** Therefore, when a state classifies in a way that disadvantages aliens, a relevant question is: Is this disadvantaging consistent with the fact that the federal government has permitted the aliens in question to reside in this country (or, in the case of "illegal" aliens, with the fact that the federal government has *not* so permitted them.)

   b. **Increasing importance:** While issues of federal supremacy have not usually been dispositive in cases involving state treatment of aliens, the supremacy aspect seems to be becoming increasingly important. For instance, both the majority and the minority in *Plyler v. Doe* (a case deciding that illegal aliens may not be barred from free state education) relied in part on their views about whether such a ban comported with congressional immigration policy. See *infra*, p. 340.

B. **General rule of "strict scrutiny":** In the early 1970's, the Court began to treat discrimination against aliens as calling for *strict scrutiny*. There were three main cases in which such scrutiny was applied, and the statute under review invalidated:

1. **Welfare benefits:** First, the Court held that states ***cannot deny welfare benefits*** to aliens. *Graham v. Richardson*, 403 U.S. 365 (1971). The opinion deemed aliens to be a "discrete and insular minority," and held that the state's fiscal interest in preserving limited resources for its citizens was not a sufficiently strong countervailing governmental interest.

   a. **Rationale:** The opinion noted that ***aliens pay taxes*** (from which the funds to pay welfare benefits come), just as citizens do.

2. **Bar admissions:** Then, the Court held that states may not prevent resident aliens from ***practicing law.*** *In re Griffiths*, 413 U.S. 717 (1973). None of the state interests supposedly served by the ban (e.g., maintaining "high professional standards" and having lawyers serve as "officers of the court") was sufficiently closely linked to exclusion of aliens to overcome strict scrutiny.

3. **Civil service:** Lastly, the Court held that a state may not bar aliens from holding positions in the state ***civil service. Sugarman v. Dougall***, 413 U.S. 634 (1973).

C. *Sugarman* **exception:** But in what was to become an extremely important dictum, the Court in *Sugarman* stated that a state ***could*** prevent aliens from holding state ***elective*** executive, legislative and judicial positions, and even important ***nonelective*** positions in any of the branches of state government.

   1. **Rationale:** The Court reasoned that such persons "perform ***functions that go to the heart of representative government***." Therefore, just as a state could exclude aliens from voting, it could exclude them from "participation in its democratic political institutions."

   2. **Consequence:** This "exception" to the principal doctrine of *Sugarman* has ***virtually swallowed the rule***. See, e.g., *Cabell v. Chavez-Salido, infra*, p. 340, placing "Spanish-speaking Deputy Probation Officers" within the *Sugarman* exception. See generally Sullivan & Gunther, pp. 812-13.

   3. *Sugarman* **exception interpreted broadly:** The trend towards interpreting the *Sugarman* exception extremely broadly, so as to bar aliens from a wide range of state employment, began with *Foley v. Connelie*, 435 U.S. 291 (1978), where the Court held that New York could prevent aliens from becoming ***state troopers***. Since state troopers were engaged in "execution of broad public policy," and since they held a large degree of ***discretion*** in doing so, they fell within the *Sugarman* exception.

   4. **Public school teachers:** The *Sugarman* exception was broadened again, when the Court permitted New York to bar aliens from becoming ***public school teachers. Ambach v. Norwick***, 441 U.S. 68 (1979), a 5-4 decision.

      a. **Facts:** The bar in *Ambach* applied to all aliens except those who had "manifested an intention to apply for citizenship." Plaintiffs refused to apply for citizenship even though they were eligible for it.

      b. **Standard:** The majority in *Ambach* expressed the test as being whether the employment was a ***"governmental function,"*** i.e., a function which was ***"bound up with the operation of the state as a governmental entity. ... " Public school teaching, in the majority's opinion, qualified under this standard.***

   c. **Application of test:**  Since public school teaching fell within the exception rather than the rule of *Sugarman*, only a mere rationality review was appropriate, and the classification passed muster under that review.

  5. **Probation officers:**  *Deputy probation officers* were added to the list of jobs from which aliens may be barred, in *Cabell v. Chavez-Salido*, 454 U.S. 432 (1982) (another 5-4 decision).

  6. **Notaries public:**  In the only post-*Sugarman* case in which the Court found *Sugarman* not applicable, the Court held that *notaries public* do *not* perform "functions that go to the heart of representative government." *Bernal v. Fainter*, 467 U.S. 216 (1984). Since the duties of a notary public are "essentially *clerical* and *ministerial*," aliens may be barred only if the state can establish a justification that survives strict scrutiny (which the state was not able to do in *Bernal*.)

  7. **Summary of present position:**  It seems clear, then, that the present majority of the Court will allow states to ban aliens from any post involving a *"political"* rather than "economic" function, and that any post *related to education or law enforcement* is likely to be found "political." In fact, it is not even at all clear that *Griffiths* (the attorney case) would be decided the same way under the present Court, though *Bernal* (the notary case) may indicate that it would.

**D. The federal government:**  Suppose a classification disadvantaging aliens is made by the *federal government*, rather than by a state. As noted, the Equal Protection Clause would not directly apply to the government's action; instead, the Fifth Amendment Due Process Clause would be interpreted to impose requirements similar to those which the Equal Protection Clause places upon the states. But because of the federal government's *exclusive responsibility for supervising immigration*, a given instance of discrimination against aliens, if made by the federal government, will be reviewed with *greater deference* than would the same type of discrimination when carried out by a state.

  1. **Balancing test:**  Roughly speaking, the Court has *"balanced"* the federal government's interest in controlling the terms of immigration against the alien's right to fair treatment.

  2. **Administrative agency action:**  The Court has granted this greater deference more readily to actions taken directly by Congress and the President than to action taken by *administrative agencies*. See, e.g., *Hampton v. Mow Sun Wong*, 426 U.S. 88 (1976) (regulation issued by the Civil Service Commission barring resident aliens from jobs in the federal Civil Service is struck down, though ban would not necessarily have been invalid if promulgated directly by the President or Congress).

  3. **Medical benefits:**  In the Court's only case where *Congress itself* discriminated against certain aliens, the Court *upheld* congressional power to do so. In *Matthews v. Diaz*, 426 U.S. 67 (1976), the Court held that Congress could impose the double requirement that aliens be both admitted for permanent residence and have resided continuously in the U.S. for five years, in order to receive Medicare. The Court (a unanimous one) stressed Congress' *full power over immigration*, a power which justified some discriminations against aliens which might not be permitted to the states.

**E. Education of illegal aliens:**  In all the cases considered in this section thus far, the aliens who claimed to be discriminated against were *legally present* in this country. But what are the rights of aliens who have not been legally admitted, i.e., so-called *"illegal"* or *"undocu-*

*mented"* aliens? The Supreme Court has not yet dealt with the rights of *adult* illegal aliens. But it has established that illegal aliens of *school age* may *not*, consistent with the Equal Protection Clause, be charged a *fee for public school education. Plyler v. Doe*, 457 U.S. 202 (1982).

1. **Facts of** *Plyler: Plyler* involved a Texas statute which: (1) denied local school districts funds for education of illegal-alien children; and (2) allowed school districts to deny free public education to such children.

2. **Majority strikes statute:** By a 5-4 vote, the Court *struck down* the statute as violative of equal protection. The majority opinion required several steps to reach this result:

   a. **Protected by Fourteenth Amendment:** First, the Court rejected Texas' argument that the Equal Protection Clause applies only to state action against "any person within [the state's] jurisdiction," and that illegal aliens are not "within Texas' jurisdiction" at all. The Court concluded, as a matter of legislative history, that the Clause was intended to cover *any person physically within a state's borders*, regardless of the *legality* of his presence.

   b. **Intermediate scrutiny applied:** The Court then devoted much of its opinion to determining the proper level of scrutiny. It concluded that *intermediate-level scrutiny* was appropriate here, since both the powerless nature of the group and the importance of education were factors.

      i. **"Not suspect class":** The Court explicitly *rejected* the suggestion that illegal aliens should be treated as a *"suspect class."* Entry into the class was a *voluntary* act (since entry into the nation was voluntary), in contrast to the involuntary nature of membership in other suspect classes. Also, illegal immigrant status was clearly not a constitutional irrelevancy, since Congress possessed, and had exercised, the power to exclude certain aliens, and the states could "follow the federal direction."

      ii. **Not mere "rational relation":** But "mere rationality" review was not sufficient, either. Although the action by adult aliens in illegally entering this country was voluntary, the action of their *children* was *not*. Also, public education, while not a "right" guaranteed by the Constitution, was certainly more important than other social welfare "benefits." Denying these children an education would render them illiterate, and would thus prevent them from advancing based on their individual merit and from becoming useful members of society.

   c. **Congressional policy:** Texas argued that Congress' failure to admit these children, and indeed its "apparent disapproval" of their presence, gave the state authority to treat them less favorably than citizens and resident aliens. The majority agreed that if Texas' denial of public education to these children was indeed in accord with an "identifiable congressional policy," Texas' action might well be valid. But, the majority believed, this denial *was not in accord with any identifiable congressional policy*. For instance, there was no evidence that Congress had ever even considered conservation of state educational resources as a reason for restricting immigration.

   d. **State interest supporting action:** Texas also asserted three interests of its own which, it believed, justified the denial of free public education. But the Court did not find any of these interests sufficiently weighty to overcome the intermediate-level scrutiny.

    **i. Prevent influx:**   First, the state contended that its statute might help ***stem the flood*** of illegal immigrants. But the Court found this a "ludicrously ineffectual" way of stemming this tide, especially in view of an alternative measure: prohibiting the ***employment*** of illegal aliens.

    **ii. Preserving high quality of education:**   Texas also contended that illegal alien children imposed an especially heavy burden on the state's ability to provide ***high quality public education***. But, the majority responded, even if excluding the children would improve the overall quality of education (an assertion as to which the Court found no evidence), Texas still bore the burden of showing why ***this particular group of aliens***, as distinguished from documented aliens, was the appropriate one to exclude. Texas was unable to discharge this burden, since documented and undocumented alien children were "basically indistinguishable" in terms of their educational needs.

    **iii. Less likely to remain resident:**   Finally, Texas claimed that illegal alien children were less likely than other children to remain within the state and therefore less likely to put their education to use there. The Court also rejected this claim, essentially because it found nothing in the record to suggest that this was true as a factual matter.

  **e. General "conservation of resources" argument:**   The majority also rejected Texas' more general claim, that it had an interest in ***preserving the state's limited educational resources*** so that it could spend these on the education of its lawful residents. The majority found it easy to dismiss this argument, by resort to precedent. Preservation of scarce resources was simply ***never a sufficient reason*** for denying those resources to one particular group; this had already been established in the case of welfare benefits (*Graham v. Richardson, supra*, p. 339).

    **i. Comparison:**   The Court's response to this "scarce resources" argument is similar to its rejection of "administrative convenience" as a grounds for discrimination against a particular group (e.g., married servicemen in *Frontiero v. Richardson, supra*, p. 323). In the most general sense, the fact that the state saves money, time, effort, etc. is ***never by itself enough to justify the selection of a particular group to bear the brunt of the state's conservation efforts*** (at least where the group is one which receives the benefit of intermediate-level or strict scrutiny).

**3. Dissent:**   Justice Burger dissented in *Plyler*, joined by three other members of the Court (White, Rehnquist and O'Connor).

  **a. Unduly result-oriented:**   First, Burger objected to the general way in which the majority arrived at the decision to use intermediate-level scrutiny. Since the majority was not treating illegal aliens as a suspect class nor education as a fundamental right, the Court was "[p]atching together bits and pieces of what might be termed quasi-suspect-class and quasi-fundamental-rights analysis [making the Court] guilty of an unabashedly result-oriented approach. ... " In the dissent's view the majority's theory had so little generality that it established "little more than that the level of scrutiny employed ... applies only when illegal alien children are deprived of a public education."

  **b. Voluntariness irrelevant:**   Burger also objected to the fact that the majority took into account the "involuntariness" of the children's presence in this country. For Burger, it was simply irrelevant that the trait upon which the discrimination was based (illegal presence) was involuntary. For instance, the state could distinguish between mentally-ill persons and mentally-healthy ones, even though the condition of the former might be beyond their control. Nor was it relevant that the Court had previously given inter-mediate-level scrutiny to classifications based on illegitimacy; here, the discrimination was not based merely on "status of birth" but on a congressionally-unsanctioned ille-gal presence.

c. **Education:** Burger also objected to the extra weight that the majority gave to the interest in education, as distinguished from other governmental benefits. He con-tended that *Rodriguez (infra*, p. 351) had definitively established that education was not a "fundamental right," and that therefore, the fact that it was education which was being denied (as opposed to, say, welfare, medical care or housing) could not make any difference to the level of scrutiny applied.

d. **Rational relations:** Since neither the plaintiff's illegal alien status nor the nature of education should, in Burger's opinion, trigger any special scrutiny, he believed that the ***"mere rationality" test was the appropriate one.***

    i. **Application of test:** Not surprisingly, Burger found that denial of free public education to these children was rationally related to legitimate interests held by Texas. The state had an interest in preserving its fiscal resources, and could rea-sonably conclude that it had no obligation to spend those resources on education for persons illegally in the country. Also, the state had a legitimate interest in attempting to curb the influx of illegal immigrants; denial of public education might not be the most effective way of accomplishing this end, but that means was not completely irrational.

    ii. **Congressional policy:** The dissent also argued that the ***federal*** government's exclusion of illegal aliens from various social welfare programs (e.g., the food stamp and AFDC programs) supported the rationality of a state's excluding such aliens from state programs.

4. **Scope of case unknown:** Because the majority, in deciding to apply intermediate-level scrutiny in *Plyler*, relied upon the ***combination*** of a disadvantaged group (illegal aliens) and an unusually important interest (education), the Court avoided the need for deciding whether ***either*** of these factors ***by itself*** might justify intermediate scrutiny.

a. **Intermediate review for illegal aliens:** Thus it remains a possibility that ***other types of discrimination against illegal aliens*** (even if not involving something as basic as the complete denial of education) ***might nonetheless trigger intermediate-level scru-tiny.***

b. **Complete denial of education:** Similarly, it is possible that the ***complete denial of education*** to any group (even one without the special powerlessness that marks illegal aliens) might be given intermediate-level or even strict scrutiny, despite the fact that lesser variations in the furnishing of education are subjected only to "mere rationality" review (under *Rodriguez, infra*, p. 351).

## VII.  ILLEGITIMACY

    **A.  Discrimination against illegitimates:**   Many states have statutes which disadvantage illegitimate children. The discrimination may take the form of ineligibility to take by intestate succession, inability to sue for the parent's wrongful death, disentitlement to claim a presumption of dependency (relevant for receipt of certain government benefits, such as social security survivors' benefits), etc.

    **B.  Present state of the law:**   The Supreme Court has vacillated considerably over the years on how classifications based on legitimacy should be treated. Here is a summary of the present state of the law:

        **1.  Mid-level review:**   *Mid-level review* is used. That is, the classification disadvantaging illegitimates must be substantially related to an important governmental objective. *Clark v. Jeter*, 486 U.S. 456 (1988).

        **2.  Claims can't be flatly barred:**   Consequently, the state cannot simply bar unacknowledged illegitimate children from bringing wrongful death actions, from having any chance to inherit, etc. Such children must be given at least *some reasonable opportunity* (typically, via a proceeding brought by their mother) to obtain a *judicial declaration of paternity.* Once they obtain such a declaration, they must be *treated equivalently to children born legitimate.*

            **a.  No short statutes of limitation:** Furthermore, the statute of limitations on paternity claims must be no longer than is reasonably needed to fulfill the state's interest in, say, weeding out stale or fraudulent claims.

                **Example:** Pennsylvania passes a statute of limitations saying that no action for child support may be brought on behalf of an out-of-wedlock child unless the action is brought before the child turns 6. *Held,* the statute violates the child's equal protection rights. Since the classification is based on out-of-wedlock status, it will be upheld only if it is substantially related to an important governmental objective. Concededly, Pennsylvania has an interest in avoiding the litigation of stale or fraudulent claims. But the 6-year statute of limitations is not "substantially related" to the achievement of that interest. *Clark v. Jeter, supra.*

## VIII.  MENTAL RETARDATION AND MENTAL ILLNESS

    **A.  Mental retardation:**   The Supreme Court has refused to treat *mental retardation* as a quasi-suspect classification. ***City of Cleburne v. Cleburne Living Center***, 473 U.S. 432 (1985).

        **1.  Rationale:**   The Court in *Cleburne* advanced four reasons why it would not be appropriate to accord heightened scrutiny to classifications based on mental retardation:

            **a.  Judicial second-guessing undesirable:**   First, the states have a legitimate interest in giving special treatment to the mentally retarded, because of their "reduced ability to cope with and function in the everyday world." The treatment to be given to the mentally retarded is "a difficult and often a technical matter, very much a task for legislators guided by qualified professionals and not by the perhaps ill-informed opinions of the judiciary." If heightened scrutiny were given to classifications based on mental retardation, the judiciary would be more likely to be required to make "substantive judgments" about the legislative handling of the retarded, judgments which it is ill-equipped to make.

    **b. No antipathy by lawmakers:** Secondly, the array of national and state legislative responses to the plight of the mentally retarded (responses which, in general, ***benefit*** the retarded) show that there is no "continuing antipathy or prejudice" on the part of lawmakers.

    **c. Not politically powerless:** Thirdly, the very fact that these legislative responses have occurred "negates any claim that the mentally retarded are politically powerless in the sense that they have no ability to attract the attention of the lawmakers."

    **d. Other groups:** Finally, if quasi-suspect status were given to the "large and amorphous class" of the mentally retarded, there would be no "principled way" to deny quasi-suspect status to a number of other groups, including the aging, the disabled, the mentally ill, and the infirm. And this kind of expansion is something the courts should be "reluctant" to embark upon (though the Court did not say why).

**2. Rational relation "with bite":** As it happened, the fact the retarded were not given quasi-suspect status in *Cleburne* did not mean that the retarded plaintiffs lost the case. Although the Court applied only the "mere rationality" standard (by which the classification would be upheld so long as it was rationally related to some legitimate governmental objective), the particular governmental classification at issue in *Cleburne* was struck down. The defendant municipality's refusal to grant a "special use permit," required by the municipal zoning ordinance before a group home for the mentally retarded could be operated, was found not to be even rationally related to any legitimate state purpose. Rather, the denial of the permit seemed to "rest on an irrational prejudice against the mentally retarded."

    **a. Rigorous application of test:** The Court appeared to be applying the "mere rationality" test with considerably more rigor than it has done in most recent cases involving that test; see *supra*, p. 248.

**3. Dissent:** Three members of the Court (Marshall, Brennan, and Blackmun) disagreed with the Court's refusal to give the mentally retarded quasi-suspect status. They contended that the mentally retarded have been subject to a " 'lengthy and tragic history' ... of segregation and discrimination that can only be called grotesque." They argued that at least where what is at issue is the right of the retarded to establish a group home (the right to "establish a home" being clearly a "fundamental liberty"), heightened scrutiny should be given to any regulation that burdens their right to do so.

    **a. Majority's rationale rejected:** The three Justices dissenting on this point also contended that the majority's reasoning was illogical:

        **i. Legislation irrelevant:** For instance, the fact that extensive legislation had recently been enacted to protect the retarded did not mean that there was no ongoing discrimination against the retarded, or that this group was necessarily less needful of the benefits of heightened scrutiny. The dissenters pointed out that "race-based classifications [did not become] any less suspect once extensive legislation had been enacted on the subject."

        **ii. Relevance of trait:** The dissenters also could not see why the fact that retardation was relevant to *some* types of regulation should mean that it was relevant to the kind of regulation here. "That a characteristic may be relevant under some or even many circumstances does not suggest any reason to presume it relevant under other circumstances where there is reason to suspect it is not. A sign that says 'men only' looks very different on a bathroom door than a courthouse door." For the dissenters, the fact that retardation is irrelevant in some circumstances, when coupled with a history of discrimination against the retarded, was enough to require heightened scrutiny.

4. **Significance:**   Beyond establishing that mental retardation will not be treated as a quasi-suspect classification, *Cleburne* appears significant for at least two other reasons:

   a. **Hostility to heightened scrutiny:**   The case probably indicates that a majority of the present Court is ***reluctant*** to establish ***additional "quasi-suspect" classes.*** The majority went out of its way to indicate that it thought quasi-suspect status should not be given to certain other classifications that arguably merit it, such as "the aging, the disabled, the mentally ill, and the infirm." Therefore, few if any new entries into the catalogue of quasi-suspect classes can be expected from the present Court.

   b. **Burdens vs. benefits:**   The case also seems to confirm the Burger/Rehnquist Court's reluctance to treat a classification as more suspicious when it is used to ***burden*** the historically-disadvantaged group than where it is used to ***benefit*** that group. Recall that in the case of gender-based classifications, the Court gives the same level of review (intermediate scrutiny) to such classifications whether they purport to benefit women or not. Similarly, in the case of mental retardation, the Court will apparently apply the same level (rigorous "mere rationality" review, but not intermediate-level scrutiny) to the classification, regardless of whether the particular classification in question appears to have been motivated by a desire to benefit or to burden the retarded.

B. **Mental illness:**   The Court has never explicitly decided whether classifications based on ***mental illness*** should be treated as quasi-suspect.

   1. **Unlikely to be quasi-suspect class:**   However, in light of *Cleburne*, it seems very unlikely that the Court would give the mentally-ill quasi-suspect status.

   2. **"Mere rationality with bite":**   However, the mentally ill, like the mentally retarded, have often been discriminated against, and do bear some of the traits of a "discreet and insular minority." (See *U.S. v. Carolene Products Co., supra*, p. 259.) Therefore, although the Court would probably give to classifications based on mental illness only low-level "mere rationality" review, it may apply that level of review in the same fairly stringent way that it did to the mental-retardation classification in *Cleburne*.

## IX.  GENERAL PRINCIPLES OF MIDDLE-LEVEL SCRUTINY

A. **General principles:**   Once a court decides that traditional deferential, "mere rationality" review is appropriate, it is almost a foregone conclusion that the statute will be upheld. Conversely, if the court decides to apply strict scrutiny, the statute will almost invariably be struck down. Thus in these two situations, it is not usually important to focus on exactly how the review takes place; the important thing is how the choice of standards gets made. By contrast, the decision to apply "middle-level" or "intermediate" review does not by any means dispose of the matter; the precise way in which the court applies the middle-ground scrutiny thus becomes extremely important. This section reviews briefly some of the principles that seem to be guiding the courts in applying intermediate-level review.

**B. Importance of objective:**   The *objective* sought to be achieved by the statute must be *"important,"* even if it need not be "compelling" (as required in strict scrutiny situations).

   **1. Little "bite":**   However, this requirement has not proven to have a lot of bite, since most asserted state objectives have been found to be "important." However, there are some exceptions, such as "administrative convenience" and "conservation of scarce resources" (see *supra*, p. 342).

**C. Close means-end fit:**   The *means* chosen by the state must be *"substantially related"* to achieving the important objective. That is, the *means-end fit* must be a *reasonably tight one*.

   **1. Less-restrictive alternatives:**   Looking at this requirement another way, the demands of intermediate scrutiny are more likely to be satisfied if there are *no available alternatives* that would carry out the asserted objectives as well or better, without causing needless disadvantage to anyone.

   **2. Smoking out bad motivation:**   One reason for requiring a close means-end fit is that it furnishes a way of *"flushing out" unconstitutional motivation*. See Ely, p. 146 (regarding strict scrutiny); see also *supra*, pp. 260-260. That is, if the state claims that a particular objective was the motivation behind the statute, yet the means is not closely related to the ends, the court will be justified in suspecting that the asserted motivation was not the real one (which may have been an unconstitutional one.)

**D. Refusal to hypothesize state purpose:**   Recall that in the area of general social and economic welfare legislation, where "mere rationality" review is all that is applied, the Court seems to be willing to consider possible objectives to which the means chosen by the legislature are rationally related, even though there is no evidence that this objective *in fact* motivated the legislature. (*supra*, p. 243.) In the intermediate-review area, however, the Court *will not hypothesize a state objective*; only those objectives which are shown (by the terms of the statute, legislative history, or otherwise) to have *actually motivated the legislature* will be considered. If none of these actual objectives is sufficiently "important," or sufficiently tightly related to the means chosen, the statute will be struck down.

> **Example:** In *Trimble v. Gordon*, 430 U.S. 762 (1977), the state argued that one purpose of its ban on intestate succession by illegitimates was to enforce the "presumed intention" of intestate decedents. The Court rejected this asserted objective, stating "[we] do not think [the law] was enacted for this purpose [and] we will not hypothesize an additional state purpose. ... "

---

*Quiz Yourself on*
## EQUAL PROTECTION — ALIENAGE AND ILLEGITIMACY

**41.** The state of Pacifica enacted a statute providing that no person who is not a U.S. citizen could hold title to beach-front land located in the state. Pacifica's west coast consists entirely of ocean-front property. The statute was enacted in part because state residents were annoyed that Japanese nationals and citizens of other Pacific rim countries were paying high prices for Pacifica beach-front property, making it harder for U.S. citizens living in Pacifica to compete for ownership of that property. Yukio, a Japanese citizen who resides permanently in the United States, and who wishes to buy ocean-front property in Pacifica, has sued to have the statute overturned on the grounds that it violates her equal protection rights.

   **(a)** What standard of review should the court give to the Pacifica statute? _____

   **(b)** Will Yukio's attack succeed? _____

**42.** The city of Xenon was concerned that many applicants for posts as public school teachers in the town, and some hires, were foreigners who spoke with a hard-to-understand accent. Therefore, the Xenon school board enacted a regulation that henceforth, all new hires for the post of school teacher in the local school system must at the time of their application be United States citizens. Ted, an Englishman married to an American citizen, was a permanent resident of the U.S. but had no desire to become a U.S. citizen (even though his marital status entitled him to become one). Ted sued Xenon to have its citizens-only rule overturned, on the grounds that it violated his equal protection rights.

   **(a)** What standard should the court use in reviewing the Xenon citizens-only provision? _____

   **(b)** Will Ted's attack on the provision succeed? _____

**43.** The village of Tesla had a fine school system, generally believed to be better than that of surrounding towns. Tesla is located less than 100 miles from the border with Mexico, and has a large number of both Mexican Americans as well as undocumented aliens from Mexico. In order to discourage enrollment by students who in fact reside in other towns, the village enacted a set of strict regulations providing that only students who satisfied two conditions could attend the village's schools: (1) they had a bona fide residence within the village limits; and (2) they were either U.S. citizens or resident aliens. One effect of this regulation, as intended by the town elders, was to make undocumented aliens unable to attend the village schools even if they resided in the village. The principal motive for the no-illegal-aliens rule was to conserve tax dollars, because undocumented aliens on average pay lower property taxes, and education in the state is financed principally through property taxes. The village allowed an exception to its enrollment restrictions for anyone willing to pay a tuition fee of $4,000 per year.

   Pedro, a resident of Tesla who was undocumented, sued the village, arguing that as applied to him the enrollment restrictions violated the Equal Protection Clause.

   **(a)** When the court reviews Pedro's challenge to the enrollment restrictions, what standard of review should it use? _____

   **(b)** Will Pedro's attack succeed? _____

**44.** The state of Rigor provides that no illegitimate child may receive any part of his or her father's estate if the father dies intestate. This statutory exclusion applies even if there has been a judicial finding of paternity prior to the father's death. When Stuart was 11, he was found (in a proceeding brought on his behalf by his mother) to be the illegitimate son of David. Two years after this finding, David died intestate. Stuart has sued for a declaratory judgment that the state's exclusion of him from an intestate share of David's estate violates his, Stuart's, equal protection rights.

   **(a)** What standard of review should the court use in examining the exclusion of illegitimate children from the intestacy scheme? _____

   **(b)** Will Stuart's attack succeed? _____

*Answers*

**41. (a) Strict scrutiny.**

**(b) Yes, probably.** Discrimination against aliens (at least aliens who are legally in this country) is to be strictly scrutinized, because aliens as a class are politically powerless and frequently discriminated against). Therefore, any statute that discriminates against aliens on its face, or whose purpose is to disadvantage aliens, will be struck down unless it is necessary to achieve a compelling governmental interest. Here, the state's interest in keeping land prices low for American citizens is almost certainly not "compelling." In any event, discrimination against aliens is not a "necessary" way to achieve that objective, since there are other less-discriminatory options available (e.g., price controls that apply to everybody).

**42. (a) The mere rationality standard.**

**(b) No.** As noted in the answer to the prior question, discrimination against aliens is generally subjected to strict scrutiny. However, under the so-called "*Sugarman* exception," this strict scrutiny does not apply to discrimination against aliens who apply for jobs that ***"go to the heart of representative government."*** The Court has held that the post of public school teacher falls within this "heart of representative government" exception, because of a teacher's opportunity to "influence the attitudes of students towards government, the political process, and a citizen's social responsibilities." *Ambach v. Norwick*. Therefore, only a mere rationality review is used, and the regulation will be upheld if it is rationally related to the achievement of a legitimate state objective. Here, the regulation almost certainly satisfies this standard. Hiring teachers who can be easily understood is surely a legitimate state objective, and there is at least a rational relation between citizenship and ease of understanding (since non-citizens on average probably have harder-to-understand accents than citizens).

**43. (a) Intermediate-level review, under which the measure will be invalidated unless it is "substantially related" to the achievement of an "important" governmental objective.**

**(b) Yes, probably.** The Court held in *Plyler v. Doe* that intermediate-level review should be given to any state law denying free public-school education to illegal aliens of school age. In *Plyler*, the Court held that the various state interests advanced there (e.g., preventing an influx of illegal immigrants, conserving tax dollars, etc.) were not sufficiently weighty to overcome this mid-level review. The enrollment restriction here is essentially identical to that struck down in *Plyler*. The fact that non-residents of the village are also excluded is irrelevant — the key fact is that among residents of the village, those who are illegal aliens are excluded, whereas those who are citizens or resident aliens are allowed. Even if the village shows that it has to spend tax dollars on educating these additional students, and even if it is able to show that it does not get state aid to compensate it for these incremental burdens, the interest in conservation of resources is likely to be found insufficient to overcome the mid-level review (and similar fiscal interests were found insufficient in *Plyler* itself).

**44. (a) Mid-level review.**

**(b) Yes, probably.** After waffling a lot about what the appropriate level of review is for classifications that disadvantage illegitimates, the Supreme Court has finally held that intermediate scrutiny should be used. That is, the statutory classification that disadvantages illegitimates must be ***substantially*** related to an ***important*** governmental objective." Here, the state's total exclusion of illegitimates from intestate succession, even those who have been found by a reliable court proceeding to be the decedent's child, is very unlikely to be found to be substantially related to the achievement of an important state objective. (For instance, while the state may have an important objective of repelling false claims of paternity, this objective is not advanced at all by excluding one who has, during the decedent's lifetime, been found to be truly his child.) See *Trimble v. Gordon*, 430 U.S. 762 (1977), roughly matching the facts of this case, and striking down the total exclusion.

# X.  FUNDAMENTAL RIGHTS

A. **Introduction:**  In the equal protection cases which we have discussed so far, the decision to apply more than extremely deferential "mere rationality" review was made because of the peculiar nature of the *group* burdened by the statutory classification. But there is another way in which more-than-deferential equal protection review may be triggered: If the classification burdens a *"fundamental right"* or "fundamental interest," the classification will be subjected to strict scrutiny, *regardless of the characteristics of the people who are burdened*.

1. **Meaning of "fundamental":**  There are two general classes of rights which are deemed "fundamental," so that any interference with them will give rise to strict equal protection scrutiny. The first consists of rights which are *independently and explicitly guaranteed by some other constitutional provision* (distinct from the Equal Protection Clause). The second consists of rights which are not independently and explicitly given by other constitutional provisions, but which are felt to be both important and implicitly granted by the Constitution, so that large deviations in equality as to them are viewed as suspect.

    a. **Example of first class:**  A primary example of the first type of "fundamental right," one independently guaranteed by constitutional provisions apart from the Equal Protection Clause, is the right of *interstate migration* (see *infra*, p. 367). While there is some dispute as to exactly which part of the Constitution guarantees this right, it is clear that the right exists apart from the Equal Protection Clause. Nonetheless, the Equal Protection Clause will be used to strictly scrutinize a classification which restricts the migration rights of some but not all citizens. See *Shapiro v. Thompson, infra*, p. 367.

    b. **Example of second class:**  As an example of the second type of fundamental right, one which does not exist outside the Equal Protection Clause and therefore relies entirely on that clause for its vindication, consider substantial interferences with the *right to vote* in state elections (see *infra*, p. 355). Thus a law imposing a $1.50 poll tax on anyone who wished to vote was strictly scrutinized and invalidated under the Equal Protection Clause, in *Harper v. Virginia Board of Elections, infra*, p. 355.

2. **Developed by Warren Court:**  Strict scrutiny of classifications impairing fundamental rights began in the Warren Court. The three principal areas in which that Court found fundamental rights to be at stake were: (1) the *right to vote* (and the related right to participate as a candidate); (2) the right to *use the courts*; and (3) the right of *interstate migration*. (Each of these is considered in its own section below).

    a. **Proposals for extensions:**  Proponents of a broad reading of the fundamental rights doctrine argued that that doctrine should also be applied in a number of other contexts; most interestingly, they contended that this treatment should be used to strictly scrutinize legislation impairing equal access to *"necessities"* (e.g., welfare, housing, and education). The Warren Court never dealt with the fundamental rights doctrine's applicability to such necessities.

3. **The Burger/Rehnquist Court:** The Burger/Rehnquist Court has resolutely refused to expand the list of fundamental rights beyond the broad areas recognized by the Warren Court. For instance, *"necessities"* like *welfare* and *education*, despite their conceded societal importance, are *not fundamental*, the Burger Court has held.

4. **Education:** The prime example of the Burger Court's refusal to treat "necessities" as fundamental rights was *San Antonio Ind. School Dist. v. Rodriguez*, 411 U.S. 1 (1973), in which the Court held (by a 5-4 vote) that there was no fundamental right to equality in *public-school education*.

   a. **Facts:** In *Rodriguez*, the plaintiffs claimed that Texas' system of financing public education violated equal protection, because it relied principally on local property taxes. Although there were other state and federal funds which remained available to each school district, districts with a high property tax base per pupil consistently spent more on education than those with a low base were able to do.

   b. **Majority's holding:** The majority rejected the plaintiffs' two main arguments: (1) that residents of property-base-poor districts formed a "suspect class," especially since (the plaintiffs contended) poorer families tended to live in districts with smaller property tax bases; and (2) that education was a fundamental right, inequalities in the distribution of which must be strictly scrutinized.

   c. **Not suspect class:** The "suspect class" theory was rejected in large part because the majority simply disagreed that the poorest families lived in the districts with the smallest tax bases. The Court conceded the validity of the plaintiff's contention that districts with smaller property tax bases spent less money per pupil on education; but this fact did not make residents of those districts a suspect class.

      i. **Rationale:** These residents had "none of the traditional indicia of suspectness." The class was "large, diverse, and amorphous … unified only by the common factor of residence in districts that happen to have less taxable wealth. … " Members of the class had not been subjected to a history of "purposeful unequal treatment," or relegated to a position of political powerlessness so as to require "extraordinary protection from the majoritarian political process."

      ii. **Wealth:** The Court implied, though did not state, that even a class composed entirely of poor people would not by that fact alone be "suspect." See *infra*, p. 370, for additional discussion of the Court's refusal to treat wealth as a suspect classification.

   d. **Not fundamental interest:** Most of the majority's opinion, however, was devoted to explaining why the deviations in per pupil expenditures did not constitute interference with a fundamental right. Most critically, the majority stated that the *"importance"* of a service performed by a state does not determine whether it is "fundamental" for equal protection purposes. "Relative societal significance" of an interest is irrelevant. Rather, the issue is whether *the right is "explicitly or implicitly guaranteed by the Constitution."*

      i. **Education not guaranteed:** By this standard, education was not "fundamental." It was certainly not explicitly guaranteed by the Constitution. The plaintiffs argued that a right to education was implicitly guaranteed by the Constitution, because education was essential to effective exercise of First Amendment freedoms and the right to vote. The majority responded that ***absolute equality*** in education was certainly not guaranteed, even implicitly, by the Constitution.

e. **Absolute deprivation issue not addressed:**  But the Court in *Rodriguez* seemed to acknowledge the possibility that an ***absolute deprivation*** of education, if imposed on some group, might nonetheless be found to be an impairment of a fundamental right: "Even if it were conceded that some identifiable quantum of education is a constitutionally protected prerequisite to the meaningful exercise of either [the First Amendment or the right to vote], we have no indication that the present [Texas] system fails to provide each child with an opportunity to acquire the ***basic minimal skills*** necessary." Only the less-than-absolute ***differences*** among districts were at issue in *Rodriguez*.

   i. ***Plyler* leaves door open:**  That a complete denial of education may constitute an interference with a fundamental right appears to remain a possibility even following the post-*Rodriguez* case of *Plyler v. Doe (supra*, p. 341). In *Plyler*, the majority paid lip service to the *Rodriguez* conclusion that public education was not a "right" granted to individuals by the Constitution. But it stressed that education was not merely "some governmental 'benefit' indistinguishable from other forms of social welfare legislation," and that it was vital to achievement of "one of the goals of the Equal Protection Clause: the abolition of governmental barriers presenting unreasonable obstacles to advancement on the basis of individual merit." While denial of public education to illegal aliens was held not to be an infringement of a fundamental right, the Court may well hold that denial of such education to a ***U.S. citizen does*** constitute such an infringement. For instance, Justice Blackmun, concurring in *Plyler*, seemed to believe this to be true. (Similarly, charging ***tuition*** for public elementary or high school education might be held to violate a fundamental right.)

f. **Rational relation test:**  Since neither a suspect class nor a fundamental right was at issue, the majority held in *Rodriguez*, the traditional "mere rationality" test applied. The Texas system passed this test. The scheme had been enacted (the majority appeared to find) for the purpose of giving each ***local district*** a large ***measure of control*** over the education given to its residents, a goal which the majority found legitimate.

   i. **Imperfect means-end fit not fatal:**  The Court conceded that some districts (the ones with a lower property tax base) had less control over spending than others. But this was merely a slight imperfection in the means-end fit, an imperfection which did not negate the existence of a "rational relationship" between the means chosen (use of local property taxes) and the ends sought (local control). It was not mandatory that the "least restrictive alternative" be selected.

g. **Dissents:**  Four Justices dissented; the two longest opinions were by White and Marshall.

h. **White's dissent:**  Justice White's dissent stressed that the property-tax-based scheme offered the low-tax-base districts virtually no ability to increase their per-pupil expenditures, and did give such a choice to the districts that were richer in property. Therefore, he argued, the scheme was not even rationally related to Texas' asserted goal of giving local districts control over the size of per-pupil education expenditures.

i. **Marshall's dissent:** Justice Marshall's dissent swept much more broadly. Most importantly, he disagreed with the majority's view that only those rights that are "explicitly or implicitly guaranteed by the Constitution" should be treated as "fundamental" for equal protection analysis. He claimed that at least three of the rights previously found "fundamental" (the right to procreate, recognized in *Skinner v. Oklahoma, supra,* p. 157, the right to vote in state elections, discussed *infra,* p. 354, and the right to appeal from a criminal conviction, discussed *infra,* p. 366) were not guaranteed in other constitutional provisions, but that discriminatory state treatment in these areas nonetheless received strict scrutiny.

  i. **Marshall's proposed test:** Marshall then proposed his own test for "fundamentality." The issue should be "the extent to which constitutionally guaranteed rights are ***dependent on interests not mentioned in the Constitution.*** As the nexus between the specific constitutional guarantee and the non-constitutional interest draws closer, the non-constitutional interest becomes more fundamental. … " For instance, the right to appeal from a criminal conviction was "fundamental" because of its close interrelationship with the Fourteenth Amendment's specific guarantee of due process of law.

  ii. **Education as "fundamental":** By this test, education was a fundamental right, since it "directly affects the ability of a child to exercise his First Amendment interests. … " Similarly, educated persons exercise the right to vote more frequently than those who are not educated.

  iii. **Wealth as suspect classification:** Marshall also contended that the Texas statute in *Rodriguez* classified by ***wealth,*** and did so in a manner that merited "careful judicial scrutiny." That the classification was based on "group wealth" (i.e., each district's taxable property) rather than the wealth of the individual did not make the classification less objectionable to Marshall. In one respect it was *worse*: since the individual had no control over the wealth of his district, the classification ran afoul of what Marshall described as the Court's precedent of "treat[ing] discrimination on a basis which the individual cannot control as constitutionally disfavored." (citing, e.g., *Levy v. Louisiana,* 391 U.S. 68 (1968)). Furthermore, here the ***government,*** by its zoning and other land use policies, had helped allocate particular areas for residential or commercial use, and had therefore ***contributed significantly*** to the fact that districts differed in their property wealth. Thus unlike the usual wealth classification, which is based upon inequality not created by the government, here the government had actually helped create the inequality, and had then discriminated based upon that inequality.

  iv. **Sliding scale:** Throughout his dissent, Justice Marshall was apparently not suggesting that full-fledged "strict scrutiny" should be given to the Texas statute. Rather, he was apparently arguing in favor of a ***"sliding scale"*** of review (a concept he had pioneered in his dissent in *Dandridge v. Williams, infra,* p. 370), whereby the degree of scrutiny in equal protection cases, rather than being a rigid two-pole scheme, would vary along a continuum depending on the importance of the interest and the suspectness of the classification. Since education was highly important, and since the wealth classification was at least somewhat suspect, this combination required substantially more than "mere rationality" review, even if traditional strict scrutiny was not merited (a point he did not address explicitly).

**j.  Significance of *Rodriguez:*** We will discuss *Rodriguez* again in the treatment of wealth classifications *infra*, p. 370. For now, several significant principles may be deduced from the case: (1) whether a right or interest is "fundamental" is determined by whether it is ***expressly or impliedly guaranteed by the Constitution, not*** by its ***"societal importance"***; (2) by this standard, the right to public education (or, at least, the right to ***equality in the expenditures made for one's public education***) is ***not fundamental***; and (3) for a classification related to wealth to be "suspect," it must probably both be against a discrete, insular, historically-discriminated-against and powerless class, and involve an almost total deprivation of the good in question, not mere inequality in the amount of that good given.

**B.  Adult sexual relations:**  An interesting question is whether the Court will come to recognize certain forms of ***adult sexual relations*** as being fundamental rights for equal protection purposes. The Court has not yet done so. Indeed, in the now-overruled case of *Bowers v. Hardwick* (*supra*, p. 185), the Court held that there was ***no*** "fundamental right [of] homosexuals to engage in sodomy" (a due-process decision that seemed to have implications for equal protection analysis as well). Even when *Bowers* was overruled by *Lawrence v. Texas* (*supra*, p. 185), the Court still did not recognize the interest in adult same-sex sexual relations as being "fundamental." But *Lawrence*'s use of unusually-rigorous rational-relation review, and that case's striking down of statutes criminalizing gay sodomy, suggest that a majority of the present Court may well view adult sexual expression — whether same-sex or different-sex — as effectively being of ***"quasi-fundamental"*** importance for both substantive-due process and equal-protection purposes.

**C.  Voting rights:**  The Constitution does not place any explicit limits on the power of states to control state and local elections. Relying in part on this constitutional silence, the Court has held over the years that the states may exercise substantial control over the ***right to vote.***

**1.  State right to regulate voter qualifications:**  For instance, the states have the right to determine ***voter qualifications*** for state elections, so long as they do not exercise that right in a way which violates any specific constitutional prohibitions (or any statute which Congress has enacted pursuant to a constitutional provision). Thus states may require that voters be of ***reasonable age***, and that they be ***citizens and residents*** of the state.

**a.  State regulation of federal voter qualifications:**  Interestingly, the Constitution indirectly gives the ***states*** the right to set voter qualifications not just for state elections but for ***federal*** ones. Article I, §2 provides that voters in House of Representatives elections shall have the same qualifications as such voters need for voting in elections for the state legislature, and the Seventeenth Amendment, §1, provides the same for election of U.S. Senators. (Article I, §4 gives Congress the right to ***override*** these state-created voter qualifications for federal elections. But Congress has no such right of override of qualifications for state elections, so that state power there is exclusive.)

**2.  Voting as fundamental right:**  Yet voting is integrally related to the First Amendment right to free speech, including political expression. Furthermore, maintenance of other constitutionally-guaranteed civil rights and liberties depends on public officials' accountability to the electorate. Therefore, the Court has labelled the ***right to vote*** in state and local (as well as federal) elections as ***"fundamental."***

a. **Strict scrutiny:** Because the right to vote is "fundamental," the Supreme Court has — but only in some circumstances — subjected laws that impair some group's right to vote to ***strict scrutiny***. The Court's cases are quite jumbled in this area, and it's hard to articulate a single standard for when the Court will use strict scrutiny. It's also hard to predict whether a particular measure will ***survive*** that strict scrutiny, an outcome that happens more often in voting-rights cases than in other areas.

b. **The "unrelated to voter qualifications" test:** In deciding whether to use strict scrutiny, the Court seems to place great weight on whether the voting regulation is reasonably ***"related to voter qualifications."***

   i. **Not reasonably related (strict scrutiny):** If the Court decides that the regulation is *not* "reasonably related to voter qualifications," then the Court ***uses strict scrutiny***, and will probably strike down the regulation. As we'll see below, poll taxes, property-ownership requirements and duration-of-residence requirements fall into this strictly-scrutinized-and-generally-struck-down category.

   ii. **Reasonably related (intermediate review):** If, on the other hand, the Court decides that the regulation *is* reasonably related to voter qualifications, then the Court generally does ***not*** use strict scrutiny. Instead, it uses some less stringent review method (typically, an intermediate-level ***balancing test***), and is likely to ***uphold*** the measure. Basic residency requirements, voter ID requirements, and regulations disenfranchising felons all fall into this category; see *infra*, p. 357.

3. **Not reasonably related to voter qualifications:** Let's first look at various types of regulations that the Court has found to be ***not reasonably related to voter qualifications***, and as to which it has therefore ***applied strict scrutiny.***

   a. **Poll tax:** The seminal area in which regulations have been found not to be reasonably related to voter qualifications is the imposition of a ***poll taxes***. A poll tax, no matter how minor, creates an inequality in the right to vote that must be strictly scrutinized, and struck down as an Equal Protection violation. Thus in ***Harper v. Virginia Board of Elections***, 383 U.S. 663 (1966), the Court struck down an annual poll tax of only $1.50, imposed as a prerequisite for voting.

      i. **Rationale:** The Court began by holding that the right to vote was fundamental, because it was "preservative of all rights." Therefore, inequality in its distribution was to be "closely scrutinized" (i.e., strictly scrutinized).

         (1) **Application of strict review:** The tax in *Harper* could not survive such scrutiny, even though the state clearly had a right to charge standardized fees for the exercise of other types of rights (e.g., a fee for a driver's license). The means-end link there did not have the requisite tightness, because "wealth, like race, creed, or color, is not germane to one's ability to participate intelligently in the electoral process."

      ii. **Dissent:** Three dissenters in *Harper* contended that a "mere rationality" rather than "strict scrutiny" standard should be applied. If this were done, they argued, the statute should be upheld, since it was rationally related to several legitimate state objectives, including promotion of civic responsibility (on the theory that "people with some property have a deeper stake in community affairs … ").

**b. Ballot restricted to "interested voters":**   Another type of inequality which has often (but not always) been strictly scrutinized and invalidated is the requirement that voters *own property* or otherwise have some *"special interest"* entitling them to vote. Such requirements tend to exist not in general elections, but in elections on *special issues* (e.g., bond issues) or for *special boards* (e.g., water districts).

   **i. Summary:**   The law in this area is somewhat confused. In general, the Court has been suspicious of state claims that only a certain group is "interested" in the results of an election. If, however, the state proves that only members of that group do indeed have a major objective interest or "stake" in the issue (as opposed to a subjective curiosity about it), the limitation may be upheld. But if the state doesn't succeed in making that proof, then the Court will strictly scrutinize, and probably invalidate, the limitation.

   **ii. School board elections:**   Thus in *Kramer v. Union Free School District No. 15*, 395 U.S. 621 (1969), the Court *struck down* a New York statute which limited *school district* elections to persons who either: (1) owned or leased property within the district; or (2) were parents of children in the district's public schools. The Court said that any requirement which had the effect of giving the franchise to some residents but not others (apart from reasonable requirements of age and citizenship) must be *"carefully scrutinized"* to determine whether the scheme was *"necessary* to *promote* a compelling state interest."

   **(1) Means not sufficiently tailored:**   By this standard, the statute here was inadequate. The state's asserted interest in limiting elections to persons "primarily interested" in, or "primarily affected" by, the elections might be a legitimate objective (the Court did not decide). However, the *means chosen* (property ownership or rental) was an inadequate way of reaching that goal, since some people who had a substantial interest in the outcome of the elections were excluded (e.g., plaintiff, who was a 31-year-old bachelor stockbroker living with his parents), while other people without a real interest could vote (e.g., "an uninterested unemployed young man who pays no state or federal taxes, but who rents an apartment in the district[.]") The means was "not sufficiently tailored" to the goal of limiting the vote to people "primarily interested" in school affairs.

   **(2) Dissent:**   The three dissenters in *Kramer* argued that some linedrawing was essential to lawmaking, and that discrepancies like the one here were the inevitable results of such linedrawing.

   **iii. Exception for "special purpose" body:**   However, if the Court finds that the governmental unit for which elections are being held has a *limited purpose* which *disproportionately affects* only one group, the franchise may be limited to that group. Thus *"special purpose bodies"* may restrict the vote to persons who are directly affected by the body's activities.

   **(1) Water district:**   For instance, votes for a special-purpose *"water storage district"* can be *limited to landowners*, and can be on a "one acre, one vote" basis. See, e.g., *Ball v. James*, 451 U.S. 355 (1981) (even though water district finances its operations by selling electricity to hundreds of thousands of residents, the vote can be limited to landowners because the district can't enact laws, and doesn't perform "normal functions of government.")

c. **Duration-of-residence requirements:** Requirements that voters have *resided within the state* for *more than a certain time* prior to Election Day are strictly scrutinized.

   i. *Dunn v. Blumstein:* Thus in *Dunn v. Blumstein*, 405 U.S. 330 (1972), Tennessee's duration-of-residency requirements (one year in the state and three months in the county) were struck down, both on the ground that they interfered with the fundamental right to vote and on the ground that they impaired the right to travel. (The "right to travel" aspects of the case are discussed briefly *infra*, p. 369.)

      (1) **Fifty-day statutes:** But *shorter* residency requirements have been *upheld*, on the theory that these are merely methods of ensuring that the person *really is a resident.* Thus the Court has twice *upheld fifty-day* residency requirements, on the grounds that such a period is needed to allow the state to maintain accurate voting lists. See, e.g., *Marston v. Lewis*, 410 U.S. 679 (1973).

4. **Reasonably related to voter qualifications:** Let's look now at some types of regulations that the Court has found to be *reasonably related to voter qualifications*, and thus to be reviewed by a *less-than-strict-scrutiny* standard. Typically, the standard the Court uses is some form of *intermediate-level* review. As the Court said in the leading case in this area, "When a state election law provision imposes only *'reasonable, nondiscriminatory restrictions'* upon the First and Fourteenth Amendment rights of voters, the state's important regulatory interests are generally sufficient to justify" the restrictions. *Burdick v. Takushi*, 504 U.S. 428 (1992).

   a. **Voter identification requirements:** For example, a state requirement that every voter *present a photo ID* was *upheld* under this non-strict-scrutiny standard, in *Crawford v. Marion County Election Board*, 128 S.Ct. 1610 (2008).

      i. **Facts:** In *Crawford*, Indiana required any voter casting a physical (as opposed to absentee) ballot to *present a government-issued photo ID at that time.* The state offered a free qualifying photo ID to anyone who could prove residence and identity.

      ii. **Challenge:** The plaintiffs brought a "facial" Equal Protection challenge to the statute. That is, they argued that the statute should be struck down for *all* voters, not just for particular voters to whom they posed especially great burdens. The plaintiffs argued that the photo ID requirement was analogous to a poll tax, and should thus be subjected to strict scrutiny and invalidated as the poll tax was in *Harper v. Virginia Bd. of Elections* (*supra*, p. 355).

      iii. **Challenge rejected:** A 6-member majority *rejected* the facial challenge, and the argument that the statute should be strictly scrutinized. There was no majority opinion, because the six Justices split on the proper rationale. But all six Justices who voted to uphold the statute agreed that *strict scrutiny was not appropriate.*

         (1) **Plurality:** An opinion signed by three of these six Justices (Stevens, joined by Roberts and Kennedy) asserted that prior cases had held that *"evenhanded restrictions* that *protect the integrity and reliability of the electoral process*

*itself"* are not "invidious" and therefore should not be strictly scrutinized. Instead, these three said, a ***"balancing approach"*** should be used, under which the interests being pursued by the state in making the regulation must be balanced against the burdens imposed. (We'll call this the plurality opinion.) At least for this facial attack, the plaintiffs had not carried their burden of showing that ***enough voters were significantly burdened*** by the photo-ID requirement, or that the burdens on those voters were sufficiently great and unfair, as to outweigh the state's interest in combatting in-person voter fraud. (But the plurality seemed to leave open the possibility that in a later ***"as applied"*** suit, particular voters without photo IDs might show that *as to them*, the ID requirement *did* constitute an unconstitutionally great burden.)

(2) **Concurrences:** In a separate concurrence in the judgment, three more justices (Scalia, joined by Thomas and Alito) agreed with the plurality opinion that strict scrutiny should not be given to any voter regulation that imposes what the concurrence called "nonsevere, nondiscriminatory restrictions." And, the concurrence said, a regulation that places "ordinary and widespread burdens, such as those requiring 'nominal effort' of everyone, are not severe" (and therefore should not trigger strict scrutiny). The photo ID requirement here was the sort of "non-severe" widespread burden that should be judged even more deferentially than the plurality opinion would have judged it. The state's burden of justification should be ***"minimal,"*** Scalia said, so that the state's interests ***merely needed to be "reasonable,"*** a standard which Scalia thought was easily met here.

iv. **Dissent:** There were three dissenters (Souter, joined by Ginsburg, in one dissent, and Breyer in another).

(1) **Souter:** Souter contended that even if the plurality opinion's balancing test was used, the photo ID requirement here should be struck down, because a significant number of voters lacked the requisite photo ID and would therefore be seriously burdened. By contrast, the state's main interest — its need to combat in-person voter fraud — had not been demonstrated to be a significant one. (Souter pointed out that Indiana had ***"not come across a single instance*** of in-person voter impersonation fraud in all of [the state's] history.")

(2) **Breyer:** Breyer's dissent asserted that the photo ID requirement had the effect of imposing on a significant number of voters — those without a driver's license or other valid form of photo ID, a group largely made up of the poor, elderly or disabled — a disproportionate burden, perhaps more severe than the $1.50 poll tax struck down in *Harper*. And, he believed, a statute that placed a "disproportionate burden" on a class of voters (here, the class without photo IDs) should be struck down.

v. **Summary:** So as the result of *Crawford*, at least six members of the Roberts court are on record as believing that as long as a restriction on voting rights is an ***"even-handed*** [one] that ***protect[s] the integrity and reliability*** of the electoral process itself," ***strict scrutiny should not be used.*** And these six further agree that the requirement of a photo ID for all persons casting physical ballots is an evenhanded restriction that should not be strictly scrutinized. But these six are evenly split about whether the standard of review that should be used is (1) a moderately-severe balancing test (the plurality's view) or (2) a very deferential standard under which, when the impact of the restriction is "not severe," the state's burden of justification should be *"minimal"* so that the state's interests merely need to be *"reasonable"* (the Scalia concurrence's view).

b. **Denial of vote to felons:** Many states deny the vote to *felons*, even ones who have served their sentence and finished any parole. It's clear that such measures won't receive strict scrutiny, and will at least as a general matter be upheld. Such disenfranchisement was **upheld** by the Court in *Richardson v. Ramirez*, 418 U.S. 24 (1974). The Court relied on the rarely-invoked §2 of the Fourteenth Amendment, which calls for reduced representation for states which deny the vote to residents, but which makes this sanction inapplicable in cases of "participation in rebellion, or *other crime*." The majority in *Richardson* felt that §2 demonstrated Congress' intent to permit disenfranchisement as a sanction for crime.

c. **Burden on right to vote by limiting voter's choices:** The restrictions we have examined so far typically had the effect, where they applied at all, of *preventing the voter from voting at all*. But suppose the state regulation of voting merely has the effect of *"burdening"* the right to vote, by *limiting the voter's choices*. Here, as in the voter-ID and disenfranchisement-of-felons scenarios just discussed, the Court does *not* use strict scrutiny; instead, the Court balances the degree of burden against the magnitude of the state's interest, and the Court is slow to strike down the regulation. It was in such a case involving a voter-choice-limiting regulation that the Court first articulated the rule relied on by the plurality in *Crawford*, supra, that "When a state election law provision imposes only *'reasonable, nondiscriminatory restrictions'* upon the First and Fourteenth Amendment rights of voters, the state's important regulatory interests are **generally sufficient** to justify" the restrictions. *Burdick v. Takushi*, 504 U.S. 428 (1992).

   i. **Ban on write-in votes:** For example, in *Burdick*, the Court held that Hawaii could *completely ban* all *write-in votes*. So long as the state gave candidates reasonable access to the ballot (thus preserving each voter's interest in having a reasonable choice of candidates), the state was not required to protect each voter's interest in being able to vote for *any* candidate of his choosing.

5. **Inequality in ballet-counting procedures:** As the result of the Court's decision that effectively handed the 2000 presidential election to George W. Bush over Al Gore, voters now seem to have some sort of equal protection right to have their votes *counted according to uniform standards*. *Bush v. Gore*, 531 U.S. 98 (2000).

a. **Facts:** The election came down to the vote in Florida. The Florida Supreme Court ordered that a statewide recount of all "undervotes" be conducted. ("Undervotes" are ballots on which, according to the machine tabulation, no candidate was selected.) The U.S. Supreme Court issued a stay blocking the continuation of this recount, then decided that no constitutionally-acceptable recount could be completed within the time available.

   i. **Chads:** Most Florida counties had a punch-card system which required a voter to perforate the ballet by a stylus. The ballots in dispute were mainly ones in which the voter did not completely perforate the ballot, making the vote uncountable by machine. Many of these ballots left a piece of the card hanging by one, two, or three corners (a "hanging chad") or contained mere indentations indicating perhaps that the voter had tried but failed to punch the card (an "indented chad.")

ii. **No uniform standards:** The Florida Supreme Court ordered a hasty manual statewide recount of all of these undervotes, without specifying uniform standards for determining when a vote should count. For example, it was left to each county's election commissioners to decide whether an indented chad should count.

iii. **Partial counts accepted:** The Florida Supreme Court also ordered that in those instances where counties had reported partial counts from recounts that had not been finished by the prior state-law deadline, those partial recount totals be accepted as legal votes.

b. **Holding:** By a 5-4 vote, the U.S. Supreme Court ruled that the entire recount procedure violated voters' equal protection rights. The Court's conservative bloc (Rehnquist, Scalia, Thomas, O'Connor and Kennedy) voted together to form a majority, and the liberal bloc (Stevens, Souter, Breyer and Ginsburg) dissented.

i. **Rationale:** The unsigned per curiam opinion for the Court said that "The right to vote is protected in more than the initial allocation of the franchise ... Having once granted the right to vote on equal terms, the state may not, by later arbitrary and disparate treatment, value one person's vote over that of another." To the majority, the recount mechanisms "do not satisfy the *minimum requirement* for *non-arbitrary treatment of voters* necessary to secure the fundamental right [to vote]. ... The formulation of uniform rules to determine intent ... is practicable and, we conclude, necessary." The majority pointed out that "the standards for accepting or rejecting contested ballots might vary not only from county to county but indeed within a single county from one recount team to other."

ii. **Not enough time:** Normally, the equal protection problem would have been taking care of by ordering the Florida Supreme Court to issue uniform standards for the recount. But the high court was ruling on Dec. 12th, and the 12th was already the last day on which the state could certify its vote and still be certain that that vote would not be challenged in Congress. That is, Dec. 12 was the last day to use the "safe harbor" built into the federal system. The five members of the majority believed that holding a fresh constitutionally-adequate recount, and requiring Florida to miss the safe harbor, would have violated Florida's own election code, made binding upon the presidential election by the Constitution. Therefore, there could be no recount, and the original Florida certification of Bush as the winner stood.

c. **Dissent:** Of the four dissenters in *Bush v. Gore*, two (Souter and Breyer) believed that the lack of uniform standards indeed raised serious equal protection problems. But those two believed that the way to handle the problem was to remand to the Florida Supreme Court with instructions that the state could try to get the recount done, with uniform standards, by the Dec. 18 final deadline. The other two dissenters (Stevens and Ginsburg) believed that the equal protection problem was not substantial.

d. **Significance:** *Bush v. Gore* probably does not have much significance for future elections. The majority took pains to observe that "[o]ur consideration is *limited to the present circumstances*, for the problem of equal protection in election processes generally presents many complexities." However, the case probably does stand for at least the vague proposition that there are some equal-protection limits to how much variation is tolerable in the standards for determining whether a ballot is a legal vote.

6. **Dilution of votes:** The Court has also recognized a voter's *fundamental right* not to have his vote *diluted* by use of electoral districts that are not constructed strictly on the basis of *population*. The "reapportionment" cases (especially *Reynolds v. Sims*, the case establishing "one man, one vote" as a constitutional principle) are discussed as part of the treatment of political questions, *infra*, p. 733.

7. **Fifteenth Amendment:** When you analyze a governmental action that arguably restricts of the right to vote, do not overlook the *Fifteenth Amendment*, which in §1 says that "The right of citizens of the United States to *vote* shall not be denied or abridged by the United States or by any State on account of *race, color, or previous condition of servitude.*" (§2, a provision analogous to §5 of the Fourteenth Amendment, see *infra*, p. 441, gives Congress the power to "enforce this article by appropriate legislation.") As we have already seen, most restrictions on the right to vote are given Fourteenth Amendment due process/ fundamental rights analysis. But occasionally, a direct limit on the right to vote on racial grounds will be found to violate the Fifteenth Amendment.

> **Example:** The Hawaiian Constitution provides that the trustees of the Office of Hawaiian Affairs (OHA) may be elected solely by persons who are descendants of the original Native Hawaiians who inhabited the island prior to Captain Cook's arrival in 1778. *Held*, this provision constitutes racial discrimination in voting, and therefore violates the Fifteenth Amendment. *Rice v. Cayetano*, 528 U.S. 495 (2000).

D. **Access to the ballot:** Related to the "right to vote" is the right of a person to *be a candidate*, and of members of a *political party* to *place their candidate on the ballot.*

1. **State interest in regulating elections:** Before we look at whether these "rights" to ballot access really exist in a constitutional sense, consider the state's interest in *limiting* the presence of candidates and parties on a given ballot. There are two main interests which a state may be pursuing when it attempts to control the number of candidates or parties listed: (1) the interest in *reducing voter confusion*; and (2) the interest in maximizing the probability that the winning candidate will have received a *majority* of the *popular vote*. See N&R, p. 877. If these goals are not met, there is a danger that the result will be "only the cacophony of an atomized body politic, not the orchestrated voice of an electorate." Tribe, p. 1097.

2. **Interest of candidates, parties and voters:** However, there are a number of countervailing interests in easy ballot access, on the part of: (1) individuals who wish to be candidates; (2) members of minor or newly-formed parties; and (3) the voters themselves. These interests may be summarized as follows:

   a. **Interest in being a candidate:** Individuals clearly have an *interest in being a candidate*. While the Supreme Court has never recognized this interest as being a "fundamental right" (and has probably implicitly decided that it is not), the interest clearly has some constitutional weight. It is related to the First Amendment right of free speech, and to the general right to participate in the political process.

   b. **Party's right of association:** A group of individuals has a strong interest in being able to *band together to form a political party*. In fact, *freedom of association*, guaranteed by the First Amendment (see *infra*, p. 608) clearly requires that they be permitted to do so. It is less clear, however, that freedom of association requires that they be permitted to be an *effective* party, in the sense of being able to place their candidates on the ballot. In general, the Supreme Court has held that this right of association does mean that parties with *significant popular support* must be given *reasonable opportunities to appear on the ballot.*

c. **Voters' interest in suitable candidate:** The *voters* have an interest in being offered a variety of candidates representing a *range of political views*. While there is certainly no constitutional requirement that every voter be offered a candidate matching the voter's own views, a system which consistently prevented participation by candidates representing particular controversial views (at least if shared by a significant part of the electorate) would probably be constitutionally suspect. See Tribe, p. 1100, n. 13.

3. **Candidate eligibility rules:** Some requirements concern the *eligibility* of the *individual candidate*. Since there is no general "right to be a candidate" which the Supreme Court has been willing to recognize as fundamental, these restrictions are generally reviewed under the highly deferential "mere rationality" standard. Thus *minimum age* requirements, and requirements that the candidate have *resided for a certain period of time* in the state or district where he is seeking office, have generally been *upheld*, on the grounds that they are rationally related to a legitimate state interest (e.g., the interest in having elected officials who have reasonable experience and maturity, and who have an interest in matters concerning their constituency). See Tribe, pp. 1100-01.

a. **Violation of other constitutional right:** Candidate eligibility requirements may not, of course, violate any other *independent* constitutional right. For instance, if a state imposed an unusually long *state residency* requirement for candidacy (e.g., four years), a strong argument could be made that such a requirement violates the individual's *right to interstate migration* (*infra*, p. 367), or at least that the requirement should be given scrutiny. See Tribe, p. 1101.

4. **Party organization and popular support:** Many states require candidates to be *affiliated with a political party* in order to obtain a place on the ballot. (Special rules, usually fairly burdensome, govern independent candidacies.) Yet only those parties that have demonstrated a certain amount of *popular support* are generally entitled to place their candidates on the ballot. In some states, the popular support requirements (perhaps coupled with requirements of an elaborate party structure, and use of nominating conventions) are quite burdensome; in such states, candidates from the two major parties have an even greater than usual advantage.

a. **Overall Supreme Court view:** The Supreme Court has decided several major cases concerning the extent to which such popular-support and organizational requirements may be placed upon newly-formed or minor parties. These cases do not yield an easily-stated unified principle. However, the cases taken together do seem to hold that: (1) states may, in order to keep ballots from becoming confusingly large, require parties (or independent candidacies) to show a *significant amount of community support*; but (2) the restrictions may not be so great that minority parties or independent candidates have *no realistic chance* of getting on the ballot. See Tribe, p. 1110-01.

b. *Williams* **case:** The first of the cases, *Williams v. Rhodes*, 393 U.S. 23 (1968), was quite easy to decide, since the ballot access restrictions there were so severe that even a party with significant popular support stood almost no chance of getting on the ballot.

    **i.**   **Facts:**   The Ohio law struck down in *Williams* required a minor party (defined as one which had not received 10% of the votes in the previous gubernatorial election) to meet, as a condition to getting on the presidential ballot, three stringent requirements: (1) the filing, earlier in the election year, of petitions signed by *15%* of the number of votes cast in the prior gubernatorial election; (2) the creation of an *elaborate party structure*; and (3) the conducting of *primaries*. The statute also *forbade independent* and *write-in* candidacies. The law was challenged by the American Independent Party, whose candidate, George Wallace, was blocked from the 1968 presidential ballot.

**c.**   **Statute struck down:**   A majority of the Court found that the scheme violated the equal protection rights of minority parties, since it made it *"virtually impossible"* for a new party, even one with hundreds of thousands of members, to get a place on the ballot, and therefore gave a large advantage to the two existing major parties.

    **i.**   **Interests implicated:**   The majority found that two specific constitutional interests were impaired by the statute: (1) the right of individuals to *associate* for advancement of their political beliefs; and (2) the right of *voters* to *"cast their votes effectively."* These interests were sufficiently important that *strict scrutiny* should be applied to the state law.

    **ii.**   **State interests inadequate:**   None of the state's asserted interests was sufficiently compelling, when measured under this strict test. For instance, the state's desire to promote the two-party system might be legitimate (the Court did not decide), but giving a permanent monopoly to two *particular* parties, Republicans and Democrats, was clearly not.

**d.**   *Jenness:*   The next case, *Jenness v. Fortson*, 403 U.S. 431 (1971), marks the other end of the spectrum, i.e., a set of restrictions so lenient that they were clearly constitutional.

    **i.**   **Facts:**   *Jenness* was a challenge to a Georgia rule which permitted independent candidates (i.e., ones with no party affiliation) to appear on the ballot, but only if they filed petitions with the signatures of at least 5% of the number of votes in the previous election. Petitions could be filed later in the election year than they could in *Williams.*

    **ii.**   **Holding:**   The Court found this situation vastly different from that in *Williams*, and quickly upheld the scheme. A key distinction was that Georgia, unlike Ohio, "in no way freezes the status quo, but implicitly recognizes the potential fluidity of American political life."

**e.**   **Middle-ground cases:**   If *Williams* and *Jenness* represent two ends of the spectrum of ballot-access restrictions, later cases discuss restrictions that are somewhere in the middle. In these later cases, the Court has seemed to apply a kind of mid-level review: The Court upholds the ballot-access measure as long as it is a *"reasonable and non-discriminatory"* way of achieving an *"important"* state interest, such as the maintenance of "ballot integrity" or "political stability."

     **i.  Organization requirement:**  For instance, a Texas requirement that minor parties hold precinct, county and state ***nominating conventions*** was ***upheld***, in *American Party of Texas v. White*, 415 U.S. 767 (1974). The key factor was the lack of discrimination against minor parties; since *major* parties in Texas were required to hold these three types of conventions in order to promulgate party platforms, the minority parties were not placed at a relative disadvantage. (But in a state where the major parties do ***not*** hold such conventions, presumably the requirement that minority parties do so would be a violation of their right to equal protection.)

     **ii.  Ban on fusion candidates:** Similarly, the Court has held that a state may prohibit a party from putting a *"fusion"* candidate on the ballot, i.e., a candidate who has ***already been nominated by another party***. *Timmons v. Twin Cities Area New Party*, 520 U.S. 351 (1997). The minor party in *Timmons* argued that the rule against fusion candidates abridged its freedom of association (mostly by giving popular candidates a large disincentive to accept the minor party's early nomination). But the Court upheld the rule, on the grounds that it was a "reasonable [and] nondiscriminatory" way of achieving the state's "important regulatory interests" in "ballot integrity" and "political stability."

   **f.  Empirical test:**  In gauging the effect of signature requirements, organizational requirements, etc., the Court generally takes into account the ***actual historical success or failure*** that minor parties have had in getting on the ballot. Obviously, the more often minor parties or independent candidates have in fact succeeded in getting on the ballot, the less likely the Court will be to find a violation of equal protection. See Tribe, p. 1111.

  **5.  Filing fees:**  *Filing fee* requirements imposed on candidates will be struck by the Court, if they prevent ***indigent*** candidates from appearing on the ballot. In *Lubin v. Panish*, 415 U.S. 709 (1974), the Court unanimously invalidated a California filing fee set at a percentage of the salary for the position being sought (a $700 fee in plaintiff's situation). The Court reasoned that a state may not charge a candidate filing fees which he is incapable of paying, unless it gives him alternative means of getting on the ballot (e.g., by filing a petition demonstrating popular support).

  **6.  Right to be a candidate:**  *Lubin* spoke in terms of the right of an indigent candidate to get on the ballot, not the right of ***voters*** to choose an indigent candidate. This seems to be the closest the Court has come to suggesting that there may be ***an independent constitutional right to be a candidate***. See Tribe, p. 1111. However, the existence of such a right is not at all clear, in light of the Court's failure to find such a right in other cases.

 **E.  Access to courts:**  Existence of a classification based on ***wealth*** has never, by itself, been enough to trigger strict scrutiny. But where the state ***imposes fees*** which have the effect of preventing the poor from gaining access to a significant constitutionally-protected right, the Court has sometimes been willing to apply strict scrutiny. This was the case, for instance, with respect to the poll tax and with respect to candidate filing fees (*supra*, p. 355 and 364). The Court has at times made the ***litigation process*** another such area; state-imposed fees or other economic barriers which prevent the poor from ***gaining access to the courts*** may be subjected to strict scrutiny, if the particular type of judicial access being sought is found to be sufficiently important.

1. **No general principle:** The Court's course in the area of judicial access has been confused and changing, so that it is difficult to state a general principle. Generally, the Court has shown a greater likelihood of striking down barriers to the pursuit of judicial remedies in *criminal cases* than it has in most *civil* contexts.

2. **Equal protection vs. due process:** Nor is it clear whether equal protection or due process is the relevant doctrine in these cases. Sometimes, the Court has seemed to hold that *due process* is what matters: if fundamental procedural fairness requires that all persons, rich or poor, be given a particular type of judicial access, the Court will order this to be done, without focusing on the distinction between rich and poor. In other cases, however, the issue has been one of equal protection: if the type of access sought is judged to be highly important, the Court has decided that what the rich are permitted to pay for, the poor must be given, in order to avoid what the Court sees as the unfairness which would inhere in making the access in question available only to those who can pay for it.

    a. **Equal protection dominant:** The *equal protection* aspect appears to have *dominated* the Burger/Rehnquist Court's decisions. However, the due process aspect crops up from time to time (e.g., in *Little v. Streater, infra*, p. 367, involving an indigent paternity defendant's right to blood-grouping tests).

3. **Not "fundamental" rights:** The Court has generally *not* labeled the rights at issue in these judicial-access cases as *"fundamental"* ones. But it has conceded that the rights at issue are highly important, and that they merit at least some extra measure of constitutional protection. Unlike the right-to-vote cases, where the right itself was "fundamental," and therefore was sufficient to trigger strict scrutiny, the judicial-access cases have generally involved strict scrutiny only where there was a *combination* of a *"quasi-suspect" wealth classification* (usually in the form of a state-imposed *fee*) *and* an *important interest.*

4. **Cutting back by Burger/Rehnquist Court:** The most important cases giving special protection to judicial access by the poor came during the Warren era. In both the criminal and civil areas (probably more so in the latter), post-Warren Courts have curtailed, though not completely overturned, the Warren-era results.

5. **Transcripts:** The first Warren-era case involved the right of indigents to a *trial transcript* in *criminal appeals*. In *Griffin v. Illinois*, 351 U.S. 12 (1956), the Court held that the state *must provide indigent criminal defendants with a trial transcript*, if such a transcript is *necessary for effective appellate review.*

    a. **Rationale:** *Griffin* was decided on both equal protection and due process grounds. In ringing rhetoric (which was never taken to its logical conclusion in subsequent, harder cases), the Court observed that "[t]here can be no equal justice where the kind of trial a man gets depends on the amount of money he has."

    b. **Harlan dissent:** But Justice Harlan, in dissent, made a point which has had continued relevance in cases involving wealth criteria. He observed that in the usual equal protection case, the state *makes a classification*, and places disabilities upon persons falling on one side of the classifying line. Here, by contrast, by charging a fee for transcripts the Court was *not making any classification at all*; it was simply failing to "alleviate the consequences of differences in economic circumstances that exist wholly apart from any state action."

    **i.**    **Consequence:**   Consequently, Harlan argued, the majority was imposing on states "an affirmative duty to lift the handicaps flowing from differences in economic circumstances" and was interpreting equal protection to require that "Illinois must give to some what it requires others to pay for." This was not the meaning of the Equal Protection Clause, Harlan contended.

   **c.**   **No "right" to an appeal:**   Even the majority agreed with Harlan that there was *no "right" to an appeal*; the state could, for instance, provide that a criminal trial was simply the final judicial event. But what the states could not do, in the majority's view, was to grant an appeal to some (those who could pay for a transcript) and not to others.

**6.**   **Counsel during appeal:**   Then, the Warren Court held that indigent criminal defendants had the right to the *assistance of counsel* on appeal, at least if: (1) this was the first appeal taken in the case; and (2) the appeal was granted as a matter of right (not judicial discretion) to all persons. *Douglas v. California*, 372 U.S. 353 (1963). The decision was, like *Griffin*, based on both equal protection and due process grounds.

**7.**   **Discretionary appeals:**   *Douglas* did not deal with the right to appointed counsel in *discretionary* appeals. But in the later case of *Ross v. Moffitt*, 147 U.S. 600 (1974), the Court explicitly *refused* to find such a right in discretionary appeals.

   **a.**   **Rationale:**   Most of the majority's opinion was addressed to the equal protection argument. The majority distinguished *Douglas*, on the grounds that the interest in equal access to appellate review was "one of degrees," and that denial of counsel's assistance in discretionary appeals (e.g., appeals to the highest state court or petitions for *certiorari* to the U.S. Supreme Court) was only a "relative handicap," much less severe than lack of counsel during the initial appeal of right.

   **b.**   **Dissent:**   Three dissenters, Douglas, Brennan and Marshall, contended that the *Douglas* rationale should be applied even with respect to discretionary appeals.

**8.**   **Civil litigation:**   Indigents have also argued that filing fees and other payments to the state should be waived for them in *civil litigation*. But such arguments have generally been *unsuccessful*; in only one category of action, loosely *"family law,"* has the Court agreed that indigents are entitled to access to the civil courts.

   **a.**   *Boddie:*   The main family-law decision involved *divorce*. That case was *Boddie v. Connecticut*, 401 U.S. 371 (1971). The parties seeking divorce were welfare recipients who could not pay the $60 filing fee. The Supreme Court agreed that *denial of access to divorce was a violation of the plaintiffs' due process rights.*

      **i.**   **State monopolization as factor:**   Two factors were found by the Court to be basic to this due process conclusion: (1) marriage occupies a *fundamental place* in our society's scheme of values; and (2) the *state* has a *monopoly* on the means for dissolving this relationship. Thus access to divorce is quite different from use of the civil courts for the *resolution of private disputes*; in the latter situation, other, nonjudicial, means of resolution are generally available.

   **b.**   **Not applicable to bankruptcy:**   Post-Warren Courts have taken an extremely narrow view of what other situations, apart from family law, entitle indigents to civil court access. For instance, indigents do *not* have a right to a waiver of the $50 filing fee for *bankruptcy*, the Court held in *U.S. v. Kras*, 409 U.S. 434 (1973).

**c. Review of welfare terminations:** Similarly, the Court has held that indigents could be forced to pay a $25 filing fee in order to gain judicial review of ***welfare-benefit terminations.*** *Ortwein v. Schwab*, 410 U.S. 656 (1973). By the same 5-4 majority as in *Kras*, the Court held that welfare payments were in the area of "economics and social welfare," and thus had "far less constitutional significance" than the interest in divorce.

**d. Other family-law contexts:** But the Court *has* granted fee relief to indigents in two contexts that are theoretically civil, but that have a ***family-law*** dimension:

    **i. Paternity suits:** First, in *Little v. Streater*, 452 U.S. 1 (1981), the defendant was an indigent against whom a ***paternity action*** had been brought. The Court held that he was entitled to ***state-subsidized blood grouping tests*** to determine whether he could have been the child's father.

    **ii. Termination of parental rights:** Then, the Rehnquist Court held that where a child's father successfully sued to have the child's mother's ***parental rights terminated*** so that the child could be adopted by the father's wife, the state had to pay for a ***trial transcript*** to be used by the mother on ***appeal***. *M.L.B. v. S.L.J.*, 519 U.S. 102 (1996). In that case, the decision seemed to turn more on the "quasi-criminal" nature of the proceeding than on the fact that it involved family-law matters. But the Court characterized "the interest of parents in their relationship with their children" as being "fundamental."

**e. Summary:** So where the proceeding is nominally *"civil,"* an indigent has ***no general right to fee relief.*** Thus actions for ***bankruptcy*** and for review of ***welfare terminations*** fall into this general "no equal protection right to fee relief" category. But an indigent *does* have an equal protection right to fee relief in three situations falling within the family-law area: actions for ***divorce***, for ***determinations of paternity***, and for ***termination of parental rights***.

**F. The right to travel:** We live in a federal system, one of the basic principles of which is that ***any American is free to travel from state to state***, and to ***change his state of residence*** or employment whenever he desires. This ***"right to travel"*** (or, a better way of putting what is usually being litigated, this ***"freedom of interstate migration"***) is not explicitly given by any one constitutional provision. But the Court has nonetheless treated the right as ***"fundamental."*** Consequently, when a state treats ***newly-arrived residents*** significantly *less favorably* than those who have lived in the state longer, strict equal protection scrutiny may be triggered.

**1. *Shapiro v. Thompson:*** The classic case applying strict equal protection scrutiny to classifications penalizing the "right to travel" (or to migrate interstate) is ***Shapiro v. Thompson***, 394 U.S. 618 (1969). In that case, the Court invalidated the denial by two states and the District of Columbia of ***welfare benefits*** to residents who had ***not resided in the jurisdiction for at least a year.***

**a. "Right to travel" rationale:** By requiring the one-year waiting period, the states were impairing the "fundamental right of interstate movement," the Court held. The Court declined to locate this right in any particular constitutional clause. Rather, the right derived from the fact that "the nature of our federal union and our constitutional concept of personal liberty unite to require that all citizens be free to travel throughout the length and breadth of our land. … "

b. **Severe impact:** Furthermore, what was being denied to newly-arrived residents was something of *extreme importance* — welfare aid "upon which may depend the ability of the families to obtain the *very means to subsist* — food, shelter, and other *necessities of life."*

c. **Strict scrutiny:** Because of this major interference with freedom to travel, the Court applied *strict scrutiny*, requiring that the one-year waiting period be *necessary* to achievement of a *compelling governmental interest*. None of the interests asserted by the state was sufficient.

   i. **Unconstitutional objectives:** In fact, several of the asserted state interests were flatly unconstitutional. For instance, the state's argument that it wished to preserve the financial integrity of the state welfare program by preventing an influx of indigent newcomers was itself flatly inconsistent with the newcomers' right to travel interstate.

   ii. **Other interests:** Other interests asserted (e.g., providing an "objective test of residency," discouraging fraudulent collection of payments from more than one state, etc.) were legitimate. But these interests were not "compelling," and could in any event have been served by less drastic means.

d. **Dissent:** There were three dissenters in *Shapiro*. The most important of the dissents was by Justice Harlan, who was especially concerned about the importance the majority attached to the fact that the newcomers might be deprived of "food, shelter, and other necessities of life" — Harlan feared that the Court might ultimately apply strict scrutiny to any classification bearing on the availability of such "necessities," an exception which he said would "swallow the standard equal protection rule" and make the Court a "super-legislature."

   i. **Fifth Amendment:** Harlan also thought that the right of interstate movement, which he conceded was an independently-valid constitutional right, could be and should be protected by resort to the *Fifth Amendment's Due Process Clause* rather than by the Equal Protection Clause.

e. **Aftermath of *Shapiro:*** Justice Harlan's fear that the Court would find a generalized fundamental right to the *"necessities of life*," triggering strict equal protection scrutiny whenever the state failed to guarantee those necessities to all citizens, never materialized. The Court's subsequent treatment of "necessities" is discussed in the section on wealth classifications, *infra*, p. 370-371. But the Court's recognition in *Shapiro* of a fundamental right to interstate travel, and its application of strict equal protection scrutiny of any classification impairing that right, have remained good law.

2. **Deterrent or penalty:** The *Shapiro* Court did not make clear exactly what sort of effect on the right to interstate travel must occur before that right would be impaired sufficiently so as to trigger strict scrutiny. The Court might have meant that the right was impaired only where the residency requirement was so obviously burdensome that it had a *deterrent effect* on interstate migration. But later cases have construed *Shapiro* to mean that the right to travel is impaired wherever it is *"penalized*," even if there is no actual deterrence. Thus since the one-year residency requirement for welfare payments caused substantial hardship to those who moved to the state (as the *Shapiro* Court found), this would be sufficient to trigger strict scrutiny, *even if there was no showing that anyone actually declined to migrate* because of the requirement.

a. **Medical benefits:** The principle that merely a "penalty," not an actual deterrent effect, is required to trigger strict scrutiny, was illustrated in the post-*Shapiro* case of ***Memorial Hospital v. Maricopa County***, 415 U.S. 250 (1974). That case struck down an Arizona requirement of one year's residence as a condition for indigents to receive free non-emergency *medical care*. The ability to receive such care was clearly not a significant deterrent to interstate migration, since it was unlikely that people would change or decline to change their state of residence to receive such care. Nonetheless, denial of the medical care was a "penalty" on the right to migrate, the Court held. As such, it was to be subjected to strict scrutiny, which it did not survive.

   i. **Definition of "penalty":** But, the Court in *Memorial Hospital* held, not all differences in treatment between residents and non-residents are "penalties"; only inequalities in distribution of ***"vital government benefits and privileges"*** are sufficiently severe to be considered penalties. The right to medical care was as much a "basic necessity of life" as were the welfare payments in *Shapiro*, so inequality in their distribution was a penalty.

b. **Divorce:** Other government-supplied benefits have been found to be less important, so that their denial to newcomers does ***not*** trigger strict scrutiny. For instance, Iowa's requirement that a person reside in that state for one year before suing a non-resident there for *divorce*, was *upheld*, in *Sosna v. Iowa*, 419 U.S. 393 (1975).

   i. **Rationale:** The majority did not speak in terms of "penalties." But it held that a requirement that a person wait one year for a divorce was a ***less severe hardship*** than waiting one year for medical benefits or welfare assistance — in the latter situation, some part of what was being sought would never be obtained (benefits applicable to the one year wait). In the divorce situation, by contrast, the plaintiff would ultimately end up with the very thing sought, i.e., an adjudication of divorce.

   ii. **Stronger state interest:** Furthermore, the countervailing state interest was much stronger in the divorce situation. In the welfare benefits and medical care cases, the state's interests were largely those of budget concerns and administrative convenience. Here, by contrast, the state had a strong interest in ***not becoming a "divorce mill"*** whose divorce decrees might be susceptible to collateral attack.

3. ***Bona fide* residence requirements:** Nothing in the Constitution, however, prevents the state from requiring that persons show that they are ***bona fide residents*** before receiving public services or benefits.

4. **Voting rights:** Some cases previously discussed in the ***voting rights*** area involve a right-to-travel component. For instance, in *Dunn v. Blumstein*, 405 U.S. 330 (1972) (*supra*, p. 357) Tennessee's duration-of-residency requirements for voting were strictly scrutinized not only because they burdened the fundamental interest in voting, but also because they impaired the interest in interstate travel.

5. **Privileges & Immunities Clause as alternate rationale:** Recall that there has been some confusion about just where in the Constitution the "right to travel" is granted. For instance, *Shapiro v. Thompson* (*supra*, p. 367) failed to specify where in the document the right was provided. But a 1999 case suggests that the "right to travel" should be founded upon the ***Fourteenth Amendment's Privileges and Immunities Clause,*** which prohibits

any state from abridging "the privileges or immunities of citizens of the United States." That case, *Saenz v. Roe*, 526 U.S. 489 (1999), is discussed *infra*, p. 383.

**G. Wealth classifications:** During the Warren Court, there were some indications that a broad range of government programs which arguably failed to take account of the special needs of the *poor* might be subjected to strict scrutiny.

1. **Possibility of suspect class:** Some observers expected this to happen by the placing of "wealth" on the list of *suspect classifications*.

2. **Possible "fundamental interest" in "necessities":** Alternatively, there were hints that the Warren Court might find a fundamental right or interest in the *"necessities of life,"* like food, shelter or clothing.

3. **Burger/Rehnquist Court declines to expand view:** But the Warren Court never explicitly held either that wealth without more was a suspect classification or that statutes impairing the right to "necessities" of life, without more, impaired a fundamental interest. The Burger/Rehnquist Court has explicitly *refused to support either of these propositions*.

4. **Not suspect classification:** For instance, in *James v. Valtierra*, 402 U.S. 137 (1971), the majority held that *wealth classifications*, unlike, say, racial ones, *simply do not trigger any heightened scrutiny.* The Court therefore upheld a California constitutional amendment providing that no low-income housing projects could be built in any community without achieving majority support in a popular referendum. The non-suspect nature of wealth classifications seems to have been reiterated (though this is not completely clear) in the school financing case, *San Antonio Ind. School Dist. v. Rodriguez, supra*, p. 351.

5. **No fundamental interest in "necessities":** Similarly, in a series of cases the Court also rejected claims that various *"necessities of life"* were fundamental interests whose impairment should trigger strict scrutiny.

   a. **Welfare benefits:** The first such area was that of *welfare benefits*. In ***Dandridge v. Williams***, 397 U.S. 471 (1970), the Court upheld a Maryland welfare scheme which set a maximum monthly payment of $250, regardless of family size or need.

      i. **Rationale:** The majority reasoned that the statute, like all welfare schemes, lay in the area of "economics and social welfare" and therefore called only for "mere rationality" review. The scheme satisfied this deferential standard, since it bore a rational relation to several legitimate state objectives (e.g., encouraging employment by prohibiting payments that might compare favorably with what a job would provide.)

      ii. **Marshall's "sliding scale" dissent:** Justice Marshall dissented in *Dandridge*. He conceded that strict scrutiny was not appropriate. But he also disagreed with the majority's finding that the traditional, deferential, "mere rationality" test was the correct one. Instead, he gave the first major exposition of his *"sliding scale"* theory: Rather than a rigid "two-tier" standard, by which all statutes are given either extreme deference or strict scrutiny, the degree of review should be adjusted along a *spectrum*, depending on: (1) the type of classification; (2) the *"relative importance* to individuals in the class discriminated against of the governmental benefits that they do not receive;" and (3) the strength of the interests *asserted by the state* in support of the classification. When this analysis was applied to the facts of *Dan-*

*dridge*, Marshall concluded that a significant degree of scrutiny should be given, since the welfare recipients' interest in the benefits was large, and (Marshall believed) the state's asserted interest in its scheme relatively weak. The scheme was not sufficient to withstand this significant scrutiny, he contended.

    **b. Housing:** Similarly, the right to ***housing*** is ***not*** a constitutionally fundamental one. See *Lindsey v. Normet*, 405 U.S. 56 (1972), where the Court applied deferential "mere rationality" review to a state statute making it relatively easy for landlords to evict tenants if the landlord claimed that the rent had not been paid.

    **c. Difficulties with contrary approach:** A contrary approach, holding that there *is* a fundamental interest in necessities, would pose large problems.

        **i. Extension of state's role:** It is true that the Court has required states to pay for certain goods rather than charging indigents for them (e.g., trial transcripts in *Griffin* and appellate counsel in *Douglas*). But the goods there, as well as in the "right to vote" cases, were used in ***areas in which the state is already dominant***. An extension of the fundamental rights doctrine to include necessities like food and shelter would expand the state's obligations into huge new areas, which until now have been left ***principally to the private sector***.

        **ii. Other difficulties:** Furthermore, there would be major difficulties in having courts determine issues like: (1) What level of food, shelter, clothing, etc. is so essential that one has a fundamental right to it? and (2) Does the claimant already have the resources to be able to purchase these goods? (and if he has part of the resources needed, what part?) Nor would it be appropriate for the court to be deferential to the legislature's statutes or regulations governing these matters, since the very idea of a fundamental right is that it is one as to which claims of impairment must be strictly scrutinized by the judiciary.

    **6. Procedural safeguards:** Keep in mind that in the welfare context and in cases involving other governmental benefits, ***procedural safeguards*** may accomplish part of the protection of the poor that the Burger/Rehnquist Court has been unwilling to impose in the name of equal protection. See, e.g., *Goldberg v. Kelly*, 397 U.S. 254 (1970) (*supra*, p. 213), holding that a person's welfare benefits may not be terminated without an administrative hearing at which certain procedural standards are adhered to.

---

*Quiz Yourself on*

## EQUAL PROTECTION — FUNDAMENTAL RIGHTS

**45.** The state of Booth has enacted a statute governing the issuance of absentee ballots in state elections. Under the statute, any male under the age of 65 will be issued an absentee ballot only upon written proof that the applicant will be unable to be present at the voting place on the scheduled day for the election. If the applicant is a female, however, no written proof is required, and the applicant's statement that she cannot be present at the polling place is accepted at face value. The motivation for the statute was the legislature's belief that many women voters are the mothers of infants, who cannot easily get to the polling place to vote. Marvin, a male resident of Booth, has attacked the requirement of written proof on the grounds that it violates his Fourteenth Amendment equal protection rights.

(a) What standard should the court use in reviewing the requirement of written proof? _____

(b) Will Marvin's attack succeed? _____

46. The county of Gardenia has established a Forest Conservation District. The purpose of this district is to levy a special tax on owners of forested property, and to use these funds to buy certain parcels of forested property in the county from willing sellers so that the property can remain forested. The ultimate purpose of the District is to ensure that there is enough forested land that erosion will not get a foothold locally, something that would happen if many forested parcels become denuded by logging. The district is to be administered by a Board of Directors having five members. The five members are to be elected annually. Only owners of forested property in the county are permitted to vote in the election for directors. Bruce, the owner of non-forested real estate, has sued for a declaration that the "one person, one vote" principle has been violated by this arrangement.

(a) What standard of review should the court use in deciding Bruce's challenge? _____

(b) Will Bruce's attack succeed? _____

47. The state of Illowa provided that in order for a "minor" party to have its presidential candidate appear on the ballot, the party must file petitions containing the signatures of 15% of all eligible voters in the state. (A party was defined as "minor" if it had not received at least 10% of the votes cast in the state in the previous presidential election.) The petition had to be filed nine months before the general election. Also, a minor party did not qualify for the ballot unless it conducted a primary election. Other Illowa electoral provisions prevented anyone from running for president as an independent, and did not allow for write-in candidacies for president. The Anti Washington Party, a newly-formed party dedicated to "throwing the rascals out of Washington," wished to have its candidate appear on the Illowa presidential-election ballot. The AWP sued on the grounds that these restrictions violated the equal protection rights of minority parties, as well as the freedom-of-association rights of party members.

(a) What standard should the court use in hearing this challenge? _____

(b) Will the AWP's attack on the restrictions succeed? _____

48. The state of Amazonia has a program called MedAmaz, which provides emergency medical assistance for indigent citizens. Under the rules for the program, a person who has moved to Amazonia is not eligible to receive emergency medical care until he or she has resided in the state for at least one year. Penelope, who moved to Amazonia three months ago from Ohio, needed an emergency appendectomy. The hospital refused to perform it because she did not meet the residency requirement, and Penelope almost died. Now, she has sued the state for damages, arguing that the residency requirement violated her right to equal protection of the laws.

(a) What standard of review should the court use? _____

(b) Will Penelope's attack succeed? _____

49. The state of New Canada has set its maximum welfare payment at $1,250 per month. For families of one child through three children, extra sums are paid for each additional child (with the $1,250 figure being paid for a family with three children). The net effect of the scheme is that a family does not receive any extra money for children after the first three. A further effect is that for a family of five children, the maximum paid by the state is 25% less than the federal poverty level. Hilda, a single mother of five children, whose only income comes from New Canada welfare payments, has sued the state, arguing that her fam-

ily's equal protection rights have been violated, in that the state has discriminated against large families such as hers.

(a) What standard of review should the court use in evaluating the statute? _____

(b) Will Hilda's attack succeed? _____

———————————

*Answers*

**45. (a) Strict scrutiny — the differential treatment must be necessary to achieve a compelling govern-mental interest.**

(b) **Yes.** Normally, a statutory scheme that distinguishes on the basis of gender must undergo merely mid-level review, i.e., it must be "substantially related" to the achievement of an "important" governmental interest. However, because the right to vote is **"*fundamental,*"** classifications disadvantaging this right are subjected to strict scrutiny. Therefore, unless the state can show that distinguishing between men and women in issuance of absentee ballots is necessary to achieve a compelling governmental interest, the restriction must fall. Here, even if the state is pursuing some kind of compelling interest (perhaps the need to avoid the fraudulent use of absentee ballots), it is highly unlikely that the gender-based discrimination chosen here is a "necessary" means to achieve that interest. For example, a provision that *each* person who wants to use an absentee ballot must furnish a written excuse would appear to be a satisfactory way to handle the fraud problem.

**46. (a) "Mere rationality" review.**

(b) **No, probably.** Normally, any deviation from the "one person, one vote" principle, will be strictly scrutinized, and will probably be found to violate the Equal Protection Clause. But the Supreme Court has made a limited exception for **"*special purpose*"** bodies, that is, governmental units having a strictly lim-ited purpose which disproportionately affects only one group. In that situation, the right to vote may be limited to the disproportionately-affected group. Here, since all funds disbursed by the district come from taxes on the owners of forested lands, and only such owners can receive the disbursed funds, this standard is probably satisfied. If so, the court will only give mere rationality review to the arrangement. Since lim-iting votes for a body to those who have some interest in the body's actions is a rational way to achieve the body's purposes, the mere rationality standard is probably satisfied. See *Ball v. James.*

**47. (a) Strict scrutiny.**

(b) **Yes, probably.** States are certainly entitled to impose ballot restrictions to ensure that only parties with a certain degree of popular support appear on the ballot. However, where ballot restrictions are so severe that they prevent virtually any but the two established parties from getting candidates on the ballot, these restrictions will be strictly scrutinized and probably struck down. The restrictions here seem to be so severe that they would be almost impossible to meet, so the court will probably invalidate the restrictions. See *Williams v. Rhodes,* one of the few ballot-access cases containing a restriction so severe that the stat-ute was struck down; the restrictions here are virtually identical to those in *Williams.*

**48. (a) Strict scrutiny.**

(b) **Yes, probably.** Normally, when the state furnishes free goods or services, and does not discriminate against a suspect class, only a "mere rationality" level of review is used. But when the state is dispensing a **"*vital government benefit or privilege,*"** *and* the state treats **newly-arrived resident**s significantly less favorably than those who have lived in the state longer, strict scrutiny is used. The Supreme Court has held that even non-emergency medical care is a "vital government benefit or privilege" (*Memorial Hospi-*

*tal v. Maricopa County*), so emergency care certainly would be. The one-year residency requirement has the effect of treating recently-arrived people less favorably, so the conditions for strict scrutiny are met. It is doubtful that there is any state interest here that is "compelling" (the state's fiscal interest probably is not), and even more doubtful that a flat ban on any assistance to those who have not yet lived in the state for a year is a "necessary" method of achieving the state's objectives.

**49. (a) The "mere rationality" standard.**

**(b) No.** First, large families (or any particular family size) have has never been found to constitute a "suspect" or "semi-suspect" class. Nor are poor people members of such a class. Hilda's only hope would be to establish that one has a "fundamental interest" in the "necessities of life." However, the Supreme Court has explicitly held that welfare benefits and other "economic necessities" are *not* fundamental interests. See, e.g., *Dandridge v. Williams* (no fundamental interest in welfare benefits). Therefore, any classification system used by the state in allocating such economic necessities is judged by the easy-to-satisfy "mere rationality" standard. Here, the state's scheme bears a rational relation to several legitimate state objectives (e.g., encouraging employment by prohibiting payments that might compare favorably with what a job would provide).

---

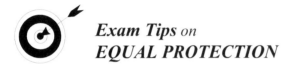

*Exam Tips on*
*EQUAL PROTECTION*

Equal protection issues, like due process ones, are often hidden, and are likely to be part of almost any complex fact pattern. It is not uncommon for 20-25% of a total Con. Law exam to consist of equal protection issues, scattered throughout multiple fact patterns. Here's what to look for:

☛ Above all else, anytime you see a legislative *classification* — a placement of people or businesses into *two or more groups* — think about the possibility that the classification might violate equal protection.

    ☞    For there to be an equal protection problem, the issue must be whether the government has behaved reasonably in *setting up* the classes in the first place. If the issue is whether the government has correctly placed an *individual* into the "right" group or class, you have a problem of procedural due process, not equal protection. (*Example:* If the government says, "All firefighters must retire at age 55," there is an EP problem because the issue is whether the government can set up the classes in this way. But if the government says, "Any firefighter too weak to do the work will be discharged," and the government then says, "Norman, you are too weak," the issue of whether Norman has been treated fairly is a procedural DP issue, not an EP issue, because the issue is whether the government has given Norman procedural regularity in deciding which class he falls into.)

    ☞    For there to be an EP problem, there must be *"discrimination"* against members of one of the classes, i.e., one class must be treated intentionally less favorably than the other. Use the adjective *"invidious"* to describe the required discrimination.

☞ If you state that P can make an EP attack on the classification at issue, state whether the attack would be "on the statute's *face*" or "*as applied*." Remember that a "facial" attack is used where the statute itself in its text discriminates against a class; an "as applied" attack is used where discrimination against one class stems from how the statute or regulation is *carried out*. (*Examples:* If government imposes a literacy test, or allows public prosecutors to use peremptory challenges, you're likely to be dealing with an "as applied" test.)

☞ Examine whether the discrimination is being practiced by a *state/local* government, or by the *federal* government. If it's the state or local government, then you're using the Fourteenth Amendment's EP Clause. If it's the federal government, you're using the Fifth Amendment's Due Process Clause, which by the process of "reverse incorporation" includes the principle of equal protection. (Especially in multiple choice tests, Profs like to give you an instance of federal discrimination and then try to tempt you to make a choice that involves "the Fourteenth Amendment's Due Process Clause," which is the wrong answer for the reason just stated.)

☞ Once you have identified an EP problem, devote extreme efforts to choosing the correct *level of review*. Remember that there are three levels used in evaluating EP situations:

☞ *Strict scrutiny* is used where either a classification is based upon a *suspect class* (race, national origin or alienage) or where the classification impairs the exercise of a *fundamental right* (e.g., the right to vote or the right to change your state of residence).

☞ *Mid-level* review is used for two "semi-suspect" classifications, those based on *gender* and *illegitimacy*.

☞ The *"mere rationality"* standard is used for all other types of classifications.

*Suggestion:* After you identify the issue, immediately state what the likely standard of review is, including details of that test. (*Example:* "Since the classification here is on the basis of gender, the Court will use a mid-level standard of review. That is, the Court will strike down the statute unless it is shown to be important to the achievement of a substantial governmental objective.")

☞ Here are the main things to remember about the *"mere rationality"* standard, and the places where it is used:

☞ If the classification relates to *economic* regulation, you will almost certainly be using "mere rationality." (*Examples:* The state says no one can put a sign on a rooftop, but gives an exception for a sign advertising goods produced by the owner of the building. Or, the state taxes one group more heavily than another (e.g., there's a sales tax on "refined petroleum," but not on "unrefined petroleum"). )

☞ Most types of *"social welfare"* classifications will also be judged by the "mere rationality" standard. (*Examples:* Discrimination based on *age*; discrimination against *aliens* where the function relates to the heart of representative government (see further discussion of aliens below); discrimination in the issuance of *licenses* or *permits*; discrimination against *out-of-staters*; discrimination against the *poor* (in the sense that government fails to pay for things the poor need that the rich can pay for themselves).

☞ If there's no suspect or semi-suspect class or fundamental right, and the government is trying to **combat an evil**, you'll probably note that the government has only attacked **part** of that evil. The question becomes whether the government has violated EP by not attacking the other evil. Here, you should say something like: "The regulation is valid, because the government is entitled to combat evils **one step at a time**." You might then want to cite to *Williamson v. Lee Optical Co.* (*Example:* The government requires lawyers, but not doctors, to take mandatory continuing education — this is OK, because the government may combat the evil of non-up-to-date professionals one step at a time.)

☞  If the government is trying to **single out an unpopular group** (but one that doesn't get suspect or semi-suspect status) for unfavorable treatment, indicate that although only "mere rationality" review is used, that review will be applied "with bite," and the scheme may well be struck down. Unequal treatment of **gays** and the **mentally retarded** seems to fall into this category.

☛ If the classification has to do with **race**, here are the key things to remember:

☞  Race is a **"suspect class."** Therefore, any intentional discrimination based on race — either in the face of the statute/regulation, or in the way it is applied — must be **strictly scrutinized**. That is, the classification must be struck down unless it is **necessary** to achieve a **compelling governmental interest**. You should almost always conclude that this standard is **not** satisfied. Typically, your reason will be because there is some alternative non-race-conscious method of handling the problem, so the race-conscious means are not "necessary."

☞  Remember that race as a suspect classification will not be deemed to be involved unless government is acting with the **purpose, not just the effect**, of classifying based on race. (*Example:* If government takes an action which happens to disadvantage more blacks than whites, there's no suspect class, and thus no strict scrutiny, unless there's evidence that government acted with the purpose of disadvantaging blacks.) **This is the single most commonly tested aspect of strict scrutiny.**

☞  Your fact pattern will usually **not** contain a racial classification "on its face." Yet, the facts will indicate to you that some racial group is affected more than other groups. This should be your tip-off that you have an " 'effect' vs. 'purpose' " problem.

☞  Keep in mind, however, that **circumstantial evidence** can always be used to show that government has the **intent** to discriminate against the unfavored group, and that the effect is not merely an unintended by-product. (*Example:* If government chooses grand jurors from the rolls of registered voters, the fact that this produces far fewer black grand jurors than other methods would is admissible as circumstantial evidence that the government really intended to discriminate against black grand jurors.)

☞  Remember that the discrimination must be **"invidious."** That is, there must be an attempt to treat some racial group in a **less favorable**, stigmatizing, way. You will want to examine whether this element of "invidiousness" is present whenever the governmental scheme tends to merely **record** racial differences, or to impose some kind of racial *"matching."* (*Examples:* If the government publishes the race of each political candidate, or the government requires that the race of an adoptive parent match the child's race, or the government imposes a sickle-cell test applicable only to African Americans, you'll want to examine whether there is a "stigmatizing" or "invidious" discrimination. Often, but not always, you will conclude that the answer is "yes.")

☞ Be on the lookout for *segregation* — any government program that intentionally *separates* the races, or intentionally encourages the races to separate themselves, is likely to be invidious and thus needs to be strictly scrutinized. (*Example:* If a state university allows dormitories to classify themselves, by vote of the existing residents, as "primarily black" or "primarily white," this probably represents intentional governmental support of segregation, and probably requires strict scrutiny.)

☛ Special rules apply to race-conscious *affirmative action*:

☞ *Strict scrutiny* is applied to the affirmative action situation just as much as to the "invidious" situation. Cite to *Richmond v. Croson* when you have a race-conscious affirmative action program.

☞ Typically, the only governmental objectives that are strong enough to overcome strict scrutiny in the affirmative action context are: (1) the eradication of *past discrimination* by government (and only if the discrimination is shown by *clear evidence*) and (2) the pursuit of *diversity* in a *student body*.

☞ The fact that it's *Congress*, rather than state or local government, that's doing the affirmative action now makes *no* formal difference — strict scrutiny is still applied. (Cite to *Adarand* if a congressional act is at issue.) However, you may want to allude to the possibility that even though the Court applies strict scrutiny, it may end up giving *slightly greater deference* to Congress' conclusion that race-conscious measures are needed, than it would to a similar conclusion by a state or local body.

☞ Be on the lookout for race-conscious affirmative action in *university admissions*. Here, say that this is OK (because student-body diversity can be a compelling objective) as long as the school (1) evaluates each applicant as an *individual*; (2) treats minority-race as merely *one "plus factor" among others*; and (3) *doesn't use mechanical means* (like *quotas* or a fixed number of "points") to obtain the desired number of minority-group admittees. Cite to the twin cases of *Grutter v. Bollinger* (race as an individualized "plus factor" is OK) and *Gratz v. Bollinger* (mechanical point systems are not OK) on this issue.

☞ Also, be on the lookout for race-conscious *pupil-assignment plans* for *public elementary or high schools.* Here, any plan that classifies each student's race, and makes any pupil assignment based on whether the student's presence would improve or worsen the target school's racial imbalance, will almost certainly flunk the requisite strict scrutiny. Cite to *Parents Involved v. Seattle School District* on this point.

☞ Here are some contexts in which race-conscious affirmative action programs may pop up on exams:

☞ preferential *admissions* to universities and public schools (see above);

☞ minority set-asides in the award of public *construction* and other *contracts*;

☞ allocation of public-sector *jobs* (including layoffs and promotions as well as original hiring);

☞ the drawing of *election districts*.

☛ The drawing of classifications based on *national origin* is also to be strictly scrutinized. However, exams rarely pose a national-origin problem.

☛ Here's what to look for when there is a classification based on *gender*:

☞ Remember that *mid-level* review is used for gender-based classifications. That is, the governmental objective must be *"important,"* and the means must be *"substantially related"* to that objective. (But note that this mid-level review is now a pretty tough standard, with the court requiring an "exceedingly persuasive justification," and giving "skeptical scrutiny." Cite to *U.S. v. Virginia*, the VMI case, as the source for these new descriptions of how the mid-level review is to be conducted.)

☞ Remember that the same review standard is in theory used whether the sex-based classification is "invidious" (intended to harm women) or "benign" (intended to help women). Any classification that derives in part from "stereotypical" views about women (e.g., that women's place is in the home, or that women are physically weak) is especially likely to be struck down.

☞ Where the classification disadvantages *men*, the same rules apply: mid-level review is used.

☞ As with race-conscious discrimination, only governmental action whose *purpose*, not mere effect, is to discriminate against one gender, will be considered. (*Example:* A strength requirement for paramedics would not be subjected to mid-level review, if the requirement's purpose was not to discriminate against women, and it was merely an unintended effect that fewer women than men could qualify.)

☞ Here are some areas where gender-based classifications have popped up on exams:

☞ (1) The government provides that pregnant women in the work force are to be treated differently than all others, e.g., with respect to exposure to toxic substances. (This is not necessarily true gender discrimination, since women who are not pregnant are not impacted, so probably you don't apply mid-level review, just "mere rationality" review);

☞ (2) Women are given different school activities than men. (*Example:* Women are not allowed to play football. Probably it's appropriate to use mid-level review, but the classification system will probably survive that review in light of the different average size and strength of women).

☛ Classifications based on *illegitimacy* are also "semi-suspect" and thus get mid-level review. Most commonly, you would be tested on a state statute that discriminates against illegitimates with respect to the right to *inherit*.

☛ Discrimination against *aliens* is very frequently tested.

☞ As a *general* rule, remember that discrimination against aliens is subjected to **strict scrutiny**. (*Examples:* A state's refusal of welfare benefits to aliens, or its refusal to let an alien practice a profession, will be strictly scrutinized.)

   ☞ Note that discrimination against "aliens" typically refers to discrimination against *legal* aliens. Probably strict scrutiny is *not* used for discrimination against *illegal* or "undocumented" aliens.

☞ Remember that there is a key *exception* to the general rule of strict scrutiny: where the alien has applied for a *job* that goes to the *"heart of representative government,"* only mere rationality review is used. Most government jobs that have a *policy*, *law enforcement* or *education* component fall within this "representative government" exception. (*Examples:* Jobs as a public school teacher, police officer, or probation officer are all within the exception, so the state merely has to be rational in its decision to close these positions off from foreigners.)

   ☞ But there are some jobs that are sufficiently ministerial that they do not fall within the "representative government" exception. (*Examples:* Secretary in a governmental agency; meter reader for a publicly owned electric utility.)

☛ Classifications impairing a *"fundamental right"* are tested less frequently than those involving a suspect or semi-suspect class. Nonetheless, these classifications sometimes pop up on exams.

   ☞ Any impairment of the right to *vote* is an impairment of a fundamental right, and thus strictly scrutinized, if it is *not reasonably related to determining the voter's qualifications.*

   *Examples:* (1) Poll taxes; (2) a requirement that the voter have resided in the jurisdiction for one year before the election; and (3) a requirement that the voter be a landowner or tenant, are generally not reasonably related to determining the voter's qualifications. Therefore, they'll be strictly scrutinized and struck down.

      ☞ But if the measure *is* reasonably related to determining the voter's qualifications, then it will be subjected only to *mid-level review*, and probably upheld.

      *Examples:* (1) A requirement that a voter present a government-issued photo ID; and (2) A requirement that a voter prove that he's a bona fide resident (e.g., by having lived in the jurisdiction for 50 days) won't be strictly scrutinized, and will probably be upheld.

      ☞ A person's right to be a *candidate* seems to be "semi-fundamental," and thus gets more-than-mere-rationality review. (*Example:* A high candidate filing fee that is imposed even on indigent candidates violates EP.) Similarly, restrictions that unfairly keep *new, not-yet-established, political parties* off the ballot get this semi-fundamental review.

   ☞ Access to the *courts* is sometimes a "fundamental interest." Look for situations where the state imposes a *fee* that it refuses to waive for indigents. The two contexts that count are *criminal* cases (so that the state may not charge an indigent for a trial transcript or for counsel) and *family law* cases (so that the state may not charge a filing fee to indigents who want a ***divorce***). But other types of civil access (e.g., small claims court or bankruptcy court) are not deemed "fundamental," so the state's refusal to subsidize indigents gets only mere rationality review.

☞ The ***"right to travel"*** (really the right to ***change*** one's state of ***residence*** or ***employment***) is "fundamental."

   ☞ Therefore, look for patterns where the state imposes a substantial ***waiting period*** on newly-arrived residents: if they have to do this wait before they get some ***vital governmental benefit*** (e.g., ***welfare***), a fundamental right has been impaired. But non-vital benefits are not "fundamental" (so that there's only mere rationality review where the state makes newcomers wait for, say, low in-state university tuition rates).

☞ The right to ***"necessities"*** is ***not*** fundamental. So if your fact pattern involves the state's refusal to equalize the right of indigents to such items as ***public school education, food, shelter or medical care***, you probably need to apply only "mere rationality" review, not strict scrutiny fundamental interest review.

Chapter 11

# MISCELLANEOUS CLAUSES: 14TH AM. PRIVILEGES & IMMUNITIES; TAKING; CONTRACTS; RIGHT TO BEAR ARMS; EX POST FACTO; BILL OF ATTAINDER

## *ChapterScope*

This chapter considers several clauses that have little in common except that they protect individuals against specific types of government conduct. The most important concepts in this chapter are:

- **Privileges and Immunities:** The 14th Amendment has a "Privileges and Immunities" Clause. But this clause is very narrowly interpreted: it only protects the individual from state interference with his rights of *"national"* citizenship (principally the right to *travel from state to state* and the right to *vote in national elections.*)

- **"Taking" Clause:** The Fifth Amendment's "Taking" Clause provides, essentially, that the government may take private property under its power of "eminent domain," but if it does take private property, it *must pay a fair price*.

  - **Land use regulations:** What the government calls mere "regulation" may occasionally amount to a "taking" for which compensation must be paid. This happens mostly in cases of *land-use regulation*. For a land-use regulation to avoid being a taking, it must satisfy two requirements: (1) it must *"substantially advance legitimate state interests"*; and (2) it must *not "deny an owner economically viable use of his land."*

- **"Contract" Clause:** The "Contract" Clause provides that "no state shall... pass any... law impairing the obligation of contracts." The meaning of this Clause depends on whether the government is impairing its own contracts or contracts between private parties:

  - **Public contracts:** If the state is trying to escape from its *own financial obligations*, then the Court will *closely scrutinize* this attempt: the state's attempt to "weasel" will be struck down unless the modification is *"reasonable* and *necessary* to support an *important* public purpose".

  - **Private contracts:** But when the state is re-writing contracts made by *private parties*, the state merely has to be acting *"reasonably"*, a much easier-to-satisfy standard. (And if the state's action is a *generally applicable* rule that has only the incidental effect of impairing contracts, the Contract Clause does not apply at all.)

- **Right to Bear Arms:** The Second Amendment has been held to guarantee private individuals the right to keep firearms at home for purposes of self-defense.

- **Ex Post Facto Laws:** Both the state and federal governments are prohibited from passing any "ex post facto" law. An ex post facto law is a law which has a *retroactive punitive effect*. So government may not impose a punishment for conduct which, at the time it occurred, was *not punishable*. Nor may government *increase* the punishment for an offense over what was on the books at the time of the act.

■ **Bills of Attainder:** Both state and federal governments are prohibited from passing any "bill of attainder". A bill of attainder is a legislative act which "applies either to **named individuals** or to **easily ascertainable** members of a group in such a way as to **punish** them without a **judicial trial**."

# I.   THE 14TH AMENDMENT'S PRIVILEGES AND IMMUNITIES CLAUSE

A.   **"Privileges and Immunities" Clause:** The *"Privileges and Immunities"* Clause of the Fourteenth Amendment comes at the beginning of the second sentence of Section I: "No State shall make or enforce any law which shall **abridge** the privileges or immunities of citizens of the United States. ... " At least some of the members of Congress who participated in the drafting of the Fourteenth Amendment expected and hoped that this Clause would constitute a substantial restraint on state government action against individuals. See Tribe, p. 550.

1.   *Slaughterhouse* **Cases:**   But the Supreme Court did not take this view. In the ***Slaughterhouse Cases***, 83 U.S. (16 Wall.) 36 (1873), the Court held (5-4) that the Fourteenth Amendment's Privileges and Immunities Clause merely forbade state infringement of the rights of **national** citizenship, not the rights of state citizenship.

   a.   **Facts of *Slaughterhouse* Cases:**   The *Slaughterhouse Cases* arose when Louisiana passed a law giving a monopoly on New Orleans-area slaughterhouses to a particular company. Butchers not included in the monopoly claimed that the statute deprived them of the opportunity to practice their trade, and thereby violated the Thirteenth and Fourteenth Amendments. The plaintiffs' most serious argument was that the statute was a denial of the privileges and immunities of Louisiana citizenship, including the right to practice one's calling.

   b.   **Argument rejected:**   But the Supreme Court rejected all of the plaintiffs' contentions, including the privileges and immunities argument. The Court observed that the first sentence of the Fourteenth Amendment distinguishes between U.S. citizenship (for which one need merely be born or naturalized in the United States) and state citizenship (for which residence is required). "Fundamental" civil rights, including the right to practice one's calling, were the domain of the states, not the federal government. Therefore, the plaintiffs should look to Louisiana law for protection; if there was no protection under Louisiana law (as apparently there was not), the plaintiffs were out of luck, since the Privileges and Immunities Clause added nothing to their rights in this area.

      i.   **Rights of national citizenship:**   The *Slaughterhouse* majority attempted to rebut the suggestion that under its interpretation, the Privileges and Immunities Clause accomplished nothing. The majority observed that there were several rights of "national" (as opposed to state) citizenship. The majority's short catalogue of "national" citizenship rights included "free access to ... seaports," federal protection "when on the high seas or within the jurisdiction of a foreign government," and a few other limited rights. These rights, the majority acknowledged, could not be infringed by any state, by virtue of the Fourteenth Amendment Privileges and Immunities Clause.

   **c. Minority view:** The four-Justice minority in the *Slaughterhouse Cases* flatly rejected the majority's limited reading of the Fourteenth Amendment Privileges and Immunities Clause. Even without the Fourteenth Amendment, the dissent argued, the privileges and immunities of national citizenship were already protected against state action (by virtue of the Supremacy Clause). Thus the majority view made the Clause utterly useless. The correct view, the dissent contended, was that the Clause guaranteed to every U.S. citizen that his "fundamental rights," rights which "belong to the citizens of all free governments," would not be infringed by any state. These fundamental rights included the right to "pursue a lawful employment in a lawful manner."

**2. View of clause until 1999:** Until 1999, the *Slaughterhouse* majority's view of the Fourteenth Amendment Privileges and Immunities Clause prevailed. For 125 years after that decision, only one state law was ever invalidated under the clause, and that decision was soon overruled. Only a few rights of "national" (as opposed to "state") citizenship were deemed protected, such as the right to **travel physically from state to state**, to petition Congress for redress of grievances, to **vote in national elections**, to enter federally-owned lands, and to be protected while in the custody of U.S. marshall (see *Twining v. New Jersey*, 211 U.S. 78 (1908)), and these were rarely even claimed to be abridged by state laws.

**3. View expanded in *Saenz*:** But then, a surprising 7-2 decision in 1999 breathed dramatic new life into the Fourteenth Amendment Privileges and Immunities Clause. In **Saenz v. Roe**, 526 U.S. 489 (1999), the Court held that the clause protects a particular and important aspect of the so-called "right to travel," namely the right of a person who has **recently become a citizen** of a state to the same privileges enjoyed by **longer-standing citizens** of that state. *Saenz* became only the second case in 125 years to strike down a state law on Fourteenth Amendment P&I grounds.

   **a. Welfare rights:** *Saenz* involved the right of a newly-arrived resident in California to receive the same state **welfare benefits** as a person who had been in the state longer. California, acting under express congressional authority, said that anyone who had resided in the state for less than one year would receive welfare benefits no greater than the level of benefits the person had received in her prior state of residence. (45 of the 49 other states had lower benefit levels than California.) Although California denied that the purpose of its provision was to deter the migration of poor people into California, the lower federal courts in *Saenz* found that this was indeed the statute's purpose.

   **b. Struck down:** The Court found that California's rule setting welfare benefits based on the recipient's state of prior residence violated the Fourteenth Amendment P&I Clause: ***"[T]he Clause does not tolerate a hierarchy of 45 subclasses of similarly situated citizens based on the location of their prior residence."*** Even if California was acting for the purpose of reducing expenditures (rather than in order to deter in-migration of poor people), using a means predicated on length of state citizenship was not acceptable, since a family's financial needs were not dependent on how long it had been in the state or where it had previously resided.

     **i.**  **Strict scrutiny:** The Court in *Saenz* seems to have applied ***strict scrutiny*** to California's rule disfavoring recent newcomers: the Court said that "[n]either mere rationality nor some intermediate standard of review should be used to judge the constitutionality of a state rule that discriminates against some of its citizens because they have been domiciled in the State for less than a year." California's fiscal justification did not come even close to satisfying this strict standard of review.

    **c.**  **Significance:** So *Saenz* probably means that the Fourteenth Amendment Privileges and Immunities Clause requires the states to ***satisfy strict scrutiny*** before they may ***treat newly-arrived residents less favorably than those of longer standing.***

        **i.**  **Bona fide residence requirements:** One last note: *Saenz* probably does not change the rule that a state is entitled to impose a ***requirement of bona fide residency as a pre-condition to receiving state benefits***.

  **4.**  **Distinguished from Article IV Clause:** It is important to distinguish the Fourteenth Amendment Privileges and Immunities Clause from the Privileges and Immunities Clause of Article IV, §2 (described *supra*, p. 100). To summarize the distinction: The Fourteenth Amendment Clause bars a state from abridging any U.S. citizen's rights of "national" citizenship (of which the most important now seems to be the right to travel, and relocate, from one state to another). The Article IV Clause protects rights of "state" citizenship, but only when a non-resident of the state is not treated the same as a resident with respect to an important state right, essentially a right involving commerce.

# II.   THE "TAKING" CLAUSE

**Introductory Note:** We turn now to two other specific constitutional protections of private (usually economic) interests: (1) the ban on the taking of private property for public use, without just compensation; and (2) the prohibition on the impairment of contracts. These two protections are related to the same concern which gave rise to the substantive due process doctrine, the danger that public action will interfere with private property rights. But the "taking" and "contract" clauses also protect an additional interest: the interest in "settled expectations," or as they are sometimes called, "vested rights." See Tribe, p. 587. The rationale behind the two clauses is that pre-existing interests in physical property and in contracts should not be disturbed by the government except under certain limited conditions.

**A.**  **The Taking Clause generally:** Governments, both state and federal, have the right to take private property for public use, provided that "just compensation" is paid. This power is known as the right of ***"eminent domain."*** Nothing in the Constitution explicitly confers this eminent domain power upon either the federal or state governments. But the Fifth Amendment, originally intended to apply solely to the federal government, provides that "private property ***[shall not] be taken for public use, without just compensation."*** This so-called Taking Clause is at least a "tacit recognition that the power to take private property exists." N&R, pp. 438-440.

1. **Two major issues:** A full discussion of the eminent domain power, and the accompanying obligation to pay just compensation, is beyond the scope of this outline. (The subject is treated more extensively in *Emanuel on Property.*) For present purposes, we are interested in the general aspects of two issues: (1) what is the borderline between a "taking" (for which compensation must be paid) and a mere "regulation" (for which no compensation is due)? and (2) when is a taking made for "private" rather than "public" use, so that there is no right of eminent domain, even if compensation is paid? The first of these issues is the more important.

2. **States subject to rules:** The federal government, as noted, is explicitly bound by the Fifth Amendment's ban on the taking of private property for public use without just compensation. The Supreme Court has repeatedly held that ***state governments*** are similarly prohibited, by the Fourteenth Amendment's Due Process Clause, from taking private property without paying for it. But since the Fourteenth Amendment Due Process Clause does not refer explicitly either to takings or to compensation, the theory by which the just compensation requirement is imposed on the states is not clear.

   a. **Competing views:** One view is that the Fifth Amendment just compensation requirement is directly incorporated into the Fourteenth Amendment Due Process Clause. An alternate view (which produces essentially the same result) is that the Fourteenth Amendment Due Process Clause, although more general, implicitly contains the same ban on takings of private property without just compensation as does the more explicit Fifth. See N&R, p. 440. In any event, essentially the same standards for determining when there has been a taking, and what constitutes just compensation, are applied to the states as to the federal government.

**B. The taking/regulation distinction:** If the court finds that private property has been "taken" by the government, compensation must be paid. But if the state merely ***regulates*** property use in a manner consistent with the state's "police power," then no compensation needs to be paid, even though the owner's use of his property, or even its value, has been substantially diminished. It thus becomes crucial to distinguish between a compensable "taking" and a non-compensable "regulation." Most of the cases requiring a distinction between taking and regulation have involved ***land use regulations***; these include zoning regulations, environmental-protection rules, landmark preservation schemes, and other schemes by which the government does not attempt to take title to a landowner's property but does regulate his use of that property.

Here are some of the principles governing when a land-use regulation will become a taking for which compensation must be paid.

1. **Physical use:** If the government makes or authorizes a ***permanent physical occupation*** of the property, this will ***automatically*** be found to constitute a taking, no matter how minor the interference with the owner's use and no matter how important the countervailing governmental interests. In ***Loretto v. Teleprompter Manhattan CATV Corp.***, 458 U.S. 419 (1982), the Court formulated this *"per se"* rule, and applied it to invalidate a statute which required landlords to permit cable television companies to install their cable facilities on the landlord's rental property. (The scheme permitted landlords to charge the cable companies what was in most instances a maximum one-time fee of $1.)

**a. Easement is physical occupation:** A post-*Loretto* case shows that the Court will take an expansive view of what kind of regulation constitutes a "physical occupation" of the owner's property. In that case the Court held that a state's refusal to grant a building permit except upon the transfer to the public of a permanent ***easement*** for the public to pass along a strip of the owners' property constituted a "permanent physical occupation" of that property. See *Nollan v. California Coastal Commission*, discussed more extensively *infra*, p. 391. The easement in *Nollan* would simply have permitted members of the public to walk along the owner's sandy strip parallel to the ocean on their way from one public beach to another. Even though this easement would not have permitted any given individual to remain on the owner's land, a physical occupation was found to exist, so that there was a taking of the owners' property.

2. **Diminution in value:** The more drastic the ***reduction in value*** of the owner's property, the more likely a taking is to be found. For instance, in ***Pennsylvania Coal Co. v. Mahon***, 260 U.S. 393 (1922), a landowner had bought the surface rights to land, and the house on it, under a chain of title which reserved to a coal company the right to mine coal from under the property. Thereafter, Pennsylvania enacted a statute preventing subsurface mining where a house might be caused to sink. The effect of the statute was to bar the coal company completely from mining under the owner's land.

   **a. Holding:** The Supreme Court held that the regulation so utterly impaired the right to mine coal that it was nearly the equivalent of an appropriation or destruction of the coal. Therefore, the regulation was a taking, which could not be carried out without compensation to the coal company. The Court, in a majority opinion by Justice Holmes, noted that "while property may be regulated to a certain extent, if regulation goes too far it will be recognized as a taking."

   **b. Dissent:** But a dissent, by Justice Brandeis, argued that the regulation was merely "the prohibition of a noxious use," and therefore did not require compensation. (The "noxious use" factor is discussed immediately below.)

   **c. Result may no longer be valid:** The result in *Pennsylvania Coal* may no longer be valid. In *Keystone Bituminous Coal Ass'n v. DeBenedictis*, 480 U.S. 470 (1987), the Court by a 5-4 vote upheld a modern (1966) Pennsylvania version of the statute struck down in *Pennsylvania Coal*. The 1966 statute required that 50% of the coal beneath existing public buildings and dwellings be left in place to provide surface support. The majority made some efforts to distinguish *Pennsylvania Coal*, but there is so little difference between the two statutes that it seems likely that *Pennsylvania Coal* would turn out the other way if decided today. However, the general principle for which the case is cited — that the more drastic the reduction in value of the owner's property, the more likely a taking is to be found — remains valid. (*Keystone* also illustrates that where the state is acting to prevent ***harm to the public***, the courts will be very reluctant to invalidate the regulation as a "taking." See the discussion of the "prevention of harm" rationale, *infra*.)

3. **Denial of all economically viable use of land:** Since (as just noted) the more drastic the reduction in value of the owner's property, the more likely a taking is to be found, it's not surprising that the Court has imposed a flat rule that a taking occurs where an owner has

been deprived of ***all economically viable use*** of his land. See *Agins v. Tiburon*, 447 U.S. 255 (1980).

a. **Particular use eliminated:** Cases in which such an extreme taking by deprivation of economically viable use is found are very rare. The fact that the ***particular*** use made by the plaintiff has been completely foreclosed will not be enough. For instance, suppose a parcel contains an aluminum smelter worth $100 million, and the city where the smelter is located then bans all smelting. The fact that P's *particular* land use — operation of the smelter — has been totally foreclosed will not be enough to make the regulation a "taking"; P is still free to convert the smelter to other uses, or even to raze it and put up some other structure (or sell it to someone who will).

b. **Total ban:** On the other hand, a ***total and permanent ban*** on the building of ***any structure*** on property *is* likely to be enough to deny the owner "all economically viable use" of his land, and thus to constitute a taking automatically. See, e.g., *First English Evangelical Lutheran Church v. Los Angeles County*, 482 U.S. 304 (1987) (*held*, a permanent ban on building any dwelling on the property constitutes denial of all economically viable use, and is thus a taking).

**Example:** South Carolina, in order to protect its coastline from continued erosion, enacts the Beachfront Management Act, which defines certain "critical areas" of erosion danger, and bars any owner of a lot in a critical area from building any permanent habitable structure on the parcel. P is the owner of two parcels which, at the time he bought them for nearly $1 million, were allowed to have houses built upon them; passage of the Act has the effect of preventing P from building any permanent structure on either lot. P contends that this "regulation" deprives him of all economic use of his property, and thus constitutes a taking. A lower state court agrees that P has been deprived of all economically viable use, but the South Carolina Supreme Court reverses on the grounds that even if this is true, the state may regulate to preserve its citizens' health and safety, and that such regulation is not a taking.

*Held* (by the U.S. Supreme Court), if P has truly been deprived of all economically viable use of his property, a "taking" has occurred. It is up to the South Carolina courts to decide whether P has really been deprived of all economically viable use. If he has been, a taking exists even though the state is trying to protect the health and safety of residents (unless the state already had, under the "background principles of the state's law of property and nuisance" the right to prevent the particular use by P, an issue to be decided by the state courts on remand; this aspect of the case is described *infra*, p. 389, Par. 6). ***Lucas v. South Carolina Coastal Council***, 505 U.S. 1003 (1992).

c. **Temporary moratorium on development:** In *Lucas*, the ban on all economically viable use of P's property purported to be permanent. What happens if the government merely imposes a *temporary* delay on all economically viable use of property, as where a planning board institutes a ***"moratorium"*** on development of certain property — is the government automatically required to pay just compensation for this delay? As a result of a post-*Lucas* case decided in 2002, the answer is ***"not necessarily"*** — the court will instead consider ***all the surrounding circumstances*** to determine whether the delay of all economically viable use was so severe as to require that compensation be paid. ***Tahoe-Sierra Preservation Council, Inc. v. Tahoe Regional Planning Agency***, 535 U.S. 302 (2002).

    **i.**  **Categorical ruling rejected:** The Supreme Court, by a 6-3 vote, ***refused*** to find a categorical right to compensation for such a temporary delay in the right to make any economically-viable use of one's property. In an opinion by Justice Stevens, the court said that "the answer to the abstract question whether a temporary [development] moratorium effects a taking is neither 'yes, always' nor 'no, never'; the answer depends upon the ***particular circumstances*** of the case."

        **(1) Distinction:** The Court distinguished sharply between physical takings and regulatory takings. Even a temporary physical occupation of P's property entitles him to compensation. But a similar rule for temporary regulatory takings would wreak havoc: "Land-use regulations are ubiquitous and most of them impact property values in some tangential way — often in completely unanticipated ways. Treating them all as *per se* takings would transform government regulation into a ***luxury few governments could afford.*** By contrast, physical appropriations are relatively rare, easily identified, and usually represent a greater affront to individual property rights."

        **(2) *Lucas* marginalized:** So as the result of *Tahoe-Sierra*, the *Lucas* decision is ***marginalized***. As Justice Stevens put it in *Tahoe-Sierra*, "the categorical rule in *Lucas* was carved out for the 'extraordinary case' in which a regulation ***permanently*** deprives property of all value; the ***default rule*** remains that, in the regulatory taking context, we require a more ***fact specific*** inquiry."

    **ii. Significance:** *Tahoe-Sierra* does *not* mean that a ban on all economically-viable use of one's property need not be compensated merely because it turns out to be temporary. The case merely means that there is no *automatic* right to compensation — instead, the surrounding circumstances must be considered in deciding whether there has been a taking. For example, if the property actually ***increased in value*** during the moratorium, that would probably strongly cut against a finding that there had been a taking.

**4.**  **"Prevention of harm" or "noxious use" rationale:**  A regulation rather than a taking is likely to be found where the property use being prevented is one that is ***harmful*** or "***noxious***" to others. For instance, a zoning ordinance may properly prevent the operation of a steel mill in the middle of a residential neighborhood; in general, anything which the common law would recognize as a public or private ***nuisance*** may be barred by regulation, without the need for compensation.

    **a.**  **Favoring one private interest over another:**  Occasionally, a zoning or other public decision that a land use is "noxious" will be the product of a clear decision to ***favor one private interest over another***. Nonetheless, the fact that a private interest, rather than the "public interest" as a whole, is being benefitted, will not render the regulation a compensable taking.

    **Example:** Many red cedar trees in the state of Virginia are infected with cedar rust, a disease that is highly dangerous to apple orchards. Virginia passes a law requiring the destruction, as a public nuisance, of all red cedar trees within a prescribed distance from an apple orchard. Cedar owners are paid only the cost of removing their trees, not the value of the trees.

*Held*, the ordinance, and the consequent uncompensated destruction of the cedars, were not a compensable taking. The state had the right to conclude that apple orchards were more important to the state economy than cedars, and its decision to sacrifice the latter to save the former did not violate due process. *Miller v. Schoene*, 276 U.S. 272 (1928).

b. **Bar must fall within common-law nuisance principles:** However, the mere fact that the legislature has labeled a certain use as being "harmful" or "noxious" is ***not enough*** to ensure that the land use restriction will be found to be a regulation rather than a taking. If a land use regulation is so severe that it deprives the owner of "all economically beneficial use of his land," then the restrictions must "do no more than duplicate the result that could have been achieved in the courts — by adjacent land owners ... under the State's law of ***private nuisance***, or by the State under its complementary power to abate nuisances that affect the public generally. ... " In other words, the legislature cannot suddenly decide that a particular use is so harmful that it should be immediately banned, if the ban will deprive an owner of all economically viable use of his land, and if the common law principles of nuisance would not allow the state to get the use forbidden by a court.

**Example:** Recall the *Lucas* case, *supra*, p. 387: South Carolina bans P and similarly-situated coastal land owners from building any permanent habitable structure on their property. *Held* (by the Supreme Court), given that the state courts have decided that this ban deprives P of all economically viable use of his land, then P has suffered a "taking" unless, under South Carolina law, the state could have achieved the same total ban on dwellings by use of the common law of nuisance. Furthermore, "it seems unlikely that common-law principles would have prevented the erection of any habitable or productive improvements on [P's] land; they rarely support prohibition of the 'essential use' of land." However, resolution of this issue is up to the South Carolina courts. *Lucas v. South Carolina Coastal Council*, *supra*, p. 387.

5. **Zoning regulation:** In cases where *zoning regulations* impair an owner's use of his property, the Court has been especially reluctant to find a compensable taking. A zoning ordinance will not be stricken as violative of due process unless it is ***"clearly arbitrary and unreasonable***, having no substantial relation to the public health, safety, morals or general welfare." *Moore v. East Cleveland*, 431 U.S. 494 (1977).

a. ***Moore:*** *Moore* itself was an extremely rare invalidation of a zoning ordinance. The ordinance there allowed only members of a "family" to live together, and defined "family" so narrowly that a grandmother was barred from living with her two grandchildren, one by each of two different children.

6. **Other environmental regulation:** Regulations designed to protect the ***environment*** are usually similarly subjected to only mild review, even if the property owner's ability to use his land is substantially circumscribed. See, e.g., *Goldblatt v. Hempstead*, 369 U.S. 590 (1962), upholding a town "safety regulation" preventing a property owner from continuing to mine a sand and gravel pit as he had done for 30 years; the ban was justified as a

"reasonable" exercise of the "police power," and the Court contended that the diminution in the value of the property, although relevant, was not conclusive. (But again, remember that if the regulation completely deprives an owner of economically viable use of his land, and that regulation could not be justified under common-law nuisance principles, a "taking" will occur even if the government's objective is to protect the environment. See *Lucas v. South Carolina Coastal Council, supra*, p. 387.)

7. **Landmark preservation:** *Landmark preservation* schemes, like zoning and environmental regulations, will *seldom* constitute a taking. In *Penn Central Transportation Co. v. New York City*, 438 U.S. 104 (1978), the Court found that the New York City Landmarks Preservation Law did not effect a taking of plaintiff's property.

   a. **Facts:** Plaintiff was the owner of Grand Central Terminal, which was designated as a "landmark" under the Law. As a consequence, the building's exterior was required to be kept "in good repair," and administrative approval was necessary for any alteration. Plaintiff sought such approval to construct a 55-story office building above the Terminal, but this request was denied on the grounds that the new structure would clash with the Terminal's beaux arts facade.

   b. **Holding and rationale:** A six-Justice majority held that so long as landmark preservation is carried out as part of a *comprehensive* preservation scheme, development of individual landmarks may be curtailed without effecting a taking. The New York City statute met the requirement of comprehensiveness. The opinion found landmark preservation schemes to be akin to zoning laws (although the Court conceded that the effect of a preservation scheme typically falls heavily upon a few, in contrast to the widespread impact of a zoning scheme.)

      i. **Use of "transferable development rights":** In determining that there was no taking, the Court took into account the fact that New York City gave the owners of landmark buildings so-called "transferable development rights" (TDRs), which could be used to increase the permissible size of other, non-landmark, buildings owned by the same owner. Because, in the Court's opinion, these TDRs had value, the economic impact on the owner of a landmark building fell short of what would be required before a taking could be found.

   c. **Dissent:** Justice Rehnquist, joined by two other members of the Court, dissented from the *Penn Central* holding. The regulation here was a taking, the dissent contended, because it was a serious destruction of property, and was not justified either under the "nuisance" rationale (see *supra*, p. 388) or the rationale of zoning-type laws. The latter are not takings, the dissenters argued, only because they apply to a broad cross-section of land, and thereby materially benefit as well as restrict the affected landowners. In the case of a landmark preservation scheme, by contrast, an extreme sacrifice is made by a small number of landowners, who receive only a negligible benefit.

8. **Tight means-end fit required:** The Supreme Court has since the 1980s required, in at least some kinds of cases, a *very close fit* between the *means* chosen by the state (i.e., the particular land use regulation selected) and the governmental *objective* being pursued. In this category of cases, even a compelling state interest will be to no avail if the means cho-

sen by the government are not quite closely tailored to advance that interest. This approach in certain land use regulation areas contrasts quite sharply with the Court's general approach in other economic regulation contexts, where all that is required is that there be a "minimally rational relation" between the means chosen and the end being pursued (see *supra*, p. 154).

This new approach to the means-end fit stems from two cases decided since 1987. Both cases involved government's attempts to require property owners to ***"dedicate"*** (i.e., give away) some part of their property to the public in return for some land-use right. It now appears that as the result of the 2005 decision in *Lingle v. Chevron U.S.A.* (*infra*, p. 392), the requirement of a tight means-end fit will be largely ***limited*** to this "dedication" situation.

a.   **The "substantially advance" requirement:**   The first case of the pair was ***Nollan v. California Coastal Commission***, 483 U.S. 825 (1987). There, the Court required that the means chosen by the government (the land-use regulation) ***"substantially advance"*** the governmental objective being pursued.

   i.   **Facts:**   The land use regulation at issue in *Nollan* prevented the Ps from rebuilding their house on their beach front property unless they first gave the public an easement across a sandy strip of the property adjacent to the ocean. The government body that issued the regulation was mainly concerned that the Ps would replace their small bungalow with a much bigger house, thus blocking the public's view of the beach.

   ii.   **Holding:**   By a 5-4 vote, the Court held that the Commission's refusal to issue the building permit except upon transfer of the easement amounted to a taking, for which compensation must be paid. In arriving at this conclusion, the majority opinion (written by Justice Scalia), reasoned as follows: (1) if the government had simply required the Ps to give the public an easement over their property, this would clearly have been a taking, since it would be a "permanent physical occupation" (even though no particular individual would be permitted to station himself permanently on the property); (2) an outright refusal by the government to grant the permit would not constitute a taking if it "substantially advanced a legitimate state interest" and did not "deny an owner economically viable use of his land"; and (3) the conditions attached to the permit must be evaluated by the same standard, so that ***only if those conditions "substantially advanced" the legitimate state interests being pursued*** would the conditions be valid.

   iii.   **Loose means-end fit:**   Requirement (3) was not satisfied, in the majority's view, because the harms feared by the government would not be cured or even materially lessened by the means chosen (the easement). For instance, there was no reason to believe that the easement would reduce obstacles to viewing the beach created by the new house, since the easement would only help people already on public beaches north or south of the Ps' property. In the majority's view, the building restriction was "not a valid regulation of land use but 'an out-and-out plan of extortion.' "

iv. **May apply only to "give-back" ("exaction") situations:** But a post-*Nollan* decision seems to mean that *Nollan*'s "substantially advance" requirement will apply only to the narrow class of cases involving **"exactions"** or **"dedications,"** i.e., situations in which government conditions a land-use benefit on the owner's **give-back** of a significant part of her right to use her property, as happened in *Nollan* itself. See *Lingle v. Chevron U.S.A. Inc.*, 544 U.S. 528 (2005), saying that the Court's formerly-announced principle — that application of a general zoning law to particular property will effect a taking if the ordinance "does not substantially advance legitimate state interests" — will apply only where government requires "dedications of property so onerous that, outside the exactions context, they would be deemed per se physical takings."

So in the garden-variety land-use regulation context (e.g., "no commercial structures permitted in this district"), the Court will *not* check to see whether some legitimate state interest is being substantially advanced. Only where the government requires that the owner "dedicate" part of his property to public uses (such as the compulsory beach-access easement in *Nollan*) will this "substantially-advances" test be applied.

b. **The "rough proportionality" requirement:** Then, in an even more striking use of rigorous review following *Nollan*, the Court held that when a city conditions a building permit on some **"give back"** by the owner, there must be a **"rough proportionality"** between the burdens on the public that the building permit would bring about, and the benefit to the public from the give back. This "rough proportionality" standard was announced in **Dolan v. City of Tigard**, 512 U.S. 374 (1994).

i. **Facts:** In *Dolan*, P was a property owner who wanted to enlarge the plumbing and electric supply store she ran on the property. D, the city of Tigard, issued her a permit to do this, but conditioned the permit on P's willingness to (among other things) convey a 15-foot strip of land on her property to the city, to be used as a bicycle pathway. (She would have been required to convey approximately 10% of the property.) The city, at the time it asked for the trade-off, asserted two reasons for it: (1) P would be paving over a larger part of her property, thus expanding the "impervious surface" and worsening the danger of flooding from a nearby creek; the unpaved pathway would help soak up some of the flood waters; and (2) P's bigger store would increase automobile traffic to her site; the bike path, by increasing the attractiveness of biking, might result in a countervailing decrease in car traffic.

ii. **P's attack:** P attacked the requirement that she convey the 15-foot strip as an unconstitutional taking of her property without compensation.

iii. **Court agrees:** The Court, by a 5-4 vote, agreed that the trade-off requirement was an unconstitutional taking of P's property. The Court first noted that under *Nollan*, there had to be an "essential nexus" between the permit condition exacted by the city, and the "legitimate state interest" being pursued; the Court found this requirement satisfied here (since there was a nexus between preventing flooding from the creek and limiting development on P's property; similarly, there was a nexus between reducing traffic congestion and providing for an alternative means of transport, biking).

    **iv.** **"Rough proportionality":** But the novel part of the Court's holding came in the imposition of a *second* requirement that any permit condition must meet: there must be a *"rough proportionality"* between the trade-off demanded by the city and the burden to the public from P's proposed development. The Court found that the city here had not satisfied this requirement. For example, although the city had calculated somewhat precisely the number of additional car trips per day that would be caused by P's expansion, the city had not tried to show how much of this traffic would be reduced by the proposed bikeway — it was not enough for the city to conclude, as it had, that the proposed bikeway *"could"* offset some of the traffic demand (though a finding that the bikeway "would" or "was likely to" offset some of the demand would apparently have sufficed).

  **c.** **Significance:** *Nollan* and *Dolan* demonstrate a much harsher review by the Court of land use regulations. We now have a scheme whereby, at least when government conditions some land-use permission on the owner's "give-back" of a significant property right, two conditions must be met:

    ❏ the means chosen by the local government unit must *"substantially advance"* a legitimate aim; and

    ❏ the "give back" required of the property owner must be *"roughly proportional"* to the harm caused by the new land use.

**9.** **Subsequent owner who takes with notice of restriction:** Suppose the case is one of those relatively uncommon ones in which the land-use restriction is so great that a taking will be deemed to have occurred. What happens if the person who owns the property at the time the regulation is put into effect does not sue, but a *subsequent buyer* — who buys the property *with knowledge* of the restriction — then sues on a takings theory? The Supreme Court has held that the subsequent buyer *may proceed* with the suit just as the original owner could have. A contrary rule, the Court held, would enable the state in effect "to put an expiration date on the Takings Clause." This ought not to be the rule, the Court continued, because "[f]uture generations, too, have a right to challenge unreasonable limitations on the use and value of land." *Palazzolo v. Rhode Island*, 533 U.S. 606 (2001).

**C.** **Requirement of "public" use:** Recall that the Taking Clause says that private property shall not be taken *"for public use"* unless just compensation is paid. This language has been interpreted by the Supreme Court as prohibiting the taking of private property for *private use, even if just compensation is made*. Thus the federal government (and, under an analogous interpretation of the Fourteenth Amendment, a state government) cannot simply take private property from one person, and give it to another, without any public purpose.

  **1.** **"Public use" construed broadly:** However, the Supreme Court has construed the requirement of a "public use" quite *broadly*. Here are two principles illustrating just how broadly the Court stretches the phrase:

    ❏ So long as the state's use of its eminent domain power is *"rationally related* to a *conceivable public purpose,"* the public use requirement is satisfied. *Hawaii Housing*

*Authority v. Midkiff*, 467 U.S. 229 (1984).

❏ The property ***need not be open to the general public after the taking.*** As the first rule above suggests, all that "public use" means is that the property be used for a "public purpose." *Kelo v. New London*, 545 U.S. 469 (2005). Therefore, the fact that the property is ***turned over to some private user*** does not prevent the use from being a public one as long as the public can be expected to derive some benefit (e.g., economic development) from the use. *Midkiff, supra.*

2. **Transfer to private owner:** The principle that there can be a public use even though the property is ***turned over to a private user*** is illustrated by ***Hawaii Housing Authority v. Midkiff***, *supra*. There, the Court upheld a scheme whereby Hawaii used its eminent domain power to acquire lots owned by large landowners, and transferred them to the tenants living on them, or to other non-landowners. Since there was tremendous inequality in land ownership (on Oahu, the most urbanized island, 22 landowners owned 75.5% of the privately-owned land), and since thousands of homeowners had been forced to lease rather than to buy the land under their homes, the state's scheme was a rational attempt to remedy a social and economic evil. As with any other state conduct sought to be justified as an exercise of the police power, all that was required was that the legislature "rationally could have believed" that the act would promote a legitimate objective; the scheme here easily passed this test.

3. **Urban renewal and economic development:** Similarly, the public use requirement can be met even though the government is pursuing the diffuse goal of ***"economic development,"*** and even if it is doing so by condemning parcels in ***non-blighted*** areas. This was the controversial result in a 5-4 decision in the 2005 case of ***Kelo v. New London***, *supra*.

    a. **Facts:** In *Kelo*, the long-struggling city of New London, Connecticut wanted to revitalize itself economically by carrying out a redevelopment plan that included building a $300 million research facility for the Pfizer pharmaceutical company, plus an adjacent conference hotel, residences and pedestrian "riverwalk" along the Thames River. The city believed that the development plan would create jobs, generate tax revenue, and revitalize the downtown. The plaintiffs were the owners of about 15 properties condemned by the city. These properties were mostly owner-occupied houses; none was in poor condition, but all were in the development area.

    b. **Ps' claim:** The plaintiffs claimed that a city's decision to take non-blighted property for the purpose of economic development was not a "public use."

    c. **Majority upholds taking:** By a 5-4 vote, the Supreme Court disagreed with the plaintiffs and upheld the condemnation. Justice Stevens wrote for the majority.

        i. **Only a "public purpose" is required:** Stevens began by saying that the requirement of public use did ***not mean that the property had to be made open to, or used by, the public at large.*** All that was required was that there be a ***"public purpose"*** behind the taking. Furthermore, the concept of "public purpose" was to be broadly defined, reflecting the court's "longstanding policy of ***deference to legislative judgments*** in this field."

ii. **Application:** Stevens then quickly concluded that New London's plan here met the requirement of public purpose. The city's economic development plan was "carefully formulated," and "comprehensive in character." The city believed that the plan would create new jobs and increased tax revenue. Therefore, Stevens concluded, it easily met the requirement that it serve a public purpose.

d. **Dissent:** Justice O'Connor **dissented**, joined by Chief Justice Rehnquist and Justices Scalia and Thomas. She would have held that takings for the purpose of economic development are simply not constitutional, because they are not for public use. "Under the banner of economic development, all private property is now vulnerable to being taken and transferred to another private owner, so long as it might be upgraded — i.e., given to an owner who will use it in a way that the legislature deems more beneficial to the public[.]" Indeed, O'Connor could not see **any logical limit** on government's power under the majority's approach: "For who among us can say she already makes the most productive or attractive possible use of her property? **The specter of condemnation hangs over all property.** Nothing is to prevent the State from replacing any Motel 6 with a Ritz-Carlton, any home with a shopping mall, or any farm with a factory."

i. **Justice Thomas' dissent:** Justice Thomas dissented separately. He would have gone even farther than O'Connor, allowing a taking "only if the government or the public **actually uses** the taken property." Thomas also warned that the majority's rule allowing economic-development takings "guarantees that [the] losses will fall disproportionately on **poor communities**."

e. **Raw transfer to the politically favored:** After *Kelo*, does the "public use" requirement have any bite at all? The answer seems to be "very little." One sliver of continuing significance is hinted at by a concurrence by Justice Kennedy, in supplying the fifth vote to uphold New London's plan. Kennedy asserted that if a taking were clearly shown to have been **"intended to favor a particular private party**, with only **incidental or pretextural public benefits,"** it would be invalid. (That obviously hadn't happened in *Kelo*, since New London's plan was a comprehensive one, and since the identity of most of the private beneficiaries was unknown at the time the plan was formulated.)

i. **Conclusion:** Since four members of the Court would not allow economic-development takings at all, Kennedy's opinion makes it clear that a transfer whose only real purpose is shown to be to take *A*'s property for the purpose of advantaging the politically powerful *B* would be invalid for failing to serve a public purpose. However, it will be a rare case indeed when the government acts so crudely (and with such poor legal advice) that such a conclusion of no-public-purpose will be reached. For all practical purposes, the public use provision **no longer meaningfully binds government.**

# III. THE "CONTRACT" CLAUSE

A. **The "Contract" Clause generally:** One of the few protections against state action given to individuals in the body of the Constitution (as distinguished from the Bill of Rights or other amendments) comes in Article I, §10: "No State shall ... pass any ... Law impairing the Obligation of Contracts. ... " This so-called Contract Clause by its terms applies only to the states. But a similar or identical rule has been held applicable to the federal government, by virtue of the Fifth Amendment's Due Process Clause. See *Lynch v. U.S.*, 292 U.S. 571 (1934); see also Tribe, p. 613.

1. **Purpose:**  The Contract Clause was enacted principally for the purpose of protecting creditors against **debtor relief laws**, by which the obligations of debtors were often postponed or even completely lifted. Such protection of creditors' rights was thought to be necessary for the economic development of the country. See N&R, p. 406.

2. **Extension to public grants:**  But the Clause was quickly extended to include the prevention of the impairment of "public" contracts, i.e., contracts between the government and private parties.

3. **Two-part discussion:**  Our discussion below is divided into two aspects: (1) the use of the Contract Clause to protect **public** agreements, i.e., those to which government is a party; and (2) the use of the Clause to protect agreements between private parties. There is reason to believe that the Supreme Court today favors stricter review of cases falling within (1) than of those coming within (2).

B. **Protection of public agreements:**  Until 1977, it appeared that the Supreme Court had virtually abandoned the Contract Clause as a limitation on states' rights to modify "public" contracts.

1. **Some elements remain (*U.S. Trust* case):**  But the Clause has turned out to have some real bite left in it, due in large part to **U.S. Trust Co. v. New Jersey**, 431 U.S. 1 (1977). That case marked the first time in almost four decades that the Supreme Court invalidated a state law on Contract Clause grounds. The case indicates that the Court will scrutinize somewhat closely a state's attempt to **escape** from its **financial obligations**, and will only permit such an escape where a **significant public need** exists that cannot be reasonably handled in any other way.

   a. **Facts of *U.S. Trust*:**  In a 1962 bond issue, the Port Authority of New York and New Jersey promised bondholders that certain revenues pledged as security for the bonds would not be used to finance unprofitable passenger railroad systems in the future. In 1974, New York and New Jersey retroactively repealed this covenant, so that the pledged revenues (including bridge and tunnel tolls) could be used to improve rail service. U.S. Trust Co., one of the bondholders, sued on the grounds that the repeal violated the Contract Clause.

   b. **Contract Clause found violated:**  The Supreme Court found, by a 4-3 majority, that the repeal violated the Contract Clause. The majority opinion, by Justice Blackmun, stated the following test: an impairment of contractual obligations will be constitutional only if it is "**reasonable** and **necessary** to support an **important public purpose**."

      i. **"Necessity" defined:**  A contractual impairment was "necessary" only when the state's public interest objectives could not be met by **less drastic** modification of the contract. Here, alternative means existed for improving mass transit (and also of discouraging automobile use, a second major state goal).

    **ii. "Reasonable" defined:** An impairment was "reasonable," as the Court used the term, only if the modification was induced by ***unforeseen developments*** occurring after the original contract was made. In contrast to the situation in *El Paso v. Simmons*, 379 U.S. 497 (1965), where the dramatic increase in land values stemming from the discovery of oil and gas was unforeseeable, the public need for mass transit improvements was quite foreseeable at the time the covenant to bondholders was made in 1962. Indeed, it was precisely to forestall use of pledged revenues to cope with concerns like those motivating the Port Authority here, that had led to the making of the covenant.

**C. Protection of private contracts:** The principal purpose of the Contract Clause was to curtail populist ***debtor-relief*** laws. The Framers' fears of such laws seem to have been justified; most of the private-agreement cases under the Contract Clause have indeed involved debtor relief. The development of Contract Clause doctrine in private-agreement cases has been roughly similar to that in the public-agreement situations discussed above: originally a fairly broad use of the Clause to strike down legislation, a near abandonment of the Clause during the 20th century, and a resuscitation by the Burger/Rehnquist Court.

    **1. Debtor relief laws:** The Court has steadily cut back on the use of the Contract Clause as a limitation on debtor relief laws. It remains the case that a state legislature may not completely absolve debtors of obligations incurred prior to the legislature's action. But whereas the Contract Clause was once a barrier to any impairment of creditors' rights, the impact of the Clause has been curtailed in a number of ways.

    **2. Prospective only:** Insolvency laws may relieve debtors from obligations contracted ***after*** the law is enacted. That is, only ***retroactive*** laws are barred by the Contract Clause. *Ogden v. Saunders*, 25 U.S. (12 Wheat.) 213 (1827).

    **3. Remedies:** Although a creditor's basic rights may not be impaired, his "***remedies***," i.e., the means by which he enforces those rights, may be modified. For instance, extensions of time can be given. This distinction between rights and remedies is an obscure and difficult one; but the basic idea is that the underlying obligation may not be impaired, although the creditor's right to strict compliance with all aspects of the contract may be modified.

    **4. Protection of public interest:** An even broader exception to the Contract Clause is that debtors' obligations may be modified where a ***vital public interest***, especially an economic emergency, so demands.

        **a. *Blaisdell* case:** One of the best known modern Contract Clause cases, ***Home Building & Loan Ass'n v. Blaisdell***, 290 U.S. 398 (1934), involved such an emergency modification of debtors' obligations. That case involved a Minnesota statute, enacted at the height of the Depression, which allowed local courts to give relief from mortgage foreclosure sales. The courts were permitted to give extensions from such sales, provided that the mortgagor paid "all or a reasonable part" of the property's fair income or rental value. The measure was intended to apply to mortgages issued prior to the date of the law; i.e., the statute was retroactive.

i.   **Right to protect public interest:**   The Supreme Court ***upheld*** the statute, on the theory that the state had at least the right to temporarily delay enforcement of a mortgage's literal terms, where "vital public interests" would otherwise suffer. In view of the enormous economic emergency which gave rise to the statute, the modification was a limited and reasonable one. The Court stressed that principal remained due, interest continued to run, the right of foreclosure would ultimately be restored, and the statute would (the Court assumed) be rescinded once the economic emergency was over.

ii.  **Implied power to modify:**   In justifying this limited right to modify contracts in order to protect the public interest, the *Blaisdell* Court noted that "[t]he reservation of ***essential attributes of sovereign power*** is ... read into contracts as a postulate of the legal order." As Tribe (p. 616) interprets this statement, it means that "[o]ne of the 'rules' that may be read into every contract at its inception is the rule that all ***other*** rules are subject to change if and when the legislature reasonably concludes that such change is needed."

5.  **Renaissance of the Clause (The *Allied Structural Steel* case):**   The Contract Clause has been saved from extinction in private-agreement cases, just as *U.S. Trust Case* (*supra*, p. 396) did this in public-contract cases. In ***Allied Structural Steel Co. v. Spannaus***, 438 U.S. 234 (1978), the Supreme Court invalidated an attempt by Minnesota to expand the pension obligations of certain Minnesota employers who closed a plant in the state. Perhaps even more than the *U.S. Trust* decision, the *Allied Structural* holding seems to indicate that the Contract Clause may now be used as a significant weapon against state police power regulations which affect contracts.

a.  **Facts:**   The Minnesota statute provided that when certain Minnesota employers closed down their operations in the state, or terminated a pension plan, any employee who had worked for the firm for more than ten years became "vested" in (i.e., entitled to benefits under) any pension plan the company might have. Allied's pension plan did not provide, in most cases, for vesting until long after ten years; the plan also provided that it could be terminated at any time, with no obligation to those employees who had not yet vested. When Allied closed its plant (which it had planned to do even before the statute was enacted, and which it did shortly thereafter), it was therefore required to pay pensions to workers who would not have been covered by the plan absent the statute.

b.  **Holding:**   By a 5-3 majority, the Supreme Court found that the Minnesota statute violated the Contract Clause. The majority opinion, by Justice Stewart, conceded that the police power allowed the states to make minor, and in a few circumstances substantial, modifications to contracts.

i.  **Strict requirements:**   But the Court held that the modification here was a substantial one, and that it could therefore be sustained only if a series of factors like those existing in *Blaisdell* (*supra*, p. 397) also existed. The Court read these to include: (1) that there be an ***emergency***; (2) that the measure be enacted to protect a "***basic societal interest, not a favored group***"; (3) that the relief be "appropriately ***tailored***" to the emergency; (4) that the modifications be "***reasonable***" in scope; and (5) that the statute be limited to the duration of the emergency. The

Court found that factors (1) and (2) were not present, since the legislative history did not disclose any major emergency to which the statute was a response, and since, in the Court's view, only a very limited number of employers and employees would be affected. The Court also implied that the effect on a company like Allied was also so drastic and permanent that conditions (3), (4) and (5) were not met either.

      **ii. Violation of reasonable expectations:** The majority also objected to the fact that the statute imposed a "sudden, totally unanticipated, and substantial ***retroactive*** obligation." This, coupled with the fact that Minnesota had never regulated the area of pensions previously, seemed to the majority to violate Allied's ***reasonable expectations*** about what it was getting into when it started a pension plan.

   **c. Dissent:** Justice Brennan dissented (joined by Justices White and Marshall). Brennan argued that the Minnesota statute simply created an "additional, supplemental duty of the employer," and that the Contract Clause, in its prohibition on the "impairment" of contractual duties, did not prohibit the creation of new duties.

**D. More deferential standard:** The *U.S. Trust* and *Allied Steel* cases represent significant revitalizations of the Contract Clause, in the case of public and private agreements, respectively. However, developments following these two decisions indicate that the Court will probably not embark on a course of wholesale invalidation of state legislation on Contract Clause grounds. The Court articulated a new standard of review for Contract Clause challenges, a standard which is apparently applicable to both public and private agreements. Although the Court claimed to be relying principally on *U.S. Trust* and *Allied Steel*, this newly-formulated standard of review seems to be ***significantly more deferential*** to state legislative judgments. ***Energy Reserves Group, Inc. v. Kansas Power and Light Co.***, 459 U.S. 400 (1983).

   **1. Three-part test:** In *Energy Reserves*, the Court articulated the following three-step test for evaluating Contract Clause challenges:

      **a. Threshold inquiry:** First, the court must make a "threshold inquiry" as to "whether the state law has, in fact, operated as a ***substantial impairment*** of a contractual relationship."

      **b. Legitimate public purpose:** If this threshold inquiry yields an affirmative result (i.e., the court finds that there has been a "substantial impairment"), the state must demonstrate that it has a ***"significant and legitimate public purpose"*** which the regulation is intended to serve.

      **c. "Reasonable and appropriate":** If the state does show such a "legitimate public purpose," the court must then take the final step of determining "whether the adjustment of 'the rights and responsibilities of contracting parties [is based] upon ***reasonable conditions*** and [is] of a character ***appropriate to the public purpose***'" asserted in support of the regulation.

   **2. Distinction between public and private contracts:** The three-part *Energy Reserves* test is, as noted, apparently now applicable both to contracts in which the state is a party and to purely private contracts. However, the Court will undoubtedly apply that test with ***significantly greater strictness*** where the state is attempting to make ***its own contractual obliga-***

*tions less burdensome*. In a footnote, the *Energy Reserves* Court cited approvingly the statement in *U.S. Trust* that when the state is a party to the contract, "complete deference to a legislative assessment of reasonableness and necessity is not appropriate because the State's self-interest is at stake."

**E. Incidental effect on contracts:** Even the relatively deferential standard now in force as the result of *Energy Reserves* is applicable only where the state takes an action that is *specifically directed* at contractual obligations. If the state applies a *"generally applicable rule of conduct"* which has the *incidental by-product* of impairing contractual obligations, the Contract Clause *does not apply at all*. This rule was stated and applied in *Exxon Corp. v. Eagerton*, 462 U.S. 176 (1983).

    **1. Facts:** In *Exxon*, Alabama increased its severance taxes on oil and gas, and prohibited oil and gas producers from passing on the increase directly or indirectly to consumers. This prohibition had the effect of blocking Exxon from taking advantage of clauses in its existing contracts permitting it to pass on tax increases to its customers.

    **2. Regulation upheld:** The Court unanimously upheld the Alabama pass-through prohibition. The Alabama law "did not prescribe a rule limited in effect to contractual obligations or remedies, but instead imposed a generally applicable rule of conduct." Therefore, the law did not trigger Contract Clause analysis at all.

**F. Other retroactivity issues:** The notion of retroactivity has been a strong theme in the Contract Clause cases discussed above — one could argue that the very idea behind the Contract Clause is that contractual obligations, once fixed, will not be retroactively upset by legislative action. Retroactivity is similarly a key theme of the *Ex Post Facto* and Bill of Attainder Clauses (discussed *infra*, p. 408 and p. 409 respectively).

    **1. Use of Due Process Clauses:** Still other possible sources of protection against retroactive legislative action are the *Due Process* Clauses of the Fifth and Fourteenth Amendments. Because these clauses are less specific than the Contract, Bill of Attainder and *Ex Post Facto* Clauses, it is a rare retroactive act which will be invalidated by use of due process analysis.

        **a. Rational relation test:** In most situations, the Supreme Court now seems to require merely that there be a *rational relation* between the retroactive legislation and a legitimate government objective.

        **b. Modification of government's own obligation:** But where the government *modifies its own contractual obligations*, the standard for judicial review is likely to be somewhat more stringent than that of the "mere rationality" test.

## IV. THE SECOND AMENDMENT "RIGHT TO BEAR ARMS"

**A. Text of the Amendment:** The Second Amendment provides: "A well regulated Militia, being necessary to the security of a free State, the right of the people to *keep and bear Arms*, shall *not be infringed*."

**B. Applicable to private individuals (the *Heller* case):** Until recently, the Amendment had never been recognized by the Supreme Court as giving *private citizens* the right to keep firearms. But in a stunning 2008 case, decided by a 5-4 vote, ***District of Columbia v. Heller***, 128 S.Ct. 2783 (2008), the Court struck down the District of Columbia's strict gun-control laws on Second Amendment grounds. The majority asserted that "the inherent right of self-defense has been central to the Second Amendment right," and concluded that the ***Amendment confers on private individuals a right to keep basic firearms, including handguns, at home for self-defense.***

1. **Significance of *Heller*:** The only significant prior Supreme Court decision on the meaning of the Second Amendment, a 1939 case, had been widely interpreted as saying that the Second Amendment gave no rights to private individuals, and merely protected the right of "well regulated militias" (now known as state National Guard units) to keep their members armed while on duty. But *Heller* concluded that this was not the correct reading of the 1939 case, and that the Amendment confers on private citizens, not just militias, the right to keep at least some kinds of weapons for self-defense and recreational purposes.

2. **D.C. statute:** The D.C. gun-control statute at issue in *Heller* was among the two or three strictest such statutes in America. The statute contained two distinct prohibitions that were challenged:

   ❏ First, the statute effectively ***banned the possession of handguns in the home*** — only registered firearms could be kept, and handguns could not be registered.

   ❏ Second, the statute required that firearms other than handguns (e.g., ***rifles*** and shotguns) could only be kept in the home if they were kept ***unloaded*** and either ***disassembled or disabled*** by a trigger lock.

3. **Challenge by P:** The plaintiff, Dick Heller, was a police officer who wanted to keep a handgun in his house. He asserted that each of the above two prohibitions violated his Second Amendment right to bear arms.

4. **Majority upholds:** By a 5-4 Vote, the court ***agreed*** that ***both provisions*** of the D.C. statute violated P's Second Amendment rights. The majority opinion was by Justice Scalia, and is probably his most important opinion since he joined the Court in 1986. Four members of the majority were those generally considered the conservative bloc of the court — in addition to Scalia they included Chief Justice Roberts and Justices Thomas and Alito. The critical fifth vote was supplied by Justice Kennedy, as has so often been the case in the Rehnquist and Roberts courts.

   a. **Language and history:** Scalia's opinion began by considering the history and language of the Second Amendment. He separately analyzed the "prefatory" clause ("A well regulated Militia, being necessary to the security of a free State...") and the "operative" clause ("the right of the people to keep and bear Arms shall not be infringed").

      i. **Operative clause:** As to the meaning of the *operative* clause, Scalia pointed to several elements that he said demonstrated that the clause was intended to give rights to ***individuals***, not just to members of state militias. First, the operative clause codified a ***"right of the people,"*** and the use of this phrase by other constitutional provisions (e.g., the First Amendment's assembly-and-petition clause) demonstrated that the phrase customarily referred to individual rights, not collective ones, he said. Second, historical and linguistic analysis showed that the phrase "keep and bear arms" was "unambiguously used to refer to the carrying of weapons outside of an organized militia." In summary, he said, the text and history of the operative clause "conferred an individual right to keep and bear arms."

    **ii.  Prefatory clause:** Next, Scalia analyzed the ***prefatory*** clause, that is, the reference to "a well regulated militia, being necessary to the security of a free State..." As to the meaning of a "well regulated militia," Scalia rejected the dissent's reading of this term as being limited to officially-organized state-militias. For Scalia, the term "the militia" referred to ***"all males physically capable of acting in concert for the common defense,"*** and the adjective "well-regulated" implied merely "the imposition of proper discipline and training." The reference to "security of a free State" referred merely to a "free country" or "free polity," not to states as the operators of state militias. So the prefatory clause was not inconsistent with Scalia's "individual rights" interpretation, he argued.

    **iii.  Historical purpose:** Scalia then analyzed the ***historical purpose*** of the Amendment. The history behind the enactment of the Second Amendment, he said, was that English tyrants had eliminated the ability of "the militia" (i.e., able-bodied men) to resist tyranny "not by banning the militia but simply by taking away the people's arms," enabling a standing army supporting the tyrant to "suppress political opponents." Consequently, Scalia asserted, "[t]he threat that the new Federal Government would destroy the citizens' militia by taking away their arms was the reason that right ... was codified in a written constitution."

    **iv.  Summary of history and language:** In sum, the history leading to the enactment of the Second Amendment, and the common 18th-century meaning of the phrases used in it, convinced Scalia that the framers intended to grant individual citizens the right to bear arms for self-defense, not merely to confer such a right upon official state militias.

  **b.  Later interpretations:** Scalia then argued that ***post-enactment interpretations*** of the Second Amendment had reached this same conclusion, that the Amendment conferred an individual right to bear arms for self-defense.

    **i.  Distinguishing *Miller*:** Scalia paid special attention to *U.S. v. Miller*, 307 U.S. 174 (1939), the Supreme Court's principal prior case on the meaning of the Second Amendment. In *Miller*, two criminal defendants charged with transporting an unregistered short-barreled shotgun, in violation of a federal statute, argued that their conduct was protected by the Second Amendment. The Supreme Court rejected this argument, saying that "In the absence of any evidence tending to show that the possession or use of a [short-barreled shotgun] at this time has some reasonable relationship to the preservation or efficiency of a well regulated militia, we cannot say that the Second Amendment guarantees the right to keep and bear such an instrument." The question in *Heller* became what this statement meant about private (non-military) possession of guns.

      **(1)  Dissent's view rejected:** The dissent in *Heller* contended that in *Miller*, the Court had meant that ***only military uses of guns were protected by the Amendment.*** But Scalia disagreed about what *Miller* said: *Miller* said "only that the Second Amendment does not protect those weapons not typically possessed by law-abiding citizens for lawful purposes, such as short-barreled shotguns." So for Scalia, *Miller* was not inconsistent with the *Heller* majority's conclusion that the Amendment protects the rights of law-abiding citizens to possess guns for self-defense.

c. **What the amendment protects:** Having concluded that the Amendment protects at least some right on the part of non-military individuals to bear arms, Scalia now turned to the *scope* of the right. On this score, he indicated merely that the right was *not absolute or unlimited.* The majority was not, he said, "cast[ing] doubt on long-standing prohibitions on the possession of firearms by *felons* and the *mentally ill,* or laws forbidding the carrying of firearms in *sensitive places such as schools and government buildings,* or laws imposing *conditions and qualifications* on the *commercial sale* of arms." Furthermore, he said, the Amendment protects only the carrying of weapons that were *"in common use at the time"* the Amendment was enacted, so that *"dangerous and unusual weapons"* (quoting an 18th century commentator) would *not* be protected. In an ambiguous sentence, Scalia seemed to be saying that what he called "weapons that are most useful in military service — M-16 rifles and the like," may be banned because they were not in common use at the time the Amendment was enacted.

d. **Application to D.C. statute:** Scalia then applied his reading of the Second Amendment to the D.C. statute before the Court. He addressed both of the District's bans: the complete ban on handgun possession, and the requirement that any non-handguns kept at home be kept in unloaded and inoperable form.

   i. **Ban on handguns:** As to the absolute handgun ban, Scalia asserted that "the *inherent right of self-defense* has been *central* to the Second Amendment right." And, he said, D.C.'s complete ban on handgun possession in homes "amounts to a prohibition of an *entire class of 'arms'* that is *overwhelmingly chosen by American society* for that lawful purpose." Since handguns were the favored method of self defense in the home, a complete ban on them violated the Amendment. But Scalia did not specify what precise standard should be used, reserving that issue for future cases. The choie of standard was unnecessary to make here, he said, because the handgun ban was unconstitutional "under *any of the standards of scrutiny* that we have applied to *enumerated constitutional rights*." (In a footnote, Scalia explained that he was not asserting that the handgun ban would violate *rational-basis* review. But he seemed to be saying that under any of the more stringent standards used by the Supreme Court, such as intermediate-level review and strict scrutiny,[1] the complete handgun ban would be invalid.)

   ii. **Requirement that guns be unloaded and trigger-protected:** Scalia then turned to the requirement that any gun the possession of which is not completely forbidden (e.g., rifles and shotguns) be kept *unloaded and inoperable* in the home. This requirement, he said, "makes it impossible for its citizens to use [such

---

1. However, Scalia did not mention either of these standards by name.

guns] for the core lawful purpose of self-defense and is hence unconstitutional." Therefore, this requirement, too, violated the Second Amendment.

**e.   Rejects "interest-balancing" approach:**   As noted, Scalia did not specify exactly *what standard of review* should be used in evaluating government actions that impact Second Amendment rights. But Scalia did reject the standard proposed by Justice Breyer in his dissent (see *infra*, p. 405). Breyer proposed an *"interest-balancing inquiry"*; for any regulation that significantly implicated competing constitutionally-protected interests, Breyer would ask merely whether the statute burdens a protected interest in a way or to an extent that is *"out of proportion"* to the statute's beneficial effects on some other protected interest. But Scalia dismissed this approach, saying that "a constitutional guarantee subject to future judges' assessments of its usefulness is no constitutional guarantee at all." In any event, he said, the Second Amendment "surely elevates above all other interests the *right of law-abiding, responsible citizens to use arms in defense of hearth and home."*

**f.   Application to *Heller*:**   Scalia then wrapped things up by saying that so long as the plaintiff (Heller) was not "disqualified from the exercise of Second Amendment rights,"[2] the District of Columbia *"must permit him to register his handgun* and must *issue him a license* to *carry it* in the home."

   **i.   Handgun violence:**   Scalia conceded that *handgun violence* was a serious problem in America, and that "some measures *regulating* handguns" would be constitutionally acceptable methods of dealing with the violence problem. But, he said, "the enshrinement of constitutional rights necessarily *takes certain policy choices off the table.* These include the *absolute prohibition of handguns held and used for self-defense in the home."*

**5.   Dissents:** Four Justices *dissented,* in two separate opinions.

**a.   Stevens' dissent:**   The principal dissent was by Justice Stevens (joined by Justices Souter, Ginsburg and Breyer). Stevens reached a completely opposite conclusion from Scalia's as to the purpose and intent of the Second Amendment. The Amendment, he said, "was adopted to protect the right of the people of each of the several States to *maintain a well-regulated militia.* It was a response to concerns ... that the power of Congress to disarm the state militias and create a national standing army posed an intolerable threat to the sovereignty of the several states." The framers had not evidenced "the slightest interest in limiting any legislature's authority to regulate *private civilian uses* of firearms."

   **i.   *Miller* case:** Stevens relied heavily on the 1939 *Miller* decision. "[The] view of the amendment we took in *Miller* — that it protects the right to keep and bear arms for certain military purposes, but that it does *not curtail* the Legislature's power to *regulate the nonmilitary use and ownership of weapons* — is both the most natural reading of the Amendment's text and the interpretation most faithful to the history of its adoption."

---

2. Scalia seemed to be referring to classes of people whose right to possess arms may be nullified, such as felons and the mentally ill.

ii. **Burden on the Judiciary:** Stevens then issued the kind of warning that in recent decades has usually been made by conservatives: that the majority's approach would *encourage judicial activism*. That approach "will surely give rise to a far more active judicial role in making vitally important national policy decisions than was envisioned at any time in the 18th, 19th and 20th centuries."

b. **Breyer's dissent:** Justice Breyer wrote a separate dissent, in which Stevens, Ginsburg and Souter joined. Breyer fully agreed with Stevens' argument that the Second Amendment only protects militia-related, not self-defense-related, interests. But, he said, even if the Amendment *were* read to protect self-defense-related interests, the D.C. statute should be found not to violate the Amendment.

   i. **Interest-balancing:** Whenever a governmental regulation "significantly implicates *competing constitutionally protected interests* in complex ways," Breyer said, the Court does and should use an explicit *"interest-balancing inquiry."* That is, the Court asks "whether the statute burdens a protected interest in a way or to an extent that is *out of proportion to the statute's salutary effects upon other important governmental interests."*[3]

   For instance, Breyer said, a proportionality approach is often used by the Court in free-speech and due process cases. Since gun control statutes, by reducing violence, have beneficial effects on citizens' constitutionally-protected interest in their lives and physical safety, the interest-balancing approach should be used here.

   ii. **Deference to legislature's empirical judgment:** A key feature of the interest-balancing approach advocated by Breyer is, he said, that the Court *"defers to a legislature's empirical judgment* in matters where a legislature is likely to have *greater expertise and greater institutional fact-finding capacity."* Thus here, the legislature (of D.C.) concluded that a handgun ban would meaningfully reduce crime, and did so after a careful consideration by the relevant committee of extensive evidence about the link between handguns and urban violence. The only role of the courts should be to "assure that, in formulating its judgments, the legislature has *drawn reasonable inferences based on substantial evidence."* And D.C. had easily met this standard here, Breyer said.

   iii. **Summary:** In sum, Breyer believed the District's gun-control law was "a *proportionate*, not a disproportionate, response to the compelling concerns that led the District to adopt it." Therefore, even if the Second Amendment were read to apply to the keeping of arms for self-defense purposes, the measure would be valid.

6. **Significance:** There is no way to know how broadly important *Heller* will prove to be. That's because the case leaves a number of vital questions unanswered.

   a. **Applicability to states and cities:** At the most fundamental level, *Heller* does not even address the question of *whether the Second Amendment is applicable to states and cities.* The District of Columbia is part of the federal government, so *Heller*

---

3. This is essentially a form of intermediate scrutiny, as Breyer correctly characterizes it.

merely illustrates that the *federal government* is bound by what the Court has now found to be a Second Amendment right to keep weapons in the home for self-defense. It is possible that the Court will conclude that this is one of the few Bill of Rights guarantees that does not apply to the states or their sub-divisions by virtue of being selectively incorporated into the meaning of 14th amendment due process.[4]

    **i.** **Likely applicable to states:** But in view of the great importance that the *Heller* majority ascribes to the Second Amendment, and the majority's relatively absolutist view of what that Amendment protects, it is highly probable that the Court will ultimately conclude that the Amendment is ***incorporated*** into the meaning of due process for purposes of the 14th Amendment, and is thus ***applicable to the states and their sub-divisions (i.e., counties and cities).***

  **b.** **Standard to be used:** It is also unclear what ***standard*** the court will use for reviewing governmental restrictions that impair Second Amendment rights. As noted (see p. 403), Justice Scalia avoiding answering this question in *Heller*, saying merely that "under any of the standards of scrutiny that we have applied to enumerated Constitutional rights," the District's complete ban on handguns in the home would "fail constitutional muster."

    **i.** **Possible strict scrutiny:** It is possible that the *Heller* majority will ultimately decide that some form of ***strict scrutiny*** is appropriate. However, Scalia indicates that prohibitions on the possession of firearms by felons and the mentally ill, and prohibitions on carrying of firearms and sensitive places like schools and governmental buildings, are valid; the upholding of such prohibitions does not seem consistent with a very rigorous form of strict scrutiny.

    **ii.** **Not mere-rationality:** At the other end of the spectrum, it's quite clear that ***something more demanding than rational-basis review*** will be used. Justice Scalia says in a footnote that Justice Breyer "correctly notes that this law, like almost all laws, would pass rational-basis scrutiny." So for the majority that decided *Heller*, something more rigorous than rational-basis review must be used.

    **iii.** **Intermediate-level review:** That leaves some form of ***mid-level scrutiny*** as the most likely alternative.

      **(1)** **Interest-balancing rejected:** But Scalia's opinion in *Heller* explicitly ***rejected*** at least one version of intermediate-level scrutiny, namely the ***"interest balancing"*** approach advocated by Justice Breyer, under which the Court should ask "whether the statute burdens a protected interest in a way or to an extent that is out of proportion to the statute's salutary effects upon other important governmental interests."

      **(2)** **Substantial-relation-to-important-interest:** However, Scalia did not comment on the more ***traditional*** form of mid-level review, under which the question is whether the means chosen by government is ***"substantially related"*** to the achievement of an ***"important"*** governmental interest (a standard used in

---

4. Other examples include the right to a grand jury indictment for felonies, and the right to a civil jury trial in cases brought at common law. See *supra*, p. 147.

several free-speech areas such as regulation of commercial speech; see *infra*, p. 573). Therefore, there is a good chance that this version of mid-level review will prove to be the ultimate standard.

**c. Effect on gun laws:** Even assuming that *Heller* and the Second Amendment turn out to apply to state and local gun laws, it's not clear that governments will lose very much of their practical power to regulate gun use.

**i. Handgun bans:** If the Second Amendment applies to state and local governments, then presumably it will apply exactly the same way as it applies to the federal government under *Heller*. This means that a ***total ban on handgun possession*** in the home would be unconstitutional, as would a requirement that non-handguns be stored in an interoperable and unloaded manner. So, for instance, Chicago's virtually complete ban on handguns would be vulnerable. But few cities, and no states, regulate handguns nearly as extensively as D.C. and Chicago do, so their restrictions may well survive.

**ii. Licensing:** It seems likely that ***licensing requirements*** will ***not*** be found to violate the Second Amendment as long as the procedures for obtaining a license are not unreasonably burdensome, and are directed towards keeping guns out of the hands of people who do not have a Second Amendment right to possess them. So, for instance, since *Heller* it makes it clear that government may ban felons and the mentally ill from possessing guns, a licensing requirement that would deny permits to such people — and that would give government a reasonable amount of time to check whether the applicant fell into these categories — would presumably be ***valid*** even if some form of strict scrutiny were used.

**iii. Concealed-carry permits:** Similarly, it seems likely that the Amendment will be found not to prohibit governments from banning the ***carrying of concealed weapons in public places.*** The majority opinion in *Heller* commented, seemingly approvingly, that "the majority of the 19th century courts to consider the question held that prohibitions on carrying concealed weapons were lawful under the Second Amendment or state analogues." Furthermore, if as the *Heller* majority asserts the thrust of the Second Amendment is to protect citizens' right of self-defense at home, it's hard to see how the Amendment is violated by prohibiting the carrying of concealed weapons outside the home.

**iv. Barring certain types of weapons:** One last open question is the ***types of weapons*** the possession of which is guaranteed by the Second Amendment. Scalia's opinion seems to agree that the 1939 *Miller* opinion was correct in holding that only those weapons that were ***"in common use at the time"*** the Amendment was adopted are protected, and that (in the words of an 18th Century commentator) ***"dangerous and unusual weapons" may be prohibited***. So presumably governments may ban the possession of modern weapons that are much more advanced and dangerous than those existing in 1791, such as ***machine guns, assault rifles*** and the ***sawed-off shotguns*** at issue in *Miller*.

**v. Summary:** So although the Second Amendment now recognizes some sort of individual right to bear arms, that right is likely to be found to be subject to ***heavy***

***governmental regulation.*** At the end of the day, it may well be the case that of gun regulations actually adopted by states or cities somewhere, only the very most extreme measures found in the D.C. statute — like the virtually-total ban on handguns, and the requirement of trigger-locking of guns stored at home — will be struck down.

# V.  *EX POST FACTO* LAWS

**A.  Constitutional prohibition of *ex post facto laws:*** The Constitution prevents both the federal and state governments from enacting ***ex post facto*** laws. See Article I, §§ 9 and 10, respectively. An *ex post facto* law is one which has a ***retroactive punitive effect***. This can happen in any of four ways:

1.  **Definition altered:** The law retroactively ***alters the definition*** of a crime, so that an act that wasn't a crime at all at the time it was committed is now defined as a crime; or

2.  **Aggravation:** The law retroactively ***aggravates a crime***, re-defining it so as to make it a greater offense than it was when it was committed (e.g., by transforming what would have been manslaughter into murder);

3.  **Increased punishment:** The law ***increases the punishment*** for an act that was a crime when it was committed; or

4.  **Rules of evidence:** The law ***alters the rules of evidence***, by allowing a conviction based on lesser evidence than was required at the time the act was committed.

*Calder v. Bull*, 3 U.S. 386 (1798) .

**B.  Criminal conduct only:** The ban on *ex post facto* laws applies only to measures which are ***criminal*** or ***penal.***

1.  **Ambiguity:** However, the dividing line between criminal and civil penalties is not always clear. The following are major illustrations of what measures have and have not been considered criminal (and therefore barred or not barred by the *ex post facto* clause when applied to conduct occurring before enactment of the measure).

   a.  **Criminal:** The following have been found to be criminal measures:

      i.  **Imprisonment:** Any measure calling for ***imprisonment;***

      ii. **Criminal fine:** Any other punitive measure which the government identifies as being part of its system of criminal punishment. For instance, if the statute defining a particular crime states that violators will be ***fined*** upon conviction, the fine will be treated as a criminal measure falling within the *ex post facto* clause.

   b.  **Not criminal:** Conversely, other types of measures, even though they may be "punitive" in the broad sense, are deemed civil rather than criminal, and therefore ***not*** subject to the ban on *ex post facto* laws.

      i.  **Professional disqualification:** Thus laws disqualifying convicted felons from certain ***professions*** (e.g., the practice of medicine) are not deemed penal, usually on the theory that such measures are a reasonable way of ensuring that the professions are practiced only by those who are fit for them.

    **ii. Deportation:** Similarly, laws providing for the ***deportation*** of persons based on certain acts committed before the enactment of the deportation measure are not penal, and therefore not subject to the *ex post facto* ban.

**C. Increase in punishment:** Any ***increase*** in the ***severity*** of a criminal punishment, compared with that authorized at the time the act was committed, violates the *ex post facto* clause. (But a retroactive ***reduction*** of a penalty does not.)

    **1. "Prior offense" measures:** But ***"prior offense"*** measures (i.e., measures providing for ***more severe criminal penalties*** for a given crime if the offender has been previously convicted of ***other offenses***) are ***not*** subject to *ex post facto* laws merely because the prior convictions occurred before the measure was enacted.

        **Example:** D is convicted of burglary in 2000, and again in 2001. In 2005, the legislature enacts a statute providing that robbery shall carry a prison term of one to five years, but that where the defendant has been previously convicted of two other felonies, the term shall be one to fifteen years. D is convicted of robbery in 2007 for a robbery he committed in 2006. He may be sentenced to fifteen years, even though the only grounds for the harsher-than-ordinarily-permitted sentence is criminal activity (the first two burglaries) committed before the increased-penalty statute was enacted. Cf. Tribe, p. 637.

**D. Rationale for ban:** The usual rationale for the *ex post facto* ban relates to the concept of ***"fair notice"*** — it is felt to be unfair to punish a person for an act which, at the time he committed it, he could not have known was subject to such a penalty.

    **1. Knowledge of who will be affected:** But another possible rationale is that the legislature should not be permitted to act "with knowledge of whom [the new measures] would adversely affect and how." Tribe, p. 640, n. 26. This rationale is similar to that behind the ban on bills of attainder, discussed immediately *infra*.

# VI. BILLS OF ATTAINDER

**A. Constitutional provision:** The Constitution prohibits both the federal government and the states from passing any ***"bill of attainder"***. Article I, §§ 9 and 10, respectively. The term "bill of attainder" has been interpreted to include not only the English bill by that name (which condemned named individuals to death and prohibited inheritance of their property) but also the English "bill of pains and penalties," which included lesser penalties. See Tribe, pp. 641-42

    **1. Coverage:** Thus the prohibition covers any legislative act which "appl[ies] either to ***named individuals*** or to ***easily ascertainable members of a group*** in such a way as to ***inflict punishment*** on them without a judicial trial … " *U.S. v. Lovett*, 328 U.S. 303 (1946).

        **Example:** In response to charges made by the House Un-American Activities Committee, Congress passes a measure which prohibits the payment of salaries to three named federal agency employees, on the grounds that they are engaged in "subversive activities."

*Held*, the act is invalid as a bill of attainder, since it applies to named or easily-identified individuals, and punishes them without a judicial trial. *U.S. v. Lovett, supra.*

**B. Rationale for clause:** The rationale for the ban on bills of attainder rests in the concept of *separation of powers*. The process of deciding which individuals should be subject to punishment is inherently a judicial process, and must be performed by the judicial branch, not by the legislature. Because of the political non-independence of the legislature, and its extreme responsiveness to popular will, it must act by rules of *general applicability*, not ones directed at specific individuals (at least where matters of punishment are concerned).

**C. Definition of "punishment":** The Bill of Attainder Clause applies only to legislative *"punishment"* of specific individuals or narrowly-defined groups. But recent cases have defined "punishment" somewhat broadly, to include measures having not only a "retributive" function, but also measures whose purpose is "rehabilitative," "deterrent" or "preventative." Thus a ban on union participation by Communist Party members was deemed "punishment" (and was thus a bill of attainder) even though the ban's purpose was to prevent strikes. See *U.S. v. Brown*, 381 U.S. 437 (1965).

    **1. Pure regulation not covered:** However, measures which are taken solely for the purpose of *regulation*, and which have no substantial stigmatizing element, are not prohibited by the Bill of Attainder Clause, even though they may contain aspects that are unfavorable to certain individuals. For instance, in *Hawker v. New York*, 170 U.S. 189 (1898), a ban on the practice of medicine by convicted felons was justified on the grounds that it was solely a regulatory measure.

---

*Quiz Yourself on*
## MISCELLANEOUS CLAUSES *(ENTIRE CHAPTER)*

**50.** The state of Okansas has a state-paid health plan, whereby the state pays the medical bills of indigent families after a $1,000-per-family annual deductible. Because of the generosity of this plan, the state has become concerned that some impoverished residents of other states offering less-generous (or no) medical coverage have been moving to Okansas to take advantage of the plan. Therefore, the Okansas legislature has provided that a family moving to Okansas from another state shall, for its first year of genuine residence in Okansas, be entitled only to those medical-bill payments that the family would have received in the state in which it previously resided.

    **(a)** You represent a poor family that has just moved to Okansas from Nebraska, which has no indigent medical coverage at all. What is the best constitutional argument you can make that Okansas' provision violates your client's rights? _____

    **(b)** Will the claim you make in (a) succeed? _____

**51.** Mill Co. has operated a steel mill in the Township of Fuschia for many years. Mill Co. owns both the factory and the land on which it is located. The mill has always obeyed all state and federal pollution control requirements. However, operation of a steel mill is inevitably a somewhat messy enterprise, with a fair amount of noise, smoke, etc. As the township has become more affluent and residential in character, the inhabitants have become increasingly unhappy with having a steel mill in their midst. Now, the township has amended its zoning ordinance so as to provide that no "heavy industry" (defined in a way that includes Mill Co.'s steel mill and a variety of other manufacturing operations) shall be permitted to operate anywhere in the town after four years from the ordinance's adoption. The effect of the ordinance is that Mill Co. or the next owner of its property may build houses, stores or warehouses on the site, but not operate a heavy manufacturing plant. Although the end of the four-year period is still two years away, Mill Co. wishes to challenge the ordinance.

**(a)** Assuming that the ordinance was enacted in a procedurally satisfactory manner, what is the strongest argument that Mill Co. can make attacking the constitutionality of the zoning ordinance as applied to it? _____

**(b)** Will this argument succeed? _____

52. The village of Green Valley wished to incinerate its trash and garbage in an ecologically sound way, rather than using up scarce landfill. It also wished to raise revenue as part of the process. Therefore, it entered into an arrangement with Waste Co., a trash management company. The arrangement provided for Waste Co. to build an incinerator in Green Valley, and for Waste Co. to pay Green Valley a 50¢ per ton "franchise fee" for every ton of trash or garbage processed by the plant over a 15-year period. (Waste Co. would make money by charging the public a fee for each load processed.) In return, Green Valley agreed to require by law, for the 15 years, that all trash and garbage produced in the town be sent to the Waste Co. facility. The arrangement operated as expected for the first five years, during which time Waste Co.'s fees to the town averaged about $2 million per year.

Then, New Co., another waste company that competed with Waste Co., proposed a new deal to Green Valley. New Co. asked Green Valley to require that trash (i.e., dry refuse) but not garbage (wet refuse, such as food remains) be sent to *its* facility. In return, New Co. would pay Green Valley a minimum of $1.5 million per year. Green Valley agreed, and changed its laws so that now, the Waste Co. plant would only get garbage, and the New Co. plant would get the trash. The net effect was that Green Valley's receipts went from $2 million a year to $3 million per year. (Green Valley, like most municipalities, could certainly benefit from the extra $1 million per year, but the town is not faced with extreme financial hardship.) The effect on Waste Co. was to reduce its profits by $500,000 per year.

**(a)** If Waste Co. wishes to challenge Green Valley's conduct on constitutional grounds, what is its best argument? _____

**(b)** Will this attack succeed? _____

53. In 1993, Byer purchased a small shopping center in the town of Happy Farms. There were several other similar shopping centers in town, as well as various other types of retail stores. At the time of the purchase, Happy Farms allowed retail stores to operate seven days a week, 24 hours a day, if they wished. At the time of the purchase, the shopping center had so called "percentage leases" with its tenants, whereby the rent paid was a percentage of the retail sales generated by the stores. Each percentage lease required the store owner to maintain hours on Sunday from noon to 6:00 p.m. Byer computed the amount that it was appropriate for him to pay for the center based on this flow of percentage rent. Six months after Byer made the purchase, Happy Farms changed its zoning ordinance to prohibit any retail store from opening on Sunday. This action (taken at the request of certain small store owners who wanted to be able to take Sundays off without losing sales to their competitors), caused Byer's tenants to suffer a 10% drop in revenues, which translated into a substantial loss of rent for Byer.

Byer now asserts that the Sunday closing law constitutes an impairment of his contractual rights, in violation of the Obligation of Contracts Clause. Is Byer's assertion correct? State your reasons.

**54.** In 1992, Dennis had sex with a 14-year-old girl, who purported to give consent. However, the state's criminal statutes regarded sex with a female under the age of 15 as statutory rape, regardless of ostensible consent. The penalty for rape was a prison sentence of up to five years. In 1993, the state legislature changed the penalty for statutory rape from a maximum of five years to a maximum of 10 years. Dennis was tried and convicted in 1994, and was sentenced to a prison term of seven years.

(a) If Dennis wishes to attack his conviction and/or sentence on constitutional grounds, what is his strongest argument? _____

(b) Will this argument succeed? State your reasons. _____

**55.** The Phrenic Brotherhood is a small, dedicated group of religious fundamentalists, located throughout the United States, whose stated mission is to dissuade the U.S. from opposing the rise of the religion of Phrenology throughout the world. Certain acts of terrorism have been traced to the Brotherhood, though it is not known who in particular committed these acts. The state of New Righteous, in response to a recent act of terrorism in the state thought to be associated with the Brotherhood, passed the following statute: "No member of the group known as the Phrenic Brotherhood shall be hired or retained on the payroll of any branch of the government of this state." Oren, who was employed as a file clerk at the New Righteous Department of Social Security, was known to his superior to be a member of the Brotherhood. The superior, citing the newly enacted statute, fired Oren.

(a) If Oren wishes to attack the statute on constitutional grounds, what argument (putting aside any argument based directly upon the First Amendment) has the best chance of success for him?

_____

(b) Will this attack succeed? _____

*Answers*

**50. (a) That it violates the "right to travel," a right protected by the 14th Amendment's Privileges & Immunities Clause.**

**(b) Yes, probably.** The Court held in *Saenz v. Roe* that a state may not provide that when a family moves into the state, for one year after arrival the family's welfare payments shall be limited to the amount that the family would have received in their prior state of residence. The Court reasoned that this violates the "right to travel" — one of the rights of "national citizenship" guaranteed by the 14th Amendment's P&I clause — because the state's action was irrational except as an attempt to carry out the forbidden objective of discouraging poor people from moving into the state. There is no reason why the same principle shouldn't apply here, since we're told the state's action is based upon this same unlawful motive.

**51. (a) That the ordinance constitutes a "taking" in violation of the Fifth Amendment.**

**(b) No, probably.** The Fifth Amendment provides that "nor shall private property be taken for public use, without just compensation." This clause, though by its terms applies only to the federal government, also applies to states and municipalities via the Fourteenth Amendment's Due Process Clause. An enactment that is labelled a "land use regulation" will generally not constitute a "taking," unless it "den[ies] an owner economically viable use of his land." Here Mill Co. is not being deprived of *all* economically viable use of its land — it is free to build houses, stores or warehouses on the site. The fact that the *particular* use being made of the property at this moment is now being foreclosed is not enough to meet this "no economically viable use" standard. See, e.g., *Goldblatt v. Hempstead* (town does not commit a "taking" where it bans the continued operation of a sand and gravel pit). If the ordinance had ***immediately*** taken effect, without any "amortization" period (here, four years), this might have tipped the balance in favor of a finding that a taking had occurred. But the amortization period, together with the fact that the mill owners had already had many years to derive value from the plant, remove this difficulty.

**52. (a) That it violated the Obligation of Contracts Clause.**

**(b) Yes, probably.** Art. I, Section 10, provides that "no State shall … pass any … Law impairing the Obligation of Contracts. … " This provision applies both to states and to municipalities. The Clause has been interpreted by the Supreme Court to mean that a state's attempt to ***escape from its financial obligations*** will be sustained only where a ***significant public need*** exists that cannot be ***reasonably handled*** in any other way. Here, Green Valley has in effect modified the terms of its agreement with Waste Co., by changing the law so that Waste Co. no longer gets the town's trash. The fact that Green Valley is somewhat better off financially as a result of this decision, and even the fact that the gain to Green Valley is greater than the loss to Waste Co., will not be enough to meet the requirement that there be a significant public need that cannot be reasonably handled in any other way. Court decisions show that an impairment will be "reasonable" only if it was induced by ***unforeseen developments*** occurring after the original contract was made; here, it was certainly foreseeable that some other waste management company might come along with a more financially attractive deal. Also, the Court has refused to merely balance the benefit to the public against the damage to the other party to the contract. See *U.S. Trust Co. v. New Jersey*. If Green Valley had been on the verge of insolvency, with this modification able to make the difference, then the impairment might stand; however, the facts do not indicate this level of hardship. Therefore, the Court would probably find that the Obligations of Contracts Clause was violated.

**53. No.** The Obligation of Contracts Clause applies only where the state takes an action that is ***specifically directed*** at contractual obligations. If the state applies a ***"generally applicable rule of conduct"*** which has the ***incidental by-product*** of impairing contractual obligations, the Contract Clause does not apply at all. See *Exxon Corp. v. Eagerton*. Here, Happy Farms has enacted a generally applicable rule, one requiring Sunday closings. The fact that certain contractual obligations (the store owners' contractual duty to remain open on Sundays) happen to be impaired is irrelevant. Therefore, we never get to the point of even determining whether the impairment here was justified by pressing needs of public policy (as we would have to do in a situation where the state specifically directed its new law at contractual obligations).

**54. (a) That it is an *ex post facto* law.**

**(b) Yes.** The Constitution prevents a state government from enacting an *ex post facto* law; see Art. I, Section 10. An *ex post facto* law is one which has a retroactive punitive effect. Some *ex post facto* laws are ones which outlaw conduct that was not criminal at the time it was committed. But there is a second kind of *ex post facto* law: one which ***increases*** the ***severity*** of a criminal punishment, compared with that authorized at the time the act was committed. Here, Dennis could not have been sentenced to more than five years in prison at the moment he committed the offense, so his sentence now constitutes a violation of the *ex post facto* ban.

**55. (a) That the statute violates the prohibition on bills of attainder.**

**(b) Yes, probably.** The Constitution prohibits both the federal government and the states from passing any "bill of attainder." (See Art. I, Section 10, for the provision as it applies to states.) The term covers any legislative act which "applies either to ***named individuals*** or to ***easily ascertainable members of a group*** in such a way as to ***inflict punishment*** on them without a judicial trial. … " Here, since the Phrenic Brotherhood is a relatively small group, and its members are fairly easily ascertained, the requirements seem met. Assuming that dismissal from the state payroll is found to be "punishment," the law seems to be a bill of attainder. Measures taken solely for the purpose of *regulation*, and which have no substantial stigmatizing element, are not prohibited by the Bill of Attainder Clause. Here, however, since the law applies to all state government jobs, and applies without respect to whether the individual has a specific intent to espouse the terrorist beliefs of some Brotherhood leaders, the law seems more like punishment than regulation. Especially since there is a risk that freedom of association values will be infringed, the Court will probably conclude that the law is a bill of attainder. See, e.g., *U.S. v. Brown* (law making it a crime for a Communist Party member to serve as an officer of a labor union is struck down as a bill of attainder).

## Exam Tips on
## MISCELLANEOUS CLAUSES

The Clauses covered in this chapter are easy to miss on an exam, because each applies to fairly specialized facts and is likely to be buried within a much larger fact pattern. Most of your work will therefore consist of spotting the issue; once you do so, analyzing it correctly shouldn't be too hard. Here are some things to look for:

☞ If your fact pattern happens to involve a person who is prevented from *travelling* from state to state, or blocked from *voting* in a national election, consider whether the *14th Amendment's Privileges and Immunities Clause* has been violated. A 1999 decision (*Saenz v. Roe*) makes questions on this Clause more likely — if the state is discriminating against people who recently moved into the state, the clause is probably violated. (But if your fact pattern involves a target state that discriminates against out-of-staters who have not moved into the target state, probably it's the *Article IV* P&I Clause, *not* the 14th Amendment P&I Clause, that's been violated.)

☞ If you have a fact pattern that involves *land-use regulation* by the state or federal government, be alert to a *Takings* Clause issue.

   ☞ The main kinds of regulations that should put you on notice to look for a Takings problem are: (1) *zoning* regs; (2) *environmental-protection* regs; and (3) *landmark-protection* regs. In general, if government is telling the owner, "You can't do such-and-such with your property" or "If you want to do such-and-such with your property, you'll have to submit to the following conditions ... ," there is likely to be a Takings issue.

   ☞ Remember that for a land-use regulation to avoid being a taking it must *not deprive an owner of all economically viable use* of his land.

      ☞ The typical zoning regulation, which is generally-applicable and leaves the owner with at least some reasonable alternative uses of the property, will *not* normally be a "taking."

      ☞ But a *permanent ban* on constructing any building on a lot *would* be a "taking," if there was no economically attractive use of the property (e.g., recreational) that did not involve construction.

☞ Also, if you have a fact pattern in which the government has clearly exercised its *eminent domain powers*, don't forget to say that the taking must be for a *"public use."* But "public use" is a very watered-down standard — there must merely be some "public benefit," and almost anything qualifies (e.g., economic development such as more jobs or tax revenues). It can still be a public benefit even though the condemned property is turned over to private developers. Cite to *Kelo v. New London* on this point.

☞ If your fact pattern has the government *"rewriting the rules"* in a way that seems to *change previously-executed contracts*, consider whether the *"Contract"* Clause has been violated. It's important for you to distinguish between government's attempt to re-write contracts to which it's a party, and government's attempt to re-write contracts between private parties:

☞ Where government is trying to escape from *its own "bad deals,"* you should be quick to find a Contract Clause violation. Remember that the Court scrutinizes this type of government action closely, and will allow it only if a *"significant public need"* exists that cannot be reasonably handled in any other way. (*Example:* If a state government faces bankruptcy unless it re-writes the payment schedule on some bonds, and the problem can't be handled by borrowing fresh funds, this might be sufficient)

☞ Where government is re-writing contracts made by *private parties*, remember that the judicial review is not so tough. So long as the government is dealing with an emergency, and protecting broad social interests (rather than a narrow, favored group), the Court will tend to uphold any contract-rewriting that is *"reasonable"* in the circumstances.

☞ If the state applies a *"generally applicable* rule of conduct" that merely has the *incidental by-product* of impairing contractual obligations, the Contract Clause *doesn't come into effect at all*. This element is perhaps the most frequently tested aspect of the Contract Clause — fact patterns typically involve some general environmental or other regulatory change that happens to make one party's promised performance under a private contract no longer legal. Here, you should conclude that the Contracts Clause never comes into play, because the government action wasn't "directed at" (enacted for the purpose of affecting) the contractual obligation.

☞ *Ex post facto* laws are fairly easy to spot — whenever you see government *making something a crime* that wasn't a crime when it was done, or *increasing the penalty* for something beyond what was on the books when it was done, you may have an *ex post facto* violation.

☞ Remember that only *"criminal"* penalties, not "civil" or "regulatory" ones, are covered. Often this distinction is what's being tested.

☞ *Bill of attainder* issues are rare. Only when you see the legislature trying to punish a group that is so *narrowly-defined* that it's possible to name all the affected people in advance, should you even think about bill of attainder. Typical example: The legislature holds that members of a particular named *organization* may not hold a certain post or receive a certain benefit.

# Chapter 12

# STATE ACTION

## *ChapterScope*

Nearly all of the rights guaranteed by the Constitution to individuals are protected only against interference *by government*. This is sometimes called the requirement of *"state action."* However, sometimes even a private individual's actions are found to be "state action," and thus subject to the Constitution. Here are the main concepts in this Chapter:

- ■ **"Public function" doctrine:** Under the *"public function"* doctrine, if a private individual or group is entrusted by the state to perform functions that are traditionally viewed as *governmental in nature*, the private individual becomes an agent of the state, and he constitute "state action." Therefore, his acts must obey the Constitution.

- ■ **"State involvement" doctrine:** Alternatively, a private individual's conduct may be transformed into "state action" if the state is *heavily involved* in those activities. This is the *"state involvement"* branch of state-action doctrine. Examples are where:

  - ❏ the state *"commands"* or *"requires"* the private person's action;

  - ❏ the state *"encourages"* the private party's actions;

  - ❏ the state and the private actor have a *"symbiotic"* or *"mutually beneficial"* relationship;

  - ❏ the state is *"entangled"* with the private actor (e.g., they act together to carry out the action being challenged).

## I. INTRODUCTION

- **A. Only state conduct covered:** Nearly all of the rights and liberties which the Constitution guarantees to individuals are protected only against interference *by governmental entities*. For instance, the guarantees of due process and equal protection, given by §1 of the Fourteenth Amendment, are introduced by the words "No State shall. ... "

  - **1. Self-executing rights:** In fact, of the constitutional rights which are "self-executing" (i.e., capable of enforcement by courts even without specific congressional legislation enacted to enforce the right), *only* the Thirteenth Amendment's prohibition on slavery (discussed *infra*, p. 444) includes private as well as governmental conduct. See Tribe, p. 1688, n. 1.

  - **2. Need for "state action" doctrine:** Therefore, in virtually every litigation in which an individual argues that his constitutional rights have been violated, the court can grant relief only if it finds that there has been *state action*, i.e., some sort of *participation by a governmental entity* sufficient to make the particular constitutional provision applicable. This chapter examines the various ways in which the Supreme Court has gone about determining whether state action exists.

  - **3. Sometimes apparent:** In many instances, the existence of state action will be so apparent that this will not be a real issue. For instance, whenever the constitutional claim is that a ***statute or regulation itself*** violates the Constitution (e.g., by being racially discriminatory), the existence of state action is apparent. Similarly, the existence of state action is clear in the case of a claim that a state official, while engaged in performance of his duties, has violated the plaintiff's constitutional rights. The issue arises only where the specific action alleged to interfere with a constitutional right is taken by a ***private individual***, i.e., one not acting on behalf of the government.

    **a.** **Two sides:** In this situation, the defendant typically argues that there cannot have been a constitutional violation because there has been no state action. The plaintiff, in contrast, typically contends that the state has in some way encouraged, benefitted from, or at least acquiesced in the private individual's conduct, thereby furnishing the requisite state involvement.

**4.** **Governmental units:** Putting aside the ***degree*** of governmental action required, the term "government" is broadly defined for purposes of determining the existence of "state action." Not only actions taken by the state, but those taken by any of its ***subdivisions***, will count as state action. Thus actions by a ***city, county, municipally-owned utility***, etc., will all qualify. Furthermore, in the case of those constitutional rights which are protected against interference at the hands of the federal government, ***any federal instrumentality*** (e.g., any federal agency or commission) will be included.

    **a.** **Government-run corporation:** In fact, even a ***corporation*** will be treated as a governmental entity, if it's set up by the government, remains under governmental control, and furthers governmental objectives. Thus ***Amtrak*** was found to be part of the federal government, for First Amendment purposes, because it was created by the U.S., the President appoints a majority of its board of directors, and it carries out the federal mission of avoiding the extinction of private passenger-train service. *Lebron v. National Railroad Passenger Corp.*, 513 U.S. 374 (1995).

**5.** **Confusing doctrines:** The Supreme Court has been largely unable to formulate rules about when the degree of state involvement is sufficiently great to convert a private person's conduct into "state action." Instead, the Court has said, in essence, that each case must be judged on its own facts. The result is a series of cases that are difficult or impossible to reconcile, and a consequent inability of observers to predict how the next case will be decided.

**B.** **Early interpretations of "state action":** The greatest importance of the state-action requirement is in connection with the Fourteenth Amendment's equal protection and due process guarantees.

**1.** ***The Civil Rights Cases:*** The first significant articulation by the Supreme Court that these Fourteenth Amendment rights are applicable only where state action is present was in the ***Civil Rights Cases***, 109 U.S. 3 (1883).

    **a.** **Facts:** The *Civil Rights Cases* involved the Civil Rights Act of 1875, in which Congress prohibited all persons from denying, on the basis of race, any individual's equal access to inns, public transportation, theaters and other places of public accommodation. The statute was clearly applicable to private conduct. The question before the Court was whether Congress had the ***power*** to enact such a statute.

    **b.** **Holding:** In deciding the case, the Court made three main holdings, which have varying degrees of acceptance today.

c. **Applicable solely to state action:** First, the Court held that the guarantees of equal protection and due process, given by §1 of the Fourteenth Amendment, apply by their own terms *solely to state action*. This holding remains valid today, at least in the sense that, in the *absence* of congressional legislation, the courts *will not find conduct that is exclusively private to be violative of these Fourteenth Amendment guarantees.*

d. **Congress without power:** Secondly, the Court held that the grant to Congress in §5 of the Fourteenth Amendment of the power to enforce these guarantees did *not authorize Congress to regulate solely private conduct*. §5 "does not authorize Congress to create a code of municipal law for the regulation of private rights. ... " The only law-making power given to Congress under §5 of the Amendment, the Court held, was the ability to pass laws to prevent the *states, by their own action*, from interfering with these rights.

   i. **Probably no longer the law:** It is not clear whether this aspect of the *Civil Rights Cases* remains good law, but it probably does not. There is no case in which a majority of the Court has held, in a single opinion, that §5 of the Fourteenth Amendment allows Congress to reach purely private conduct. But six Justices in *U.S. v. Guest*, 383 U.S. 745 (1966), in two separate opinions, argued that Congress has such power. See the fuller discussion of this issue *infra*, p. 442.

e. **Thirteenth Amendment inapplicable:** Lastly, the Court held that the statute could not be justified as an exercise of the *Thirteenth* Amendment. The Court conceded that that Amendment is *applicable to private as well as state conduct*, since it prevents private individuals from holding others in slavery. But the Amendment by its terms bars only "slavery [and] involuntary servitude," and the Court took a narrow view of this phrase. Refusal to allow blacks to use public accommodations was simply not a "badge of slavery."

   i. **Overruled:** This narrow view of what constitutes a "badge of slavery" prohibited under the Thirteenth Amendment has clearly been overruled, at least with respect to Congress' power to enact *legislation* to enforce that Amendment (an enforcement power given in §2 of the Amendment.) See, e.g., *Jones v. Alfred H. Mayer Co.*, 392 U.S. 409 (1968), discussed *infra*, pp. 444. But the Court has continued to take a narrow view of the definition of slavery when analyzing state or private conduct directly, where there is no relevant congressional statute. Only conduct involving *actual peonage* (e.g., state laws imprisoning workers who violate labor contracts) has so far been held directly violative of the Amendment itself. See Tribe, p. 1688, n. 1.

f. **Statute invalidated:** Since there was, in the majority's view, no satisfactory constitutional basis for the 1875 Civil Rights Act, the Act was *invalidated.*

g. **Dissent:** Justice Harlan, in dissent, objected to the majority's view of both the Thirteenth and the Fourteenth Amendments.

   i. **Broad view of Thirteenth:** As to the Thirteenth, he believed that freedom from slavery necessarily entailed not only the liberation from physical bondage, but also the eradication of all *"burdens and disabilities"* suffered by black people because of their race. Therefore, he believed that Congress could prevent black people from being denied, on grounds of race, those *"civil rights"* which white people have. In his opinion, these civil rights included the right to use inns, public transport, and other public facilities.

ii. **Harlan's Fourteenth Amendment view:** With respect to the Fourteenth Amendment, Harlan pointed to a part of §1 that the majority ignored, the provision that "[a]ll persons born or naturalized in the United States and subject to the jurisdiction thereof, are citizens of the United States and of the State wherein they reside." He believed that this section gave blacks *state citizenship*, and that this grant of state citizenship in turn entitled them to "exemption from race discrimination in respect of *any civil right belonging to citizens of the white race* in the same State." As in the case of the Thirteenth Amendment, he believed that these civil rights included access to public accommodations. (Apart from this argument, Harlan also contended that railroad companies, innkeepers, etc., since they serve the public and are subject to state regulation, should be viewed as *agents of the state*, so that their conduct constitutes state action for equal protection and due process purposes.)

2. **Consequence of case:** The *Civil Rights Cases*, and other cases decided shortly thereafter which took an equally narrow view of congressional power, had a devastating effect on Congress' ability to prevent the emergence of virtual apartheid in the South. It was not until the 1940s that some meaningful limits on unofficial racial discrimination were imposed; this happened principally through a broadening of the concept of "state action," a process described below.

C. **Modern approach to state action:** The narrow view of what constitutes "state action," implicit in the *Civil Rights Cases*, remained in force until the 1940s. Then, the Court began to broaden the concept of state action, with the result that various acts that were carried out by private persons, not state officials, were nonetheless attributed to the state. The Court has used a number of theories (or, perhaps "descriptions" is a better term) to explain why particular private conduct is so closely linked to official conduct that it should be considered state action. The cases generally seem to fall into two main groups: (1) those in which the private activity is attributable to the government because the private actor is fulfilling a *"public function"*; and (2) those in which the various connections (the *"nexus"*) between the state and the private actor are sufficiently great that the state can be said to be *involved in*, or even to have *"encouraged,"* the private activity which is being complained of. We will consider each of these lines of cases in turn.

1. **Limitations by Burger/Rehnquist Court:** In both of these areas, the broadening of the state action concept culminated during the Warren era. The Burger/Rehnquist Court has clearly stopped the state action concept from further expansion, and in numerous respects appears to have in fact narrowed it. At the very least, the modern Court has clearly disproved predictions made by some during the Warren era, that nearly all private conduct might come to be viewed as somehow linked with the state and therefore subject to constitutional prohibitions. See Gunther (12th Ed.), p. 889.

2. **Relation between two doctrines:** The relation between the "public function" doctrine and the "nexus" doctrine remains somewhat obscure. Apparently, the party who is attempting to show that his adversary's conduct constitutes state action will prevail if he can show *either* that that adversary performed a "public function" *or* that there was a suf-

ficient "nexus" of contacts between the state and the adversary to justify subjecting the latter to constitutional prohibitions.

## II.  THE "PUBLIC FUNCTION" APPROACH

A. **The "public function" approach generally:**  The "public function" doctrine holds that when a private individual (or group) is entrusted by the state with the performance of functions that are *governmental in nature*, he becomes an agent of the state and his acts constitute state action. This public function analysis at one time appeared to be potentially extremely broad-sweeping. But the Burger/Rehnquist Court has cut back the doctrine substantially, principally by insisting that the function be one that is normally "exclusively" reserved to the state. See *infra*, p. 423.

B. **The *White Primary Cases*:**  The "public function" analysis seems to have had its start in the so-called *White Primary Cases*. In a series of decisions, the Court held that despite state attempts to delegate more and more of the nominating process to private political parties, the *entire electoral process is a public function* and the political parties are acting as agents of the state. Therefore, they may not practice racial discrimination.

    1. **Discrimination by political parties:**  For instance, where a state convention of Democrats established a rule that only whites could vote in the Texas Democratic Primary, the racial restriction was held to be violative of the Fifteenth Amendment, in *Smith v. Allwright*, 321 U.S. 649 (1944).

    2. **Extended to pre-primary:**  This rationale was carried even further in *Terry v. Adams*, 345 U.S. 461 (1953), where state action was found even in the racially-restrictive "*pre-primary*" elections held by the Jaybird Democratic Association, a group whose candidate almost always won the ensuing Democratic Primary (usually unopposed).

      a. **Rationale:**  There was no majority opinion, but the prevailing rationale appeared to be that the state, by inaction, had permitted this unofficial pre-election to *usurp the role of the official primary* (which, under *Smith*, was itself an integral part of the election process). Several of the Justices seemed to rely on the fact that the state's tolerance of private discrimination reflected a *purposeful* decision to maintain a racially discriminatory system of elections. See Tribe, p. 1708.

    3. **Scope of rationale:**  It is not clear how broadly applicable the rationale of the *White Primary Cases* is. It does not seem likely that all or most other conduct by political parties will be deemed to be state action; for instance, the selection of party chairmen would probably not be held to be the performance of a public function. Nor is it clear that discrimination based on grounds other than race, even in the primary process, would necessarily be held to be state action; the *White Primary Cases* were founded on the Fifteenth Amendment, which applies only to racial discrimination. Thus a party which limited its membership solely to men, or solely to Protestants, might well be found not to be engaged in state action. See Tribe, p. 1119, n. 11.

C. **Company towns and shopping centers:**  A second major area in which "public function" analysis developed concerned actions taken by the owners of *company towns* and *shopping centers.*

1. **Issue:**   The issue in these cases was whether the owner of the property had the right to use *state trespass laws* to keep out people who wished to *speak* or *distribute literature* on the property. Where operation of the property was held to be a public function, First Amendment guarantees became applicable, barring the use of state trespass laws. By contrast, where there was no public function, there were no First Amendment rights and the owner therefore had the ability to keep the outsiders off his property.

2. **Company town:**   The first of this line of cases involved a company town. In *Marsh v. Alabama*, 326 U.S. 501 (1946), a Jehovah's Witness was charged with criminal trespass for distributing religious literature in the town of Chickasaw, Alabama, a town *wholly owned* by the Gulf Shipbuilding Corporation. The Court held that, since the town was just like any other town (except for the fact that title to the real estate was vested in a private company), *operation of the town was a public function*. Prior cases had held that ordinary non-private towns could not bar distribution of religious literature, under First Amendment principles; these principles were therefore applicable to Chickasaw as well.

   a. **Public access:**   The *Marsh* Court attached some importance to the fact that the town was not limited to housing, but also included a downtown shopping district, which was accessible to and freely used by outsiders. The Court's stress on this fact may mean that privately-owned communities that are *purely residential*, as well as *camps for migrant workers*, are *not* fulfilling public functions, since these are typically not used by outsiders. Later cases, discussed *infra*, holding that shopping centers are not by themselves engaged in public functions, seem to buttress this more limited view of what types of property will be found to be used for public functions.

   b. **Balancing:**   Strict logic would indicate that, since Chickasaw fulfilled a "public function," *any activity* taken in connection with its administration would be subjected to constitutional scrutiny. For instance, by this analysis, any person hired as a *sanitation worker* under a contract would presumably have the right to procedural due process before being discharged. Yet the *Marsh* Court's analysis leaves open the possibility that the operation of a town may be a public function only for *some, but not all*, purposes. The opinion seems to call for a *balancing test*, whereby "the constitutional rights of owners of property" are balanced against the right of the people to "enjoy freedom of the press and religion."

      i. **Application:**   Under such a balancing test, the right of a town worker not to be discharged without a fair hearing might be found to weigh less heavily on the scale than did the right to distribute literature, and might lead to a decision that such firings are not part of the town's public function. A similar holding might be made in response to charges that the town refused to hire, say, women for sanitation positions.

3. **Shopping centers:**   For a while, it appeared that *shopping centers* would also be treated as engaged in a public function, so that First Amendment guarantees, at least, would be applicable to activities there. But cases so indicating were overruled in 1976 by *Hudgens v. NLRB*, 424 U.S. 507 (1976).

   a. **Facts and holding:**   In *Hudgens*, union members who were engaged in a labor dispute with one of the stores in a shopping mall attempted to picket in the open area and the parking lot of the mall. A majority of the Court held that, prior cases to the contrary notwithstanding, a large self-contained *shopping center* was *simply not the*

***equivalent of the company town*** in *Marsh*, and that ***no First Amendment guarantees were applicable to activities in it.***

  **b.** **State of company-town cases:** *Marsh* itself presumably remains good law. But the effect of *Hudgens* is to limit *Marsh* to its own facts; thus operation of a company-owned town will be deemed a public function, but operation of property that supplies less than a full range of municipal services will not be.

**D. Parks and recreation:** Operation of a ***park*** has been considered the exercise of a "public function."

  **1.** ***Evans case:*** Thus in *Evans v. Newton*, 382 U.S. 296 (1966), a park in Macon, Georgia had been left in trust by Senator Bacon, with the proviso that it be used only for whites. At first, the City of Macon acted as trustee and enforced the proviso; then, it was replaced by private trustees who did the same.

    **a.** **Holding:** The Supreme Court held that operation of the park in a racially discriminatory manner violated the Fourteenth Amendment. One reason for this conclusion was that the services rendered even by a private park were ***"municipal in nature"***; like fire and police departments, a park ***"traditionally serves the community."***

    **b.** **Aftermath of case:** The Supreme Court was subsequently required to decide whether the reverter in Senator Bacon's will, which was to be triggered if the park was no longer racially restricted, could constitutionally be enforced by the state. It concluded that it could, in *Evans v. Abney*, discussed *infra*, p. 427.

  **2.** **Present status:** It is unlikely that the "public function" analysis of *Evans v. Newton* will be extended to include other types of recreational facilities, such as country clubs or amusement parks. The Burger/Rehnquist Court has held that only those functions which are traditionally ***"exclusively"*** performed by the state will be deemed public functions. A footnote to Justice Rehnquist's majority opinion in *Flagg Bros., infra*, below, suggests that "parks for recreational purposes" do not fit into this category, and that the real explanation for *Evans* lay in the city's day-to-day involvement in the park's maintenance. Thus if the issue were to arise again, purely private operation of even an ordinary park might no longer be held to be a public function.

**E. The requirement of state "exclusivity":** In the Burger/Rehnquist years, the Court has dramatically narrowed the situations in which "public function" analysis will apply, by requiring that the function be one which has traditionally been ***exclusively*** the domain of the government. The Court has used this exclusivity requirement on at least four occasions to reject the application of the public function doctrine.

  **1.** **Utilities:** Operation of a ***privately-owned utility*** licensed and regulated by the state was held ***not*** to be performance of a public function, in ***Jackson v. Metropolitan Edison Co.***, 419 U.S. 345 (1974).

    **a.** **Rationale:** Public function analysis is applicable, the Court said, only where a private entity exercises "powers traditionally ***exclusively reserved*** to the State." This exclusivity requirement was not met by operation of the utility in *Jackson*, the Court concluded; this was demonstrated by the fact that state law did not ***obligate*** the state to furnish power.

    **i.** **"Public interest" rationale rejected:**  The *Jackson* Court explicitly rejected the argument that all heavily regulated businesses "affected with a public interest" should be treated as exercising public functions.

  **b.** **Dissent:**  Justice Marshall, in dissent, would have treated as state action the provision of any service *"uniquely public in nature,"* which in his view included operation of a utility. The mere existence of governmental regulation of an enterprise was not sufficient, he conceded; but in the case of a utility, the state invariably either provided the service itself, or so heavily regulated it that the private enterprise in effect had "surrender[ed] many of the prerogatives normally associated with private enterprise and behave[s] in many ways like a government body."

**2.** **Warehouseman's lien:**  The impact of the exclusivity requirement was still more evident in a case in which the Court held that sale by a *warehouseman* of goods stored with him in which he had a *warehouseman's lien* for unpaid storage charges was not a public function. *Flagg Bros., Inc. v. Brooks*, 436 U.S. 149 (1978).

  **a.** **Rationale:**  The majority, in an opinion by Justice Rehnquist, rejected the contention that resolution of private disputes was traditionally an exclusive government function. Here, for instance, Rehnquist argued, the dispute need not have been settled by the warehouseman's sale: the owner of the goods could have brought a replevin action, or could have sued for damages based on her claim that she had not authorized the storage.

    **i.** **Application to other areas:**  Yet the majority seemed to be slightly uncomfortable with its rigid holding that only functions traditionally reserved exclusively to the state would be deemed "public" ones. In certain areas, the majority opinion said, there was a "greater" degree of exclusivity than that involved in the dispute-resolution situation; these areas included "education, fire and police protection, and tax collection." The majority expressly declined to say whether performance of these functions would be deemed "public"; yet it was also unwilling to characterize them as manifesting complete (as opposed to "greater") exclusivity. Thus the public function doctrine's application in these areas remains uncertain.

  **b.** **Dissent:**  Three dissenters, in an opinion written by Justice Stevens, objected to the majority's imposition of an exclusivity requirement. The dissenters believed that such a requirement was not imposed by prior cases; they pointed to *Evans v. Newton (supra,* p. 423), for instance, and insisted that that was a case in which the activity (operation of a park) was found to be a public function even though it was *not* "exclusive." (The majority claimed that the case had really been decided in reliance on the city's day-to-day involvement in maintaining the park.)

    **i.** **Exclusivity satisfied:**  The dissenters also objected to the majority's conclusion that the debt-resolution mechanism at issue was not an exclusively public one; the fact that the owner of the goods could sue the warehouse for damages for wrongfully disposing of them did not make the lien foreclosure itself any less an exclusively public function (any more than allowing a citizen to sue a policeman for false arrest transformed the arrest into a private rather than a public act.)

  **c.** **Encouragement theory:**  In *Flagg Bros.*, the owner of the goods also claimed that there was state action because the state, by statutorily authorizing the warehouseman to impose a lien and foreclose on it in these circumstances, was "encouraging" the warehouseman's conduct. This aspect of the case is discussed in the treatment of the "encouragement" or "involvement" cases *infra*, p. 432.

3. **Nursing homes:** Operation of *nursing homes*, including the making of decisions about patient care, was found *not* to be a public function, in *Blum v. Yaretsky*, 457 U.S. 991 (1982). The majority seemed to be imposing still another requirement for application of the public function doctrine: that the activity be one which the state is *required* to provide by statute or by the state constitution. Since the state was not required to supply nursing home, or other medical, care, no public function was involved. (Other aspects of the case are discussed *infra*, pp. 427.)

4. **Private school:** One of the issues expressly left open in *Flagg Bros.* was resolved when the Court held that operation of a *private school*, even one whose income comes primarily from public grants, is *not* a public function. *Rendell-Baker v. Kohn*, 457 U.S. 830 (1981). Provision of education was not the "exclusive" prerogative of the state, even though it was a function normally provided by the state out of public funds.

F. **Future of "public function" doctrine:** In summary, the "public function" doctrine has been *substantially narrowed* by the Burger/Rehnquist Court. It will probably only be applied where two quite stringent conditions are met: (1) the function is one which is *traditionally the exclusive prerogative* of the state; and (2) some statute or state constitutional provision *in fact requires the state* to perform the function.

1. **Where satisfied:** The present Court seems to regard only two groups of prior cases as meeting these requirements: the maintenance of *streets* (in *Marsh v. Alabama*, the company-town case) and the maintenance of an *electoral system* (in the *White Primary Cases*.)

# III. "NEXUS" — THE SIGNIFICANCE OF STATE INVOLVEMENT

A. **The "nexus" theory generally:** The second broad branch of the state action doctrine relates not to the type of activity carried out by the private actor, but to the *conduct of the government*. If the government is sufficiently *"involved"* in the private actor's conduct or *"encourages"* that conduct, or *benefits from* it, the private party's acts will be deemed state action, and subjected to constitutional review. A common catch-all way of referring to this branch of state-action analysis is to call it the *"nexus"* approach; that is, the issue is the nexus, or *points of contact*, between the state and the private actor.

B. **"Commandment":** One way in which the state can become responsible for a private party's conduct is by *commanding* that conduct. Some examples of commandment are so obvious that no one would dispute the presence of state action; for instance, if the state ordered private restaurant owners to serve only white customers, both the order, and the private owners' execution of it, would be state action.

1. **Facially neutral law:** Much more interesting are those situations where the state, by *applying facially neutral laws, enforces private agreements* with the result that one person is judicially ordered to discriminate against another. Even the application of such neutral laws may be construed as a commandment to discriminate, and therefore state action.

2. ***Shelley v. Kraemer:*** The classic illustration of this principle is ***Shelley v. Kraemer***, 334 U.S. 1 (1948).

    **a. Facts of *Shelley*:**  *Shelley* involved the enforceability of ***racially restrictive covenants***. Most homeowners in an area had entered into a covenant that their property would not be owned by anyone but Caucasians for 50 years. When blacks bought homes from willing white owners despite the covenants, other whites, who were owners of properties also subject to the covenants, sued to block the blacks from taking possession. The issue before the Supreme Court was whether the state courts could award the white plaintiffs the relief they sought, without violating the Fourteenth Amendment.

    **b. Holding:**  The Supreme Court held that ***judicial enforcement*** of the restrictive covenant ***would constitute state action***, and would therefore violate the Fourteenth Amendment. "[B]ut for the active intervention of the state courts, supported by the full panoply of state power, [defendants] would have been free to occupy the properties in question. ... " Nor was it relevant that enforcement by the state occurred because of a longstanding ***common-law***, rather than ***statutory***, policy of granting such enforcement.

        **i. Not inaction:**  The Court also noted that this was not a case in which the state was simply remaining ***inactive***, while one private person discriminated against another. The *Shelley* Court stressed that the case involved ***willing sellers*** as well as buyers, so that it was only the state's coercive judicial machinery which would cause the discrimination to occur.

**3. Damage actions:**  Suppose the white plaintiffs in *Shelley* had sought not an injunction against the black purchasers, but ***money damages*** against the ***white sellers***. Granting this relief, too, would be state action and a violation of the Fourteenth Amendment, the Court held in ***Barrows v. Jackson***, 346 U.S. 249 (1953).

    **a. Rationale:**  The Court's rationale was that awarding such relief would impede an agreement between an otherwise willing seller and buyer just as the injunction sought in *Shelley* would have, since the seller would be either completely dissuaded from selling to a black by the possibility of a damage action, or at least motivated to charge black buyers a higher price to cover a possible damage award.

**4. Scope of *Shelley* uncertain:**  The scope of *Shelley* (and *Barrows*) is highly unclear.

    **a. Broad reading:**  A broad reading of *Shelley* would be that anytime a person's decision to discriminate, or an agreement between two or more people to discriminate, is enforced or left undisturbed by the state's legal system (even pursuant to a facially neutral legal rule), state action exists.

        **i. Refusal to sell:**  By this reading, if a white homeowner who had signed a racially restrictive covenant like the one in *Shelley* simply ***refused to sell*** to a black in reliance on the covenant, the judiciary's refusal to ***prevent*** the white from relying on the agreement would be state action and thus unconstitutional.

        **ii. Refusal to serve:**  Similarly, by this reading of *Shelley*, a restaurant owner's decision not to allow black civil rights workers to conduct a sit-in on his premises could not constitutionally be backed up by use of the state's trespass laws, even though this law was a facially neutral provision that entitled any property owner to decide who may come on his property.

    **b. Narrower reading:**  But a strong case can be made that the proper reading of *Shelley* is much ***narrower***. For instance, there is reason to believe that the rationale of *Shelley* was meant to apply *only* to those situations where there are a *willing seller and buyer*, and the state is asked to use its power affirmatively to prevent them from consummating their sale. (This reading is suggested by the *Shelley* Court's statement that this was not a case "in which the states have merely abstained from action, leaving private individuals free to impose such discriminations as they see fit.")

> **i.** **Narrower view probably accurate:** Subsequent Supreme Court cases certainly have not disproved the narrower view of *Shelley*. For instance, the great lengths to which the Court has gone to develop other theories for finding state action (such as the "symbiosis" rationale of *Burton v. Wilmington Parking Authority, infra*, p. 429) suggest that mere invocation of neutral state laws to preserve individuals' "right" to discriminate probably does not constitute state action. The Court's refusal to rely on the broader reading of *Shelley* in sit-in cases decided in the 1960s also lends some support to this narrower view of *Shelley*.

5. **Not truly neutral:** The *Shelley* Court, and most commentators, have assumed that the rule of law which the plaintiffs there tried to have applied (that covenants regarding land use, including racial restrictions, shall be enforced) was a *neutral* one, in the sense that the source of the rule did not lie in a desire to discriminate against non-whites. But Tribe (p. 1714-15) argues that this rule of law *was not really neutral at all*. He notes that many other sorts of restraints on land (e.g., grants that would violate the Rule Against Perpetuities) are *not* enforced by the courts. Therefore, the common-law decision to enforce *racial* restrictions without enforcing other sorts of restraints can be seen as *not racially neutral*. Imposition by the government of a non-racially-neutral rule of law (even one developed under the common law) can easily be seen as state action violative of the Fourteenth Amendment.

6. **Reverter in deed:** In any event, if a private agreement calls for discrimination, it is not unconstitutional state action for a court to enforce a provision in the agreement dealing with the contingency that the discrimination is held unenforceable. This was demonstrated by *Evans v. Abney*, 396 U.S. 435 (1970), a further development in the litigation of which *Evans v. Newton (supra*, pp. 423) was a part.

   a. **Facts:** After *Evans v. Newton* established that Baconsfield Park could not be operated in a racially discriminatory way, the state trial court determined that, since fulfillment of Senator Bacon's intent was no longer possible, the trust should *terminate* (presumably causing the property to close as a park), and the property should revert to the Senator's heirs. This reversion was called for by operation of Georgia law in the event of a trust's termination.

   b. **Ruling upheld:** The Supreme Court held that this state ruling did *not violate* the Fourteenth Amendment. The only discrimination was by Senator Bacon, not by the state's laws calling for reversion. This situation was distinguishable from *Shelley*, the majority held, because in *Shelley*, the state court was called upon to *enforce* a private scheme of discrimination; here, the state ruling, rather than enforcing discrimination, in fact nullified discrimination by preventing the park from being used by either blacks or whites.

7. **Delegation:** The Court since the '80s has taken a quite narrow view of the circumstances in which the state will be deemed to have "*commanded*" particular actions by private persons. If any real degree of *discretion* is delegated to the private party, this will probably be

enough to relieve the state of responsibility for those private actions, even though they take place within a fairly rigid framework of state-created rules. For instance, in *Blum v. Yaretsky*, 457 U.S. 991 (1982), a class of Medicaid patients in private nursing homes unsuccessfully claimed that decisions by the homes to discharge them or send them to facilities giving less extensive (and less costly) service constituted state action.

    **a.  Facts:** The patients contended that the decisions on level-of-care, although made in individual cases by the nursing home's staff, were tightly circumscribed by the state rules, and that the state therefore bore responsibility for these decisions.

    **b.  Claim rejected:** But a majority of the Court, in an opinion by Justice Rehnquist, disagreed. The actual discharge or transfer decisions were based on "medical judgments," which were made by independent nursing home professionals who were not controlled by the state. Therefore, these decisions were not state action.

**C.  "Encouragement" by the state:** If *Shelley v. Kraemer* may be seen as a case where the state "commanded" the discrimination (by attempting to enjoin the willing white sellers from selling to the black purchasers), other cases have found that the state has *"encouraged"* discrimination. Such encouragement, too, will constitute state action, and may thus trigger a constitutional violation.

    **1.  Repeal of civil rights laws as "encouragement":** Such an "encouragement" theory was used in ***Reitman v. Mulkey***, 387 U.S. 369 (1967). In *Reitman*, the Court found state action where California voters amended their constitution to prohibit the government from interfering with any private individual's right to discriminate in the sale or lease of residential real estate. An immediate effect (and purpose) of the constitutional amendment was to overturn two statutes which barred some sorts of private residential housing discrimination. The California Supreme Court, in striking the constitutional amendment, found that its purpose and effect would inevitably be to encourage private discrimination. The U.S. Supreme Court, in affirming, agreed that this was *encouragement* by the state, *not even-handedness*.

        **a.  Deference to state court finding:** The U.S. Supreme Court, in agreeing that the constitutional amendment would have the effect of encouraging private discrimination, gave deference to the California court's finding that, "in the California environment," the amendment would have this effect.

        **b.  Scope of *Reitman*:** Even giving *Reitman* a broad reading, it seems extremely *unlikely* that the *mere failure by a state to forbid private discrimination constitutes state action*. Thus had California simply never enacted any legislation or regulation dealing with private housing discrimination, its inaction would almost certainly not be deemed state conduct. Even had it enacted legislation, the *mere repeal* of the statute(s) by the legislature would probably not have been state action, since a strong argument could be made that such a repeal merely restored the status quo. It was probably only the fact that the change was made to the state's *constitution*, and thus acted as a bar to enactment of fair housing legislation in the future, that state "encouragement" was found.

**D.  "Symbiosis" between state and private actor:** Another way in which the state can become so involved with private discrimination that the latter will be subjected to constitutional scrutiny is if there is a "symbiotic," i.e., *mutually beneficial*, relation between the state and the private discriminator. That is, if there are *extensive contacts* between the state and the private party, in such a way that each benefits from the other's conduct, the requisite state involvement may be found.

1.  **The *Burton* case:**   The classic example of such a symbiotic relationship is ***Burton v. Wilmington Parking Authority***, 365 U.S. 715 (1961).

    a.  **Facts:**   *Burton* involved the relationship between a parking building owned and run by the Wilmington Parking Authority (a state agency) and a restaurant run by a private company within the building, under a 20-year lease between the Authority and the company. The restaurant refused to serve blacks. (No provision in Delaware or federal law at the time required private companies to do so.) A black who was refused service contended that the Authority's involvement with the restaurant was sufficiently great as to make the private discrimination "state action" violative of the Fourteenth Amendment.

    b.  **State action found:**   The Supreme Court agreed that *state action was present*. The Court relied heavily on various indications that the restaurant was essential to successful operation of the overtly public facility (the parking portion). For instance, the project could not have been financed without rents from commercial tenants like the restaurant. Furthermore, since the restaurant claimed that its business would be hurt if it were forced to serve blacks, the "profits earned by discrimination" were indispensable elements in the project's financial success.

    c.  **No relevant lease provision:**   Unlike the constitutional amendment in *Reitman*, nothing the state did in *Burton* expressly conferred on the restaurant the right to discriminate. The lease was completely silent on the issue of discrimination. But the Supreme Court held that, in view of the symbiotic relation between the parties, the state had an ***affirmative obligation*** to insert a non-discrimination requirement in the lease (which, under state law regarding leases of public property, it had the power to do). This obligation could not be avoided even upon a showing by the state of perfect good faith, and of a complete absence of desire to encourage discrimination.

    d.  **Scope of *Burton*:**   As with many of the other state action decisions, it is difficult to gauge the scope of *Burton*. The case probably does ***not*** stand for the proposition that any time the state has the power to prevent discriminatory use of public property, it must exercise that power. For instance, if the Authority had ***sold*** the entire building as surplus, it seems unlikely that an anti-discrimination clause in the deed would be constitutionally required. A key aspect of *Burton* is undoubtedly that the state ***benefited*** heavily from the lease, and may in fact have benefited from the discrimination itself (since the absence of an anti-discrimination clause probably made the restaurant willing to pay higher rents). In fact, *Burton* may be seen as a case in which there was ***circumstantial evidence*** that the ***government itself had racially discriminatory motives*** in failing to prohibit the private discrimination. See Tribe, p. 1701, n. 13.

E.  **Involvement or "entanglement" by state:**   There are some situations in which the state is so heavily ***involved*** in or "entangled with" private action that, even though the state does not ***benefit*** from or encourage the private conduct (thus ruling out the "symbiosis" approach, *supra*, p. 428) the court will nonetheless attribute to the state the private conduct.

1.  **Licensing by the state:**   Where the state ***licenses*** a private entity to perform a particular function, it is often claimed that the act of licensing is sufficient state involvement to make

the private conduct state action. But in general, the Supreme Court has ***rejected*** such claims.

   **a.   Liquor license:**   The best-known case on state action through licensing is ***Moose Lodge No. 107 v. Irvis***, 407 U.S. 163 (1972), involving a liquor license.

       **i.   Facts:**   In *Moose Lodge*, the Lodge, a private club, refused service to the black guest of a member. The guest contended that, since the state had given the club one of a limited number of liquor licenses, this act of licensing was sufficient to render the club's discrimination state action.

       **ii.   Claim rejected:**   The Supreme Court disagreed, holding that the mere fact that a state grants a license to an entity does not transform the latter's conduct into state action, ***even where the number of licenses is limited***. (But the majority hinted that the result might have been different if the licenses were limited in such a way that clubs holding them had a "***monopoly***" in the dispensing of liquor.")

       **iii.   "Significant involvement" standard:**   The majority phrased the issue as being whether the state was ***"significantly involved"*** with invidious discrimination. The mere fact of licensing did not constitute such significant involvement. The Court distinguished this situation from that in *Burton*, where there was a "symbiotic relationship" between a public restaurant and a public building; here, by contrast, there was a ***private*** club in a private building.

       **iv.   Dissent:**   Three Justices dissented. One of the dissents, written by Justice Douglas, conceded that as a general rule, the activities of a private club were beyond the reach of the Constitution, even if the club operated pursuant to some sort of license. But this case was different, he contended, because there was a "state-enforced ***scarcity of licenses***" that restricted the ability of blacks to obtain liquor. If individuals wanted to form a club that would serve blacks, they would have to buy an existing club license, and would have to pay a ***monopoly price***; the creation of this monopoly scheme was directly attributable to the state. Therefore, Douglas contended, the Lodge's discrimination was state action.

**2.   Grant of monopoly:**   Related to the problem of licensed businesses is that of "natural monopolies," i.e., areas of commerce where, usually because of high capital requirements, only one business can profitably exist. Such natural monopolies are usually ***highly regulated***, since there is no competition to keep their charges reasonable. Yet despite this intense regulation, actions by these monopolies will ***not*** generally be deemed state action. The classic example is conduct of a public ***utility***.

   **a.   *Jackson v. Metropolitan Edison*:**   The Court refused to find that the conduct of an electric utility, which had a monopoly in its area, constituted state action, in ***Jackson v. Metropolitan Edison Co.***, 419 U.S. 345 (1974). Consequently, plaintiff's claim that her electric service should not have been turned off for nonpayment without notice and fair hearing was unsuccessful. The Court was not convinced that the state had really "granted" the utility a monopoly (since the monopoly was a "natural" one). But even if it had, this was not sufficient to transform the utility's activities into state action, because there was an "insufficient relationship between the challenged actions of the [utility] and [its] monopoly status."

**b. Dissent:** Three Justices dissented in separate opinions. Two of them believed that the state *had* conferred a monopoly on the utility, and appeared to believe that this fact justified subjecting the utility's actions to constitutional review. One of the dissenters, Justice Marshall, pointed out that an important part of the state's regulatory program was its decision not to have the state itself *compete* with private utilities, and to regulate the latter "in a multitude of ways to ensure that the [utilities'] service will be the functional equivalent of service provided by the State." (See the discussion of the majority and dissent's viewpoints on this "public function" issue *supra*, p. 424.)

3. **State funding:** The fact that a private entity *receives substantial state funding* will not by itself convert its activities into state action. Thus in *Rendell-Baker v. Kohn*, 457 U.S. 830 (1982), the Court held that a *private school*, whose income came primarily from public funding, and which was regulated by public authorities, was not committing state action when it fired employees.

4. **"Joint participation":** The necessary state involvement with a private party *will* be found where the private party and a state official have *jointly participated* in the activity being challenged. This "joint participation" theory was used to find state action in *Lugar v. Edmondson Oil Co.*, 457 U.S. 922 (1982).

   **a. Facts:** *Lugar*, like *Flagg Bros. (supra*, p. 424), involved a creditor's right to summarily seize or dispose of his debtor's property. In *Lugar*, the creditor (Edmondson) sued to collect a debt, and obtained a pre-judgment attachment against the property of the debtor, Lugar, which had the the effect of preventing Lugar from being able to sell it (though he remained in possession). To obtain the attachment, Edmondson was required only to file an *ex parte* petition stating a belief that Lugar might dispose of the property in order to defeat his creditors; a clerk of the court then issued a writ of attachment, which was executed by the sheriff.

   **b. Holding:** The Court held that because the clerk and sheriff acted *together with* Edmondson, Edmondson's conduct in obtaining the attachment was state action. Therefore, Edmondson could be held liable for violating Lugar's constitutional rights if (as Lugar alleged) the attachment statute failed to comply with the requirements of due process.

   **c. Limited scope:** But only Lugar's allegation that the *statutory procedure itself* was unconstitutional, *not* Edmonson's alleged *misuse* of the statute, was held to involve state action. Misuse of a properly-drafted statute was not "conduct that can be attributed to the state," because such misuse did not give rise to a "[constitutional] deprivation … caused by the exercise of some right or privilege created by the state or by a rule of conduct imposed by the state. … "

   **d. Peremptory challenges as joint participation:** For another illustration of the principle that joint participation between the state and a private party can be enough to transform the private party's action into state action, consider the use of *peremptory juror challenges* in trials. The Court has held that when a *private litigant* — either a civil litigant or a defendant in a criminal case — uses peremptory challenges to exclude jurors on racial grounds, this conduct constitutes state action and therefore violates the Equal Protection Clause. See *Edmonson v. Leesville Concrete Co.*, 500 U.S. 614 (1991) (in a civil case, private litigants cannot exercise their peremptory challenges in a racially discriminatory manner); *Georgia v. McCollum*, 505 U.S. 42 (1992) (same rule for criminal defendants).

e. **Regulation of interscholastic athletics:** For yet one more illustration of how joint participation between the state and a private party can constitute state action, consider the regulation of *interscholastic athletics* within a state. In a 2001 decision, the Court held that although high school interscholastic athletics within a state were regulated by a nominally private association, the association was a state actor due to the extensive participation of state entities in the association's affairs. The fact that 84% of the association's members were public high schools, and the fact that educators from those public schools were fulfilling their own job responsibilities when they worked with the association, contributed to the Court's conclusion that the association was a state actor. See *Brentwood Academy v. Tenn. Secondary School Athletic Assoc.*, 531 U.S. 288 (2001), discussed more extensively *infra*, both immediately below and on p. 433.

5. **"Entwinement":** A 2001 decision suggests that where the links between a state entity and a private group are so extensive that the two can fairly be said to be *"entwined,"* this entwinement will itself be strong evidence that the private group should be deemed to be a state actor. In *Brentwood Academy v. Tenn. Secondary School Athletic Assoc.*, 531 U.S. 288 (2001) (also discussed immediately *supra*, and *infra* at p. 433), the majority said that "Entwinement will support a conclusion that an ostensibly private organization ought to be charged with a public character and judged by constitutional standards; entwinement to the degree shown here requires it."

   a. **Facts:** *Brentwood* involved the question whether an Association regulating secondary-school athletics within a state should be treated as a state actor. The Court found two types of public-private entwinement in *Brentwood*. First, the State Board of Education was intertwined with the Association in numerous ways (e.g., the Board appointed non-voting members to the Association's committees). Second, most of the public secondary schools within the state not only belonged to the Association but performed some of their official functions (e.g., the running of interscholastic sports programs) in close conjunction with the Association. These two forms of entwinement justified the conclusion that the Association's conduct constituted state action.

6. **Acquiescence by the state not enough:** Mere *acquiescence* by the state in the private individual's conduct is not enough to make the latter "state action." The government must *actively encourage* or *facilitate* the private conduct, not merely *tolerate* it. This is true even where the state has the clear power to *prevent* the challenged private conduct, but chooses not to exercise that power.

   **Example 1:** A utility files with the State Public Utilities Commission a tariff, which among its terms states a right to terminate a customer's service for nonpayment. The Commission does not object to this provision.

   *Held*, the utility's practice of terminating service for nonpayment, without giving notice or an opportunity for a hearing, is not transformed into state action merely because the Commission (a state agency) allowed it. (A prior case in which a utility's conduct was carefully scrutinized by a utilities commission, and in which the commission ultimately praised the practice as improving service, was distinguishable, since there, the state placed its "imprimatur" on the practice). *Jackson v. Metropolitan Edison Co.*, 419 U.S. 345 (1974), also discussed *supra*, p. 423.

**Example 2:** The state, by enacting the Uniform Commercial Code, grants a warehouseman a lien for unpaid storage charges against goods deposited with him, and permits him to sell these goods to satisfy the lien. Plaintiff, whose goods are about to be sold in this manner, argues that the sale constitutes state action, and that its terms must therefore satisfy procedural due process.

*Held*, the carrying out of the sale does ***not*** constitute state action. The state has merely ***permitted, not encouraged***, such sales by warehousemen. Plaintiff's claim is merely that the state has refused to act (i.e., that it has refused to bar the sale), and mere inaction by the state cannot transform private acts into state acts. *Flagg Bros., Inc. v. Brooks*, 436 U.S. 149 (1978) (also discussed *supra*, p. 424).

**Note:** A dissent by Justice Stevens in *Flagg Bros.* argued that the majority's distinction between "permission" and "compulsion" cannot be the determining factor in state-action analysis. Under the majority's rationale, the state could also pass a statute providing that "any person with sufficient physical power [may] acquire and sell the property of his weaker neighbor"; such sales would then not be state action. Justice Stevens instead believed that state action was present, because the state had delegated to a private party what was essentially a state function, the non-consensual transfer of property to satisfy debts. (See the discussion of this portion of his dissent *supra*, p. 424.)

7. **Recognition by state:** If a state ***formally recognizes*** the role played by a private association in a particular type of state-organized activity, that recognition will itself make it more likely that the association will be deemed to be a state actor. Thus in a 2001 case in which the Court found that a state association regulating interscholastic secondary-school athletics was a state actor, the Court relied heavily on the state's recognition of the association's special role as regulator of the athletic activities of public junior-high and high schools. *Brentwood Academy v. Tenn. Secondary School Athletic Assoc.*, 531 U.S. 288 (2001).

*Quiz Yourself on*
**STATE ACTION (ENTIRE CHAPTER)**

56. Pablo, an American of Hispanic origin, attempted to receive treatment at Green Valley Hospital. He believes that he was denied admission solely because he was Hispanic. Green Valley Hospital is owned by the Little Sisters of Green Valley, a private religious order. Pablo has brought suit against the Little Sisters, arguing that they have violated his right to equal protection under the Fourteenth Amendment. Assuming that the facts are as asserted by Pablo, will his suit succeed? _____

57. A statute enacted by the state of Albatross makes it a felony for any individual to "interfere with any right guaranteed by the Equal Protection Clause of the Fourteenth Amendment of the U.S. Constitution." Delbert was the manager of a housing project funded and operated by a federal housing agency. Delbert refused to rent to a family solely because they were black. If Delbert is charged with violating the Albatross statute, should he be convicted? _____

58. Ninety percent of the kindergarten-through-twelfth-grade students who attend school in the state of Mongoose attend public schools. The other 10% attend private schools, some of which are parochial and some of which are not. Beaver Academy is a non-sectarian private school, 40% of whose operating funds are supplied by the state as part of an innovative program to encourage excellence in education. The state does not prescribe any aspect of the Beaver curriculum, beyond checking to make sure that students

achieve a minimum level of competency in core subjects like reading. Pamela, a sixth-grade student, has brought suit against Beaver Academy, asserting that she was denied admission to Beaver solely on the grounds that she is black. Because Mongoose has extremely limited civil rights statutes, Pamela's suit consists solely of the assertion that the school's failure to admit her violated her Fourteenth Amendment equal protection rights. Assume that Pamela's factual assertions are true.

(a) When Pamela attempts to prove the presence of state action, what doctrine offers her the best chance of success? _____

(b) Will Pamela's suit succeed? _____

59. State U is a large public university located in the fairly small town of Arborville. Students at the university represent a substantial share of the local demand for housing. Much of the housing stock in Arborville consists of two-family homes, in one part of which the owner lives and the other part of which is rented to students. State U's housing department maintains a list of local homeowners who have such housing to offer to students. State U allows a homeowner to indicate his or her racial or ethnic preferences on the listing; thus one who prefers whites may request that a "W" designation be affixed, one who prefers blacks that a "B" be affixed, etc. The university does not charge for these listings. Because State U does not have enough dormitory space to house all students, the availability of private housing like that contained in the list is an important resource for the university. There is evidence that some homeowners who have participated in the list would not do so if they were not able to indicate their racial preferences and thus reduce the possibility of an embarrassing face-to-face refusal to rent to minorities.

Bernard, a black student at State U, has been unable to find what he considers suitable housing. He believes that there are substantially fewer housing units available to black students than to white students, and that on average the ones that are available to blacks are either more costly or less attractive. Assume that no federal or state statute bars discrimination by an owner/occupier of a two-family house in the selection of a tenant. Bernard has sued State U for an injunction against continued use of the racially-coded housing list, on the grounds that the U's maintenance of that list violates his equal protection rights.

(a) What is the best argument Bernard can make as to why maintenance of the list violates his equal protection rights? _____

(b) Assuming that many private landowners on the list are in fact discriminating against black students, and that black students on average have to pay more for less attractive accommodations than whites when they rent from the list, should Bernard's request for an injunction be granted? _____

---

*Answers*

56. **No.** The Fourteenth Amendment, like all aspects of the Constitution (except the Thirteenth Amendment) only restricts **government** action. Here, the facts tell us that Green Valley Hospital is operated by a private religious order. Since there is no government involvement, there cannot be an equal protection violation.

57. **No.** This is essentially a "trick question." The Fourteenth Amendment applies only to conduct by **state** and **local** governments. Therefore, any conduct by or on behalf of the housing agency here could not have violated the Equal Protection Clause, because it was conduct of the federal government, not the state government. Delbert therefore did not cause any interference with equal protection rights. (Equal protection **principles** are binding on the federal government via the Fifth Amendment's Due Process Clause, and these equal protection principles are interpreted the same way as are the Fourteenth Amendment's equal protection principles. But the question here has been carefully worded to refer only to conduct that violates the Fourteenth, not the Fifth, Amendment.)

**58. (a) The "public function" doctrine.**

**(b) No.** The "public function" doctrine holds that when a private actor (or group) is entrusted by the state with the performance of functions that are governmental in nature, that actor or group becomes an ***agent of the state*** and his/their acts constitute state action. However, for the "public function" doctrine to apply, the function must be one which has traditionally been ***exclusively*** the domain of the government. The Court has held that the providing of education is ***not*** the exclusive prerogative of the state, even though it is a function normally provided by the state out of public funds. Therefore, the "public function" doctrine will not apply to Beaver. See *Rendell-Baker v. Kohn*, refusing to treat a private school as involving a public function, even where the school's income came primarily from public grants. (It is also conceivable that the state might be found to have been so heavily "involved" or "entangled" in the private school here that state action should be found, but the Court has held that mere government funding of a private actor's operations does not convert those private operations into state action, so this argument, too, would almost certainly fail.)

**59. (a) That there is a symbiotic relationship between State U and the private landowners, sufficient to turn the private acts of discrimination into state action.**

**(b) Yes, probably.** If the state is deeply involved with private discrimination, that private discrimination can sometimes be viewed as itself being state action. One of the ways this can happen is if there is a ***"symbiotic,"*** i.e., mutually beneficial, relation between the state and the private discriminator. Here, a strong argument can be made that the university is benefitting greatly from private acts (the rental of housing to State U students), and that the private discriminators are receiving important benefits from the state (free listings and a free flow of potential tenants).

To the extent that the pool of homeowners willing to list their properties has been increased by the coding option, it can be argued that State U has actually achieved a benefit not just from the overall listing program, but from the very acts of discrimination being complained of; if so, this makes it even more likely that state action would be found. All in all, there is a better than even chance that State U would be found to be so heavily involved with the private acts of discrimination that state action should be found in the maintenance of the list. The symbiosis here is reminiscent of that in *Burton v. Wilmington Parking Authority* (where restaurant paid rent for space in publicly-owned building, discrimination by restaurant was state action).

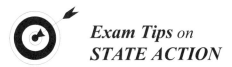

# *Exam Tips* on *STATE ACTION*

You need to be on the lookout for State Action problems in any question that involves the rights of individuals (i.e., due process, equal protection, freedom of expression, freedom of religion, etc.) Remember that these constitutional guarantees only come into play when government is acting. Here are some specific things to watch for:

☛ Before you start to write about how the due process, equal protection, or other guarantee has been violated, make sure that there is "state action," i.e., that the challenged action is really ***action by the government***, or at least that the challenged action can somehow be ***ascribed*** to the government.

☛ If a private individual is doing something that would clearly pose constitutional problems were it done by government, that's a tip off to a state action problem. Examples:

A private apartment owner refuses to rent to a black;

A private employer refuses to hire a person because of her gender;

A private shopping center refuses to allow P to distribute political campaign literature.

☞ In all of these situations, there will be no state action (and thus no constitutional violation), unless additional facts are presented that somehow tie the state in to the private actor's conduct.

☛ Be alert to situations where the only action is by a private individual, but the activity in question is one that is a *"public function,"* i.e., a function *"traditionally" done by the states.* Thus you may have at least an issue of whether a "public function" is being performed if your facts involve any of the following:

a private (but partly state-funded) *school*;

a privately-operated *park*;

a *political party* conducting a primary or other party business;

a *"company town;"*

a person taking some action typically done by the *judicial system* (e.g., a seller or lender foreclosing on collateral).

☞ Remember that today, the "public function" doctrine applies only where the function has traditionally been done *"exclusively"* by the states. This requirement knocks out a large percentage of the cases (including at least the private-school situation referred to above).

☛ Also, be on the lookout for situations where the state is somehow heavily *"involved"* in the private actor's actions. The common scenarios for this are:

☞ The state has *"commanded"* or *"required"* the private action. (*Example: Shelley v. Kraemer*, where the state, by enforcing restrictive covenants, in effect commanded private individuals not to sell their homes to blacks.)

☞ *Testable issue:* May the state enforce some *neutral state law* where this has the effect of facilitating private discrimination? (*Example:* Where a private store owner refuses to serve blacks and wants them evicted, does the state's use of its trespass laws turn the property owner's action into "state action?" The answer is probably "no," as long as the state is evenhanded in how it uses the trespass law.)

☞ The state has *"encouraged"* the private action.

☞ The state has a *"symbiotic relationship"* with the private action, i.e., the state and the private actor *benefit from each other's conduct*. Classic illustration: *Burton v. Wilmington Parking Authority* — the state builds a state-operated building, and rents space in it to a restaurateur who discriminates; because the state is getting major benefits from the restaurateur's operations, his conduct is transformed into "state action."

☞ The state is heavily *"involved," "entangled"* or *"entwined"* in the activity.

> ☞ Where the state merely *licenses* the private activity, that's not enough involvement or entanglement to produce state action. (*Example:* Where government gives a liquor license to a private club, that's not enough to turn the club's discriminatory actions into state action. *Moose Lodge v. Irvis.*)
>
> ☞ But where state entities *participate* heavily in the private activity, and the state *recognizes* that activity as being closely related to important state concerns, this will probably be enough entanglement to make the activity state action.
>
> **Example:** A state statute provides that a private association of high schools, all of which are located within a single state, has the role of regulating interscholastic sports in the state. Most association members are public high schools, and nearly all public high schools are members. The association's activities will probably found to be so entwined with state concerns as to make the association a state actor. (*Brentwood Academy.*)

# CHAPTER 13

# CONGRESSIONAL ENFORCEMENT OF CIVIL RIGHTS

*ChapterScope*

This Chapter involves several aspects of Congress' power to enforce the post-Civil War Amendments. The main concepts are:

■ Congress has special powers to enforce the post-Civil War Amendments, i.e., the 13th, 14th, and 15th Amendments.

■ Congress probably can't prohibit *purely private discrimination* under the 14th and 15th Amendments.

❏ But Congress *can* prohibit purely private discrimination under the *13th* Amendment, if it finds that the discrimination is a *"badge or incident of slavery."*

■ Congress does not have power to *define the scope* of the post-Civil War Amendments. Only the federal courts may do this.

❏ So Congress may not *"expand"* the meaning of these Amendments, i.e., define them in a way that causes more government action to run afoul of these Amendments.

❏ Nor may Congress *"reduce"* the scope of these Amendments. Thus once the Supreme Court says for instance, that the Equal Protection Clause prohibits a certain kind of government action, Congress can't use its enforcement powers to say, in effect, "The conduct shall no longer be deemed to be a violation of the Equal Protection Clause."

## I. INTRODUCTION

A. **Issues presented:** This chapter examines Congress' power to *enforce* the post-Civil War Amendments, i.e., the Thirteenth, Fourteenth and Fifteenth Amendments. There are two main issues regarding this power:

1. **Reaching private actors:** To what extent may Congress enact legislation pursuant to these Amendments so as to reach *purely private conduct*, given that these Amendments (at least the Fourteenth and Fifteenth) only refer to conduct *by the states?*

2. **Interpreting the Amendments:** What power does Congress have to *interpret* these Amendments *differently from the Supreme Court*, with respect to: (i) *remedies* to impose for what the Court and Congress both would agree constitutes violations of these Amendments; and (ii) the *substantive content* of these rights?

B. **Applicable statutes:** Our focus will be upon the constitutional boundaries of Congress' power to enforce the amendments, not upon the precise interpretation of the statutes which Congress has in fact enacted. Nonetheless, a brief overview of the existing statutory framework is helpful. Our summary of this framework is done from the perspective of statutes now on the books.

1. **Civil provisions:**   A number of statutes *grant civil rights* as distinguished from those imposing criminal penalties:

   a. **General equal rights:**   The most general grant of civil rights is made under what is today 42 U.S.C. §1981. That section gives all persons within the United States the same right "as is enjoyed by white citizens" to *make and enforce contracts*, to sue, and to be subject to identical punishments, taxes, and other treatment by the government. This statute was originally enacted as part of the Civil Rights Act of 1866, which was premised on the Thirteenth Amendment (since the Fourteenth did not yet exist).

   b. **Property rights:**   What is now 42 U.S.C. §1982 gives all United States citizens the *same property rights* as whites have, including rights of inheritance, purchase and sale and lease. This provision, too, was part of the 1866 Civil Rights Act, and was given a broad reading by the Court in *Jones v. Alfred H. Mayer Co., infra,* p. 444.

   c. **Deprivations "under color of law":**   42 U.S.C. §1983 allows a private suit for damages to be brought against any person who, *"under color of any statute"* or other law, deprives the plaintiff of *"any rights, privileges or immunities secured by the Constitution and laws."* §1983, one of the best-known of all federal statutory provisions, has often been used to bring suit against *state and local government officials who violate individuals' civil rights.* It derives from the 1871 Civil Rights Act, and relies on at least the Fourteenth Amendment, and perhaps the Thirteenth, for constitutional authority.

   d. **Private conspiracies:**   Two or more persons who *conspire* to deprive anyone of *equal protection* or *equal privileges and immunities under the law*, may be subjected to civil suit under 48 U.S.C. §1985(c). This provision, which derives from the 1871 Civil Rights Act, appears to be applicable *even where there is no state action*, so long as access to a federally-guaranteed right is infringed or sought to be infringed. The constitutionality of this statute's application to conduct involving only private persons is suggested, but not made explicit, in *U.S. v. Guest, infra,* p. 442.

2. **Criminal statutes:**   Two statutory provisions, deriving (like the ones above) from the post-Civil War period, provide *criminal penalties* for roughly the same types of conduct for which private civil actions are permitted by those provisions summarized in (c) and (d), respectively, above.

   a. **Color of law:**   Thus the criminal analog to §1983's civil "color of law" provision is 18 U.S.C. §242, which imposes a fine or imprisonment upon any person who *"under color of any law*, statute, ordinance, regulation or custom," willfully deprives another of any rights protected by the Constitution or federal statutes, on account of *color, race or alienage*. If death results from the deprivation, life imprisonment is authorized.

   b. **Private conspiracies:**   The criminal analog to §1985(c)'s civil conspiracies provision is 18 U.S.C. §241, setting criminal penalties for *conspiring* to "injure, oppress, threaten, or intimidate any citizen in the free exercise or enjoyment of any right or privilege secured to him by the Constitution or the laws of the United States."

3. **Modern statutory additions:**   Major civil rights laws enacted in the 1960's have added some important new provisions. Among these are the following:

   **a. Public accommodations:** Discrimination in the furnishing of *public accommodations* is banned, and made subject to private and governmental civil suits in the Public Accommodations Title of the Civil Rights Act of 1964, 42 U.S.C. §2000a *et seq*. This title was based on Congress' power to regulate interstate commerce, not its power to enforce the Civil War Amendments. See *supra*, p. 46.

   **b. Voting:** Various provisions to ensure *the right to vote* were contained in the 1965 Voting Rights Act, 42 U.S.C. §1973, including measures to restrict the discriminatory use of literacy tests and other voter registration requirements. The Act is discussed in the treatment of *South Carolina v. Katzenbach, infra*, p. 448.

   **c. Fair housing:** Important restrictions on the ability of private entities and individuals to discriminate in the sale or rental of *housing* were contained in Title VIII of the 1968 Civil Rights Act, the Fair Housing Title.

   **d. Violence:** *Violent interference* with a person's enjoyment of his civil rights, even if it is not part of a conspiracy (as is required for application of 18 U.S.C. §241) and even if it involves no state action (as is required for 18 U.S.C. §242) is prohibited by 18 U.S.C. §245, part of the 1968 Civil Rights Act.

## II. CONGRESS' POWER TO REACH PRIVATE CONDUCT

**A. Purely private conduct:** The Fourteenth and Fifteenth Amendment, by their terms, apply only to *state* interferences. As we saw in the previous chapter, the Court has (especially in recent years) read this state action requirement to impose substantial "bite." But §5 of the Fourteenth Amendment, and §2 of the Fifteenth Amendment, explicitly grant Congress the power to *enforce* each of those amendments *"by appropriate legislation."* Thus the issue arises, to what extent may Congress "appropriately" enforce the Fourteenth and Fifteenth Amendments by *proscribing conduct which the Court would not construe to be "state action?"*

   **1. Some latitude:** While the precise answer to this question has never been decided, it seems clear that Congress has at least some latitude, and that certain types of private conduct unaccompanied by state involvement may nonetheless be prohibited.

      **a. Link to state conduct:** For instance, private conduct which *prevents state officials* from giving equal protection or due process to others may clearly be prohibited by Congress. Similarly, private conduct which intentionally interferes with rights guaranteed to an individual by federal constitutional provisions *other than* the Fourteenth Amendment (e.g., the *right to travel interstate*) may be barred by Congress.

      **b. Gray area:** The principal gray area is the extent to which Congress may prevent *purely private discrimination* by one individual against another, where no state facilities, programs or rights are directly involved. For instance, may Congress prohibit discrimination by small private social clubs that hold no state licenses?

**B. Early decision:** The first time Congress' power to regulate private discrimination was considered, that power received an extremely narrow reading by the Court. Recall that in the *Civil Rights Cases*, 109 U.S. 3 (1883), discussed *supra*, p. 418, a majority of the Court held that, since only state action could violate the Fourteenth Amendment, Congress' enforcement power *only permitted it to restrict state action*, and not private conduct.

1. **Consequence:** Under the logic of the *Civil Rights Cases* (though this was not made explicit in the opinion), Congress did not even have the power to prevent one private individual from forcibly blocking another's exercise of the right to vote in state elections, the right to attend public schools, or other exercises of state rights. Such private conduct would presumably be in violation of state law, but it would not itself be a violation of "equal protection of the [state] laws;" only action **by** the state could be that. And Congress' enforcement power was limited to enactment of those statutes which were needed to **prevent the state** from abdicating its equal-protection obligations.

C. **The *Guest* case:** This extremely narrow view of congressional power under the Fourteenth Amendment was not re-examined until the 1960's. Then, in **U.S. v. Guest**, 383 U.S. 745 (1966), six members of the Court stated that Congress could, under §5 of the Fourteenth Amendment, reach a substantial range of **private racially discriminatory conduct**. But since three Judges did so in one concurring opinion and the other three in another, *Guest* did not produce a single majority articulation of the scope of Congress' right to reach private conduct.

   1. **Facts of *Guest*:** *Guest* concerned a prosecution for criminal conspiracy under 18 U.S.C. §241 (see *supra*, p. 440). The defendants were private individuals. The first count of the indictment charged them with conspiring to interfere violently with the rights of several blacks to use state-owned facilities.

   2. **Court's opinion:** The opinion for the Court, written by Justice Stewart, avoided deciding whether §241 could constitutionally be applied to racially discriminatory, but entirely private, interference with the use of public facilities, as charged in the first count. It did so by pointing to the possibility that the indictment might be claiming, although ambiguously, that **state officials participated** in the interference.

   3. **Concurrences:** Six Justices, in two concurrences, were willing to go further. They thought that the first count of the indictment was constitutional even if it charged only purely-private conduct, with no participation by state officials.

      a. **Clark's concurrence:** One concurrence, by Justice Clark, reasoned that "[t]he specific language of §5 [of the Fourteenth Amendment] empowers the Congress to enact laws punishing all conspiracies — **with or without state action** — that interfere with Fourteenth Amendment rights." But he gave no explanation of *why* §5 should be read so as to dispense with any requirement of state action.

      b. **Brennan's concurrence:** Justice Brennan's separate concurrence, however, *did* deal with the question Justice Clark ducked. Brennan believed that §5 gave Congress the power to make any law which it concluded was **"reasonably necessary** to protect a right created by and arising under" the Fourteenth Amendment. Thus he would apply the same standard as applied by Chief Justice Marshall in *McCulloch v. Maryland*, in interpreting "the Necessary and Proper" Clause.

         i. **Application of test:** In Brennan's view, Congress could reasonably have concluded that prevention of **private** interference with access to state-owned facilities was a reasonably necessary means toward preventing **governmental** interference with that access. In fact, he believed that Congress could punish **all** conspiracies that interfered with Fourteenth Amendment rights, even if no state officers were involved.

**D.** ***Morrison* wipes out the expansive interpretation of *Guest*:** For 34 years after *Guest*, no one knew whether the views of the six concurring justices in *Guest* — that Congress could use its §5 remedial powers to reach purely private conduct that interfered with Fourteenth Amendment rights — represented good law. But in a case decided in 2000, ***U.S. v. Morrison***, 529 U.S. 598 (2000) (also discussed *supra* p. 39), the Court decided by a 5-4 vote that the concurrences in *Guest* did *not* represent a holding of the Court, and should be disregarded. Consequently, it is now clear that ***it is not within Congress' §5 powers to reach purely private conduct***, even if that conduct interferes with rights protected by the Fourteenth Amendment.

    **1. Context:** *Morrison* involved a federal statute, the Violence Against Women Act, which allowed women who had been the victims of gender-motivated violent crimes to sue the perpetrator in federal court. When the defendant attacked the statute as beyond Congress' powers, the plaintiff argued (among other things) that even if the statute reached purely private conduct, that private conduct consisted of attempts to violate women's equal protection rights, and was therefore reachable on the theory of the six concurring justices in *Guest*.

    **2. Claim rejected:** But the five-justice majority in *Morrison* squarely *rejected* this argument. The Court conceded that the three-Justice concurrence authored by Justice Brennan in *Guest* represented a real view on the merits that Congress could use its §5 powers to reach purely private conduct that interfered with 14th Amendment rights. But the *Morrison* majority pointed out that the other three concurring justices in *Guest*, led by Justice Clark, had given no explanation at all for their similar views. Consequently, Clark's statement that Congress could reach purely private conduct was ***"naked dicta"*** that could not be added to the opinions of the Brennan group for pruposes of deriving a constitutional holding.

        **a. Conclusion:** Therefore, the *Morrison* majority concluded, *Guest* said nothing authoritative about whether Congress could reach purely private conduct, and the *Civil Rights Cases* still represented prevailing law. Under the *Civil Rights Cases*, purely private action that interferes with rights protected by the Fourteenth Amendment is simply beyond Congress' §5 remedial powers.

**E. Current state of the law:** So here's what the present law seems to be regarded Congress' use of its Fourteenth Amendment §5 powers to reach conduct by private individuals:

    **1. Conduct not relating to public officials:** Where Congress tries to reach purely private conduct that has ***nothing to do with state officials***, it's now clear as the result of *Morrison* that Congress cannot do this under its §5 enforcement powers.

        Example: In *Morrison* itself, we saw that Congress could not use its §5 remedial powers to give private citizen *A* a federal cause of action against private citizen *B* merely because *B* practiced gender discrimination against *A* of a sort that would have been a 14th Amendment violation had *B* been acting under color of state law. The same would clearly be true if *B* was a private individual who practiced *racial* discrimination against *A* (e.g., *B* refused to rent an apartment to *A* on racial grounds, and Congress tried to use its §5 powers to give *A* a federal cause of action against *B*).[1]

    **2. Interference with state officials:** On the other hand, suppose that Congress merely prohibits private individuals from ***interfering with state officials' attempts*** to furnish equal protection or due process. Here, it seems clear that Congress' action *does* fall within its §5 remedial powers, notwithstanding *Morrison*.

**Example:** Suppose that Congress makes it a federal crime for a private individual to prevent or attempt to prevent a public School Board official from complying with a federal court's school-desegregation order. Since the private action being regulated is closely tied to state action (the school board desegregation efforts), it seems clear that Congress has acted validly under its 14th Amendment §5 remedial powers.

3. **Private-state interaction:** Finally, where a private party acts in ***conjunction with a state official***, it is quite clear that Congress may punish the private conduct. In fact, 18 U.S.C. § 242 (the statute preventing discriminatory action committed "under color of law") is applicable even to the private actors in this situation.

   a. ***Price* case:** For instance, in *U.S. v. Price*, 383 U.S. 787 (1966), the Court held that private individuals who acted together with local law enforcement officials in the infamous 1964 murder of three civil rights workers near Philadelphia, Mississippi, acted "under color of law" (and could therefore be charged under § 242) even though they themselves were not law enforcement officers.

F. **The Thirteenth Amendment and private conduct:** §1 of the ***Thirteenth*** Amendment provides that "[n]either slavery nor involuntary servitude, except as a punishment for crime … shall exist within the United States. … " §2 gives Congress the power to "enforce this [amendment] by appropriate legislation." Because the Thirteenth Amendment, unlike the Fourteenth and Fifteenth, is ***not explicitly limited to governmental action***, the Amendment has proved to be a useful source of congressional power to reach certain private conduct.

1. **Originally narrowly construed:** The Court has always conceded that Congress could reach purely private conduct under the Thirteenth Amendment; this was one of the holdings of the *Civil Rights Cases*, discussed *supra*, p. 418. However, the Court, beginning with those cases, took a very narrow view of the ***type*** of conduct which the Thirteenth Amendment forbade. The Amendment, and any congressional statutes enforcing it, could only deal with slavery and its ***"badges and incidents"***; private ***discrimination***, even in the furnishing of transportation, hotels and other accommodations, did not constitute a badge of slavery prohibited by the Thirteenth Amendment.

2. **Broadened in *Jones v. Mayer*:** This narrow view of the Thirteenth Amendment's scope was dramatically broadened in a startling case, ***Jones v. Alfred H. Mayer Co.***, 392 U.S. 409 (1968). That case held that Congress had the power, under the Thirteenth Amendment, ***"rationally to determine what are the badges and incidents of slavery."*** Furthermore, it held, Congress' definition of those badges and incidents could rationally be a very ***broad*** one, broad enough to encompass private racial discrimination in ***real estate transactions***.

   a. **Facts:** In *Jones*, plaintiffs complained that defendant (a private developer) refused to sell them a house solely because they were black. Plaintiffs claimed that this was a violation of 42 U.S.C. §1982, which provides that "[a]ll citizens of the United States

---

1. Remember, we're talking here only about whether Congress' *14th Amendment* enforcement powers can be used. In the rental situation, other congressional powers, such as the Commerce power and the *13th* Amendment's enforcement power (see *infra*, p. 444), could clearly be used. That's why, for instance, 42 U.S.C. §1982's grant of equal rights to "inherit, purchase, lease, sell, hold, and convey real and personal property" without racial discrimination is clearly still valid notwithstanding *Morrison* — it's almost certainly valid under the Commerce power, and certainly valid under the 13th Amendment (see *Jones v. Alfred H. Mayer Co.*, *infra*, p. 444).

shall have the same right, in every State and Territory, as is enjoyed by white citizens thereof to inherit, purchase, lease, sell, hold, and convey real and personal property." §1982 derives from the 1866 Civil Rights Act, which was enacted solely in reliance on the Thirteenth Amendment, since the Fourteenth had not yet been enacted. Defendant argued that even if §1982 was not intended to apply to private conduct (which Defendant claimed it was not), such conduct could not constitutionally be reached under the Thirteenth Amendment.

   b. **Holding:** The Supreme Court disagreed, finding that the statute was ***within Congress' power under the Thirteenth Amendment***. §2 of the Amendment, giving Congress enforcement powers, allowed Congress to pass "all laws necessary and proper for abolishing all badges and incidents of slavery in the United States" (quoting the *Civil Rights Cases*). And this section gave Congress the right rationally to determine ***what the badges and incidents of slavery are***. This "rationality" test was satisfied here, since it was not irrational of Congress to conclude that barriers to enjoyment of real property were badges of slavery; "when racial discrimination herds men into ghettos and makes their ability to buy property turn on the color of their skin, then it too is a relic of slavery."

   c. **Potentially broad impact:** *Jones* seems to acknowledge Congress' power to define the "badges and incidents of slavery" in almost any way it wishes, so long as the definition is rational.

   d. **Possible limitations:** However, this view of *Jones* seems unduly broad. For instance, while Congress' power to define "slavery and its incidents" may indeed be broad, it is not clear whether Congress may treat anything other than ***racially motivated*** (or ***ethnically*** motivated) discrimination as coming within the Amendment.

      i. **Protection of whites:** It does seem clear that Congress may use its Thirteenth Amendment enforcement powers to protect ***groups other than blacks*** against racial discrimination.

      ii. **Non-racial discrimination:** Apart from discrimination based on race, Congress may probably use the Thirteenth Amendment to prohibit private discrimination on grounds of ***ancestry***, or ***ethnic characteristics***. However, the Court has never squarely addressed the issue of whether the Thirteenth Amendment can support legislation banning these types of discrimination.

      iii. **Other types of discrimination:** The Court has never explicitly indicated that Congress may use the Thirteenth Amendment to prohibit invidious discrimination on ***grounds other than race, ancestry, or ethnic background***. So, for instance, it is highly questionable whether Congress could, say, ban purely private discrimination against ***gays***, lawyers, or other unpopular groups under authority of the Thirteenth Amendment.

      iv. **Purposeful discrimination:** In any event, whatever discrimination is banned under authority of the Thirteenth Amendment must probably be ***purposeful*** and ***invidious***.

3. **Self-executing scope of amendment:** Keep in mind that this broad view of the "badges and incidents of slavery" applies only where Congress has enacted a ***statute*** under its powers to enforce the Thirteenth Amendment. Where the ***direct***, self-executing meaning of the

Amendment itself, absent any statute, is concerned, the Court gives a very narrow reading to "badges and incidents of slavery" — perhaps only peonage is included.

> **Example 1:** Suppose that a state passes a law stating that "any owner of residential real estate may discriminate on the basis of race in the sale or lease of that property." Assume that Congress has not passed any statute which would conflict with this state statute. A court probably could *not* strike down the state statute on the grounds that it violated the Thirteenth Amendment — that Amendment has practically no self-executing scope.

> **Example 2:** Suppose that a state passed a statute providing that where one person owes a debt to another and cannot pay, the former may be required to work at minimum wage for the latter until the debt is paid off, and that a person who refuses to do such mandatory labor shall be sent to prison. Even in the absence of a federal statute prohibiting this kind of compulsory work, a court probably would hold that the state statute violates the Thirteenth Amendment — the self-executing scope of the Thirteenth Amendment, while very narrow, probably does cover true "peonage," and this state statute would probably be held to involve peonage.

**G. Violation of other constitutional rights:** So far, we have considered only private conduct which may be barred by congressional statutes relying on the Civil War Amendments. But there are also some rights which are secured by *other constitutional provisions* (that is, apart from the Thirteenth, Fourteenth and Fifteenth Amendments) which are applicable against private, not just state, interference.

1. **Right to travel:** Perhaps the most important of these is the *right to travel from state to state*. See, e.g., *U.S. v. Guest*, 383 U.S. 745 (1966) (other aspects of which are discussed *supra*, pp. 396-98), in which the Court held that Congress was authorized to punish purely private conspiracies to interfere with the exercise of this right (although the Court did not point to any specific constitutional provision as being the source of this right).

2. **Other examples:** Other constitutional rights which are applicable against private interference include: the right to *vote* in *federal primary* and *general elections*, the right to *inform federal officials of violations of federal law*, and the right to *assemble to petition Congress* for a redress of grievances. See Justice Harlan's concurrence in *U.S. v. Guest*, 383 U.S. 745 (1966), for his catalogue of such rights.

    a. **Tie-in with civil rights statutes:** These rights are *not* necessarily *self-executing*. That is, it is not clear that one private citizen may recover damages against another, or obtain an injunction against him, for violation of any of these rights, unless a congressional statute so provides. But the post-Civil War civil rights statutes, especially the criminal and civil conspiracy provisions, 18 U.S.C. §§241 and 1985(c) respectively, authorize the federal courts to give civil and criminal relief for certain types of violations of *any* constitutional provision, not merely the provisions of the Thirteenth, Fourteenth and Fifteenth Amendments.

# III. CONGRESS' POWER TO REMEDY CONSTITUTIONAL VIOLATIONS, OR TO MODIFY CONSTITUTIONAL RIGHTS

**A. General problem:** We turn now to three questions about how far Congress' powers to enforce the post-Civil War amendments extends:

(1) What kinds of explicitly "remedial" actions may Congress take?

(2) If Congress disagrees with the Supreme Court about the ***proper scope*** of the rights guaranteed by the Thirteenth, Fourteenth or Fifteenth Amendment, may Congress use its remedial powers to ***change the scope*** of these guarantees?

(3) Under what circumstances may Congress ***stop a state*** from engaging in conduct that Congress thinks may violate these Amendments?

As to (1), the brief answer is, "a very broad range of measures." As to (2), the brief answer is "no." As to (3), the brief answer is, "only if Congress' response is proportional to the state's threatened constitutional violations"; this topic so so important that we devote an entire section to it (see "IV" beginning on p. 451).

**B. Broad "remedial" powers:** It is clear that congressional power to adopt ***"remedial"*** legislation concerning the Thirteenth, Fourteenth and Fifteenth Amendments is ***extremely broad.*** For example, Congress may prohibit states from enacting a particular facially-constitutional law (e.g., a literacy test for voting) if Congress merely has a reasonable fear that the ***effect*** (not the purpose) of the law will be to interfere with a right guaranteed by one of these Amendments.

1. **Voting rights:** The broadening of Congress' "remedial" powers occurred largely within the framework of voting-rights measures adopted during the 1960's.

   a. **Historical background:** Reconstruction-era efforts by Congress to eradicate racial discrimination in voting in the South were only marginally successful, and most of the statutory provisions were repealed in 1894. Meanwhile, many of the southern states enacted ***literacy tests*** and other tests which were often used to deny blacks the franchise. The Fifteenth Amendment was of course theoretically available for relief in these situations, but litigation under it was generally time-consuming and difficult. Even when states or counties *were* ordered by the courts to eliminate one discriminatory practice or another, they were often able to devise some new scheme by which to perpetuate racial discrimination in voting. Initial statutory efforts by Congress in 1957, 1960, and 1964 proved largely ineffective.

   b. **Voting Rights Act of 1965:** Therefore, Congress enacted the Voting Rights Act of 1965, designed to eradicate racial discrimination in voting by dealing with it prophylactically rather than on a case-by-case basis.

   c. **Suspension of any "test or device":** The most important aspect of the Act, from the perspective of Congress' power to enforce the Fifteenth Amendment, was its treatment of ***literacy tests*** and other ***voter eligibility standards***. The Act ***suspended***, for a period of five years, literacy and similar voting tests in any state or political subdivision as to which the following ***administrative findings*** were made: (1) the Attorney General found that the jurisdiction maintained a ***"test or device"*** for voter eligibility (including not only literacy tests, but requirements of good moral character, knowledge of particular subject matter, etc.) in November 1964; and (2) less than 50% of the jurisdiction's voting-age residents were registered in November 1964.

    **i.**  **No judicial review:**  These findings were ***not judicially reviewable*** in the normal manner. The only way in which a jurisdiction found to fall within the Act's provisions could escape coverage was by obtaining a declaratory judgment from the federal district court for the District of Columbia stating that the jurisdiction had not used tests or devices for the purpose of racial discrimination in the previous five years.

    **ii.**  **Procedure summarized:**  Thus the statutory scheme was in the first instance one of administrative fact-finding, with ***no requirement that those findings include discriminatory intent***. Only thereafter did the jurisdiction have the right to seek judicial review in Washington, in a proceeding in which ***it***, not the federal government, ***bore the burden of proof.***

2.  **Upheld in *South Carolina* case:**  This scheme was ***upheld*** by the Supreme Court in ***South Carolina v. Katzenbach***, 383 U.S. 301 (1966).

    **a.**  **"Rationality" standard:**  The Court construed Congress' power to enforce the Fifteenth Amendment broadly. It held that ***"any rational means"*** could be used to enforce that Amendment's ban on racial discrimination in voting.

    **b.**  **Ban on tests rational:**  The particular scheme chosen by Congress here, that of banning tests or devices where they coincided with less-than-50% registration, satisfied the rationality standard. This was so because there was evidence presented to Congress that all of the areas known to have practiced racial discrimination in voting shared these two characteristics. Also, the use of tests or devices clearly furnished a means of carrying out racial discrimination, and low registration figures were an obvious symptom of such discrimination.

    **c.**  **Court's own view of literacy tests:**  *South Carolina v. Katzenbach* demonstrates that Congress' remedial powers under §2 of the Fifteenth Amendment permits it to ***outlaw practices which the Court would not on its own find to violate §1 of that Amendment,*** as long as these practices are reasonably closely related to practices that *would* violate §1.

3.  **Nationwide suspension of tests:**  Congress wielded its remedial powers under §2 of the Fifteenth Amendment even more broadly as part of the ***1970 Amendments*** to the Voting Rights Act. The Amendments included a suspension of literacy tests ***nationally***, not just in the areas covered in the '65 Act. This step, too, was approved by the Court, in *Oregon v. Mitchell*, 400 U.S. 112 (1970).

4.  **Provisions upheld:**  This broad view of Congress' remedial powers under the Fifteenth Amendment has continued during the Burger/Rehnquist era. In fact, ***Rome v. U.S.***, 446 U.S. 156 (1980), upholding certain provisions of the Voting Rights Act, probably represents an ***expansion*** of the Court's view of these powers.

    **a.**  **Facts:**  The state of Georgia had been made a covered jurisdiction under the 1965 Act. Therefore, none of its political subdivisions was permitted to change its voting procedures without obtaining clearance from the Attorney General; he could clear the change only if he found that it would not have ***either*** the purpose ***or effect*** of restricting the right to vote on account of race. The Attorney General found that the changes which the City of Rome, Ga. wanted to make in the way its city commissioners were elected would have a discriminatory effect on blacks, even though there was no evidence that the changes were motivated by a discriminatory purpose. Rome claimed that these 1965 Act provisions could not be constitutionally applied to it.

    **b. Act and application upheld:** The Court *rejected* all of the city's claims.

        **i. Discriminatory effect:** Most importantly, the Court held that Congress had the constitutional power to ban practices that were discriminatory *only in their effect*, not their purpose, under its §2 remedial powers. This was true even if §1 of the Fifteenth Amendment barred only purposeful discrimination (an issue the Court did not decide). Any remedial method that was "appropriate" could be used, and the prohibition of measures whose effect would be discriminatory was an appropriate way of barring purposeful discrimination, at least in those jurisdictions (such as Georgia) where there was already evidence of *past* intentional discrimination.

    **c. Significance of *Rome*:** The Court's opinion in *Rome* gives an extremely generous reading to Congress' powers to "remedy" past or anticipated discrimination. In essence, the Court seems to be saying that wherever a practice (whether at-large voting districts, literacy tests, or other practice) has a discriminatory *impact* on minorities, and *might* be used for discriminatory purposes, Congress may ban that practice (at least in states that have in the past purposely committed racial discrimination in voting). This is true even if the jurisdiction responds with compelling evidence that the practices are *not* being used for discriminatory purposes.

**5. Limits to Congress' remedial powers:** Sometimes, Congress claims to be using its remedial powers, but the Court decides that Congress' "remedy" was out of all proportion to any likely state violation of constitutional rights, and was therefore not a proper use of the remedial powers. We discuss this scenario extensively beginning *infra*, p. 451.

**C. Substantive modifications:** *South Carolina v. Katzenbach* and *Rome v. U.S.*, although they interpret broadly Congress' remedial powers under the post-Civil War Amendments, do so explicitly on a remedial theory. That is, Congress' actions were viewed there as being designed to combat what, by the Court's own opinions, constituted past or prospective violations of the post-Civil War Amendments. But other legislation enacted by Congress from time to time under its Thirteenth, Fourteenth and Fifteenth Amendment enforcement powers is harder to justify on a "remedial" theory. This latter type of legislation seems to constitute an attempt by Congress to *redefine the meaning and scope of constitutional guarantees themselves*. Can Congress do this?

**1. Congress may not redefine scope of guarantees:** After decades of uncertainty, the Court in 1997 finally decided that Congress may *not* do this — *it's up to the Court alone, not Congress, to define the scope of Constitutional rights,* even rights (such as those given by the Fourteenth Amendment) as to which Congress has an explicit remedial power.

**2. *Boerne v. Flores*:** The landmark case in which the Court found that Congress has no right to specify the substantive contours of constitutional rights was *City of Boerne v. Flores*, 117 S. Ct. 2157 (1997). In that case, the Court held that Congress could not use its Fourteenth Amendment remedial powers to prevent local governments from unintentionally burdening individuals' religious freedom in certain ways. The decision's effect was to prevent Congress from effectively overruling a prior Supreme Court decision about the meaning of the Free Exercise clause.

a. **Statutory and caselaw background:** Before we can understand *Boerne*, we have to understand a bit about that prior Court decision, and Congress' response to it.

   i. **Prior Court decision:** In 1990, the Supreme Court decided *Employment Division v. Smith* (*infra*, p. 696), a case about the meaning of the First Amendment's guarantee of the free exercise of religion. The Court reversed its prior doctrine, and held that where a state enacts a criminal ban that is generally applicable, the state may automatically enforce that ban — without any balancing of the government's interest against the individual's interest — even where the ban has the effect of substantially interfering with an individual's exercise of his religion. (The ban at issue in *Smith* prevented Native Americans from making their traditional religious use of the drug peyote.)

   ii. **Congress' response:** The *Smith* decision was very unpopular. Congress responded in 1993 by overwhelmingly passing the "Religious Freedom Restoration Act" (RFRA). The RFRA forced federal, state and local governments to apply pre-*Smith* law, by which no government action that had the effect of "substantially burdening" a person's exercise of religion could be taken unless that action was the least restrictive means of accomplishing a "compelling governmental interest." (In other words, Congress was effectively saying that any governmental action that substantially burdened the exercise of religion had to survive strict scrutiny.)

   iii. **Based on Congress' 14th Amendment remedial power:** In applying its new rule to state and local governments, Congress relied on its Fourteenth Amendment remedial powers: since the First Amendment (including the guarantee of free exercise of religion) is made applicable to the states through the Fourteenth Amendment's guarantee of due process (see *supra*, p. 143), Congress reasoned that it could tell the states how to enforce that free-exercise guarantee as a means of "enforcing" due process.

b. **Result:** In *Boerne v. Flores*, the Supreme Court held that the RFRA was ***unconstitutional***. Writing for a 6-3 majority, Justice Kennedy said that "[Congress] has been given the power 'to enforce,' ***not the power to determine what constitutes a constitutional violation.***" (In fact, even the three dissenters agreed that Congress did not have the power to define substantive aspects of the 14th Amendment.)

   i. **Rejection of *Katzenbach v. Morgan*:** Justice Kennedy admitted that there was language in a prior Court opinion, *Katzenbach v. Morgan*, 384 U.S. 641 (1966), which he said "could be interpreted as acknowledging a power in Congress to enact legislation that expands the rights contained in §1 of the Fourteenth Amendment." But he said that this was not the best interpretation of what *Katzenbach* was saying.

   ii. **Effects would be unbounded:** Kennedy then argued that allowing Congress to expand or contract the scope of constitutional guarantees would produce an unstable, easily-changed Constitution: "If Congress could define its own powers by altering the Fourteenth Amendment's meaning, no longer would the Constitution be 'superior paramount law, unchangeable by ordinary means.' It would be 'on a level with ordinary legislative acts, and, like other acts, . . . alterable when the legislature shall please to alter it' [citing *Marbury v. Madison*]. Under this approach, it is difficult to conceive of a principle that would limit congressional power. . . . Shifting legislative majorities could change the Constitution and effectively circumvent the difficult and detailed amendment process contained in Article V."

iii. **RFRA struck down:** Justice Kennedy then concluded that the RFRA in fact modified the scope of the free exercise clause, rather than merely enforcing that clause.

   (1) **Congress can sometimes prohibit state statutes:** Kennedy acknowledged that Congress could, in certain circumstances, prevent states from enacting certain types of statutes that were not facially unconstitutional, as a method of preventing likely constitutional violations. For instance, in the Voting Rights Act provision upheld in *Katzenbach v. Morgan*, Congress could, and did, prohibit states with a history of voting-rights violations from applying literacy tests.

   (2) **The "congruence and proportionality" test:** Kennedy then set forth a new test for when Congress has gone beyond its Forteenth Amendment §5 remedial powers: He conceded that Congress must have "wide latitude" in determining where the line is between an appropriate remedial provision and an improper substantive re-definition of a 14th Amendment right. But, he said, "there must be a ***congruence and proportionality*** between the injury to be prevented or remedied and the means adopted to that end."

   (3) **RFRA out of proportion:** But the RFRA, Kennedy said, flunked this "congruence and proportionality" test. It was "so ***out of proportion*** to [any] supposed remedial or preventive object that it cannot be understood as responsive to, or designed to prevent, unconstitutional behavior. It appears, instead, to attempt a substantive change in constitutional protections." Therefore, it was invalid.

iv. **Dissent:** Three Justices dissented in *Boerne*. But even the three dissenters agreed that Congress can't expand or contract the scope of constitutional guarantees, even the scope of the Fourteenth Amendment guarantees as to which Congress has an explicit remedial power. (These Justices dissented only because they disagreed with the *Smith* decision, and therefore didn't believe that Congress was in fact modifying the scope of the Free-Exercise clause from what these dissenters believed that scope should be.)

# IV. FEDERAL ATTEMPTS TO STOP STATES FROM DISCRIMINATING

A. **Federal attempts to stop states from discriminating:**   The federal government sometimes tries to argue that a federal statute that purports to tell the states how to behave is ***not a redefinition*** of a constitutional right, but rather merely a prophylactic ***"remedy"*** to prevent constitutional ***violations by the state***. In recent years, the Court has ***rejected*** this argument, in several cases involving the states' ***11th Amendment immunity*** from federal-court damage suits.

1. **11th Amendment:** The 11th Amendment says, in brief, that the states are immune from being sued for money damages by private citizens in federal court. We discuss the Amend-

ment much greater detail later in this outline (see p. 725). But for now, you need to know only that Congress has the power to **override this state immunity** when it does so by using its 13th, 14th or 15th Amendment remedial powers to create a valid remedy against state violations of the rights protected by those amendments.

B.  **Effect of *Boerne v. Flores*:** Well, suppose Congress purports to rely on its post-Civil-War-Amendment remedial powers to pass a general anti-discrimination or other statute, and wants to make the states — not just private individuals — subject to the statute. If the statute is a valid exercise of the remedial powers, then Congress can in fact let private individuals bring damage suits against the states in federal court for violating it. But if the statute goes beyond Congress' remedial powers — in other words, if it violates the **"congruence and proportionality"** requirement of *Boerne v. Flores*, *supra* — then the private suits against the states are **not proper**, and the states have **immunity** from the suits. This may sound like only a theoretical possibility, but in fact in the first few years after the 1997 decision in *Boerne*, the Court quickly found that the states were immune from several important federal statutes because Congress went beyond its 14th Amendment remedial powers.

   1.  **Why this happened only recently:** Why did this federal-state battle erupt only relatively recently, beginning in the late 1990's? The answer is that originally, practically everyone thought that Congress could use its *Commerce* powers to abrogate the states' 11th Amendment immunity, so it didn't matter whether Congress could also abrogate the immunity under its 14th Amendment remedial powers. But in the 1996 case of *Seminole Tribe of Florida v. Florida* (see *infra*, p. 727), the Court held that *only* the post-Civil-War-Amendment remedial powers, not the Commerce clause, could serve as the basis for a congressional abrogation of the 11th Amendment. So now, if Congress wants to subject the states to federal-court damage actions by private individuals, Congress *must* rely exclusively on its 13th, 14th or 15th Amendment remedial powers as the source for the legislation creating the private rights being sued on. And it didn't take very long for the Court to find that various congressional enactments went beyond those post-Civil-War remedial powers.

C.  **Age and disability discrimination:** For instance, in a pair of decisions the Court held that when Congress tried to make the states (acting as employers) liable in federal court for **age and disability discrimination**, Congress **exceeded** its Fourteenth Amendment §5 remedial powers. **Kimel v. Florida Bd. of Regents**, 528 U.S. 62 (2000) and **Bd. of Trustees of Univ. of Alabama v. Garrett**, 531 U.S. 356 (2001). We'll discuss *Kimel* first.

   1.  **The ADEA statute (*Kimel*):** Back in the 1960s, Congress passed the Age Discrimination In Employment Act (ADEA), which prohibits various forms of age discrimination in employment. Congress expressly subjected the states to the ADEA's requirements when they act as employers. And for quite awhile, state employees often successfully sued the states in federal court for damages for age-discrimination based on ADEA violations.

      a.  **State arguments after *Seminole Tribe* and *Boerne*:** But after the 1996 decision in *Seminole Tribe* and the 1997 decision in *Boerne v. Flores*, states started defending these private ADEA suits with the following pair of arguments:

         [1]  the states can be liable for ADEA violations only if Congress was acting properly under its power to enforce the equal protection clause of the 14th Amendment (since that's the only clause of the 13th, 14th or 15th Amendments that even arguably has anything to do with age discrimination); and

[2] Congress didn't find that the states were major violators of equal protection when they discriminated on the basis of age, so making the states obey the ADEA as a means of combating equal protection violations was not a "congruent and proportional" response to an equal protection problem, as required by *Boerne v. Flores*.

b. **States win:** In *Kimel*, the state of Florida ***prevailed*** with this 2-pronged argument. The only real question was whether argument (2) would convince the court. Five members of the court concluded that the argument had merit. The majority noted that prior to passage of the ADEA, older persons were not commonly the victims of equal protection violations at the hands of state or local governments. Older workers had not been subjected to a "history of purposeful unequal treatment," and were not "discrete and insular minority." Therefore, as the Court had previously decided in *Mass. Ret. Bd. v. Murgia* (*supra*, p. 249), discrimination on the basis of age need only survive mere rationality review, not some form of a ban scrutiny. Consequently, any attempt by Congress to subject the states to extensive age-discrimination rules could not possibly have been a "congruent and proportional" response to equal protection violations, as required by *Boerne*. This meant that individual employees could not constitutionally be permitted to recover damages for ADEA violations against state or local employers.

2. **Same result for disability discrimination under ADA (*Garrett*):** Then, a year after *Kimel*, the Court reached a similar conclusion about Title I of the Americans with Disabilities Act (ADA). Just as *Kimel* found that Congress did not have §5 remedial power to subject the states as employers to age discrimination rules, the Court held in a 5-4 ruling in *Bd. of Trustees of Univ. of Alabama v. Garrett*, 531 U.S. 356 (2001) that Congress did not have §5 power to bar the states from discriminating against ***employees with disabilities***, as it tried to do in Title I.

   a. **Lack of adequate proof:** The ADA was a more modern statute than the ADEA (at issue in *Kimel*), and Congress tried hard to document, through extensive hearings, that the states as employers often discriminated unconstitutionally against the disabled. But this showing, too, failed to satisfy a majority of the Court. The majority conceded that the states may often have discriminated against disabled employees. But since the disabled were not a suspect or semi-suspect class, the only discrimination against them that would be a violation of the Fourteenth Amendment was ***"irrational"*** discrimination. (See *City of Cleburne*, *supra*, p. 344, where the Court found that discrimination against one type of disability, mental retardation, was to be judged by the mere-rationality standard.) And, the majority found, Congress despite its efforts failed to identify "a pattern of irrational state discrimination in employment against the disabled."

   b. **Lack of congruence:** Furthermore, the majority concluded in *Garrett*, the ***remedy*** chosen by Congress in the ADA lacked "congruence and proportionality" to any equal protection violations that the states may have been guilty of, just as had been the case in *Kimel*. For the ADA required states to spend hard dollars to modify existing facilities to make them readily accessible to disabled employees; that duty of accommodation went far beyond what could possibly have been required to address whenever small equal protection violations the states may have been guilty of.

c. **Significance:** So the Eleventh Amendment means that a state, when it acts as an employer, is not liable for money damages if it discriminates against a disabled employee or applicant in a way that would violate the ADA.

D. **Other areas:** The principle that Congress can only use its § 5 powers to make the states liable to private parties in federal damage-suits if Congress acts in a congruent-and-proportional way is not limited to the areas of age and disability discrimination.

1. **Patent violations:** For instance, the Court has held that Congress cannot use its 14th Amendment remedial powers to make states defend *private patent-infringement suits.* There was no evidence that the states had engaged in widespread infringement of patent rights (which if it had occurred could have been a 14th Amendment due process violation), so Congress' attempt to hold states liable in private patent enforcement suits was not a proportional response to a constitutional violation, as required by *Boerne.* See *Florida Prepaid Postsecondary Education Expense Board v. College Savings Bank*, 527 U.S. 627 (1999), discussed further *infra*, p. 728.

E. **Significance of class or right requiring heightened review:** All of the cases we've examined so far involving the "congruence and proportionality" requirement — that is, the cases discussing when Congress may abrogate the 11th Amendment and make the states defend private damage suits in federal court — have involved Congress' efforts to legislate in areas where the states' actions, if challenged on constitutional grounds, would receive *only mere-rationality review.* For instance, when a state is alleged to have discriminated in employment on the basis of age or disability — the types of discrimination at issue in *Kimel* and *Garrett* — equal protection review of the states' conduct would involve just the easy-to-satisfy mere-rationality level of review, since neither age nor disability has ever been found to be a suspect or semi-suspect category, and employment is not a fundamental right.

1. **Class or right triggering heightened scrutiny:** But now, suppose that Congress is trying to combat state discrimination either based on a *suspect or semi-suspect category*, or involving a *right that is "fundamental"* for due process or equal protection purposes. Does the fact that a *heightened level of review* gets used in these contexts[2] entitle Congress to act *more aggressively* when it tries to include states in a private-damages remedy for the discrimination in question? The answer that emerged in a pair of recent cases, one from 2003 and one from 2004, seems to be *"yes"* — if the discrimination involves a suspect or semi-suspect category, or a fundamental interest, the court will apparently be *quicker to conclude* that when Congress gave individuals a right to sue the states in federal court for this type of discrimination, Congress acted in a way that *was* "congruent and proportional," and thus proper under § 5, than where the area requires only mere rationality review.

2. **The Family and Medical Leave Act and gender discrimination:** The first of the cases was *Nevada Department of Human Resources v. Hibbs*, 538 U.S. 721 (2003). There, the issue was whether Congress could use its powers under § 5 of the 14th amendment to allow individuals to sue the states in federal court for violations of the *Family and Medi-*

---

2. Remember that for suspect categories like race and alienage, the Court uses strict scrutiny (see *supra*, p. 252, 253), and for a semi-suspect category like gender the Court uses mid-level review (*supra*, p. 322). Similarly, when an equal protection or due process violation is alleged regarding a right that the court deems to be "fundamental," the Court uses strict scrutiny here as well. See, e.g., equal protection challenges involving voting rights (*supra*, p. 355) or access to courts (*supra*, p. 364).

*cal Leave Act* of 1993 (FMLA). FMLA lets an eligible employee take up to 12 weeks of unpaid leave for any of several reasons, including a serious health condition in the employee's spouse or child. Congress clearly intended to allow state employees to sue the employer in federal court for violating FMLA rights, so the question was whether Congress' decision to let them do so was a "congruent and proportional" response to discrimination in this area by the states.

    **a. Majority finds Congress acted properly:** The 5-justice majority, in an opinion by Chief Justice Rehnquist, concluded that the congruent-and-proportional standard was *met*. In so deciding, the Court for the first time took the view that the ***presence or absence of heightened review for the type of discrimination in question makes a difference.*** Rehnquist distinguished the *Kimel* and *Garrett* decisions on the grounds that the types of discrimination at issue there (age discrimination in *Kimel* and workplace-disabilities discrimination in *Garrett*) receives only rational-basis review. In passing FMLA, on the other hand, Rehnquist concluded, part of what Congress was trying to do was to redress ***gender*** discrimination, a type of discrimination that is subject to heightened scrutiny.

       **i. Consequences:** Therefore, when Congress attacked gender discrimination in FMLA, "because the standard for demonstrating the constitutionality of a gender-based classification is more difficult to meet than our rational-basis test [it] was ***easier for Congress to show a pattern of state constitutional violations***." And, Rehnquist concluded, Congress had found enough evidence of this easier-to-show pattern of gender discrimination by state employers that subjecting such employers to the FMLA rules was a "congruent and proportional" response.

**3. Court access for disabled:** Then, in *Tennessee v. Lane*, 541 U.S. 509 (2004), another 5-Justice majority used similar reasoning to conclude that Congress had power to permit federal court suits against the states for money damages under Title II of the Americans with Disabilities Act (ADA), at least for activities relating to ***access to courts.***

    **a. Court access:** Title II provides that no disabled person can be excluded from participating or getting the benefits of any "***services***, programs or activities of a ***public entity***," or be discriminated against by such an entity. The plaintiffs in *Lane* were paraplegics who sought damages because they did not have adequate access to court services. One plaintiff, for instance, was required to crawl up stairs to answer criminal charges, because the county courthouse had no elevator.

    **b. Compared with Title I of ADA:** Recall that in *Garrett* (*supra*, p. 453), a narrow majority of the court held that Congress could not authorize damage suits against states for violations of Title I of the ADA, which covers employment discrimination. But Justice O'Connor changed sides from *Garrett* to *Lane*, forming a majority for the proposition that Congress had power to allow damages for Title II violations, at least in the court-access area. The majority reasoned that the ***right of access to courts*** is subject to ***"more searching judicial review"*** than the rational-relation review used in disability-discrimination-in-employment cases like *Garrett*. Furthermore, there was much clearer evidence before Congress that the states had failed to ensure equal treatment for the disabled in the provision of state services (Title II) than there was that the states as employers had discriminated against disabled employees (Title I).

**F. Right to allow damages for actual constitutional violations:** Cases like *Kimel* and *Garrett* — finding that Congress did not have constitutional power to authorize damage suits in the areas in question — involved private damage suits for ***state action that did not itself violate anyone's constitutional rights.*** (For instance, in *Kimel* the plaintiffs who were seeking money damages against Florida for age discrimination were not arguing that their constitutional rights had been violated, merely that their rights under the ADEA statute had been violated.) But if particular action by a state *would* directly violate the ***constitutional rights*** of a person, Congress *does* have power under § 5 of the 14th Amendment to authorize the injured person to recover damages against the state in federal court. This proposition became clear in *U.S. v. Georgia*, 126 S.Ct. 877 (2006).

   **1. Prisoner's right:** *U.S. v. Georgia* involved claims by a disabled inmate that the Georgia prison system had violated his constitutional rights, and his rights under Title II of the ADA, in various ways (e.g., by keeping him all day in a cell that was too narrow for him to turn his wheelchair around). The Court's opinion (by Justice Scalia) said that "While the members of this Court have disagreed regarding the scope of Congress' 'prophylactic' enforcement powers under § 5 of the 14th Amendment, no one doubts that § 5 grants Congress the power to 'enforce ... the provisions of the Amendment' by creating private remedies against the states for ***actual violations*** of those provisions." Therefore, he concluded, if the conduct that the plaintiff was complaining of actually violated his 14th Amendment rights, Congress had the § 5 power to give him the right to recover damages against the state in federal court.

      **a. Significance:** So Congress is always free to give private individuals a right to sue the states in federal court for damages for ***actually violating the individual's constitutional rights***, and when Congress does so it doesn't have to worry about the "congruent and proportional" rule. It's only when Congress acts "***prophylactically***" — when it forbids the states from taking some action that wouldn't necessarily violate anyone's constitutional rights, but which action is somehow related to possible constitutional violations that Congress is trying to prevent before they occur — that Congress' response must be "congruent and proportional" to the constitutional violations that Congress is trying to stamp out.

**G. 3-step analysis:** So to summarize this welter of cases regarding Congress' power under § 5 of the 14th Amendment to authorize federal-court damage suits against states, you should follow a three-level analysis:

   ❑ First, ask whether the state conduct that the plaintiff is complaining of was an ***actual violation*** by the state of the plaintiff's ***constitutional rights.*** If the answer is yes, then Congress can clearly grant the plaintiff the right to recover damages against the state in federal court, without worrying about whether its response is congruent-or-proportional to the violation. Cf. *U.S. v. Georgia, supra.*

   ❑ Now, assuming that the state conduct complained of by the plaintiff was not an actual constitutional violation, ask whether the federal statute that creates the private right of action (i.e., the right of the plaintiff to sue for damages) deals with an area that involves ***either a suspect or semi-suspect class or a fundamental right.*** If the answer is yes, then, since the Court applies some form of ***heightened scrutiny*** to this area, the Court will be quite likely to find that Congress' decision to allow a damages suit ***meets the "congruent and proportional" requirement*** and is thus constitutional. (See, e.g., *Nevada v. Hibbs, supra*, p. 454, finding that Congress' decision to let state employees sue for violations of the disability-leave provisions of the FMLA was constitutional because FMLA attempts to combat gender discrimination, a semi-suspect class that receives mid-level scrutiny.)

❏ Finally, assume that the answer to both of the above questions was "no." Now, Congress has power under § 5 of the 14th Amendment to allow the plaintiff to sue the state *only if Congress found widespread unconstitutional state conduct in the area in question.* And even if such widespread conduct was found, Congress must choose *narrowly-tailored methods* for combating the state conduct. This is all captured in the slogan that Congress' response must be "congruent and proportional" to the pattern of unconstitutional state actions relied on by Congress. (See, e.g., *Garrett*, supra, p. 453, holding that Congress did not have § 5 power to let state employees sue for violations of Title I of the Americans with Disabilities Act, because Congress did not have evidence of widespread discrimination by states against disabled employees).

---

*Quiz Yourself on*
## CONGRESSIONAL ENFORCEMENT OF CIVIL RIGHTS *(ENTIRE CHAPTER)*

**60.** The U.S. Congress has decided that it would now be desirable to extend the reach of federal anti-discrimination laws to the rental of units in 1-4 family homes, which have previously been exempt from such laws. Therefore, Congress proposes to make it a crime for any homeowner, regardless of the size of his dwelling or the number of units in it, and regardless of whether the owner resides in the dwelling, to decline to rent to another person on the grounds of the latter's race, ethnic group or national origin. The Chief Counsel to the Senate Judiciary Committee has expressed her opinion that Congress' remedial powers under the Fourteenth Amendment furnish adequate constitutional support for this statute. Is she correct? _____

**61.** Same facts as prior question. Now, however, assume that you are asked to find a constitutional basis for the proposed statute other than the Fourteenth Amendment and other than the Commerce Clause. What provision would you point to? _____

**62.** After a sharp right-ward shift in the politics of the nation, Republicans and conservative Democrats gained a majority in both houses of Congress. They passed, and the President signed into law, a statute providing as follows: "It shall be a federal felony for any person to perform an abortion on a woman who is more than three months pregnant, unless the pregnancy was caused by rape or incest or the abortion is necessary to save the woman's life." Assume for purposes of this question that if a state passed a comparable statute, Supreme Court precedents already on the books would compel the conclusion that the state statute was an unconstitutional violation of women's right of privacy. A woman and her doctor have challenged the federal statute on the grounds that it is a violation of the right to privacy, as embodied in the Fifth Amendment's Due Process Clause. Will this attack on the statute succeed? _____

---

*Answers*

**60. No, probably.** The Fourteenth Amendment is generally triggered only where there is "state action." Thus the clause dealing with equal protection provides that "[n]o State shall make or enforce any law which shall … deny to any person within its jurisdiction the equal protection of the laws." On the other hand, §5 of the Fourteenth Amendment grants Congress the power to enforce that amendment "by appropriate legislation." The issue is whether Congress may "appropriately" enforce the Equal Protection Clause by proscribing private, as opposed to governmental, conduct.

Certainly some types of private conduct may be reached under Congress' remedial powers. For instance, Congress may prevent a private person from interfering with a state official's attempts to furnish equal protection (e.g., Congress may punish private individuals to who prevent local school board officials from carrying out desegregation). But where the conduct being proscribed is *purely* private, involving the interaction of one private individual with another, it is clear that Congress' power to enforce the Equal Protection Clause does not extend that far; see *U.S. v. Morrison*.

**61. The Thirteenth Amendment.** The Thirteenth Amendment provides that "[n]either slavery nor involuntary servitude, except as a punishment for crime … shall exist within the United States. … " The Thirteenth Amendment, unlike the Fourteenth and Fifteenth, is thus not explicitly limited to governmental action. Section 2 of the Thirteenth Amendment gives Congress the power to "enforce this [amendment] by appropriate legislation." This §2 remedial power has been construed to mean that Congress has the right to decide what the ***"badges and incidents of slavery"*** are. If Congress makes a finding that one of the badges and incidents of slavery is the refusal of private homeowners to rent to others on the basis of race, the Court would uphold the proposed statute here as a valid exercise of this remedial power. All that is required is that Congress act "rationally" in determining that a particular aspect of private conduct is indeed a badge or incident of slavery, and Congress' conclusion here would certainly be found to be "rational." See *Jones v. Alfred H. Mayer Co.* (Thirteenth Amendment is broad enough to let Congress conclude that private racial discrimination in real estate transactions is a badge or incident of slavery).

**62. Yes, probably.** The question boils down to, "May Congress reduce the substantive content of individuals' constitutional rights?" The answer to this question is "no." The Court held in *Boerne v. Flores* that Congress' power to enforce the post-Civil War Amendments does not include the power to redefine the substantive boundaries of the rights given by those Amendments. Here, Congress has tried to reduce the substantive contours of a woman's substantive due process right to abortion, and under *Boerne* (and other Court cases), Congress may not do this.

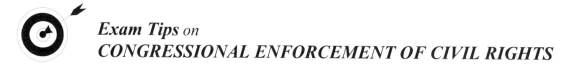

### *Exam Tips on* ***CONGRESSIONAL ENFORCEMENT OF CIVIL RIGHTS***

Exam questions on the subjects covered in this Chapter are relatively rare. Here are the few things to keep in mind:

☛ Probably most important, the 14th and 15th Amendments cannot be used to reach ***purely private conduct***, i.e., conduct not involving the state in any way. (This is another way of stating that "state action" is required.) But where government action and private action ***combine***, then Congress can reach this activity. (*Example:* Congress can make it a crime for a private citizen to interfere with government desegregation efforts.)

☛ Sometimes tested: The ***13th*** Amendment is the only Amendment that can reach ***purely private conduct***. That is, Congress gets to say what is a "badge or incident of slavery," and to then forbid it. *Example:* Congress can ban purely private discrimination in housing, under authority of the 13th Amendment. *Jones v. Alfred H. Mayer Co.*

☞ This means that the 13th Amendment can be the basis for federal anti-discrimination legislation that would otherwise have to be based on the Commerce Clause.

☞ The 13th Amendment can be used to ban racial discrimination against ***non-blacks*** (e.g., whites, Asians, etc.)

☞ Testable issue: Can Congress ban, under the 13th Amendment, discrimination on ***other than racial grounds***? Probably Congress can attack discrimination based on ***national origin*** and ***ethnicity***, but not on other characteristics (e.g., gender or sexual orientation). Also, probably only ***purposeful*** discrimination can be reached.

☛ Where Congress is trying to combat a clear problem of ***discrimination by a state***, its ***remedial*** powers are ***relatively broad***. So as long as Congress is behaving rationally in combatting discrimination, you should conclude that it is acting constitutionally under its power to enforce the 13th, 14th and 15th Amendments.

☞ But even where Congress is combatting state discrimination, Congress' response must be ***"congruent and proportional"*** to the discrimination — Congress can't choose methods that are much ***broader*** than the discrimination being cured. (*Boerne v. Flores*.) So Congress can't ban certain state discriminatory conduct, and then make the states liable in damages to private plaintiffs for that conduct, unless Congress had evidence that the states frequently violated people's constitutional rights in that area.

**Example:** Suppose Congress rationally concludes that states, acting as employers, occasionally (but not frequently) violate the constitutional rights of disabled employees. Congress still can't give state employees the right to sue the state for damages for violating the statute -- the states have Eleventh Amendment immunity from private damage suits, and that immunity can be overcome only by proof that Congress' response was congruent and proportional to widespread state discrimination of the type being addressed, something not present here. (*Bd. of Trustees of Ala. v. Garrett*.)

☞ But where the area of discrimination that Congress is trying to prevent is one that gets ***heightened scrutiny*** (i.e., involves a ***suspect or semi-suspect class***, or a ***fundamental right***), then Congress can allow private damages based on a ***lesser showing*** of that the states have discriminated.

**Example:** Congress orders state and private employers to give employees various rights to take unpaid leave to care for sick family members. In doing so, Congress is acting to combat gender discrimination. Even if the states have practiced only occasional leave-related gender discrimination against their employees, Congress can still let state employees sue for violations of the state, because gender-discrimination gets heightened (mid-level) review. (*Nevada Dept. of Hum. Res. v. Hibbs*)

☛ Occasionally, you'll notice buried in a fact pattern that Congress is arguably ***expanding*** or ***contracting*** the ***scope*** of a right guaranteed under one of the post-Civil War Amendments. Say that under *Boerne v. Flores*, Congress may ***neither*** expand nor contract the boundaries of any constitutional right, even under Congress' power to "enforce" the post-Civil War Amendments.

CHAPTER 14

# FREEDOM OF EXPRESSION

## *ChapterScope*

The First Amendment provides, in part, that "Congress shall make no law ... abridging the freedom of speech, or of the press. ... " These rights (plus the accompanying "freedom of association") are often grouped together as "freedom of expression." Here are the key concepts relating to freedom of expression:

- **Content-based vs. content-neutral:** Courts distinguish between *"content-based"* and *"content-neutral"* regulations on expression.

  - ❏ **Content-based:** If the government action is *"content-based,"* the action will be generally subjected to *strict scrutiny*, and the action will usually be struck down.

  - ❏ **Content-neutral:** On the other hand, if the government action is *"content-neutral,"* the government's action is subjected to a much easier-to-satisfy test, and will usually be upheld.

  - ❏ **Classifying:** A governmental action that burdens expression is "content-based" if the government is *aiming* at the *"communicative impact"* of the expression. By contrast, if the government is aiming at something other than the communicative impact, the action is "content-neutral," even if it has the *effect* of burdening expression.

- **Analysis of content-based government action:** Where a government action impairing expression is "content-based," here's how courts analyze it:

  - ❏ **Unprotected category:** If the speech falls into certain pre-defined *unprotected* categories, then the government can more or less completely ban the expression.

    - ❏ **Listing:** The main "unprotected" categories are: (1) obscenity; (2) fraudulent misrepresentation; (3) defamation; (4) advocacy of imminent lawless behavior; and (5) "fighting words."

  - ❏ **Protected category:** All expression not falling into one of these five categories is "protected." If expression is protected, then any government ban or restriction on it based on its content is *presumed to be unconstitutional*. The Court subjects any such regulation to *strict scrutiny* — the regulation will be sustained only if it (1) serves a *compelling governmental objective*; and (2) and is *"necessary,"* i.e., drawn as *narrowly as possible* to achieve that objective.

- **Analyzing content-neutral regulations:** If the government restriction is *content-neutral*, then here is how the Court analyzes it:

  - ❏ **Three-part test:** The government must satisfy a *three-part test* before the regulation will be sustained, if the regulation substantially impairs expression:

    - ❏ **Significant governmental interest:** First, the regulation must serve a *significant governmental interest*;

    - ❏ **Narrowly tailored:** Second, the regulation must be *narrowly tailored* to serve that governmental interest; and

❑ **Alternative channels:** Finally, the state must *"leave open alternative channels"* for communicating the information.

■ **Overbreadth:** A person whose expression is impaired by the government may make use of the doctrine of *"overbreadth."* A statute is "overbroad" if it bans speech which could constitutionally be forbidden but *also* bans speech which is protected by the First Amendment. Overbreadth doctrine lets a litigant prevail if he can show that the statute, applied according to its terms, would violate the First Amendment rights of *persons not now before the court*.

■ **Vagueness:** A second important First Amendment doctrine is that of *vagueness*. A statute is unconstitutionally vague if the conduct forbidden by it is so *unclearly defined* that a reasonable person would have to *guess at its meaning*.

■ **Advocacy of illegal conduct:** The government may ban speech that *advocates imminent illegal conduct*. To be banable, the speech must satisfy two requirements: (1) the advocacy must be *intended* to incite or produce *"imminent lawless action"*; and (2) the advocacy must in fact be *likely* to incite or produce that imminent lawless action.

■ **Time, place and manner regulations:** The government frequently tries to regulate the *"time, place and manner"* of expression.

❑ **Three-part test:** A "time, place and manner" regulation of speech or expressive conduct has to pass the *three-part test* summarized above, i.e., (1) it has to be *content-neutral*; (2) it has to be *narrowly tailored* to serve a *significant governmental interest*; and (3) it must "leave open *alternative channels*" for communicating the information.

❑ **Licensing:** There are special limits on the government's right to require a *license* or *permit* before expressive conduct takes place.

 ❑ **No excess discretion:** Most importantly, the licensing scheme must set forth the grounds for denying the permit *narrowly* and *specifically*, so that the *discretion* of local officials is curtailed.

❑ **Fighting words:** Expression that constitutes *"fighting words"* can be flatly banned or punished by the state. "Fighting words" are words which are likely to make the person to whom they are addressed commit an *act of violence*, probably against the speaker.

 ❑ **Limits:** But the "fighting words" doctrine is tightly limited. For instance, the police must *control* the angry crowd instead of arresting the speaker, if they've got the physical ability to do so.

❑ **Offensive language:** Language that is *"offensive"* is nonetheless protected by the First Amendment. (Thus language that is *profane*, or language that preaches *racial or religious hatred*, is protected.)

■ **The public forum:** Speech that takes place in a *"public forum"* is harder to regulate.

❑ **Content-based:** If a regulation is *content-based*, it makes no difference whether the expression is in a public forum: strict scrutiny will be given in any event.

❑ **Neutral "time, place and manner":** If a regulation is content-neutral, then the fact that the speech does or does not take place in a public forum makes a difference. Usually, we're talking about "time, place and manner" restrictions here.

❑ **Non-public forum:** When expression takes place in a ***non-public forum***, the regulation merely has to be ***rationally related*** to some ***legitimate*** governmental objective, as long as equally effective alternative channels are available.

❑ **Public forum:** But where the expression takes place in a ***public forum***, the regulation has to be ***narrowly drawn*** to achieve a ***significant*** governmental interest (roughly ***intermediate-level*** review). It is still necessary (but not sufficient) that the government leaves alternative channels available.

❑ **What are public forums:** "True" public forums are: (1) streets; (2) sidewalks; and (3) parks. Also, places in which a public government ***meeting*** takes place are probably true public forums.

❑ **Designated-public:** There are also *"designated-public"* forums. These are locations where the government has decided to open the place to particular open-expression purposes. The rules are essentially those for true public forums, except that government may at any time decide to close the forum.

❑ **Non-public forums:** Other public places are "non-public forums." Here, government regulation merely has to be rationally related to some legitimate governmental objective, as long as alternative channels are left open. (*Examples:* Airport terminals, jails, military bases, courthouses, schools used after hours, and governmental office buildings.)

■ **Access to private property:** In general, a speaker does not have any First Amendment right of access to another person's private property to deliver his message. Thus there is no First Amendment right to speak in a private ***shopping center***.

■ **Defamation:** The First Amendment places limits on the extent to which a plaintiff may recover tort damages for ***defamation***.

❑ **Plaintiff as public official or public figure:** Where P is a ***public official*** or ***public figure***, he may only win a defamation suit against D for a statement relating to P's official conduct if P can prove that D's statement was made with either *"**knowledge** that it was false"* or *"**reckless disregard**"* of whether it was true or false.

■ **Obscenity:** Expression that is *"obscene"* is simply ***unprotected*** by the First Amendment. For a work to be "obscene," all three parts of the following test must be met:

❑ **Prurient interest:** First, the average person, applying today's community standards, must find that the work as a whole appeals to the *"**prurient**"* (i.e., sexual) interest;

❑ **Sexual conduct:** Second, the work must describe or depict in a "patently offensive way" particular types of ***sexual conduct*** defined by state law; and

❑ **Lacks value:** Finally, the work taken as a whole must lack "serious literary, artistic, political or scientific value."

*Note:* But the mere ***private possession*** of obscene material by an adult may ***not*** be made criminal.

■ **Commercial speech:** Speech that is *"commercial"* gets First Amendment protection. But this protection is more limited than protection given to non-commercial speech:

❏ **Truthful speech:** Content-based restrictions on truthful commercial speech get only mid-level review: the government must be: (1) *directly advancing* (2) a *substantial* governmental interest (3) in a way that is *reasonably tailored* to achieve the government's objective. (This compares with strict scrutiny of content-based restrictions on non-commercial speech.)

❏ **False, deceptive or illegal:** False or deceptive commercial speech, or speech proposing an *illegal transaction*, may be forbidden by the government.

■ **Freedom of association:** First Amendment case law recognizes the concept of *"freedom of association."* If an individual has a First Amendment right to engage in a particular expressive activity, then a *group* has a "freedom of association" right to engage in that same activity as a group.

❏ **Illegal membership:** The freedom of association means that *mere membership in a group or association may not be made illegal*. Membership may only be made part of an offense if: (1) the group is *actively engaged* in unlawful activity, or incites others to imminent lawless actions; and (2) the individual *knows* of the group's illegal activity, and specifically *intends* to *further* the group's illegal goals.

❏ **Denial of public benefit or job:** The government may not deny a *public benefit or job* based on a person's protected associations. If a person's activities with a group could not be made *illegal*, then those activities may generally not be made the basis for denying the person the government job or benefit.

❏ **Loyalty oath:** Similarly, the government may generally not require a job applicant to sign a *loyalty oath*, unless the things the applicant is promising not to do are things which, if he did them, would be grounds for punishing or denying him the job.

# I.  GENERAL THEMES

A. **Text of First Amendment:**  The First Amendment provides that "Congress shall make no law ... abridging the *freedom of speech*, or of *the press*; or the right of the people peaceably to assemble, and to petition the Government for a redress of grievances."

 1. **Related rights:**  There are thus several distinct rights which may be grouped under the category "freedom of expression": freedom of *speech*, of the *press*, of *assembly*, and of *petition*. Additionally, there is a well-recognized "freedom of association" which, although it is not specifically mentioned, is derived from individuals' rights of speech and assembly.

B. **Two broad classes:**  When government "abridges" freedom of speech, its reasons for doing so can be placed into two broad classes. The first is that the government is restricting the speech *because of its content*, that is, because of the *ideas or information contained in it*, or because of its general subject matter. The second reason for abridgment has nothing to do with the content of the speech; rather, the government seeks to avoid *some evil unconnected with the speech's content*, but the government's regulation has the *incidental by-product* of interfering with particular communications.

1. **Two tracks:** The Supreme Court has implicitly recognized that the dangers posed by governmental action taken for the first reason are different (and generally more severe) than those posed by regulation carried out for the second reason. Therefore, the Supreme Court's rules for determining whether the government has violated the First Amendment differ depending on whether the governmental control falls within the first class or the second.

   a. **Track one (communicative impact):** Where the government's conduct falls within the first class, which Tribe summarizes as governmental actions "aimed at *communicative impact*," he has labeled the appropriate analysis *"track one"* analysis. (Tribe, p. 791).

   b. **Track two (noncommunicative impact):** Where the government's conduct falls within the second class (which Tribe describes as government actions "aimed at *noncommunicative impact* but nonetheless having *adverse effects on communicative opportunity*"), he calls the relevant analysis *"track two."* Tribe, p. 792.

   c. **We adopt terms:** For ease of labeling, we will follow the same "track one" and "track two" terminology.

2. **Some examples:** Following are some examples of governmental actions punishing or restricting speech, and the track into which each falls:

   **Example 1:** The state forbids pharmacists to advertise the prices of prescription drugs, because it is afraid that the public will buy drugs at the lowest available price and will therefore receive low-quality goods and service. This case falls within "track *one*," since the speech is being regulated because of the government's fears about consumers' reaction to the speech's **content**. See *Virginia Pharmacy Board v. Virginia Consumer Council*, 425 U.S. 748 (1976) (invalidating the restriction, as discussed *infra*, p. 567).

   **Example 2:** The state forbids "maliciously and willfully disturb[ing] the peace or quiet of any neighborhood or person [by] offensive conduct." D is convicted under the statute for wearing a jacket bearing the words "Fuck The Draft" in a corridor of the county courthouse. The case should be analyzed under "track *one*," since the asserted offensiveness caused by D results *solely from the content* of his communication. (To see this, observe that bystanders who *could not read English* would *not* have been offended.) See *Cohen v. California*, 403 U.S. 15 (1971) (reversing D's conviction, as discussed *infra*, p. 506).

   **Example 3:** The federal Espionage Act of 1917 forbids anyone from obstructing the draft or causing insubordination in the military. D, as part of a speech deploring the U.S.'s participation in World War I, praises draft resisters and tells his audience that they are "fit for something better than slavery and cannon fodder." He is convicted under the statute. The case should be analyzed under "track *one*," since the harm which the government claims resulted (interference with the draft) resulted from the *content* of D's speech. See *Debs v. U.S.*, 249 U.S. 211 (1919) (upholding the conviction, as discussed *infra*, p. 475).

   **Example 4:** A city prohibits the use of sound trucks which emit "loud and raucous noises" while operating on the streets. The ordinance should be analyzed under "track two," since the harm which the government seeks to prevent is *independent of the* *content* of the messages being amplified — even a listener who *could not understand English* would be a victim of the harm. See *Kovacs v. Cooper*, 336 U.S. 77 (1949) (upholding such a ban, as discussed *infra*, p. 499).

**Example 5:** A city forbids distribution of leaflets, because it wishes to prevent littering. The case should be analyzed under "track *two*," since the harm sought to be avoided exists regardless of what information is contained on the leaflets. (In fact, even *blank* leaflets could end up being litter.) See *Schneider v. State*, 308 U.S. 147 (1939), striking the ban (on the grounds that the First Amendment requires a less restrictive alternative, such as only punishing actual littering; the case is discussed *infra*, p. 491).

C. **Analysis of "track one" cases:**   If a case falls within "track *one*," that is, if the government objects to the *communicative impact* of the expression, a very rigid analysis must be followed. The most important general rule is the following (as phrased by Tribe, pp. 833-34): *"whenever the harm feared could be averted by a further exchange of ideas, governmental suppression is conclusively deemed unnecessary."*

1. **Marketplace of ideas:**   This rule reflects the view, implicit in the First Amendment, that it is not the government's place to suppress ideas because they are "wrong"; rather, as Justice Holmes put it in his dissent in *Abrams v. U.S.*, 250 U.S. 616 (1919) (discussed more extensively *infra*, p. 476), there is to be *"free trade in ideas,"* and truth will become accepted through "the *competition of the market.*" Only where the circumstances are such that there is *no time to expose evil ideas* (and to prevent their harmful effect) through *more speech* may the government bar expression.

2. **Unprotected categories:**   Furthermore, in "track one" cases, it is generally not open to the government to argue that *in the particular case at hand*, the feared harm cannot be avoided by more speech. Instead, the Court has defined certain *established categories* of speech, which are deemed not protected by the First Amendment. The creation of a given category amounts, in effect, to a finding by the Court that that *type* of speech is harmful, not valuable under the First Amendment, and not "nullifiable" by more speech; these categories have traditionally included *obscenity, fraudulent misrepresentation, advocacy of imminent lawless behavior, defamation, "fighting words,"* etc. *Unless the speech falls within one of these previously-fixed categories*, it is simply *not open to the government to argue that the speech is harmful* because of its content, and that it should be suppressed or punished.

   **Example:** Consider Example 1, *supra*, p. 465, in which the state prohibited pharmacists from advertising their prices for prescription drugs. The state contended that barring this information would be in the public interest, since a contrary policy would lead people to be interested only in price, and therefore to receive low-quality goods or services. The Court conceded the plausibility of the state's claim. But it held that the weighing of the state's interest in protecting its citizens versus the value of free-flowing information was *not the Court's or the Virginia legislature's to make*. "It is precisely this kind of choice between the dangers of suppressing information, and the dangers of its misuse if it is freely available, *that the First Amendment makes for us*." *Virginia Pharmacy Board v. Virginia Consumer Council*, 425 U.S. 748 (1976) (discussed more extensively *infra*, p. 567).

a. **Rationale for making category unprotected:** When the Court decides whether to *create an entire category* of unprotected speech, it generally does take into account the harmfulness of the types of messages being conveyed, and the ability or inability of more speech to cure the harm. For instance, advocacy of imminent lawless action is unprotected in large part because such speech may result in a crime before other speakers have had a chance to respond. (See the treatment of such advocacy *infra*, p. 474.)

    i. **Only "dialogue" valued:** More generally, the formation of unprotected categories stems from the fact that "free speech" has value only in the context of *"dialogue,"* that is, communication that concerns beliefs and ideas, and involves "persuasion." The Court will make into an unprotected category those types of "utterances [that] are no essential part of any exposition of ideas [and] of ... slight social value as a step to truth." *Chaplinsky v. New Hampshire*, 315 U.S. 568 (1942) (discussed further *infra*, p. 503). Speech in the unprotected categories (e.g., fraudulent misrepresentations of fact, "fighting words," obscenity, libelous statements) can be viewed as *"projectiles"* whose effect cannot be prevented by more speech, rather than as part of an exchange of views. See Tribe, p. 837-38.

b. **Significance of categories:** By generally allowing government to suppress for "track one" reasons only if the speech falls in a previously-defined unprotected category, the Court has made it less likely that governments, or popular majorities, will be able *intentionally to stifle dissent*.

    i. **Alternative is unsatisfactory:** To see this, consider the alternative, a system in which government could prohibit a particular message on the ground that the dangers posed *by that particular message* are greater than the benefits (both to the speaker and to his listeners) of allowing the idea to be expressed. In such an *ad hoc* balancing system, unpopular ideas would be quite likely to be suppressed, by legislatures in the first instance (who directly represent the majority), and by judges in the second instance (who, although presumably somewhat more independent, are nonetheless not immune to the sentiments of the majority.) In times of national crisis, the tolerance for dissent would be even less.

    ii. **Categories approach:** An "unprotected categories" approach, by contrast, at least means that "consideration of likely harm takes place at *wholesale, in advance*, outside the context of specific cases." Ely, p. 110.

    iii. **Not totally unprotected:** By the way, even speech falling within an "unprotected category" is *not completely* unprotected by the First Amendment. Even as to such speech, government must regulate in a basically *content-neutral* way, the Supreme Court has recently held. See *R.A.V. v. City of St. Paul*, discussed *infra*, p. 510. For example, the state may not criminalize just those libels that are directed towards government officials.

3. **Cases outside of unprotected categories:** If content-based regulations are imposed in a situation that does *not* fall within one of these pre-existing "unprotected categories," there is a *strong presumption* that the regulation is *unconstitutional*. In this situation, the Court will *strictly scrutinize* the regulation: the government bears the burden of showing "that its regulation is necessary to *serve a compelling state interest* and that it is *narrowly drawn* to achieve that end." *Widmar v. Vincent*, 454 U.S. 263 (1981). The techniques of

strict scrutiny here are therefore comparable to those in the due process (*supra*, p. 156) and equal protection (*supra*, p. 260) contexts.

a. **Consequences:** Use of strict scrutiny to cover content-based restrictions not involving an unprotected category entails the following consequences:

   i. **Effect of more speech:** Any time ***more speech*** could eliminate the evil feared by the state, the Court will conclude that the regulation is ***not "necessary"*** to prevent that evil (no matter how serious the evil is). This is simply an application of the general principle, previously noted, that whenever possible, "harmful" speech must be fought by more expression, not by government-imposed silence.

   ii. **Other speakers' opportunities irrelevant:** The government may not claim that the content of the expression has been adequately articulated by ***other speakers***, and that proponents of ***different viewpoints*** on the issue should be given a chance to speak instead (see Tribe, p. 834).

   iii. **Other times and places irrelevant:** The government may not claim that the speaker can make his point just as well in ***some other place***, at ***some other time***, or in ***some other manner.*** *Id.* Once the government is seen to be objecting to a message based on its content, ***not even a "trifling" or "minor" interference with expression will be tolerated by the courts***.

b. **Illustration:** A case involving the right to put up ***billboards*** illustrates the strict (and usually fatal) scrutiny given to non-content-neutral regulations where the expression does not fall into an "unprotected category." In ***Metromedia, Inc. v. San Diego***, 453 U.S. 490 (1981), the Court struck down a San Diego ordinance which, *inter alia*, ***prohibited all billboards*** containing ***non-commercial messages***, except for those messages falling within certain defined categories (e.g., temporary political campaign signs, signs carrying news items or telling the time or temperature, etc.) The Court objected to this handling of non-commercial speech, on the grounds that "[t]he city may not choose the appropriate subjects for public discourse"; the city was required to either allow ***all***, or ***no***, non-commercial messages. (The Court did not reach the issue of whether other First Amendment principles might prevent a ***total*** ban on billboards. However, in a later case, the Court concluded that a city could totally ban the posting of signs on public property. See *Los Angeles v. Taxpayers For Vincent*, 466 U.S. 789 (1984).)

c. **Another illustration:** Strict scrutiny for content-based restrictions was also fatal in ***Widmar v. Vincent***, 454 U.S. 530 (1981).

   i. **Facts:** A state university made its facilities generally available for registered student groups, but refused to allow a student religious group to meet anywhere on the campus. This refusal was part of a general policy prohibiting the use of university facilities "for purposes of religious worship or religious teaching."

   ii. **Holding:** The Supreme Court held that the ban violated the religious group's First Amendment right of free speech and association. Because the denial of facilities was content-based, it could be upheld only if shown to be: (1) necessary to serve a compelling state interest, and (2) narrowly drawn to achieve that interest. Here, the university could not make the required showing. (The university's main defense, that its policy was justified as a promotion of the separation of church and state, is discussed *infra*, p. 659.)

d. **Final illustration:** Similarly, strict (and fatal) scrutiny was applied to a content-based statute in *Boos v. Barry*, 485 U.S. 312 (1988). The statute prohibited the display of any sign within 500 feet of a foreign embassy if that sign tends to bring that foreign government into "public odium" or "public disrepute."

    i. **Facts:** The statute, applicable to the District of Columbia, prohibited such signs in order to serve the governmental interest in protecting the dignity of foreign diplomatic personnel. Since only signs bearing certain messages were prohibited (those bringing the foreign government into "public odium" or "public disrepute"), the regulation was clearly not content neutral. Therefore, it had to be subject to strict scrutiny, and could be upheld only if it was necessary to serve a compelling state interest and narrowly drawn to achieve that interest.

    ii. **Result:** The statute failed that test, according to the Court. Even if the interest in preserving the dignity of foreign diplomats was "compelling" — which the Court did not decide — more narrowly-drawn measures (e.g., a ban on harassing foreign officials) would have protected that interest adequately.

4. **Content-based regulation of unprotected categories:** Until relatively recently, by contrast, if speech fell *within* one of the pre-defined "unprotected categories," even a non-content-neutral regulation abridging that speech was generally subjected only to *"mere rationality"* review, not "strict scrutiny." But a majority of the Court now seems to have abandoned this distinction between the protected-categories situation and the unprotected-categories situation: in *either* case, *viewpoint-based restrictions will now be strictly scrutinized.* See *R.A.V. v. St. Paul*, 505 U.S. 377 (1992) (discussed further *infra*, p. 509), in which the Court held that a city may not differentiate between racially-based "fighting words" (an unprotected category, see *infra*, p. 503) and fighting words on other topics. (The Court did allow government to regulate unprotected categories based on content where the content-based regulation is "because of [the expression's] constitutionally proscribable content," a somewhat vague phrase.)

a. **Significance of categories:** In light of *R.A.V.*, what significance remains to the fact that particular speech does or does not fall within an "unprotected category"? The main significance of the unprotected/protected distinction is probably now that: (1) government may *completely proscribe* materials falling in an unprotected category (so long as government acts in a content-neutral manner within the category), and may obviously not enact such a total ban on materials not falling within an unprotected category; and (2) *time/place/manner* restrictions on speech in public forums will be *presumptively valid* when applied to unprotected categories, but will be subjected to careful review (see *infra*, p. 492) in the case of protected categories.

5. **Distinction between subjects or between types of speech:** The normal requirement of content-neutrality clearly means that the government may not show favoritism as between differing points of view on a particular subject. But it also means that the state *may not place a particular issue off-limits while allowing other subjects to be discussed.*

a. ***Con Edison* case:** For instance, in *Consolidated Edison v. Public Serv. Commission*, 447 U.S. 530 (1980), the Court prevented the New York Public Service Commission from ordering utilities not to discuss, as part of their monthly billing materials, the desirability of nuclear power. The Court reasoned that "[t]he First Amendment's hostility to content-based regulation extends not only to restrictions on particular viewpoints, but also to prohibition of public discussion of an entire topic."

b. **"Son of Sam" law:** Similarly, the government may not penalize a speaker based on the particular *topic* of the speech. Consider New York's "Son of Sam" law, which required that an accused or convicted criminal's income from works *describing his crime* be deposited in an escrow account and made available to the victims of the crime. This statute was ruled a First Amendment violation in *Simon and Schuster Inc. v. New York State Crime Victim's Board*, 502 U.S. 105 (1991). The statute was content-based, in that it "singles out income derived from expressive activity for a burden the State places on no other income, and it is directed only at works with a specified content."

c. **Differing types of speech:** However, it is not clear whether the requirement of content-neutrality sweeps so broadly as to prevent the government from distinguishing between different **broad categories** or **types** of speech.

   i. **Political vs. commercial speech:** On the one hand, a plurality in *Lehman v. Shaker Heights*, 418 U.S. 298 (1974) upheld Shaker Heights' right to accept commercial advertising on city-owned buses while rejecting political advertising. The four Justices in the plurality denied that the buses constituted a public forum, and argued that they were, rather, part of a "commercial venture"; requiring the city to accept short-term political advertising might have interfered with long-term lucrative contracts, and would also have raised "lurking doubts about favoritism, and sticky administrative problems … in parcelling out limited space to eager politicians." Thus, judging by *Lehman*, a near-majority of the Court **would allow political speech to be discriminated against vis-a-vis commercial speech**. (But four other members of the Court, dissenting, argued that this constituted discrimination "solely on the basis of message content," in violation of the First Amendment. Justice Douglas cast the deciding vote, but he did so on the basis that bus riders formed a "captive audience," and that no advertiser, commercial or political, had a constitutional right to address that audience.)

   ii. **Billboard case:** On the other hand, a different four-Justice plurality, in *Metromedia, Inc. v. San Diego*, 453 U.S. 490 (1981), asserted that the government **may not prefer commercial to non-commercial speech**. That plurality concluded that such was the forbidden effect of an ordinance which barred all billboards containing commercial messages except "on-site signs," but which barred **all** non-commercial billboards with **no** on-site exception. Two concurring Justices, Brennan and Blackmun, seemed also to agree that commercial speech may not be preferred to non-commercial speech; they objected to any scheme which would even give the city officials the power to *determine* whether a message is "commercial" or "non-commercial" — "Cities are equipped to make traditional police power decisions, not decisions based on the content of speech."

   iii. **Conclusion:** Thus a majority of the Court now seems to be on record as believing that commercial speech may not be preferred to non-commercial speech (and perhaps, by extension, that no broad category of speech may be preferred to another.) Therefore, the *Lehman* plurality apparently remains at best just that, a plurality. (Conversely, other Court decisions make it clear that commercial speech *may* be **disfavored** vis-a-vis non-commercial speech; in fact, only recently has commercial speech been granted *any* First Amendment protection at all. See *infra*, p. 567.)

    **iv. Public forum:** In any event, government's possible right to discriminate between broad classes of speech exists only where **no public forum is involved**. Where expression takes place in a **public forum**, not even content-**neutral** restrictions will be tolerated unless they are **closely-tailored** to serve significant governmental interests. (See *infra*, p. 492.) For this reason, the plurality in *Lehman, supra*, p. 470, found it necessary to conclude that the city-owned buses were not a public forum, before concluding that political speech could be banned on them.

  **d. Taxation:** A *tax*, like a regulation, may be found to be directed at the communicative impact of speech, and therefore presumptively invalid. Thus in *Minneapolis Star & Tribune Co. v. Minnesota Comm'r of Revenue* (discussed further *infra*, p. 626), the Court concluded that a special Minnesota "use tax" applicable only to the cost of **paper and ink** consumed in the production of **publications**, violated the First Amendment.

    **i. Rationale:** The Court did not find any indication in the legislative history of any "impermissible or censorial motive on the part of the legislature." But by enacting the tax (which was a special one, not part of the state's generally-applicable use tax), the state had **"singled out the press for special treatment."** Therefore, the tax could not stand unless it was "necessary to achieve an overriding governmental interest" (i.e., "track one" strict scrutiny.)

  **e. Religious speech gets equal protection:** The requirement of content-neutrality is so strong that it will apparently now take precedence over the **Establishment Clause** (designed to protect separation of church and state; see *infra*, p. 657). That is, if the government allows private speech in a particular forum, government may not treat religiously-oriented speech less favorably than non-religiously-oriented speech.

    **Example:** If a public university gives funding for student publications on various topics, the requirement of content-neutrality means that the university must give the same funding to a student publication whose mission is to proselytize for Christianity. See *Rosenberger v. University of Virginia*, 515 U.S. 819 (1995), discussed further *infra*, p. 660.

**6. Ascertaining government's motive:** The government, in justifying its prohibition of a certain type of speech, will rarely admit to being non-content-neutral. For instance, it will virtually never admit that it is trying to suppress speech merely because it doesn't like the content of what is being said. The government will almost always point to some danger beyond the speech itself — for instance, the danger of unlawful activity which the speech may incite, or the listener's reliance to his detriment on the speaker's misstatement of fact. Furthermore, the government will often claim that the evil is **independent** of the speech's content; thus the state will frequently claim that it is merely regulating the "time, place or manner" of the speech, not its content. Despite such justifications, the Court will look at two aspects of the regulation in order to determine whether it is in reality aimed at the communicative impact of the expression (and therefore calls for "track one" analysis):

a.  **Facial review:**  First, the Court will examine the statute *on its face*. If this facial review discloses that the regulation is targeted at the content of the speech, "track one" analysis will be used.

**Example:** D peacefully pickets near a school, carrying a sign protesting discrimination. He is convicted under a local ordinance prohibiting all picketing near school buildings during school hours; however, the ordinance exempts "the peaceful picketing of any school involved in a labor dispute." On these facts, the Supreme Court in effect applied "track one" analysis, and invalidated the ordinance: "Government may not prohibit [persons] from assembling or speaking on the basis of what they intend to say." *Chicago Police Department v. Mosley*, 408 U.S. 92 (1972).

b.  **Intent:**  Second, even if the governmental regulation is found to be content-neutral on its face, the Court may conclude that it was *motivated* by an intent to single out certain types of subject matter for suppression or penalty. A facially-neutral regulation which the state justifies, for instance, on the grounds that it is merely a regulation of "time, place or manner," may be found by the Court to have really been motivated by a desire to suppress certain types of communicative content.

**Example:** A school district forbids the wearing of armbands in school; the armbands are being worn as a symbol of opposition to the Vietnam War. Despite the district's claim that the ban was merely a regulation on the "manner" of expression, the Supreme Court concluded that it was really motivated by the district's desire to avoid dealing with the controversial nature of the subject matter (anti-war sentiment). In reaching this conclusion, the Court relied on the fact that other ideological symbols that could be or were worn by students (e.g., political buttons) were not proscribed. *Tinker v. Des Moines School District*, 393 U.S. 503 (1969) (discussed further *infra*, p. 543).

i.  **Mere effect:** But the mere fact that the regulation has a greater *effect* on one type of subject matter or idea will *not* be enough to put the regulation into "track one." (However, the differential impact might be circumstantial *evidence* that government had an intent to classify based on the content of the speech.)

7.  **Some speech of "lesser value":**  The normal rule, as noted, is that unless material falls within a pre-defined "unprotected category," the government will find it virtually impossible to suppress on the basis of its content, even if there is a strong state interest in doing so. There are some signs, however, that certain types of speech, although still entitled to First Amendment protection, may be found to be *"less important,"* and therefore more closely regulable, even though not completely suppressible. For the first time, a majority of the Supreme Court seems to have taken this view in a case involving non-obscene (and therefore protected) child pornography. See *New York v. Ferber, infra*, p. 563. The permissibility of "content discrimination" is discussed more generally *infra*, p. 517.

D.  **Analysis of "track two" cases:**  Let us turn now to the analysis of a case which belongs on "track *two*," that is, one in which the government's interest in regulation *does not relate to the communicative impact of the expression*. Regulations of the *"time, place or manner"* of speech (assuming that they do not mask discrimination based on the communicative content of the speech) fall within "track two."

1. **General principles:** Analysis on "track two" depends on whether or not the expression takes place in a ***"public forum."*** (This term includes traditional public places like streets and parks, and is further defined *infra*, p. 526.)

   a. **Public forum:** Where the expression takes place in a public forum, the regulation must not only be ***content-neutral*** (which it must be no matter what the forum, unless the expression falls within an "unprotected category" as discussed above), but it must also ***not close adequate alternative channels*** for communications, and it must be ***narrowly-tailored*** to serve a ***significant governmental interest.*** Tribe, p. 992. Regulations that impair the use for expressive purposes of such public forums may ***not*** be justified merely by the government's ***convenience*** (e.g., a ban on handbills to prevent littering).

      i. **Balancing test:** This is a ***"balancing test"*** of sorts, but a strict one. The individual's interest in free expression in the public forum is deemed to be sufficiently important that only governmental interests that are not merely equally important, but that ***cannot be achieved by less restrictive alternatives***, will be deemed to outweigh that interest in expression.

   b. **Private places:** Where the expression takes place in a location that is ***not*** a public forum, a balancing test is also used. But this test is a much easier one for the state to satisfy:

      i. **Insubstantial restraint:** If the impairment of expression is ***not substantial***, the state must merely show that its regulation is ***rational*** (assuming, as always, that the restraint is content-neutral).

      ii. **Substantial:** If the impairment of expression *is* "substantial," the state must show that its own interest is even more substantial. But in contrast to the public-forum situation, the state can prove that a restraint on expression in a non-public-forum is not substantial by showing that there are ***alternate channels*** by which the speaker can reach the same audience with the same message. Tribe, p. 982.

E. **Regulation of "pure conduct":** So far, we have assumed that "expression" is somehow being regulated by the government. But how do we decide whether what is being regulated *is in fact "expression"*? The fact that what is being regulated is "conduct" rather than "pure speech" is not dispositive — a long line of Supreme Court cases holds that "expressive conduct" receives First Amendment protection just as "pure speech" does. (For instance, marching down the street in a protest is in a sense "conduct," but it is also clearly "expression." See the discussion of this conduct/speech distinction *infra*, p. 492.) But some conduct may contain such a ***small*** component of expression that it is found to be ***not protected by the First Amendment at all***.

1. **Supreme Court's test:** The Supreme Court has articulated a two-part test for determining whether conduct possesses sufficient ***"communicative elements"*** to trigger the First Amendment protection: it must be the case that ***both***: (1) an "intent to convey a ***particularized message*** was present"; and (2) "the likelihood was great that the message would be ***understood*** by those who viewed it." *Spence v. Washington*, 418 U.S. 405 (1974).

   **Example:** A court might hold that panhandling on the street has so little expressive content that it gets no First Amendment protection at all. The court might reason that the express or implied statement "Please give me money" (or even "Please give me money because I'm poor") does not really convey any communicative element that would be so understood by the people to whom it is addressed. (The Supreme Court has never decided whether panhandling gets any First Amendment protection.)

## II.  ADVOCACY OF ILLEGAL CONDUCT

A.  **Introduction:**  If any kind of speech can lay claim to special constitutional protection, it is probably speech of a *political* nature. Our entire system of representative government operates on the assumption that political and social change will come about peacefully, through public discussion, rather than through violence.

1.  **Dangerous speech:**  Yet, certain types of political speech may seem to most of us to pose a threat to the very system of representative democracy which freedom of speech is supposed to ensure. For instance, speech calling for immediate assassination of the President, or the institution of a military coup, seems dangerous to tolerate. However, once the government is permitted to prevent or punish some types of political speech, there arises the threat that those in power may also ***stifle legitimate dissent.***

2.  **Advocacy of illegal conduct:**  During the approximately 65 years since the Supreme Court first began grappling with the limits of valid political speech, the Court has generally tried to distinguish between, on the one hand, general political dissent and advocacy of abstract theories (which may not be punished), and, on the other hand, ***incitement*** of ***particular illegal acts*** (which constitutes an "unprotected category," and may therefore be punished). But the Court has vacillated dramatically during this period in drawing the line between these two types of speech. Most commentators agree that the current standard, articulated in 1969 in *Brandenburg v. Ohio*, 395 U.S. 444 (1969) (discussed *infra*, p. 481) gives substantially greater protection to political speech than the various tests in force before it.

B.  **The "clear and present danger" test:**  For most of this century prior to *Brandenburg*, the dividing line between legal advocacy and illegal incitement of criminal acts was drawn by use of the ***"clear and present danger"*** test. Under this test, speech could be punished as an attempt to commit an illegal act if the speech created a "clear and present danger" that the illegal act ***would come about*** (even if it never in fact occurred).

1.  *Schenck:*  The test was first articulated by Justice Holmes (speaking for a unanimous Court) in ***Schenck v. U.S.,*** 249 U.S. 47 (1919). The case arose in a wartime context, and involved the degree to which citizens had a constitutional right to oppose the First World War.

    a.  **Facts:**  In the 1917 Espionage Act, Congress made it a crime, *inter alia*, to "willfully cause or attempt to cause insubordination, disloyalty, mutiny, or refusal of duty, in the military or naval forces of the United States," or to "willfully obstruct the recruiting or enlistment service" of the U.S. The defendants were not charged with violating the Act, but rather, with ***conspiring*** to violate it. The defendants had sent two draftees a document opposing the draft, calling it "despotism," and urging the draftees, "[d]o not submit to intimidation." But the document ***did not explicitly advocate illegal resistance*** to the draft; it merely advocated ***peaceful measures,*** such as petitioning for repeal of the Conscription Act.

    b.  **Holding:**  Nonetheless, the Court unanimously found that the defendants could constitutionally be convicted of conspiracy to violate the statute. Whether or not a given utterance is protected by the First Amendment depends, Holmes wrote, on the circumstances; the defendants' document might have been constitutionally protected, for instance, in time of peace. The issue was "whether the words used are used in such circumstances and are of such a nature as to create a ***clear and present danger*** that they will ***bring about the substantive evils*** that Congress has a right to prevent." Whether the defendants' conduct in fact posed a "clear and present danger" was a factual issue, the jury's disposition of which the Court refused to disturb.

c. **Crying "fire" in theater:** In his *Schenck* opinion, Holmes illustrated his assertion that not all speech was constitutionally privileged by posing the now-famous example of ***falsely crying "fire!" in a crowded theater.***

    i. **Criticism:** However, the nature of crying "fire!" in a crowded theater seems dramatically different from the speech in *Schenck*; for one thing, the false cry of "fire" is clearly understood by its listeners to be a statement of ***fact,*** not an exhortation or expression of opinion as the *Schenck* document obviously was. Also, if one believes that the best way to combat false speech is by combatting it in the "marketplace of ideas" (a view espoused by Holmes himself in *Abrams v. U.S., infra,* p. 476), the two situations are clearly different: there is not time to argue with the cry of "fire!", but probably ample time to argue about the merits of conscription.

2. ***Frohwerk*** **and** ***Debs:*** Very shortly after *Schenck,* Justice Holmes wrote two more opinions, for a unanimous Court, upholding Espionage Act convictions against First Amendment arguments.

    a. ***Frohwerk:*** One of these, *Frohwerk v. U.S.,* 249 U.S. 204 (1919), involved writers of editorials criticizing the draft in a German-language newspaper. Holmes' opinion seemed to shift the burden of proof to the defendants — because of the lack of clarity of the record on appeal, it was "impossible to say that it might not have been found" that the publication might have been enough to "kindle a flame" of draft resistance.

    b. ***Debs:*** The other case, ***Debs v. U.S.,*** 249 U.S. 211 (1919) is perhaps even more disturbing to those who believe that general opposition to government policies, unaccompanied by explicit advocacy of illegal acts, ought to be protected by the First Amendment. The defendant in *Debs* was the well-known socialist and presidential candidate Eugene V. Debs, who made a speech opposing the First World War. Debs' conviction of obstructing military recruitment was upheld by the Court.

    i. **Weak standard:** Although Holmes purported to be applying the "clear and present danger" standard, he phrased it as merely requiring that the words have as their ***"natural tendency and reasonably probable effect"*** the obstruction of recruitment. As in *Schenck,* the Court refused to reject the jury's finding that Debs' speech met this test.

    ii. **Criticism of *Debs*:** The "clear and present danger" standard which the *Debs* opinion purported to apply obviously gave very little protection to Debs. The paucity of First Amendment protection which he received is shown by the fact that far from exculpating Debs because he did not explicitly advocate illegal resistance to the draft or recruitment, the Court instead held against him the fact that he told his audience "that he had to be prudent and might not be able to say all that he thought, thus intimating to his hearers that they might infer that he meant more. ...

" There was no showing that anyone in the audience *in fact* inferred "more" (e.g., a call to illegal action); nor was there any evidence that any obstruction of recruitment actually occurred as a result of the speech. Holmes did not acknowledge that there was a difference between mailing anti-draft leaflets *directly* to draftees (as in *Schenck*) and addressing a general audience. Debs' conviction was "somewhat as though George McGovern had been sent to prison for his criticism of the war [in Vietnam]." 40 U. CHI. L. REV. 237 (quoted in L,K&C, p. 653, n.a.)

3. **Holmes' dissent in *Abrams*:**  It was not until ***Abrams v. U.S.,*** 250 U.S. 616 (1919) that application of the "clear and present danger" standard was sufficient to produce even so much as a dissent against a conviction for anti-war speech. In that case, Justice Holmes' dissent (joined by Justice Brandeis) finally placed some First Amendment "bite" into the standard; *Abrams* is one of his best-known dissents.

   a. **Facts:**  The defendants in *Abrams*, American socialists of Russian-Jewish birth, were convicted of violating a newly-added section of the Espionage Act, which prohibited the urging of any curtailment of war production with intent to hinder the United States' prosecution of the War. The defendants had published two pro-Bolshevik leaflets, which attacked the United States' production and supplying of arms that might be used against Russia (against whom the U.S. had not declared war); neither leaflet was pro-German, and in fact one was violently against German militarism. The leaflets urged workers not to make bullets which would be used not only against Germans but Russians as well.

   b. **Majority view:**  The key factual issue in the case was whether the defendants had the requisite intent to interfere with the war effort ***against Germany***. The majority conceded that the defendants' *primary* purpose may have been only to aid the Russian Revolution. But "[m]en must be held to have intended ... the effects which their acts were ***likely to produce***." Curtailment of production to protect Russians could not have been accomplished except by also impairing the war effort against Germany, the majority believed, so that the intent requirement was satisfied. (The majority also went out of its way to emphasize, repeatedly, that the defendants were self-proclaimed "anarchists.")

   c. **Holmes' dissent:**  Much of Holmes' dissent was on the fairly pedestrian issue of intent. Unlike the majority, he believed that an actor does not "intend" a consequence "unless that consequence is the aim of the deed." By this standard, the defendants simply had no intent to interfere with the war effort against Germany, however likely that possible outcome may have seemed to them.

      i. **Immediacy of danger:**  The place of "clear and present danger" in Holmes' opinion is unclear. He stated that Congress was justified in limiting expressions of opinion on public matters only where there was a "present danger of immediate evil *or* an intent to bring it about. ... " Holmes seemed to be saying that *either* intent *or* immediate (but unintended) evil was sufficient; however, it is possible that Holmes was careless in his use of "or," and meant to require both elements. See Tribe, p. 843, n. 16. In any event, Holmes felt that what he characterized as "the surreptitious publishing of a silly leaflet by an unknown man" posed no danger of immediate hindrance of the war effort.

ii. **Value of free speech:** But Holmes' dissent is best known for its more general words about the value of free speech. He articulated what could be called the "marketplace of ideas" theory: he urged *"free trade in ideas,"* and argued that "[t]he best test of truth is the power of the thought to get itself accepted in the competition of the market. ... " The importance of allowing ideas to compete with each other, he argued, was so great that even opinions which we "loathe and believe to be fraught with death" should not be suppressed, "unless they so imminently threaten immediate interference with the lawful and pressing purposes of the law that an immediate check is required to save the country."

4. **Criticism of "clear and present danger" doctrine:** Holmes' "clear and present danger" doctrine has been criticized on a number of grounds.

a. **Not very protective:** First, at least as it was applied in early cases, the doctrine obviously did not give very much protection to freedom of speech, since the defendants in *Schenck, Frohwerk, Debs*, and *Abrams* were all convicted, without a showing that the words of any of them actually brought about a substantive evil.

b. **Opinion about threat:** Second, the test, since it relies upon the fact-finder's opinion about the immediacy of a specific threat (e.g., obstruction of military recruitment), makes political speech particularly vulnerable to the mass hysteria which tends to strike in times of national crisis. For instance, the test gave the least protection to speech during the First World War and during the McCarthy anti-Communist scare, as discussed below.

c. **Vague standards:** Third, the test requires the jury to make a factual determination (as to the cause and effect relationship between words and potential events), the standards for which are *so vague* that the trial or appellate judges will have little ability to overturn a jury verdict resulting from such mass hysteria (or "patriotism").

d. **Ineffectiveness rewarded:** Finally, the test seems to say that any kind of speech is permissible *as long as it is ineffective*, making the test a very peculiar way of carrying out the First Amendment notion of political change through peaceful speech rather than through violent action.

C. **The Learned Hand test:** Because of these weaknesses in the "clear and present danger" test, Judge Learned Hand, one of the greatest federal district and appeals court judges in our history, articulated a different test, one focusing *solely on the words spoken, not on the surrounding circumstances*. Hand's test was put forth in *Masses Publishing Co. v. Patten*, 244 F. 535 (S.D.N.Y. 1917), a pre-*Schenck* decision.

1. **Terms of test:** Hand believed that words could be punished if they "counsel or advise others to *violate* the law as it stands," but not if they are merely *critical* of the law.

a. **Application:** The speech at issue in *Masses* consisted of anti-war cartoons and text which criticized the War and the draft, and which expressed great sympathy for draft resisters. Yet for Hand, this was still only *abstract advocacy* of the anti-war position, not a direct call to violate the law. Consequently, he found the materials beyond Congress' power to prohibit or punish.

2. **Significance:** The main significance of Hand's test is that it makes the *likely effects* of the speech *completely irrelevant*. Even if it were shown that the materials in fact caused many readers to resist the draft illegally, the publication would still be beyond Congress'

reach. By the same token, if the publication *did* constitute a **direct call** to violate the law, it would be punishable **even if it was utterly ineffectual**.

3. **Fate of Hand test:** Hand's test was immediately rejected; not even the federal court of appeals in *Masses* itself was willing to affirm it. Instead, the "clear and present danger" test prevailed for the next 50 years. But the Hand approach has ultimately had its day; *Brandenburg v. Ohio (infra*, p. 481) incorporates the main aspects of that test, though it adds aspects of "clear and present danger" as well.

D. **Statutes directly proscribing speech:** In the cases considered thus far, the legislature proscribed *acts*, not speech; speech became relevant only because the prosecution claimed that the speech constituted an attempt, or conspiracy, to bring about the forbidden act. Later, however, legislatures began enacting statutes which *directly forbade* certain types of speech. A major debate erupted on the Court about whether the "clear and present danger" test applies to prosecutions under such statutes as well.

1. **Test not applied:** The argument was won, at least temporarily, by those who claimed that the "clear and present danger" test had *no application* in this instance, and that the legislature's *own conclusion* that certain types of speech were *intrinsically dangerous* was to be respected.

2. *Gitlow:* Thus in *Gitlow v. New York*, 268 U.S. 652 (1925), the Court construed the New York "criminal anarchy" statute, which banned advocating (orally or in writing) the overthrow of a government by assassination or other violent means. The defendant, a socialist, was involved in the publication of a "Left-wing Manifesto," which advocated establishment of a dictatorship of the proletariat through mass strikes and other "revolutionary mass action."

     a. **Majority view:** There was no showing at trial that the publication had posed any present danger of governmental overthrow or other substantive evil. Nonetheless, the majority *upheld* the defendant's conviction.

         i. **Rationale:** The "clear and present danger" test of *Schenck* was only to be applied "in those cases where the statute merely prohibits certain *acts* involving the danger of substantive evil, *without any reference to language* itself. … " Here, by contrast, the legislature had *already* determined that *certain types of language* (advocacy of violent overthrow of the government) posed a risk that substantive evils would result. It was not open to the Court to dispute the legislature's judgment and to conclude that, in a particular case, utterances coming within the statute were not dangerous.

         ii. **No immediacy requirement:** Furthermore, there was no requirement that the legislature proscribe only speech advocating *definite* or *immediate* action. Thus the defense that the Manifesto called only for action at some indefinite time in the future was unavailing.

     b. **Dissent:** A dissent by Justice Holmes (joined by Justice Brandeis) argued that the "clear and present danger" test *should* be applied on these facts. Under this test, he argued there should be no conviction because the Manifesto "had *no chance* of starting a *present conflagration*." But Holmes did not respond directly to the majority's argument that the test should not be applied where the legislature has directly forbidden certain types of speech.

3. ***Whitney:*** The legislature's right to ban a certain type of speech, regardless of the substantive dangers posed by it, was presented again in ***Whitney v. California,*** 274 U.S. 357 (1927).

    **a. Facts:** The California Criminal Syndicalism Act forbade the knowing membership in any organization advocating the use of force or violence to effect political change. Miss Whitney, who did not deny being a member of the Communist Labor Party, was convicted even though she did not agree with the Party's advocacy of violent means of change, and had in fact voted for a more temperate plank.

    **b. Holding:** But a majority of the Court upheld the conviction, believing that the legislature's conclusion that mere knowing membership in an organization advocating criminal syndicalism was substantively dangerous, "must be given great weight."

    **c. Brandeis' dissent:** Justice Brandeis' concurrence in *Whitney* (joined by Holmes) is one of his most eloquent on free speech.

        **i. Legislature's power:** Brandeis disagreed with the majority about how the validity of a statute forbidding certain types of speech should be evaluated. The legislature, by passing a statute, "***cannot alone establish the facts*** which are essential to [the law's] validity." The relevant test continued to be, in Brandeis' opinion, whether the speech or assembly posed a clear and present danger of a substantive evil; ***only the court***, not the legislature, could determine whether a particular utterance or meeting posed such a danger. The legislature's proscription of an entire class of speech or assembly created merely a "rebuttable presumption" that, in the particular time and circumstances, such dangers were presented.

        **ii. The value of free speech:** Brandeis also spoke more generally about the value of free speech. An orderly society ***cannot be maintained merely through fear and enforced silence***, for "fear breeds repression ... repression breeds hate ... [and] hate menaces stable government." On the contrary, "the path of safety lies in the opportunity to discuss freely supposed grievances and proposed remedies. ... *[T]he fitting remedy for evil counsels is good ones.*" This might be thought of as the ***"safety valve"*** theory of free speech (in contrast to the view that human expression is an end in itself, not merely a means to maintenance of order.)

        **iii. Emergency:** For Brandeis, it followed that anytime bad ideas could be combatted by good ones, this combat, rather than suppression of the bad ideas, must be allowed to take place. Only where "the incidence of the evil apprehended is so imminent that it may befall ***before there is opportunity for full discussion***" may speech be prohibited or punished. Furthermore, even if the danger is imminent, it may not be suppressed unless it is ***"relatively serious"***; for instance, advocacy of the right of pedestrians to cross unfenced vacant lands could not be prohibited, even if there were imminent danger that such advocacy would lead to trespass.

        **iv. Concurrence:** However, Brandeis' opinion was cast as a concurrence, not a dissent, because in Brandeis' opinion the defendant had not raised the appropriate constitutional claims at the trial level.

    **d. Overruled:** *Whitney* was explicitly overruled in *Brandenburg v. Ohio*, 395 U.S. 444 (1969), discussed extensively *infra*, p. 481.

**E. Threat of communism and the Smith Act:** During and immediately following the Second World War, fears of an international communist threat became even more pronounced. One response was the passage by Congress in 1940 of the Smith Act, which was similar to the New York Criminal Anarchy Statute upheld in *Gitlow (supra*, p. 478).

1. **The *Dennis* case:** The most important Smith Act case was ***Dennis v. U.S.***, 341 U.S. 494 (1951), in which the Court purported to apply the "clear and present danger" standard, but did so in a manner that gave dramatically *less First Amendment protection* to political speech than Holmes or Brandeis would presumably have wanted.

   a. **Facts:** The defendants were convicted under the Smith Act of conspiring to advocate the overthrow of the United States Government, and of conspiring to reorganize the U.S. Communist Party, which the prosecution claimed was a group that advocated such overthrow.

   b. **Majority upholds:** A majority of the Court *upheld* the conviction. The opinion, by Justice Vinson, purported to be applying the "clear and present danger" test. However, the majority refused to interpret the test as requiring that there have been a clear and present danger of an *actual attempt* to overthrow the government; the Holmes test "cannot mean that before the Government may act, it must wait until the putsch is about to be executed, the plans have been laid and the signal is awaited."

      i. **Adoption of Hand balancing test:** Instead, the majority applied a test which had been formulated by Learned Hand, writing for the appeals court below: the test was "whether the *gravity* of the 'evil', *discounted by its improbability,* justifies such invasion of free speech as is necessary to avoid the danger." (Hand thus abandoned his *Masses* test, and instead tried to reshape the Holmes test.) Here, the evil (violent overthrow of the government) was so great that even a *small, non-imminent*, chance of success justified curtailing the speech.

      ii. **Danger determined by judge, not jury:** Also, the majority held that the issue of whether the requisite danger did indeed exist (as determined under the Hand test) was to be decided *by the trial judge*, not the jury; this was an issue of constitutional law, not of fact.

   c. **Concurrences:** There were two concurrences.

      i. **Frankfurter's view:** In the more significant one, Justice Frankfurter stated his belief that the test should not be the existence of "clear and present danger," but rather, performance of a "candid and informed weighing of the competing interests. ... " This *balancing test* should be performed *by Congress*, not by the judiciary; only if Congress acted without any reasonable basis should its determination be reversed. Here, Congress could reasonably have concluded that recruitment of members for the Communist Party posed a substantial danger to national security, and should be forbidden. The majority's version of "clear and present danger" required a "judicial reading of events still in the womb of time," a task which required "knowledge of the topmost secrets of nations" and was beyond the judiciary's capacities.

   d. **Dissents:** Only two Justices, Black and Douglas, dissented. Black objected that the majority, instead of giving First Amendment freedoms the *"high preferred place"* to which they are entitled in a free society, had "watered down" the Amendment so that it was "little more than an admonition to Congress." Douglas did not object to "clear and present danger" as the test, but believed that the majority had misapplied it. Only if conditions were so critical that there was "no time to avoid the evil that the speech threaten[ed]" could free speech be limited. Also, he thought that the jury, not the trial judge, should decide the issue of clear and present danger.

e. **Significance of *Dennis*:** *Dennis* represents "the temporary eclipse of the Holmes-Brandeis formulation of the clear and present danger test." Tribe, p. 846. Once the evil's *seriousness* became a *substitute* for its *immediacy,* speech could be restricted *no matter how remote its anticipated consequences*.

   i. **Criticism:** This test gave especially little protection to radical political speech, since such speech would always seem to be a threat to the nation and thus the most serious evil imaginable. Shapiro, *Freedom of Speech: The Supreme Court and Judicial Review*, p. 65 (quoted in L,K&C, p. 713). Furthermore, the test seemed to balance the seriousness of the evil against "not the improbability that the speech in question will bring the evil about, but that it will occur from *any* cause." *Id.* Thus even if one were convinced that the speech or association charged in *Dennis* was itself highly unlikely to contribute to overthrow of the government, the fact that such overthrow might occur from *any* cause would be enough to justify restricting or punishing the speech.

F. **The modern standard:** Today, the Supreme Court gives *greater protection to free speech*, at least in the political area, than at any previous time.

   1. ***Brandenburg:*** The present status of freedom of political speech is best expressed in ***Brandenburg v. Ohio***, 395 U.S. 444 (1969), a case in which the Court combined the most speech-protective aspects of *both* the *"clear and present danger"* test and the *"advocacy/incitement"* distinction.

      a. **Facts:** Defendant was a leader of an Ohio Ku Klux Klan group. He was charged with violating Ohio's Criminal Syndicalism Statute, which (like that of California, sustained in *Whitney v. California, supra*, p. 479) forbade the advocacy of crime or violence as a means of accomplishing industrial or political reform.

      b. **Holding:** The Court (in a unanimous *per curiam* opinion) *struck down* the Ohio statute, without considering whether the defendant's actual speech could have been properly proscribed.

         i. **New test:** In so doing, the Court articulated new requirements which a statute proscribing speech must meet. Speech advocating the use of force or crime could only be proscribed where two conditions were satisfied: (1) the advocacy is *"directed to inciting or producing imminent lawless action"; and* (2) the advocacy is also *"likely to incite or produce such action."*

   2. **Significance of new test:** The two-part *Brandenburg* standard is usually viewed as combining aspects of both the Holmes and Hand tests, in a way that gives "double protection" to speech.

      a. **Holmes aspect:** The Holmes "clear and present danger" legacy is reflected in the requirement that the speech be *"likely* to incite or produce" *imminent* unlawful action. Thus the concern with immediate, likely, consequences remains.

**b.   Hand aspect:**   But *Brandenburg* also reflects Hand's insistence that what should be restricted is only direct advocacy of ***action***, not mere advocacy of ***abstract doctrine***. This distinction is imposed by the requirement that the speech be ***"directed"*** (i.e., ***intended***) to ***"inciting*** or ***producing"*** an unlawful response.

**c.   Consequence:**   Apparently, therefore, no speech that would have been protected by ***either*** the Holmes or Hand tests may be prohibited under *Brandenburg*.

**d.   Application to Ohio statute:**   The significance of the *Brandenburg* test is illustrated by the way the Court applied it to the Ohio statute at issue there. The Ohio act punished all advocacy of the "duty, necessity or propriety of crime [or] violence … as a means of accomplishing industrial or political reform. … " This language was sufficiently broad that it forbade advocacy of the ***abstract doctrine*** of violent political change, as well as incitement to imminent unlawful action. Therefore, it was held unconstitutional, even though some applications of it might have been constitutional (an illustration of the "overbreadth" doctrine, discussed below).

**3.   Severity of harm:**   The *Brandenburg* test does not explicitly take into account the ***severity*** of the harm which is threatened. Reading *Brandenburg* literally, a speaker who advocated use of nuclear weapons for terrorist purposes, but only after a one-year moratorium, could not be punished (since the harm would not be "imminent"). Conversely, one who incited his listeners to jaywalk immediately could be punished. Tribe (p. 849, n. 59) advocates taking into account seriousness, at least on the less-serious side of the spectrum.

**4.   *Whitney* overruled:**   *Brandenburg* explicitly overruled *Whitney v. California, see supra*, p. 479, which had upheld a Criminal Syndicalism statute nearly identical to that struck down in *Brandenburg*.

**5.   Other modern cases:**   Other cases decided in the late 60's or later present additional illustrations of the twin modern requirements of: (1) ***incitement*** (as distinguished from abstract advocacy); and (2) harm that is ***imminent*** (as distinguished from remote).

**a.   *Bond*:**   The Court held that the Georgia House of Representatives' exclusion of Julian Bond from membership violated his First Amendment rights, in *Bond v. Floyd*, 385 U.S. 116 (1966). Bond, an opponent of the war in Vietnam, had joined a statement of "sympathy with, and support [of] the men in this country who are unwilling to respond to a military draft." The Georgia House reasoned that Bond could not truthfully swear to "support the Constitution of this State and of the United States." But the Court held that Bond could not be penalized for his statement, since it did not constitute a call for unlawful draft resistance, but was merely a ***general, abstract***, declaration of opposition to the war.

**b.   *Watts*:**   A black anti-war activist, in a speech, said "[i]f they ever make me carry a rifle, the first man I want to get in my sights is L.B.J. They are not going to make me kill my black brothers." He was convicted under a law making it a crime intentionally to threaten to kill the President. In *Watts v. U.S.*, 394 U.S. 705 (1969), the Court reversed the conviction, on the grounds that the circumstances showed that the speaker did not intend to make a ***"true threat"*** but rather, to state his ***political opposition*** to the President (albeit in a "very crude, offensive" way). The Court relied especially on the fact that the "threat" was conditional, and that the audience responded by laughter.

c. ***Hess:*** *Bond, Watts* and *Brandenburg* were all decided during the Warren era. But the post-Warren Court has also applied the *Brandenburg* standard. One instance is *Hess v. Indiana*, 414 U.S. 105 (1973), growing out of a campus anti-war demonstration in which demonstrators blocked a street until they were moved off it by the police. Defendant then said "We'll take the fucking street later [or again]." (The record was ambiguous as to the precise word used.) The Court found this to be protected speech, rather than an unprotected incitement to illegal action. Construed least favorably to the defendant, the statement was "nothing more than advocacy of illegal action at ***some indefinite future time***"; only words intended to produce (and also likely to produce) ***imminent*** disorder could be punished.

d. **NAACP boycott:** The Court again demonstrated that the Brandenburg "incitement" test will be rigorously applied, in *NAACP v. Claiborne Hardware Co.*, 458 U.S. 886 (1982).

   i. **Facts:** The case (other aspects of which are discussed *infra*, p. 604) involved efforts by black citizens in a Mississippi county to boycott white merchants until certain demands for racial equality were satisfied. One of the defendants was Charles Evers, an NAACP leader, who in speaking in favor of the boycott said that blacks who violated the boycott would be "disciplined" by their own people.

   ii. **Holding:** The Supreme Court reversed a lower court verdict against Evers and others for the lost earnings of the white merchants. In so doing, it concluded that Evers speech ***did not constitute incitement***, and was therefore protected by the First Amendment. Evers used "strong language," but, the Court held, "[a]n advocate must be free to stimulate his audience with spontaneous and emotional appeals for unity and action in a common cause." Evers' language did not cross over the line into incitement of imminent violence.

   iii. **Result taken into account:** In reaching this conclusion, the Court also relied on the fact that unlawful acts ***did not in fact result*** from Evers' speech. The Court implied that when speech *is* followed by violent or otherwise illegal acts, the requisite "intent to incite" is more likely to be found, than where no such acts follow.

# III.  OVERBREADTH AND VAGUENESS

A. **Overbreadth:** Because of the especially great importance of freedom of expression in our constitutional scheme, the Supreme Court has developed several techniques of statutory analysis to make sure that that freedom gets the extra protection it requires. One of these techniques is the use of the doctrine of *"overbreadth."*

1. **Definition:** A statute is overbroad if, in addition to proscribing activities which may constitutionally be forbidden, it *also* sweeps within its coverage speech or conduct which is ***protected by the guarantees of free speech or free association***. See *Thornhill v. Alabama*, 310 U.S. 88 (1940).

2. **Significance:** There are two respects in which the doctrine of statutory overbreadth changes the usual rules of constitutional litigation:

a. **Standing:** First, a litigant who is attempting to have a statute ruled unconstitutional must normally show that it is unconstitutional ***in its application to him.*** For instance, in a First Amendment case that does not involve overbreadth, the challenger to a statute must show that his own speech or conduct was protected by the First Amendment. But the overbreadth doctrine permits the challenger to prevail if he can show that the statute, applied according to its terms, would violate the First Amendment rights of persons not now before the Court. Thus overbreadth can be viewed as an ***exception to the usual requirements of "standing"*** (see *infra*, p. 711), by which a person is not normally permitted to assert the constitutional rights of others, only his own. Or to put it in terms of the usually-employed set of labels, most constitutional attacks are required to be ***"as applied"*** attacks (the plaintiff is saying that the statute is unconstitution "as applied" to her, i.e., the statute violates her own rights), whereas an overbreadth attack is a ***"facial"*** attack, i.e., an attack ***"on the face"*** of the statute.

    **i.  Statute's application to challenger:**  In fact, where overbreadth analysis is applied, the Court simply ***assumes*** that a more narrowly-drawn statute *could* constitutionally proscribe the challenger's own conduct. Ordinarily, the Court never even decides this question explicitly; by deciding to apply overbreadth analysis, it is able to decide instead the usually *easier* question of whether the statute by its terms covers hypothetical constitutionally-protected conduct by third parties.

  **b.  Statute found void on its face:**  Secondly, in the usual situation, where a court finds a statute to be unconstitutional it will simply *excise* the statute's unconstitutional applications, ***leaving the statute in force*** as to those situations where its application would be constitutional. But where overbreadth is applied, the statute is ***completely struck down***. That is, the statute is found to be ***void "on its face."*** Until a different statute is enacted (a more limited one, applying only where it may constitutionally do so), or until another court with authority construes the statute more narrowly (in a way that forbids only constitutionally-proscribable speech or conduct), the statute is simply unenforceable against ***anyone.***

  **3.  Rationales:**  There are two main rationales for using the overbreadth doctrine in First Amendment cases:

  **a.  "Chilling effect" on speech:**  First, the mere existence of an overly broad statute (that is, a statute which by its terms forbids some protected speech) is likely to have a ***"chilling effect"*** on free speech. Some people whose speech the statute could ***not*** constitutionally reach (and who thus would presumably prevail in court if they spoke and then litigated the statute's application to them) might simply be ***intimidated*** into ***not exercising their right to speak.***

    **i.  Explanation:**  As Justice Marshall put it in a dissent to *Arnett v. Kennedy*, 416 U.S. 134 (1974), an overbroad statute "hangs over [people's] heads like a Sword of Damocles. … That this Court will ultimately vindicate [a person] if his speech is constitutionally protected is of little consequence — for the value of a sword of Damocles is that it hangs — not that it drops." He added that the focus of the overbreadth doctrine "is not on the individual actor before the court but on others who may forego protected activity rather than run afoul of the statute's proscriptions."

  **b.  Selective enforcement:**  Secondly, an overly-broad statute is highly vulnerable to ***selective enforcement*** by the authorities, i.e., enforcement that discriminates against certain classes of people or certain points of view. The problem of selective enforcement exists in any statute. But the risk is greater in the case of an overbroad one, since the statute gives officials, by hypothesis, not only the opportunity to treat people differently (a problem with any statute, since it is always possible to prosecute only one of two people who may constitutionally be prosecuted), but also the chance to ***violate the constitutional rights*** of one person without violating those of another.

> **Example:** Assume that a town ordinance proscribes "all demonstrations, involving 100 or more persons, held in public streets." This ordinance by its terms applies both to activity which may constitutionally be proscribed (e.g., demonstrations that include violence or a substantial breach of the peace) as well as to those which may ***not*** be constitutionally prohibited (peaceful demonstrations, conducted at an appropriate time, without causing major interference with traffic.)

Within the class of activities to which the statute may ***not*** constitutionally be applied, there is an open invitation to the police to allow their own views about acceptable content to color their decision. For instance, they may "look charitably at a post game victory celebration in the streets of a college town [but] not feel the same way about an antiwar demonstration." See 43 CHI. L. REV. 38 (quoted in L,K&C, p. 733). Therefore, the statute will be found to be overbroad, and thus void "on its face"; that is, it may not be applied even to activity which ***could*** constitutionally be proscribed by a more narrowly-drawn statute (e.g., demonstrations that include violence to bystanders.)

4. **Doctrine cut back — "substantial" overbreadth now required:** However, the Burger/Rehnquist Court has significantly **curtailed** the use of overbreadth analysis in First Amendment cases. It has done so principally by requiring that the overbreadth be ***"substantial,"*** compared with the legitimate applications of the statute. This requirement was first set forth in ***Broadrick v. Oklahoma***, 413 U.S. 601 (1973), a case which remains the best statement of the modern Court's view on overbreadth.

   a. **Facts:** §818 of Oklahoma's Merit System Act prohibited civil servants from engaging in certain political activities, including taking part in the management or affairs of any political party or campaign, and soliciting for campaign contributions. Broadrick, who had campaigned for a superior and had solicited money for him, challenged §818 on overbreadth (as well as vagueness) grounds. He pointed out that §818 had been construed as applying to such political expression as the wearing of political buttons and the displaying of bumper stickers, which (he asserted) were constitutionally-protected free speech activities. Therefore, he contended, the section must be struck down, regardless of whether his own activity could have been constitutionally proscribed by a more narrowly-drawn statute.

   b. **Holding:** By a 5-4 vote, the Court ***rejected*** Broadrick's claims, spending most of its time on the overbreadth one.

   c. **Speech vs. conduct:** The opinion distinguished between statutes primarily regulating conduct and those directly governing speech. In situations involving the latter, the Court did not modify the overbreadth rule. But in the case of statutes ***governing conduct***, where the conduct happens to have an expressive content, the "strong medicine" of complete invalidation of the statute should not invariably be applied. Instead, the majority believed, for facial invalidation to be appropriate, "the overbreadth of a statute must not only be real, but ***substantial*** as well, judged in relation to the statute's plainly legitimate sweep." Where the overbreadth is not substantial, unconstitutional applications should be rooted out one at a time, by analysis of the particular fact situations in which successive litigants find themselves.

d. **Application:**   The Oklahoma statue, under this analysis, ***did not call for overbreadth treatment***. The statute was primarily directed at **conduct** (taking part in a political campaign), not at pure speech. The statute was ***not "substantially overbroad,"*** since in the majority's judgment, it applied to a "substantial spectrum of conduct" that could constitutionally be subjected to state regulation.

  i. **Some protected applications:**   The Court conceded that the statute by its terms could be applied to the wearing of political buttons or the use of bumper stickers, and that these might be constitutionally-protected expressions. But such potential unconstitutional applications of the statute were ***not numerous enough compared with the body of permissible applications***, so there was no "substantial overbreadth."

  ii. **Applied to litigant:**   Since Broadrick's own conduct was clearly regulable rather than protected, the statute was upheld as applied to him.

e. **Pure speech:**   Even after *Broadrick*, statutes directed at ***"pure speech,"*** rather than at conduct, presumably continue to be subjected to overbreadth analysis even where the overbreadth is not "substantial."

f. **Makes hard cases easy:**   The overbreadth doctrine, even with its requirement of "substantial" overbreadth, often has the effect of ***making "hard" cases into "easy" ones***. That is, a case that would be a difficult one if it had to be decided on its own facts often becomes easy once the statute can be taken literally and applied to other hypothetical situations, as to which it would clearly be unconstitutional. See Sullivan & Gunther, p. 1346.

B. **Vagueness:**   The doctrine of ***"vagueness"*** is similar, but not identical, to that of overbreadth. A statute will be held void for vagueness if the conduct forbidden by it is so ***unclearly defined*** that persons "of common intelligence must necessarily ***guess at its meaning*** and differ as to its application." *Connally v. General Construction Co.*, 269 U.S. 385 (1926).

1. **Constitutional basis:**   Theoretically, the proscription against vagueness stems from the Due Process Clause's requirement that people be given ***fair notice*** of what conduct is prohibited. But many void-for-vagueness holdings stem more from violations of other constitutional provisions, particularly the First Amendment. In the First Amendment area, an unduly vague statute has the same ***"chilling"*** effect on speech or association as does an overbroad one: a person does not know whether or not his conduct will ultimately be held to be constitutionally protected, so he declines to exercise his right of speech or association.

2. **Curbing discretion:**   The other main function of the vagueness doctrine is to ***curb the discretion*** afforded to law enforcement officers or administrative officials. Observe that this danger, too, is also a danger posed by an overbroad statute (*supra*, p. 484).

3. **Distinguished from overbreadth:**   Yet vagueness and overbreadth are quite distinguishable doctrines. Their differences can be illustrated by the following example:

**Example:** Statute I prohibits anyone from "publicly display[ing] a red flag [as] a sign, symbol or emblem of opposition to organized government." Statute II prohibits anyone from "publicly displaying a red flag for any purpose whatsoever."

Statute I is unconstitutionally *vague*, because there is no way to tell whether it is meant to apply to peaceful displays of opposition to the political party currently in office, or to other constitutionally-protected expressions of political opposition. (See *Stromberg v. California*, 238 U.S. 359 (1931), so holding.)

Statute II is unconstitutionally overbroad. It is obviously not "vague," since its meaning is perfectly clear. But since by its terms it appears to apply to constitutionally-protected conduct, and since there is no "bright line" rule to separate out the constitutional from unconstitutional applications, neither a member of the public nor a court has an easy way to articulate what the statute may constitutionally cover.

**Note:** These two statutes show that vagueness and overbreadth are both, in part, attempts to deal with the same problem. Both statutes leave the user uncertain about which applications of the statute may *constitutionally* be imposed. The main difference is that in the overbreadth situation, the vagueness is "latent"; for this reason, overbreadth has been called "really a special case of the problem of vagueness." See Freund, *The Supreme Court of the United States* (quoted in L,K&C, p. 732).

*Quiz Yourself on*
# FREEDOM OF EXPRESSION — GENERAL THEMES; ADVOCACY OF ILLEGAL CONDUCT; OVERBREADTH AND VAGUENESS

**63.** Darwin and 10 others were all members of the basketball team of State U, a public university. The Chancellor of State U had recently suspended Xavier, one of the members of the team, from both the team and the school for alleged cheating in an exam. At 10:00 a.m. on a Tuesday morning, Darwin and his 10 teammates stood in front of the University administration building, which contained the Chancellor's office. They carried signs saying, "Reinstate Xavier"; they also chanted and sang. The Chancellor happened to be away from the office that day (unbeknownst to Darwin and his friends), and nobody in the building was considering Xavier's case at the time.

A statute of the state in which State U is located provides as follows:

> "No group of 10 or more persons shall demonstrate on the sidewalk or other public way in front of a state or local government office building during business hours, unless the demonstration is related to matters currently under consideration by government officials working in the building. Violation of this provision shall be punishable as a misdemeanor."

Darwin has been charged with violating this section. He wishes to defend on the grounds that the section violates his First Amendment freedom of expression.

**(a)** What is the best argument he can make as to why his First Amendment rights would be violated by a conviction? _____

**(b)** May Darwin constitutionally be convicted of violating the provision? _____

**64.** The city of Munford has enacted the following ordinance: "No person shall attempt to give to passersby on any sidewalk or public thoroughfare any handbill during a Restricted Time Period. 'Restricted Time Period' shall mean the hours between 8:00 and 9:30 a.m. and the hours between 4:30 and 6:00 p.m., Monday through Friday. 'Handbill' is defined to include any piece of printed literature, four pages or less, dealing with a single topic." The purpose of the definition is to cover advertising circulars and brochures, but not to cover newspapers and magazines. The ordinance was enacted in response to two fears: (1) that during the busy rush hour, people were handing out so many handbills that the flow of pedestrian traffic was frequently impaired; and (2) that an extraordinary amount of litter was being generated when people who had handbills thrust into their hands dropped them on the sidewalk. Kermit, a political candidate who was giving out brochures in support of his own candidacy, was charged with violating the statute. Kermit now argues that a conviction would violate his First Amendment rights. Should the Court agree?

_____

**65.** Leonard was a self-styled "gay revolutionary." One day he went to a park that was frequented by both gays and non-gays. Before a moderately interested audience of about 20 people, all of whom had come to the park for other purposes, Leonard began to make a speech. He said, "If the government won't cure AIDS, we'll have to make 'em do it. Let's start by building up an arsenal of automatics and machine guns. Eventually, we'll have guerilla cells throughout the city to make the government's life such a hell they'll put the money we need into research programs." A few of the listeners applauded, one asked a question, but no one took any other action in apparent response to Leonard's speech. Immediately after his speech, Leonard was arrested by the police for violating §123 of a state statute. That statute provided that it is a felony to "advocate insurrection against the state government or any local subdivision thereof." Leonard now defends on the grounds that a conviction would violate his First Amendment rights. May Leonard constitutionally be convicted of violating the statute? _____

**66.** Robert was a tenured teacher in a public high school, in the state of Cartesia. He was also a member of NAMBLA, the National Association of Man Boy Love Affairs. NAMBLA's charter says that it is dedicated to the furtherance of social and sexual interaction between men and boys. Cartesia makes it a crime for an adult male to have sexual relations with a boy under the age of 17. Robert knows the aims of NAMBLA, and supports those aims; in fact, he himself has in the recent past had sexual relations with a boy. School officials, worried about recent publicity concerning teachers who belong to NAMBLA, asked Robert and all other teachers at the school to sign an affidavit stating that "I am not now nor have I ever been a member of NAMBLA." (The affidavit said nothing else.) School officials announced that if a teacher did not sign the affidavit, they would consider that refusal to sign presumptive evidence of unfitness to be a teacher. Robert has so far refused to sign the affidavit. He wishes to challenge the constitutionality of the school's insistence that he sign.

**(a)** What is the strongest argument Robert can make as to why the affidavit requirement is unconstitutional? _____

**(b)** Will Robert's attack on the requirement's constitutionality succeed? _____

**67.** Becky, a young woman, walked topless on the boardwalk of Straitsville. She was arrested for violating a town ordinance that banned "lewd or lascivious public conduct." The statute contains no other relevant language, and there is no legislative history. For purposes of this question, assume that it would be possible to draft a statute in such a way that it could constitutionally proscribe appearing topless in public. Instead, concern yourself only with whether Becky may be convicted for violating *this* statute.

**(a)** What is Becky's strongest argument as to why she cannot constitutionally be convicted of violating the statute? _____

**(b)** Will Becky's argument succeed? _____

*Answers*

**63. (a) That the section is a content-based regulation on speech, and is thus invalid unless necessary to achieve a compelling state interest.**

**(b) No.** Government may impose reasonable regulations on the time, place and manner of speech that takes place on public forums. However, government's right to do this is contingent on its behaving in a *content-neutral* way. If government chooses to allow some messages and not allow others based on the content of the speech, then the restriction will be strictly scrutinized, and will be struck down unless it is: (1) necessary to achieve a compelling objective; and (2) narrowly drawn to achieve that objective. See, e.g., *Widmar v. Vincent*.

Here, government allows messages that pertain to matters under discussion inside the office building, but not messages pertaining to other matters. The government might defend on the grounds that it has not objected to the content of the messages, but has merely allowed some whole "categories" of speech while not allowing other whole categories. However, even distinctions between topics or categories is likely to be found to be content-based. See, e.g., *Consolidated Edison v. Public Serv. Comm.* (state may not prevent utilities from discussing the issue of nuclear power's desirability, because "[t]he First Amendment's hostility to content-based regulation extends not only to restrictions on particular viewpoints, but also to prohibition of public discussion of an entire topic.") In any event, the speech here is taking place in a public forum, so the court will be especially reluctant to allow such a broad interference with it.

**64. Yes.** First, we need to analyze whether the restriction is content-neutral. In contrast to the restriction in the prior question, the one here probably *is* content-neutral; that is, the government truly does not seem to be interested in what topics are described in the materials being given out, so long as the materials are essentially single-topic short pieces, rather than newspapers and magazines. Although it could be argued that distinguishing between newspapers/magazines on one hand and all other communications on the other is not content-neutral, the court would probably conclude that the distinction here is at such a high level of generality that there is no attempt to suppress a particular message or group of messages.

Assuming content-neutrality, the regulation here must be evaluated by the standards for testing "time, place and manner" restrictions. In general, such restrictions must be *"narrowly tailored"* to serve a *"significant governmental interest,"* and must *"leave open alternative channels"* for communicating the information. The restriction here probably *fails* to satisfy the "narrowly tailored" requirement. That is, the city could probably find methods that are less intrusive of freedom of expression than the total ban on handbills for large parts of the day. For instance the city could strictly enforce its ordinary anti-littering laws, or could prohibit anyone from blocking other pedestrians' right of easy passage on the street or sidewalk. It is important to note that the communication here is occurring in a *public forum* (the street or sidewalk), and the availability of different public forums or the present public forum at a different time, usually will not be enough to constitute an "alternative channel." (This is especially true here, where large segments of the population, i.e., commuters, will be on the street *only* during rush hours, and will thus never get to hear Kermit's message if the regulation is enforced.)

**65. No.** The government may forbid a person from advocating illegal conduct, such as insurrection or overthrow of the government. However, speech advocating such illegality may only be proscribed if two conditions are satisfied: (1) the advocacy is directed to inciting or producing *imminent* lawless action; and (2) the advocacy is *likely* to incite or produce such action. Here, neither of these requirements seems to be met. Leonard is not calling for *imminent* illegality — he says "let's start ... ," but he does not indicate that action should take place immediately. Furthermore, although his statement about having guerilla cells could probably be interpreted as a call for illegality, his statement about "building up an arsenal" is not necessarily a call for illegality, since there are many legal ways to buy guns, even automatics and machine guns. Even if the court decides that Leonard was attempting to incite imminent lawless action, it is pretty clear that there was very little risk that his speech was ***likely*** to produce that effect, since he had only a small crowd in front of him, they were in the park for other reasons, and they did not in fact respond with immediate illegal actions.

**66. (a) That it is overbroad.** A statute or regulation is overbroad if, in addition to proscribing activities which may constitutionally be forbidden, it also sweeps within its coverage future conduct which is protected by the guarantees of free speech or free association.

**(b) Yes, probably.** The government is clearly entitled to insist that Robert not commit crimes, and that he not advocate that others imminently commit crimes. However, the government may ***not*** make mere membership in an organization, without more, a crime, and it may not deprive a person of a government job or benefit for being merely a member or for refusing to say that he is not a member. Here, the affidavit merely requires Robert to say that he has not been a member; since Robert would be entitled to be a mere member of NAMBLA, so long as he did not agree with its aim of advocating imminent commission of the crime of man-boy love, the affidavit requirement would punish some membership that is constitutional. Robert's own membership here is ***not*** constitutionally protected, since he in fact knows of NAMBLA's stated aims and supports those (illegal) aims. But under the overbreadth doctrine, Robert is permitted to say, in effect, "The affidavit requirement would be unconstitutional if applied to (hypothetical) other people who merely belong to NAMBLA without supporting its criminal aims, so it should be struck down as facially invalid."

Under the requirement of ***"substantial* overbreadth,"** the overbreadth doctrine would not be applied unless the invalid applications of the requirement are substantial compared to the legitimate applications. Here, however, this requirement of substantial overbreadth is probably satisfied, since quite a number of people are likely to belong to NAMBLA just to get information about the law and politics surrounding this question rather than to advocate or practice illegal man-boy sex. Therefore, Robert's overbreadth attack will probably succeed.

**67. (a) That the statute is unconstitutionally vague.**

**(b) Yes, probably.** A statute will be held void for vagueness if the conduct forbidden by it is so unclearly defined that a person of ordinary intelligence would not know what is forbidden.

Here, the statute uses the words "lewd or lascivious," but furnishes no further information about what type of conduct is being forbidden. A reasonable observer would probably be in doubt as to whether it is necessarily lewd for a woman to appear topless. Because of the ordinance's lack of specificity, undue discretion is given to local law enforcement officials, who depending on how they felt about Becky or toplessness generally could decide to look the other way rather than making an arrest. Therefore, while the city might be entitled to ban women from appearing topless in public if the ordinance specifically applied to toplessness, the formulation here is probably unconstitutionally vague.

---

## IV.   REGULATION OF CONTEXT — "TIME, PLACE AND MANNER"

**A.   Context regulations generally:**   Recall that the state is somewhat more free to regulate expression when it does so for reasons independent of the speech's communicative content (a "track two" situation) than where the regulation is motivated by the expression's content (the "track one" case). Or, to put it another way, the state is substantially freer when it acts in a *content-neutral* manner. This section discusses various factual settings in which the state has claimed (not always successfully) that it is merely regulating the ***"time, place and manner"*** of speech and is therefore entitled to "track two" analysis.

1. **Rules for "track two" cases:**   In general, the Court has applied a ***balancing test*** to determine whether the government's interest in content-neutral regulation of speech-related conduct outweighs the speaker's (or his listeners') interest in a particular form of communicative activity. But in performing this balancing test, the Court in effect places a "thumb on the scale" on the side of free expression, to reflect the exceptional importance of such expression.

2. **Disproportionate impact:**   In performing the balancing test, the court will take into account the extent to which the regulation "falls ***unevenly upon various groups*** in … society." Tribe, p. 980. For instance, the poor cannot generally afford television spots or full-page newspaper announcements; they must use cheaper means such as demonstrations, leafletting and door-to-door canvassing. Therefore, regulations which inhibit these economical forms of expression will be especially closely scrutinized because of their unequal impact.

3. **Public forum:**   Speech in a ***"public forum"*** (defined *infra*, p. 526) may not be restricted, even in a content-neutral way, unless the restriction is a ***narrow one*** which is ***necessary*** to serve a ***significant governmental interest***. Tribe, p. 982. Thus citizens have in essence a ***"guaranteed access"*** to streets, parks and other public forums. See *Hague v. CIO*, 307 U.S. 496 (1939): "The privilege [to] use the streets and parks for communication of views on national questions may be regulated in the interest of all; [but] it must not, in the guise of regulation, be abridged or denied."

    a. **Mere inconvenience:**   This "guaranteed access" to public forums is implemented by several rules not applicable to non-public-forum situations. In a public forum context, ***mere inconvenience*** to the government will ***not suffice*** to outweigh the interest in public expression. Also, the government must use the ***least restrictive means*** of achieving its legitimate content-neutral objectives.

       **Example:** Ordinances in several cities completely forbid distribution of leaflets. The cities claim that the bans are necessary to prevent littering.

       *Held*, the flat bans violate the First Amendment. The objective of keeping the streets clean is insufficiently substantial to justify preventing a person with a right to be on a public street from giving literature to one who wants to receive it. Also, the state's objective can be met by means which place less of a burden on the freedom of expression (e.g., punishing only those who actually litter). *Schneider v. State*, 308 U.S. 147 (1939).

    b. **Alternative places or times:**   Similarly, where a public forum is involved, the fact that the same message may be expressed by the speaker at a ***different place*** or time, or in a different manner, will not by itself suffice to validate a content-neutral restriction on the expression.

4. **Non-public forum:**   By contrast, where the expression does ***not*** take place in a "public forum," the analysis depends on whether the regulation constitutes a ***substantial interfer-***

*ence* with communication. Here, the existence of alternatives is relevant — the availability of a different place, time or manner for expressing the same message is likely to mean that the regulation's interference with speech is not substantial. If there is no substantial interference with expression, the state must merely show a ***rational justification*** for the regulation (assuming that it is content-neutral). Tribe, p. 982.

5. **General rule for "time, place or manner" rules:**   Where a regulation is claimed to be a valid ***"time, place or manner"*** regulation, the Court now applies the following ***three-part test.*** The regulation will not be valid unless it satisfies ***all*** of these these three requirements:

❏ It must be "justified without reference to the content of the regulated speech"; that is, it must be ***content-neutral*** (thus avoiding "track one" analysis);

❏ It must be ***"narrowly tailored"*** to serve a *"**significant** governmental interest."* (The requirement that the regulation be "narrowly tailored" to serve the interest means that it must be the case that the interest cannot be equally well-served by a means that is substantively less intrusive of First Amendment interests. See *Clark v. Community For Creative Non-Violence*, 468 U.S. 288 (1984));

❏ It must *"**leave open alternative channels** for communication of the information." Metromedia, Inc. v. San Diego*, 453 U.S. 490 (1981).

**Note:** The above test does not explicitly distinguish between speech which takes place in public forums and that which does not. However, the second and third of the above requirements are interpreted more stringently in the public forum situation. As noted, "mere governmental convenience" (e.g., prevention of littering) is not treated as a "significant governmental interest" where a public forum is involved, and availability of other public forums or other times for using the one at issue are not deemed to be adequate "alternative channels."

B. **Speech vs. conduct:**   In many cases, especially those which should properly be analyzed under "track two" principles, the Court has instead purported to focus on a distinction between ***"pure speech"*** and ***"speech plus conduct."*** In upholding governmental restrictions as valid regulations on the "time, place or manner" of speech, the Court has, in these cases, claimed that the restriction is justified because what is being regulated is "conduct" rather than pure speech.

1. **Criticism:**   However, this "speech vs. conduct" distinction is not very helpful in predicting whether a regulation will be upheld or stricken, for virtually all speech is accompanied by action. In fact, there have been numerous cases in which the Court granted extensive First Amendment protection to a completely nonverbal act, recognizing that it was nonetheless expressive; examples include the wearing of an armband (*Tinker v. Des Moines School District, infra*, p. 543) and the refusal to engage in compulsory flag salutation (*West Virginia State Board of Education v. Barnette*, 319 U.S. 624 (1943)). Thus when the Court has labeled a particular expressive activity as being "speech plus conduct," this "must be seen at best as announcing a ***conclusion*** of the Court, rather than as summarizing in any way the analytic processes which led the Court to that conclusion." Tribe, p. 827.

2. **Alternative analysis:**   The use of two separate "tracks" of analysis, based on whether or not the perceived harm flows from the communicative impact of the expression, furnishes a much better way of predicting how the case will be decided.

a. **Illustration:** For instance, if an anti-war activist breaks the windows of an induction center in protest against the draft, the state should be able to punish this act with only a rational justification. This is so because, although the act is expressive, the harm which the state seeks to prevent (the breaking of windows) *does not flow from the content of the protester's message* — the same harm would be present if the window was broken by apolitical vandals. See Ely, p. 113. Therefore, the case is suitable for "track two" analysis; since there is no public forum, a mere "rational justification" for punishing the act is all that is needed.

   i. **Use of "speech vs. conduct" role:** By contrast, if the "speech vs. conduct" distinction were used, it would be hard to punish this conduct yet explain why staging of a peaceful *protest march* outside that same draft center should not be punished — these activities are both "conduct" rather than "pure speech." Use of the "two track" theory, however, does allow the protest march to be distinguished from the window-breaking. The government's objection to the march, assuming that it does not physically disrupt the functioning of the center, must relate to the communicative impact of the march, i.e., to the possibility that it may induce others to oppose the draft; the restriction therefore belongs on "track one," and will be subjected to strict scrutiny and probably invalidated.

C. **Meaning of "narrowly tailored":** As we noted above (*supra*, p. 492), the regulation of "time, place, or manner" must not only be serving a significant government interest, but must be *"narrowly tailored"* to serve that interest. However, this "narrowly tailored" requirement does *not* mean that the state must choose the *least-restrictive* or least-intrusive means of achieving its objective. Instead, the state must merely avoid choosing means that are *"substantially broader* than necessary to achieve the government's interest." *Ward v. Rock Against Racism*, 491 U.S. 781 (1989). In other words, the fact that an alternative method would have interfered somewhat less with expression while still fulfilling the government's objectives, is irrelevant — all that is required is that the means-end fit be *fairly close*, not perfect.

   1. **Illustration:** The facts of *Ward*, *supra*, illustrate this principle. To cut down on complaints by citizens that rock concerts in the city's parks were too loud, New York City imposed a requirement that rock performers use only city-provided sound equipment and sound technicians. The Court upheld this requirement as a valid "time, place, and manner" restriction. The Court conceded that the city might have found a less-restrictive means of solving the loudness problem. (For instance, it could have monitored the performances, and punished the performers who exceeded pre-defined sound limits.) But the availability of less-restrictive means of regulating volume was irrelevant — since the means chosen by the city were not *"substantially* broader than necessary" to keep sound low, the requirement that the means be "narrowly tailored" to serve the government's interest was satisfied.

      a. **Dissent:** Three justices dissented in *Ward*. They argued that the majority was eviscerating the "narrowly tailored" requirement. For instance, if the city did not have to choose the least-restrictive means of regulating loudness here, the dissenters argued, a city could also ban all handbill distribution as a way of controlling litter (rather than using the less-restrictive method of punishing litterers directly, a method that prior decisions had required cities to use; see *supra*, p. 491).

**D. "Leave open alternative channels" requirement:** The third and final requirement for a "time, place and manner" regulation is that it "*leave open alternative channels* for communication of the information." See *supra*, p. 492. Usually, a regulation that satisfies the other requirements (content-neutral, and narrowly tailored to serve a significant governmental interest) will also satisfy this final requirement. But occasionally, the requirement does turn out to make a difference. It is especially likely to do so where the government tries to foreclose an *entire medium* or *method* of communication, and the method is so easy-to-use or inexpensive that other channels simply are not substitutes.

1. **Use by individuals:** In general, the more a particular method is likely to be used by *individuals* who are trying to disseminate core political messages without spending a lot of money, the more likely the method is to be found so vital that its prohibition fails to leave open "alternative channels." Thus complete bans on *handbills* (see *supra*, p. 491) or on the display of *homemade signs* are likely to be struck down as not leaving open alternative channels.

   **Example:** The City of Ladue, Missouri generally prohibits "signs," and defines that term broadly. All residential signs are prohibited except for "identification signs" and "for sale" signs. P places an 8.5 x 11 inch sign in the second story window of her home, stating "For Peace in the Gulf." The city asserts that P's sign must come down, and defends its ordinance on the grounds that it is merely a "time, place and manner" regulation whose purpose is to minimize the visual clutter associated with signs.

   *Held*, for P. By forbidding residents from displaying virtually any "sign" on their property, the city "has almost completely foreclosed a venerable means of communication that is both unique and important." The city has not "[left] open ample alternative channels for communication. … Displaying a sign from one's own residence often carries a message quite distinct from placing the same sign someplace else, or conveying the same text or picture by other means. … Residential signs are an unusually cheap and convenient form of communication. Especially for persons of modest means or limited mobility, a yard or window sign may have no practical substitute." Therefore, even though the city's ordinance may be content-neutral, and even assuming that the ordinance is narrowly tailored to serve a significant governmental interest, it unconstitutionally infringes P's free speech. *City of Ladue v. Gilleo*, 512 U.S. 43 (1994).

**E. Licensing:** One way in which governments often attempt to regulate speech or expressive conduct is through *licensing* or *permit* requirements, by which official permission is required *in advance* of a public address, march, solicitation campaign, or other expressive activity.

1. **Multiple techniques:** The Court has used a number of techniques to ensure that such requirements will not stifle the freedom of expression:

   a. **Content-neutrality:** The government must apply the permit requirement in a *content-neutral* manner. If, for instance, a permit is required before any parade, the officials charged with granting or denying permit requests *may not take into account the ideas or politics being espoused* by the paraders. (Only if the content of the expression places it within an "unprotected category," such as "advocacy of imminent illegal activity," may this content be taken into account.)

i. **Consequence:** Thus if the government wishes to have its advance-permit requirement sustained in a particular fact situation, it will almost certainly have to show either that the case belongs on "track two" rather than "track one," or that the speech's content falls into an unprotected category.

ii. **Fee based on content of speech:** For example, the government almost certainly cannot charge a ***different fee*** for the license or permit, based on the content of the speech. In fact, the Court has held that the government may not vary the fee according to the ***costs of security*** that the government will bear in connection with the expression, because such costs will inevitably depend on the content of the speaker's message, and the hostility generated by that message.

**Example:** A Forsyth County, Georgia, ordinance requires a permit for any public parade, assembly or demonstration. Permit applicants are required to pay a fee, not to exceed $1,000 per day; the county administrator is permitted under the ordinance to "adjust the amount to be paid in order to meet the expense incident to the administration of the Ordinance and to the maintenance of public order in the matter licensed." A white supremacy group which wishes to conduct a demonstration challenges the statute as being on its face a violation of the First Amendment.

*Held,* the ordinance violates the First Amendment on its face. Because unpopular speech will be met with greater audience hostility than will popular speech, police expenses in providing security for the demonstration will be higher for unpopular speech than popular speech. Listeners' reaction to speech is not a content-neutral basis for regulation. *Forsyth County v. The Nationalist Movement,* 505 U.S. 123 (1992).

b. **Excessive administrative discretion:** The grounds upon which a permit may be denied must be set forth ***specifically***, and ***narrowly***, in the ordinance. If the official charged with granting or denying permit applications is given ***too much discretion***, the ordinance will be voided for overbreadth, vagueness, or both (see *supra*, p. 483).

**Example 1:** A municipal ordinance forbids the distribution anywhere within the town of "literature of any kind," unless a permit has first been obtained from the City Manager. D is convicted of violating the ordinance for distributing religious literature published by the Jehovah's Witnesses.

*Held,* the ordinance is an unconstitutional violation of freedom of speech. It gives a censor's power to the City Manager, since his right to deny a permit is not tied to the avoidance of littering or disorderly conduct, or to regulation of time and place. Because the ordinance is void on its face (for what would today be called overbreadth), D was not required to seek the permit and then challenge its denial in court; she was free to disregard the permit requirement and to challenge the ordinance after her arrest. *Lovell v. Griffin,* 303 U.S. 444 (1938).

**Example 2:** A municipal ordinance allows newspaper vending machines to be placed on public property only after the granting of a permit by the Mayor. The ordinance recites no standards for determining when a permit shall be granted, and specifies that any permit actually granted shall be on any "terms and conditions deemed necessary and reasonable by the Mayor."

*Held*, the ordinance is unconstitutional, because it places no explicit limits on the Mayor's discretion, and therefore renders the guarantee against censorship "little more than a high-sounding ideal." The Court is unwilling to presume that the Mayor will act in good faith and adhere to standards that are absent from the statute's face. *Lakewood v. Plain Dealer Publishing Co.*, 468 U.S. 750 (1989).

    **i.  Variable fee:** Similarly, if the official charged with granting or denying permit applications is given too much discretion in the *amount of the fee*, the ordinance will be struck down.

  **c.  Narrow tailoring of means to end:** The permit *mechanism* must be *closely tailored* to the *objective* that the government is trying to achieve. Thus if the government says that it is trying to avoid harm X, but the permit scheme either (1) seriously burdens speech that poses no danger of harm X, or (2) fails to deter speech and related conduct that *does* pose a danger of harm X, the court is likely to strike the scheme on the grounds that it is not closely tailored to the achievement of an important governmental interest (the intermediate-level scrutiny that the Court tends to use in permit cases.)

    **Example:** D, an Ohio village with 278 residents, passes an ordinance that prohibits any "canvasser," "solicitor," or various others from going onto private residential property for the purpose of promoting any "cause" without first having obtained a "Solicitation Permit" from the mayor. The permits are issued without charge, but only after the applicant fills out a detailed registration form that includes the registrant's name, his address for the past five years, the purpose of the solicitation, the name of the registrant's employer or organization, the "specific address of each private residence" at which solicitation will occur, etc. The Ps (Jehovah's Witnesses, who distribute religious materials door-to-door throughout the U.S.) challenge the ordinance on its face. In litigation, D defends the statute on the grounds that it prevents fraud and crime, and protects the privacy of residents.

    *Held*, the ordinance is invalid on its face, in part because it is "not tailored to [D's] stated interests." The interest in combating fraud might support the permit requirement as to commercial transactions and fund solicitation, but the anti-fraud interest does not support such a requirement as to the kind of religious proselytizing done by the Ps, or as to political campaigns. With respect to the interest in preventing "crime," the permit requirement is not much of a deterrent, since criminals could knock on doors and then have conversations not covered by the ordinance (e.g., asking to use the phone, or posing as surveyors or census takers). Conversely, the interest in protecting privacy could be adequately protected by other means, such as by allowing residents to post "No Solicitation" signs and making the ignoring of such a sign an offense (as a different provision of the ordinance, not challenged in this case, does.) Consequently, the fit between the means chosen here (the permit scheme) and the Village's stated objectives is too imprecise. *Watchtower Bible and Tract Soc. of N.Y. v. Village of Stratton*, 536 U.S. 150 (2002).

  **2.  Prior restraint:** One of the reasons the courts look with particular disfavor on permit requirements is that these amount to *prior restraint* on the freedom of speech. That is, in contrast to statutes which merely *punish* certain types of expressive conduct *after* they have occurred, the permit requirement, if enforced, prevents the expression from ever taking place at all.

a. **Illustration:** This hostility to prior restraints is illustrated by *Kunz v. New York*, 340 U.S. 290 (1951), where a permit requirement was combined with a provision making it unlawful "to ridicule or denounce any form of religious belief" or to "expound atheism or agnosticism [in] any street." The Court held that the use of these provisions to deny a permit to a Baptist minister who had previously made verbal attacks on Catholics and Jews was "clearly invalid as a prior restraint on the exercise of First Amendment rights." If the speaker's words resulted in disorder and violence on a particular occasion, *that* would be the time for the government to take action (presumably by ordering him to stop and/or punishing him.)

b. **Restraint of press:** The Court's hostility to prior restraints on free expression is even more noteworthy in the case of the press. See, e.g., *Near v. Minnesota*, discussed *infra*, p. 628.

3. **General right of regulation:** However, if the statute or ordinance *does* adequately constrain administrative discretion, does require content-neutrality, and does have an adequate means-end fit, it will be upheld if it is a ***reasonable means of ensuring that public order is maintained.***

   a. **Illustration:** For instance, in *Cox v. New Hampshire*, 312 U.S. 569 (1941), a municipal ordinance requiring a permit for all parades and public meetings was sustained, where it was enacted in accordance with a state statute setting forth elaborate procedural requirements for the hearing of such permit requests.

      i. **Reliance on state procedures:** The Supreme Court relied upon the state court interpretations of the licensing procedures; the state courts had found: (1) that ***content-neutrality*** was required by the statute; and (2) that the defendants (again, Jehovah's Witnesses) would, had they applied for a permit, have had an unqualified right to a permit so long as their proposed parade was to be at a time and place where it would not unduly disturb public use of the streets. The municipality's interest in not having overlapping parades, and in having advance notice so as to be able to ensure proper policing, furnished adequate justification for the permit requirement.

   b. **Strong procedural safeguards not required:** As long as the court is convinced that the permit system is truly content-neutral, the strong ***procedural safeguards*** that are required in cases of *content-based* prior restraint will ***not*** be required. For instance, advance licensing requirements for motion pictures, which are designed to protect against obscenity and are thus inevitably content-based, must allow for ***immediate judicial review*** of a license denial, and must put the ***burden of proof*** in that judicial review on the censor. But the Court has held that a permit scheme for large-scale events in public parks need *not* meet these same procedural safeguards, as long as the permit scheme is truly content-neutral. *Thomas v. v. Chicago Park Dist.*, 534 U.S. 316 (2002).

4. **Right to ignore requirement:** When a permit requirement exists, may the speaker decline to apply for a permit (or apply for one and be turned down), speak anyway, and then attack the constitutionality of the permit requirement if he is prosecuted? The answer depends on the respect in which the permit requirement is unconstitutional.

   a. **Invalid on its face:** If the permit requirement is unconstitutional *on its face*, because it is overbroad or vague, the speaker is ***not required*** to apply for a permit; he may decline to apply, then speak, and avoid conviction on the grounds of the permit requirement's unconstitutionality. This is, for instance, exactly what happened in *Lovell, supra,* p. 495. Similarly, he may apply unsuccessfully, then speak, and later challenge the ordinance if he is prosecuted.

b.  **Unconstitutional as applied:**  But where the permit requirement is ***not facially invalid*** (i.e., not unduly vague or overbroad), and the speaker's claim is merely that he has been ***wrongfully denied a permit*** (or that had he applied, he would have been constitutionally entitled to one), a different result occurs. The speaker ***must seek judicial relief before speaking***. If he simply ignores the denial of the permit and speaks without trying to obtain judicial relief, he ***loses the right to object*** to the permit scheme's unconstitutionality as applied to him. See, e.g., *Poulos v. New Hampshire*, 345 U.S. 395 (1953). (But an exception exists where the applicant shows that he ***could not obtain prompt judicial review*** of the administrative denial of the permit. Tribe, p. 1044.)

c.  **Injunctions:**  When a person is judicially ***enjoined*** from speaking, marching, etc., he generally may ***not*** ignore the injunction and then attack its constitutionality in a subsequent contempt proceeding. Instead, he must seek prior judicial relief. For instance, in *Walker v. Birmingham*, 388 U.S. 307 (1967) the defendants were charged with contempt of court for violating an *ex parte* injunction directing compliance with an ordinance that the defendants claimed was overbroad. Even though the injunction merely repeated the words of the ordinance, the Court (by a 5-4 vote) held that the defendants could not defend against the contempt proceedings by arguing the injunction's unconstitutionality; they were required to seek "orderly review" of the injunction before violating it.

   i.  **Delay of review:**  But if, in an injunction situation like that of *Walker*, the defendant can show that he ***tried unsuccessfully to obtain a prompt judicial hearing*** of his constitutional claim before violating the injunction, then a subsequent collateral attack during the contempt proceeding will be permitted. Tribe, pp. 1044-45.

F.  **Intrusive speakers vs. right to be left alone:**  One way in which the state has sometimes justified content-neutral regulations on expressive activity is by claiming that the would-be audience has an interest in ***not being forced to listen*** to the speaker's message. The Court has not been completely unsympathetic to this "right to be left alone." But it has generally held that it is ***up to the unwilling listener*** (or viewer) to ***avoid the undesired expression***, and that the state may not issue a blanket proclamation shielding both the willing and unwilling from the expression.

1.  **Loudspeakers:**  Thus the Court has carefully scrutinized restrictions on ***loudspeakers*** and ***soundtrucks***. Where such restrictions give ***uncontrolled discretion*** to local officials, they will be struck down (just like other types of overbroad or vague permit schemes, discussed above).

   a.  *Saia:*  For instance, in *Saia v. New York*, 334 U.S. 558 (1948), the Court by a 5-4 vote struck down an ordinance which prohibited use of amplification systems without the police chief's permission. The majority believed that the ordinance was invalid on its face; because it was subject to the police chief's uncontrolled discretion, it was a standardless "previous restraint" on free speech.

    **i.  Less restrictive alternatives:** Also, the Court in *Saia* relied on the existence of *less restrictive alternatives*; a statute could have been more narrowly drawn to prohibit only noise above a certain decibel level, and to bar the use of the sound devices outside of certain hours and places. By instead giving the police uncontrolled discretion, there was a *risk of censorship*: "[a]nnoyance at ideas can be cloaked in annoyance at sound."

  **b.  "Loud and raucous noises" prohibitable:** But if administrative discretion is sufficiently restricted, and the statute is not overbroad or vague, regulation of amplification devices will be permitted, as a valid regulation of the "time, place or manner" of expression.

    **i.  Loudspeakers:** For instance, in *Kovacs v. Cooper*, 336 U.S. 77 (1949), the Court *upheld* a ban on all amplification devices operated in public places which emit *"loud and raucous noises."* The municipality's interest in avoiding distractions to traffic, and in protecting the "quiet and tranquility" of its inhabitants, was sufficient to justify the regulation, despite the "preferred position of freedom of speech." (It is not clear whether the logic of the majority opinion in *Kovacs* would allow a city to ban *all* public amplification devices, since it is not clear whether all such devices make "loud and raucous noises." A concurring Justice, and three dissenters, all believed that the majority's opinion would allow a complete ban on such devices.)

    **ii.  Regulating sound equipment:** Similarly, the Court held that New York City could require that any musician performing in a public forum (the bandshell in Central Park) use city-provided sound-amplification equipment and sound technicians. The city had a significant governmental interest in protecting citizens from unduly loud sounds, and the regulation was not substantially broader than necessary to achieve that interest. *Ward v. Rock Against Racism* (other aspects of which are discussed *supra*, p. 493).

  **c.  Distinction:** An additional important difference between *Saia* and *Kovacs* is that in *Saia*, the ordinance acted as a *prior restraint* (since it called for a permit); in *Kovacs*, by contrast, the scheme merely called for a subsequent punishment. In general, the Court has been considerably more tolerant of subsequent-punishment schemes than it has been of those that constitute prior restraints.

**2.  The captive audience:** Whenever speech is directed towards a *captive audience*, that is, one which *cannot easily avoid exposure* to the speech, this is a factor which the Court will weigh in favor of *allowing restriction* on that form of expression. A number of cases show how the presence of a captive audience is a factor making the Court more willing than usual to allow restrictions on expression:

  **a.  Print advertising on city buses:** For instance, in *Lehman v. Shaker Heights*, 418 U.S. 298 (1974), the Court upheld restrictions on some but not all types of print advertising on city-owned buses. The Court held that the fact that commercial advertising was accepted did not give political candidates a right to have *their* advertising accepted; the majority relied in part upon the city's interest in limiting access so as to reduce "the risk of imposing upon the captive audience."

  **b.  Picketing in front of residence:** Similarly, the Court has held that a municipality may ban all *picketing* in front of a *particular residence*, in order to protect the inhabitants of that house from hearing or seeing unwanted messages. *Frisby v. Schultz*, 487 U.S. 474 (1988), also discussed *infra*, p. 527.

c. **Women visiting abortion clinics:** Finally, **women** who are **visiting abortion clinics** or other healthcare offices now seem to get significant protection from unwanted expression. The Court held in an especially contentious 6-3 decision, *Hill v. Colorado*, 530 U.S. 703 (2000) that a state may create a **"buffer zone"** around the entrance to any healthcare facility, in which no one may make an unwanted approach to another person to counsel, pass out a leaflet, or picket.

   i. **Majority supports right to be left alone:** The majority viewed the law as a **valid regulation** on time, place, and manner. It found the law to be **content-neutral**, since it prohibited all unwanted approaches, regardless of the topic. The majority stressed the captive-audience aspect, saying that the Court had "repeatedly recognized the interests of unwilling listeners in situations where the 'degree of captivity makes it impractical for the unwilling viewer or auditor to avoid exposure'."

      (1) **Narrowly tailored:** The majority then found the statute to be **narrowly tailored** to protect the state's interest in protecting citizens from unwanted speech. (Remember that narrow tailoring is a requirement for time, place and manner restrictions under *Ward v. Rock Against Racism*; see *supra*, p. 493). According to the majority, protesters could still deliver their message effectively across the buffer zone.

d. **No general rule:** Don't let *Hill* make you that that the Court has adopted a broad rule that the public has an absolute **"right to be left alone."** The interest in avoiding unwanted intrusion is merely **one factor** to be placed into the balance. Even in the abortion context, it is clear that citizens in public places must tolerate some unwanted messages — the listener's remedy is generally to avert his eyes and ears, not to have government forbid or restrict the delivery of the message.

G. **Canvassing and soliciting:** The interest in being left alone also plays a role in the case law on **canvassers and solicitors**. Here, too, however, this interest has been merely one factor in the balancing of society's interest in regulating the form of expression against the speaker's interest in unrestrained communication.

1. **Significance of place:** The **place** in which the canvassing or solicitation occurs is important; the Court has granted greater weight to the rights of canvassers and solicitors in **public places** than at **private residences** (though even as to the latter, access may not be completely cut off by a blanket ban.)

2. **Mailboxes:** The Court's concern with the sanctity of the home has led it to be sympathetic to legislative acts which restrict access to **home mailboxes.**

   a. **Homeowner's right to block receipt:** Thus a congressional provision allowing a homeowner who has received what he (in his sole judgment) believes to be "erotically arousing or sexually provocative" material to obtain a post office order requiring the mailer to remove the homeowner's name from its mailing lists, was upheld in *Rowan v. Post Office Dept.*, 397 U.S. 728 (1970). The Court found that "[t]he right of every person 'to be let alone' must be placed in the scales with the right of others to communicate." Whatever rules might apply outside the home, "[a] mailer's right to communicate **must stop at the mailbox** of an unreceptive addressee."

b. **Not public forum:**   The mailer's "right of access" to home mailboxes was further undermined when the Court upheld a federal statute which prohibited depositing ***unstamped materials in home mailboxes,*** in ***U.S. Postal Service v. Greenburgh Civic Assns.***, 453 U.S. 114 (1981). There, several civic groups argued that they had a constitutional right to deliver messages to local residents by placing unstamped pamphlets and notices in such mailboxes. But the Court held that ***home mailboxes do not constitute a "public forum,"*** even though they are in effect controlled by the government; therefore, any reasonable, content-neutral, regulation of their use was permissible.

3. **Personal visits at home:**   Those who wish to solicit or canvass by making ***personal visits*** to homes have received substantial First Amendment protection from the Court, notwithstanding the homeowner's interest in being left alone. In general, the Court has taken the view that ***it is up to homeowner himself to indicate his desire to be left alone*** (in which event the state may enforce that desire); the state may not simply ***assume*** that all homeowners wish to be undisturbed.

> **Example:** An ordinance prohibits anyone from distributing handbills to residents by either ringing their doorbell or otherwise calling them to the door. (Nor is there any way to get a permit that would allow this.) The town defends this prohibition on privacy grounds. *Held*, this flat ban on canvassing is unconstitutional, because less restrictive alternatives are available (e.g., letting a homeowner post a no-soliciting sign, and then making it an offense for anyone to ring the bell of such a person.) *Martin v. Struthers*, 319 U.S. 141 (1943).

4. **Heightened scrutiny:**   Even where an ordinance regulating canvassing is written in a way that does not give officials undue discretion, it will not pass constitutional muster if it: (1) directly and substantially impairs protected First Amendment expression; and (2) is not substantially related to achievement of a ***"strong, subordinating interest."*** This two-part test was applied to invalidate an ordinance barring door-to-door or in-the-street solicitation by charitable organizations that do not use at least 75% of their receipts for "charitable purposes" (defined to exclude overhead and solicitation expenses). *Schaumburg v. Citizens For Better Environment*, 444 U.S. 620 (1980).

5. **Solicitation in public places:**   Where canvassing or solicitation occurs in ***public places***, essentially the same constitutional standards apply as in the door-to-door situation. That is, the regulation must be content-neutral, and authorities may not be given excessive discretion in determining who may solicit, or in what manner. Reasonable "time, place and manner" regulations which satisfy both of these requirements will be upheld, so long as they serve a ***significant governmental interest*** and ***leave open ample alternative channels*** for communicating the same information.

   a. **Less judicial tolerance:**   But since the "governmental interest" and "alternative channel" factors inevitably involve a kind of balancing, the Court has been ***less tolerant*** of regulations on solicitation done in public forums than in the door-to-door situation (where the governmental interest in having citizens be left alone is stronger.)

   b. **State fair grounds:**   The precise nature of the public forum where the solicitation occurs is likely to be important. For instance, the government was found to be entitled to make greater regulation of solicitation on ***the grounds of a state fair*** than on city streets, in *Heffron v. Int'l Soc. For Krishna Consciousness (ISKCON)*, 452 U.S. 640 (1981).

**i.**  **Facts:**  In *Heffron*, the state provided that anyone who wished to sell or distribute merchandise (including literature) or solicit funds at the Minnesota State Fair must do so only from an ***assigned booth***. ISKCON, a Krishna religious group, contended that the regulation impaired its ritual of sending its members into public areas of the Fair to sell or distribute religious literature and to solicit contributions.

**ii.**  **Regulation upheld:**  A majority of the Court upheld this regulation as it applied to all three of ISKCON's activities: distribution of literature, sales of it, and solicitation of contributions. Since the regulation was content-neutral (all commercial and non-commercial enterprises were equally regulated, and assigned-booth space was given out on a first-come, first-served basis), and since there was no sign of excessive discretion given to fair officials, the only issues were: (1) whether the restriction served a "significant governmental interest;" and (2) whether adequate "alternative channels" for the communication were left. The Court believed that the answer to each of these issues was "yes."

**iii.**  **Interest in crowd control:**  The majority relied principally on the state's interest in protecting the "safety and convenience" of fairgoers, which it accomplished by maintaining the "orderly movement of the crowd" (containing up to 150,000 members.) This interest in crowd control was stronger, the majority asserted, in the fair context than it would be on city streets. Also, the relevant danger was not merely the disorder which ISKCON would cause by being allowed to solicit throughout the fairgrounds, but rather, the disorder which would result if ***all*** persons who wanted to do this were permitted to do so.

**6. Anonymous solicitation:**  One component of the right to canvas and solicit is the right to do so ***anonymously***. "An author's decision to remain anonymous, like other decisions concerning omissions or additions to the content of a publication, is an aspect of the freedom of speech protected by the First Amendment." *McIntyre v. Ohio Elections Comm'n*, 514 U.S. 334 (1995). Any limitation on this right of anonymity will be ***strictly scrutinized***, and probably struck down. Both broad prohibitions on anonymous handbills, and narrower ones limited to electoral literature, have been struck down by the Court.

> **Example:** Ohio prohibits the distribution of campaign literature that does not contain the name and address of the person issuing the literature. P, a private citizen not running for office, distributes handbills opposing the waste of tax dollars; she signs them "Concerned Parents and Taxpayers," and does not list her name or address. P is fined for violating the statute. The state claims its prohibition is necessary to prevent campaign "dirty tricks" and other electoral fraud.
>
> *Held*, the ordinance abridged P's freedom of speech. The right to write anonymously is important, both so that writers may escape persecution for unpopular ideas, and so that a writer who is personally unpopular may "ensure that readers will not prejudge her message simply because they do not like its proponent." Any limitation of "core political speech" — of which Ohio's statute is an example — must be strictly scrutinized. It is true that Ohio has an important interest in preventing electoral fraud. But the extremely broad prohibition here (which, for instance, applies to private individuals not running for office who are spending only their own money) goes far beyond anything necessary to combat fraud. *McIntyre, supra*.

**Note:** The Court in *McIntyre* left open the possibility that a narrower rule might survive strict scrutiny. For instance, it's possible that a state might be allowed to require that where literature is published by a *candidate* for office and is paid for by *campaign donations* solicited from others, the material must contain the author's name and address.

**H. The hostile audience and "fighting words":** One of the "unprotected categories" of speech consists of so-called *"fighting words,"* that is, words which are likely to make the person to whom they are addressed *commit an act of violence* (probably against the speaker). "Fighting words" receive no First Amendment protection, because, like other unprotected categories (e.g., defamation, obscenity, etc.) they are not normally part of any "dialogue" or "exposition of ideas." But the Supreme Court today keeps this exclusion within tightly circumscribed bounds.

1. *Chaplinsky:* The "fighting words" doctrine originated in *Chaplinsky v. New Hampshire*, 315 U.S. 568 (1942).

   a. **Facts:** The defendant in *Chaplinsky* was a Jehovah's Witness who called the city marshall a "goddamned racketeer" and "a damned fascist," and then got into a fight with him on the sidewalk. He was convicted under a broadly-worded statute, which provided that "no person shall address any offensive, derisive or annoying word to any other person who is lawfully in any street or other public place ... " But the New Hampshire Supreme Court had interpreted the statute to bar only "words *likely to cause an average addressee to fight.*"

   b. **Conviction upheld:** The conviction was *upheld*. The Supreme Court believed that the defendant's words were indeed ones which would *likely provoke the average person to retaliate*. It then held that among the classes of speech which are not protected by the First Amendment are "fighting words," which the Court defined as "those which by their very utterance *inflict injury* or *tend to incite an immediate breach of the peace*." Such words are "*no essential part of any exposition of ideas*, and are of such *slight social value as a step to truth* that any benefit that may be derived from them is clearly outweighed by the social interest in order and morality."

   c. **Two branches:** Observe that this *Chaplinsky* formulation defines "fighting words" quite broadly — in addition to words which are likely to incite an immediate fight, words are also included which "inflict injury." This latter branch of *Chaplinsky*, which is part of the problem of offensive words and the sensitive audience, is discussed *infra*, p. 506. Here, we are concerned only with words likely to provoke a fight or other breach of the peace.

2. **Limitations on doctrine:** The Court realized, soon after *Chaplinsky*, that giving a broad scope to the "fighting words" doctrine would lead to the swallowing up of important First Amendment protections. Therefore, the Court has *limited* the "fighting words" doctrine in a number of ways.

   a. **"Stirring to anger" not enough:** To constitute "fighting words," it is not enough that the speaker's words *make the listeners angry; incitement to violence* (whether or not the violence actually ensues) is required. For instance, in *Terminiello v. Chicago*, 337 U.S. 1 (1949), D made a race-baiting speech, which attracted an angry crowd; the speaker then denounced the crowd as "snakes" and "slimy scum." The Supreme Court reversed D's conviction under a breach-of-the-peace statute which the trial court had interpreted to include speech which "stirs the public to *anger* [or] *invites dispute*," as well as speech which creates a disturbance.

    **i.   Rationale:**  The Supreme Court reasoned that speech which "stirs the audience to anger" or "invites dispute" is *protected* under the First Amendment and that, in fact, *the most valuable expression may well be that which, because it is provocative and challenging, produces these emotions.* Therefore, the statute (as interpreted by the trial judge) was *overbroad* on its face; D's conviction had to be reversed, regardless of whether *his actual words* could have been made criminal under a more narrowly-drawn statute covering only words likely to incite violence.

  **b.  Crowd-control required:**  Wherever the police have the physical ability to *control the angry crowd* as a means of preventing threatened violence, they *must do so* in preference to arresting the speaker for using "fighting words." For instance, in *Cox v. Louisiana (Cox I)*, 379 U.S. 536 (1965), 2,000 civil rights demonstrators picketed a courthouse; about 75 policemen separated the demonstrators from 100-300 whites gathered on the other side of the street. The Court, in reversing the breach of peace conviction of the demonstration's leader, rejected the state's claim that the conviction was justified because "violence was about to erupt" — the Court relied in part on the fact that the police could have "handled the crowd."

    **i.   "Heckler's veto":**  Observe that a contrary rule, allowing the police to silence a speaker whenever the audience threatens violence, would legitimate what has been called the *"heckler's veto."* That is, members of the audience would gain the right to silence any speaker with whose ideas they did not agree.

  **c.  Generalized fears insufficient:**  It is not sufficient that the police have *generalized fears* that there may be violence. Only if *specific words or acts* by the speaker (or demonstrator), or by the audience, threaten violence, will the "fighting words" doctrine apply (assuming, also, that control of the crowd cannot be accomplished). See, e.g., *Edwards v. South Carolina*, 372 U.S. 229 (1963), where 187 black students demonstrated at the State House, before a crowd of 200-300 onlookers; the Supreme Court reversed their breach of peace conviction on the grounds that there was no violence or specific threat of violence from either the demonstrators or the crowd (as well as on the grounds that an adequate number of police were present).

  **d.  Mere dislike of speaker's identity not sufficient:**  If it is the *mere identity* or lawful acts of the speaker or demonstrator, *not his threatening words or actions*, which lead the police to believe that violence is imminent, the "fighting words" doctrine may *not* be applied.

    **i.   Civil rights sit-ins:**  For instance, in several breach-of-peace cases involving civil rights sit-ins of segregated facilities, the state was able to justify its fear of imminent violence only by asserting that the *mere fact that blacks were using segregated facilities* made whites likely to attack them. Even if this anticipation of whites' response was accurate, it was constitutionally irrelevant, since the blacks' use of these facilities was not evidence of any crime. See *Garner v. Louisiana*, 368 U.S. 157 (1961). See also Tribe, p. 854.

 **3.  Doctrine sometimes applicable:**  But these *are* occasional situations in which none of these exceptions or limitations applies, and the "fighting words" doctrine is applicable.

These will be those situations in which "imminent spectator violence cannot be satisfactorily prevented or curbed by means of crowd control techniques, and ... the speech itself is the apparent cause of the impending disorder." Tribe p. 855.

**a.** *Feiner:* The last true "fighting words" conviction sustained by the Court was in *Feiner v. New York*, 340 U.S. 315 (1951).

   **i. Facts:** D, a left-wing college student, made a street-corner speech in which he called President Truman a "bum" and the American Legion a "Nazi Gestapo," and said that blacks should "rise up in arms and fight for [legal rights]." One member of the racially-mixed crowd said that if the police did not get that "son of a bitch" off the stand he would do it himself. D refused to heed requests from the police to stop speaking, and was then arrested for disorderly conduct.

   **ii. Conviction upheld:** A majority of the Court believed that D's conduct constituted *incitement to riot*, and that his arrest was motivated by the police's legitimate desire to prevent a fight, not by disagreement with the content of D's message. The Court conceded that "the ordinary murmurings and objections of a hostile audience cannot be allowed to silence a speaker," but implied that the crowd response here went beyond that. Therefore, the Court *upheld* D's conviction.

   **iii. Black's dissent:** But Justice Black dissented, disagreeing with the majority's view of both the facts and the law. As a factual matter, he did not agree that violence was imminent; he believed that D had in reality been arrested and convicted for the unpopularity of his views, not the tendency of his speech to induce violence. He also believed, as a legal principle, that the police must, before interfering with a lawful speaker, make "*all reasonable efforts to protect him ... even to the extent of arresting the man who threatened to interfere.*" (Black believed that the majority's opinion implied that there was no such requirement.)

   **iv.** *Feiner* **to be read narrowly:** However, the present Court would probably construe *Feiner* quite *narrowly*, and it is not at all clear that the case would be decided the same way if it arose today. In particular, the Court is probably less inclined to accept the police's self-justifying rationales for their action ("We didn't think we could control the crowd.") See Tribe, p. 855.

**4. Relation to "clear and present danger":** The problem of "fighting words" is similar to, and in some ways a subset of, the problem of advocacy of illegal conduct (*supra*, p. 474). Just as under *Brandenburg, supra*, p. 481, only speech which is intended to advocate *imminent* lawless action, and which is in fact *likely* to result in such action, may be punished, so only those words which are likely to result in violence that cannot be prevented in any other way (e.g., by controlling the crowd) will be preventable or punishable under the "fighting words" doctrine.

   **a. Perhaps no longer valid:** This requirement of imminent unpreventable violence is so strict that many commentators doubt that the fighting words doctrine has much real practical value today. For instance, it is probably the case that there are no words which by themselves are "automatically" fighting words — each utterance has to be evaluated *in context* to determine whether there were actual listeners who were likely to resort to violence. This, coupled with the fact that no regulation has been upheld under the fighting words exception since *Feiner* in 1951, may render the doctrine largely irrelevant.

    **i.**   **Effect of hate-speech case:**   However, the Supreme Court's hate-speech decision, *R.A.V. v. St. Paul* (*infra*, p. 510), suggests that there may be some life in the fighting words doctrine after all. In that case, a St. Paul, Minn. ordinance was construed to ban all fighting words motivated by race, religion or other specified factors. The Supreme Court struck down the statute as being impermissibly content-based. However, the majority opinion observed in dictum that if the city had banned **all** fighting words, not just those based on the enumerated biases, the regulation would have been valid. So judging by *R.A.V.*, a government may still ban all words tending to incite the listener to immediate violence. Whether such a ban would reach very much real-world speech (especially "hate speech," see *infra*, p. 509) is another matter.

**I.**  **Offensive words and the sensitive audience:**  A related issue is whether the government may prevent or punish words which listeners will find **offensive**, even though these words are not likely to lead to actual violence. In general, the Court has not allowed government to suppress speech or expressive conduct on the grounds that others would find it "offensive," unless **substantial privacy interests** are at stake (most notably, when those offended form a "captive audience"). See Tribe, pp. 948-49.

    **1.**  **Second branch of *Chaplinsky:***  Initially, the Court seemed to take the view that "offensive" speech was **not necessarily protected by the First Amendment**. The Court so hinted in *Chaplinsky v. New Hampshire, supra*, p. 503, where, distinct from the lack of protection given to "fighting words," words which "by their very utterance inflict injury" were also placed outside the First Amendment. *Chaplinsky* did not give examples of such utterances; perhaps the Court had in mind foul and disgusting language, statements which reveal another's secrets and therefore invade his privacy, and any other verbal expression which inflicts psychological injury even though it does not necessarily threaten to provoke violence.

    **2.**  **Reluctance to exclude offensive speech:**  But this "offensive language" branch of *Chaplinsky* was really *dictum*, and it is not clear that the law has ever been that offensive language in general falls outside of the First Amendment. For instance, in *Cantwell v. Connecticut*, 310 U.S. 296 (1940), decided two years before *Chaplinsky*, the Court reversed the conviction of a Jehovah's Witness who played a record which attacked all organized religions as instruments of Satan, and singled out Catholicism as particularly evil. The reversal occurred despite the fact that, in the Court's opinion, listeners were "in fact highly offended."

    **3.**  **Foul language:**  Most of the cases involving "offensive language" have focused upon *profanity*. Generally, the Court has held that statements **may not be punished merely because they are profane** and are therefore offensive to their listeners. These cases, even though they involve "four-letter-words" with a sexual connotation, must be sharply distinguished from speech that is "obscene"; here, we deal with statements whose tone is **not erotic**, so that the law of obscenity is irrelevant.

    **4.**  ***Cohen v. California:***  The most important case involving the state's right to ban offensive language (in this case, a profane utterance) is ***Cohen v. California***, 403 U.S. 15 (1971). The case stands basically for the proposition that **profane, offensive language is nonethe-**

*less First Amendment speech*, and may not be suppressed under the guise of regulating the "manner" of speech.

a. **Facts:** Cohen wore a jacket bearing the legend "Fuck the Draft" in a corridor of the Los Angeles County Courthouse, where women and children were present. He was convicted of violating a statute prohibiting the intentional "disturb[ing] the peace or quiet of any ... person [by] offensive conduct."

b. **Conviction reversed:** The Court, in a classic opinion by Justice Harlan, *reversed the conviction* on First Amendment grounds. In so doing, Harlan rejected a number of arguments advanced by the state.

c. **Not obscene:** Harlan found that the legend on the jacket was *not obscene*. An expression is obscene only if it is "in some significant way, erotic." No erotic "psychic stimulation" could reasonably have been expected to result when anybody read the jacket.

d. **Not "captive audience":** The state claimed that *Cohen's* message had been "thrust upon unwilling or unsuspecting viewers," and that the state had the power to protect such *"captive audiences"* from offensive language. But Harlan's opinion took a narrow view of what constitutes a true "captive audience." He quoted a prior case in which the Court had noted that "[w]e are often 'captives' outside the sanctuary of the home and subject to objectionable speech." The situation here was quite different from that of, for instance, a person forced to listen to noisy soundtrucks outside his residence. Here, those in the courthouse could have "avoid[ed] further bombardment of their senses simply by *averting their eyes*." (Harlan also found it significant that there was no evidence that any unwilling viewer was *in fact* offended.)

e. **Right to purge offensive language:** Lastly, Harlan rejected the state's most general claim, that it had the right to ban certain expletives in order to "maintain what [officials] regard as a *suitable level of discourse* within the body politic." He stressed that the First Amendment's general function is to *"remove governmental restraints for the arena of public discussion."* Only where speech falls within relatively narrow preestablished categories may government regulate its form or content; none of these exceptions was applicable here. But Harlan also found more specific reasons for finding that the state could not ban expressions like Cohen's from public discourse:

    i. **No stopping point:** First, there was no principled way to distinguish "fuck" from other words. Yet the state clearly did not have the right to "cleanse public debate to the point where it is grammatically palatable to the most squeamish among us." The preferable constitutional result was simply to *leave matters of "taste and style" to the individual*, especially since "[o]ne man's vulgarity is another's lyric."

    ii. **Emotional content:** Secondly, this was not simply a situation in which Cohen chose vulgar words to express an idea that could have been equally well expressed by more polite language. The language chosen by Cohen, like much expression, conveyed not only an intellectual idea, but also *"otherwise inexpressible emotions."* The Constitution protects this *"emotive function"* of speech just as much as the cognitive content of expression.

    iii. **Smokescreen for censorship:** Finally, governments might often ban particular words as a *smokescreen* for banning the *expression of unpopular views*. "One [cannot] forbid particular words without also running a substantial risk of suppressing ideas in the process."

5. **Nazi-Skokie dispute:** The proposition that expression may not be banned merely because it will be "offensive" to those who are exposed to it, was put to a stern test in a confrontation between an *American Nazi group* and the Village of Skokie, Illinois. The resulting judicial opinions suggest that even speech which will undeniably cause *psychic pain* to listeners must not be suppressed, so long as the pain comes from the content of the speech.

   a. **Facts:** The Nazi group planned to demonstrate in front of the Skokie Village Hall. Skokie is a predominantly-Jewish community, and about 5,000 of its residents are survivors of the concentration camps. Just before the scheduled demonstration, the village enacted several ordinances designed to neutralize the demonstration, including one forbidding the dissemination of any materials which promote or incite racial or religious hatred. These materials were defined to include "public display of markings and clothing of symbolic significance," which the village would apparently have interpreted to include swastikas and military uniforms.

   b. **Holding:** Both the federal district and appeals courts reviewing this ordinance on the merits found it *unconstitutional*. (The case never reached the Supreme Court.) The court of appeals explicitly rejected the argument that the village had the right to prevent a substantive evil, the "infliction of psychic trauma on resident Holocaust survivors." *Collin v. Smith*, 578 F.2d 1197 (7th Cir. 1978).

      i. **Rationale:** The court noted that although the demonstration might be shocking to the village's residents, any shock effect would be due to the *content of the ideas expressed*, and "public expression of ideas may not be prohibited merely because the ideas are themselves offensive to some of their hearers."

      ii. **Not captive audience:** The court also stressed that the village's residents would not form a captive audience, since they could simply avoid the village hall area during the demonstration.

6. **Strict scrutiny to be used:** If the state *does* want to regulate speech on the grounds of its offensive content, the courts will use *strict scrutiny*. And that's true even if government is merely burdening the offensive speech rather than banning it outright. This was illustrated by a case involving the regulation of adult programming distributed on cable TV, *U.S. v. Playboy Entertainment Group, Inc.*, 529 U.S. 803 (2000).

   a. **Facts of *Playboy Entertainment*:** *Playboy Entertainment* involved a federal statute that had the effect of completely barring cable TV operators from broadcasting sexual explicit materials before 10 PM (a "time blocking" system). The industry wished to use a "signal scrambling" system instead of a time-blocking one, but Congress did not regard signal scrambling as sufficient to protect minors, because of the risk of "signal bleed" (a viewer's ability to hear the audio track, or see brief images, even when the signal was scrambled).

   b. **Playboy's argument:** Playboy, which operated the leading adult-programming channels, argued that the statute constituted content-based regulation and thus required strict scrutiny. Because less-restrictive alternatives were available (e.g., signal scrambling), Playboy contended, the statutory scheme must flunk that scrutiny.

**c.** **Court strikes down:** By a 5-4 vote, the Court agreed with Playboy that strict scrutiny must be used, and that the measure could not survive because of the availability of less-restrictive alternatives.

    **i.** **Content-based:** This was, the Court said, clearly "content-based" regulation, since Congress had chosen to regulate signal bleed only when it occurred in the transmission of sexually explicit adult programming, not other types of programming. The majority noted that "It is rare that a regulation restricting speech because of its content will ever be permissible."

    **ii.** **Less-restrictive alternative:** The majority then found that there was a ***less-restrictive alternative available***, causing the statute to fail strict scrutiny. That alternative was a scheme under which the default arrangement would be a not-quite-perfect scrambling (in which there might be some signal bleed some of the time), coupled with a right of any household to demand complete time-blocking of the signals to that home.

        **(1)** **Must tolerate some loss of effectiveness:** The Court seemed to be saying that a less-restrictive alternative must be used ***even if that alternative would not be quite as effective in achieving the government's goals*** — the chance that some parents might not learn about the voluntary time-blocking option, and their children might therefore be exposed to signal bleed, was not enough to prevent this alternative from being preferable to Congress' content-based scheme.

**d.** **Significance:** So *Playboy Entertainment* establishes clearly that when government regulates — not just bans — speech on the basis of its offensive content, strict scrutiny will apply.

**J.** **Regulation of "hate speech":** As we just saw, government may generally not prevent or punish words on the grounds that listeners will find them offensive. Groups interested in eliminating discrimination against ***minorities*** have argued that an exception should be made for ***"hate speech"*** directed against racial minorities, women, homosexuals, and other traditionally disfavored groups. State legislatures have generally agreed — all but four states have some form of "hate crime" law criminalizing bias-motivated speech or acts.

However, if government ***singles out bias-motivated speech***, criminalizing it while not criminalizing other types of angry speech, the government can properly be accused of acting in a forbidden ***content-based*** rather than content-neutral way. In a series of three cases since 1992, the Supreme Court has tried to lay out some rules for when government may single out hate speech and punish it specially. Two of the three cases have involved ***cross burning***, a particular form of hate speech that has a long history of expressing racial hatred (and, often, of preceding racial violence).

**1.** **Three rules:** These three cases stand for the following main propositions, which represent a general rule about what the state may not ban, and three exceptions to that major rule:

    ❑ **General ban:** A ban on speech or conduct intended or likely to incite anger or violence based solely on ***particular listed topics or motives*** — such as race, color, religion or gender hatred — is ***impermissibly content-based***. That's true even if all the speech/conduct banned falls within an ***"unprotected"*** category such as, here, ***"fighting words."*** (See *R.A.V., infra.*)

❏ **Worst examples:** However, a state *may* impose a content-based ban on *particular instances* of unprotected speech if the ban forbids *only the very worst examples* illustrating *the very reason the particular class of speech is unprotected.* (Thus the state may choose to criminalize just the very most dangerous "fighting words," the very most obscene obscene images, etc.) (*R.A.V.*)

❏ **Penalty-enhancement statutes:** Also, a state may identify particular generally-applicable criminal proscriptions, and may then choose to punish *more severely* those criminal acts that happen to be motivated by hate than those not motivated by hate. This is called the *"penalty enhancement"* approach. For instance, from within the overall class of acts that constitute criminal vandalism or arson, the state may punish vandalism or arson more seriously if it's motivated by bias against particular groups. (*Wisconsin v. Mitchell, infra,* p. 513.)

❏ **All intimidating acts:** Finally, a state may select a particular type of expressive act (e.g., cross-burning), and punish *all instances* where that act is done with a purpose of *intimidating or threatening* someone, even though the state doesn't punish other types of intimidating or threatening acts. (*Virginia v. Black, infra,* p. 513.)

2. **The general principle of *R.A.V. v. St. Paul*:** The first of this trio of Supreme Court cases on hate-speech was *R.A.V. v. City of St. Paul*, 505 U.S. 377 (1992). The case involved a *cross-burning*, but seems applicable to anti-hate-speech laws in general.

   a. **Facts:** In *R.A.V.*, D and several other teenagers allegedly burned a homemade cross inside the fenced yard of a black family that lived across the street from D; the incident took place in the middle of the night. D was prosecuted under the St. Paul "Bias-Motivated Crime Ordinance," which provided that "whoever places on public or private property a symbol, object, appellation, characterization or graffiti, including, but not limited to, a burning cross or Nazi swastika, which one knows or has reasonable grounds to know arouses anger, alarm or resentment in others on the basis of race, color, creed, religion or gender commits disorderly conduct and shall be guilty of a misdemeanor." D contended that the ordinance violated the First Amendment in two respects: (1) it was substantially overbroad; and (2) it was impermissibly content-based.

   b. **Court agrees:** The Court unanimously agreed that the ordinance, on its face, violated the First Amendment. However, the Court was bitterly split, 5-4, on the proper rationale.

   c. **Opinion of the Court:** Justice Scalia, joined by four other Justices (Rehnquist, Kennedy, Souter and Thomas), wrote the opinion for the Court. Scalia concluded that the law was *impermissibly content-based*, because "it prohibits otherwise permitted speech solely on the basis of the subjects the speech addresses."

      i. **Only applicable to "fighting words":** The Minnesota Supreme Court, in construing the ordinance, had concluded that it was intended to apply only to *"fighting words"* (see *supra*, p. 503), not to bias speech that would not threaten an immediate breach of the peace. Scalia believed that he had no choice but to accept the Minnesota court's construction of the statute.

      ii. **No content-based regulation of unprotected categories:** The Supreme Court had previously held, as noted (see *supra*, p. 503) that fighting words are an "unprotected category" under the First Amendment. But Scalia's opinion asserted that ***even when government is regulating a supposedly "unprotected" category, it may not do so in a content-based manner.***

**(1) Examples:** Scalia gave two examples of what he considered to be impermissibly content-based regulations of "unprotected" categories: The government may proscribe libel, but it may not make the further content discrimination of proscribing ***only*** libel critical of the government. Similarly, a city council may not enact an ordinance prohibiting only those legally obscene works that contain criticism of the city government.

**(2) Content based on "very reason for proscription of class":** Scalia acknowledged that there is an ***exception*** to the rule that even unprotected categories enjoy complete freedom from content-based regulation: when "the basis for the content discrimination consists ***entirely of the very reason the entire class of speech at issue is proscribable***, no significant danger of idea or viewpoint discrimination exists," and the content discrimination is allowed. Thus the state could choose to prohibit only "the most lascivious displays" of sexual activity, rather than all constitutionally-obscene materials; or, the federal government can (as it does) criminalize only those threats of violence that are directed against the President — in each case, the proscribed speech represents the most extreme instance of the reason why the whole category is unprotected in the first place (e.g., it is the "most obscene," or it is the "most dangerously violent").

iii. **Ordinance unconstitutional:** By Scalia's standard, the St. Paul ordinance was clearly ***unconstitutional***, even though applicable only to generally-unprotected "fighting words." The ordinance was certainly content-based, because it applied only to fighting words that insult or provoke violence "on the basis of race, color, creed, religion or gender" — abusive language, no matter how vicious or severe, was permitted under the ordinance unless it was addressed to one of the "specified disfavored topics"; fighting words used to express hostility based on political affiliation, union membership or homosexuality, for instance, were not covered by the ordinance.

**(1) Viewpoint based:** In fact, Scalia said, the ordinance was not only content-based but "***viewpoint*** based." That is, where two opposing sides had a confrontation concerning a matter of race or religion, one side could use fighting words while the other could not. "One could hold up a sign saying, for example, that all 'anti-catholic bigots' are misbegotten; but not that all 'papists' are, for that would insult and provoke violence 'on the basis of religion.' " St. Paul has no authority, Scalia asserted, "to license one side of a debate to fight free-style, while requiring the other to follow Marquis of Queensbury Rules."

iv. **Remedy:** Proponents of the ordinance argued that even if it was content-based, it could survive the strict scrutiny given to content-based regulations because it was necessary to serve a compelling state interest. Scalia conceded that the state had a compelling interest in safeguarding the rights of traditionally-disfavored groups, including their right to live in peace where they wish. But he argued that the ordinance was not *"necessary"* to achieve this state interest, because there were *"adequate content-neutral alternatives."* In particular, St. Paul could enact an ordinance prohibiting *all* fighting words, not merely fighting words motivated by racial, religious or other specifically-enumerated biases. To Scalia, burning a cross in someone's front yard is "reprehensible," but St. Paul had "sufficient means at its disposal to prevent such behaviour without adding the First Amendment to the fire."

    **d. Concurrence:** The main concurrence in *R.A.V.* (by Justice White, joined by Blackmun, O'Connor and, in most respects, Stevens) read more like a dissent.

        **i. Unprotected categories:** Justice White believed that where a category is "unprotected," the states are *not* prevented from regulating it on the basis of content. "It is inconsistent to hold that the government may proscribe an entire category of speech because the content of that speech is evil … but that the government may not treat a subset of that category differently without violating the First Amendment; the content of the subset is by definition worthless and undeserving of constitutional protection."

        **ii. Strict scrutiny:** Second, White contended, even if the principle of content-neutrality should be applicable to unprotected categories (which, of course, White thought that it should not), the principle merely required strict scrutiny, not a total ban. In White's view, the ordinance here could *survive* strict scrutiny. But White disagreed even with the use of strict scrutiny at all — he argued that the only test that regulation of "unprotected speech" should have to satisfy is that it be "rationally related to a legitimate government interest" (a test imposed, he argued, by the Equal Protection Clause, not the First Amendment). By this standard, the St. Paul ordinance was clearly valid.

            **(1) Overbreadth:** White asserted that the case should instead have been decided on *overbreadth* grounds. He interpreted the Minnesota court to have ruled that the ordinance prohibited expression that "by its very utterance" causes "anger, alarm or resentment." By this interpretation, the ordinance reached not only words tending to incite an immediate breach of the peace (words which may constitutionally be proscribed), but also words and expressive conduct that cause *only* hurt feelings, offense, or resentment (words and conduct which may not be constitutionally proscribed). Since the ordinance reached both protected and unprotected speech, it was overbroad, and thus invalid.

    **e. Effect on other provisions:** The Court's approach in *R.A.V.* *invalidates* many anti-hate crime statutes that, like St. Paul's, define certain activities as a *new, separate, crime*. These statutes typically turn on the offender's *motive* for the conduct — thus an epithet, a cross-burning, or act of intimidation becomes criminal if it is committed "on account of" the victim's race, religion, gender, etc. Since the legislature has chosen to proscribe expression motivated by some types of animus (e.g., race) but not other types of animus (e.g., sexual orientation), these statutes are invalid in the same way that the St. Paul ordinance was invalid, as being non-content-neutral.

    **3. Enhancement-of-penalty statutes are still valid:** But *R.A.V.* does *not invalidate* statutes that approach the hate-speech problem in a quite different way: these statutes punish *existing crimes* like vandalism and arson *more seriously* if the prosecution shows that the crime was motivated in part by one of the listed types of bias. The Court found such a ***"penalty enhancement"*** statute to be ***valid***, in ***Wisconsin v. Mitchell***, 508 U.S. 476 (1993). This unanimous decision seems to validate all of the dozens of state and local hate-crime laws of the "penalty enhancement" variety throughout the country.

   **a.**  **Facts:**  In *Wisconsin v. Mitchell*, D, a black teenager, was convicted of aggravated battery, a crime that in Wisconsin ordinarily carries a maximum sentence of two years in prison. However, there was strong evidence that D had selected his victim, V, based on race; for instance, he pointed to V, told his friends, "There goes a white boy; go get him," then led them in a severe beating of V. Under Wisconsin's statute, the maximum sentence for aggravated battery was increased to seven years because of D's race-based selection of a victim.

   **b.**  **Statute upheld:**  The Court unanimously held that this penalty-enhancement scheme did not violate D's First Amendment rights, and thus ***upheld*** the statute.

      **i.**  **Defendant's argument:**  D argued in *Mitchell* that since the only reason for the enhanced sentence was his discriminatory motive for selecting his victim, the statute punished his beliefs. Therefore, he argued, the penalty-enhancement statute was no more constitutionally acceptable than the ban on certain "fighting words" struck down in *R.A.V.*

      **ii.**  **Speech/ conduct distinction:**  But the Court rejected this argument. In doing so, the Court relied heavily on the old distinction between speech and conduct. The ordinance struck down in *R.A.V.* was explicitly directed at expression, whereas the penalty-enhancement statute here was aimed at conduct, and this conduct was completely unprotected by the First Amendment. (That is, there is no constitutional protection for the act of battery, whatever the actor's motive.)

      **iii.**  **Analogy to anti-discrimination laws:**  The Court also observed that many other statutes punish a defendant based on his motive for acting. For instance, federal Title VII makes it unlawful for an employer to discriminate against an employee "because of such individual's race, color, religion, sex, ... ", yet that statute has always been found to conform with the First Amendment.

**4.**  **Ban on all acts intended to intimidate:**  Finally, in the most recent cutting back on the general rule of *R.A.V.*, the Court has held that ***all instances*** of a certain type of expressive act — such as cross-burning — may be prohibited if done for the purpose of ***intimidation or threat***, even if other intimidating acts with expressive content are not prohibited. ***Virginia v. Black***, 538 U.S. 343 (2003).

   **a.**  **Statute:**  The statute at issue in *Black* made a crime to burn a cross in a public place or on the property of another, if done "with the intent of ***intimidating any person or group of persons.***" The statute also added a clause (we'll refer to it here as the "prima facie" clause) saying that "Any such burning of a cross shall be prima facie evidence of an intent to intimidate[.]"

   **b.**  **Two sets of defendants:**  Two different criminal cases were consolidated by the Supreme Court for review in *Black*; the two cases differed from each other with respect to use of the prima facie clause. In one case, Barry Black, a Ku Klux Klan member who supervised a cross burning in an open field, was convicted after the jury was instructed based on the prima facie clause. (The jury was told that "the burning of a cross by itself is sufficient evidence from which you may infer the required intent [to intimidate]".) In the other case, the two defendants, Elliott and O'Mara, attempted to burn a cross in the yard of Elliott's next-door neighbor. O'Mara pled guilty; Elliott was convicted by a jury that was not told of the prima facie clause and that was told merely that they must find that the defendant had intended to intimidate another person when he burned the cross. Thus Black's conviction was dependent upon use of the prima facie clause, but Elliott's and O'Mara's were not.

c.  **Main provision upheld:**  The Court's opinion in *Black* was fragmented — there was no opinion that spoke for a majority on all points. But there were separate majorities for two propositions: (1) that government may *single out cross burning* as a particularly virulent form of intimidation, and may thus *ban all cross burnings done with intent to intimidate* even while not banning other expressive acts intended to intimidate; and (2) that the statute here was *unconstitutional* (though no majority agreed about why). Let us examine these two propositions one at a time.

   i.  **Government may single out cross-burning:**  Six justices believed that Virginia could *ban any cross-burning done with intent to intimidate another,* even if the state did *not criminalize other intimidating messages.* On this point, Justice O'Connor wrote for all six of these justices (all Justices but Souter, Ginsburg and Kennedy). Cross burning is "a particularly virulent form of intimidation." Therefore, "[i]nstead of prohibiting all intimidating messages, Virginia may choose to *regulate this subset of intimidating messages* in light of cross burning's long and pernicious history as a *signal of impending violence.*"

      **(1) State may prohibit worst instances:**  To O'Connor, singling out cross burning was merely an application of *R.A.V.*'s prior holding that a state may choose to criminalize just those instances that represent the *very worst illustrations* of the *very reason why an entire category is unprotected* by the First Amendment. "Just as a State may regulate only that obscenity which is the most obscene due to its prurient content, so too may a State choose to prohibit only those forms of intimidation that are most likely to inspire fear of bodily harm."

      **(2) Thomas' dissent:**  Justice Thomas's position on this issue was noteworthy. He believed that O'Connor's view did not go far enough. Thomas summarized the history of the Ku Klux Klan's use of cross burning, and concluded that "In our culture, cross burning has almost invariably meant lawlessness and understandably instills in its victims well-grounded fear of physical violence." Consequently, he said, in those cases covered by the statute — that is, those in which cross burning was done for the purpose of intimidation — the statute "prohibits *only conduct*, not expression." Therefore, the statute *should not trigger First Amendment analysis at all.* "Just as one cannot burn down someone's house to make a political point and then seek refuge in the First Amendment, those who hate cannot terrorize and intimidate to make their point."

   ii.  **Prima facie clause unconstitutional:**  Four justices (O'Connor, joined on this point by Rehnquist, Stevens and Breyer) believed, however, that the *prima facie clause* rendered the statute *unconstitutional*, at least as applied to Black's case, where the jury was instructed on the clause's effect. (Remember that this clause said that any cross burning "shall be prima facie evidence of an intent to intimidate.") For O'Connor, the clause "strips away the very reason why a state may ban cross burning with the intent to intimidate." A burning cross is not always intended to intimidate, O'Connor said — for instance, a cross is sometimes burned at Klan gatherings as a "symbol of group solidarity," rather than as an attempt to intimidate. Therefore, the prima facie clause ***"chills constitutionally protected political speech*** because of the possibility that a State will prosecute — and potentially convict — somebody engaging only in *lawful political speech* at the core of what the First Amendment is designed to protect." The clause "ignores all of the ***contextual factors*** that are necessary to decide whether a particular cross burning is intended to intimidate."

(1) **Souter's dissent:**  Although only three other justices joined O'Connor's opinion that the prima facie clause rendered the statute unconstitutional, another three (Souter, joined by Kennedy and Ginsburg) believed that the statute was probably an unconstitutional content-based distinction within the category of intimidating or threatening expressions, even in the absence of the prima facie provision. But these three agreed with O'Connor that the prima facie clause made matters worse.

iii. **Outcome:**  In terms of the fates of the particular parties in *Black*, the outcome was split. Black's conviction was overturned with no possibility of retrial, because he wasn't charged with intimidating anyone, and his conviction depended on the unconstitutional prima facie clause. But Elliott and O'Mara could be retried, since their convictions did not depend on the prima facie clause.

d. **Significance:**  *Black* is significant mainly for the proposition that a properly-constructed statute may ***ban a particular type of intimidating expression*** — such as cross burning — while ***declining to ban other types of intimidating expressions***.

i. **Ruling on prima facie clause:**  The Court's ruling striking down the ***prima facie clause*** is of much less practical importance, since a state will be able to draft a statute without that type of clause and still get convictions as long as there is some evidence — even if circumstantial — that the defendant intended to intimidate another. Indeed, by the time *Black* was decided by the court, Virginia had already amended its statute to remove the prima facie provision.

5. **University codes:**  Many ***colleges*** and ***universities*** have enacted campus hate speech regulations, which generally forbid one student from insulting or harassing another based on race, ethnicity, religion, sexual orientation, or other enumerated factors. It seems likely that ***public*** universities, as the result of *R.A.V.* and its progeny, may not single out particular types of "hate message" for proscription.

a. **The Michigan regulation:**  For example, the University of Michigan prohibits "physical acts or threats or verbal slurs, invectives, or epithets referring to an individual's ***race, ethnicity, religion, sex, sexual orientation, creed, national origin, ancestry, age or handicap*** made with the purpose of injuring the person to whom the words or actions are directed and that are not made as part of a discussion or exchange of an idea, ideology or philosophy." The Michigan regulation is probably too broad, in light of *R.A.V.* To the extent that this regulation singles out ***only certain topics or messages*** (it does not, for example ban one person from calling another a "grade grubber" or a "male chauvinist pig") it seems vulnerable to exactly the sort of objection that brought down the St. Paul ordinance in *R.A.V.* — the objection of being non-content-neutral where a content-neutral alternative (banning *all* speech in a broad category) was available. After *R.A.V.*, University of Michigan officials were reported to be considering changing the regulation to ban all violence and intimidation against any person, without reference to the actor's motivation or the content of his speech. See *New York Times*, June 24, 1992, B13, col. 4. Such a ban on all violence and intimidation seems perfectly fine in light of *Virginia v. Black, supra.*

6. **"Unprotected" categories now partly protected:**   One aspect of *R.A.V.* that is especially surprising is that a majority of the Court has given a major degree of First Amendment protection to so-called ***"unprotected"*** categories. Prior to *R.A.V.*, nothing in any opinion by the Court signaled that speech falling into categories like defamation, fighting words or obscenity was protected in any way. Now, under *R.A.V.*, we have the principle that the state must behave in a content-neutral manner even with respect to speech falling into these categories, unless the expression is regulated in a content-based way "because of [the expression's] constitutionally proscribable content" (as the majority put it in *R.A.V.*).

   a. **Illustration:** Thus the state may choose to ban only those obscene works that are in some sense "especially prurient," or only those libelous works where the defamation is especially untrue or especially hurtful to the target. But the state may not ban only libels directed at the government, and presumably may not punish libels of political figures more heavily than libels against, say, private citizens.

K. **Injunctions against expressive conduct:**   So far, when we have looked at restrictions on speech or on expressive conduct, we have been assuming that the restrictions come either in the form of a generally-applicable statute, or in the form of a permit or license requirement. There is an additional form of government restriction on expression: the ***injunction*** issued by a judge. But when a court issues an injunction that serves as a kind of "time, place and manner" restriction, the injunction will be subjected to slightly more ***stringent*** review than would a generally-applicable statute containing the same substance. *Madsen v. Women's Health Center, Inc.*, 512 U.S. 753 (1994). The test is whether the injunction "burdens ***no more speech than necessary*** to serve a significant governmental interest."

1. **"Buffer zone" around abortion clinic upheld:** Injunctions will certainly sometimes survive this level of scrutiny. For instance, in *Madsen, supra*, abortion protesters had — in defiance of an earlier injunction — repeatedly blocked access to an abortion clinic and had harassed patients and doctors both at the clinic and at their homes. The trial court then issued a second injunction that, *inter alia*, created a 36-foot ***"buffer zone"*** around the entrance to the clinic. In this buffer zone, which covered the street and sidewalks near the clinic, protesters were prohibited from demonstrating. The Supreme Court ***upheld*** this buffer zone, finding that it "burden[ed] no more speech than necessary" to accomplish the state's interests in safeguarding the safety and health of clinic staff and patients and in maintaining traffic flow.

   a. **"Floating" buffer zone struck down:** But not every buffer zone ordered to allow access to a facility will be upheld. For instance, in another post-*Madsen* case, the Court ***struck down*** a ***"floating"*** buffer zone, under which abortion protesters were ordered not to approach ***within fifteen feet of any person or vehicle*** entering or leaving an abortion clinic. This floating zone, the Court held, would unduly interfere with protesters' attempts to demonstrate peacefully. *Schenck v. Pro-Choice Network of Western New York*, 519 U.S. 357 (1997). (On the other hand an ***eight-foot*** floating zone, applicable within 100 feet of any abortion clinic or other healthcare facility, was ***upheld*** by the Court, in *Hill v. Colorado, supra*, p. 500. This was not an injunction case.)

**L. All speech not necessarily created equal (the disfavoring of indecent speech):** Implicit in *Cohen v. California, supra*, p. 506, is the principle that all constitutionally-protected expression is ***created equal*** in the eyes of the First Amendment, so that the government ***may not prefer certain ideas or subject matter to others.*** But a number of cases suggest that a majority of the present Court believes that certain types of expression, while not directly suppressible on the grounds of their content, are inherently ***less valuable*** and may therefore be ***regulated more extensively*** than speech closer to the "core" of First Amendment values, such as political speech. This less-favored of speech seems to include mainly speech that is "*indecent*."[1] This is sometimes referred to as the ***"two-tier"*** theory of First Amendment protection.[2]

    **1.** *American Mini Theatres,* **and the two-tier theory:** The first case strongly suggesting a possible "two-tier" theory of First Amendment protection was ***Young v. American Mini Theatres***, 427 U.S. 50 (1976), an indecent-speech case.

        **a. Facts:** The case presented the constitutionality of Detroit's ***"anti-skid row ordinance,"*** which required theaters specializing in "adult movies" to be geographically dispersed from each other and from "adult bookstores." The city defended the ordinance on the grounds that it was merely a zoning law, which grew out of the tendency of red-light districts to have high crime rates and low property values.

        **b. Lesser value:** A plurality opinion by Justice Stevens ***upheld*** the ordinance against several constitutional attacks, including the contention that the ordinance impaired certain protected speech (non-obscene "adult" films and books) based on its content. In rejecting this argument, Stevens (speaking for four Justices) contended that the sort of expression involved here was of ***lesser value*** than other types of speech, especially political debate. The need for free political speech is clear to all of us, yet "few of us would march our sons and daughters off to war to preserve the citizen's right to see 'Specified Sexual Activities' exhibited in the theaters of our choice." Such sexually-explicit, but non-obscene, materials could not be completely suppressed, but they could be ***regulated to an extent to which political speech could not.***

            **i. Two-tier theory:** Thus Stevens seemed in *American Mini Theatres* to be advocating a ***"two-tier"*** approach to First Amendment speech, by which some types of speech are less deserving of full First Amendment protection than are others.

        **c. Dissent:** The four dissenters objected strongly to the plurality's "lesser value" theory. "[I]f the guarantees of the First Amendment were reserved for expression that more than a 'few of us' would take up arms to defend, then the right of free expression

---

1. *Commercial* speech also seems to be somewhat less-favored. See *infra*, p. 567.

2. Don't confuse this "two-tier" theory with the "two track" analysis on p. 465 *supra*. "Two-tier" refers to the Court's distinction based on the "value" of the speech. "Two track" refers to two ways of analyzing restrictions on speech, one track for content-based regulations and the other for content-neutral time-place-and-manner regulations.

would be defined and circumscribed by ***current popular opinion***. ... " The dissent believed that time, place and manner regulations must be strictly content-neutral except in the "limited context of a captive or juvenile audience."

    **d.  Powell's "swing vote":**  The ordinance was upheld only because of Justice Powell's "swing vote," expressed in a separate concurrence. Powell declined to join Stevens' "lesser value" rationale. Instead, he believed that the ordinance's effect on First Amendment interests was "incidental and minimal." Also, here the city was not acting for the purpose of regulating the ***content*** of the films (as, in his opinion, it had in *Erznoznik*); instead, it was acting in pursuit of governmental interests "wholly ***unrelated to the regulation of expression.*** "

**2.  Ban on child pornography:**  A ***majority*** of the Court eventually endorsed Justice Stevens' view that some types of speech, although they are entitled to some First Amendment protection, may have such slight value that they can be regulated, or even prohibited, based on their content, if the state has a sufficiently strong interest for doing so. See *New York v. Ferber*, 458 U.S. 747 (1982) (discussed *infra*, p. 563), holding that the distribution of non-obscene materials showing ***children engaged in sexual conduct*** could be barred, in view of the "exceedingly modest, if not *de minimis*" First Amendment value of the speech, and the state's countervailing, compellingly strong interest in stopping sexual exploitation of child actors.

**3.  The "secondary effects" doctrine:**  So in what way may lesser-valued speech like indecent speech be more extensively regulated than high-value speech? An important difference between the two types of speech is that the ***"secondary-effects"*** doctrine seems to apply to this lesser-valued speech.

    **a.  Nature of the doctrine:**  Under the secondary-effects doctrine, if the court is satisfied that the government was merely trying to eliminate the undesirable ***non-content-related consequences*** of an expressive activity — things like increased crime, or declining property values — the regulation will be found to be ***content-neutral*** and will be given only relatively un-strict "track two" review. Furthermore, in cases qualifying for the secondary-effects doctrine, the Court seems unusually willing to find that the measure *passes* that track two review. That is, the Court typically accepts that the government is indeed pursuing an important interest, and that the regulatory means being chosen appropriately further that interest while leaving open adequate alternative channels for communication.

    **b.  *Renton,* and the operation of adult theaters:**  The case that gave birth to the secondary-effects doctrine was ***Renton v. Playtime Theatres, Inc.,*** 475 U.S. 41 (1986). There, a four-Justice plurality upheld a municipal zoning ordinance that prohibited adult movie theaters from locating in about 94% of the city's land.

        **i.  Rationale:**  The plurality reasoned that because the city's "predominant intent" was to combat the secondary effects of adult theaters — the ordinance recited that it was designed to ***prevent crime***, protect the city's retail trade, maintain property values and protect the quality of the city's neighborhoods — the ordinance was ***content-neutral***. Therefore, it could be upheld as long as it was "designed to serve a substantial governmental interest and allows for reasonable alternative avenues of communication." The Court then quickly found that the ordinance satisfied this test, especially since "some 520 acres, or more than 5% of the entire land area of [the city]," was left open for use as adult theater sites.

ii. **Blackmun's concurrence:** Justice Blackmun furnished the fifth vote in *Renton*, by concurring in the result without opinion. Therefore, it is plausible to interpret *Renton* as five votes for the proposition that statutes that regulate indecent or otherwise-low-valued expressive conduct in order to combat the conduct's secondary effects will be viewed as content-neutral and not strictly scrutinized.

iii. **Same result under 2002 case:** A 2002 case has seemed to produce exactly the same result as in *Renton*: five votes for the proposition that statutes that regulate indecent conduct for the purpose of combating the conduct's secondary effects (e.g., extra crime) will be treated as content-netural and therefore given ***intermediate scrutiny,*** rather than strict scrutiny for being content-based. See *Los Angeles v. Alameda Books*, 535 U.S. 425 (2002).

iv. **Summary:** So as the result of *Renton*, where a city regulates indecent expression for the ***purpose*** of ***combatting secondary effects*** rather than trying to suppress messages it doesn't like, the regulation will not be strictly scrutinized so long as the regulation ***does not substantially reduce the amount of such speech***. Instead, the regulation will be given ***mid-level review***, and will be upheld if substantially related to the goal of combatting secondary effects (like an increase in crime).

c. ***Erie v. Pap's* expands the doctrine to allow a complete ban:** *Renton* seemed to say merely that government may combat the secondary effects of undesirable expressive conduct by limiting the ***geographic location*** in which that conduct occurs. But a 2000 case seems to dramatically ***expand*** the impact of the secondary effects doctrine, by holding that the doctrine may result in a ***complete ban*** (not just a geographical limitation) on the disfavored expressive conduct. The case is ***Erie v. Pap's A.M.***, 529 U.S. 277 (2000).

i. **Facts:** *Pap's* was a ***"nude dancing"*** case. The city of Erie, Pa. passed an ordinance that required live dancers to wear at least "pasties" and a "G-string." (Neither the city nor anyone else claimed that nude dancing was obscene and therefore constitutionally unprotected.) The city said that it was attacking not the expressive content of nude live entertainment, but rather its secondary effects, such as violence, sexual harassment, public intoxication, prostitution, and the spread of sexually transmitted diseases. The ban applied throughout the city, not just in an delimited area. A nightclub that presented live nude dancers attacked the ordinance.

ii. **Plurality:** The Court ***upheld*** the ordinance. However, there was no majority opinion on the underlying constitutional issues. As in *Renton* and *Los Angeles v. Alameda Books*, a four-Justice plurality (opinion by O'Connor, joined by Rehnquist, Kennedy and Breyer) found that the secondary-effects doctrine applied, so that the ordinance should be judged by the more-forgiving track two analysis for ***content-neutral*** time-place-and-manner regulations.

(1) **Bad motivation irrelevant:** In fact, to the plurality it didn't even matter that the city may have been ***motivated in part*** by a desire to ***suppress particular expression***. According to the plurality, as long as *one* of the purposes of the

regulation was to combat secondary effects, it didn't matter that government also had the motive of suppressing speech.

**(2) Passes track-two analysis:** The plurality then found it easy to conclude that the ordinance satisfied the track-two time-place-and-manner standard.

iii. **Additional votes:** Justices Scalia and Thomas concurred. They believed that because the ordinance was a "general law regulating conduct and not specifically directed at expression," the ordinance was *not subject to First Amendment scrutiny at all.* Therefore, they agreed that the ordinance easily passed constitutional muster.

iv. **6 votes for using secondary-effects analysis:** So there now seem to be at least six votes on the Court for holding that even an *absolute government ban* on a particular form of expressive conduct motivated by a desire to combat the conduct's secondary effects is to be viewed as *content-neutral*, and may be upheld if the ban is a reasonably effective means of combating those effects. Thus the secondary-effects doctrine will now apparently justify a much *broader range* of regulation, not just the geographic limitations for which the doctrine had previously been used.

v. **Limited to indecency or other less-favored speech:** So far, the secondary-effects doctrine has not been applied outside of the *indecency* context. Thus as far as we know, government can't attack what it says are the bad secondary effects of protected speech other than indecency (e.g., *core political speech*) except by surviving strict scrutiny.

**M. Regulation of indecency in media:** A number of cases have dealt with *indecency in the media.* A brief summary of the Court's holdings is that the government has substantial latitude in regulating indecent expression on the *public airwaves* (over-the-air *TV and radio* broadcasts) but much less latitude when it tries to carry out such regulation in media that are more one-on-one, such as *phone systems,* modern individually-addressable *cable TV systems,* and *computer networks* such as the *Internet.*

1. **Over-the-air broadcasts (the *Pacifica* case):** The main case on when government can combat indecency in radio and TV broadcasting is *FCC v. Pacifica Foundation*, 438 U.S. 726 (1978). There, a 3-Justice plurality advanced the view (deriving from *Young v. American Mini Theatres*, *supra*, p. 517) that not all First-Amendment-protected speech is precisely equal in its susceptibility to context-regulation (the "two-tier" theory). The plurality opinion was written by Justice Stevens.

a. **Facts:** WBAI, a listener-supported radio station, broadcast early one weekday afternoon a monologue by satirist George Carlin. The monologue, which was broadcast as part of a WBAI program on attitudes toward language, was about the seven dirty words which "you definitely wouldn't say ever" on the public airwaves (listed by Carlin as including "fuck," "cocksucker" and "cunt," among others.) The FCC, responding to a single complaint from a motorist who claimed that he had heard the broadcast while driving with his young son, concluded that the broadcast was "indecent" (though not obscene), and claimed that it had authority to issue sanctions against the station (though it did not do so).

i. **FCC's rationale:** The FCC did not assert that it could ban non-obscene but "indecent" language from all airwaves at all times. Rather, it contended that principles analogous to those of ***nuisance*** could be applied, making ***context*** all-important. Therefore, the FCC believed, it could keep this kind of language off the airwaves in early afternoon, when children were likely to be in the audience.

b. **FCC upheld:** The Court ***upheld*** the FCC's view, though there was no majority opinion on the constitutional issues. Justice Steven's three-justice plurality on the core First Amendment questions called the seven words "obnoxious, gutter language" which "ordinarily lack[s] literary, political, or scientific value. ... " While these words are entitled to some First Amendment protection, their ***"social value"*** depends on the ***context*** in which they are used. Therefore, the FCC had the ***right to take context into account***, and to hold that even First-Amendment-protected language may be prohibited in contexts where it is especially offensive, just as a "nuisance may be merely a right thing in the wrong place — like a pig in the parlor instead of the barnyard" (quoting a prior Supreme Court nuisance case).

   i. **Context:** In Stevens' view, there were two ways in which the context of the WBAI broadcast was especially inappropriate for these indecent words: (1) the broadcast media are a "uniquely pervasive presence," and confront the citizen in the ***"privacy of the home."*** A person who stumbles upon language like Carlin's is in effect a ***captive audience*** for at least that instant until he can switch to another station; thus prior warnings of the material's offensive nature (which were in fact given by WBAI) were insufficient to nullify this assault on privacy; and (2) broadcasting is "uniquely ***accessible to children,"*** even those too young to read. The ***early-afternoon time*** of the broadcast made this problem particularly acute.

c. **Disagreement with Stevens' view:** Four members of the Court explicitly rejected Justice Stevens' assertion that this kind of language was of lesser value, and therefore more regulable, than other types of speech. (Two did so in a concurrence and the other two in a dissent.) Two more Justices dissented on grounds of statutory interpretation. But the Commission's order was upheld because the concurring Justices agreed that protection of children from inappropriate broadcast materials was more difficult than in the case of other materials, since there can be no physical separation of audiences; they also agreed that the fact that broadcasting comes directly into the home made a significant difference.

   i. **Dissent:** The two dissenters on constitutional grounds, Brennan and Marshall, did not object only to Justice Stevens' two-tier First Amendment theory. They also disagreed that the fact that broadcasting comes into the home makes a constitutional difference; the radio can be turned off with a minimum of effort, and the listener who stumbles onto offensive material for a few seconds is no worse off than the unsuspecting passers-by in *Cohen v. California* — both groups can, and are required to, simply ***avert their attention.***

      (1) **Minors:** These two dissenters also contended that the government may not shield minors from "indecent" language, unless that language is ***constitutionally obscene as to them;*** the Constitution leaves the protection of juveniles from non-obscene language ***to their parents***, not to the government.

**(2) Emotive power of words:**   Finally, the dissenters disagreed with Stevens' argument that the FCC was objecting not to Carlin's "point of view" (that our attitude towards these words is silly), but to the "way in which it is expressed." A given word may have a "unique capacity to capsule an idea, evoke an emotion, or conjure up an image." The dissenters saw this decision as being "another of the dominant culture's inevitable efforts to force those groups who do not share its mores to conform to its way of thinking, acting and speaking."

d.  **Significance:**   Superficially, the result in *Pacifica* may not seem any more hostile to "offensive" language than, say, *American Mini Theatres or Pap's*. But in reality, it is probably much more so. The ordinances in *American Mini Theatres* and *Pap's* were aimed at the "secondary effects" (increased crime, neighborhood deterioration, etc.) accompanying the concentrated display of certain types of films or live nude dancing; in *Pacifica*, by contrast, the harm that the FCC was aiming at was the ***speech itself.***

e.  **Criticism:**   The case has provoked criticism by a number of commentators.

   i.  **Gunther's view:**   Gunther, for instance, states that the case comes down to "majority support of a prohibition of speech because it is offensive to the audience. [And] that is startlingly bad news." Gunther (12th Ed.), p. 1163. He points out that under *Pacifica's* rationale, the FCC ought to stop announcers on southern radio stations who use the word "nigger." And ultimately, he argues, the same logic would permit the Village of Skokie to ban the swastika (see *supra*, p. 508). *Id.*

   ii.  **Self-censorship:**   Since most broadcasters (and virtually all commercially-supported ones) engage in "self-regulation" to start with, which prevents them from doing anything that might offend majoritarian tastes, only "maverick" stations like WBAI, usually listener-supported ones, would be likely to defy majoritarian tastes; *Pacifica* may remove the last traces of non-majoritarian programming.

2.  **Regulation of indecency on phone, cable and computer systems:** *Pacifica, supra,* indicated that the government could restrict non-obscene "indecent" material broadcast over the air. But several post-*Pacifica* cases have made it clear that when government tries to limit indecency in ***other media*** that are not as intrusive and widely-disseminated, the limits will be ***strictly scrutinized.*** These cases have involved ***phone networks*** ("dial-a-porn") ***cable TV*** systems, and the ***Internet.***

   a.  **Phone networks (the "dial-a-porn" case):** The case involving indency on ***phone networks*** is a ***"dial-a-porn"*** case, *Sable Communications, Inc. v. FCC*, 492 U.S. 115 (1989). There, the Court struck down a federal statute that made it a crime to make "any obscene or indecent communication for commercial purposes" by interstate telephone call, even if the defendant is the callee rather than caller.

      i.  **Government's argument:** Congress' intent was to prohibit dial-a-porn services, i.e., those that charge callers to hear pre-recorded sexually-oriented messages. The government conceded that as to messages that were "indecent" (but not "obscene"), a ban directed at adults would not be constitutional. But the government argued that the interest in preventing ***children*** from hearing indecent messages justified a total prohibition (i.e., one applicable to adults as well as children).

ii. **Holding:** However, the Court disagreed with the government. The Court agreed that preventing access by minors was an important interest. But the situation was different from the over-the-air broadcasts at issue in *Pacifica*: "[Placing] a telephone call is not the same as turning on a radio and being taken by surprise by an indecent message." Therefore, the government's total prohibition was ***insufficiently closely tailored*** to achieving the governmental interest, in view of other technological solutions that were available (e.g., requiring payment by credit card, access codes, scrambling, etc.). The Court appeared to be applying strict scrutiny, though it did not use that phrase.

b. **Cable programming:** When government tries to perform content-based regulation of indecent speech on ***cable TV systems***, the court will use ***strict scrutiny,*** just as it does in the dial-a-porn situation. Thus a federal statute effectively requiring that cable systems completely block transmission of sexually-explicit material except during late-night hours was strictly scrutinized, and struck down, in *U.S. v. Playboy Entertainment Group, Inc.*, 529 U.S. 803 (2000). The case is more extensively discussed *supra*, p. 508.

   i. ***Denver Area* case:** Similarly, the Court struck down aspects of a prior congressional attempt to regulate indecency in cable TV, in *Denver Area Educational Telecommunications Consortium v. FCC*, 518 U.S. 727 (1996). This was a highly technical and complex holding that doesn't merit a detailed discussion.

   ii. **Less restriction permissible:** *Playboy Entertainment* and *Denver Area* make it clear that much less regulation of indecency will be tolerated in the cable TV area than in the broadcast area, because of cable's technological ability to ***block access on a household-by-household basis.*** Since content-based restrictions will be strictly scrutinized, any reasonably-effective less-restrictive alternative must be used. Therefore, government, instead of curtailing transmission of indecent material to *all* households, must instead give cable operators the right to offer blocking to ***just those households that want it.***

c. **Indecency on the Internet:** What about ***"cyberspace,"*** and in particular the ***Internet***? Is the Internet more like over-the-air broadcasting (as to which the Court has traditionally allowed substantial government regulation), or is it more like books and newspapers (which receive the greatest First Amendment freedom)? The Supreme Court has answered this question by saying that the Internet ***more closely resembles books and newspapers,*** and is therefore deserving of the ***utmost freedom from content regulation***. The Court did so in two major opinions concerning Congress' efforts to restrict the access of ***minors*** to ***indecent content*** over the Internet.

   i. ***Reno v. ACLU*:** The first of the two cases was ***Reno v. American Civil Liberties Union***, 521 U.S. 844 (1997). The plaintiffs attacked two provisions of the federal Communications Decency Act (CDA). The first provision made it a crime to use a "telecommunications device" to transmit any communication which is "obscene or ***indecent***," while "***knowing that the recipient*** of the communication is under 18 years of age." The second made it a crime to "use any interactive computer service" to "display in a manner ***available to a person under 18***," any communication that uses ***"patently offensive"*** language or images. (For easy reference, we'll call the first provision the "knowing transmission" provision and the second the "make available" provision.) Both provisions were directed mainly at the Internet.

(1) **Unanimously struck down:**   All nine Justices agreed that at least parts of the CDA were *unconstitutional*. All nine agreed that the "make available" provision violated the First Amendment, and seven believed that the "knowing transmission" one did as well. The Court's opinion was by Justice Stevens, who found the CDA to be both overly vague and overbroad.

(2) **Less risk of intrusion:**   Stevens concluded that the burden on government to justify content regulation of the Internet was much greater than for such regulation of over-the-air broadcasting. Over-the-air broadcasting merited regulation in part because there was no way to adequately *protect the listener from unexpected messages.* By contrast, the risk that a computer user would *stumble upon* indecent material by accident was *"remote,"* because "a series of affirmative steps is required to access specific material." So cases like *Pacifica* furnished no support for a finding that the CDA was constitutional.

(3) **Statute found overbroad:**   Stevens concluded that the statute was *overbroad*, because it restricted the free-speech rights of *adults*. "In order to deny minors access to potentially harmful speech, the CDA effectively suppresses a large amount of speech that *adults have a constitutional right to receive* and to address to one another." For instance, if one member of a 100-person chat group was a minor, the entire group would be foreclosed from discussing an "indecent" topic, even though the 99 adults clearly had a right to discuss that topic.

(4) **Fails strict scrutiny:**   This suppression of protected adult speech had to survive *strict scrutiny*, Stevens said. Therefore, the government had to show that there was *no less restrictive alternative* that would accomplish the same ends. The government had failed to carry this burden, he concluded. For instance, the government might have just imposed the less-restrictive alternative that indecent material be "tagged" so that user-installed filters could block it.

ii.  **Replacement statute is also found invalid:**   After *Reno*, Congress tried to fix the CDA's constitutional problems by enacting a replacement statute, the *Child Online Protection Act (COPA)*. But in *Ashcroft v. American Civil Liberties Union*, 542 U.S. 656 (2004), the Court found that COPA, too, was very likely a violation of the First Amendment. (Because of the preliminary-injunction posture of the case, the Court did not definitively decide the statute's constitutionality.)

(1) **Terms of statute:**   COPA made it a crime to put on to the Web content that was "harmful to minors." Material was deemed "harmful to minors" if it was either obscene or was designed to appeal to minors' prurient interests in a "patently offensive" way that lacked serious literary or other value to such minors. (Minors were defined as persons under 17.)   Web operators were given an affirmative defense if they screened minors from access by some *age-verification mechanism*, such as by requiring a credit card or by "any other reasonable measures that are feasible under available technology." So basically, COPA said that anyone who wanted to operate a commercial Web

site containing material that might be harmful to minors had to impose a mechanism for checking that only adults used the site.

**(2) Lower court issues injunction:**  A federal district court issued a preliminary injunction against COPA, on the grounds that it, like the CDA before it, violated the First Amendment rights of adults.

**(3) Supreme Court agrees with Injunction:**  By a 5-4 vote, the Supreme Court held that the lower-court had ***not abused its discretion in entering the injunction.*** Justice Kennedy's opinion for the majority began by repeating *Reno*'s holding that if a statute suppresses a large amount of speech that adults have a constitutional right to receive, the government must bear the burden of showing that there are no less-restrictive alternatives that would be at least as effective.

**(4) Filtering not shown to be less effective:**  Kennedy concluded that the government had not born this burden of proof here. In particular, he focused on ***"blocking and filtering software"*** that could voluntarily be installed by users on their own computers. Such filtering software would clearly be less restrictive than the age-verification scheme required by COPA; for instance, an adult with children could simply turn off the filter when the adult wanted to use the computer. And, Kennedy asserted, user-installed filters might well prove more effective than COPA — for instance, filters could block ***foreign-hosted material*** (which COPA could not effectively reach). Therefore, the injunction should be permitted to stand while the case was tried on the merits, and the statute would be found valid only if the government could show (as seemed very unlikely) that the statute was in fact the ***least-restrictive available means of effectively blocking minors*** from accessing indecent Internet material.

**(5) Dissent:**  The four dissenters, led by Justice Breyer, believed that COPA did indeed satisfy the least-restrictive-alternative requirement. They believed that COPA blocked very little content that was not in fact obscene (and thus forbiddable even to adults).

iii. **Significance:**  Here are some of the things that *Reno v. ACLU* and *Ashcroft v. ACLU* seem to establish:

**(1) Broad protection for Internet:** The Internet, and publicly-available computer networks in general, deserve the same ***very broad First Amendment protection as books and newspapers,*** not the lesser protection given to scarce over-the-air broadcast media. (*Reno.*) This means that any time-place-and-manner restriction on the Internet will have to be very closely linked to the achievement of an important governmental interest.

**(2) Protection of rights of adults:** When government tries to protect minors from non-obscene material, government must make great efforts to see to it that the ***rights of adults*** to access material that they have a constitutional right to access are not inadvertently hampered. *Reno.* (So a ban on putting non-obscene "indecent" material in any place where minors might see it infringes the rights of adults, since adults have a right to see the material and the ban will dissuade people from making the material broadly available.)

**(3) No-restrictive available alternatives:** Indeed, if government *is* going to make it harder for adults to access material that they have a First Amendment right to see — even if "harder" means imposing a hurdle as relatively small as requiring the user to prove that she is in fact an adult — government must bear the burden of proving that there are ***no less-restrictive available alternatives.*** For example, if Congress wants to impose an age-verification requirement, Congress would have to prove that this device is less restrictive, or more effective, than filtering software voluntarily installed by private (adult) users, clearly a hard-to-make showing. (*Ashcroft.*)

**N. The public forum:** We turn now to a detailed discussion of the ***public forum*** as a factor in determining whether governmental regulation that purports to be merely of the "time, place or manner" of expression nonetheless violates the First Amendment.

1. **Recap of rules:** To recapitulate briefly how the status of a place as a public or non-public forum fits into the constitutional analysis, here is a summary of the relevant rules:

   a. **Content-neutrality:** If the regulation occurs because the government objects to the ***communicative impact*** of the expression (i.e., the government is not being content-neutral), it ***does not make a difference*** whether the expression takes place in a public forum or not; in either event, the governmental regulation is presumptively invalid, unless the expression falls in a pre-defined "unprotected category" (or, apparently now, if it falls within a class of speech that has "lesser social value," such as the "offensive" or "indecent" speech in *American Mini Theatres* and *Pacifica* or the child pornography in *Ferber).*

   b. **Public forum:** Assuming content-neutrality, if the speech occurs in a ***public forum***, it (and conduct related to it) can only be regulated in ***narrow ways*** which the government shows to be ***necessary*** to serve ***significant governmental interests***. Tribe, p. 982. The availability of ***alternative channels*** for the communication will ***not*** by itself be enough to make the regulation valid.

   c. **Designated public forum:** Some government-owned property is viewed as a ***"designated public forum."*** This happens where government makes the decision to open non-public-forum property to broad expressive uses. (*Example:* Government decides to let any student group use its classrooms for any expressive activity.) The same rules (given in (b) above) apply to designated public forums as to true public forums, but government can at any time change its mind and remove the designation, making the site or use a non-public forum.

   d. **Non-public forum:** Where the speech does ***not*** occur in a public (or designated public) forum, the state's right to regulate it in a content-neutral manner depends on whether the regulation's interference with expression is ***"substantial"*** or not.

      i. **Substantial interference:** If the interference *is* substantial, the same rule applies as in the public-forum situation: the regulation must be narrowly drawn, and necessary to serve some significant government interest.

      ii. **Insubstantial interference:** But if the interference is ***not substantial***, the government must only show a ***rational justification*** for its regulatory scheme. Tribe,

p. 982. The government's scheme may allow access to some speakers and some subject matters while excluding others, "so long as the distinctions drawn are reasonable in light of the purpose served by the forum and are viewpoint neutral." *Cornelius v. NAACP Legal Defense and Educational Fund*, 473 U.S. 788 (1985), discussed further *infra*, p. 532.

   **iii. Alternative channels:**  One significant difference between expression occurring in a public (including designated public) forum and that occurring in a non-public forum is that in the latter situation, the *availability of equally effective alternative channels* is *sufficient to make the interference "insubstantial"* (so that the "rational relation" test is all that has to be met.) Tribe, p. 982.

2. **Necessary for significant state interest:**  In applying the requirement that public-forum regulations must be narrow ones that are necessary to serve significant governmental interests, the Court has held that *mere administrative convenience does not suffice* as a governmental interest. Recall, for instance, that a city's interest in keeping its streets clean was held not to constitute a sufficient justification for a ban on distribution of handbills, in *Schneider v. State*, 308 U.S. 147 (1939) (*supra*, p. 491).

   **a. Safety:**  But a need to *control crowds* to prevent *physical danger* from say, demonstrators or their audience, *will* suffice, provided that the Court is convinced that the crowd-control justification is not really a smokescreen for censorship (non-content-neutrality), and provided that there is no problem of vagueness or overbreadth (so that administrative discretion is held within acceptable limits.)

   **b. Protection of unwilling listener:**  Similarly, the need to protect an *unwilling listener* against being forced to hear or see a message is a sufficiently strong governmental interest. For instance, a municipality may ban all picketing in front of a single residence, in order to protect the inhabitants' right to be free of unwanted messages while at home. See *Frisby v. Schultz*, 487 U.S. 474 (1988), so holding. (In *Frisby*, the Court upheld such an ordinance, whose effect was to prevent anti-abortion activists from picketing the residence of a doctor who performed abortions.)

   **c. Access to public and private places:**  The need to allow *access* to public and private buildings will clearly justify some regulation of demonstrators. For instance, at least where less-intrusive measures have not worked, a judge may enjoin protesters or picketers from blocking access to the place that they are picketing. See *Madsen v. Women's Health Center, Inc., supra,* p. 516, upholding a 36-foot "speech free" buffer zone on the street and sidewalks surrounding an abortion clinic, so that staff and patients of the clinic could come and go without any possibility of interference.

   **d. Traffic flow:**  Even the need to keep streets *free for ordinary traffic* may justify *limited* regulation of marchers or demonstrators (e.g., a requirement that they use a street that is not a main thoroughfare). This is the implication of *Cox v. Louisiana [Cox I]*, 379 U.S. 536 (1965), where the Court stated that one could not, "contrary to traffic regulations, insist upon a street meeting in the middle of Times Square at the rush hour as a form of freedom of speech or assembly. Governmental authorities have the duty and responsibility to keep their streets open and available for movement." (But the Court reversed the defendants' conviction for obstructing public passages, on the grounds that officials were left with uncontrolled discretion, and used it in a discriminatory manner.)

e.  **Total closing of streets and parks:**  In *Cox I*, the Court explicitly declined to decide whether a statute which flatly forbade ***all access*** to streets and other public facilities for parades and meetings, applied in a uniform, non-discriminatory manner, might be constitutional. But more recent cases make it highly ***unlikely that the streets may be completely closed to this sort of activity***, even if such closure is done in a non-discriminatory way. The modern rationale of the public forum is that ***access to such a forum is a key aspect of the freedom of expression***, and that such access, not merely uniform non-access, is ***required*** in order for the First Amendment to be satisfied. See Tribe, p. 986, n. 3.

3.  **Private places:**  Even where expression takes place in a ***private*** place, content-neutral regulations may be found to so impair the freedom of expression that the First Amendment has been violated. This will be true where the channel of communication being impaired ***has no adequate substitutes.***

> **Example:** The City of San Diego bans all billboards containing non-commercial messages, apart from a few narrowly-defined exceptions. The City raises the defense (among others) that the ordinance is a reasonable "time, place and manner" restriction.
>
> *Held*, the ban is not a valid "time, place and manner" restriction; such restrictions, to be valid, must not only be content-neutral, but must also serve a significant governmental interest and ***"leave open ample alternative channels for communication of the information."*** Here, the parties stipulated that many advertisers rely on outdoor advertising because other forms of advertising are "insufficient, inappropriate and prohibitively expensive." Thus these other forms of advertising do not represent adequate alternative channels. *Metromedia, Inc. v. San Diego*, 453 U.S. 490 (1981).

a.  **Other locations:**  In private-forum situations, there is no general rule to predict when alternative channels will be found to be "adequate." One rule of thumb that seems to have emerged, however, is that a different ***location*** (as distinguished from a different medium) is much more likely to be an adequate substitute when it is in the ***same city*** as the location which has been placed under restriction, than where this alternative location is in a neighboring city.

b.  **Ban on posting of signs on public property:**  The Burger/Rehnquist Court seems to be quite quick to conclude that adequate alternative channels are available. For instance, the Court upheld a city's ***total ban*** on the posting of signs on public property. See ***Los Angeles v. Taxpayers For Vincent***, 466 U.S. 789 (1984). The Court conceded that the posting of signs might be a convenient and inexpensive way to send a message to the public at large (e.g., an electioneering message, as in *Taxpayers for Vincent*). Nonetheless, the Court pointed out, speakers could get their message across by speaking orally, or by distributing literature. *Taxpayers For Vincent* indicates that it will be rare that an individual will be able to show that a particular channel of communication not involving a public forum is so important that adequate alternative channels do not exist.

  i.  **Dissent:**  Three dissenters in *Taxpayers For Vincent* took strong exception to the majority's conclusion that there were adequate alternative channels. For instance, handbills were not an effective substitute, in the dissenters' view, because they must be printed in large quantity and because far more hours must be spent distributing them than are required to post signs on, say, telephone poles.

4. **"True" or "traditional" public forums:** Let us now consider in more detail the various types of forums. First, and easiest to analyze are *"true" public forums,* sometimes referred to as *"traditional"* public forums. These are forums that by custom, rather than by any explicit government decision or designation, are completely public.

 The clearest examples of a completely public forum, recognized as such since the 1930's, are **streets, sidewalks and parks**. See *Hague v. C.I.O.*, 307 U.S. 496 (1939) ("Use of the streets in public places [for assembly and debate of public questions] has, from ancient times, been a part of the privileges, immunities, rights and liberties of citizens.") Even a **quiet street** in a **residential neighborhood** is a true public forum. See *Frisby v. Schultz, supra*, p. 527, so holding (but concluding that the state nonetheless was entitled to ban all picketing on a residential street in front of a particular house).

 a. **Rules:** Remember the *rules* applicable to true public forums:

 ❏ any content-based regulation will be strictly scrutinized (regulation must be necessary to achieve a compelling governmental interest); and

 ❏ any content-neutral "time, place and manner" regulation must be **narrowly drawn** to serve **significant governmental interests**, while leaving open adequate **alternative channels** for the communication.

5. **Designated public forums:** An additional class consists of what are called *"designated public forums."*[3] These are public facilities as to which the government **has made the decision to open the place up to a broad range of expressive activities.** (As we explain below, these are treated essentially the same way as true public forums.)

 a. **Municipal theater:** For instance, a **municipal theater** held open as a place where **any group** may put on productions becomes a designated public forum, and certain groups or productions may not be excluded merely because a different theater is available. See *Southeastern Promotions, Ltd. v. Conrad*, 420 U.S. 546 (1975) (city theater may not exclude production of "Hair," even though some other, privately-owned theater in the city was available.)

 b. **School classrooms:** The same would be likely to be true of **school classrooms**, if the school district has decided to let practically any community group or school group use the premises **after hours.** Such a decision makes the classrooms (at least after hours) a designated public forum, at which point the government can't allow or disallow partic-

---

3. The Court has sometimes used the phrase *"limited public forum,"* to describe a **sub-group** within the class of designated public forums. The governmental unit that creates the designated public forum may decide to open it to all speakers, on all or nearly all subjects. (That's the situation we're talking about in the main text when we use the phrase "designated public forum.") Alternatively, however, government may decide that the designated public forum should be open *only to certain types of speakers or subjects* (e.g., a school forum that is open only for the discussion of current events). The Court sometimes uses the phrase "limited public forum" to describe this latter type of designated public forum. In the relatively few cases in which the Court has classified a forum as a limited public one, the Court has allowed government to **restrict access based on subject matter**, so long as the subject matter distinctions are **reasonable** and **viewpoint-neutral**. In other words, a "limited public forum" is to be treated essentially *like a non-public forum* (see *infra*, p. 530). We will not use the phrase "limited public forum" further here. You should understand, however, that in the discussion beginning on p. 530 concering regulation of non-public forums, a few of the forums being discussed are ones that the Court might call "limited public forums"; in that event the treatment will be the same as for a non-public forum.

ular groups to use the rooms based on agreement/disagreement with the group's message.

c. **Rules:** Once a place becomes a designated public forum, the ***same rules apply as apply to true public forums:*** (1) content-based regulation will be strictly scrutinized; and (2) content-neutral "time, place and manner" regulation must be narrowly drawn to serve significant governmental interests, while leaving open adequate alternative channels for the communication.

   i. **Government may change its mind:** The only difference between a true public forum and a designated public forum is that with a designated forum, government may at any time ***change its mind,*** and ***remove the designation*** — at that point the forum becomes a non-public forum (see immediately below), which may be subjected to much greater "time, place and manner" regulation.

   **Example:** Suppose that a school board allows all classrooms at the local high school to be used by any community group after hours. At this point, the classrooms after hours constitute a designated public forum. The board then changes its policy, in response to complaints about damage to school property. Under the new policy, only student groups, not community groups, may use the rooms. A court would hold that the district was entitled to make this change (removal of the public-forum designation), at which point the rooms became a non-public forum. Now, the board's student-use-only policy will be upheld as long as it is content-neutral and "reasonable" in light of the classroom's purposes.

6. **Non-public forums:** A final category consists of those public facilities which are used for purposes ***not particularly linked to expression.*** Such a facility is usually referred to as a ***"non-public forum."*** Of the three categories of public areas, this group offers the ***least*** constitutionally-protected access for First Amendment expression. The government regulation of expression in a non-public forum must merely be: (1) ***reasonable*** in light of the ***purpose served*** by the forum; and (2) ***viewpoint neutral.*** See, e.g., *Int'l Soc. for Krishna Consciousness, Inc. v. Lee*, 505 U.S. 672 (1992).

   a. **Reasonableness:** The requirement of ***"reasonableness"*** has relatively little bite here, as in the due process and equal protection areas. Government may limit speech in the non-public forum even if ***less restrictive alternatives are readily available***, and even if the restriction chosen is not the ***"most reasonable."***

   **Example:** The public authority that operates the three major New York City airports bans all repetitive solicitation of money within the terminals, and all distribution of literature.

   *Held*, because airport terminals are not public forums, the regulation of expression within them must merely be reasonable. The ban on face-to-face solicitation of money is reasonable, because "passengers who wish to avoid the solicitor may have to alter their path, slowing both themselves and those around them [with the result that] the normal flow of traffic is impeded." Also, face-to-face solicitation presents risks of duress and fraud. (But, a different majority of the Court holds, the sale and distribution of literature may ***not*** be banned; at least one member of the Court believes that such regulation is not even "reasonable.") *Int'l Soc. for Krishna Consciousness, Inc. v. Lee*, *supra*.

**b. Viewpoint neutrality:** But the requirement of *viewpoint neutrality* has a real impact in these non-public-forum cases. The government can restrict speech across the board in these forums, but it can't restrict speech by *preferring some messages or perspectives over others.*

    **i. Can't bar religious viewpoint, even if it involves worship:** The most dramatic example of the requirement of viewpoint-neutrality for non-public forums comes from a trio of cases saying that when a school district allows after-hours use of *school facilities* by a variety of community groups, *religious groups* must be given *equal access*.

        **(1) Showing of religious film:** In the first of these cases, *Lamb's Chapel v. Center Moriches Union Free School Dist.*, 508 U.S. 384 (1993), a school district allowed school property to be used after-hours for "social, civic and recreational activities," but not for "religious purposes." P, an evangelical church, wanted to publicly exhibit at the school a concededly-religious film dealing with family and child-rearing issues. The school district refused to allow the showing. The Supreme Court held that the ban on showing the film was not viewpoint neutral, and thus violated the First Amendment — the district was allowing the presentation of all views about family issues and child-rearing except for those views dealing with these issues from a religious standpoint, so viewpoints were not being treated equally.

        **(2) Funding of student activities:** Next, the Court held that where a public university funds a broad range of student publications, it may not exclude publications on the grounds that they are religiously-oriented. *Rosenberger v. Univ. of Virginia*, discussed *infra*, p. 532.

        **(3) Religious club for elementary school students:** Most dramatically, and most recently, the Court held that where a school district allowed various community groups to offer a broad range of after-school activities at elementary schools, the district could not exclude the "Good News Club," an evangelical group that wished to "teach moral lessons from a Christian perspective through live storytelling and prayer." *Good News Club v. Milford Central School*, 533 U.S. 98 (2001). To the five-justice majority, neither the fact that the activity included prayer, nor the fact that the attendees would be impressionable elementary-school children (rather than the adult audience at issue in *Lamb's Chapel, supra*) made any difference — the district was excluding speech on the grounds that it "use[s] a religious viewpoint," and that exclusion constituted "unconstitutional viewpoint discrimination." (The Court also rejected the school district's argument that allowing the activity would violate the Establishment Clause; this aspect of the case is discussed *infra*, p. 659.)

    **ii. Candidate forums on government-owned TV:** Similarly, government must be viewpoint-neutral when it organizes a debate or forum for *competing political candidates*. See *Arkansas Educational Television Comm'n v. Forbes*, 118 S. Ct. 1633 (1998), holding that a state-owned TV station which held a candidates' forum was not entitled to choose which candidates to invite based upon the candidate's political views (but also holding that the station did not violate this principle).

iii. **Even spending must be viewpoint-neutral:** The requirement of viewpoint-neutrality is so strict that it applies even to activities that are *funded by the government*. Thus government may *not* choose to *fund some third-party activities and not others, based on the viewpoints expressed*.

**Example:** The University of Virginia (a public university) funds certain student publications, by paying for their printing costs. The University disqualifies from this funding any publication that "primarily promotes or manifests a particular belie[f] in or about a deity or an ultimate reality." P is the publisher of *Wide Awake*, a student newspaper that gives a "Christian perspective" on the University, and that challenges students "to live, in word and deed, according to the faith they proclaim and to encourage students to consider what a personal relationship with Jesus Christ means." P argues that the University's refusal to fund *Wide Awake* violates his free-speech rights. The University concedes that its policy puts a whole subject — religion discussed from a proselytizing perspective — off limits, but claims that its policy is viewpoint-neutral. (For instance, the university points out that those opposing the practice of religion are equally excluded.)

*Held*, for P (by a 5-4 vote). The regulation here was not viewpoint-neutral. "The University does not exclude religion as a subject matter but selects for disfavored treatment those student journalistic efforts with religious editorial viewpoints." (The case is thus similar to *Lamb's Chapel*, *supra*.) Nor does the fact that the University is spending money make any difference. If the University were disseminating only its own messages, it would not have to fund opposing viewpoints. But once it chooses to fund some *third-party viewpoints* (i.e., some student-run publications), it may not choose which ones to fund based on the viewpoint of the speaker. (Also, requiring the University to fund publications like P's does not violate the Establishment Clause. See *infra*, p. 660.) *Rosenberger v. University of Virginia*, 515 U.S. 819 (1995).

**Note:** For another case in which the Court has held that even government-funded activities must be handled in a viewpoint-neutral way, see *Legal Services Corp. v. Velazquez*, discussed *infra*, p. 605. There, the Court held that Congress could not, as a condition of giving federal funding to legal clinics for the indigent, prevent the clinics' lawyers from taking certain litigation positions (e.g., that a particular welfare law was unconstitutional).

c. **"Subject neutrality" not required:** But the requirement of neutrality in non-public forum cases seems to be merely one of "*viewpoint* neutrality," *not "subject neutrality."* Thus "[a] speaker may be excluded from a non-public forum if he wishes to address a *topic* not encompassed within the purpose of the forum … or if he is not a member of the class of speakers for whose special benefit the forum was created. … [But] the government violates the First Amendment when it denies access to a speaker solely to suppress the *point of view* he espouses on an otherwise includable subject." *Cornelius v. NAACP Legal Defense and Educational Fund, Inc.*, 473 U.S. 788 (1985). The *Cornelius* case illustrates the great flexibility that the lack of a requirement of "subject neutrality" gives the government in regulating access to a non-public forum.

i.  **Facts:** *Cornelius* involved the Combined Federal Campaign (CFC), which is a collective charity drive targeted at federal employees, and administered by the federal government. Those charities permitted to participate submit a 30-word written statement about their goals and how they spend their contributions. The statements from the participating charities are then circulated to federal employees at the workplace, and many employees contribute to one or more of them. Only "voluntary, charitable, health and welfare agencies that provide or support direct health and welfare services to individuals or their families" are permitted to participate — specifically excluded are "agencies that seek to influence the outcomes of elections or the determination of public policy through political activity or advocacy, lobbying, or litigation on behalf of parties other than themselves." The NAACP Legal Defense Fund, the Sierra Club Legal Defense Fund, and a number of other advocacy and litigation-oriented charitable groups were refused the right to participate.

ii. **Holding:**   The Supreme Court ***upheld*** (though only by a 4-3 vote) the government's right to exclude the litigation and advocacy organizations. Since the CFC was a non-public forum, "the Government's decision to restrict access ... need only be *reasonable*; it need not be the most reasonable or the only reasonable limitation. In contrast to a public forum, a finding of strict incompatibility between the nature of the speech or the identity of the speaker and the functioning of the nonpublic forum is not mandated ... nor is there a requirement that the restriction be narrowly tailored or that the Government's interest be compelling."

iii. **Application to facts:**   Here, there were reasonable justifications for the exclusion. For instance, "the President could reasonably conclude that a dollar directly spent on providing food or shelter to the needy is more beneficial than a dollar spent on litigation that might or might not result in aid to the needy." Also, "avoiding the appearance of political favoritism" was a valid justification. (But if, despite these rational justifications, there was evidence that the government's choice of rule "conceal[s] a bias against the viewpoint advanced by the excluded speakers," the regulation could nonetheless be struck down. The excluded organizations would be given a chance to come up with such evidence on remand.)

**Note:** However, the borderline between "subject neutrality" (not required) and "viewpoint neutrality" (required) can be quite blurry. Recall, for instance, that in *Rosenberger, supra*, p. 532, the Court held that when the university funded all student-run publications except essentially "preaching" ones, it was engaging in forbidden "viewpoint" discrimination rather than allowable "subject" discrimination. In general, the Court today seems eager to stretch to find that the lines government has drawn are of the forbidden "viewpoint-based" type; this is especially true where government tries to treat religiously-oriented activities or messages less favorably than all other types.

d.  **Total ban on expression:**   Are there some non-public forums whose nature is such that First Amendment expression may be ***totally banned*** within them? The Supreme Court has never found this to be true of any particular non-public forum, and it seems probable that *some* expressive activity (e.g., political speech by employees who work in that forum) will always be allowable under the "reasonableness" test. For example, even though the Court has held that a public airport is not a public forum (see *Int'l*

*Soc. for Krishna Consciousness v. Lee, supra*, p. 530), the Court also held in that case that a ***total ban on literature distribution*** in airports violated the First Amendment; the deciding vote on this issue was cast by Justice O'Connor, who believed that a total ban on what she called "leafletting" in a non-public forum like an airport was "unreasonable."

**Note:** The Court in *Krishna* left open the interesting question of whether ***"begging,"*** i.e., asking for money for oneself, is protected by the First Amendment at all. *Krishna* and other cases involving organized charities make it clear that the conduct of seeking funds for a *charity **is*** protected First Amendment activity. (See, for instance, *Schaumburg v. Citizens for Better Environment, supra*, p. 501.) But at least one prestigious federal court has held that begging for funds for one's own use is not protected by the First Amendment at all.

e.   **Particular types of places that are non-public forums:**   The Court is increasingly quick to find that particular publicly-owned places are not public forums. The test is whether the government has intended to create ***"general access for a class of speakers"*** (in which case the forum is true public or designated public) or, instead, "selected access for individual speakers" (in which case the forum is probably nonpublic.) *Arkansas Educational Television Comm'n v. Forbes*, 118 S. Ct. 1633 (1998).   In most cases where the issue has been discussed by the Court, a nonpublic forum has been found.

   i.   **Airport terminals:** Most dramatically, the Court has held that an ***airport terminal*** is not a public forum. ***Int'l Soc. for Krishna Consciousness v. Lee***, 505 U.S. 672 (1992).

      (1) **Rationale:**   Six members of the Court believed that an airport terminal was a non-public forum. The majority opinion, by Chief Justice Rehnquist, asserted that public forums have two principal characteristics: they have *traditionally* been used for purposes of assembly and expression, and they have as a "*principal purpose … the free exchange of ideas."* Airports do not satisfy either of these tests: only recently have they been made available for speech activity, and their principal purpose is to facilitate travel and make a regulated profit, not to facilitate free expression. Justice O'Connor, in a concurrence, agreed that publicly-owned airports are not public forums.

      (2) **Dissent:**   Four members of the Court (Kennedy, Blackmun, Stevens and Souter) dissented from the majority's conclusion that airports are not public forums. Kennedy, in one of the two opinions on this point, argued that tradition should not be the principal test of determining whether something is a public forum: "Open, public spaces and thoroughfares which are suitable for discourse may be public forums, whatever their historical pedigree. … " Today, "an airport is one of the few government-owned spaces where many persons have extensive contact with other members of the public." For Kennedy, the factors should be: "Whether the property shares physical similarities with more traditional public forums, whether the government has permitted or acquiesced in broad public access to the property, and whether expressive activity would tend to interfere in a significant way with the uses to which the government has as a factual matter dedicated the property." By this standard,

the broad publicly-accessible areas of an airport terminal (including the areas dedicated to shops, as opposed to those where access requires a security check) should be considered public forums. "It is the very breadth and extent of the public's use of airports that makes it imperative to protect speech rights there." And the problem of congestion, relied on by the majority, was no more severe than in the case of streets or parks.

(3) **Result of case:** *Krishna* is quite clear on the public-forum issue: a majority of the Court has now held that airports are not public forums. The case is more confusing as to its ultimate result. By a 6-3 vote, the government may ban face-to-face *solicitation of funds* at the terminal, because of its non-public forum status. But by a different 5-4 vote, a total ban on *distribution of literature* violates the First Amendment. (Four members of the Court believed that this result stemmed from the fact that airports *are* public forums; the fifth, Justice O'Connor, believed that even though airports are not public forums, a total ban on literature distribution failed to meet even the easier "reasonableness" standard applicable to non-public forums.)

(4) **Other transportation hubs:**  What about *subways, bus stations, railroad stations,* and other publicly-owned and operated parts of transportation systems? The rationale of the majority's opinion in the *Krishna* case suggests that these, too, will be found to be non-public forums — they have not traditionally been used for purposes of free expression (with the possible exception of big-city subways), and their principal purpose is transportation, not expression.

ii. **Jails:**  Another good example of a non-public forum is the *jailhouse.* Jailhouses serve the limited function of housing prisoners, and nearly any type of expressive conduct, whether by prisoners or members of the public, is likely to be seen as incompatible with this basic purpose. Thus in *Adderley v. Florida*, 385 U.S. (1966), the Court, by a 5-4 vote, sustained the trespass convictions of civil rights demonstrators who protested segregation at a county jail. The majority distinguished between the state capital grounds at issue in *Edwards v. South Carolina (supra*, p. 504), which were open to the public, and jails, which because they are built for security purposes, are not.

iii. **Military bases:**  Similarly, *military bases* may be placed off-limits to political speakers. In *Greer v. Spock*, 424 U.S. 828 (1976), a majority of the Court so held, reasoning that the purpose of a military base is to "train soldiers, not to provide a public forum." The policy against political campaign appearances was also justified by the "American constitutional tradition of a politically neutral military under civilian control."

(1) **Dissent:**  Two dissenters, Justice Brennan joined by Marshall, took a much broader view of the right of access to public facilities other than traditional public forums. Even where a governmental facility was not a "public forum" at all, expressive activity should be permitted on it, they argued, as long as the form of expression was compatible with the activities occurring there. By this standard, political rallies whose time and location within the base were carefully regulated so as to prevent disruption of military training should have

been allowed. (However, there is no sign that a majority of the Court is likely to go along with this broad view of the right of access to all public facilities.)

iv. **Courthouse:** The Court has indicated that it will regard a ***courthouse*** and its grounds as falling within this category of public places that have "not been traditionally held open … for expressive activities" and are therefore not public forums. In *U.S. v. Grace*, 461 U.S. 171 (1983), the Court suggested in *dictum* that the Supreme Court Building and its grounds are like the military base in *Greer v. Spock*, and are not a public forum merely because the public has virtually unlimited access to the grounds and access during certain hours to the building.

  (1) **Sidewalk:** But the Court held that the ***sidewalk*** abutting the grounds *is* a public forum. Consequently, the Court invalidated, as applied to the sidewalk, a federal statute banning the display on the grounds of the Supreme Court of "any flag, banner" or other sign. The Court found it of critical importance that there was no "separation" or "fence" which made the sidewalk in front of the Court grounds different from other sidewalks; thus the case was distinguishable from the streets in the military base in *Greer*, which were clearly part of an "enclosed military reservation." (But a post-*Grace* case suggests that some special-purpose sidewalks may ***not*** be public forums. See *U.S. v. Kokinda, infra*, where a plurality held that a sidewalk linking a post office parking lot to the post office itself was not a public forum.)

v. **Post office:** A ***post office***, like a courthouse, probably falls within the group of public places that are not public forums. The Court has never decided the status of post office property generally. But a plurality of the Court has held that the ***sidewalk*** in front of the post office falls within this non-public-forum category, at least where the sidewalk serves only to link the post office's parking lot with the main postal building. See *U.S. v. Kokinda*, 497 U.S. 720 (1990), holding that such a sidewalk is a non-public forum because it has not been intentionally opened for public discourse, and that the U.S. government can therefore ban certain types of expression there (e.g., solicitation of cash charitable donations).

vi. **School mail system:** A ***school system's*** internal ***mail*** system, including teachers' mailboxes, was held to fall into this non-public-forum category, in *Perry Education Ass'n v. Perry Local Educators' Ass'n*, 460 U.S. 37 (1983). The fact that the official teachers' union, as well as a number of other outside organizations (e.g., YMCA and Cub Scouts) were permitted to use the mail system was not enough to convert the system into a public forum. Therefore, the school district's rule that no "school employee organization" except the official union could use the system was valid.

vii. **Governmental workplace:** A ***governmental workplace*** will apparently be treated as a non-public forum. In *Cornelius v. NAACP Legal Defense and Educational Fund, supra*, p. 532, the Court held that a charitable campaign held at federal workplaces fell into the non-public forum category. While the Court refrained from holding that the workplace as a whole was for all purposes non-public, it appears that during the time when the workplace is being used to perform government business (especially during the ordinary workday), this non-public categorization will control. Thus had the government permitted some speakers but not others to give face-to-face speeches to workers during the workday, this scheme, like the printed-matter charitable solicitation campaign involved in *Cornelius*, would be evaluated under the unstringent "rational relation" test.

viii. **Candidates' debates or fora:** When government organizes a *forum or debate for political candidates,* this will often be a nonpublic forum. For instance, in a case in which a state-owned TV station organized a televised debate to which the two leading candidates for a congressional seat were invited, the court found that the forum was a nonpublic one, because the debate "did not have an open-microphone format," i.e., the station did not make its debate "generally available to candidates" for that seat. Therefore, the station was within its rights not to invite plaintiff, a minor candidate (so long as the station made its decision based upon an objective determination of the plaintiff's lack of strength rather than upon lack of enthusiasm for his views.) *Arkansas Educational Television Comm'n v. Forbes*, 118 S. Ct. 1633 (1998).

ix. **Internet connections in libraries:** *Internet connections at public libraries* appear not to constitute public forums. Therefore, the government may require libraries receiving federal funding to install anti-pornography filters on any computer connected to the Internet. See *U.S. v. Amer. Library Ass'n*, 539 U.S. 194 (2003) (4-justice plurality holds that "a public library does not acquire Internet terminals in order to create a public forum for Web publishers to express themselves, any more than it collects books in order to provide a public forum for the authors of books to speak." A fifth Justice, Breyer, in concurring, says he agrees with this determination.)

x. **Buses:** *Buses* that are part of a municipally-owned transit system also appear to fall within the category of non-public-forum facilities. See *Lehman v. Shaker Heights*, 418 U.S. 298 (1974), where a plurality reached this conclusion.

xi. **Utility poles:** *Utility poles* owned by the government are not a public forum, so that a city may prevent the posting of signs on them, in order to reduce "visual blight." See *Los Angeles v. Taxpayers For Vincent*, 466 U.S. 789 (1984).

O. **Right of access to private places:** In most of the First Amendment cases which we have examined so far, the speaker sought to use *public property* to deliver his message. In a few of the other cases above, he sought to use his own property, or that of a willing owner (e.g., billboard advertisers in *Metromedia v. San Diego, supra*, p. 528). We turn now to the rights of a speaker to use *private property, against the owner's will*, for expressive purposes. In this group of cases, speakers have in effect argued that there should be recognized certain *"private forums,"* to which the government should guarantee speakers access, just as it guarantees access to public forums like streets and parks.

1. **Rationale:** The main argument in support of recognizing a guaranteed right of access to certain private forums is that a contrary view would *close off many important channels of communication*. The mere fact that government itself has not closed down these channels is of small consolation, "[f]or if no one will rent an unpopular speaker a hall or print the speaker's views, it may be of little use that the government has not gone out of its way to muzzle the speech." Tribe, p. 998.

2. **Two main contexts:** There are two main types of "private forums" to which speakers have asserted a guaranteed right of access: (1) *shopping centers*; and (2) the *media*, both

print and broadcast. Under present law, ***only broadcast media*** are treated as a forum to which speakers have certain rights of access.

3. **Shopping centers:**  Speakers asserting a right to access to privately-owned shopping centers were, initially, partly successful. Relying on a prior Court decision that the "business district" of a "company town" should be treated as the equivalent of "public property" for First Amendment purposes (*Marsh v. Alabama, supra*, p.422 ), the Court in *Amalgamated Food Employees Local 590 v. Logan Valley Plaza*, 391 U.S. 308 (1968) held that a privately-owned shopping center was the "functional equivalent" of the business district in *Marsh*. Therefore, the *Logan Valley* Court held, the center's owner could not constitutionally be permitted to use state trespass law to bar peaceful union picketing of a store in the center.

   a. **Subject-matter dependence:**  But then, the Court held that *Marsh* and *Logan Valley* were not relevant to First Amendment rights in a shopping center if the speech did not ***relate to the center's operations***. See *Lloyd Corp. v. Tanner*, 407 U.S. 551 (1972) (barring anti-war activists from distributing leaflets at the center.)

   b. ***Logan Valley* overruled:**  Finally, the Court concluded that *Lloyd* had in fact really overruled *Logan Valley*, and that the First Amendment did not guarantee a right of access to privately-owned shopping centers, whether or not the speech related to the center's operations. ***Hudgens v. NLRB***, 424 U.S. 507 (1976).

      i. **Rationale:**  In *Hudgens*, the Court ruled that the distinction drawn in *Lloyd* between *Lloyd* and *Logan Valley* was not a valid one. That distinction (the *Hudgens* Court asserted) permitted a speaker's right of access to a shopping center to depend on the ***content of the speech*** (since only speech related to the center's operation was constitutionally guaranteed). Yet under First Amendment principles, the content of the speech ***could not make a difference.***

      ii. **Conclusion:**  The *Hudgens* Court then elected to follow *Lloyd* rather than *Logan Valley*, and held that there was no right of access. Apparently the choice of *Lloyd* rather than *Logan Valley* was made simply because *Lloyd* was the more recent case.

   c. **Present rule:**  In any event, the present rule at least has the merit of clarity: neither labor picketers, anti-war activists ***nor any other citizens have a First Amendment right to express themselves in shopping centers over the property owner's objection***. (It is not clear whether the same rule applies to the business district of a modern-day company town, or to other types of privately-owned communities, such as migrant labor camps.)

   d. **Access guaranteed by state constitution:**  Although there is no right of access to a shopping center under the First Amendment to the federal constitution, at least one state, California, has interpreted ***its own constitution*** as guaranteeing such a right. In *Pruneyard Shopping Center v. Robins*, 447 U.S. 74 (1980), the Court held that this interpretation of the California State Constitution did not violate a shopping center owner's federal right of free speech, nor his right not to have his property taken without just compensation.

4. **The media:**  Claims of a guaranteed right of access to the ***media*** have fared much better in the case of the ***broadcast*** media than in the case of newspapers and magazines.

5. **Print media:** The Court has *never recognized any First Amendment-based right of access to the print media.*

    a. **"Right of reply" law invalidated:** Such a right of access was explicitly rejected in *Miami Herald Pub. Co. v. Tornillo*, 418 U.S. 241 (1974). In *Tornillo*, the Court held unconstitutional a Florida statute that forced newspapers to print the replies of political candidates whom the paper had attacked. Supporters of the statute argued that the present-day concentration of ownership in the newspaper business now prevents a wide variety of views from reaching the public, and contended that only affirmative action by the government could remedy the situation. But the Court (with the Justices unanimous in the result) held that the statute violated the paper's freedom of the press. Newspapers would tend to avoid subjects that would trigger the right of reply, thus dampening the vigor of press coverage of public events; also, the statute was an unwarranted "intrusion into the function of editors."

       i. **Defamation retraction statutes:** Two Justices, concurring in *Tornillo*, observed that the Court was not expressing any opinion about the constitutionality of so-called "*retraction*" statutes, whereby those who have been *defamed* may sue to require the paper to publish a retraction. Thus such statutes may well be constitutional despite *Tornillo*.

    b. **Right to put message in utility bill:** Similarly, third persons may not be given the right to insert their own messages into utility bills over the utility's objection. In *Pacific Gas & Electric Co. v. Public Utilities Comm'n. of California*, 475 U.S. 1 (1986), the Court held that a utility could not be compelled to disseminate in its billing envelopes the views of a ratepayers' group with which it disagreed. The Court relied on *Tornillo*, and held that forcing the utility to disseminate the views of those with whom it disagreed impermissibly burdened the utility's own freedom of speech — the utility would be forced to choose between appearing to agree or responding, and "the choice to speak includes within it the choice of what not to say."

6. **Broadcasting:** The Supreme Court has always drawn a sharp distinction between the right of access to print-based media and the right of access to *broadcast media*. In theory, the number of newspapers and magazines that are publishable is infinite. In contrast, the radio and television spectrums are *limited*, and the airwaves are thus *"technologically scarce."* For this reason, the Court has always assumed that, just as Congress (through delegation to the Federal Communications Commission) had the right to carve up the broadcast spectrum in making original grants of licenses, so it may, consistent with the First Amendment, *grant the public certain rights of access to the airwaves*. Only a *"limited"* right of access has been recognized, and its precise contours are still being developed.

    a. **"Fairness" doctrine:** The Court has approved aspects of the FCC's "Fairness" doctrine, under which broadcasters are required to grant individuals the right to reply to *personal attacks* broadcast on the station, and the right to reply to the station's political editorials. *Red Lion Broadcasting Co. v. FCC*, 395 U.S. 367 (1969).

       i. **Rationale:** The *Red Lion* Court relied on the "spectrum scarcity" theory outlined above, and held that broadcasters could be required to share their frequency with others, at least in a limited way. It is "the right of the viewers and listeners, not the right of the broadcasters, which is paramount."

7. **Criticism of distinction:** The basic distinction between *print* media (as to which there is absolutely no constitutional right of access) and *broadcast* media (as to which there is a limited right of access) is frequently criticized. This distinction may have made sense at a time when most communities had several daily newspapers, and there were few radio or TV stations. But today, the pendulum has swung quite far in the other direction: many markets have only one major daily newspaper, yet the proliferation of AM and FM radio, plus UHF and cable television, means that a variety of views are likely to find their way onto the airwaves even without governmental intervention. Thus the traditional distinction seems at serious odds with today's economic realities.

   a. **Benefits:** However, it has been argued that there are nonetheless substantial benefits from having one branch of the media regulated and the other unregulated. Such a system is reasonably effective at making sure a broad range of viewpoints is presented to the public. Yet it does not run as great a risk of government-imposed censorship as would a completely regulated system (since the unregulated press is always an available outlet for the "truth," even if government succeeds in muzzling broadcasters or if broadcasters become timid and engage in self-censorship).

# V. SYMBOLIC EXPRESSION

A. **Problem generally:** Just as expression may consist of speech accompanied by conduct (e.g., a protest march), so expression may sometimes consist solely of *non-verbal actions*. The Supreme Court has for a long time been willing to recognize that certain non-verbal conduct is protected by the First Amendment (e.g., *Stromberg v. California*, 283 U.S. 359 (1931), striking a statute prohibiting display of a red flag as a symbol of opposition to organized government.) Yet the Court has been wary of giving generalized First Amendment protection to any act which is an attempt to convey a message; this reluctance stems principally from the fear that granting such protection would legitimatize actions like political assassinations, Patty Hearst-type bank robberies, pouring blood on draft records, and other violent actions. See Tribe, p. 601.

   1. **Two-track analysis:** The Court's recent cases on symbolic expression seem to have implicitly followed the Tribe "two-track" method of analysis. That is, where the Court believes that certain symbolic expression is prohibited because the government objects to the *communicative content* of the expression (Tribe's "track one"), the Court applies *strict scrutiny*. Conversely, where the Court believes that the government's interest in regulating the conduct has nothing to do with the conduct's expressive content (Tribe's "track two"), a more-easily-satisfied balancing test is applied, in which the interest being pursued by the state may well be found to outweigh the individual's interest in using that particular mode of expression.

   2. **Draft card burning:** The Court's choice of "track two" rather than "track one" analysis seems to have been dispositive in the well-known case involving a conviction for *draft card burning, U.S. v. O'Brien*, 391 U.S. 367 (1968).

      a. **Facts:** O'Brien and several others burned their draft cards in public, as part of a protest against the war in Vietnam. They were convicted of violating an amendment to the draft laws making it a crime to "knowingly destroy [or] mutilate" a draft card.

**b. Court finds right to regulate:** O'Brien contended that the burning was "symbolic speech" protected by the First Amendment. But the Court held that even if this were true, conduct combining "speech" and "non-speech" elements could be regulated if four requirements were met:

[1] the regulation was within the constitutional power of the government;

[2] it furthered an *"important or substantial governmental interest"*;

[3] that interest was *"unrelated to the suppression* of free expression"; and

[4] the *"incidental restriction"* on First Amendment freedoms was *"no greater than is essential* to the furtherance" of the governmental interest.

The *O'Brien* Court found that all of these requirements were satisfied.

**Note:** This four-part test continues to be the one used by the Court for analyzing time, place and manner regulations. Therefore, it's worth memorizing.

    **i. "Track two" analysis:** The four-part test turns out to be indistinguishable from what we've been calling "track two" analysis (see *supra*, p. 472). The requirement that the governmental interest be "unrelated to the suppression of free expression" is a somewhat clumsy and conclusory way of saying that the harm which the regulation seeks to avoid must not stem from the communicative content of the conduct; this is the key finding of "content neutrality" that places a case on "track two" rather than "track one." Requirement (4) is equivalent to the "track two" requirement that content-neutral regulations of conduct in public forums must not close alternative channels for communication. See Tribe, p. 992.

**c. Content neutrality:** The Court in *O'Brien* identified several governmental interests served by the prohibition on draft-card destruction — which were *"limited to the non-communicative aspect* of O'Brien's conduct." For instance, the government had an interest in making sure that all draft-age males had in their possession a document indicating their availability for induction in an emergency. This and the other governmental interests were "important and substantial," and could not have been achieved with any less impact on O'Brien's freedom of expression. Therefore, his conviction did not violate the First Amendment, the Court concluded.

**d. Relevance of motive:** O'Brien argued that Congress' *"purpose"* or *"motive"* in enacting the statute was the improper one of suppressing dissent. But the Court rejected this argument, concluding that *congressional "purpose" was simply irrelevant to a statute's constitutionality, so long as there was a legitimate governmental interest which could support the statute* (whether or not Congress actually relied on it).

    **i. Still a rule:** It apparently remains the case that in First Amendment cases, the existence of a legitimate non-content-based government interest can save a statute that burdens expressive conduct, even if one of the government's motives is to suppress or oppose the message being communicated.[4]

---

4. Notice, though, that the same "motive irrelevant" rule doesn't apply to at least some constitutional rules outside the First Amendment area. For instance, the legislature's motivation is often relevant in *equal protection* cases; see, e.g., *Washington v. Davis*, 426 U.S. 229 (1976), *supra*, p. 255, holding that the absence or presence of government intent to commit racial discrimination is relevant in equal protection cases.

e.  **No less-restrictive alternatives:**  Assuming that the Court's analysis was correct, and that the relevant governmental interests served by the statute were the content-neutral ones relating to smooth functioning of the registration system, the rest of the Court's analysis (its application of "track two" principles) seems reasonable. Assuming that making sure all draft-age males possessed unmutilated draft cards was an important governmental objective, there was ***no less restrictive way of accomplishing this objective.*** (For instance, merely requiring each person to keep the card in his possession, as the pre-1965 law did, would not be enough to prohibit A from destroying B's draft card.)

   i.  **Alternatives narrowly defined:**  But observe that this manner of applying the less-restrictive-alternatives test will generally be ***extremely difficult for any challenger of a statute's constitutionality to meet.*** The government's interest was defined extremely ***narrowly***, and an alternative qualified as less-restrictive only if it satisfied this interest ***exactly as well*** as the regulation actually chosen, not merely "***almost as well***" (as the original requirement of continued possession did). See 88 HARV. L. REV. 1484-89 (quoted in L,K&C, pp. 1109-10). This is quite different from the usual less-restrictive-alternatives analysis performed in public-forum cases, where an alternative merely has to be ***nearly*** as effective as the original; for instance, the state must prosecute individual litterers, rather than banning distribution of handbills to avoid littering, even though the former method is obviously a more costly means of litter control and will miss many offenders. See *Schneider v. State, supra*, p. 491.

   ii.  **Approach reaffirmed:**  A more recent case reaffirms the *O'Brien* view that a less-restrictive alternative should be should be deemed available only if it accomplishes the government's objective ***as well*** (not merely almost as well) as the means under challenge. In *Rumsfeld v. FAIR*, 547 U.S. 47 (2006), the issue was the constitutionality of the "Solomon Amendment," under which Congress said that any university could receive certain federal funding only if all parts of the university, including its law school, gave the same on-campus access to military recruiters as to recruiters from other employers.

      (1)  **The claim:**  Prior to the Solomon Amendment, a number of law schools had barred any employer that discriminated against gays and lesbians (including the military) from recruiting on campus; after the Amendment, an association of such schools sued the federal government, arguing, *inter alia*, that the schools' recruitment-hosting activities were expressive conduct under *O'Brien*, and that the Solomon Amendment failed to satisfy *O'Brien*'s requirement that there be no available less-restrictive alternative. A lower court agreed with the plaintiff schools, holding that because the military had ***ample resources to recruit through alternative means*** (e.g., radio and TV advertisements), the Solomon Amendment was not the least restrictive method of accomplishing the military's recruitment objectives.

      (2)  **Argument rejected:**  But the Supreme Court in *FAIR* ***rejected*** this least-restrictive alternative argument. If military recruiters did not have equal campus access, the military's attempts to raise armed forces would be ***"less effective,"*** the Court said. The fact that other means of raising an army and navy

might be *"adequate"* was *irrelevant* — as long as the means chosen by Congress *"add to the effectiveness"* of military recruitment, the no-less-restrictive-alternatives requirement of *O'Brien* was *satisfied*.

3. **Protest in schools:** That the Court's initial judgment about whether or not the government's regulation of symbolic expression is targeted at the expression's communicative impact will usually be dispositive, is also shown by another Vietnam-War-protest case. In ***Tinker v. Des Moines School District***, 393 U.S. 503 (1969), several high school and junior high school students were suspended for wearing black armbands as a symbol of opposition to the War; a rule forbidding the wearing of such armbands had been adopted by school officials two days before, in anticipation of the protest.

   a. **Free expression right upheld:** The Court held that the prohibition on armbands *violated* the students' First Amendment rights. What was being suppressed was not "actually or potentially disruptive conduct," but rather, something that was nearly "pure speech."

      i. **Wish to avoid controversy:** The authorities seem to have acted out of a wish to *avoid controversy* which might stem from the students' silent expression of opinion about the War. But this fear was not a valid reason for banning the expression: "Undifferentiated fear or apprehension of disturbance is not enough to overcome the right to freedom of expression."

      ii. **Other symbols not barred:** The lack of content-neutrality in the school officials' conduct was also shown by the fact that they did not prohibit the wearing of *all* political or other controversial symbols; buttons for national political campaigns, and even the Nazi iron cross symbol, were permitted.

   b. **"Track one" analysis:** Thus the *Tinker* Court seems to have applied conventional "track one" analysis, under which any regulation of expression which is done because of the communicative impact of the expression will be strictly scrutinized, and allowed only if necessary to serve a compelling governmental interest.

      i. **Possibility of "track two":** But, the Court indicated, had the students' act "materially and substantially interfere[d] with the requirements of *appropriate discipline* in the operation of the school," the officials would have been justified in preventing it. If the officials had been able to show that they acted for this reason, this presumably would have been the equivalent of showing that they were content-neutral, and would thus have entitled them to the less stringent review of "track two."

4. **Regulation of hair and clothing:** The Court in *Tinker* explicitly declined to deal with the constitutionality of school regulations dealing with *hair length, clothing type*, and other aspects of *personal appearance* which arguably have an expressive content. Nor has the Court ever been willing to confront this issue after *Tinker*.

   a. **Lower courts:** Most lower courts have held that such aspects of personal appearance are not sufficiently communicative as to be entitled to full First Amendment protection. However, particular regulations have sometimes been struck down on the grounds that they infringe the personal liberty protected by the *Fourteenth* Amendment. See Tribe, p. 1386. See also *supra*, p. 194.

**5. Sleeping in park:** The low level of scrutiny given to content-neutral regulations that affect symbolic expression was again demonstrated in **Clark v. Community For Creative Non-Violence**, 468 U.S. 288 (1984). There, the Court held that a National Parks Service **ban on sleeping in public parks** did **not** violate the First Amendment rights of demonstrators who wished to sleep in tents in two Washington D.C. national parks in order to dramatize the plight of the homeless. (The Court assumed, without deciding, that sleeping in connection with the demonstration constituted symbolic expression.)

    **a. Application of test:** The Court found that the regulation was valid under the four tests of *U.S. v. O'Brien, supra*, p. 540. Most significantly, the Court found a substantial governmental interest in "maintaining the parks in the heart of our capital in an attractive and intact condition," and concluded that the ban on sleeping furthered this interest by limiting the extent and duration of demonstrations like the one involved here.

**6. Conduct must be "inherently expressive":** Conduct will receive even the limited protection that *O'Brien* confers only if the conduct is ***"inherently expressive."*** This principle is illustrated by **Rumsfeld v. FAIR**, 547 U.S. 47 (2006) (also discussed *supra*, p. 542), where the issue was whether Congress could, by means of the "Solomon Amendment," force law schools to allow equal access to military recruiters even though the military discriminated against gays and lesbians. The law schools argued that when Congress required the schools to host military recruiters on campus on the same basis as private non-discriminating-against-gays employers, Congress was regulating the schools' expressive conduct, in a way that entitled the schools to the protection of *O'Brien*.

    **a. Court rejects:** But the Supreme Court unanimously ***rejected*** even the applicability of *O'Brien* to the Solomon Amendment. In an opinion by Chief Justice Roberts, the court noted that "Unlike flag burning [see *Texas v. Johnson, infra*, p. 545, applying *O'Brien* to the flag-burning scenario], the conduct regulated by the Solomon Amendment is ***not inherently expressive.***" When, prior to the enactment of the Solomon Amendment, schools barred military recruiters from campus, the expressive content of the schools' conduct was evident only because the schools ***"accompanied their conduct with speech explaining it."*** For instance, an observer who simply saw a military recruiter recruiting off-campus wouldn't know whether this was because the school was expressing its disapproval of the military or because, say, all classrooms were full. Therefore, the fact that the expressive content of the schools' conduct could not be understood without accompanying speech was "strong evidence that the conduct at issue here is ***not so inherently expressive that it warrants protection under O'Brien.***"

        **i. No ability to transform conduct into speech by talking about it:** And, Roberts continued, "If combining speech and conduct were enough to create expressive conduct, a regulated party could ***always transform conduct into 'speech' simply by talking about it.***" For instance, he said, "If an individual announces that he intends to express his disapproval of the Internal Revenue Service by refusing to pay his income taxes, we would have to apply *O'Brien* to determine whether the tax code violates the First Amendment." *O'Brien* did not require this absurd result.

        **ii. Significance:** So, *FAIR* makes clear, to be covered by *O'Brien* the conduct must be ***"inherently expressive"*** — conduct that gets expressive meaning from ***accompanying speech doesn't qualify***, unless the government is also regulating the accompanying speech.

**B. Flag desecration:** One context in which the right of symbolic speech is important is the area of *flag desecration*: nearly all states (as well as the federal government) make it a crime to mutilate or otherwise desecrate an American flag. Most such statutes seem to have been enacted for the purpose of preserving the flag as a symbol of *national unity*, or some similar rationale. If such a statute, either on its face or as applied, applies to some flag-related conduct but not others based on the actor's *message*, the Court will presumably apply strict scrutiny, and will therefore probably strike the statute.

    **1.** *Texas v. Johnson:* This is what happened in *Texas v. Johnson*, 491 U.S. 397 (1989), the first of the Court's two highly controversial decisions on flag burning.

       **a. Statute:** The Texas statute at issue in *Johnson* made it a crime to "intentionally or knowingly desecrate … a state or national flag." "Desecrate" was defined to mean "deface, damage, or otherwise physically mistreat in a way that the actor knows will *seriously offend* one or more persons *likely to observe* or discover his action."

       **b. Facts:** Johnson, the defendant, participated in a political demonstration outside the 1984 Republican National Convention in Dallas. At the end of the demonstration, he unfurled an American flag, doused it with kerosene, and set it on fire. While the flag burned, the protestors chanted, "America, the red, white, and blue, we spit on you." Johnson was charged with violating the desecration statute; at his trial, several witnesses testified that they had been seriously offended by the flag burning, and he was convicted.

       **c. Holding:** By a 5-4 vote, the Court held that the Texas statute violated the First Amendment as applied to Johnson's acts. The majority opinion was written by Justice Brennan.

          **i. "Track one" analysis:** The key to the result reached by the majority was that the Court applied what we have called "track one" analysis. That is, the majority determined that the prosecution of Johnson was *"directly related to expression."* In reaching this conclusion, the Court reviewed the two objectives that Texas asserted it was pursuing: (1) preventing breaches of the peace; and (2) preserving the flag as a symbol of nationhood and national unity. As to objective (1), the majority simply disbelieved that preventing breaches of the peace was what had motivated Texas on these facts (since no disturbance of the peace either actually occurred or was threatened by this particular flag burning). As to objective (2), the need to protect the flag as a symbol of national unity would only be implicated if the defendant's conduct had a contrary message associated with it, so this objective was "directly related to expression" and thus called for track one scrutiny. The content-based nature of the statute was illustrated by the fact that particular conduct was covered only if an observer's likely reaction would be to be "seriously offended" — the offense could only flow from the message accompanying the act. (For instance, if D had burned the flag as a means of respectfully disposing of it because it was dirty or torn, he would not have offended anyone, and he would not have been convicted under the statute.)

          **ii. Strict scrutiny applied:** Since Johnson was prosecuted only because of the content of the particular message he was conveying, the Court applied strict scrutiny to the statute. "If there is a bedrock principle underlying the First Amendment, it is that the Government may not prohibit the expression of an idea simply because society finds the idea itself offensive or disagreeable." Here, Texas's objective — preserving the flag as a symbol of national unity — may have been worthy, even "compelling." But the means chosen by Texas to serve that objective were not necessary ones. First, the majority didn't believe that the nation's belief in the cherished significance of the flag would be undermined by acts of mutilation; indeed, these acts might produce the opposite result. Second, the government could combat such acts by acts of its own, such as giving the remains of the flag a respectful burial (as one witness to Johnson's burning did).

   **d. Dissent:** Four members of the Court bitterly dissented. The principal dissent was by Justice Rehnquist (joined by White and O'Connor). The dissenters thought that a state could prohibit the burning of a flag without violating the First Amendment prohibition on suppression of ideas. "The flag is not simply another 'idea' or 'point of view' competing for recognition in the market place of ideas." Also, the dissenters thought that flag burning is so inherently inflammatory that it inevitably threatens a breach of the peace, and thus could be analogized to "fighting words" and deprived of First Amendment protection entirely. In a separate dissent, Justice Stevens thought that the flag, even though it is in a sense an intangible asset, could be protected from desecration just as, say, the Lincoln Memorial could be protected from having a political message spray-painted upon it.

2. **The federal statute:**   The problem with the Texas statute in *Texas v. Johnson* seemed to be the statute's proscription of flag burning that would "seriously offend" observers — this reference to "offensiveness" made it clear that only flag burning intended to convey a particular message (disrespect) was proscribed by the statute. Therefore, immediately after the *Johnson* decision, the U.S. Congress tried to enact a *federal* flag burning statute that would ban all or most flag burning without being content-based and thus unconstitutional. This federal statute, the Flag Protection Act of 1989, punished anyone who "knowingly mutilates, defaces, physically defiles, burns, maintains on the floor or ground, or tramples upon any flag of the United States. ... " However, even though the statute avoided any reference to conduct that would "offend" an observer, the Supreme Court, by a 5-4 vote, found that this statute, too, was a violation of the First Amendment. ***U.S. v. Eichman***, 496 U.S. 310 (1990).

   **a. Rationale:**   The five-justice majority in *Eichman* found that despite the more careful wording, this statute, like the one in *Johnson*, was content-based. "Although the [Act] contains no explicit content-based limitation on the scope of prohibited conduct, it is nevertheless clear that the government's asserted *interest* is 'related to the suppression of free expression' ... and concerned with the content of such expression." The majority noted that the government was asserting its interest in preserving the flag as a *symbol for certain national ideals*; this goal was intimately related to the content of the burner's message (so that, for instance, a person's secret burning of the flag in his basement would not threaten this symbolic meaning of the flag). Since Congress was attempting to "suppress ... expression out of concern for its likely communicative impact," the statute had to be strictly scrutinized. It failed that scrutiny. (Interestingly, Justice Scalia was part of the five-member majority voting to strike down the statute, a surprise given his generally conservative views.)

3. **Significance:**   As a result of *Johnson* and *Eichman*, there is probably no way for government (whether state or federal) to "wipe out flag burning." Even if the statute uses the

most content-neutral language (e.g., "No one may burn a flag under any circumstances"), the statute will presumably be struck down so long as the Court believes that it was ***motivated*** by a desire to preserve the symbolic value of the flag. Therefore, a constitutional amendment is probably the only way to prevent such acts.

*Quiz Yourself on*

## TIME, PLACE & MANNER RESTRICTIONS; SYMBOLIC EXPRESSION

**68.** Centerville is a small town. Its two biggest streets are Broadway and Main. After several recent parades and demonstrations that badly snarled traffic, Centerville's City Council enacted an ordinance that forbade all parades from taking place on either Broadway or Main. The ordinance did not forbid parades on the other, smaller streets in town. There is no evidence that the ordinance was motivated by hostility to particular types of parades, and the ban has been enforced even-handedly as to all parades. Citizens Against Corruption, a group wishing to protest what it believed was corruption in the mayor's office, paraded in an organized way down Broadway, and its leaders were arrested. The city has asserted that its ban on parades is a valid "time, place and manner" regulation.

   **(a)** What standard should the court use in evaluating the ordinance as applied here?

_____

   **(b)** Should the court uphold the ordinance, and convict the marchers, under the test you specified in (a)? _____

**69.** An ordinance in the town of Harmony provides that "no demonstration or parade involving more than 20 persons shall take place on the town's streets, parks or other city-owned property without the prior issuance of a permit." The permit is free, and is to be granted by the mayor's office, "if the mayor concludes, acting in a reasonable manner, that the proposed activity would not be detrimental to the overall community, taking into account the time, place and manner of the activity." Firebrand, the head of a local group of anarchists, wished to conduct a demonstration in the park, at which he planned to urge his followers to immediately attempt a "sit in" of the mayor's office. The mayor, without knowing the precise purpose of the demonstration and knowing only that it was to be a demonstration against the local government, refused to issue the permit. In announcing the refusal, the mayor stated that "there has been too much demonstration, and not enough cooperation, around here recently." Firebrand then brought suit for an injunction against continued application of the permit requirement, and for a declaratory judgment that the permit requirement as drafted was unconstitutional. Should the court find the ordinance unconstitutional on its face? _____

**70.** Same facts as prior Question. Now, however, assume that Firebrand ignored the ordinance, did not ask for a permit, and held a demonstration involving 30 people in a city park. He was arrested and charged with violating the ordinance. He now wishes to defend on the grounds that the ordinance is overbroad and thus facially invalid. Assuming that the ordinance is indeed overbroad, should the court acquit Firebrand?

_____

**71.** Same facts as Question 70. Now, however, assume that before Firebrand ever considered speaking, the Supreme Court of the state in which Harmony is located interpreted the Harmony ordinance in a very narrow way, so as to make it not overbroad. In particular, the court said that the mayor should adopt regulations stating with precision the grounds for granting or denying a permit, and the mayor did this. As in Question 70, Firebrand has ignored the requirement, has demonstrated, was arrested, and is now defending on the grounds that the statute itself is overbroad. Should the court acquit Firebrand?

_____

72. The town of Lawton had a very carefully worded permit requirement. For any demonstration or parade involving more than 30 people, a permit was required, application for which must be made at least one hour prior to the close of business on the day before the proposed activity. Under the terms of the ordinance, the police commissioner was required to issue the permit, subject only to the rule that if in the commissioner's reasonable judgment, a breach of peace would be likely to occur which could not be controlled with the manpower available to the Lawton Police Department, the permit could be denied until such later date as proper police protection could be arranged (by borrowing from other police departments, if necessary).

Rouser, a radical, applied late on Friday afternoon to make a speech on Saturday. Because past speeches by Rouser had led to skirmishes, and because the commissioner believed that under weekend police schedules only three officers would be available (a number which the Commissioner believed would not be sufficient if problems should occur), the Commissioner turned down the request for a permit, and suggested that Rouser wait until the following Saturday. A local Justice of the Peace Court was open Friday night, and the Justice would have had jurisdiction to issue an injunction against the permit requirement. However, Rouser did not seek an injunction. Instead, Rouser gave his speech anyway, and no violence occurred. Rouser was charged with violating the permit requirement. He is now defending on the grounds that he was wrongfully denied the permit, because there was not in fact a serious threat of a breach of the peace, and that even if there was one, the presence of three officers would have been sufficient.

Assuming that the court agrees with Rouser's factual contentions about the danger of breach of the peace, should Rouser be acquitted? _____

73. The city of Blue Bell has enacted an ordinance providing as follows: no "canvasser or solicitor" may ring the doorbell of a private home, or knock on the door of a private home, where her purpose is to distribute handbills or to solicit an order for goods, services or charitable contributions. The ban does not prevent a person from simply sticking advertising material under the door or into the mail slot, so long as there is no bell-ringing or door-knocking. The purpose of the ordinance is to avoid disturbing residents (including those who work nights and sleep days), and also to prevent crime (e.g., people who want to see into the residence to "case the joint" for a later burglary).

Delrina, a Jehovah's Witness, was charged with violating the statute in that she rang doorbells so that she could personally hand inhabitants the literature requesting donations to the Jehovah's Witness organization. She has defended on the grounds that the ordinance represents an unconstitutional infringement of her right to free expression. May Delrina be convicted? _____

74. The city of Crooklyn had two substantial ethnic populations that were frequently at odds with each other, Middle-eastern Moslems and Orthodox Jews. After complying with a city requirement calling for a permit before the making of a public address, Mohammed, a self-proclaimed Islamic Fundamentalist, gave a speech in a park in Crooklyn. There were approximately 100 Islamic followers in the audience, as well as a group of about 30 Orthodox Jews. The Jews carried signs opposing Mohammed. Mohammed then made various anti-Semetic inflammatory statements, such as "Jews are corrupt" and "Jews control the U.S. government." He also addressed the Jews in the audience, saying, "You Jews in the audience today, you're not fit to kiss the dung-stained shoes of my poorest follower." At no time did Mohammed urge his audience to attack any of the Jewish onlookers or to otherwise commit immediate illegal acts.

Some of the Jews in the audience began to shake their fists and yell back at Mohammed; five of them then began to move towards the podium with upraised fists. There were 15 police officers at the scene to prevent disturbances, most of them ringed around the podium. They immediately arrested Mohammed and charged him with violating an ordinance prohibiting anyone from inciting a riot or causing a breach of the peace. Mohammed has defended on the grounds that his arrest violated his freedom of expression.

**(a)** What doctrine can the prosecution point to as justifying the arrest?  _____

**(b)** Do First Amendment principles prevent Mohammed's conviction?  _____

**75.** The Women's Health Alliance is a clinic that principally performs abortions. Abortion protesters decided to demonstrate outside the clinic. The protesters waved signs containing messages such as "Abortion Equals Murder." Whenever the protesters saw a woman leaving the clinic, they shouted, "Baby Killer," at her. The protesters remained at least 20 feet away from the front door of the clinic, and they did not block anyone's access to or from the clinic. All protesting took place on public property. A local ordinance forbids "the making of any public statement or the showing of any sign where the speaker knows the statement or sign is likely to be offensive to the person to whom it is addressed." May a protester who has waved the sign and shouted the epithet described above be convicted of violating the statute?

_____

**76.** State U, a public university, recently added the following provision to its Student Code: "No student or faculty member shall address to any other student or faculty member any verbal slur, invective, insult or epithet based on the addressee's race, ethnicity, gender, handicap or sexual orientation." The penalty for a first offense is suspension, and for the second offense is expulsion. Desmond, a white student at the university, addressed the following remark to Vera, a black student, "You nigger, go back to Africa where you belong." State U has commenced disciplinary proceedings against Desmond. You are the university's general counsel. The president has asked you the following question: "May the university constitutionally suspend Desmond for making this remark?" If your answer is "no," please describe the types of changes that might be made in the Code to alleviate the problem.  _____

**77.** The state of Morality makes it a crime to post any "indecent" photo on a computer system located in the state, if the computer is connected by means of a physical wire or a telephone line to any other computer. "Indecent" is defined to include "any photo of a naked man or woman that would be offensive when measured by local community standards." The legislature means for its prohibition to apply even to pictures that would not be "obscene," including photos having significant artistic value. The legislature's purpose is to prevent minors from seeing indecent material. *Playpen* magazine puts a photo of a naked woman (which is not obscene under U.S. Supreme Court rulings) on its dial-in computer, located in Morality. Peter, a 16-year-old, dials in and retrieves the photo. A local prosecutor in Morality prosecutes the owner of *Playpen*, Hugh, and shows that Hugh had ordered that the photo be placed on the system. May Hugh constitutionally be convicted?  _____

**78.** The Grand Union Station is a large train station owned and run by a public agency, the Tri-State Transit Authority. The Authority has enacted a "policy statement," prominently posted on the walls of the Station, which says, in part, that "no person or organization shall solicit for funds within this Station." Hussan, a member of the Hari Krishna religious sect, approached numerous passengers in the Station one day, asking each one, "Would you like to contribute to my religious organization?" Authority police stopped him and politely but forcibly removed him from the station for violating the no-solicitation policy. The police appear to enforce the no-solicitation rule uniformly, i.e., they stop everyone from soliciting, regardless of whether the solicitation is religiously-oriented, regardless of whether it appears to be "begging" or on behalf of an organized charity, etc.

    **(a)** Is the Station a "public forum" for purposes of First Amendment analysis? _____

    **(b)** Was the police's treatment of Hussan constitutional? _____

**79.** For many years, Acadia High School, a public high school, has had a School Dress and Appearance Code. The Code provides that, among other things, no student may go barefoot, hair must be worn in a way that will not interfere with school functions (including getting caught in machinery in shop and home economics classes), and that girls may not wear skirts more than one inch above the knee. One of the purposes behind the Code (including specifically the skirt-length provision) was to avoid dress or appearance that might distract other students or cause discipline problems. Alicia is a member of an informal group of girls who call themselves the "Sexed Up Girls." The members of this group, all of whom attend Acadia High School, wish to dress in a way that expresses their notion of themselves as sexually active women who are aware of that fact and wish other students to know it. Alicia came to school wearing an extremely short and tight mini skirt, four inches above the knee. She was suspended for violating the Code. She has defended on the grounds that the Code, as applied to her, violates her First Amendment rights.

    **(a)** Does the application of the Code to Alicia's skirt impair any expression on her part (putting aside the issue of whether any interference is justified)? _____

    **(b)** Assuming, for purposes of this part only, that some expression by Alicia has been interfered with, is the application of the Code to Alicia's skirt constitutionally permissible? _____

---

*Answers*

    **68. (a) The ban must be: (1) content-neutral; (2) narrowly tailored to serve a significant governmental interest; and (3) leave open alternative channels for communication of the information.**

    **(b) No, probably.** The facts indicate to us that the ban is content-neutral both in terms of the purposes for which it was enacted and the way in which it is applied. However, it seems not to be "*narrowly tailored* to serve a *significant* governmental interest." Since the proposed speech would take place in the most traditional of all public forums — the streets — mere convenience, such as avoiding traffic obstructions, probably does not qualify as a "significant governmental interest." Also, there are more narrowly-tailored restrictions that could be used, such as an advance permit requirement which would give the police time to detour traffic and thereby reduce disruption. Finally, the requirement that alternative channels be left open is strictly construed in a public-forum context; the fact that there may be other public places (e.g., smaller streets) where the same expression is allowed will not generally be enough to qualify as an adequate alternative channel.

    **69. Yes.** An advance permit requirement will be upheld if it is content-neutral, adequately constrains administrative discretion, and is a reasonable means of insuring that public order is maintained. However, in order to avoid giving the official charged with granting or denying permit applications too much *discretion*, the grounds upon which a permit may be denied must be set forth *specifically* and *narrowly* in the ordinance. Here, the standard given for granting or denying a permit — that the proposed activities "not be detrimental to the overall community" — gives the mayor virtually uncontrolled discretion, and acts as an invitation to him to behave in a content-based way. This excessive discretion makes the statute overbroad and vague. Therefore, even though Firebrand's own proposed conduct might be capable of being prohibited by an appropriately-drawn ordinance, the ordinance here must be struck down as invalid on its face.

**70. Yes.** If a permit that is required prior to the exercise of First Amendment rights is unconstitutional *on its face*, the speaker is *not required* to apply for a permit. He may decline to apply, then speak, and avoid conviction on the grounds of the permit requirement's unconstitutionality. See, e.g., *Lovell v. Griffin*. Because a statute that is overbroad is facially invalid, this rule applies to overbreadth claims. Therefore, Firebrand may assert overbreadth even though he failed to ever apply for a permit.

**71. No.** A statute which appears to be overbroad may be saved from that fate by a state court *interpretation* cutting back the statute's scope so as to cover only constitutional applications. In the case of an apparently overbroad permit requirement, if such a state court interpretation occurs before a particular speaker flouts the ordinance, he will lose his overbreadth claim. See, e.g., *Cox v. New Hampshire*. (But if the narrowing court interpretation only occurred *after* the speaker spoke, the speaker will probably *not* lose the overbreadth claim.)

**72. No.** Where a permit requirement is not facially invalid (e.g., not unduly vague or overbroad), and the speaker's claim is merely that he has been wrongfully denied a permit, the speaker *must seek judicial relief* before speaking. That is, for an "as applied" as opposed to "facial" challenge to a permit requirement, one who ignores the denial of the permit loses the right to object to the permit scheme's unconstitutionality. There is an exception where the applicant shows that he could not have obtained prompt judicial review of the administrative denial of the permit; however, the facts here tell us that Rouser could have obtained judicial review prior to the time for the speech, if he had wanted to do so.

**73. No.** As with any "time, place and manner" restriction, the ordinance will be valid only if it is content-neutral, is narrowly tailored to serve a significant governmental interest, and leaves open alternative channels for communicating the information. Here, probably the requirement of content-neutrality is satisfied (unless there is evidence that, say, Jehovah's Witnesses were a special target of the ordinance). The government probably has a significant government interest in preventing homeowners from being disturbed at home when they do not want to be. However, it is doubtful that the ordinance is "narrowly tailored," since there are less restrictive alternatives (e.g., permitting a homeowner to indicate on his door that he does not wish to be disturbed by solicitors) — when the city makes a blanket assumption that *no* homeowner wishes to receive a solicitor, this is probably not a sufficiently narrowly tailored approach. Furthermore, it is doubtful whether alternative channels have been left open, since for many types of organizations, door-to-door and face-to-face is the only affordable means, given the large expense associated with, say, newspaper and TV advertising. Upon facts similar to these, the Court struck down a blanket ban. See *Watchtower Bible and Tract Soc. v. Stratton* (ban on solicitation without prior permit is unconstitutional).

**74. (a) The "fighting words" doctrine.**

**(b) Yes, probably.** Among the classes of speech which are not protected by the First Amendment are "fighting words," which the Court has defined as "those which by their very utterance … tend to incite an immediate breach of the peace." *Chaplinsky v. New Hampshire*. However, there are several exceptions and clarifications to the "fighting words" doctrine, which make it seldom applicable. One of those exceptions is that if the police have the physical ability to *control the angry crowd* as a means of preventing threatened violence, they *must do so* in preference to arresting the speaker for using "fighting words." *Cox v. Louisiana*. Here, it seems probable that the 15 police officers could have either arrested or at least restrained those Jews who were moving forward towards the podium, and probably any other hostile Jew in the audience. At the very least, the police needed to make some effort to do this, rather than immediately arrest the speaker.

75. **No.** In general, government may not forbid speech merely because it would be *"offensive"* to the listener. For example, language cannot be forbidden merely because it is profane. *Cohen v. California* (D cannot be punished for wearing a jacket bearing the legend "Fuck the Draft"). Here, the statute is phrased specifically to reach only "offensive" conduct, so it runs afoul of this principle. Furthermore, the statute is probably unconstitutionally vague, since a reasonable reader of it would not know exactly what types of language would be forbidden.

76. **No.** The problem is that the ban here is *content-based*. That is, it proscribes only certain types of speech, based on the content or message of that speech. Thus insults based on race, ethnicity and three other attributes are banned, but insults based on other attributes are not (e.g., the addressee's politics, intelligence, short or tall stature, etc.). Even if the university interprets the ban so as to bar only "fighting words," this will not be enough to save the statute, because *R.A.V. v. City of St. Paul* (striking down an anti-cross-burning statute) establishes that government may not ban some fighting words but not others, based on the words' precise message. The best way for State U to solve the problem is to amend its code so as to ban "all slurs, invectives, insults or epithets that would have the likely effect of either inducing the listener to respond with violence, or which would be likely to create in the listener an apprehension of imminent physical harm." Such a formulation would essentially ban all fighting words, plus all words that would constitute an assault; these two categories may clearly be constitutionally proscribed, as long as the proscription occurs in a content-neutral way. (Of course, this re-write would fail to prohibit a lot of hate speech, so it would not be a perfect solution, but at least it would be content-neutral.)

77. **No.** The Supreme Court has held that computer networks are more like newspapers than like broadcast TV, and that content-based restrictions on what is placed on such networks must therefore be strictly scrutinized. See *Reno v. ACLU*. Applying strict scrutiny, the measure is clearly unconstitutional, since it's content-based (only materials with an "indecent" message are proscribed), and it's not narrowly tailored towards the (admittedly "compelling") objective of keeping indecent materials away from minors — for instance, the state could give parents free filtering software that would block access to these materials by minors. See *Ashcroft v. ACLU*. Furthermore, the statute is overbroad: it applies to viewing by adults (who have a right to see the photo), as well as to viewing by minors (who probably don't have a First Amendment right to see such a photo, though this is not completely clear). Since the rights of adults are being curtailed in a content-based way, the statute will surely fail strict scrutiny. *Reno v. ACLU*.

78. **(a) No.** The Supreme Court has held that airport terminals are not "public forums," even though they are public places. *Int'l Soc. for Krishna Consciousness, Inc. v. Lee.* Assuming that train stations are analyzed the same way as are airport terminals — which seems virtually certain — the terminal here falls into the category of "non-public forum." Non-public forums are public facilities that are used for purposes that are not especially linked to expression; thus the terminal here is primarily linked to transportation, and has never historically been viewed as a center for expression.

**(b) Yes.** A non-public forum offers the *least* constitutionally-protected access for First Amendment expression. Government regulation of expression in a non-public forum must merely be: (1) *reasonable* in light of the *purpose* served by the forum; and (2) *viewpoint neutral*. See *Krishna v. Lee, supra*. The Court in *Krishna* held that these tests were met by a ban on funds solicitation in airport terminals; presumably the same analysis would apply to the fund solicitation in the train station here. The ban on face-to-face solicitation of money was found to be reasonable in *Krishna* because such solicitation might slow pedestrian traffic within the terminal, interfering with its transportation-related function. (But a ***total ban*** on ***literature distribution*** was found not to be even "reasonable" in *Krishna*.)

79. **(a) Yes, probably.** The Supreme Court has never spoken on whether a public school student's choice of clothing or other aspects of appearance is sufficiently "communicative" that the choice receives First Amendment protection. (The only relevant case is *Tinker v. Des Moines School District*, holding that the wearing of a black armband as a protest was expressive conduct.) However, a majority of the Court believes that "nude dancing" contains enough expressive content to be protected by the First Amendment. See *Barnes v. Glen Theatre*. Regardless of whether a typical student's selection of clothing would be found to be sufficiently communicative to be covered by the First Amendment, Alicia's selection here has a clear expressive component, in that she is trying to make a statement about her sexuality. Therefore, Alicia probably would receive some First Amendment protection for her choice of skirt (though, as described in the answer to the next part, the fact that she receives some protection does not mean that the Code is invalid as applied to her).

**(b) Yes, probably.** The first question is whether the restriction is "content neutral." If there were evidence that the skirt-length provision was enacted principally for the purpose of suppressing statements about the wearer's sexuality or sexual availability, then we would have a content-based regulation, which would have to survive strict scrutiny (which it probably could not). However, on the facts here, all aspects of the Code seem to be directed at the maintenance of discipline and order, and not at the suppression of any particular type of message. Therefore, the Code is probably content-neutral. If so, we apply the standard "track 2" analysis: the regulation must be ***narrowly tailored*** to serve a ***significant governmental interest***, and must leave open ***"alternative channels"*** for communicating the information. Probably all parts of this test are satisfied. The school district certainly has a significant interest in maintaining discipline and avoiding distraction. Assuming that there is at least some evidence that short mini skirts would lead other students to gawk, make sexual propositions to the wearer, or otherwise be distracted, the requisite "narrow tailoring" is probably present. And there probably are adequate alternative channels for women such as Alicia to communicate their sexual availability (e.g., by making verbal statements of availability, by wearing tight-fitting sweaters, etc.).

# VI. DEFAMATION AND INVASION OF PRIVACY

A. **Initially no protection:** Initially, the Supreme Court took the view that any language treated as ***defamatory*** under state law was not entitled to First Amendment protection. For instance, in *Chaplinsky (supra*, p. 503), the Court included libelous statements in the list of categories which are "no essential part of any exposition of ideas," and as to which there is therefore no First Amendment protection.

1. **Group libel:** The class of statements that are unprotected because they are libelous was even extended to include those that defame ***groups*** as well as individuals, in *Beauharnais v. Illinois*, 343 U.S. 250 (1952), a 5-4 decision. The Court seemed to be saying that the states could define libel however they wished (for instance, by including groups as victims), without raising a constitutional issue; the only restriction was that the extended definition must be "related to the peace and well-being of the state." But the four dissenters

argued that such a broadening of state libel rules impaired the expression protected by the First Amendment, at least where the "group libel" did not present a "clear and present danger" of breach of the peace.

    **a. Probably not law today:** *Beauharnais* has never been explicitly overruled by the Supreme Court. However, ***New York Times Co. v. Sullivan** (infra)* and its progeny, insofar as they have placed clear First Amendment limits on the states' freedom to define and punish libel and slander as they wish, probably mean that *Beauharnais* is no longer good law.

**B. *New York Times v. Sullivan:***    The Court concluded that the First Amendment protections for speech and the press place at least ***some limits on state rules for defamation actions***, in *New York Times Co. v. Sullivan*, 376 U.S. 254 (1964). In particular, these constitutional protections require that a defense for ***"honest error"*** be allowed in the case of statements made about ***public officials*** relating to their ***official conduct.***

    **1. Facts:**    Plaintiff in *New York Times* was a public official one of whose duties was supervising the Montgomery, Alabama Police Department. He alleged that the *Times* had libeled him by printing an advertisement that stated that the Montgomery police had attempted to terrorize Martin Luther King and his followers. (Plaintiff was not even named in the advertisement; but under Alabama libel law, criticism of the department of which he was in charge was deemed to reflect on his reputation.)

        **a. Truth as affirmative defense:**    The libel law of Alabama, like that of most states at the time, provided for ***strict liability***. That is, a publisher could not avoid liability by showing that he reasonably believed his statement to be true, if it was in fact false. Furthermore, although "truth" was an available defense under Alabama law, it was an ***affirmative defense*** as to which the defendant bore the burden of proof. Therefore, although the factual errors in the *Times* ad were minor (e.g., that Dr. King had been arrested seven times, rather than the actual four times), and even though there was no showing that the *Times* ought to have known that the ad prepared by others contained falsehoods, the paper was nonetheless subjected to a $500,000 libel judgment. The net result was that familiar rules of libel gave Alabama's "white establishment" a formidable weapon with which to punish the *Times*, and any other proponents of civil rights. See Tribe, p. 863.

    **2. Libel judgment reversed:**    A unanimous Supreme Court ***reversed*** the damage award. In so doing, the Court for the first time established that ***state defamation rules are limited by First Amendment principles.***

        **a. Robust debate:**    The Court viewed this case as one involving ***criticism of government policy***, not merely factual statements about an individual. Debate on public issues must be "uninhibited, robust, and wide open," and may often include "vehement, caustic, and sometimes unpleasantly sharp attacks on government and public officials." Requiring critics of official conduct to guarantee the truth of all their factual assertions would lead to ***self-censorship***, rather than free debate.

            **i. Sedition Act:**    The Court found that the effect of Alabama's libel rules was similar to that of the original federal Sedition Act of 1798. The Sedition Act made it a crime to publish any "false scandalous and malicious writings" against the federal government with intent to bring it into "contempt or disrepute." Although the Act expired before the Supreme Court determined its constitutionality, the view that the Act violated the First Amendment had "carried the day in the court of history," according to the *New York Times* Court. So, here, criticism of government public officials could not be curtailed, without violating the First Amendment.

3. **Formal rule:** The Court was not content merely to strike the libel judgment as a disguised ban on criticizing the government. Instead, it articulated a formal rule, so that future speakers would not have to worry about liability for libel in similar circumstances: the First Amendment prohibits a ***public official*** from recovering damages for a defamatory falsehood ***relating to his official conduct*** unless he proves that the statement was made with ***"actual malice"*** — that is, ***"with knowledge that it was false*** or with ***reckless disregard of whether it was false or not."*** The case thus establishes a ***"constitutional privilege for good faith critics of government officials."*** Tribe, pp. 864-65.

   a. **Knowing or reckless falsity:** *New York Times* requires the public official to prove that the defendant ***knew*** his statement was false, or ***recklessly disregarded*** whether it was true or not. It is ***not*** enough for the official to show that a ***"reasonably prudent man"*** would not have published the statement, or would have investigated further before publishing. Rather, there must be evidence to permit the conclusion that "the defendant ***in fact entertained serious doubts*** as to the truth of his publication." *St. Amant v. Thompson*, 390 U.S. 727 (1968). Thus at least with respect to statements published about public officials relating to their duties (and also statements about "public figures," see *infra*), ***"ignorance is bliss."*** Tribe, pp. 870-71.

C. **Extension to "public figures":** The *New York Times* "actual knowledge or reckless disregard of the truth" test was extended to include ***"public figures"*** in *Curtis Pub. Co. v. Butts* and *Associated Press v. Walker*, both reported at 388 U.S. 130 (1967). In these cases both the University of Georgia football coach and a prominent retired Army General were held to be public figures.

   1. **"Public figure" narrowly defined:** However, the Court has read the "public figure" category ***narrowly*** in cases since *Butts* and *Walker*. The Court has recognized three classes of public figures: (1) those who have ***"general fame*** and notoriety in the community," who are public figures for ***all*** purposes; (2) those who have "voluntarily ***injected themselves*** into a ***public controversy*** in order to influence the resolution of the issues involved," who are public figures ***only*** with respect to ***that controversy***; and (3) ***"involuntary*** public figures," who are directly ***affected*** by the actions of public officials, such as a ***defendant in a criminal case*** (who would be an involuntary public figure with respect to news items concerning that case.) See *Gertz v. Robert Welch, Inc.,* 418 U.S. 323 (1974) (discussed extensively *infra*.)

   2. **Meaning of "voluntarily injected":** The Court will not be quick to conclude that a person has "voluntarily injected" himself into a controversy (required for category (2) above). For instance, in *Time, Inc. v. Firestone*, 424 U.S. 448 (1976), *Time* incorrectly reported that one of the grounds for Ms. Firestone's divorce was adultery. The Court found that she was not a "public figure," even though she had held some press conferences during the divorce trial, and even though the trial itself had been widely reported in the Miami newspapers. (Nor did Ms. Firestone's extensive activities before the trial as a prominent member of Palm Beach society make her a public figure.)

3. **"Involuntary" class narrow:** Similarly, category (3), that of "involuntary public figures," has also been narrowly construed by the Court; such involuntary figures will be relatively rare.

D. **Private figures:** The *New York Times* standard does *not* apply to suits by *private figures*. That is, where the plaintiff is neither a public official nor a public figure, there is *no constitutional requirement* that he prove that the defendant *knew his statement to be false or recklessly disregarded the truth. Gertz v. Robert Welch, Inc.,* 418 U.S. 323 (1974).

   1. **Facts:** The plaintiff, Gertz, was a locally well-known lawyer who represented the family of a youth who was killed by a policeman. Defendant, publisher of a John Birch Society magazine, falsely attacked Gertz as having helped "frame" the policeman and as being a communist.

   2. **Negligence standard permitted:** The Supreme Court held, 5-4, that in libel actions brought by *private figures*, the First Amendment *does not forbid use of a simple negligence standard*. The states are free to decide whether they wish to establish negligence, recklessness or knowing falsity as the standard (but they *may not impose strict liability).*

      a. **Reasoning:** The majority reasoned that private individuals are both more vulnerable, as well as more deserving of recovery for defamation, than public figures. They are more *vulnerable* because public figures generally have "significantly greater access" to the media, and can use that access to counteract false statements. They are *deserving* of extensive protection against defamation, because public figures have generally "voluntarily exposed themselves to increased risk of injury from defamatory falsehoods," unlike private persons.

   3. **Punitive damages not allowed:** The majority also held that, if a private figure shows only negligence on the part of the defendant, rather than recklessness or knowing falsity, he *may not recover presumed or punitive damages*. ("Presumed" damages are ones awarded where there is no proof of actual harm, but the jury believes that damage would ordinarily result from a defamatory communication like the one in issue.) The Court imposed this limitation because the state's interest in giving broader protection to private figures only justified awarding "compensation for *actual* injury."

   4. **Who is private figure:** In holding that Gertz himself was a private figure, the Court implicitly took a narrow view of the term "public figure." Gertz was a well-known lawyer locally, and had agreed to take a case which he knew would attract substantial publicity. Nonetheless, Gertz had not achieved "general fame or notoriety in the community" (so that he was not public figure for all purposes); similarly, he was not a public figure for the limited purposes of this case, because he had played only a "minimal role" in it.

   5. **Dissents:** The four dissenters differed significantly among themselves in reasoning. For instance, Justice Brennan continued to believe (as he had in *Rosenbloom v. Metromedia,* Inc., 403 U.S. 29) that the *New York Times* standard should be applied to private-person libel actions arising out of events of "public or general interest." But Justice White argued the quite opposite position that the *Gertz* majority should not even have stripped the states of their right to apply *strict liability* in suits brought by private persons.

   6. **Proof of falsity:** As noted, one aspect of *Gertz* is that the states may not impose strict liability, even in cases brought by private figures. This aspect of *Gertz* was broadened in the later case of *Philadelphia Newspapers, Inc. v. Hepps,* 475 U.S. 767 (1986), where the

Court held that the private figure suing a media defendant must bear the burden of proving not only "fault," but also the *falsity* of the defendant's statement. That is, *Gertz* has been held to replace the common-law rule *presuming* falsity. (This holding applies only where the suit involves a matter of "public interest"; the presumption of falsity is probably constitutional where there is no matter of public concern, in light of *Dun & Bradstreet, Inc. v. Greenmoss Builders, Inc., infra*, p. 557.)

**E. Non-media defendants:** Both *New York Times* and *Gertz* involved *media* defendants, and in those cases the Court relied heavily on freedom-of-the-press considerations, especially the need to prevent media self-censorship. It is not clear whether the public-figure standard of *New York Times* and the private-figure standard of *Gertz* also apply where the *defendant* is a *private person* or other *non-media defendant.*

    **1. Possibility of different standard:** Thus it is possible that such defendants might be liable *without* a showing of reckless disregard or knowledge of falsity when they defame a public official or public figure. Similarly, they might even be *strictly liable* where they defame a *private* figure.

        **a. Unlikely:** However, a post-*Gertz* case makes it less likely that the Court will distinguish between media and non-media defendants. In that case, *Dun & Bradstreet, Inc. v. Greenmoss Builders, Inc.,* discussed further, *infra*, D was a credit reporting agency (that is, a non-media defendant) which falsely reported that P, a corporation, was insolvent. The legal issue in the case was whether presumed and punitive damages (see *infra*, p. 557) could be awarded. Rather than deciding whether the distinction between media and non-media defendants was constitutionally significant, a plurality of the Court distinguished between matters of "public interest" and those of merely private interest. (It permitted presumed and punitive damages to be recovered without a showing of reckless disregard for the truth where only matters of private concern are involved.) Thus it appears unlikely that the distinction between media and non-media defendants will assume constitutional significance within libel law.

        **b. Criticism:** In any event, a distinction between media and non-media defendants would seem to be unfair. For instance, although it is conceivable that the Court might theoretically allow strict liability to be imposed for defamation of private figures if the defendant is not part of the media, "[I]t would seem strange to hold that the press, composed of professionals and causing much greater damage because of the wider distribution of the communication, can constitutionally be held liable only for negligence, but that a private person, engaged in a casual private conversation with a single person, can be held liable at his peril if the statement turns out to be false, without any regard to his lack of fault." Rest. 2d, Torts, §580B, Comment e.

**F. Statements of no "public interest":** If the communication does *not involve any matter of "public interest,"* special constitutional rules apply. These were laid down in *Dun & Bradstreet, Inc. v. Greenmoss Builders, Inc.,* 472 U.S. 749 (1985).

    **1. Facts:** D was a credit reporting agency which falsely reported to several subscribers that P, a small corporation, was insolvent. The issue in the case was whether presumed and punitive damages could be awarded without a showing of reckless disregard for the truth or actual knowledge of falsity.

    **2. Result:** Although no opinion commanded a majority of the Court, the divided Court affirmed an award of both types of damages. Three Justices thought that presumed and punitive damages could be awarded even without a showing of reckless disregard for the truth or knowledge of falsity if the statements did not involve any issue of "public interest"; two more Justices thought that *Gertz* was entirely wrongly decided (and thus that presumed and punitive damages should be allowed to all private plaintiffs, regardless of whether an issue of public interest was involved).

   **3. Consequences:**   Thus *Dun & Bradstreet* seems to put a majority of the Court behind two or three constitutional principles:

   **a. Presumed and punitive damages:**   First, where a private plaintiff sues concerning statements that involve no issue of public interest, he can recover ***presumed and punitive damages without*** a showing that the defendant recklessly disregarded the truth or knew of the falsity of his statement. This is the actual result of *Dun & Bradstreet*.

   **b. Strict liability:**   Secondly, *Dun & Bradstreet* probably means that where a private figure sues on a statement relating only to matters of private concern, ***he is not constitutionally required to show even ordinary negligence*** in order to recover. (At least one member of the Court that decided *Dun & Bradstreet*, Justice White, stated that he believed this result to follow from *Dun & Bradstreet*. See his concurrence in the judgment in that case.)

**G. Statements of opinion:**   The Supreme Court has refused to give special First Amendment protection for statements of *"opinion."* So some statements, even though they express opinions, may be the subject of defamation actions. But only when a statement contains or implies a statement of ***provably false fact*** may the suit proceed. *Milkovich v. Lorain Journal Co.*, 497 U.S. 1 (1990).

   **1. Holding:**   In *Milkovich*, the Supreme Court held that statements of opinion ***get no special First Amendment protection***. However, the majority opinion in *Milkovich* makes it clear that the Court's prior First Amendment rulings will ensure that statements of ***pure*** opinion are not found to be defamatory. The Court observed that these prior cases require any libel plaintiff to prove: (1) that the statement is "***false***"; and (2) that the statement can be reasonably interpreted as stating ***"actual facts"*** about an individual. A pure statement of opinion (e.g., "In my opinion Mayor Jones shows his abysmal ignorance by accepting the teachings of Marx and Lenin.") would not be actionable, because it: (1) is not provably false; and (2) cannot reasonably be interpreted as stating actual facts about the plaintiff.

**H. Intentional infliction of emotional distress:**   The *New York Times* standard also now applies to actions for ***intentional infliction of emotional distress***. That is, a public figure or public official may recover against the publisher who causes such distress only if he can prove that the publication contained a false statement of fact published either with knowledge that the statement was false or with reckless disregard as to whether it was true or not. The Supreme Court so held in *Hustler Magazine v. Falwell*, 485 U.S. 46 (1988).

   **1. Facts:**   The facts of *Hustler* vividly illustrate this extension of *New York Times* to suits for emotional distress. Hustler Magazine published a parody of an advertisement for Campari Liqueur, which portrayed P (the Reverend Jerry Falwell) as a drunken hypocrite who had sex with his mother. The ad contained a legend at the bottom, "Ad parody, not to be taken seriously." A jury found that the parody could not reasonably be understood as describing actual facts about Falwell; the jury therefore rejected his libel claim, but gave him an award for intentional infliction of emotional distress.

**2. Holding:** All eight members of the Court who heard the case agreed that Falwell could **not** receive such an award consistent with the First Amendment. The Court observed that "even when a speaker or writer is motivated by hatred or ill-will, his expression [is] protected by the First Amendment." The Court noted that political parody and satire is an important element of political speech, and believed that there is no way to distinguish such "core" political speech from the kind of satire involved here. The "outrageousness" of the speech here did not furnish an acceptable distinction, because that term is inevitably highly subjective.

**I. Invasion-of-privacy actions:** Actions brought against media defendants for *"invasion of privacy"* raise similar First Amendment questions. The extent to which the constitutionally-based rules of *New York Times* and *Gertz* apply to such actions remains quite unclear.

**1. "False light" cases:** Probably the most common kind of invasion-of-privacy claim is the sort which has been called a *"false light"* action. In such an action, the plaintiff claims that he has been presented to public view in a *misleading way*, and that the erroneous presentation would be *highly offensive* to a reasonable person. What distinguishes such "false light" actions from defamation claims is that for the former, the plaintiff need **not** show that his *reputation has been damaged* — in fact, even the portrayal of a plaintiff as courageous, or dashing and romantic, could give rise to a "false light" action, if the presentation contains substantial misstatements of fact.

**a. New York Times standard applied:** Prior to *Gertz*, the plaintiff in a "false light" action arising out of a matter of "public interest" was required to satisfy the *New York Times* standard; that is, he was required to prove that the defendant published the report with *knowledge of its falsity* or *in reckless disregard of the truth*. This was the holding of *Time, Inc., v. Hill*, 385 U.S. 374 (1967).

**i. May not survive Gertz:** But it is not at all clear that *Time v. Hill* remains good law following the *Gertz* decision. Since *Gertz* represents the majority's repudiation of the view that the *New York Times* standard must apply to **all** defamation actions arising out of a matter of "public interest," even ones brought by private figures, it can be plausibly argued that the reasoning of *Gertz* also applies to "false light" actions brought by private persons.

**b. Suit by public figure:** On the other hand, if a *public* figure or public official brings a "false light" suit, it seems highly probable that he will have to show that the defendant knew the falsity of its account or recklessly disregarded the truth. *Hustler v. Falwell* (*supra*, p. 558) establishes that the *New York Times* "actual malice" requirement applies to claims for intentional infliction of emotional distress. That being so, the Court would almost certainly hold that the same standard applies to a public figure's suit claiming that he has been put in a false light.

**2. "True" privacy actions:** Another type of action for invasion of privacy, sometimes called a "true" privacy action, contends that the plaintiff's right of privacy has been violated by *accurate* disclosure of *highly personal facts* in which the public has no legitimate interest. The Court has never decided what limitations, if any, the First Amendment places upon states' ability to grant relief in such actions. Since a "true" privacy case concedes that the disclosures are accurate, the constitutional issue becomes: must truth be recognized as a defense in this type of action?

a. **"More speech" no remedy:**  Clearly, in this type of action, more so than even in the "false light" situation, the remedy of "more speech" (e.g., granting the plaintiff the right to publish a "rebuttal") will be utterly useless as a remedy; in fact, it will simply draw more attention to the original damaging disclosure. Also, since by hypothesis "true" privacy claims will be allowed only where the material disclosed is found to be so highly personal that the public has no legitimate interest in it, the basic rationale behind the First Amendment — that comment and debate on matters of public interest must be unimpeded, is only weakly applicable if at all. These two considerations thus suggest that, assuming "true" privacy actions are indeed limited to those cases that involve materials not of legitimate public concern, ***truth should not be a constitutionally-required defense*** in such privacy suits, and state tort rules allowing recovery should not be disturbed in the name of the First Amendment.

# VII.  OBSCENITY

A. **Generally unprotected:**  Obscenity, like defamation and "fighting words," was listed in *Chaplinsky (supra,* p. 503) as being a type of speech **unprotected by the First Amendment**. But again, as with defamation, the states are no longer completely free to define obscenity however they wish, and to then punish the distribution or sale of the material so defined.

1. **Attempt to define:**  Instead, the Supreme Court has attempted to lay down specific guidelines for what materials may, compatibly with the First Amendment, be punished as "obscene." However, none of these attempts to define "obscenity" has turned out to be specific enough to give legislatures and lower courts reliable guidance about what materials are covered. Therefore, the Supreme Court has remained very much in the business of deciding, case by case, whether given materials meet the Court's definition.

2. *Roth:*  The first case which required the Court to face directly the issue of whether obscene materials are protected by the First Amendment was ***Roth v. U.S.***, 354 U.S. 476 (1957). In *Roth* (in an opinion by Justice Brennan), the Court confirmed what its dictum in *Chaplinsky* had suggested — that "obscenity is not within the area of constitutionally protected speech or press." But the Court also held that First Amendment concerns **limit the acceptable definition of "obscenity."**

   a. **Definition of "obscene":**  The Court formulated its own definition of "obscenity": ***"whether to the average person, applying contemporary community standards, the dominant theme of the material taken as a whole appeals to prurient interest."*** The Court purported to be repeating the definition of obscenity laid down in certain prior lower-court cases. However, the definition seems to have been intended as a ***minimal constitutional standard***; that is, the state could not, consistent with the First Amendment, ban a given item as obscene unless it satisfied this *Roth* definition.

   b. **Meaning of "prurient":**  The Court defined "prurient" as "material having a tendency to excite lustful thoughts." (But in a much later case, the Court interpreted this definition of "prurient" to *exclude* materials which, although they "excite lustful thoughts," provoke "only normal, healthy sexual desires." *Brockett v. Spokane Arcades, Inc.*, 472 U.S. 491 (1985). However, the *Brockett* Court did not define its phrase "normal, healthy sexual desires.")

c. **Redeeming social value:** Of primary importance to the *Roth* Court was distinguishing between obscenity and "the portrayal of sex ... in *art, literature and scientific works.*" The latter must be given full constitutional protection. It is not clear from the Court's opinion whether, apart from the definition cited above, there is an *additional* requirement for obscenity that the work not constitute art, literature, or other category having social value. But the Court did say that "all ideas having even the *slightest redeeming social importance*" are to be protected (and, implicitly, are to be judged not obscene).

   i. **Ambiguity:** If a work had some serious social value (e.g., of a literary nature), but its dominant theme was nonetheless one which "excites lustful thoughts" and is therefore "prurient," it is simply not clear whether the material could be obscene under *Roth*. (In any event, the presence of a small amount of "redeeming social importance" is *no longer sufficient* to prevent a work from being obscene, under *Miller v. California*, the presently-applicable test, discussed *infra*, p. 561.)

3. **Post-*Roth* cases:** In a long string of post-*Roth* cases, the Court was forced to decide whether particular materials were obscene under the *Roth* definition. In many instances, no majority of the Court could agree on a single rationale, though of course there was always either a majority of the Court believing that the materials were obscene or a majority believing that they were not. From *Roth* until 1973, in fact, no majority of the Court ever agreed on a definition of obscenity.

   a. **Stewart's remark:** Perhaps the most candid, and certainly the most famous, comment made during the post-*Roth* period on the difficulties of defining "obscenity," was that of Justice Stewart. Concurring in *Jacobellis v. Ohio*, 378 U.S. 184 (1964), he conceded that he might never be able intelligibly to describe "hard core pornography," which he believed to be the only type of material bannable under *Roth*. However, he observed, *"I know it when I see it*, and the motion picture involved in this case is not that."

B. ***Miller:*** Finally, in ***Miller v. California***, 413 U.S. 15 (1973), five Justices agreed on a *new definition* of "obscenity," one which was built upon the *Roth* definition but which also resolved some additional issues.

1. ***Miller's* definition:** *Miller* laid out the following three-part test (all parts of which must be met) for identifying material which may be banned as obscene:

   a. the *"average person*, applying *contemporary community standards"* would find that "the work, *taken as a whole*, appeals to the *prurient* interest" (citing *Roth*);

   b. the work "depicts or describes, in a *patently offensive way, sexual* conduct specifically defined by the applicable state law" and

   c. the work, taken as a whole, *lacks "serious literary, artistic, political, or scientific value."*

2. **Changes:** This definition changes or clarifies prior law in two major respects:

   a. **"Community" standards:** The *Miller* majority explicitly *rejected* the argument that what appeals to the "prurient interest" or is "patently offensive" should be determined by reference to a *national standard*. What counts are the standards of the *local community* where the prosecution is taking place. Thus "the people of Maine or Mississippi [need not] accept the public depiction of conduct found tolerable in Las Vegas, or in New York City."

**b. Limited to "hard core" sex:** *Miller* also establishes that the states may ban as obscene only depictions or descriptions of **"hard core"** sexual conduct. Since the states must **be specific** about what sexual conduct is being banned (in order to satisfy the First Amendment need for "fair notice" of what is forbidden, and in order to avoid a chilling effect on expression), the Court provided several examples of materials which could be banned:

   **i. Ultimate sexual acts:** "Patently offensive representations or descriptions of **ultimate sex acts**, normal or perverted, actual or **simulated**";

   **ii. Other:** "Patently offensive representations or descriptions of **masturbation, excretory functions**, and **lewd exhibition** of the **genitals**."

   **Note:** Later Court cases show that mere *nudity*, by itself, is *not obscene*, and indeed gets some First Amendment protection. For instance, in *Erie v. Pap's A.M.*, *supra*, p. 519, the Court assumed that nude dancing was not obscene. As a 4-Justice plurality said in that case, nude dancing is "expressive conduct," although these Justices added that "we think that [such dancing] falls only within the outer ambit of the First Amendment's protection."[5]

**3. Dissents:** Four Justices dissented in *Miller*. The reasoning of three of them was more fully expressed in their dissent to a companion case decided the same day, *Paris Adult Theatre I v. Slaton*, discussed *infra*.

**4. Some limits on right to define terms:** Notwithstanding *Miller's* "community standards" approach, the Court will impose some limits on the right of the local community to apply its own interpretation of the meaning of terms like "patently offensive" or "prurient interest." For instance, the Court has made it clear that the definition of "prurient interest" (part of the definition of obscenity in *Miller*, and in *Roth, supra*, p. 560) **may not include** a concept of lust that encompasses "only normal, healthy sexual desires." *Brockett v. Spokane Arcades, Inc.*, 472 U.S. 491 (1985). That is, the community is not free to say, in effect, that material that excites "normal, healthy sexual desires," and that does not incite sexual responses above and beyond these normal ones, is "prurient" or "offensive."

**5. No exception for consenting adults:** Prior to *Miller* and its companion case, *Paris Adult Theatre I v. Slaton*, 413 U.S. 49 (1973), the Court had carved out an exception to the government's power to ban concededly obscene materials: *private possession* of such materials may not be made a crime. See *Stanley v. Georgia*, discussed *infra*, p. 562. The Court might plausibly have extended *Stanley* to include a freedom from total suppression for all materials exhibited only to *consenting adults*, even in places of public accommodation. But in *Paris Adult Theatre*, a majority of the Court *refused* to grant an exception for such consenting-adult-only displays.

**C. Private possession by adults:** The mere *private possession* of obscene material by an adult *may not be made criminal. Stanley v. Georgia*, 394 U.S. 557 (1969).

---

5. However, 7 members of the Court held in *Pap's* that totally nude dancing could nonetheless be prohibited as part of a content-neutral attempt to combat nude dancing's "secondary effects." See *supra*, p. 519.

1. **Rationale:** In reaching this conclusion, the Supreme Court relied both on the weakness of the state's interest in controlling private possession of obscenity, and on the strength of the individual's interest in not being forbidden such private usage. The state's interest was only the weak one of "protect[ing] the individual's mind from the effects of obscenity." The individual's interest was directly contrary, and much stronger: that of *not having his thoughts controlled*. "If the First Amendment means anything, it means that a State has *no business telling a man, sitting alone in his own house, what books he may read or what films he may watch*."

    a. **Two interests:** Thus the *Stanley* rule relied on two distinct interests held by individuals: the First Amendment interest in having free access to ideas, and a distinct *privacy* interest in not having what one does in one's own home made the subject of government scrutiny.

2. **Possession of child pornography:** There is one important exception to *Stanley's* rule that private possession of obscene material by an adult may not be made criminal: the states may criminalize even private possession of *child pornography*. See *Osborne v. Ohio*, discussed *infra*, p. 564.

3. **No right to supply consenting adults:** Since *Stanley* recognized a right held by consenting adults to possess and use obscenity in their homes, it would not have been illogical for the Court also to conclude that there was a right to *supply* obscene materials to such adults. But the Court has refused to extend the rationale of *Stanley* in this manner.

    a. **Mailing of obscene material:** For instance, government may make it a crime to *mail* obscene materials to consenting adults. *U.S. v. Reidel*, 402 U.S. 351 (1971). *Reidel* concluded that the focus on *Stanley* had been on "freedom of mind and thought and on the privacy of one's home" (the privacy strand of *Stanley*), and that *Stanley* did not recognize any First Amendment right to acquire obscene materials from commercial suppliers.

    b. **Adult movie theaters:** Similarly, the holding of *Paris Adult Theatre, supra*, p. 562, that there is no right to show obscene movies to consenting adults, represents an unwillingness to carry the rationale of *Stanley* beyond its immediate facts.

D. **Protection of children:** The Court has developed special doctrines to give the states additional authority to protect *children* from pornography. Two sorts of dangers are involved: (1) that children may read, view or listen to pornography; and (2) that children may be induced to take part in sexual conduct in order to be *filmed* for pornographic pictures and movies.

1. **Protection of children as audience:** A state may prohibit the distribution of sexually explicit materials to children, even though those materials would not be obscene if distributed to an adult.

    a. **Can't impair access of adults:** But if the state wants to keep materials that are sexually explicit (but not obscene) out of the hands of minors, it must do so in a way that does *not substantially impair* the access of *adults* to those materials. That is, the state must *narrowly tailor* its regulations so that the materials are forbidden *only* to minors.

2. **Children as photographic subjects:** A state may also ban the distribution of materials *showing children engaged in sexual conduct, even though the material is not legally obscene*. In reaching this conclusion, the Court in *New York v. Ferber*, 458 U.S. 747 (1982) relied on the state's "compelling," surpassingly important, interest in *preventing*

*the sexual exploitation and abuse of children* who are photographed for production of such materials.

    **a.**   **Private possession may also be banned:**   The state's interest in preventing the sexual exploitation and abuse of children is so strong that even the *private possession* of sexually explicit nude pictures of children may be prohibited. In the post-*Ferber* case of *Osborne v. Ohio*, 495 U.S. 103 (1990), the Court upheld a statute criminalizing most private possession of nude pictures of children. Even though *Stanley v. Georgia* (*supra*, p. 562) had held that adults have a First Amendment right to privately possess pornography, the *Osborne* Court held that materials showing children are different: the state's interest in preventing the pornographic exploitation of children is much stronger than the interest in protecting the minds of adults, so any First Amendment interest in possessing nude pictures of children is outweighed by this anti-child-exploitation interest. And this is true even if the materials are not "obscene," merely "indecent."

  **3.**   **Virtual child pornography:** On the other hand, government may *not* ban non-obscene *"virtual child pornography,"* by forbidding either *computer-generated images* that appear to be of children having sex, or explicit images of *young-looking adults posing as minors*. In *Ashcroft v. Free Speech Coalition*, 535 U.S. 564 (2002), the Court rejected the federal government's argument that barring such virtual images was necessary to restrain the market for actual child pornography, and therefore necessary to protect children.

    **a.**   **Facts:** Congress passed the Child Pornography Prevention Act of 1996 (CPPA). §2256(8)(B) of that act prohibited any "visual depiction," regardless of how it is produced, that "is, or appears to be, of a minor engaging in sexually explicit conduct." The section covered (and was intended to cover) *computer-generated images* produced without any live actors. A different section, §2256(2), prohibited movies made with adult actors rather than minors, if the jury believed that an actor *"appears to be"* a minor engaging in "actual or simulated ... sexual intercourse." Finally, a third section, §2256(8)(D), a "pandering" provision, prohibited as child pornography any sexually explicit image that was *"advertised*, promoted, presented, described or distributed" in such a manner that *"conveys the impression"* that the image depicts a minor engaging in "sexually explicit conduct." All three of the sections were designed to include works that would not be "obscene" under the standard *Miller v. California* definition.

    **b.**   **All sections found unconstitutional:** The Court, in an opinion by Justice Kennedy, found that all three of the sections were *unconstitutionally overbroad*. The CPPA "prohibits speech that records no crime and creates no victims by its production." Because the Act contained no exception for works of serious literary, artistic, political or scientific value, it would apply to "a picture in a psychology manual," "a movie depicting the horrors the sexual abuse," and perhaps even such Hollywood blockbusters as *Traffic* and *American Beauty*, since these films each contained scenes in which teenage characters appeared to be having sex. The vote to overturn the ban on youthful-appearing adult actors was 7-2, as was the vote to overturn the "pandering" provision; the vote as to computer-generated images was 6-3.

**E.**  **Pornography as subordination of women:**   In the last couple of decades, an attack on sexually explicit materials has been led by a group not previously especially active in that effort: feminists. Asserting that pornography promotes a view of women as inferior sex objects and thus is a type of *sex discrimination*, feminist groups have promoted anti-pornography ordinances that have been enacted by, among other cities, Minneapolis and Indianapolis. These ordinances distinguish between those sexually explicit materials that *subordinate* or degrade women and those that do not; only the former are banned.

1. **Unconstitutional:** In the most serious test thus far of such ordinances, a federal court of appeals struck down the Indianapolis ordinance, in *American Booksellers Assoc., Inc. v. Hudnut*, 771 F.2d 323 (7th Cir. 1985).

   a. **Facts:** The Indianapolis ordinance treated "pornography" as a practice that discriminates against women, and that is to be redressed through the same administrative and judicial means as other discrimination. It defined pornography to include "graphic sexually explicit subordination of women" that also includes the presentation of: women as "sexual objects who enjoy pain or humiliation [or] who experience sexual pleasure in being raped;" women being "penetrated by objects or animals;" women as being "sexual objects for domination, conquest … ," etc.

   b. **Holding:** The Court of Appeals struck down the ordinance on the ground that it was *not content-neutral*. Under the ordinance, "[s]peech that 'subordinates' women … is forbidden, no matter how great the literary or political value of the work taken as a whole. Speech that portrays women in positions of equality is lawful, no matter how graphic the sexual content. *This is thought control*. It establishes an 'approved' view of women, of how they may react to sexual encounters, of how the sexes may relate to each other. Those who espouse the approved view may use sexual images; those who do not may not."

   c. **Effect on conduct:** Supporters of the ordinance had argued that the way women are portrayed in pornography affects society's view of women and increases discrimination against them. The court agreed that this may well be true; but this "simply demonstrates the power of pornography as speech. All these unhappy effects depend on mental intermediation." Just as speech that encourages racial bigotry or anti-semitism is protected under the First Amendment, so is speech that furthers the view of women as subordinate.

F. **Other issues:** A number of other substantive issues raised by obscenity laws may be briefly summarized:

1. **Book without pictures:** A book without pictures, in which sexual acts are *verbally described*, may nonetheless be obscene under the *Miller* test.

2. **Role of jury limited:** Several of the issues raised whenever the *Miller* test is applied are "factual" ones (e.g., whether the material is "patently offensive" under local community standards). Therefore, these factual issues may be resolved by the jury. But the jury does *not have unbridled discretion*; appellate courts, including the Supreme Court, will review these findings of fact and will reverse if the findings *could not have been made by a reasonable jury*.

   a. **Illustration:** For instance, *Jenkins v. Georgia*, 418 U.S. 153 (1974), concluded that the movie "Carnal Knowledge" could not reasonably be found to show sexual conduct in a "patently offensive" way, as the jury found that it did. (The Court found it significant that the camera did not focus on the bodies of the actors during the sex scenes, and that there was no exhibition of genitals, even though there was some nudity.)

3. **Community standards:**   In *Miller*, the Court held that the "community standards" by reference to which terms like "patently offensive" should be defined did not have to be national. In *Jenkins v. Georgia*, and its companion case, *Hamling v. United States*, both reported at 418 U.S. 87 (1974), the Court *rejected* the argument that the standards should have to be at least *statewide*. Thus an obscenity case can be tried in a small, conservative rural town, and the *standards of that town* may be made the relevant ones (though the judge is not *precluded* from allowing evidence of standards in other communities.)

   a. **Venue for federal suits:**   Permitting local community standards to control becomes especially significant in view of state and federal prosecutors' ability to pick as the venue for trial *any town through which the allegedly obscene materials have passed*. The federal statute prohibiting the mailing of obscene matter, for instance, has been held to allow venue *anywhere along the route that the mailed material travels*, not just the point of mailing or receipt.

      i. **Consequence:**   Thus a publisher or distributor who wishes to sell his materials nationally must face the possibility that any small town anywhere in the country through which a mail train or truck carrying one copy of the materials passes may be selected by federal prosecutors as the venue for a criminal trial. That place's local standards for determining what is "patently offensive," "prurient," etc. will then control.

4. **Standards for determining "value":**   On the other hand, when it comes time to determine the *"value"* of a work (the third prong of the *Miller* test), this determination is made *not* by reference to the standards of the applicable community but rather, by reference to whether a *reasonable person* would conclude that the entire work has social value. *Pope v. Illinois*, 481 U.S. 497 (1987). "Just as the ideas a work represents need not obtain majority approval to merit protection, neither, insofar as the First Amendment is concerned, does the value of the work vary from community to community based on the degree of local acceptance it has won."

5. **"Thematic obscenity":**   The Court has distinguished between obscenity on the one hand and *advocacy* of certain types of sexual conduct on the other. Such advocacy, sometimes called *"thematic obscenity,"* is an expression of *ideas*, and is therefore *protected* by the First Amendment. For instance, in *Kingsley International Pictures Corp. v. Regents*, 360 U.S. 684 (1959), the Court struck down a New York movie licensing law which, in effect, barred any movie which presented adultery or fornication as *acceptable behavior* (and which was used to ban the film of "Lady Chatterley's Lover"). The licensing scheme allowed censorship for "advocat[ing] an idea," and thus was no more valid under the First Amendment than a ban on the advocacy of, say, socialism.

6. **Scienter:**   The seller of an obscene work may not be convicted unless the prosecution proves *scienter*, that is, knowledge by the defendant of the *contents* of the materials. *Smith v. California*, 361 U.S. 147 (1959). (But there is no requirement that the prosecution prove that the defendant knew, as a conclusion of law, that the materials were obscene. Thus "ignorance of the law is no excuse" in obscenity prosecutions, any more than it is in most other contexts. See *Hamling v. U.S.*, 418 U.S. 87 (1974).)

# VIII. COMMERCIAL SPEECH

**A. Overview:** Like libel, obscenity and a few other types of speech, most kinds of *"commercial speech"* were traditionally viewed as being an "unprotected category" totally outside the scope of the First Amendment. But just as the Court in recent decades has held that the states do not have an unlimited right to ban or regulate speech merely by labeling it "libelous" or "obscene," so the Court has now given substantial First Amendment protection to speech which can be described as "commercial."

   **1. Extensive change:** In fact, in some senses this change towards more extensive First Amendment protection has been even greater in the commercial-speech area than in the areas of defamation and obscenity: in the latter two areas, the Court has simply limited governments' ability to define these areas as broadly as they wish. Once speech falls within the allowable definition of "libel" or "obscenity," it is completely without First Amendment protection. But most types of commercial speech, by contrast (all types except those that are misleading or that propose illegal transactions), are now *entitled to some First Amendment protection*. However, this protection is generally not as extensive as that reserved for speech nearer the "core" of First Amendment values, especially "political" speech.

   **2. Traditional view:** The traditional view was that "purely commercial advertising" was not entitled to any First Amendment protection, and could therefore be subjected to governmental regulation in the same way as any other type of business activity. *Valentine v. Chrestensen*, 316 U.S. 52 (1942).

      **a. Difficulties with doctrine:** But this traditional view posed difficulties from the very beginning. For instance, did the fact that speech took the form of a paid advertisement automatically remove its First Amendment protection? The Court answered "no," in *New York Times v. Sullivan, supra,* p. 554; the fact that the advertisement in *New York Times* was "political" was enough to qualify it for First Amendment protection. Other cases also limited *Valentine's* exclusion of commercial speech from First Amendment protection.

**B. The *Virginia Pharmacy* revolution:** Then, in a 1976 case, the Court formally abandoned the *Valentine* rule, and held that *even "purely commercial" speech is entitled to First Amendment protection. Virginia Pharmacy Bd. v. Virginia Consumer Council*, 425 U.S. 748 (1976).

   **1. Facts:** *Virginia Pharmacy* involved a state statute making it "unprofessional conduct" for a pharmacist to *advertise prescription drug prices.*

   **2. Statute stricken:** This ban was held by the Court to violate the First Amendment. The Court conceded that this case involved speech that was *purely* commercial, and that the only "idea" expressed was "I will sell you the *X* prescription drug at the *Y* price." Nonetheless, the Court held, such wholly commercial speech was protected by the First Amendment.

      **a. Informational value:** In reaching this conclusion, the Court relied on society's strong interest in "the free flow of commercial information." Here, for instance, consumers, especially poor ones, had a compelling interest in who was charging how much for what drug.

b.  **Weak state interest:**  The countervailing state interest in suppressing price advertising was that of maintaining "a high degree of professionalism on the part of licensed pharmacists," an interest implicated by the possibility that advertising might lead to aggressive price competition, which might in turn lead to shoddy services. But this interest amounted to saying that consumers would be best protected *if kept in ignorance*. And, the Court concluded, the First Amendment *flatly forbids the state from deciding that ignorance is preferable to the free flow of truthful information.*

3.  **Exceptions:**  However, the Court hinted that although purely commercial speech is entitled to First Amendment protection, that protection might be *less extensive* than for other types of speech. *False or misleading* advertising could clearly be prohibited (whereas such statements when made about public figures cannot be, unless there is actual malice — see *New York Times v. Sullivan, supra*, p. 554). Similarly, *broader regulation of "time, place and manner"* might be justified, and the strong *presumption against prior restraints* might not apply.

4.  **Rehnquist dissent:**  The only dissenter was Justice Rehnquist, who argued that the First Amendment was designed to protect discussion of "political, social and other public issues, rather than the decision of a particular individual as to whether to purchase one or another kind of shampoo." He thought that Virginia had a strong interest in combatting drug abuse, a danger to which unregulated advertising of prescription drugs and their prices might lead (e.g., "Pain getting you down? Insist that your physician prescribe Demerol.").

5.  **Audience's right to information:**  Apart from the fact that it recognizes purely commercial speech as being entitled to First Amendment protection, *Virginia Pharmacy* is of interest because it demonstrates the Court's recognition of a First Amendment right to *receive* information. Prior First Amendment cases had almost all involved the right to *express* oneself, that is, to be a *disseminator* rather than a recipient of information.

   a.  **Third-party rights:**  The plaintiffs in *Virginia Pharmacy* were in fact consumers, not pharmacists. It is not yet completely clear whether disseminators of information may assert the third-party rights of their audiences in First Amendment cases, though it seems probable that they may. This would be an exception to the usual rules of standing (discussed *infra*, p. 711), which normally permit a litigant to assert only that his *own* rights have been violated.

6.  **No right to ban "For Sale" signs:**  The rationale of *Virginia Pharmacy*, especially the principle that dissemination of even purely commercial information may not be barred because that information would be "harmful," was later applied in *Linmark Associates, Inc., v. Willingboro*, 431 U.S. 85 (1977). There, the Court unanimously held that a racially-integrated town's prohibition on *real estate "For Sale" and "Sold" signs* violated the First Amendment, despite the town's interest in stemming "white flight."

   a.  **Suppression of truthful information:**  The fatal flaw of the *Linmark* ordinance was that it, like the ban in *Virginia Pharmacy*, was an attempt to protect the public (residents of the town) by *keeping them in ignorance*. The town's claim that the information about sales might cause residents to act "irrationally" would, if accepted, permit "every locality in the country [to] suppress any facts that reflect poorly on the locality."

7. **"Track one"**: *Virginia Pharmacy* and *Linmark* can be viewed as classic "track one" cases, using Tribe's term (see *supra*, p. 465). That is, in those cases the government tried to suppress information based on the chance that the **communicative impact** of the message might cause harm. Such "track one" abridgements will be allowed only where they either fall into pre-defined "unprotected categories" or survive strict scrutiny; the point of *Virginia Pharmacy*, of course, is that "commercial speech" is no longer such an unprotected category.

   a. **Later case:** But the later case of *Central Hudson Gas, infra*, p. 571, indicates that such content-based restrictions may be upheld if they are a narrow and direct means of pursuing substantial governmental interests, probably a variant of "intermediate" scrutiny.

C. **Regulation of lawyers:** First Amendment protection for commercial speech has also been conferred by the Court in several cases involving regulation of the way in which *lawyers* acquire clients.

   1. **Newspaper advertising in general:** The first of these cases established that states *may not ban all newspaper advertising of legal services*. In *Bates v. State Bar of Arizona*, 433 U.S. 350 (1977), the Court upheld by a 5-4 vote the right of a "legal clinic" to offer in newspaper advertisements certain routine services at "very reasonable fees."

   2. **In-person solicitation:** The majority in *Bates* explicitly excluded considerations of whether lawyers could be barred from *in-person solicitation* of clients. But in a pair of 1978 cases, the Court held that some (though not all) types of in-person solicitation of clients may be banned. The two cases were at absolute opposite ends of the spectrum in terms of the acceptability of the lawyer's conduct. Therefore, it is hard to know where the line will be drawn between solicitation that may constitutionally be prohibited and that which may not.

      a. **Pecuniary gain:** *Ohralik v. Ohio State Bar Ass'n*, 436 U.S. 447 (1978) represented the most prohibitable kind of solicitation, classic **"ambulance chasing."** There, the Court held that a state may forbid *in-person solicitation* for *pecuniary gain*. So a state may forbid the kind of conduct at issue in *Ohralik*, in which the lawyer solicited accident victims in person, to induce them to let him represent them for a contingent fee.

      b. **Right of association:** The other case, *In re Primus*, 436 U.S. 412 (1978), represented the kind of solicitation that is least objectionable and most worthy of protection.

         i. **Facts:** Primus, a South Carolina lawyer who did occasional work without pay for the ACLU, wrote a letter to a woman who had allegedly been illegally sterilized as a condition to her further receipt of Medicaid benefits; the letter offered the ACLU's free services in filing a lawsuit on her behalf. Primus, like Ohralik, was disciplined for violating anti-solicitation rules.

         ii. **Punishment reversed:** But the Supreme Court held that Primus *could not constitutionally be punished* for what she did. Her letter, and the ACLU litigation itself, were attempts to further her *political and ideological goals*. Therefore, her conduct implicated her interest in *free "political expression"* as well as *freedom of association*, both core First Amendment values. (This was the same sort of associational activity that the Court had earlier protected in *NAACP v. Button*, *infra*, p. 603.) These First Amendment interests were sufficiently strong that the state could **not** use **prophylactic measures** because of the mere potential for over-reaching, fraud or other abuse; instead, Primus could only be disciplined if there was a showing that her solicitation had **in fact** led to one of these harms.

c. **Some in-person solicitation allowed:**  A much more recent case suggests that some types of **in-person solicitation** by professionals will be **allowed**, and that it was the unusually **vulnerable and susceptible condition** of the prospective clients in *Ohralik* that made the difference there. See *Edenfield v. Fane*, 507 U.S. 761 (1993), striking down Florida's ban on direct, in-person uninvited solicitation of business owners by Certified Public Accountants.

3. **Advertising for particular type of case:**  While *Bates* gave general First Amendment protection to newspaper advertising by lawyers, it did not say anything about whether a lawyer could advertise for cases against a **particular defendant**, or having to do with a **specific legal problem**. In *Zauderer v. Office of Disciplinary Counsel*, 471 U.S. 626 (1985) the Supreme Court held that the states may not institute a blanket ban on print advertising oriented toward a particular legal problem or potential defendant.

a. **Facts and holding of *Zauderer*:**  In *Zauderer*, the Court upheld a lawyer's use of a newspaper advertisement soliciting as clients women who had been injured by the Dalkon Shield intrauterine device (a birth control device which had been proven in many lawsuits to be dangerously defective, and which was manufactured by only one defendant).

4. **Targeted direct-mail advertising:**  Similarly, states may not completely ban **targeted direct-mail** advertising of legal services. See *Shapero v. Kentucky Bar Assoc.*, 486 U.S. 466 (1988), holding that the state may not ban letters written to people against whom foreclosure proceedings have been instituted, offering legal help for this specific problem.

a. **May require "cooling off" period for tort victims:** On the other hand, where targeted direct mail would be likely to cause direct **mental anguish** to the recipient, the state may be able to ban it, or at least delay it. Thus the state may require a **30-day "cooling off" period** before lawyers may send targeted direct mail solicitations to **tort victims** and their relatives following an accident or disaster. See *Florida Bar v. Went For It, Inc.*, 515 U.S. 618 (1995).

i. **Rationale:** *Went For It* was a close (5-4) decision. The majority acknowledged that the free speech rights of tort lawyers were being restricted, but found that these rights were outweighed by two countervailing state interests: (1) the interest of victims or their relatives in being spared a personalized sales pitch "while **wounds are still open**" (something that couldn't be completely eliminated by the "short ... journey from mail box to trash can"); and (2) the interest of the bar in forestalling **the public's outrage** over this kind of conduct.

ii. **Dissent:** The four dissenters argued that the 30-day rule in fact hurt accident victims, because it "deprives [them] of information which may be critical to their right to make a claim for compensation," such as the need to assemble evidence quickly and the need to avoid uncounselled settlements.

**D. Commercial speech doctrine curtailed:** *Virginia Pharmacy* seemed to hold that the states may not suppress even "purely commercial" speech, so long as the speech was not false or misleading and did not propose an illegal transaction. But later cases show that *Virginia Pharmacy* cannot be read this broadly. While purely commercial speech is entitled to First Amendment protection, it ***does not receive the full range*** of that Amendment's protection.

1. **"Common sense distinction":** For instance, in *Ohralik, supra,* p. 569, the Court noted that it was not discarding "the 'common sense' distinction between speech proposing a commercial transaction, which occurs in an area traditionally subject to government regulation, and other varieties of speech." The Court was giving commercial speech "a ***limited measure of protection***, commensurate with its ***subordinate position*** in the scale of First Amendment values, while allowing modes of regulation that might be impermissible in the realm of non-commercial expression."

2. **The *Central Hudson* case:** Then, in *Central Hudson Gas v. Public Service Commission,* 447 U.S. 557 (1980), the Court laid down a formal ***four-part test*** to determine whether a given regulation of commercial speech violates the First Amendment. This test indicates that, even apart from the states' right to prevent misleading speech or speech that proposes illegal transactions, the government has significantly more power to regulate commercial speech than might have been supposed from a simple reading of *Virginia Pharmacy.*

   a. **Facts:** In *Central Hudson Gas,* the New York State Public Service Commission (PSC) banned all "promotional advertising" by electric utilities. The stated purpose of the ban was to conserve energy; "promotional advertising" was defined as advertising intended to stimulate the purchase of utility services (so that all other types of advertising by utilities, including "institutional" ads, were permitted).

   b. **Four-part test:** Before analyzing the ban, the Court reviewed prior commercial speech cases, and derived for the first time a ***four-part test*** for determining whether a given regulation abridges the First Amendment.

      [1] **Protected speech:** First, courts must determine whether the commercial speech is protected ***at all*** by the First Amendment. All commercial speech receives at least partial protection except for: (1) speech that is ***"misleading"***; and (2) speech which ***concerns unlawful activity.*** (The contours of these two exceptions are discussed further, *infra,* p. 573.) Speech which falls into one of these exceptions raises no First Amendment issues at all, and may thus be fully regulated by the government.

      [2] **Substantial government interest:** Second, the court must ask whether the ***governmental interest*** asserted in support of the regulation is ***"substantial."*** If not, the regulation will be struck down without further inquiry. If the interest is substantial, the government must still meet the final two parts of the test.

      [3] **Interest "directly advanced":** Third, the court will decide whether the regulation ***"directly advances"*** the governmental interest evaluated in part (ii) of the test. If it does not, the regulation will be struck down. If it does, it will still have to meet the fourth part of the test.

      [4] **Means-end fit:** Finally, the court will ask whether the regulation is ***"not more extensive than is necessary"*** to serve the government interest. If it *is* more extensive than necessary, the regulation will be struck down. (But a post-*Central Hud-*

*son Gas* case has watered down this "not more extensive than is necessary" test. Today, all that is required of the fit between the means and the end is that the means be ***"reasonably tailored"*** to serve the governmental objective, so that some looseness in the means-end fit will be tolerated where what is regulated is commercial speech. See *Edenfield v. Fane*, discussed further, *infra*, p. 574.)

c. **Application to facts:**  The Court then applied its test to the facts of *Central Hudson Gas*.

   i. **Protected speech:**  Utilities' promotional advertising was clearly speech ***protected*** by the First Amendment, satisfying part (i). The Court rejected the argument that advertising by a monopolist has no value; for one thing, even a monopolistic electric utility faces competition from alternative energy sources.

   ii. **State interests:**  The state asserted two interests in support of its ban: conservation of energy and maintenance of a fair and efficient rate structure (which, the state contended, would have been impaired by an increase in usage, because of the peculiarities of the rate structure.) The Court agreed that each of these interests was ***substantial***.

   iii. **Direct link:**  The Court found that there was a ***direct link*** between the ban and one (but not the other) of the asserted state interests, that of energy conservation. (The link between promotional advertising and inequitable rates was, by contrast, too speculative to satisfy the "direct link" requirement.)

   iv. **Least-restrictive alternative:**  With respect to the ban as a way of promoting energy conservation, part (iv) was ***not satisfied***; the ban was ***more extensive than needed*** to further that interest. For instance, it prevented a utility from promoting the use of electricity even for those applications where it was a more efficient power source than that currently being used.

d. **Concurrences:**  There were two concurrences.

   i. **Blackmun:**  Justice Blackmun conceded that what he termed the majority's "intermediate level" scrutiny was appropriate where commercial speech was potentially ***misleading*** or ***coercive***. But he thought that test gave too little protection against ***content-based regulation***. The regulation here was content-based, he contended; it was a "covert attempt by the state to manipulate the choices of its citizens ... by depriving the public of the information needed to make a free choice." And in his view, cases like *Virginia Pharmacy* and *Linmark* were not based on the lack of a sufficiently direct and narrow link between the regulation and the asserted state interest; rather, they were based on the broader principle that the state "may not [pursue its goals] by ***keeping the public in ignorance.***"

   ii. **Stevens' concurrence:**  Justice Stevens also concurred. Stevens agreed that the ban should be struck down, but reserved judgment on whether the majority's four-part test gave adequate protection to properly-defined commercial speech.

e. **Rehnquist dissent:**  Justice Rehnquist was the sole dissenter. He thought that the majority's four-part test did not give the government enough power to regulate commercial speech, and that the test gave commercial speech falling within the First Amendment protection that was "virtually indistinguishable" from that given to non-commercial speech. Rehnquist believed that the regulation here was more an economic regulation than a restraint on "free speech." Therefore, he would have given it "virtually complete deference," in contrast to what he viewed as the majority's resurrection of the discredited doctrine of *Lochner v. New York* (see *supra*, p. 150).

**E. Current status:** The *current status* of the protection given to "commercial speech" may be summarized as follows:

1. **Misleading or deceptive statements:** Commercial speech which is *misleading* or *deceptive*, or which *proposes an illegal transaction*, is *not* entitled to *any* First Amendment protection at all.

    a. **Potential to mislead:** Even speech which merely has a *potential* to mislead may be regulated. But if information may be presented in *either* a misleading or a non-misleading way, the state must attempt to prohibit *only* the misleading method (i.e., it must use the *least-restrictive alternative*). *In re R.M.J.*, 455 U.S. 191 (1982).

    b. **Proposing illegal transaction:** As an illustration of speech which does not receive First Amendment protection because it proposes an illegal transaction, see *Pittsburgh Press Co. v. Human Relations Commission*, 413 U.S. 376 (1973). That case upheld an order forbidding newspapers from publishing sex-designated help-wanted columns, on the theory that such columns act as an "aid" to illegal sex discrimination in employment.

2. **Three-part test:** If the commercial speech is covered by the First Amendment, then it may be regulated only if the state shows that the regulation (1) *directly advances* (2) a *substantial governmental interest* (3) in a way that is *reasonably tailored* to achieve that objective (the last three prongs of *Central Hudson Gas*). This is essentially "mid-level" review.

3. **Definition of commercial speech:** The Court has not agreed on precisely how "commercial speech" should be defined.

    a. **"Proposing commercial transaction":** Clearly, any expression which merely *"proposes a commercial transaction"* will be deemed "commercial speech" by the Court, and will therefore be given at most the limited protection implied by the four-part *Central Hudson Gas* test.

    b. **Economic interests:** The majority in *Central Hudson Gas* indicated that it would also consider to be commercial speech any speech which is *"related solely to the economic interests* of the speaker and its audience." However, it is not clear whether this definition will be adhered to, since it would include within the less-protected area speech having strong political or other public-interest dimensions (e.g., the union leader's strike call, hypothesized by Justice Stevens' concurrence in *Central Hudson)*.

    c. **Advertisement status not dispositive:** The fact that speech is in the form of a *paid advertisement* does *not* by itself make it commercial speech. Recall, for instance, that the speech in *New York Times v. Sullivan (supra*, p. 554), to which full First Amendment protection was given, was an advertisement, but one on a clearly political subject.

    d. **Reference to public debate:** The fact that speech "links a product to a *current public debate"* is *not* enough automatically to remove it from the commercial-speech classification. For instance, in *Bolger v. Youngs Drug Products*, 463 U.S. 60 (1983), the defendant drug company mailed consumers unsolicited advertisements for contraceptives. Even though the mailings contained discussions of important public issues such as venereal disease and family planning, they were nonetheless held to constitute commercial speech.

4. **"Reasonably tailored means"**: Part (3) of the *Central Hudson Gas* test requires that the regulation of commercial speech be "no more restrictive than necessary" to achieve the government's objective. But several post-*Central Hudson Gas* cases show that the Court is not taking the phrase "no more restrictive than necessary" literally, as if it meant "least restrictive possible alternative." Instead, all that is required of the means-end fit is that the means be *"tailored in a reasonable manner"* to serve the government objective, i.e., that the means advance the objective in a *"direct and material way."* *Edenfield v. Fane*, 507 U.S. 761 (1993). The fact that there may be some other means that would serve the government interest as well, while restricting the commercial speech less, will not be fatal. In other words, some degree of looseness in the means-end fit will be tolerated when what is being regulated is commercial speech. See *Board of Trustees of SUNY v. Fox*, 492 U.S. 469 (1989).

   a. **Can still have "bite"**: But the not-so-demanding means-end test still has considerable *"bite"* — If the Court is convinced that there is some alternative method of achieving the same end as well or almost as well, with *significantly less interference* with protected speech, the Court will not hesitate to *strike down* the restriction. Indeed, the Court will generally place upon the government the burden of *showing* that *proposed less-restrictive alternatives would not adequately fulfill* the governmental objective being sought.

      **Example:** The FDA allows "drug compounding," a process by which a pharmacist combines various drugs to produce a medication that is customized for the needs of a particular patient. The process is generally used only when the product is not commercially available. A key benefit of drug compounding is that the usual FDA new-drug-approval process does not need to be complied with. However, the FDA exempts drug compounding from the new-drug-approval requirement only if the pharmacist does not advertise or otherwise promote any particular compounded drug. P, a hospital, attacks the no-advertising rule as a violation of its rights of commercial speech.

      *Held* (by a 5-4 vote), for P. The FDA is attempting to draw a line between small-scale compounding (which must be allowed so that drugs the demand for which is so small that they cannot go through the expensive new-drug-approval proces, but that are needed by patients who have no alternative treatment, remain available) and large-scale compounding (which is dangerous because it may lead to wholesale evasion of the new-drug-approval process, necessary for protecting public safety). That line-drawing is a legitimate governmental objective.

      However, the government has failed to demonstrate that the no-advertising rule is "not more extensive than is necessary to serve" this interest in preventing large-scale compounding. Several non-speech-related means of achieving that same objective "might be possible" here. For instance, government could (i) ban the use of "commercial scale manufacturing" for compounded drugs; (ii) prohibit pharmacists from compounding drugs in advance of the receipt of an actual prescription for the drug; or (iii) cap the amount of any particular drug that a pharmacist may make or sell in a given period of time. Since the government has failed to demonstrate why these methods would not be adequate to prevent large-scale compounding, it loses. *Thompson v. Western States Medical Center*, 535 U.S. 357 (2002).

b. **Internal consistency required:** An important factor in whether the means will be found not to be uncessarily restrictive is whether the means selected by the government are *internally consistent* — where the means are not self-consistent, the Court is likely to find that the scheme is too irrational to advance the stated objective sufficiently.

**Example:** A federal statute prohibits beer manufacturers from listing their beverage's alcohol content on the label. The federal government defends the ban on the grounds that it's needed to prevent brewers from engaging in "strength wars," in which each maker increases its beer's alcohol content and then tries to lure drinkers by advertising the high content.

*Held*, the statute violates the brewers' free speech rights. The federal government does not prohibit alcohol strength listings in advertising, only on labels. Similarly, the government doesn't ban such listings for the labels of wines and spirits, only beer. These inconsistencies make the scheme so irrational that it does not "directly and materially advance" the objective of preventing strength wars. *Rubin v. Coors Brewing Co.*, 514 U.S. 476 (1995).

c. **Some chance of success:** A second factor in determining whether the means are reasonably tailored to the government objective is whether the means have a *reasonable probability of achieving the objective* at least some of the time. The means-end fit will be too loose if it "provides only *ineffective or remote support* for the government's purpose" (*Edenfield*, *supra*), or if there is *"little chance"* that the restriction will advance the state's goal (*Greater New Orleans Broadcasting Assoc.*, *infra*, p. 578).

**Example:** Massachusetts regulates indoor advertising for smokeless tobacco and cigars in a number of ways. One restriction is that advertising for such products cannot be placed lower than five feet above the floor of any retail establishment located within 1000 feet of any school or playground. The purpose of the regulation is to make tobacco products less appealing to minors, by limiting minors' exposure to advertising about the products.

*Held*, the restriction is unconstitutional. The five-foot rule "does not seem to advance" the state's goal. "Not all children are less than five feet tall, and those who are certainly have the ability to look up and take in their surroundings." Therefore, the height restriction "does not constitute a reasonable fit" with the state's goal. *Lorillard Tobacco Co. v. Reilly*, 533 U.S. 525 (2001) (also discussed *infra*, p. 578).

5. **Advertising of lawful but harmful products:** Advertising of unlawful products may clearly be prohibited under *Central Hudson Gas*. But what about the advertising of products or services that are *lawful*, but believed by the legislature to be *harmful*? Examples include **cigarettes**, **liquor**, and **gambling**. A 1986 decision seems to give legislatures greater power to regulate advertising of such *"vice"* products than ordinary products, but a 1996 decision casts doubt on the continued vitality of the 1986 case.

a. **"Power to ban includes power to regulate" theory:** The 1986 case was *Posadas de Puerto Rico Associates v. Tourism Company of Puerto Rico*, 478 U.S. 328 (1986), in which the Court held that Puerto Rico could ban advertising for casino gambling aimed at Puerto Rican residents.

    **i.   Nature of regulation:**   Puerto Rico wanted to fill its gambling casinos with tourists from the mainland, and to keep participation by residents to a minimum. Rather than prohibiting residents from playing, Puerto Rico vastly curtailed the right of casino owners to advertise directly to residents. Regulations specified which words could not be used in such advertising (e.g., the word "casino"); ads had to be cleared by the government before running.

    **ii.   Holding:**   By a 5-4 vote, the Court ***upheld*** the regulatory scheme. Since the commercial speech at issue — regulatory advertising of casino gambling aimed at Puerto Rican residents — concerned a lawful activity and was not misleading or fraudulent, the final three steps of the *Central Hudson Gas* analysis were relevant. The majority found that all three were satisfied by the regulation.

        **(1) No narrower means:**   Most importantly, the regulations were "no more extensive than necessary to serve the government's interest." In particular, Puerto Rico was ***not*** required, in lieu of banning pro-gambling advertising, to run ***"counterspeech"*** advertising designed to discourage gambling. "The legislature could conclude … that residents of Puerto Rico are already aware of the risks of casino gambling, yet would nevertheless be induced by widespread advertising to engage in [it]."

    **iii.   Significance:**   *Posadas de Puerto Rico* seemed to mean that if an activity could be ***completely banned***, advertising of it could be completely banned, or tightly regulated. This has been referred to as the ***"greater includes the lesser"*** theory.

**b.   Probably no longer valid:** But a 1996 case suggests that a majority of the present Court would no longer endorse this "greater includes the lesser" theory. In ***44 Liquormart v. Rhode Island***, 517 U.S. 484 (1996), all nine Justices agreed that a Rhode Island statute forbidding the advertising of liquor prices violated the First Amendment. Four Justices explicitly said that *Posadas'* "greater includes the lesser" theory should be overruled, and another four suggested that they didn't like the theory much.

    **i.   Facts:** Rhode Island absolutely prohibited ***all advertising of liquor prices***, except for price tags displayed with the merchandise and not visible from the street. Even in-state ads referring to sales outside of the state were prohibited if they listed prices. The state defended the prohibition on the grounds that price advertising would lead to ***lower prices***, and lower prices would lead to ***increased consumption***, a result that was at odds with the state's interest in "temperance."

    **ii.   Struck down:** All 9 Justices agreed that the Rhode Island statute could not stand, but no rationale commanded a majority on most points.

    **iii.   The Stevens bloc:** The principal opinion was by Stevens, who was joined by various members on varying points of his analysis.

        **(1) More rigorous review:** Stevens acknowledged that where a state regulates commercial messages to protect against misleading, deceptive, or aggressive sales practices, or requires the disclosure of "beneficial consumer information," "less than strict review" is appropriate. (The phrase "less than strict review" apparently refers to the *Central Hudson Gas* standard.) But he argued that "when a State ***entirely prohibits*** the dissemination of ***truthful***, nonmisleading commercial messages for reasons ***unrelated to the preservation of a fair bargaining process***, there is ***far less reason to depart*** from the ***rigorous review*** that the First Amendment generally demands." Such complete bans "usually rest solely on the ***offensive assumption that the public will respond 'irrationally' to the truth.***" In the part of his opinion seemingly saying that traditional strict scrutiny should apply to such complete prohibitions, Stevens was joined by two other Justices (Kennedy and Ginsburg).

**(2) Rhode Island's ban fails review:** Stevens then concluded that Rhode Island's ban on liquor price advertising failed this stricter review, and in fact failed even the less-stringent *Central Hudson Gas* standard. In particular, the ban flunked prong three of *Central Hudson Gas* (see *supra*, p. 571, sub-par iii), the requirement that the regulation ***"directly advance"*** the state's interest. Stevens interpreted prong three to require that the regulation ***"materially"*** or "significantly," not just slightly, advance the state interest. And here, there was no evidence that prohibiting price advertising *significantly* curtailed alcohol consumption. Furthermore, the ban flunked prong four of *Central Hudson Gas*: the ban failed to be ***"no more extensive than necessary"*** (since the state could have limited alcohol consumption by increased taxation, limits on per capita purchases, or educational campaigns.) On this analysis of prongs three and four, Stevens was joined by three other Justices.

**(3) *Posadas* rationale rejected:** Stevens then turned to *Posadas'* theory that if a state could completely ban a particular product, it could instead choose to ban or tightly regulate advertising for that product because this would be a lesser intrusion (the "greater includes the lesser" theory). Stevens said that this theory should be ***abandoned***, because it was ***illogical***: "We think it quite clear that banning speech may sometimes prove ***far more intrusive*** than banning conduct. . . . [A] local ordinance banning bicycle lessons may curtail freedom far more than one that prohibits bicycle riding within city limits. . . . The text of the First Amendment . . . presumes that attempts to regulate speech are more dangerous than attempts to regulate conduct." (Only three other Justices joined directly with Stevens in rejecting *Posadas*, but at least four, if not all five, of the remaining members seemed to agree that the reasoning in *Posadas* should no longer be followed.)

**(4) 21st Amendment irrelevant:** Lastly, Stevens dealt with Rhode Island's argument that its ban was rendered constitutional by the 21st Amendment, which in repealing Prohibition gave each state the right to ban the use or sale of alcoholic beverages within the state. Stevens rejected this argument, too. The 21st Amendment gives the states substantial authority to regulate alcohol, Stevens concluded, but was not intended to change the way the First Amendment applies to the states. On this point, all members of the Court apparently agreed.

iv. **O'Connor's concurrence:** Justice O'Connor (joined by Rehnquist, Souter and Breyer) concurred in the result and in most of Stevens' reasoning. She agreed with

Stevens' conclusion that the ban couldn't even satisfy the fourth prong of *Central Hudson Gas*, because the availability of less intrusive methods, like higher taxes or an educational anti-drinking campaign, meant that the fit between Rhode Island's method (ban on all price advertising) and its goal (reducing drinking) was not "reasonable." But O'Connor would not have gone beyond this to say, as Stevens did, that a more rigorous scrutiny should be used where the state is pursuing goals that don't relate to combatting deception or unfair bargaining. And she wasn't willing to say that *Posadas'* "greater includes the lesser" rationale should be completely overruled, though she did say that later cases required a "closer look" at the fit between the state's methods and its goals than *Posadas* implied.

v.  **Thomas' absolutist view:**   Justice Thomas, in a separate concurrence, went further towards giving commercial speech the same protection as political speech than anyone else on the Court. He wrote that in cases "in which the government's asserted interest is to ***keep legal users of a product or service ignorant in order to manipulate their choices in the marketplace***, the balancing test adopted in *Central Hudson Gas . . .* should not be applied. . . . Rather, such an 'interest' is ***per se illegitimate***, and can no more justify regulation of 'commercial' speech than it can justify regulation of 'noncommercial' speech."

c.  **No right to ban advertisement of legal gambling:**   A post-*44 Liquormart* case indicates that a majority of the present Court (indeed, perhaps every member of the Court) now agrees with Justice Stevens' statement in *44 Liquormart* that the right to ban an activity ***does not carry with it the right to allow it regulate or prohibit advertising of that activity.*** In *Greater New Orleans Broadcasting Assoc., Inc. v. U.S.*, 527 U.S. 173 (1999), the Court unanimously agreed that a federal statute violated the First Amendment when it prohibited radio and television advertising of private casino gambling in states where such gambling is legal. No member of the Court dissented from Justice Stevens' statement for the Court that "the power to prohibit or to regulate particular conduct does not necessarily include power to prohibit or regulate speech about that conduct" (citing *44 Liquormart*).

d.  **Cigarettes and other tobacco products:** Ever since the Court indicated in *44 Liquormart* that the right to ban a harmful product did not include the right to regulate speech about it, observers have wondered most of all whether several decades of federal and state restrictions on ***tobacco advertising*** would pass constitutional muster. As the result of a 2001 decision, it seems likely that much of this regulation will ultimately be found to violate the commercial free speech rights of tobacco producers and retailers. ***Lorillard Tobacco Co. v. Reilly***, 533 U.S. 431 (2001). The majority opinion was by Justice O'Connor.

i.  **Massachusetts' regulations:** Massachusetts decided in the late 1990s to regulate tobacco advertising extensively, perhaps more extensively than any state had ever done. The regulations were principally addressed to advertising that might be enticing to ***minors***. The state banned various methods of advertising cigarettes, smokeless tobacco and cigars,[6] including: (1) all outdoor advertising (not just bill-

---

6. The ban applied to locations less than 1,000 feet from a school or playground. Although the precise impact of the 1,000-foot limit was uncertain, it was clear that many if not most urban locations in the state would be covered by the ban.

boards but shop windows visible from the outside of the store); (2) all point-of-sale advertising lower than five feet from the floor; and (3) all self-service displays.

**ii. Preemption:** As to the cigarette advertising, the Court avoided the constitutional issue, by concluding that everything Massachusetts had done was ***preempted*** by a 1965 federal statute that regulated advertising on cigarette packages (the famous "Surgeon General's warnings" statute). (See *supra*, p. 88 for a discussion of how preemption works.)

**iii. Smokeless tobacco and cigars:** But the Court did reach the First Amendment issue with respect to smokeless tobacco and cigars (these were not covered by the 1965 labeling statute), and, in a major victory for the tobacco industry, ***voided*** most of the restrictions on these products.

**(1) Outdoor advertising:** As to the ban on ***outdoor advertising***, Justice O'Connor, speaking for five members of the Court, found that the prohibition was overbroad. She readily conceded that the state had a strong interest in reducing minors' exposure to tobacco advertising. But tobacco manufacturers and retailers, and their adult consumers, had a significant countervailing First Amendment interest in the exchange of truthful information about the products. The state had failed to show that the outdoor advertising ban was "***not more extensive than necessary*** to advance the State's substantial interest" in combating underage tobacco use.

**(2) The 5-foot rule:** O'Connor similarly found unconstitutional the rule that all tobacco advertising within a retail establishment be at least ***five feet above the floor***. The idea was to make the advertising less enticing to minors. But O'Connor found that the fit between this means and the prevention-of-usage-by-minors objective was simply too loose, since even the shortest of minors could look up to see the ads anyway. (See *supra*, p. 575, for more about this aspect of the case.)

**(3) The ban on self-service:** On the other hand, the Court found that the ban on a ***self-service displays*** *was* constitutional. The ban basically required tobacco retailers to put tobacco products behind counters, and required customers to have contact with a salesperson before purchasing. This regulation left open "ample channels of communication" (e.g., retailers could put empty packaging on open display, and could put actual products behind a visible but locked display case). Therefore, the rule did not "significantly impede" adult access to tobacco products.

**iv. Dissent:** What may be most interesting about *Lorillard* is that on the core question of whether the bans on outdoor advertising and low-hanging in-store displays violated the First Amendment, there was not a lot of real disagreement on the court. Justice O'Connor, speaking for five justices, believed that these restrictions should be struck down even without a trial. There were four dissenters, led by Justice Stevens, but the dissenters did not disagree with O'Connor's conclusion that the measures presented serious First Amendment issues. As Stevens put it, "Noble ends do not save a speech-restricting statute whose means are poorly tailored." However,

Stevens would not have decided the issue on summary judgment as O'Connor did; he would instead have remanded for a trial on such issues as what other avenues of communication were available to tobacco manufacturers and retailers. So the Court now seems to be *unanimously* of the belief that broad restrictions on commercial advertising will often thwart the First Amendment rights of businesses and consumers to disseminate truthful information.

    **v.**  **Ban on broadcast advertising:** The 1965 federal law prohibiting tobacco companies from *advertising on radio and TV* is clearly in serious *jeopardy* as the result of *Lorillard* — it's hard to believe that the present Court would find that this ban is sufficiently closely tailored to the government's interest in preventing the harms of smoking as to justify depriving the tobacco companies and their adult consumers of such an important means of communicating truthful information about a lawful product.

  **e.**  **Present state of the law on regulating "vice" advertising:** So in light of *44 Liquormart, Greater New Orleans Broadcasting* and *Lorillard*, here's where the law seems to stand on state regulation of the advertising of "vice" products like cigarettes, liquor, and gambling:

    **i.**  **"Consume less" objective will fail:** If the government's sole justification for limiting advertising of the legal-but-assertedly-harmful product is that the limitation will cause people to *consume less* of the item, it will be extremely difficult for the limitation to pass muster. First, the government will have to show that the limit "significantly" reduces consumption, and this will generally be quite hard to do. Second, the government will have to show that no means are available that are significantly less intrusive; since the government will almost always be free to increase taxes on the item, or to regulate how and where it can be sold, or to conduct an educational campaign showing its dangers, it's again unlikely that the government will succeed in making the required showing that materially less restrictive alternatives don't exist.

    **ii.**  **Protect minors:** If the government's principal justification is to prevent *minors* from gaining access to, or being enticed by, the "vice" product, government will have to *tailor its methods very tightly* so that there is no undue interference with the rights of *adults* to obtain or learn about the product. For instance, no matter how laudable the state's interest in preventing minors' access to tobacco products, the state may not regulate advertising in a way that interferes materially with the legitimate rights of the tobacco industry, and its adult customers, to exchange truthful information (*Lorillard*).

**6.**  **Constitutionally-protected products:**  The use of some products is so tightly tied in with the *exercise of constitutional rights* that sale of the product could *not* constitutionally be banned; therefore, advertising of these products may also not be banned or heavily regulated. For instance, since there is a constitutional right to use *contraceptives*, a ban on the advertising of contraceptives would not be any more constitutional than would a ban on the sale of them. Indeed, the Court held this to be the case, in *Bolger v. Youngs Drug Products Corp.*, 463 U.S. 60 (1983).

**7.**  **Limited protection:**  The requirement of *Central Hudson Gas* that regulations of commercial speech be a direct and least-restrictive method of advancing "substantial" governmental interests, by itself demonstrates that commercial speech now receives less First Amendment protection than speech closer to the First Amendment's core values (especially "political" speech). Content-based suppression of purely political speech would never be permitted merely because the suppression satisfied this "intermediate" level of scrutiny. There are a number of other respects, as well, in which the government may regulate commercial speech more broadly than non-commercial expression. These include the following:

   **a.**   **No overbreadth doctrine:**   The ***overbreadth doctrine*** will ***not*** be applied in commercial-speech cases. Thus A will not be able to claim that a regulation should be struck down because it infringes upon the commercial-speech rights of B, who is not before the court. The Court in *Bates, supra,* p. 569, explained that the rationale behind the overbreadth doctrine, that of preventing a chilling effect on speech, is normally not applicable in the commercial-speech context, since a business needs to advertise in order to remain commercially healthy; its commercial speech, therefore, will not be likely to be "chilled" by overbroad regulations.

   **b.**   **"Time, place and manner" regulations:**   The state has a somewhat freer hand in regulating the ***"time, place and manner"*** of commercial speech. The state has especially broad freedom to impose such regulations where they are reasonably needed to prevent speech from being misleading.

   **c.**   **Less tolerance for inaccurate statements:**   Commercial speech is generally more ***objectively verifiable*** than political speech. Furthermore, the facts needed to determine whether speech is accurate or not normally are in the control of the advertiser. Therefore, government ***need not tolerate inaccurate statements*** to the same extent that it must in the non-commercial context.

   **d.**   **Prior restraint:**   The heavy presumption against the validity of ***prior restraints*** does ***not*** apply in commercial speech cases. For instance, the state may require that certain types of advertisements be ***submitted for previewing*** before they are published; see *Central Hudson Gas,* indicating that such a previewing system would be constitutional.

---

*Quiz Yourself on*
## DEFAMATION, OBSCENITY AND COMMERCIAL SPEECH

**80.** Joe was the owner of "Joe's Jewelry," a jewelry store that was the only such store in the town of Liberty. Since Liberty was a small town, most people knew who Joe was, but they didn't know much about his personal life, and he had never been involved in politics. One day, the local newspaper, the *Liberty Post,* reported that Joe had shot Tim, a shopper in the store, based on Joe's mistaken belief that Tim was attempting to rob the store. In fact, Tim was shot in Joe's store, but by Pete, Joe's employee, who Joe then immediately fired. (Tim was not in fact trying to shoplift, and Pete simply made a bad mistake.) Joe has brought a libel action against the *Post.* The state's policy is to allow a libel recovery whenever such a recovery would be allowed at common law and would not be forbidden by the U.S. Constitution. At the end of the case, the judge charged the jury that Joe could recover against the *Post* if the jury found that the *Post* had been negligent, but not if it found that the *Post* had made a non-negligent error as to the underlying facts. Does this charge correctly reflect the relevant constitutional principles? _____

**81.** After Emilio failed to pay numerous traffic tickets, the police came to his house to arrest him on a bench warrant. While they were standing inside the foyer of his house making the arrest, they saw copies of two unusual publications. One was *Kiddie World*, which contained pictures of nude adolescents; the adolescents were suggestively posed, but were not engaged in real or simulated sexual activities. The second publication was *Barnyard Illustrated*, which consisted exclusively of pictures of men and women having real or simulated sex with a variety of barnyard animals, including sheep and goats. A state ordinance forbids the sale or possession of "any pictorial material containing sexually explicit photographs that are obscene under prevailing constitutional standards." Assume that Emilio can be shown to have known the contents of both of these magazines.

   **(a)** Can Emilio be convicted for violating the ordinance as to *Kiddie World*? _____

   **(b)** Can Emilio be convicted for violating the ordinance as to *Barnyard Illustrated*? _____

**82.** Congress has concluded that the nicotine used in cigarettes is "highly addictive." Congress has also concluded that cigarette advertising causes many minors (who under federal and state laws can't legally buy the product) to take up smoking. Therefore, Congress has now banned all print advertising for cigarettes. Together with a prior ban on broadcast advertising for cigarettes, this means that billboards and handbills are now the only allowable means of advertising cigarettes. The cigarette industry asserts that this near total ban violates its right of free expression.

   **(a)** What is the test that the Court will use in evaluating the constitutionality of the ban? _____

   **(b)** Is the statute constitutional? _____

————————

*Answers*

**80. Yes, probably.** The first question is whether Joe is a *"public figure."* If he is a public figure, he may not be permitted to recover unless he shows "actual malice" on the part of the *Post*, i.e., that either the *Post* had knowledge that its statement about who did the shooting was false, or that the *Post* acted with "reckless disregard" of whether the statement was false or not. So if Joe is a public figure, then the judge's instruction is wrong. Joe might be held to be an "involuntary public figure" because of his involvement in this matter of obvious public interest; however, since he is not a criminal defendant, and since the Court has construed the "involuntary public figure" category narrowly, probably Joe does not fall into this category. Joe is certainly not a generally famous person (even locally), nor one who has voluntarily injected himself into a public controversy, so he probably doesn't fit into either of the other public figure categories recognized by the Court.

   If Joe is in fact a "private figure," then the judge's charge is correct. Under *Gertz v. Robert Welch*, where P is neither a public official nor a public figure, there is no constitutional requirement that he prove that the defendant knew his statement to be false or recklessly disregarded the truth. (On the other hand, the state would not be permitted to grant Joe a recovery based on strict liability; the First Amendment requires that the *Post* be proven to be at least negligent, even in a suit brought by a private figure.)

**81. (a) Yes.** On these facts, Kiddie World is probably not, strictly speaking, "obscene" under Supreme Court definitions. The reason is that mere nudity, without any attempt to portray sexual activity, is not considered "obscene." However, the state's interest in preventing the sexual exploitation and abuse of children is so strong that states may prohibit the sale, and even the private possession, of sexually explicit nude pictures of children, even though these are not strictly speaking "obscene." *Osborne v. Ohio*.

**(b) No.** The material here is almost certainly "obscene." Under *Miller v. California*, material is obscene if it depicts "patently offensive representations or descriptions of ultimate sex acts, normal or perverted. ... " It must be the case that the average person, applying contemporary community standards, would find that the work taken as a whole appeals to the prurient interest, and that the work taken as a whole lacks serious literary, artistic, political or scientific value. These tests all seem to be satisfied by the material here. However, the mere *private possession* of obscene material by an adult may not be made criminal. *Stanley v. Georgia*. Therefore, even though the state might be able to punish the person who sold the magazine to Emilio, it may not punish Emilio for knowingly possessing the material in his house. (As noted in part (a), possession of material showing sexually explicit photos of children does not come within the purview of *Stanley*.)

82. **(a) In theory, the four-part test of *Central Hudson Gas v. Public Service Comm.***, as modified by later cases. First, the Court will determine whether the commercial speech is protected at all by the First Amendment; commercial speech receives at least partial protection so long as it is not "misleading" and does not propose unlawful activity. Next, the Court asks whether the governmental interest in support of the regulation is ***"substantial."*** Third, the Court decides whether the regulation ***"directly advances"*** the governmental interest being sought. Finally, the Court asks whether the restriction is ***"not more extensive than is necessary"*** to serve the governmental objective. (But *44 Liquormart v. Rhode Island* shows that at least 4 Justices would apply strict scrutiny, not the mid-level standard of *Central Hudson Gas*, when a ban on advertising is premised on the idea that less advertising of a harmful product will lead to less consumption; so the *Central Hudson Gas* test might not be applied here.)

**(b) Unclear, but it's slightly-more-likely-than-not that the statute would be struck down.** Even if the not-so-hard-to-satisfy *Central Hudson Gas* test were applied, it's not clear whether the restriction would survive. General cigarette advertising is not "misleading" and does not propose unlawful activity (since Congress has not outlawed the sale of cigarettes), so the speech gets some First Amendment protection. The government's interest in preventing additional people (especially minors) from becoming "addicted" certainly seems to be "substantial." A ban on all print advertising certainly seems to "directly advance" the objective of preventing the creation of new smokers, given the power of advertising; however, *44 Liquormart* says that the anti-consumption impact of the regulation must be "significant," and it's not clear that the impact here would qualify. Finally, it's not clear whether the ban is "not more extensive than is necessary" to serve this interest, since there are some less-restrictive methods (e.g., a broader anti-smoking campaign, or higher taxes) that haven't been tried yet.

However, it may be that the fact that the users that Congress is targeting are *minors*, who under state and federal law can't be legal purchasers of the product, may lead the Court to give more deference to the restriction here than it did to the no-liquor-price-ads restriction struck down in *44 Liquormart,* or to the no-broadcast-gambling-ads restriction struck down in *Greater New Orleans*. The outcome of a suit on this fact pattern would probably be very close.

# IX. REGULATION IN THE CONTEXT OF POLITICAL CAMPAIGNS

A. **Money in political campaigns, generally:** In the modern political campaign, speech and the expenditure of money seem inevitably to go hand in hand. Whether money is spent by a private citizen who is contributing to a candidate, by a political action committee which runs advertisements backing or opposing certain candidates, or by a candidate himself, campaign spending has a strong expression component. Yet if corruption and the appearance of corruption are to be curbed, and if the cynical view that the richest candidate generally wins is to be proved wrong, some sorts of limits on campaign spending are probably necessary.

1. **General principles:** In a series of cases beginning in 1976, the Supreme Court has attempted to work out a line dividing those types of election spending which the states or the federal government may prohibit from those which are constitutionally-protected. While this line is a somewhat blurry one, several basic principles have emerged:

  ❏ ***Contributions*** made by individuals or groups to individual candidates, to Political Action Committees (PAC's) or to political parties, may be ***limited in dollar amount***, so long as the limits are not so low as to substantially interfere with candidates' and parties' ability to ***run a competitive election campaign.***

  ❏ On the other hand, ***independent expenditures by individuals***, and expenditures by ***candidates from their own funds***, may ***not*** be limited at all;

  ❏ Contributions that are made in support of or in opposition to ***ballot measures*** (as opposed to candidacies) may ***not*** be limited; and

  ❏ Congress may require that corporations (even non-profit ones) and unions, if they want to take out ***broadcast ads for or against particular federal candidates*** near election time, must do so via highly-regulated PACs.

B. ***Buckley v Valeo:*** The first, and most important, of this line of cases is ***Buckley v. Valeo***, 424 U.S. 1 (1976), in which the Supreme Court upheld some but not all provisions of the Federal Election Campaign Act of 1971 (FECA), as amended in 1974 (shortly after Watergate).

  1. **Statutory provisions:** Of the several provisions of the Act whose constitutionality the Court reviewed in *Buckley*, two are of concern to us here: (1) the Act's limitation on ***individual political contributions*** to $1,000 to any single candidate per election (with a corollary $25,000 limit on ***aggregate*** contributions by any one individual in any year); and (2) its limitations on ***expenditures***, including a $1,000-per-year limit on ***independent*** expenditures by individuals and groups on behalf of a "clearly identified" candidate, various limits on expenditures ***by a candidate*** from personal or family funds, and various limits on ***total*** campaign spending.

  2. **Result:** In brief, the Court's *per curiam* decision ***sustained*** the contribution limits, but found ***unconstitutional*** the limits on independent expenditures by individuals, on expenditures by a candidate from personal or family funds, and on aggregate campaign spending.

  3. **Contribution limits upheld:** The Court applied what it called its "closest scrutiny" to the ***contribution*** limits. But despite the close scrutiny, the Court ***upheld*** the limits, on the following analysis:

     a. **Marginal restriction:** Although these limits placed some quantity restriction on political expression, the restriction was only ***"marginal."*** Since a dollar contribution does not communicate the "underlying basis" for the contributor's support of the candidate, the amount of "communication" being done by the contributor ***does not increase*** as the size of the contribution increases — whatever expression takes place when a contribution is made derives from the "undifferentiated, symbolic act of contributing," whose symbolism is largely independent of dollar amount.

    b.   **Strong governmental interest:**  On the other side of the scale, the governmental interest supporting the limits was a powerful one, that of limiting the ***actuality and appearance of corruption*** resulting from large individual contributions, which are sometimes made to secure a political *quid pro quo* from the candidate. ***No less restrictive alternative*** would have been adequate; for instance, anti-bribery and disclosure laws could not deal fully with the need to root out all apparent as well as actual opportunity for corruption.

4.   **Expenditures by individuals:**  By contrast, the Court found that the limitations on ***expenditures*** by ***individuals acting independently*** from candidates imposed "***direct and substantial restraints*** on the quantity of political speech," and limited political expression "at the core ... of First Amendment freedoms." For instance, the restrictions would have made it impossible for an individual or association legally to take out a single quarter-page advertisement backing a particular candidate in a big-city newspaper.

    a.   **State interest insufficient:**  When viewed with the requisite "exacting scrutiny," the governmental interest in combatting corruption, asserted in support of the limits on expenditures by individuals, was ***inadequate***. First, not all apparent or actual *quid pro quo* deals would be eliminated, since the limits applied only to expenditures "advocating the election or defeat" of a "clearly identified candidate," so that ads could be run supporting the candidate's ***views*** (as part of a *quid pro quo*), without expressly advocating his election. Secondly, the expenditure limits only applied where the expenditures were made ***totally independently*** of the candidate and his campaign; spending which was controlled by or coordinated with the campaign was treated as a contribution. Where such complete independence existed, a carefully-orchestrated *quid pro quo* was less likely, the Court concluded.

5.   **Spending of candidate's own money:**  The Court also struck down limits on the amount that a ***candidate*** may spend from his ***own personal or family funds***. The interest in preventing actual or apparent corruption did not apply to this situation, since obviously a candidate would not bribe himself. And the interest in ***equalizing the resources*** of competing candidates was not well served by the spending limit, since a candidate who spent less of his own money than his opponent could nonetheless outspend the latter by raising more money from outside sources. Therefore, no state interest was sufficient to outweigh the candidate's own "First Amendment right to engage in the discussion of public issues and vigorously and tirelessly advocate his own election. ..."

    a.   **Still valid:**  This principle that the amount a candidate may spend from his own resources may not be capped remains intact — and indeed has since been expanded — in the Roberts court. See the discussion on p. 589 of *Davis v. FEC*, where the Court struck down a federal "Millionaire's Amendment" that had provided that if a rich candidate spent more than a certain amount of his own funds, the candidate's adversary would be freed from certain limits on third-party campaign donations.

6.   **Limits on total campaign spending:**  Finally, the Court struck down limits on what a candidate could ***spend from all sources combined***. Candidates have a First Amendment right to spend as much as they wish to promote their own political views, and the governmental interest in curbing the skyrocketing costs of political campaigns is not sufficient to

outweigh that right, the Court held. (But Congress may create a scheme for ***publicly funding*** elections, in which case the candidate *may* be required to choose between respecting an aggregate spending limit and losing the public subsidy.)

7. **Other opinions:** Only three Justices joined the Court's opinion in its entirety. Five others concurred only in part, and one did not participate.

   a. **Burger's concurrence:** Justice Burger dissented from the plurality's upholding of the contribution limits. In his view, contributions, no less than expenditures, were ways of communicating. Contributions were simply a way of "pooling" money, and were thus associational activities comparable to, say, volunteer work; therefore, freedom of ***association*** as well as freedom of speech required that these not be restricted unless there was no less-restrictive satisfactory alternative. In Burger's view, anti-bribery laws and disclosure requirements could solve the corruption problems inherent in large contributions just as they could in the expenditure context.

   b. **White's concurrence:** Justice White, like Justice Burger, saw no principled distinction between expenditures and contributions. But in sharp contrast to Justice Burger's view, White believed that ***both*** the contribution and expenditure limits were ***valid***. He disagreed with the plurality's equation of money with speech. Also, he would have deferred much more completely to Congress' superior knowledge of what motivates politicians, and to its conclusion that expenditure limits on both private citizens and candidates are needed to accomplish the goals of preventing bribery and corruption and equalizing "access to the political area."

8. ***Buckley* remains valid (*Randall v. Sorrell*):** A 2006 decision involving Vermont's campaign-finance reform statute shows that ***Buckley's general approach remains valid*** in the Roberts Court. That case, ***Randall v. Sorrell***, 126 S.Ct. 2479 (2006), held that:

   ❏ limits on ***candidate expenditures*** remain flatly ***unconstitutional***, as *Buckley* had held them to be; and

   ❏ limits on ***contributions*** will often be constitutional (as the ones in *Buckley* had been held to be), but the particular Vermont limitations at issue were so low that they ***interfered with candidates' ability run a competitive election***, and thus ***violated*** the First Amendment.

*Randall* was a 6-3 vote, but there were so many different opinions and alliances that there was apparently no majority of the Court standing for any particular rationale for judging either expenditure limits or contribution limits.

   a. **Expenditure limits:** On the ***candidate-expenditure*** front, Vermont prevented candidates for governor from spending more than $300,000 in any two-year primary-plus-general-election cycle. Limits for candidates for other offices were even lower, such as $4,000 for a state senator.

      i. **Struck down:** By 6-3, the Court ***invalidated*** these expenditure limits.

         (1) **Breyer's opinion:** The main opinion on the expenditure limits was by Justice Breyer. Breyer (joined by Chief Justice Roberts and Justice Alito), concluded that such expenditure limits had been made unconstitutional by *Buckley*, and that there was no reason to overrule this aspect of *Buckley*. Defenders of the Vermont statute had asked the Court to consider a rationale

for candidate-expenditure limits that they said *Buckley* had not considered: that such limits protect candidates from **spending too much time raising money**. But Breyer believed that the *Buckley* court *had* considered, and had implicitly rejected, this rationale.

    **(2) Three more votes:** Justices Kennedy, Thomas and Scalia, concurring in separate opinions, agreed with Breyer's conclusions that (i) *Buckley* had properly found that candidate-expenditure limitations violated the First Amendment, and (ii) Vermont's limitations here fell within the scope of *Buckley*. This made six votes for striking the expenditure limits.

  **ii.** **Dissent:** Three Justices (Stevens, Souter and Ginsburg) dissented from the Court's striking of the expenditure limits. Stevens believed that expenditure limits were "far more akin to **time, place and manner restrictions** than to restrictions on the content of speech," and that such limits should therefore be upheld "so long as the purposes they serve are legitimate and sufficiently substantial," a standard he thought was met here. Souter and Ginsburg would not have gone that far, but they thought the case should be remanded to the lower court for consideration of the state's "prevent candidates from spending too much time raising money" rationale.

**b.** **Contribution limits:** Unlike the expenditure-limit ruling, the Court's decision on the Vermont contribution limits made new law — it marked **the first time the Court had ever found a contribution limit to be unconstitutionally low.** That finding was made by the same 6-3 lineup as on the expenditure limits.

  **i.** **Low limits:** The state's contribution limits were, overall, the lowest in the nation. For instance, the most that any individual could give to a candidate for governor during a two-year primary-plus-general-election cycle was **$400**. Even more stringently, a **political party's** contribution to any gubernatorial candidate was limited to this same $400 per two-year cycle, and all affiliates of a party (e.g., the local, state and national Democratic Party) were lumped together as a single contributor for purposes of the $400 limit.

  **ii.** **Breyer's opinion:** Justice Breyer (joined again by Chief Justice Roberts and Justice Alito) believed that these limits were **simply too low to pass constitutional muster.**

    **(1) Recap of the rules of *Buckley*:** Breyer noted that *Buckley* had upheld a $1,000 contribution limit (in 1976 dollars), and that that case had held that contribution limits were permissible as long as the government demonstrated that the limits were **"closely drawn"** to match a **"sufficiently important interest."** He then repeated *Buckley*'s more specific test for evaluating contribution limits: such limits must not be so low that they prevent candidates from **"amassing the resources necessary for effective [campaign] advocacy,"** and must not **"magnify the advantages of incumbency** to the point where they **put challengers to a significant disadvantage."** In sum, Breyer pointed out, *Buckley* had acknowledged that there was **"some lower bound,"** below which the danger to democratic electoral processes would simply be "too great."

**(2) Five factors:**  Breyer then identified *five factors* in the Vermont statute that convinced him that the contribution limits here were so low that they were not "closely drawn" to further the state's legitimate interest in preventing corruption:

❏ the limits were so low that they would "significantly restrict the amount of funding available for challengers *to run competitive campaigns*";

❏ the application of the low limits to *political parties* threatened "harm to a particularly important political right, the *right to associate in a political party*";

❏ the statute aggravated the problem by treating as a "contribution" *expenses borne by volunteers* in the course of campaign activities;

❏ the statute's limits would *not be adjusted for inflation over time*, unlike some of the contribution limits previously upheld by the Court.

❏ there was *no "special justification" advanced* by the state in support of such restrictive limits, merely the same basic justifications that had been considered in *Buckley*.

These five factors persuaded Breyer that the contribution limits were not "narrowly tailored," and that they *"disproportionately burden[ed]"* the First Amendment interests of candidates, political parties and volunteers.

iii. **Concurrences by Kennedy, Thomas and Scalia:**  Three additional Justices, Kennedy, Thomas and Scalia, *concurred* in the judgment on contribution limits, though they did not agree with Breyer's rationale. This made six votes to strike the contribution limits. Justice Thomas, in an opinion joined by Justice Scalia, argued that contribution limits infringe as directly and seriously on First Amendment freedoms as do expenditure limits. Therefore, Thomas would have overruled *Buckley*'s deferential treatment of contribution limits, and would have strictly scrutinized Vermont's limits here, a scrutiny which he was certain those limits would fail.

iv. **Three dissenters:**  Justice Souter (joined by Justices Stevens and Ginsburg), *dissented* from the striking of the contribution limits as they had done regarding the expenditure limits. Souter believed that Vermont's limits were "not remarkable departures" from either limits previously approved by the Court or limits recently enacted by other states. Souter conceded that some per-capita limitations might be so low that "aggregated donations simply could not sustain effective campaigns," in which case the limits would be unconstitutionally low. But he was not convinced that this was true of Vermont's scheme. Souter believed the contribution limits were constitutional because they were *not* "so radical in effect as to *render political association ineffective, drive the sound of a candidate's voice below the level of notice, [or] render contributions pointless."*

c. **Significance of *Randall*:**  Here is what *Randall* seems to demonstrate:

❏ On the *candidate-expenditure* front, the case proves that *Buckley*'s total ban on all expenditure limitations not only remains *valid*, but has a robust six-member majority of the newly-constituted Roberts Court behind it. Therefore, there seems little prospect of campaign-finance reform that works by placing limits on how much candidates may spend. (But nothing in *Randall* prevents government from instituting **public funding** of campaigns, and then forcing the candidate to choose between taking the public funding or being free to spend without limit.)

❏ As to **contribution** limits, a six-Justice majority seems to believe that the basic approach of *Buckley* — that contribution limits should be deferentially reviewed and **rarely struck down** — remains **sound**. Only in the quite unusual case in which contribution limits are **so low that they make it extremely hard for a challenger to mount a serious campaign against incumbent,** will the contribution limits be struck down. So the actual result in *Randall* — contribution limits found to be unconstitutionally low — probably **won't often be repeated** when the schemes of other jurisdictions are evaluated.

❏ But there does not seem to be anything close to a majority in agreement on any particular **test** for determining **"how low is too low"** when it comes to contribution limits. For instance, Breyer's elaborate five-factor test was able to get the votes of only two other Justices.

9. **Candidates' personal-expenditure limits remain unconstitutional (*Davis*):** In the decades after *Buckley*'s ruling that limits on a candidate's expenditure of her own personal funds violated her First Amendment rights, Congress sought to find other ways to reduce the advantages held by wealthy candidates willing to spend their own funds. One result was the so-called **"Millionaire's Amendment,"** passed by Congress in 2002. This amendment said that when a candidate for the House of Representatives spent more than $350,000 of his own funds, the candidate's **adversary** could receive individual contributions at **three times the usual rate** (i.e., subject to a per-donor limit of $6,900 rather than the usual $2,300). The idea was to "even the playing field," so that the millionaire candidate wouldn't have an unfair advantage from his ability to self-fund without limit. But in ***Davis v. F.E.C.***, 128 S.Ct. 2759 (2008), the Court by a 5-4 vote found that the Millionaire's Amendment **violated the First Amendment rights of wealthy candidates.**

a. **Burden on speech:** The majority agreed with the plaintiff (a wealthy candidate) that the amendment required candidates to "choose between the First Amendment right to engage in unfettered political speech and subjection to discriminatory fund-raising limitations." Therefore, the amendment imposed a **"substantial burden"** on the exercise of the First Amendment right to use personal funds for campaign speech, triggering strict scrutiny.

   i. **Flunks strict scrutiny:** The measure could not survive that strict scrutiny, the majority held. The measure did not further the governmental interest in eliminating corruption, because a candidate's use of his own funds **reduces** the threat of corruption rather than increasing it. And as for the asserted interest in **"level[ing] electoral opportunities** for candidates of different personal wealth," this was **not a legitimate governmental objective** because it would "permit Congress to arrogate the voters' authority to evaluate the strengths of candidates competing for office."

b. **Dissent:** The four dissenters in *Davis* believed that the plaintiff candidate could not show that he had suffered **any First Amendment injury** whatsoever — the amendment merely amplified the voice of the wealthy candidate's opponent, and "this amplification in no way mutes voice of the millionaire, who remains able to speak as loud and as long as he likes in support of his campaign." Furthermore, the dissenters believed, the amendment was closely tailored to furthering the government's strong interest in "reducing both the ***influence of wealth*** on the outcomes of elections, and the ***appearance*** that wealth alone dictates those results."

C. **Contributions to Political Action Committees:**  The election statute reviewed in *Buckley* also prohibited individuals and associations from contributing more than $5,000 per year to any "multi-candidate political committee" (commonly called a ***Political Action Committee*** or ***PAC***). This limitation was ***upheld*** in *California Medical Assn. v. FEC*, 453 U.S. 182 (1981).

   1. **Contributions by Political Action Committees:**  But a $1,000 limitation on the amount that may be contributed ***by*** a PAC to a Presidential candidate was ***struck down,*** in *FEC v. National Conservative Political Action Committee*, 470 U.S. 480 (1985).

D. **"Soft money" and pre-election "issue ads" (*McConnell* and *Wisconsin Right to Life*):**  The federal campaign finance reform measures approved by the Court in *Buckley* turned out not to be tremendously effective over the several decades that followed. Sophisticated and wealthy donors and advocacy organizations — and the national political parties — bypassed these measures by various devices, most notably the institutions of ***"soft money"*** and ***"issue ads."*** Finally, Congress responded by enacting the Bipartisan Campaign Reform Act of 2002 ("BCRA"), popularly known as the ***McCain-Feingold Act*** after its chief Senate sponsors. In an important pair of decisions, the Court first approved the key measures of the BCRA, but then (after a switch in Court personnel) reversed itself by striking one of the key measures.

The two cases are: ***McConnell v. Federal Election Comm.***, 540 U.S. 93 (2003) (approving both key measures, mostly by a 5-4 vote) and ***Federal Election Commission v. Wisconsin Right to Life***, 127 S.Ct. 2652 (2007) (largely invalidating the ban on election-time issue ads, also by a 5-4 vote). *McConnell* and *Wisconsin Right to Life* are probably the most important campaign-finance decisions by the Court since *Buckley* itself.

   1. **Twin targets of the BCRA:**  The BCRA addressed the two practices that Congress believed were the most egregious ways in which wealthy donors and special-interest groups were corrupting and distorting the federal election process:

      a. **Soft money:**  First was the giving of ***"soft money"*** donations. Political contributions whose amounts were regulated by the FECA (the act upheld in *Buckley*) were and are known as ***"hard money"*** donations. But the FECA as interpreted by the Federal Election Commission treated certain donations and expenditures as not falling within this regulated, hard-money classification; these unregulated sums are what is known as soft money. For instance, donors could contribute ***unlimited soft-money sums to the Democratic and Republican national parties*** (or special committees run by those parties), and the parties could then ***re-spend the money*** however they wanted as long as the funds were not used to expressly advocate the election or defeat of a particular candidate. Such large soft-money donations could be given by wealthy individuals, corporations, labor unions, and anyone else, as long as the funds were used in this no-advocacy-of-election-or-defeat-of-a-specific-candidate manner.

         i. **Get-out-the-vote and other uses of soft money:**  So, for instance, political parties could raise large sums from wealthy donors, then spend those sums on activities like ***get-out-the-vote drives*** (directed at voters expected to vote for the party putting on the drive), and ***generic party advertising*** (e.g., "Vote for the Democratic ticket this November 2nd.")

**b.  Issue ads:**  The second practice that was upsetting Congress was the use of ***special-issue broadcast ads*** by groups like corporations and labor unions. If a corporation or union wanted to buy an ad expressly advocating the election or defeat of a particular candidate, that ad had to be paid for with hard (and thus tightly-regulated) dollars, and lots of information about the sponsor of the ad had to be disclosed. But if the sponsor avoided the "magic words" — i.e., words expressly advocating a particular candidate's election or defeat — then the ad could be funded by ***unlimited sums furnished by the corporation or union,*** and with no disclosure of the sponsors' identity.  These ads are generically known as ***"issue ads"*** (and ones attacking rather than supporting a particular candidate are known as ***"attack ads"***).Thus a Republican-leaning advocacy group might purchase ads attacking Democratic Congressman Joe Smith's voting record on Social Security, and then conclude, "Call Joe Smith and tell him to stop weakening Social Security." These attack ads were in fact often ***more effective*** than direct "vote for [or against] Jane Doe" ads.

**2.  Congress attacks the twin evils:**  So by enacting the BCRA, Congress tried to curb the abuses associated with both unregulated soft money and with issue ads purchased by that unregulated money. In doing so, Congress believed that it was acting to reduce not only corruption but the ***appearance*** of corruption, stemming from wealthy donors' apparent attempt to purchase access to office holders.  The heart of the BCRA consisted of Titles I and II.

**a.  Title I on soft money:**  Title I of the BCRA was Congress' attempt to plug the soft-money loophole. The main provision in Title I ***prohibited the national political parties and their committees from soliciting, receiving or spending any soft money.*** As the *McConnell* majority later summarized this provision, Title I "takes national parties out of the soft-money business."

**b.  Title II on issue ads:**  Title II mainly prohibited corporations and labor unions from using their general funds for ***broadcast advertisements naming specific candidates for federal office near election time.***

    **i.  Electioneering Communications:**  Title II defined a new category called ***"Electioneering Communications,"*** which consisted of ***TV and radio ads***, broadcast within 60 days before a general election or 30 days before a primary, and referring to an ***identified candidate*** for federal office.

    **ii.  Ban on ads:**  Title II then said that ***corporations and labor unions may not use their general funds to pay for Electioneering Communications,*** and must instead pay for these with money from their Political Action Committees (see *supra*, p. 590).

    **iii.  Significance:**  Since PACs are ***subject to contribution limits*** and other types of regulation (e.g., the requirement that the names of individual donors be ***publicly disclosed***), Title II significantly restricted the ways in which corporations (including ***non-profit advocacy corporations*** like the ACLU and the NRA) could pay for and carry out their own election-time broadcast advertising. In enacting Title II, Congress seems to have been especially angry at "attack ads," in which special-interest advocacy groups attack a particular candidate for her stand on a particular issue (e.g., "Tell Senator Jones to stop voting to weaken our nation's defenses.").

3. **Attacked by odd grouping:** In *McConnell*, a consortium of non-profit groups attacked the statute's constitutionality, including such unlikely allies as the American Civil Liberties Union and the National Rifle Association.

4. **Court upholds both Title I and II in *McConnell*:** The *McConnell* Court **upheld the constitutionality of both Title I and Title II**, and thus upheld virtually all of the BCRA.[7] The majority opinion on Titles I and II was jointly authored by Justices Stevens and O'Connor (joined by Souter, Ginsburg and Breyer). Most of the case was decided on a 5-4 vote.

   a. **Title I upheld:** As to Title I, the majority wrote that soft money had enabled candidates and parties to **circumvent** FECA's limits. The majority agreed with the congressional drafters of Title I that there was ample evidence to support the conclusion that large soft-money contributions to the national political parties had had a corrupting influence, or at the very least had given rise to the **appearance** of corruption. It was not a violation of donors' First Amendment rights for Congress to regulate donations so as to curb the reality or appearance of that corruption.

   b. **Title II also upheld :** The majority also thought that **Title II** was constitutional. Those attacking Title II argued that under *Buckley*, speakers had an absolute First Amendment right to engage in "issue advocacy" (as opposed to express advocacy of the election or defeat of a particular candidate). But the majority disagreed: broadcast ads near the time of an election, mentioning specific candidates, were just as clearly intended to influence the election as were the type of express-advocacy ads regulated under *Buckley*. Therefore, it did not violate the First Amendment for these issue ads to be regulated in the same way.

   c. **Dissents in *McConnell*:** Four justices — Kennedy, Scalia, Thomas and Rehnquist — **dissented** from the majority's wholesale upholding of Title I and Title II in *McConnell*.

      i. **Kennedy's dissent:** The longest dissent was by Justice Kennedy, who was joined in part by the other three. Kennedy thought that the majority's opinion replaced traditional First Amendment principles with "new, amorphous, and unsound rules, rules which **dismantle basic protections for speech**."

         (1) **PACs not a substitute:** Kennedy particularly objected to what he said was the majority's minimizing of Title II's impact on corporations' and unions' free-speech rights. The majority thought that corporations and unions could almost as easily use PACs to make the kind of Electioneering Communications that Title II prevented them from doing directly. But Kennedy believed that ads by PACs were a poor substitute for direct corporate or union speech, because PACs require major amounts of **planning and paperwork**. Smaller entities would be the most burdened; for instance, "for an organization that has not yet set up a PAC, **spontaneous speech** that 'refers to a clearly identified candidate

---

7. The one part of the Act that was struck down was a ban on contributions by **minors** — Congress was worried that rich parents would funnel, through their minor children, contributions in excess of the hard-money limits. But the Court said that there was no evidence that such evasions were occurring.

for federal office' becomes ***impossible***, even if the group's ***vital interests are threatened*** by a piece of legislation ***pending before Congress*** on the eve of a federal election."

    **ii. Scalia's dissent:** Justice Scalia's dissent said that the majority had "smiled with favor upon a law that cuts to the heart of what the First Amendment is meant to protect: the right to ***criticize the government***." In particular, he thought the law improperly allowed Congress to ***insulate its own incumbent members against criticism*** by political parties and corporations. The BCRA might be "evenhanded" in the sense that it similarly prohibited criticism of those running *against* incumbents. But "this is an area in which ***evenhandedness is not fairness***. [If] incumbents and challengers are limited to the same quantity of electioneering, ***incumbents are favored.***"

**5. Title II largely struck down in *Wisconsin Right to Life*:** But four years after *McConnell* was decided, and following a change in the Court's membership, the Court effectively ***reversed itself*** as to Title II's ban on ***issue ads*** near election time, in *FEC v. Wisconsin Right to Life*. Justice O'Connor's replacement by Justice Alito produced a switch to 5-4 the other way, under which the Court did not expressly overrule this part of *McConnell* but so narrowed the permissible scope of the issue-ad ban that that ban effectively no longer exists.

    **a. Possibility of "as applied" attack left open:** In *McConnell*, the attack on Title II had been "on its face" — the plaintiffs claimed that Title II's ban on "electioneering communications" was substantially overbroad in that it improperly restricted lots of protected speech as well as some non-protected speech, and that the Title should therefore be struck down in its entirety, even if the plaintiffs could not show that their own speech had been improperly restricted. (See the discussion of facial attacks and the overbreadth doctrine *supra*, p. 484). The *McConnell* majority, as noted, rejected this facial attack; but it left open the possibility that some later plaintiff might be able to bring a successful "as applied" attack, that is, be able to show that when the statute was applied to the conduct of that particular plaintiff, the statute violated the plaintiff's own freedom of speech because the plaintiff was engaging in a protected "genuine issue ad" as opposed to an unprotected disguised-electioneering ad.

    **b. As-applied attack by WRTL:** The *Wisconsin Right to Life* suit involved just such an as-applied challenge to Title II's ban on electioneering communications. Wisconsin Right to Life (WRTL), a small nonprofit "ideological advocacy" corporation, wanted to run, just before a senatorial primary election, an ad criticizing both of Wisconsin's incumbent senators for supporting a filibuster intended to delay consideration of several of President George W. Bush's judicial nominees. The ad did not urge voters to vote any particular way in the upcoming Democratic primary, but it urged listeners to "Contact Senators Feingold and Kohl and tell them to oppose the filibuster." The ad would clearly have violated Title II, because it was an "electioneering communication" (i.e., it mentioned a particular candidate) by a corporation, paid for out of its general funds, run within 30 days of a primary. WRTL claimed that the ad was a genuine issue ad, the banning of which violated the organization's free-speech rights.

    **c. Majority upholds challenge:** Five members of the Court agreed that the application of Title II to this ad ***violated WRTL's freedom of speech.*** Justices Kennedy, Scalia and

Thomas thought Title II was unconstitutional, just as they had thought in the case of the facial attack in *McConnell*. Chief Justice Rehnquist had in the interim left the Court and been replaced by Roberts, who took essentially the same the-statute-is-unconstitutional approach as Rehnquist had done in *McConnell*. On the other side of the ledger, Stevens, Souter, Ginsburg and Breyer thought Title II was fully constitutional, as they had thought in *McConnell*. So the question was which way Alito, who had replaced O'Connor, would vote. He voted with the strike-the-statute group, making a majority.

i.   **Two blocks:** But although five justices agreed in *Wisconsin Right to Life* that WRTL's rights had been infringed, they could not agree on a rationale, or on the correct procedural solution. Roberts and Alito formed one bloc, and Kennedy, Scalia and Thomas formed another.

ii.  **The Roberts bloc:** Chief Justice Roberts, in an opinion joined only by Alito, thought that: (1) *McConnell*'s holding on Title II should be kept in force rather than overruled; (2) *McConnell* had held that Title II is constitutional only to the extent that it "regulates express advocacy or its functional equivalent"; (3) an ad should be deemed to be the "functional equivalent" of express advocacy (and thus regulable by the FEC) only if "the ad is *susceptible of no reasonable interpretation other than as an appeal to vote for or against a specific candidate.*" This was a tough standard, which the FEC would rarely if ever be able to meet in a real-world situation. Roberts liked this test because he thought the Court should "give the benefit of any doubt to protecting rather than stifling speech."

     **(1) Application to WRTL's ad:** By this standard, WRTL's ad was clearly *not* the "functional equivalent of express advocacy," because it focused on a legislative issue, took a position on that issue, and did not mention an election, candidacy, political party or challenger. Therefore, Roberts believed, Title II's ban on the running of electioneering communications was unconstitutional as applied to the ad here.

iii. **The 3-vote bloc:** Justice Scalia, joined by Kennedy and Thomas, concurred in the result, but disagreed with Roberts' rationale. Scalia thought that *McConnell*'s holding that Title II was not facially invalid was wrong and should be flatly overruled, not just de facto overruled via an as-applied decision, as Roberts' opinion would do.

iv.  **Dissent:** The four dissenters (Souter, joined by Stevens, Ginsburg and Breyer), thought that *McConnell* had correctly upheld the constitutionality of Title II, and should not be surreptitiously overruled as the majority was doing. Roberts' opinion effectively deprived the FEC of the right to regulate any ad that did not contain the "magic words" of expressly advocating the election or defeat of a particular candidate, Souter said. This view would force regulation back to the "toothless" state that had led Congress to enact the BCRA in the first place, and would deprive Congress of the power to make "a realistic response when corporations and labor organizations commit the concentrated monies in their treasuries to electioneering." Souter also objected to the majority's approach on *stare decisis* grounds: "the price of *McConnell*'s demise ... seems to me to be a high one. The Court (and, I think, the country) loses when important precedent is overruled without good reason[.]"

6. **Prognosis:** So here is where federal regulation of soft money and issue ads seems to stand after *Wisconsin Right to Life*'s retrenchment of *McConnell*:

❑ Title I's ban on *soft money contributions to the national political parties* remains *constitutional*, at least for now. There is no indication that a majority of the Roberts Court disagrees with *McConnell*'s conclusion that Congress can constitutionally fight the appearance of corruption by tightly regulating the making of cash contributions to candidates or parties.

❑ But Title II's ban on *"electioneering communications"* is basically *defunct*. As long as an issue ad avoids expressly advocating that voters vote for or against a particular candidate — and instead uses an indirect phrase like "Tell [the candidate] to stop jeopardizing our national defense" — the ad *cannot be regulated,* even if the organization taking the ad subjectively *intends to affect* the election, and *explicitly mentions* the candidate's name.

❑ Consequently, corporations, unions and *non-party special-interest groups* (like Wisconsin Right to Life) will all likely have *more influence* on elections than they used to have, because of their ability to spend limitless sums on issue ads. Conversely, the *national political parties* may lose influence relative to these other kinds of groups, since the political parties' fundraising abilities have been restricted and the independent entities' fundraising and fund-spending abilities have not.

E. **Campaign spending by political parties:** Campaign spending by *political parties* on behalf of congressional candidates *may not be limited*, as long as the party is working *"independently"* of the candidate rather than in "coordination" with her. This was the result of the pre-*McConnell* case of *Colorado Republican Federal Campaign Committee v. Federal Election Commission*, 518 U.S. 604 (1996) (*"Colorado Republican I"*).

1. **Limited by BCRA:** But the BCRA (*supra*, p. 590) means that such spending by political parties will be limited, because the parties are now restricted to raising only tightly-regulated hard-money donations from which to make even such candidate-independent expenditures.

2. **Limits on coordinated spending are constitutional:** Furthermore, it is *constitutional* for Congress to limit campaign spending by parties that *is coordinated* with the candidate. The court so concluded in *Federal Election Commission v. Colorado Republican Federal Campaign Committee*, 533 U.S. 431 (2001) (*"Colorado Republican II"*), a later stage of the same *Colorado Republican* litigation. In a preview of *McConnell*'s "avoidance of circumvention" rationale, the Court reasoned that if coordinated-expenditure limits on the parties did not exist, candidates could easily bypass the (constitutional) limits on direct-to-candidate contributions by routing such contributions through the parties.

F. **How low can limits be set:** We know from *Buckley* that government can set a dollar limit on campaign contributions, and we also know from that case that a $1000 limit (in 1976 dollars) per-contributor/per-candidate is valid. But may the limits constitutionally be *set even lower*? As the result of a 2000 case, *Nixon v. Shrink Missouri Government PAC*, 523 U.S. 666 (2000), we know that the answer is *yes*: as long as the limitation is not so radical as to *"render contributions pointless,"* it will be *sustained* even though it buys far less campaign speech than

$1000 did in 1976. (So, for instance, a limit of $1,075 in donations for statewide offices was upheld in *Nixon*.)

1. **Applies to states:** Notice that *Shrink Missouri* means that the ***states*** may limit campaign contributions for state elections, just as *Buckley* and *McConnell* said that Congress may do for federal elections.

2. **Some limits are too low:** In only one case has the Court concluded that contribution limits were ***unconstitutionally low.*** In *Randall v. Sorrell*, *supra*, p. 586, the Court concluded that Vermont's limits — for instance, a $400 limit on what an individual or party could contribute to a candidate for governor during a two-year election cycle — were so low as to "disproportionately burden" the First Amendment rights of candidates, parties and volunteers. Only in a truly extraordinary case — where the limits are so low that they prevent challengers from making an effective campaign against incumbents, for instance — will the Court find that the limits are unconstitutionally low. (No majority of the Roberts Court has been able to agree on a standard for determining when contribution limits are "too low.")

G. **Ballot measures:** The "anti-bribery" and "anti-corruption" rationales relied upon in *Buckley* and *McConnell* to sustain limits on contributions are ***not as readily applicable*** where a ***referendum*** or other ***ballot measure***, rather than an election of ***candidates***, is at issue. Therefore, the government will have a harder time showing the need to curb contributions and expenditures in connection with such measures than in the partisan-election area. This distinction explains why the Court struck down a Berkeley, California ordinance placing a $250 limit on personal contributions to committees formed to support or oppose ballot measures, in *Citizens Against Rent Control (CARC) v. Berkeley*, 454 U.S. 290 (1981). The net result is that states and local governments may not impose ***any contribution limits*** in ***ballot-measure elections***.

1. **Can't ban paid campaign workers:** Similarly, in a post-*CARC* case, the Court held that a state may not prohibit the ***payment*** of people who ***circulate petitions*** in connection with a ballot measure. *Meyer v. Grant*, 486 U.S. 414 (1988). "The First Amendment protects appellees' right not only to advocate their cause but also to select what they believe to be the ***most effective means*** for so doing."

H. **Corporate and judicial expression during campaigns:** So far, our discussion of free speech and campaigns has focused mostly on money. We turn now to two other issues involving regulation of campaign speech: (1) to what extent may political expression be regulated on account of the fact that the speaker is a ***business*** or ***corporation***?; and (2) in places where ***judges*** must run for office, what restrictions may be placed upon the candidates' campaign speech? The Supreme Court has issued one decision on each of these questions; in each case, the Court has ruled in favor of the First Amendment claim by the speaker or candidate.

1. **Corporate political expression:** On the issue of campaign-related speech by ***businesses*** and ***corporations***, the Court has held that political expression may not be denied Fourteenth Amendment protection merely because its source is a ***corporation*** rather than an individual. In *First National Bank of Boston v. Bellotti*, 435 U.S. 765 (1978) the Court, by a 5-4 vote, struck down a Massachusetts ban on ***corporate political advocacy***. The decision relied on the ***public's right to know***, rather than on the corporation's right to speak.

   a. **Facts:** Massachusetts passed a law prohibiting corporations from spending funds to influence the vote on any ***referendum*** which did not materially affect the corporation's business.

   **b. Statute struck down:** The majority, in striking down the statute on First Amendment grounds, declined to consider whether corporations always have First Amendment rights identical with those of individuals. Instead, the majority reasoned that the speech here, because it *informed the public* on a political matter, was protected by the Fourteenth Amendment *regardless of whether its source was corporate or individual*.

2. **Campaign speech in judicial elections:** As to campaign speech by those seeking election to *judgeships*, the Court has struck down a Minnesota rule that a candidate for judicial office shall not "announce his or her views on disputed legal or political issues." *Republican Party of Minn. v. White*, 536 U.S. 765 (2002).

   **a. Purpose of the rule:** Drafters of the rule reasoned that when a candidate publicly makes known her views on issues that may come before her court, the *due process rights* of later litigants are likely to be abridged.

   **b. Struck down:** By a 5-4 vote, the Court struck down Minnesota's rule on the theory that it violated the First Amendment rights of judicial candidates. The opinion, by Justice Scalia, conceded that opposition to judicial elections "may be well taken." But, he said, "the First Amendment does not permit [opponents of judicial elections] to achieve [their] goal by leaving the principle of elections in place while preventing candidates from discussing what the elections are about."

   **c. Dissent:** The four dissenters contended that the Minnesota rule was a reasonable way for Minnesota to pursue its legitimate goal of maintaining judicial impartiality.

# X. SOME SPECIAL CONTEXTS

**A. Scope:** We now examine several particular contexts in which special First Amendment problems have arisen. Generally, these special problems arise because the First Amendment comes into conflict with unusually strong "public policy" interests, for instance, the interest in running an effective public-school system, or in the smooth administration of justice.

**B. Schools:** The conflict between First Amendment values and society's substantial interest in pursuing other important values can be seen clearly in the *public school* context. On the one hand, the public school system is the community's principal means for transmitting knowledge and values from one generation to the next; this process unavoidably involves teaching students how, and sometimes what, to think. See 96 HARV. L. REV. 151. Yet students and teachers have First Amendment rights, which they do not completely surrender when they enter the school.

1. **Reluctance to intervene:** The Supreme Court has generally been reluctant to intervene in school authorities' handling of school operations. The Court will not intervene in those operations unless "basic constitutional values" are "directly and sharply implicate[d]." *Epperson v. Arkansas*, 393 U.S. 97 (1968).

2. **Illustrations of interference:** But the Court has, nonetheless, occasionally held that school authorities have violated the First Amendment or other constitutional rights of students or teachers. For instance, the Court has held that the state *may not forbid* the *teaching of foreign languages*; see *Meyer v. Nebraska*, 262 U.S. 390 (1923) (decided on substantive due process grounds; see *supra*, p. 157). Similarly, the Court has held that school children *cannot be required to salute the flag; West Virginia Bd. of Ed. v. Bar-*

*nette*, 319 U.S. 624 (1943). And recall that a student's right to wear an armband and to protest symbolically against the Vietnam War was not permitted to be suppressed by school authorities, at least where this was done to suppress a particular point of view; *Tinker v. Des Moines School District*, 393 U.S. 503 (1969) (*supra*, p. 543).

   **a. Permissible purposes:** However, school authorities may act to preserve *discipline*, the *rights of other students*, and the *educational function of the school*. For instance, the Court in *Tinker* indicated that the armband display could have been prohibited if there had been a showing that it did or would substantially interfere with school work or discipline.

**3. Choice of materials to be taught:** Perhaps the most difficult First Amendment issue in the school context is the extent to which that Amendment restricts educators' choices of *curriculum* and *teaching materials*. Educators must of course be given the right to determine what is to be taught in the public schools. Yet there is a potential conflict between this right and the First Amendment principle that "no official, high or petty, can prescribe what shall be orthodox in politics, nationalism, religion, or other matters of opinion. ... " *West Virginia Bd. of Ed. v. Barnette, supra.*

   **a. School libraries:** The only Supreme Court case to deal directly with this conflict did so in a limited context, the right of school authorities to *remove books from a school library*. In *Board of Education v. Pico*, 457 U.S. 853 (1982), a plurality of the Court held that such a removal must not be carried out in a *"narrowly partisan or political manner,"* or for the purpose of denying students access to *ideas with which the authorities disagree.*

      **i. Facts:** The school board in *Pico* ordered nine books to be removed from its high school and junior high school libraries, including Richard Wright's *Black Boy* and Eldridge Cleaver's *Soul on Ice*. The books were all on a list published by a conservative parents' group and were labelled by the board as "anti-American, anti-Christian, anti-Semitic, and just plain filthy."

      **ii. Holding:** Because of the procedural posture, the Supreme Court did not directly decide whether the school board had violated the Constitution in ordering the removal of the books. The plurality did, however, articulate what it saw as the appropriate constitutional standard: a school board has wide authority in determining what books to remove from a library, but it may not remove books for the purpose of *denying access to ideas for political or partisan reasons*. As an extreme example, the plurality noted that a Democratic school board could not, motivated by party affiliation, order the removal of all books written by Republicans.

   **b. Curriculum and textbooks:** It is hard to know what standard the Court will apply to the issue of school authorities' discretion to select the *curriculum* and *required textbooks*. Although, as noted, the Court will probably recognize greater discretion here than in the library-book-removal situation of *Pico*, it is not clear that this discretion will be much broader. Something like *Pico*'s ban on "narrow partisan or political motives" will probably be applied in this situation as well. For instance, it is doubtful that a majority of the Court would uphold a school board's rule that no teacher may express in class the opinion that the war in Vietnam was morally and legally wrong.

      **i. Teacher's own expression of views:** At the same time, *individual teachers* may probably take actions which a school board would not be permitted to take on a system-wide basis. For instance, a teacher may certainly constitutionally express to his students a view about the morality or legality of the Vietnam War, whether or not the school system may formulate an "official" view on the same subject; this distinction is appropriate because an individual teacher's views do not represent an "official" or "orthodox" position in the same way that a system-wide position does.

4. **Speech by students:** What about *speech by students?* Students do not "shed their constitutional rights to freedom of speech or expression at the schoolhouse gate." *Tinker v. Des Moines School District*, 393 U.S. 503 (1969), discussed more extensively, *supra*, p. 543. Thus in *Tinker*, the Court held that the First Amendment rights of several high school and junior high school students were abridged when they were suspended for wearing black armbands in school as a symbol of opposition to the Vietnam War.

However, the Supreme Court has recognized some important *limits* on *Tinker*. Two of the more important are that school authorities are free to limit student speech when:

[1] this is needed to *maintain school discipline* and fulfill the school's *educational mission*; or

[2] the speech *advocates illegality*, at least in the special case of *drug use*.

Let's examine each of these exceptions in more detail.

a. **Maintenance of discipline and the school's mission:** Notwithstanding *Tinker*, school authorities have a strong and valid interest in *maintaining school discipline and in carrying out their educational mission.* Pursuit of these goals will sometimes entitle the authorities to regulate speech in a way that would not be permissible outside the school context. The cases of *Bethel School District No. 403 v. Fraser* and *Hazelwood School District v. Kuhlmeier* illustrate this principle.

   i. **Speech at a school assembly (*Bethel*):** In *Bethel School District No. 403 v. Fraser*, 478 U.S. 675 (1986), a high school student addressing a high school assembly gave a speech that school authorities found to be lewd. The speech, made in support of a candidate for a student government office, contained an elaborate sexual metaphor (e.g., "Jeff Kuhlman is a man who takes his point and pounds it in. … He doesn't attack things in spurts — he drives hard, pushing and pushing until finally — he succeeds.") School authorities suspended the speaker and removed him from the list of candidates for commencement speaker.

      (1) **Disciplinary action upheld:** The Court *upheld* the disciplinary actions over the student's claim that they violated his freedom of expression. "The undoubted freedom to advocate unpopular and controversial issues in schools and classrooms must be balanced against society's countervailing interest in *teaching students the boundaries of socially appropriate behavior.*" When balanced in this way, the school's interest in prohibiting "vulgar and lewd speech" outweighed whatever First Amendment interests the student might have had, especially since the penalties were *"unrelated to any political viewpoint," i.e., they were content-neutral.*

   ii. **Student newspaper (*Hazelwood*):** Similarly, school officials may exercise editorial control over the contents of *student newspapers* if they do so in a way that is *reasonably related to legitimate pedagogical concerns. Hazelwood School District v. Kuhlmeier*, 484 U.S. 260 (1988).

**(1) Facts:**   Thus in *Hazelwood*, the Court upheld a school principal's decision to remove two articles from the student newspaper: (1) a story describing three students' experience with pregnancy; and (2) a story discussing the impact of divorce on students at the school. The principal believed that the first story might indirectly identify the students (even though their names weren't used), and that its references to sexual activity and birth control were inappropriate for some of the younger students at the school. He believed that the second article, which in the draft the principal saw identified a student who blamed her father for her parents' divorce, unfairly denied the father the chance to respond.

**(2) Holding:**   A majority of the Court held that where a school a **sponsors an activity**, in such a way that students and others may reasonably perceive the activity as **bearing the school's imprimatur**, the school's right to restrict student speech is much greater than in the *Tinker* situation (*supra*, p. 543). In *Tinker*, the students who wore armbands were not in any school-sponsored activity; they merely happened to be on school property, but did not forfeit their right of free speech. But expression that occurs during the course of a school-sponsored publication, theatrical production, or other school-sponsored activity may be subject to school authorities' control "so long as [the authorities'] actions are **reasonably related to legitimate pedagogical concerns.**"

**(3) Application:**   Applying this "reasonable relation" test, a majority found that the school principal acted reasonably: based on the facts as the principal then knew them, suppression of the articles was reasonably related to the school objectives of protecting privacy, shielding younger students from inappropriate subject matter, and teaching journalistic fairness.

**b. Advocacy of illegal drug use:** Both of the above cases (*Bethel* and *Hazelwood*) were ones in which either school discipline or the school's pedagogic mission was at stake, so it seemed realtively painless for the Supreme Court to carve out an exception from *Tinker* to justify the regulation of student speech.  Where the student speech does *not* place discipline or the school's pedagogic mission in danger, the Court has been less likely to approve regulation. Thus in the core scenario typified by *Tinker* — student engages in political or social expression in a way that cannot plausibly be thought to pose discipline or pedagogic problems – *Tinker* remains the law, and restraints on student expression will be strictly scrutinized. But the Court has recently carved out one special **exception** to this general rule: speech **advocating the use of illegal drugs** may be restricted. That was the holding of **Morse v. Frederick**, 551 U.S. __ (2007)

**i.   Facts:** In *Morse*, students at a public high school were permitted to leave school to observe the carrying of the Olympic Torch; the excursion was treated as a school trip. One of the students, Frederick, while watching the Torch procession, unfurled a banner that said "BONG HiTS 4 JESUS." (No one seems confident of what the banner was supposed to mean, though it seemed to express the owner's view that marijuana use was a good thing.) The principal demanded that Frederick take down the banner, because she thought it encouraged illegal drug use in violation of school policy; she also suspended him from school.

    **ii. Action upheld:** The Court held that the confiscation of the banner and suspension of Frederick *did not violate* his First Amendment rights. The Court concluded that "a principal may, consistent with the First Amendment, restrict student speech at a school event, when that speech is reasonably viewed *as promoting illegal drug use.*" That was true even though the speech here could not reasonably be viewed as a threat to the school's discipline or mission. The Court reasoned that schools have "an important, perhaps compelling" interest in deterring drug use by school-children.

        **(1) Narrow exception:** The exception carved out in *Morse* seems to be pretty *narrow.* Nothing in the opinion suggests that the Court will allow censorship of student speech merely on the grounds that it advocates some sort of illegality. So, for instance, a sign that said, "Let's get drunk" would not seem to fall within the case's rationale even though the sign promotes illegal underage drinking. So at least for now, as long as discipline and educational mission are not put in jeopardy, the only kind of advocacy of illegality that can be restricted is the very special case of illegal drug use.

**C. Interference with administration of justice:** The state obviously has a strong interest in the fair and efficient *administration of justice*. While a judicial proceeding is still going on, statements made either in court or out of court may pose a danger to that administration. Judges have sometimes used their power to issue a *contempt citation* in order to punish statements which have had or may have such an effect. But the Supreme Court, in its sensitivity to First Amendment concerns, has generally upheld the constitutionality of contempt citations in this situation only if the situation poses a *"clear and present danger"* to the administration of justice in a pending proceeding.

    **1. Cases tried by judge:** Where the case is being tried by a *judge*, the Court is especially slow to find a clear and present danger to justice. This is due in large part to the Court's assumption that judges will not (and should not) be swayed by public criticism, that they are "supposed to be men [sic] of fortitude, able to thrive in a hardy climate." *Craig v. Harney*, 331 U.S. 367 (1947).

        **a. Attacks on judge:** Thus oral statements or publications *attacking a judge's integrity*, or criticizing the administration of justice generally, will *not* be punishable by contempt. This is especially true where the attack is upon a decision which has already been made, but the presumption against the constitutionality of such contempt citations also applies where the case is still *sub judice*.

            **i. Illustration:** For instance, in *Bridges v. California*, 314 U.S. 252 (1941), the Court struck down a contempt citation based on a union leader's public release of a telegram to the Secretary of Labor threatening a crippling strike if an "outrageous" lower-court decision were not reversed.

        **b. *Landmark Communications* case:** That protection of a judge's reputation will rarely by itself be a state interest strong enough to justify suppression of free expression is also illustrated by *Landmark Communications, Inc. v. Virginia*, 435 U.S. 829 (1978). There, a newspaper had accurately reported that a judge (whom the paper identified) was under investigation by a state judicial review commission; the paper was convicted under a state law which made it a crime to breach the confidentiality of the commission's proceedings.

    **i.  Holding:**  The Supreme Court reversed the conviction on First Amendment grounds. The Court conceded that the state had an interest in protecting against injury to judges' reputations by maintaining the confidentiality of these proceedings (and could, for instance, punish staff members who breached that confidentiality). But once the information came ***into the hands of a newspaper or other member of the public***, that person's interest in free expression ***outweighed the state's interest in confidentiality***. The Court had some doubts about whether the traditional "clear and present danger" test was the appropriate one; but even if it was, the danger here was not sufficiently direct or substantial to satisfy that test.

  **2.  Case tried to jury:**  Where a case is currently being tried before a ***jury***, the courts seem to have somewhat greater freedom to punish for contempt statements which may interfere with the jury's just consideration of the case; juries are presumably less resistant to public criticism than are judges.

    **a.  Gag order:**  Perhaps the most troubling situation is that in which a defendant is currently or will soon be on trial before a jury on a criminal charge, and a newspaper or other source disseminates ***prejudicial*** information about him, which may make it difficult to hold a ***fair trial***. Even in this situation, however, the Supreme Court has come down on the side of free expression; in ***Nebraska Press Association v. Stuart***, 427 U.S. 539 (1976), the Court held unconstitutional a so-called ***"gag order"*** prohibiting reporting of any confessions or other material "strongly implicative" of the defendant, who was on trial for a brutal mass murder. (The case is discussed more extensively *infra*, p. 632).

        **i.  Alternative means:**  In striking the gag order, the Court indicated that other means (e.g., change of venue, postponement of trial, sequestration of jurors, etc.) should have been considered and eliminated before such a drastic measure was used.

        **ii.  Prior restraint:**  However, observe that *Nebraska Press* involved a ***prior restraint***, which is normally even more constitutionally-suspect than an after-the-fact contempt-of-court citation.

    **b.  Reporting of court testimony:**  In any event, it is quite clear that one may not be punished for reporting ***events or testimony*** which occurred in ***open court***, even if these took place ***outside the presence of the jury***. See Tribe, pp. 859-61. Matters transpiring in open court are by that fact alone made public, and there can be no penalty imposed for further publicizing them. See, e.g., *Cox Broadcasting Corp. v. Cohn*, 420 U.S. 469 (1975) (state may not punish the broadcasting of the name of a rape victim, learned from the reading of a publicly-filed indictment.)

**D.  Furnishing of legal services by lay groups:**  As part of their interest in regulating the ***legal profession***, states have a strong interest in preventing any conduct which interferes with the relationship between a client and his attorney. One concern which many states have had is that people or organizations might ***stir up litigation*** in which they have no direct pecuniary interest, and might then exercise control over the handling of the law suit, control which should normally be solely in the hands of the lawyer and client. Most states would, for instance, prohibit the creation of a for-profit corporation whose purpose is to advertise to personal-injury victims the availability of contingent-fee representation, and to receive a commission, or "forwarding fee" from the lawyer to whom the corporation assigns a case; even under the modern Court's relaxed view of lawyer advertising, such prohibitions would almost certainly be upheld.

1. **Rights and political expression:** However, these valid state interests may sometimes conflict with the interests of an organization in *furthering political goals* or obtaining economic benefits for its members, by notifying individuals of their legal rights, referring them to lawyers, or paying their legal bills. In general, where a *lay organization* (i.e., one not composed solely of lawyers) is able to make a respectable claim that it is engaged in *associational activities* when it gives such advice, referrals or funding, these freedom-of-association rights will *prevail* over the state interest in regulating the attorney-client relationship.

2. *NAACP v. Button:* The classic case demonstrating the strength of such associational interests is *NAACP v. Button*, 371 U.S. 415 (1963), in which the Supreme Court upheld the NAACP's right to refer to lawyers individuals who were willing to become plaintiffs in public school desegregation cases, and to pay these plaintiffs' litigation expenses.

   a. **Facts:** In *Button*, Virginia made it a crime for any organization to employ or compensate any attorney "in connection with any judicial proceeding in which [the organization] has no pecuniary right or liability." The state also forbade any organization to "control" or "exploit" the lawyer-client relationship, or to "intervene between client and lawyer." The Virginia NAACP brought about school desegregation cases by encouraging parents to become plaintiffs, by referring them to non-NAACP-staff lawyers, and by paying all litigation expenses. The Virginia courts held that these activities violated both the anti-control and anti-compensation rules.

   b. **Activities held protected:** But the Supreme Court held that the NAACP's activities were "modes of expression and association protected by the First and Fourteenth Amendments," and *could not be prohibited* under the state's power to regulate the legal profession. The Court reasoned that the litigation promoted by the NAACP was not a "technique of resolving private differences," but was rather a means for achieving equal treatment for blacks, and was thus a *"form of political expression."*

   c. **Strict scrutiny:** The Court held that "only a *compelling state interest*" in the regulation of an activity subject to the state's power could justify limiting First Amendment freedoms. *Button* is thus one of the earliest examples of the Court's *strict scrutiny* of state regulations which impair First Amendment rights. Neither of the asserted state interests was compelling here. The state's traditional interest in preventing maintenance and champerty was applicable only where "malicious intent" was present, which was not the case here. Similarly, the prohibition on payment to lawyers by non-litigants was justified only by the "danger that the attorney will desert or subvert the paramount interests of his client to enrich himself or an outside sponsor"; there was no showing of any such conflict between the NAACP and the individual plaintiffs.

3. *Primus:* *Button* has been extended, to allow an *individual lawyer* to solicit clients as part of her *pro bono* work on behalf of the ACLU. See *In re Primus*, 436 U.S. 412 (1978) (discussed more extensively *supra*, p. 569).

**E. Group economic activity for political ends:**   Where group economic activity linked with speech is carried out for purely economic ends, the state may regulate that activity as part of its general economic regulatory power. But where *group economic activity* with an expressive component is done for *political purposes*, the state will have to satisfy a somewhat higher standard before it may regulate that activity, since political speech is at the core of First Amendment values.

   1. **Economic boycott for political end:**   The substantial protection given to politically-motivated expression is illustrated by *NAACP v. Claiborne Hardware Co.*, 458 U.S. 886 (1982), in which the Supreme Court refused to allow civil liability to be imposed on a civil rights organization for a largely non-violent *politically-motivated economic boycott.*

      a. **Facts:**   Black residents of Claiborne County, Mississippi, in an attempt to get white government and business leaders to bring about racial equality, launched a *boycott of white merchants* in the County. The boycott was basically peaceful, but there were some episodes of violence, as well as some attempts to enforce the boycott by threatening those who violated it with social ostracism. Some of the merchants sued to recover economic damages they sustained as the result of the boycott; there were 148 defendants, including the NAACP. The Mississippi courts held that because there were some acts of violence, the *entire boycott* was a tortious malicious interference with the plaintiffs' businesses; these courts also held that because the defendants conspired to carry out the boycott, they were each *jointly and severally liable* for all economic losses suffered by the plaintiffs.

      b. **Protected activity:**   The Supreme Court reversed, holding that those boycott activities which were *non-violent* were entitled to First Amendment protection, so that only losses *proximately caused* by the few violent episodes could be recovered for. The other boycott activities, such as peaceful picketing and even the use of threats of social ostracism, were constitutionally protected. As to the latter, the Court observed that "[s]peech does not lose its protective character … simply because it may embarrass others or coerce them into action."

      c. **Result:**   The net result was that only those who had themselves engaged in acts or threats of violence could be held liable, and only for losses stemming directly from those acts or threats.

**F. Government as speaker or as funder of speech:** So far, nearly everything we have said in this chapter concerns the role of government as the regulator of speech by non-government actors. But sometimes, *government itself wishes to speak.*   And sometimes, government wishes to give *financial support* to certain speech by others.  In these two contexts — government as speaker, and government as funder of speech — government seems to have at least somewhat greater ability to prefer one viewpoint over another than it does when it merely regulates.  However, the law governing these two special contexts is far from settled.

   1. **Government as speaker:** When government wishes to *be a speaker itself*, it is pretty clear that government may *say essentially what it wants*, and is not subject to any real rule of viewpoint neutrality.

      a. **Rationale from abortion-counselling case:** There is not much Supreme Court precedent directly on point on this issue. But in a case in which the court held that Congress could condition grants to family planning clinics upon the clinics' agreement not to recommend abortion, the majority observed that "When Congress established a National Endowment for Democracy to encourage other countries to adopt democratic principles, it was not constitutionally required to fund a program to encourage competing lines of political philosophy such as communism and fascism." *Rust v. Sullivan*, 500 U.S. 173 (1991) (also discussed *infra*, p. 624). This seems to mean that government can espouse, essentially, any viewpoint it wants.

**Example:** Even Justice Souter, who takes an expansive view of the First Amendment's scope, has said, "[I]f the Food and Drug Administration launches an advertising campaign on the subject of smoking, it may condemn the habit without also having to show a cowboy taking a puff on the opposite page." *National Endowment for the Arts v. Finley*, 524 U.S. 569 (1998) (dissent).

2. **Government as funder of third-party speech:** But a much tougher question arises when government *funds speech by third parties*, who are essentially expressing their own beliefs rather than the government's. Here, may government be non-viewpoint-neutral, by funding only those viewpoints of which it approves? The answer now appears to be mostly *"no"* — when government funds third-party speech, it must generally (but subject to some exceptions discussed below) do so in a *viewpoint-neutral way*.

   a. **Funding of student publications:** One indication that this is so is *Rosenberger v. University of Virginia* (*supra*, p. 532), where the Court held that once a public university chose to fund various student publications, it could not exclude publications that had a religious content.

   b. **Attacks on welfare laws:** Another demonstration of this viewpoint-neutrality requirement comes from a case involving federal funding of the Legal Services Corporation (LSC), which supplies legal representation to indigent people in certain types of civil cases. In *Legal Services Corp. v. Velazquez*, 531 U.S. 533 (2001), the Court held by a 5-4 vote that Congress violated free speech when it put limits on the types of litigation positions that LSC lawyers could take.

      i. **Facts:** Congress had funded the LSC, but only on condition that LSC lawyers not attempt to "reform a Federal or State welfare system." Congress also said that in welfare litigation, LSC's work could not "involve an effort to amend or otherwise challenge existing law."

      ii. **Rationale:** In an opinion by Justice Kennedy, the majority concluded that what Congress had done was to impose a viewpoint-based restriction, and the fact that government was paying for the speech did not avoid the First Amendment problem. Just as the Court had held in *Rosenberger* (supra, p. 532) that a public university that funds student publications could not discriminate against certain viewpoints, so Congress here could not fund expressive activities by lawyers and then say that certain ideas — arguments in favor of welfare reform — must not be expressed. Kennedy was especially troubled by the fact that the restriction here "threatens severe *impairment of the judicial function*" — the restriction "operates to insulate current welfare laws from constitutional scrutiny and certain other legal challenges, a condition implicating central First Amendment concerns."

      iii. **Not government speech:** The government had argued that the speech by the LSC lawyers that was being regulated was in effect the *government's own speech*.

When a government-funded LSC lawyer was restricted in what she could say on behalf of a welfare client in litigation, the government contended, this was no different than when a doctor in a government-funded family-planning clinic was told she could not counsel abortion, something the court had approved in *Rust v. Sullivan* (*infra*, p. 624). But Kennedy found the cases quite different, ruling that in *Rust* the clinic members had been delivering a government-sponsored message, whereas here, "the LSC program was designed to facilitate private speech, not to promote a governmental message." Since the present case fell on the "government-funded private speech" rather than "government-funded governmental speech" side of the line, strict scrutiny of the government's actions was required.

   iv. **Dissent:** In dissent in *Legal Services*, Justice Scalia disagreed with Kennedy's distinction of *Rust* from the present case. Scalia believed that the two cases were completely indistinguishable. Neither case, in his opinion, involved subsidized government speech, so they could not be distinguished on that basis: "If the private doctors' confidential advice to their patients at issue in *Rust* constituted 'government speech,' it is hard to imagine what subsidized speech would *not* be government speech." In Scalia's view, *Rust* established the proposition that government could selectively fund a program to encourage certain speech-related activities it believed to be in the public interest, without at the same time funding alternative speech-related conduct that sought to deal with the problem another way. Such selective funding was what was involved here in *Legal Services*, he said, and did not constitute forbidden viewpoint discrimination.

   v. **Significance:** It is hard to know how broad a principle *Legal Services* establishes. The case may stand for the proposition that if the government funds private speech, the requirement of viewpoint-neutrality means that government may not put certain classes of disfavored expression off-limits. But there is a good chance that a narrower reading will turn out to be the correct one: that it was the special role of lawyers involved in *litigation* — and their right to frame constitutional arguments — that made the difference in there.

c. **Government as subsidizer of a few parties' expression:** *Rosenberger* and *Legal Services* involved subsidies paid by government to a fairly **broad** group of third-party recipients (in *Rosenberger*, all non-religiously-oriented student publications, and in *Legal Services*, all Legal Services lawyers who didn't try to change existing law). Singling out an unfortunate few speakers for non-subsidies based on the content of their expression seems like censorship, so it's not surprising that the Court has blocked this. But now, suppose that government acts a ***"patron"*** by giving subsidies to a ***select number*** of speakers. In this context, it appears that the Court will ***not*** require government to remain rigidly viewpoint-neutral. In this situation, the government cannot be expected to fund every speaker, so it is entitled to some degree of discretion in what speakers, and messages, it wishes to fund. However, the limits of that discretion are very unclear.

   i. **Arts funding:** As an illustration of government's partial discretion about what speech to fund, see *National Endowment for the Arts v. Finley*, 524 U.S. 569 (1998). There, Congress passed a statute saying that when federal NEA ***artistic grants*** are doled out to applicants, the NEA should "tak[e] into consideration general standards of decency and respect for the diverse beliefs and values of the

American public." The Ps (various artists and an artists' organization) claimed that the requirement that the standards be taken into account was a violation of the principle applied in *Rosenberger* that when a public university university funded certain student publications, it could not exclude those with religious content. But the Court found that *Rosenberger* was ***inapplicable***, and that the NEA statute was ***constitutional*** on its face: "[Any] content-based considerations that may be taken into account in the grant-making process are a consequence of the ***nature of arts funding***. ... The 'very assumption' of the NEA is that grants will be awarded according to the 'artistic worth of competing applications,' and ***absolute neutrality is simply 'inconceivable.'***"

ii. **Internet connections at libraries:** Another indication that government will be permitted at least a mild degree of content-discrimination when it funds third-party speech comes from *U.S. v. Amer. Library Ass'n., Inc.*, 539 U.S. 194 (2003). There, a four-justice plurality held that Congress could constitutionally require that any public *library* receiving federal funds and making Internet access available to patrons must ***install an anti-pornography filter*** on each Internet-connected computer, even though the filter would inevitably block some protected speech as well. The plurality relied in part on the ***constitutional-condition*** cases like *Rust v. Sullivan, infra*, p. 623: quoting *Rust*, the plurality said that "[W]ithin broad limits, 'when the Government appropriates public funds to establish a program it is entitled to ***define the limits of that program***.' " Here, since Congress was helping libraries fulfill their traditional role of obtaining appropriate materials, Congress was entitled to impose the "permissible condition under *Rust*" that filtering software be used to ensure that no pornography be included. (It was central to the plurality's analysis that the statute authorized librarians to turn off the filtering on a case-by-case basis if requested by a patron.)

iii. **Summary:** So where government funds the dissemination of ideas, government is permitted some degree of discrimination based on a viewpoint or subject matter, but how much is very unclear. Where government is funding a few projects based on some concept of excellence (as in *N.E.A. v. Finley*), there is no constitutional problem when a certain degree of content-non-neutrality creeps in. And at the other end of the spectrum, where government funds the availability of an extremely wide range of expressions — as where government funds libraries with Internet connections (as in *Amer. Library Ass'n*) — the government is permitted to use methods that may filter out some constitutionally-protected viewpoints, as long as that filtering can be readily turned off when a member of the public so requests. But in cases not involving either of these two special situations — i.e. situations in which the government funds a broad range of expressions one category at a time (as in the student-publications scenario in *Rosenberger*) — Government may apparently *not* pick and choose which constitutionally-protected third-party expressions or topics it wants to fund. For instance, it's pretty clear that just as a public university may not fund all student publications except those dealing with religion (*Rosenberger*), so a university or city may not fund, say, the speech of Democrats (or heterosexuals) while refusing to fund the speech of, say, Republicans (or homosexuals).

# XI. FREEDOM OF ASSOCIATION, DENIAL OF PUBLIC JOBS OR BENEFITS, AND UNCONSTITUTIONAL CONDITIONS

**A. Freedom of association generally:** The First Amendment does not explicitly mention the freedom of *association*. But in numerous cases, the Supreme Court has held that that freedom derives by *implication* from the explicitly-stated right of speech, press, assembly and petition.

1. **Limited scope:** However, the freedom of association has not been broadly construed by the Court. For instance, the Court has never held that any activity which an individual may lawfully do by himself, he is constitutionally entitled to do in concert with others. Rather, all that has been recognized is "a right to join with others to pursue goals *independently protected* by the First Amendment." Tribe, p. 1013. These goals include *political advocacy*, *literary expression* and *religious worship*, among others.

   a. **Litigation:** The pursuit of *litigation* has also been regarded by the Court as an activity which generally receives First Amendment protection where carried out by an individual, and which therefore may be carried out jointly as well. Recall, for instance, the Court's recognition of the NAACP's right to group legal action in *NAACP v. Button*, *supra*, p. 603. Cases following *Button*, principally ones involving unions, have established that the freedom of association protects group pursuit even of litigation on non-political topics (e.g., workmen's compensation or personal injury claims). See *supra*, p. 604.

   b. **No general right of "social association":** Since there is a special freedom of association only where the goals being pursued are independently protected by the First Amendment, there is no special freedom to engage in *"social association."* That is, a group of people do not have any specially-protected First Amendment right to gather together for social purposes such as dancing, partying, watching a sporting event, etc. These events are not primarily expressive events, so there is no special First Amendment right to *gather* for purposes of engaging in these events.

2. **Strict scrutiny:** Government is not absolutely forbidden to impair the freedom of association, just as it is not absolutely forbidden to interfere with freedom of speech. However, before the government may significantly interfere with protected associational activity, two showings must be made: (1) that the governmental interest being pursued is a *compelling* one; and (2) that that interest cannot be achieved by means *less restrictive* of the freedom of association. In other words, *strict scrutiny* is normally applied. See *NAACP v. Alabama*, 357 U.S. 449 (1958) (discussed further *infra*, p. 621), holding that "[s]tate action which may have the effect of curtailing the freedom to associate is subject to the closest scrutiny."

   a. **Anti-discrimination measures:** One governmental interest that is almost always found to be compelling, and that often cannot be achieved without restrictions on First Amendment freedoms, is the interest in *preventing discrimination* based on race, sex, or other suspect criterion. For instance, the Supreme Court has held that Minnesota could constitutionally require the Jaycees to admit women members, even though there might be some impairment of existing members' freedom of association or freedom of speech. *Roberts v. United States Jaycees*, 468 U.S. 609 (1984).

      i. **Rationale:** Minnesota's desire to eliminate discrimination in "places of *public accommodation*" (found as a factual matter to include quasi-commercial organizations like the Jaycees) was a compelling interest which the state was achieving through the least restrictive available means.

    **ii. California Rotary case:** Similarly, the Court has held that California was constitutionally empowered to force Rotary Clubs in that state to admit women, because "the relationship between Rotary Club members is not the kind of intimate or private relation that warrants constitutional protection." *Board of Directors of Rotary International v. Rotary Club of Duarte*, 481 U.S. 537 (1987).

**B. Right not to associate:** The Court has also recognized, in effect, a right *not* to associate. That is, individuals have a constitutional right *not to be compelled to support*, either financially or otherwise, most types of expressional activities by organizations of which they do not approve. Additionally, an association or other *group* has a right not to be *compelled to accept unwanted members* whose presence would significantly interfere with the group's message.

    **1. Right to avoid compulsory financial support:** An important aspect of the "right not to associate" is the right not to be compelled to give *financial support* to organizations or activities where the money will be used to disseminate messages with which one disagrees.

        **a. Union service fee:** For instance, *union members* have a first amendment right not to have their compulsory union dues used to support causes or ideas of which the member disapproves. The main case so holding is *Abood v. Detroit Board of Education*, 431 U.S. 209 (1977). There, public-school employees were not required to join the union, but anyone who did not join was required to pay a "service fee" equal in amount to union dues. The Court held that non-union employees had a constitutional right not to have their service fees used for *support of ideological causes* of which they disapproved. (But they had no right to refuse to have their service fees used for the costs of maintaining a collective bargaining system.)

        **b. Compulsory advertising:** Similarly, government cannot force all *participants in a particular industry* to contribute a percentage of their sales so that the money can be spent on an industry-wide *advertising campaign*. In *U.S. v. United Foods*, 533 U.S. 405 (2001), the Court held that when the U.S. Agriculture Dept. created a such a mandatory-assessment program for the mushroom industry, the program violated the First Amendment protection, recognized in *Abood*, for those who are legally required to maintain membership in a group yet do not wish to be compelled to give financial support to speech by the group.

            **i. Limitation:** But the result in *U.S. v. United Foods* seems to apply only to a mandatory assessment that is used *solely to fund advertising*, and does not apply where an advertising program is part of an *overall pattern of regulation* and collective acttivities paid for by the assessment. Thus in the earlier case of *Glickman v. Wileman Bros.*, 521 U.S. 457 (1997), the Court upheld a government program that forced every grower of California nectarines to contribute to a fund for generic advertising of the product; according to the later opinion in *United Foods*, the difference between the two outcomes was due to the fact that the compelled contributions for advertising in *Glickman* were "part of a far broader regulatory system that does not principally concern speech." (The California nectarines at issue in *Glickman* were not individually marketed by the growers, but were instead marketed through a single cooperative, and the group-funded advertising there grew out of the cooperative's need to merchandise its product.)

c. **Protection is not absolute:** However, a person's right to not be required to give financial support to the expression of ideas with which she disagrees is ***not an absolute right***. Essentially, the rule seems to be that a member of a group (even if the membership is compulsory rather than voluntary) may be required to give financial support to expressive activities of the group that are highly ***germane*** to the group's purposes, but not required to support expression that is less germane to those purposes. And, if the germane/non-germane distinction is too hard to draw in a particular case, there may be no right to withhold one's support at all. Several cases help illustrate how the protection against compulsory support of unwanted ideas is not absolute:

   i. **Union dues and the collective bargaining system:** *Abood, supra,* held that although teachers have the right not to have their union dues used for the support of ideological causes (since these were not germane to the union's function), the members had no right to refuse to have these fees used for the costs of maintaining a collective bargaining system (germane).

   ii. **University activity fees:** A more recent case holds that a public ***university*** may require all students to pay a ***"student activity fee"*** which is then used to fund various student expressive activities. In that case, *Board of Regents of the University of Wisconsin System v. Southworth,* 529 U.S. 217 (2000), the Court declined to use the germane/non-germane distinction, because it would be too difficult to apply in the university student-activity context (which student activities are germane to the university's function, and which are not?)

      (1) **Viewpoint-neutrality required:** Instead, the Court decided the case by merely requiring ***viewpoint-neutrality*** in the allocation of student dollars. That is, instead of giving each student a First Amendment right to withhold her dollars from causes she disapproved of, the Court decided, all the student was constitutionally entitled to was that the dollars be allocated in a viewpoint-neutral way, i.e., in a way that would not differentiate based on the messages spread by the various funded activities.

   iii. **Marketing messages that are part of a system of regulation:** Finally, recall *Glickman v. Wileman Bros.,* 521 U.S. 457 (1997), *supra,* p. 609, where the Court upheld a mandatory assessment on all California nectarine growers, even though part of the funds were used for a generic advertising campaign. The fact that the message was not political or ideological, and grew out of an ***overall system of regulation*** of the industry in question, was enough to save the program from First Amendment attack.

2. **Veto on unwanted participants:** The "right not to associate" extends well beyond the right not to have to give financial support to groups or causes of which one disapproves. An other important aspect of the right is that a group has a First Amendment right ***not to be forced to accept participants whose presence would interfere with the group's expressive activities.***

   a. **Parade:** For instance, private parties who conduct a ***parade*** may exclude unwanted members — or at least unwanted messages — from the parade. Thus in *Hurley v.*

*Irish-American Gay, Lesbian, and Bisexual Group of Boston*, 515 U.S. 557 (1995), the Court held unanimously that Massachusetts could not require a private group that conducts a St. Patrick's Day parade in Boston to include gay and lesbian marchers marching under their own banner.

    **i. Expressive conduct:** The "right not to associate" is closely related to the ***"right not to speak,"*** which the Court has also long recognized. Thus in *Hurley*, the parade organizers were in fact willing to have gays and lesbians in the parade — the fight was about whether the gays should be allowed to march in their own unit ***under their own banner.*** The Court found that a parade inevitably has expressive content, and that gays marching under a banner would be sending a message (presumably a message supporting gay rights and gay lifestyles) that the parade organizers had a right to refuse to endorse. "It boils down to the choice of a speaker not to propound a particular point of view, and that choice is presumed to lie beyond the government's power to control," the Court said in *Hurley.*

  **b. Must be perceived as group's own speech:** But the right of a group not to be forced to accept co-participants of whose message the group disapproves applies ***only*** where the ***group's own "message" will be affected by the unwanted participation.*** This principle is demonstrated by ***Rumsfeld v. FAIR***, 547 U.S. 47 (2006), where the Court upheld the constitutionality of the "Solomon Amendment," under which Congress said that any university could receive certain federal funding only if all parts of the university, including its law school, gave the same on-campus access to military recruiters as to recruiters from other employers.

    **i. The claim:** A group of law schools argued in *FAIR* that since the military discriminates against gays, the Amendment unconstitutionally forced the schools to support a message they abhorred; the plaintiffs contended that by forcing the schools to serve as host for on-campus military recruiting, the Solomon Amendment infringed the schools' freedom not to associate with the military just as directly as the forced participation of gays in *Hurley* infringed the rights of the St. Patrick's Day parade organizers.

    **ii. Argument rejected:** But the Court in *FAIR* ***disagreed*** with the plaintiffs' assertion that the two cases were the same. The compelled-speech cases like *Hurley* turned on the fact that "the ***complaining speaker's own message was affected*** by the speech it was forced to accommodate." Thus in *Hurley* itself, the parade was expressive, and a law forcing the inclusion of an unwanted group altered the expressive content of the parade. In *FAIR*, by contrast, "[A]ccommodating the military's message ***does not affect the law schools' speech,*** because ***the schools are not speaking when they host interviews and recruiting receptions.*** Unlike a parade organizer's choice of parade contingents, a law school's decision to allow recruiters on campus ***is not inherently expressive*** ... Nothing about recruiting suggests that law schools agree with any speech by recruiters, and nothing in the Solomon Amendment restricts what the law schools may say about the military's policies."

**3. Right to exclude from membership in group:** Perhaps most significantly, the "right not to associate" also means that an association has a First Amendment interest in ***not being forced to accept unwanted members.*** For instance, the rights of a Democratic club would probably be impaired if the government forced the club to admit registered Republicans as members, and the rights of NAACP members would be impaired if the organization were forced to admit, say, Nazi supremacists or Ku Klux Klanners.

**a. Gays in the Boy Scouts:** The most dramatic example of this "right not to associate" came in ***Boy Scouts of America v. Dale***, 530 U.S. 640 (2000), where the Court held that because opposition to homsexuality was part of the Scouts' "expressive message," the Scouts' freedom of association was violated by a state anti-discrimination law that barred the group from excluding gays as members.

  **i. Facts:** The case arose when Dale, an assistant Scoutmaster who had been an Eagle Scout as a youth, was expelled from the organization after the Scouts learned from a college newspaper article that he was an avowed homosexual and gay-rights activist. Dale objected that his ouster violated a New Jersey anti-discrimination law which prohibited discrimination on the basis of sexual orientation in any "public accommodation" (which the state determined the Scouts to be). The Scouts responded that the state law was trumped by the organization's freedom of association rights, given the Scouts' opposition to homosexuality.

  **ii. Ouster upheld:** By a 5-4 vote, the court found for the Scouts. The majority, in an opinion by Justice Rehnquist, concluded that the Scouts had an "official position" that avowed homosexuals should not be Scout leaders, and that homosexual conduct was in the Scouts' view incompatible with the requirement that a Scout be "morally straight." Given this viewpoint, Rehnquist wrote, requiring that the Scouts keep Dale as a member would "at the very least, force the organization to ***send a message***, both to the youth members and the world, that the Boy Scouts ***accept homosexual conduct*** as a legitimate form of behavior." It didn't matter that the Scouts were not formed "for the purpose" of opposing homosexuality — as long as being forced to admit a practicing homosexual would ***impair the organization's message***, this was enough to trigger a strong first Amendment interest, one which the state's anti-discrimination interest could not overcome.

    **(1) Strict scrutiny:** Chief Justice Rehnquist didn't expressly say that he was using strict scrutiny. But he rejected the *O'Brien* content-neutral standard, which he characterized as an "intermediate standard of review," and he appears to have in fact used a variant of strict scrutiny.

  **iii. Dissent:** The four dissenters did not disagree with the general proposition that an organization cannot be forced to accept members whose presence would materially impair the group's message. But they disagreed about the application of this test here. As Justice Stevens' principal dissent put it, the Scouts had never — at least outside of various litigations — made a ***"clear, unequivocal statement"*** of opposition to homosexuality. And such a clear statement, in his view, was necessary before an organization could claim an infringement of its associational rights. All the Scouts had done was to "adopt[] an exclusionary membership policy" without any "shared goal of disapproving of homosexuality."

**b. Compulsory membership won't necessarily interfere with expression:** As *Boy Scouts* implies, the more central and unequivocal the organization's views on a particular matter, the greater the interference with associational rights if the organization is forced to accept a member with opposing views. If a particular point of view is not clearly articulated by the organization, or not especially central to the organization's mission, compulsory membership by one with opposing views or conduct may cause so little harm that a countervailing governmental objective may outweigh the associational interest. And where that governmental interest is the possibly-compelling interest of reducing discrimination, the government is especially likely to prevail.

   i.   **Illustration:** This is what happened, for instance, in *Roberts v. United States Jaycees, supra,* p. 608: the originally all-male membership of the Jaycees had a First Amendment interest in not being required to accept women as members, but the organization's no-women stance was (the Court found) not very central to the organization's purposes. Consequently, this relatively weak interest was outweighed by the state's compelling interest in banning discrimination in places of public accommodation, an interest which could not be fully achieved by narrower measures.

C.  **Ways of interfering with right:**   The right of association may be interfered with in a number of different ways. Forcing a person or group to support (or accept as a member) an unwanted message or individual is one way, which we've already discussed above. We now consider several other types of interference:

   ❏   government makes it ***illegal to be a member*** of a group (see *infra,* this page);

   ❏   government ***withholds public jobs and benefits*** from members of particular groups or associations (see *infra,* p. 613); and

   ❏   government requires that an individual ***disclose*** his organizational affiliations (or, conversely, that a group disclose its members) (see *infra,* p. 620).

D.  **Illegal membership:**   Mere membership in an association or group may not be made ***illegal***. Membership in a group may only serve as an element of a criminal offense if the following additional requirements are satisfied:

   [1]   the group is ***actively engaged in unlawful activity***, or ***incites*** others to ***imminent lawless action*** (in such a way that the incitement is punishable as a "clear and present danger" under the modern *Brandenburg* test, *supra,* p. 481); and

   [2]   the individual member ***knows*** of the group's illegal activities, and has the ***specific intent*** of furthering the group's illegal goals.

See Tribe, p. 1015. This series of requirements evolved through the case law on subversive advocacy and the "clear and present danger" text, a subject treated in detail *supra,* p. 474.

E.  **Denial of public job or benefit:**   The freedom of association may be unconstitutionally abridged if a ***job in the public sector***, or a license or benefit issued by the government, is denied because of the applicant's associational activities. This possibility arises most commonly where a job or license is denied on the grounds of the applicant's membership in the ***Communist Party*** or other subversive group.

   1.   **No ban based solely on membership:**   A public job or other public benefit ***may not be denied merely on the basis of the applicant's constitutionally-protected membership in a group or organization***.

   2.   **Subversive group:**   Therefore, unless an individual's group activities could be made ***illegal***, those group activities cannot be grounds for denying him a job, license to practice law, or other public benefit.

a. ***Elfbrandt case:*** Thus the two-part test discussed above, in connection with the outright outlawing of subversive group activity, is in essence the test applied in the public-benefits context as well. For example, in *Elfbrandt v. Russell*, 384 U.S. 11 (1966), the Court struck down a state statute providing for the discharge of any public employee who knowingly becomes a member of the Communist Party or of any party whose purposes include overthrow of the state government, if the employee has knowledge of this unlawful purpose. The statute was found invalid because it did not also require that the employee have the "specific intent" to further the organization's illegal aims.

3. **Vagueness:** Statutes making associational activities grounds for non-hiring or dismissal are also susceptible to being struck down because of ***vagueness***. Standards for precision in drafting are especially stringent in the First Amendment area, since a vague statute is likely to have a ***"chilling effect"*** on the exercise of First Amendment rights — an individual who does not know precisely which conduct is forbidden will err on the side of safety, by declining to exercise his First Amendment rights to the fullest. (See the discussion of vagueness *supra*, p. 486.)

   a. **Illustration:** Thus in *Keyishian v. Board of Regents*, 385 U.S. 589 (1967), the Court struck down, *inter alia*, a statute requiring the removal of public university professors for "treasonable or seditious" utterances or acts, on the grounds that the teacher had no way of knowing where the line was to be drawn between permitted statements about abstract doctrine and forbidden incitement to action.

4. **Patronage hirings and dismissals:** The use of ***political patronage*** presents special free association problems: when a person or party who controls public-sector jobs gives those jobs out as a means of rewarding faithful party workers, applicants without political connections can plausibly claim that they have been discriminated against based on their political affiliation (or lack of one). In general, the Supreme Court has ***agreed*** with such claims. The rule is that when ***hiring, promotion and dismissal*** decisions are made concerning ***low-level public jobs***, party affiliation may ***not*** be a factor. *Rutan v. Republican Party of Illinois*, 497 U.S. 62 (1990).

   a. **Massive patronage rejected:** The facts of *Rutan, supra,* show the kind of patronage scheme that will ***not*** be allowed. Plaintiffs alleged that the Republican governor of Illinois prohibited any hiring, firing or promotions for any state office except on his "express permission," and that only those who had voted for or supported the Republican party in past years were favored. The Court held that these employment practices, if proven, violated the First Amendment free association rights of those not given special treatment.

   b. **High-level posts:** On the other hand, some government posts are sufficiently ***high level*** that party affiliation ***may*** be considered in hiring and firing. For instance, "Democrats have no right to consideration on equal terms with Republicans when the newly elected Republican government of a state is choosing a speech writer or a high-level special assistant." Tribe, p. 1018. The test is "whether the hiring authority can demonstrate that party affiliation is an ***appropriate requirement*** for the ***effective performance*** of the public office involved." *Branti v. Finkel*, 445 U.S. 507 (1980).

      i. **Public defender:** It is unclear where the dividing line is between high-level posts for which patronage may be used, and low-level "ordinary" government jobs where it may not be. The one Supreme Court case that sheds some light on this dividing line is *Branti, supra*. There, the Court held that two Republican assistant *public defenders* could *not* be discharged on party-affiliation grounds when a Democrat was named to head the public defender's office. The majority reasoned that a public defender's *effectiveness* depends on how he handles his client's needs, not on any partisan political interests. (The *Branti* Court rejected a prior doctrine which had made patronage dismissals available only in "policy-making positions." To the *Branti* Court, the issue was not policy-making, but effective performance of the job. Thus a governor's speech writer usually must, to be effective, have political beliefs comparable to the governor's; therefore, his party affiliation may be considered, even though he is not in any "policy-making" role.)

    c.  **Independent contractors:** The same rule — that party affiliation may be considered only if it's an appropriate requirement for effective performance — is used where the government work is being done by an *independent contractor* rather than an employee. *O'Hare Truck Svc. v. Northlake*, 518 U.S. 712 (1996).

        i.  **Large impact on patronage:** The *O'Hare* decision makes *huge inroads on traditional patronage.* Legal work, construction and architectural contracts, cable TV franchises — all of these are often awarded by local and state governments on a "help your friends and not your enemies" basis. Apparently government will now have the burden of demonstrating that either it would have reached the same contracting decision regardless of the plaintiff's affiliations, or that consideration of affiliation is an "appropriate requirement for effective performance," something that will typically be hard to establish.

**5.**  **Loyalty oaths:** Normally, denial of a job or license based on associational activities does not occur as the result of extensive investigation by the government. Rather, such denials have generally occurred where the applicant or employee is required to take an *oath* that he has not belonged to certain types of organizations, or engaged in other activities, and he is unwilling or unable to take such an oath.

    a.  **Rule:** In general, the rule regarding such *"loyalty oaths"* is that one may not be required to state that one has not performed a certain act, or that one will not perform it in the future, unless actual *performance* of that act would be grounds for discharge. That is, the permissible scope of such oaths is co-extensive with the scope of grounds for *non-hiring or discharge.* See *Cole v. Richardson*, 405 U.S. 676 (1972).

        i.  **Illustration:** For instance, recall that one may not be discharged for membership in an organization advocating overthrow of the government, unless one had knowledge of the organization's purpose and specific intent to further that purpose. Consequently, one may not be required to swear a blanket oath that one has never been a member of an organization advocating such overthrow — language referring to the affiant's knowledge of the illegal purposes, and to his specific intent to further them, must be inserted into the oath itself.

**6.**  **Speech critical of superiors:** Thus far, we have examined the denial of public jobs and benefits for *associational* activities. Similar issues arise when the government attempts to deny a public job or benefit because of a person's *speech*-related activities. For instance, under what circumstances may a government employee be fired for *criticizing his superiors?*

**a.** ***Connick case:*** The free speech rights of government employees were the subject of ***Connick v. Myers***, 461 U.S. 138 (1983). The case illustrates that governmental attempts to fire or otherwise penalize its employees for speech on matters of ***"public concern"*** will be ***strictly scrutinized***, but that speech on matters that are not within this category will receive substantially less protection.

    **i.** **Facts:** The plaintiff in *Connick*, Myers, was an assistant D.A. After learning that she had received an unwanted transfer to a new post within the D.A.'s office, she gave her co-workers a questionnaire soliciting their views on a number of matters concerning the office, including whether they had "confidence in" particular superiors, and whether they ever "feel pressured to work in political campaigns on behalf of office supported candidates." The D.A., upon learning of the questionnaire, viewed it as an act of insubordination, and fired Myers for both the questionnaire and for refusing to accept the transfer.

    **ii.** **Firing upheld:** The Court, by a 5-4 vote, sustained the D.A.'s decision to fire Myers. The Court distinguished sharply between employee speech on matters of "public concern," and speech involving only private matters.

    **iii.** **Public concern:** Where speech involves a matter of ***"public concern,"*** the Court held, the judiciary must carefully examine the justification given by the state for penalizing the speech, and must strike a ***balance*** between the free speech rights of the employee and the "interest of the State, as an employer, in promoting the efficiency of the public services it performs. … " Only one of the numerous questions on the questionnaire was found by the Court to involve a matter of public concern (the question regarding pressure to work in political campaigns).

    **iv.** **Matters not of "public concern":** Where the matters discussed by the employee are ***not*** ones of public concern, the court should give "a wide degree of ***deference*** to the ***employer's judgment.***" The employer's interest in, for instance, avoiding "the disruption of the office and the destruction of working relationships" should be weighed heavily.

    **v.** **Striking of balance:** The Court concluded that the questionnaire as a whole touched only slightly on matters of "public concern." Therefore, the firing was sustained, because the D.A. "reasonably believed [that Myers' actions] would disrupt the office, undermine his authority and destroy close working relationships." Had matters of public interest been more plainly implicated in the questionnaire, the Court indicated, less deference would have been due the D.A.'s judgment, and a much stronger showing of danger to the efficiency of the office would have been required.

    **vi.** **Dissent:** The four dissenters (in an opinion by Justice Brennan), attacked the majority opinion in several respects. First, the dissenters contended that the majority was taking an unduly narrow view of what matters are of "public concern"; any matter that could reasonably be expected to be of interest to persons wanting to know how the D.A.'s office was functioning should have been included in this category. Numerous questions, insofar as they involved morale in the office, fell within this category, the dissenters believed. Also, the dissent criticized the deference paid by the majority to supervisors' judgment. Such deference will, the dissent predicted, have the result that "public employees will not speak out when what they have to say is critical of their supervisors." Instead, the dissent argued, a court should make its own appraisal of the likely effects of the speech.

**b. Expansive reading to "public concern":** The *Connick* standard was applied in a more recent case, *Rankin v. McPherson*, 483 U.S. 378 (1987), in which the Court gave a surprisingly broad reading to the definition of "public concern." In *Rankin*, the Court decided by a 5-4 vote that McPherson, a clerical employee in the county constable's office, could not be dismissed for saying in the office, in response to hearing of John Hinckley's attempted assassination of President Reagan, "If they go for him again, I hope they get him." The remark was made to a co-worker who happened to be McPherson's boyfriend, but was overheard by another co-worker who informed the Constable, who fired McPherson.

    **i. Matter of public concern:** The majority opinion, by Justice Marshall, found that McPherson's comment was on a matter of "public concern," thus satisfying the first prong of the *Connick* test. Taken in the context in which it was made, the remark was essentially a commentary on the President's policies and the attempted assassination, both of which were matters of public concern.

    **ii. State loses on second prong:** Since the statement touched on a matter of public concern, the dismissal could only be upheld if the State bore the burden of justifying the discharge on legitimate grounds. Any justification had to take into account the context in which the statement was made, including time, place, and manner. Here, McPherson had no policy-making or law-enforcement responsibilities and her statement had no discernible impact on the functioning of the constable's office, so the State failed to justify the dismissal.

    **iii. Dissent:** Justice Scalia dissented, joined by Chief Justice Rehnquist and Justices White and O'Connor.

**c. Need not have "property" interest:** Observe that in the "speech critical of superiors" cases (*Connick*, for instance), the employee has a qualified right not to be fired for First Amendment activity even if she has no ***"property"*** interest in the job. This is very different from the rule in cases brought under the Due Process Clause.

    **i. Illustration:** For instance, if P in *Connick* had been fired simply because the head prosecutor didn't like her, P would have had the right to procedural safeguards (e.g., a hearing or statement of reasons) only if she showed that she had a "property" interest in the job, i.e., that she was, under state law, something more than an at-will employee. But because P was fired for reasons of speech, she had a qualified right not to be fired for her speech activities even if she was a completely at-will employee who could have been fired at any time for no reason at all. (In fact, of course, the Court held in *Connick* that P could be fired anyway, because her speech did not touch on matters of "public concern"; but the point is that P got some First Amendment protection against firing even though she had no "property" interest in her job.)

**d. No balancing if speech not on matter of public concern:** Recall that under *Connick*, if the matter discussed by the employee is *not* one of public concern, the court will give great deference to the employer's judgment, and to the employer's conclusion that the speech would disrupt the functioning of the government office for whom the speaker works. See *supra*, p. 616. In this the-speech-is-not-a-matter-of-public-concern scenario, the court will ***not even conduct a Connick-type balancing*** between the employee's free-speech rights and the state's interest in promoting efficiency. This principle was illustrated in *City of San Diego v. Roe*, 543 U.S. 77 (2004).

    **i.**   **Facts:** *Roe* involved a San Diego police officer (Roe) who made a video showing himself stripping off a police uniform and masturbating. Roe sold copies of the video on the adults-only section of ebay, and maintained an ebay user profile identifying him as employed in the field of law enforcement. The police department terminated him for conduct unbecoming of an officer. Roe responded by suing the department on a claim that his firing violated his right to free speech.

    **ii.**   **Court rejects claim:** The Supreme Court unanimously ***rejected Roe's free-speech claim***. In doing so, the Court held that Roe was not even entitled to a *Connick*-style balancing of the employee's free-speech rights against the employer's interest in promoting the efficiency of the public services it performs. The *Connick* balancing test applies only, the Court wrote, when the employee's speech touches upon a "matter of ***public concern***." A matter of public concern is one that is "a subject of ***legitimate news interest***; that is, a subject of general interest and of value and concern to the public at the time of publication." Roe's speech here did not satisfy this standard: his activities "did nothing to inform the public about any aspect of the [police department's] functioning or operation."

        **(1)**   **Consequence:** Consequently, the courts were not required to do any balancing at all. Instead, they were required to give extreme deference to the police department's decision to fire Roe for conduct detrimental to the mission and functions of the department.

**e.**   **Speech must not occur as part of job responsibilities:** In order for speech on matters of public concern to get the protection of *Connick*, the speech ***must not be made "pursuant to the employee's official duties."*** So speech on matters of public concern made in furtherance of the public employee's ***job functions*** receives ***less First Amendment protection*** than speech the employee makes as a "citizen" acting outside of his job. The Court announced this principle in ***Garcetti v. Ceballos***, 126 S.Ct. 1951 (2006).

    **i.**   **Facts:** The plaintiff in *Garcetti* was a supervising lawyer in the L.A. County District Attorney's Office. P was called on to investigate whether an affidavit prepared by a deputy sheriff to obtain a search warrant was properly done. After his investigation, P wrote a memo to his supervisor concluding that the affidavit had been improperly done, and recommending dismissal of the criminal case premised upon it. This memo precipitated a chain of events at the end of which, P claimed, his superior retaliated against him for writing the memo. The D.A.'s office retorted that P's act of writing the memo was not entitled to First Amendment protection because the memo was created as part of P's job responsibilities.

    **ii.**   **Court agrees:** By a 5-4 vote, the Court agreed with the D.A.'s position: "[W]hen public employees make statements ***pursuant to their official duties,*** the employees are ***not speaking as citizens*** for First Amendment purposes, and ***the Constitution does not insulate their communications from employer discipline.***" Here, because P's investigation and the ensuing memorandum were part of his job responsibilities, the employer had the right to regulate the content and manner of P's speech.

    **(1) Rationale:** The majority reasoned that "employers have heightened interests in controlling speech made by an employee in his or her professional capacity ... Supervisors must ensure that their employees' official communications are accurate, demonstrate sound judgment, and promote the employer's mission."

  **iii. Dissent:** The four dissenters conceded that the majority was correct to recognize a government employer's important interest in ensuring that employees who speak for it while doing their work have competence, honesty and good judgment. But the dissenters, led by Justice Souter, would nonetheless apply a *Connick*-style ***balancing*** when on-the-job speech implicates matters of public concern — they thought that the government's interest in job performance could sometimes be ***outweighed*** by the employee's interest in speaking (and the public's interest in hearing the speech) on matters of public concern. For Souter, such a balancing was appropriate, for instance, "when a public auditor speaks on his discovery of embezzlement of public funds, when a building inspector makes an obligatory report of an attempt to bribe him, or when a law enforcement officer expressly balks at his superior's order to violate constitutional rights he is sworn to protect."

 **f.** **Independent contractor has same right:** The same free-speech limits imposed by cases like *Connick* apply when government wants to discharge or stop using a person or company as an ***independent contractor*** rather than employee. So if the contractor speaks out on a matter of public concern (e.g., by criticizing the government), the government can't retaliate against the contractor unless the government's interests outweigh the contractor's free-speech interests. *Board of County Commissioners v. Umbehr*, 518 U.S. 668 (1996).

**7.** **Ban on payments for outside speech:** *Connick* and the other cases discussed just previously focus on the problem of speech by government employees that occurs ***in the workplace***, or that ***directly concerns*** that workplace. Government has a ***lesser*** right to regulate speech that occurs ***outside*** the workplace and has little to do with the employee's own conditions of employment. Here, government will have to show that its interest in maintaining control over its employees clearly outweighs their free-speech rights, and that there is a relatively tight fit between the means of control chosen and the governmental objective being pursued. Thus in *U.S. v. Nat'l Treasury Employees Union*, 513 U.S. 454 (1995), the Court partially struck down a federal statute that barred most federal employees from receiving ***payments*** ("honoraria") for ***outside speeches and articles***.

  **a.** **Nature of the ban:** Congress became sensitive to public complaint that members of Congress and other federal employees were abusing their office by accepting honoraria for outside speeches and articles; often, the speeches and articles were addressed to and paid for by businesses who were regulated by Congress. Congress responded by banning not only its own members, but nearly all federal employees, from receiving any outside payment for speeches or non-fiction articles. The ban applied even to speech or writing that had ***no connection to the employee's work***.

  **b.** **Challenge:** The ban was challenged by a union representing federal Civil Service employees below the relatively high rank of GS16 (i.e., the challengers were roughly those earning less than $87,000 in 1995).

   c. **Struck down:** By a 6-3 vote, the Court struck down the statute as it applied to employees below the rank of GS16.

      i. **Poor means-end fit:** A key reason was that the scheme here was ***"crudely crafted"*** and ***overbroad***, according to the majority. For instance, it applied even to speech that was not related to the speaker's federal work, as to which impropriety was unlikely. And it was internally inconsistent — for example, it applied to all single articles (work-related or not), but only to "series" of articles if the series was work-related. Because of this poor means-end fit, the measure was not a "reasonable response to the posited harms" (e.g., the appearance of impropriety).

8. **Imposition of burdens:** So far, we have talked about the award by the government of ***benefits*** (e.g., public-sector jobs). But a similar rule applies where the government metes out ***burdens***. That is, the government may not use as a basis for selecting which individuals are to be burdened the individuals' exercise of constitutionally-protected rights (or any other constitutionally-illicit criterion, e.g., race). This is true even if the government would otherwise have the right to place that burden upon the individuals in question. For instance, "there are First Amendment problems if only Democrats, or only critics of government, or only Socialists, are selected for ***income tax audit***." Gunther, 1985 Supp., p. 66. The same is true of any other government prosecution or penalty.

F. **Compulsory disclosure:** Frequently, interference with associational freedoms will be alleged where the government does not deny a job or benefit based on organizational membership, but rather ***inquires*** of an employee or applicant about the organizations to which he belongs (or, conversely, asks an organization who its members are.) Typically, this is done by requiring the filling out of a questionnaire or affidavit detailing all of one's associational memberships. (Use of a "loyalty oath" sometimes fulfills the same function; see the discussion of such oaths *supra*, p. 615.) Ordinarily, refusal to submit the required document is made grounds for non-hiring or discharge.

   1. **Evolution of law:** The principles governing such compelled disclosure have changed dramatically in the last thirty years. Whereas in the 1950's broad inquiry was permitted, today inquiry must be restricted to little more than matters which would constitute substantive grounds for non-hiring or firing.

   2. **Original view:** In the 1950's, when fear of Communism was at its height, the Court permitted government to conduct inquiries about organizational memberships which, even if they existed, would ***not necessarily have been grounds for disqualification from employment.*** See, e.g., *Garner v. Los Angeles Board of Public Works*, 341 U.S. 716 (1951) (Government may require all municipal employees to sign an affidavit stating whether they have ever been members of the Communist Party, even though such membership, without more, does not necessarily justify discharge.)

   3. **Evidence of poor reliability:** The broad use of such compelled disclosure was buttressed by decisions holding that the ***refusal to answer*** questions could be taken as evidence of unfitness, not because the refusal justified the presumption that the undisclosed information was unfavorable, but on the theory that the refusal to answer was ***itself*** evidence of ***unreliability*** or insubordination.

   4. **Closer scrutiny of means-end link:** Today, government's right to compel a person to disclose his associations is much ***narrower*** than it was in the 1950's. The trend towards narrowing the permissible scope of compulsory disclosure has been brought about partly

through increasingly close scrutiny of the ***link*** between the ***governmental interest*** being pursued by the inquiry, and the ***means chosen*** to carry out that inquiry (i.e., the particular information sought).

The test now applied is essentially that of ***strict scrutiny***: if the governmental interest sought through mandatory disclosure is not a ***compelling*** or "subordinating" one, or if that interest could be attained by means ***less restrictive*** of associational or expressional freedoms, the mandatory disclosure will not be upheld.

    **a. NAACP membership lists:** The classic illustration of this new heightened means-end scrutiny is a case involving compulsory disclosure of NAACP membership lists, ***NAACP v. Alabama***, 357 U.S. 449 (1958).

        **i. Facts:** Alabama demanded the names and addresses of all the NAACP's Alabama members. The demand was part of a request made by the state for an injunction against the organization, to stop it from conducting activities in Alabama on the grounds that it had not satisfied a requirement that foreign corporations qualify before doing business there.

        **ii. Holding:** In holding that compulsory disclosure of the membership lists would ***violate members' associational rights***, the Court emphasized that "privacy in group association may in many circumstances be indispensable to preservation of freedom of association, particularly where a group espouses ***dissident beliefs***." Here, the NAACP showed that on past occasions, members whose names were publicly released had been subjected to loss of jobs, physical threats, economic loss and other public hostility. Therefore, this was clearly one of those situations where disclosure would impair the freedom of association.

        **iii. Balancing:** Only a compelling, ***"subordinating"*** state interest could outweigh the harm to freedom of association that compulsory disclosure would bring about. The names of the NAACP's rank and file members, the Court concluded, did not have the requisite "substantial bearing" on the state's interest in preventing unregistered foreign corporations from conducting intrastate business. (The Court emphasized that the NAACP was willing to supply other data relevant to the business it was doing in the state, such as names and addresses of its employees and officials.)

**5. Modern Court's approach:** The Court has continued the modern approach of substantially restricting the scope of compulsory disclosure, if there is a significant risk of impairing associational freedom. In general, it remains the law that compulsory inquiry may be made only into those matters which ***could provide substantive grounds for disqualification*** for the job or benefit at issue. (Also, the Court has continued the Warren Court's policy that one may not be required to promise, in a loyalty oath, to refrain from specified activities, unless carrying out those activities would be grounds for disqualification. See *supra*, p. 615.)

    **a. Narrow construction of statute:** But the modern Court has shown some tendency to construe disclosure provisions and loyalty oaths ***narrowly***, if by so doing their constitutionality can be preserved. For instance, in *Cole v. Richardson*, 405 U.S. 676 (1972), the Court used such a narrowing technique to uphold a loyalty oath which Massachusetts required all public employees to take. One part of the oath was a promise to "oppose the overthrow of the government. ... " The Court rejected the claim that this promise imposed "vague, undefinable responsibilities actively to combat a potential overthrow of the government." The Court construed the promise as not requiring "specific action in some hypothetical or actual situation," but rather as merely calling for a commitment not to use illegal force to change the system.

6. **Disclosure of campaign contributions:** Compulsory disclosure of *campaign contributions* has been upheld over the objection that such disclosure violates the freedom of association. *Buckley v. Valeo*, 424 U.S. 1 (1976) (other aspects of which are discussed *supra*, p. 621).

   a. **Disclosure requirements:** The federal statute construed in *Buckley* required candidates to disclose the source of any contribution over $10, and also required individuals who made political contributions or independent expenditures of more than $100 per year to itemize their spending. The *Buckley* plaintiffs claimed that these disclosure rules violated the associational freedoms of *minor parties* and of *small contributors.*

   b. **Strict scrutiny standard:** The Court concluded that the compulsory disclosure provisions did indeed encroach significantly on First Amendment rights; in this respect, the Court held, compulsory disclosure of spenders was no different from compelled disclosure of members (found to impinge on associational freedoms in such cases as *NAACP v. Alabama, supra*, p. 621). Therefore, such compulsory disclosure must be subjected to *strict scrutiny*, the Court held.

   c. **Scrutiny survived:** But the Court then concluded that the disclosure provisions *survived* this strict scrutiny. Three governmental interests were sufficiently important, and closely enough linked to the means chosen, to outweigh the interference with associational freedoms. These interests were: (1) helping the electorate evaluate the candidate by disclosing who his supporters are; (2) avoiding corruption, and the appearance of corruption, by exposing contributions to public scrutiny; and (3) gathering data needed to enforce the contribution limits set forth in other provisions of the statute.

G. **The bar membership cases:** Cases on qualifications for *admission to the bar* are a kind of hybrid, raising problems both as to the grounds for denial of publicly-conferred benefits (the license to practice) as well as issues of the scope of required disclosure. Most of the bar cases have involved state qualification procedures designed to deal with *subversive* activities. Here's what seems to be the present state of affairs about bar-admission inquiries:

1. **No disqualification:** The state cannot ask the candidate a question whose *sole function* is to determine whether the candidate has been a knowing member of an organization which advocates forcible overthrow of the government. Thus *knowing membership* in such an organization, without more, *can't be the basis* for denying admission. *Baird v. State Bar of Arizona,* 401 U.S. 1 (1971).

2. **Screening device:** However, the state *can* use a *two-part question*, where the first part acts merely as a *screening device.* Thus the state can ask the initial question, "Have you ever been a member of an organization which advocates forcible overthrow of the government, while knowing that that was the organization's aim?" Then, if the answer is "yes," the state can ask the follow-up question, "Do you *support* this aim?" An affirmative answer to this second question (or a refusal to answer it) can apparently then be grounds for denying bar admission. *Law Students Research Council v. Wadmond,* 401 U.S. 154 (1971).

**H. Legislative investigations:** Issues about the scope of compulsory disclosure also arise in the context of *legislative investigations*. Such investigations, carried out by *committees* of Congress or state legislatures, have the right to subpoena testimony in matters relevant to contemplated legislation; witnesses who refuse to give relevant testimony may be subjected to criminal contempt proceedings.

    **1. Conflict with right of association:** Such legislative investigations have sometimes come into conflict with the freedom of association. Typically, this conflict has arisen where the investigation concerns subversive activities, and the witness is asked either about his own associational activities or about those of other persons.

    **2. Modern strict scrutiny:** In recent decades, the Court has applied *strict scrutiny* to all legislative questioning which impairs freedom of association or expression. The application of strict scrutiny occurred most notably in *Gibson v. Florida Legislative Comm.*, 372 U.S. 539 (1963).

        **a. Facts:** In *Gibson*, a committee of the Florida legislature, claiming suspicions that Communists had infiltrated the NAACP, demanded that the association produce its state-wide membership lists. The association refused, and its local president was convicted of contempt.

        **b. New test stated:** In reversing the contempt conviction, the Court articulated a strict scrutiny standard for judging any investigation which intrudes upon First Amendment rights: the state must "convincingly show a *substantial relation* between the information sought and a subject of *overriding and compelling state interest.*"

        **c. Application of test:** Here, this test was not met. This was a very different case from earlier ones in which member lists of the Communist Party or other subversive organizations were sought; here there was no suggestion that the NAACP *itself* was a Communist organization, merely that there might have been some *infiltration*. Only a connection between the NAACP and Communist *activities* would suffice to establish the required compelling state interest.

**I. Unconstitutional conditions:** The Supreme Court sometimes applies the doctrine of *"unconstitutional conditions"*. This doctrine holds that "government *may not grant a benefit on the condition that the beneficiary surrender a constitutional right*, even if the government may withhold that benefit altogether." 102 HARV. L. REV. 1415. The idea behind the doctrine is that what the government may not do directly, it may not do indirectly either. *Id.* However, the Supreme Court has chosen to apply the unconstitutional conditions doctrine in only a few of the many situations where it might logically apply. As the result of a 1991 decision, *Rust v. Sullivan, infra*, p. 624, use of the doctrine will probably remain rare.

    **1. Places where applied:** We have already seen one instance where the Court has applied the doctrine of unconstitutional conditions — recall that government may not condition a public job or benefit on the applicant's surrender of her constitutionally-protected membership in a group or organization. (For instance, the state may not refuse to hire workers who decline to swear an oath that they will not join the Communist Party.) See *supra*, p. 615. Similarly, the government may not condition an applicant's receipt of unemployment benefits on the worker's willingness to work on his sabbath day. (See *Sherbert v. Verner, infra*, p. 692.) And a decision in which the Court struck down a congressional prohibition on editorializing by federally-funded public broadcasters can be viewed as an application of the doctrine. See *FCC v. League of Women Voters, infra*, p. 641.

2. **Doctrine rejected:** But the Court has probably ***rejected*** the doctrine more than it has accepted it. For instance, the Court has held that government may subsidize the medical expenses of childbirth but not of abortion (see *Harris v. McRae* and *Maher v. Roe*, *supra*, p. 172 and p. 171 respectively), a pair of holdings arguably allowing the government to condition a poor woman's receipt of medical assistance upon her surrender of her right to an abortion. Similarly, the Court has held that the First Amendment is not violated by a federal statute giving public funds to political candidates only if the candidate promises not to spend more than a certain amount on constitutionally-protected campaign speech. See *Buckley v. Valeo*, *supra*, p. 584.

3. **Abortion counseling:** The 1991 decision in ***Rust v. Sullivan***, 500 U.S. 173 (1991), suggests that the modern Court is very hostile to unconstitutional-condition arguments in most contexts. In *Rust*, the Court held that Congress may in effect say to federally-funded "Title X" family planning clinics, "If you accept federal money, you may not give your clients abortion advice." (For a more complete description of the restrictions at issue in *Rust*, see *supra*, p. 172.)

   a. **Majority:** At least five members of the Court in *Rust* believed that putting federally-funded clinics and the doctors working in them to this choice — give up the money or give up advocacy of abortion — was ***not*** an unconstitutional condition. The majority relied principally on a distinction between a Title X "project" and a Title X "grantee." It is true, the majority wrote, that a Title X *project* may not give abortion counselling or referral to an abortion provider. But a Title X *grantee* may do so, so long as it conducts these activities through a separate, and separately funded, program. Since Title X employees are free to pursue abortion-related activities when they are not acting under the auspices of the Title X project, they are not being forced to choose between receiving the funding and exercising the constitutionally-protected right.

   b. **Dissent:** But the two justices who dissented on the unconstitutional-condition argument — Blackmun and Marshall — argued that the majority's project/grantee distinction should not make a difference. The majority's view amounted to the proposition that "the First Amendment could be read to tolerate *any* governmental restriction upon an employee's speech so long as that restriction is limited to the funded workplace." The dissenters believed that the government could restrict workplace speech only if the restriction was narrowly tailored to serve a compelling governmental interest. The dissenters cited cases in which limits on government-funded workplace speech had been struck down, despite the employee's freedom to speak outside of work; for instance, in *Rankin v. McPherson* (*supra*, p. 617), a public clerk was not permitted to be dismissed for saying on the job that she hoped President Reagan would be assassinated.

   c. **Significance:** The rationale of *Rust* seems to give the federal government (and perhaps the states) extensive rights to ***use their power of the purse to influence the way in which citizens exercise their constitutional rights***. The majority's thinking in *Rust* would seem to validate the following kinds of governmental "strings":

      i. The federal government pays schools money so that poor kids can have lunch, but only if the school agrees that it will not provide sex education;

      ii. A state denies welfare payments to any poor woman who declines to get sterilized and who then gives birth to a third or later child; or

**iii.** Each federally-chartered bank is told that in exchange for federal deposit insurance, no official of the bank may criticize the actions of the Fed while on the job.

**d. Possible cutting-back of case:** On the other hand, a post-*Rust* case seems to cut back considerably on the significance of *Rust*. In *Legal Services Corp. v. Velazquez*, 531 U.S. 533 (2001), discussed more extensively *supra*, p. 605, Justice Kennedy, speaking for five members of the Court, characterized *Rust* as having been a case in which the government "used private speakers to transmit information ***pertaining to its own program***." *Rust* therefore involved, he said, a form of "governmental speech," rather than private speech that was being influenced by the government. So *Rust* now seems to stand merely for the quite limited proposition that when the government funds a third party to speak ***about a government program***, the government has extensive power to put particular topics off-limits.

**4. Doesn't apply where government could compel result directly:** A 2006 case demonstrates another important limitation on the unconstitutional-conditions doctrine: if government could ***directly compel the constitutionally-related objective*** it seeks, there is ***no unconstitutional condition when government offers a benefit to induce a person to help bring about that result.*** The case was ***Rumsfeld v. FAIR***, 547 U.S. 47 (2006)

**a. Issue:** The issue in *FAIR* was the constitutionality of the "Solomon Amendment," under which Congress said that any university could receive certain federal funding only if all parts of the university, including its law school, gave the same on-campus access to military recruiters as to recruiters from other employers. The purpose of the Amendment was to prevent the schools from denying on-campus recruitment slots on account of the schools' disapproval of the military's anti-gay recruitment policies.

**i. Claim by universities:** The plaintiff association of law schools claimed that the Solomon Amendment was an unconstitutional condition: a government benefit (funding) was being granted on condition that the law schools give up what they characterized as their free-speech right to express disapproval of the military by denying it on-campus access.

**b. Rejected by Court:** The Court, perhaps surprisingly, conceded that the Solomon Amendment would indeed impose an unconstitutional condition "if Congress could not directly require universities to provide military recruiters equal access to their students." But, the Court unanimously concluded, Congress' Art. I powers to "provide for the common Defense" and to raise and maintain an army and a navy gave Congress the power ***unconditionally to compel schools to give access to military recruiters.*** Since Congress could simply ***force*** schools to admit recruiters, it was not imposing an unconstitutional condition by offering an incentive (funding) instead of using straight compulsion.

# XII. SPECIAL PROBLEMS CONCERNING THE MEDIA

**A. Summary of issues:** Certain First Amendment problems arise only where the First Amendment right is being asserted by a member of the ***media***, i.e., professional ***publishers*** and ***broadcasters***. The four issues which we address that pertain specially to the media are:

**1.** Does the press have a special role to play under the First Amendment, so that it has ***rights*** which an ***ordinary member of the public would not?***

2. Under what circumstances, if any, may the media be *restrained* from publishing or broadcasting material (as distinguished from being punished after such dissemination has already occurred)?

3. Does a journalist have any greater rights to *resist governmental demands for information* known to the journalist, than does an ordinary member of the public? and

4. Do the media have any First Amendment *right of access* to information *within the government's possession* or control?

B. **Special role for the press:** The First Amendment explicitly prohibits abridgment of the freedom "of the press," in addition to protecting the freedom "of speech." On its face, this language suggests that the organized press is entitled to somewhat greater First Amendment protection than are ordinary members of the public; otherwise, the explicit reference to the press would seem to be redundant.

  1. **Not yet recognized:** However, in no case has a majority of the Court ever recognized the Press Clause of the First Amendment as having independent constitutional significance. Yet, neither has the Court ever squarely held that the Clause is redundant.

  2. **Laws of general applicability:** The Court has heard a number of cases in which the press argued that it should receive an *exemption* from rules of general applicability. The Court has virtually always *denied* any special exemption for the press. For instance, if a state's generally applicable procedural rules allow a person to be forced to give *testimony* to a grand jury or petit jury, then the press must obey those rules like anyone else. See *Branzburg v. Hayes, infra*, p. 633. Similarly, the same rules apply to the issuance of *search warrants* to search a publisher's premises as apply to searches of a non-publisher. *Zurcher v. Stanford Daily, infra*, p. 635. And newspapers may be made to pay damages for violating contractual promises of *confidentiality*, the same as any private citizen may be. See *Cohen v. Cowles Media Co., infra*, p. 637.

     a. **Access right:** There is one situation in which the press may have rights superior to those of the public at large. The press may have a right of *access* to newsworthy information within the government's control — such a right of access for the press, based on general free-expression principles, may have been recognized by the Court in the *Richmond Newspapers* case, *infra*, p. 639.

  3. **Government can't single out press:** Regardless of whether the press has special rights, what is clear is that government may not *single out* the press for *unfavorable* treatment.

     a. **Taxation:** This has been clearest in cases involving *taxation*. The government may not impose a tax that applies to newspapers (or all media) but that is not generally applicable. Thus in ***Minneapolis Star & Tribune Co. v. Minnesota Comm'r of Revenue***, 460 U.S. 525 (1983), the Court held that a special Minnesota "use tax" applicable only to the cost of *paper and ink* consumed in the production of *publications*, violated the First Amendment.

        i. **Rationale:** The Court did not find any evidence that the Minnesota legislature had tried to censor or chill the press. But the tax was a special one, not part of the state's generally-applicable use tax. Therefore, the Court concluded, the state had "singled out the press for special treatment." Consequently, the tax had to be strictly scrutinized — it would be invalid unless "necessary to achieve an overriding governmental interest."

    **ii. "Chilling" effect:** There was evidence that the particular tax here was not especially burdensome to the press (since it was at the same percentage rate as the general state sales and use taxes, and applied only to paper and ink, not to the total price of the newspaper). Nonetheless, because the state had singled out the press, the "*political constraints* that prevent a legislature from passing crippling taxes of general applicability are weakened, and the threat of burdensome taxes becomes acute." The *mere threat* of crippling taxes might well have a censorial effect, the Court argued.

    **iii. Strict scrutiny test failed:** The statute was not able to withstand the strict scrutiny to which the Court subjected it. The state's interest in raising revenue might be a compelling one (the Court did not say); but the singling out of the press for a special tax was *not a necessary means* of achieving that objective. The state could, for instance, simply have made newspaper sales part of the *general state sales tax* already in force.

    **iv. Dissent:** Justice Rehnquist, in dissent, argued that not all "differential treatment," but only that differential treatment which *burdens* the press, should be strictly scrutinized. Here, he calculated, the use tax was *more favorable* to the press than, say, a sales tax set at the same percentage, but applicable to the newspaper's gross revenues. Therefore, there was a "benefit" to the press, not a "burden."

  **b. Taxation based on content:** Where a tax operates differently upon different members of the press depending on the *content* of a publication, it is even more likely to be found invalid. In the post-*Minneapolis Star* case of *Arkansas Writer's Project, Inc. v. Ragland*, 481 U.S. 221 (1987), an Arkansas statute that taxed general interest magazines, but exempted newspapers and other special-interest publications, was invalidated by the Court. The fact that the tax did not discriminate among particular *views*, merely among subject areas, was not sufficient to save the statute.

    **i. Exemption that is denied to large category:** On the other hand, where a generally-applicable tax is applied to most media as well as to non-media, and an exemption is given to a certain media segment, denial of the exemption to the rest of the media seems *not* to be unconstitutional. Thus if a state has a generally-applicable sales tax on goods and services, it may decide to cover cable TV services while continuing to exempt newspapers, magazines, and satellite broadcast services. *Leathers v. Medlock*, 499 U.S. 439 (1991). The idea seems to be that as long as it is not the case that a small segment of the media is singled out for negative treatment, the fact that some segment of the media *is* given an exemption is irrelevant.

**C. Prior restraints:** A key aim of the drafters of the First Amendment was to forbid any system of *prior restraints*, similar to the English licensing scheme, by which nothing could be published without government or church approval. This aim remains a vital part of modern First Amendment doctrine, so that any governmental action which prevents expression from occurring (as distinguished from punishing it once it has occurred) is *presumed to be constitutionally invalid*. This is all the more true where the prior restraint is directed against the organized press. See Tribe, p. 1041.

  **1. Procedural obstacles:** The dangers of prior restraints also stem from the fact that procedural rules applied in American courts make such restraints more likely to *"chill"* the exercise of First Amendment rights than would a subsequent punishment. Where a person is sought to be punished *after* his speech-related conduct, he is completely free to raise the claim that the statute at issue is unconstitutional, either on its face or as applied to him. But where a person is enjoined *prior* to his expressive act, and yet goes ahead and does that act anyway, he will not be permitted to argue that either the underlying statute or the injunction was unconstitutional as applied to him (though he may argue that the statute was void on its face). See, e.g., *Walker v. City of Birmingham, supra*, p. 498. Thus an unconstitutionally-imposed prior restraint is likely to cow the defendant into foregoing his First Amendment rights, at least during the length of time it takes to conduct an appeal. See Tribe, pp. 1042-45.

2. **Examples of prior restraints:**   There are two basic types of pre-publication restraints. One consists of governmental orders and court injunctions telling a particular person that he cannot engage in a certain type of communication. The other consists of a scheme requiring a ***license or permit*** before a particular type of expression may be engaged in. Movie-censorship schemes are illustrations of the latter category. All of the cases involving the organized press, with which we are concerned here, are of the governmental-order or court-injunction type.

3. *Near v. Minnesota:*   The classic case articulating the heavy presumption against prior restraints is ***Near v. Minnesota***, 283 U.S. 697 (1931).

   a. **Facts:**   In *Near*, a state procedure for closing down as a public nuisance any "malicious, scandalous and defamatory newspaper" was used to permanently enjoin the publication of a newspaper which criticized local officials.

   b. **Holding:**   In striking the injunction as an unconstitutional infringement of free speech, the Court held that the primary aim of the First Amendment was to prevent pre-publication restraints. The proper remedy for false accusations against public officials was by a post-publication libel action, not by a pre-publication procedure which the Court found to be tantamount to censorship.

      i. **Exceptional cases:**   The prohibition on prior restraints, in the *Near* Court's view, was almost, but not quite, complete. There could be a few "exceptional cases" in which prior restraint would be permissible; the Court gave as illustrations actual obstruction of recruitment for the armed forces, and publication of "the sailing dates of transports or the number and location of troops."

      ii. **Burden of proof:**   One aspect of the Minnesota statute to which the Court took particular exception was that the ***burden of proof*** was placed ***upon the publisher*** to show his truthfulness or good faith, rather than on the party seeking the injunction to show falsity or malice. However, nothing in the *Near* opinion (or in subsequent case law) suggests that placing the burden of proof in these issues on the party seeking the injunction would validate such a generalized prior restraint scheme.

4. **Pentagon Papers case:**   The only other case to reach the Court on the issue of prior restraint of political speech is the famous ***Pentagon Papers*** case, ***New York Times Co. v. U.S.***, 403 U.S. 713 (1971). This case establishes that the press has ***almost absolute immunity*** from pre-publication restraints. See Tribe, p. 1039.

a. **Facts:** *The New York Times* and *The Washington Post* began publishing portions of a secret Defense Department study (popularly known as the "Pentagon Papers") of U.S. policy in Vietnam. The government sought an injunction against the two papers to prevent further publication. The government conceded that the Papers discussed only historical events which transpired prior to 1968, but argued that publication would prolong the War by giving the enemy information useful to it and would embarrass our diplomatic efforts.

b. ***Per curiam* opinion:** The opinion of the Court was a brief *per curiam* one, which recited prior case law that there is a heavy presumption against the constitutionality of prior restraints, but which contained no other reasoning. By a 6-3 vote, the Court determined that the government was ***not entitled*** to the injunctions.

c. **Nine separate opinions:** *Every member* of the Court wrote a separate opinion, and no majority of the Court agreed on a precise rationale for the decision. The opinions fell into three broad categories: Justices Black and Douglas argued that there could ***never*** be a prior restraint on the press; Justices Brennan, White, Stewart and Marshall contended that there could be prior restraint in extraordinary circumstances, but that the present case did not qualify; and Justices Burger, Harlan, and Blackmun believed that prior restraint was appropriate here.

d. **Absolutist view:** Justices Black and Douglas appeared to be saying that ***ever*** to permit the publication of news to be enjoined would "make a shambles of the First Amendment."

   i. **Criticism:** But as Professor Cox has pointed out, in 94 HARV. L. REV. 6, "Surely [Black and Douglas] would not have ruled during World War II that a newspaper had a constitutional right to publish for Nazi eyes the knowledge that, because of … cryptographic work … British authorities were reading the orders of the Nazi High Command."

e. **Possible restraints:** The four other Justices in the six-man majority believed that prior restraint of news publication could sometimes occur, but not in this case. This group, consisting of Brennan, Stewart, White and Marshall, argued that there must be a ***virtual certainty*** that grave damage to the country would result if publication were not enjoined; as Justice Stewart, joined by White, expressed the test, there must be a showing that disclosure "will ***surely result*** in ***direct, immediate, and irreparable damage*** to our Nation or its people."

   i. **Danger not substantially certain:** Most or all of these Justices seemed to believe that publication would ***probably*** damage the nation. It was only because there was not a ***substantial certainty*** of such damage that they voted to strike the injunction.

   ii. **Absence of statutory authorization:** To all of these four Justices except Brennan, an important weakness of the government's position was that ***no statute*** provided for an injunction against news publication in circumstances like these. Separation of powers principles made it impermissible for the Court to issue an injunction where Congress had declined to act. (But Justices Stewart and White seemed to say that even in the ***absence*** of statutory authorization, a certainty of direct, immediate and irreparable damage to the country might permit issuance of an injunction. This view would probably command a majority of the Court today. See 94 HARV. L. REV. 7.)

**f.   Dissent:**   Three Justices, Harlan, Burger and Blackmun, dissented. They criticized the haste with which the Court heard and decided the case. (Less than one week elapsed between filing of the case and announcement of the decision.) Only one Justice, Harlan, formulated a test for evaluating the constitutionality of such injunctions.

  **i.   Harlan's test:**   In Harlan's view, the Court's role should be limited to determining: (1) whether the subject matter of the dispute lies within the ***proper scope*** of the ***President's foreign relations power***; and if the answer is "yes," (2) whether the determination that disclosure would irreparably impair the national security was personally made by the head of the relevant executive department, here, the Secretary of State or Secretary of Defense. If the answer to this question, too, was "yes," the injunction should be upheld.

  **ii.   Rationale:**   Harlan argued that it was a violation of separation of powers principles for the judiciary to go beyond these two inquiries and to "redetermine for itself the probable impact of disclosure on the national security."

**g.   Receipt of stolen goods:**   As is well known, the newspapers' source for the Pentagon Papers was Daniel Ellsberg, who was given them in confidence while he did work for the government. Had the government been able to show that the newspapers were ***receivers of stolen goods***, by showing that the newspapers were aware that Ellsberg's making and distributing copies was a violation of his obligation of confidentiality, it is possible that the Court might have found this to be grounds for an injunction. No subsequent case to reach the Court has faced this question squarely.

  **i.   Difficulty:**   One difficulty with allowing an injunction based on such a receivership-of-stolen-goods theory is that "requiring a newspaper to decide at its peril whether information that it has received about an official proceeding is confidential would have a chilling effect upon the publication of legitimate news." 94 HARV. L. REV. 12.

**h.   Injunction on initial distribution:**   Another unanswered question is whether, had the government discovered that Ellsberg was ***about*** to give copies of the Papers to the media, it could have enjoined ***him*** from doing so, even though it would not have been able to enjoin the media from publishing once they had the material. If an oral or written contract existed which would be violated by such a distribution by Ellsberg, general equitable principles would seem to permit an injunction, even though some impairment of Ellsberg's First Amendment rights might occur.

  **i.   Subsequent punishment:**   In any event, someone who violates an employment agreement or other contract by causing confidential materials to be published may clearly be subjected to ***subsequent punishment***. See, e.g., *Snepp v. U.S.*, 444 U.S. 507 (1980), permitting the CIA to collect all royalties due to Snepp, a former agent, for writing a book containing non-classified information, without subjecting the book to agency pre-publication clearance procedures as he was obligated to do under his CIA employment contract.

**5.   The *Progressive* H-bomb case:**   At least one court has interpreted the *Pentagon Papers* case to ***permit*** an injunction against publication of newsworthy information if a statute so authorizes, and if the danger is sufficiently compelling. In *U.S. v. The Progressive, Inc.*, 467 F. Supp. 990 (W.D. Wis. 1979), the district court enjoined a magazine from publishing an article containing **technical information about the H-bomb**. At least some of the materials had previously been declassified. But the U.S. convinced the court that these materials, taken together with other classified information (also sought to be released by the magazine), could pose a direct threat to national security by possibly "allow[ing] a medium size nation to move faster in developing a hydrogen weapon."

    **a. Rationale:** The judge reasoned that two main considerations made this case distinguishable from the *Pentagon Papers* case: (1) here, a statute, the Atomic Energy Act, authorized an injunction against publication of certain information relating to the use or manufacture of nuclear weapons (including some of the information in the proposed article); and (2) publication might well lead to nuclear proliferation, which in turn might lead to "thermonuclear annihilation for us all."

    **b. Balancing test:** The court then balanced the dangers to the paper's First Amendment rights against the danger to the nation. As to the former, although the injunction might interfere with the magazine's broadly-defined First Amendment rights, it would not interfere with its "laudable crusade to stimulate public knowledge of nuclear armament and bring about enlightened debate on national policy questions." The balance was struck in favor of the injunction; the "disparity of risk" between the danger to the nation and the damage to the paper's First Amendment rights justified what the court conceded was "the first instance of prior restraint against a publication in this fashion in the history of this country."

    **c. Outcome:** Before the paper's appeal could be heard, the government's attempt to get a permanent injunction against it was dropped, because the information was published elsewhere.

6. **"Gag orders" and preservation of fair trials:** The media's exercise of its First Amendment rights may sometimes come into conflict with a **criminal defendant's right to a fair trial**. Extensive pre-trial publicity, including disclosure of confessions (possibly inadmissible) by the defendant, may make it much more difficult to find jurors who can be impartial. Nonetheless, the United States has never gone even a single step towards the English rule, which makes illegal the pre-trial publication of information that might cause prejudice.

    **a. Standard for biased jury:** If the defendant can show that the jury was biased against him, he is entitled to a **reversal** of his conviction. But it is **not** sufficient for him to show that the jurors had **knowledge before they were sworn in about the facts and issues involved in the case** — requiring complete ignorance would be virtually impossible in important trials, given today's mass communications. Rather, the defendant must show that the jury was **prejudiced** against him as the result of pre-trial publicity.

    **b. Publicity during trial:** Similarly, publicity **during** the trial may be so great that, if the jury is exposed to it, the defendant's right to a fair trial will be found to have been violated. See, e.g., *Sheppard v. Maxwell*, 384 U.S. 333 (1966), the famous Sam Sheppard murder case, where massive prejudicial publicity during the trial, to which the jury was exposed, was held to be grounds for reversal; the Court observed that the problem could have been avoided by **sequestering** the jury for the length of the trial.

c.  **Gag orders:**  Because of these dangers of publicity, especially before the trial begins, trial judges have sought ways of assuring that they will be able to find an unbiased jury. One appealing method that some seized upon is the ***"gag order,"*** a pre-trial order ***prohibiting the press from publishing certain types of information*** about the case. But as the result of the one case involving a gag order to reach the Court, such orders will ***almost never be constitutionally permissible***. That case is ***Nebraska Press Ass'n v. Stuart***, 427 U.S. 539 (1976).

    i.  **Facts of *Nebraska Press:***  In *Nebraska Press*, a man was about to be tried for a heinous mass murder, which had attracted widespread media attention. The trial judge, in order to assure his ability to select an unprejudiced jury, issued an order prohibiting the press from reporting any confessions or admissions by the defendant, or any other fact "strongly implicative" of him, until after impaneling of the jury.

    ii.  **Holding:**  The Supreme Court held unanimously that the gag order ***violated*** the press' First Amendment rights.

    iii.  **Majority opinion:**  The majority opinion was written by Chief Justice Burger, with whom four other Justices joined. Burger declined to hold that a ban on pre-trial publicity could ***never*** be constitutional. Instead, he applied a test long ago advocated by Learned Hand for subversive-advocacy cases: the restraint should be allowed only if the "gravity of the 'evil,' discounted by its improbability" is greater than the damage from impairment of First Amendment rights.

        **(1) Standard not met:** Here, Burger said, this test was not satisfied. The trial judge's conclusion that pretrial publicity would impair the defendant's rights "was of necessity ***speculative***," rather than certain. Furthermore, the trial judge should have considered ***other alternatives*** for reducing the harmful effect of such publicity (e.g., change of venue, postponement of trial, careful *voir dire*, restricting statements by the lawyers, police and witnesses, etc.) Finally, the trial judge should have considered whether his gag order would even be effective, in view of the rumors which usually circulate in a sensational case. On balance, then, it was not sufficiently established that the benefits of the gag order outweighed its First Amendment dangers.

d.  **Significance:**  *Nebraska Press* probably presents about the strongest case imaginable for a gag order furthering the right of fair trial. Therefore, the result of that decision is that such orders will virtually never be constitutional, at least as long as the press acquires its information without violating the law.

e.  **Distinguished from subsequent punishment:**  What made the order in *Nebraska Press* a "prior restraint" was not simply that it forbade publishing a certain type of material; it was that the restriction took the form of an order applicable to one particular, specifically-identified factual setting (this particular trial). Had the ***legislature*** made it a ***crime*** to publish prejudicial information in advance of *any* criminal trial, such a statute could ***not properly be termed a prior restraint***, and would ***not*** necessarily be unconstitutional.

    **i. Analysis:** General First Amendment principles might be interpreted to make such a statute violative of freedom of expression, but the heavy presumption against prior restraints would have nothing to do with the decision.

    **f. Silencing the lawyer:** The "gag order" in *Nebraska Press* was directed at the media; the case establishes that such press-directed orders will rarely be constitutional. But courts have a far greater ability to issue a constitutional gag order against the *lawyers* in the case, as the result of a post-*Nebraska Press* case decision. In *Gentile v. State Bar of Nevada*, 501 U.S. 1030 (1991), the Court held that states may prevent a lawyer from making any statement that would have a ***"substantial likelihood of materially prejudicing"*** an adjudicative proceeding. The Court upheld a Nevada rule patterned on the American Bar Association's Model Rule (prohibiting statements posing a substantial likelihood of material prejudice) over the lawyer's claim that a "clear and present danger" standard should be used.

    **g. Closure orders:** Since trial judges will almost never be permitted to use a pre-trial gag order directed at the press, an obvious alternative is for them simply to ***close pre-trial proceedings to the public (and press)***. The use of such closure orders, at least where they are limited to pretrial proceedings and are not opposed by either the prosecution or the defense, was upheld by the Supreme Court, in *Gannett Co. v. DePasquale*, discussed *infra*, p. 639.

**D. Governmental demands for information held by press:** First Amendment issues may arise when the government seeks ***disclosure*** of information ***obtained by the press*** during its news-gathering activities, but not yet published. Typically, the government seeks such disclosure as part of its ***law enforcement*** efforts. The two Supreme Court cases on point, one involving a grand jury investigation and the other the use of an *ex parte* search warrant, indicate that the press is ***not entitled to any special First Amendment protection*** against what would otherwise be proper compulsory disclosure of information obtained during news-gathering.

    **1. Indirect impact on First Amendment rights:** Observe that the nature of the interference with First Amendment expression is quite different in this compulsory-disclosure setting than in the prior restraint area. In the latter setting, restraint is almost always sought ***because of the communicative impact*** which publication would have; thus prior restraints almost always call for "track one" analysis (to use Tribe's term), and strict scrutiny is obviously appropriate. But in the compulsory disclosure area, any interference with First Amendment expression (e.g., the drying up of information from informants, because they are afraid their confidentiality will not be preserved) is ***incidental to,*** not the purpose of, the disclosure. Therefore, these cases call for "track two" analysis, which as noted (*supra*, p. 472) is handled by a much less stringent balancing of harms and benefits. Therefore, it is not surprising that the Supreme Court has been much less quick to accept the press' arguments in the compulsory-disclosure area than in the context of prior restraints. See 94 HARV. L. REV. 55.

    **2. *Branzburg* and grand jury investigations:** In ***Branzburg v. Hayes***, 408 U.S. 665 (1972), the Court held by a 5-4 vote that requiring newsmen to testify before ***grand juries*** concerning ***information obtained from confidential sources*** during news-gathering does ***not*** violate the First Amendment. In so deciding, the Court ***rejected*** journalists' requests for at least a ***qualified privilege*** to refuse to disclose the ***identities of confidential sources*** or the ***information*** received from them.

a. **Journalists' argument:**  The argument raised by Branzburg and two other journalists was that news-gathering often requires confidential sources, who agree to supply the journalist with otherwise unavailable information only if non-disclosure of the informant's name and/or some of the information is promised. If a grand jury could compel disclosure, the journalists argued, not only the source of the particular information sought, but other confidential sources in the future, would be dissuaded from talking to journalists.

b. **Holding:**  In rejecting the claim for a privilege, the Court held that such a privilege had never been found to exist, and that journalists had always been viewed as having the ***same duty as any other citizen*** to disclose to grand juries information about crime. The majority was not convinced that a significant portion of information supplied by confidential sources would dry up, especially since such information was widely available to newsmen even though no privilege had ever been recognized.

   i. **Balancing:**  Even if significant impairment of confidential sources did occur, the majority saw no reason why "[t]he public interest in possible future news about crime from undisclosed, unverified sources" should take precedence over the governmental interest in prosecuting crimes about which journalists possess evidence.

   ii. **Definitional problem:**  Also, the majority saw a ***definitional*** problem: recognition of a privilege would require the courts either to decide that only the "organized press" should be protected (and to define that term), or to make the privilege dangerously broad by protecting "lectures, political pollsters, novelists, academic researchers, dramatists" and anyone else claiming to be informing the public and to be relying on confidential sources.

c. **Qualified privilege rejected:**  The majority also rejected even a ***qualified*** privilege, by which disclosure of confidential information could not be compelled unless the state showed that a crime had been committed and that the journalist possessed relevant information not available from other sources.

d. **Protection against harassment:**  But the majority preserved the right of a journalist to obtain relief against ***harassment***, e.g., a subpoena issued not to pursue law enforcement ends but for the purpose of disrupting the reporter's relationship with his news sources (perhaps because of official displeasure with the newsman's work). However, so long as the questions were relevant and material, and were part of a good faith grand jury investigation, the newsman could not decline to answer.

e. **Powell's concurrence:**  The crucial fifth vote was supplied by Justice Powell, who although he joined the Court's opinion submitted a separate concurrence as well; this concurrence made the result of the case somewhat ambiguous. Whereas the other four members of the majority rejected a qualified privilege, and left room only for a defense of harassment, Justice Powell's concurrence stated that claims of privilege should be decided on a ***case-by-case basis***, by balancing freedom of the press against the obligation of all citizens to give relevant testimony. Powell suggested, for instance, that a newsman may obtain relief if he can show that he has been asked for information bearing "only a remote and tenuous relationship to the subject of the investigation," or that his confidential sources would be compromised "without a legitimate need of law enforcement."

**f. Dissent:** Three of the four dissenters in *Branzburg* did not argue for an absolute privilege against grand jury disclosure of confidential sources. But they did support a type of *strict scrutiny* of such compulsory disclosure, by which the government would have to make three showings before a reporter could be required to reveal confidences: (1) that there is "probable cause to believe that the newsman has information which is *clearly relevant* to a *specific probable violation of law*;" (2) that the information cannot be obtained by "*alternative means* less destructive of First Amendment rights"; and (3) that the government has a "compelling and overriding interest" in the information.

> **i. Relation to Powell's view:** As the dissenters pointed out, this type of qualified privilege may not be so different from the position taken by Justice Powell. The absolute position taken by the other four members of the majority, by contrast, would "annex the journalistic profession as an investigative arm of government," the dissenters argued.

**3. Limited scope of ruling:** In addition to grand jury proceedings, the rationale of *Branzburg* obviously applies to *criminal trials* as well. But it is not clear that the theory of *Branzburg* also deprives newsmen of a constitutional privilege regarding testimony in *civil suits*. Some lower courts have granted a *qualified privilege* in this situation, which may be overcome only by a showing that the confidentially-obtained information is not available from other sources. See N&R, p. 1051.

**4. Shield laws:** The majority in *Branzburg* noted that Congress and state legislatures are free to enact *statutes* granting to newsmen a privilege against disclosure of confidential sources or information in grand jury or other proceedings. More than half of the states have, either before or after *Branzburg*, conferred such a privilege by means of so-called *"shield laws."*

**a. No Court decisions:** The Supreme Court has not yet had occasion to determine whether some applications of such a shield law unconstitutionally interfere with other constitutional rights, most notably a criminal defendant's Sixth Amendment *right to a fair trial.*

**b. *Farber* case:** One well-known state court case, involving a trial judge's order to a reporter to produce interview notes in connection with a murder case, concluded that such a shield law *must yield to the defendant's Sixth Amendment rights. In re Farber*, 394 A.2d 330 (N.J. 1978).

**5. *Ex parte* search warrants:** Another press claim for special protection against compelled disclosure for law enforcement purposes failed in *Zurcher v. Stanford Daily*, 436 U.S. 547 (1978). There, the Court upheld an *ex parte warrant* for the search of a student newspaper's offices, based on probable cause to believe that photographs of a riotous demonstration might be found there.

**a. Usual rules applied:** The majority opinion spent most of its time talking about the Fourth Amendment, not the First, and saw no reason to depart from usual principles allowing the issuance on probable cause of *ex parte* warrants (that is, warrants issued without notice to the person whose property is to be searched).

**b. Qualified privilege rejected:** As in *Branzburg*, the Court *rejected* the press' request for at least a *qualified* privilege, under which an *ex parte* warrant would be issued only where there was reason to believe that a *subpoena* might lead to the destruction of the evidence.

**E. Disclosure of confidential or illegally-obtained information:** To what extent may government prohibit the media from *disclosing information* that government believes ought to be *secret*? The interests that government may be trying to protect can include the *privacy of individuals*, the *rehabilitation of juvenile offenders*, or the maintenance of *national security*, among others. A good summary of the Court's decisions in this area is that "[i]f a newspaper *lawfully obtains truthful information* about a matter of *public significance* then [government] officials may not constitutionally punish publication of the information, absent a *need … of the highest order.*" *Smith v. Daily Mail Publishing Co.*, 443 U.S. 97 (1979).

1. **Information about legal proceedings:** A number of the Court's decisions concerning publication of "secret" material have involved information about *legal proceedings* or *law enforcement*. Here, government has almost always been *unsuccessful* in *making it a crime to publish* legally-obtained truthful information. Here are some examples:

   ❏ A broadcaster may not be held civilly liable for *publishing the name of a rape victim*, if the name is learned from the reading of a publicly-filed indictment. *Cox Broadcasting Corp. v. Cohn*, 420 U.S. 469 (1975).

   ❏ A state may not make it a crime for a newspaper to report (accurately) that a state judicial commission is contemplating an *investigation of a particular sitting judge*. *Landmark Communications, Inc. v. Virginia*, 435 U.S. 829 (1978).

   ❏ A newspaper cannot be punished for publishing the *name and photo of a juvenile offender*, where the newspaper obtained the name from witnesses to the crime and from law-enforcement officers who investigated it. *Smith v. Daily Mail Publishing Co.*, 443 U.S. 97 (1979).

2. **Information obtained by means of a crime:** An important sub-question is whether this rule — that publication of newsworthy confidential information may not be criminalized absent an extremely strong state interest — applies even to *illegally-obtained* information.

   a. **Where publisher has acted illegally:**    If the *publisher itself* has *acted illegally* in obtaining the information, then it is quite clear that government *may make it a crime* to punish the information, no matter how newsworthy it is.

   **Example:** Suppose that, in 1974, a reporter for the *Washington Post* broke into the White House and found a tape that recorded White House officials conspiring to burglarize the Democratic National Committee's offices. If the *Post* published a transcript of that tape, it's quite clear that a state could constitutionally punish the paper for the publication (apart from the break-in), because the newspaper obtained the information as a result of a crime by its own employee.

   b. **Where private party has acted illegally but publisher has not:** On the other hand, the fact that the secret information was originally obtained illegally by a person *acting independently* of the eventual publisher is *not* enough to allow publication to be made criminal, at least where the material has significant newsworthiness.

      i. **Illegal interception of cellphone calls:**    A vivid illustration of this principle occurred in a 2001 case in which a radio station played a tape of a cellphone conversation that had been intercepted in violation of a federal wiretapping law.

Because the interception occurred without the participation of the station, and because the conversation involved important public events, the station could not be prosecuted for the broadcast. *Bartnicki v. Vopper*, 532 U.S. 514 (2001).

**(1) Facts:** In *Bartnicki*, the conversation was a cellphone conversation between two officials of a teachers union, who were discussing a bitter contract negotiation that they were having with the local school board. During the conversation, one of the officials said that if the board remained intransigent, it might be necessary for the union to go to board members' homes and "blow off their front porches." An unknown person intercepted the conversation in violation of federal law and sent it anonymously to a radio station, which broadcast it. The two officials sued the station for damages, as allowed by federal and state wiretap statutes prohibiting the disclosure of intercepted telephone conversations.

**(2) Holding:** By a 6-3 vote, the Court held that the station could not constitutionally be held liable for damages — the extreme newsworthiness of the conversation outweighed the strong governmental interest in protecting the privacy of electronic communications. The majority conceded that the government had a strong interest in deterring illegal interceptions, but believed that barring publication by a third person who did not participate in the interception would not significantly deter the illegal conduct.

**(3) Newsworthiness:** It seems clear that the extremely strong ***newsworthiness*** of the conversation in *Bartnicki* — which contained not only news about the bitter negotiation but a possible threat to people's physical safety — played a key role in the Court's decision.

**(4) Significance:** So what we know from *Bartnicki* is merely that where a publisher innocently comes into possession of illegally-intercepted conversations, and those conversations involve matters of unusually great public interest, the publisher may not be punished for disseminating them. There is a good chance that where the conversation involves matters that are ***not*** of major public interest (e.g., trade secrets or personal gossip), publication *can* be criminalized. And, of course, the person who does the illegal intercepting may be punished for publishing, no matter how great the public interest in the intercepted conversation.

3. **Enforcement of confidentiality promises:** Now consider one last aspect of government's power to enforce the confidentiality of information: if a journalist promises confidentiality to a source and then breaches that promise by publishing the confidential information, may the state allow the source to recover damages? The brief answer is "yes" — the Supreme Court has held that the states may ***enforce such confidentiality promises*** as they would any other contract, without thereby running afoul of the First Amendment. *Cohen v. Cowles Media Co.*, 501 U.S. 663 (1991). *Cohen* allowed recovery for breach of the promise not to disclose the source's ***identity***, but the rationale of the decision would allow contract damages to be awarded for breach of other promises by journalists as well (e.g., a promise to use the information only for background rather than on the record).

a. **Facts:**   In *Cohen*, P, a Republican campaign worker, offered reporters for two newspapers (the defendants) information about the criminal record of an opposing candidate for lieutenant governor. P offered the information only if the reporters promised not to name him as the source. The reporters turned over the information to their editors, who decided that the bigger story was not the information itself (the offenses were extremely minor), but rather the fact that an opposing campaign worker was attempting to leak that information. Over the reporters' objections, the two newspapers identified P, who was immediately fired from his full-time job.

b. **State court recovery:**   The Minnesota courts allowed P to recover damages based on a promissory estoppel theory.

c. **Damages upheld:**   The Supreme Court, by a 5-4 vote, held that the First Amendment did not bar the Minnesota courts from awarding P damages in this situation. The majority viewed this as a situation in which a generally applicable law — the law of promissory estoppel — happened to have some application to a news-gathering event. Any impact on freedom of expression was ***unintended*** and ***incidental***.

d. **Extension:**   *Cohen* directly dealt only with disclosure of the identity of a source. But the logic of the decision seems equally applicable to almost any promise made between a journalist and a news source. So a damage action is probably constitutionally allowable where: (1) the reporter promises the source that the information will be "for background only," rather than "on the record"; (2) the reporter promises that the story will be a "favorable" one; or (3) the reporter promises that the source will get to see the story — and confirm or deny its accuracy — before it is printed.

F. **Right of access to government-held information:**   Much newsworthy information is ***within the government's possession*** or control. Until recently, nothing in any Supreme Court decision supported any First Amendment right on the part of the press to have ***access*** to this newsworthy information. Thus although the press has long been recognized to have a broad First Amendment right to publish information which it obtains, the press has ***not*** been constitutionally entitled to ***assistance in obtaining information.*** Such a right of access has still not been explicitly recognized by the Court, but the decision in *Richmond Newspapers, Inc. v. Virginia*, discussed *infra*, p. 639, upholding a right of access to criminal trials, may presage some form of right of access to government-controlled newsworthy material.

1. **Access to jails:**   Several cases have established that the press has little or no special right of access to information about ***prison conditions***.

a. ***Pell* and *Saxbe*:**   In the companion cases of *Pell v. Procunier*, 417 U.S. 817 (1974) and *Saxbe v. Washington Post Co.*, 417 U.S. 843 (1974), the Court upheld state and federal regulations prohibiting press interviews with any specific prisoner. The Court rejected First Amendment claims raised by both the media and by prisoners. The majority opinion in both cases, by Justice Stewart, relied mainly on the fact that the regulations ***treated the press no worse than they did members of the general public.*** While the First Amendment prevents the government from interfering with the media's attempt to gather news, it does ***not*** "require government to accord the press special access to information not shared by members of the public generally."

b. **Marginally different treatment for press:**   In a later case, *Houchins v. KQED, Inc.*, 438 U.S. 1 (1978), a majority of the seven Justices participating reaffirmed the general *Pell* and *Saxbe* principles that the press has no special right of access beyond that granted to the general public. But because of an unusual alignment, a different major-ity held that *slightly different rules* might be required to be applied to the press, *even in the absence of a superior right of access*. This result was a consequence of Justice Stewart's view that the press is entitled to *"effective* access" to all publicly-accessible parts of a prison.

    **i.**   **Rationale:**   Stewart argued that merely permitting reporters to sign up for the same monthly tours as were available to the general public did not give them the requisite "effective" access; he indicated that press access "on a more flexible and frequent basis than scheduled monthly tours," and the right to use cameras and recording equipment, were necessary to make the access effective.

    **ii.**   **Right-of-access issue avoided:**   *Houchins*, like *Pell* and *Saxbe*, did not resolve the issue of whether the *public itself* has any *right of minimal access* to prisons. This issue is still an undecided one, though the *Richmond Newspapers* case, *infra*, p. 639, may indicate that the Court is now prepared to recognize a limited right of access, on the part of both public and press, to information about the operations of government.

**2.**   **Access to pretrial proceedings:**   Since trial judges are not permitted to issue pretrial "gag orders" in order to preserve the defendant's right to an unbiased jury (see *Nebraska Press Ass'n v. Stuart, supra*, p. 602), some have instead *closed pretrial proceedings to the public*. In *Gannett Co. v. DePasquale*, 443 U.S. 368 (1979), the Court held that such pre-trial closure orders are at least *sometimes constitutional*, and may even have held that the press and public *never* have a First Amendment right to attend such pretrial proceedings.

**3.**   **Closure of criminal trials:**   One key question left unresolved by *Gannett* was whether a criminal defendant's interest in a fair trial could be preserved by *closing the entire trial* to the public. In *Richmond Newspapers, Inc. v. Virginia*, 448 U.S. 555 (1980), the Court answered this question largely in the negative, holding that "absent an *overriding interest* articulated in findings," the First Amendment requires that "[t]he *trial of a criminal case must be open to the public*." Although the vote was 7-1, there was no majority opinion, and the precise scope of the decision remains unclear.

    **a.**   **Significance of case:**   At a minimum, *Richmond Newspapers* establishes that the public and press have a First Amendment right to attend criminal trials, and that entire trials can be closed only if that right is outweighed by *overriding* interests which *cannot be satisfied by less restrictive means*. Whether the decision means more than that is not clear.

       **i.**   **Civil trials:**   It seems probable that the decision is also applicable to *civil trials*, since such trials, like criminal ones, have traditionally been open to the public, and since there is a strong public interest in observing the administration of civil jus-tice. Several of the Justices in *Richmond Newspapers* specifically stated that they believed the decision to be applicable to such civil proceedings.

       **ii.**   **Pretrial context:**   The First Amendment right of access to criminal trials recog-nized in *Richmond Newspapers* has been extended to certain *pretrial proceedings*. For instance, the public has a right to attend the *voir dire* of the jury; see *Press Enterprise Co. v. Superior Court*, 467 U.S. 501 (1984).

iii. **Closure of portions of trial:** Trial judges presumably retain their traditional power to close *certain portions* of a criminal trial in order to protect the integrity of the proceedings. For instance, testimony of a particular witness might be held outside of the presence of the public, in order to prevent other witnesses from hearing his testimony and adjusting their own to match it (though sequestration of subsequent witnesses is a preferable technique for solving this problem). Also, any trial proceedings *not held in the presence of the jury* (e.g., discussions of the admissibility of evidence) probably may be closed to the public.

iv. **Limited seats:** Also, the right of access to public trials does not mean that *every* person who desires to see a particular trial has a right to do so. Obviously, courtrooms have limited seating, and a trial judge may use a reasonable scheme of allocating seats. However, the First Amendment right recognized by *Richmond Newspapers* probably does require that *at least some seats be given to media representatives*.

4. **Less-restrictive alternative required:** Although *Richmond Newspapers* established that there is a First Amendment right to access to criminal trials, *no* Justice suggested that that right is an *absolute* one. The test for determining when that right is outweighed by other countervailing interests has been developed in later cases.

a. *Globe Newspapers:* In *Globe Newspapers v. Superior Court*, 457 U.S. 596 (1982), the Court applied what amounted to a traditional *strict scrutiny* standard: access to criminal trials may be denied only if the denial is "necessitated by a *compelling governmental interest*, and is *narrowly tailored to serve that interest*." Under this test, a Massachusetts statute was unconstitutional in *requiring* the exclusion of the press and public from the courtroom during the testimony of any minor who is allegedly the victim of a sex offense.

G. **Regulation of broadcast media:** The Supreme Court has always recognized that the *broadcast* media may be subject to *closer regulation* than newspapers and other non-broadcasters. As noted *supra*, p. 539, the closer regulation of broadcasters derives from the fact that broadcast frequencies are a *naturally scarce* commodity — whereas there can in theory be an unlimited number of newspapers serving any particular market, the technology of broadcasting is such that there could only be a strictly limited number of television and radio stations serving any particular market. (This distinction is, in practical terms, much less convincing in today's world of cable television, UHF television, massive FM as well as AM radio, etc., than it was when broadcasting was largely limited to VHF television and AM radio. But the Court has not fundamentally altered its willingness to tolerate closer regulation of the broadcast media.)

1. **Means of regulation:** This regulation has generally been carried on through the Federal Communications Commission (FCC). The Court has several times sustained the FCC's power to ensure various types of *public access* to the broadcast media. See, e.g., *Red Lion Broadcasting Co. v. FCC, supra*, p. 539, in which the Court upheld the FCC's "fairness" doctrine, by which broadcasters are compelled to grant individuals the right to reply on the air to political editorials or personal attacks. Similarly, the Court is probably more willing to tolerate closer regulation of *context* where the source of speech is a broadcaster; this is indicated by the *Pacifica* case (*supra*, p. 520), in which the Court permitted the FCC to

ban language that was "indecent" (but not "obscene") from the airwaves during afternoon hours when children were likely to be in the audience.

2. **"Mere rationality" review for content-neutral regulations:**  Where regulations against broadcasters are *content-neutral*, these regulations are judged very deferentially, essentially according to the "mere rationality" standard. For instance, *Red Lion, supra*, seems to have applied "mere rationality" review to the FCC's fairness doctrine, on the theory that that doctrine is essentially content-neutral.

3. **Middle-level scrutiny for content-based restrictions:**  However, where the regulation against broadcasters is *content-based*, the Court seems to apply a *middle-level scrutiny*, more stringent than "mere rationality." But even here the standard of review reflects the Court's view that broadcasters should be subjected to tighter regulation because of their access to scarce airwaves: the mid-level review given to content-based broadcasting regulations is clearly less stringent than the "strict" (and almost always fatal) review given to content-based regulations against newspapers and other non-broadcasters. (See *supra*, p. 467.) This middle-level scrutiny was demonstrated in *FCC v. League of Women Voters*, 468 U.S. 364 (1984), a 5-4 decision.

   a. **Ban on editorializing struck down:**  In *League of Women Voters*, the Court struck down (by a 5-4 vote), a congressional prohibition on *editorializing* by public broadcasters who receive federal funding. The majority viewed the ban as being non-content-neutral. The test set forth by the Court was that such restrictions impinging on broadcasters' First Amendment rights will be upheld only if they are *"narrowly tailored* to further a *substantial governmental interest*, such as ensuring adequate and balanced coverage of public issues. … "

   b. **Test not satisfied:**  The Court concluded that the ban on editorializing could not survive this middle-level review. For instance, Congress may have had a substantial governmental interest in making sure that public broadcasters did not become "vehicles for governmental propagandizing" as the result of federal funding, but there were other, more narrowly-tailored, ways of making sure that government did not interfere with the broadcasting judgment of station officials.

4. **Cable gets greater free speech:**  The Court has held that *cable* television is, in effect, *somewhere between broadcast TV and newspapers* in terms of the amount of government regulation of speech that operators must tolerate.

   a. **Content-neutral regulation:** Thus where the regulation of cable TV is *content-neutral*, *mid-level review* is to be used. In *Turner Broadcasting System, Inc. v. FCC*, 512 U.S. 622 (1994) (*"Turner I"*), the Court held that where cable TV operators are subjected to content-neutral regulations, mid-level review, not the easy-to-satisfy "mere rationality" standard used in the over-the-air broadcast cases, should be used.

      i. **Regulations upheld:**  But content-neutral governmental regulation of cable TV certainly can sometimes *pass* constitutional muster, even though mid-level rather than rational-relation review is used. For instance, Congress has enacted "must carry" provisions, which require cable TV systems to devote some of their channels, free of charge, to the retransmission of local broadcast TV stations. In a successor to *Turner I, supra*, the Court upheld these must-carry rules after mid-level review. The Court gave special deference to Congress' legislative findings on the need for must-carry, because Congress was better equipped than the judiciary to "amass and evaluate the ***vast amounts of data***" bearing on legislative questions, especially ones concerning "regulatory schemes of the ***inherent complexity***" and "assessments about the likely interaction of ***industries undergoing rapid economic and technological change***." *Turner Broadcasting System Inc. v. FCC*, 520 U.S. 180 (1997) (*"Turner II"*).

b. **Content-based regulation:** Where cable TV operators and programmers are regulated in a ***content-based*** way, ***strict scrutiny*** must be used. See *U.S. v. Playboy Entertainment Group, Inc.*, 529 U.S. 803 (2000), discussed *supra*, p. 508.

*Quiz Yourself on*

## FREEDOM OF ASSOCIATION; DENIAL OF PUBLIC JOBS OR BENEFITS; SPECIAL PROBLEMS OF THE MEDIA

**83.** There have been several bombings of government office buildings on the island of Puerto Rico recently. After each bombing, an anonymous caller has told the local newspaper that the bomb was planted by "People for a Free Puerto Rico" (PFPR), an organization dedicated to using any means necessary to end Puerto Rico's status as a United States territory and establishing it as a sovereign nation. There is evidence that the PFPR was able to plant the bombs so successfully inside the buildings because its members or sympathizers have jobs in government agencies located in those buildings, who could furnish information and access for placement of the bombs. To deal with the threat, the territorial government of Puerto Rico has now imposed a requirement that any new applicant for any government position must before being hired sign a loyalty oath stating, among other things, that "I am not a member of the People for a Free Puerto Rico or of any group advocating the use of force to alter the territorial status of Puerto Rico." Ramona, an applicant for a position as a clerical worker in the Puerto Rican government, has declined to sign the oath, without specifying her reasons. Can the government constitutionally decline to hire her on the grounds that she has refused to sign? _____

**84.** Sheryl was a low-level clerk in her state's Department of Motor Vehicles. News reports were published stating that Horace, the Commissioner of the Department of Motor Vehicles (and thus, ultimately, Sheryl's boss) may have taken payments from Computer Systems Inc. in return for helping Computer Systems get a contract to install a large new computer system at the Department. Horace protested his innocence, and the District Attorney eventually decided that no charges should be brought. Shortly thereafter, Sheryl said to a co-worker, while on the job, "I still think Horace took the money, and I think he's a crook." Another employee who overheard the remark reported it to Horace, who immediately fired Sheryl for insubordination and fomenting discord in the Department. Under the relevant Civil Service rules, Sheryl was an at-will employee who had no reason to expect continued employment. Sheryl now seeks a court order restoring her position, on the grounds that she was fired in violation of her First Amendment rights. Should the court grant reinstatement to Sheryl? _____

**85.** The cable TV franchise for the town of Harmony was up for award. No state or municipal statute prescribed procedures by which the franchise was to be awarded. The Town Council decided to authorize the Mayor to negotiate a contract that would "deliver good TV service to the people of Harmony"; the Mayor was not required to make his selection based on who would deliver the cheapest service, or any other specific criteria. The mayor awarded the contract to Harmony Cable, a company newly set up by Norman, one of the Mayor's most fervent campaign supporters. Harmony Cable and Norman had no pertinent cable TV expertise, though Norman owned a local radio station. Experienced Cable Co., which held the cable franchise for a neighboring town, also sought the Harmony contract. However, the Mayor declined to award Experienced the contract even though (he conceded) it had more expertise than Harmony Cable; he explained his decision by saying, "I don't think the owners of Experienced will back my next re-election campaign, and I know Norman will." Experienced now brings a federal-court suit for damages against the town and the Mayor, alleging that its First Amendment rights of association have been violated under color of law. Will Experienced win? _____

**86.** P.J. Summers, a former football player turned sports announcer, was charged with the brutal murder of his wife. While in police custody, Summers gave a confession. In pretrial hearings, the trial judge determined that the *Miranda* rules had not been complied with, and decided that the confession would not be admissible at the trial. The press learned of the confession through pretrial proceedings in open court, and did not act improperly in obtaining this information. Prosecutors decided to try Summers as a principal in the murder, and also decided to charge B.C. Scowling, a long-time friend of Summers, as an accomplice. Both trials were to be held simultaneously (but in front of separate juries) in proceedings conducted by Judge Jones.

Judge Jones was very worried that disclosures about the confession might make it difficult or impossible to impanel a jury that would be fair to Summers. Therefore, several days before jury selection was to start, Jones issued two orders from the bench: (1) he ordered that no newspaper, magazine or broadcaster report the existence or details of the inadmissible confession until after the jury had been picked (once the jury was picked, it could be sequestered, so that prejudicial disclosures would not matter anymore); (2) he also ordered that no lawyer on the case, including the lawyer for Scowling, disclose to the press or to anyone else the existence of Summers' confession. (There was reason to believe that Scowlings' lawyer planned to say in a public press conference, "My client is innocent; P.J. confessed, and in his confession he said that he acted alone").

   **(a)** Is the judge's order in part (1) constitutional? _____

   **(b)** Is the judge's order in part (2) constitutional? _____

**87.** Roger is a reporter for the Hillsdale Star, a local newspaper. In the most celebrated crime to hit Hillsdale in many years, Joshua, an eight-year-old boy, was found strangled in front of his house. The police have not found any suspects. One week after the killing, Roger published an article saying, "A source that I cannot identify saw the crime from a distance, and believes that the perpetrator was a young white male about 22 years old, six feet tall, weighing about 175 pounds." In the ensuing months, the police have never been able to find this or any other witness to the crime. The prosecutor called Roger in front of a grand jury, and demanded that he identify the witness who served as his source. Roger stated under oath that the witness was fearful that the killer would kill her to silence her. Roger further stated that he had signed a written pledge to the witness that he would never reveal her name; only in response to this pledge did the witness agree to speak to him. Roger did say, however, that the witness lived in the neighborhood and that in his opinion, she could be identified by good police work. The judge then ordered Roger to disclose the witness' identity, or be found in contempt of court. Roger refused. There is no state law relevant to the issue. Can Roger constitutionally be found in contempt and imprisoned until he divulges the name of the witness? _____

---

## Answers

**83. No.** One may not be required to state in a loyalty oath that one has not performed a certain act (or that one will not perform it in the future) unless *actual performance* of that act would be grounds for discharge. One may not be discharged for membership in an organization advocating overthrow of the government or other illegality, unless one has ***knowledge*** of the organization's purpose and ***specific intent*** to further that purpose. Consequently, one may not be required to swear a blanket oath that one has not been a member of such an organization — language referring to the swearer's knowledge of the illegal purposes, and to her specific intent to further them, must be inserted into the oath. Since the oath here does not refer to Ramona's specific intent to use force to alter the Puerto Rican government, she cannot be penalized for refusing to sign it. See *Cole v. Richardson*.

84. **Yes, probably.** When government attempts to deny a public job or benefit because of a person's speech-related activities, the level of judicial review depends on whether the speech related to matters of ***"public concern."*** If the speech did relate to matters of "public concern," then the Court gives something like strict scrutiny to the situation, striking a balance between the free speech rights of the employee and the state's interest as an employer in conducting its activities efficiently. *Connick v. Myers*. Here, the speech is clearly relating to a matter of public concern, i.e., whether the head of the department took a bribe. Since Sheryl was engaging in core political speech, her interest in being allowed to do so was a strong one. On the other side of the equation, Sheryl was a low-level clerk, not a policy-making official; therefore, her speech was unlikely to have created a severe additional threat to the department's efficiency, especially since other people inside and outside the department were undoubtedly discussing the same much-publicized issue anyway. *Rankin v. McPherson*. Consequently, a court would probably conclude that Sheryl's free speech interest outweighed the department's interest in maintaining smooth operations; if so, the court should order Sheryl reinstated.

By the way, it makes a difference that here, Sheryl's statement was ***not required as part of her job duties.*** *Garcetti v. Ceballos* establishes that where an employee speaks as part of her official duties, what she says ***gets no First Amendment protection at all.*** So if, say, Sheryl's official duties had included the obligation to make a report about any conflicts-of-interest she observed on the job, her statement, "Horace took money from Computer Systems in violation of our Department's conflict-of-interest rules," made in her officially-required report, would not get First Amendment protection, and Sheryl would now not be entitled to reinstatement. So it's only because Sheryl was speaking "as a citizen" (not as an employee) to her co-worker that she gets protection under *Connick v. Myers*.

Lastly, observe that because Sheryl was an at-will employee, she could be fired at any time for "no reason"; even so, under *Connick* she had a First Amendment right not to be fired for the ***particular*** reason that she was exercising her free speech rights.

85. **Yes, probably.** *O'Hare Truck Svc. v. Northlake* establishes that the same rules restricting when party affiliation or the like can be considered for purposes of public employment also apply to the awarding of ***independent contracts*** between government and private parties. Therefore, the rule that party affiliation may only be considered if it's an "appropriate requirement for effective performance" (*Branti v. Finkel*) applies. Here, it's very unlikely that the political affiliation of the cable TV franchisee is an "appropriate requirement" for effectively delivering cable TV services. So unless the town can show that the Mayor would probably have reached the same decision had he not considered the political affiliations of the two bidders (something it's unlikely to be able to show on these facts), Experienced will win.

86. **(a) No.** "Gag orders" — that is, pretrial orders prohibiting the press from publishing certain types of information about the case — are virtually never constitutionally permissible. See *Nebraska Press Ass'n v. Stuart*. A gag order is a species of prior restraint, so it can be allowed only if its benefits substantially outweigh its First Amendment dangers, something that will virtually never happen. Here, there are other methods available to the judge to help assure a fair trial (e.g., careful *voir dire* to make sure that each juror has either not heard about the confession or understands that it is to be absolutely disregarded). (A gag

order might be allowed if the press had ***illegally*** gotten the information, e.g., by bribing a member of the police department to release sealed information; but where the press comes by the information legally, a gag order preventing it from disseminating the material will almost never be upheld.)

**(b) Yes, probably.** States may prevent a lawyer from making any statement that would have a ***"substantial likelihood of materially prejudicing"*** an adjudicative proceeding. *Gentile v. State Bar of Nevada.* The state must give guidelines that are reasonably specific about what kinds of disclosures are and are not allowed. The ban here, which refers specifically to the facts of the confession, seems to have adequate specificity. While some sorts of gag orders might unconstitutionally restrict a defense lawyer's right to defend his client in the public eye (e.g., the states probably can't prevent a lawyer from asserting that his client is innocent, or from generally describing the client's proposed defense), references to a co-defendant's inadmissible confession are probably the sort of unduly prejudicial remarks that a lawyer falling within the court's jurisdiction may be barred from making.

**87. Yes.** The First Amendment is not violated when a reporter is required to testify before a grand jury concerning information obtained from confidential sources during newsgathering. In fact, reporters are not even entitled to a ***qualified privilege*** to refuse to identify their sources or information received from those sources — thus a reporter, like any other citizen, may be required to divulge information that could be obtained by police or prosecutors from other sources. *Branzburg v. Hayes.* (Over half of the states have enacted ***statutes*** that grant reporters a privilege against disclosure of confidential sources or information. If such a "shield law" existed here, it would prevent Roger from being held in contempt on these facts.)

## *Exam Tips* on *FREEDOM OF EXPRESSION*

Freedom of expression typically makes up a larger portion of a full-year Con. Law exam than does any other single topic. Almost any regulation of an individual's conduct may pose a free expression issue, so think very broadly. Here are some particular things to keep in mind:

☛ Remember that free expression issues are posed not just where government is regulating "speech" but also where government is regulating ***"conduct"*** that includes an ***expressive component***. So for each activity that's being restricted, first deal with the issue: "Is there an expressive component to the activity?" If you answer "yes," you've got a free expression issue. (*Example:* Panhandling on the subway has been held to be expressive — and thus protected — conduct.)

☛ Once you've identified a situation where government is "substantially impairing" speech or expressive conduct, decide whether the regulation is ***"content-neutral"*** or not.

    ☞ A tip to help you decide: Ask whether the harm the government is trying to prevent would exist to the same degree if the listener/reader didn't understand English. If the answer is "no," the government's action is probably content-based.

    ☞ Always consider the government's ***motive*** in regulating the speech — the issue is what the government wished to do: did it want to suppress/control ideas, or did it really want to regulate "secondary" concerns not related to the expressive content?

☛ If you decide that the regulation is "content-based," apply ***strict scrutiny***. That is, write that the regulation must be struck down unless the government shows that the restriction is ***necessary*** to achieve a ***compelling*** governmental purpose. You should almost always then conclude that the government restriction can't survive. (Usually, the key reason will be that there is some less restrictive way to deal with the problem, even if that less restrictive way is not an absolutely perfect way of handling the problem.)

  ☞ One commonly-tested scenario: A public school district allows community groups to use the school for their own purposes after hours. A particular group is denied access because of the type of activity, or because of the group's controversial views. (Typically, you should conclude that the restriction here is content-based, and therefore apply strict scrutiny.)

  ☞ For a regulation to be "content-neutral," the regulation must be more than just ***"viewpoint"*** neutral. "Content neutral" means "without reference to the content." For instance, restrictions that put ***whole topics*** off limits usually are not content-neutral. (*Example:* If a city requires a permit for political demonstrations, but does not require one for sports victory celebrations, then the distinction is not content-neutral, because the general type of speech or emotion being expressed serves as the basis for imposing or not imposing the permit requirement.)

☛ If you conclude that the regulation is truly "content-neutral," use a three-part test. For instance, any regulation of the ***"time, place and manner"*** of demonstrations or other expressive conduct will be analyzed by this test if you find that it is content-neutral. Here are the three parts (***all*** of which must be satisfied):

  ☞ The regulation must serve a "***significant*** governmental interest";

  ☞ The regulation must be ***narrowly tailored*** to achieve that objective; and

  ☞ The regulation must leave open adequate ***alternative channels*** for communication.

*Note:* Of these three, the "narrowly tailored" requirement is the one most commonly violated — if there is some ***less restrictive means*** available for dealing with the problem, that means must usually be selected. (However, the less restrictive means probably counts only if it is truly ***"as effective,"*** not just "almost as effective," as the means chosen by government. This makes it hard for the plaintiff challenging the restriction to establish that the "narrowly tailored" requirement has been violated. Cf. *Rumsfeld v. FAIR*.)

*Note:* In assessing a "time, place and manner" restriction, consider whether a ***public forum*** is involved. The "narrowly tailored" and "alternative channels left open" requirements are ***more strictly construed when a public forum is involved.*** (The public forum is discussed further below.)

☛ Always consider whether either of two key First Amendment doctrines applies:

  ☞ First, ***overbreadth***. Remember that most litigants in Con. Law are not permitted to assert the rights of others. But under First Amendment overbreadth, P is allowed to assert that the government regulation violates the rights of a person who is not now before the court. (*Example:* A city bans the sale of "sexually explicit" materials. P is charged with violating the statute. The materials sold by him are clearly obscene. Yet, he can defeat the prosecution by showing that the ban also applies to non-obscene sexually explicit materials, which cannot be constitutionally prohibited.)

☞ Second, *vagueness*. Remember, a statute or regulation is unconstitutionally vague if a person of normal intelligence wouldn't know whether the action in question was forbidden or not. (*Examples:* Statutes forbidding conduct that is "demeaning," "offensive," or "disruptive to public order" might all be found to be unconstitutionally vague, because it is not clear where the line is between what they do and do not proscribe.)

☛ Many exam questions involve a speaker who tries to rouse the crowd to take *subversive* or *illegal action*. Be on the lookout for persons charged with "inciting to riot," "urging the overthrow of the government," "advocating illegal conduct," or the like. When you have such a fact pattern, check for three things:

☞ Was the riot or illegality *imminent*, as opposed to something that would take place at a later date? Only speech urging imminent illegality may be punished. (*Example:* If the speaker says, "Start thinking about forming guerrilla units … ," the required imminence is not present.)

☞ Was the advocacy *intended* to produce illegality? (If illegality was the *unintended by-product* of the speaker's speech, he can't be punished for it.)

☞ Was the advocacy *likely* to produce the illegality? Ineffectual efforts don't count. (*Example:* If people are in a park for other purposes, happen to listen to the speaker, and then go about their business, the "likely to produce illegality" requirement probably is not met.)

☛ When government attempts to require a *license* or *permit* before expressive activity (typically a speech or demonstration) may occur, here are the things to check for:

☞ Make sure that the license/permit requirement is truly *content-neutral*, both as written (i.e., "on the face" of the statute) and as applied (i.e., as the permits are actually handed out by officials). A permit/license requirement cannot be used as a smoke-screen for suppressing unpopular views or unpopular topics.

☞ Make sure that the scheme does not give *excessive discretion* to the official charged with issuing the permit. (*Example:* If the fact pattern tells you that the permit is to be issued "based on the Police Commissioner's overall assessment of the good of the community," that's excessive discretion.) This is a commonly tested aspect.

☞ Profs frequently test on whether a speaker has a right to *ignore* a permit requirement.

☞ If the permit requirement is unconstitutional *on its face* (e.g., it's content-based, in that it requires a permit for certain topics but not others), the speaker is *not* required to apply for a permit. He may decline to apply, speak, and then defend on the grounds of the permit requirement's unconstitutionality.

☞ But if the permit is not facially invalid, only unconstitutional *as applied* to the speaker, then the speaker generally does *not* have the right to ignore the requirement. He must apply for the permit, then seek prompt judicial review rather than just going ahead and speaking. (But an exception exists where the applicant shows that *sufficiently prompt judicial review* of the denial was not available.)

☞ When the speaker is judicially *enjoined* from speaking, marching, etc., he generally may *not* ignore the injunction and then raise the constitution as a defense in a subsequent contempt proceeding. Instead, he must seek prior judicial review.

☞ If the above requirements are satisfied, then the permit requirement is valid. (*Example:* A permit will not be invalid merely because it is issued upon conditions that the marchers or demonstrators not block the public's access to a particular place, e.g., an abortion clinic or government building.)

☞ Be on the lookout for expression that may constitute *"fighting words."* These are words that are likely to induce the addressee to *commit an act of violence*, typically against the speaker. Government may forbid fighting words, or punish them after they are spoken.

☞ But be skeptical of claims by the government that the speech in question really constituted "fighting words." Most importantly, remember that the police must *control the crowd* if they have the ability to do so — they can't stand back, then punish the speaker for rousing the crowd to violence.

☞ Also, distinguish fighting words from mere *"offensive speech."* Speech may not be forbidden merely because the listeners are likely to find it offensive. (*Examples:* Nazis demonstrating in front of Holocaust survivors, or black students calling white students "honkey" at a public university, are probably not using "fighting words," merely "offensive speech" — unless the circumstances made violence very likely, the speech cannot be forbidden.)

☞ Look out for attempts to restrict *"hate speech."* A *broad ban* on *all fighting words* is OK. So is a broad ban on all words or acts intended to *harass* or *intimidate* others. Government can even single outs certain intimidating acts and forbid them (e.g., *cross burnings*, when done as a threat or intimidation), while declining to forbid other intimidating acts (e.g., burnings in effigy). But government *can't forbid just those fighting words or threats that are motivated by particular kinds of hatred* (e.g., racial or gender hatred). (Cite to *R.A.V. v. St. Paul* on this point.)

**Example:** University, a public university, passes a speech code that says "All students are forbidden to harass or threaten other students on the basis of race, gender, or sexual orientation. Violations are punishable by suspension." Since the code bans just certain types of harassment or threats (those based on race, gender and sexual orientation) and not others (e.g., those based on political affiliation), the code is a content-based regulation, and must be strictly scrutinized. It will probably fail that scrutiny, since there are content-neutral alternatives that are less restrictive of speech and will do the job almost as well (e.g., a code banning *all* harassments and threats, regardless of the speaker's motive).

☞ Speech cannot be banned on the mere grounds that it is *profane*. This merely makes it "offensive," not "obscene" or "fighting words." (*Example:* D can wear a jacket saying, "Fuck the Draft." Cite to *Cohen v. California*.)

☞ Whenever you're dealing with a ban on "offensive" conduct or "harassment," consider the possibility that there may be a *vagueness* problem with the regulation.

☛ Whenever your fact pattern involves a restriction on speech that takes place in a *public forum*, note this fact, and try to explain what difference it makes.

☞ The fact that the expressive conduct is taking place in a public forum only makes a difference if the regulation is content-neutral. Assuming that it is content-neutral, the principal difference is that we use *mid-level review* (the restriction must be narrowly drawn to serve a significant governmental interest, while leaving open adequate alternative channels for the communication) as opposed to "mere rationality" review for non-public-forum speech.

☞ The classic *"traditional"* public forums are: *streets*, *sidewalks*, *parks*. There are also *"designated"* public forums, where government has decided to open the place to a broad range of expressive activity (e.g., an open City Council meeting or a school whose classrooms are made available after hours to any community group); the same rules apply to designated forums as to true forums, except that government can change its mind and make the place a non-public forum.

☞ The mere fact that something is public property does not mean it is a public or designated-public forum. There are public spaces that are *"non-public forums,"* as to which "mere rationality" review is all that is used. (*Examples:* Airport terminals, jails, military bases, courthouses, government office buildings.)

☞ But even in a non-public forum, regulation must still be *rational* and *viewpoint-neutral*. Be especially alert for a violation of viewpoint-neutrality when government *excludes religious groups* from benefits that it gives to a wide range of non-religious groups.

**Example:** A school district allows a variety of local community groups to use elementary school classrooms after hours to run programs promoting the "general welfare." However, the district excludes from this program any activity or group that is "primarily of a religious nature." This will be unconstitutional viewpoint-based discrimination, even though school classrooms used this way are probably a non-public forum.

☛ Fact patterns often involve speech that takes place on *private property*. Here are the two aspects that are most frequently tested:

☞ The *public* has no First Amendment right of access to private property. (*Example:* A person does not have a First Amendment right to distribute literature in a privately-owned shopping center.)

☞ Government may limit an owner's right to use, or to rent his property to others, for expressive purposes. Here, use standard "time, place and manner" analysis, except that no public forum is involved. Therefore, the regulation will usually be upheld if it is content-neutral and other avenues are left for the message. (*Example:* Government may prevent owners from putting signage on their property advertising their wares, as long as the ban applies to all types of signage, and there are other advertising channels available.)

☞ The same rules apply to regulation of *"symbolic* expression" as apply to speech and speech-mixed-with-conduct. "Symbolic expression" refers to *non-verbal acts*.

   ☞ For instance, if government wants to ban destruction of the flag, it must do so in a content-neutral way (e.g., it cannot ban flag burning that is intended as a means of political dissent while allowing flag burning that is intended as a means of destroying worn-out flags).

☞ Remember that when the government regulates *defamation*, there are First Amendment limitations:

   ☞ Most important, under *New York Times v. Sullivan*, if P is a **public official** or **public figure**, he may only win a defamation suit against D for a statement relating to P's official conduct if P can prove that D's statement was made either "with *knowledge* that it was false" or "with *reckless disregard*" of whether it was true or false. Use the phrase "actual malice" to describe this requirement.

   ☞ Be sure to examine whether the plaintiff is truly a public or, rather, private figure. If P is a private figure, he merely has to prove negligence rather than "actual malice."

   ☞ Remember that in an action for "intentional infliction of emotional distress," P must, similarly, follow *New York Times v. Sullivan* and prove "actual malice," if P is a public figure.

☞ *Obscenity* is frequently tested. Here are some of the most commonly-tested sub-issues:

   ☞ The relevant standard is the *"community"* standard — if the relevant sale and trial take place in a small town in Kansas, what counts is whether the average member of that town would find that the work as a whole appeals to the "prurient" interest.

   ☞ The fact that the work shows *nakedness* is not enough — there must be real or simulated sex that is described or portrayed.

   ☞ The fact that D, the seller of the obscene material, has engaged in *"pandering"* is relevant on the issue of whether the material appeals primarily to "prurient interests." D has "pandered" if he has marketed the goods by emphasizing their sexually provocative nature (e.g., by using sexually explicit advertising, packaging materials, etc.).

   ☞ Remember that no matter how obscene the work is, its *private possession* by an adult in the privacy of his own home cannot be punished. (But the *seller* can still be punished.)

   ☞ Be sure to distinguish between material that is truly "obscene," and material that's merely *"indecent."* Mere nakedness, for instance, doesn't make something obscene (e.g., because of the possibility that the material may have artistic or social value, or because the material may not be "patently offensive.")

      ☞ So if government tries to regulate "indecency," indicate that the material gets First Amendment protection and that government has to satisfy strict scrutiny.

      *Example:* Congress prohibits the furnishing of "indecent" material on the Internet, hoping to keep this stuff away from minors. You should apply strict scrutiny, and strike down the restriction, because the total ban is overbroad — the ban covers material that could be proscribed because it's obscene, but also material that's not obscene and thus protected as to adults. Cite to *Reno v. ACLU.*

Same analysis if Congress, trying to avoid having minors access indecent material, says that a Web site can show such material only if the user is required to provide proof that he is an adult; this will flunk strict scrutiny if a less-restrictive and equally-effective alternative — say, user-installed filtering — is available. Cite to *Ashcroft v. ACLU.*

☞ But government has a relatively free hand to regulate the *"secondary effects"* of indecent speech. (*Example:* A town can ban live nude dancing if it reasonably believes that nude dancing establishments contribute to increased drug use, prostitution, etc.)

☛ Ascertain whether the regulated speech is *"commercial"* (as opposed to core political) speech. Commercial speech is speech proposing a sale or other commercial transaction. Here are the things to remember about regulation of commercial speech:

☞ If the commercial speech is truthful and proposes a *legal* transaction, the Court uses mid-level review. The restriction survives only if it: (1) *directly advances* (2) a *substantial* governmental interest (3) in a way that is *"not more extensive than is necessary"* to achieve the government's objective. This is true even if the regulation is *content-based*. (So it's somewhat easier for government to do content-based regulation of commercial speech than of non-commercial speech, as to which strict scrutiny has to be used.)

☞ If the speech is *false, deceptive* or proposes an *illegal transaction*, government can *flatly ban* it.

☞ Profs frequently test on whether the government may prohibit or regulate truthful advertising about products that are *harmful* but *lawful*. Generally, this regulation gets mid-level review, which it will often *flunk* because *substantially less-restrictive means are available*. (*Examples:* If government tries to prohibit or tightly regulate truthful advertising for *cigarettes*, *liquor* or *gambling*, the Court is likely to say that less-restrictive means like educational campaigns, or higher taxes, must first be tried. Cite to *Lorillard*, the Mass. case that banned outdoor tobacco advertising, on this point.)

☞ Restrictions on *lawyer advertising* are often tested. Except for some *in-person solicitation* by profit-motivated lawyers seeking clients, states generally can't block truthful advertising. (*Example:* States can't block a public interest lawyer or advocacy group from soliciting clients, even through direct mail or in-person contacts.)

☛ If the regulation is of *public school students*, state that the courts apply a "balancing" test: the student has a limited right of free speech, to be balanced against the administration's right to carry out its educational mission and to maintain discipline. (So officials may not suppress students' speech merely because they disagree with it on ideological or political grounds, but they may ban profanity, or ban school-newspaper stories that would disturb the school's educational mission, such as stories about sex.)

☞ If you have a fact pattern that involves ***group activity*** of an expressive nature, refer to the protected ***"freedom of association."*** (*Example:* If a group gets together and pursues class action litigation, their right to do so is protected by the associational freedom.)

  ☞ Remember that there's also a "right ***not*** to associate"; for instance, a group can't be required to take unwanted members whose presence will detract from the group's expressive activities. (*Example:* The NAACP can't be forced to accept white supremacists as members.)

☞ Many fact patterns involve the denial of ***public jobs or benefits*** to persons based upon their expressive conduct. This is a very commonly tested area. Here are some key aspects to keep in mind:

  ☞ In general, the standard for whether government may refuse to hire, or may fire, based on expressive conduct is the same as for when government may ***prosecute***. (*Example:* Since a person may not be prosecuted for belonging to an organization unless there is a showing that he had the specific intent to further the organization's illegal aims, so a person may not be fired for belonging to the organization without such a showing of specific intent.)

  ☞ A person may be required to sign a ***loyalty oath*** as a condition for getting or keeping a public job, but he may not be forced to promise to refrain from doing anything that he would be constitutionally permitted to do. (*Example:* You may be forced to sign a loyalty oath that you have not belonged to the Communist Party while specifically intending to further the overthrow of the government, but you may not be required to sign a loyalty oath stating simply that you do not belong to the Communist Party — since you can't be prosecuted for mere membership without specific intent to further illegal aims, you can't be forced to sign a loyalty oath that you won't be a mere member.)

  ☞ There is an ***exception*** to these limits: you can be deprived of expressive freedom where the expression would truly interfere with your ***job performance***. (*Example:* Civil servants can be forced to choose between their jobs and engaging in partisan political activities, since there's a strong governmental interest in making sure that civil servants don't get coerced into campaigning for their elected bosses.)

    ☞ Where a public ***benefit*** as opposed to a job is at stake, there is no "performance" exception, and it's hard for government to restrict free speech. (*Example:* A person's right to continue as a tenant in public housing, or to receive welfare payments, generally can't be made contingent upon their forfeiting their freedom of expression, because they generally don't have a "performance" obligation that would be impaired by pursuit of expressive conduct or speech.)

    ☞ If the plaintiff does work as an ***independent contractor*** of government, instead of as an employee, indicate that the ***same rules apply*** (i.e., P can't be deprived of the contract unless P's speech or association would ***interfere with his/its performance***). (*Example:* If P is a corporation with a garbage-hauling contract with City, the contract can't be terminated because P criticizes the mayor, or because P's president does not belong to the same political party as the mayor.)

☞ If your question involves restrictions placed on the ***media*** (publishers or broadcasters), there are some special considerations:

☞ If the governmental action consists of a ***prior restraint***, you should almost certainly conclude that the restraint is not valid. For instance, if the government is trying to get an injunction against a newspaper that will publish a story, it's almost impossible for the government to succeed.

☞ The media must obey a ***subpoena*** (e.g., to give information to a grand jury) pretty much the same as a private citizen must.

☞ The press does not get any special ***right of access*** to government-held information, beyond what the public as a whole has.

☞ Some issues turn on the ***type of media***:

    ☞ ***Over-the-air broadcast radio and tv*** may be subjected to somewhat greater ***time-place-and-manner regulation*** than print media, because these are scarce resources, and they are potentially intrusive (someone may stumble upon unwanted content while dial-turning).

    ☞ ***Print publications***, and the ***Internet***, by contrast, are neither scarce nor intrusive. So these media get ***very great freedom*** from time-place-and-manner regulation.

CHAPTER 15

# FREEDOM OF RELIGION

## *ChapterScope*

Here are the key concepts involving "freedom of religion":

- **Two clauses:** There are two distinct clauses in the First Amendment pertaining to religion:

  - **Establishment Clause:** First, there is the ***Establishment Clause***. That clause prohibits any law "respecting an establishment of religion." The main purpose of the Establishment Clause is to prevent government from ***endorsing*** or ***supporting*** religion.

  - **Free Exercise Clause:** The second clause is the ***Free Exercise*** Clause. That clause bars any law "prohibiting the free exercise of religion." The main purpose of the Free Exercise Clause is to prevent government from ***outlawing*** or seriously ***burdening*** a person's pursuit of whatever religion (and whatever religious practices) she chooses.

- **Applicable to states:** Both religious clauses, by their terms, apply only to action taken by ***Congress***. However, both clauses are interpreted to apply also to the ***states***, by means of the Fourteenth Amendment's Due Process Clause.

- **Establishment Clause:** The purpose of the Establishment Clause is to put a ***wall between church and state***. Mainly, this means that government must stay out of the business of religion. (*Example:* Government can't intentionally prefer one religion over another religion.)

  - **Three-part test:** Government action that has some relationship to religion will violate the Establishment Clause unless it satisfies ***all three parts*** of the following test:

    - **Purpose:** First, the government action must have a ***secular legislative purpose***.

    - **Effect:** Second, the government action's principal or ***primary effect*** must ***not be to advance*** religion. (But ***incidental effects*** helpful to religion do not violate this prong.)

    - **Entanglement:** Finally, the governmental action must not foster an ***excessive government entanglement*** with religion.

- **The Free Exercise Clause generally:** Under the Free Exercise Clause, the government is barred from making any law "prohibiting the free exercise" of religion. The Free Exercise Clause prevents the government from getting in the way of people's ability to practice their religions.

  - **Includes conduct:** The Free Exercise Clause prevents the government from unduly burdening both a person's abstract "beliefs" as well as a person's religiously-oriented ***conduct***. Most real-world problems relate to regulation affecting conduct.

    - **Non-religious objectives:** Free exercise problems most typically arise when government, acting in pursuit of ***non-religious objectives***, either: (1) forbids or burdens conduct which happens to be ***required*** by someone's religious beliefs; or (2) conversely, compels or encourages conduct which happens to be ***forbidden*** by someone's religious beliefs.

    - **Intentional vs. unintentional burdens:** The Free Exercise Clause prevents the government from unduly interfering with religion whether the government does so *intentionally* or *unintentionally.*

❏ **Intent:** If the interference is *intentional* on government's part, then the interference is subjected to the *most strict scrutiny*, and will virtually never survive.

❏ **Unintentional burden:** If the government *unintentionally burdens* religion, the Free Exercise Clause is still applied. Here, however, the Court uses a somewhat less stringent form of strict scrutiny. (In fact, if the government makes certain conduct a *crime*, and this unintentionally burdens the exercise of religion, the Court does not use strict scrutiny at all, and instead uses "mere rationality" review.)

❏ **Coercion required:** The Free Exercise Clause only gets triggered where government in some sense *"coerces"* an individual to do something (or not to do something) against the dictates of his religion. If the government takes an action that unintentionally happens to make it harder for a person to practice his religion — but without coercing him into taking or not taking some action as an individual — the Free Exercise Clause does not apply.

❏ **Exemptions required:** Because strict scrutiny is traditionally given even to unintentional impairments of religion, government *must give an exemption* to avoid such an unintentional interference with religion, if this could be done *without seriously impairing some compelling governmental interest.* (*Example:* The state may not deny unemployment benefits to a person who refuses to work on his religion's holy day.)

❏ **Criminal prohibition:** But a generally applicable *criminal law* is *automatically enforceable*, regardless of how much burden it causes to an individual's religious beliefs (assuming that the government did not *intend* to disadvantage a particular religion or religious practice when it enacted its law).

# I. INTRODUCTION

A. **Two clauses:** The First Amendment contains two distinct clauses designed to protect religious freedom. One is the *Establishment* Clause, which prohibits any law "respecting an establishment of religion." The other is the *Free Exercise* Clause, which bans laws "prohibiting the free exercise" of religion.

B. **General function of clauses:** These two clauses are designed to protect the same basic value, the freedom of every individual to worship (or not worship) as he wishes, without governmental interference. The two clauses have been summarized as requiring "that government neither engage in nor compel religious practices, that it effect no favoritism among sects or between religion and nonreligion, and that it work deterrence of no religious belief." *Abington School District v. Schempp*, 374 U.S. 203 (1963) (Goldberg, J. concurring).

C. **Conflict between clauses:** However, in some contexts the two clauses *conflict.*

1. **Illustration:** Consider, for instance, state financial assistance to private schools, including parochial schools. If such aid is given, a strong argument can be made that the Establishment Clause is violated, since government is assisting parochial schools in an activity that has a strong religious component. Yet if such aid is not given, while public schools are given large amounts of assistance, a claim can be made that students' free exercise of reli-

gion is infringed, because economic burdens force them to abandon parochial schools for public ones.

2. **No solution:** The Supreme Court has not yet found a precise way of harmonizing the two clauses. The Court has asserted that government rules must be *"neutral"* towards religion. But the Court has used the concept of neutrality in such a vague way that the term does not aid in the solution of any of the difficult cases of conflict between the clauses.

3. **Zone of permissible accommodation:** Tribe suggests that the Court's cases recognize a *"zone of permissible accommodation,"* a zone which "the Free Exercise Clause carves out of the Establishment Clause for permissible accommodation of religious interests." Tribe, p. 1169. Under this view, if any governmental action is *"arguably compelled"* by the Free Exercise Clause, then that action is *not forbidden by the Establishment Clause.* Tribe, p. 1168. Thus wherever one action might violate the Free Exercise Clause and a contrary action might violate the Establishment Clause, *it will always be safe for the government to elect the course whose threat is to the Establishment Clause.* To put it another way, "[t]he free exercise principle should be dominant in any conflict with the anti-establishment principle." Tribe, p. 1201.

D. **Application of clauses to states:** Although the First Amendment by its terms only restricts legislative action by *Congress*, the two religion clauses, like most of the other guarantees of the Bill of Rights, have been incorporated into the Fourteenth Amendment's due process guarantee, and thereby made *applicable to the states*. See, e.g., *Everson v. Board of Education*, 330 U.S. 1 (1947) (application of Establishment Clause to states).

# II. THE ESTABLISHMENT CLAUSE

A. **Background:** The basic purpose of the Establishment Clause is, in the words of Thomas Jefferson, to erect "a *wall of separation* between church and state." However, the image of a "wall" does not help very much in determining what types of state actions violate the Clause.

1. **Specific prohibitions:** There are some types of governmental actions which clearly violate the Establishment Clause. The majority catalogued some of these in *Everson v. Board of Education, supra*:

   a. **No official church:** Neither a state nor the federal government may *set up an official church.*

   b. **No coercion:** Government may not *"force* [or] *influence* a person *to go to* or to *remain away* from church against his will or force him to *profess a belief* or *disbelief* in any religion."

   c. **Punishment for beliefs:** No one may be *"punished* for entertaining or professing *religious beliefs or disbeliefs*, for church *attendance* or *non-attendance."*

   d. **No preference:** Government may not *prefer* one religion over another. Also, government may not prefer religion to non-religion.

   e. **Participation:** Government may not *participate in the affairs* of religious organizations, and such organizations may not *participate* in the affairs of government.

   **Note:** Some of these prohibitions (e.g., the right not to be punished for one's religious beliefs) are also protected by the Free Exercise Clause, perhaps even more directly than by the Establishment Clause. Nonetheless, the *Everson* Court purported to be list-ing solely those prohibitions stemming from the Establishment Clause.

2. **Three-part test:** The modern Court applies a ***three-fold test*** to determine whether gov-ernmental action violates the Establishment Clause. See ***Lemon v. Kurtzman***, 403 U.S. 602 (1970). Only if the action satisfies ***each*** of the following conditions will it be valid:

    a. **Purpose:** It must have a ***secular legislative purpose***;

    b. **Effect:** Its principal or ***primary effect*** must neither ***advance*** nor ***inhibit*** religion; and

    c. **Entanglement:** It must not foster an ***excessive government entanglement*** with reli-gion.

    d. **Political division:** Also, the law must not create an ***excessive degree of political division*** along religious lines. (However, this seems to be simply an aspect of the requirement of no "excessive entanglement"). See N&R, p. 1262.

3. **Possible single "endorsement of religion" standard:** There are some hints that the present Court may be unhappy with this *Lemon* three-part test, and that the Court may be moving to a single test: Does the state's conduct amount to an ***"endorsement of religion"***? See, e.g., *Texas Monthly, Inc. v. Bullock*, 489 U.S. 1 (1989), where the majority stated the main test as being whether the legislation "constitutes an endorsement of one or another set of religious beliefs or of religion generally."

    a. **May fall into disuse:** The Court may well overrule *Lemon* at some point. Alterna-tively, the Court may simply stop using it, without overruling it. This is in effect what happened in a recent major Establishment Clause case, *Board of Education of Kiryas Joel v. Grumet*, discussed *infra*, p. 678. The majority found that the challenged prac-tice there (the establishment of a school district consisting solely of members of a par-ticular Jewish sect) violated the Establishment Clause, but the majority opinion referred only briefly to *Lemon* and did not purport to apply the *Lemon* test.

B. **Religion and the public schools:** The extent to which the government may accommodate religion in operating the ***public schools*** has provoked much controversy and several important cases. The primary areas of concern are the extent to which the state may: (1) accommodate students' desire to ***receive religious instruction*** during school hours, or on school property; (2) allow the ***reading*** of state-composed ***prayers*** or the Bible, as part of a daily ritual; and (3) ***modify the curriculum*** in order to accommodate the religious views of some. In general, the Court has permitted the public schools ***very little leeway*** in pursuing these objectives.

1. **Religious instruction:** In two cases, the Court has analyzed the extent to which public schools may accommodate religion by ***releasing students*** for ***optional religious instruc-tion.***

    a. **Instruction on public school premises:** In the first of these, *McCollum v. Board of Education*, 333 U.S. 203 (1948), the public school allowed privately-employed reli-gious teachers to conduct classes ***on the public school's premises, during school hours***. While attendance was voluntary, students who did not attend the religious classes studied secular subjects elsewhere in the building. The Court ***struck down*** this scheme as a violation of the Establishment Clause, on the theory that the program helped religious groups obtain pupils "through the use of the state's compulsory public school machinery."

**b. Release for classes held elsewhere:** But the Court then, in *Zorach v. Clauson*, 343 U.S. 306 (1952), upheld a program which was quite similar to the one struck down in *McCollum*, except that the students who elected to participate were released to receive religious instruction ***away from the public school's physical facility.***

**c. Use of college facilities by student groups:** Notwithstanding *McCollum*, a state-supported school's policy of allowing religious groups to use its physical facilities does not violate the Establishment Clause if the policy is ***truly neutral*** as between religious and non-religious groups. Thus in ***Widmar v. Vincent***, 454 U.S. 263 (1981) (also discussed *supra*, p. 468), a state university banned the use of its facilities for purposes of worship by student-run religious groups, but allowed all non-religious student groups to use them. In holding that this policy was unconstitutional on free speech grounds, the Court rejected the university's claim that an equal-access policy would have violated the Establishment Clause.

     **i.** ***McCollum* distinguished:** It was precisely the fact that the facilities were also available to ***non-religious*** groups that made the situation in *Widmar* distinguishable from the use of school facilities for religious purposes in *McCollum*. Here, equal access would not "confer any imprimatur of state approval on religious sects or practices," and the advancement of religion would not be the "primary effect" of such a policy.

     **ii. Possibility of dominance by religion:** However, the majority in *Widmar* put aside the issue of whether a different result would be required if there were evidence that religious groups would ***dominate*** the use of facilities under an open-access scheme. Arguably, such dominance would cause the scheme to run afoul of the requirement that the state not pursue policies whose ***"primary effect"*** is to advance religion.

**d. Use of school facilities by student groups:** Congress has made the result of *Widmar* applicable to ***high schools*** receiving federal financial assistance. The ***Equal Access Act***, 20 U.S.C. §§4071 et seq., enacted in 1984, requires public high schools receiving federal financial assistance to allow ***student religious groups*** to ***hold meetings*** before and after school hours, if other extra-curricular groups are given similar rights. The bill applies only to meetings that are ***student-initiated, voluntary***, and carried out ***without sponsorship by the school*** or its employees (who may be present only as non-participants).

     **i. Constitutional:** The Equal Access Act was found ***constitutional***, in *Board of Education v. Mergens*, 496 U.S. 226 (1990). A majority of the Court agreed that where a public high school allows student religious groups to meet outside of school hours on the same basis that non-religious extracurricular groups are allowed to meet, this does not violate the Establishment Clause any more than does a similar policy at the university level.

     **ii. Religious groups in elementary schools:** Even if it is a public *elementary* school that allows religious groups to meet on the same after-school basis as non-religious groups, there is no Establishment Clause problem, the Court has held. *Good News Club v. Milford Central School*, 533 U.S. 98 (2001) (also discussed *supra*, p. 531). And this is true even if the attendees will be ***elementary school students***. The five-justice majority that decided *Good News* was not worried that young children might think that the school was endorsing a religious message, because "we cannot say the danger that children would misperceive the endorsement of religion is any greater than the danger that they would perceive a ***hostility*** toward the religious viewpoint if the [religious group] were ***excluded*** from the public forum."

**iii. Prayer no problem:** The equal access principle of *Widmar* is now so powerful that even if the religious group wants to conduct activity that is essentially a ***prayer service***, there is apparently no Establishment Clause problem with allowing the group to do so, as long as the facilities are equally opened to non-religious groups. Thus in *Good News, supra*, the majority was not troubled by the fact that the program in question "chooses to teach moral lessons from a Christian perspective through live storytelling and prayer" (the majority's characterization). Nor did the majority seem to disagree with the dissent's characterization of the program as "an evangelical service of worship calling children to commit themselves in an act of Christian conversion" — however the speech was labeled, it could be permitted without Establishment Clause problems as long as non-religious speech was allowed on the same basis.

   **(1) Worship services:** So apparently, after *Good News*, if government opens a particular public facility to wide community use, the fact that one of those uses is the conducting of ***traditional religious worship services*** will not pose an Establishment Clause problem, as long as the religious group is given no favoritism or endorsement by the government.

**iv. School-initiated:** But if attendance at a religious meeting at a public school is ***not truly voluntary***, or if ***school officials actively participate***, this would almost certainly be sufficient governmental "sponsorship" to make the meeting a violation of the Establishment Clause. Similarly, if meetings are held ***during school hours***, even the lack of participation by school officials, and the theoretical "voluntariness" of the meetings (in the sense that students could pursue alternate activities) would probably not be enough to save the meeting's constitutionality; this situation would seem to fall within *McCollum v. Board of Education's (supra*, p. 658) ban on programs which help religious groups obtain pupils "through the use of the state's compulsory public school machinery."

**v. Rights for non-religious groups:** Similarly, if a school allowed religious groups to conduct voluntary meetings outside of school hours, but ***did not grant this right to non-religious groups***, there would probably be an Establishment Clause violation, on the theory that this type of conduct had the purpose and effect of primarily aiding religion; such a policy would also arguably offend the free speech rights of the non-religious groups. (Paradoxically, the surest way for a school system to stay clear of both Establishment Clause and free speech problems, as well as problems under the Equal Access Act, may be to ban ***all*** extracurricular activities!)

**e. Funding of student activities:** The "equal access" principle of *Widmar* — that a school must treat religious and non-religious activities equally — now applies even where what the school is supplying is ***funding*** for activities, rather than merely access to pre-existing facilities. In ***Rosenberger v. University of Virginia***, 515 U.S. 819 (1995), the Court held by a 5-4 vote that it would not be an Establishment Clause violation for the University of Virginia to fund an evangelical Christian student publication on the same basis it funded other student publications, so long as the funds were paid to third parties (e.g., the printer) rather than to the students running the publication. (The Court also said that the University's failure to treat the Christian publication equally was a *free speech* violation; see *supra*, p. 532).

    **i.**   **Dissent:** A four-member dissent in *Rosenberger* vehemently objected, arguing that the Court "for the first time, approves direct funding of core religious activities by an arm of the State. ... Using public funds for the direct subsidization of preaching the word is categorically forbidden under the Establishment Clause, and if the Clause was meant to accomplish nothing else, it was meant to bar this use of public money." In the dissenters' opinion, the fact that the government was neutral as between religious and non-religious publications could not overcome this problem — the requirement of evenhandedness should be in *addition* to the requirement that religion not be directly advanced by the expenditure of public funds.

**2.**  **Prayer reading:**  The official *reading of prayers* in the public schools has several times been held by the Court to *violate* the Establishment Clause.

    **a.**  **State-composed prayer:**  First, the in-classroom reading of a *state-composed* "non-denominational" prayer was held to violate the Establishment Clause, in *Engel v. Vitale*, 370 U.S. 421 (1962). The Court reached this determination even though *no child was compelled to recite the prayer.* Neither this non-compulsory aspect, nor the non-denominationality, saved the scheme, because it was clearly part of a "religious program carried on by government."

    **b.**  **Reading from Bible:**  Similarly, a daily classroom ritual of *reading from the Bible* was struck down in *Abington School Dist. v. Schempp*, 374 U.S. 203 (1963). As in *Engel*, it made no difference that no child was compelled to participate.

        **i.**   **Rationale:**  The Court for the first time articulated in *Schempp* two prongs of the present three-prong test for determining whether governmental action violates the Establishment Clause: (1) the *purpose* of the action must be secular, rather than advancing or inhibiting religion; and (2) the *primary effect* of the action must also not be to advance or inhibit religion.

        **ii.**  **Application:**  The Bible readings were clearly "religious exercises," and thus failed at least the "primary effect" prong. Because of this primarily religious effect, it was no defense for the state to argue (even if accurately) that its *purposes* were the secular ones of promoting morality, anti-materialism, tradition and great literature.

        **iii.** **Dissent:**  The sole dissenter in *Schempp*, Justice Stewart, contended that a completely non-compulsory scheme of Bible reading, which provided alternative activities for non-participating students, was not violative of the Establishment Clause, and might even be compelled by the Free Exercise Clause.

    **c.**  **Voluntary silent prayer:**  A state statute that explicitly authorizes *"voluntary" silent prayer* in the public schools will not be saved from constitutional problems merely because the prayer is silent and non-compulsory. Any such statute is to be analyzed according to the three-prong *Lemon* test (*supra*, p. 658) — if the provision has no secular purpose, or has the primary effect of aiding religion, or results in excessive government entanglement with religion, it will be struck down even though each student is given the freedom not to participate in the prayer. Thus the Supreme Court has struck down an Alabama statute which authorized a ***one-minute silent period*** at the start of each school day which was to be used "for meditation or voluntary prayer." ***Wallace v. Jaffree***, 472 U.S. 38 (1985). The vote was 6-3.

  **i.    Rationale of majority:**   The *Wallace* majority concluded from various pieces of evidence that the legislature's ***sole purpose*** in enacting the statute was to endorse religion, a violation of the first prong of *Lemon*. (For instance, the bill's chief sponsor testified that the bill's purpose was to return voluntary prayer to the schools.) Since the first prong of *Lemon* was not satisfied, the Court did not need to reach the issue of the statute's conformance with the second and third *Lemon* prongs (primary effect and state entanglement).

 **d.  Academic study:**   The school prayer decisions do not prohibit the ***study*** of the Bible in public schools, as long as this study takes place in a purely ***academic manner***. The issue is whether the school, by including Bible study in the curriculum, intends to (or does in fact materially) advance religious beliefs.

 **e.  Ceremonies:**   So far, we have considered only prayers that take place in ***classrooms***. Suppose that a school conducts an official ***ceremony*** or ritual outside the classroom, and prayer is part of that ceremony. At least where school officials can fairly be said to be ***sponsoring*** the religious message, a prayer will be found to be a ***violation*** of the Establishment Clause. The Court so held in ***Lee v. Weisman***, 505 U.S. 577 (1992). *Lee* also establishes that even a completely ***non-denominational*** school prayer will violate the Establishment Clause if it is state-sponsored.

  **i.    Facts:**   *Lee* involved prayers at public middle-school and high-school graduation ceremonies. In one instance, a middle-school principal invited a rabbi to deliver a prayer, told him the prayer should be non-sectarian, and gave him a pamphlet (prepared by the National Conference of Christians and Jews) detailing the kinds of prayers that would be appropriate at a public civic occasion. The prayers delivered by the rabbi were indeed non-denominational, and consisted mainly of thanks to God (e.g., "Oh, God, we are grateful to You for having endowed us with the capacity for learning which we have celebrated on this joyous commencement. … Send Your blessings upon the teachers and administrators who helped prepare [the students]"). P was a graduating student who argued that she shouldn't be required to listen to a prayer as part of her graduation ceremony.

  **ii.   Practice struck down:**   By a 5-4 vote, the Court ruled that the delivery of the prayer in this context violated the Establishment Clause. The five-Justice majority, in an opinion by Justice Kennedy, held that the state here effectively ***coerced*** students into participating in, or at least supporting, the prayers. The school district had argued that attendance at the commencement ceremony was voluntary, in the sense that P could have received her diploma even without attending. But this argument ignored reality, Kennedy said; "To say each student has a real choice not to attend her high school graduation is formalistic in the extreme. …   Everyone knows that in our society and in our culture high school graduation is one of life's most significant occasions. …   The Constitution forbids the State to exact religious conformity from a student as the price of attending her own high school graduation." Nor was it a defense that P was not required to specifically *partici-pate* in the prayer — the combination of school supervision and peer pressure effectively required her to stand or at least maintain respectful silence, and this was tantamount to requiring her to participate in the religious exercise. Finally, the fact that the prayer was non-sectarian was irrelevant; there is no such thing as an "official" or "civic" religion which, because it is non-sectarian, is exempt from the Establishment Clause.

**iii. Dissent:** Four Justices (Scalia, joined by Rehnquist, White and Thomas) dissented. The dissenters principally argued that there was *no official compulsion* here — P was not required to attend the graduation ceremony at all (thus distinguishing the case from the in-classroom prayer cases), and certainly was not required to join in the prayers in any way, merely to accommodate others who wished to pray. Also, the dissenters contended, invocations and benedictions at public ceremonies, such as the prayers here, were part of an old *tradition* dating back to Jefferson's inauguration; "The long-standing American tradition of prayer at official ceremonies displays with unmistakable clarity that the Establishment Clause does not forbid the government to accommodate it." Finally, the dissenters believed that there was an important national objective to be served by group prayer in public settings, the objective of *unifying* participants of different backgrounds. "To deprive our society of that important unifying mechanism, in order to spare the nonbeliever of what seems to me the minimal inconvenience of standing or even sitting in respectful nonparticipation, is as senseless in policy as it is unsupported in law," Scalia concluded.

**iv. Incidental references to religion:** Suppose that an official ceremony or ritual contains mere *occasional* references to God, which are *incidental* to the ceremony. In this situation, it seems likely that the majority of the Court would *allow* the reference, despite its religious content. For instance, a majority of the Court has indicated in dictum that the use in public schools of the *Pledge of Allegiance*, with its reference to God, does not violate the Establishment Clause, because this is merely a "reference to our religious heritage," rather than an endorsement of religion. *Lynch v. Donnelly*, discussed *infra*, p. 675(the Nativity Scene case). (But see our further discussion of the Pledge issue *infra*, p. 670.)

**f. "Student-sponsored" speeches:** A key aspect of the Establishment Clause problem in *Lee v. Weisman* was that the school clearly endorsed the prayer — the principal invited a rabbi to give the prayer, and gave him instructions about what type of prior to use, making the prayer effectively school-sponsored. In part to get around *Lee*, a number of school districts after *Lee* put in place procedures whereby a *student* can be *elected by the student body* to be a speaker at a school-sponsored event. If the speaker then chooses on her own to give a prayer, the school can plausibly claim that the speech is private speech — posing no Establishment Clause problem — rather than school-sponsored speech. But a post-*Lee* case, in which the Court struck down a pre-football-game prayer delivered by an elected student speaker, suggests that this technique will rarely be successful. *Santa Fe Independent School Dist. v. Doe*, 530 U.S. 290 (2000).

**i. Facts:** Prior to the litigation, the Sante Fe, Tex., school district elected a *"Chap-lain"* of the high school student council each year, whose function was to deliver a prayer over the public address system before each varsity football game. After this practice was challenged on Establishment Clause grounds, the school instead instituted a formal written "policy" for dealing with the issue.

**(1) Two-election procedure:** The policy provided for two elections. First, the class would vote by secret ballot whether a "statement or invocation" should be delivered before each game, to "solemnize the event." If the vote was yes, a second election would be held to choose the spokesperson to deliver the invocation/statement.

**(2) Prayers delivered:** The student body in fact voted to have the invocations, and those invocations turned out to be, the lower court later found, prayers that appealed to "distinctively Christian beliefs."

ii. **Struck down:** By a 6-3-vote, the Court found that the school policy ***violated*** the Establishment Clause.

**(1) Not private speech:** The majority rejected the school district's claim that the pregame invocations should be regarded as ***"private speech."*** The school policy itself encouraged religious messages (e.g., by providing that the purpose of the message must be to "solemnize the event"). And the fact that the invocation was delivered at a school-sponsored event, over a school-owned public address system, added to the impression that this was school-sponsored, not private, prayer.

**(2) Sham:** An important aspect of the majority's reasoning in *Santa Fe* was that the ***real*** governmental purpose, not the stated one, should prevail. Thus the majority found it highly significant that the current policy had evolved from the prior practice of having a "Student Chaplain," and that prior versions of the policy had candidly included the title "Prayer at Football Games." In sum, the ostensibly religious-neutral policy was a ***sham***, an unsuccessful attempt to disguise a government desire to promote prayer.

iii. **Dissent:** The three dissenters in *Santa Fe*, led by Chief Justice Rehnquist, agreed with the district's argument that the prayers should be viewed as private speech, because it was up to the elected students to decide what to say in the pre-game speech.

3. **Modification of curriculum:** The state may not design or modify the ***curriculum*** of its schools in order to further religion at the expense of non-religion, or one set of religious beliefs over others.

a. **Anti-evolution laws:** This principle is most vividly demonstrated by the Court's invalidation of an Arkansas ***"anti-evolution"*** *statute*, which forbade public school teachers from teaching "the theory or doctrine that mankind ascended or descended from a lower order of animals." ***Epperson v. Arkansas***, 393 U.S. 97 (1968). (This statute was an offshoot of a comparable Tennessee statute, which was the subject of the famous 1927 Scopes trial.)

i. **Rationale:** The *Epperson* Court concluded that the statute violated the Establishment Clause because its ***sole purpose*** was a religious one: to bar the teaching of a theory that was at odds with the "fundamentalist sectarian conviction" that man was created in the manner described in the Bible. Even if the statute was intended only to prohibit teaching Darwinian theory as "true" (rather than barring even any *explanation* of what the theory says), the law's solely religious motivation was sufficient to make it unconstitutional.

**b. Requirement that Bible be taught:** May the state require that the biblical theory of creation be taught *in addition to* the theory of evolution? Such a requirement could, of course, be defended on the grounds that it preserves neutrality as between religion and non-religion, and presents all viewpoints. However, if such a requirement were imposed solely or primarily for the same religious *purpose* as the *Epperson* statute, it would violate the Establishment Clause. Thus in one case, the Supreme Court held that a Louisiana statute, the "Balanced Treatment for Creation-Science and Evolution-Science in Public School Instruction" Act, was motivated solely by religious purposes, and therefore violated the Establishment Clause. *Edwards v. Aguillard,* 482 U.S. 578 (1987).

  **i. Facts:** The Louisiana Act forbade the teaching of evolution in public schools unless that teaching was *accompanied by instruction in "creation science."* No school was required to teach evolution or creation science, but if either was taught the other must also be taught.

  **ii. Statute stricken:** The outcome of the case essentially turned on the extent to which one believed that the Louisiana legislature could have had a valid secular purpose in enacting the statute. Seven members of the Court, represented in a majority opinion by Justice Brennan, concluded that there *could not have been such a secular purpose*. Brennan concluded that "[t]he preeminent purpose of the Louisiana legislature was clearly to advance the religious viewpoint that a super-natural being created humankind." In reaching this conclusion, Brennan relied heavily upon the *legislative history* of the statute, including statements made by the bill's sponsor and testimony at the legislative hearings by the leading expert on creation science; both of these sources indicated that the theory of creation science includes a belief in the existence of a "supernatural creator," and is thus a religious doctrine.

  **iii. Dissent:** Justice Scalia, joined by Chief Justice Rehnquist, issued a forceful dissent that challenged the majority's analysis on both factual and legal grounds. Factually, Scalia disagreed that the record was adequate to allow the Court to conclude that the principal or sole motivation for the statute was to advance religious beliefs. Scalia noted that the act recited a secular purpose ("protecting academic freedom") and that the act was endorsed by a vast majority of legislators, only a small minority of whom were members of fundamentalist religious denominations. Furthermore, he stressed, the issue was not whether the statute would actually achieve the purpose of enhancing academic freedom, but merely whether the legislators were *sincere* in believing that it would have this outcome.

    **(1) Disagreement on standard:** The dissenters also disagreed about what the proper standard should be in determining whether a statute violates the Establishment Clause. They contended that the first prong of *Lemon* (*supra*, p. 658) — that the act have a secular legislative purpose — should be abandoned. "[D]iscerning the subjective motivation of those enacting the statute is, to be honest, almost always an impossible task." So long as the statute satisfied the second and third *Lemon* prongs — that it not have the primary effect of either advancing or inhibiting religion, and that it not foster an excessive government entanglement with religion — the dissenters would uphold it.

    **iv. Significance:** Observe that the majority approach in *Edwards* — that a religious motivation will invalidate the statute — can mean that when two states adopt an identically-worded statute, the statute may be ***valid in one state and invalid in the other***, since the two legislatures may have been differently motivated. It is, therefore, at least possible (though in practice unlikely) that the same statute invalidated in *Edwards* might be upheld in some other state, if the Court were convinced that *those* legislators, unlike the ones in Louisiana, were really motivated by a non-religious intent.

    **c. No secular purpose:** *Epperson* and *Edwards* are two of the few cases in which the religious purpose of a law was dispositive. The "purpose" prong of the three-prong Establishment Clause test is that there must be *a* "secular purpose," not that there may not be a religious purpose. Thus if there is ***both a religious and secular purpose***, the prong is ***not violated***. The statutes in *Epperson* and *Edwards* are two of the few legislative enactments as to which members of the Court could find no conceivable secular purpose. (For another such statute, see the Alabama "voluntary prayer" statute struck down in *Wallace v. Jaffree, supra*, p. 661.)

**C. Sunday closing laws:** Laws requiring merchants to be ***closed on Sunday*** do ***not*** violate the Establishment Clause. ***McGowan v. Maryland***, 366 U.S. 420 (1961).

    **1. Rationale:** The Court reasoned in *McGowan* that, as these statutes are administered today, they have a ***secular purpose and effect:*** providing a ***uniform day of rest for all citizens***. (The Court believed it irrelevant that the laws were originally enacted for purely religious reasons.)

    **2. Overlapping of secular and religious purposes:** Of course, the fact remains that the day chosen for this uniform day of rest is Sunday, the day of religious observance for most Americans. The case therefore illustrates the rule that a statute does not violate the Establishment Clause if it has ***both a religious and secular purpose***. See Tribe, p. 1205-06.

    **a. Effect:** Similarly, the fact that the law had both a secular and religious ***effect*** did not cause a violation of the Establishment Clause, since the religious effect was not the primary, or even major, one. The Court seems correct in viewing the Sunday closing laws as having merely an ***incidental*** unofficial effect of advancing religion.

    **3. Employees' right not to work on Sabbath:** But if a statute relating to Sabbath observance *does* have the primary effect of advancing religion, it will be found to violate the Establishment Clause. For instance, a Connecticut statute requiring all employers (including private employers) to give any employee the day off on that employee's Sabbath, was struck down as violative of the Establishment Clause, in ***Thornton v. Caldor, Inc.***, 472 U.S. 703 (1985).

    **a. Rationale:** The statute in *Thornton* went beyond the government's right to "accommodate" the needs of religious observers. There, the preference given to Sabbath observers was an ***absolute*** one. For instance, suppose that an employer is faced with having to choose which of two employees should have Sunday off: one employee points to Sunday as his Sabbath; the other, who has more seniority, has a pressing and legitimate, but non-religious need for Sundays off (e.g., to have the same day off as his working spouse and school-aged children). The Connecticut statute mandated an absolute preference for the former. The statute thus had the primary effect of "impermissibly advanc[ing] a particular religious practice" (namely, Sabbath observance).

b. **Non-absolute preference:** But a statute that merely required an employer to make "reasonable attempts" to accommodate the religious interest of workers probably would ***not*** violate the Establishment Clause.

**Note:** There is often a tension between Establishment Clause and Free Exercise principles. See *infra*, p. 692, for several cases in which government was *required* to accommodate the needs of individuals to observe the Sabbath.

**D. Property-tax exemptions for churches:** The granting of ***property tax exemptions*** to churches generally does ***not*** violate the Establishment Clause. *Walz v. Tax Commission*, 397 U.S. 664 (1970).

1. **Sales tax exemption violates clause:** On the other hand, some kinds of tax exemptions given to religious groups ***will*** be held to violate the Establishment Clause. For instance, Texas exempted from ***sales tax*** all (and only) periodicals "published or distributed by a religious faith and [consisting] wholly of writings promulgating the teaching of the faith and books that consist wholly of writings sacred to a religious faith." This exemption was struck down by the Court in *Texas Monthly, Inc. v. Bullock*, 489 U.S. 1 (1989).

2. **Distinction:** How was the property tax exemption in *Walz* different from the sales tax exemption in *Texas Monthly*? The main difference seems to be that the exemption in *Walz* was part of a ***broader scheme*** that did not prefer religion over non-religion — property owned by most types of non-profit organizations (including hospitals, libraries, patriotic groups, etc.) was also exempted. In *Texas Monthly*, by contrast, ***only*** religious writings published by religious groups were exempted, so the exemption's sole purpose (and apparently its principal effect) was to advance religion.

**E. Military and prison chaplains:** Recall that government has some ability to ***accommodate*** the religious needs of citizens, so long as government is not "sponsoring" official religious practices. The right of public schools to release their students so that they can receive religious instruction outside of the school is one illustration of this principle. The "accommodation" principle is also applicable when government supplies ***military chaplains*** or ***prison chaplains*** to soldiers or prisoners who wish to use them, or otherwise accommodates the religious needs of solders or prisoners.

1. **Religious accommodation to prisoners:** For instance, the Court has upheld the Religious Land Use and Institutionalized Persons Act (RLUIPA), which essentially requires all prison systems to accommodate the religious needs of prisoners unless refusing to do so would further a compelling governmental interest by the least restrictive means. See *Cutter v. Wilkinson*, 544 U.S. 709 (2005), discussed *infra*, p. 680. Even though RLUIPA clearly prefers religion over non-religion (e.g., by effectively requiring that prisoners be given the right to attend organized group prayer meetings and the right to wear religiously-dictated non-standard apparel while prisoners who wish to engage in these activities for non-religious reasons are not given the right to do so), the Court found no Establishment Clause violation.

**F. Helping religious groups spread their message:**   Recall that one of the prongs of the *Lemon v. Kurtzman* test (*supra*, p. 658) is that the governmental action's principal effect must not be to *advance* religion. Thus government actions whose primary effect is to help religious organizations *spread a religious message* or *obtain converts* would presumably fail this prong and thus violate the Establishment Clause.

> **Example:** Suppose that Congress passed a law providing grants to religious (and only religious) organizations, for the express purpose of giving them the financial resources to run expanded membership drives and to explain their beliefs to the general population. This statute would almost certainly violate the "primary effect" prong of *Lemon*.

**1. Incidental effect:**   But if grants are made to a wide variety of institutions, only some of which are religiously-affiliated, the fact that some of the recipients happen to be religious organizations who use the funds to spread the organization's religious message will not lead to a striking down of the entire statute (though it may cause grants to the particular organizations who use the funds in this way to be struck down). Only if a *significant portion* of the government funding flows to institutions that are *"pervasively sectarian"* will the entire funding scheme be a violation of the Establishment Clause.

> **Example:** Congress enacts the Adolescent Family Life Act (AFLA), which is mainly a scheme for giving grants to public or non-profit private organizations so that the organizations can give adolescents counseling about sex and pregnancy. In order to receive a grant, an organization may (but need not) be religiously-affiliated; every grant recipient must, even if not itself religious, describe how it will "involve religious … organizations in its activities."
>
> *Held* (by a 5-4 vote), the AFLA is not unconstitutional on its face. It does not have the primary effect of advancing religion because: (1) a wide variety of organizations is eligible to receive funding under the Act, only some of which are religious; and (2) there is no reason to believe that any significant proportion of the funds will flow to "pervasively sectarian" institutions. *Bowen v. Kendrick*, 483 U.S. 1304 (1988).

**G. Judicial inquiry into doctrines and belief:**   Recall that the third prong of the test for Establishment Clause violations is that the governmental action must not give rise to *excessive entanglement* on the part of government in the affairs of religion, or vice versa. This anti-entanglement policy is reflected in the principle that courts will strenuously avoid inquiry into the *truth* of particular religious doctrines and practices.

**1. Truth vs. sincerity:**   While courts are unwilling to adjudicate the truth of religious beliefs, they are sometimes willing to consider the *sincerity* of professed beliefs.

    **a. *Ballard*:**   The truth/sincerity distinction was made in *U.S. v. Ballard*, 322 U.S. 78 (1944), where the defendants, self-professed *faith healers*, were charged with fraudulently soliciting donations. The Court held that the Free Exercise Clause barred the submission to the jury of the truth or falsity of the defendants' faith healing claims: "Men may believe what they cannot prove. They may not be put to the proof of their religious doctrines or beliefs." However, the Court held, a jury could be required to decide whether the defendants were *sincere* in their claims, that is, whether they genuinely (whether or not reasonably) believed these claims.

        **i. Criticism:**   But it is hard to see how a jury could evaluate sincerity of belief without at least some consideration of the truth or falsity of belief. For instance, the prosecution in a case like *Ballard* would probably try to prove insincerity by showing that the alleged acts of faith healing did not take place, so that the defendants could not have in fact believed their claims; yet such evidence would inevitably reflect on the truth, not just the sincerity, of the claims. See L,K&C, p. 1232.

**H. Entanglement by church involvement in government:** The anti-entanglement principle will also be violated by the converse problem, that of excessive involvement *by the church in affairs of government.*

1. *Larkin:* For instance, in *Larkin v. Grendel's Den, Inc.*, 459 U.S. 116 (1982), the Court struck down a Massachusetts statute prohibiting issuance of a liquor license to any premises located within 500 feet of a church or school if the church or school makes a written objection to the issuance of the license.

    a. **Rationale:** Giving such a veto provision to churches "enmeshes churches in the exercise of substantial governmental powers," the *Larkin* Court held, and therefore runs afoul of the anti-entanglement principle of the Establishment Clause.

**I. Ceremonies and displays:** When the government conducts a *ceremony* or puts on a *display*, and the ceremony or display refers to a religious subject, Establishment Clause problems will often result.

1. **Ceremonies:** First, consider ceremonies. The fact that God is *occasionally referred to* in a ceremony put on by the government will usually *not* cause the ceremony to violate the Establishment Clause.

    a. **Legislative chaplain:** For instance, the practice of opening each daily session of a state *legislature* with a *prayer* by a state-paid chaplain does not violate the Establishment Clause, the Court held in *Marsh v. Chambers*, 463 U.S. 783 (1983).

        i. **Rationale:** The Court relied principally on the theory that such practices have deep *historic roots*, going back to the First Congress; this fact demonstrated that the congressmen who approved the First Amendment must have believed that use of a chaplain did not violate principles of church-state separation.

        ii. **Dissent:** But Justice Stevens, one of three dissenters, argued that the Nebraska legislature's choice of a Presbyterian to hold the position of chaplain for sixteen years, probably in order to reflect the state's primary sect, constituted an illegal "preference of one faith over another."

        iii. **Distinguished from prayer at school commencement:** Recall that it *is* a violation of the Establishment Clause for a school district to sponsor a prayer during *high school commencement* ceremonies (see *Lee v. Weisman, supra*, p. 662). What is the constitutional difference between a prayer before the opening of a state legislative session and one before a school commencement? The majority in the school-commencement case distinguished the two as follows: "The atmosphere at the opening of a session of a state legislature where adults are free to enter and leave with little comment and for any number of reasons cannot compare with the constraining potential of the one school event most important for the student to attend." The Court has always been quicker to find Establishment Clause violations in the context of public schools than in other contexts, so the distinction between prayer at a legislative session and prayer during a school commencement is not surprising.

**b. Pledge of Allegiance:** What about the Pledge of Allegiance? The Pledge contains the phrase, "One nation, under God, indivisible, with liberty and justice for all." Probably this brief reference to God will not be held (at least by the Rehnquist Court) to be a violation of the Establishment Clause. The Pledge would probably be viewed as a whole, and when so viewed would probably not be found to have the sole purpose of, or the primary effect of, advancing religion.

   **i. Tradition:** Also, as *Marsh v. Chambers*, *supra*, p. 669, shows, the Court seems more inclined to allow references to religious themes when the reference is part of a ***long-standing tradition*** or ***historical practice***. The Pledge certainly seems to qualify on this ground. Similarly, the Court's recent decision in *Van Orden v. Perry*, *infra*, p. 671 — where the Court upheld a monument of the Ten Commandments on the Texas State Capitol grounds in major part because the monument had stood for 40 years without complaint — reinforces the likelihood that the Court will uphold public use of the Pledge as a long-standing tradition.

**2. Religious displays:** Great controversy can arise when the government either puts on, or makes its property available for private groups to put on, some sort of ***display*** or presentation that involves religious themes. For instance, suppose the government allows a private religious group to display a copy of the Ten Commandments, a nativity scene, a Hanukkah menorah, or some other symbol that has great religious significance. Does the fact that the government is making its property available for such a display violate the Establishment Clause? The test now seems to be this: Would a reasonable observer seeing the display conclude that the government was ***endorsing*** religion in general, or endorsing a particular religion? If the answer is "yes," the display violates the Establishment Clause. If the answer is "no," it does not.

   **a. Context:** This means that the constitutionality of a given Ten Commandments display, nativity scene, etc., will be a question of fact. The most important single factor seems to be the ***context*** in which the religious symbol is displayed. If the religious symbol is presented ***by itself*** in what is clearly a space reserved by the government for its own property and its own messages, the Court is likely to conclude that a "reasonable observer" would believe that the government was endorsing the religious message. Conversely, the presence of ***other non-religious symbols nearby***, or the existence of a ***sign*** indicating that the display was furnished by private parties without governmental approval, or evidence that the religious material was provided for its historical rather than religious value — any of these factors may well be enough to lead a reasonable observer to the conclusion that government was ***not*** endorsing religion.

   **b. Intent:** Government's ***intent or motive*** in establishing the display is also of vital importance. If the court believes that the government's principal purpose in establishing the display was to ***promote or endorse religion*** (or some particular religion), this fact by itself will probably lead to a finding of unconstitutionality. *McCreary County v. ACLU*, a Kentucky Ten Commandments case which we'll be reviewing in detail *infra*, p. 672, illustrates how a governmental purpose to advance religion will be fatal.

   **c. Five cases:** There have been five cases since 1984 in which the Court has considered whether religiously-oriented displays in public space violate the Establisment Clause.

Two involved the Ten Commandments, two involved nativity scenes, and the fifth involved a cross.

**d. The Ten Commandments cases:** Two 2005 companion cases involving public displays of the text of the *Ten Commandments* are the Court's most recent rulings on religiously-oriented displays in public spaces. The two cases went in opposite directions, with one finding a display at the Texas State Capitol to be constitutional, and the other finding a display in two Kentucky courthouses to be unconstitutional. The Texas case was *Van Orden v. Perry*, 545 U.S. 677 (2005) and the Kentucky one was *McCreary County v. ACLU of Kentucky*, 545 U.S. 844 (2005).

   **i. Two 5-4 decisions:** In each case, the decision was 5- 4. Four members of the court (Rehnquist, Scalia, Thomas and Kennedy) believed both displays were constitutional; four other members (Souter, Stevens, O'Connor and Ginsburg) believed both displays were unconstitutional. The swing vote was Justice Breyer, who therefore made a majority for upholding the Texas display and a different majority for striking down the Kentucky one.

   **ii. The Texas case (*Van Orden*):** In the Texas case (*Van Orden*), the display was a six-foot high monument containing the text of the King James version of the Ten Commandments. The monument was one of 17 monuments and 21 historical markers installed in 22 acres on the grounds of the Texas Capitol. The monument was contributed to the state in 1961 by Texas branch of the Fraternal Order of Eagles, which during that era contributed similar monuments to state legislatures around America in the hopes of reducing juvenile delinquency. Apparently there was little if any public Establishment-Clause objection to the monument for 40 years, until plaintiff Van Orden, a former lawyer, brought suit.

   **(1) Rehnquist's opinion upholds the display:** Chief Justice Rehnquist, in a plurality opinion joined by Scalia, Kennedy and Thomas, concluded that the monument ***did not violate*** the Establishment Clause. With Justice Breyer's vote concurring in the result, this provided the five votes needed to uphold the display. Rehnquist believed that although the Ten Commandments "are religious," they also "have an undeniable historical meaning," since "Moses was a lawgiver as well as a religious leader." He continued, "Simply having a religious content or promoting a message consistent with a religious doctrine does not run afoul of the Establishment Clause." Acknowledgments of the role played by the Ten Commandments in the country's heritage are common throughout America, he said — for instance, the Supreme Court itself has had for many years a frieze showing Moses holding the two tablets containing the Hebrew text of the commandments. So Texas' "passive use" of the text of the Commandments, placed alongside many other monuments representing "the several strands in the state's political and legal history," did not violate the Establishment Clause.

   **(2) Breyer supplies the fifth vote:** Justice Breyer concurred in the result and thus supplied the needed fifth vote for upholding the Texas display's constitutionality. For Breyer, this was "a borderline case." The Commandments' text had an undeniable religious message. But the display of which they were part conveyed a secular message as well, a message about the historical relation between this religious text and the development of law. To Breyer, the physical setting of the display — among 17 monuments and 21 historical markers, all illustrating the "ideals" of Texas' settlers and later residents — "suggests little or nothing of the sacred[,]" but rather, suggested that the "moral message" of the display was intended to predominate over its religious message.

Perhaps even more important to Breyer, the fact that ***40 years had passed without a challenge*** to this monument suggested that "few individuals [are] likely to have understood the monument as amounting [to] a government effort to favor a particular religious sect, primarily to promote religion over nonreligion, [or] to 'work deterrence' of any 'religious belief.'" In fact, Breyer worried that if the display was found *in*valid, that very result might "lead the law to exhibit a ***hostility toward religion*** that has no place in our Establishment Clause traditions" and that might "create very kind of religiously based divisiveness that the Establishment Clause seeks to avoid."

**(3) Dissents:** Justices Stevens, Souter, O'Connor and Ginsburg dissented in the Texas case.

Stevens asserted that the message transmitted by Texas's display was that "this state ***endorses the divine code of the 'Judeo-Christian' God.***" (He noted that the Texas monument displayed the words "I AM the LORD thy God" in especially large letters.) The Establishment Clause, he said, ***"demands religious neutrality*** — Government may not exercise a preference for one religious faith over another." The Ten Commandments state the message that "there is one, and only one, God," namely a Judeo-Christian God. Since this message is ***"rejected by prominent polytheistic sects***, such as Hinduism, as well as ***nontheistic religions***, such as Buddhism," Stevens continued, allowing government to propagate this message "would have the tendency to make nonmonotheists and nonbelievers *'feel like [outsiders] in matters of faith* and [strangers] in the political community.'"

In a separate dissent sounding similar themes, Justice Souter said that the Ten Commandments "constitute a religious statement" and that Texas's purpose in singling them out was a religious one. The state capitol building is the "civic home of every one of the State's citizens"; therefore, "if neutrality in religion means something, any citizen should be able to visit that civic home without having to confront religious expressions clearly meant to convey an official religious position that may be at odds with his own religion, or with rejection of religion."

**iii. The Kentucky case (*McCreary County*):** In the Kentucky case (*McCreary County v. ACLU of Kentucky*), Justice Breyer joined the four dissenters from *Van Orden* to **strike down** two counties' posting of the Ten Commandments. The ***history*** of that posting — a history that convinced a majority of the Court that government's primary purpose was to endorse religion — was dispositive.

**(1) Facts:** The two counties, McCreary and Pulaski, initially ordered large framed copies of the King James version of the Ten Commandments posted on a stand-alone basis in their courthouses. In Pulaski County, the ceremony in which the document was hung was presided over by a pastor from the county executive's church. The ACLU sued both counties almost immediately on Establishment Clause grounds. The legislature of each county, acting on legal advice, then ordered the display expanded to add, in smaller frames, various other religiously-oriented portions of historical documents (e.g., the passage from the Declaration of Independence saying that all men are "endowed by their Creator" with inalienable rights).

The trial court in the ACLU action issued an injunction requiring that the displays be removed. The counties did so, but then installed a new display — the third within a year — consisting of framed copies of the Ten Commandments plus various other historical documents (e.g., the Magna Carta, the Declaration of Independence and the Bill of Rights), each accompanied by a statement about its historical and legal significance. For the Ten Commandments, the accompanying statement said that the Commandments "provide the moral background of the Declaration of Independence, and the foundation of our legal tradition." The trial judge concluded that this last display, too, violated the Establishment Clause.

(2) **Majority strikes down:** Justice Souter, writing for himself and for Stevens, O'Connor, Ginsburg and Breyer, concluded that the third display *violated the Establishment Clause*. Souter relied on the *"purpose"* prong of *Lemon v. Kurtzman* (p. 658) — the display was invalid because it was *not supported by any genuine "secular legislative purpose."* Souter quoted a prior holding, that "The First Amendment *mandates governmental neutrality* between religion and religion, and *between religion and nonreligion*[,]" and added that when government acts with the predominant purpose of advancing religion, it "violates that central Establishment Clause value of official religious neutrality[.]"

Souter then turned to the facts. He looked first at the original display, in which the Ten Commandments were displayed alone. Given the Commandments' status as a "central point of reference in the religious and moral history of Jews and Christians," given the absence of any "context plausibly suggesting a message going beyond an excuse to promote the religious point of view," and given the presence of a pastor who testified at the Pulaski County display ceremony as to the certainty that God existed, any "reasonable observer could only think that the Counties *meant to emphasize and celebrate the Commandments' religious message."*

Souter then considered the second and third displays. As to the third display -- the one expressly under litigation — he concluded that the same religious purpose that had motivated the Counties in making the prior displays had continued: "No reasonable observer could swallow the claim that the Counties had cast off the [religious] objective so unmistakable in the earlier displays." In reaching that conclusion, Souter rejected the Counties' argument that in evaluating government's purpose only the final display should be considered; "reasonable observers have reasonable memories, and our precedents sensibly forbid an observer 'to turn a blind eye to the context in which [the] policy arose.' "

Finally, Souter argued that in close cases, the Establishment Clause should be interpreted in a way that achieves the ***"principle of neutrality"***: the framers intended to "guard against the **civic divisiveness** that follows when the Government weighs in on one side of religious debate."

**(3) O'Connor's concurrence:** Perhaps surprisingly, Justice O'Connor concurred in *McCreary County.* She wrote that "At a time when we see around the world the violent consequences of the assumption of religious authority by government, Americans may count themselves fortunate ... Those who would renegotiate the boundaries between church and state must therefore answer a difficult question: why would we trade a system that has served us so well for one that has served others so poorly?" She added that "it is true that many Americans find the Commandments in accordance with their personal beliefs. But **we do not count heads before enforcing the First Amendment."**

**(4) Dissent:** Justice Scalia wrote the only dissenting opinion in *McCreary County* (in which Chief Justice Rehnquist and Justice Thomas joined in full and Justice Kennedy in part). Scalia's main objection was to the majority's view that the establishment clause requires ***neutrality between religion and nonreligion,*** and to what he characterized as the majority's view that ***acknowledging society's belief in God*** violates this neutrality principle. "Nothing stands behind the Court's assertion that governmental affirmation of the society's belief in God is unconstitutional except the Court's own say-so[.]" Scalia argued that the Court had often violated the no-preference-for-religion neutrality principle, as when it approved property tax exemptions for church property (*Walz v. Tax Comm., supra*, p. 667).

Scalia conceded that the Establishment Clause means, generally, that government cannot favor one religion over another. But this principle, he said, "necessarily applies in a more ***limited sense*** to ***public acknowledgement of the Creator."*** Historical practices, he argued, "demonstrate that there is a distance between ***acknowledgement of a single Creator*** and the establishment of a religion." He noted that the three most popular religions in the U.S. — Christianity, Judaism and Islam — account for 97.7% of all believers, and that these three religions are not only all monotheistic but believe that "the Ten Commandments were given by God to Moses, and are divine prescriptions for a virtuous life." Therefore, he said, the practice of publicly honoring the Ten Commandments, like that of ***publicly honoring God***, is "recognized across such a ***broad and diverse range of the population*** ... that [it] ***cannot reasonably be understood as a government endorsement of a particular religious viewpoint."***

Scalia also objected to the majority's preoccupation with the "purpose" underlying a particular display. He thought this preoccupation ***"ratchet[s] up the Court's hostility to religion."*** Under the majority's approach, "displays erected in silence (under the direction of good legal advice) are permissible, while those hung after discussion and debate are deemed unconstitutional." Making purpose so central "trivializes the [Establishment] Clause's protection against religious establishment; indeed, it may inflame religious passions by making the passing comments of every government official the subject of endless litigation."

e. **The nativity cases:** Before the two Ten Commandments cases were decided, the Court's most important opinions on religious displays were two cases involving ***nativity scenes.***

   i. **Rhode Island case:** The earlier of the two nativity-scene cases was ***Lynch v. Donnelly***, 465 U.S. 668 (1984), involving the city of Pawtucket, Rhode Island.

      (1) **Facts:** Pawtucket put up a Christmas display every year in a public park near the city's shopping district. The display included several symbols traditionally associated with Christmas, but not having much, if any, overtly religious significance (e.g., Santa Claus, a reindeer, a Christmas tree, and a banner reading "Seasons Greetings"). The display also included a creche, or nativity scene, depicting the birth of Christ.

      (2) **Holding:** A majority of the Court (in a 5-4 vote) concluded that this nativity display did ***not*** violate any of the three traditional tests, especially when considered "in the context of the Christmas season." There was a secular purpose ("to celebrate the Holiday and to depict the origins of that Holiday"); the primary effect was not to benefit religion in general, or Christianity in particular (since any advancement of religion was "indirect, remote and incidental," just like exhibition of religious paintings in a government-owned museum); and there was no undue "administrative entanglement" (since the city erected and maintained the display without any contact with religious authorities).

      (3) **Acknowledgment of holidays:** More generally, the majority in *Lynch* believed that the display was allowable because it was merely one of many illustrations of "the Government's acknowledgment of our religious heritage and governmental sponsorship of graphic manifestations of that heritage." This display was no different from: (1) federal proclamations making Christmas a national holiday; (2) statutory establishment of "In God We Trust" as our national motto; and (3) the display in government museums of "masterpieces with religious messages."

      (4) **Dissent:** The four dissenters believed that the display violated all three prongs of the test of *Lemon v. Kurtzman* (*supra*, p. 658). As to purpose, the dissenters pointed to evidence that the creche was motivated in part by popular desire to "keep Christ in Christmas." The primary effect of the display was "to place the government's imprimatur of approval on the particular religious beliefs exemplified by the creche" and to convey to minority religious groups and atheists "the message that their views are not similarly worthy of public recognition nor entitled to public support." And, the dissenters argued, significant political divisiveness on the issue had occurred after the suit was filed. The dissenters disagreed with the majority's argument that this creche was no

different from the accompanying Santa Claus and reindeer — to the dissenters, the creche was neither secular nor historical, but rather a "mystical re-creation of an event that lies at the heart of Christian faith. ... "

**ii. Pittsburgh case:**   But contrast the holding in *Lynch* with the second, later, case involving a nativity scene, *Allegheny County v. American Civil Liberties Union*, 492 U.S. 573 (1989). Here, the Court (again by a 5-4 vote) found that the nativity scene *violated* the Establishment Clause.

   **(1) Facts:**   The creche in *Allegheny County* was displayed in the county courthouse during the Christmas season. The creche was owned and put up by a private Catholic group (not by the city itself, as was the case in *Lynch*). In addition to the usual figures of Jesus, Mary, Joseph, shepherds, wise men, etc., the creche contained a banner proclaiming, "Gloria in Excelsis Deo!" ("Glory to God in the Highest"). The creche occupied a prominent position on the Grand Staircase of the courthouse. Unlike the creche in *Lynch*, there were no significant other nearby symbols such as Santa Claus, reindeer, or "Seasons Greetings" banners — the creche stood by itself.

   **(2) Holding:**   The five-justice majority believed that this creche violated the Establishment Clause. The test was whether a reasonable observer seeing the display would believe that the government was endorsing a religious or sectarian message. Here, there were several factors not present in *Lynch* that would lead an observer to believe that the government was endorsing a Christian message. For instance, there were no other non-religious symbols nearby as there had been in *Lynch* (like the Santa Claus and reindeer), so an observer would not think that the city was merely celebrating the holiday season.

   **(3) Hanukkah menorah:**   But a different five-justice majority in *Allegheny County* thought that an 18-foot-high *Hanukkah menorah*, placed next to a 45-foot Christmas tree in a different part of Pittsburgh, did *not* violate the Establishment Clause. These justices reasoned that the menorah was near the tree, the tree was primarily secular, the tree was much bigger than the menorah, and the two symbols taken together as part of a single display therefore conveyed primarily the message of celebrating the secular Christmas holiday season, not the message of celebrating the religious significance of Hanukkah.

**f. Display of cross:**   The Court's final religious-display case of recent years involved the Ku Klux Klan's attempt to display a *cross* in a state-owned park immediately in front of the Ohio statehouse. By a 7-2 vote, the Court held that the display did *not* violate the Establishment Clause. *Capitol Square Review Board v. Pinette*, 515 U.S. 753 (1995).

   **i. Facts:**   The park in question had long been made available to a wide variety of public groups who wanted to conduct expressive activities, or erect unattended displays, there. The question was whether the state could deny the Klan's attempt to put up a cross — which the Court treated as being a religious (as opposed to political) symbol — on the ground that to allow the cross would be a violation of the Establishment Clause.

ii. **7 members find no violation:** 7 Justices believed that it would ***not*** violate the Establishment Clause for the state to allow the cross. But they differed sharply as to the rationale.

iii. **Plurality's view:** A 4-Justice plurality, led by Justice Scalia, thought that where the speech was that of a private party rather than the government, the "reasonable observer" test should be ***rejected*** entirely. In the plurality's opinion, only if government ***intentionally "fostered or encouraged"*** the belief that government was endorsing religion, could there be an Establishment Clause violation. So here, where the government had always applied an "equal access" policy toward displays in the park, a policy that was neutral as between religion and non-religion, there was no Establishment Clause violation whether or not a reasonable observer might have (mistakenly) believed that the government was endorsing religion.

iv. **3-Justice bloc:** Another bloc of three Justices, led by O'Connor, believed that the ***"reasonable observer"*** test was the ***correct*** one. To this bloc, "Where the government's operation of a public forum has the effect of endorsing religion, even if the governmental actor neither intends nor actively encourages that result ... the Establishment Clause is violated." But these three Justices agreed with the plurality that there was no Establishment Clause violation here. This bloc reasoned that the "reasonable observer" should be one who is "deemed aware of the ***history and context*** of the community and forum in which the religious display appears," not a "casual passerby." Since such an observer would have known that the park was essentially open to any private display meeting simple content-neutral permit requirements, he or she would not have concluded that government was endorsing religion by allowing the cross to be displayed.

g. **Synthesis:** The law in this "religious display" area is confused and probably still shifting. Here's what we can say:

i. **Government vs. private speech:** Where the display is owned and put on by the ***government***, it is of course more likely to be found to be an Establishment Clause violation than if it is put on by a private speaker who is permitted to do so by the government. (But if the display is viewed as a "holiday season" or other "cultural" message rather than a specifically religious message, it can still survive, as the nativity scene in *Lynch* did.)

ii. **Context:** ***Context*** remains very important. The presence of non-religious symbols nearby, for instance, makes it more likely that even a usually-religious symbol like like a creche or a copy of the Ten Commandments will be found not to violate the Clause. Thus in *Van Orden, supra*, the fact that a display of the Ten Commandments was only one of 17 monuments and 21 historical markers installed throughout a 22-acre public site helped convince a majority of the Court that a reasonable observer wouldn't conclude that the Ten Commandments display was intended as a governmental endorsement of religion.

iii. **History:** The ***history*** behind the display is important — the longer the display has been around without objection or controversy, the less likely it is to be an Establishment Clause violation. Thus contrast *Van Orden, supra*, with *McCreary County*: In *Van Orden*, the display had existed for 40 years without objection, helping the Court find it not a violation. But in *McCreary County*, the display was a substitute for two clearly-religious prior displays, with all three posted during a short period, and with all three raising Establishment Clause objections from the start; this brief and controversial history helped the Court find a primary government purpose to promote religion, and thus to find an Establishment Clause violation.

iv.  **"Reasonable observer" test:** There remains a bare 5-justice majority in favor of using the *"reasonable observer"* test, by which the Clause is violated when a reasonable observer would believe (even if mistakenly) that government was endorsing religion.

v.  **Sign as disclaimer:** The government is free to require that any display contain a *sign* or other *disclaimer* to make it clear that the display was placed by private parties; the displayer's free speech rights are not violated where government requires such a disclaimer.

vi.  **Close property entirely:** Also, the government can avoid constitutional controversies by making the property completely *off-limits* to *all* privately-placed unattended displays, whether religious or not. This is apparently true even where the property is a traditional public forum (e.g., a park) — the government couldn't bar all "live speech" by human beings, but it's entitled to bar all unattended signs or displays.

J.  **No preference for one sect over others:**  Just as the Establishment Clause is violated when government prefers religion over non-religion, so is it violated when the government *favors a particular sect over other sects*, or over non-religious interests.

1.  **Accommodation vs. favoritism:** However, one of the core principles of the Free Exercise Clause is that government must sometimes *"accommodate"* the religious needs of a particular person or group. But government action may sometimes *cross over the line* from "accommodation" into forbidden favoritism. This happened in *Board of Education of Kiryas Joel Village v. Grumet*, 512 U.S. 687 (1994). The case also illustrates that where a state *delegates governmental power* directly to a religious group, a violation of the Establishment Clause is almost certain to be found.

a.  **Facts:**  The *Kiryas Joel* case had its origins when a group of Satmar Hasidim, fundamentalist Jews, moved from Brooklyn to upstate New York, to the Town of Monroe. In 1977, taking advantage of a New York State law that allows groups of residents within a town to form a smaller village, the Satmars formed the Village of Kiryas Joel. The village was drawn to include just the 328 acres owned and inhabited by Satmars. The village has a population of about 8,500 today.

i.  **Isolated:**  The 8,500 Satmars are vigorously religious and deeply insular. They speak Yiddish as their primary language, segregate the sexes outside the home, forbid TV and radio, and dress distinctly. Except for the handicapped children who were the focus of the suit, all children in the village attend private Jewish schools.

ii.  **Handicapped children:**  Under state and federal laws, all *handicapped* children are entitled to special publicly-funded education services. The Satmars wanted to receive these services without having to send their handicapped children to a neighboring district's public schools (where there were almost no Satmar students).

iii. **Special district:** The New York Legislature tried to give the Satmars what they wanted, by passing a special statute that provided that "the territory of the Village of Kiryas Joel ... shall be ... a ***separate school district.***" The effect of the statute was to allow a locally-elected board of education to open schools, hire teachers, and impose property taxes to fund the operation. The resulting Kiryas Joel Village School District in fact used its powers very narrowly; the only school or program it ever ran was a special-education program for handicapped children, mostly paid for by state funds. At the time the suit was heard by the Court, the new district served only 40 full-time students, of whom two-thirds were Hasidic children who commuted from outside the village.

b. **Holding:** By a 6-3 vote, the Court held that the establishment of the Kiryas Joel Village School District violated the Establishment Clause. The majority opinion, by Justice Souter, seemed to say that there were two distinct problems with the way the district was created: (1) ***religious criteria*** were used to ***draw the boundary lines*** of the district; and (2) the creation of the district was a ***special favor*** for a particular religious sect, with no assurances that other similarly-situated groups would receive the same benefits.

c. **Status of *Lemon* questionable:** The *Kiryas Joel* case raises doubts about the continued viability of the *Lemon* three-part test for Establishment Clause violations. The majority opinion did not rely on *Lemon*, and mentioned it only briefly in the form of two "see also" cites. Justice O'Connor, in her concurrence, welcomed this fact, and urged that the Court's jurisprudence be "freed from the *Lemon* test's rigid influence." Even if a majority does not explicitly overrule *Lemon*, something that many think will happen, *Lemon* may simply fade into disuse.

d. **Another illustration:** *Kiryas Joel* is not the only case in which the Court has found a forbidden preference for one sect over another. The Court also found such an unconstitutional preference in a Minnesota law which originally exempted all religious organizations from registration and reporting requirements applicable to other types of charitable organizations, but which was amended to remove the exemption for any religious organization receiving less than half of its total contributions from members. ***Larson v. Valente***, 456 U.S. 228 (1982). One of the first religious groups to be disadvantaged by the amendment was the Unification Church ("Moonies"), who brought the suit giving rise to the Court's decision.

i. **Strict scrutiny:** For perhaps the first time in an Establishment Clause case, the Court in *Larson* applied ***strict scrutiny*** analysis, rather than the three-prong test (*supra*, p. 596). The three-prong test was appropriate in cases where religion as a whole was arguably benefitted *vis-à-vis* non-religion; where ***one religion*** is ***preferred over another***, the more demanding strict scrutiny analysis must be applied, the Court held. Such an inter-denominational preference could be sustained only if it was "justified by a ***compelling governmental interest*** and ... ***closely fitted*** to further that interest."

ii. **Result of test:** Whether or not Minnesota's asserted interest in guarding against abusive solicitation practices was a compelling one (the Court declined to decide), the means chosen here were ***not "closely fitted" to further that interest.*** Nothing suggested that the likelihood of solicitation abuse was closely related to the ratio of member contributions to total contributions.

**2. Accommodation found not to be a violation:** In *Kiryas Joel* and *Larson v. Valente*, one religion or sect was accommodated in preference to another, and the accommoation was found to be an Establishment Clause violation. However, where what is being accommodated is not a particular religion or sect, but rather, the ***practice of religion generally***, the Court is much ***less likely*** to find an Establishment Clause violation. For example, the Court recently held that a federal statute requiring accommodation of the ***religious practices of prisoners*** — greater accommodation than given to non-religious practices of prisoners — did not on its face violate the Establishment Clause. See ***Cutter v. Wilkinson***, 544 U.S. 709 (2005).

    **a. RLUIPA:** Congress passed a statute, the Religious Land Use and Institutionalized Persons Act of 2000 (RLUIPA), which says in part that "No government shall impose a substantial burden on the religious exercise of a person residing in or confined to an institution," unless the burden furthers "a compelling governmental interest" and does so by "the least restrictive means."

    **b. Suit by prisoners:** The plaintiffs in *Cutter* were several prisoners in the Ohio State Penal system who belonged to "nonmainstream" religions like Satanist and Wicca. They claimed that Ohio prison officials were violating RLUIPA by denying them religious rights given to members of mainstream religions, such as opportunities for group worship and the right to adhere to the dress mandates of their religion. Ohio defended by claiming that RLUIPA on its face violated the Establishment Clause by improperly advancing religion.

    **c. Court strikes down challenge:** The Court unanimously held that RLUIPA ***did not violate*** the Establishment Clause on its face. Even if RLUIPA gave prisoners' rights beyond what would be required to protect their Free Exercise interests, this was a permissible accommodation because " 'there is room for play in the joints' between the [Free Exercise and Establishment] Clauses ... some space for legislative action neither compelled by the Free Exercise clause nor prohibited by the Establishment Clause." Prisoners are unable to attend to their religious needs without government accommodation, so having government give them that accommodation is not the sort of preference for religion over non-religion that would violate the Establishment Clause, the Court said.

        **i. As-applied challenge:** But it's important to note that the attack on the statute in Cutter was a "facial," not an "as applied," attack. (See *supra*, p. 236, for an explanation of the distinction.) The Court observed that if in a *particular case* RLUIPA caused religious accommodation to override other significant governmental interests, such as security, then on an ***as applied*** basis the statute might still be found to be an unconstitutional preference for religion. In this case, because the state's attack on the statute was a facial one, the state could only win if it showed that there was ***no scenario*** in which the statute could be constitutionally applied; the state had not met this heavy burden.

**K. Financial aid to religious schools:** Probably the most important and sensitive issue in the Establishment Clause area is whether, and to what extent, the government may give ***financial assistance*** to religious schools, or to students at these schools.

1. **Three-prong test:** The Court applies the three-prong test in these financial-assistance cases, and in fact it was in such a case that the test was originally formulated. Thus such a program must satisfy each of the following requirements in order to avoid violating the Establishment Clause: (1) it must have a ***secular legislative purpose*** (though it may also have a religious purpose, as long as at least one secular purpose exists); (2) its "principal or primary ***effect***" must neither advance nor inhibit religion; and (3) it must not foster "an excessive government ***entanglement*** with religion." Also, as either an additional requirement or as a sub-requirement of (3), the Court has disallowed programs which are likely to be ***"politically divisive."***

2. **Broad themes:** Before we turn to consideration of particular assistance programs, it is worthwhile to summarize some of the broad themes that have characterized the Court's handling of attacks on financial aid schemes.

    a. **Lower vs. higher education:** The Court has been much less likely to sustain programs which aid ***elementary and secondary*** parochial schools, than it has been to uphold those aiding sectarian ***colleges and universities***. This distinction stems from the belief that in the elementary and secondary setting, religious instruction ***permeates every aspect*** of the educational process, whereas in the higher education context, it is possible to identify and support those aspects of the institution which are devoted to purely secular objectives. Most of the discussion which follows relates to elementary and secondary contexts; separate consideration is given to the higher education area beginning *infra*, p. 688.

    b. **Direct vs. indirect aid:** Assistance programs are more likely to be upheld if the aid is given to ***students and their parents***, rather than directly to the school, and each parent or student gets to decide at which school to use the benefit. (See, e.g., *Zelman v. Simmons-Harris*, the tuition-voucher case, *infra*, p. 684, making this distinction.) This distinction is based on the theory that it is easier to ensure that the aid is used to fulfill secular objectives if the parents and students, rather than the school, are given control of the money or items being furnished.

    c. **All students:** A program which by its terms assists ***all students***, both in public and private schools, is much more likely to be sustained than one which is addressed solely to religious-school students. Also, a program which is ***in fact*** utilized by a significant number of students in public schools, or in non-sectarian private ones, is more likely to be upheld than one which, although theoretically available to all, is overwhelmingly used by parochial school pupils. (However, the fact that the overwhelming majority of users of a program are religious schools or their students is not automatically fatal, if the program is theoretically available to all.)

    d. **Secular effect:** All three of these broad principles can be seen as deriving from the basic requirement that the financial assistance have a ***primary effect*** that is ***secular***. For an effect to be secular, the Court has insisted that it be ***clearly separable*** from any religious effects. Also, the ***breadth*** of the ***benefitted class*** (i.e., the extent to which beneficiaries are not just parochial school students) is an important index of secular effect. See Tribe, pp. 1215-16.

3. **Particular programs:** We turn now to consideration of particular programs aiding parochial schools or their students.

4.  **Transportation:**   A program by which parents were reimbursed for the money spent to *transport* their children to school on *public buses* was upheld, in *Everson v. Board of Education*, 330 U.S. 1 (1947).

    a.  **Public school students included:**   A key feature of the plan approved in *Everson* was that parents of *public school students* were *included* in the reimbursement scheme. It is highly unlikely that a transportation-reimbursement scheme applicable only to religious-school students would be approved by the Court today. The key difference is that the *Everson* scheme can justly be viewed as supplying the secular benefit of "transportation to one's school," and as supplying that benefit in a way that is completely neutral as between religious and secular institutions.

    b.  **Advancement of religion:**   Of course, the argument can be made that at least some parents who send their children to parochial schools under an *Everson*-like scheme might send them to public schools instead if only transportation to public schools were reimbursed by the state. In this sense, an effect of the scheme is to advance religion. The majority in *Everson* dealt with this argument by asserting that the scheme was neutral as between religion and non-religion. Today, the Court would probably dispose of this argument by saying that any benefit to religion was an *incidental* and remote effect, rather than the "principal" or "primary" one.

5.  **Textbooks and other materials:**   *Textbooks* may be loaned to parochial school students, as long as: (1) a similar policy is followed with respect to public-school and private-non-parochial students; and (2) the textbooks are themselves secular rather than religiously-oriented. See *Board of Education v. Allen*, 392 U.S. 236 (1968).

    a.  **Computers and other non-textbook materials:** Similarly, non-textbook materials and equipment, such as *computers*, *audio-visual equipment,* and the like, may be given or lent to religious schools as long as: (1) the materials are themselves non-religious in nature; (2) the materials are *not diverted* for religious purposes (e.g., computers are not used to run religiously-oriented programs); and (3) *all schools* — religious or not — are eligible for the aid on the *same terms*. *Mitchell v. Helms*, 530 U.S. 793 (2000).

        i.   **4 votes for disregarding diversion:** In fact, four members of the Court that decided *Mitchell* believed that even if the non-religious materials *were* diverted for religious use at the school, this would not make any difference. To these four, as long as the government is *evenhanded* in how it treats religious and non-religious schools, there can be no Establishment Clause violation. In other words, these four would not impose requirement (2) above — they would, for instance, allow religious schools to use publicly-funded computers to run religiously-oriented programs.

        ii.  **5 members disagree:** But the other five Justices in *Mitchell* disagreed with this extreme view. Justice O'Connor, who contributed the fifth vote needed for the upholding of the program in *Mitchell*, did so even though she thought diversion was impermissible, because she didn't think substantial diversion had actually occurred in the case and she believed that a theoretical risk of diversion or a few isolated actual instances of it did not create a problem.

6.  **Salary supplements:**   The state may not subsidize parochial education by reimbursing parochial schools for a portion of *teachers' salaries*, even where this reimbursement is

theoretically for the teaching of secular subjects. See, e.g., *Lemon v. Kurtzman*, 403 U.S. 602 (1971). Again, the problem is that there is no way to make sure that these funds are not used for religious purposes, at least not without such surveillance of the teachers' actual conduct that the monitoring itself would constitute excessive entanglement between church and state. *Id.*

7. **Furnishing of teachers:** Suppose the state takes ***public-school teachers*** (i.e., teachers who are on the public payroll and who do most of their teaching in the public schools) and ***sends them into parochial schools*** to teach special subjects. As the result of a major 1997 shift in case law, this will ***no longer be deemed to violate*** the Establishment Clause, if the public-school teachers teach in a secular manner and without curricular interference by the parochial school. ***Agostini v. Felton***, 117 S. Ct. 1997 (1997).

   a. **Rationale:** The 5-Justice majority in *Agostini* made these major points:

      i. **Direct aid not necessarily invalid:** It is not true (as the Court had previously thought it was) that "all government aid that directly aids the educational function of religious schools is invalid."

      ii. **No "symbolic union" problem:** It's also not true that the presence of public-school teachers in parochial school classrooms "will, without more, create the impression of a *'symbolic union'* between church and state."

      iii. **No distinction from sign-language-interpreter situation:** The provision of the educational programs here — remedial courses in basic school subjects, given to those in danger of failing — was "indistinguishable" from the provision of ***sign-language interpreters*** in parochial schools, something that the Court had previously approved.

      iv. **No excessive-entanglement problem:** There was simply no reason to believe that the monitoring needed to ensure that the in-school programs didn't inculcate religion would cause an ***excessive entanglement*** between government and religion. ***Unannounced monthly visits*** by public supervisors would probably be enough to fulfill this need for monitoring, and would not result in any greater "entanglement" than other programs that the Court had previously approved.

   b. **Dissent:** The four ***dissenters*** in *Agostini* strenuously objected. The principal dissent was by Justice Souter.

      i. **Subsidy problem:** First, Souter argued that allowing publicly-funded teachers to teach basic subjects inside the parochial school amounted to a ***"subsidy"*** of the school — the school was relieved of the need to teach core subjects, thus ***freeing up funds*** that could then be used to fulfill the school's religious mission. This violated the "flat ban on subsidization" that, he said, had been an "unwavering rule in Establishment Clause cases."

      ii. **Impression of public endorsement:** Second, he thought that in-school publicly-funded teaching was substantially more likely to give the impression of ***public endorsement*** of religion than such teaching delivered outside the school. "Sharing the teaching responsibilities within a school having religious objectives is far more likely to ***telegraph approval of the school's mission*** than keeping the State's distance would do."

8. **Services:** Publicly-funded *services* (e.g., testing and counseling) may be supplied to parochial school students. Apparently the only present limitations on such services are that: (1) they must be *offered to all schools* in a way that does not intentionally favor parochial schools; and (2) they must have an exclusively secular content. So if, for instance, the state offers testing, counseling, remedial education or other specialized services to all non-public schools, with the quantity of services keyed to the size of the school's enrollment, and with the services having no direct religious content, there is apparently no Establishment Clause problem. That seems to be true even if the principal *effect* of the services is to aid religion.

    a. **Source of this principle:** This principle — that the presence of a principal effect of aiding religion is not fatal when services are provided — seems to follow from two of the recent cases that we've already discussed, *Agostini v. Felton* (*supra*, p. 683) and *Mitchell v. Helms* (*supra*, p. 682). In *Agostini*, the Court held that the state may supply teachers to teach even basic remedial courses in the parochial schools as long as the curriculum is carefully kept secular. There seems to be no reason why specialized services such as testing and counseling can't also be supplied on this basis. And *Mitchell* establishes that the government may give or lend schools educational equipment and materials subject only to the requirements of even-handedness and secular-content, so this case, too, suggests that services may be furnished to parochial schools on the same basis as to public and non-religious private schools.

9. **Tuition vouchers:** *Tuition vouchers* may be given to parents to enable them to pay religious-school tuition, if the vouchers may also be used in non-religious private schools. In *Zelman v. Simmons-Harris*, 536 U.S. 639 (2002), the most controversial and important Establishment Clause case in years, the Court held by a 5-4 vote that such a tuition voucher plan *did not violate the Clause.* The majority reasoned that any "advancement of a religious message" that the plan facilitated was an "incidental" one that resulted from *"the deliberate choices of numerous individual recipients,"* not from the government. The Court seems to have announced a new approach to cases involving government funding that finds its way to religious institutions — so long as private citizens make individual choices about how to use the funding, the fact that the great majority of the funding ends up being used in religious institutions, for pursuit of religious ends, does not seem to matter.

    a. **Facts:** In *Zelman*, the state of Ohio set up a program under which any Cleveland student in kindergarten through 8th grade could receive a voucher of up to $2,250 to attend private school. In the most recent year, 3,700 of the 75,000 students in the Cleveland school district took advantage of the program. Although the program let both religious and non-religious private schools participate, 96% of participating students enrolled in religious schools. The principal purpose of the program seems to have been to enable students in a failing public school system (a federal judge had placed the entire Cleveland system under state supervision on account of its failure to educate students) to afford a private alternative. However, the federal Court of Appeals found the program to violate the Establishment Clause, on the grounds that it had the primary effect of advancing religion.

    b. **Majority upholds:** Chief Justice Rehnquist was joined by Justices O'Connor, Scalia, Kennedy and Thomas in upholding the constitutionality of the program.

**i.** **Reliance on precedent:** The Chief Justice began by reviewing earlier cases that, he said, had distinguished between "government programs that provide aid directly to religious schools" and "programs of true private choice, in which government aid reaches religious schools only as a result of the genuine and independent *choices of private individuals*." Programs falling into this latter category — ones that implement private choices — had been consistently upheld, he said. For instance, in *Mueller v. Allen*, 463 U.S. 388 (1983), the Court rejected an Establishment Clause attack on a Minnesota program that gave tax deductions for certain private school tuition costs, even though 96% of the program's beneficiaries were parents of children in religious schools. In *Mueller*, the Court reasoned that where public funds were made available to religious schools "only as a result of numerous, private choices of individual parents," "no imprimatur of state approval can be deemed to have been conferred on any particular religion, or on religion generally."

**ii.** **Private choices here:** Consequently, Rehnquist wrote, the voucher program here was constitutional because it, too, was a "program of *true private choice*," one that was "neutral in all respects toward religion." Rehnquist noted that not only non-parochial private schools, but also public schools from adjacent (non-Cleveland) school districts, were eligible to participate in the voucher program. Therefore, the mere fact that most participating students attended parochial schools did not indicate any preference for religion, especially in view of the fact that 81% of private schools in Ohio were religious schools.

**iii.** **Percentage disputed:** Rehnquist also disputed the significance of the fact that 96% of voucher users attended religious schools. The proper way to look at the issue, he said, was to consider what percentage of all students using *any kind of alternative publicly-funded educational program* attended religious schools. If one added to the voucher users those Cleveland children enrolled in "alternative community schools," "alternative magnet schools" and "traditional public schools with [separately funded] tutorial assistance," fewer than 20% of those receiving alternative public funding used that funding to attend religious schools. In sum, the Ohio program permitted "a wide spectrum of individuals" to "exercise genuine choice among options public and private, secular and religious." Such a program of "true private choice" did not have the primary effect of aiding religion, and therefore did not violate the Establishment Clause.

**c.** **O'Connor concurrence:** Justice O'Connor, in a concurrence, agreed particularly with this last point of Rehnquist's — in deciding whether the program was neutral between religion and non-religion, the Court was required to make "an evaluation of *all reasonable educational options* Ohio provides the Cleveland school system, regardless of whether they are formally made available in the same section of the Ohio Code as the voucher program." By this test, which would include the magnet schools, alternative community schools and the like, the Ohio program met the test of being religiously neutral.

**d.** **Dissents:** The four dissenters (Stevens, Souter, Ginsburg and Breyer) wrote three dissents. All viewed the majority's opinion as a major and regrettable change to the Court's prior Establishment Clause doctrines, and all warned that this new approach would likely *trigger major social conflicts.*

i. **Stevens:**  In a brief dissent, Justice Stevens warned that "whenever we remove a brick from the wall that was designed to separate religion and government, we *increase the risk of religious strife* and weaken the foundation of our democracy."

ii. **Souter:**  Justice Souter warned that the voucher program here gave far more extensive aid to religion than the "isolated and insubstantial" aid allowed by prior decisions. Here, the money would pay for instruction not only in secular subjects but in *religious ones as well*, "in schools that can fairly be characterized as founded to teach religious doctrine and to imbue teaching in all subjects with a religious dimension."

    **(1) Not true private choice:**  Souter also rejected the majority's core assertion that the voucher program was merely a neutral implementation of private choices. He said that "the question is whether the private hand is *genuinely free* to send the money in either a secular direction or a religious one." To him, the answer was "no" — the $2,250 cap on tuition reimbursement was *significantly lower than the tuition typically charged* by nonreligious private schools, but fit comfortably with the typical tuition at religious schools in Cleveland (e.g., an average tuition at participating Catholic schools of $1,592). Consequently, it was not surprising that only three secular private schools in Cleveland enrolled more than eight voucher students. "For the overwhelming number of children in the voucher scheme, *the only alternative to the public schools is religious.* And it is entirely irrelevant that the state did not deliberately design the network of private schools for the sake of channeling money into religious institutions."

iii. **Breyer:** Justice Breyer warned that the majority was violating the primary principle behind the court's Establishment Clause cases, the principle of *"avoiding religiously based social conflict."* For instance, he noted that the voucher program here required that no participating school "advocate or foster unlawful behavior or teach hatred of any person or group on the basis of race, ethnicity, national origin, or religion." It is, he said, "difficult to imagine a more divisive activity than the appointment of state officials as referees to determine whether a particular religious doctrine 'teaches hatred or advocates lawlessness.' "

    **(1) Funding of religious teaching:** Furthermore, Breyer pointed out, the vouchers here would be used to *fund primary religious education*. For instance, some of the schools participating in the program had announced that their goals were to "communicate the gospel" and to "provide instruction in religious truths and values." He argued that "history suggests ... that government funding of this kind of religious endeavor is far more contentious than providing funding for secular textbooks, computers, vocational training, or even funding for adults who wish to obtain a college education at a religious university." The "parental choice" aspect of the program, he said, did not cure the problem. For instance, "parental choice cannot help the taxpayer who does not want to finance the religious education of children."

e. **Significance:**  *Zelman* suggests that a majority of the Court will henceforth take a significantly less rigorous view of government programs whose benefits flow to religious organizations. So long as the funding program is facially neutral as between religious and non-religious organizations, and so long as the program relies upon individual citizens to make their own decisions about which organization shall receive the funding, the fact that the vast majority of the total funding directly advances organizations' religious objectives seems not to matter. Here are two examples of how *Zelman* may be interpreted:

❏ Suppose a student wants to use a ***state-funded scholarship*** to study for the priesthood at a religious seminary. Presumably *Zelman* means that so long as the scholarship program is facially neutral — i.e., it allows the funds to be used, at the student's discretion, in both religious and non-religious programs — there's no Establishment Clause problem, even if most students who get such scholarships use them for religious training. (See the discussion of scholarship, Par. 10 below.)

❏ Suppose the federal government adopts a bond program, whereby any organization meeting certain financial criteria can issue ***tax-free bonds to construct buildings***. Suppose further that 90% or more of the buildings so built are houses of worship. As long as the eligibility criteria are facially neutral (i.e., non-religious organizations in theory have an equal opportunity to participate), the fact that the vast majority of the tax-subsidized funds are used to support directly a core mission of worship probably won't matter.

10. **Scholarships for religious study:** Even before *Zelman, supra*, it was clear that a generalized program of awarding **scholarship money** or other grants to students would not run afoul of the Establishment Clause, even if some students used the funds to attend religious institutions that would prepare them for a religious calling. Thus in *Witters v. Washington Dept. of Services for the Blind*, 474 U.S. 481 (1986), the Court unanimously held that the Establishment Clause was not violated by a state's grant of funds under a vocational rehabilitation assistance program to a blind student who would use the funds to attend a private Christian school, where he would train to be a "pastor, missionary, or youth director."

   a. **Effect of *Zelman*:** *Zelman* seems to add to this result in *Withers* the further rule that there is no Establishment Clause violation even if the ***vast majority*** of those participating in the scholarship program use the scholarship for religious-education purposes, as long as the program is equally open to those who want to pursue non-religious study.

   b. **Scholarships for ministry-study not required by Free Exercise clause:** By the way, *Witters* and *Zelman* do not mean that a state *must* include scholarships or vouchers for ministry study if the state gives scholarships for study in all other fields. In other words, the mere fact that a state is free under the Establishment clause to give scholarships that will be used for religiously-oriented purposes does *not* mean that it ***violates the Free Exercise clause*** if it excludes ministry studies from a generally-applicable scholarship program.

      i. ***Locke v. Davey*:** This result was announced in *Locke v. Davey*, 540 U.S. 712 (2004). There, the state of Washington awarded merit scholarships that could be used in any accredited college, and for any field of study, except the pursuit of a degree in "theology."[1] By a 7-2 vote, the Court concluded that this exclusion of theology studies did not violate the Free Exercise clause. The Court stressed that "there are some state actions permitted by the Establishment Clause but not required by the Free Exercise Clause," and said that this case fell into that category. For more about *Locke*, see *infra*, p. 691.

11. **Aid to higher education:** Public financial assistance to sectarian *colleges* raises *fewer Establishment Clause problems* than does aid to elementary and secondary schools. Although the Court has applied the usual three-prong test in the aid-to-colleges context, it has found that test to be much more readily met. This has been especially true of the "primary secular effect" and "no excessive entanglement" prongs, which have often tripped up schemes for aiding lower education.

   a. **General subsidies:**  For instance, in *Roemer v. Maryland Public Works Bd.*, 426 U.S. 736 (1976), the Court upheld a scheme of subsidies to private colleges, including religious ones, even though the subsidies were not earmarked for particular uses (though they were not permitted to be used for "sectarian purposes.")

      i. **Rationale:**  The Court in *Roemer* reasoned that unlike church-related elementary and secondary schools, the colleges performed *"essentially secular educational functions."*

   b. **Construction of chapels:**  However, it is possible to imagine programs assisting colleges which might nonetheless violate the Establishment Clause. For instance, a college's use of public funds (paid directly from the government to the college) to *build chapels* would probably be unconstitutional, as would direct governmental assistance to seminaries whose sole function was to train priests or ministers.

## III.  THE FREE EXERCISE CLAUSE

A. **Introduction:**  The First Amendment bars government from making any law *"prohibiting the free exercise"* of religion. The Free Exercise Clause, like the Establishment Clause, applies not only to the federal government but also to the states, via the Fourteenth Amendment.

   1. **No forbidding of belief:**  The Free Exercise Clause flatly forbids the outlawing of any religious *belief.*

   2. **Conduct:**  The difficult issues arise not in connection with pure beliefs, but in connection with *conduct* that is related to beliefs. Normally, free exercise problems arise when the government, acting in pursuit of *non-religious objectives*, either: (1) forbids or burdens conduct which happens to be dictated by someone's religious belief; or (2) compels or encourages conduct which is forbidden by someone's religious belief.

      **Example:** The state awards unemployment compensation only to those jobless workers who make themselves available for work Monday through Saturday. Although this rule has a non-religious purpose (making sure that only those whose unemployment is involuntary collect aid), the statute strongly encourages conduct which is violative of the religious beliefs of some persons (e.g., Seventh Day Adventists, whose religion

---

1. The provision was intended to comply with a state-constitutional prohibition on the provision of public funds used towards degrees that are "devotional in nature or designed to induce religious faith." So a student could use the scholarship to take some theology courses, but could not use the scholarship for a degree in theology, since that would be a "devotional" degree.

makes Saturday the day of rest). Therefore, the act raises significant free exercise problems. (In fact, the act was held to violate the Free Exercise Clause as applied to Seventh Day Adventists, in *Sherbert v. Verner, infra*, p. 692.)

3. **General principles:** However, not all statutes which forbid conduct required by religious beliefs or which compel conduct forbidden by religious beliefs are automatically violative of the Free Exercise Clause. The Court has not developed a clear test for determining when such a violation exists (in contrast to the three-prong standard in Establishment Clause cases). But the following principles seem to be generally applied:

   a. **Intent:** Whenever the ***purpose*** of a governmental action is to negatively effect a particular type of conduct ***because*** it is dictated by religion, that act will almost automatically be found to violate the Free Exercise Clause. Such purposeful interference with religion will be ***strictly scrutinized***, and almost never upheld. However, situations where such an illicit motive can be proved rarely arise. For one illustration, see *Church of the Lukumi Babalu Aye, infra.*

   b. **Burdensome effect:** Where the statute is not motivated by an intent to interfere with religiously-related conduct, but the statute nonetheless has that ***effect***, the Court has applied a ***heightened scrutiny***: the state must demonstrate "first, that the regulation pursues a ***particularly important governmental goal***, and, second, that an ***exemption*** would ***substantially hinder*** the fulfillment of that goal." Tribe, p. 1251.

      i. **Exemptions required:** Thus even if the state is pursuing a very important non-religious end, but that end could be achieved as well or almost as well by granting an ***exemption*** to those whose religious beliefs dictate non-compliance, such an exemption ***must be given.***

      ii. **Cutting back:** However, a recent case suggests that this rule requiring exemptions to be given where feasible will be dramatically ***cut back*** by the Rehnquist Court. *Employment Division v. Smith*, a 1990 case discussed *infra*, p. 696, seems to mean that only in the very limited case of ***unemployment benefits*** will the Court give heightened scrutiny to government's refusal to grant an exemption from laws that burden religious beliefs.

      iii. **Criminal prohibition:** Also, if the government act that burdens religious beliefs takes the form of a generally applicable ***criminal prohibition***, and if the burden on religious belief is merely an incidental (not intended) effect, the *Smith* case holds that there can be no violation of free exercise principles and the prohibition is automatically valid. Thus in *Smith* itself, the Court held that Oregon did not have to give an exemption from the general rule against use of the drug peyote to American Indians who used the drug in their religious rituals. See *infra*, p. 696.

B. **Intent to interfere with religion:** As noted, where government takes an action whose ***purpose*** is to forbid or interfere with particular conduct ***because*** the conduct is dictated by a religious belief, the governmental action will be strictly scrutinized and almost always struck down as a violation of the Free Exercise Clause. Cases in this category rarely arise, however.

   1. **Animal sacrifice case:** Virtually the only modern Supreme Court case in which government was shown to have had such an illicit intent to disfavor a particular religion is ***Church of the Lukumi Babalu Aye, Inc. v. Hialeah***, 508 U.S. 520 (1993), involving ***ritual animal sacrifice*** by practitioners of the Santeria religion.

a.  **The Santeria religion:**   The plaintiffs in *Lukumi* were members of a church following the Santeria religion. Santeria, found most often in Cuba, is a religion whose members perform ritual sacrifices of chickens, pigeons and other animals as part of rites for birth, marriage and death, for cure of the sick, and at other times. The animal is killed by the cutting of its carotid arteries, and is usually (but not in all instances) cooked and eaten.

b.  **Government's response:**   The city of Hialeah, Florida, where the Ps' church was located, enacted a series of ordinances that, taken together, outlawed religious animal sacrifice. One ordinance, for instance, made it unlawful to "sacrifice any animal" within the city limits, and defined "sacrifice" as "to unnecessarily kill, torment, torture, or mutilate an animal in a public or private ritual or ceremony not for the primary purpose of food consumption.  ...  " The ordinances were written so that their sole effect would be to ban sacrifices by Santeria practitioners; for instance, Kosher slaughter was carefully exempted by defining "sacrifice" so as to exclude slaughter that is "for the primary purpose of food consumption."

   i.   **Motive:**   The history behind the ordinances' enactment — such as the supporting statements by Council members, and the public debate concerning the issue — made it clear that the community as a whole ***disliked the practice of Santeria***, and wanted to ***abolish sacrificial rituals*** by Santeria practitioners.

c.  **Ordinance struck down:**   *All members* of the Court agreed that the Hialeah ordinances should be struck down as a ***violation of the Free Exercise Clause***. Seven Justices believed that the intent of the City Council in enacting the ordinances was to suppress the ritual portion of the Santeria religion, and agreed that governmental action that is intended to disfavor a particular religious practice will almost always violate the Free Exercise Clause.

d.  **Rationale:**   Writing for the Court on most points, Justice Kennedy explained that government action that affects religion will be subjected to the ***"most rigorous of scrutiny"*** (which it will rarely survive) unless the government act is both: (1) ***"neutral"***; and (2) of ***"general applicability."***

   i.   **Not "neutral":**   Here, Kennedy found, the ordinances were clearly ***not "neutral"*** since they were transparently enacted for the ***purpose*** of disfavoring a particular religious practice.

   ii.  **Not "generally applicable":**   Nor was the ordinance of ***"general applicability."*** Kennedy seemed to say that the more ***"underinclusive"*** (see *supra*, p. 238) a governmental action is, the less likely it is to manifest the required "general applicability." Here, the ordinances were very underinclusive. For instance, the city claimed that the ordinance was necessary to protect the public health, since sacrificed animals were frequently not properly disposed of. Yet the city did not regulate the disposal of animals that had been killed by hunters, or the disposal of leftover food by restaurants.

e.  **Net result:**   *Lukumi* makes it clear that in those very rare instances where government is shown to have acted for the ***purpose*** of burdening a particular type of conduct because that conduct is dictated by religion, the governmental act will be subjected to such ***strict scrutiny*** that it will almost never survive.

**f.** **Not applicable to withholding of rewards rather than giving of punishment:** *Lukumi* involved a government-imposed *punishment* of a religiously-motivated practice; the case says that strict scrutiny will be given to that government punishment unless the punishment was both "neutral" and "of general applicability." What if the government disfavors a religious practice not by imposing an affirmative punishment, but rather by ***withdrawing a benefit*** that is given to otherwise-similar non-religious practices? A 2004 case seems to mean that *Lukumi **does not apply*** to this "withdrawal of benefits" scenario.

    **i.** ***Locke v. Davey:*** The case was *Locke v. Davey*, 540 U.S. 712 (2004) (also discussed *supra*, p. 687), in which the state of Washington gave merit scholarships to all eligible college students, with the one exception that the scholarship could not be used to pursue a degree in "devotional theology" (i.e., training for the ministry). The Court held that this carve-out of a generally-applicable government benefit did not violate the Free Exercise clause. Justice Scalia (joined by Justice Thomas) argued in dissent that *Lukumi* required that this carve-out be strictly scrutinized, and struck down, as being facially discriminatory towards religion. But the majority responded that *Lukumi **did not apply***, because the state's disfavor of religion here was of a ***"far milder kind"*** than in *Lukumi*,[2] and imposed ***"neither criminal nor civil sanctions*** on any type of religious service or right." Also, majority said, "training someone to lead a congregation is an essentially religious endeavor" that has "no counterpart with respect to other callings or professions"; therefore, *Lukumi* did not require equal treatment of that essentially-religious endeavor.

    **ii.** **Limited scope of *Lukumi*:** So perhaps *Locke* means that *Lukumi* will apply only to criminal or civil ***"sanctions"*** — in essence punishments — that are imposed for the purpose of disfavoring religious practices, not to government conduct that merely withholds some generally-applicable benefit so the benefit cannot be used in connection with a religiously-motivated activity. At the very least, *Locke* seems to mean that *Lukumi* won't apply — and the Free Exercise clause won't be violated — where the government intentionally withdraws funding from an "essentially religious endeavor," like training for the ministry, while funding otherwise-comparable endeavors.

**C.** **Incidental burdensome effect:** Now, let us turn to the more usual type of Free Exercise case, that in which governmental action has the ***unintended effect*** of burdening religiously-motivated conduct. Our discussion is divided into "traditional approach" and "modern approach."

**D.** **Traditional approach to "unintended effect" cases:** The principle described in "Burdensome effect" (*supra*, p. 689) — that where a law has the unintended effect of burdening religiously-related conduct, an exemption must be given where feasible — has only been applied since the 1960's. Prior to that time, the Court took the view that so long as the state was acting in pursuit of non-religious ends, and was regulating conduct rather than pure beliefs, the Free Exercise Clause served as little or no barrier.

---

2. For instance, the scholarship could be used at a sectarian college, and could even be used for the taking of a limited number of theology courses, as long as the student was not pursuing a devotional-theology degree.

1. **Polygamy:** For instance, the federal government's right to make ***bigamy*** a crime in federal territories was upheld in *Reynolds v. U.S.*, 98 U.S. 145 (1878), over the Free Exercise objection of a Mormon who claimed that polygamy was his religious duty. The Court saw the practice of religiously-related polygamy as no different from the practice of religiously-motivated human sacrifice; each was conduct "in violation of social duties," and therefore prohibitable by the state.

2. **Use of Free Speech Clause:** Prior to the 1960s, whatever protection of religious liberty did come from the Court tended to come from the ***Free Speech*** rather than Free Exercise Clause.

   a. **Compulsory flag salute:** For instance, in *West Virginia State Board of Ed. v. Barnette*, 319 U.S. 624 (1943), a group of Jehovah's Witnesses attacked regulations requiring students to salute the flag. The Court invalidated the regulations, but on free speech rather than free exercise grounds — the state had no power to "force citizens to confess by word or act" their faith in any particular view of "politics, nationalism, religion or other matter of opinion," and the right not to be subjected to such compulsion existed whether one's disagreement came from religion or from other sources.

   b. **"Live Free or Die" license plates:** Free speech rather than free exercise principles were again used in the more recent case of *Wooley v. Maynard*, 430 U.S. 705 (1977), where the Court struck down New Hampshire's requirement that the state motto "Live Free or Die" be displayed on car license plates; what the Court found to be violated was the broad First Amendment right to "refrain from speaking."

E. **Modern approach to "unintended effect" cases:** The ***modern approach*** to situations where state regulations have the unintended effect of burdening religious beliefs is, as noted, to uphold such laws only when they are the ***least restrictive means*** of accomplishing a ***compelling*** state objective. In particular, where the state's objective could be served as well, or almost as well, by granting an ***exemption*** to those whose religious beliefs are burdened by the regulation, ***such an exemption must be given.*** (But as is discussed *infra*, p. 696, as the result of a 1990 decision the Court seems to be dramatically cutting back this principle that an exemption must be given where feasible.)

1. **Accommodation for Sabbath:** The most important case demonstrating the "give an exemption where feasible" approach is ***Sherbert v. Verner***, 374 U.S. 398 (1963). Sherbert, a Seventh Day Adventist, was fired for being unwilling to work on Saturdays, her religion's day of rest. All other available jobs required willingness to work on Saturdays. The state refused to give her unemployment compensation benefits, on the grounds that she had declined to accept "suitable work when offered." But the Supreme Court held that the state's refusal violated Mrs. Sherbert's right to the free exercise of her religion.

   a. **Rationale:** The Court reasoned that South Carolina's policy burdened Sherbert's free exercise of her religion, since it forced her to choose between receiving benefits and following her religion. This choice placed "the same kind of burden upon the free exercise of religion as would a fine imposed against [her] for her Saturday worship." Furthermore, there was a ***discriminatory*** component to the state's action, since Sunday worshippers were not put to this choice.

   b. **Strict scrutiny:** But the fact that Sherbert's free exercise rights were burdened was not by itself enough to gain her a victory. Rather, the issue became whether there was a compelling state interest justifying the governmental policy, which could not be satisfied by means placing less of a burden upon the exercise of religion. Here, no showing was made by the state that an ***exemption*** for Sabbatarians would prevent the state from achieving its objective (assuring that payments go only to those who were involuntarily unemployed).

    **c.**   **Dissent:**   A dissent argued that the majority's holding amounted to a rule that the state "must single out for financial assistance those whose behavior is religiously motivated, even though it denies such assistance to others whose identical behavior (in this case, inability to work on Saturdays) is not religiously motivated." In the dissent's view, such "financial assistance to religion" might not violate the Establishment Clause if voluntarily given by the state, but it was certainly not ***compelled*** by the Constitution. In the dissent's view, the effect of South Carolina's rule on Sherbert's practice of religion was "indirect, remote and insubstantial." (Justice Stewart, although he concurred in the result, believed that that result did violate the Court's prior Establishment Clause decisions, in that it preferred a religious over a secular ground for being unavailable for work; but Stewart believed that the prior Establishment Clause decisions were wrong.)

    **d.**   **Sunday closing laws:**   The rationale of *Sherbert* may be at odds with a prior case involving a similar issue, *Braunfeld v. Brown*, 366 U.S. 599 (1961). There, the Court upheld the application of a state Sunday closing law to orthodox Jewish merchants, who argued that their ability to earn a livelihood was impaired by the law, since their religious beliefs prohibited Saturday work.

      **i.**   **Standard used:**   The Court articulated much the same standard later used in *Sherbert*: "If the State regulates conduct by enacting a general law within its power, the purpose and effect of which is to advance the State's secular goals, the statute is valid despite its indirect burden on religious observance unless the state may accomplish its purpose by means which do not impose such a burden."

      **ii.**   **Application of standard:**   Here, however, granting an exemption for those whose religious beliefs forbade Saturday work would (in the Court's view) have undermined the state's secular purpose: the purpose of assuring a ***uniform day of rest.***

    **e.**   **Difficulty of reconciling:**   The three Justices who concurred or dissented in *Sherbert* believed that the majority's rationale was inconsistent with the result in *Braunfeld*, and that *Sherbert* thus effectively overruled *Braunfeld*. In both cases, the state's policy put the individual to the hard choice between following a religious conviction and avoiding financial suffering. Indeed, it can be argued that the hardship in *Braunfeld* was greater than that in *Sherbert*, since the hardship in *Sherbert* lasted only during the limited unemployment compensation period, while that in *Braunfeld* would theoretically continue throughout the merchant's working career.

    **f.**   **Modern Court's view:**   The ruling and rationale of *Sherbert* — at least when applied to the same narrow context of unemployment benefits — have remained good law under the Burger and Rehnquist Courts. See, e.g., *Frazee v. Illinois Dept. of Employment Security*, 489 U.S. 829 (1989).

    **g.**   **Tension with Establishment Clause rules:**   Cases like *Sherbert* and *Thomas* (as well as *Yoder, infra*) demonstrate that the Free Exercise Clause sometimes requires government to accommodate the religious interests of private citizens. Yet, the Establishment Clause clearly places limits on the extent to which government can carry out this accommodation. There is, therefore, an obvious tension between the two clauses.

> **i.   Connecticut Sabbath case:**  For instance, the Court has held that a Connecticut statute requiring private employers to give every worker a day off on his day of Sabbath observance violated the Establishment Clause. See *Thornton v. Caldor, Inc.*, 472 U.S. 703 (1985) (discussed more extensively *supra*, p. 666). Thus it can be argued that the very thing that South Carolina was required to do in *Sherbert* (protect an employee from being burdened by the consequences of refusing to work on his Sabbath day) was something that Connecticut was prevented from doing in *Thornton*. It could even be argued that *Sherbert* and *Thornton* are inconsistent.

**2.   Compulsory education:**  Where interference with religious freedom exists, it is not quite sufficient for the state to show that there are no less-restrictive alternatives for fully achieving its goals. If granting an exemption will *almost* fully achieve these goals, the state will generally be required to grant it even at this slight sacrifice to its objectives. This is implicitly illustrated by ***Wisconsin v. Yoder***, 406 U.S. 205 (1972), where the Court invalidated Wisconsin's refusal to exempt 14- and 15-year-old Amish students from the requirement of attending school until the age of 16.

> **a.   Rationale:**  The parents of the Amish students satisfied the Court that it was an essential element of the Amish religion that members be informally taught to earn their living through farming and other rural activities, and that compulsory high school education was at odds with that belief. Applying strict scrutiny, the Court concluded that an exemption must be granted unless the state could show an interest "of the highest order," which could not be served by means other than denial of an exemption.

> **b.   Harm not sufficiently great:**  The state's interest, of course, was in having all of its citizens be reasonably well-educated, so that they could participate intelligently in political affairs and become economically self-sufficient. The Court implicitly conceded that Amish children who failed to attend high school would not receive the same level of intellectual learning; in other words, the state's objective would not be as fully realized if an exemption were given. But the Court considered it crucial that nearly all Amish children continued to live in the Amish community throughout their lives, and that the informal vocational training they received seemed to prepare them well for that life.

> **c.   Significance:**  Thus the Court in *Yoder* seemed to hold that the state's interest must be read ***broadly and flexibly***, not narrowly and rigidly, in determining whether that interest could still be fulfilled if an exemption were given.

> **d.   Dissent:**  Justice Douglas, the sole dissenter in *Yoder*, argued that the majority was wrong to decide the case without determining whether each of the ***children*** involved desired to attend high school over the objections of his parent; Douglas contended that the child's desires should be preeminent.

**3.   Denial of exemption survives strict scrutiny:**  Not every governmental refusal to allow an exemption from regulations which burden a genuinely-held religious belief will be struck down, even though strict scrutiny is applied. For instance, the federal government's refusal to exempt Amish employers from paying ***social security taxes*** on wages paid survived strict scrutiny in *U.S. v. Lee*, 455 U.S. 252 (1982).

a. **Rationale:** Unlike the situation in *Sherbert* and *Yoder*, an exemption would, the Court reasoned, significantly impair government's achievement of its objective, "the fiscal vitality of the social security system," since **mandatory participation** is indispensable to attainment of that objective.

b. **Other cases not distinguishable:** Also, the Court argued, if an exemption were made in the social security tax context, it would be hard to justify not allowing a similar exemption from **general** federal taxes where the taxpayer argues that his religious beliefs require him to reduce or eliminate his payments (e.g., so that he will not contribute to the government's war-related activities.)

c. **Stevens' view:** Justice Stevens, concurring in *Lee*, went even further. He did not believe that strict scrutiny was warranted at all. Rather, he contended, "it is the objector who must shoulder the burden of demonstrating that there is a **unique reason** for allowing him a special exemption from a valid law of general applicability."

    i. **Incentives:** He also suggested that the situation here was quite different from that in *Sherbert* and *Thomas*, since the incentives were very different: the individuals in *Sherbert* and *Thomas* gave up jobs, and sought only less-profitable unemployment compensation; they thus made a real sacrifice for their asserted religious beliefs. Here, by contrast, Lee's refusal to pay social security taxes was not a sacrifice by him at all, and would in fact be beneficial to him if allowed. Allowance of such an exemption would give "every citizen … an economic motivation to join the favored sects," thus destroying the constitutional ban on preference of one religion over another.

4. **Combatting race discrimination as compelling interest:** The government's interest in **preventing racial discrimination** is one interest which is **so compelling**, and so unlikely to be satisfactorily achieved if exemptions are given, that the government may forbid such discrimination **even where the ban conflicts with genuine religious beliefs**. Thus in *Bob Jones University v. U.S.*, 461 U.S. 574 (1983), the Court upheld the IRS' denial of tax-exempt status to the university because of its white-only admissions policy. Even though that policy was the product of university officials' "genuine belief that the Bible forbids interracial dating and marriage," the policy was in conflict with the state's compelling interest in banning privately-practiced discrimination, and that interest could not be satisfied by less-restrictive means.

5. **Wearing of yarmulke in military:** Where a Free Exercise claim is asserted by a person in active **military service**, a refusal by military authorities to accommodate that claim will *not* be subject to strict scrutiny. Indeed, as a case involving military dress shows, a majority of the Court will give **great deference** to the military's determination that accommodation would be unwise. In ***Goldman v. Weinberger***, 475 U.S. 503 (1986), the Court held that an Orthodox Jewish Air Force captain did not have a Free Exercise right to wear a yarmulke while on duty, in contravention of an Air Force regulation requiring uniform dress. (A yarmulke is a head-covering that Orthodox Jewish men are required by their religion to wear at all times.)

a. **Rationale:** A deeply divided Court, by a 5-4 vote, held that the military context requires a far different balance between the interests of the government and the individual than does the civilian context. Although a person in military service is not completely without First Amendment rights, the majority said, "when evaluating whether military needs justify a particular restriction on religiously motivated conduct, courts must give great deference to the professional judgment of military authorities concerning the relative importance of a particular military interest."

    **i.**   **Interest in standardized uniform:** Here, the Air Force made a judgment that the use of *standardized uniforms* "encourages the *subordination of personal preferences and identities* in favor of the *overall group mission*." Even though the rule banning the wearing of religious headgear would cause Captain Goldman to violate the tenets of his religion, "the First Amendment does not require the military to accommodate such practices in the face of its view that they would detract from the uniformity sought by the dress regulation."

  **b.**   **Concurrence:** In a separate concurrence, three Justices indicated that the principal problem with allowing Captain Goldman to wear the yarmulke was not the need for standardized dress, but the need for "*uniform treatment* for the members of *all religious faiths*."

**6.**   **Prisoner's claim:** Where a Free Exercise claim is raised by a *prisoner*, a refusal by prison authorities to accommodate that claim will be *even more deferentially* reviewed than a comparable refusal by military authorities (see *supra*).

  **a.**   *O'Lone* **case:** Thus in *O'Lone v. Shabazz*, 478 U.S. 342 (1987), the prisoners, Muslims, contended that they had a Free Exercise right to attend Jumu'ah, a congregational service held at mid-day on Fridays, and that the prison authorities' refusal to modify the prisoners' work schedules to permit them to attend the service violated that right.

  **b.**   **Action upheld:** A five-justice majority, in rejecting the prisoners' arguments, applied an extremely deferential standard, under which the authorities must *merely behave "reasonably"* — the same weak standard applied to a variety of other prisoners' rights claims. In particular, the majority refused to impose upon prison officials the burden of "disprov[ing] the availability of alternatives."

**7.**   **Generally-applicable criminal rule:** Suppose that the government enacts a *criminal prohibition* on a certain type of activity. Suppose further that the government does not intend to burden religious beliefs, but that some people's religious beliefs are in fact seriously burdened by the proscription. In this situation, the Court articulated a new rule in 1990 that seems to be a stunning reversal of past theory. In *Employment Division v. Smith*, 494 U.S. 872 (1990), the Court, by a 5-4 vote, held that such a generally-applicable criminal law is automatically *enforceable*, apparently regardless of the degree of burden it causes on an individual's religious beliefs. The majority wrote that "the right of free exercise does not relieve an individual of the obligation to comply with a valid and neutral law of *general applicability* on the ground that the law proscribes ... conduct that his religion prescribes. ... "

  **a.**   **Facts:** In *Smith*, the issue was whether Oregon could criminalize the possession of the drug peyote, and refuse to give an exemption to American Indians whose use of the drug is a central part of their religious rites. The majority not only held that Oregon could refuse an exemption, but also held that *no balancing* of the state's interest in its prohibition against the burden on the individual's religious beliefs need be carried out — so long as the ban on peyote was generally applicable, and not motivated by a governmental desire to affect religion, the law was fully enforceable despite the burden on the plaintiffs.

b. **Dissents and concurrences:** The other four members of the Court disagreed with this test. In a concurrence by Justice O'Connor, and a dissent by Justice Blackmun (joined by Brennan and Marshall), these four argued that *strict scrutiny* should be applied wherever a generally-applicable law burdened the free exercise of religion. As Justice Blackmun put it, "A state statute that burdens the free exercise of religion ... may stand only if the law in general, and the state's refusal to allow a religious exemption in particular, are justified by a compelling interest that cannot be served by less restrictive means." These four Justices also asserted that the Court's prior cases — cases like *Wisconsin v. Yoder, supra,* p. 694— did *not* turn (as the majority claimed) on the fact that other constitutional interests, like the right of free speech, were present in addition to the religious interests.

c. **Significance:** At the very least, *Smith* seems to mean that any generally-applicable criminal proscription may be enforced even against a person on whom it causes an extreme religious burden, so long as this consequence was not intended by government. But the Court, from the tone of its majority opinion, seems likely to go even further: probably *Smith* will be extended to mean that *any* generally-applicable regulation, *whether criminal or civil*, and whether it requires conduct or forbids conduct, will be fully enforceable and upheld despite the burden on individuals' Free Exercise beliefs. If so, this would mean that the traditional strict scrutiny given to government's refusal to grant an exemption would be *abolished*. Probably the Court will maintain a narrow exemption for unemployment compensation payments, like those in *Sherbert, supra,* p. 692. Probably it will also maintain an exception where rights of free speech, free assembly, or other separate constitutional interests are present in addition to the Free Exercise claim; thus cases like *Wisconsin v. Yoder* (holding that the state must exempt Amish students from the requirement of attending school) will not be overruled.

   i. **Trend:** *Smith* is part of a strong trend on the part of the Rehnquist Court to curtail Free Exercise rights. Cases like *Goldman* (*supra,* p. 695, holding that servicemen do not have a free exercise right to wear a yarmulke while on duty), *O'Lone* (*supra,* p. 696, holding that prisoners do not have the right to have their work schedules modified to permit them to attend religious services), and *Lyng* (see *infra,* holding that government may destroy a group's traditional ritual grounds), also illustrate this trend.

d. **Not applicable to intentional discrimination against religion:** Don't forget that *Smith,* though it makes it dramatically tougher for the plaintiff to win a free exercise challenge to government action, only applies where the government action has the *unintentional effect* of burdening religion. In those rare instances where government acts for the *purpose* of disfavoring a particular religious practice, the most rigorous strict scrutiny will still be applied, and the government action will almost always be struck down. See, e.g., *Church of the Lukumi Babalu Aye, supra,* p. 689, where the Court found that an ordinance forbidding animal sacrifice was exactly such a government action intended to disfavor religion, and thus struck it down.

**8. Government action that makes exercise more difficult:**   Most of the free exercise claims we have considered so far involved some degree of *"coercion"* by the state against the individual religious adherent — thus a person is ordered to do something (e.g., send a child to school, as in *Yoder*), or not to do something (e.g., not wear a yarmulke in the military, as in *Goldman*). Suppose, however, that the government takes an action that does not "coerce" the individual to do or not do something, but that nonetheless happens to have the *effect of making it much more difficult for him to practice his religion.* A majority of the Court now seems to believe that the government may take such actions even where the governmental interest in carrying out the action is *very weak*, and the burden to the individual's practice of his religion is *very great*. This seems to be the result of the case of *Lyng v. Northwest Indian Cemetery Protective Ass'n*, 485 U.S. 439 (1988), in which the Court held that the federal government could construct a road through federal land, even though this would destroy certain American Indians' traditional rituals, with only a slight gain to any federal interest.

    **a. Rationale:**   The Court in *Lyng* (by a 5-3 vote) apparently conceded that the damage to the Indian religion from the proposed road would be extreme, and that the federal interest supporting construction of the road was relatively weak. Nonetheless, the majority concluded that *"incidental effects* of government programs, which may make it more difficult to practice certain religions but which have *no tendency to coerce individuals* into acting contrary to their religious beliefs, [do not] require government to bring forward a compelling justification for its otherwise lawful actions." A contrary rule, the majority wrote, would unduly burden government.

    **b. Significance:**   A concept of *"coercion"* now seems to be central to Free Exercise law: *no matter how much governmental action burdens an individual's practice of his religion,* if the individual is not being "coerced" (i.e., ordered or intentionally induced to do or not do something), there is simply *no Free Exercise claim*, and the government need not come up with any particular justification for its acts.

        **i. Illustration:**   Thus had the federal government *ordered* the Indian tribes not to use the federal lands for religious rituals, the case would probably have turned out differently; at the least, the Indians' free exercise right would have been at stake, and probably only a compelling countervailing governmental interest would have sufficed to outweigh that free exercise right. Here, the Indians were not told that they could or could not do something; rather, external reality was simply changed in a way that happened to make the doing of something difficult or impossible.

**F. Military service and conscientious objection:**   There are many who hold the religious belief that *all war is evil*. Since the advent of the selective service system, Congress has always made available to such *"conscientious objectors"* an *exemption from military service.*

    **1. Not necessarily required under Free Exercise Clause:**   However, the Court has *never* held that such an exemption is *required* by the Free Exercise Clause. In fact, the Court has generally assumed, without deciding, that the exemption is *not* constitutionally required.

        **a. Possibly required today:**   However, the development of case law like that of *Sherbert* and *Yoder*, requiring the government to show that its compelling objectives cannot be met if exemptions are given to those whose religious beliefs are burdened by a regulation, makes it likely that the Court would now hold some sort of conscientious-objector exemption to be *required* by the Free Exercise Clause. See Tribe, p. 1266. It is hard to see how an exemption from combat for what would almost certainly be a limited number of objectors would interfere with the safeguarding of our national security, especially if alternative service were required (as it is today) in order to reduce the incentive to make false claims of conscientious objection.

2.  **Selective conscientious objection:**  *"Selective"* conscientious objectors are those who do not believe that all wars are unjust, but do contend that they should be exempted from service in any *particular* war which they believe to be unjust. If such selective conscientious objection is based upon religious beliefs, may Congress constitutionally deny an exemption while granting an exemption for "non-selective" objection? The Court answered *"yes"* to this question in *Gillette v. U.S.*, 401 U.S. 437 (1971).

    a.  **Rationale:**  The Court conceded that the congressional requirement that conscientious objection be total burdened some types of religious beliefs more than others. But the Court applied the familiar principle that such disparate effect is permissible if there is an important governmental interest which cannot be achieved by means less burdensome to religious beliefs. Here, the government satisfied this test. One governmental interest was that in *fairness*; if selective conscientious objection were allowed, there would be a danger that "as between two would-be objectors, [that] objector would succeed who is more articulate, better educated, or better counselled." Also, the government's interest in procuring militarily-necessary manpower might not be fulfillable if selective conscientious objection were permitted.

G.  **Public health:**  Another category of regulation sometimes attacked on Free Exercise grounds is that of *public health* rules. The individual raising the Free Exercise claim has generally lost when the health or welfare of others was at issue, but has usually won where *only his own health* or well-being would be jeopardized by an exemption.

    1.  **Vaccinations and drugs:**  Thus the Court has held that an individual may be required to *receive a vaccination* against disease, even if his religion prohibits such procedures. *Jacobsen v. Massachusetts*, 197 U.S. 11 (1905). Even under the broadest reading of the Free Exercise Clause, the government's secular objective (prevention of epidemics) probably cannot be fully achieved if exemptions are granted. Similarly, the Court has held that a state may ban *drugs* that it considers dangerous (e.g., the drug peyote) in order to fulfill its general purpose of combatting narcotics, even though this may heavily burden an individual's observance of the rituals of his religion. See *Employment Division v. Smith*, *supra*, p. 696.

    2.  **Life-saving medical treatment:**  Where an adult refuses on religious grounds to receive a *blood transfusion* or other *life-saving medical care*, the issues are complex. If the adult is competent and has no minors dependent upon him, it seems probable that forcing him to submit to such care violates his Free Exercise rights.

        a.  **Child or parent of minor:**  But where the patient is a *child* whose parents object on religious grounds, or the patient is a *parent with minor children*, most courts have *compelled* the treatment, on the theory that the state's interest in safeguarding minors outweighs whatever rights of religious liberty are at stake.

H.  **What constitutes a "religious belief":**  A Free Exercise claim, to be valid, must of course involve a "religious belief." Thus the courts are forced to consider not only whether a belief is genuinely held, but whether it is "religious." The Supreme Court has never articulated a formal definition of "religious belief" or of "religion." However, several things are clear about how the Court determines the religiosity of a belief:

1.  **Not necessarily theistic:** The belief, and the system of beliefs of which it is a part, ***need not necessarily recognize a Supreme Being***. That is, non-theistic as well as theistic religions may receive Free Exercise protection. See, e.g., *Torcaso v. Watkins*, 367 U.S. 488 (1961), striking down a state requirement that all holders of public office declare their belief in the existence of God.

2.  **Organized vs. unorganized religion:** The Court will try hard to avoid preferring ***"organized"*** religions (i.e., ones that are well-established, with large numbers of adherents and conventional practices) over ones that are new, unconventional or sparsely-followed.

    a.  **Religion practiced by a single person:** In fact, a person's religious beliefs are entitled to the protection of the Free Exercise Clause even if those beliefs are held by a ***single person*** rather than being part of the teachings of any kind of group or sect. See *Frazee v. Illinois Dept. of Employment Security*, 489 U.S. 829 (1989).

3.  **Sincerity:** Obviously, a court should not sustain a Free Exercise claim unless it is convinced that the belief is ***genuine***. However, in making this determination the court will strive mightily to avoid considering the "truth" or "reasonableness" of that belief. See *U.S. v. Ballard, supra*, p. 668.

4.  **Centrality:** A belief which is claimed to be in conflict with a particular governmental rule must also be ***central*** to the individual's religion; the government should not be required to grant an exemption from a regulation which merely ***inconveniences*** a believer. However, as in the case of gauging whether a belief is "sincerely" held, this decision should be based in part on subjective criteria: if an individual genuinely feels that the conflict is with a belief central ***for him***, his claim should be upheld even though most members of the same sect would consider the belief to be peripheral. Tribe, p. 1249. See, e.g., *Thomas v. Review Bd. Ind. Empl. Sect. Div.*, 450 U.S. 707 (1981), where a Jehovah's Witness' refusal to work in a munitions factory was held to require an exemption from unemployment compensation rules under the Free Exercise Clause, even though there was evidence that another Jehovah's Witness *was* willing to work in the same factory.

---

*Quiz Yourself on*

**FREEDOM OF RELIGION** *(ENTIRE CHAPTER)*

88. The town of Amity has a religiously diverse population. In October, the mayor announced that he and the City Council believed it would be nice to have some sort of public display celebrating the upcoming holiday season. Therefore, he said, a small area would be set aside in Amity's biggest and most centrally-located park, in which a display could be assembled. He established a "Committee for a Happy Holiday," to which he appointed several eminent local citizens. Anyone else who wished to join the committee was permitted to do so. The purpose of the committee was to design and assemble a display. The committee put together a display consisting of: (1) a crèche or nativity scene, portraying the birth of Christ in the manger; (2) a Christmas tree; (3) a Menorah; (4) a Santa Claus riding reindeer; and (5) a banner reading, "Have a Happy Holiday." There was no instance in which a citizen (whether a member of the committee or not) proposed a figure or item that was rejected.

    **(a)** You are volunteer counsel to the local branch of the ACLU. Your members wish you to bring suit attacking the constitutionality of this display. What constitutional provision should you base your suit on?

**(b)** Will your attack succeed? _____

89. The state of Carginia requires every religious organization operating in the state to register with the state Attorney General, and to submit financial statements, if the institution wishes to be exempt from state property taxes and state income taxes. (An institution is always free to forego these tax advantages, in which case it need not register or submit financial statements.) After numerous small community churches, synagogues and mosques claimed that the paperwork involved was terribly burdensome to them, the registration and financial-statement provisions were amended to grant an exemption for any institution "50% or more of whose financial support derives from donations by persons who consider themselves members of the institution."

   The state legislature considered eliminating the registration/financial-statement requirement altogether, but did not do so because of a fear that groups that solicit donation from non-members are likely to practice fraud, harassment, and other abuses. There is evidence that the legislature was especially concerned about groups that did their fund-raising by ringing doorbells at private homes, such as "Moonies" and Jehovah's Witnesses. A local group of Jehovah's Witnesses gets most of its financial support by selling Bibles door-to-door to non-members. This group has sued to overturn the statutory scheme as a violation of its Establishment Clause rights. Should the court find in favor of the plaintiff? _____

90. The legislature of the state of Largesse was concerned that students in the state's biggest and most financially-troubled city, Bigtown, were not getting a good public-school education. To increase school competition, and to give parents of Bigtown students a choice of schooling options, the Largesse legislature enacted the "Tuition Voucher Plan of 2002." Under this plan, the parents of any elementary- or middle-school student living in Bigtown could attend any licensed private school (including parochial schools) in or near Bigtown, and receive a state voucher worth $2,000 to be used towards the private school's annual tuition. Mostly because the average non-religious private school's annual tuition in Bigtown is $15,000, and the average religious school's annual tuition is just $2,500, about 95% of the students who took advantage of the voucher program in its first year attended religious schools, where they were given intensive instruction in religious subjects (e.g., Roman Catholic catechism) as well as secular subjects. There are no other special programs in Bigtown designed to solve the educational problems that the Largesse legislature has identified. A parent of a public-school attendee, Paul, has sued the state, arguing that the voucher program violates the Establishment Clause. Should the court find in Paul's favor?

91. The religion of Weejun is practiced primarily on a small island in the South Pacific Ocean. A number of adherents have made their homes in the West Coast town of Pacifica. The Weejuns speak their own language, and practice their own rituals in a church located in the town. As part of their rituals, the Weejuns drink a beverage called nectaria, made from fermented nectarines. The beverage is smelly and of quite high alcoholic content. Practitioners sometimes get drunk from using it in their rituals. The Weejuns are, in general, relatively uneducated, of lower income status, and seem quite strange to most non-Weejun residents of Pacifica. For some time, non-Weejun Pacificans had been complaining at Town Council meetings that the Weejuns and their nectaria-based rituals were leading to public drunkenness, and a consequent burdening of the police and lowering of Pacifica's "image." The Town Council then enacted an ordinance whose sole provision was to ban the sale or public use of nectaria. "Public use" was defined to include the use in any gathering of more than three people who were not related to each other and who were not meeting in a private home. Since the Weejun church was a free-standing building, the sole effect of the ordinance was to ban the use of nectaria as part of the Weejun church rituals.

(a) If the members of the Weejun congregation wish to attack the constitutionality of the Pacifica ordinance, what constitutional provision should they rely upon? _____

(b) What test or standard of review should the court apply in evaluating the challenge you referred to in (a)? _____

(c) Is the ordinance constitutional, when judged by that standard of review? _____

**92.** Practitioners of the religion of Parentism believe that it is up to the parents of the child to carry out that child's education, and that the teaching of the child by strangers (i.e., non-parents) is against God's will. Consequently, each child born to parents who practice Parentism is schooled at home, and no private religious schools following the Parentism religion exist. The state of Gomorra has been worried that students who are taught at home by their parents fail to receive necessary socialization, and frequently don't learn needed skills like cooperation, as well as knowledge of more advanced subjects like trigonometry. Therefore, the state has recently enacted a ban on any kind of home education (though parents are free to send their children to any private or religious school they wish, so long as children from more than one family attend). There is no evidence that the Gomorra regulation was motivated by any particular dislike, or even awareness, of Parentism; in fact, the practitioners of Parentism are so few that state education officials are barely aware that they exist. Priscilla, an adherent of Parentism who has been teaching her child Pamela at home, has applied to the state for an exemption from the no-home-schooling requirement, on the grounds that the ordinance would otherwise violate Priscilla's and Pamela's free exercise rights. Must the state grant an exemption so that Pamela may be schooled at home? _____

**93.** A central element of the Sharkist religion is to possess and pray to a piece of a fin from a Great White Shark. Because the Great White Shark is a nearly extinct species, and because it has been relentlessly hunted as a source of shark fin soup and other delicacies, the U.S. (acting together with other western nations) has recently enacted a ban on the possession or importing of any fin or other body part from Great White Sharks. When Congress enacted this ban, few if any members of Congress were aware of the existence of the Sharkist religion, which has very few adherents. The federal legislation makes it a felony, punishable by up to five years in prison, to knowingly possess a Great White Shark's fin. Samark, a practitioner of Sharkism, has petitioned the U.S. for an exemption from the ban, contending that the ban violates his free exercise rights. Religious experts estimate that there are fewer than 100 Sharkists in the United States, and that granting them an exemption would have no material effect on the rate at which Great White Sharks are hunted. Must the U.S. grant the exemption? _____

**94.** The Reverend John Butcher was a self-proclaimed "faith healer." Through programs paid for by his ministry on radio and television, he gave notice to the world that if a person was physically or mentally ill, Butcher would lay hands upon that person and, in most cases, could cure them. Butcher charged a "donation" for each attempt at faith healing, which he said should normally be about equal to one month's wages, payable in advance. Butcher performed dozens of attempted acts of faith healing. Of the first 30 such attempts, 29 ended with the patient/worshipper believing that he or she had not been helped at all; the other one believed that there had been some slight improvement. Butcher's 31st patient, Jones, had cancer; she relied on Butcher's laying on of hands and did not seek medical treatment, which could have cured her. She died of the cancer.

Butcher was prosecuted for the manslaughter of Jones, as well as for financial fraud in her case. The essence of the prosecution was that Butcher did not in fact believe that he had faith healing powers, and purported to have them only as a means to make money. At the trial, the prosecution was permitted to show that 29 of the first 30 patients believed that they had not been helped by Butcher. The judge then charged the jury, "The issue is not whether Butcher's treatments worked, but whether Butcher sincerely believed that they might work. In making this determination of sincerity, you may consider evidence that they did not in fact work, as bearing circumstantially on whether Butcher believed that they might work." Butcher has objected to this charge on the grounds that it infringes upon his free exercise of religion. Is Butcher's argument correct? _____

*Answers*

88. **(a) The Establishment Clause.** The Establishment Clause of the First Amendment prohibits any law "respecting an establishment of religion." In a general sense, its purpose is to erect a wall between church and state.

**(b) No, probably.** The Establishment Clause prevents government from **sponsoring** or **endorsing** one religion over another, or religion over non-religion. A display of religiously-oriented materials at holiday time might indeed be found to constitute an implicit endorsement or sponsorship by the government of religion or of a religious message. In evaluating whether a particular display or ceremony violates the Establishment Clause, the Court generally uses a three-part test (derived from *Lemon v. Kurtzman*). Only if the action satisfies **each** of the following conditions will it be valid: (1) it must have a **secular legislative purpose**; (2) its principal or **primary effect** must neither advance nor inhibit religion; and (3) it must not foster an **excessive governmental entanglement** with religion.

On facts very similar to these, the Court held by a 5-4 vote that the display did **not** violate any of these three tests. *Lynch v. Donnelly.* Here, a court would probably find a secular purpose (to celebrate the holiday, which is a secular government-observed holiday in addition to being one with religious significance). The primary effect of the display would probably not be found to benefit religion in general or Christianity specifically (since the non-religious "holiday spirit" was also being benefitted, and any advancement of religion was somewhat indirect). And there would probably not be found to be undue entanglement between government and religious institutions, since government basically left the space available and allowed citizens to do what they wished without further government intervention. The most important factor would probably be **context**: here, there were at least some non-religiously-oriented items in the display (e.g., the banner, and the reindeer), so that a reasonable observer would probably not conclude that the display was, overall, a government endorsement of religion. (Observe, however, that *Lynch* was a 5-4 decision, and even a small variation in the items displayed, or in how they came to be displayed, might have resulted in a shift of one vote and thus a change in result.)

89. **Yes.** The facts are similar to those in *Larson v. Valente.* The Court held that this type of scheme benefited one religion or group of religions over another. Therefore, the Court applied **strict scrutiny**, not the *Lemon* three-prong test. Such a preference of one religious group over others could be sustained only if it was "justified by a compelling governmental interest and … closely fitted to further that interest." Although the state may have an interest in guarding against "abusive solicitation practices," the means selected here are not "closely fitted" to furthering that interest, since there is no reason to believe that the likelihood of solicitation abuse is closely related to the ratio of member contributions to total contributions.

The conclusion that the legislature has "played favorites" here is buttressed by the evidence that the legislature knew it was disfavoring Jehovah's Witnesses and other residential-doorbell-ringers. If there were evidence that the disfavoring of Jehovah's Witnesses was entirely **incidental**, perhaps strict scrutiny would not be called for.

**90. No, probably.** The main issue is whether the program here has the "primary effect" of advancing religion (since if it does, it's a violation of the Establishment Clause.) The facts here are quite similar to those in *Zelman v. Simmons-Harris*, where a bare majority of the Court held that the program was constitutional because any funding that went to religious education resulted from the "deliberate choices of numerous individual recipients," not from any legislative desire to aid religion. One difference between the facts here and those in *Zelman* is that in *Zelman*, there were other "alternative" educational programs paid for by the state that didn't even arguably aid religion (e.g., special public magnet schools and tutoring programs), and these alternative programs had more participants than the private-school-voucher program — so viewed in the aggregate, the total alternative programs didn't primarily advance religion. Therefore, it's possible that a court would rule that the absence of such alternatives here makes a difference. But probably, the result here would be the same as in *Zelman* — because (a) each parent is making her own decision about whether to use the voucher at a religious or non-religious school, (b) the voucher program is open to students and private-schools regardless of whether they do or don't have a religious affiliation; and (c) there's no evidence that the legislature was intending to advance religion, the program will probably pass muster.

**91. (a) The Free Exercise Clause.** The First Amendment bars government from making any law "prohibiting the free exercise" of religion. The clause can apply to regulations that are directed at religious beliefs or, more commonly, directed at religiously-oriented *conduct*. Here, we have a regulation that is directed at conduct (the consumption of a particular beverage).

**(b) Strict scrutiny.** Where government takes an action whose *purpose* is to forbid or interfere with particular conduct *because* the conduct is dictated by a religious belief, the government action is strictly scrutinized and almost always struck down. Here, all the evidence is that the Pacifica Town Council was motivated principally by members' dislike of the Weejun religion and its practitioners, not by a generally-applicable dislike of drunkenness. The facts are roughly analogous to those of *Church of the Lukumi Babalu Aye, Inc. v. Hialeah*, where the Court struck down a ban on ritual animal sacrifice on the theory that the ban was motivated by hostility to practitioners of the Santeria religion. When the Court is deciding whether governmental regulation is designed for the purpose of interfering with a particular religious practice, the extent to which the ordinance is of "general applicability" will be considered; here, the ordinance speaks solely of nectaria, not other beverages of equal alcohol content, and the ordinance affects nobody but practitioners of Weejun. Therefore, a court would almost certainly conclude that there was an intent to interfere with the religious practice, not merely an unintended effect upon religion. Consequently, strict scrutiny must be used.

**(c) No.** Strict scrutiny in the free exercise context, as in other constitutional contexts, means that the regulation will be struck down unless it is *necessary* to achieve a *compelling* governmental interest. The government's interest here in cutting down on public drunkenness might be "compelling," but the means selected are certainly not "necessary" to achieving that end. For instance, the town could simply have banned public drunkenness, or banned all substances of sufficiently high alcohol content that were very likely to produce drunkenness. The ordinance here is extremely underinclusive (it deals with only one source of drunkenness), demonstrating that it is not "drawn in narrow terms" to accomplish the objective.

**92. Yes, probably.** In general, where a law has the unintended effect of seriously burdening religiously-related conduct, the state must give an *exemption* where feasible. Only if strict compliance with the state regulation is the *least restrictive means* of accomplishing a *compelling state objective* is the state free to not give an exemption. Here, although insuring the adequate education of children is perhaps a compelling state objective, a scheme that totally refuses to allow home schooling probably is not the least restrictive means of accomplishing that objective. The facts are similar to those of *Wisconsin v. Yoder*, where the Court held that a state must exempt Amish teenage students from the requirement of attending school until the age of 16. Here, while it is true that home schooling may have certain inadequacies, the Court would probably hold that the state must tolerate some slight sacrifice to its objective (fully adequate education) where a religious belief would otherwise be severely burdened. Therefore, the state probably must give an exemption from the home-study ban.

**93. No.** Where government enacts a generally-applicable ***criminal prohibition*** on a certain type of activity, and government does not intend to burden religious beliefs, government does not have to grant an exemption to those whose religious beliefs or practices are burdened by the prohibition. The facts are analogous to those of *Employment Division v. Smith*, where a state was allowed to refuse to grant American Indians an exemption from the ban on peyote, even though use of the drug was a central part of their religious rites. *Smith* establishes that government does not have to engage in any ***balancing*** of its interests in its prohibition against the burden on the individual's religious beliefs — so long as the ban is generally applicable, and not motivated by a governmental desire to affect religion, the law is fully enforceable no matter how large the burden on the plaintiff or how small the benefit to the state. Therefore, even though an exemption would not meaningfully interfere with the goal of safeguarding Great White Sharks, no exemption needs to be given.

**94. Unclear.** The facts are analogous to those of *U.S. v. Ballard*, where the defendants were faith healers charged with fraudulently soliciting donations. The Court held that the Free Exercise Clause barred the submission to the jury of the truth or falsity of the defendants' faith healing claims. Here, the prosecution is entitled to prove that Butcher did not in fact believe his claims, but it is not clear that the prosecution should be entitled to show in detail that they were false, as a means of making a circumstantial case that Butcher believed his claims were false — a court might well conclude that, as in *Ballard*, the evidence as to truth or falsity was prejudicial, given that the only ultimate issue properly before the jury was the genuineness of Butcher's belief.

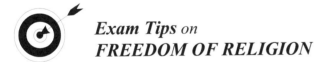

# *Exam Tips on* FREEDOM OF RELIGION

Issues involving freedom of religion are usually easy to spot: the fact pattern has to refer to religion, religious beliefs, church, parochial school, God, prayer, or some symbol commonly associated with religion (e.g., a creche, a Star of David, etc.). So the trick with freedom of religion issues is to analyze them correctly, not to spot them. Here's what to concentrate on:

☛ Of utmost importance: decide whether the issue poses an *Establishment* Clause or a *Free Exercise* Clause problem. A given governmental action will rarely pose the danger of both (though the government will often have a ***choice*** of two actions, each posing the risk of violating a different clause).

    ☞ Here's a tip for deciding which Clause is involved: if government seems to be *favoring* religion generally, or favoring a particular religion over the "rest of society," you probably have an Establishment Clause problem. If government seems to be *disfavoring* a particular person relative to the rest of society, in a way that is related to that person's religious beliefs, then you probably have a Free Exercise Clause problem. Classic illustration of Establishment Clause problem: school prayer. Classic illustration of Free Exercise Clause problem: P can't get unemployment benefits if she doesn't make herself available for Saturday work forbidden by her religion.

☞ In analyzing an *Establishment Clause* problem, the first thing to do is to recite the three-part test (which you should cite as the *"Lemon v. Kurtzman"* test):

☞ First, the government action must have a *secular legislative purpose* (but it's OK if there is *also* a religious purpose);

☞ The act must have a *primary secular effect*; and

☞ The government action must not involve *undue entanglement* of government in religious affairs, or religion in government affairs.

☞ Of these three prongs, the one that is most likely to be violated in your fact pattern is probably the "primary secular effect" prong, since a large variety of government programs seem to assist religious groups more than they benefit other groups.

☞ The most common type of Establishment Clause problem that you will see on an exam involves *religion in the public schools*. Typically, the state gives some sort of financial aid to religious schools or to students who attend religious schools. Here are some rules of thumb in analyzing these:

☞ If the program benefits *all students*, or even all *private-school* students (including non-parochial students), the fact that the biggest beneficiaries are religious students is not fatal. (*Example:* Tuition vouchers which can be used to send a student to any private school, religious or non-religious, are allowable — *Zelman v. Simmons-Harris.*)

☞ If the assistance is being rendered to a *college or university*, it's more likely to pass muster than where it is rendered to a secondary or elementary school.

☞ Loans of *tangible objects* (e.g., text books or school buses) are easier to justify than loans of *personnel*, since the loans of tangible objects involve fewer supervisory/entanglement problems for government. But even a loan of personnel to teach inside the religious school is OK, so long as the religious school authorities don't have any influence over the curriculum or the style of teaching.

☞ A common type of fact pattern involves a school district that makes school premises available *after hours* to various groups. The issue becomes, "Must religious groups be excluded?" The correct answer: religious groups typically need *not* be excluded, as long as the government does not get entangled with what the group is doing, as by having public officials co-sponsor the activity. In fact, exclusion of religious groups from a program open to other sorts of groups generally violates the religious groups' free exercise rights.

**Example:** A school district opens elementary school classrooms after hours to various community groups. If religious groups are allowed to participate (even if their programs are worship services), this is not an Establishment Clause program, because the religious groups are just getting equal treatment. (And if the religious groups were excluded, this would violate their free expression rights. *Good News Club.*)

☞ Another common fact pattern occurs where government gives funds to some religious organization for use in some theoretically non-religious "socially beneficial" charitable purpose. (*Example:* Government gives grants to religious and non-religious groups for use in running family planning clinics, legal services clinics, etc.) In this type of fact pattern, use the three-part *Lemon* test. Pay special attention to the risk of entanglement: how does government know that the particular religious organization isn't using the funds to advocate religious doctrine, or to favor its co-religionists? But say that the present Court seems inclined to find that there is no Establishment Clause violation in this type of fact pattern.

☞ A special type of establishment problem is posed where government *favors one sect* or religion over another. (*Example:* Government gives tax breaks to certain religions, or gives certain sects free time on government-owned broadcast stations.) This kind of preference is virtually per se violative of the Establishment Clause.

☞ In analyzing *free exercise* problems, be on the lookout for two different kinds of scenarios:

☞ In one scenario, P wants to do something that is required by P's religion, and the government blocks him from doing so.

☞ In the other scenario, P doesn't want to do something that is forbidden by her religion, and the government requires her to do so (typically, as a condition to the receipt of some kind of government benefit).

☞ If government's interference with a religious practice or belief is *intentional* (i.e., motivated by government's desire to interfere with the religion), the interference is virtually per se illegal. This kind of fact pattern is rare on exams. One example: government bans animal sacrifices, in circumstances showing that government is acting out of dislike of an unpopular minority religion (*Lukumi*, the Santeria Case).

☞ But this principle probably applies only to *serious "sanctions" — punishments —* intentionally directed against religion, not to minor withdrawals of generally-applicable government *benefits*. (*Example*: If government funds college scholarships, but doesn't let the scholarship be used for training for the ministry, this is not a Free Exercise violation, because there is no "sanction" or punishment intended here, just avoidance of church-state conflicts. *Locke v. Davey.*)

☞ In the more usual free exercise case, the government interference with religious practices or beliefs is *unintended* and *incidental*. Here's what to look for in this usual situation:

☞ Look for *"coercion"* by the government. It's only a violation of free exercise if the government is "requiring" a person to do or not do something. If government simply happens to make it more difficult for a person to do something, that's not a violation. (*Example:* If a public school happens to schedule graduation on P's holy day, and the graduation ceremony is voluntary, P will lose her free exercise challenge, because she is not being "coerced" or "forced" to do anything.)

☞ If the government really *is* using coercion of some sort, then apply *strict scrutiny*. This means that the government must give an *exemption*, unless the granting of an exemption would impair some compelling governmental interest. The classic scenario: government denies a benefit because a person can't or won't do something. *Examples:* (1)

government says that no practicing clergymen may be elected to public office; (2) government says that no person may get unemployment benefits without making herself available to work on Sunday; (3) a school district says that no teacher may pray on the job. In all of these situations, government probably has to give an exemption unless some compelling governmental interest would be impaired (which it probably would not be).

☞ Remember that there is now a key exception to this general rule requiring an exemption, an exception so large that it almost swallows the rule. The exception is that a generally applicable *criminal law* is *automatically enforceable* without need for an exemption, regardless of how great the burden is on the individual, and regardless of the ease with which the government could give an exemption. Cite to *Employment Division v. Smith* for this principle. Some examples:

❏ Government bans all cruelty to animals, defined to include any death not administered in a painless manner. Assuming that there is no motive to disfavor particular religions, this ban may be applied to groups sacrificing animals as part of a religious ritual, since the ban is a rule of general applicability.

❏ Government bans group sex. Again, since this is a generally-applicable criminal rule, government need not give an exemption to groups for whom group sex is a religious ritual.

❏ A zoning ordinance prohibits any "neon signs" on the rooftops of buildings. This rule can probably be applied to churches, since it's a generally-applicable ban.

☞ Also, remember that government need not grant an exemption where this would *impair* a *compelling* state interest. (*Example:* Government can grant funds to universities on condition that they not practice racial discrimination; government need not exempt universities having a religious belief that God doesn't want the races to mix.)

☛ In any free exercise case, be on the lookout for an issue concerning, *"What is a religious belief?"* Here are the key aspects of this issue:

☞ The courts may insist that the belief be *"bona fide."* So the court is permitted to gauge the *"genuineness"* or *"sincerity"* of the individual's belief.

☞ But the court is *not* permitted to gauge the *"truthfulness"* or *"reasonableness"* of the belief. No matter how bizarre or out-of-the-ordinary the belief, only sincerity counts.

☞ Even *unorganized* beliefs, and beliefs practiced by just a *single person*, are protected. Thus the court may not consider that a particular practice is "not traditional" — if it's part of P's own practice of the religion, it doesn't matter that it's a deviation from the general practices of the sect to which P belongs.

# Chapter 16

# JUSTICIABILITY

## *ChapterScope*

In order for a case to be heard by the federal courts, the plaintiff must overcome a series of procedural obstacles that we collectively call the requirements of *"justiciability."* Here is an overview of each of these obstacles:

- **Advisory opinion:** The federal courts may not issue opinions based on **abstract** or **hypothetical** questions. This is known as the prohibition of *"advisory opinions."* It stems from the fact that the Constitution limits federal court jurisdiction only to "cases and controversies."

- **Standing:** The most important single justiciability requirement is that the federal courts may hear a case only when the plaintiff has *"standing"* to assert his claim. By this, we mean that the plaintiff must have a significant **stake** in the controversy.

   - **Requirement of "injury in fact":** That is, P must show that he has suffered an *"injury in fact."* That is, P must show that **he has himself been injured** in some way by the conduct that he complains of.

   - **Three requirements:** Generally, there are three standing requirements that the plaintiff must meet: (1) he must show that he has suffered (or is likely to suffer) an *"injury in fact"*; (2) the injury he is suffering must be **concrete** and *"individuated"*; and (3) the action being challenged must be the *"cause in fact"* of the injury.

   - **Rights of third persons:** A key function of the standing doctrine is that it prevents a litigant from asserting the constitutional rights of *"third persons" not before the court*. (However, there are several exceptions to the rule that P may not assert third-party rights; First Amendment overbreadth is an example.)

- **Mootness:** A case may not be heard by the federal courts if it is *"moot."* A case is moot if **events occurring after the filing** have deprived the litigant of an **ongoing stake** in the controversy.

- **Ripeness:** A case is not yet *"ripe,"* and therefore not yet decidable by a federal court, if it has **not yet become sufficiently concrete** to be easily adjudicated. For instance, if a criminal statute is almost never enforced, P's challenge to the constitutionality of the statute may be found not to be ripe if it is unlikely that the statute will be enforced against P.

- **The 11th Amendment and suits against the states:** The 11th Amendment bars certain types of suits against states. In particular, the amendment bars most types of **damage suits** against the state, including suits where the plaintiff is a citizen either of the defendant's state or some other state.

- **Political questions:** Certain issues are held to involve non-justicable *"political questions."*

   - **Commitment to another branch:** For instance, a case will be found to pose a non-justicable political question if it raises an issue whose determination is clearly committed by the Constitution to **another branch** of the federal government rather than the judiciary. Many issues concerning **impeachment** fall into this category.

❏ **Lack of manageable standards:** Alternatively, an issue may be found to be a non-justiciable political one if there are *"no manageable standards"* to guide the judiciary in deciding that issue.

## I. INTRODUCTION

**A. Scope:** This chapter discusses preconditions which must be satisfied before a federal court will adjudicate a lawsuit, including a suit raising a constitutional claim.

    **1. Source of preconditions:** Some of these preconditions come from Article III, §2's limitation of federal jurisdiction to "cases and controversies." Others come from non-constitutional discretionary policies implemented by the Supreme Court, sometimes called *"prudential"* considerations. Only if a case satisfies *all* of these preconditions will it be deemed *"justiciable,"* i.e., suitable for being disposed of on the merits.

    **2. Summary of topics:** The preconditions discussed in this chapter include:

        **a.** that the suit involve a concrete controversy, so that the court will not be issuing an *"advisory opinion;"*

        **b.** that the plaintiff have *"standing,"* i.e., an appropriate interest or stake in the matters under suit;

        **c.** that the suit not be *"moot"* because of events which have occurred following institution of the action;

        **d.** that the suit be *"ripe,"* i.e., sufficiently well-developed and specific to merit adjudication;

        **e.** that the suit (or appeal to the Supreme Court) not be one from which the federal courts should *abstain* for the sake of certain discretionary policies (e.g., non-interference with state court proceedings in order to promote federalism); and

        **f.** that the case not present a non-justiciable *"political question."*

**B. Policies served:** Most of these requirements for justiciability further one or both of the following policies, implicit within the constitutional requirement of a "case or controversy":

    **1.** the limitation of federal court jurisdiction to issues presented in an *adversary context* and capable of being resolved by the judiciary; and

    **2.** the maintenance of the *separation of powers*, by assuring that the federal courts do not intrude into areas reserved for the two other branches of government. See Tribe, p. 67.

## II. ADVISORY OPINIONS

**A. "Case or controversy" requirement:** Article III, §2 of the Constitution limits federal court jurisdiction to "cases" and "controversies." The federal courts are thus prevented from issuing opinions on *abstract* or *hypothetical* questions. An important consequence of this limitation is that federal courts *may not give "advisory opinions,"* that is, opinions which give advice about particular legislative or executive action, when no party is before the court who has suffered or imminently faces specific injury.

**Example:** Secretary of State Jefferson, on behalf of President Washington, writes to the Supreme Court asking it to give informal advice on various legal issues, such as the rights and duties of the United States under a treaty with France during the 1793 European War.

*Held* (in a return letter to the President), the Constitution's separation-of-powers principles limit the President, when he wants to solicit opinions, to calling on members of the Executive Branch. Therefore, the Court may not give the requested opinions. *Letter from the Justices to President Washington,* August 8, 1793 (reprinted in Hart and Wechsler, *Federal Courts,* 1973 Ed., pp. 64-66).

1. **Need for focused controversy:** In addition to the separation-of-powers rationale relied on by the Justices in response to Washington's request, the ban on advisory opinions is also frequently justified by the need to have the judiciary decide only *focused, specific conflicts*, in which adversaries *explore every aspect* of the situation. Otherwise, it is feared, the court will not be adequately briefed, and may make an unwise or unduly broad pronouncement which it will then have to revise when confronted with a specific, and real, conflict. (But this problem could probably be overcome if the Court were to assign "friends of the court" or other interested parties to brief and argue the issues, even in the absence of a concrete dispute. See Tribe, p. 74, n. 7.)

2. **"Strict necessity":** The ban on advisory opinions also reflects the general policy of *judicial restraint* in deciding constitutional issues; such issues will not be decided unless *"strictly necessary."* (Most of the other preconditions for justiciability, considered later in this chapter, similarly reflect this policy of avoiding constitutional adjudication whenever possible.)

B. **Declaratory judgments:** A *declaratory judgment* is one in which the court is not requested to award damages or an injunction, but rather, requested to state what the legal effect would be of proposed conduct by one or both of the parties.

1. **Some actions allowed:** The Court has permitted federal court decision or review of at least those declaratory judgment actions which are reasonably *concrete*.

2. **Insufficiently concrete:** But if a declaratory judgment action presents only questions which are unduly *hypothetical* or *abstract*, the federal court may conclude that it is being called upon to issue an illegal advisory opinion, not because the action is for a declaratory judgment, but simply because no specific, concrete controversy exists.

   a. **Criminal statutes:** A plaintiff seeking a declaratory judgment that a *criminal statute* is unconstitutional must generally show *either*: (1) a sometimes-enforced prohibition which *on its face clearly applies* to conduct in which the plaintiff has regularly engaged or will engage; or (2) an *actual threat* that the statute will be enforced *against the plaintiff* (in the case of a statute which on its face does *not* unambiguously cover the plaintiff's conduct). See Tribe, p. 78. If neither showing is made, the declaratory judgment action will be dismissed as being unduly hypothetical.

# III. STANDING

A. **Nature of "standing" generally:** When we say that a litigant must have "standing" to assert his claim, we mean that he must have a significant *stake* in the controversy to merit his being the one to litigate it. Thus standing focuses mostly on the *party* asserting the claim, whereas most other elements of justiciability focus upon the nature of the *issue* being litigated. See Tribe, p. 107. The study of standing is thus the study of *what kind of interests in the outcome of a controversy* are sufficient.

1. **Policies behind doctrine:** The requirement of standing reflects principally the policy against allowing federal courts to act like a *"roving commission"* whose purpose is to enforce judges' own views of legality or the interests of "bystanders" in having constitutional or statutory principles adhered to.

2. **Special relevance to constitutional issues:** In most civil actions, the existence of standing is quite clear. The tort plaintiff who alleges personal injury, for instance, and the contract plaintiff who alleges economic damages from a breach, clearly have a sufficiently direct and personal stake in the suit's outcome that they should be permitted to litigate it. But in much *constitutional* litigation, where a plaintiff alleges that the government has acted in an unconstitutional manner, it will be much less clear that the governmental action has affected the plaintiff *more directly* than any other citizen, or that resolution of the dispute in his favor will be of special benefit to him.

   a. **No general interest in constitutional government:** The Court has never been willing to hold that the *generalized interest* of a *citizen* in having his government *behave constitutionally* is a sufficient "stake" to permit the litigation. Therefore, in most of the cases below, the plaintiff tries to show (sometimes successfully, often not) that his interest in the controversy is somehow *more direct* and *individualized* than that of the citizenry at large.

3. **Article III vs. prudential limitations:** The Supreme Court's rules on standing are a blend of: (1) requirements deemed to be imposed by the Article III "case or controversy" requirement; and (2) so-called *"prudential"* considerations, i.e., non-constitutional judgments about what constitutes wise policy in administering the judiciary. The principal consequence of the distinction is that Congress is *not free to override* the Supreme Court as to an element of standing found by the Court to fall within the "case or controversy" requirement, but it *is* free to override the prudential considerations.

4. **Two-part discussion:** Our discussion of standing is divided into two main parts: (1) cases brought by plaintiffs alleging that their rights as *taxpayers* or (less successfully) their rights as *"citizens"* have been infringed; and (2) cases claiming other, usually more individualized, types of injury. The Supreme Court has applied different rules in the two contexts; generally, but not always, the requirements are easier to fulfill for type (2) suits.

5. **Requirement of "injury in fact":** The standing doctrine boils down to just one requirement, in most instances: the requirement that the litigant have suffered an *"injury in fact."*

   a. **"Nexus" requirement in taxpayer cases:** In cases where the plaintiff sues *as a federal taxpayer*, claiming that his taxes are being spent in a way that violates the Constitution or a federal statute, the Court imposes an additional requirement: that there be a certain type of *"nexus"* between the taxpayer's status and the claim sought to be litigated. See *infra*, p. 713.

   b. **"Causation in fact" requirement:** In *non-taxpayer* cases, the modern Court has imposed what might be thought of as a corollary to the "injury in fact" requirement: the injury must be one which was *caused by the act being complained of* (typically a violation of the Constitution or of a federal statute), and there must be a significant possibility that this injury will be *redressed* by giving the litigant the relief he seeks. These two causal aspects may be summarized by saying that the asserted wrongdoing must be the *"cause in fact"* of the injury. See *infra*, p. 717.

6. **Significance:** The standing doctrine tends to keep out of the federal courts two main classes of suits:

   a. **Non-individuated harm:** Cases in which the harm complained of by the plaintiffs is *no different from that suffered by very large numbers of people* not before the court. The prime example is the harm claimed to be suffered by *"citizens" at large* when government does not act according to constitutional or statutory dictates. See, e.g., *Schlesinger v. Reservists to Stop the War, infra*, p. 715.

   b. **Third parties' rights:** Cases where the rights claimed to be violated are those of *third parties* not before the court. (But the general rule against assertion of third parties' rights has numerous exceptions; see *infra*, p. 721.)

B. **Federal taxpayer and citizen suits:** The assertion that the plaintiff's harm is no different from that suffered by lots of others arises most often where the plaintiff is claiming that his rights as a *federal taxpayer* or *federal citizen* have been abridged.

1. **Rule before 1968:** Until the late 1960's, the Supreme Court took a completely hostile view towards actions brought by plaintiffs claiming that their rights as federal *taxpayers* or as federal *citizens* had been abridged. A federal taxpayer could, of course, bring suit on a claim that *his own taxes* had been improperly assessed. But a taxpayer simply had no standing to assert that *taxpayers' funds in general* were being improperly collected or spent. See *Frothingham v. Mellon*, 262 U.S. 447 (1923), reasoning that the plaintiff-taxpayer's "interest in the moneys of the Treasury [is] shared with millions of others [and] is comparatively minute and indeterminable."

2. **Exception in *Flast*:** But in a 1968 case, the Court finally made an exception to *Frothingham*'s general rule that taxpayers do not have standing to attack the validity of government spending. In *Flast v. Cohen*, 392 U.S. 83 (1968), the Court held that a taxpayer may challenge the constitutionality of a federal taxing or spending program if there is a *"logical nexus* between the status [of taxpayer] and the claim."

   a. **What "nexus" requires:** The requisite nexus will be found to exist, the Court held, only where two showings are made: (1) that the statute relies on Congress' power under the *Taxing and Spending Clause* of Article I, §8, rather than being merely "an incidental expenditure of tax funds in the administration of an essentially regulatory [law];" and (2) that the challenged law violates *"specific constitutional limitations"* imposed *on that Taxing and Spending power*, not simply that the statute is "generally beyond the powers delegated to Congress by Article 1, §8."

   b. **Test satisfied in *Flast*:** The claim in *Flast*, the Court found, *passed* the two-part test. Mrs. Flast's claim was that a federal-aid-to-education act, by giving financial aid to religious schools, violated the First Amendment's Establishment Clause. This Clause, the Court held, operates as a *"specific constitutional limitation"* upon Congress' Taxing and Spending powers.

3. **Modern Court's view:** The Burger, Rehnquist and Roberts Courts have never overruled *Flast*. But they have stubbornly refused to allow any broadening whatsoever of the *Flast*

exception to *Frothingham*'s general rule against taxpayer actions, and in fact **no case** after *Flast* has been able to come within that exception.

a. **Must be limit on "taxing and spending" power:**  Thus the Court has continued to insist that, in a taxpayer action, only those constitutional provisions which act as **"specific"** limitations on the "Taxing and Spending" power of Congress may be relied upon. *U.S. v. Richardson*, 418 U.S. 166 (1974).

> **Example:**  President George W. Bush, by executive order, sets up the Faith-Based and Community Initiatives Program.  Under that program, money supplied by the Executive Branch is used to fund conferences at which the merits of faith-based non-profit social-service programs are extolled by government speakers. The Ps are taxpayers who argue that the purpose and effect of the conferences is for the federal government to promote religion. Congress has not separately authorized any funds for the Faith-Based Program; any funds expended are spent by the Executive Branch from the general (non-earmarked) funds appropriated by Congress for the running of the executive branch.
>
> *Held*, the *Flast* exception does not apply, and the Ps therefore do not have standing. The expenditures here were made by the Executive Branch, not by Congress. *Flast* allowed taxpayer standing to attack violations of the Establishment Clause that occur as the result of Congress' use of its Art. I § 8 power to tax and spend for the general welfare. Therefore, *Flast* will be confined to suits alleging Establishment Clause violations that are funded by a "specific congressional appropriation and undertaken pursuant to an express congressional mandate[.]" *Hein v. Freedom from Religion Foundation*, 551 U.S. ___ (2007).

   i. **Significance:** So today, only suits that are virtually **identical** to *Flast* (i.e., suits claiming that congressional action taken under the "Taxing and Spending" power violates the Establishment Clause) may be brought by taxpayers.

b. **Suits by state and local taxpayers:** What about federal suits by **state** and **local** taxpayers?

   i. **State taxpayers:**  As to **state taxpayers**, the same no-standing rule applies as to suits by federal taxpayers — "**state taxpayers have no standing** ... to challenge state tax or spending decisions simply by virtue of their status as taxpayers." *DaimlerChrysler Corp. v. Cuno*, 126 S.Ct. 1854 (2006).

   > **Example:** The Ps are citizens of Toledo, Ohio, who pay state income taxes. They bring a federal suit against state officials and DaimlerChrysler, arguing that tax benefits given by the state to Daimler violate the Commerce Clause. The Ps claim that they have standing because the tax breaks leave the state with less money, increasing the Ps' own taxes and financial burdens.
   >
   > *Held*, for the Ds — the Ps have no standing to raise this claim. "Affording state taxpayers standing to press such challenges simply because their tax burden gives them an interest in the state treasury would interpose the federal courts as 'virtually continuing monitors of the wisdom and soundness' of state fiscal administration, contrary to the more modest role Article III envisions for federal courts." *DaimlerChrysler Corp. v. Cuno, supra.*

    **ii. Municipal taxpayer:** **M**unicipal taxpayers, on the other hand, clearly *do* have federal-court standing to assert that their tax dollars are being improperly spent. A municipality is viewed as being sufficiently smaller than a state that a municipal taxpayer is deemed to be ***directly injured*** by an improper expenditure of the town's tax dollars.

**4. Citizenship suits:** The Court has ***never*** been willing to recognize standing on the part of individuals ***as citizens*** to object to unlawful or unconstitutional conduct. This refusal has been based upon the view that one citizen's interest in lawful government is no different from that of any other citizen, and that an individual litigant relying upon citizenship has not shown the ***"individualized"*** injury-in-fact required for standing. *Schlesinger v. Reservists to Stop the War*, 418 U.S. 208 (1974).

**C. Standing not based on taxpayer or citizen status:** Somewhat different rules have evolved for actions in which the standing claim is ***not*** based on taxpayer or citizen status.

**1. Summary:** The rules presently imposed may be summarized as follows:

    **a. Injury in fact:** The litigant must have suffered (or be likely to suffer) an ***"injury in fact."***

    **b. Must be "individuated":** The injury suffered must be concrete and ***"individuated."*** That is, it must not be precisely the same harm as is suffered by an extremely large group of others (so that harms suffered by every "citizen" as the result of, say, violation of the Establishment Clause do not qualify, as noted above). However, the injury in fact need not be ***economic***; for instance, damage to environmental conditions where one lives or pursues recreation qualifies.

    **c. Causation in fact:** The action challenged must be the ***"cause in fact"*** of the injury. This means both that the challenged action was a "but for" cause of the injury, and that the relief being sought, if granted, has a reasonable likelihood of ***redressing*** the injury. (No comparable causation requirement is imposed in taxpayer suits.)

    **d. No nexus requirement:** No requirement of a "nexus" between the injury and the challenged action, comparable to that imposed in taxpayer suits (e.g., *Flast*) is imposed outside the taxpayer context.

**2. The "injury in fact" requirement:** Although the plaintiff must show that he has suffered or will probably suffer some concrete, "individuated," ***"injury in fact,"*** this requirement is interpreted quite liberally.

    **a. Non-economic harms:** The harm need not be ***economic*** in nature. For instance, in *Sierra Club v. Morton*, 405 U.S. 727 (1972), the environmental group claimed that construction of a recreation area in a national forest would violate federal laws. The Court held that injury to "aesthetic and environmental well-being" could constitute injury in fact, so that people who use national forests would have standing.

    **b. Must be "actual or imminent":** The "injury in fact" must, however, be ***"actual or imminent."*** Thus if the threatened harm is too ***far in the future***, or too ***speculative***, the "actual or imminent" element will not be satisfied, and standing will not be found.

    **Example:** The Ps challenge certain federal agency action that, they say, will have the effect of endangering certain species abroad. D (the United States government) argues that the Ps do not have standing. The Ps retort that they have in the past, and will again, travel abroad to the habitats of the potentially affected species, in order to observe and study those species.

*Held*, for D. The Ps have not shown the requisite actual or imminent harm. "Such 'someday' intentions — without any description of concrete plans, or indeed any specification of *when* the someday will be — do not support a finding of the 'actual or imminent' injury that our cases require." *Lujan v. Defenders of Wildlife*, 504 U.S. 555 (1992).

3. **Harm suffered by many:** As long as the litigant (or the group representing him) alleges the requisite "concrete" and "individuated" harm, standing will not be denied merely because there is a *large number* of people suffering the harm.

   a. **Citizenship:** But there are limits on how widespread the class may be. Thus the interest of all "citizens" in having their government operate constitutionally and according to statute is so diffuse that actions based on citizenship will not be allowed. See *Schlesinger v. Reservists*, *supra*, p. 715.

      i. **No interest in avoiding abstract "denigration":** Similarly, *members of a minority group* will not from that membership alone derive standing to litigate against governmental conduct which *denigrates* that minority group. For instance, in *Allen v. Wright*, 468 U.S. 737 (1984) (discussed more extensively *infra*, p. 718), parents of black public school children sued the IRS, claiming that the latter was not effectively carrying out its obligation to ensure that discriminatory private schools do not receive tax- exempt status. The parents' interest in avoiding the "stigmatizing injury" generally caused by racial discrimination was insufficient to establish standing — only those who were *"personally denied equal treatment"* by the challenged discriminatory conduct had standing.

   b. **No interest in avoiding "institutional" loss of power:** Similarly, members of a *political body*, such as a *legislature*, do *not* have standing to litigate against an action that they say *takes away the political power of that body*. Thus members of Congress who unsuccessfully voted against a bill allowing line-item vetoes by the President were held not to have standing to litigate the constitutionality of the resulting statute, where their only claim was that the bill "causes a type of *institutional injury* (the diminution of legislative power), which necessarily damages all Members of Congress and both Houses of Congress equally." *Raines v. Byrd*, 117 S. Ct. 2312 (1997).

   c. **Organizations and associations:** On the other hand, the Supreme Court is perfectly willing to grant standing to *associations* in some circumstances. An association has standing not only where its own interests are at stake, but in some cases where it is suing solely as a *representative* of its members. An association has standing to sue on behalf of its members if three conditions are met:

      (1) its members would "otherwise have standing to sue *in their own right*";

      (2) the interests the association seeks to protect are "germane to the organization's *purpose*; and

      (3) "neither the claim asserted nor the relief requested requires the participation of *individual members* in the lawsuit."

   *Hunt v. Washington Apple Advertising Comm.*, 432 U.S. 333 (1977).

4. **Causation:** Outside of the taxpayer-suit context, the Court has required that the litigant show that the challenged governmental action ***"caused"*** the injury of which he complains. This causation requirement has two components; the litigant must show that: (1) the challenged action was a "but for" cause of the injury, in the sense that the injury ***would not have occurred unless the challenged action had taken place***; and (2) a favorable decision in the suit will ***redress*** the injury. (Requirement (2) is called the ***"redressability"*** requirement.)

    a. **Confusion as to "redressability" standard:** It is not clear whether, to satisfy the redressability requirement, it is sufficient to show that a favorable decision will ***probably*** redress the harm. Sometimes, the Court has indicated that a ***probability*** of redress is sufficient; at other times, however, it has suggested that there must be a ***virtual certainty*** that redress will follow a favorable decision. See Tribe, pp. 129-30.

       i. **Potential easier standard:** But the 2007 decision in *Massachusetts v. EPA* (*infra*, p. 719) suggests that in some circumstances, even a ***less-than-50/50 chance*** that the sought-for relief will redress the problem may be enough, if the severity of the problem is great enough. In that case, Massachusetts tried to require the EPA to regulate U.S. automobile emissions so as to reduce global warming; the majority found that the redressability requirement was met, even though the harm feared by Massachusetts (flooding of its coastal lands) was nearly all yet-to-occur, and even though there was little concrete showing that if the requested relief were granted, the threatened harm would be averted. But *Mass. v. EPA* probably represents merely a weakening of the redressability requirement for the special case of ***state-as-plaintiff***, not a general weakening for all plaintiffs.

    b. ***Warth v. Seldin:*** The leading case illustrating how the Court applies the two causation requirements — the "but-for" requirement and "redressability" requirement — is ***Warth v. Seldin***, 422 U.S. 490 (1975). The plaintiffs in *Warth* failed to satisfy ***either*** part of the causation test.

       i. **Facts:** The plaintiffs in *Warth* were a number of parties who claimed to have been injured by the zoning rules of Penfield, New York. They claimed that these rules had been imposed for the purpose of excluding the building of low- and moderate-income housing in the town. The plaintiffs fell into a number of categories, two of which were:

          (1) **Low-income seekers of housing:** Low- and moderate-income individuals who had never lived in Penfield, but who alleged that they had sought housing there and would have moved there had affordable housing been available; and

          (2) **Real estate developers:** Two groups of entities, including real estate developers, who claimed that they would have participated in building affordable housing in Penfield had the zoning rules so permitted.

       ii. **Standing rejected:** The Supreme Court found that all of the plaintiffs ***lacked standing***. Most standing claims were rejected for failure to meet the "but-for" aspect of the causation requirement.

          (1) **Individuals:** For instance, the ***individuals*** who ***sought to live*** in Penfield lacked standing because they were unable to show that, had the restrictive zoning practices not existed, there was a ***"substantial probability*** that they would

have been able to purchase or lease in Penfield." They failed in this showing, the Court held, because construction of the appropriate housing would require not merely removal of the zoning laws but also a ***third party willing actually to build*** the projects, and there was no showing that such third parties would indeed have built projects which these particular individual plaintiffs could have afforded.

> **(2) Developers:** Conversely, the entities which wanted to ***participate in building*** such housing failed to show the requisite injury because they could not point to any ***specific project*** which had been precluded by the zoning rules.

**c. Article III basis for cause-in-fact rule:** In *Warth*, the majority did not make it clear whether its entire holding was dictated by the Article III "case or controversy" requirement, or rather, stemmed in part from "prudential" considerations. But in the later case of *Simon v. Eastern Ky. Welfare Rights Organization (EKWRO)*, 426 U.S. 26 (1976), the Court held that the requirements that the challenged action be the cause of the injury, and that the sought-for relief would remove that injury, are ***imposed by Article III.***

**d. Government allows injury by third party:** *A* plaintiff will generally find it hard to establish the cause-in-fact aspect of standing for a claim that ***government action or inaction*** has caused some ***third party not before the court*** to injure him. The difficulty of establishing standing for such a claim was illustrated when the Court found the cause-in-fact requirement unsatisfied in a case in which ***parents*** of black public school pupils attacked the IRS's ***grant of tax-exempt status*** to ***discriminatory private schools. Allen v. Wright***, 468 U.S. 737 (1984).

> **i. Facts:** In *Wright*, the parents claimed that the tax breaks enabled discriminatory private schools to offer cheaper tuition, thus inducing more parents of white students than would otherwise be the case to withdraw their children from the public schools to place them in these private schools. These withdrawals in turn deprived the black students of their constitutional right to attend integrated public schools, the parents claimed.

> **ii. Holding:** But the Court, by a 5-3 vote (with Justice Marshall not participating), concluded that the line of causation from the IRS's conduct to the continued segregation of the public schools was ***so attenuated*** that the latter was ***not*** "fairly traceable" to the former.

> > **(1) Speculative elements:** For there to have been standing, the majority indicated, the parents would have had to make three showings: (1) that "there were enough racially discriminatory private schools receiving tax exemptions in [plaintiffs'] communities for withdrawal of those exemptions to make an appreciable difference in public-school integration;" (2) that a significant number of schools would, if threatened with loss of the tax exemption, change their policies; and (3) that a significant number of parents of children attending such schools would transfer their children to public school if the exemption were withdrawn. According to the majority, plaintiffs had not alleged any of these three elements.

**5. Special deference when plaintiff is a state acting for its citizens:** When the plaintiff is a ***state*** acting on behalf of its citizens, the usual rules of standing will apparently be ***relaxed,***

as a result of a recent and controversial 5-4 decision by the Court in a case involving global warming. The case, ***Massachusetts v. EPA***, 549 U.S. __ (2007), seems to mean that the ***individuated-harm*** and ***causation*** requirements are especially likely to be relaxed where the plaintiff is a state suing in an ombudsman-like manner.

a. **Facts:** Massachusetts and ten other states sued the EPA, arguing that the agency was required under a congressional statute to issue regulations that would limit automobile emissions of carbon dioxide and thus reduce global warming. The agency, which under the George W. Bush administration did not want to (or believe that it had authority from Congress to) issue the regulations, argued that the states did not have standing to bring the suit, in part because they had not met the injury-in-fact or causation requirements.

b. **Holding:** The four liberal members of the court (Stevens, Ginsburg, Souter and Breyer) joined with Justice Kennedy to form a majority that concluded that Massachusetts, at least, ***had the requisite standing*** on account of the danger that ***rising sea levels*** would pose to its ***coastal areas.*** The opinion was by Justice Stevens.

   i. **State as sovereign:** Stevens seemed to be saying that Massachusetts' status in the suit as a ***sovereign representing the interests of its citizens*** justified some relaxation of the usual standing requirements imposed on private plaintiffs. The only authority cited by Stevens on this point was a 100-year-old case in which Georgia had been found to have standing to sue a private mining company for emitting pollutants outside Georgia's borders that threatened the quality of air and water inside the state. Massachusetts today, like Georgia then, had a "well-founded desire to preserve its sovereign territory," Stevens said.

   ii. **Injury in fact:** Stevens said that Massachusetts had met the ***injury in fact*** requirement because global warming had already caused a slight rise in sea level, and the rising seas "have already begun to swallow Massachusetts' coastal land." The injury suffered by Massachusetts was in both its quasi-sovereign capacity as representative of its citizens, and in the state's own capacity as owner of much of the coastal land. Furthermore, he said, this injury would grow only worse ***over "the course of the next century"*** if sea levels continued to rise, as generally predicted, from global warming.

   iii. **Causation:** A bigger issue for the Court was the causation requirement.

      (1) **The EPA's argument:** The EPA claimed that (1) automobile emissions in the U.S. accounted for only a very small portion of present global warming; (2) even if the EPA regulated emissions, this would reduce total worldwide emissions by only a tiny fraction, and thus reduce global warming by only a tiny proportion; and (3) any EPA-caused reduction in emissions would likely be swamped by ever-growing emissions from outside the U.S. Therefore, the EPA said, Massachusetts could not meet the ***"redressability"*** portion of the causation requirement (see *supra*, 717) – that is, it could not show that if it got the requested relief, there was even a reasonable prospect that the claimed injury would be redressed.

      (2) **Court rejects:** But Stevens ***rejected*** all parts of this syllogism, and held that the causation requirement was met by Massachusetts. As to part (1), the US

transportation segment accounts for 6% of worldwide carbon oxide emissions, not such a miniscule portion. And as to parts (2) and (3), the fact that any regulation on transportation emissions by the EPA would at most slow or reduce global warming – not reverse it – did not matter, because "a reduction in domestic emissions would *slow the pace* of global emissions *increases*, no matter what happens elsewhere."

(3) **Summary:** In sum, Stevens said, Massachusetts had standing because "the risk of catastrophic harm, though remote, is nevertheless *real* [and] that risk would be *reduced to some extent* if [Massachusetts] received the relief [it] seek[s]."

c. **Dissent:** Chief Justice Roberts dissented, joined by Scalia, Thomas and Alito. Roberts argued that states, like private plaintiffs, were required to satisfy "the bedrock requirement of showing injury, causation, and redressability to satisfy Article III." He believed that Massachusetts had failed to satisfy any of these three requirements.

   i. **Injury:** As to the requirement of injury, for instance, Roberts contended that Massachusetts had not shown any evidence of actual loss of its coastal land, and that with respect to the prospect of future loss, the majority's acceptance of a *"century-long time horizon* and a series of compounded estimates" rendered the traditional requirement that future harm be imminent and immediate "utterly toothless."

   ii. **Causation:** Likewise, Roberts believed that Massachusetts had not proved that US transportation-sector emissions had played a major role in the global warming crisis. More significantly, he believed that the relief Massachusetts was requesting – regulation leading to lesser U.S. automotive emissions – would not meaningfully reduce the harm Massachusetts was complaining of (which he defined as the loss of coastal land). Precedent required a showing that the requested relief would be "likely" to redress the claimed injury, something Massachusetts hadn't shown, especially given the probable rise in non-U.S. emissions whatever the EPA did.

d. **Significance:** *Massachusetts v. EPA* seems to mean that states will find it meaningfully easier than private parties to bring federal suits, especially in the environmental area. It is doubtful that a private citizen – even a coastal landowner – would have been found to have standing to attack the EPA's lack of steps to prevent global-warming.

D. **Third-party standing:** One of the principal functions of the standing doctrine is to implement the general rule that a litigant may normally ***not assert the constitutional rights of persons not before the court.*** This principle is also sometimes referred to as the rule against assertion of "constitutional *jus tertii*" ("rights of third persons" in Latin).

   **Example:** Recall that in *Warth v. Seldin, supra,* p. 717, residents of Rochester claimed that, because nearby Penfield had refused to allow low- and middle-income housing, their own taxes were higher since Rochester had had to grant tax abatements to encourage construction of more such housing than it otherwise would. The Rochester residents were denied standing; although their higher taxes constituted an "injury in fact," the zoning laws did not apply to them and thus did not violate *their* rights. Their claim thus fell within the general rule that one may not assert the rights of third persons (e.g., those who were excluded from Penfield by the zoning laws) except under special situations, none of which existed here.

1. **Rule is prudential, not constitutional:** The general rule against third-party standing is founded upon *discretionary* or *"prudential"* considerations, and is *not mandated by the Article III "case or controversy" requirement.*

    a. **Exceptions:** Therefore, the Court has been free to develop what has turned out to be a confused patchwork of judge-made *exceptions* to the no-third-party-standing rule.

2. **Relation to overbreadth doctrine:** The First Amendment *"overbreadth"* doctrine can be viewed as an exception to the rule against assertion of a third party's rights. Recall that by the overbreadth doctrine (discussed *supra,* p. 483), a party to whom a criminal statute clearly and constitutionally applies may be permitted to argue that the statute is applicable to some types of conduct which, if engaged in by third parties, would be constitutionally protected. In the overbreadth context, the third parties are hypothetical, and the litigant is *also* asserting his *own* constitutional right not to be convicted under a broadly-drawn statute which may chill his (as well as others') freedom of expression.

E. **"Prudential" standing:** We just saw that the rule against third-party standing is not dictated by the Article III "case or controversy" requirement, and is instead the result of *"prudential"* considerations (i.e., considerations "dictated by prudence"). More generally, the federal courts retain the right refuse to hear *any* case on such prudential-standing grounds, even cases falling outside the pure third-party-standing area.

For instance, in a well-publicized 2004 case a majority of the Court concluded that prudential standing considerations should prevent the federal courts from hearing a father's challenge to the constitutionality of a public-school recitation of the Pledge of Allegiance, because the suit affected *both* the plaintiff's own rights and his minor daughter's rights and also because the challenge raised questions of state domestic relations law that the federal courts have traditionally tried to avoid. The case was *Elk Grove Unified School Dist. v. Newdow,* 542 U.S. 1 (2004), in which five Justices thought that the prudential-standing doctrine dictated that the federal courts not hear the case, while three sharply disagreed (and the ninth recused himself).

1. **Facts:** The substantive issue in *Elk Grove* was whether group recitation of the Pledge of Allegiance in a public elementary school was a violation of the First Amendment. The plaintiff, Michael Newdow, was an atheist whose daughter attended the school in question. Newdow contended that his First Amendment rights (not his daughter's) were violated by the Pledge, because the Pledge interfered with his right to inculcate in his daughter, free from government interference, his own atheistic beliefs. But the posture of the case was complicated by the fact that Newdow was divorced from the child's mother, Ms. Banning, who under California law had the right to make final legal decisions about the daughter's upbringing if the two parents disagreed. Banning opposed Newdow's suit.

2. **Court of Appeals finds constitutional violation:** The Ninth Circuit Court of Appeals reached the merits, and found that the Pledge indeed violated Newdow's rights.

3. **Supreme Court reverses on standing grounds:** But a majority of the Supreme Court *reversed,* concluding that the lower courts should *never have reached the merits.* This was a case in which the prudential standing doctrine should be applied, the Court said.

    a. **Abstention from domestic relations cases:** First, the majority said, it was "in general ... appropriate" for the federal courts to *"leave delicate issues of domestic relations to the state courts."*

b.  **Rights of others:**   Second, any decision in the case would necessarily affect not only Newdow's rights, but also the rights of Banning (the mother) and, most of all, their daughter, "a young child who finds herself at the center of a highly public debate over her custody, the propriety of a widespread national ritual, and the meaning of our Constitution." These three sets of interests were potentially in conflict.

c.  **Rule of prudence:**   Finally, the Court summarized its conclusion: "It is improper for the federal courts to entertain a claim by a plaintiff whose standing to sue is founded on *family law rights that are in dispute* when prosecution of the lawsuit may have an *adverse effect on the person who is the source* of the plaintiff's claimed standing." The Court continued, "When hard questions of domestic relations are sure to affect the outcome, the *prudent course* is for the federal court to *stay its hand* rather than *reach out to resolve* a weighty question of federal constitutional law."

d.  **Dissent:**   Three dissenters disagreed. To the dissent, the daughter was not the source of Newdow's standing; instead, the relationship between daughter and father was what was providing Newdow with his own standing. That is, what Newdow claimed was being infringed was *his own right* to expose his daughter to his religious views without government interference. And that, to the dissenters, was enough to confer standing. The dissenters ridiculed the majority's rule as so narrow as to "be, like the proverbial excursion ticket — good for this day only." Instead, the dissenters would have applied "general principles, rather than ad hoc improvisations," and would have heard the case on the merits.

4.  **Struggle to avoid tough case:**   The majority in *Elk Grove* seems to have gone out of its way to avoid deciding an extremely controversial case. As one casebook says, *Elk Grove* can be viewed as a "case in which the Court attempted to ... avoid a contestable constitutional ruling that would undoubtedly have divided the nation, especially but not only if the Court had accepted Newdow's argument." S,S,S,T&K, p. 118. In other words, *Elk Grove* illustrates that the prudential standing doctrine is one of those elastic doctrines that can be used to sidestep a difficult or controversial decision.

# IV.  MOOTNESS

A.  **Mootness generally:**   A case is not justiciable if it is *"moot."* A case is moot if it raised a justiciable controversy at the time the complaint was filed, but *events occurring after the filing* have deprived the litigant of an ongoing stake in the controversy.

> **Example:** P sues D, a state university, claiming that its law school admissions program is racially discriminatory. He is permitted to attend the law school while the case is being litigated. By the time the case arrives at the Supreme Court for review, P is in his final year of law school, and the university says that he will be allowed to graduate.
>
> *Held*, the case is moot, and determination of the legal issues in the suit is no longer necessary. Therefore, the appeal will not be decided. *DeFunis v. Odegaard*, 416 U.S. 312 (1974).

B.  **Exceptions:**   There are a number of reasons for which a case which is ostensibly moot will nonetheless be heard. The main ones, each of which is discussed below, are: (1) that the issue is *"capable of repetition, yet evading review"*; (2) that the case seems moot only because the defendant has *voluntarily*, but not necessarily permanently, changed his conduct; and (3) that there are *collateral consequences* to the defendant's action which, when considered, prevent mootness. See Tribe, p. 84.

1. **"Capable of repetition, yet evading review"**: An issue will not be treated as moot if it is *"capable of repetition, yet evading review." Southern Pacific Terminal Co. v. ICC*, 219 U.S. 498 (1911).

> **Example:** P, a pregnant woman, attacks the constitutionality of state anti-abortion laws. She brings the suit as a class action, in which she is the named plaintiff and other pregnant women desiring abortions are unnamed members. By the time the case reaches the Supreme Court, P is no longer pregnant.
>
> *Held*, the case should not be dismissed as moot. Pregnancy will almost always be completed before the usual appellate process is complete. P herself may become pregnant again, but even if she does not, obviously other women will. The issue is thus "capable of repetition, yet evading review." *Roe v. Wade*, 410 U.S. 113 (1973).

2. **Voluntary cessation by defendant**: If the defendant *voluntarily ceases* the conduct about which the plaintiff is complaining, this will normally ***not*** be enough to make the case moot. If the plaintiff seeks damages, the cessation will of course be irrelevant to the issue of mootness. But even if the plaintiff seeks an *injunction*, the cessation will not make the case moot, if there is any substantial chance that the defendant might "return to his old ways." See Tribe, p. 89.

3. **Collateral consequences**: In determining whether the plaintiff continues to have a stake in the controversy, all *collateral consequences* of the challenged conduct must be examined. If any of these collateral consequences could be adverse to the plaintiff, the case is not moot. For instance, where a criminal defendant has already *served his sentence*, his attack on the constitutionality of his conviction will not be deemed moot, because of the likelihood of collateral consequences from the conviction, such as loss of the right to vote, and damage to reputation or to employability. See Tribe, p. 92.

# V. RIPENESS

A. **Problem generally:** The problem of *ripeness* may be regarded as the opposite of that of mootness. Whereas a case is moot (and therefore not justiciable) because it *no longer* involves an actual controversy, a case will be regarded as not yet ripe (and therefore not yet justiciable) if it has *not yet become sufficiently concrete* to be worthy of adjudication.

1. **Relation to ban on advisory opinions:** The ban on adjudication of unripe matters is closely related to the ban on *advisory opinions (supra*, p. 710). Both doctrines reflect the view, based partly on the constitutional requirement of a "case or controversy," that the federal courts must not render opinions except in situations where there is a well-defined, live controversy, with specific facts, and with either an allegation of past injury or a likelihood of future injury.

2. *Mitchell* **case:** The classic illustration of a matter not yet ripe for adjudication is *United Public Workers v. Mitchell*, 330 U.S. 75 (1947).

   a. **Facts:** The plaintiffs in *Mitchell* were federal civil servants who wished to attack the Hatch Act, which prohibits federal executive-branch employees from involvement in "political management or … political campaigns." The plaintiffs claimed, in essence, that they *desired* to engage in prohibited political activities; however, all but one conceded that they had *not yet done so.*

b. **Holding:** A majority of the Court held that the claims of those plaintiffs who had not yet violated the Act were *not ripe.*

    i. **Rationale:** The Court reasoned that plaintiffs' claims were so general that they constituted "really an attack on the political expediency" of the statute, "not the presentation of legal issues." It was the province of the legislature, not the judiciary, to make such general determinations of political expediency.

    ii. **Specific conduct:** Thus the Court seems to have really been troubled not so much by the fact that the plaintiffs had not yet violated the statute and not yet been subjected to the prescribed punishment (discharge), but rather, by the fact that the plaintiffs were not *adequately specific* as to the precise acts which they wished to carry out. Had the plaintiffs set forth *in detail* what they wished to do, the ripeness doctrine might not have prevented their case from being adjudicated even though these acts had not yet been carried out. See Tribe, p. 79.

B. **Uncertain enforcement of criminal statute:** Ripeness problems also may arise where the plaintiff alleges that he has violated a statute whose constitutionality he attacks, but it is not clear that the statute is *generally enforced*, or that it will be enforced in this particular case. In this situation, the Court has often been reluctant to allow the case to be adjudicated.

1. *Poe v. Ullman:* For instance, in *Poe v. Ullman*, 367 U.S. 497 (1961), two married couples and a physician challenged Connecticut's anti-contraception law. A majority of the Court refused to hear the case on appeal, on the grounds that the statute had been on the books for 80 years with only one reported prosecution and that there was thus not the requisite "clear" threat of prosecution.

2. **Willingness to hear evolution case:** But the Court has not always held that a rarely-enforced statute fails to present a ripe controversy. For instance, in *Epperson v. Arkansas, supra,* p. 664, the anti-evolution statute struck down by the Court had not been enforced in the 40 years of its history, nor was there any showing of a specific threat of enforcement against the plaintiff. See L,K&C, p. 1682, n. 2. The Court's willingness to adjudicate *Epperson* suggests that its refusal to hear *Poe* was an exercise of its *discretion*, not the product of a lack of an Article III "case or controversy." See Hart and Wechsler, *Federal Courts*, p. 657.

C. **Requirement of specific threatened harm:** For a case to be ripe, it is not necessary that the litigant have already suffered harm; it is sufficient that there is a reasonable probability of harm. However, the anticipated harm must be *reasonably specific*.

1. *Laird v. Tatum:* For instance, in *Laird v. Tatum*, 408 U.S. 1 (1972), plaintiffs attacked an Army Intelligence scheme for *gathering data* about persons and activities who had the potential for "civil disorder." Plaintiffs claimed that this surveillance scheme had a "present inhibiting effect" on their activities, even though they had no idea what use, if any, the Army might make of the information being gathered. But the Court, by a 5-4 vote, found that a present "subjective chill" was not enough to make the case ripe; what had to be shown was a *"specific present objective harm"* or a *"threat of specific future harm."*

# VI. THE 11TH AMENDMENT, AND SUITS AGAINST STATES

A. **The 11th Amendment:** The 11th Amendment imposes limitations — increasingly important ones in the 1990s — on the jurisdiction of the federal courts.

   1. **Text of the Amendment:** That Amendment provides:

      The Judicial power of the United States shall not be construed to extend to ***any suit in law or equity***, commenced or prosecuted ***against one of the United States*** by ***Citizens of another State***, or by Citizens or Subjects of any ***foreign*** state.

   2. **Facial meaning:** So on its face, the 11th Amendment merely seems to say that one state can't be sued in federal court by a citizen of a different state, or by a foreigner. And in fact, if you were wearing your *Civil Procedure* hat, you might think that this Amendment was simply saying that suits based solely on diversity — rather than on a federal question — could not be brought against a state.

   3. **Interpreted more broadly:** But over the years, the Amendment has been interpreted much more broadly than that. We don't have space for a long explication of the Amendment, but here are the highlights of how the Supreme Court has interpreted its scope:

      a. **Suits by citizens of the defendant state:** First, the Amendment is interpreted so as to bar suits by a citizen against his or her ***own state***. *Hans v. Louisiana*, 134 U.S. 1 (1890).

      b. **Suits involving federal question:** Second, the Amendment covers ***federal question suits***, not just diversity suits. Many scholars believe that the 11th Amendment was intended only to block diversity suits against states, not federal-question suits against them. But this view has not prevailed, and the 11th Amendment is interpreted to block all suits by private citizens against states, whether based on diversity, alienage, or federal question.

      c. **Constitutional embodiment of sovereign immunity:** Third, this broad reading of the limits on suits against states — that a state may not be sued even by its own citizens, and may not be sued even in a case raising a federal question — is now held to be a core ***constitutional limitation on federal judicial power***, not just an interpretation of broad "principles" surrounding the 11th Amendment itself. The most important consequence is that ***Congress generally cannot overrule this broad reading***, and cannot authorize a state to be sued by its own citizens in federal-question suits. This is the nub of the Court's 1996 ruling in *Seminole Tribe*, discussed in detail *infra*, p. 726.

      d. **Suits in equity:** Finally, the Amendment applies not only to suits "at law," but also to suits "at *equity*." Thus a private citizen cannot sue to have a state enjoined or ordered to do something, any more than she can sue to recover damages. (But as we discuss immediately below, the Amendment does not bar suits against a state *official*, in his private capacity, seeking to enjoin him from violating federal law.)

   4. **Exclusions:** There are a number of important exclusions from the coverage of the 11th Amendment:

      a. **Suits against officials for injunctions:** Most important, the 11th Amendment does not prevent suits against ***state officials*** in which the relief sought is an ***injunction*** against the ***violation of federal law***. This principle was established in *Ex parte Young*, 209 U.S. 123 (1908). The theory behind the principle is that when a state officer's official conduct violates the U.S. Constitution or a federal statute, he is acting without true authority, and his conduct is therefore not really "state conduct" for purposes of the 11th Amendment. See Chemerinsky, §7.5.1.

b. **Suits against official for money damages:** The Amendment also doesn't bar suits against a *state official* for *money damages*, as long as the damages are to be paid out of the official's own pocket. But where a suit would if successful lead to a state's being ordered to pay damages out of its own pocket, the suit is barred by the Amendment, even if the suit is nominally filed against the official rather than the state itself. Chemerinsky, §7.5.2.

c. **Suit for injunction against violation of state law:** The 11th Amendment *does* apply to bar injunctions prohibiting state officials from violating *state* (as opposed to federal) law. *Pennhurst State School Hosp. v. Halderman*, 465 U.S. 89 (1984).

d. **Suits by federal government:** The 11th Amendment does not bar suits *by the federal government* against a state.

e. **Suits against cities:** The Amendment does not bar suits against *cities*, or other political subdivisions of a state.

f. **State agencies and other entities:** The caselaw is unclear and inconsistent as to when the Amendment bars suits against state *agencies*, boards and other entities — such as state-owned universities — associated with state government.

g. **Suits by one state against another:** The Amendment does not bar suits by *one state against another* (as long as the plaintiff state is truly suing for itself rather than merely to protect private interests of individual citizens.)

h. **Suits in state court:** The Amendment only applies in federal courts; it doesn't prevent a private individual from suing a state in *state court*, even to vindicate a federal right. (But, of course, the state court must have jurisdiction over the suit. Some state courts may not have jurisdiction because of the state's enabling statutes; also, some federal statutes that create rights provide for exclusive federal-court jurisdiction in proceedings to enforce those rights, in which case no state-court forum is available.)

    i. **Appellate jurisdiction:** Also, as long as the suit started in state court, nothing in the 11th Amendment prohibits the U.S. Supreme Court from using its *appellate jurisdiction* to review a state-court decision to see if it violates federal law. Chemerinsky, §7.4

i. **Waiver by state:** The protections of the 11th Amendment can be *waived* by a state — if the state consents to be sued in federal court, the 11th Amendment will no longer stand as a bar. Chemerinsky, §7.6.

j. **Suits under the post-Civil War Amendments:** If Congress passes a statute pursuant to its power to enforce the *post-Civil War Amendments* (13th, 14th and 15th), and that statute gives private citizens the right to sue a state in federal court, this statute will be enforced, and won't be deemed to violate the 11th Amendment.

5. **Congress' general power to allow suits against the states:** As just noted, where Congress is legislating pursuant to its special powers to enforce the post-Civil War amendments, it may abrogate the 11th Amendment and permit private citizens to sue the states in federal court. But outside this post-Civil War area, *Congress may not abrogate the 11th*

*Amendment*, no matter how explicitly it tries to do so. This is the somewhat startling holding of *Seminole Tribe of Florida v. Florida*, 517 U.S. 44 (1996), a major case that significantly hampers Congress' ability to give private citizens the ability to sue states for violations of federal law.

a. **Facts:** Congress passed a statute, the Indian Gaming Regulatory Act, to govern aspects of gambling operations run by Indian tribes. The IGRA provided that when a state allows non-Indian gambling, the state must also negotiate in good faith with any tribe located in the state to try to reach an agreement permitting the tribe to conduct comparable gambling operations. The statute also provided that if a tribe believed that the state was not negotiating in good faith, the tribe could sue the state in federal court for an order directing the state to negotiate in good faith.

b. **Split:** The Court, by a 5-4 vote, held that this statute *violated the 11th Amendment*. The split was precisely the same as in *U.S. v. Lopez*, the case restricting Congress' Commerce Clause powers (see *supra*, p. 36).

c. **Holding:** The majority opinion, by Chief Justice Rehnquist, held that "Even when the Constitution vests in Congress *complete law-making authority over a particular area*, . . . the Eleventh Amendment *restricts the judicial power under Article III*, and Article I cannot be used to circumvent the constitutional limitations placed upon federal jurisdiction." So even though Article I gives Congress full authority to "regulate commerce . . . with the Indian tribes," Congress cannot allow a tribe to sue a state in federal court.

     i. **Rationale:** The majority's rationale was that the 11th Amendment *embodies concepts of state sovereignty*. Furthermore, the principle of state sovereignty embodied in the 11th Amendment limits the Article III jurisdiction of the federal courts, and Congress cannot expand those limits just because it wants to.

     ii. **Suits based on Commerce Clause:** Even though *Seminole* itself involved congressional power based on the Indian Commerce Clause, the decision applies broadly to *all sources of congressional power other than the post-Civil War amendments*. For instance, it clearly applies to congressional action based on the *"regular" Commerce Clause*, a source that probably accounts for a majority of federal statutes enacted over the last 50 years.

d. **Dissents:** There were two dissents, one by Stevens, the other by Souter (joined by Ginsburg and Breyer). Souter's dissent was the principal one; indeed, at 92 pages it was three times the length of Rehnquist's majority opinion.

     i. **Limited view of Amendment:** To Souter, all the drafters of the 11th Amendment ever meant to do, and all the Amendment had ever been interpreted as doing, was to prevent suits based *solely on diversity*, i.e. those brought by a state against a non-citizen of that state in circumstances under which no federal question was raised.

     ii. **Destructive of ability to protect federal rights:** The dissenters believed that the majority's view was not only wrong but *highly destructive of federally-guaranteed rights*. As Stevens put it, the majority's holding *"prevents Congress from providing a federal forum* for a broad range of actions against States, from those sounding in *copyright* and *patent* law, to those concerning *bankruptcy, environmental law*, and the regulation of our vast national economy."

e. **Later illustration:**  A post-*Seminole* decision by the Supreme Court demonstrates the broad impact that *Seminole* is likely to have.  In *Florida Prepaid Postsecondary Education Expense Board v. College Savings Bank*, 527 U.S. 627 (1999), the Court held that just as Congress may not abrogate the 11th Amendment when acting under authority of the *commerce* power (the point decided in *Seminole*), Congress may not do so when acting under its *patent* power. Therefore, Congress, no matter how explicitly it tries to do so, *may not force the state to defend a private patent damage suit in federal court.*

f. **Broader significance:** The greatest significance of *Seminole* and *Florida Prepaid* may turn out to be these cases' suggestion of a radically new — and restricted — view of federal power. These cases, taken together with *U.S. v. Lopez*'s limits on the Commerce power (*supra*, p. 36), *New York v. U.S.*'s resurrection of the Tenth Amendment (*supra*, p. 50), *Alden v. Maine*'s recognition of state immunity from state-court suits based on federal rights (*infra*, p. 728), and *Federal Maritime*'s prohibition on certain federal administrative proceedings involving state defendants (*infra*, p. 729), represent the view of a 5-Justice majority that federal power is *far less extensive than had previously been thought*. As Prof. Tribe has said, "the Court's current dedication to a states' rights doctrine seems to be a rather free-floating cloud that can rain on almost any source of congressional power." *NY Times*, April 1, 1996, p. A1.

6. **States' sovereign immunity from state-court suits based on federal rights:**   Just    as *Seminole Tribe* says that Congress generally can't authorize federal-court suits against the States, so the doctrine of *sovereign immunity* generally prevents Congress from subjecting the states to private suits *in their own courts, even where the right sued on is federal*. That is the startling result of a 1999 decision, *Alden v. Maine*, 527 U.S. 706 (1999), decided three years after *Seminole* by the same 5-4 split as in *Seminole*.

a. **Facts of *Alden*:**  Congress had said that the Fair Labor Standards Act (FLSA), which governs overtime and other wage matters, applies to the states as employers, just as it does to private employers. Congress also said that a state's employees could bring FLSA suits against the state in the state's own courts. In *Alden*, workers employed by the state of Maine did just that, arguing in the Maine courts that they were entitled to certain extra pay for overtime.

b. **Struck down:**  But in an opinion by Justice Kennedy, the 5-member majority held that Congress had no constitutional authority to force the Maine courts to hear the workers' suit, *even though that suit was based upon a federal right* that (even the majority agreed) Congress had authority to confer upon the workers. For a state's immunity from private suits for money damages in the state's own courts was "a *fundamental aspect of the sovereignty which the states enjoyed before the ratification of the Constitution*, and which they *retain today*."

c. **Significance:**   *Alden* seems to mean that the states now have *full sovereign immunity from any private suit in the state's own courts seeking damages for the state's violation of federal law.* For instance, the states as employers are presumably immune to damage suits alleging that they committed *employment discrimination* (e.g., discrimination based on age or disability), and the states as market participants are apparently immune from state-court claims that they have violated federal laws governing commerce (e.g., **trademark** and **antitrust** laws). Coupled with the extensive federal-court 11th Amendment immunity recognized in *Seminole Tribe*, the states now seem to have a large zone in which, as a practical matter, they are completely insulated from congressional attempts to give private individuals a damages remedy for violations of federal rights.

7. **Complaints before federal agencies:** The latest extension of the Court's tendency to limit federal-law-related actions against the states involves federal **administrative-agency** proceedings. In a 2002 decision, the Court held that the same principle of state sovereignty cited in *Alden* bars the federal government from **requiring that states defend** against private complaints in **proceedings brought before federal administrative agencies**. *Federal Maritime Comm. v. South Carolina State Ports Auth.*, 535 U.S. 743 (2002).

# VII. POLITICAL QUESTIONS

A. **Introduction:** The final aspect of justiciability is the requirement that the case not require decision of what is commonly called a **"political question."** The scope of the "political question" doctrine is even less well-defined than the other aspects of justiciability considered above. Also, the doctrine is less important today than it was in prior periods; in only a few cases since 1970 has the Court found an issue to be a non-justiciable political question.

1. **Phrase a misnomer:** The phrase "political question" is something of a misnomer. The Court will not treat as a non-justiciable political question an issue which merely happens to **involve politics**, even if politically-related issues are at the very heart of the case. Rather, the political question doctrine seems to be a meshing of two sets of principles:

    a. **Separation of powers:** *Separation-of-powers* principles, by which, as a constitutional matter, the Court will not decide matters which it concludes are committed by the Constitution to other branches of government for decision; and

    b. **Prudential concerns:** various *"prudential"* considerations, because of which the Court concludes that it is unwise, even if not strictly unconstitutional, for it to decide the case.

2. **General unifying principle:** The factors which lead a court to conclude that an issue is a political question, factors which are discussed in detail below, are not easily summarized into one overarching principle. Perhaps the most useful formulation is that proposed by Tribe; he asserts that in deciding whether an issue is a non-justiciable political question, the court is "determin[ing] whether constitutional provisions which litigants would have judges enforce do in fact **lend themselves to interpretation as guarantees of enforceable rights**." Tribe, p. 106. (But as Tribe himself concedes, the factors which the courts must consider in making this determination are a diverse blend of constitutional and discretionary considerations. *Id.*)

B. *Baker v. Carr:* The modern Court's approach to political questions is set forth most notably in the well-known case of *Baker v. Carr*, 369 U.S. 186 (1962). That case, which held that the constitutionality of legislative apportionment schemes is not a political question, paved the way for the Court's "one person, one vote" ruling; therefore, the case is discussed more extensively in our treatment of reapportionment, *infra*, p. 733.

1. **Factors:**  For now, what is significant is that the Court in *Baker* announced a series of *factors*, at least one of which (the Court asserted) *must be present* in order to make an issue a non-justiciable political question. Each of these factors, the *Baker* Court argued, relates in some way to the *separation of powers*. The Court listed the following factors:

   a. **Commitment to another branch:**  A "textually demonstrable constitutional *commitment of the issue* to a *coordinate political department*" (i.e., to Congress or to the President);

   b. **Lack of standards:**  A "lack of judicially discoverable and manageable *standards* for resolving" the issue;

   c. **Unsuitable policy determination:**  The "impossibility of deciding [the issue] without an initial *policy determination* of a kind clearly for non-judicial discretion";

   d. **Lack of respect for other branches:**  The "impossibility of a court's undertaking independent resolution without expressing *lack of the respect due co-ordinate branches of government*";

   e. **Political decision already made:**  An "unusual need for unquestioning adherence to a *political decision already made*"; and

   f. **Multiple pronouncements:**  The potential for "embarrassment from *multifarious pronouncements* by various departments on one question."

2. **Most significant factors:**  Here, we will concern ourselves mainly with three of these factors: (1) the "commitment to other branches" factor; (2) the "lack of judicially discoverable and manageable standards" factor; and (3) the "need for a single pronouncement" factor. Additionally, we will consider the existence of a fourth factor not explicitly mentioned in *Baker*, the extent to which the issue raises a controversial question whose adjudication might lead to major, undesirable consequences. Finally, we give separate consideration to the reapportionment cases, which involve more than one of these factors.

C. **The "commitment to other branches" strand:**  As *Baker v. Carr* suggested, the Court will regard as a non-justiciable political question any issue the determination of which is clearly committed by the Constitution to *another branch of government*. The cases decided under this strand have all involved decisions arguably committed to the President or Congress (not decisions arguably committed to the states.)

1. **Impeachment:**  A strong case can be made that the House of Representatives' decision whether to *impeach* the President or other federal officer, and the Senate's decision whether to convict, are *not judicially reviewable* because these decisions are committed to those bodies by the Constitution. If this view is accepted, the Court would not have jurisdiction even to determine whether the grounds upon which, say, the President was convicted fell within the constitutionally-defined category of "high Crimes and Misdemeanors." See *supra*, p. 132.

   a. **Majority view:**  Most commentators believe that impeachment decisions do indeed fall within the "committed to other branches" category, and are therefore non-justiciable political questions. One of the difficulties with a contrary view is that the legitimacy of Supreme Court review of an impeachment conviction might not be apparent to the nation. As one author has noted, if the Senate voted to convict, and the Supreme Court ordered reinstatement, "[o]ur military commanders would have to decide for themselves which President they were bound to obey, the reinstated one or his successor." Black, *Impeachment: A Handbook*, pp. 61-62 (quoted in L,K&C, p. 50).

b. **Senate has sole power to decide what constitutes a "trial":** The Court has never had to determine whether Congress' decision to impeach or convict a federal officer is judicially reviewable. But a recent case on a different aspect of impeachment law strongly indicates that most controversies relating to impeachment will be found to fall within the "committed to other branches" category and thus to be non-justiciable political questions. In *Nixon v. U.S.*, 506 U.S. 224 (1993), Walter Nixon, a federal judge whom the House had impeached and the Senate convicted based on bribery charges, challenged the ***procedures*** used by the Senate. The Senate ***delegated to a committee*** of senators the job of holding hearings on the accusations against Nixon. The committee then gave the full Senate a transcript of the proceedings, and the Senate voted by more than the required two-thirds majority to convict Nixon.

   i. **Argument:** Nixon argued that the Senate, by having a committee rather than the full Senate hear the evidence, violated the requirement of Article I, Section 3, Clause 6 that the Senate "try all impeachments."

   ii. **Held non-justiciable:** But the Supreme Court held that Nixon's argument presented a non-justiciable political question. The Court relied mainly on the plain text of the Senate Impeachment Clause, which provides that "the Senate shall have ***sole Power*** to try all Impeachments." The Court interpreted this reference to "sole Power," along with the history behind the provision, to mean that the Senate, nor the courts, should determine what procedures could validly constitute a "trial." (The Court also reasoned that a "lack of finality" problem dictated that the courts not hear Nixon's claim: "Opening the door of judicial review to the procedures used by the Senate in trying impeachments would 'expose the political life of the country to months, or perhaps years of chaos,'" especially if it were the President who was being impeached.)

2. **Amendment of Constitution:** The process by which ***constitutional amendments*** are adopted is probably also committed to Congress for final determination, and therefore presents a non-justiciable political question. Thus in *Coleman v. Miller*, 307 U.S. 433 (1939), four members of the Court, concurring, believed that only Congress could determine whether a particular state had ratified a constitutional amendment. (The case is discussed more extensively *infra*, p. 732, because of the Court's reliance on the "lack of judicially manageable standards" strand.)

3. ***Powell v. McCormack:*** The most famous case discussing the "commitment to other branches" strand was one in which the Court concluded that at most only a ***limited*** commitment of the decision-making authority in question to another branch (Congress) was involved. In ***Powell v. McCormack***, 395 U.S. 486 (1969), Adam Clayton Powell, Jr., who had been elected to Congress from Harlem, successfully challenged the House's refusal to seat him.

   a. **Facts:** The House's refusal came after one of its committees found that Powell had dodged the process of the New York courts, had wrongfully diverted House funds, and had made false reports to a House committee. When Powell sued for a declaratory judgment that the refusal to seat him was unconstitutional, the House defended on the grounds that Article I, §5 (which provides that "[e]ach House shall be the Judge of the

... Qualifications of its own Members") gave the House the sole right to determine what qualifications are necessary for membership. Powell, by contrast, argued that that clause merely gives the House the right to determine whether a person possesses the "standing qualifications" expressly set out in the Constitution (Article I, §2's age, citizenship and residence requirements).

   b. **Victory for Powell:**   The Supreme Court agreed with Powell. Article I, §5 was at most a grant to Congress of the right to determine whether the three standing qualifications set forth in Article I, §2 were satisfied. Therefore, Congress had not been given the right to impose additional qualifications for membership.

      i. **Standing qualifications:**   But, the Court noted, it was still possible that the decision about whether a member met the three standing qualifications *was* committed to Congress, so as to bar the federal courts from reviewing that determination. The Court noted that it was not deciding this issue, which remains undecided to this day. The issue did not arise in *Powell* itself because all parties conceded that Powell met these qualifications.

D. **"Lack of judicially manageable standards" strand:**   A second major factor which may lead the Court to conclude that a case presents a non-justiciable question is that there is a "lack of *judicially discoverable* and *manageable standards* for resolving it."

   1. **Guarantee of republican form of government:**   For instance, the Court has consistently held that claims based upon Article IV, §4 (which provides that "[t]he United States shall guarantee to every State in this Union a *Republican Form of Government*") are non-justiciable political questions.

      a. ***Luther v. Borden:***   The best-known case on this so-called *Guaranty Clause* is *Luther v. Borden*, 7 How. 1 (1849). The case grew out of a rebellion by some dissatisfied Rhode Island citizens, and ultimately required the federal courts to decide which of two competing governments was the lawful government of the state. But the Supreme Court declined to make this determination, concluding that the case posed a political question. The decision seems to have been based in part upon the "lack of criteria by which a court could determine which form of government was republican" (as the decision was summarized in the later case of *Baker v. Carr, infra*, p. 733).

   2. **War Powers disputes:**   If the federal courts were called upon to referee a dispute between the President and Congress concerning whether the President had usurped Congress' *war-making powers* by *committing our armed forces to combat* without congressional approval, the "lack of judicially manageable standards" strand might cause the case to be regarded as a political question. For instance, a refusal by the President to bring American troops home from hostilities within 60 days of invocation of the War Powers Resolution of 1973 (see *supra*, p. 140) might fall into this category.

E. **The need for a unified voice (especially in foreign affairs):**   The need for the federal government to speak with a *single, unified voice* has occasionally been a factor in the conclusion that an issue presents a political question. This is more likely to happen in the area of *foreign affairs* than in the domestic area.

   1. **Treaty termination:**   For instance, the Court has refused to decide whether the President can *terminate a treaty* with Taiwan without congressional approval. *Goldwater v. Carter*, 444 U.S. 996 (1979). There was no majority in agreement on why the case was non-justi-

ciable; the four-member plurality may have had the "single voice" rationale in mind when it remarked that the case posed a political question because "it involves the authority of the President in the conduct of our country's foreign relations."

**F. Reapportionment:** Until 1962, the Court consistently refused to adjudicate claims concerning *legislative apportionment*, on the grounds that they presented political questions. See, e.g., *Colegrove v. Green*, 328 U.S. 549 (1946), in which Justice Frankfurter's plurality opinion declared that "[i]t is hostile to a democratic system to involve the judiciary in the politics of the people. ... [C]ourts ought not to enter this political thicket."

1. ***Baker v. Carr:*** But in ***Baker v. Carr***, 369 U.S. 186 (1962), the Court reversed its course. The challenge in *Baker* was to the apportionment of the Tennessee Assembly, which had not been reapportioned in 60 years, despite a state constitutional requirement that representation be on the basis of population, and despite significant changes in population over the years. The Court concluded that the claim, which was that the malapportionment violated the ***Equal Protection Clause***, did ***not*** present a political question.

   a. **Rationale:** The Court reasoned that not all cases involving "politics" present non-justiciable "political questions." The Court listed a catalogue of factors, at least one of which, it asserted, had always been present in true political-question cases. (See *supra*, p. 729.) The equal protection claim here, the majority concluded, did not involve any of these factors. For instance, the issue had not been "textually ... commit[ted] by the Constitution to another branch of government"; nor were "judicially discoverable and manageable standards for resolving it" lacking.

2. **"One person, one vote" principle (*Reynolds v. Sims*):** The conclusion in *Baker* that apportionment claims do not necessarily present non-justiciable political questions opened the door for numerous challenges to the apportionment of state legislatures and federal congressional districts. In a series of decisions, the Court developed its famous, and simple, ***"one person, one vote"*** principle. The major case in this line was ***Reynolds v. Sims***, 377 U.S. 533 (1964).

   a. **Facts:** *Reynolds* was a challenge to the apportionment of the Alabama legislature. Therefore, it posed different problems from a case decided shortly before, *Wesberry v. Sanders*, 374 U.S. 1 (1964), a challenge to a state's apportionment of its ***federal congressional districts*** — in *Wesberry*, the Court had been able to dispose of the case by interpreting Article I, §2's requirement that representatives be chosen "by the People of the several States" as requiring that "as nearly as practicable one man's vote in a congressional election is to be worth as much as another's."

   b. **Apportionment struck down:** Nonetheless, the *Reynolds* Court struck down the Alabama apportionment (or rather, malapportionment) scheme. It did so upon an ***equal protection*** theory: the Equal Protection Clause "requires that the seats in ***both houses*** of a bicameral state legislature must be apportioned ***on a population basis***. ... An individual's right to vote for state legislators is unconstitutionally impaired when its weight is in a ***substantial fashion diluted*** when compared with votes of citizens in other parts of the State."

      i. **Rationale:** The Court observed that equal protection generally requires "the uniform treatment of persons standing in the same relation to the governmental action questioned or challenged." Since "legislators represent people, not trees or acres," there was no apparent reason for making one person's vote worth more than another's in the election of those legislators.

    **ii.** **Some deviations allowed:** The Court in *Reynolds* did ***not*** require ***strict mathematical equality***. "Some deviations" from the equal-population rule would be permissible, if they were directed towards the carrying out of a "rational state policy." But "neither history alone, nor economic or other sorts of group interests, are permissible factors. ... " Furthermore, even pursuit of a "clearly rational state policy" (e.g., "according some legislative representation to political subdivisions") by an apportionment scheme would ***not*** be valid if "population is submerged as the ***controlling consideration.***"

**c.** **Disagreement:** Three members of the Court disagreed with the majority's general approach in *Reynolds*.

    **i.** **Harlan's dissent:** Only Justice Harlan dissented from the result in *Reynolds*; he argued mainly that the framers of the Equal Protection Clause simply did not intend that Clause to be used to limit the power of the states to apportion their legislatures however they wished.

    **ii.** **Stewart's concurrence:** Justice Stewart (joined by Justice Clark) agreed that the Alabama scheme was "completely lacking in rationality." However, he disagreed with the majority's general approach. He did not think that the Equal Protection Clause barred a state's divergence from mathematical equality of votes if this was done for the purpose of providing "effective and balanced representation of all substantial interests." The only limitation imposed by that Clause, he believed, was that a plan "must be such as not to permit the ***systematic frustration of the will of a majority*** of the electorate of the State." That is, so long as a majority was not consistently blocked from electing a majority of the legislators, the scheme must merely be "rational." (For instance, Stewart believed that New York's scheme, reviewed in a companion case, met this standard even though it guaranteed at least one representative to each county, and gave fewer legislators to New York City than it would have been entitled to strictly on the basis of population; Stewart thought that this was a valid attempt to "protect against overcentralization of power.")

**d.** **Justiciability of "one person, one vote" rule:** Observe that the existence of "judicially discoverable and manageable standards" for resolving apportionment questions was greatly aided by the Court's selection in *Reynolds* of the "one person, one vote" principle. For instance, had the Court accepted Justice Stewart's more limited rule that there must simply not be "systematic frustration of the will of a majority of the electorate," the Court might have been required to "canvass the actual workings of the floor leadership in the legislative branches, the mechanisms of party control not only over voters in the city government but also over elected representatives — in short, the details of the petty corruption and networks of personal influence that all too often constitute critical sources of power in municipal politics." 20 STAN. L. REV. 247 (quoted in Ely, p. 124). Thus it was "precisely because of considerations of administrability [that the Court] found itself with no perceived alternative but to move to a one person, one vote standard." Ely, p. 124.

3. **Other issues:** The companion cases to *Reynolds* settled some other issues, in addition to the basic "one person, one vote" principle. Most importantly, *Lucas v. Colorado General Assembly*, 377 U.S. 713 (1964) established that an apportionment scheme that violated the "one person, one vote" rule could not be saved by the fact that it had been **approved by the voters of the state**. A "citizen's constitutional right can hardly be infringed simply because a majority of the people choose that it be." (Similarly, the fact that the state **constitution** apportions one of the two houses on a basis other than population will not make that apportionment valid.)

4. **Local government:** Subsequent cases applied the general "one person, one vote" rule to elections for **local government** bodies. After some initial confusion, the Court settled on the rule that the "one person, one vote" standard applies whenever persons are chosen by popular election to "perform **governmental functions**," whether or not those governmental functions are **"general"** ones. Thus in *Hadley v. Junior College Dist.*, 397 U.S. 50 (1970), the case in which the Court articulated this rule, the Court required an attempt at equal-population apportionment for trustees of a junior college district, obviously not a body of general jurisdiction.

   a. **Special-purpose bodies:** However, the Court noted in *Hadley* that some bodies or officials may have "duties [that] are so far removed from normal governmental activities and [may] so disproportionately affect different groups that a popular election … might not be required." See *Ball v. James, supra*, p. 357, for an example of such a special-purpose body (a water district) not requiring application of the *Reynolds* principle.

5. **How much equality is required:** In cases following *Reynolds*, the Court was required to decide **how much** deviation from strict mathematical equality is permissible. In doing so, it established a key distinction between **congressional** districting on the one hand, and districting for state and local governmental bodies on the other.

   a. **Congressional districting:** In **congressional** districting, the rule is that **"as nearly as is practicable**, one man's vote in a congressional election is to be worth as much as another's." *Kirkpatrick v. Preisler*, 394 U.S. 526 (1969). States must make a "good-faith effort to achieve **precise mathematical equality**." *Id.*

   b. **State and local apportionment:** By contrast, the Court has been willing to allow **much greater deviation** from mathematical equality in the apportionment of **state legislatures** or **local governmental bodies**.

      i. **"De minimus" category:** First, the Court has established a **"de minimus"** category — deviations below a certain level **need not be supported by any state objective at all**. This category covers **"minor population variations,"** and seems to include all deviations of **less than 10%**.

      ii. **"Legitimate state considerations":** Second, even deviations above this roughly 10% threshold will not cause a state legislative or local governmental apportionment scheme to be invalidated, if the deviations are justified by **"legitimate state considerations." Abate v. Mundt**, 403 U.S. 182 (1971). For instance, in *Mahan v. Howell*, 410 U.S. 315 (1973), the Court approved an apportionment of one house of the Virginia Legislature having a maximum variation of 16.4% from population equality; this deviation was justified by the state's policy of "maintaining the **integrity of political subdivision lines**."

**6. Gerrymandering:**   The *Reynolds* "one person, one vote" formulation says nothing about ***how the district lines are to be drawn***; all that standard requires is that the districts end up with equal numbers of voters in each. But "one person, one vote" by itself leaves room for a maneuver which may have an even more dramatic ability to dilute some voters' strength: the ***gerrymander***.

   **a. Gerrymander defined:**   The gerrymander is a device by which the strength of a particular voting bloc is curtailed by restricting its members to carefully- and artificially-constructed districts. (For an illustration of a gerrymander, see *supra*, p. 313.)

   **b. Justiciable:**   A bare majority of the Court continues to hold that claims of unconstitutional gerrymandering are ***justiciable***.

     **i. *Davis v. Bandemer*:**   In *Davis v. Bandemer*, 478 U.S. 109 (1986), by a 6-3 vote the Court held that there were indeed "judicially discernible and manageable standards by which political gerrymander cases [may] be decided." Such cases involve the adequacy of representation, and are therefore no different in a general sense from claims involving population apportionment, found to be justiciable in the Reynods "one person, one vote" decision. (The six Justices in the majority split sharply into two camps with regard to what the substantive standards should be for deciding whether a political gerrymander violated the Equal Protection clause.)

     **ii. *Vieth v. Jubelirer* affirms this result:**   Then, in 2004, an even narrower (5-Justice) majority of the Court affirmed *Bandemer*'s ruling that political gerrymander cases could theoretically be justiciable. In ***Vieth v. Jubelirer***, 541 U.S. 267 (2004), five Justices concluded that although it is hard to figure out a standard for determining which gerrymanders are so extreme as to violate the Constitution, the Court should not hold gerrymander cases to be categorically non-justiciable. But this five-justice majority for the proposition that gerrymander cases may be justiciable was a very weak one;  for instance, one of the five, Justice Kennedy, said that he would use "great caution" in even approaching such cases, that he did not at present know of a rationale or standard for deciding such cases, and that he was merely voting in *Vieth* "not [to] ***foreclose all possibility*** of judicial relief" if an appropriate standard could be found in the future.

       **(1) 4-Justice dissent argues for nonjusticiability:**   Four Justices in *Vieth* pointed out that in the almost two decades following *Bandemer*, "no judicially discernible and manageable standards for adjudicating political gerrymandering claims have emerged." Therefore, these four said, "we must conclude that political gerrymandering claims are ***nonjusticiable*** and that *Bandemer* was wrongly decided[.]" When these four votes are added to Justice Kennedy's view that no acceptable rationale for deciding such cases has emerged yet, a majority of the *Vieth* Court could not see any concrete circumstance in which they would vote to award relief on a gerrymandering claim.

     **iii. Nearly impossible to win:**   In any event, even though as noted a bare majority of the Court continues to view partisan gerrymandering cases as being theoretically justiciable, it has proven ***virtually impossible for plaintiffs to win*** such cases. For instance, in both *Bandemer* and *Vieth*, the plaintiffs failed to convince the Supreme Court that the gerrymandered districting plans there violated the constitution. See *supra*, p. 313, for more about the Court's fierce internal disagreements about what the substantive standard for judging partisan gerrymandering claims should be.

---

## Quiz Yourself on
## *JUSTICIABILITY (ENTIRE CHAPTER)*

**95.** The President, in an attempt to restore democracy in Haiti, dispatched American troops to that island without a congressional declaration of war. The troops have now remained there for 60 days, still without a congressional declaration. Their expenses have been paid for out of the general Defense Department budget, appropriated by Congress before the troops were sent and without the expectation that they would be sent. Paul, a U.S. citizen and taxpayer, has sued the President seeking an injunction requiring the President to withdraw the troops. The substance of Paul's suit is that only Congress has the power to declare war, and that the President's action amounts to an illegal declaration of war. Paul further asserts that his federal tax dollars are being unconstitutionally spent to support this illegal action.

    **(a)** If you are the President's lawyer, what is the first defense you should assert? _____

    **(b)** Will this defense prevail? _____

**96.** Same basic facts as above question. Now, however, assume that Paul asserts that he has standing to pursue his claim in federal court, because he is a citizen of the United States, and his right to have his government not behave in an unconstitutional manner has been abridged. Is Paul correct? _____

**97.** A federal statute places restrictions on the extent to which private companies may be permitted by the U.S. government to engage in logging in national forests. Penzel, a private individual, sues the U.S. Secretary of the Interior. His suit contends that the Secretary has administered regulations on logging in a way that contravenes the statute. The suit contends that the effect will be to allow more logging in the forests than permitted by statute. Penzel asserts that he uses a particular national forest for a one-week hike twice per year, and that the unauthorized logging affects a part of the forest that he expects to hike in during the next year. At least four million hikers each year will cross through parts of federal forests that are likely to have been affected by the allegedly excessive logging. The Secretary asserts that Penzel lacks standing to make this claim. Does Penzel have standing? _____

**98.** Same facts as prior question. Now, however, assume that the plaintiff is Friends of the National Forests, Inc. (FNF), a non-profit corporation whose members are users and lovers of the national forests. No individual plaintiffs are named. Does FNF have standing to pursue the suit? _____

**99.** George Brensteiner was the owner of the New York Strikers of the National Soccer League. Brensteiner's existing stadium was about to be demolished, and he needed to pick a new site for a stadium that he would build. After some preliminary investigation, Brensteiner announced that there were three "finalist sites," of which one was Yonkers, New York. Brensteiner applied for clearances from the federal Environmental Protection Agency (EPA) for all three sites. He received quick clearances for the other two. As to Yonkers, the local EPA administrator covering Yonkers determined that the proposed stadium would be on a protected wetland, and that the stadium could not be built unless Brensteiner first filed an Environmental Impact Statement (EIS) showing that the wetlands would not be damaged. Brensteiner then announced, "Because of the expense of preparing an EIS for the Yonkers site, I have selected one of the other sites as the winner, namely, Rutherford, New Jersey." Brensteiner acquired land in Rutherford, and quickly completed about 10% of the construction. At that moment, Steve, a Yonkers resident, brought suit against the EPA. Steve's suit argued that the EPA's requirement of an EIS for the Yonkers site was in violation of federal statutes, and that the effect of this violation was to deprive him, Steve, of easy access to a soccer sta-dium (in Yonkers) in which to view Strikers games. Steve's suit asked for a declaratory judgment that an EIS was not required for the Yonkers site. The EPA has defended on the grounds that Steve lacks stand-ing. Is the EPA's contention correct? _____

100. Fred, who is black, is a police officer on the force of the town of Suburbia. Suburbia's population is 30% black, but Fred is the only black out of 15 officers on the force. Fred has sued the department, arguing that the department's failure to hire more black patrol officers is intentional, and constitutes a violation of the Equal Protection Clause. Fred asserts that this failure to hire additional black officers harms him, by mak-ing him racially isolated on the force and leading to a department that is generally insensitive to the con-cerns of the minority community, thus making Fred's own working conditions less attractive. Does Fred have standing to bring this suit? _____

101. A local school district allows non-profit community groups to use classrooms at the district's public high school at night. The Old Christians Association (OCA), a group of senior citizens who want to pray together, applied for a room. The school district turned them down on the grounds that to allow them to use the room would constitute an unconstitutional establishment of religion. The OCA began a suit in fed-eral district court against the school board, asserting that the denial of a room violated their free exercise rights. After the suit was begun, the school board issued a statement reversing its policy against allowing religious groups to use classrooms, and granted the OCA's permit request. The OCA would like to con-tinue with the suit, so that they may obtain a judicial opinion in their favor that can be cited as precedent in other school districts.

    (a) What defense should the school board defendant raise? _____

    (b) Will this defense succeed? _____

102. Pintard is a 52-year-old trooper in the police department of the State of New Spain, and is a resident of that state. New Spain has fired him because, in the department's judgment, no one over the age of 50 is physically fit enough to carry out the duties of state trooper. A federal statute, the Federal Age Discrimi-nation Act, applies to all employees and forbids firing on account of age. Pintard has sued the state of New Spain for damages. (He does not want to be reinstated, because he has found a new job.)

    (a) What defense should the state raise? _____

    (b) Will this defense succeed? _____

103. The state of Caledonia was running short of funds, due to a budget crisis. To save money, the Governor ordered that only one copy be purchased of any personal-computer software package needed by the state government, and that staff members make copies. A staffer made 2,000 copies of the "PC-Word" word-processing package (published by PC Word Corp., a Caledonia company), and distributed these to each state office, where they were used. The retail value of each copy of PC Word is $295. PC Word Corp. has sued the state in federal court for the district of Caledonia, alleging that the state has violated the federal copyright act and seeking money damages ($295 x 2000). Assume that the federal copyright act expressly allows a state to be sued in federal court (whether by its own citizen or by a citizen of another state).

    (a) What defense should Caledonia raise? _____

    (b) Will this defense succeed? _____

104. Jose won a U.S. congressional seat from a district located in New York City, in a close race against Mar-tin. The House routinely determined that Jose met the constitutional requirements to be seated (that he

was at least 25 years old, a U.S. citizen, and a resident of the state from which he had been elected). Martin then brought a federal district court suit against the House of Representatives and Jose, seeking to have Jose ruled unqualified to sit in the House. The essence of Martin's suit was that Jose really "inhabits" (as that term is used in Art. I, §2, second sentence) not the state of New York but rather, the State of Pennsylvania. Martin has come forward with evidence from voting records, state income tax filings, and other documents strongly suggesting that Jose spends the vast bulk of his time in, and considers himself a resident of, Pennsylvania.

**(a)** What defense should Jose raise to these proceedings? _____

**(b)** Will this defense succeed? _____

---

*Answers*

**95. (a) That Paul lacks standing.**

**(b) Yes.** As a general matter, federal taxpayers do not have standing to assert that taxpayers' funds in general are being improperly spent. There is an extremely narrow exception if plaintiff is able to show: (1) that the federal action complained of is an exercise of Congress' power under the Taxing and Spending Clause; and (2) that the challenged action violates some specific constitutional limitation imposed on the Taxing and Spending power. *Flast v. Cohen.* It is highly unlikely that Paul can satisfy either of these requirements for the exception. The President's dispatch of troops presumably relies upon his Commander in Chief powers, and certainly does not rely upon Congress' Taxing and Spending power. Furthermore, the requirement that only Congress may declare war is not a specific constitutional limitation on the Taxing and Spending power, merely an unrelated constitutional limit. Therefore, the general rule that there is no taxpayer standing would apply.

**96. No.** The Supreme Court has never been willing to recognize standing on the part of individuals *as citizens* to object to unlawful or unconstitutional conduct. This refusal is based on the view that one citizen's interest in lawful government is no different from that of any other citizen, and that an individual litigant relying upon citizenship has not shown the ***"individualized"*** injury-in-fact required for standing. See, e.g., *Schlesinger v. Reservists to Stop the War.*

**97. Yes, probably.** A federal-court plaintiff must show some concrete, ***"individuated,"*** "injury in fact." But this harm need ***not*** be *economic* in nature; harms to a person's esthetic enjoyment of nature, for example, will suffice. See, e.g., *Sierra Club v. Morton* (giving people who use national forests standing to protest construction of recreation area in the national forest). The threatened harm must be "actual or imminent." Since Penzel asserts that he will walk within one of the affected areas within the next year, the "imminence" requirement is probably satisfied. The fact that there are a large number of people suffering or likely to suffer the same harm as alleged by the plaintiff does not by itself remove standing from the plaintiff.

**98. Yes.** An association or organization has standing not only where its own interests are at stake, but in some cases where it is suing solely as a ***representative*** of its members. An association has standing to sue on behalf of its members if three conditions are met: (1) its members would otherwise have standing to sue ***in their own right***; (2) the interests the association seeks to protect are ***germane*** to the organization's ***purpose***; and (3) neither the claim asserted nor the relief requested requires the participation of ***individual members*** in the lawsuit. *Hunt v. Washington Apple Advertising Comm.* Here, all three of these requirements seem to be met: the prior question illustrates that individual forest-lovers would have standing; protection of the forests certainly is the core purpose of the organization; and there seems to be no reason why individuals rather than the organization need to participate in the lawsuit.

99. **Yes, probably.** One of the requirements for standing is that the challenged action must be the *"cause-in-fact"* of the injury. A sub-aspect of the "cause in fact" requirement is that the litigant must show that the relief being sought, if granted, has a reasonable likelihood of *redressing* the injury. The problem here is that even if the EPA was completely wrong in the first instance, it is far from clear that a victory by the plaintiff will result in the stadium being built in Yonkers rather than Rutherford. The ultimate decision is up to Brensteiner. Since Brensteiner has already bought the property in Rutherford and commenced construction, it is very unlikely that a declaratory judgment that the EPA should not have required an EIS for Yonkers will cause Brensteiner to stop construction and start it instead in Yonkers. Therefore, even though the other requirements of standing are met (Steve's loss of the ability to watch Strikers games near his house is certainly an "injury-in-fact" that is sufficiently concrete, individuated and imminent), the fact that victory in the suit will not redress the harm is fatal to Steve's standing. See, e.g., *Simon v. Eastern Ky. Welfare Rights Organization* (where IRS rules reduced the amount of free medical care that hospitals must donate to the poor in order to get tax breaks, a suit by poor people attacking those rules does not have standing, because the hospitals might not give the free medical care even if the rules were struck down).

100. **No, probably.** As a general rule, a litigant may normally not assert the constitutional rights of *third persons not now before the court*. This is the rule of constitutional *"jus tertii."* Fred may have been injured "in fact" by the absence of other blacks on the force. But the Equal Protection Clause protects only those applicants who would have been hired had there not been intentional discrimination. Since Fred was not part of this group, the fact that he may have suffered some incidental injury is not enough to give him standing — he must assert that the challenged governmental action violates *his* rights, not the rights of some other person not now before the court. (There are some important exceptions to the rule against third-party standing, such as where there is some legal restriction preventing the third party from exercising his own constitutional rights. But here, black applicants whom the department intentionally declined to hire because of their race clearly could bring their own suit, so neither this nor any of the other exceptions to the rule against third-party standing applies.)

101. **(a) That the action is now moot.** A case is moot if it raised a justiciable controversy at the time the complaint was filed, but *events occurring after the filing* have deprived the litigant of an ongoing stake in the controversy.

**(b) Yes.** Where the intervening event is the defendant's *voluntary* cessation of the conduct complained of, this may or may not be enough to render the case moot. If the facts show that the conduct claimed to be illegal is *very unlikely* to recur, then the voluntary cessation usually *is* enough to make the case moot. That is probably what the court would find to be the situation here. Therefore, the OCA's desire to obtain a favorable decision that it may use as precedent elsewhere will not be enough to give it an ongoing stake in the controversy, and the action will be dismissed.

102. **(a) The Eleventh Amendment.** The Eleventh Amendment excludes from the federal judicial power any suit "against any one of the States by Citizens of another State or by Citizens or Subjects of any Foreign State."

**(b) Yes.** Although on its face the Eleventh Amendment does not seem to prohibit federal-court suits against a state by a citizen of that state, the amendment has been interpreted to ban these suits as well as those by a citizen of one state against another state. See *Hans v. Louisiana*. The Eleventh Amendment applies only to suits for damages (as opposed to suits for injunctions), but the facts make it clear that money damage relief is what is sought here. Therefore, the Eleventh Amendment defense will be successful.

**103. (a) The Eleventh Amendment.**

**(b) Yes.** *Seminole Tribe v. Florida* holds that except with respect to suits brought under federal statutes supported by Congress' power to enforce the post-Civil War Amendments, Congress cannot remove the state immunity provided by the Eleventh Amendment. Therefore, even though Congress has clearly said that a state may be sued for damages for violating the copyright act, this statement of congressional intent is without effect, and the Eleventh Amendment applies to bar the suit. (But PC Word Corp. could get an *injunction* against the governor prohibiting further violations, since the Eleventh Amendment does not apply to injunction suits against state officials; see *Ex parte Young*.)

**104. (a) That the issue posed here is a non-justiciable political question.**

**(b) Yes, probably.** The Court will regard as a non-justiciable political question any issue whose determination is committed by the Constitution to **another branch** of government (i.e., the executive or the legislative). There is an excellent chance that the Court will conclude that the decision about whether a person elected to Congress meets the three standing requirements is committed by the Constitution to the House itself. The Court would point to Art. I, §5, which provides that "each House shall be the Judge of the Elections, Returns and Qualifications of its own members. … " In *Powell v. McCormack*, the Court held that the issue of whether the House could refuse to seat a Congressman who met the three standing requirements but who had, in the House's opinion, committed other infractions, was *not* committed by the Constitution to the House, and could be heard by the Court. But it seems probable that a suit involving the narrow issue of whether a person met all of the three requirements expressly listed in Art. I, §2 is committed to the House and is thus non-justiciable (though the Court has never explicitly decided that question).

---

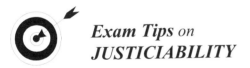

## *Exam Tips on*
## *JUSTICIABILITY*

Justiciability questions are pervasive and often hidden. Typically, your fact pattern will **not** contain the key words "standing," "ripe," "moot," "abstain," "political question," etc. — it will be up to you to spot these issues. Worse, these issues can be hidden in absolutely **any type** of fact pattern, so you can't let your guard down for a moment. Here are some specifics to watch for:

☞ Here's a brief checklist of justiciability issues:

(1) *advisory opinions;*

(2) *standing;*

(3) *mootness;*

(4) *ripeness;*

(5) *11th Amendment's* ban on certain **suits against the states;**

(6) *abstention;* and

(7) *political questions*.

☞ "Advisory opinion" problems usually arise on exams where a *state court* issues an advisory opinion (as allowed by the procedures of most states), and the loser seeks review in the U.S. Supreme Court. Typically, you'll say that even if the state court advisory opinion is based on federal law, the Supreme Court cannot hear the issue because there is no true "case or controversy" as required by Article III.

☞ The overwhelmingly most important aspect of justicability on exams is *"standing."* For *every claim* asserted anywhere on your exam, ask yourself, "Has P suffered, or is she about to suffer, a *concrete, individualized harm*, that would be *redressed* by a favorable result in the lawsuit?" Unless the answer is "yes," there's probably no standing.

    ☞ Here's a checklist for standing, with the five individual elements broken out::

        ☞ P must have suffered an *"injury-in-fact,"* or be *likely* to suffer one reasonably *soon*;

        ☞ P's harm must be *concrete*, not abstract;

        ☞ P's harm must be *"individuated,"* i.e., not the same as that suffered by every other citizen or taxpayer;

        ☞ The action that P is complaining about must have been the *"but for" cause* of P's harm; and

        ☞ A favorable decision in the suit must be likely to *redress* the injury to P.

    ☞ One common fact pattern: P has a contract with the government, and some statute or rule would prevent (or dissuade) the government from honoring the contract. Here, there's usually standing because P is likely to suffer an "injury in fact" from losing the benefit of the contract. (*Example:* P has a contract to build a school for state X; a federal statute would withdraw funds that X was expecting to receive and pay over to P. In this situation, P has standing.)

    ☞ Remember that P need not have already suffered the harm. But if not, the threatened harm needs to be pretty *imminent* and pretty likely — some small chance of harm at some indefinite future time won't suffice. (*Example:* A first-year law student doesn't have standing to challenge a state's Continuing Legal Education requirement, because that requirement won't apply to her for several years.)

    ☞ An *organization* will generally be allowed to sue *on behalf of its members*, if the members would individually have standing, and if the suit is *related* to the organization's *purposes*. Most organization-based suits you'll see on an exam will *satisfy* these conditions.

    ☞ If P is asserting rights as a *federal "taxpayer"* or as a *"citizen,"* and P is not part of the transaction in question, probably P does *not* have standing. Three special cases:

        ☞ If P is a *state* taxpayer challenging a state expenditure, then probably all that's required for standing is that there be a "direct expenditure of funds" by the state. Normally, this will be satisfied in your fact pattern.

☞ If P is a federal taxpayer who is challenging the *tax itself*, which P would have to pay unless the suit succeeds, P has standing.

☞ If P is a federal taxpayer or citizen challenging a federal expenditure that *directly violates some constitutional guarantee*, P may have standing. Probably, this exception only applies to federal expenditures that violate the First Amendment's *Establishment Clause* (e.g., the federal government pays money to private schools to be used in furthering their religious message).

☞ Regardless of whether P has standing on her own, P will *not* usually be allowed to assert the rights of *third persons* not then before the court. You can refer to this as the rule against *"jus tertii"* to sound erudite. There are three important exceptions:

   ☞ In free-expression cases, litigants get to use the First Amendment *overbreadth* doctrine. This lets P say, in effect, "This statute blocks expressive conduct of mine that may constitutionally be proscribed, but it also could be interpreted to block expressive conduct or speech on the part of others not present, for whom it would violate their free speech rights."

   ☞ The litigant can assert the third party's rights if these rights would be impaired, and it's legally or practically *difficult* for the third party to be present in the suit. (*Example:* Vendors are often permitted to assert the rights of their customers, who would each individually have too little at stake to sue.)

   ☞ Associations get to assert their members' rights, as noted above.

☛ You can spot a *mootness* problem by the fact that P "doesn't really seem to have a problem anymore." (*Example:* P has been kept out of a public university by an allegedly discriminatory policy; if the university then allows P to enroll, the case has become moot.)

   ☞ Before you conclude that P doesn't really have a problem anymore, look for *"collateral consequences."* Most common: the litigant (he can either be P or D) has been *convicted*, then paroled or discharged — there will still be collateral consequences to him from having a conviction on the books (e.g., job or voting problems), so the case is not moot.

   ☞ Look for issues that are "capable of *repetition*, yet evading review." This happens where P is one of a series of similarly-situated people, each of whom would face the same problem that would always turn out to be moot. Classic illustration: P is a pregnant woman seeking to overturn restrictions on abortion; she's no longer pregnant by the time the suit gets heard, but all other pregnant women similarly situated would have the same problem, so a court will hear the case now. Another illustration: a political group is prevented from doing something until "after the election"; the election is now over, but other political groups, or this very group, would be likely to face the same mootness problem in a future context.

☛ You can spot a *ripeness* problem by looking for a situation that's *"too early"* or *"not concrete enough."*

   ☞ Classic illustration of ripeness: there's a criminal statute on the books that P wants to violate or has violated, but there's very little risk that the statute will in fact be enforced against P. (In this scenario, P is generally seeking a declaratory judgment that the statute is unconstitutional.) This type of problem is especially acute where P **hasn't committed** the violation yet, and we're not sure that he will. (*Example:* A statute prevents people from distributing literature on private property, including shopping centers. P says he wants to do this kind of distribution, but hasn't done it yet, and it's not even clear that the owner will object or that the police will arrest. P's case is probably unripe.)

☞ Another type of scenario: the risk is too **abstract**. (*Example:* A state keeps a secret file on citizens; P, one of the monitored citizens, claims that his First Amendment rights are being "chilled." The Court will probably hold that any chilling problem is too speculative and abstract, and the case unripe, unless P can show what activity he is being dissuaded from engaging in.)

☞ Whenever a suit is brought in federal court by a **private citizen** against a **state**, there's a good chance that the suit is blocked by the **11th Amendment**. This is true whether P is a citizen of the defendant state or of some other state. (*Example:* P, a citizen of state D, is injured when a state D employee runs him over while the employee is on the job. P sues state D in federal court for damages. The suit will be blocked by the 11th Amendment.)

☞ Some **exceptions** to the 11th Amendment:

☞ Suits against a state by **another state** or by the **federal government**;

☞ Suits against **counties**, **cities**, or anything but the state itself.

☞ Suits for an **injunction** against state **officials** directing them to **cease violating federal law**. (But a suit to force a state official to obey *state* law *is* covered by the 11th Amendment and thus not allowed in federal court).

☞ Keep in mind that **Congress generally can't change** this "no federal-court suits against the states" law, even if it wants to. Cite to the *Seminole Tribe* case on this point. (*Example:* Congress passes a statute saying any state can be sued by private citizens for violating federal environmental-protection laws. This statute won't have any effect, and the federal court won't be allowed to hear a private suit against a state for damages for environmental violations.)

☞ But also remember that Congress *can* provide for federal-court suits by private citizens when the right being sued on stems from Congress' power to enforce the **post-Civil War Amendments**. (*Example:* Congress passes a broad statute banning racial and gender discrimination in employment, and says that workers can sue states in federal court for violations. The 11th Amendment won't block such suits, because Congress has the power to say that the Amendment won't apply to suits brought under federal statutes passed under Congress' authority to enforce the 14th Amendment.)

☞ If the question involves a private damages suit brought on a congressionally-guaranteed right, but brought **against a state in its own courts**, remember that the newly-recognized constitutional doctrine of **sovereign immunity** (the *Alden v. Maine* case) means that the state **doesn't have to hear the case.**

☞ Be alert to possible non-justiciable *"political questions."* Remember that there are two different ways a question can become a non-justiciable political one:

☞ First, this can happen where, at least arguably, the Constitution gives the problem to the *executive* or *legislative* branch to resolve, rather than to the judiciary. Classic illustration: anything to do with the procedures or grounds for *impeachment*. Another illustration: a federal court is asked to overrule Congress' decision that P doesn't satisfy the age, citizenship or residency requirement for Senators and Representatives.

☞ Second, a question can be a non-justiciable political one because there are *no "manageable standards"* to guide the judiciary in deciding. This type of fact pattern is relatively rare. (*Example:* P claims that a particular tax is so burdensome that it amounts to an uncompensated "taking" in violation of the Fifth Amendment. This issue is a non-justiciable political one, because no standards exist to tell the Court how to decide.)

☞ One area that you might think would fall into this "no manageable standards" category — *reapportionment* — doesn't. The Court has decided that the "one person, one vote" principle applies to virtually all federal and state elections, and that this principle can be successfully applied by the judiciary.

# ESSAY EXAM
# QUESTIONS AND ANSWERS

The following Essay Questions are taken from the Constitutional Law volume of *Siegel's Essay & Multiple Choice Questions & Answers*, a series written by Brian Siegel and published by us. The full volume contains 23 essays (with model answers), as well as 119 multiple choice questions. (The essay questions were originally asked on the California Bar Exam, and are copyright the California Board of Bar Examiners, reprinted by permission.) The book is available for $15.95 from your bookstore, or from http://lawschool.aspenpublishers.com.

**QUESTION 1:** City, a municipality of State X, has a permit ordinance that prohibits making speeches in the City-owned city park without first obtaining a permit from City's police chief. The ordinance authorizes the police chief to establish permit application procedures, and to grant or deny permits based upon the chief's "overall assessment of the good of the community." The ordinance also provides that denial of a permit may be appealed to the city council.

On Tuesday, Tom applied to Dan, City's police chief, for a permit to speak in the city park the following Saturday. Tom gave Dan his name and local address, but Dan denied Tom's application for a permit because Tom refused Dan's request for a summary of what he intended to say in his speech. When Tom told Dan that he intended to make his speech anyway, Dan immediately gave Tom's name and address to the city attorney of City.

The city attorney did nothing about the matter until Friday, when, without notice to Tom, he made application on behalf of City to a State X court of general jurisdiction for a temporary restraining order preventing Tom from speaking in the city park without a permit. The State X court issued an ex-parte temporary restraining order and an order to show cause, answerable in five days, directed to Tom. The orders were served on Tom in the city park on Saturday as he was about to speak. Despite the temporary restraining order, Tom spoke to about twenty mildly interested persons who were then in the park for various other reasons.

The essence of Tom's speech was that the federal government, "aided and abetted" by City's government, was "leading America to destruction," and that "those who would survive will eventually have to fight in the streets of City to regain their liberties." Tom urged the audience to "stockpile weapons" and to "start thinking about forming guerrilla units to take back freedom from the government."

Tom was arrested and charged in the State X court which had issued the temporary restraining order with **(a)** speaking in the city park without a permit, a misdemeanor, **(b)** contempt of court for violating the temporary restraining order, and **(c)** violation of the State X criminal advocacy statute prohibiting "advocating insurrection against local, state, or the federal governments," a felony.

Five years ago, the State X Supreme Court construed the criminal advocacy statute as applying only to advocacy that is not protected by the United States Constitution.

A week after Tom's speech, in a case unrelated to the charges against Tom, the State X Supreme Court construed City's permit ordinance as authorizing the City police chief to consider "only the time, place, and manner of the proposed speech, and not its content" in passing upon permit applications.

What rights guaranteed by the United States Constitution should Tom assert in defense to the charges brought against him, and how should the court rule? Discuss.

**QUESTION 2:** County School Board (Board) cancelled the remedial reading program in County's public schools. At the same time, Board increased funding for drama arts workshops provided for seniors in the public high schools of County. Such increased funding is about 15% of the cost of the remedial reading program.

Racial minorities comprise 10% of the County population and 50% of the students enrolled in the remedial reading program. "AB" is an organization consisting of the parents of these minority students.

Some students are enrolled in the remedial reading program because of learning disabilities or other handicaps adversely affecting reading skills. "CD" is an organization of the parents of these students.

AB objected to the cancellation of the remedial reading program on the ground that the program's termination would disproportionately affect their children adversely. CD objected to the program's termination on the ground that such action would effectively end public education for their children.

In recommending termination of the program, the Board's director had stated: "This action is a necessary economy measure. We have other educational programs, such as pre-college math, which are educationally more important. Handicapped students will simply have to be served sometime in the future when we again have sufficient financial resources. We will, even then, have to target the program so that it helps handicapped children, not children of racial minorities who just need to improve their skills in the English language." Board's actions were based on its director's recommendations.

AB and CD filed suit against Board in federal court, asserting that termination of the remedial reading program violated the constitutional right of the parents and the children represented by those organizations, and asking that Board be ordered to reinstate the program. While the suit was pending, Congress enacted a federal statute requiring school boards of all state political subdivisions to provide remedial reading courses. In passing this legislation, Congress relied upon findings derived through congressional hearings that adults without reading skills inhibit production, sales and travel in interstate commerce.

Assume that both AB and CD have standing to assert their claims.

**1.** Is the federal statute constitutional? Discuss.

**2.** If the court rules that the federal statute is unconstitutional:

   **A.** What issues under the U.S. Constitution should AB raise against the actions of Board? How should they be decided? Discuss.

   **B.** What issues under the U.S. Constitution should CD raise against the actions of Board? How should they be decided? Discuss.

**QUESTION 3:** The legislature of State A recently passed a law requiring drivers of trucks carrying explosives on roads in State A to have "Special Driving Permits." These permits are to be issued only after rigorous physical examinations and driving tests. The State A law also provides that only permits issued by State A are acceptable for truck drivers; permits issued by certain other states, all of which have less stringent requirements, are not acceptable. Under the State A law, permits cannot be issued to persons under 30 or over 60 years of age, because statistical studies have shown that drivers in these categories have higher accident frequencies.

Assume that a federal law prohibits employers from discriminating against employees on the basis of age.

Ned, who is 62 years old, is a driver for Ajax, a truck company engaged in the interstate transportation of dynamite for construction projects in various states, including State A. Ned would normally be assigned to drive dynamite shipments from Ajax's headquarters in State B, into State A, but he cannot obtain a Special Driving Permit from State A. Ned would be able to satisfy both the physical examination and driving test requirements of the State A law, but is barred solely because of his age. Ned has a driver's permit issued by State B qualifying him to drive trucks carrying explosives. As a consequence of the State A law, Ajax has been obliged to revise its normal driver assignment policy to schedule Ned on routes which do not require ingress into State A.

Ajax and Ned have brought suit in the United States District Court in State A against the appropriate State A officials, seeking to have the State A law declared invalid. The defendants have moved to have the case dismissed on the grounds that (1) the plaintiffs lack standing, and (2) State A courts have not yet ruled upon the validity of the new law.

**1.** How should the court rule on the motion for dismissal? Discuss.

**2.** Assume the motion for dismissal is denied. What rights arising under the United States Constitution should Ajax and Ned urge in support of their claims that the State A law is invalid, and what result should follow? Discuss.

# ANSWERS

## SAMPLE ANSWER TO QUESTION 1:

### (a) The misdemeanor charge:

Tom ("T") could initially contend that the misdemeanor charge should be dismissed because it was based upon a statute which was overly broad on its face (i.e., the entity charged with enforcing the law had virtually total discretion in determining whether or not it should be applied to a particular situation). Such enactments cannot serve as the basis for governmental action; *Lovell v. Griffin*, 303 U.S. 444 (1938). Since the statutory standard to be utilized in granting licenses or not is highly subjective in nature (i.e., the "overall community good"), T would argue that it was constitutionally defective. While it would be difficult for City to argue that the test for determining if licenses should be granted or not is adequate, it could assert that where the defendant should have anticipated a constitutionally curative construction, an overly broad enactment may serve as the basis for governmental action; *Shuttlesworth v. Birmingham*, 394 U.S. 147 (1969). Since the State X Supreme Court had made a proper narrowing interpretation of the criminal advocacy statute five years earlier, T should have foreseen that a constitutionally proper interpretation of the misdemeanor statute would also be rendered when it was judicially reviewed.

T could respond, however, that he could ***not*** foresee a constitutionally curative interpretation of the licensing ordinance because it appeared to be plain on its face (i.e., it would have been very difficult to anticipate that the requirement for speaking would be almost completely repudiated and the factors of time, place and manner of speech substituted in lieu thereof).

Alternatively, T could argue that, even if a proper narrowing interpretation could have been anticipated, a law which is unconstitutionally applied (i.e., the permit was rejected for T's failure to disclose the content; not time, place or manner considerations) cannot serve as the basis for a criminal conviction where no adequate opportunity for review is available. T would assert that this standard was satisfied because (1) there was no provision for independent review by a judicial body (any appeal was to be heard by the city council, presumably the same entity which enacted the law), and (2) the facts are unclear as to how often the city council met (if it was not until after T's projected speaking date, no timely appeal to that body could possibly be taken). While City could contend in rebuttal that T waived any potential constitutional defect in the prescribed review procedure by neglecting to contest the police chief's decision to deny T's request for a permit before the city council, a procedure which requires appeal to a legislative branch of local government is probably inadequate.

In summary, the prosecution of T for violation of the licensing ordinance will probably ***not*** be successful.

**(b) The contempt of court decree:**

Ex-parte orders are ordinarily not appropriate unless there was a need to act immediately and there was no opportunity to give the opposing party notice. Since the attorney for City was apparently aware of T's prospective speech on Tuesday (the facts indicate that Dan "immediately" gave the City attorney T's name and address), T probably should have been given an opportunity to contest the issuance of an injunction. While even an improper court order must ordinarily be obeyed, where an ex-parte injunction is deliberately sought and served in such a manner as to preclude effective judicial review (as was the case in this instance since City's attorney served the order upon T just as he was beginning to speak), it may be attackable in a subsequent proceeding; *Walker v. Birmingham*, 388 U.S. 307 (1967). However, since T's speech had not been preceded by extensive publicity, it would not have greatly burdened him to have sought appellate review of the injunction. Thus, a conviction for contempt would appear to be proper.

**(c) The felony charge:**

While the advocacy of ideas is protected by the First Amendment (applicable to the states via the Fourteenth Amendment), speech made for the purpose of inciting immediate unlawful conduct and which is likely to incite such action may be proscribed; *Brandenburg v. Ohio*, 395 U.S. 444 (1969). T could contend that the felony charges must be dismissed because (1) the statute in question is too vague (i.e., a person of ordinary intelligence could not determine what words constituted "advocating insurrection"), and (2) alternatively, the above cited standard is not satisfied in this instance because (i) while he advocated that the listeners "stockpile weapons" be never suggested that this be done illegally (in most states, various types of firearms can be purchased in a lawful manner), (ii) even if his words could be construed as urging illegal conduct, it wouldn't be done imminently (i.e., it would take time to aggregate these weapons), and (iii) there was little likelihood that the listeners would respond to T's speech, since they were (a) in the park for "various other reasons," and (b) only mildly interested in T's speech. Finally, T's comment to "begin thinking about forming guerilla units" obviously does not contemplate immediate unlawful conduct.

While City could respond to T's vagueness assertion by pointing out that the statute had received a constitutionally curative interpretation, there appears to be no successful rebuttal to T's argument that the *Brandenburg* test is not met. Thus, the felony charge should be dismissed.

**SAMPLE ANSWER TO QUESTION 2:**

**1.** *Is the federal statute constitutional?*

Board's strongest argument is that the statute violates the Tenth Amendment, on the theory that Congress may not compel a local school board to provide remedial reading courses. Under *Printz v. U.S. & Mack v. U.S.*, 117 S. Ct. 2365 (1997), Congress may not compel a state or local government's executive branch (which includes local school boards) to perform tasks or functions, even doing background checks on gun purchasers. A court would probably conclude that requiring particular courses in public schools is a comparable over-reaching of congressional power. Therefore, the statute will probably be held unconstitutional under *Printz/Mack*.

As a second argument, Board can contend that even if the statute was valid under the Tenth Amendment, it would be invalid under the Commerce Clause. Under Article I, Section 8 (Clause 3), of the Constitution, Congress has the right to regulate interstate commerce. There are three broad categories of activities that Congress can constitutionally regulate under its commerce power: (1) "channels" of interstate commerce; (2) "instrumentalities" of interstate commerce; and (3) those activities having a "substantial effect" on interstate commerce. *U.S. v. Lopez*; 514 U.S. 549 (1995). The federal statute falls under the third category, since it has no effect on the channels or instrumentalities of interstate commerce. Since the activity being regulated (education) is non-commercial, there must be an *obvious connection* between the activity and interstate commerce. While Congress did make legislative findings linking the regulated activity to interstate commerce, the Court no longer finds this dispositive on the constitutionality of commerce clause regulations. *Lopez*. Here, there is no jurisdictional nexus between the regulations and interstate commerce; i.e., the regulation equally affects those people traveling in, and those not traveling in, interstate commerce.

Therefore, there is no "obvious connection" between the regulation and interstate commerce, and it is likely that under *U.S. v. Lopez* the legislation will be held unconstitutional.

**2A.** *Assuming the federal statute is unconstitutional, what issues should the AB group raise against Board?*

The AB group would raise equal protection and due process objections to the Board's action.

In determining whether a law which is neutral on its face (such as the present legislation, which discontinues **all** remedial reading programs) has a discriminatory purpose, a court may consider any pertinent data (including the statements made by the Board's director). If purposeful discrimination could be shown, the County's actions would have to satisfy the strict scrutiny standard (i.e., a compelling state interest is furthered by the governmental conduct, and there is no less burdensome means of satisfying that objective). Since the termination of the program has a disproportionately adverse racial impact (while racial minorities comprise 10% of the County's population, they constitute 50% of the number of students enrolled in the program), Board would have the burden of proving that its actions were **not** racially motivated.

Board could argue that (1) its action was dictated by financial necessity, and (2) the effect of the program's termination also impacts upon non-minority students. In rebuttal, the AB group could contend that Board's purposeful discrimination is proven by the facts that (1) there were **increased** monies available for the drama arts workshops (however, the total of this amount was only 15% of the funds which had been available for the remedial reading program), and (2) the director indicated handicapped students would receive preference over minority students if adequate funding subsequently became available (although this could be defended by the fact that the latter group would completely fail to learn to read if their regular studies were not supplemented by the remedial program). Without data as to Board's financial situation, it is impossible to determine if the cessation of the program was "a necessary economy measure" or racially inspired. Assuming the court found that it was not, then County would only have to show that the program's termination had a reasonable relationship to a constitutional purpose to sustain its action. This would seem to be established by the County's showing that monetary pressures compelled cessation of the remedial reading program.

The AB group could alternatively contend that the program's closure violated their substantive due process rights. Under the Fourteenth Amendment, one cannot be deprived of fundamental "liberties" (i.e., rights recognized as essential to the orderly pursuit of happiness). The right to possess reasonably adequate reading skills is arguably "fundamental," since a failure to read proficiently inevitably results in lower paying jobs and an overall diminished ability to enjoy life. While the Supreme Court has held that there is no fundamental right to an equally financed education (i.e., all school districts within a particular county do not have to expend an equal dollar amount per child; *San Antonio School District v. Rodriguez*), it has never held that a school district can offer less than an adequate education.

Again, more facts are necessary to determine if, without the program, children of the AB group would be literate. If not, continuation of the program probably is a fundamental right, and therefore the strict scrutiny test would be applicable (i.e., Board would have to show that discontinuing the remedial reading program was virtually the only means of meeting its budgetary crisis). However, if the AB group would receive an adequate education without the program, Board's action would only have to have a reasonable relationship to a constitutional purpose. This would seem to be present in this case, since any good faith decision with respect to how a limited amount of education money is apportioned would be reasonable.

**2B.** *Assuming the federal statute is unconstitutional, what issues would the CD group raise against Board?*

The CD group would also raise the substantive due process argument described above (i.e., that the right to receive adequate reading skills is a "fundamental" one, and therefore cessation of the program is subject to a strict scrutiny analysis). The facts indicate that, given their innate learning disabilities, this group would not acquire adequate reading skills without the program. Since it is unlikely that Board could show that other programs are more important than minimal reading proficiency, it is highly doubtful that (1) cancellation of the program served a compelling state interest, and (2) there was no less burdensome means available to Board of satisfying its financial constraints. In summary, the substantive due process argument of the CD group should be successful.

Alternatively, the CD group would contend that their equal protection rights were violated. There is no case law supporting the proposition that educationally handicapped students are a "suspect" or "quasi-suspect" group. Since (1) there has probably been no history of purposeful unequal treatment with respect to educationally handicapped persons, and (2) their handicaps are (presumably) not unalterable, it appears to be doubtful that the CD group would be classified as "suspect" or "quasi-suspect." Since the program's cessation would probably meet the rational relationship test, CD's equal protection argument should be unsuccessful.

## SAMPLE ANSWER TO QUESTION 3:

### 1. The Motion for Dismissal:

#### Abstention:

A U.S. District Court may abstain from hearing a case which challenges the constitutionality of an ambiguous non-federal statute if the alleged defect might be cured by a narrowing interpretation by a state court. While State A might contend that abstention is appropriate in this instance because no state court has yet construed the statute in question, Ajax and Ned ("Plaintiffs") could probably successfully argue in rebuttal that a curative construction is unlikely since both the (1) 30-60 year parameters, and (2) specific testing requirements, leave virtually no room for a constitutionally valid interpretation.

### 2. The rights of the Constitution versus State A law:

#### Standing:

Article III of the Constitution requires that to have standing in federal court, a plaintiff must show a direct and immediate personal injury which is traceable to the challenged action; *Simon v. Eastern Kentucky Welfare Rights Organization*, 426 U.S 26 (1976). State X might contend that Ned has suffered no injury since he has not been terminated from his employment, nor is there any indication that he is receiving less compensation than he had made prior to the State A enactment. Ajax arguably lacks standing because it apparently has other drivers who are capable of obtaining the "Special Driving Permits." Assuming, however, (1) Ned's re-assignment (a) to other routes ultimately results in lessened compensation (of any amount) for him, or, (b) is disadvantageous for any other reason (i.e., the substituted routes are more physically demanding because they are longer and/or more dangerous), and (2) altering driving assignments to. comply with State A law could result in some drivers deciding to leave Ajax's employ, the Plaintiffs probably have standing.

#### The State A Statute:

Pursuant to the Tenth Amendment, a state may ordinarily enact legislation which is aimed at promoting the health, safety or welfare of its citizenry. Since the legislation in question is obviously aimed at decreasing the possibility of accidents involving explosive-carrying trucks, it would be constitutionally valid (unless it contravenes some federal interest).

#### Supremacy Clause:

Where a state statute conflicts with the language of, or purposes sought to be achieved by, a federal statute, the former enactment will be invalid under the Supremacy Clause.

Plaintiffs will contend that the State A statute is inconsistent with the purposes sought to be achieved by the federal law because it would induce age discrimination (i.e., to avoid being obliged to juggle schedules to circumvent State A, employers would (a) hire drivers within State A's age parameters, and (b) be more likely to terminate employees who could not travel within State A). However, State A could argue in rebuttal that (1) Plaintiffs' argument is premised on speculative secondary effects of its law, and (2) it is unlikely that Congress intended to preempt state legislation which was based upon bona fide occupational qualifications (statistical studies support State A's age restrictions). Unless there is clear legislative history that Congress intended to totally preclude age as a consideration for employment, Plaintiffs probably would not succeed on this argument.

**Equal Protection Clause:**

Since the elderly have not historically been subjected to purposeful unequal treatment or relegated to a position of political powerlessness, the strict scrutiny standard would probably not apply; *Massachusetts Board of Retirement v. Murgia*, 427 U.S. 307 (1976).

Plaintiffs might nevertheless contend that the rational relationship test (i.e., there must be a rational relationship between the classification drawn by the statute and the governmental object sought to be achieved) is not satisfied. This is because (1) the physical examination and driving test measure more accurately one's ability to drive safely than strict biological age, and (2) persons with perfect driving records could be excluded as a consequence of the statute, while others with negative driving histories might nevertheless qualify for a Special Driving Permit ("SDP"). However, since the classification (1) need only be rational (i.e., maybe drivers over 60 are more prone to heart attacks), and (2) is supported by empirical data, State A would probably prevail on this issue too.

**Dormant Interstate Commerce Clause:**

State legislation which unduly burdens interstate commerce (i.e., the interference with interstate commerce resulting from the local regulation outweighs the interest sought to be protected by the law) is invalid; *Bibb v. Navajo Freight Lines, Inc.*, 359 U.S. 520 (1959). Plaintiffs could contend that the State A statute imposes a substantial burden upon interstate commerce, since interstate trucking companies will now be obliged (probably at substantial inconvenience and expense) to avoid State A or be compelled to hire additional employees who can acquire a SDP. State A, however, could argue in rebuttal that it has a strong interest in the legislation (i.e., the desire to avoid catastrophic explosions which have a potential for causing great loss of lives and property).

Assuming State A could show that most truck companies have drivers within their employ who qualify for a SDP (and therefore the statute merely results in the inconvenience of having to alter job assignments), it would again prevail.

**Due Process:**

Where a state statute irrebuttably presumes that certain facts exist which result in an adverse classification, the denial of an opportunity to challenge that presumption violates an individual's Fourteenth Amendment's due process right to demonstrate that the fact presumed is not true in his/her case, some Supreme Court cases suggest. See, e.g., *Vlandis v. Kline*, 412 U.S. 441 (1973). Thus, Plaintiffs' could argue that the irrebuttable presumption that persons over 60 are more prone to accidents than others is invalid (especially since Ned was capable of satisfying the physical examination and driving test requirements of State A). However, State A could probably successfully contend in rebuttal that (1) the irrebuttable-presumption cases like *Vlandis* are probably no longer good law; (2) there is no "property" interest in private employment, and (3) statistical studies (which were presumably methodologically sound) have established that drivers over 60 have a higher incidence of accidents than others, so the classification is certainly rational, which is all that is required by either due process or equal protection.

In summary, it is unlikely that Plaintiffs would be able to invalidate the State A statute.

# TABLE OF CASES

Principal discussion of a case
is indicated by page numbers in *italics*.

# SUBJECT MATTER INDEX